The Mexican-American People

THE MEXICAN-AMERICAN PEOPLE *the nation's second largest minority*

LEO GREBLER / JOAN W. MOORE /
RALPH C. GUZMAN

with JEFFREY L. BERLANT / THOMAS P. CARTER /

WALTER FOGEL / C. WAYNE GORDON / PATRICK H. MCNAMARA /

FRANK G. MITTELBACH / SAMUEL J. SURACE

THE FREE PRESS
A Division of Macmillan Publishing Co., Inc.
New York
Collier Macmillan Publishers
London

The Free Press.
A Division of Macmillan Publishing Co., Inc.
866 Third Avenue, New York, N.Y. 10022
Collier Macmillan Canada, Ltd.

Library of Congess Catalog Card Number: 73-81931

printing number
   4 5 6 7 8 9 10

Preface

This volume is the result of a study designed by the Mexican-American Study Project at the University of California, Los Angeles, and executed in cooperation with scholars at other institutions of higher learning.

The investigation was initiated in 1963 with a prospectus for a "comprehensive study of the socioeconomic position of Mexican Americans in selected urban areas of the five Southwestern states." The actual research work began in January 1964. It was supported by a generous grant from the Ford Foundation and by a supplemental grant from the College Entrance Examination Board for special analysis of educational problems. The study was completed in the summer of 1968.

INTERDISCIPLINARY APPROACH

To comprehend the nexus of interrelated factors that impinge on the experience and position of a minority group poses well known problems. Each of the social sciences is bounded by the academic division of disciplines. For example, the economist may concern himself with the occupational structure of the group and with the variables affecting this structure, but leave to others the analysis of the consequences of increasing class differentiation for ethnic cohesiveness. The anthropologist may focus on the preservation of distinctive culture traits of the group in a specific context of time and space, without full-fledged study of the population's over-all socioeconomic conditions and their change over time. This common approach has made great contributions, but the resulting fragmentation tends to impede broader understanding.

Most of the literature on Mexican Americans is indeed unidisciplinary. The present study seeks to achieve a more integrative result through the teamwork of a group of specialized scholars, or interdisciplinary research. This approach seems to be needed despite its known difficulties and occasional failures.

Whether conducted by a team or by an individual, any research to portray and analyze the multi-faceted life of a group of people is beset with problems of selection. It would have been folly to approach this study in the spirit of writers of an earlier age who set out to offer a "compleat" analysis of one phenomenon or another. Such a goal is elusive under ideal circumstances, and it is clearly unrealistic within the constraints of a research project bounded by limits of time and budget. Our objective is rather to present a portrait of the Mexican-American minority in relation to the dominant society that is comprehensive enough in geographic coverage to lift this study from the confines of localism, and inclusive enough in content to articulate interrelationships between such matters as economic status and cultural values, style of life, educational attainment, family structure, or political participation, and between current socioeconomic conditions and their historical antecedents. But selection remains an obstinate problem. Which relationships are of greatest relevance, and how can depth in the analysis of a given subject be reconciled with the breadth sought in interdisciplinary work?

The answer will obviously vary with different analysts. Some guidelines are furnished by the rich literature on minority groups in American society, and by the concepts, theories and observations developed mainly by sociologists and anthropologists in the study of such groups throughout the world. With the caution dictated by the distinctive features and experiences of any minority, this book will indeed draw on this cumulative knowledge. Nevertheless, there is no firm model that would establish clear-cut boundaries for a study of this type or furnish any generally accepted order of priorities for the inclusion of subject matters.

To check our own judgment on the selection of topics and on other matters of research planning, we held four seminars in 1964 with groups of scholars who were drawn from many institutions of higher learning and represented a wide array of social-science disciplines. This was helpful, but the authors still had to make the ultimate decisions in light of the human and financial resources available for the project, the time allotted to the study, the extent to which a subject was researchable at the current state of the art, and the interpretative potentials of whatever data or other empirical materials could be obtained. Our decisions were not devoid of compromise.

RESEARCH PLANNING

The study started with a highly tentative and deliberately flexible design. About nine months were devoted to the development of a more structured research plan. The first step was a series of field trips throughout the Southwest. These tours were invaluable. They sharpened our awareness of the enormous diversity of both the Mexican-American population and the social settings and problems in various areas. They served to establish numerous personal contacts and helped us to discover study materials available locally and research work planned or in progress. They gave us first-hand insights into Mexican-American styles of behavior, grievances, and tensions within the community. They revealed a variety of Mexican-American views of the larger society and a variety of Anglo views about the minority group.

The field tours included some 20 cities in the Southwest as well as Chicago. Over 200 unstructured interviews were held with key persons in the Mexican-American communities, government officials, representatives of civic organizations, business and labor leaders, and scholars. These were later supplemented by field observations of Southwest school systems and of the political activity of Mexican Americans.

A list of persons interviewed informally on the field trips as well as in Los Angeles is presented in Appendix K.

The initial field tours were followed by intensive staff discussions and by the previously mentioned research seminars in which members of the UCLA Faculty Advisory Committee participated. The research plan prepared in light of these consultations was adopted with only minor exceptions. It is reflected in the scope and structure of the present volume.

One of the major issues in research planning was a familiar problem of methodology. It would have been entirely legitimate and might have enhanced the academic interest in our study if we had started with a number of general hypotheses and sub-hypotheses presumably explaining the socioeconomic condition of Mexican Americans in the Southwest. This whole volume might have been given over to hypothesis-testing or model-building. We have refrained from doing so.

Starting at the outset with generalizations may hamper rather than help the researcher when he enters uncharted territory—and, in spite of the seemingly large volume of scholarly literature, this study of Mexican Americans did embark on a new venture. Initial hypotheses may fail to include some of the variables relevant to this population, and they may stress others. Research that runs the risk of accomplishing little more than the verification of null hypotheses would be inconsistent with the purpose of the study. Whether the Mexican-American minority fits general theories of acculturation is a research question to be answered in light of empirical evidence rather than a matter of pre-judgment.

Hence it seemed to be the better part of wisdom to proceed with an analysis unrestrained by specific sets of hypotheses, although the data collection itself was unquestionably influenced by relationships presumed in theory. However, main findings are indeed interpreted in light of existing generalizations about minority groups, and an attempt is made to show how the findings contribute to the verification or modification of applicable hypotheses or to suggest new hypotheses. The research methods are varied and eclectic, ranging from aggregative statistical analysis of census data to mostly qualitative interpretation of social institutions or historical antecedents and to the use of household interview surveys for gaining insight into attitudes and values of Mexican-American individuals.

Another issue in research planning was the number and scope of original field studies. At the beginning, we contemplated intensive studies in five or six localities in the Southwest. These would include interview surveys of Mexican-American households and an examination of the structure of the entire community and the minority's place in that structure. However, we soon discovered that original surveys were even more costly than we had anticipated. In some of the cities which seemed to be good candidates for local study, competent researchers were not available. Organizational arrangements for cooperative research turned out to be highly complex. As a result, the ambitious initial program of field studies was substantially modified. Interview surveys were limited to Los Angeles and San Antonio, the two "heartland communities" of Mexican Americans. At the same time, it seemed important to investigate the allegedly distinctive "Spanish Americans" of New Mexico separately and to extend our work into at least one locality outside the Southwest. The results of these two studies were published in Advance Reports (which are listed later), and some of the findings appear in several chapters of this volume.

The interview surveys in Los Angeles and San Antonio were limited to Mexican-American households. Alternatively, of course, one might have designed surveys to include Anglos and nonwhites for "control" purposes and in order to obtain more useful data on mutual perceptions. Such a program was precluded by budgetary constraints, but we were able to derive limited information on mutual perceptions from related surveys in both cities.

STAFF AND CONTRIBUTORS

This volume is the product of a collaborative effort of the three authors, a number of scholars who contributed special analyses, and a supporting research staff. Since it was not designed as a symposium, the authors are responsible for the entire content, including the parts prepared by various specialists as well as their own work. We offer cheerfully the customary absolution from guilt by association to all those who have contributed and assume full liability for errors of omission or commission and for matters of interpretation.

To integrate the manuscripts prepared by our collaborators and by ourselves into this book and to avoid duplication and excessive length, it was usually necessary to condense the original materials and fit them into the over-all framework of the study.

The large scope of the research work called for the establishment of a special unit known as the Mexican-American Study Project. Leo Grebler, Joan W. Moore, and Ralph C. Guzman served as director, associate director, and assistant director, respectively.

Until the fall of 1966, Frank G. Mittelbach of the Graduate School of Business Administration at UCLA was a member of the Project staff. He directed the statistical unit, contributed to the initiation and general development of the study, co-authored several chapters, and supervised the sampling procedures for the Los Angeles and San Antonio household surveys. Mr. Mittelbach's careful review of draft materials is gratefully acknowledged.

Grace Marshall served effectively as statistical analyst supervising the preparation of the huge amount of census and related data for the study. She is also co-author of one of the Advance Reports.

Miriam Morton joined the staff in January 1967 as editor. We owe her sincere thanks for improving a number of Advance Reports but most importantly for editing drafts for this volume. Burton M. Moore volunteered to assist us in so many ways that the acknowledgments in various chapters cannot fully express our appreciation.

The scholars who collaborated in the study are listed below:

Jeffrey L. Berlant of the University of California, Berkeley, contributed to the study of "Protestants and Mexicans" (Chapter 20).

Richard Brymer of Wesley Community Centers and Trinity College, San Antonio, was in charge of the household interview survey in San Antonio. In this connection, we acknowledge also the generous cooperation of Wesley Community Centers under its executive director, Buford E. Farris, Jr. This organization provided not only the physical facilities for the San Antonio survey staff but also a great deal of local expertise.

Thomas P. Carter of the University of Texas at El Paso undertook a study of Southwest schools (Chapter 7) while he was on the faculty of the University of California at Riverside. The more extensive original version of his study has been published by the College Entrance Examination Board.

Walter Fogel of the University of California, Los Angeles, prepared most of the analysis in Chapters 8 to 10 and is the author of two Advance Reports.

Nancie L. González of the University of New Mexico wrote a monograph on the Spanish Americans of New Mexico which was published as an Advance Report and is used in several sections of this volume.

C. Wayne Gordon of the University at Los Angeles headed the group of scholars who designed the special study of Los Angeles schools and analyzed its results (Chapter 7). The group included David Nasatir, Audrey J. Schwartz, Gordon E. Stanton, and Robert Wenkert.

Patrick H. McNamara, now at the University of New Mexico, contributed the analysis of the role of the Catholic Church (Chapter 19). At the time, he was a member of the Society of Jesus.

Stanley Plog prepared an annotated bibliography on ethnicity, mental health, and personality characteristics while he was at the University of California, Los Angeles.

Julian Samora and Richard A. Lamanna of the University of Notre Dame conducted a field study of Mexican Americans in East Chicago, Indiana, and authored an Advance Report on the subject.

Samuel J. Surace of the University of California, Los Angeles, undertook the sociological–historical analysis incorporated mainly in Chapter 5.

Velma Montoya Thompson of the California State College at Los Angeles prepared a manuscript on the participation of Mexican Americans and Negroes in Los Angeles labor unions.

A. Taher Moustafa, M.D., and Gertrud Weiss, M.D., while attached to the School of Public Health at the University of California, Los Angeles, authored the health study published in an Advance Report.

Clifton M. Wignall, at Colorado State Hospital, Pueblo, Colorado, prepared a manuscript on "Mexican-American Usage of State Mental Hospital Facilities."

We note with satisfaction that five doctoral dissertations were generated at the University of California, Los Angeles, in conjunction with the research project; one or two additional theses may follow.

We received invaluable aid from other academic colleagues. We are greatly indebted to Eli Ginzberg of Columbia University and William Petersen of Ohio State University who responded generously to our invitation to review the entire draft of this book. Their incisive comment and criticism resulted in major revisions. At UCLA, Raymond J. Jessen was especially helpful in the preparation of the household surveys. He designed the sampling procedure and examined its execution. Helpful comments on drafts of chapters were offered by John Caughey, George Cole, Buford E. Farris, Jr., G. Shubert Frye, Edwin Gaustad, Patrick McNamara, T. Scott Miyakawa, John Modell, and Georges Sabagh. George I. Sanchez advised on the study of Southwest schools. The late Eshref Shevky participated in the research planning. Of course, the reviewers and consultants should be exonerated from any responsibility for the final product.

The research work was supported by a staff of technical specialists, research assistants, and interviewers too numerous for complete listing. Their length of service ranged from several years to a few months. Practically all of the research assistants were graduate students who worked part-time and in the process obtained a liberal education in the conduct of research. The following made notable contributions: Roy Simon Bryce-Laporte, Lorenzo M. Campbell; Joyce Chamberlain and Ronald McDaniel (who shared responsibility for computer programs and data processing); Paul Fisher, Nicandro Juarez, and Gerald Rosen. Alfredo Cuellar and Ronald Lopez were generous in offering materials and ideas. Susan L. Courtney drew the charts and maps and drafted geographical materials.

A special team of bilingual interviewers, most of them Mexican-American students, conducted the household surveys. They performed this task intelligently, energetically, and tactfully. The opportunity to visit Mexican-American homes representing a cross-section of the population motivated some of the interviewers to take a deeper and perhaps lasting interest in the community.

Among the administrative and clerical personnel, we owe an enormous debt to Rose Altman who was associated with the study from the beginning to the end. Mrs. Altman rendered outstanding service as Project secretary, especially in steering this volume through various stages of drafting to its completion. Alice Erickson handled efficiently budgetary and personnel matters as well as other administrative detail. Connie Bishop provided capable assistance.

We acknowledge gratefully the services of the UCLA Western Data Processing Center and its staff in the extensive computer analyses associated with the study.

ADVISORY COMMITTEES

The study benefited greatly from the guidance of a Faculty Advisory Committee drawn from several departments of the University of California, Los Angeles, and of Community Advisory Committees composed of distinguished Mexican Americans in Los Angeles and San Antonio. The members of these committees are listed on pages xiii–xiv. None of the committees nor any individual members bear responsibility for any of the findings or interpretations.

We are grateful to our academic colleagues who advised the staff at meetings and individually, but we owe a very special debt to the Community Advisory Committee in Los Angeles. Here was a group of persons extremely busy in important jobs and deeply involved in various activities of the Mexican-American community, yet willing to give freely of their time and energy to help in the conduct of the study. In addition to participation in committee meetings, many members provided generous assistance on an individual basis. We are particularly obliged to Congressman Edward R. Roybal for his unfailing interest in the study from its formative stage to its completion. Throughout, the Committee served as a formal link to the Mexican-American community, although the staff maintained community contacts through many additional means.

ADVANCE REPORTS

The study was scheduled for several years and its final results would therefore not be available for some time. For this reason, it seemed desirable to release preliminary or partial findings on selected subject matters in Advance Reports while the research work was proceeding. Materials presented in the Advance Reports are incorporated in the present volume, but usually in condensed as well as revised form and in a context dictated by the over-all framework of analysis.

With the publication of this volume, the Advance Reports serve an additional purpose. They become "back-up" materials which may be useful to students of particular subject matters or to those interested in more detail. In some cases the Advance Report is the only document in which the research performed by a contributing scholar or staff member is preserved in its entirety as an integral piece of work. The following Advance Reports were published:

1. *Education and Income of Mexican-Americans in the Southwest.* By Walter Fogel.
2. *Mexican Immigration to the United States: The Record and Its Implications.* By Leo Grebler, with contributions by Judge Philip W. Newman and Ronald Wyse.
3. *Revised Bibliography,* with a bibliographical essay by Ralph C. Guzman.
4. *Residential Segregation of Minorities in the Urban Southwest.* By Joan W. Moore, and Frank G. Mittelbach.
5. *The Burden of Poverty.* By Frank G. Mittelbach and Grace Marshall.
6. *Intermarriage of Mexican-Americans.* By Frank G. Mittelbach, Joan W. Moore and Ronald McDaniel.
7. *The Schooling Gap: Signs of Progress.* By Leo Grebler.
8. *Mexican-Americans in a Midwest Metropolis: A Study of East Chicago.* By Julian Samora and Richard A. Lamanna.
9. *The Spanish Americans of New Mexico: A Distinctive Heritage.* By Nancie L. González.
10. *Mexican-Americans in Southwest Labor Markets.* By Walter Fogel.
11. *Health Status and Practices of Mexican-Americans.* By A. Taher Moustafa, M.D., and Gertrud Weiss, M.D.

Copies of the Advance Reports are deposited with the Library of the University of California, Los Angeles, and a number of university and other libraries throughout the country (including the Library of Congress), especially at institutions in the Southwest.

LEO GREBLER
JOAN W. MOORE
Los Angeles　　　　　　　　　　　　　　　　　RALPH C. GUZMAN
November 1969

Faculty Advisory Committee

at the University of California, Los Angeles

RALPH BEALS   Department of Anthropology
NATHAN COHEN   School of Social Welfare
WERNER Z. HIRSCH   Department of Economics and Director, Institute of Government and Public Affairs
RAYMOND J. JESSEN   Graduate School of Business Administration
DWAINE MARVICK   Department of Political Science
FRED MASSARIK   Graduate School of Business Administration
FREDERICK MEYERS   Graduate School of Business Administration
LEO G. REEDER   School of Public Health
MILTON I. ROEMER   School of Public Health
GEORGES SABAGH   Department of Sociology
MAY V. SEAGOE   School of Education
MELVIN SEEMAN   Department of Sociology
ESHREF SHEVKY   Emeritus, Department of Sociology
GEORGE A. STEINER   Graduate School of Business Administration, and Director, Division of Research
FRANK F. TALLMAN   Department of Psychiatry
LEO GREBLER   Project Director and Chairman of Faculty Advisory Committee

Community Advisory Committee, Los Angeles*

JUAN D. ACEVEDO   Board Member, California Youth Authority
DANIEL L. FERNANDEZ   President, Council of Mexican-American Affairs
HECTOR GODINEZ   Postmaster, Santa Ana
EUGENE GONZALES   Assistant to State Superintendent of Public Instruction
GEORGE HERRERA
AUDREY KASLOW   Supervising Deputy Probation Officer, Los Angeles Probation Department
JOSEPH MALDONADO   Executive Director, Economic and Youth Opportunities Agency
MIGUEL MONTES   D.D.S. and Member of the California Board of Education
EDWARD R. ROYBAL   Member of the U.S. House of Representatives
LEOPOLDO SANCHEZ   Judge, Superior Court, Los Angeles
THOMAS TALAVERA   Deputy Labor Commissioner

* Positions listed refer to the main period of a member's service on the committee and have changed since that time in a few cases. The composition of the Los Angeles Committee changed slightly during the course of the study. The above list includes the members who served in the last two years but the majority were on the Committee from the beginning. Carlos F. Borja, Jr., who served until December 1964 and took a very helpful interest in the initiation of the study, resigned when he was appointed to the U.S. Mission to El Salvador.

Community Advisory Committee, San Antonio

JOHN C. ALANIZ   State Representative
WILLIAM ELIZANDO   Optometrist
ANTONIO GALLARDO
HIPPO GARCIA   Judge, County Court
M. C. GONZALES   Assistant District Attorney, San Antonio
HENRY B. GONZALEZ   Member of the U.S. House of Representatives
MIKE MACHADO   Judge, Corporation Court
JOSÉ SAN MARTIN   Optometrist
PHILIP J. MONTALBO   Attorney
HENRY MUNOZ   Director, Department of Equal Opportunity
JOE OLIVARES   Hotel Owner
ALBERT A. PEÑA, JR.   Commissioner, County of Bexar
JOHN SOLIS   Texas Employment Commission
FRANK VALDEZ   Architect

Contents

Contents

Part six POLITICAL INTERACTION

Part seven SUMMARY AND CONCLUSIONS

APPENDIXES

Contents

Part one

THE SETTING

ONE

Introduction

THIS book is part of the current discovery of Mexican Americans in the United States. Even the grant that made our study possible was the first of its kind. No national foundation had ever before given funds for major research on this minority group.

In national politics, Mexican Americans were discovered in the Presidential campaign of 1960. John F. Kennedy was the first national political candidate to make a serious effort to win their votes; by that time there were enough voters among them to make such effort worthwhile. The response was the *Viva Kennedy* movement that involved this minority in unprecedented political participation.

The end of the *bracero* program in 1964 signaled a significant victory for Mexican Americans in Federal legislation. Opposition to the program came from many groups. But Mexican Americans had a special interest in eliminating the job competition of Mexican nationals brought to the United States for seasonal work on the ranches and farms. This was one of the issues on which they could agree.

The discovery of Mexican Americans as a national minority is a consequence

3

of change both in the larger society and among the Mexican Americans themselves. Change in the general climate of opinion has become articulated in civil-rights legislation, antipoverty programs, and the United States Supreme Court decisions against discrimination in schools, political elections, and other spheres of life. In this atmosphere the Federal government was bound to turn its attention to the Mexican-American group sooner or later. For this is the nation's second largest minority—now well over five million people. It bears a disproportionate share of our society's problems, in addition to many problems of its own.

Mexican Americans began to discover *themselves* at about the same time that the nation noticed their existence. The changes they witnessed in the larger society solidified a growing conviction that their traditional approach of patiently waiting for recognition was unproductive. Mexican Americans formed politically oriented organizations *demanding* national attention. A new generation of leaders began to sense that the whole complex of national opinion, concern within the Federal government, and modern communications media could be used to voice and eventually redress their grievances. The concept of a "national minority" was slowly replacing the parochial orientation of earlier spokesmen who sought to solve individual problems in individual areas.

STUDYING A MINORITY IN THE 1960s

Our research work began when these changes were barely discernible. The encounter of the researcher with a minority seeking a new self-definition must be noted here because it became part of the process of redefinition. "In a general way, any minority sits inside a delicate and complicated structure of political and moral postures. Imbedded in this structure are the group's deepest aspirations and frustrations. To enter this fabric, no matter how gently, means that this structure of frustration and aspiration is somehow altered."[1] To enter this fabric in the charged social climate of the 1960s could not but intensify the issues always present when the scholar sets out to study a disadvantaged minority.

The disparity between the researcher's perception of his role and its definition by any group of people with special interests always poses difficulties. Whether the scholar will validate a group's claims is always a source of tension. Today the disparity is most acute in the case of disadvantaged minorities. The scholar's preoccupations with rules of evidence, broad abstractions, alternative interpretations, and cautious conclusions are definitely not those of the ethnic activist.[2]

This problem became immediately apparent at the beginning of our research. Our first exploratory interviews with Mexican Americans throughout the Southwest in 1964 suggested that we were defining the Mexican-American population in a particular way—as a national minority. To a leadership involved in local and regional quarrels, this was a novel interpretation. Our definition (tentative at that time)

[1] Notes for this chapter start on page 11.

seemed threatening to many leaders. It appeared to classify all Mexican Americans with the least acculturated people in the group. It appeared to slight traditional Mexican culture. It appeared to suggest the end of local autonomy. It implied unsettling comparisons with Negroes and their new militant tactics.

Although we were nearly always received with great courtesy, it became clear that our appearance in the field was causing considerable apprehension. We did not represent national attention as directly as did the investigators of the U.S. Civil Rights Commission or the members of Congressional committees. But our credentials as faculty members of a large university and researchers for a project financed by a large foundation placed us squarely with the "Anglo establishment." Understandably, the consequences of our work for the minority and its leaders, rather than its scholarly substance, was of prime concern to many of the group's spokesmen with whom we talked on our initial field tours.

The Mexican Americans' apprehension was increased by the scope of our study. There had been many researchers before us, but practically all of them were interested in local situations; thus their interests did not usually transgress the localism of the leadership. But our study encompassed the whole Southwest region; it was bound to probe conditions in areas and localities beyond the expertise of local ethnic spokesmen. The very size of our undertaking placed us in a different category: If we failed to endorse the leaders' view of the minority's grievances, if we failed to pay sufficient attention to the emotional qualities and cultural traditions of the Mexican-American people, if quantitatively minded researchers would make mere numbers of the whole group, then public policies could be seriously misguided. All these fears were augmented by our definition of Mexican Americans as a national minority.

Though this reaction made our task more difficult, it indicated a healthy development. It demonstrated that Mexican Americans no longer perceived the Anglo establishment as immune to their attempts to influence the social environment. Meanwhile, their own spokesmen were beginning to recognize that the "national minority" definition would ease rather than aggravate the group's problems, no matter how distinctive some of these problems were. The concrete gains that would result from a joint classification with other disadvantaged national minorities were increasingly seen as more than offsetting a possible loss in collective status or in the prestige of some ethnic leaders.

A FORGOTTEN MINORITY

When our research got under way, the definition of Mexican Americans as a national minority was almost as novel to the larger society as it was to the minority itself. The general public has only recently become aware of the fact that the people of Mexican descent form a sizable and also a *permanent* part of our population, and this awareness has not penetrated deeply. School textbooks at both the secondary and college level tend to ignore them.[3] Because so many Americans have a limited knowledge of their country's history, they are only dimly conscious of the early colonization of parts of the Southwest by people of Hispanic-Mexican origin. Or, if they know about it, they are inclined to shrug it off as a quaint accident of history without consequence. Because the experience of Mexican Americans in this country never included outright slavery or any other extraordinary legal status, their problems have never weighed on the national conscience as have those of the Negroes or even of American Indians.

The Mexican-American minority could escape national attention for so many years because it was, and still is, largely confined to the Southwest region. Most of the population live in five states: California, Texas, New Mexico, Colorado, and Arizona. Among other things, this concentration meant that public policy affecting these people could be considered the exclusive concern of local governments. In the Southwest, where the larger society could not avoid being aware of the Mexican-American presence, interaction of the minority with the general population was impeded by historical conflict and continuing tension between the people of Mexican descent and the Anglos (all whites who are not of such descent).[4] The traditional isolation of Mexican Americans greatly limited their chances to learn about the society in which they lived.

The national news media in recent years have reported more news about this minority than ever before. But news media deal only with exciting events, and these events happened to involve fringe problems of the Mexican-American population: for example, Cesar Chavez' organization of farm-workers in the San Joaquin Valley of California, and Reies Tijerina's crusade to regain the land which the indigenous Spanish Americans of New Mexico claimed had been taken from them illegally. The news reports served to reinforce a false national image of Mexican Americans as a rural people with special complaints that are only loosely related to the main problems of our urban society.

Other popular media also have perpetuated clichés. One stereotype portrays the Mexican American as a villainous character inclined to banditry in the old days and other forms of criminality in more recent years. Another stereotype romanticizes him as a strong peasant with a sweet disposition and the mind of a child. The former image is familiar from Western movies and television serials, the latter appears in much belletristic literature. Anglo attitudes have long included both affection for these "exotic" people and rejection of them as a strange, Latin group. These stereotypes have been sources of great frustration to Mexican Americans, who sense the condescension and hostility.

Contrary to widespread impressions, a great deal has been written about Mexican Americans by social scientists. (Our bibliography lists about 1,500 items ranging from books to magazine articles and government publications). Much of the scholarly work is valuable. However, most of it is so local in scope that its impact on even the scholarly community has been limited. Moreover, many studies have focused on the rural Mexican American, or they were conducted in remote areas and urban ghettos where isolation allowed traditional culture traits to be preserved. These studies unwittingly helped to overemphasize the notion of a highly distinctive population. Many users of such research carelessly extended the notion of cultural uniqueness to the entire Mexican-American population regardless of differences in the social setting. Policy makers embraced this notion when it would help "explain" why American institutions failed to reach the population. Few investigations have related the experience of the Mexican-American people to the richly documented experience of other minorities in the United States.

There is no Mexican-American equivalent of Gunnar Myrdal's *An American Dilemma*. Although some Mexican-American scholars have written extensively about this group, none of their publications has had the scope, significance, and recognition of E. Franklin Frazier's *The Negro in the United States*.[5] A few publicists, notably Carey McWilliams, have tried to present a broad view of the Mexican-American minority to a wider audience, but because McWilliams' insightful work of the 1930s and 1940s was intended as a call for social action, it could be easily dismissed as "reform" literature.[6]

The Federal government has been slow to recognize Mexican Americans as a nationally significant minority. The U.S. Census in both 1950 and 1960 provided valuable data on Spanish-surname people living in the five Southwest states—a statistical classification closely approximating the Mexican Americans in the region. But "white-nonwhite" has remained the standard classification in the vast array of other government statistics and official studies which often are the foundation for social action. Much less attention is given to people of Mexican descent. Characteristically, an unofficial resumé of a five-volume report of the U.S. Commission on Civil Rights, published in 1962, deals only with Negroes and Puerto Ricans—reflecting the focus of the report itself.[7] When the Federal Equal Employment Opportunities Committee in late 1963 held its first regional meeting in Los Angeles, it was clear that many Washington officials in policy-making positions had their first real encounter with the problems of Mexican Americans. Only very recently did this condition change.[8]

In 1967, the Federal government sought to give Mexican Americans a measure of recognition by organizing the Cabinet Committee Hearings on Mexican American Affairs in El Paso, which were visited briefly by President Johnson.[9] But this was an anticlimax. The meeting fell short of the more prestigious White House Conference that Mexican-American leaders had been led to expect. Because it was held in El Paso to coincide with the ceremonial cession to Mexico of the small Chamizal territory, the meeting seemed once more to relegate the group to a provincial entity.

On our field tours we encountered indifference or complacency about Mexican Americans at most state and local government offices as well. In an interview held in 1964, during the Democratic primary, Governor John Connally of Texas assured one of the authors in elaborate detail that Mexican Americans were happy Texans and had few problems of consequence not well on the way to solution.[10] Although officials in other areas exhibited greater concern, reliable information to guide state and local government programs was uniformly scarce. When we tried to obtain data ranging from employment to schooling to mental health, we met with near-total failure. In the case of health statistics, it was an investigator for this study who persuaded the California Department of Health to tabulate its data in such a manner that the condition of Mexican Americans could be analyzed.[11]

DIVERSITY OF PEOPLE AND PLACES

Perhaps enough has been said to make the purpose of this book clear. Explicitly, it aims to depict factually and analytically the present realities of life for Mexican Americans in our society. These realities depend largely on the minority's interaction with the dominant system. Hence, much of our analysis will be concerned with interaction in various spheres of life. Our study focuses on *urban* Mexican Americans. Until World War II, a large percentage of Mexican Americans were rural people. Today most of them are in the cities.

From the beginning of the research, our strongest single impression of the Mexican-American people was their exceptional *diversity*. Our findings transform this impression into a certainty. As a collectivity, Mexican Americans are sharply differentiated from the general population on almost every socioeconomic measure. But this differentiation can easily obscure their internal diversity.

We shall point up the great genetic and cultural differences among Mexican Americans. We shall discuss the implications of the different lengths of time they have been in this country—from a few months or weeks in the case of immigrants who crossed the border recently to a lifetime in the case of those whose ancestors settled here in the sixteenth century. We shall furnish evidence of increasing differentiation by social class, though the majority of Mexican Americans are poor. We shall analyze how an evolving social class structure affects ethnic identity in this minority, as it did in others. We shall observe that a fairly large and apparently increasing number of Mexican Americans have attained a wider range of options in social relations with out-group or in-group people, in the preservation or abandonment of cultural traditions, and even in primary relations involving the choice of ethnic or Anglo spouses. In sum, their isolation from the general population is diminishing.

Our analysis emphasizes *change*. One of the major stereotypes of the group, held by minority and majority alike, asserts that Mexican Americans have been extraordinarily resistant to change. The facts do not support this notion. The persistence of social problems or culture traits does not imply the absence of change. The socioeconomic dynamics of the Mexican-American population are likely to be of greater long-run importance than the persistencies, especially if the trends toward change are used as a basis for action.

The *local milieus* for the Mexican Americans of the Southwest also show striking variations, even when one ignores the rural areas where the group still tends to be in a semicaste position. Some of the region's cities are relatively "good" places for this minority, while others score low. Whether one considers occupations, income, housing conditions, residential segregation, or other indicators of the minority's position relative to the majority, the local contrasts are exceedingly strong. It is as hazardous to derive conclusions about the status of Mexican Americans as a whole from their status in Brownsville, Texas as it is to generalize from their status in the San Francisco Bay area.

ASSIMILATIVE POTENTIALS

The range of options available to the Mexican-American individual, then, varies greatly from place to place. The increased freedom of choice is far more evident in Los Angeles than in San Antonio, the two cities in which we conducted intensive research. Generally, the local variations suggest that the progress of the group will depend to some considerable extent on the speed with which the local institutions of the larger society provide Mexican Americans with access to opportunities. Some collective progress has also been achieved through internal migration to California, which offers this group the most favorable social and economic environment in the Southwest. Progress has usually been greater in the large metropolitan areas than in the smaller cities and towns.

Our evidence of the assimilative trends of the Mexican-American population is mixed—and not only because of the enormous local differences in their socio-economic standing relative to Anglos. Any study of a large group of people in a complex society will reveal ambiguities, and this is no exception. Thus, we shall discover considerable social interaction of Mexican Americans with Anglos. It is usually the greatest among the younger generation, the more well-to-do, and those who live in mixed urban neighborhoods. But we shall also see evidence of slow integration. For example, the extent to which Mexican Americans have maintained the use of their mother tongue is without contemporary parallel in the United States. And the aliens among them show a very low rate of naturalization.

Perhaps the most striking ambiguities relate to the family. On the one hand, the Mexican-American family of today is no longer a bulwark of tradition, with rigid roles and rules of behavior assigned to father, mother, and male and female children. On the other hand, the typically large size of the family is still one of the outstanding characteristics of this population. And to compound the difficulty of interpretation, our 1965–1966 surveys in Los Angeles and San Antonio revealed far greater acceptance of contraceptive devices than one would expect from an at least nominally Catholic group.

An overall appraisal of assimilative potentials must take account of the relatively recent appearance of a sizable Mexican-American population in the United States. The experience of this group cannot be compared with that of other immigrant populations which have had much more time to improve and consolidate their

9

positions. The first large wave of immigration from Mexico occurred in the 1920s. Whatever gains the newcomers could achieve in the era of prosperity were wiped out during the Great Depression. In a massive repatriation organized by hard-pressed public and private welfare agencies, many of them were forced at that time to go back "home." The next large influx of immigrants came in the 1950s and the 1960s. These people have had relatively little time to achieve material advances and to pass them along to the younger generation or to transform their style of life.

Even the indigenous "Spanish Americans" of the Southwest can be viewed as a relatively recent immigrant group when *social* rather than legal status is used as a criterion. Most of these people, especially in New Mexico and southern Colorado, lived in such geographic and social isolation that they began to move into modern America only after World War II. The experience of Mexican Americans, then, must be seen in the light of a comparatively short period of interaction with the larger society.

To discover yet another ethnic group that is showing signs of assimilation would be nothing out of the ordinary if it were not for the widespread belief that Mexican Americans were "unassimilable"—forever alien to the American way of life—and predestined for low social status. The general experience of immigrant populations in the United States was rarely if ever projected to this minority. The insistence of some Mexican-American spokesmen on the cultural distinctiveness of the group served to reinforce the majority's view that such projection would be unrealistic. On the whole, *our findings suggest that these stubborn notions are in need of revision.*

*　　*　　*

This book draws on a great variety of research materials. These include an extensive analysis of census data, both published and unpublished; household sample surveys of Mexican Americans in Los Angeles and San Antonio made especially for our study; numerous informal interviews with both Mexican Americans and Anglos throughout the Southwest; and the authors' direct observations of local conditions on field tours. We have made extensive use of the literature on the Mexican-American population, including a large number of unpublished theses and dissertations as well as the more accessible books, journal articles, and government publications. Additional materials are derived from the eleven Advance Reports issued by the Mexican-American Study Project, which are listed in the Preface, and from other extensive monographs written by our collaborators. Much of this vast research material is presented here in condensed form.

Our book also reflects the mixture of human resources drawn into the Mexican-American Study Project. The interdisciplinary approach of the study meant the involvement of scholars in various academic departments. The inter-ethnic character of our topic meant the involvement of Mexican Americans as well as Anglos in the research work. The Mexican Americans who participated included Ralph C. Guzman, one of the three senior authors (and the only professional member of the staff giving his full time to the study for about three years). They included consultants, the authors of an Advance Report, research assistants, and the large number of interviewers for the household surveys. Formal acknowledgements are made in the Preface. However, the most significant collaboration in the research work occurred between Mr. Guzman and the other authors. It provided an extraordinarily useful system of internal "checks and balances." Through a process of mutual education we saved one another from misinterpretations reflecting either a purely "outside" or a wholly "inside" view of Mexican-American life and attitudes. The results of this process permeate much of this volume.

NOTES TO CHAPTER ONE

1. Joan W. Moore, "Political and Ethical Problems in a Large-scale Study of a Minority Population," in Gideon Sjoberg (ed.), *Ethics, Politics, and Social Research* (Cambridge, Mass.: Schenkman Publishing Company, Inc., 1967), p. 225. This is a more extensive account of our experience during the first year of our project in researching the Mexican-American minority.

2. *Ibid.*, p. 242.

3. This was true in the 1960s, according to one study of secondary school texts, and must have been even more the case in earlier decades. See Lloyd Marcus, *The Treatment of Minorities in Secondary Textbooks* (New York: Anti-Defamation League of B'nai B'rith, 1961), pp. 55, 56. No systematic analysis of college textbooks was undertaken, but an examination of about a dozen in wide use shows very little on Mexican Americans. This deficiency is currently being remedied at least in the college literature.

4. As Lyle Saunders has pointed out, the Anglo as viewed by Mexican Americans is a "residual category" that includes anyone who is not identifiable as Spanish-speaking or Indian. See Lyle Saunders, *Cultural Differences and Medical Care* (New York: Russell Sage Foundation, 1954), p. 249. In the broadest sense, the term "Anglos" denotes for Mexican Americans "others." Depending on time, place, and other contexts, "Anglos" may include nonwhites as well as whites. However, since the Anglo is usually identified with the dominant society by Mexican Americans, it seems best to limit the term to whites. This definition has the additional advantage of consistency with our later use of "Anglo" for statistical purposes. Throughout this book, data for "Anglos" denotes whites other than Spanish-surname persons.

5. Gunnar Myrdal, *An American Dilemma: The Negro Problem and Modern Democracy* (New York: Harper & Row, Publishers, Inc., 1962), originally published in 1944; E. Franklin Frazier, *The Negro in the United States* (New York: The Macmillan Company, 1949).

6. Carey McWilliams, *Factories in the Field* (Boston: Little, Brown and Company, 1934); *Ill Fares the Land: Migrants and Migratory Labor in the United States* (Boston: Little, Brown and Company, 1942); "The Forgotten Mexican," in *Brothers Under the Skin*, (Boston: Little, Brown and Company, 1944); and *North from Mexico: The Spanish-speaking People of the United States* (New York: J. B. Lippincott Company, 1949). Other works, presumably designed for a wider audience, include George I. Sanchez, *Forgotten People: A Study of New Mexicans* (Albuquerque, N. Mex.: University of New Mexico Press, 1940);

and Ruth D. Tuck, *Not With the Fist: Mexican-Americans in a Southwest City* (New York: Harcourt, Brace & Company, Inc., 1956).

7. Wallace Mendelson, *Discrimination* (Englewood Cliffs, N.J.: Prentice-Hall, Inc., 1962).

8. For example, the U.S. Civil Service Commission has published data on the employment of Mexican Americans in the Federal government. These data are presented in Chapter 9. Federal government agencies have also published an increasing number of analytical articles about the Mexican-American population. Cf. Raymond F. Clapp, "Spanish-Americans of the Southwest," *Welfare in Review*, IV (January, 1966), pp. 1–12, based on government data; *Low-income Families in the Spanish-surname Population of the Southwest*, Agricultural Economic Report no. 112, U.S. Department of Agriculture, Economic Research Service (1967).

9. *The Mexican American: A New Focus on Opportunity*, testimony presented in the Cabinet Committee hearings on Mexican American Affairs, El Paso, Tex., Oct. 26–28, 1967. Inter-Agency Committee on Mexican American Affairs, Washington, D.C.

10. Moore, *op cit.*, p. 229.

11. See A. Taher Moustafa, M.D., and Gertrud Weiss, M.D., *Health Status and Practices of Mexican Americans* (Mexican-American Study Project, Advance Report 11, Graduate School of Business Administration, University of California, Los Angeles, Feb., 1968), chap. III.

TWO

A Preview of Socioeconomic Conditions

As a group, Mexican Americans in the Southwest are highly differentiated from the dominant society on nearly every yardstick of social and economic position. A profile of their main demographic characteristics, such as age, family size, fertility, and the incidence of broken families reveals large variations from the Anglo "norms." Their educational attainment shows an especially notable gap. Associated with this gap is an unfavorable occupational structure and a low average income. Their housing conditions reflect not only poor earnings but the pressures resulting from extremely large families.

A comprehensive analysis of these and related subjects is presented in Part Three. The following pages summarize that section.

CHARACTERISTICS OF THE POPULATION

Mexican Americans are a significant part of the population in the United States. On the basis of U.S. Census of Population data on Spanish-surname persons for the Southwest, we estimate the 1960 population nationally at 3,842,000. Our projection for 1970 is about 5,600,000.

Chart 2–1.
Size of Selected Disadvantaged Minority Groups in the United States, 1960

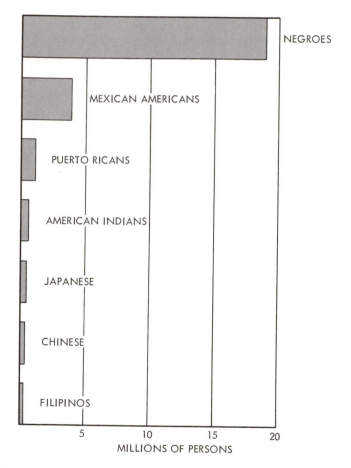

Source: *1960 U.S. Census of Population*, vol. I, part I, table 44; PC(2)–ID, table 1; and Appendix A in this volume.

Among the more visible and usually also disadvantaged minorities in the United States, Mexican Americans are the second largest group (Chart 2–1). Puerto Ricans received much attention after the sudden rush of migration after World

14

War II. But in comparison with Mexican Americans the Puerto Rican population on the mainland is quite small. The 1960 census counted 893,000 persons of Puerto Rican birth or parentage. Even the whole of Puerto Rico itself had only 2,350,000 people. Whether one thinks of American Indians (nearly 524,000 in 1960), Japanese Americans (464,000), or Chinese Americans (237,000), each of these minorities is but a small fraction of the Mexican-American population. Of course, the 18.9 million Negroes in the United States in 1960 outnumbered Mexican Americans almost five to one, but, as will be seen, the numerical relationship is quite different in the Southwest.[1]

Mexican Americans in the United States represent the largest concentration of people of Latin-American descent in the world outside of Latin America itself. In 1960, they equalled about 11 percent of the population of the Mexican Republic. The vast majority of Mexican Americans live in the five states designated here as the Southwest: Arizona, California, Colorado, New Mexico, and Texas. In 1960, about 87 percent of the estimated total resided in this region, which held only 16 percent of the entire United States population.

Within the Southwest, the vast majority of Mexican Americans live in the two biggest states, California and Texas. Each of these accounted for over 1.4 million of the nearly 3.5 million Spanish-surname persons recorded by the census in 1960.* Together, California and Texas held 82 percent of the population, and the three remaining states, Arizona, Colorado, and New Mexico, only 621,000, or 18 percent. The Los Angeles metropolitan area alone had slightly more Mexican Americans than the three small states combined. All this means that the future of Mexican Americans depends very largely on their progress in California and Texas—and, as will be seen, conditions for progress differ greatly in these two states.

Among the population characteristics shown in Table 2-1, one stands out in sharp relief: the number of Spanish-surname people in the Southwest is growing very rapidly. Between 1950 and 1960 it increased by 51 percent as against 37 percent for Anglos and 49 percent for nonwhites. Although immigration from Mexico has contributed to this growth, natural population increase has been a far more important factor—as is suggested by the extraordinary fertility of Spanish-name women. Representing 12 percent of the Southwest population in 1960, Mexican Americans now undoubtedly account for a still larger proportion of the total. Nonwhites were only 9 percent of the total in 1960. Despite the influx of Negroes to California from other parts of the nation, nonwhites probably are still less numerous in the Southwest than the Mexican Americans. And the nonwhites of the Southwest are a far more heterogeneous population than those in most other areas of the United States. They include American Indians (especially in Arizona and New Mexico) and Orientals (in California) as well as Negroes. Only in Texas can nonwhite be equated with

---

[1]Notes for this chapter start on page 33.

*The subsequent analysis draws on the census data for "white persons of Spanish surname." As shown in Appendix A, these data can be accepted as a fair equivalent for Mexican Americans. Hence, we use the terms *Spanish-surname* and *Mexican American* interchangeably.

Negro. Some of the comparisons in later chapters will show separate data for major components of the nonwhite population in the region.

Related to the high birth rate implied in the fertility data is the comparative youth of the Spanish-surname population—a median age of 20 years in 1960 as compared to 30 years for Anglos and 24 years for nonwhites. Children under 15 accounted for over 40 percent of this group but only 30 percent of the Anglos. The

Table 2–1. Major Population Characteristics, Southwest, 1960

Item	Anglo[a]	Spanish-surname	Non-white	Reference[b]
Percent of total population	79	12	9	Table 6–1
Population growth 1950–60, percent	37	51	49	Chart 6–1
Percent in urban areas	81	79	80	Table 6–6
Median age	30	20	24	Chart 6–6
Percent of children under 15	30	42	37	Chapter 6
Dependency ratio[c]				Chart 6–8
Total dependent	85	121	98	
Dependent young	68	112	87	
Dependent aged	17	9	11	
Incidence of broken families				
Percent other than husband-wife[d]	10	16	22	Table 6–10
Same, age of household head 35–44	9	14	20	
Percent separated and divorced women	7	8	15	Table 6–11
Same, age 35–44	7	9	18	
Index numbers of fertility rates				
(Anglo rates = 100)				
Fertility ratio[e]	100	156	135	Table 6–12
Children per 1,000 women,[f] urban				
Women age 25–34	100	144	115	
Women age 35–44	100	172	112	

[a] Anglo is defined statistically throughout this volume as white other than Spanish-surname.
[b] References show the detailed tables, charts or other materials that present these data in later chapters. The same guides are included in other summary tables in this chapter.
[c] Combined number of persons under 20 and 65 or over, related to the population 20 to 64 years of age.
[d] Families with female heads or "other male" heads as a percent of all families.
[e] Number of children under 5 divided by the number of women aged 15–49, multiplied by 1,000.
[f] Children ever born per 1,000 women ever married.

1,500,000 Spanish-surname children represented almost 16 percent of all children in the Southwest. This over-representation suggests a high rate of future population growth. It underscores the special impact of the minority on school systems as well as the importance of constructive measures to deal with the education of Mexican-American youth. The large number of children also accounts for an unusually high dependency ratio among Mexican Americans.

In one important respect, however, the Mexican-American people are no longer highly differentiated from the rest of the population: *They are about as urbanized as Anglos or nonwhites.* Approximately four-fifths of each of the three population segments in the Southwest were living in cities and towns in 1960. Interestingly, a trace of the previous Mexican-American orientation to rural life is still found in the fact that the occupations of Spanish-surname persons are less highly urbanized than their domicile. A relatively large number of those who live in cities have agricultural jobs, using their urban residence as a base for migratory work.

After our observations on the low median age of Mexican Americans, their great number of children, and the high fertility of their women, the prevalence of large families comes as no surprise (Chart 2–2). The detailed data will indicate that the size differences between Spanish-surname families and the reference populations exist in urban as well as in rural areas. In fact, except for Negroes in some parts of the South and American Indians (who are more concentrated in rural areas) it is difficult to find any substantial, identifiable group of people in the United States who match or approximate the typical family size of the Mexican-American population.

Chart 2–2.
Average Number of Persons in the Family, Southwest, 1960

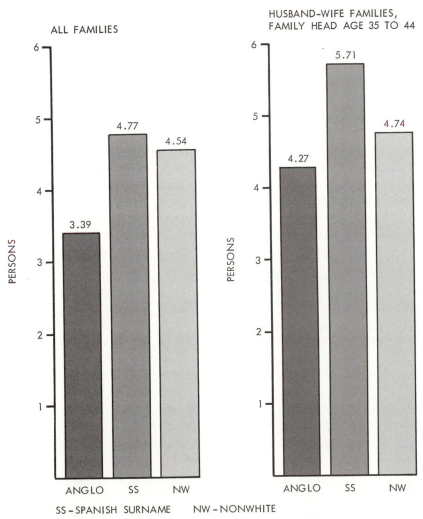

Source: Table 6–8.

17

Although the findings on family size validate a common notion, those on family stability do not—at least if one starts from the impression that the Mexican-American family represents a strong bulwark of traditional stability. The incidence of broken families exceeds the Anglo incidence by a substantial margin, and the percent of women separated or divorced from their spouses is somewhat larger than among the Anglo population. However, family instability of this kind is far more frequent in the nonwhite group. Moreover, the statistical indicators of family instability among Mexican Americans must be interpreted with caution, as will become apparent in the full analysis.

DIFFERENCES IN EDUCATIONAL
AND ECONOMIC STATUS

The Spanish-surname people in the Southwest rank low in formal education by comparison not only with Anglos but also with nonwhites (Table 2–2). *Mexican Americans 14 years and over in 1960 averaged about four years less schooling than Anglos and one and a half years less than nonwhites.* The incidence of functional illiteracy (0–4 years of school) was seven times the Anglo and nearly twice the nonwhite rate. Only 13 percent of the Spanish-surname persons had four years of high school as against 28 percent of Anglos and 19 percent of nonwhites. Less than 6 percent of the Mexican Americans had some college education—half the nonwhite and a quarter of the Anglo rate.

The record is not altogether bleak. The younger Mexican Americans show a somewhat better relative attainment than the adults. Nevertheless, the education

Table 2–2. The Schooling Gap, Southwest, 1960

Item	Anglo	Spanish-surname	Non-white	Reference
Median school years completed by persons				
14 years and over	12.0	8.1	9.7	Table 7–1
14–24	11.3	9.2	10.6	a
25 and over	12.1	7.1	9.0	Table 7–5
Difference from Anglo schooling, years				
Age 14 and over	—	3.9	2.3	
Age 14–24	—	2.1	0.7	
Age 25 and over	—	5.0	3.1	
Years of schooling completed by persons				
14 years and over[b]				Table 7–1
0–4	3.7%	27.6%	15.1%	
5–8	22.1	33.8	29.8	
9–11	24.3	20.1	24.7	
12	27.8	12.8	18.7	
Some college[c]	22.1	5.6	11.7	

[a] *1960 U.S. Census of Population*, vol. I, parts 4, 6, 7, 33, and 45, tables 47 and 103; PC(2)–1B, tables 3 and 7.
[b] Percent of each group completing their schooling at specified level (number of years of schooling).
[c] Includes complete college education (4 years or more) as well as one to three years of college.

gap remains so large that it will continue for some considerable time to impede the social mobility of Mexican Americans. In addition to the quantitative gap revealed by census statistics, one must take account of differences in the quality of education: Many schools in urban slums as well as rural areas are substandard.

According to various measures of income, Spanish-surname median earnings in 1959 were 57 to 66 percent of Anglo earnings but above nonwhite income levels (Table 2–3). The relationship between Mexican-American and nonwhite income is the reverse of their educational attainment, which is another way of saying that the same amount of schooling has paid off better for Mexican Americans than for nonwhites, especially Negroes. Obviously, education is only one of the factors accounting for the relative income status of minorities.

For the individuals in the labor force, the income gap between Mexican Americans (or nonwhites) and Anglos of comparable age was greater than the gap in family income. But the most startling differential appears in the median income per person in the family. On this yardstick, *Mexican Americans had only 47 cents for every dollar of Anglo income, and they were worse off than nonwhites.* That the educational gap explains only part of the income gap is shown directly when the median

Table 2–3. The Economic Gap, 1960

Item	Anglo	Spanish-surname	Non-white	Reference
Index numbers (Anglo = 100)				
Median family income				Table 8–1
Southwest	100	65	56	
Urban Southwest	100	66	59	
Median income per person				
in family, Southwest	100	47	51	Table 8–3
Median income of males[a]				Table 8–4
Southwest	100	57	51[b]	
Urban Southwest	100	61	53[b]	
Median income adjusted for schooling				Table 8–9
Males in California[a]	100	88	72	
Males in Texas[a]	100	72	56	
Labor-force participation rate, urban,[c] percent				Table 9–1
Males in Southwest	80.0%	78.0%	78.0%	
Females in Southwest	36.0	31.0	46.0	
Unemployment rate, urban, percent				Chapter 9
Males in Southwest	4.5	8.5	9.1	
Females in Southwest	5.0	9.5	8.1	
Occupational structure of males, urban Southwest				
Percent white collar	47.0	19.0	18.0	Table 9–3
Percent low-skill manual	26.0	57.0	60.0	Table 9–4
Overall occupational position (index: Anglo = 100)	100	84	82	Chapter 9
Housing condition in metropolitan areas				
Percent overcrowded units	8%	35%	22%	Chart 11–1
Percent substandard units[d]	7	30	27	Table 11–2

[a] Adjusted for age differentials among the three population groups. All income figures pertain to 1959.
[b] Negro.
[c] Percent of persons 14 years and older in labor force.
[d] Deteriorating and dilapidated units.

19

incomes of Mexican Americans and Anglos are adjusted for schooling. The residual income difference that is not attributable to schooling amounted to 12 percent in California and 28 percent in Texas. The detailed data will show that *income differentials tend to widen as educational attainment increases.*[2]

Mexican Americans bear a heavy share of poverty in the Southwest (Chart 2–3). In 1960, about 35 percent of the Spanish-surname families fell below the poverty line of $3,000, as against less than 16 percent of the Anglo and almost 42 percent of the nonwhite families. The incidence of poverty among the two minorities was disproportionate, but the number of poor Anglo families exceeded the combined total of poor Spanish-surname and nonwhite families two-to-one. Minority status is but one of the many factors contributing to poverty.

THE POSITION OF MEXICAN AMERICANS
IN LABOR MARKETS

The poor income of Mexican Americans reflects a highly differentiated position in labor markets. The labor force participation rate for Mexican-American males in the urban Southwest was somewhat lower than for Anglos, but their unemployment in 1960 was nearly twice the Anglo rate. The same pattern holds for nonwhites. These two phenomena are probably interrelated. Members of the minority groups may withdraw from the work force when they find their opportunities for employment to be discouragingly slim. The percent of Spanish-surname females in the labor force is small relative to Anglos and especially relative to nonwhites, with whom they share generally low income status. The relatively low proportion of working women probably reflects cultural traditions and the typically large number of children in the Mexican-American family requiring care and attention. Domestic service, long so frequent among Negro females, has only recently come to be a growing type of employment for Mexican Americans.

But a more strategic differential appears in the occupational structure. In 1960, only 19 percent of the Spanish-surname males in urban areas were in white-collar occupations as against 47 percent for Anglos. On the other hand, 57 percent of the Mexican Americans and only 26 percent of the Anglos were employed in low-skill manual work. The ranks of urban Spanish-surname men at the low end of the occupational hierarchy are swelled by an unusually high proportion of agricultural workers, reflecting the relatively large number of migratory farm laborers having an urban domicile.

An over-all occupational index for urban males shows a 16 percent gap between the minority and the majority. This gap is smaller than the comparable income difference of 39 percent for urban males. In other words, the income experience of Mexican Americans has been far less favorable than their occupational experience. Thus, their relatively poor occupational standing does not explain fully their low

Chart 2–3.
Poor Families in Various Population Groups in the Southwest, 1960

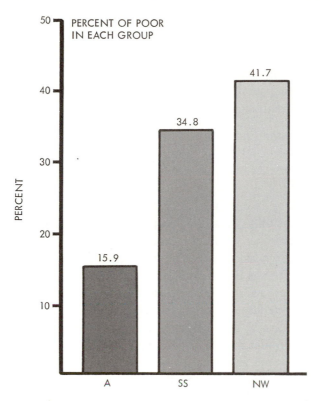

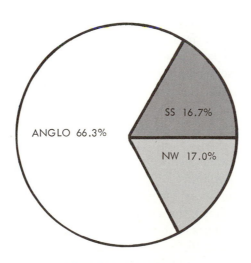

POOR IN EACH GROUP
AS PERCENT OF ALL POOR

Source: Table 8–11.

21

earning status. When education, occupation and income—the most important status indicators[3]—are arrayed in terms of differentials, even the simple figures used here exhibit the inconsistency illustrated as follows for Mexican-American males in the urban Southwest:

	Percent of Anglo
Median school years completed	64
Occupational position index	84
Median income	61

The relative schooling and income positions are broadly consistent, confirming the general though not invariable relationship between the level of education and earning capacity. Neither of these status measures, however, is consistent with the occupational index.

This discrepancy is mainly explained by the fact that the broad occupational classifications do not fully reveal the low position of the Spanish-surname group in labor markets. According to special census tabulations obtained for this study, Mexican Americans tend to hold inferior jobs within nearly each major occupational group; and their earnings in the same occupations and the same job classifications within occupations are usually smaller than those of Anglos.

After testing a variety of hypotheses related to inferior jobs or lower earnings in comparable job classes, our analysis draws a number of conclusions bearing on the presence of discrimination. Mexican Americans are disproportionately employed in low-wage or marginal firms. Firms which offer high or standard wages tend to reject job applicants from this group either because of their ethnicity or because the applicants are unable to meet job qualification standards—usually educational standards. Thus, *the employee selection process shunts disproportionate numbers of Mexican-American job seekers to businesses in highly competitive industries, to nonunion employers, and to small firms.* These three types of employers (which overlap to a considerable extent) pay typically lower wages and offer less security of employment. The standards of schooling for job qualification operate against all undereducated job applicants, whether they are Anglos or members of minority groups. But since the minorities are over-represented among the poorly educated in terms of both the quality and the quantity of schooling, they bear the brunt of these selection procedures.

Educational requirements for nonmanual employment may have a rational basis in the assumption that job performance in most cases is related to the level of education. This proposition is much more dubious in the case of manual jobs where the amount of schooling is not a clear predictor of work performance.[4] On the whole, the discriminatory effects of the allocation system are more severe in Texas than in California. Throughout the Southwest region they seem to operate against Mexican Americans in lesser degree than against Negroes.[5]

Finally, our findings point to the impact of low income on at least one aspect of consumption: housing (Table 2-3). *The percent of Mexican Americans living in*

22

overcrowded and in substandard housing units exceeds not only the Anglo share, as one would expect, but also the nonwhite share. Here, a strategic determinant seems to be the income per person in the family rather than the total family income. The full analysis will reveal that the higher incidence of poor housing among Mexican Americans extends over the whole range of incomes shown by the census. Budgetary constraints on the quantity and quality of housing, associated with the preponderance of large families, operate quite generally in this minority.

What the low earnings of most Mexican Americans mean in terms of other consumption items must be left to the reader's insight. As for their health status, the highly inadequate data for a few areas show perceptibly greater neonatal and infant death rates—always a telling indicator of depressed economic conditions. Likewise, pneumonia and tuberculosis seem to be more frequent than in the general population. But there is no evidence that Mexican Americans suffer from a higher incidence of total illness or from a greater prevalence of chronic disease.[6]

ON THE MEANING OF "DISADVANTAGE"

All in all, then, one can characterize the Mexican-American population as a large "disadvantaged group"—the term so widely adopted in recent public discussion. We have already used this term and shall refer to it again. Yet, one can legitimately ask whether this is more than a slogan or a convenient catch phrase. The meaning of "disadvantage" is not self-evident. Disadvantaged by whom and by what? The following few pages represent a modest attempt to clarify this question.

The case of disadvantage is relatively clear when *individuals* are considered. Thus, a child who through an accident or illness is physically handicapped—with a loss, say, of a limb or eyesight—or who is mentally retarded is disadvantaged in comparison with others. More effort and unusual resources will be required to compensate for the handicap. In many such cases, equalization of the afflicted person's educational and economic opportunities or even of his chances for a normal social life will be impossible, but it may at least be approximated. Likewise, if the accident of birth has placed the child in a poor or broken family, even without physical or mental handicaps, his opportunities are more limited in comparison with others; again, it will take more effort and special means to overcome the barriers inherent in such a condition. The life stories of many people attest to the fact that this can be done; poverty or other adverse elements in the home and community environment may indeed act as a spur to achievement for some individuals and as a roadblock for others—for reasons still little understood. Further, individual abilities vary a great deal even with equal "inputs" of schooling, home environment, and other identifiable factors.

When one proceeds to groups of people, the problem becomes more complex. No matter how one divides a nation's population, he finds departures from the national norm (which may either be a statistical average of one or more socioeconomic characteristics or some goal-oriented value imputed by the observer or analyst). Thus, people in regions endowed with poor natural resources have generally lower incomes than those in other regions of the country. The farm population was long believed to be more healthy than the city dwellers, although this notion has been questioned by recent studies. Or, to take an unchallenged example, the residents of rural areas generally have fewer years of formal schooling than urban residents.

A growing array of Federal policies attests to our society's acceptance of government action on behalf of segments of the population believed to be handicapped. Thus, Federal farm-support programs are at least in part based on the idea of parity (of prices for farmers' products and for nonagricultural goods purchased by farmers), which can be interpreted as an effort to narrow disadvantage.* Likewise, national policy has moved in the direction of special aids to underdeveloped areas, as in the case of the Appalachian region—with the objective of narrowing regional differences in economic growth and therefore in the opportunities available to people in the areas. The problems of the aged as a group have been increasingly recognized in public programs ranging from tax benefits to medical care and housing. The poor versus the non-poor has become another recent division of groups of people for policy purposes, and the notion of "disadvantage" has clearly emerged in this case.

It is at the point of intersection between low economic status and minority status that the problem of designating an ethnic or racial group as "disadvantaged" can be perceived most clearly. As was shown, Mexican Americans bear a disproportionate share of poverty. Knowledge has not progressed to the point where the causes of poverty can be determined by assigning weights to cultural values, home environment, historical antecedents, inhibiting factors in the larger society, and possible genetic differences. Some analysts stress the importance of subcultures and, in extreme cases, define "disadvantage" in cultural terms,[7] whereas others emphasize other variables. Nor is it necessary for the identification of a group as "disadvantaged" to quantify the causes of subordinate standing in regard to defined socioeconomic characteristics. It seems sufficient to accept two broad generalizations.

One of these is the proposition that individual capability is a social product as well as the result of other factors. Human ability has a better chance to develop when it is recognized, encouraged, and fostered by society. It has a greater chance to advance to the individual's potential capacity (whatever his aptitude may be) when the social as well as the home environment affords adequate opportunities for doing so.[8] The other proposition involves the difference between individual achievement potential and actual achievement. Many persons achieve less than they are capable of accomplishing, and, here again, the gap between potential and actual accomplishment is a social product as well as the result of other factors.

A category of people, then, can be defined as disadvantaged if society at large has acted by omission or commission to hinder a disproportionate number of its members in the development of their individual abilities. As will be seen throughout this book,

---

*We are here concerned with the existence of national policies, not necessarily with their effectiveness. In the case of farm-support programs, both the effectiveness and the equitable distribution of Federal moneys among poor farmers and well-to-do farmers have been questioned.

there is ample evidence that American society has indeed acted in such fashion with regard to Mexican Americans. So formulated, the notion of disadvantage does not necessarily imply the ultimate achievement of "parity." The point is that removing societal obstructions to the attainment of a more equal position by the minority would help individuals in the group to achievement more commensurate with their capacity, and that the standing of the group as a whole would thereby be improved. The process can be accelerated if the larger society offers compensatory opportunities in education and other parts of the system—for example, small school classes in slum areas or tutorial programs for college students drawn from minority populations. Whether or not such measures will produce parity, and in what respects, only the future can tell. Because individual abilities are unevenly distributed and because of differences in values and traditions, over-representations and under-representations of groups of people in various measures of achievement may persist even after impediments external to individuals or groups have disappeared.[9]

Nor is there any logical or operational reason why parity should be considered an upper limit for a group's achievement any more than it is for an individual. The achievement of a minority may well exceed the norm, or it may be superior on some norms while falling short on others. Thus, Japanese Americans in California showed a somewhat better educational attainment in 1960 than did Anglos (in terms of the number of school years completed), but their median income was lower.[10] The notion of "disadvantage" does not imply a goal of proportionate representation of any population group on any single or aggregate measure of achievement.

Our definition of *disadvantage* is perhaps best conceptualized in terms of statistical distributions—the kinds of distributions underlying the group averages often shown in this book as a matter of convenient shorthand expression. The accompanying chart presents a wholly hypothetical illustration (Chart 2–4). Position 1 shows how members of the majority and of a minority are distributed in terms of an abstract or composite measure of achievement at a given moment of time. Position 2 shows the distributions at a later period, on two assumptions: (*a*) the achievement norms represented by the majority population have advanced (as they did in the past on such criteria as schooling, occupations, and real income), and (*b*) the minority's achievement distributions have improved more than *pari passu* as societal impediments were removed. Since achievement seems to be a function of many factors, Position 2 indicates a remaining gap between the norm and the minority performance which may or may not be closed with the further passage of time.

Using the same abstract measure of achievement for persons in the minority and in the majority implies a general norm. However, actual achievement goals may vary between segments of the population, depending in large part on people's perception of their opportunities. For example, differences in achievement goals are often associated with differences in social-class status. Likewise, members of a minority may not accept the ideas of accomplishment prevalent in the larger society, or, more accurately, a larger proportion of the minority may reject or modify these ideas. To what extent achievement goals of Mexican Americans differ from the norm will be discussed in Chapter 14.

In terms of our illustration, a disparity in achievement goals will be merely one of the factors contributing to the remaining distribution differentials between the majority and the minority in Position 2, but it may reflect individual preferences as well as variations in the perception of opportunities. For example, significant

Chart 2–4.
Hypothetical Illustration of Achievement Distributions of Persons in Different Population Groups

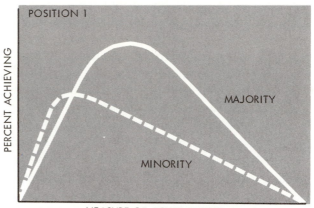

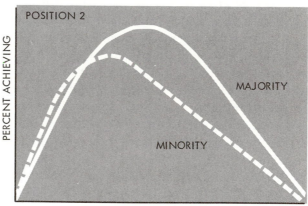

numbers of people in a group may obtain more gratification from leisure or from having large families than is the norm. As a consequence, their earnings or their income per person in the family will be lower (other things being equal); and the lower income may affect adversely the educational opportunities of their children. However, these are matters of choice rather than of economic deprivation. One of the pertinent questions for research, as well as for social action, is the *basis* for choice—

whether decisions are made with reasonable knowledge of available alternatives or because of ignorance, demoralization, or tradition.

STATUS IMPROVEMENTS OVER TIME

The foregoing discussion is directly related to the question of progress. Has the minority's disadvantage become greater or smaller with the passage of time? Has the position of Mexican Americans improved relative to that of Anglos? It would be rewarding if one could answer these questions with reference to a long period, say, several decades. Unfortunately, consistent census classifications of the Spanish-surname population exist only for 1950 and 1960. Status comparisons must therefore be limited to these years (Table 2–4). Because of statistical difficulties, they are also limited to a few selected status indicators. And one can only speculate about progress since 1960.

Table 2–4. Changes in Educational and Economic Position, 1950–1960

Item	Anglo	Spanish-surname	Non-white	Reference
Median years of school completed[a]				
Increase 1950–1960	0.8	1.7	1.2	Table 7–5
Difference from Anglo schooling, 1950	—	5.9	3.5	
Difference, 1960	—	5.0	3.1	
Percent increase in median income[b]				Table 8–6
Southwest, 1949–1959	57	69	70	
Urban Southwest, 1949–1959	56	67	59	
Occupational position index, urban males				
(Anglo = 100)				Table 9–7
California, 1950	100	81	78	
California, 1960	100	84	82	
Texas, 1950	100	74	60	
Texas, 1960	100	77	66	
Percent of home ownership[c]				Table 11–4
Urban Southwest, 1950	56	45	41	
Metropolitan Southwest, 1960	62	53	43	

[a] Persons age 25 and over (males and females combined).
[b] Males and females combined. Adjustments for age and sex composition do not change the results significantly.
[c] The available data force us to compare metropolitan-area data for 1960 with urban-area data for 1950. However, the resulting inaccuracy should be relatively small.

The educational gap between Mexican-American and Anglo adults was slightly narrowed between 1950 and 1960. The median income of Mexican-American individuals in the Southwest rose at a substantially higher rate than that of Anglos. There was also some moderate upgrading in their occupations, as indicated in the occupational position indexes for both California and Texas.

Home ownership increased more among the Mexican-American than among the Anglo population (and much more than among nonwhites). This increase is significant because the extent of home ownership is a measure of the opportunity structure of minority groups: It rests on the availability of mortgage credit, and it denotes the adoption of a national norm. Besides, owner-occupied units tend to provide housing of better quality and with more space. Limited data suggest that the 1960 Spanish-surname rate of home ownership was about identical with the Anglo rate for comparable income and age groups. On other yardsticks of housing standards, however, Mexican Americans seemed to have made no progress relative to Anglos.

The 1950–1960 advances in the educational and economic standing of Mexican Americans in the Southwest are partly attributable to migration to California from the remaining four states, especially from Texas. For example, the share of Southwest Mexican-American income earners who lived in California increased from 43 percent in 1949 to about 49 percent in 1959. The increase for all income earners was smaller—from about 54 percent to 56 percent. On practically all status measures California ranked highest in absolute terms and lowest in terms of differences between the minority and the majority. On most, Texas ranked lowest. *Thus, the shift of the Spanish-surname population toward California of itself produced or accelerated region-wide improvements in the population's relative position.*

Migration and population data attest to the magnitude of these shifts. Nearly 60 percent of the Mexican-American interstate movers between 1955 and 1960 went to California, although the state accounted for only one-third of the Spanish-name people in 1950 and two-fifths in 1960. Of those coming to the United States from Mexico, 63 percent went to California. In contrast, only 17 percent of the interstate movers and 26 percent of those migrating from Mexico went to Texas, which accounted for 45 percent of the Southwest Spanish-surname population in 1950 and only 41 percent in 1960. The three smaller states have attracted relatively few movers from other states or from Mexico. The shift to California is one of long duration. Only a little over 17 percent of first- and second-generation Mexican Americans lived in that state in 1920, but this share had increased to 40 percent by 1960 and is now likely to be still greater. In contrast, 55 percent of this population segment resided in Texas in 1920, and only 38 percent in 1960.

In conclusion, the relative status of Mexican Americans in the Southwest as a whole has improved, though at a slow rate. The gap between the minority and the majority has certainly not widened, as some observers maintain in regard to other minorities. That there has been progress is all the more remarkable in view of the relatively large volume of Mexican immigration in the decade of the 1950s, when over 293,000 persons sought permanent residence. Since most of the immigrants are under-educated and unskilled, at least by United States standards, they tend to keep the achievement averages for the Spanish-surname group down.

How much progress has occurred since 1960 is a matter of speculation. However, one can say with a fair degree of assurance that some of the factors that contributed to relative gains of the Mexican-American group in the 1950s have continued into the present decade: the shift to California, an increased share of natives in the total ethnic population, the better educational preparation of the younger members of the group, and the related improvement in the occupational structure. The closing of the border to *braceros* at the end of 1964 reduced labor-market competition that affected Mexican Americans with particular force. This will continue to benefit the group provided that illegal entries and the movement of Mexicans who commute to work in the United States are reasonably well controlled. The Great Society programs should also have helped to accelerate progress, but it is too early at this writing to express any judgments on their effects.

NATIVES AND IMMIGRANTS

We now turn from broad aggregations of people and places to strategic kinds of differentiation. One of the most conspicuous of these variations is native-born versus foreign-born Mexican Americans. At the same time, the economic standing of these groups provides insight into another dimension of progress: intergenerational gains, which can be seen in the position of different nativity classes at the same date (1960). In both respects, the analytical potential is enriched by the fact that the census shows statistics for three nativity classes, or generations: natives of native parentage, natives of foreign or mixed parentage, and the foreign born.

Table 2–5. Selected Characteristics of Spanish-surname Persons, by Nativity Status, Southwest, 1960

Item	NNP[a]	NFP[a]	FB[a]	Reference
Percent of Spanish-surname population				Table 6–2
Southwest	55	30	15	
New Mexico	87	9	4	
California	46	34	20	
Median age, Southwest	13	24	43	Chart 6–12
Median school years completed, 14 years and over				Table 7–4
Male	8.6	8.6	4.5	
Female	8.8	8.4	5.0	
Median income of urban males age 35–44[b]	100	105	83	Table 8–7
Occupational status of urban males age 35–44, percent[c]				Table 9–9
White-collar occupations	23	20	15	
Craft occupations	22	25	19	
Low-skill manual occupations	46	53	62	

[a] NNP = Native born of native parentage; NFP = Native born of foreign parentage; FB = foreign born.
[b] Indexes (natives of native parentage = 100).
[c] Because of an unusually large percentage of "occupation not reported" among natives of native parentage, the figures for this group may not be strictly comparable with the data for the two other groups.

The foreign born, or first generation immigrants, accounted for only 15 percent of the Spanish-surname population in 1960. However, the *foreign stock*, which includes the native born of foreign or mixed parentage (the second generation) as well, totaled 45 percent (Chart 2–5). In contrast, the foreign-stock portion of the entire Southwest population was only 19 percent and a little over 15 percent in the balance of the United States.[11] Here, then, is a group with an uncommonly large admixture of immigrants and their children. This admixture varies greatly from state to state, with New Mexico showing the lowest percentage of foreign stock and California the highest (Table 2–5).

The three nativity classes differ greatly in age composition, with an astonishingly low median of 13 years for *natives of natives* as against 43 years for the *foreign born* in 1960. These large age differences must be taken into account when the economic status of the three groups is compared. The economic indicators in Table 2–5 are therefore limited to males in one age class.

Chart 2–5.
Spanish-Surname Population in the Southwest, by Nativity, 1960
(Nativity groups as a percent of total)

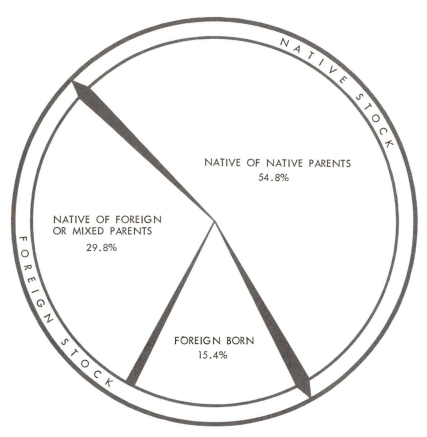

NATIVE STOCK

NATIVE OF NATIVE PARENTS
54.8%

NATIVE OF FOREIGN
OR MIXED PARENTS
29.8%

FOREIGN STOCK

FOREIGN BORN
15.4%

Source: Table 6–2.

In both education and economic condition, the natives, regardless of parentage, are far better off than the foreign born. Their schooling period was nearly twice as long as that of the foreign born. Their incomes were substantially higher, and they were better represented in the better-paid white-collar and craft occupations. However, status differences between *the two groups of native born* were relatively small and not always in favor of the natives of native parentage. The latter had a slight edge over second-generation immigrants in education and in white-collar work, but the reverse was true for income and for representation in craft occupations. The only item in the table that conforms to the notion of continuous progression from the first to the third and succeeding generations is the percent of each group in low-skill manual occupations. These data, as well as others in the more detailed analysis, suggest that *the significant contrast in economic standing is between the natives and the foreign born, while native parentage seems to convey few if any additional benefits.*

Why this is so is a matter of conjecture. One can hypothesize that the income-producing capacity of people is greatly influenced by basic values, such as attitudes toward work versus leisure or non-work attainments, and that these values do not differ substantially among native Mexican Americans regardless of whether their parents were born in the United States or in Mexico. Also, discriminatory practices in labor markets and the application of educational resources may not draw the rather fine distinction between natives of natives and those of foreign parentage.

CONTRASTS BETWEEN AREAS

Another important differentiation in the condition of Mexican Americans in the Southwest relates to local variations. In the next chapter, we shall discuss the region as the main locus of contacts between the minority and the dominant society, point up the sharp differences in environments found within the Southwest, and show how these differences bear on the position that Mexican Americans have been able to attain in various areas. The point to be made here can be summed up in the following proposition: Minority status, at least for the Spanish-surname group, is characterized not only by pervasive differentiation from the majority but also by large and disproportionate area variations in its condition relative to the status of Anglo Americans. Texas and California, or Fresno and San Francisco (both in the same state), may be different worlds for everybody, only more so for the people of Mexican descent. Demographic and economic aspects of the difference are high-lighted in Table 2–6, and other, more subtle aspects are analyzed in various parts of this book.

For one thing, the Mexican Americans of the Southwest are very unevenly distributed relative to Anglos (and, it may be added, relative to nonwhites). In New Mexico, where it was once the numerical majority, the Spanish-name group even as late as 1960 accounted for 28 percent of the state's total population. In adjoining Colorado, its share was only 9 percent, the same as in California. The Mexican-American population was nearly 15 percent of the total both in Arizona and Texas. The range is far greater for metropolitan areas: between 80 percent of the total population in Laredo and 1 percent in Tyler, both in Texas. Laredo is at the Mexican border, but its proximity to the border may not be so important as the fact that this metropolitan complex is in the lower Rio Grande Valley, whereas Tyler is located in east Texas. A very large proportion of the Mexican-American population of Texas is concentrated in the southern part of the state, which is relatively underdeveloped; low incomes prevail generally, schools are of poor quality, and the region offers few prospects for occupational upgrading and larger earnings. This concentration affects the relative position of the Spanish-surname group in Texas as a whole.

Likewise, Mexican Americans have long been concentrated in the southern part of Colorado and the northern part of New Mexico. These are depressed areas similar to the Appalachian region. Hence, the economic condition of Mexican

Table 2–6. Maximum State and Local Variations in Selected Characteristics, 1960

Item and Area[a]	Anglo	Spanish-surname	Reference
Percent of total population[b]			
New Mexico	64	28	Table 6–1
Colorado	88	9	
California	83	9	
Laredo, Texas	20	80	Chart 6–5
Tyler, Texas	72	1	
Median years of school completed, persons 25 years and over			
California	12.2	8.6	Table 7–5
Texas	11.5	4.8	
Colorado Springs	12.4	10.1	Table 7–8
Lubbock, Texas	12.1	3.1	
Index of median family income (Anglo = 100)			
California	100	79	Table 8–1
Texas	100	52	
San Antonio	100	59	Chapter 8
San Diego	100	84	
Housing conditions			Census of Housing
Percent of overcrowded units			
Lubbock	12	72	
San Francisco–Oakland	5	16	
Percent of substandard units			
Lubbock	10	56	
San Francisco–Oakland	6	14	

[a] Variations for metropolitan areas are based on the number of such areas for which relevant data are available from the 1960 census.
[b] Percentages of the two population groups do not add up to 100, because nonwhites are omitted.

Americans in the two states reflects their location in underdeveloped subregions. In contrast, Mexican Americans in California are more evenly distributed over the state. In fact, they are under-represented in the less developed northern and mountainous areas of California.

Second, the extremes shown in the table highlight the great state and local differences in relative schooling and economic standing. The schooling gap between Spanish-surname and Anglo adults in 1960 was 6.7 years in Texas but only 3.6 years in California. The gap was 9 years in Lubbock, where Spanish-surname adults had 3.1 years of schooling (which is generally considered to fall within the range of "functional illiteracy"), and the gap was only 2.3 years in Colorado Springs. For every dollar of Anglo median family income in the same area, Mexican Americans earned only 52 cents in Texas but 79 cents in California; only 59 cents in the San Antonio metropolis as against 84 cents in San Diego (which, despite the proximity of the Mexican border, showed the highest ratio).

Even greater contrasts are found in housing conditions. The incidence of overcrowding in the Spanish-surname group was three times the Anglo incidence in the San Francisco–Oakland metropolitan area but six times in Lubbock, Texas. The incidence of substandard housing units varied almost as much. Likewise, housing segregation differed greatly between individual cities (Chapter 12). The index of residential dissimilarity of Mexican Americans from Anglos ranged from a low of 30 in Sacramento, California to a high of 76 in Odessa, Texas. In each of the 35 Southwest cities analyzed, however, they were living in less segregated housing than were Negroes. This fact is significant not only in itself but also because the degree of residential segregation is an indicator of the general status of a minority in American society.

Enormous inter-area differences in the relative status of Mexican Americans have persisted despite the substantial internal migrations of Spanish-surname people within the Southwest, notably to California. Since California provides a comparatively good milieu, this movement should tend to narrow the area variations. As was mentioned, there is reason to believe that it contributed importantly to the improvement of conditions between 1950 and 1960. Yet, the role of migration should not obscure the fact that, for many years to come, the collective progress of Mexican Americans will depend on the broadening of their opportunities *throughout the Southwest*, and especially in those areas where their position is the poorest.

NOTES TO CHAPTER TWO

1. The figures for Negroes, Japanese, Chinese, and Filipinos are for all living generations, persons of mixed ancestry being classed by the census according to the race of the nonwhite parent, and mixtures of nonwhite races according to ancestry by father. Puerto Ricans on the mainland include two generations only (those born in Puerto Rico and children of persons born in Puerto Rico). American Indians counted by the census are those living on reservations or remaining on tribal or agency rolls (at least one-quarter Indian). Consequently, their number is understated, but this does not materially affect their numerical relationship to Mexican Americans.

2. This finding corresponds to similar observations for nonwhites or Negroes. Cf., among others, Rashi Fein, *An Economic and Social Profile of the Negro American*, Reprint 110 (Washington: The Brookings Institution, 1966), pp. 833–835, and Herman P. Miller, *Rich Man–Poor Man* (New York: Thomas Y. Crowell Company, 1964), p. 155.

3. In the preparation of this chapter we have given considerable thought to the computation of a simple summary measure of the socioeconomic position of Mexican Americans relative to the two reference populations. It would indeed be very desirable to present some kind of index that would express the differential condition of a population in a meaningful total fashion, in lieu of the disparate measures of educational, income, occupational, and similar differences. Such an index has been devised by sociologists and statisticians using

original field data in the form of a socioeconomic status (SES) score, and this method was for the first time applied by the U.S. Bureau of the Census to some of its data for 1960. See U.S. Bureau of the Census, *Methodology and Scores of Socioeconomic Status*, Working Paper no. 15 (1963), and *Socioeconomic Characteristics of the Population: 1960*, Series P-23, no. 12, July 31, 1964. The SES score combines measures of occupation, education, and income. The Bureau of the Census has also computed measures of status consistency among the three components of the SES score.

Upon study and some experimentation with the application of SES scores to our data, we decided to refrain from this type of presentation. For one thing, the method lends itself mainly to summary measures based on records for *individuals*. Thus, the census analysis of 1960 socioeconomic characteristics is derived from its One-in-a-Thousand Sample, and not from its regular statistics on population groups and areas. If the present study had been limited to that sample, its scope would have been severely restricted; among other things, no data could have been provided for the Southwest reference populations, and most of the detailed classifications by income, education, and other such measures would have included too few persons of Spanish surname to produce reliable results. Further, scores of this type may inject a degree of arbitrariness when relatively small populations are compared with very large populations and the dispersion of items to be measured differs greatly between the two.

We believe that our summary measures of relative position are easily comprehensible and provide some notion of the degree of consistency in the relative standing of Mexican Americans with regard to education, occupation, and income.

4. The hypothesis that there is a direct and systematic relationship between amount of schooling and work performance has even been questioned for white-collar jobs. See S. M. Miller, "Credentialism and the Education System," paper read before the American Orthopsychiatric Association, Washington, D.C., March 23, 1967

5. See Walter Fogel, *Mexican Americans in Southwest Labor Markets* (Mexican-American Study Project, Advance Report 10, Graduate School of Business Administration, University of California, Los Angeles, Oct., 1967), chap. 9.

6. See A. Taher Moustafa, M.D., and Gertrud Weiss, M.D., *Health Status and Practices of Mexican Americans* (Mexican-American Study Project, Advance Report 11, Graduate School of Business Administration, University of California, Los Angeles, Feb., 1968).

7. For example, Jerome Himmelhoch, "Delinquency and Opportunity: An End and a Beginning of Theory," in Alvin W. Gouldner and S. M. Miller (eds.), *Applied Sociology: Opportunities and Problems* (New York: The Free Press, 1965). More generally, the "culture of poverty" has become a widely used term since the appearance of the writings of Oscar Lewis.

8. See Moshe Sinilansky, "Fighting Deprivation in the Promised Land," *Saturday Review*, XLIX (Oct. 15, 1966), pp. 82, 85, 86, and 91. The article deals with experimental programs in Israel to cope with the educational problems of children of non-European origin in a Western-style system of universal education.

9. For a more extended discussion of this point, see Fein, *op. cit.*, p. 819. The paper was originally published in *Daedalus*, XCIV (Fall, 1965), pp. 815, 846. This is a time-lag analysis seeking to determine, among other things, at which periods a current position of Negroes equalled a previous position of whites. There are insufficient data for Mexican Americans to make such long-run comparisons.

10. Walter Fogel, *Education and Income of Mexican Americans in the Southwest* (Mexican-American Study Project, Advance Report 1, Graduate School of Business Administration, University of California, Los Angeles, Nov., 1965), table 5.

11. Total population: *1960 U.S. Census of Population*, vol. I, table 9. Total foreign stock: *Ibid.*, table 110.

Part two

HISTORICAL PERSPECTIVE

INTRODUCTORY NOTE

The history and nature of its early experience in the United States is important for any ethnic population and particularly important for Mexican Americans. This is a minority that was native to the Southwest long before the region became part of the United States. The demographic, economic, and political displacement of Mexicans since the middle of the nineteenth century may be without parallel in American history. The borderland remained an arena of conflict between Mexicans and Anglos many decades after the new boundaries were established. This unusual history has left its mark on mutual attitudes and perceptions among the minority and the majority.

Under these circumstances, one might be tempted to write a comprehensive history of Mexican Americans in the Southwest as a basis for understanding their present condition. But such an undertaking is beyond the scope of this volume. Instead, the following three chapters focus on three historical forces especially pertinent to the current situation. Whereas the standard historical works tend to concentrate on the early history of Hispanic-Mexican settlement, we shall deal mainly with developments after the incorporation of the Southwest in the United States.

One might be tempted also to describe the society from which the immigrants came, i.e., examine the Mexican background in some detail. To do justice to this subject, however, would require considerable resources beyond our command. *Many Mexicos*, the title of a book by Lesley Byrd Simpson, is an apt description of the problem. Moreover, few data are available on the geographic or social origin of Mexican immigrants, and most of them are out of date. Thus, which of the "many Mexicos" are represented by the immigrants of various periods is not at all clear.

One of the historical forces in American society that have greatly influenced the condition of Mexican Americans is the general milieu of the Southwest and its changes over time (Chapter 3). The region's mixture of population, its economic development, and its political systems show special features that have affected Mexicans in many ways. Despite great intra-regional diversity, these features distinguish the Southwest sharply from the Eastern environment, in which most of the European immigrant groups of an earlier era settled. For example, the presence of American Indians and Orientals in parts of the Southwest places racial issues in an almost unique framework. Because of the importance of farming and mining in the early economic growth of the region, Mexican Americans were placed in jobs and locales offering minimum contact with the larger community. The long history of conflict and tension between Mexicans and Anglos added to the distinctiveness of the Southwest milieu.

The second historical force discussed in this group of chapters is immigration from Mexico (Chapter 4). Not only does immigration account for much of the rapid growth of the Mexican-American population in the Southwest, but it shows some distinctive characteristics in comparison with the more familiar mass movements from Europe. Among other things, the migrations from Mexico have posed acute problems of control that continue to this day. The historical conflict between open-door and restrictionist sentiments (and economic interests) is compounded by the dictates of the Good Neighbor Policy. The manner in which public policy has accommodated itself to these problems over the years offers interesting insights into the changing balance of political and economic power in the Southwest.

Conflicting interests bear on an unusual range of movements from Mexico. These movements include not just regular immigrants for permanent residence but the commuters to work, the legally admitted temporary laborers, and the illegal border crossers. The potential migration from Mexico is so great that these issues will remain alive for some time to come. Only one of them was settled when the *bracero* program came to an end in 1964.

Third, we analyze the historical patterns of work and settlement of Mexican immigrants. These patterns had far-reaching effects on the assimilative opportunities available to the minority group (Chapter 5). On the whole, his work and settlement patterns tended to isolate the Mexican American from the larger society. The immigrants were concentrated in rural areas or isolated towns. More often than not their jobs were seasonal and migratory. Many of these people moved from place to place in ethnically homogeneous groups of family units or of male labor gangs. In contrast, the European immigrants in the late nineteenth and early twentieth centuries typically entered American society in cities and in industrial occupations. This initial experience afforded more contact with the larger system, better economic prospects, greater opportunities for labor organization, more regular schooling for their children, and easier access to political institutions.

The three main themes discussed here do not pre-empt our historical background materials. Thus, today's social class structure of Mexican Americans cannot be fully understood without reference to its antecedents in Colonial times and after Anglo domination. The role of churches among Mexican Americans has important historical dimensions that affect significantly the present functioning of both the Catholic Church and some Protestant denominations for this minority group. The history of Mexican-American contacts with governmental authority casts its shadow on the development of political interaction. These and other more particularized facets of history will be analyzed in later parts of this book.

THREE

The Milieu of the Southwest

Nearly all interaction between Mexican Americans and American society has taken place in the Southwest. The vast majority of people of Mexican descent have always been located principally in Texas, New Mexico, Arizona, and California, which border on Mexico, and in Colorado. Although these are highly diverse states ranging from poor to rich, from the heavily populated to the sparsely settled, and from a benign to an inhospitable climate, they are linked by the historical presence of Mexicans.[1]

The milieu of the Southwest has had an important influence on the relations between the minority and the larger society. Hence, this chapter presents a historical sketch of this region, its demographic and economic features, and the contrasts between the component states. It provides an account of past interactions between Mexicans and Anglos and of characteristics of the five states which are judged to be particularly salient for the present conditions of contact between the minority and majority.[2] Thus, this is a highly selective history.[3]

[1] Notes for this chapter start on page 55.

The historical sections of this chapter were developed from materials prepared by Paul Fisher, Burton M. Moore, and Samuel J. Surace.

EVOLUTION OF THE BORDER

The Mexican Americans, or a highly significant segment of them, have a position in American history that is almost unique among the minorities in this country. They had been native to the area for some centuries before its occupation by the United States, and had become politically subordinate to her as boundaries changed. According to the definition given to such a status by the Hugheses, the Mexicans living in what became part of the United States after the mid-nineteenth century can be characterized as a "charter member minority."[4]

Most of the Southwest was acquired from Mexico in the middle of the nineteenth century. But relationships between Mexicans and Anglos in this shifting border territory anteceded its incorporation into the United States. From the beginning the interaction between the two groups was characterized by strife. Conflict began with the adjoining Spanish possessions before the Louisiana Purchase and continued sporadically until a boundary settlement was made in 1821. By that year only a few Anglos had pushed beyond a boundary line that excluded most of modern Texas.

When Mexico achieved its independence from Spain in 1821, Stephen Austin received permission to establish colonies in east Texas. Thereafter, tens of thousands of Anglos were admitted as peaceful settlers in this outpost of Mexico. Before long Americans outnumbered Mexicans by more than five to one, and conflict followed promptly. An abortive attempt to seize control of Texas in 1826 led Mexico to prohibit further colonization by Anglos. Armed conflict reached a climax in the successful Texas Revolution of 1836. Nine years of tension and sporadic guerilla warfare followed, and Texas was always threatened by the possibility of Mexican reconquest. The struggle led to the annexation of Texas by the United States in 1845 and the outbreak of the Mexican War. Border disputes continued long after the Treaty of Guadalupe Hidalgo in 1848, for this peace treaty, like the earlier formal agreements, was merely an ineffective stopgap in a continuing history of conflict. Everyday life in what is now Texas was anything but peaceful. Political and diplomatic conflict was converted to group clashes between the conquerors and the conquered.[5]

The Texas rebellion, the Treaty of Guadalupe Hidalgo, and the Gadsden Purchase of 1853 all resulted in significant shifts of the border. But both northern Mexico and the new American Southwest were areas remote from centers of government, and the settlements were remote from each other. The lines of Spanish settlement were almost entirely south-to-north, following rivers and mountain passes through the wilderness. One line extended through El Paso to the substantial settlements of northern New Mexico and southern Colorado,[6] another led through a now unimportant Rio Grande River town to the frontier regions of east Texas, another worked up to Tucson, and the last thrust into California. There was almost no communication or passage from east to west until the Gold Rush of 1848. In effect, the 1853 border defined little more than cartographic lines as designated by the Treaties. The territory continued to be in large part a wilderness. The borderland was an arena of hostilities, with neither government in full control. Indians, Mexicans, as well as Americans conducted raids on both sides. In some cases, after the new border had been formalized, these raids took on the character of international incidents. Organized border penetrations by military units as well were quite frequent, and as late as 1879 they produced a crisis which threatened open warfare between the two countries.[7] The most recent well-known crisis was occasioned by Pancho Villa's raids, to which the United States responded with the expeditionary force led by General Pershing in 1916.[8]

In recent years the bloodshed has all but disappeared, while the social, political and cultural relations have become more intricate. The term "border" designates a complex geographic reality. Along more than half of its length, the border cuts through nearly impassable and uninhabited terrain, such as the terrifying Sonora desert and bleak mountain ranges. In Texas, the border is the Rio Grande River, which, as McWilliams observed, brings the people of both countries together in the river towns and cities rather than separating them, especially in the fertile area south of Laredo. But north and west of Laredo, the Rio Grande runs through a vast desolate landscape, with El Paso the only really important gateway between the two nations in that section.

Most of the border has presented a major geographic barrier. Except for the two states at the extreme east (Tamaulipas and Nuevo Leon), the Mexican side of the border is sparsely populated, with densities of less than ten persons per kilometer in 1965.[9] Highways and railroads provide tenuous links.

In recent decades, as immigration from Mexico became more restricted, the border acquired a new look. Would-be immigrants crowded into the cities on the Mexican side, which burgeoned as Mexican "twins" of usually much smaller American towns. Here, in places like Matamores, Juarez, and Tijuana, the border area serves a kind of "Ellis Island" function, with people waiting to enter the United States. Unlike the brief stay at Ellis Island, however, this wait is often prolonged for years. These cities have supplied the so-called "commuters"—workers for the American cities and fields a few miles away. The sojourn at the border provides an experience of anticipatory socialization for many who ultimately become immigrants to the United States. While they are waiting for their papers, Mexicans are exposed to American tourists, American jobs, American officials who work with Mexican officials, and, in some cases, American schools. Mexican and American capital alike is being invested in enterprises in these border towns.

Viewed as a social passageway between Mexico and the United States, the border has always presented a complex and often ambiguous character. Because of its geographic and ecological diversity, the border's passage function has been highly variable. Crossing is physically easy in some places but extremely hazardous in others. The extended Ellis Island function of the border cities adds to the complexity. The passage function is also varied from a formal point of view. There are many ways in which a Mexican can enter the United States legally or illegally for work and permanent residence. Also, large numbers of Mexican nationals and American citizens, some of Mexican descent, cross the border for shopping, business, and sightseeing. This great variety of movements across the border is detailed in the next chapter.

PATTERNS OF SETTLEMENT
IN THE AMERICAN SOUTHWEST

The sparseness of settlement in Mexico's northern states has been matched on the American side. All five Southwest states have been thinly populated through most of their history. Even as late as 1900, generations after their acquisition by the United States, these areas had a population density well below the national average (Table 3–1).

Table 3–1. Population Growth of the Five Southwest States
and Balance of the United States, 1900–1960

Area	POPULATION (THOUSANDS)		PERCENT INCREASE,	POPULATION RANK*a*		POPULATION PER SQUARE MILE	
	1900	1960	1900–1960	1900	1960	1900	1960
Southwest	5,392	29,304	443	—	—	7.1	38.6
Arizona	123	1,302	959	46	35	1.1	11.5
California	1,485	15,717	958	12	2	9.5	100.4
Colorado	540	1,754	225	32	22	5.2	16.9
New Mexico	195	951	338	44	37	1.6	7.8
Texas	3,049	9,580	214	5	6	11.6	36.5
Balance of U.S.	70,602	149,160	111	—	—	25.4	53.8

a Rank among 48 states.
Source: *1960 U.S. Census of Population,* vol. I, part 1, tables 9, 10, and 12; *Statistical Abstract of the United States, 1960,* table 9.

Unlike the states of northern Mexico, however, the Southwest experienced rapid growth in the twentieth century. Between 1900 and 1960, while the total United States population doubled, the Southwest states grew fourfold, and their share of the nation's population increased from 7 percent to 16 percent. Even so, the average density remained relatively low: The five states encompass 21 percent of the land of the continental United States.

Urbanization in the Southwest also outpaced the rest of the country. In 1900, its population was more rural (70 percent compared with 60 percent elsewhere). By 1960 its urban share had increased to 71 percent compared with 61 percent in the rest of the nation.[10] In general, then, the Mexican-American population of the twentieth century was caught up in the momentum of an exceedingly rapid rate of growth and of urbanization.

These broad developments have been quite uneven in the region. Thus, it was California's growth that accounted for more than half (60 percent) of the total population increase in all five states between 1900 and 1960. But the other four states also grew at a rate faster than the rest of the nation. Population density is now far more variable in the region, partly as a result of the growth disparities. The density in California is almost twice the national norm, whereas New Mexico, with fewer than eight persons per square mile in 1960, is reminiscent of the Southwest as a whole in 1900. Interstate differences in urbanization, too, have been enormous. In 1900, the populations of California and Colorado were about half urban compared with only about 15 percent of those in the remaining three states. By 1930 contrasts in urbanization were still very great, ranging between 25 percent in New Mexico and 73 percent in California. After World War II, the state differentials narrowed, and by 1960 the range was from two thirds in New Mexico to 86 percent in California.

The consequences for Mexican Americans of these patterns of settlement and their changes in the twentieth century can only be surmised. In all probability, the sparse settlement and weak linkages of these settlements in the early part of this century meant a high degree of isolation. Further, there were no compelling economic or political reasons for Mexican Americans to become involved with the larger system. Nor did the ecology of the region tend to push the poorer segments of the population into the mainstream of regional life.

THE REGION'S INHABITANTS

The people already living in the Southwest and those who came to settle differ in many respects from the population of the rest of the country.[11] The most significant difference for this analysis is the historical primacy of Mexicans. Although the majority of today's Mexican Americans are descendants of twentieth-century immigrants, there had been Mexicans throughout what are now the five Southwest states from far earlier times.

Mexicans Before the Twentieth Century

When Anglos first began to colonize Texas in 1821, Spanish or Mexican settlers were estimated to number some 4,000.[12] Anglos outnumbered Mexicans five to one by the time of the Texas Revolution, and by 1850, two years after the end of the Mexican War, when the United States census began to count Texans, its total population had reached 212,000.[13] Texas was the only area in the Southwest where Anglos vastly outnumbered Mexicans even before Mexico lost control of the territory.

New Mexico and southern Colorado represented the most successful of the Spanish and Mexican settlements. The United States census counted some 61,000 residents there shortly after the Treaty of Guadalupe Hidalgo of 1848. Some of these were Anglos, although a large majority were Hispano-Mexican. Furthermore, New Mexico remained predominantly Hispano-Mexican for a hundred years.

By contrast, Arizona was the least successful of Mexico's colonies, with perhaps less than 2,000 inhabitants[14] even after the Gadsden Purchase had extended the boundary south of the thriving city of Tucson (pop. 1,000). By 1870, when the census first counted people in Arizona, the population totaled 9,000 exclusive of Indians.[15] By 1880, as the Indians were gradually brought under control, the population increased to 40,000. By 1890, there were 88,000 persons, including Indians, in the Territory. By then, both the Santa Fe and the Southern Pacific railroads were crossing Arizona. Here it did not take many Anglos to outnumber the Mexicans, who were at that time also outnumbered (and intimidated) by the resident Indians. Arizona was still very much empty frontier country for a generation after its occupation by the United States.

California represents the greatest extreme in demographic discontinuity between the Mexican and Anglo periods, especially in the northern sector. There were perhaps 7,500 Mexicans in all of California at the time of the American takeover. The gold rush, however, sent almost 85,000 Americans into northern California in just one year—the year of the '49ers. Mexicans, both old *californios* and new immigrants to the mines from Sonora, became a numerical minority, and an even smaller one in the succeeding ten years. In southern California, a similar influx occurred much later—in the 1870s and 1880s, when the railroad made the area more accessible. The Mexicans were suddenly outnumbered ten to one in a series of land booms which attracted people from the East.

Thus, Mexicans came to be outnumbered at different times and in different fashion in the five states. In Texas, it happened during the 1820s and 1830s, when the area was still under Mexican rule. In Arizona, Mexicans were outnumbered shortly after the American takeover (although there were so few indigenous Mexicans that such reckoning is almost meaningless). In northern California, the change came with dramatic suddenness almost immediately after annexation. In southern California the population shift waited thirty years, but happened then just as abruptly. In New Mexico, only after a hundred years did Anglos outnumber the Mexicans.

Other Minorities

The Southwest states had another indigenous population: the *American Indians*. Only in coastal California and parts of New Mexico were the Indians of little hindrance and indeed an aid to the settlement of the area. In other parts of New Mexico and in Texas and Colorado the original Spanish settlements were continuously harassed by Indian attacks, and after 1848 Anglo administrators inherited the problems of the Mexicans.[16] In Arizona the Indians were so threatening that it took a full-scale war to subdue them. This was not achieved until 1886.[17] The presence of the Indians and their reputation for treachery and savagery probably had notable effects on the Anglo view of Mexicans.* A conviction that Mexican immigrants in general were "Indians in physique, temperament, character, and mentality" is reflected in public documents spanning several decades in the nineteenth and twentieth centuries.[18] The view was reflected in public debates about immigration from Mexico and in the fact that California crime reports classified Indian and Mexican arrests in a common category.[19] Whether the identification of Mexican with Indian was as complete as these reports suggest or was more of an argument by analogy—in that both had been "defeated right here in the United States"[20]—the presence of both Mexicans and Indians in the area before the influx of Anglo settlers probably had adverse implications for later Mexican arrivals.

The economic development of the Southwest also brought a succession of *non-European foreigners.* Chinese, Japanese, Filipinos, Indians from Asia, and Negroes as well as Mexicans came to fill the demand for low-wage labor. Not many European immigrants were available for such work. Most Europeans who did come to the Southwest had already lived elsewhere in the United States and acquired greater skills.

The Southwest had a more diversified and substantial non-European population (both indigenous and "imported") than any other part of the United States. And this meant a different cast to race relations than elsewhere in the United States. On the formal level, many states enacted elaborate laws designed to restrict the economic and social opportunities of one or another racially distinctive group. Special taxes, manipulation of land ownership, miscegenation statutes, and, most recently, the evacuation of the Japanese from the West Coast during World War II marked a history of racist legislation or administration spanning more than a century.[21] This kind of sentiment actually delayed by about ten years the admission of Arizona and New Mexico to statehood. Senator Albert Beveridge, the chairman of the strategic Senate Committee on Territories, argued that people in those areas were not sufficiently American in their habits and customs, and that the states were not equal in resources or population to other states in the Union.[22] Formal actions were matched by informal practices designed to minimize the social impact of the influx of badly needed non-European labor.

In more recent years, the nonwhite population of the Southwest, outside of Texas, included an increasing proportion of Negroes. Only in Texas was it always possible to equate "nonwhite" with "Negro" (Table 3–2), and Negroes still formed a higher proportion of the nonwhites of Texas in 1960 than of those in the other Southwest states. In Arizona and New Mexico, American Indians still predominated in the nonwhite group in 1960. Colorado showed the lowest proportion of nonwhites of any of the five states, and most of those have always been Negroes. California's pattern is different in every respect. Before World War II, Orientals were by far the largest nonwhite group. The growth of the Negro population, which dates back to the wartime demand for labor, accelerated so rapidly that by 1960 there were 255

*This section dealing with the implications of the presence of American Indians in the area draws on a manuscript prepared by Samuel J. Surace.

Negroes for every 100 Orientals, a ratio nearly the reverse of the 1930 figures. Despite this growth of the Negro population, the Southwest as a whole still had a substantially smaller proportion of Negroes in 1960 than the balance of the United States, and the same was true for the proportion of *all* nonwhites. It is the diversity of the nonwhite population rather than its size that has characterized these states to date.

Table 3–2. Nonwhite Population as a Percent of Total Population, Southwest and Balance of United States, 1910–1960

	1910	1920	1930	1940	1950	1960
Southwest						
Nonwhite	11.6	10.2	9.2	8.8	8.7	9.3
Negro	9.6	8.3	7.2	7.0	7.1	7.4
Indian	0.9	0.8	0.7	0.7	0.6	0.6
Oriental	1.1	1.2	1.3	1.1	1.0	1.3
Arizona						
Nonwhite	16.1	12.8	13.1	14.5	12.7	10.2
Negro	1.0	2.4	2.5	3.0	3.5	3.3
Indian	14.3	9.9	10.0	11.0	8.8	6.4
Oriental	0.8	0.5	0.6	0.5	0.4	0.4
California						
Nonwhite	5.0	4.7	4.7	4.5	6.3	8.0
Negro	0.9	1.1	1.4	1.8	4.4	5.6
Indian	0.7	0.5	0.3	0.3	0.2	0.2
Oriental	3.4	3.1	3.0	2.4	1.8	2.2
Colorado						
Nonwhite	2.0	1.7	1.6	1.5	2.1	3.0
Negro	1.4	1.2	1.1	1.1	1.5	2.3
Indian	0.2	0.1	0.1	0.1	0.1	0.2
Oriental	0.3	0.3	0.4	0.3	0.5	0.5
New Mexico						
Nonwhite	6.9	7.1	7.6	7.4	7.5	7.9
Negro	0.5	1.6	0.7	0.9	1.2	1.8
Indian	6.3	5.4	6.8	6.5	6.2	5.9
Oriental	0.2	0.1	0.1	0.1	0.1	0.2
Texas						
Nonwhite	17.8	16.0	14.7	14.5	12.8	12.6
Negro	17.7	15.9	14.7	14.4	12.7	12.4
Indian	0.0	0.0	0.0	0.0	0.0	0.1
Oriental	0.0	0.0	0.0	0.0	0.1	0.1
Balance of U.S.*a*						
Nonwhite	11.1	10.3	10.3	10.4	10.7	11.6
Negro	10.8	10.1	10.0	10.1	10.5	11.2
Indian	0.2	0.2	0.2	0.2	0.2	0.2
Oriental	0.1	0.1	0.1	0.1	0.1	0.2

a Does not include Alaska and Hawaii.
Source: *1960 U.S. Census of Population,* vol. I, parts 4, 6, 7, 33, and 45, table 15; vol. I, part 1, table 44.

The Anglos

Throughout much of this century the Southwest was distinctive because the white population was more heavily native born than the rest of the United States except the South (Table 3–3). Texas and New Mexico were the most "native," Texas following the Southern pattern in this regard as well as on other scores. New Mexico is a special case because the natives included large numbers of Spanish-American descendants of the original settlers. California was more cosmopolitan than most other parts of the region, and Arizona's and Colorado's historically low proportions of native-born inhabitants reflect the foreign workers drawn into the development of the states' natural resources.

Even the smaller proportion of foreign stock had a larger share of Anglo-Saxon, or Old Immigrants, and their children than the rest of the United States (Table 3–4). The only substantial number of immigrants from southern Europe were the Italians; in the rest of the nation, the largest New Immigrant groups were the Poles, Russians, and Austrians, as well as the Italians.

Finally, the new white settlers were heavily Protestant. Statistics on religious affiliation are notoriously imprecise, yet they permit some impressions. The number of Roman Catholics in the Southwest states has been recently estimated at 7 million. If one deducts the 3.5 million Spanish-surname persons enumerated by the 1960 census from this figure, Catholics accounted for only about 12 percent of the non-Mexican inhabitants of the Southwest. In contrast, Catholics in the balance of the United States represented an estimated 25 percent of the total population. Though state estimates are even more dubious than those for the region, Texas, like other Southern states, appears to have relatively few Catholics.[23] Texas Protestants also appear to include a disproportionate share of members of the more fundamentalist denominations; in the mid-1950s more than half were Southern Baptists.[24]

NINETEENTH-CENTURY ECONOMY:
DISPLACEMENT OF MEXICANS

The economic decline of Mexicans after coming under the hegemony of the United States differed in time and place, but it generally coincided with the advent of large-scale, highly capitalized ranching, agricultural, and mining enterprises in each area. These enterprises largely displaced small-scale ranching and mining. The end of the Mexican Colonial period was already an era of poverty, exacerbated on this remote frontier by political and economic upheavals in Spain and in Mexico. The settlements in Arizona, New Mexico, and Texas were left to their own resources in the endless war against marauding Indians. This struggle nearly strangled economic development in many areas, particularly Arizona and New Mexico.

Spanish settlement in Texas began with irrigation and field crops and some livestock. Early settlers from the United States continued this pattern, but in later years, after perhaps 1850, the land was used more profitably by running livestock, often on a vast scale. Cattle were run freely without much regard to property lines. The introduction of cheap barbed-wire fencing after 1870 meant a large-scale enclosure movement. The economic subordination of Mexicans was an inevitable

**Table 3–3. White Natives of Native Parentage as a Percent
of the Total White Population, 1910–1960**

	REGENS[a]			
Year	Southwest	Northeast	North Central	South
1910	67.3	43.7	55.6	90.3
1920	66.6	42.9	58.1	90.5
1930[b]	67.5	44.0	61.9	91.2
1940	74.1	52.2	70.0	93.4
1950	77.2	57.6	75.0	93.1
1960	79.8	64.6	80.3	92.7

	SOUTHWEST STATES				
Year	Arizona	California	Colorado	New Mexico	Texas
1910	48.1	49.0	60.6	83.9	81.2
1920	51.9	51.4	65.3	81.7	79.4
1930[b]	59.2	54.7	68.9	83.0	80.6
1940	71.2	63.5	76.5	89.0	85.2
1950	76.1	69.9	81.1	90.4	86.1
1960	80.4	74.2	85.1	91.2	87.2

[a] Southwest as defined in this book; other regions as defined by the U.S. Bureau of the Census.
[b] Estimates for the Southwest, the rest of the United States, and Arizona and New Mexico.
Source: *1960 U.S. Census of Population,* vol. I, part 1, tables 44, 156, and 162; vol. I, parts 4, 6, 7, 33, and 45, table 99; PC(2)–1A, table 2. *1950 U.S. Census of Population, Special Report:* PE no. 3A, tables 1, 3, 12, 13, 14; parts 3, 5, 6, 31, 43, table 24. *1940 U.S. Census of Population, Special Report:* Nativity and Parentage of the White Population by Country of Origin, tables 2, 5, 6. *1920 U.S. Census of Population,* vol. II, p. 915, and Abstract, pp. 99 and 107. *1910 U.S. Census of Population,* Abstract, table 15.

**Table 3–4. White Foreign-stock Population Ranked by Country of Origin,
Southwest and Balance of the United States, 1910–1960**

	Rank of Country of Origin as Contributor and Percent of Foreign-stock Population								
AREA AND	FIRST		SECOND		THIRD		FOURTH		FIFTH	
YEAR	Country	Percent	Country	Percent	Country	Percent	Country	Percent	Country	Percent
Southwest										
1910	Germany	20.3	Mexico	16.4	U.K.	11.7	Ireland	10.1	Italy	6.6
1920	Mexico	22.8	Germany	15.1	U.K.	10.7	Ireland	7.9	Italy	7.6
1930	Mexico	27.3[a]	n.a.		n.a.		n.a.		n.a.	
1940	Mexico	26.5	Germany	12.0	U.K.	10.6	Italy	8.2	Canada	7.2
1950	Mexico	27.2	Germany	10.5	U.K.	8.9	Italy	8.2	Canada	6.8
1960	Mexico	26.7	Germany	9.3	U.K.	8.2	Canada	8.1	Italy	7.3
Balance of U.S.										
1910	Germany	18.9	Russia	12.5	Ireland	10.3	Italy	10.0	Canada	9.2
1920	Germany	20.4	Ireland	11.7	Russia	11.2	Italy	9.3	Austria	9.0
1930[b]	Germany	17.2	Italy	11.4	U.K.	10.9	Canada	8.4	Poland	8.4
1940	Germany	15.5	Italy	13.9	Poland	9.2	U.K.	9.2	Canada	8.6
1950	Germany	14.5	Italy	14.3	Poland	9.2	Canada	9.1	U.K.	8.1
1960	Italy	14.7	Germany	13.5	Canada	9.6	Poland	9.4	U.S.S.R.	7.1

[a] Estimated.
[b] Data for 1930 are percent of U.S. total, since data from which to derive figures for the balance of the United States are unavailable.
Source: *1960 U.S. Census of Population,* vol. I, part 1, table 110; *1950 U.S. Census of Population,* PE no. 3A, tables 13 and 15; *1940 U.S. Census of Population,* Nativity of the White Population, tables 1, 4, and 5; *1920 U.S. Census of Population,* Abstract, tables 101, 104, and 105; *1910 U.S. Census of Population,* Abstract, tables 13, 14, 15.

consequence of the spread of fenced, Anglo-owned, large-scale ranching and farming. This pattern eliminated comparatively small operations based on ownership of cattle and sheep rather than land.[25] It also eliminated large numbers of Mexican land claimants, many of them absentee owners who competed with each other for dubious titles. Mexican land ownership was retained in a few instances, but, as the record of the growth of the King Ranch illustrates,[26] the trend toward large-scale operations was difficult to stem.

The process of economic displacement started even before the annexation of Texas into the United States, and continued late into the nineteenth century. As was already pointed out, the earlier period was one which saw considerable conflict; the later one was dominated by the struggles of the Civil War and Reconstruction in Texas (the only Southwest state to be seriously involved in that upheaval). This involvement was exacerbated by border clashes on the lower Rio Grande. Thus, the economic shifts took place in an atmosphere of hostility. Conflicts often involved Mexican-American owners of Texas land siding with Anglos, and settled or marauding Anglos siding with subgroups of Mexican nationals. It was a confused and bloody period, but by 1900 the Mexican's role in Texas as a landless and dependent wage-laborer was well established in all but a few insignificant areas.

The pattern of large-scale Anglo-owned pastoral and agricultural operations spread west into New Mexico in the last quarter of the nineteenth century. The shift was far less dramatic in New Mexico than in Texas. However, by 1900, many small holders had been forced into wage labor through overgrazing and the consequent erosion, the consolidation of larger ranches and continued division of the smaller ones among many heirs, and the rapid withdrawal of grazing land into national forests and railroad grants. Small landowners met the same fate regardless of ethnicity. The coming of the railroad in the 1880s encouraged the expansion of mining and the further consolidation—and enclosure—of big enterprises by opening up Eastern markets for the sale of wool, hides, and meat. This steady pauperization of independent pastoralists extended well into the twentieth century.

The continued presence of hostile Indians stultified Arizona's development both under Spanish or Mexican rule and during the first years of American rule. The final pacification of the Indians in the 1880s coincided with the construction of railroads and the beginning of large-scale mining in isolated company towns. "Copper, cotton, and cattle" became the three economic dominants in Arizona. As in Texas and New Mexico, these were—or became—Anglo operations on an increasing scale requiring substantial capital inputs.

In northern California, the economic subordination of the Mexicans occurred relatively quickly. A flood of immigrants attracted by the Gold Rush of 1848 soon turned to farming, often squatting on Mexican-owned land. This beginning of the family-farm system was accompanied by considerable conflict; there was open fighting as well as complicated litigation over land titles. Although the Mexican ranchers won some of the claims, the growing political influence of the huge numbers of Anglo migrants from the East soon left them in a hazardous position, economically overextended and disliked by the Anglo small farmers who were becoming a demographic and a political majority.

The situation in southern California was quite different. Here a good portion of the Mexican landowners remained in control of land and influential in politics for almost a generation. A handful of Mexican families owned almost all of the arable land in the region; the ranches were worked by Indians, and the products—largely meat—were sold in the northern part of the state. The economic collapse of these few families came largely as the result of natural catastrophies. Disastrous floods and droughts in 1862 and 1863 drove the owners into debt. Market prices declined and the land passed quite rapidly from Mexican to Anglo owners. Before 1869 most of the California land parcels worth more than $10,000 were held by Mexicans. By 1870 the same families held less than a quarter of them.[27] Economic displacement thus occurred prior to demographic subordination. The railroads did not bring their hordes of settlers into southern California until the 1880s.

Since economic displacement involved mainly control over land—the area's dominant resource—conflict in many parts of the Southwest focused to a large extent on legal rights to its ownership. The transfer of territory from Mexico to the United States left complicated problems of land titles, some of which have remained sources of friction to the present day. Reies Tijerina's *Alianza Federal de Mercedes*, the current effort of Spanish Americans in New Mexico to regain control of the land, is only the most recent and perhaps the most militant of many movements similar in nature.

Because some of the original grants had been made either by governments whose acts were no longer recognized in Mexico,[28] or under conditions that left cloudy titles, a long and acrimonious process of adjustment followed between older residents and the new government. Although the Gadsden Treaty protected land claims recognized by the earlier Treaty of Guadalupe Hidalgo, one section stipulated that "no titles shall be valid unless recorded in the Mexican archives."[29] Some of these conflicts were compounded by the question of mineral rights within the grants, which had not been clearly assigned.[30] In addition, squatters who had occupied land for many years without proof of title frequently found themselves embroiled in legal action brought against them by land speculators who had gained title or who were probing the validity of doubtful settlers' claims.

The degree of tension between old settlers and new is indicated by the fact that a special court created in New Mexico to handle land conflicts processed claims amounting to over 33 million acres between 1891 and 1904.[31] Many of these disputed lands passed into the hands of Anglos who could better afford legal counsel and who had the sympathy of the courts.[32] For Texas, Taylor's data show that in 1835 *all* of the land in Nueces County was granted to Mexicans, yet by 1883 every one of these grants had been purchased by non-Mexicans. (By 1928, twenty-nine Mexicans again owned land in Nueces County).[33]

Although the loss of land was caused by a variety of circumstances, it left great bitterness among the Mexicans. The ambiguity of many title claims, even when there was no chicanery, also left grounds for later suspicion. In many regions, in fact, ambiguity probably caused more trouble than outright chicanery. The economic result was the emergence of large-scale Anglo ownership. The land was worked by impoverished and dependent Mexicans. Another consequence was widespread and lingering mistrust and suspicion of the new, dominant population by the indigenous settlers and their descendants.

ECONOMIC DEVELOPMENT
IN THE TWENTIETH CENTURY

Throughout the nineteenth century and well into the twentieth, the five South-west states were truly an underdeveloped part of the nation, with an economic base heavily oriented to the exploitation of natural resources. Needs for large amounts of capital could be met only by "importing" funds from the East and from outside the United States. In some respects, the region is still catching up with the rest of the country. In 1960, for example, only 20 percent of the labor force was in manufacturing, compared with 29 percent in the balance of the nation. And the recency of economic development, combined with extraordinary population growth, has meant a heavy concentration of human and other resources in the region's infrastructure: railroads, highways, communications facilities, public works to bring water to desert lands, electric power plants and transmission systems, and construction.

In recent years, all five states experienced a very high rate of economic growth. They also have gone through radical shifts in economic structure. However, the diversification of activities has bypassed many subregions. The Southwest includes depressed areas on a scale reminiscent of Appalachia as well as some of the fastest growing urban-industrial complexes.

The importance of agricultural and mining activities varied greatly even in 1900.[34] The economic base of Texas was clearly agriculture, and that of New Mexico and Arizona agriculture plus mining, while California and Colorado already had more diversification.[35] These conditions affected the demand for labor when the first waves of Mexican immigrants were seeking work. For one thing, both agriculture and mining were labor-intensive rather than capital-intensive, and involved a great deal of dirty and low-wage work. For another, the labor force was organized in gangs of families (including child workers) or of single men. Jobs in agriculture and processing plants were typically seasonal and temporary housing was provided on the site. Finally, the geographic isolation of many places of employment often entailed company towns. As will be detailed in Chapter 5, these conditions tended to keep contact between laborers and the general community to a minimum.

Structural changes in the economy between 1900 and 1940 were very uneven from state to state. Though manufacturing absorbed a rapidly increasing share of the labor force of both California and Texas, the other states lagged behind. During and after World War II development tended to reduce the remaining diversity, and the 1940–1960 period saw a drastic decline in agricultural jobs. But even in 1960 there were notable differences between the states. California held the highest proportion of manufacturing jobs (24 percent—still behind the rest of the nation's 28 percent, however). New Mexico had the lowest, with only 7.5 percent in manufacturing. Mining continued to be important in New Mexico, along with government employment which provided relatively more jobs than in other states in the region. Texas continued to have a relatively high proportion (9 percent) in agriculture, as did Arizona (8 percent). Arizona also had very few jobs in manufacturing.

Just as agriculture generally declined, the most rapid growth almost everywhere occurred in distribution and government, and in business, consumer, and professional services. This modern growth sector of the economy, with its demands for a highly educated labor force, followed quite suddenly an economy that emphasized the infrastructure and thus demanded many unskilled laborers.

Diversity between the states is also mirrored in per-capita personal income. Here again, California has been in a class by itself (Table 3–5). Although over-all

Table 3–5. Per-capita Personal Income in the Southwest and in the United States, Selected Dates, 1929–1965 (Dollars)

	1929	1939	1949	1959	1965
Southwest (weighted average)	711	580	1,504	2,328	2,862
Arizona	591	477	1,245	1,923	2,370
California	995	775	1,725	2,648	3,258
Colorado	637	516	1,385	2,204	2,710
New Mexico	407	352	1,113	1,837	2,193
Texas	478	409	1,283	1,928	2,338
United States^a	703	556	1,382	2,163	2,746
			Rank Among 48 States		
Arizona	26	26	26	27	30
California	4	5	4	5	6
Colorado	19	21	18	14	18
New Mexico	39	36	35	29	38
Texas	33	31	25	26	32

a Does not include Alaska and Hawaii prior to 1960.
Source: U.S. Department of Commerce, Personal Income by States (supplements to the *Survey of Current Business*).

per-capita personal income in the Southwest was slightly higher than in the United States as a whole, this is because California is part of the region. Three of the states, Arizona, New Mexico and Texas, ranked well below the national average.

The economic variations would be even sharper if the analysis included subareas, with their pockets of ethnic settlement, within the five states. Thus depressed South Texas, where Mexican Americans are concentrated, contrasts with more prosperous parts of the giant state. Southern Colorado is a world apart from Denver. Mexican

Americans are found in backward rural areas of California as well as in wealthy Los Angeles and San Francisco, in the depressed northern part of New Mexico as well as in Albuquerque. One of the most significant over-all consequences of the persistent economic variations within the Southwest has been intra-regional migration. California has become the magnet attracting Mexican Americans from poorer states and subareas and increasing proportions of immigrants from Mexico (Chapter 4).

SOME FEATURES OF THE POLITICAL MILIEU

Institutional resources are important for subordinate populations. Some institutions are critical in the life of Mexican Americans and are discussed in later chapters. Here, we note that in the nineteenth century the institutions of the area shifted from Hispano-Mexican to American with comparative ease in some areas and with great discontinuity in others.

In Texas, neither Mexican political institutions nor meaningful Mexican political participation on a state-wide level survived the Texas Revolution. The emergence of the one-party system after the Reconstruction period, together with the poll tax and the "wide-open primary" dating from the World War I era, further militated against Mexican political participation in all but a few areas.

In New Mexico, the Spanish-Mexican political institutional structure was not changed significantly after the conquest of the state in 1848.[36] The original leadership in the state remained largely intact and assumed a place alongside the Americans in ruling the region. Both Anglos and Hispanos profited from the complicated and profitable intrigues of the Santa Fe Ring, an ethnically integrated group of business-men, lawyers, and politicians. For the poorer Spanish Americans of northern New Mexico, the shift of political control meant not much more than a shift in names among an elite.

In northern California, the influx of Americans and their institutions was accompanied by sometimes violent outbreaks of anti-Mexican feeling and a barrage of anti-Mexican legislation. The *californios* originally welcomed the annexation but soon lost control over their own fortunes and all their political influence as well.

For a long time state governments in the Southwest were dominated by a few large economic enterprises. These were the railroads, highly capitalized farms, mining interests, and big land-development companies. The domination and blatant corruption of the California state government by the railroad interests are well documented.[37] But only in New Mexico were the native Mexicans participants in the political domination by economic enterprises. In the other states the business interests that controlled governments were owned by Anglos, and none were responsive to the welfare of the subordinate populations who were in large measure their employees.

The power structure has changed in the Southwest as in other regions. In some states, such as California, vigorous reaction against the political-business alliance resulted in a grass-roots reform movement. And throughout the region economic development meant that business influence lost its monolithic quality. Railroads lost dominance; a greater variety of manufacturing interests replaced mining; and financial institutions became more important. Labor unions were also a growing force, although a latecomer generally on the Southwest political scene. A telling indicator of changes in the distribution of power appears with the termination of the *bracero* program (the government-controlled recruitment of Mexicans for agricultural work in the United States) at the end of 1964. The action involved national policy as well as the Southwest. For many years after World War II the highly developed agribusinesses of the region succeeded in having the Congress extend Public Law 78 on which the contract labour agreement with Mexico initiated during the war was based. They were no longer able to do so by 1964 in the face of opposition from organized labor, civic and church groups, and Mexican-American organizations. The demise of the *bracero* program symbolized the end of an era, and it is particularly meaningful for Mexican Americans.

State-to-state differences in the political influence of Mexican Americans have, of course, continued to exist to the present day. As later chapters will show, this influence is still quite large in New Mexico, and it is almost nil in California (at least in terms of representation in state government). But what such contrasts have meant to the welfare of the Mexican-American population is by no means clear. On a variety of indexes of the quality of life, California ranks high nationally as well as in the region. New Mexico and Texas generally rank low. Arizona is also below the national average, and Colorado has a mixed rating.[38] Given the increasing dependence of the poor on the welfare state, it would appear that only in California and Colorado do minorities such as the Mexican Americans have a better-than-average chance of help from public and private sources. Interestingly, New Mexico, with its high order of political participation of its Spanish-surname residents, is so poor that the quality of life remains low. California, a state in which Mexican Americans are politically under-represented, is a good place to live even for the poor.

SUMMARY

The characteristics of the five states in which Mexican Americans are concentrated have importantly conditioned their lives in this country.

All but one of the states borders on Mexico. Historically, these border territories were areas of conflict, some of it violent, between Anglo settlers and Mexicans and Indians. The border itself has played a major and complex role. Its functioning as a social passage between Mexico and the United States has varied not only over time but, because of geographic and ecological diversity along its great length, in space as well.

Both sides of the border were sparsely settled at the beginning of this century. But the American side has been growing faster than the rest of the United States and has also been urbanizing more rapidly, although both population growth and urbanization have been quite unevenly distributed.

From Colonial times, Mexicans have shared the Southwest area with the Indians. Also, many parts of the region have been characterized by the presence of non-European immigrants more numerous and more diverse than in most other regions of the United States. The white settlers tended to include more native born people, more Anglo-Saxons among the foreign stock, and more Protestants than most other areas.

The economic impact of American settlement in the nineteenth century was of critical importance to Mexican life. Large-scale mining and ranching displaced the small farming and livestock agriculture of the native Spanish-surname population. Increasingly, in all five states, the new economy used Mexicans as wage laborers. The speed and extent of their loss of economic independence varied greatly from state to state.

In recent decades, as the largely underdeveloped region experienced rapid economic growth, structural changes in the economy required even more wage labor. Mexicans, both indigenous and immigrant, were readily available to help meet this demand. However, economic growth has been very uneven. This unevenness is reflected in the rate of Mexican absorption into the economic life of the region.

The political milieu of these five states has worked generally to the disadvantage of minority groups, though the degree of disadvantage has varied from state to state. Mexican Americans have retained a political voice in New Mexico to the present day. But New Mexico is a very poor state, and so it offers little in the way of institutional amenities to promote the welfare of the indigenous population. In California, on the other hand, Mexican Americans have been highly ineffective politically, but the state's wealth has meant considerable development of its welfare and educational activities. It seems that ecological and economic factors have been strategic determinants of the position of Mexican Americans in the changing environment of the Southwest.

NOTES TO CHAPTER THREE

1. Though in some respects the five states do not meet the criteria of a region, nevertheless, as John W. Caughey has said, "For the United States there has always been a Spanish Southwest." See his "Spanish Southwest: An Example of Subconscious Regionalism," in Merrill Jensen (ed.), *Regionalism in America* (Madison, Wis.: University of Wisconsin Press, 1951), p. 180. In the U.S. Census Bureau classification of the states in this region, Texas is part of the South and the other four states are part of the West, with California assigned to the Pacific division and Arizona, Colorado and New Mexico to the Mountain division. Historians have sometimes included other states—for example, Kansas, Oklahoma, Utah, and Nevada—in their "Southwest." Colorado is often excluded. See also Rupert N. Richardson and Carl C. Rister, *The Greater Southwest* (Glendale, Calif.: The Arthur H. Clark Co., 1934).

2. For an application of the concept "conditions of contact" to Mexican Americans, see Leonard Broom and Eshref Shevky, "Mexicans in the United States: A Problem in Social Differentiation," *Sociology and Social Research*, XXXVI (Jan-Feb., 1952), pp. 150–158.

3. Carey McWilliams, *North From Mexico* (Philadelphia: J. B. Lippincott Company, 1949) remains the best general history of Mexican Americans in the border states despite the author's tendency to ascribe "progressive" aspirations to the past, particularly the more recent past. Other sources include Leonard Pitt, *The Decline of the Californios* (Berkeley, Calif.: University of California Press, 1966) on California till 1890; Paul Horgan, *Great River: The Rio Grande in North American History* (New York: Rinehart & Company, Inc., 1954), vols. I and II on Texas, New Mexico, and Colorado till World War I; Nancie L. González, *The Spanish Americans of New Mexico: A Distinctive Heritage* (Mexican-American Study Project, Advance Report 9, Graduate School of Business Administration, University of California, Los Angeles, Sept., 1967) on New Mexico up to contemporary times; and Edwin Corle, *The Gila: River of the Southwest* (New York: Rinehart & Company, Inc., 1951) for a chatty treatment of Arizona up to the late 1930s. General sources on the history of the region include Howard Roberts Lamar, *The Far Southwest, 1846–1912: A Territorial History* (New Haven, Conn.: Yale University Press, 1966) and W. Eugene Hallon, *The Great American Desert* (New York: Oxford University Press, 1966).

4. Everett C. Hughes and Helen MacGill Hughes, *Where Peoples Meet: Racial and Ethnic Frontiers* (New York: The Free Press, 1952), p. 23. This theme of historical primacy has been important in the ideology of Mexican Americans. Only descendants of those who were in the territory before its acquisition by the United States, of course, are a charter-member minority; these are especially the Mexican Americans living in northern New Mexico and southern Colorado. The ideology, however, has blurred the distinction between those individuals and descendants of twentieth-century immigrants from Mexico.

5. For sources of this brief account, see H. H. Bancroft, *Works* (San Francisco: The History Co., Publishers, 1889), vol. XVI.; J. Fred Rippy, *The United States and Mexico* (New York: Alfred A. Knopf, Inc., 1926), pp. 8, 9. See also Samuel H. Lowrie, *Culture Conflict in Texas, 1821–1835* (New York: Columbia University Press, 1932), and Rudolph L. Biesele, *The History of the German Settlements in Texas, 1831–1861* (Austin: Von Boeck-mann-Jones, 1930). An excellent concise history of the war is in Otis A. Singletary, *The Mexican War* (Chicago: The University of Chicago Press, 1960).

6. See George I. Sanchez, *Forgotten People: A Study of New Mexicans* (Albuquerque, N. Mex.: University of New Mexico Press, 1940); Carolyn Zeleny, "Relations Between the Spanish-Americans and the Anglo-Americans in New Mexico: A Study of Conflict and Accommodation in a Dual Ethnic Relationship" (unpublished Ph.D. dissertation, Yale University, 1944); McWilliams, *op. cit.*, pp. 63–80; Paul A. Walter Jr., "A Study of Isolation and Social Change in Three Spanish-speaking Villages of New Mexico" (unpublished Ph.D. dissertation, Stanford University, 1938), pp. 40ff and *passim*; and González, *op. cit.*

7. The history of these later border tensions is detailed in Rippy, *op. cit.*, pp. 168–185, 282–310.

8. Practically all of the border "adjustments," which transferred large areas of land to the United States, resulted in the intensification of hostile national feelings on both sides. Spokesmen in the United States, for example, frequently declared "that the Mexican people were incapable of self-government, and that the only solution of the frontier problems was to be found in the annexation to the United States of the 'whole country' north of the Sierra Madre range and extending from the Gulf to the Pacific" (*ibid.*, p. 283). Within Mexico, the stability of the government often depended upon its assuming aggressive, intransigent positions with respect to border situations, and both supporters and opponents of particular regimes stimulated national sentiments hostile to the presence of the American power

pressing against the country's border. A summary of the background for the residual bitterness in Mexican national sentiment over the border's evolution is given in Howard F. Cline, *The United States and Mexico* (New York: Atheneum Publishers, 1963), pp. 10–14. See also Rippy, *op. cit.*, 320–331 and *passim*.

9. The six Mexican states among the eight on the border had less than 16 percent of Mexico's population in 1960. *Estados Unidos Mexicanos, Secretaria de Industria y Comercio, Direccion General de Estadistica, VIII Censo General de Poblacion, 1960, Resumen General* (Mexico, D.F., 1962).

10. Because of changes in urban and rural classifications over the decades the percentages are not precise, although the comparison between the Southwest and the balance of the United States is consistent for each census year. Sources: U.S. Bureau of the Census, *Historical Statistics for the United States* (1960), and *Statistical Abstract of the United States*.

11. Martin Katzman has pointed out the possible general significance of what he terms "ethnic geography." Noting that, despite recent shifts, the geographical distribution of ethnic groups in the United States in 1960 was remarkably similar to that of 1880, Katzman suggests a reciprocal economic dependency between region and ethnic group, the one offering a special set of labor demands and the other a special labor supply. Differences in income opportunities among ethnic groups reflect largely differences in regional development. The differences in opportunities facing ethnic groups have persisted despite labor migration. Katzman's analysis generally supports our emphasis on the importance of the Southwest as a milieu. See Martin T. Katzman, *Ethnic Geography and Regional Economies, 1880–1960* (Institute of Government and Public Affairs, University of California, Los Angeles, Reprint no. 47, 1969).

12. The estimate of the Texas population in 1821 is made in Lewis W. Newton and Herbert P. Gambrell, *Texas Yesterday and Today* (Dallas, Tex.: The Turner Company, 1949).

13. Although the share of Mexican Americans in this total is unknown, there is little probability that they had increased much over the 4,000 in 1821. Only one generation had passed, and this was a period of bitter strife not likely to attract people from Mexico. The population of the border counties was about 8,000 in 1850; San Antonio had a total of about 3,500. Data are derived from the *Texas Almanac* (Dallas: A. H. Belo Corporation, 1963).

14. Derived from Corle, *op. cit.*, p. 183.

15. At the same time, there were an estimated 40,000 Indians in the Arizona Territory. Indians were excluded from the census count until 1890. Other figures are from U.S. Bureau of the Census, *Historical Statistics of the United States* (1960).

16. Of course, there were variations. Many of the Spanish mountain towns were comparatively easily defended and remained relatively safe. Some of the Indian tribes formed alliances with the Spanish settlers against other tribes. But the generalization stands despite exceptions. See González, *op. cit.*

17. The war cost the lives of more than 1,000 United States soldiers and cost $40,000,000 between 1861 and 1870 alone for the Arizona Indians. The Apache Wars of 1882–1886 are not included in the financial estimate. See McWilliams, *op. cit.*, p. 66.

18. For example, in the 1845 debates of the Texas Constitutional Convention, the question of voting rights involved the status of the Mexican American. A delegate to that convention stated:

> I shall welcome the Norwegian and Spaniard alike. . . . It is not these I fear. . . . Hordes of Mexican Indians may come in here from the West, and may be more formidable than the enemy you have vanquished. . . . I fear not the Castilian race, but I fear those who, though they speak the Spanish language, are but the descendants of that degraded and despicable race which Cortez conquered.

Cited in Paul S. Taylor, *An American-Mexican Frontier* (Chapel Hill, N.C.: The University of North Carolina Press, 1934), p. 232. The ideology of this racial mystique as related to the conquest of Mexico is noted in Richard Hofstadter, *Social Darwinism in American Thought* (Boston: Beacon Press, 1955), pp. 171 ff., and *passim*.

In later years, when national and state governments, as well as public and private bodies, began to consider immigration policy, specific identification with "half-breed" *mestizo* races promoted the notion that the incoming Mexicans were unassimilable and unable "to sustain or advance the civilization already established in the U.S." Discussion of these ideas received national circulation in Kenneth L. Roberts, "Wet and Other Mexicans," and "Mexicans or Ruin," *The Saturday Evening Post*, CC (Feb. 4, 1928), p. 10, and (Feb. 18, 1928), p. 14. The quoted material is from the issue of Feb. 4, p. 11.

For treatment in public documents, see, for example, *Mexican Labor in the United States*, U.S. Bureau of Labor Bulletin 78 (1908), and *Seasonal Agricultural Laborers from Mexico*, House Committee on Immigration and Naturalization, 69th Congress, first session, 1926, pp. 92, 144.

19. See Paul S. Taylor, "Crime and the Foreign Born: The Problems of the Mexican," U.S. National Commission on Law Observance and Enforcement, *Reports*, no. 10 (June 24, 1931), p. 201.

20. For these general community sentiments see Ruth D. Tuck, *Not With the Fist: Mexican-Americans in a Southwest City* (New York: Harcourt, Brace and Company, Inc., 1956). The quotation is from pp. 24 and 25.

21. Only a few examples will be given here. During the California gold rush, a special tax was imposed on foreign miners; this measure was intended especially for the many Mexicans and Chileans who had joined the search for the precious metal, and little if any distinction was made between those who had come north from Sonora or were United States citizens and indeed *Californios*, the natives of Hispano-Mexican stock. And Anglo miners often took the enforcement of the law into their own hands by ousting Mexicans, some of whom retaliated in bandit groups. Another case in point is the California Land Law of 1851, which contributed to the erosion of the Hispano-Mexicans' main economic base in agriculture, as did a variety of Anglo manipulations of land ownership in New Mexico. See Pitt, *op. cit.*

22. Both Beveridge and President Theodore Roosevelt, after the acquisition of Puerto Rico and the Philippines as a result of the Spanish-American War, "appear to have viewed Arizona and New Mexico somewhat as they did the new 'empire,'"—as backward areas which had been stifled by their Spanish heritage. Lamar, *op. cit.*, pp. 17 and 491.

23. Estimates prepared by Patrick H. McNamara from the *Catholic Directory* (New York: P. J. Kenedy & Sons, 1967). The figures derived from this source should be considered rough approximations; the accuracy of the figures varies from diocese to diocese. There is no uniform procedure for taking a census by Roman Catholic dioceses. Estimates are prepared about every five years, but not at the same time in each diocese. Consequently, the data published in 1967 probably refer to the first half of the 1960s. The estimated 7 million Roman Catholics in the Southwest (including Mexican Americans and others) represented 20 percent of the total Southwest population in 1960. The estimated 40 million Roman Catholics in the balance of the United States accounted for nearly 25 percent of the population outside the Southwest. As for Texas, the number of Catholics in Texas and in the El Paso diocese is estimated at 1.9 million: There were 1.4 million Spanish-surname persons in Texas, leaving 500,000 other Catholics. The latter composed little more than 5 percent of the Texas population other than Spanish-surname persons.

24. *Churches and Church Membership in the United States*, National Council of Churches of Christ in the U.S.A., Division of Home Missions, Series B, "Denominational Statistics by Regions, Divisions, and States," Bulletin no. 8 (New York: National Council of Churches, 1956).

25. Patterns of land and livestock ownership and grazing rights are complicated, but an understanding of them is essential for understanding the economics of the West. For the definitive treatment, see Ernest Staples Osgood, *The Day of the Cattlemen* (Chicago: The University of Chicago Press, 1929).

26. Tom Lea, *The King Ranch*, vol. I (Boston: Little, Brown and Company, 1957).

27. Pitt, *op. cit.*, p. 248.

28. H. H. Bancroft, *op. cit.*, vol. XVII, p. 601.

29. *Ibid.*, p. 601.

30. *Ibid.*, p. 766.

31. Zeleny, *op. cit.*, p. 166.

32. For a history of these land-title difficulties in the Southwest, see Bancroft, *op. cit.*, vol. XVII, pp. 598–600, 646–648, 756–766; vol. XXIII, pp. 529–581.

33. Taylor, *op. cit.*, p. 179.

34. The data underlying this section come from two different sources and are not strictly comparable. One, used for earlier decades, is Harvey Perloff et al., *Regions, Resources, and Economic Growth* (Baltimore: The Johns Hopkins Press, 1960). The other is the *U.S. Census of Population*, 1940 and 1960.

35. However, much of the manufacturing activity in Colorado (as well as Arizona and New Mexico) was tied to mining and was located in relatively isolated places near the resource base. Therefore the apparent economic diversification in Colorado may be deceptive in terms of potential interaction.

36. In the isolated frontier communities of New Mexico, simplified forms of Spanish political institutions had developed to deal with the maintenance of trade routes, defense against Indians, and the administration of justice—the problems basic to the survival of the province. See Jack E. Holmes, "Party, Legislature, and Governor in the Politics of New Mexico, 1911–1963" (unpublished Ph.D. dissertation, University of Chicago, 1964), p. 20. The American takeover was not welcomed officially as it had been in California, but many Mexican merchants involved in trade along the Sante Fe Trail looked forward to it as promising more business and better protection from the Indians. The governor of the province, Manuel Armijo, reflected these two attitudes. He assembled an army of 4,000 volunteers to resist Stephen W. Kearny, but because he was also a businessman with large investments in the Taos trade he disbanded the army at the last minute without firing a shot.

37. Andrew F. Rolle, *California: A History* (New York: Thomas Y. Crowell Company, 1963), pp. 443–445.

38. John O. Wilson has devised multifactor indexes measuring, among other things, "living conditions," "health and welfare," and "equality." Among all 50 states, California ranked third, Colorado twenty-fourth, Arizona thirty-first, New Mexico thirty-second, and Texas fiftieth in living conditions. These rankings were based on total state technical assistance expenditure per poor person, economic opportunity assistance per poor person, percent of families with income under $3,000, percent of housing units deteriorating and dilapidated, per capita general expenditure of state and local government for housing and urban renewal, weighted index of crime rates, weighted index of median family income in central cities as a percent of SMSA median family income, and per-capita recreation area.

Among all 50 states, Colorado ranked sixth, California fourteenth, Arizona thirty-eighth, New Mexico forty-third, and Texas forty-ninth on the index of health and welfare. This index was based on number of doctors, dentists, and nurses, per 100,000 population; number of acceptable general and mental hospital beds per 1,000 population; number of beds for long-term care for the aged per 1,000 population over 65; special and general patient-days of care and mental-patient–days of care per 1,000 population; state and county mental hospital admissions per 100,000 population; state and county mental hospital releases per 1,000 average daily patients; percent population served by fluoridated water supply; infant deaths per 1,000 live births; child welfare expenditure per child under 21; mothers receiving medical-clinic services; crippled children served; children receiving child welfare services; full-time caseworkers per 10,000 children; vocational rehabilitants per 100,000 population, cases per counsellor and per capita expenditures; old-age assistance; and aid to families with dependent children.

Wilson's measure of inequality pertains to discrimination on the basis of race, sex, and religion. The measure includes nonwhite-white ratios for income, occupation, education, housing density and quality, and mortality rates. Colorado ranked second among the 40 states for which data were available, California held third place, Arizona and New Mexico ranked twenty-third and twenty-fourth, respectively, and Texas twenty-ninth.

From John Oliver Wilson, *Quality of Life in the United States: An Excursion into the New Frontier of Socio-Economic Indicators* (Kansas City, Missouri: Midwest Research Institute, no date but apparently issued in late 1968 or early 1969). Data for each indicator appear to have been the most recent available to the author.

FOUR

The Ebb and Flow of Immigration

ACROSS a border of great length, easy to cross in numerous places, and quite unreal to many living in its vicinity, a traditional pattern of migration continued unhampered long after the boundary was established. Since 1900, nearly 1.4 million Mexican immigrants were admitted legally. Many others entered illegally or with permits for temporary employment. This mass movement has been part of an experience intrinsic to the development of our society—peoples coming to the United States from many lands. As Oscar Handlin put it, "Once I thought to write a history of the immigrants in America. Then I discovered that the immigrants *were* American history."[1] But the Mexican movement across the border reveals quite distinctive characteristics when compared with immigration from Europe.

[1] Notes for this chapter start on page 77.

DISTINCTIVE FEATURES

OF MIGRATION FROM MEXICO

First, immigration from Mexico is a late chapter in the history of immigration to the United States. Significant numbers of legal immigrants were first recorded in 1909 and 1910, at the beginning of the Mexican Revolution. About this time, total immigration to the United States had reached its peak and started to decline. The influx from Mexico gathered momentum in the 1920s, with nearly half a million legal immigrants, although by then *total* immigration was sharply reduced from pre-World War I levels.

Second, migration across the Mexican border shows an unusual variety of movements. There are permanent legal immigrants as well as people who come for temporary employment but manage to stay. Mexican and United States citizens who live south of the border commute regularly for work in the United States. Agricultural workers come and go with the seasons. In addition there is the usual array of businessmen, visitors, tourists, students, shoppers, and others entering for limited periods. The Canadian border, too, is traversed by varied traffic, but the pull of economic opportunity drawing Mexicans across the boundary—and hence their incentive to enter the United States by any available means—has been much greater than for Canadians.

Third, movements across the Mexican border have been unusually intensive. In the second half of the 1920s, and again in the period from 1955 to 1964, Mexican immigrants accounted for more than 15 percent of all immigrants coming to the United States. Between 1957 and 1966, more people arrived on visa from Mexico than from any other country. Mexico has long been the largest single source of aliens for temporary farm work. To judge from statistics on expulsions, which show Mexicans consistently at or near the top, Mexico has also been the main single source of illegal entrants. Its great length and generally harsh terrain make the border difficult to control. The problems of control have been compounded by the recruiting efforts of Southwest employers, by pressures on the Border Patrol from growers and other businesses to relax its vigilance,[2] and by the availability of friendly hiding places in the *barrios* of the border states.

Fourth, the intentions of Mexicans coming to this country generally seem to have been less certain and more varied than those of the many millions who came from other lands. Physical proximity, the relatively low cost of movement after railroad and highway connections were established, and the varied opportunities for crossing the border made it easier for many Mexicans to view migration to this country as an experiment, an adventure, or a temporary expedient without a momentous commitment. If a Mexican entered on a regular immigration visa, he could return without incurring great emotional or monetary cost. If he came for temporary employment and liked the experience, he often found it easy to stay. The Mexican on the move might even come and go more than once before he decided to accept or reject the new land permanently. As a result, there has been a large volume of return movements from the United States to Mexico, augmented by forced repatriations which at times reached large proportions.[3]

THE RECORD OF IMMIGRATION

The Period Before 1920

Literature ranging from folklore to historical treatises testifies to substantial movements of people across the Mexican border long before such movements were controlled, classified, and measured. Even in the late years of the nineteenth century, migration was still informal. Controls were so minimal that no records whatever were kept from 1886 to 1893, and even the statistics for subsequent years were rough approximations. This was still the period of our "open door" immigration policy, modified only by some qualitative restrictions and a small "head tax."[4] Admission to the United States was arranged at the border station, and no visa from an American consulate was required.

Mexican nationals came to the United States under a variety of arrangements. About 24,000 were reported as immigrants in the first decade of this century. But many more crossed the border for temporary work.[5] Mexican laborers were employed not only in agriculture but in mining, railroad construction and maintenance, and other jobs. Around the turn of the century, railroads had been built from the interior of Mexico to the United States. Thus, migration became much easier and cheaper. Yet, recorded (presumably permanent) immigration in the 1900–1909 period was of moderate proportions. Most of the foreign labor employed in Southwest agriculture was still supplied by earlier immigrants from Asia. The vast majority of Mexico's population was immobile geographically as well as socially. Nearly nine-tenths lived in rural areas, and large numbers of agricultural workers were held in peonage, which of course restricted their freedom to move.

The Mexican revolutionary period beginning in 1909–1910 spurred the first substantial and permanent migration to the United States (Table 4–1). The immigrants of this time had backgrounds probably more differentiated than the backgrounds of those who entered before and after this era. They included upper- and middle-class refugees who felt threatened by the Revolution, as well as many others who simply sought escape from a bloody and protracted conflict. The Revolution also had a more important and durable indirect effect on the movement to the United States. By liberating masses of people from social as well as geographic immobility, it served to activate a latent migration potential of vast dimensions.

How many refugees of the revolutionary era went back to Mexico is not known, but family histories show that quite a few decided to stay in the United States. It is perhaps characteristic that a Mexican American in Texas, whose parents had immigrated during this period, remembers continual family discussion of an early return to the homeland, until he himself, at the age of eighteen, recognized that "he was here to stay."

With the advent of World War I, the "push" of the Mexican Revolution was reinforced by the "pull" of American labor requirements. The shortage of domestic workers meant that growers could make a good case for opening the southern border.

Table 4–1. *Number of Mexican Immigrants Compared with All Immigrants,*
1900–1968[a]

Period[b]	Mexican[c]	Total	Mexican as percent of Total
1900–1904	2,259	3,255,149	.07
1905–1909	21,732	4,947,239	.44
1910–1914	82,588	5,174,701	1.60
1915–1919	91,075	1,172,679	7.77
1920–1924	249,248	2,774,600	8.98
1925–1929	238,527	1,520,910	15.68
1930–1934	19,200	426,953	4.50
1935–1939	8,737	272,422	3.21
1940–1944	16,548	203,589	8.13
1945–1949	37,742	653,019	5.78
1950–1954	78,723	1,099,035	7.16
1955–1959	214,746	1,400,233	15.34
1960–1964	217,827	1,419,013	15.35
Annual figures			
1960–1964 (av.)	43,565	283,803	15.35
1965	37,969	296,697	12.79
1966	45,163	323,040	13.98
1967	42,371	361,972	11.71
1968	43,563	454,448	9.59

[a] The reported figures for the earlier periods should be considered approximations. All of them refer to persons who were legally admitted for permanent residence.
[b] Fiscal years.
[c] Classified by country of birth, except for the periods 1935–1939 and 1940–1944, in which the data refer to Mexico as the country of last permanent residence. This classification had to be adopted because the reports for several years in these periods do not furnish data by country of birth. The statistics for periods for which both classifications are reported indicate that numerical differences are relatively small. The "country of birth" classification was adopted here as the basic one not only because it is definitionally superior, but also because characteristics of immigrants are reported on this basis.
Source: Annual Reports of the U.S. Immigration and Naturalization Service and its predecessor agencies.

Mexicans were close at hand. The economic distress of the Revolution meant that a great many of them were willing to work in American agriculture. The labor shortage opened up opportunities in non-agricultural employment as well, and special regulations issued in 1917 to admit temporary farm workers from Mexico were quickly extended to cover jobs in railroad maintenance and mining.[6] Hence, this period witnessed substantial temporary as well as increased permanent immigration.

The Mass Migration of the 1920s

Immigration from Mexico reached a peak in the 1920s. Close to 500,000 were reported as entering on permanent visas. Mexican immigrants accounted for 9 percent of all immigrants to this country in the first half of the decade, and nearly 16 percent of the total in the second half when the quota system, European prosperity, and emigration restrictions in fascist Italy and communist Russia reduced the movement of people from Europe.

In the 1920s, too, migration from Mexico to the United States reached a peak relative to Mexico's own population (Table 4–2). Mexican literature of this period

Table 4–2. Emigration from Mexico to the United States as a Percent of Mexico's Population, 1900–1960

Year	Mexican Population[a]	Mexican Population, Decade Average[a]	Emigration During Decade[b]	Emigrants as percent of Population
1900	13,607			
		14,383	23,991	0.17
1910	15,160			
		14,747	224,705	1.52
1921[c]	14,335			
		15,444	436,733	2.83
1930	16,553			
		18,103	27,937	0.15
1940	19,654			
		22,722	54,290	0.24
1950	25,791			
		30,357	293,469	0.97
1960	34,923			

[a] In thousands.
[b] Emigration figures as reported in the United States immigration statistics.
[c] The census was taken in 1921 rather than 1920. The corresponding emigration data cover the 11 years from 1910 through 1921. The emigration data for 1921–1930 cover nine years.
Sources: Mexican population: *Censos Generales de Población.* Immigration: Annual Reports of the U.S. Immigration and Naturalization Service and its predecessor agencies.

began to reveal the first fears that Mexico was losing too many of her energetic, skilled, and ambitious people to the big northern neighbor.[7] On the other hand, apprehensions in the United States about the volume and composition of Mexican immigration led to a vigorous Congressional debate over the extension of the quota system to Mexicans and to stricter administrative controls in the late 1920's.[8]

Immigration reached high levels despite the increased difficulty of entry. American consulates were designated as visa-issuing agencies, and entry could no longer be arranged at the border station. Costs also rose. Many Mexicans wishing to emigrate now had to incur travel expenses to file their application, in addition to the fees for Mexican passports and United States visas. That immigration during the 1920s reached such proportions in the face of these obstacles reflected great pressures.

In Mexico, the economic consequences of the civil war continued well into the

1920s. North of the border, the new era of prosperity acted as a strong magnet. The supply of Asian farm laborers had already dried up in the previous decade. In 1930, an official report to the Governor of California stated that the Mexican "is today a principal source of farm labor in California." The report listed certain qualities of this labor supply that would often be repeated for more than a generation. "He does tasks that white workers will not or cannot do. He works under . . . conditions that are often too trying for white workers. He will work in gangs. He will work under direction, taking orders and suggestions."[9]

Also, nonagricultural labor requirements of the rapidly developing Southwest increased sharply. In other parts of the country, the demand for unskilled labor in manufacture and service industries was met in part by Negroes who migrated from the South. Outside Texas, however, the Southwest's Negro population remained quite small. Mexican immigrants provided a growing part of the low-wage work force. The dependence of the Southwest on Mexican labor was reflected in stepped-up solicitation of Mexican workers by farm and other enterprises through middlemen— a practice already adopted in earlier periods. It was also reflected in the renewal of World War I arrangements for the admission of temporary workers, although the immigration authorities pointedly stated that "so far as the records indicate, many of the laborers never returned to Mexico."[10] Border control was strengthened in 1924.[11] Nevertheless, illegal immigration seems to have reached large dimensions during the decade. The illegal border crosser could save the head tax, the bother and expense of obtaining a visa from an American consulate, and the cost of waiting at border stations; and he could avoid the literacy test. Manuel Gamio has written a graphic description of the ways of the illegal immigrant during this period, of the strategic role of the "coyotes," or professional smugglers and labor contractors, of document forgery, and of American enterprises enticing immigrants and paying commissions to the smugglers.[12]

The Great Depression and World War II

Beginning in 1928, immigration from Mexico dropped sharply as economic conditions in the United States deteriorated. Large segments of American agriculture were in trouble long before the general slump in business. As the Depression took its toll and soil erosion in the Dust Bowl displaced farmers, rural tenants, and workers, Western agriculture found a new source of low-wage labor supply among the "Okies" and the urban unemployed who sought refuge in temporary farm work. During the 1930s only 27,900 Mexicans entered on permanent visas. The share of Mexicans in total immigration was less than 4 percent as against more than 11 percent in the previous decade. But the outstanding feature of this troubled era was substantial net out-migration, caused in large part by forced repatriation (Chapter 21).

The manpower emergency of World War II made the Mexicans welcome again. However, legal immigrants from Mexico were slow in responding. Mexico enjoyed increased prosperity, and she needed more workers as world demand for some of her export products rose. Besides, immigrants to this country faced the prospect of service in the United States armed forces when they were of draft age, and some of Mexico's manpower was drawn into her own army when she declared war against the Axis nations in 1942.

But the small figures for visa immigrants during the war tell only part of the story, for this was when the *bracero* program was born. A *bracero* is a person who works with his arms [*brazos*]; the word has become the Spanish equivalent of farm hand. The program provided for the government-regulated recruitment of temporary workers. Initiated under an executive agreement between the United States and Mexico and ratified by Congress in August 1942, it included guarantees on working and living conditions and steady employment, which had been lacking in previous arrangements for Mexican field workers. Conceived as a war-emergency measure, it was to be 22 years before the agreement was terminated, in December 1964. It was replaced by the (sharply reduced) importation of agricultural workers under general provisions of the immigration law.

Immigration Since 1950

Immigration on permanent visa began to accelerate in the early fifties, increasing steadily from 6,372 in 1951 to over 65,000 in 1956. Nearly 293,500 were recorded in the decade as a whole, and the share of Mexican in total immigration exceeded 15 percent in the second half of the 1950s. The increased volume did not reflect a relaxation of the law or its administration; the Immigration and Nationality Act of 1952 recodified existing statutes and introduced changes affecting mainly Europeans, but left the position of Mexican immigrants essentially unchanged.

Temporary migrations, too, increased sharply during the 1950's. For a time after World War II, the *bracero* program was inoperative, but American growers made such a persuasive case for its resumption that Congress, in 1951, enacted Public Law 78, which replicated the earlier arrangement. The familiar arguments for the need to draw on Mexican workers were reinforced by the manpower shortage of the Korean War. In fact, however, the peak of contract labor was reached in the late 1950s (Table 4–3). The volume declined gradually over several years before the program ended. This served to soften the impact of its termination on the Mexican economy as well as on United States agriculture.

The flood of wetbacks continued even after the 1951 legislation. Although the *bracero* program offered a legal alternative to men sneaking across the border for temporary work, the number of Mexicans who could participate was limited. Moreover, through illegal employment both Mexican laborers and American ranchers could save money, time, and inconvenience, and avoid regulation. *Braceros* and wetbacks often worked side by side in the fields. In the early postwar years, the situation became so confused that an administrative solution was devised by transporting the illegal migratory workers back across the border and then readmitting them as "legally contracted."[13] The process was, perhaps inevitably, called the "drying-out" of wetbacks.

It became clear that the attempt to channel the irresistible wave of temporary farm workers into the orderly and regulated *bracero* program had failed. The Annual Report of the Immigration and Naturalization Service for the fiscal year 1953 referred to the human tide of wetbacks as the most serious problem of the agency: "For every agricultural laborer admitted legally, four aliens were apprehended by

Table 4–3. Number and Annual Average Employment of Mexican Contract Workers Admitted for Temporary Work in U.S. Agriculture, 1942–1967[a]

Calendar Year	Number Admitted	Annual Average Employment[b]
1942	4,203	1,300
1943	52,098	15,600
1944	62,170	18,600
1945	49,454	14,800
1946	32,043	9,600
1947	19,632	5,900
1948	35,345	10,600
1949	107,000	32,100
1950	67,500	20,200
1951	192,000	57,600
1952	197,100	59,100
1953	201,380	70,700
1954	309,033	85,300
1955	398,650	112,800
1956	445,197	125,700
1957	436,049	132,200
1958	432,857	131,800
1959	437,643	135,900
1960	315,846	113,200
1961	291,420	95,700
1962	194,978	59,700
1963	186,865	45,900
1964	177,736	42,300
1965	20,284	2,200
1966	8,647	1,000
1967[c]	6,125	600

[a] Numbers of *braceros* and others admitted as reported by the U.S. Department of Agriculture for 1942–1947 and by the Bureau of Employment Security, U.S. Department of Labor, thereafter. The figures vary from those reported by the Immigration and Naturalization Service partly because the latter are for fiscal years. The data of the U.S. Department of Labor are used here because they have been converted by the Bureau of Employment Security to annual average employment for the period 1953–1967. See House Committee on the Judiciary. *Study of Population and Immigration Problems*, Special Series No. 11 (1963), appendix for part II, table 3; and the current reports *Farm Labor Developments* by the U.S. Department of Labor. For the years before 1953, the above data on annual average employment are estimates constructed as follows: The above source shows annual average employment of temporary Mexican workers in agriculture in the 1953–1962 period to equal 30.1 percent of the number of workers admitted. A ratio of 30 percent was applied to the years prior to 1953. This procedure assumes a constant relationship between admissions and duration of employment.
[b] Total man-months for the year divided by 12. The figures are rounded.
[c] No Mexican workers were reported in this category for 1968.

the Border Control." Of the 875,000 persons apprehended during the fiscal year, 30,000 were found to hold industrial and trade rather than agricultural jobs, and 1,545 were smugglers of alien labor.[14] This situation led to "Operation Wetback" of 1954–1955, which rounded up and returned many thousands (Chapter 21).

Legal immigration continued at high levels in the early 1960s and was rising— from less than 33,000 in 1960 to over 55,000 in 1963. At this juncture, the U.S. Department of Labor intervened through an administrative act. In a routine press release of July 1, 1963, the Department announced that job offers to Mexican immigrants would henceforth need to be "certified". The state employment services were required to verify the legitimacy of the prospective employer and of the job, as well as the permanence of employment. No job could be certified if it could be filled by domestic workers or if the alien's employment would adversely affect domestic wages and working conditions.[15] The immediate result was a sharp drop in legal immigration to 33,000 in 1964. The number increased again in subsequent years, but it levelled off at an annual average of about 44,000 in 1966–1968, far below previous peaks. (For annual immigration figures, see Chart 4–1.)

Although the job-certification procedure was authorized in the 1952 Immigration and Naturalization Act for broad classes of immigrants from any country, it was implemented in 1963 against Mexicans only. Thus, the 1963 restriction and the end of the *bracero* program in 1964 fundamentally altered the conditions under which Mexicans could come to the United States.

COMPOSITION OF IMMIGRANTS

Immigration statistics show only a limited number of characteristics of people who come to the United States: age, sex, and occupation. (The last item may not be fully descriptive, because it relies solely on the immigrant's designation.) Nevertheless, it is instructive to compare the composition of Mexican immigrants with that of all immigrants and with certain characteristics of the Mexican population itself. Broadly speaking, the Mexican immigrant has been younger than his counterpart from other countries, less skilled (as revealed by his occupation), and more likely to be a male. In recent years, however, there have been some notable changes, probably associated with the job-certification procedure of 1963.*

The younger age of Mexican immigrants has persisted, and probably reflects the unusual prevalence of large families in the population of Mexico and a shorter life expectancy in that country. The youthfulness of the group became even more pronounced in 1965–1968, when children and adolescents represented a much greater

*For the full array of data on the composition of Mexican and of all immigrants and for comparative figures on the Mexican population, see Leo Grebler *et al.*, *Mexican Immigration to the United States: The Record and Its Implications* (Mexican-American Study Project, Advance Report 2, Graduate School of Business Administration, University of California, Los Angeles, January, 1966), Chaps. 5 and 8. Our description here is based on this source, and the accompanying tables are merely designed to show recent changes.

Chart 4–1.
Number of Mexican Immigrants Compared with All Other Immigrants, 1910–1967

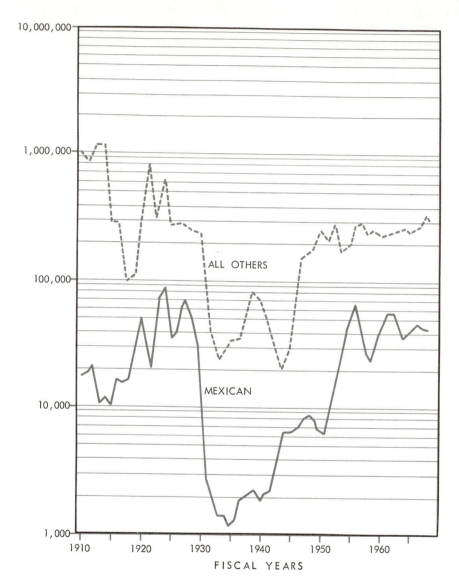

FISCAL YEARS

Source: Leo Grebler et al., Mexican Immigration to the United States: The Record and Its Implications (Mexican-American Study Project, Advance Report 2, Graduate School of Business Administration, University of California, Los Angeles, January, 1966), Table 25.

70

proportion of Mexican immigrants than of all immigrants, with the reverse true for the people in "productive" age brackets (Table 4–4). The breadwinners in the latter segment needed the job certificate, whereas the children of previous immigrants who had left their families behind could enter under preference provisions. The sex ratio of Mexican newcomers has also changed. In 1960–1964 the ratio still showed the historical majority of men, especially in the productive age groups. In recent years,

Table 4–4. Age Distribution and Sex Ratio of Mexican Immigrants Compared with All Immigrants, 1960–1964 and 1965–1968[a]

| Age Group | Age Distribution | | | | Sex Ratio[b] | | | |
| | 1960–1964 | | 1965–1968 | | 1960–1964 | | 1965–1968 | |
	Mexican, %	All, %	Mexican, %	All, %	Mexican	All	Mexican	All
Under 10	20.3	16.3	25.4	16.8	101.3	103.0	103.5	103.2
10–19	18.4	15.9	27.4	17.4	96.0	76.0	108.6	83.1
20–29	30.5	33.0	23.2	28.1	134.0	67.2	63.2	59.0
30–39	16.2	17.4	10.5	17.1	162.9	96.0	54.7	87.7
40–59	11.7	13.8	10.1	15.8	116.5	85.5	57.0	77.2
60 and over	2.9	3.5	3.4	4.8	96.8	68.3	83.6	66.0
All ages	100.0	100.0	100.0	100.0	119.5	81.0	82.1	77.4

[a] Fiscal years.
[b] Males per 100 females.
Source: Annual Reports of the U.S. Immigration and Naturalization Service, 1960–68, tables 9 and 10.

however, the sex ratio shows a drastic reversal in favor of women. Again, it seems that wives of previous immigrants have recently accounted for a larger percentage of all admissions, because the entry of male workers has been restricted by the job certification program. It is also possible that the program made it easier for female domestics to immigrate because local supplies in this occupation often fall short of demand.

Mexican immigrants have always been more concentrated in low-grade occupations than other immigrants entering *at the same time*, as is shown in Table 4–5 for recent periods. On the whole, the occupational distribution of Mexican immigrants of the past few decades resembles that of the European immigrants of *an earlier era* rather than of their counterparts arriving from Europe in the same period.[16] This is a distinction of considerable consequence. In the late decades of the nineteenth century and the early years of this century, the American economy could easily absorb millions of unskilled Irish, Polish, Italian, and Scandinavian immigrants. But since the 1920s (when mass immigration from Mexico began) and particularly since World War II the absorption of people with low-grade job qualifications has become increasingly difficult. The mechanization of industry, the more recent automation of manufacturing and other processes, and the growing importance of consumer and business services have placed a high premium on skills.

The recent occupational distribution of Mexican immigrants shows notable shifts. One is a sharp increase in the percentage of people without occupation, largely women and children (Table 4–5, Section *A*). The other is an occupational upgrading of those immigrants whose occupation is reported (Section *B* of the table). There are fewer laborers in the total. White-collar workers have increased—without, however, reaching parity with the occupational composition of all immigrants. The percentage of household workers among Mexican immigrants has risen. These changes seem to be largely attributable to the job certification program.

According to studies conducted over many years, migration is a selective process. People who move differ from those who do not in such matters as age, sex, education and even in personality characteristics.[17] From a Mexican perspective, one can say that until recent years the United States attracted a disproportionate number of Mexicans of productive age.[18] The emigration rates shown in Table 4–2 could

Table 4–5. Occupational Distribution of Mexican Immigrants Compared with All Immigrants,[a] 1960–1964 and 1965–1968

OCCUPATIONS	1960–1964		1965–1968	
	MEXICAN	ALL	MEXICAN	ALL
A. Over-all Distribution				
Professional, technical, etc.	1.3%	8.7%	1.5%	10.4%
Farmers and farm managers	0.5	0.8	0.5	0.8
Managers, officials, and proprietors	0.6	2.0	0.7	2.2
Clerical, sales, etc.	2.2	9.4	1.2	7.0
Craftsmen, foremen, etc.	3.1	6.3	2.8	5.7
Operatives, etc.	1.9	4.9	1.5	5.0
Private household	6.6	3.2	6.0	4.4
Service workers except household	1.0	3.3	1.4	3.5
Farm laborers and foremen	9.5	2.3	3.0	1.3
Laborers except farm and mine	17.3	5.1	7.6	3.0
All others[b]	56.1	54.0	73.8	56.8
B. Distribution of Those Reporting Occupation				
Professional, technical, etc.	3.0%	19.0%	5.7%	24.0%
Farmers and farm managers	1.3	1.7	1.8	1.7
Managers, officials, and proprietors	1.4	4.4	2.6	5.0
Clerical, sales, etc.	4.9	20.5	4.7	16.3
Craftsmen, foremen, etc.	7.0	13.7	10.8	13.2
Operatives, etc.	4.0	10.8	5.7	11.6
Private household	15.1	6.8	23.0	10.2
Service workers except household	2.2	7.2	5.5	8.1
Farm laborers and foremen	21.6	5.0	11.3	2.9
Laborers except farm and mine	39.5	10.9	29.0	6.9

[a] Mexican immigrants in each occupational class as a percent of all Mexican immigrants, and total immigrants in each class as a percent of all immigrants.
[b] Housewives, children, and others with no reported or classified occupation.
Source: Annual Reports of the Immigration and Naturalization Service 1960–68, table 8.

probably be doubled for persons in the "best years of their lives." Because Mexican immigrants have historically included more men than women, the movement to the United States drained off manpower. Skilled and unskilled industrial workers have been over-represented among immigrants compared to their share in the *Mexican* labor force. However, the net effect of the movement has probably benefited Mexico, first, by relieving her problems of unemployment and under-employment, especially in agriculture; second, through the earnings that the visa immigrants and temporary workers sent home; and third, through the training of those who returned to Mexico.[19]

Next to nothing is known about the geographic origin of the immigrants. Earlier writings on this subject assert that the majority have come from Mexico's central plateau, which comprises largely agricultural states. A secondary locus of migration is said to be the region bordering on Texas. Information on the geographic origin of *braceros* seems to confirm these statements, but only on the assumption that *braceros* and permanent immigrants have largely come from the same areas.[20] Much of the evidence is not only meager but out of date. According to Mexican observers, the more recent immigrants include a growing proportion of city dwellers. Long waiting periods in Mexican border cities also confound the problem of ascertaining the geographic origin of many immigrants.

COMMUTERS: A GROWING PROBLEM

Visa entry has been complicated since 1963 by the requirement of a job certificate, and the *bracero* program was abandoned in 1964, but there remains one special issue affecting border-state conditions and border-state sentiment on immigration matters: the commuters who live in Mexico but work in the United States. Commuters may be Mexican nationals, or they may be United States citizens (including naturalized Mexican Americans) who live south of the border. If they are aliens they are usually "green-card holders," that is, at each crossing they present an alien registration card which evidences that they are legally admitted immigrants and can therefore work (and live) in the United States. Some of the commuters are "blue-card holders," who are permitted to cross the border for periods not to exceed 72 hours and to perform temporary work.

The whimsical aspect of this issue begins with the legal construct under which green-card holders are considered regular immigrants without meeting the criterion of continuous *residence* in the United States. A court decision refers to it as an "amiable fiction."[21] The fictional content is increased by the apparently widespread practice of commuters to establish residence addresses in the American border cities while continuing to live in Mexico.[22]

The volume of commuting traffic is not known. The regular statistics of the Immigration and Naturalization Service cover all legal border-crossers—shoppers, entertainment seekers, people visiting their relatives, and those on business trips, as well as workers. And each entry is counted separately without recording repeated crossings by the same individual or his purpose. Thus, United States officials have not produced any continuous, reliable data on the number of Mexicans who commute to *work*.[23] It is astonishing to find that this statistics-minded nation has failed to develop measurements of important border transactions that could be easily supplied by means of modern data-gathering and -processing methods.

In the absence of data, private groups have made widely varying guesses without any firm basis. The estimates (for unspecified recent periods) vary between 30,000 and 100,000 alien commuters to work.[24] The U.S. Department of Labor, in a presentation to a Congressional Committee in 1963, referred to estimates ranging "from about 9,000 to 50,000."[25] The best figures have come from a Mexican government source—the reports of the *Programa Nacional Fronterizo* on Mexican border towns—and they pertain to 1960. On the basis of these reports, we estimate that a minimum of 60,000 persons crossed the border regularly in 1960 from Mexico for employment in the United States. The Immigration and Naturalization Service reported that 40,176 aliens were in this category in November-December 1967, exclusive of commuters who were United States citizens.[26]

Both citizens and aliens, of course, are drawn into international commuting from home to job by higher wages in the United States (even though the earnings may be low by this country's national or regional standards) and by lower living expenses in Mexico (even though prices there may be inflated by the very presence of commuters).

The policy issues posed by this movement are highly complex, and the commuter problem has accordingly received Congressional and other public attention. A drastic curtailment of commuting would have serious repercussions on the economic base of some American border cities. For example, El Paso and Brownsville would probably not be logical locations for garment factories in the absence of the low-wage workers commuting from Mexico. If such businesses closed, the adverse multiplier effects on the entire local economy could reach considerable proportions. Moreover, commuters are important customers of retail stores on the American side of the border. If commuting were blocked, the Mexican government might make it more difficult for Mexican nationals to cross the border for shopping. Thus, on balance the local economy might be stronger with than without the commuting system even if it involved spending more tax money to support unemployed domestic workers and their families.

On the other hand, commuters displace domestic labor, largely Mexican Americans, and depress wages and working conditions. The opposition to the system by organized labor is now reinforced by the antipoverty programs. There seems to be no point in spending public funds to alleviate poverty when the effort is undercut by allowing commuters to take jobs at substandard wages. The employment of Mexican commuters may be considered an indirect form of foreign aid, but the opposition questions the equity of such an arrangement. In this instance, the burden of foreign aid falls mainly on domestic workers competing in local job markets, instead of being distributed more widely.

The commuter system, then, is increasingly under fire from organized labor and welfare groups,[27] particularly since farm enterprises along the border seem to have replaced *braceros* with commuters. For diplomatic if no other reasons, the government will resist the attacks as long as it can, for United States immigration policy vis-à-vis Mexico has always taken international implications into account, perhaps more than for other countries; and the commuter issue is a case in point. In a suit brought in 1962 by the Texas AFL–CIO against the Attorney General of the United States for failure to enforce the immigration law, the Secretary of State intervened by filing an affidavit in which he cautioned that "a sudden termination of the commuter system as the result of a court decision would have a serious deleterious effect upon our relations with Mexico." Meanwhile, Mexico's border development program attempts to anticipate trouble by augmented investment and the establishment of bonded manufacturing districts in Mexican border cities. The objective is to have labor-intensive operations performed south of the border and other operations on United States territory, without customs interference. American firms are increasing their plant investment in Mexican border areas to take advantage of these possibilities. Thus, the free movement of goods and capital could in time replace the movement of workers.

THE OUTLOOK

Future Mexican movements to the United States will depend on the migration pressure south of the border and on our own policy. The pressure in Mexico remains high—caused as it is by a compound of fast population growth, low per-capita income, slow if any progress toward more equal income distribution, continued under-employment in the country's large rural sector, and great difficulty in absorbing the migrants into the urban economy.[28] For some time Mexico has been one of the leading countries in terms of over-all economic growth, with a steady increase of about 6 percent per year after adjustment for price changes. But much of this gain has been canceled by the rapid population growth, recently about 3.5 percent per year; and abject poverty is still so widespread that the pressure for emigration is likely to persist for many years to come.[29]

Turning to United States policy, we note that it is clear from the job certification procedure of 1963 and the end of the *bracero* program in 1964 that immigration policy has entered a new, more restrictive era. This is a remarkable change. Until very recently, employers have been able to convince policy makers of the desirability of an ample supply of workers from Mexico; the opposition of labor and civic organizations was to no avail.[30] Now business interests are counterbalanced by considerations of levels of domestic employment, protection of wages and labor standards, and the implications of immigration for antipoverty programs. Under these circumstances, the volume of immigration will unquestionably depend far more on United States policy than on the Mexican migration potential.

The growth of restrictionist sentiment appears in the legislative history and in some of the provisions of the Immigration and Nationality Act of 1965. The original bill was designed mainly to abolish the 41-year-old quota system based on national origin. The position of immigrants from Western Hemisphere countries remained largely unchanged. But in the hearings and congressional debates on the bill, the immigrant from New World countries became a major concern. The outcome was an amendment, taking effect in mid-1968, to allow no more than 120,000 persons a year to enter from Western Hemisphere nations.[31] Thus, the legislators and the

75

Administration who pressed for the abandonment of the traditional quota system could achieve their goal only by yielding to a new regional quota for the Western Hemisphere.

Among the main arguments for the imposition of a maximum was the sharp increase in total immigration from Central and South American countries in recent years, and especially from the Caribbean area (Table 4–6). Without a maximum, the population pressures associated with the extraordinarily high birth rates in practically all the economically underdeveloped Western Hemisphere nations would produce a flood of immigrants. Other arguments revolved around the difficulty of assimilating people coming from different cultures and absorbing them in an economy in which skills are increasingly essential. These points were often reminiscent of the contentions of the restrictionists on earlier occasions. However, it is notable that the Congressional debates hardly touched on immigration from Mexico or Canada.

Table 4–6. Number of Immigrants from Western Hemisphere Countries, 1955–1968[a]

FISCAL YEAR	MEXICAN	CANADIAN[b]	ALL OTHER	TOTAL
1955	50,772	23,091	22,468	96,331
1956	65,047	29,533	31,683	126,263
1957	49,154	33,203	33,587	115,944
1958	26,712	30,055	35,060	91,827
1959	23,061	23,082	28,389	74,532
1960	32,684	30,990	34,449	98,123
1961	41,632	32,038	45,188	118,858
1962	55,291	30,377	53,150	138,818
1963	55,253	36,003	61,368	152,624
1964	32,967	38,074	73,034	144,075
1965	37,969	38,327	81,395	157,691
1966	45,163	28,358	71,390	144,911
1967	42,371	23,442	90,842	156,655
1968	43,563	27,662	178,811	250,036

[a] By country or region of birth.
[b] Including Newfoundland.
Source: Annual Reports of the U.S. Immigration and Naturalization Service.

The effect on Mexican immigration of the ceiling on admissions from Western Hemisphere countries cannot be assessed at this point, but it is safe to predict a continuous tendency toward tighter control of both legal and illegal movements and a policy to reduce the volume of commuting to work. But control will remain a difficult problem. The history of Mexican immigration provides ample evidence that the various kinds of movement across the border are highly interdependent. Thus, when hundreds of thousands of wetbacks were sent home in 1954–1955, many of them returned with "clean papers" or came back as *braceros*. When immigration was curtailed in 1963 and the *bracero* program terminated, one of the immediate results was an increasing number of illegal migrants.[32]

If control were more effective, it would profoundly influence labor-intensive industries in the border states and the Mexican Americans themselves. Agriculture would be forced into increasingly rapid mechanization, thus hastening the migration of Mexican Americans to the cities. Industries would face more effective labour organization. More limited immigration would allow Mexican Americans to consolidate social and economic gains somewhat faster. Their persistent general problem of being identified as an alien and lower-class element would be alleviated. The distance between the minority and the dominant population in education, skills, social status, and English-language competence would probably be reduced more rapidly.

NOTES TO CHAPTER FOUR

1. Oscar Handlin, *The Uprooted* (Boston: Little, Brown and Company, 1951), p. 3.

2. For examples of informal cooperation between border patrol inspectors and farmers interested in obtaining Mexican labor, see Ernesto Galarza, *Merchants of Labor: The Mexican Bracero Story* (San Jose, Calif.: The Rosicrucian Press, Ltd., 1964), pp. 10 and 14; also Lyle Saunders and Olen E. Leonard, *The Wetback in the Lower Rio Grande Valley of Texas*, Inter-American Education, Occasional Papers no. VII (Austin, Tex.: University of Texas Press, July 1951), p. 80.

3. Return movements of earlier immigrants from other countries were also large at times, although the data are difficult to interpret. See Simon Kuznets and Ernest Rubin, *Immigration and The Foreign Born*, Occasional Paper 46 (New York: National Bureau of Economic Research, 1954). To reconcile the statistics on immigration from Mexico with the census figures on the number of Mexican-born persons is a tortuous exercise complicated by the large volume of illegal entries. For example, the number of Mexican-born persons in the United States declined from 639,017 in 1930 to 377, 433 in 1940 (See E. P. Hutchinson, *Immigrants and Their Children, 1850–1950* [New York: John Wiley & Sons, Inc., 1956], table 3). This sharp drop occurred in spite of the fact that nearly 488,000 Mexican immigrants had entered the United States legally in the decade of 1920–1930. Also, the number of Spanish-surname persons in the Southwest who reported in 1960 to the Census Bureau that they had lived in Mexico in 1955 totaled 103,000. Yet, 214,746 immigrants from Mexico were recorded in the 1955–1959 period. These figures are beset with reporting errors and problems of definition and interpretation. Nevertheless, they indicate substantial attrition of reported immigration, probably due to remigration. For earlier attempts to reconcile United States immigration figures with census data or with Mexican estimates of emigration, see Manuel Gamio, *Mexican Immigration to the United States* (Chicago: The University of Chicago Press, 1930) and Paul S. Taylor, *Mexican Labor in the United States—Migration Statistics* (University of California Publications in Economics, vol. 6, no. 3, Berkeley, 1929).

4. The qualitative controls were designed to keep out persons classified as feeble-minded, destitute, seriously ill, or morally undesirable. The head tax, for example, was raised successively and amounted to $8 in 1917. For details, see Leo Grebler et al., *Mexican Immigration to the United States: The Record and Its Implications* (Mexican-American Study Project, Advance Report 2, Graduate School of Business Administration, University of California, Los Angeles, Jan., 1966), Appendix D.

5. The *Annual Report of the Commissioner General of Immigration* for the fiscal year 1911, p. 160, refers to at least 50,000 "nonstatistical" aliens arriving annually in "normal" years from Mexico.

6. *Annual Report of the Commissioner General of Immigration* for the fiscal year 1918, pp. 15, 16.

7. See, for example, Enrique Santibanez, *Inmigración Mexicana en Los Estados Unidos* (San Antonio: The Clagg Co., 1930). The author had been Mexican Consul General at San Antonio.

8. The control operated mainly through stricter standards for determining whether a visa applicant would become a "public charge" in the United States. The requirement was usually met by affidavits of United States citizens or residents that they would support the applicant in case of need. A series of press releases in 1929 and 1930 by the White House and the State Department indicates the importance of the issue. The policy of the Executive Branch was apparently designed to fend off Congressional restrictions which would interfere with relations with Mexico. See *Publications of the Department of State*, press releases of October 1929–June 1930 and July–December 1930.

9. *Mexicans in California*, Report of Governor C. C. Young's Mexican Fact-finding Committee (Sacramento, Calif., 1930), p. 171.

10. *Annual Report of the Commissioner General of Immigration* for the fiscal year 1923, p. 28.

11. *Annual Report of the Commissioner General of Immigration* for the fiscal year 1924, p. 23.

12. Gamio, *op. cit.*, especially appendix 2.

13. For a comprehensive discussion of the *bracero* program and related migrations, see Galarza, *op. cit.*

14. *Annual Report* of the U.S. Immigration and Naturalization Service for the fiscal year 1953, p. 3.

15. For the text of the press release, see Grebler et al., *op. cit.*, Appendix B.

16. See Brinley Thomas, *Migration and Economic Growth* (London: Cambridge University Press, 1954), pp. 141–144. According to figures derived by Thomas from the U.S. censuses, 64 to 67 percent of the British-born employed persons were manual workers or servants in 1870, 1890, and 1900. For the Irish born, the figures varied between 74 and 78 percent.

17. For the large literature on this proposition and on its verification for both international and internal migrations, see, among others, Dorothy S. Thomas, *Research Memorandum on Migration Differentials* (New York: Social Science Research Council, 1938); *Selected Studies of Migration since World War II* (New York: Milbank Memorial Fund, 1958); Albert H. Hobbs, "Differentials in Internal Migration" (Ph.D. dissertation, University of Pennsylvania, 1942); E. W. Hofstee, *Some Remarks on Selective Migration* (The Hague: Nijhoff, 1952), Brinley Thomas, *op. cit.* There are also many journal articles on the subject, but they deal largely with internal migration.

18. Grebler et al., *op. cit.*, chap. 6.

19. Mexican observers attribute considerable value to this training, especially the exposure of temporary workers to work organization and methods as well as the use of machinery in agriculture. (Interview Notes.)

20. See Gamio, *op. cit.*, chap. 2 and appendix IX; Leonard Broom and Eshref Shevky, "Mexicans in the United States—A Problem in Social Differentiation," *Sociology and Social Research*, XXXVI (Jan.–Feb., 1952), pp. 152 and 153; and Saunders and Leonard, *op. cit.* For Mexican sources, see Gloria R. Vargas y Campos, *El Problema del Bracero Mexicano* (thesis published by the School of Economics, University of Mexico, 1964), tables 7 and 7-a; Ernesto Lopez Malo, *Emigrantes, El Problema de los Trabajadores Mexicanos* (Universidad de Mexico, VIII, February, 1954), which pertains to the 1942–1950 period and is based on official figures, presumably for *braceros*; and Moises de la Peña, *El Pueblo y su Tierra Mito y Realidad de la Reforma Agraria en Mexico* (Cuadernos Americanos, Mexico,

D.F., 1964), which provides data for temporary migrants from 1957 to 1961 as well as for 1942 to 1952.

21. This term was used by District Judge Luther Youngdahl in *Amalgamated Meat Cutters v. Rogers*, 186 F. Supp. 114, 119 (1960), quoting Gordon and Rosenfield, *Immigration Law and Procedure* (Albany, N.Y.: Banks, 1959), p. 127.

22. See the statement by the District Director of the Immigration and Naturalization Service, El Paso, Texas, quoted in *Texas State AFL-CIO et al. v. Robert F. Kennedy et al.* Brief for Appellants, U.S. Court of Appeals for the District of Columbia Circuit, No. 17,976, filed September 10, 1963, p. 5.

23. The Immigration and Naturalization Service reported data on alien and United States citizen commuters for employment in the fiscal years 1945 to 1951 for persons commuting at least four times a week. The annual numbers vary between 2,143 and 4,151 for aliens and 3,093 and 6,283 for citizens. The series was discontinued. No information was provided on the method used for obtaining the data. Because the results appear highly dubious, it is inadvisable to use them for estimating the volume of commuting in subsequent years. The Immigration and Naturalization Service presented 1963 figures to a Congressional committee. These figures are based on counts taken on two days, May 8 and May 17, 1963. They show a total of little over 34,000 "commuters" for the following Southwest districts: El Paso, Los Angeles, Phoenix, Port Isabel, and San Antonio. There is no indication of how "commuters" was defined. See *Study of Population and Immigration Problems*, House Committee on the Judiciary, Special Series no. 11, 1963, p. 181. The Service, in a personal communication to Fred H. Schmidt at UCLA, provided a table showing 42,641 commuters over the southern border on January 11, 1966. Although this figure is an apparent increase over the 1963 figure, interpretation is impossible in the absence of information on method and definition and in view of the inadequacy of a statistic for merely a single day.

24. In early 1965, the AFL-CIO estimated that "as many as 100,000 Mexican citizens fall into the commuter category" along the entire border. This statement by the American Section of the Joint United States–Mexico Trade Union Committee was included in a news release of February 10, 1965 issued by the California Labor Federation, AFL-CIO. In a lawsuit against the U.S. Attorney General (note 22), the AFL–CIO complaint mentioned a range of 30,000 to more than 50,000.

25. House Committee on the Judiciary, *op. cit.*, p. 156.

26. For the underlying data of our estimate and other details, see Grebler et al., *op. cit.*, Chap. 7. The 1967 figure is from a letter to the Mexican-American Study Project from the U.S. Immigration and Naturalization Service dated Feb. 21, 1968.

27. In 1959, when the strike-bound Peyton Packing Company in El Paso replaced domestic workers with commuters from Juarez, the Amalgamated Meat Cutters brought suit against the immigration authorities for allowing the strikebreakers to enter the United States. *Amalgamated Meat Cutters v. Rogers*, 186 F. Supp. 114 (1960). In 1962, the Texas AFL-CIO joined with individual Mexican-American and other union members in a lawsuit in which it claimed that the United States Attorney General, by permitting commuters to take jobs in this country, failed to enforce the immigration law (see note 22). One interesting aspect of the case was that commuters intervened and took a position against the plaintiffs. The case was appealed in 1963, but the original judgment that the plantiffs had no standing to bring this action was upheld, and the substantive issues were left undecided. Early in 1965, the California Labor Federation, AFL-CIO, announced an intensified drive to "protect workers on both sides of the California-Mexican border from exploitation." The drive was mapped at a conference of the Joint United States–Mexico Trade Union Committee and was aimed mainly at organizing the commuters. News release of the California Labor Federation, AFL-CIO, dated Feb. 10, 1965.

For more recent materials on the commuter issue, see *The Impact of Commuter Aliens along the Mexican and Canadian Borders*, Hearings before the Select Commission on Western Hemisphere Immigration (Washington, D.C.: U.S. Government Printing Office), Parts I to IV, various dates, 1968. After the hearings, two members of the Select Commission expressed their personal views in a letter to the President, dated July 22, 1968 and reproduced in Part I of the Hearings, pp. V–VIII. They recommended a new form of border crossing authorization for non-citizens who wish to work in the United States, to be issued only if a government agency certifies that the work permit would not adversely affect wages and working conditions of resident workers; and that the commuter status of green-card holders be terminated after a "grace period." The commuter issue is also discussed in the broader context of border area development in *Industrial and Employment Potential of the United States-Mexico Border* (U.S. Department of Commerce, Economic Development Administration, December 1968). This is a study prepared for the Economic Development Administration by Robert R. Nathan Associates, Inc.

28. Annual population growth in the 1950s averaged 3 percent. See Frank R. Brandenburg, *The Making of Modern Mexico* (Englewood Cliffs, N.J.: Prentice-Hall, Inc., 1964), p. 234. See also *50 Años de Revolución Mexicana en Cifras* (p. 21), a document issued by the Office of the President of the Republic of Mexico in March 1963 on the occasion of the fiftieth anniversary of the Revolution. Unpublished work by demographers at the Colegio de Mexico indicates an annual growth rate of about 3.5 percent in the 1960s (personal communication to the author). As for income, per-capita gross domestic product for 1963 was estimated at a "parity rate" of $394, or 14.1 percent of the United States figure. See *Yearbook of National Accounts Statistics* (New York: United Nations, 1964). Concerning income distribution, see Ifigenia M. deNavarrete, *La Distribucion del Ingreso y el Desarrollo Economico de Mexico* (Instituto de Investigaciones Economicas, Universidad Nacional Autonoma de Mexico, Mexico D.F., 1960), especially chap. 4, p. 89. See also Adolph Sturmthal, "Economic Development, Income Distribution, and Capital Formation in Mexico," *Journal of Political Economy*, LXIII, June, 1955, pp. 183–201. For problems in agriculture, see Brandenburg, *op. cit.*, chap. 9.

29. Because census statistics reveal the subject matters of national concern, it is pertinent to observe what kinds of poverty-related data are reported in the Mexican census of 1960. This census presents figures on the number of persons whose diet has been improved by the inclusion of bread, meat, fish, milk, and eggs (instead of being limited to beans, corn, and other traditional staples). In 1960, close to 11 million people, or 30 percent of those reporting, did not eat bread, and more than 8 million, or 23 percent of the total, did not have a diet enriched by the other kinds of food. Most of these poor were in rural areas. The Mexican census also reported that nearly 5 million people, or 14 percent, went barefoot, nearly 9 million wore sandals or *huaraches*, and 21 million had shoes. Among the rural population 23 percent went barefoot and 39 percent wore sandals or *huaraches* (*Censo General de Poblacion, 1960, Resumen General*, table 16). These figures represented considerable improvements over previous conditions. For example, in 1940 only half the population wore shoes, whereas nearly 27 percent went barefoot and 23 percent wore sandals or *huaraches*. Nathan L. Whetten, *Rural Mexico* (Chicago: The University of Chicago Press, 1948), p. 37.

30. Mexican-American labor organizations have historically been opposed to immigration, as have labor unions generally. For example, the job and wage threat posed by immigration was a major reason for the formation of the Confederation of Mexican Labor Unions in Los Angeles in 1928. The first general convention of the organization considered and apparently approved an anti-immigration platform. See *Mexicans in California* (San Francisco: California State Department of Industrial Relations, 1930), p. 127.

31. This amendment has a somewhat involved history. It was adopted in 1965 but made contingent upon subsequent legislation in response to recommendations of the

Select Commission on Western Hemisphere Immigration, which was established in the 1965 act. The commission filed its report in January 1968. The report recommended that the effective date for the imposition of the 120,000 ceiling on Western Hemisphere immigration be extended from July 1, 1968 to July 1, 1969. The recommendation was made to allow more time for judging the effects of the labor certification provisions of the 1965 legislation. However, the Congress failed to take legislative action in 1968. As a result, the ceiling became effective July 1, 1968 under the terms of the 1965 act. Among other things, this means that no legislative guidelines are provided on the administration of the 120,000 ceiling. The commission had recommended that no national-origins quotas be adopted, but that an annual maximum limitation of no more than 40,000 per country be established. See the *Report of the Select Commission on Western Hemisphere Immigration* (Washington, D.C., Jan., 1968).

32. The number of deportable Mexican aliens located by the Border Patrol increased from 55,349 in the fiscal year 1965 to 89,751 in 1966, 108,327 in 1967, and 151,705 in 1968 (*Annual Reports* of the U.S. Immigration and Naturalization Service).

FIVE

Patterns of Work
and Settlement

WHAT kinds of work Mexican immigrants could find and where they settled had very considerable consequences for the assimilative opportunities available to them. This chapter will follow the immigrants of the first half of this century to their places of work and settlement. It will show that their work and settlement patterns varied significantly from those of most European immigrant groups. On the whole these patterns tended to retard the assimilation of Mexican Americans.

Of course, patterns of work and patterns of settlement are closely related. Work and residence impose limits one upon the other. A census official of the 1870s spoke of "those who are where they are, because they are doing what they are doing; and those who are doing what they are doing, because they are where they are."[1]

[1] Notes for this chapter start on page 95.
Arthur Gerst assisted in the preparation of materials used in this chapter.

The work experience and settlement patterns of immigrant groups are deeply (but not exclusively) affected by the structure of the economy of the receiving country. In the Southwest economy during the twentieth century large parts of the region were underdeveloped when mass migrations from Mexico began (Chapter 3). Workers were in relatively great demand for ranching, agriculture, mining, railroads, irrigation works, and construction. Much of the growing industrial activity was initially related to farming (such as the processing of agricultural products) or to mining. Both the location and type of jobs bore a close resemblance to rural work away from urban concentrations. The rapid growth of the region was made possible, in part, by importing foreign workers—first Asians and then Mexican Americans. These workers did the dirty and low-wage chores which most natives could afford to shun. By contrast, the earlier European immigrants to the East took up their new life in a more highly industrialized as well as urbanized economy, which provided far greater opportunities for material gains and assimilation.

Compared with twentieth-century immigrants to the East, Mexican Americans were largely confined to rural areas for several decades during the early peak years of immigration (Table 5–1). This had much to do with the nature of the region at the time.

CONTRASTS BETWEEN MEXICAN AND EUROPEAN IMMIGRANTS

For many European immigrants their first view of the United States was New York as seen from Ellis Island; for Mexican newcomers it was more likely to be the vast expanse of Texas seen from El Paso, not unlike the rural areas from which they came. Before World War II, few if any cities of the Southwest matched the strong industrial, diversified base of Eastern cities. The initial points of entrance were not the teeming urban areas filled with opportunity but rather points of departure or bases of operation for the primary sources of employment, such as mining, railroads, and agriculture. All of these are non-urban industries, and the last two require a mobile labor force—the former for constantly moving construction gangs and more or less stable section (maintenance) crews, and the latter for work at various peak seasons on various crops. Railroads were particularly important employers of Mexican labor in the early decades of the twentieth century.[2] Agricultural and railroad work also accounts for the Mexican-American settlements outside the Southwest. In Chicago, Kansas City, Detroit, St. Louis and other midwest cities, Mexican-American *barrios* developed around railroad *secciones*, packing-houses, or other work camps. Widespread networks of family and friendship communication reaching to Mexico as well as the Southwest aided in maintaining this mode of life through information about employment opportunities in a large part of the country. As both travel and settlement were mostly ethnically homogeneous activities, geographic mobility did little to enhance opportunities for assimilation. In addition, when Mexicans did go to cities in the Southwest, they were likely to be cities in which there had always been large concentrations of Mexicans.

Ethnic groups that develop within an already existing community of the same ethnic background have a real advantage in settling in a social environment approaching relatively more "institutional completeness."[3] Such groups have less reason to rely on the host society for the satisfaction of needs. This suggests that for urbanizing Mexican Americans the social and cultural uprooting may have been less severe than for other immigrants to the United States. Although Mexican-American communities often lacked a formal complex of ethnic school, work, welfare and political institutions,

Table 5–1. Percent Urban of Selected Foreign-stock Subpopulations in the United States, 1920–1950

Country of Origin[a]	1920		1930		1940		1950	
	FB[b]	FP[c]	FB[b]	FP[c]	FB[b]	FP[c]	FB[b]	FP[c]
Mexico	47	40	57	51	63	58	69	72
Italy	84	84	88	87	88	88	91	91
USSR	89	83	90	84	90	85	92	89
Poland	84	n.a.	86	83	86	84	89	88
Austria	75	71	83	79	80	76	85	83
Hungary	80	70	83	80	82	80	n.a.	n.a.
France	74	68	77	72	78	71	n.a.	n.a.
Belgium	66	53	73	61	73	62	n.a.	n.a.
Canada (French)	79	75	79	75	79	75	81	79
Canada (other)	72	64	77	68	75	69	80	74
Total percent	75	69	79	72	80	74	84	80

[a] The countries included in the table are those which sent to the United States their greatest number of immigrants in a decade close to the period of greatest Mexican immigration. Thus, Ireland, Great Britain, Norway, Sweden, and Germany are excluded, because their respective decades of greatest immigration were far removed from the Mexican decade. Canada and Mexico reached their peak in the 1921–1930 decade, whereas for all the remaining nations the peak decade was 1901–1910. Further, with the exception of Canada, the peak decade coincides with the decade by which the corresponding country had already sent 50 percent of its immigrants for the 1851–1950 period. Canada's peak decade was 1921–1930, but the 50 percent point was reached in the previous decade. Peak decades and percentages were derived and partially computed from W. S. Woytinsky, *World Population and Production* (New York: The Twentieth Century Fund, 1953), p. 83. This manner of selection reduces the bias of comparing Mexican Americans with groups which had been in the United States for much longer periods. However, Mexican peaks came still later in this immigration surge.
[b] Foreign born.
[c] Foreign or mixed parentage.
Source: E. P. Hutchinson, *Immigrants and Their Children* (New York: John Wiley & Sons, Inc., 1956), p. 26. Figures are rounded.

their informal networks were strong. Whether the urbanizing Mexican American came from Mexico or from rural settlements in the United States, he had greater relative opportunity to become imbedded in a familiar pre-established social structure. Consequently, adaptation and adjustment problems undoubtedly required less inter-ethnic contact.[4]

Interaction and involvement with institutions of the host society are important steps toward assimilation and acculturation. To the extent that the receiving ethnic community provides new members with a prepared institutional structure, furnishing both protection and isolation, a significant opportunity for assimilation becomes relatively weak or ineffective. According to Eisenstadt, absorption is less likely to occur when communication with the surrounding host society is restricted. Communication constitutes a process through which new values, goals, and aspirations are transmitted, and which eventually undermines the original primary group structure.[5] Mexican "institutional completeness" thus tended to hamper communication with the dominant white society. Furthermore, apparently Mexicans were not defined by the core society as particularly salient targets for communication. In Los Angeles, for example, a growing political machine in the early part of this century excluded Mexicans along with other "colored populations" from their efforts.[6]

There is even some evidence to suggest that the presence of an established Mexican-American nucleus which attracted urbanizing Mexican Americans probably acted to frustrate their politicization and their utilization of other urban institutions. The relatively sudden and massive urbanization of the other nationality groups implies that large proportions of each group faced similar problems simultaneously, before internal differentiation of interests could produce serious divisions. In the Mexican-American pattern, many of the towns possessed an established and "advanced group of Mexican Americans with traditions of family and culture."[7] Drawn to these segregated ethnic enclaves, later arrivals either from Mexico or rural areas in the United States faced problems which were not identical with those of the more experienced earlier residents, despite the identity in culture and traditional institutions. The newcomers often encountered greater internal differentiation of class, status, and interest. Among other national groups the relative suddenness of their urbanization suggests that an overwhelming proportion started out occupying approximately equal status and were confronted by common problems of adjustment, with differentiation developing later.

As for the comparatively large percentage of Mexican-American farm workers who lived at least part of the year in cities,[8] the intensity and range of their orientation to urban institutions may have been less than for those who worked as well as lived in the city.

Work experience and work patterns of an immigrant group may be significantly affected not only by the structure of the receiving country's economy but also by its degree of prosperity. One of the great setbacks in the American economy occurred shortly after the 1920–1929 wave of Mexican immigration, which brought almost half a million legal and many illegal entrants to this country. It is quite likely that the Great Depression inhibited the initial economic progress of this large group of immigrants. The small advances, if any, of the Mexican Americans up to the 1930s may have been easily wiped out, impeding the transfer to the second generation of skills, aspirations, and improved levels of living. It is possible that this effect of the Depression restricted the opportunities for assimilation or delayed them by a whole generation. The next wave of immigration did not occur before the 1950s and 1960s. Thus this new group has had comparatively little time to make appreciable progress, although the economy as a whole has been prosperous. Possibly a successful preparatory period (of unknown length) is necessary before immigrant groups can "take off" into self-sustained assimilative job careers. The timing of Mexican immigration may have served to lengthen this period.

Further, the assimilative opportunities of Mexican immigrants were narrowed by their concentration in dead-end agricultural jobs. Industrial work, besides being more steady and better paid, has always provided a more promising avenue to social mobility. To make matters worse, the proximity of the border made it easy to expand (and contract) the supply of agricultural labor, with the result that wages could be held at low levels.

Finally, the general economic context has important consequences for the competitive relations between immigrant and native groups. European immigrants settling in Eastern cities competed with one another but competed less directly with the more established natives, who were settled in higher status positions.[9] For example, Italian immigrants, eager to seize opportunities, competed with and were compared with other immigrants of nearly equal status. In the case of Mexicans there was an historical exception to this common situation. In the 1930s, California attracted natives from other parts of the country who migrated to escape disaster produced by the Depression or by farm erosion in Oklahoma, Arkansas, and elsewhere. Thus, Mexican Americans were competing directly with natives for opportunities at the same economic levels. Consequently, the normal struggle of immigrants was relatively more intense for the large number of Mexican Americans who had arrived in this country during the 1920s.

SPECIAL ASPECTS OF WORK PATTERNS

Associated with the historical concentration of Mexican immigrants in rural areas was their unusually great involvement in agricultural work. Although the statistical evidence for the early part of this century is meager, estimates indicate, for example, that in Texas 46 percent of all foreign-born Mexicans were employed in agriculture in 1900, and 49 percent in 1910.[10] But the work experience of the newcomers from Mexico shows still other distinctive characteristics.

Discontinuity in Immigrants' Work Patterns

Discontinuity in the types of work performed by Mexicans in the home country and in the new country seems to have differed from the discontinuity experienced by the other immigrant groups included in our comparative analysis. A relatively large percentage of European immigrants who entered nonagricultural work here had agricultural backgrounds. In contrast, Mexican immigrants included a relatively small percentage of persons with agricultural backgrounds, but upon arrival a high percentage were inducted into agricultural jobs. In the four half-decades starting with 1910 and ending with 1929, Mexican farm laborers and foremen were only 2.2, 1.6, 1.2, and 6.7 percent, respectively, of the total. Percentages computed for all immigrants in the same four periods were 32.9, 11.1, 6.6, and 11.0, respectively. Of the

Mexican immigrants between 1910 through 1929, about 70 percent were in the nonfarm, non-mine laborer category. For all immigrants in the same period, the proportion was about 30 percent.[11] In view of the highly informal movements of people across the Mexican border during the early part of the twentieth century, the occupational classifications of immigrants may be quite imperfect. Mexican immigrants may have been motivated to list nonagricultural occupations. Besides, many of the Mexican immigrants who reported that they were engaged in nonfarm work probably came from small towns and other places with a rural orientation, and it would be erroneous, in light of Mexico's economic structure before World War II, to equate nonagricultural with industrial occupations. Consequently, it would be perhaps an overstatement to say that Mexican and non-Mexican immigrants experienced opposite discontinuity in work patterns at home and in the new country. It suffices for this analysis to suggest that the kind of discontinuity typical for many Europeans—from farm to urban work—was not duplicated in the case of many Mexicans.

Migratory Jobs

Another distinctive pattern of work is the migratory character of agricultural jobs held by Mexican immigrants—again a fact of history, though not as important today in the total employment pattern of the group as it was in the past. In comparison to most other immigrant groups, Mexicans were highly concentrated among *migrant* farm workers. The literature describing their migratory routes is abundant. For example, Menefee's study of the work histories of 300 Mexican-American families in Crystal City in 1938 found a neat dovetailing of season, crop, and migratory movement:

> More than nine-tenths of the families worked in spinach . . . from late November to the end of March. When all the spinach was cut and shipped, 19 out of 20 families migrated north or east to work in other crops. Almost a third got in a few weeks' work in the Texas onion harvest before going on to beets or cotton. Over 60 percent of the families worked in the sugarbeet fields throughout an area extending from Michigan to Montana. A third of all the families worked at picking cotton from July until late autumn. Almost half of this latter group found work in chopping cotton before the picking season started.[12]

Similar migratory patterns have been described for California in the 1930s, where Mexican-American families worked on truck crops in the Imperial Valley in January, moved northwest for pea-picking in March, traveled farther north for apricots in June, then worked in vineyards during the summer in San Bernardino County. The migratory routes extended from El Centro to north of Fresno. Taylor estimated that one-half or more of the 20,000 Imperial Valley Mexican Americans "join in the great migration to the San Joaquin Valley to work in grapes, cotton, apricots, peaches and prunes."[13] Using data from sugar-beet companies, Taylor shows that in 1927 over 10,000 Mexican-American farm workers migrated into Colorado beet fields; these workers came mostly from Colorado, but a large number migrated from New Mexico, Texas, and California.[14] Taylor's study of Dimmit County, Texas, also reports on migratory movements of Mexican-American families: "A majority of the Mexicans pick cotton in south, central, and west Texas. Most of them begin near Corpus Christi, some go as far north as Dallas and west to Amarillo."[15]

Two related aspects of these migratory work patterns deserve emphasis. First, many of the migrants moved from place to place in family units, a phenomenon infrequently encountered in other new immigration groups. A number of studies confirm Taylor's observation that "many of those [Mexicans] going into the cotton fields of Texas are accompanied by their entire families. This is to the liking of the planters, for it is maintained that children as a rule will pick as much cotton as the grown-ups."[16] Extensive use was made of child labor in Colorado beet fields.[17] For the most part, the family units moved and worked in ethnically homogeneous groups, as did the gangs of single men involved in migratory farm labor. This pattern of employment served, of course, to reinforce their isolation.

Second, as mentioned earlier, many of the migratory workers resided in urban centers and worked for part of the year in nonagricultural jobs. Urban places were often a winter haven or convenient job market to which farm workers returned during off seasons. For these workers and their families, then, there was less differentiation between urban and rural residence or farm and nonfarm work than there was for most other immigrant groups. Theirs was a more transitional type of social organization, not completely developed into one or the other form. Many studies show this fluctuation,[18] but its significance can easily be obscured by employment surveys taken at particular times of the year. For example, the 1930 report of Governor C. C. Young of California stresses the wide range of occupations held by Mexican Americans and their involvement in nonagricultural work. The data were derived from a survey reporting employment and wage data for Mexican Americans as of May 15, 1928.[19] Because of this date, the mixed rural-urban work pattern was probably not revealed in its true proportions. The survey most likely caught many workers in jobs which were exchanged for agricultural labor several months later.[20]

The study of pecan shellers by Menefee and Cassmore illustrates the continuing links between farm work and work normally recorded as nonagricultural.[21] From 1933 to 1938, pecan shelling in San Antonio employed from 10,000 to 20,000 workers annually, almost all of them Mexican Americans. The study excluded families whose principal income was from work outside the pecan industry. About 68 percent of the 512 family heads surveyed were either born in San Antonio or had arrived there nearly 20 years before the time of the study. Most of these people, then, would be classified in official statistics as urban and nonagricultural. Yet, despite the exclusion of workers whose principal income was outside the industry, the study reported that 23 percent of the surveyed families followed the crops in Texas, Michigan, and Minnesota.[22] Shifts from urban to agricultural work, and vice versa, were necessary because of seasonal or intermittent employment in both, and because wages were so low that neither rural nor city earnings alone could sustain life. Thus, the wages of pecan shellers "were unbelievably low"—estimated at $2.00 a week in 1934, and their median annual income was estimated at $251 in 1938 (for a family of 4.6 persons).[23]

Isolating Effects of Work Patterns

The mixed patterns of work and residence—a high incidence of farm employment and migratory jobs, families as work units, incomplete differentiation of agricultural from industrial occupations—have almost no twentieth-century counterpart among European immigrant groups. The resulting restraints on assimilative opportunities were reinforced by the fact that some of the nonagricultural jobs typically held by Mexican Americans also tended to insulate them from contacts with the larger community.

This was true for mining—an industry traditional to members of the group and one usually located in remote, isolated places. And it was also true for railroad workers, who were often housed in old railroad cars or other makeshift accommodations near the tracks or on the wrong side of the tracks. In fact, some of the urban places to which Mexican Americans gravitated for steady employment had originated as one-industry railroad towns and, since railroad trains in earlier days required more frequent service stops, small isolated settlements, neither urban nor rural, were developed along the tracks. Barstow, California, was such a town that attracted Mexican immigrants. "Section houses" composed of two-room units arranged in six- to eight-unit buildings were constructed by the Santa Fe Railroad along the tracks at five- to ten-mile intervals and were provided rent-free for its workers. Single-family units were built in Barstow for personnel with higher occupational status. Single men lived in railroad bunk houses or roomed in Barstow or nearby Daggett.[24]

There were still other urban industries with a Mexican-American labor force which afforded minimal scope for assimilation. The brickyard, typically located at the edge of a town, is a case in point. Isolation was carried to an extreme in a settlement in Los Angeles County just outside of Montebello, where the Simons Brick Company erected a walled, wholly Mexican company town—complete with church, school, store, and other community facilities. The company was managed in a spirit of paternalistic benevolence, but its workers were effectively isolated from the larger community.[25]

IMPLICATIONS

FOR ASSIMILATIVE OPPORTUNITIES

In comparison to other immigrant groups, the historical work and settlement patterns of Mexican Americans tended to retard the rate at which they were able to develop a base of welfare and power from which further gains could be achieved,

89

consolidated, and transmitted to the next generation. Although it is difficult to differentiate clearly between the settlement pattern and the work pattern as causative forces, the one probably compounded the influence of the other in inhibiting assimilation. However, some specific implications of work patterns merit elaboration.

Time and Place

One of these implications pertains to the timing and destination of immigration. During the nineteenth century it was easier for newcomers who entered agricultural work in low-level jobs to use this start as a basis for further gains. Proprietorship in land was not difficult to achieve and, through homesteading and other tax benefits, was encouraged by the government. Of course, many Mexican Americans participated in the industrial expansion of the Southwest, but the relatively larger proportions engaged in farm work entered a system where it was almost impossible to convert hard work into a stable base for gain. The organization of agriculture in the Southwest, which was closely linked to Mexican immigration, did not result in the type of system where hard work near the bottom facilitated access to higher levels. Most of Southwest agriculture was always the province of big business and vast financing that people with modest means could not enter or even influence. New immigrant groups entering the United States at about the same time as the Mexicans but settling in the cities and industries of the East and Midwest had far better opportunity to acquire the skills and experience promoting upward movement. When compared with these groups, the discontinuity in work patterns experienced by Mexicans acted to locate more of them in sectors of the economy where status improvement was relatively difficult.

Effects of Work Patterns on Unionization

Another implication of the work patterns is related to labor-union organizations. For one thing, union organization generally occurred relatively late in the Southwest, and, as shown in Chapter 9, it is even now less developed in major parts of the region, notably Texas, than in other areas of the nation. The open shop was pervasive through World War II and is still widespread, with right-to-work laws in Arizona and Texas. Hence, the labor union in the Southwest has only in recent years begun to perform the assimilative function that it served earlier for immigrant groups in the East.

Further, labor unions have historically discriminated against Southwest Mexican Americans. Discriminatory ideologies in labor unions extend back to the first wave of Mexican immigration in the 1920s, and are interwoven with the traditional union opposition to immigration and the frequent use of Mexicans as strike breakers. In 1925 the California Federation of Labor convention went on record as recognizing a definite "Mexican immigration problem."[26] In 1926, the California delegation to the national AFL convention spearheaded an effort to have the federation adopt an exclusionist plank regarding Mexican immigration. In 1928, the Oil Workers of Ventura, a labor union in a community north of Los Angeles, called the Mexican "inassimilable," and Paul Scharrenberg, Secretary-Treasurer of the California State Federation of Labor, appealed for support of the Box Bill, which would have placed a quota on Mexican immigration.[27] The pattern was repeated at every convention of the Federation until 1932. Resolutions were introduced by various AFL locals, many from southern California (such as the San Diego construction locals), to exclude the Mexicans, and they were adopted by the convention with the approval of all the Los Angeles locals. A California labor official warned in 1928 that "If we do not remain on guard it is not going to be our country," and added that there was danger that governmental institutions would eventually be dominated by "a mongrel population consisting largely of Mexicans."[28] In 1930, the California State Federation of Labor pledged to wage "a constant, increasing contest . . . in the direction of effecting legislation which is calculated to stop the influx of nationals from Mexico."[29] Shapiro also reports that San Antonio's few and weak unions had an "openly hostile attitude toward minority groups, who provided scab labor in strikes and were generally willing to work for lower wages."[30]

Craft unions usually excluded ethnic or racial minorities from the better jobs. Records indicate discrimination against Mexican Americans in the Boilermakers, Machinists and Railway Carmen unions.[31] Labor organizations in the Texas oil industry were repeatedly struggling against access for Mexican Americans, invoking the dangers of lowered standards of living and unstable wages. An official union publication in 1921 commended "international officers [who] have done everything in their power to eliminate this undesirable element from the oil fields."[32] Even in 1945 it was possible for a wildcat strike to be precipitated by Anglo refinery workers after the Federal Fair Employment Practice Commission forced upgrading in the seniority of three Mexican Americans and directed the company and the union to eliminate contract conditions making the best jobs the exclusive right of Anglos.[33]

However, Mexicans were importantly involved in some labor activity. In Los Angeles the first union to strike under the National Recovery Act, which included the famous Section 7(a) guaranteeing the right to organize and bargain collectively, was the International Ladies Garment Workers Union. About half of the garment workers were Mexican Americans. The strike began on October 12, 1933, and lasted until November 6. Mexican women were the most militant group on the picket lines, prompting the official publication of the Central Labor Council, the *Los Angeles Citizen*, to say that "to the surprise of everyone" the Mexican girls were "flocking into the union."[34] In a subsequent garment-industry strike, in 1936, Mexican women were again in the forefront of picket activity. Subsequent efforts to form a Spanish-speaking local in the ILGWU were, however, frustrated. Two other locals with large Mexican-American memberships in Los Angeles, the Butchers' Local 563 and Upholsterers' Local 15, also organized during the early 1930s in conjunction with strikes. In San Antonio, the pecan shellers struck in 1938 in protest against a penny-a-pound pay reduction. This major dispute was long (30 days) and violent, involving tear gas, jailings, government intervention, and the support of national CIO officials.

The historical role of union restrictions in retarding the economic progress of Mexican Americans and the associated assimilative opportunities is difficult to assess. In the earlier decades of this century, labor organization in the Southwest was generally weak. Unions which typically control job entry and promotion were found in the construction trades, but their effectiveness at that time was questionable. Railroad workers were already well organized, and although Mexican Americans were accepted, their employment was usually confined to common labor or other low-paid jobs.[35] That not all unions practiced or condoned restrictions is exemplified by the case of the mine workers, who in 1944 brought charges against employers discriminating against Mexican Americans, and struck mining companies in 1946 largely because the companies had not complied with a corrective order by the National War Labor Board.[36] Apart from the mixed evidence, the effect of labor unions and their ethnic policies on opportunities has remained a controversial issue.[37]

More important, the absence of viable and permanent unions in agriculture has meant that the relatively large numbers of Mexican Americans in farm work were barred from whatever economic and social opportunities labor organization could provide. Not until the mid-1960s did any agriculturally based unions in the Southwest, notably California, show promise of sustained operation. Mexican Americans were involved in efforts during the 1920s and 1930s to establish farm labor unions. These efforts resulted in dramatic and partially successful strikes, but they were episodic and without organizational continuity. In a thorough and comprehensive study of agricultural unionism, Jamieson concluded in 1945 that it consisted of "hundreds of organizations that were sporadic, scattered and short-lived," and that "the few attempts to organize agricultural and allied workers in nationwide unions affiliated to the leading labor federations were on the whole unsuccessful."[38]

The migratory work pattern compounded the problem of labor organization. A dispersed population in motion is not an easy target for organizational appeals, and a temporary success is difficult to consolidate when workers are continuously migrating. Industrial unionism had the advantage of mobilizing workers who were more concentrated in work place and residence. It was easier to organize a work force whose members filed in and out of the work place at fixed locations and at fixed times and who were exposed to daily contact with organizers. In agricultural work, both migratory and non-migratory, seasonal work place and home are essentially one, thus isolating workers on private property away from the public staging areas of organizational efforts. In addition, the multiple employer structure of farm work, partially a function of labor mobility, made it less likely that union gains in one area could be transferred to another, especially when a considerable part of the work group consisted of family units.[39]

Finally, ethnicity posed a special problem in agricultural unionization. Mexican Americans contributed disproportionately large numbers to farm labor, and the relatively high mobility of this group led to public overestimates of their number.

The actual concentration, combined with an inflated estimate of concentration, probably reinforced their identification as unfriendly aliens knocking at the door of American society through agitation.[40] That farm labor agitation could be countered by threats of deportation complicated the task of union organizers. Deportation threats had public appeal because they were aimed at an easily discernible and relatively homogeneous population, and they facilitated control over a low-status group regarded as being outside the established system.[41] Oriental farm workers, especially in California, had experienced this type of antagonism earlier. At the California Fruit Growers Convention in 1907 Japanese were accused of being a "tricky and cunning lot . . . they are not organized into unions, but their clannishness seems to operate as a union would."[42] In a similar vein, farm employers could warn against letting "a bunch of Mexicans tell us what to do. [The unions] have organized a bunch of foreigners."[43]

The ethnic identification of labor movements was reinforced by the practice of giving Spanish names to organizations of Mexican-American farm workers and by the tendency of "a few race-conscious Mexican unions to function separately."[44] The ethnic linkage with union organization also contributed to inter-union rivalry and discrimination in cases like the shed workers who refused to work with nonwhites because of their tendency to "stick together."[45] Equally important in this respect was the direct involvement, probably unique in the United States, of Mexican Consuls in the affairs of Mexican-American workers. Mexican diplomats played an extensive role in worker organizations, including conciliation and arbitration in labor disputes, sponsorship of unions, and establishment of anti-communist associations.[46] It is very likely that this involvement served to reinforce the notion that Mexican Americans were difficult to assimilate.[47]

Normally, an ethnically based organization may provide a source of unity and solidarity. But the most fertile ground for the development of such solidarity is found in the more diversified industrial world, where ethnic unions have entered into coalitions with other organized groups. Ethnically homogeneous groups may gain solidarity, and thus a measure of power, by isolating their members from the appeal of competitive groups; but they sustain and expand their power usually by participating in a network of changing group coalitions. Without coalitions, organized groups attain isolation and independence, but they do not develop deployable power.[48] Mexican-American unions participated in tactical and sporadic collaboration with Filipino, Japanese and Anglo organizations, and at various times there were flexible but unsuccessful coalitions with communist political groups. But until recent years none of the agricultural unions succeeded in developing effective coalitions with the more powerful industrial organizations, even though they tried to do so.[49]

Thus, the symbolic solidarity of ethnically homogeneous Mexican-American organizations was not conducive to the establishment of relations with broader areas of the dominant social structure, and may have acted against it. Unionization campaigns in Southwest agriculture were part of a national effort to widen the base of labor organization, especially in the 1930s when the labor movement was struggling to win public acceptance. Unions of Mexican Americans had to contend not only with the regular opposition to the labor movement but also with hostility and prejudice against their ethnicity.

Effects of Work Patterns on Education

Finally, work patterns had profound and long-range significance for assimilative opportunities provided by schooling. Not only did school segregation and discrimination play an important role in the persistently low order of education achieved by this group (Chapter 7), but work patterns intervened to produce differential and independent effects upon education. The relative concentration of Mexican Americans in agriculture and the unique pattern of migratory work in family units acted to remove large proportions of children from social contexts facilitating educational achievement. The use of Mexican-American children in farm work, both migratory and residential, restricted educational opportunities. Various local studies show that fluctuations in attendance were correlated with fluctuations in agriculture. According to Taylor, the months requiring heavy farm work coincided with low enrollment levels.[50] When cotton acreage in California declined, school attendance of Mexican-American children increased.[51] Wharburton's data for Texas show for migratory families that 16 percent of the children 6 to 15 years of age attended school for 24 to 35 weeks; for children of non-migratory families the attendance was 63 percent.[52] Menefee found in Crystal City, Texas, that 65 percent of the children aged 7 to 18 of Mexican-American migrant families did not attend school at all in 1938; 16 percent attended part time, and 19 percent attended full time.[53]

School systems added to the adverse effects of work patterns upon educational opportunity by relaxing the standards for enforcing school attendance in the case of Mexican-American children, especially in rural areas. Taylor's finding that "they just never have enforced the law on the Mexicans"[54] was probably characteristic of many places in the Southwest. Colorado beet growers "who are frequently members of the rural school boards, and who employ large numbers of families which work in beets" were probably not zealous champions of enforcement.[55] Objections to the use of child farm labor were "rarely raised against Mexicans," but complaints concerning German-Russian families were frequent, because they competed "with resident American growers."[56]

Children in urban places who do not attend a school are more conspicuous in their truancy, as well as more accessible to school authorities. There are countless cases of Mexican-American families whose children went to school irregularly not because of work but because of lack of knowledge regarding compulsory attendance, or because of various family needs, values and beliefs. Of course, some urban children were kept out of school because they had to work or because they were needed to help with household responsibilities. Yet, children of the urban ghettoes were relatively easier to locate and influence than those in rural areas.

Still another, related consequence of work patterns to educational opportunities is more elusive. The work patterns which reduce the proportion of children system-atically involved in schooling also deprive the parents of an assimilative opportunity. Children of immigrants carry the content of socialization from school to home, and this content may become the seedbed of social change among the adults. The role models, aspirations, and orientations imparted in the school context often produce conflict in the traditional household, but in coping with the tension thus created, parents are often influenced to perceive and accept the possibility of change in their own life plans as well as in those of their children. A multiplier effect may be pro-duced in the sense that children become agents of parental socialization, which in turn reinforces the assimilative influences of the school on the children. Because so many Mexican-American children were exposed to a highly erratic school experience, the younger generation could not perform this function as effectively as did their counterparts among other immigrant groups.

In all probability, the work patterns analyzed here retarded the differentiation between family and school, thus weakening the assimilative opportunities normally accompanying educational experience in immigrant families.

*   *   *

Both the settlement and the work patterns of Mexican Americans—patterns which are interrelated and probably mutually reinforcing in their effects—have historically restricted this group's chances for assimilation. In contrast to European immigrants in the late nineteenth and the early twentieth centuries who typically entered our society in urban places and industrial occupations, Mexican immigrants were more concentrated in rural areas and agricultural jobs. Besides, much of their farm work was seasonal and migratory, with people moving from area to area in ethnically homogenous groups of family units or individuals and a large admixture of child labor. For many members of the minority, urban employment and residence were not clearly differentiated from rural. Among the consequences were a degree of residential and work instability not encountered by major European immigrant groups, far greater isolation from the community-at-large and its social institutions, and specific educational handicaps. All these factors made it difficult to achieve a base of economic security and influence in the community from which initial gains could be expanded, consolidated, and transmitted to the next generation. Work patterns, combined with ethnic orientation of efforts to organize farm labor, con-tributed to the problems of using unionization as a means of economic and social improvement.

NOTES TO CHAPTER FIVE

1. E. P. Hutchinson, *Immigrants and Their Children: 1850–1950* (New York: John Wiley & Sons, Inc., 1956), p. 68, note.

2. McWilliams quotes a Department of Labor investigator in 1912 to the effect that "most of the Mexicans then in the United States had at one time or another worked for the

railroads." Carey McWilliams, *North from Mexico* (Philadelphia: J. B. Lippincott Company, 1949), p. 168.

3. "Institutional completeness would be at its extreme whenever the ethnic community could perform all the services required by its members. Members would never have to make use of native institutions for the satisfaction of any of their needs." Raymond Breton, "Institutional Completeness of Ethnic Communities and the Personal Relations of Immigrants," *American Journal of Sociology*, LXX (Sept., 1964), p. 194.

4. *Ibid.*, p. 201–203.

5. See S. N. Eisenstadt, *The Absorption of Immigrants* (London: Routledge & Kegan Paul, Ltd., 1954), pp. 6–10.

6. Robert M. Fogelson, *The Fragmented Metropolis: Los Angeles, 1850–1930* (Cambridge, Mass.: Harvard University Press, 1967), Chap. 10, p. 203.

7. O. Douglas Weeks "The League of United Latin-American Citizens: A Texas-Mexican Civic Organization," *Southwestern Political and Social Science Quarterly*, X (Dec., 1929), p. 258. Weeks mentions especially Brownsville, Rio Grande City, Roma, and Laredo, in Texas, but there are many others.

8. Large-scale commercialized ranching and farming required a labor force which could be expanded and contracted with seasonal demands. Especially in California, agriculture had little need for a work force permanently settled on the land. In his study of Wasco, California, Goldschmidt found that industrialized agriculture, despite its reliance on traditional types of agricultural labor, is consistent with the kind of structural and cultural differentiation characteristic of urban communities. Walter Goldschmidt, *As You Sow* (New York: Harcourt, Brace and Company, Inc., 1947). See also Carey McWilliams, *Factories in the Field* (Boston: Little, Brown and Company, 1939), and Ernesto Galarza, *Merchants of Labor: The Mexican Bracero Story* (San Jose, Calif.: The Rosicrucian Press, Ltd., 1964), pp. 22–26

According to census data, 28.6 percent of California's paid farm workers lived in urban areas in 1930, increasing to 30.0 percent by 1950. When just Spanish-surname workers are examined (possible only for 1950), the proportion increases to 35.5 percent. The other Southwest states fall short of these figures, with 25.4 percent in 1950 for Arizona, 13.3 percent for Colorado, 10.9 percent for New Mexico, and 19.4 percent for Texas (for all farm workers, including Spanish surname). However, Arizona and Texas remain in advance of the United States average of 13.9 percent for the same year. In 1930, figures include 8.3 percent for Arizona, 14.2 percent for Colorado, 6.7 percent for New Mexico, and 13.3 percent for Texas. For 1930, see *1930 U.S. Census of Population*, vol. III, part 1, tables 30 (U.S.) and 10 (states); part 2, table 10 (states). Data are for workers 10 years and older. For 1950, *1950 U.S. Census of Population*, vol. II, part 1, table 126; parts 3, 5, 6 and 31; and part 45, table 75. Because of a new definition of "urban," the 1950 data are not strictly comparable with the 1930 figures. Also, data are for workers 14 years and older. For Spanish surname, see U.S. Census of Population, 1950, v. IV, Special Reports, part 3, *Persons of Spanish Surname*.

9. See Milton Gordon, *Assimilation in American Life* (New York: Oxford University Press, 1964), pp. 42 ff.

10. For 1920 the estimate is 29.8 percent in Texas. Estimates were also made for New Mexico (where in 1900 29.1 percent, in 1910 35.9 percent, and in 1920 26.0 percent of all foreign-born Mexicans were employed in agriculture) and for Arizona (where in 1900 18.3 percent, in 1910 65.8 percent, and in 1920 10.1 percent of all foreign-born Mexicans were employed in agriculture, though the 1910 figure is questionable). These were estimated by first computing the absolute number of foreign-born in agriculture (using percentages derived from Varden Fuller, "Occupations of the Mexican-born Population of Texas, New Mexico and Arizona," *American Statistical Association*, XXIII [Mar., 1928], pp. 64–67). Second,

we calculated what percentage this number was of foreign-born Mexicans, using *Abstract of the Twelfth Census*, p. 85; *Thirteenth U.S. Census*, Occupation Statistics, p. 44; *Abstract of the Fourteenth Census*, p. 500. The exclusion of California and Colorado in these early statistics compiled by Fuller eliminates important information. More adequate data, however, are available for 1930, and they shows that 32.9 percent of the Mexican-American males in the Southwest at that time were farm laborers. See Walter Fogel, *Mexican Americans in Southwest Labor Markets* (Mexican-American Study Project, Advance Report 10, Graduate School of Business Administration, University of California, Los Angeles, Oct., 1967), table 23.

11. Leo Grebler et al., *Mexican Immigration to the United States: The Record and Its Implications* (Mexican-American Study Project. Advance Report 2, Graduate School of Business Administration, University of California, Los Angeles, Jan. 1966), table 8.

12. Selden C. Menefee, *Mexican Migratory Workers in South Texas*, Works Progress Administration (Washington, D.C., 1941), p. xiv.

13. Paul S. Taylor, *Mexican Labor in the United States: Imperial Valley* (Berkeley, Calif.: University of California Press, 1928), p. 40.

14. Paul S. Taylor, *Mexican Labor in the United States: Valley of the South Platte, Colorado* (Berkeley, Calif.: University of California Press, 1929), p. 135. See also Allen G. Harper et al., *Man and Resources in the Middle Rio Grande Valley* (Albuquerque, N. Mex.: The University of New Mexico Press, 1943), pp. 66–79.

15. Paul S. Taylor, *Mexican Labor in the United States: Dimmit County, Winter Garden District, South Texas* (Berkeley, Calif.: University of California Press, 1930), p. 308. For earlier migratory movements, see Paul S. Taylor, *An American-Mexican Frontier* (Chapel Hill, N.C.: University of North Carolina Press, 1934), pp. 102 ff.

16. *Ibid.*, p. 102. See also Menefee, *op. cit.*, pp. 15 ff., and Amber Wharburton et al., *The Work and Welfare of Children of Agricultural Laborers in Hidalgo County, Texas* (U.S. Department of Labor, Children's Bureau, 1943).

17. Sara A. Brown, *Children Working in the Sugar Beet Fields of Certain Districts of the South Platte Valley, Colorado* (New York: National Child Labor Committee, 1925), *passim*, especially pp. 54 and 162, 163

18. See California. Legislature. Joint Committee on Agricultural and Livestock Problems. *The Recruitment and Placement of Farm Laborers in California, 1950*, California State Senate (Sacramento, 1951), pp. 195-198, 206–215, 266–340 *passim*; Taylor, *Imperial Valley*, pp. 27–29; Harper et al., *op. cit.*, pp. 66–69.

19. *Mexicans in California*, Report of Governor C. C. Young's Mexican Fact-finding Committee (Sacramento, Calif., 1930). Almost 11 percent of the workers in the 975 firms sampled were Mexican Americans working in manufacturing establishments. For all gainful workers in California in 1930, about 26 percent were in manufacturing and mechanical industries (calculated from *Abstract of the Fifteenth Census*, pp. 321–324).

20. California labor needs in agriculture are relatively low in May. The heaviest demand occurs from July to October (Report of Governor Young's Committee, *op. cit.* p. 157). The same report includes a survey of almost 800 households in southern California, in which 72 percent of the male heads "gave their occupation as laborers, most of whom were doing agricultural work" (*ibid.*, pp. 209, 214).

21. Selden Menefee and Orin Cassmore, *The Pecan Shellers of San Antonio* (Works Progress Administration, 1940).

22. *Ibid.*, pp. 2, 4, and 26.

23. Harold A. Shapiro, "The Workers of San Antonio, Texas, 1900–1940" (unpublished Ph.D. dissertation, University of Texas, 1952), pp. 119–121; based on Menefee and Cassmore, *op. cit.*

24. Joan Teplow, "The Mexican Americans of Barstow, California" (unpublished manuscript).

25. Lorenzo M. Campbell, "Simons: The Brickyard Hacienda" (unpublished manuscript).

26. *Proceedings of the 26th Annual Convention*, California State Federation of Labor (San Diego, Calif., Sept. 21–25, 1925), p. 78.

27. *Proceedings of the 29th Annual Convention*, California State Federation of Labor (Sacramento, Calif., Sept. 17–21, 1928), pp. 29, 51, 65.

28. Testimony in 1928 by Edward H. Dowell, Vice-President of the California State Federation of Labor, before the United States Senate Committee on Immigration; cited in Robert J. Lipshultz, "American Attitudes Toward Mexican Immigration, 1924–1952" (unpublished Ph.D. dissertation, University of Chicago, 1962), p. 61.

29. *Proceedings of the 31st Annual Convention*, California State Federation of Labor (Marysville, Calif., Sept. 15–19, 1930), p. 79.

30. Shapiro, *op. cit.*, p. 333.

31. H. R. Northrup, "Race Discrimination in Trade Unions: The Record and Outlook," *Commentary*, II (Aug., 1946), p. 128.

32. Ruth Allen, *Chapters in the History of Organized Labor in Texas* (Austin, Tex.: University of Texas Press, 1941), 233. The publication referred to was the *International Oil Worker*.

33. Pauline R. Kibbe, *Latin-Americans in Texas* (Albuquerque, N.Mex.: The University of New Mexico Press, 1946), p. 161. However, this was not a union-sponsored strike.

34. *Los Angeles Citizen.* Oct. 6, 1933, p. 6.

35. Even as late as 1946, it was reported that some of the rail unions classified Mexicans as nonwhite and excluded them, along with Negroes and Indians. Complaints were filed with the Federal Equal Employment Opportunities Committee that the Brotherhood of Railway Carmen had prevented Mexican Americans from obtaining jobs other than as common laborers on the Union Pacific. The Brotherhood of Maintenance-of-Way Employees, which had jurisdiction over most of the Mexican-American railroad workers, required United States citizenship as a prerequisite for holding a union office. See Northrup, *op. cit.*, p. 128.

36. The case involved the International Union of Mine, Mill and Smelter Workers, CIO, and three mining companies. The National War Labor Board found that the companies classified employees as "Anglo-American Males" and "Other Employees." Included in the latter classification were all females, "Latin-Americans," Negroes, Filipinos, and Indians. If a Mexican with no experience was hired, he was classified as a common laborer and paid $5.21 for a shift; but if an Anglo-American with no experience was hired, he was classified as a helper and paid $6.36 per shift. The board also found that there was no apparent relationship between the length of service of an employee and his wage rate. Workers classified in the "Other Employees" group who had been employed for ten years rarely received more than the starting rate for Mexican labor. From McWilliams, *North From Mexico*, *op. cit.*, pp. 197–198.

37. One of the few comprehensive studies of the subject states that "the job level of an ethnic minority is likely to be an indirect result of hiring practices in the industry, rather than the ethnic policies of the labor union . . . " Scott Greer, *The Participation of Ethnic Minorities in the Labor Unions of Los Angeles County* (unpublished Ph.D. dissertation, University of California, Los Angeles, 1952), p. 144. According to one student of unionism, however, unions have had most effect, both positive and negative, upon labor mobility, of which access to jobs is a part. See George H. Hildebrand, "American Unionism, Social Stratification, and Power," *American Journal of Sociology*, LVIII (Jan., 1953), especially pp. 385, 386. For further discussion of this subject, see chapter 9.

38. Stuart Jamieson, *Labor Unionism in American Agriculture*, U.S. Bureau of Labor Statistics Bulletin 836 (1945), p. 406. Extensive documentation on Southwest agriculture is in pp. 15–30, 80–149, 164–188, and 270–282.

39. *Ibid.*, pp. 101, 102, and pp. 104, 105.

40. See Alexander Morin, *The Organizability of Farm Labor in the United States* (Cambridge, Mass.: Harvard University Press, 1952), p. 35. An exhibit submitted to United States Senate hearings in 1937 stated that "The common estimate of farm employers during the late twenties was that the ... Mexican laborers constituted 70 to 80 percent of the casual labor supply." The actual figure was about 21 percent. See United States Senate Hearings, *Violations of Free Speech and Rights of Labor*, part 52 (1940), p. 19859.

41. Jamieson, *op. cit.*, p. 102

42. *Ibid.* p. 52. For even earlier sentiments, see *ibid.*, pp. 46 ff.

43. *Ibid.*, p. 227.

44. *Ibid.*, pp. 122 ff. and p. 128.

45. *Ibid.*, p. 199.

46. *Ibid.*, pp. 90–92 and pp. 108, 109. It should be recalled that these observations pertain to the period following the Mexican Revolution.

47. For other types of relations between the Consulate and Mexican Americans, see Emory S. Bogardus, "The Mexican Immigrant and Segregation," *American Journal of Sociology*, XXXVI (July, 1930), pp. 74–80.

48. The successes of Cesar Chavez's National Farm Workers Association, strongly identified as Mexican American, would probably not have occurred without the extensive cooperation of liberal urban groups and of the AFL-CIO, notably of Walter Reuther.

49. Jamieson, *op cit.*, pp. 122–133

50. Taylor, *A Mexican-American Frontier*, p. 194; *Dimmit County*, p. 372.

51. Taylor, *Imperial County*, p. 76.

52. Wharburton et al., *op. cit.*, p. 38.

53. Menefee, *Mexican Migratory Workers*, p. 44.

54. Taylor, *Dimmit County*, statement by a school principal, p. 373.

55. Taylor, *South Platte Colorado*, pp. 195, 196 ff.

56. *Ibid.*, p. 201.

Part three

SOCIOECONOMIC

CONDITIONS:

A DETAILED PORTRAIT

INTRODUCTORY NOTE

This group of chapters describes (1) the demographic characteristics of Mexican Americans, their educational attainment, and their economic position; (2) the status differences within the population, especially the differences between generations; and (3) the local variations in the condition of this minority.

The highlights of the analysis were presented in Chapter 2. We shall now probe the reasons for the generally low status of Mexican Americans, as well as portray their conditions in more detail. *Why* does their average schooling lag so much behind that of the general population? *Why* is their average income so low in comparison with Anglos? To what extent is the income gap explained by the educational gap? *Why* do Mexican Americans earn less than Anglos even when sex, age, occupation, and urban–rural residence are held as constant as the data and statistical techniques permit? *Why* is their residential segregation from Anglos (and from nonwhites) greater in some Southwest cities than in others?

To try to answer such questions means entering hazardous territory. The available data or the "state of the arts," or both, are often too limited to yield wholly satisfactory results. In some cases, it is possible to identify and even quantify correlates of a given condition that have varying degrees of explanatory power. This is true, for example, for residential segregation, though the multiple regression analysis involved in such an effort to pin down causes leaves unexplained variance. Discrimination in housing markets is probably one of the factors hidden in such variance. However, our findings indicate that the residential segregation of Mexican Americans is less severe than that of Negroes in all cities.

In other cases, as in the analysis of the Mexican-Americans' position in urban labor markets, we examine a number of hypotheses to explain why Mexican Americans earn less than Anglos in identical job classifications. We shall show how the job allocation system places Mexican Americans at a disadvantage even when no discrimination is intended. Among other things, the system tends to channel minority workers into highly competitive industries, non-union employers, and small firms. Wage rates are low and jobs unsteady in these three types of business.

The discussion of housing conditions points up the influence of the large Mexican-American family on consumption patterns. Minority households occupy housing inferior to that of Anglos and are more crowded regardless of whether they are well-to-do or poor. The size of Mexican-American families exceeds the size of Anglo families in each income bracket.

The greatest difficulty is encountered when one tries to explain the educational gap—unquestionably an important factor in the low economic status of this minority, and of growing importance in a modern economy in which good jobs increasingly require high skills. In addition to a statistical analysis of educational attainment, Chapter 7 presents the results of two special studies designed to investigate *why* the average schooling of Mexican Americans is so poor. One was a review of school practices, policies, and philosophies throughout the Southwest. The other study, limited to Los Angeles schools, was quantitative and more intensive. Here, an effort was made to discover the influence on pupils' achievement of the school itself and its environment, of the students' peer group, of the parents' socio-economic status, and of other measurable factors. Both home and school environment seem to be important, but many questions remain unanswered.

In addition to *de facto* school segregation, intra-school segregation continues to prevent interaction between Mexican-American and Anglo students. That this is a real dilemma rather than a wholly contrived policy to keep the minority pupils apart is illustrated by the fact that even the recent programs of bilingual instruction or remedial education tend to separate Mexican-American students from the majority.

* * *

The statistical materials included in this group of chapters warrant some comment. Most of the data are from the U.S. Census of Population, and the last census available for this study was taken in 1960. Although the figures are several years old, we believe that they depict a reasonably current situation for the analysis of *structural relationships,* which is the focus of these chapters. To be sure, the number of Mexican Americans has increased since 1960, probably at a greater rate than did the rest of the population, and their residential distribution may have changed. However, we are mainly concerned with *differentials*—for example, the

103

income of Mexican Americans relative to that of the reference populations, income differences between the native-born and the foreign-born persons in the group, and inter-area variations in the relative income of Mexican Americans.

As the comparisons of 1950 and 1960 data will show, differentials of this kind changed slowly in a decade. The relative position of the minority improved on most scores. There is no reason to believe that changes since 1960 accelerated to such an extent that the structural relationships shown in the 1960 census are no longer broadly representative. This is an unhappy fact of life when the speed of progress of Mexican Americans is considered, but it means that the 1960 census still provides the most reliable and comprehensive information on their position in the Southwest. The generally available census statistics are supplemented here by special unpublished tabulations obtained for this study.

The reference populations selected for the analysis include Anglos, that is, all whites other than Spanish-surname persons; nonwhites; and, in some cases, subgroups of nonwhites such as Negroes, Orientals, and American Indians. The nonwhite population is unusually heterogeneous in some areas of the region. Therefore, separate statistics are shown for subgroups when they are particularly relevant and data are available. However, a systematic disaggregation of nonwhites would take us too far afield and would in any event be difficult for lack of adequate comparable data.

The census figures pertain to "white persons of Spanish surname" rather than Mexican Americans. As is shown in Appendix A, these figures nevertheless can be considered reasonably representative of the Mexican-American population. However, the user of the census data must be mindful of the technical limitations discussed in Appendix A.

SIX

Distinctive Population Patterns

As the result of a high birth rate and continuous immigration, the Mexican-American population of the Southwest has been growing at a fast pace. Between 1950 and 1960 the rate of increase (compounded annually) was 4.1 percent as against less than 3.1 percent for Anglos and 3.3 percent for the total population. The regional growth rate, in turn, greatly exceeded that of the nation (1.7 percent). The Mexican-American population was an important contributor to the regional growth. Spanish-surname people were 10.9 percent of all persons in the Southwest in 1950 and 11.8 percent in 1960. They accounted for 14.2 percent of the *increase* in the region's total population during the decade. Their share in the total is unquestionably greater at the present time. Nonwhites in 1960 were 9.3 percent of the Southwest population. Thus, Spanish-surname persons and nonwhites together accounted for well over one-fifth of all people in the region (Table 6–1). Few if any large areas of the United States show a comparable constellation of two large, though differentiated, minority groups that comprise such a high proportion of the total population.

The rapid growth of the Mexican-American population continued in the 1960s. Our projections for 1970 in Appendix A indicate a range of 4.7 to 5.2 million people in the Southwest, compared to 3.4 million in 1960; and a range of 5.3 to 5.8 million in the United States as against 3.8 million in 1960. Throwing caution to the wind, we estimate Mexican Americans at 5 million in the Southwest and 5.6 million in the United States. The latter estimate is broadly consistent with the results of a sample survey by the U.S. Bureau of the Census for November 1969, as explained at the conclusion of Appendix A.

Table 6–1. Spanish-surname Population Compared with Other Population Groups, Five Southwest States, 1950 and 1960

AREA AND STATE	TOTAL POPULATION	White		NONWHITE
		ANGLO	SPANISH-SURNAME	
1950				
Southwest	21,053,280	16,933,532	2,289,550	1,830,198
Arizona	749,587	526,193	128,318	95,076
California	10,586,223	9,154,720	760,453	671,050
Colorado	1,325,089	1,178,522	118,131	28,436
New Mexico	681,187	381,331	248,880	50,976
Texas	7,711,194	5,692,766	1,033,768	984,660
United States	150,216,110	134,478,365		15,737,745
1960				
Southwest	29,304,012	23,111,042	3,464,999	2,727,971
Arizona	1,302,161	975,161	194,356	132,644
California	15,717,204	13,028,692	1,426,538	1,261,974
Colorado	1,753,947	1,543,527	157,173	53,247
New Mexico	951,023	606,641	269,122	75,260
Texas	9,579,677	6,957,021	1,417,810	1,204,846
United States	178,466,736	158,460,699[a]		20,006,037

[a] Of the white population in the United States, 3,842,000 persons were estimated to be Mexican Americans in 1960 (Appendix A).
Source: *1960 U.S. Census of Population*, vol. I, part 1, table 158; parts 4, 6, 7, 33, and 45, table 15; and PC(2)–1B, table 1. *1950 U.S. Census of Population*, PE no. 3C, table 1.

The vast majority of the Spanish-surname people were native born in both 1950 and 1960, and the percentage of natives increased during the decade despite substantial immigration (Table 6–2). The foreign born represented the largest portions of the population in California, Arizona, and Texas, in that order. In contrast, nearly all Mexican-American residents in Colorado and New Mexico were natives. These are the two states in which the descendants of the Hispano-Mexican settlers have always been concentrated. Moreover, the economic development of New Mexico and Colorado has offered relatively few inducements for immigrants.

When first- and second-generation persons of Spanish surname are considered together (foreign stock), it is apparent that the children of immigrants represent a sizable portion of the total. The foreign stock accounted for about 45 percent of the Mexican Americans in the Southwest in 1960 and more than half in 1950. In this regard, the Spanish-surname group has remained very differentiated from the rest of the population. People of foreign stock other than Mexican represented only 16 percent of the Anglo and nonwhite population of the Southwest in 1960. The national proportion of foreign stock was 19 percent.

Nonwhites in the Southwest are not only more highly differentiated than in most parts of the country but also quite unevenly distributed over the region. As shown in Table 6–3, Orientals and American Indians in 1960 represented 20 percent of all nonwhites in the region. American Indians accounted for the largest share of nonwhites in Arizona and New Mexico. In California, 27 percent of the nonwhites were Orientals, and 70 percent Negroes. Only in Texas was the nonwhite group almost exclusively Negro.[1]

Table 6–2. Distribution of Spanish-surname Persons by Nativity Status, Southwest and Five States, 1950 and 1960
(Percent of total in each area)

AREA AND STATE	NATIVE OF NATIVE PARENTAGE		NATIVE OF FOREIGN PARENTAGE[a]		BORN IN MEXICO	
	1950	1960	1950	1960	1950	1960
Southwest	48.8	54.8	34.0	29.8	17.2	15.4
Arizona	41.5	49.3	40.4	33.1	18.1	17.6
California	35.2	46.0	42.8	34.0	22.0	20.0
Colorado	83.2	86.1	12.6	10.4	4.2	3.5
New Mexico	87.2	87.4	8.6	8.6	3.9	3.9
Texas	46.5	54.8	35.3	31.2	18.2	14.0

[a] Includes natives of Mexican and mixed parentage and the relatively small group, "other and not reported."
Source: *1960 U.S. Census of Population*, PC(2)–1B, table 1. *1950 U.S. Census of Population*, PE no. 3C, table 5.

Table 6–3. Components of the Nonwhite Population, Five Southwest States, 1960
(Percent)

POPULATION GROUP	ARIZ.	CALIF.	COLO.	NEW MEXICO	TEXAS	SOUTH-WEST	UNITED STATES
Negro	32.7	70.0	75.1	22.7	98.5	79.6	92.1
Indian	62.9	3.1	8.1	74.7	0.5	6.9	2.6
Japanese	1.1	12.5	12.9	1.2	0.3	6.3	2.3
Chinese	2.2	7.6	1.4	0.5	0.3	3.8	1.2
Filipino	0.7	5.2	1.1	0.3	0.1	2.5	0.9
Other	0.4	1.6	1.5	0.6	0.2	0.9	1.1

Source: *1960 U.S. Census of Population*, vol. I, part 1, table 44; parts 4, 6, 7, 33, and 45, tables 15 and 96; PC(2)–1B, table 1.

MIGRATIONS: THE SHIFT TO CALIFORNIA

California has grown so rapidly that one is not surprised to find the largest 1950–1960 increase of Mexican Americans in that state, both in numbers and in percentage (Chart 6–1). The gain was more than twice the rate for Anglos, but it was

[1] Notes for this chapter start on page 138.

Chart 6–1.
Growth of the Spanish-surname Population Compared with Other Population Groups, Five Southwest States, 1950–1960

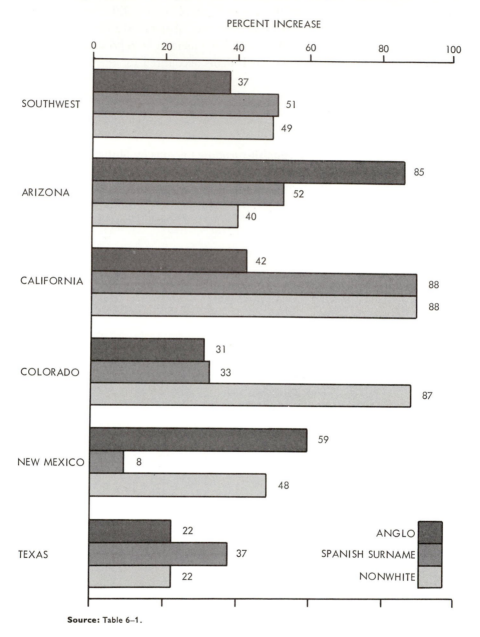

PERCENT INCREASE

Source: Table 6–1.

matched by nonwhites. The growth of the Spanish-name population in California accounted for nearly three-fifths of the growth in the entire Southwest. The absolute and relative increase in Texas was much smaller. Among the other states in the region, New Mexico shows the slowest growth of the Spanish-surname population in the face of a substantial and continuous influx of Anglos. This trend has been under way for considerable time and has profoundly altered the ethnic composition of this state, where only a few decades ago Spanish-surname people held a numerical majority. A relative decline in the Mexican-American population occurred in Arizona as well as in New Mexico.

In part, these shifts reflect migrations of major magnitude. Nearly 60 percent of the Mexican-American interstate movers between 1955 and 1960 went to California, although the state accounted for only one-third of the Spanish-surname population in the Southwest in 1950 and two-fifths in 1960. Of those coming from abroad in the 1955–1960 period, 63 percent were located in California in 1960, though some of them may have first resided in other states. In contrast, only 17 percent of the Spanish-surname interstate movers between 1955 and 1960 went to Texas, and few went to the smaller Southwest states. It seems that all states in the region except California experienced some net out-migration of Spanish-surname persons.[2]

The direction of migrations—both internal and international—can also be inferred from the fact that only 55 percent of California's Mexican Americans in 1960 were born in that state. The corresponding figures for Texas and New Mexico were 81 percent and 87 percent, respectively, with the remaining states between these extremes.[3]

We know little about the characteristics of Mexican Americans who migrated. The census data on 1955–1960 changes in residence show only small differences by sex for internal migration, whereas males have predominated in immigration from Mexico.[4] Movers are heavily concentrated in the 20- to 40-year age bracket (Chart 6–2). Also, Mexican Americans show greater mobility the further they are removed from the immigrant generation. Only 8 percent of the foreign born went to a different county between 1955 and 1960, as against 12 percent of the natives of foreign parentage and 15 percent of the natives of native parentage.[5]

The intra-regional redistribution of the Spanish-surname people between 1950 and 1960 conforms broadly to a long-term trend in the Mexican-stock population (Table 6–4). In 1910, over 60 percent of all persons of Mexican stock in the United States resided in Texas; 50 years later it was only 38 percent. Arizona and New Mexico, which were never centers of attraction for immigrants from Mexico, also show marked relative declines. California is the one state with a steadily increasing share of all persons of Mexican stock in the United States. Two-fifths of the first- and second-generation Mexican Americans in the United States lived in California in 1960. The percentage is surely larger at the present time.[6]

The vast majority of people of Mexican descent have always lived in the Southwest. In 1910, only 5.7 percent had their residence outside the region. This proportion had doubled by 1950 and reached 12.8 percent in 1960. But this is still a very small share of the total. The Mexican–American population in the Southwest remains one of the most conspicuous examples of geographic concentration among national minorities in the United States. One can only speculate about the reasons. Immigrants are always attracted to places where they can find relatives or large numbers of their

Chart 6–2.

Long-distance and Short-distance Movers Among the Spanish-surname Population, by Age, Five Southwest States Combined, 1955–1960

(Percent of all persons 14 years and over in 1960 moving between 1955 and 1960)

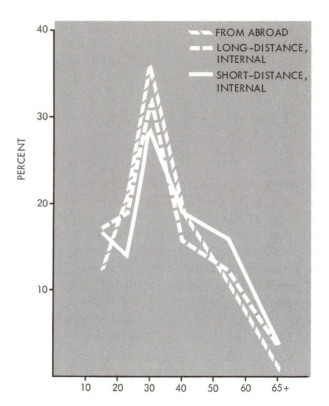

SHORT-DISTANCE: DIFFERENT HOUSE, SAME COUNTY
LONG-DISTANCE: DIFFERENT COUNTY

Source: *1960 U.S. Census of Population,* PC(2)–1B, table 7.

own group; speak their mother tongue without embarrassment; rely on fellow countrymen for employment, housing, and help in orienting themselves to a strange environment; and use community organizations. For Mexican immigrants, a natural base was provided by the early colonial settlers and by long acquaintance with the

110

area through informal border-crossings. Thus, their continued concentration in this region appears to be a self-reinforcing process.

The Southwest also offers a climate and landscape compatible with the experience and preferences of many Mexican immigrants. Physical proximity to the homeland may have tended to keep them in the area. In many cases, ignorance of opportunities

Table 6–4. Geographic Distribution of Persons of Mexican Stock, by Region and State, 1910–1960[a]

Area	1910	1920	1930	1940	1950	1960
A. BORN IN MEXICO						
Arizona	13.4	12.6	7.6	6.6	5.5	6.2
California	15.2	18.1	31.2	35.6	36.0	43.2
Colorado	1.2	2.3	2.1	1.7	1.2	0.8
New Mexico	5.4	4.2	2.6	2.4	2.1	1.9
Texas	56.5	52.2	41.6	42.2	43.5	35.3
Southwest	91.7	89.3	85.1	88.4	88.4	87.4
Other	8.3	10.7	14.9	11.6	11.6	12.6
U.S. Total	100.0	100.0	100.0	100.0	100.0	100.0
B. MEXICAN OR MIXED PARENTAGE						
Arizona	13.3	12.5	8.9	7.7	6.4	5.9
California	10.8	16.1	27.3	31.5	35.7	38.6
Colorado	0.5	1.5	2.2	2.1	1.7	1.3
New Mexico	6.2	5.7	3.6	3.0	2.4	2.1
Texas	67.0	59.2	49.7	46.5	42.4	39.3
Southwest	97.9	95.0	91.6	90.8	88.7	87.1
Other	2.1	5.0	8.4	9.2	11.3	12.9
U.S. Total	100.0	100.0	100.0	100.0	100.0	100.0
C. MEXICAN STOCK (A PLUS B)						
Arizona	13.4	12.6	8.2	7.3	6.1	6.0
California	13.4	17.4	29.3	32.9	35.8	40.1
Colorado	0.9	2.0	2.1	2.0	1.5	1.2
New Mexico	5.7	4.7	3.1	2.8	2.3	2.0
Texas	61.0	54.6	45.5	45.0	42.8	37.9
Southwest	94.3	91.3	88.2	90.0	88.6	87.2
Other	5.7	8.7	11.8	10.0	11.4	12.8
U.S. Total	100.0	100.0	100.0	100.0	100.0	100.0

[a] Over the decades the Bureau of the Census has reported only on the parentage of the *white* foreign stock, except for some censuses in the early 1900s. In 1930 the Bureau of the Census changed its definition of Mexicans and classified them as nonwhite. As a consequence, the number of persons counted in the white foreign stock declined drastically. In 1940 the census again classified Mexicans as white and issued revised 1930 figures on the white foreign stock from Mexico as well as for the total white foreign stock. However, no corrected numbers were published for Arizona and New Mexico. In the above table, the 1930 figures for these two states are estimates based on the relationships in 1920 and 1940.
Source: *U.S. Census of Population.*

elsewhere was probably a roadblock to further costly moves. Perhaps most importantly, it was unnecessary for Mexican Americans to reach beyond the Southwest for better socioeconomic opportunities. Because of its high rate of economic development and its superior social environment, California was the natural intra-regional magnet.

The Southwest ever since World War I has also been a gateway through which some Mexican Americans have moved into other areas, partly of their own volition, partly in response to labor recruitment, and quite often through a process of "peeling off" the migratory stream of farm workers that extended to the Northwest and Middle West or beyond.[7] Others went directly from Mexico to such industrial centers as Chicago.[8] Table 6–5 shows that the people of Mexican stock outside the Southwest region are greatly concentrated in the Middle West and especially in Illinois. In 1960, Illinois had more Mexican Americans of foreign stock than Colorado and New Mexico combined. Among the Midwest cities with sizable Spanish-surname populations are Chicago, Kansas City, Detroit, and Milwaukee.

Table 6–5. Number of Persons of Mexican Stock in Selected States Outside the Southwest, 1960[a]

State	Number	Percent of U.S. Total	State	Number	Percent of U.S. Total
Illinois	63,063	3.6	Ohio	9,960	0.6
Michigan	24,298	1.4	Missouri	8,159	0.5
Indiana	14,041	0.8	Wisconsin	6,705	0.4
Kansas	12,972	0.7	Nebraska	5,858	0.3
Washington	11,084	0.6	Utah	5,557	0.3
New York	10,074	0.6	All others[b]	53,163	3.1

[a] Persons born in Mexico or of Mexican or mixed parentage in states having 5,000 or more such persons.
[b] States with less than 5,000 persons of Mexican stock.
Source: *1960 U.S. Census of Population*, vol. I, table 110.

THE FAST PACE OF URBANIZATION

Between 1950 and 1960 *Mexican Americans urbanized more rapidly than Anglos or nonwhites.* By 1960 the percent of the urban population in the group's total approximated parity with the two reference populations (Table 6–6). Among non-whites, however, Negroes, Japanese and Chinese showed above-average proportions of city dwellers. Urbanization of Mexican Americans between 1950 and 1960 exceeded the Anglo rate in all Southwest states except Arizona.

A population once dependent largely on agriculture is now so greatly linked with city life that many of its problems mirror the problems of urban America. And although on balance the group has benefited from the rural-urban shift, the transition has been associated with the usual personal stresses of adjustment to the city, and compounded by the problems of minority status and often by language handicaps. Formal and impersonal controls enforced by an anonymous urban officialdom have replaced the informal and person-to-person contacts with authority in rural areas. There is a world of perplexing and ego-wounding forms and documents. City living compounds the problems of transportation and schooling. The new urban milieu often has a disruptive influence on family life.

The movement to cities has been so strong that rural areas showed a net decline of Spanish-surname people between 1950 and 1960, as was true for the general population. This trend has probably continued since 1960. The rural Mexican-

American population dropped only slightly in the Southwest as a whole, but the decline was about 23 percent in New Mexico and 17 percent in Colorado.[9] Many of the agricultural communities in northern New Mexico and southern Colorado have become ghost villages.

When residence in a *metropolitan area* is used as a yardstick of urbanization,[10] Mexican Americans in the Southwest were still the least metropolitan of the three population groups (Chart 6–3). By inference, a larger percentage of the urban Spanish-surname population live in small non-metropolitan cities. In many cases, such cities have a more traditional social structure and are more oriented to agricultural or food and fiber processing jobs. But Mexican Americans are increasingly

Table 6–6.   Urban Population as a Percent of Total Population, Spanish-surname Group Compared with Other Population Groups, Five Southwest States, 1950 and 1960[a]

| | 1950 | | | | 1960 | | | |
| | | WHITE | | | | WHITE | | |
Area	Total	Anglo	Spanish-surname	Non-white	Total	Anglo	Spanish-surname	Non-white
Southwest	71.1	72.0	66.4	68.2	80.7	81.1	79.1	79.8[b]
Arizona	55.4	60.0	61.3	22.7	74.5	79.7	74.9	36.2
California	80.7	80.7	75.8	85.6	86.4	86.0	85.4	91.4
Colorado	62.7	63.6	49.7	82.5	73.7	73.8	68.7	86.4
New Mexico	50.2	59.8	41.0	23.3	65.9	73.6	57.7	32.7
Texas	62.7	61.8	68.1	62.6	75.0	74.3	78.6	75.1
United States	64.0	64.3		61.6	69.9	68.4		72.5

[a] According to the 1960 census, the urban population includes persons living in urbanized areas and in places of 2,500 or more inhabitants outside urbanized areas. An urbanized area consists of at least one city of 50,000 or more inhabitants and the surrounding closely settled areas, whether incorporated or not. This is essentially the same as the 1950 definition.

[b] The urban component was 83.5 percent for Negroes, 85.3 percent for Japanese, and 96.3 percent for Chinese. Negroes show a higher rate of urbanization than the Spanish-surname population in all five states except Texas, and so do Orientals in California, the only state with a large Oriental population.

Source: *1960 U.S. Census of Population*, vol. I, part 1, table 158; parts 4, 6, 7, 33, and 45, tables 15 and 96; PC(2)–1B, table 1. *1950 U.S. Census of Population*, vol. II, part 1, table 38; vol. II, parts 3, 5, 6, 31, and 43, tables 13 and 14; PE no. 3C, table 2.

pulled into the metropolitan trend. Nearly three-quarters of the 1950–1960 *increase* in the Spanish-surname population occurred in the metropolitan areas, as against 46 percent for Anglos.[11]

Mexican Americans were more heavily represented in the smaller metropolitan areas than either Anglos or nonwhites. Nearly 18 percent of all Mexican Americans living in Southwest metropolitan areas in 1960 were in places of less than 250,000 people, as against 11 percent of all Anglos or of nonwhites. Places with 250,000 to 1 million inhabitants accounted for 41 percent of the metropolitan Mexican Americans compared with 29 percent of Anglos and 21 percent of nonwhites. At the other end of the scale, in areas of 1 million people or more, the percentages were 41 for Mexican Americans but 59 for Anglos and 68 for nonwhites.

The distribution of Spanish-surname people over the 37 metropolitan areas of the Southwest varied somewhat from the total population (Chart 6–4). The Los

Angeles metropolis ranks first in size for both the Spanish-surname and the total population. The San Francisco complex holds third place for the total and second for persons of Spanish surname. But the rankings differ substantially in other cases. San Antonio, El Paso, Albuquerque, Corpus Christi, Brownsville, and Laredo have many more Mexican Americans than one would expect from their total size. The reverse is true for the rapidly growing metropolises of east Texas—Houston, Dallas,

Chart 6–3.
Percent of Spanish-surname Population in Metropolitan Areas Compared with Other Population Groups, Southwest, 1950 and 1960

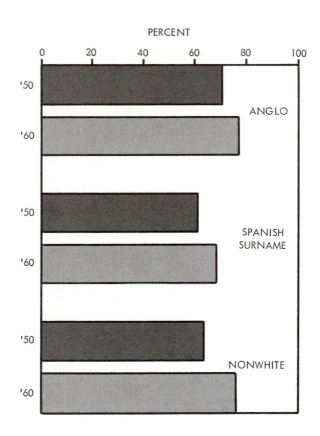

Source: *1960 U.S. Census of Population*, vol. I, part 1, table 36; vol. I, parts 4, 6, 7, 33, and 45, tables 20 and 21; PC(2)–1B, tables 1, 9, and 13; and *Census Tracts*, PHC(1) nos. 15, 50, 157, and 163, tables P–1 and P–5. *1950 U.S. Census of Population*, vol. II, parts 3, 5, 6, 31, and 43, tables 33 and 41; PE no. 3C, tables 1, 8, and 9.

Fort Worth, and Beaumont. In California, Sacramento and San Diego (despite the latter's proximity to the Mexican border) rank substantially lower in the size of the Spanish-surname population than in total size. So does Denver.*

The number of Mexican Americans in metropolitan Los Angeles exceeded the population of some major cities—for instance New Orleans, Pittsburgh, and Seattle.

*The Spearman correlation for the rankings in Chart 6–4 is +.74.

114

Chart 6–4.
Metropolitan Areas in the Southwest,[a] Ranked by Size of Spanish-surname and Total Population, 1960

SPANISH–SURNAME PERSONS		TOTAL POPULATION

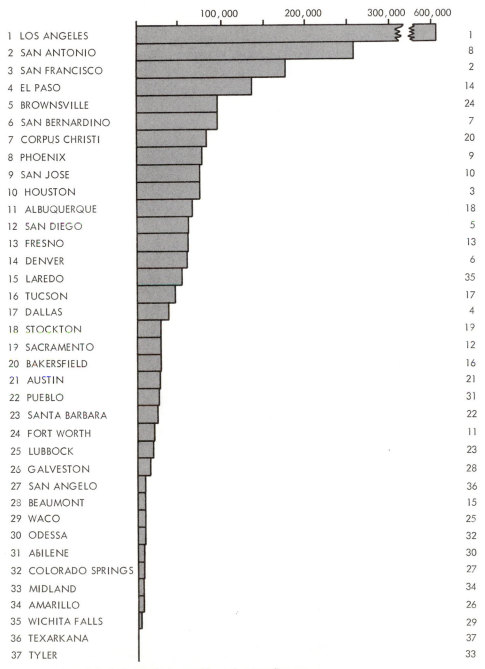

		TOTAL POP. RANK
1	LOS ANGELES	1
2	SAN ANTONIO	8
3	SAN FRANCISCO	2
4	EL PASO	14
5	BROWNSVILLE	24
6	SAN BERNARDINO	7
7	CORPUS CHRISTI	20
8	PHOENIX	9
9	SAN JOSE	10
10	HOUSTON	3
11	ALBUQUERQUE	18
12	SAN DIEGO	5
13	FRESNO	13
14	DENVER	6
15	LAREDO	35
16	TUCSON	17
17	DALLAS	4
18	STOCKTON	19
19	SACRAMENTO	12
20	BAKERSFIELD	16
21	AUSTIN	21
22	PUEBLO	31
23	SANTA BARBARA	22
24	FORT WORTH	11
25	LUBBOCK	23
26	GALVESTON	28
27	SAN ANGELO	36
28	BEAUMONT	15
29	WACO	25
30	ODESSA	32
31	ABILENE	30
32	COLORADO SPRINGS	27
33	MIDLAND	34
34	AMARILLO	26
35	WICHITA FALLS	29
36	TEXARKANA	37
37	TYLER	33

[a] Only the largest city is named for each metropolitan area.
[b] The number of Spanish-surname persons in Texarkana (652) and Tyler (613) is too small to indicate on a graph of this scale.
Source: *1960 U.S. Census of Population*, vol. I, part 1, table 36; PC(2)–1B, tables 9 and 13; and *Census Tracts*, PHC(1) nos. 15, 50, 157, and 163, tables P–1 and P–5.

Chart 6–5.
Metropolitan Areas of the Southwest, Ranked by Percent Spanish-surname Population and Showing Percent Nonwhite Population, 1960

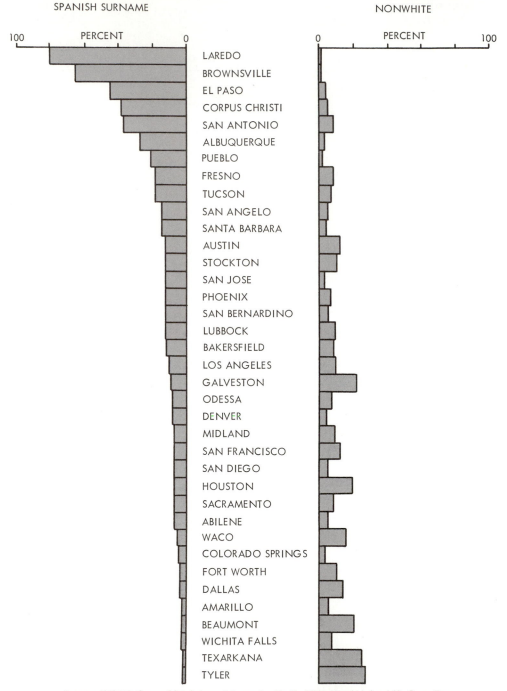

SPANISH SURNAME

NONWHITE

| 100 | PERCENT | 0 | | 0 | PERCENT | 100 |

LAREDO
BROWNSVILLE
EL PASO
CORPUS CHRISTI
SAN ANTONIO
ALBUQUERQUE
PUEBLO
FRESNO
TUCSON
SAN ANGELO
SANTA BARBARA
AUSTIN
STOCKTON
SAN JOSE
PHOENIX
SAN BERNARDINO
LUBBOCK
BAKERSFIELD
LOS ANGELES
GALVESTON
ODESSA
DENVER
MIDLAND
SAN FRANCISCO
SAN DIEGO
HOUSTON
SACRAMENTO
ABILENE
WACO
COLORADO SPRINGS
FORT WORTH
DALLAS
AMARILLO
BEAUMONT
WICHITA FALLS
TEXARKANA
TYLER

Source: *1960 U.S. Census of Population,* vol. I, part 1, table 36; PC(2)–1B, tables 6 and 13; *Census Tracts,* PHC(1) nos. 15, 50, 157, and 163, tables P–1 and P–5; and vol. I, parts 4, 6, 7, 33, and 45, table 13.

116

It exceeded the total Mexican-American population of Arizona, Colorado, and New Mexico. Los Angeles is still often said to have the largest concentration of people of Mexican descent in the world after Mexico City. But this was no longer true by 1960, when Guadalajara had overtaken the Mexican-American population of Los Angeles.[12]

The share of Spanish-surname people in the population of metropolitan areas shows a striking range (Chart 6–5). Some of these populations are predominantly Mexican-American; some have scarcely any members of this ethnic group. The range extends from nearly 80 percent in Laredo and 64 percent in Brownsville to less than 1 percent in Tyler. As it happens, the extremes are all in Texas. The largest relative concentrations are in south central and southwest Texas, and the smallest in east Texas. For California metropolitan areas, the range is much more narrow— between 17 percent in Fresno and 6 percent in Sacramento. In the three remaining states, Albuquerque, Pueblo, and Tucson have substantial proportions of Mexican Americans, ranging from 26 percent to 17 percent of the total.

Metropolitan concentrations in 1960, measured by percent of total population, differed markedly between Mexican Americans and nonwhites. There seems to be an inverse relationship.* Where Spanish-surname people represent a large part of the population, the share of nonwhites is relatively small, and vice versa. Only in a few cities does one find an approximate balance. Among these few are Los Angeles, Sacramento, and San Diego; Austin and Lubbock; and Colorado Springs. The largely inverse relationship is also found in the 1950 data and appears to be a pattern of long standing. Possibly much of the demand for menial labor was met in past years in different areas either by some nonwhite group or by Mexican Americans. With one minority already entrenched in low-paid jobs, the other had little incentive to gravitate to the same locale.

SUBREGIONAL PATTERNS

OF POPULATION DISTRIBUTION†

Additional Mexican-American population clusters can be seen when the 421 counties in the five states are identified in terms of numbers of Spanish-surname persons (Map *A*) and of the proportion of such persons in the total population (Map *B*). Each method of portraying subregional distributions has its advantages and limitations. Together, they provide a more comprehensive picture.

Heavy concentrations of Spanish-surname persons are found in larger urban centers, in regions of intensive truck-crop agriculture, and in areas of older Spanish-Mexican colonization. Also apparent is the small number of Spanish-surname people in rural areas originally settled by Anglos and in areas of very sparse settlement (for example, mountain regions and deserts). As one would expect, Mexican Americans

---

*The Spearman correlation for the rankings in Chart 6–5 is −.61.
†Materials for this section were prepared by Susan Courtney.

MAP A. NUMBERS OF PERSONS WITH SPANISH SURNAME, BY COUNTIES.

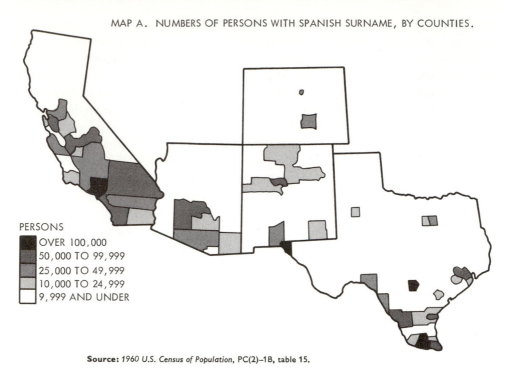

PERSONS

- OVER 100,000
- 50,000 TO 99,999
- 25,000 TO 49,999
- 10,000 TO 24,999
- 9,999 AND UNDER

Source: *1960 U.S. Census of Population*, PC(2)–1B, table 15.

MAP B. PERSONS WITH SPANISH SURNAME AS PERCENT OF THE
TOTAL POPULATION, BY COUNTIES.

PERCENT

- 0 TO 5
- 5 TO 10
- 10 TO 20
- 20 TO 50
- OVER 50

Source: *1960 U.S. Census of Population*, PC(2)–1B, table 15; vol. I, parts 4, 6, 7, 33, and 45, table 28.

118

cluster in some of the border areas, but heavy concentrations are seen at a considerable distance from the border as well. These generalizations are elaborated in the following paragraphs.

Urban Areas

Only four counties in the entire Southwest have more than 100,000 Spanish-surname persons, and three of these are major urban centers: Los Angeles, El Paso, and Bexar County (San Antonio). (The fourth, Hidalgo County, being agricultural, is discussed later). Cameron County, which includes the city of Brownsville, Texas, just barely misses this category (97,000), but this is an important agricultural as well as urban area. Other urban counties with high numbers of Spanish-surname residents are those which include the cities of Corpus Christi, Houston, Laredo, Albuquerque, Phoenix, San Diego, San Francisco, and some parts of the southern California metropolitan complex.

Agricultural Areas

Three areas of intensive, irrigated agriculture show large concentrations of Spanish-surname population: the lower Rio Grande Valley—Hidalgo and Cameron Counties, Texas—which is an important citrus and winter truck-crop producer; the Salt and Gila River Valleys of Arizona (including the urban complex of Phoenix); and Fresno County, California (including the urban complex of Fresno). Moderately high concentrations occur in the other Central Valley counties of California; and they would probably have been recorded as much greater had the 1960 census been taken in the midsummer, the height of the agricultural season, when the migrant workers are most numerous.

California

A moderately high to very high concentration of Spanish-surname persons characterizes all of southern California. Few Mexican Americans are found in the northern part of California, a generally sparsely populated area settled after the Mission and Mexican periods and traditionally Anglo-Saxon. Mexican Americans are practically absent in the mountains of the Sierra Nevada. The inclusion of a considerable area of mountainous terrain within the borders of Fresno and Tulare Counties might make it appear otherwise on Map *A*, but the Spanish-surname persons reside almost exclusively in the lowlands. Few are found in the northern part of the deserts. These areas are characterized by a low share of Spanish-surname people in a small total population, as shown in Map *B*. The apparent exception of San Bernardino

119

County (in both maps) is due to the fact that its boundaries include the lowland extension of the Los Angeles complex as well as a great expanse of barren desert.

San Benito County presents a curious case. The number of Spanish-surname persons is small, but it represents a very high percentage of the total population. This is sparsely populated hill country, with many small farms and ranches held by Mexican Americans, two small towns (Hollister and San Juan Bautista), and a large cement plant.

Arizona

Northern Arizona has few Spanish-surname residents. This is a thinly populated area to begin with, and it has a disproportionately high Indian population. Southern Arizona, an area of old Spanish settlement that later became mining country, has a moderate concentration. An interesting example is that of Santa Cruz County, on the Mexican border. Small and consisting mostly of desert land, it ranks very high on a percentage basis (Map *B*), but on the basis of total numbers it ranks very low (Map *A*). The high concentration in Maricopa County (Map *A*) is due to the combination of intensive irrigated agriculture of the Gila and Salt River Valleys, mining and smelting activity in which Mexicans have long been prominent, and the developing industrial base of the city of Phoenix and its suburbs.

New Mexico

The area of old Spanish colonization in north-central New Mexico shows a moderate concentration of Spanish-surname persons, with a strong nucleus in Albuquerque, whose industrial growth has attracted people from the northern part of the state (Map *B*). Lack of rainfall and irrigation and a paucity of irrigable land have limited the development of the area. Total population remains rather low; hence no county except Bernalillo (Albuquerque) has a large number of Spanish-surname people (Map *A*). A second area of moderate concentration is found along the lower reaches of the Rio Grande in the state, where irrigated agriculture is well developed, with large numbers of small subsistence holdings by Spanish Americans.

Colorado

Considerable numbers of Spanish-surname people are recorded only in two counties—in the urban areas of Pueblo and Denver (Map *A*). Because of the sparseness of any other population element in southern Colorado, the few Spanish-surname residents there constitute a very high percentage of the total (Map *B*).

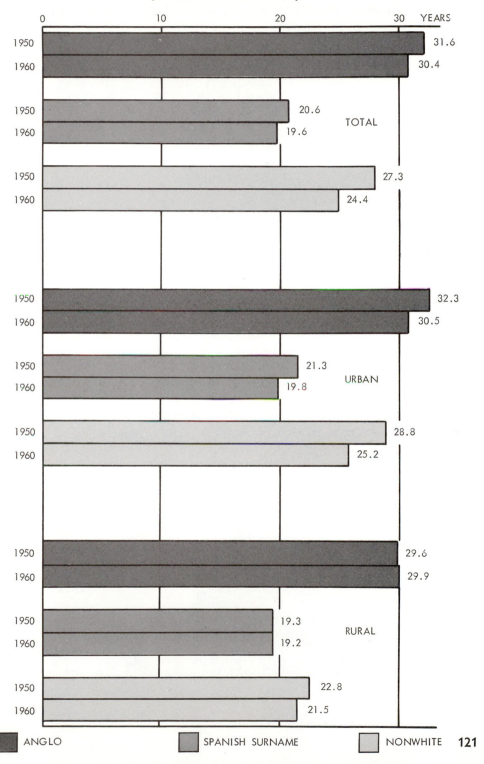

Chart 6–6.
Median Age of the Spanish-surname Population Compared with Other Population Groups, Five Southwest States Combined, 1950 and 1960
(Urban and rural areas)

0   10   20   30   YEARS

TOTAL
1950 31.6
1960 30.4
1950 20.6
1960 19.6
1950 27.3
1960 24.4

URBAN
1950 32.3
1960 30.5
1950 21.3
1960 19.8
1950 28.8
1960 25.2

RURAL
1950 29.6
1960 29.9
1950 19.3
1960 19.2
1950 22.8
1960 21.5

ANGLO   SPANISH SURNAME   NONWHITE   **121**

Source: *1950 U.S. Census of Population*, vol. II, parts 3, 5, 6, 31, and 43, table 15; PE no. 3C, table 3. *1960 U.S. Census of Population*, vol. I, parts 4, 6, 7, 33, and 45, table 96; PC(2)–1B, table 2.

Chart 6–7.
Population Pyramids for Urban Anglo and Spanish-surname Populations in the Southwest and Urban Population in Mexico, 1960

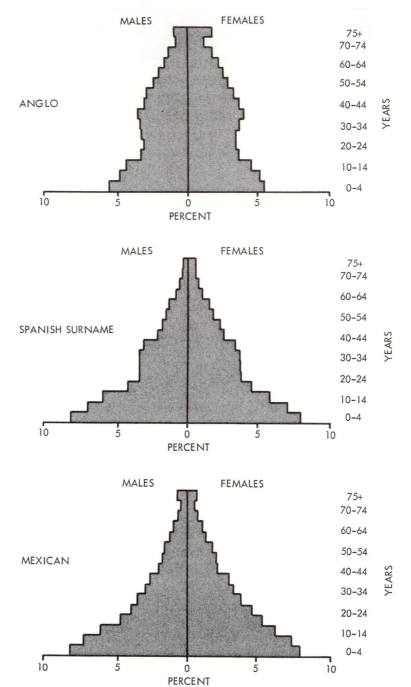

Source: 1960 U.S. Census of Population, vol. I, parts 4, 6, 7, 33, and 45, table 96; PC(2)–1B, table 2. Mexico: VIII Censo General de Población, 1960, table 8.

Texas

Except for El Paso, west Texas is similar in all respects we are considering here to the adjacent parts of New Mexico, with their low populations. One finds few Spanish-surname residents in each county (Map *A*), but these constitute a high percentage of the total population (Map *B*). South Texas displays a high concentration, particularly in the cities and in the agricultural areas of the lower Rio Grande. Throughout the remainder of the state, agrarian counties are so small in area and in total population that none show large numbers of Spanish-surname persons (Map *A*), although in many cases their proportion to the total population is high (Map *B*). Anglos and Negroes predominate in the north and northeast.

AGE AND SEX COMPOSITION

One of the most distinctive characteristics of the Mexican-American population is its *low median age*. The median for Spanish-surname persons in the Southwest in 1960 was nearly 11 years lower than for Anglos and six years lower than for nonwhites (Chart 6–6). The age contrast holds for urban and rural areas alike, and it is highlighted by the fact that children under 15 years accounted for 42 percent of the Mexican Americans but only 30 percent of Anglos and less than 37 percent of nonwhites. Spanish-surname males and females were of about the same median age (19.7 and 19.5 years, respectively), whereas the median for Anglo females exceeded that of Anglo males by almost two years. According to limited studies, Spanish-surname women have a less favorable mortality record compared to men than do Anglo women.[13] But comprehensive vital statistics on Mexican Americans that could throw light on longevity differences are unavailable. This deficiency limits the interpretation of population data at many critical points.

The age distribution of the Spanish-surname population in the urban Southwest resembles more closely that of the urban people in the Republic of Mexico than of the Southwest Anglos (Chart 6–7). This is confirmed by dissimilarity indexes.*

The dependency ratio for the Mexican-American population is unusually high in comparison with Anglos and substantially greater than that of nonwhites (Chart 6–8). Only in rural farm areas do nonwhites show a still higher ratio than the Mexican Americans. The disproportionately large number of dependents among the latter are primarily children and adolescents. In the Southwest as a whole in 1960, there were 112 persons under 20 for every 100 Mexican Americans 20 to 64 years old, as against

---

*The dissimilarity index for urban Anglos versus urban Spanish-surname persons in the Southwest is 15.7. The index for the latter versus urban Mexicans is 4.7. Urban populations have been selected for this comparison because the marked difference in the Mexican and the American Southwest urban–rural "mix" could affect the results for the total populations. (An *index of dissimilarity* indicates the percentage of one population that would have to be redistributed in order to have the same distribution with regard to the characteristic being measured as another population. Complete dissimilarity would yield the maximum index value of 100. Complete similarity, or no difference whatever in distribution, would yield an index value of zero. The above index numbers on age distributions are calculated from data for five-year age groups in each population.)

Chart 6–8.
Dependency Ratios for the Spanish-surname Population Compared with Other Population Groups, Five Southwest States Combined, 1960
(Urban and rural areas)

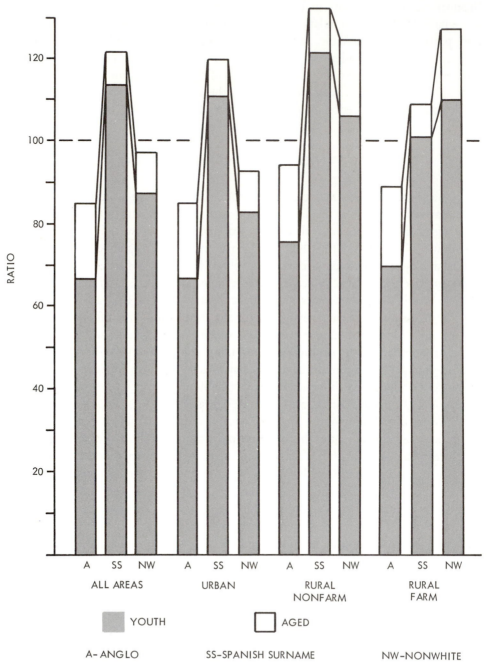

Source: *1960 U.S. Census of Population*, vol. I, parts 4, 6, 7, 33, and 45, table 95; PC(2)–1B, table 2.

68 for every 100 Anglos and 87 for every 100 nonwhites of comparable age. For the dependent aged, the Spanish-surname group shows the lowest ratio (8.9), and the Anglos the highest (16.6).*

Another distinctive feature of the Mexican-American population is the sex ratio. In the United States generally, males are less numerous than females. In 1960, for example, there were only 97 males for every 100 females. As shown in Table 6–7,

**Table 6–7. Sex Ratios for the Spanish-surname Population
Compared with Other Population Groups,
Urban and Rural Areas, Southwest, 1950 and 1960
(All ages: males per 100 females)**

	1950			1960		
	Anglo	Spanish-surname	Nonwhite	Anglo	Spanish-surname	Nonwhite
All areas	99.6	104.3	102.4	98.6	102.6	99.5
Urban	95.8	99.0	98.4	96.1	98.8	96.6
Rural	110.7	115.6	111.4	109.4	118.6	110.8
Rural nonfarm	—	—	—	109.8	112.8	110.7
Rural farm	—	—	—	107.9	138.0	111.6

Source: *1950 U.S. Census of Population*, vol. II, parts 3, 5, 6, 31, and 43, table 15; PE no. 3C, table 3. *1960 U.S. Census of Population*, vol. I, parts 4, 6, 7, 33, and 45, table 96; PC(2)–1B, table 2. Because of a major reclassification by the census of the rural farm population between 1950 and 1960, total rural only is shown for 1950.

the same pattern prevailed in the Southwest for both Anglos and nonwhites. In the case of Mexican Americans, however, there were almost 103 males for every 100 females. The 1950 census revealed an even higher sex ratio for this group. The sex ratios of the three populations do not differ very much in the urban places of the Southwest. The intergroup differences are still small in rural-nonfarm areas but become magnified in the rural-farm segment. Here, the excess of males over females in the Spanish-surname group is extreme—with a ratio of 138 in 1960. Thus, the unusual sex ratio of Mexican Americans emerges as a predominantly rural phenomenon. Detailed data on sex ratios by age suggest that this pattern is explained in large part by the presence of migrant workers from Mexico, mostly men, who were included in the census count. Another factor is the disproportionately large share of males among pre-1960 immigrants.

*The *dependency ratio* is defined as the ratio of the combined number of persons under 20 and 65 or over to the population 20 to 64 years of age. Any such yardstick leaves much room for argument. In the case of the aged, increasing government support has lightened the burden of the family. The cutoff at age 65 may be too high for the many members of minority groups who hold manual jobs, and possibly too low for others. As for the young, the group between 15 and 20 years includes persons with jobs as well as students, and the proportion of earners among the youth is greater for the two minorities than among Anglos. Also, the position of the aged may differ with ethnicity as well as social class, depending on variations in peoples' sense of family obligation for support of the elderly and in their access to social security and welfare agencies. Nevertheless, the dependency ratio describes differential family burdens in various groups of the population with a fair degree of accuracy.

LARGE FAMILIES

Mexican-American families are very large. In the Southwest, the 1960 average was 4.77 persons for Spanish-surname families as against 3.39 for Anglos and 4.54 for nonwhites. The differentials are pervasive, whether all families or only urban families are considered, or regular husband–wife versus broken families, or families headed by persons in the relatively homogeneous age group of 35 to 44 years (Table 6–8). The rank order of family size is clearly Mexican American, nonwhite, Anglo.

Table 6–8. *Average Number of Persons per Family:*
Spanish-surname Families Compared with Other Families,
Southwest, 1960

	Total	Anglo	Spanish-surname	Nonwhite
All families				
Southwest	3.61	3.39	4.77	4.54
Urban Southwest	3.57	n.a.	4.68	n.a.
By type of family				
Husband-wife	3.68	3.50	4.92	4.16
Other male head	2.89	2.66	3.69	3.25
Female head	3.14	2.82	4.00	3.84
Family head age 35–44				
All families	4.33	n.a.	5.53	n.a.
Husband-wife	4.44	4.27	5.71	4.74
Other male head	3.03	n.a.	3.74	n.a.
Female head	3.51	3.17	4.52	4.20

Source: *1960 U.S. Census of Population*, vol. I, parts 4, 6, 7, 33, and 45, table 110, and special census tabulations for the Spanish-surname population.

About 31 percent of all Spanish-surname families, over one-fifth of the nonwhite families, and only one-tenth of the Anglo families had six persons or more.

Except for Negroes in some parts of the South, it is difficult to point to any substantial identifiable group in our society that is characterized by a similar prevalence of large families. In this respect, Mexican Americans in the Southwest stand about midway between the family in the Republic of Mexico and the Anglo family in the Southwest. The dissimilarity index for the Mexican and the Spanish-surname family size distribution in 1960 is 12.6, or about half the index for the Anglo and the Spanish-surname distributions (24.3).[14] This finding does not necessarily imply an exclusively cultural explanation. Other factors such as education and income are also significantly related to the size of family. However, as will be shown in Chapter 8, the size of Mexican-American families exceeds by wide margins the size of all other families in the Southwest in each income bracket. Thus, the differential family size does not seem to be mainly a function of low income status.

Large families are especially common among Mexican Americans in the *rural* areas of the Southwest (Chart 6–9). But in each of the three types of areas shown in the chart there emerges something like a scissor pattern. Spanish-surname families of two to four persons are under-represented in comparison with the total population,

Chart 6–9.
Distribution of Families by Number of Persons in Family, Spanish-surname Population Compared with Total Population, Urban and Rural Areas in the Southwest, 1960

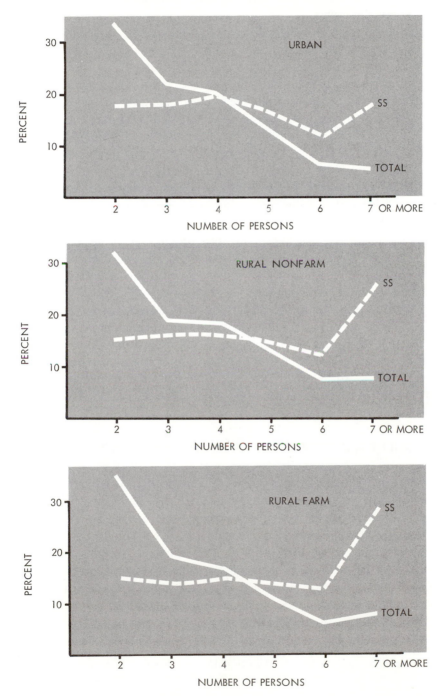

Source: *1960 U.S. Census of Population*, vol. I, parts, 4, 6, 7, 33, and 45, table 110; PC(2)–1B, table 5.

and the units with five or more persons are over-represented. The aggregate figures for the rural Southwest obscure some startling local variations. About half the Spanish-surname families in the rural-farm areas of Arizona and nearly this many in Texas had six or more persons. In the comparable areas of California, less than 29 percent were in this group.

A great deal has been written about the *extended family* among Mexican Americans and other national minorities in the United States, and about its importance in Latin and other cultures. In this country, the *nuclear family* composed of parents and children or a married couple has long been the norm. The extended family may include one or more relatives—the wife's unmarried sister or widowed father, for instance, or even another nuclear family related to the head of the household. This may be a matter of choice, tradition, or economic necessity. It is therefore relevant to note that the *subfamily*, a convenient statistical proxy for the extended unit,* is indeed more frequent among Mexican Americans than among the reference populations. In the Southwest, 5.2 percent of the Spanish-surname primary families had subfamilies living with them in 1960, as against 2.0 percent for Anglos and 5.3 percent for nonwhites; and the incidence was as great in urban as in rural areas. Nevertheless, a figure of little over five percent does not seem to validate the notion of the widespread persistence of the extended family living under one roof. And the fact that the incidence of subfamilies among nonwhites is equally high suggests poverty as an important determinant in this case.

That the extended family among Mexican Americans is not as common as might be expected from previous studies in small and isolated communities is also indicated by another set of data. Only one-quarter of the difference in average family size between Spanish-surname families and all families is attributable to the larger number of "other relatives" (the census term) in the household and of children over 18 years of age. Most of the difference is due to the larger number of children under 18.[15]

MARITAL STATUS AND FAMILY STABILITY

The marital status of females shows a rather special distribution between single women and those ever married in the Spanish-surname population. The percentage of single females 14 years and over is much larger than among the reference populations. And this is true for the young, the middle-aged, and the elderly, except that the incidence of spinsters among Anglo women 65 years and over is somewhat greater than among Mexican-American women in the same age class (Table 6–9). According to detailed census data, the differential in marital status between Spanish-surname and other females holds, irrespective of urban or rural location.

*A *subfamily* is a married couple with or without children, or one parent with one or more of his or her own children under 18 years, living in the housing unit of another family (the *primary family*) and related to the head of the primary family or his wife. This Census Bureau definition excludes single relatives living with a primary family and therefore may understate the presence of extended families.

The percentage of widows among Spanish-surname women ever married is remarkably small in comparison to the reference populations, though this is not true for the three age groups selected in the table. Here again, the lack of vital statistics for Mexican Americans makes it impossible to determine whether the low incidence of widowhood is associated with differential longevity. The incidence of remarriage is also much lower among Spanish-surname women than among either Anglo or non-white females. This difference is probably related to the fact that there are fewer widows and fewer divorcees among Mexican-American women.[16]

The subject of family stability is usually explored statistically through *indicators of instability*. One such indicator is the percentage of families which are not of the common husband–wife type but which have as the family head a person other than the father—either a female (usually the mother) or, to use the census term, some "other male." Another indicator is the percentage of married women who are separated or divorced from their husbands. Since they supplement one another,

Table 6–9. Marital Status of Spanish-surname Females Compared with Other Females Age 14 and Over, by Selected Age Groups[a], Southwest, 1960

| Population and Age Group | Percent of Total | | Percent of Ever Married[b] | |
	Single	Ever Married[b]	Widowed	Married More Than Once
All ages				
Anglo	15.6	84.4	14.1	20.3
Spanish-surname	24.6	75.5	10.8	14.1
Nonwhite	18.7	81.3	15.3	27.3
20–24				
Anglo	21.3	78.7	0.3	7.8
Spanish-surname	31.3	68.7	0.5	4.9
Nonwhite	30.2	69.8	1.2	6.4
35–44				
Anglo	4.0	96.0	2.4	22.4
Spanish-surname	6.5	93.5	3.9	16.9
Nonwhite	4.4	95.6	6.2	29.5
65 and Over				
Anglo	6.6	93.4	56.6	21.1
Spanish-surname	5.4	94.6	58.6	18.4
Nonwhite	2.8	97.2	61.8	38.0

[a] In this table, as well as elsewhere, age groups have been selected to represent the young, the middle-aged, and the elderly.
[b] Includes married spouse present, spouse absent, and separated.
Source: *1960 U.S. Census of Population*, vol. I, parts 4, 6, 7, 33, and 45, table 105; and PC(2)–1B, table 7.

both sets of statistics are presented.[17] Both are at variance with the widespread notion of especially strong family stability in the Mexican-American population.

The incidence of families other than the husband–wife type among the Spanish-surname population in 1960 was far greater than among Anglos, though smaller than among nonwhites (Table 6–10). This was true for the Southwest as a whole as well as in its urban areas. The only exceptions occur in the relatively small group of "other male" family heads. The data for separate age classes suggest that intergroup contrasts in the incidence of unstable families are not a function of age differences. However, *the broken family may have different implications in different cultures or ethnic communities.* In the case of Mexican Americans, the deserted wife's brother or another close relative may more often represent the "other male" and assume the absent husband's role in the family; or the core family may be reconstituted by grandparents living with the woman and her children. If so, the psychological and economic effects of a broken family on mother and children may be substantially modified.

Table 6–10. Families Other than Husband–Wife as a Percent of All Families, Spanish-surname Population Compared with Other Population Groups, Total and Urban Southwest, and for Selected Age Classes of Family Head, 1960

Family Head and Age Class	Anglo	Spanish-surname	Nonwhite[a]
Southwest, all ages			
Female head	7.7	11.9	18.1
"Other male" head[b]	2.2	3.8	3.8
Female and "other male"	9.9	15.7	21.9
Urban Southwest, all ages			
Female head	8.4	12.8	18.9
"Other male" head[b]	2.2	3.7	3.7
Female and "other male"	10.6	16.5	22.6
Age 14–34			
Female head	5.7	8.6	19.7
"Other male" head[b]	1.6	2.5	3.1
Female and "other male"	7.3	11.1	22.8
Age 35–44			
Female head	7.2	11.0	17.3
"Other male" head[b]	1.9	2.7	3.2
Female and "other male"	9.1	13.7	20.5
Age 65 and over			
Female head	13.1	19.8	21.9
"Other male" head[b]	3.7	8.8	6.6
Female and "other male"	16.8	28.6	28.5

[a] Data for California, the only state for which sufficient information on subgroups of nonwhites is available, show that the higher rate for nonwhites is attributable largely to Negroes. In urban California, for example, families other than husband-wife accounted for 24.6 percent of all Negro families, but only 12 percent of all Japanese or Chinese families.
[b] Other than husband with wife present.
Source: *1960 U.S. Census of Population,* vol. I, parts 4, 6, 7, 33, and 45, tables 50, 109, 111; PC(2)–1B, table 3.

Table 6–11 affords a closer view of family instability. Among women ever married, divorcees are less frequent in the Spanish-surname group than in either the Anglo or the nonwhite population. However, the incidence of separations (without divorce) is substantially greater than among Anglos, though far smaller than among nonwhites. Restraints on divorce among the predominantly Catholic Mexican Americans probably account for much of this difference between divorces and separations. When separations and divorces are combined, Anglo women show the lowest incidence, Spanish-surname females rank next, and nonwhites by far the highest. Again, these observations hold more or less for each of the three age groups shown in the table.

Thus, the data tend to modify the cliché of the Mexican-American family as a unit largely untouched by modern trends, urbanization, and increased contact with the Anglo world; but, just the same, these figures must be placed in their proper perspective.

Table 6–11. Separated and Divorced Women as a Percent of Women Ever Married, Spanish-surname Females Age 14 and Over Compared with Other Females, by Selected Age Groups, Southwest, 1960

Population and Age Group	Separated	Divorced	Separated and Divorced	Married, Spouse Absent[a]	Total[b]
All Ages					
Anglo	1.5	5.1	6.6	2.0	8.6
Spanish-surname	3.7	4.3	8.0	3.2	11.2
Nonwhite[c]	7.7	7.4	15.1	5.4	20.5
Age 20–24					
Anglo	2.3	3.8	6.1	3.8	9.9
Spanish-surname	3.9	3.3	7.2	4.9	12.1
Nonwhite	9.8	4.5	14.3	7.6	21.9
Age 35–44					
Anglo	1.5	5.6	7.1	1.8	8.9
Spanish-surname	3.9	5.2	9.1	2.6	11.7
Nonwhite	8.6	9.2	17.8	3.2	21.0
Age 65 and over					
Anglo	0.9	3.8	4.7	1.7	6.4
Spanish-surname	2.3	2.4	4.7	1.9	6.6
Nonwhite	2.4	3.7	6.1	1.8	7.9

[a] Separated physically for reasons other than marital discord, such as military service, imprisonment, employment in another area, or immigration without spouse.
[b] Sum of "separated and divorced" and "married, spouse absent."
[c] Data for California indicate that the high nonwhite rate is explained largely by the incidence of separation and divorce among Negroes. The Negro rate was 20.9 percent as against 2.6 percent for Japanese and Chinese.
Source: *1960 U.S. Census of Population*, vol. I, parts 4, 6, 7, 33, and 45, table 105; PC(2)–1B, table 3.

In the case of all three populations, the statistics refer to relatively small segments of the universe. Moreover, they do not reveal anything about the quality of family life among the 90 or 85 or 80 percent of the units in each population which the statistical evidence indicates to be stable. It is entirely possible for a category of people to have a large incidence of family instability, as here measured, and at the same time to include a high proportion of families rated as exceptionally cohesive and strong.

THE FERTILITY DIFFERENTIAL

The previous discussion of the age composition of the Mexican-American population and the size of families has given more than a hint of extraordinary fertility. The data confirm this impression—and they are especially significant in the absence of statistics on birth rates for the Spanish-surname population.

In both 1950 and 1960 the fertility ratios were much greater for Spanish-surname females than for Anglos and even for nonwhites in the Southwest (Table 6–12). Only in Arizona and New Mexico, with their relatively large component of American Indians, did the 1960 nonwhite ratios exceed those for Mexican Americans. California showed the lowest Spanish-surname ratio, and New Mexico the highest. It is

Table 6–12. *Fertility Ratios of Spanish-surname Women Compared with Others, Five Southwest States, 1950 and 1960*[a]

State and Population Group	*1950*	*1960*	*Percent Change, 1950–1960*
Southwest			
All	430	499	16.0
Anglo	399	455	14.0
Spanish-surname	655	709	8.2
Nonwhite	451	612	35.7
Arizona			
All	488	554	13.5
Anglo	422	481	14.0
Spanish-surname	660	753	14.1
Nonwhite	661	846	28.0
California			
All	401	472	17.7
Anglo	386	442	14.5
Spanish-surname	574	657	14.5
Nonwhite	422	569	34.8
Colorado			
All	448	516	15.2
Anglo	420	491	16.9
Spanish-surname	762	738	−3.1
Nonwhite	416	621	49.3
New Mexico			
All	561	618	10.2
Anglo	464	543	17.0
Spanish-surname	713	754	5.8
Nonwhite	664	793	19.4
Texas			
All	449	520	15.8
Anglo	410	459	12.0
Spanish-surname	691	745	7.8
Nonwhite	445	624	40.2

[a] The fertility ratio is the number of children under 5 years old divided by the number of women aged 15–49, multiplied by 1,000.
Source: Spanish surname: 1960: *1960 U.S. Census of Population*, PC(2)–1B, table 2; 1950: *1950 U.S. Census of Population*, PE no. 3C, table 5. Total: *1960 U.S. Census of Population*, 1960 state volumes, table 17; *1950 U.S. Census of Population*, 1950 state volumes, table 17. Nonwhite: same as for Total.

noteworthy, however, that the fertility ratios of Mexican-American females increased much less between 1950 and 1960 than those in the two reference populations.* Much of the decade of the 1950s, of course, was characterized by high birth rates among the general population—the late phase of the postwar baby boom which affected the 1960 fertility ratios. It seems that Mexican Americans, with an already high

*Changes in fertility ratios over time may be influenced by changes in infant mortality. A decline of infant mortality between 1950 and 1960 could bring about an increase in the fertility ratio if levels of fertility remained constant, or it could counteract a decline in fertility.

Chart 6–10. **Measures of Fertility: Spanish-surname Women Compared with Others, 1960**

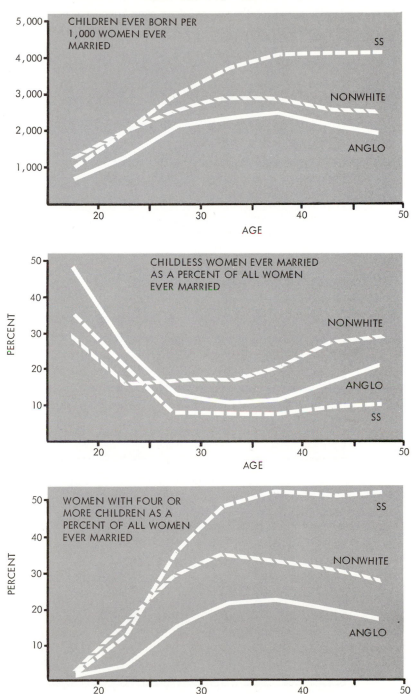

Source: *1960 U.S. Census of Population*, PC(2)–3A, table 11; vol. I, parts 4, 6, 7, 33, and 45, table 113.

133

Chart 6–11. Fertility of Spanish-surname and of All Women in the Urban Southwest and of All Women in Urban Mexico, 1960

(Women with specified number of children ever born as a percent of all women with children, by selected age groups)

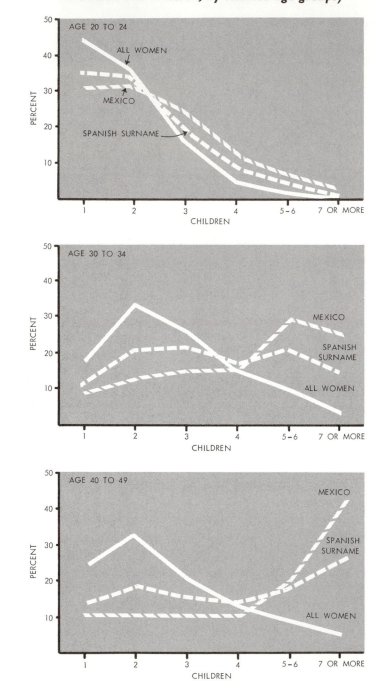

Source: *1960 U.S. Census of Population,* vol. I, parts 4, 6, 7, 33, and 45, table 113; PC(2)–3A, table 11; for Mexico, *VIII Censo General de Población,* 1960, Resumen General, Cuadro 37.

fertility, did not share proportionately in this general trend. Also, our household surveys of 1965–1966 in Los Angeles and San Antonio indicate that the principle of family planning has come to be rather widely accepted in this group, at least in large urban centers (Chapter 15). Thus, the fertility differential may be somewhat narrowed in the future.

The more refined measures provided by age-specific data and by statistics for urban areas alone reinforce the evidence of an exceedingly high fertility of Mexican-American women.* The fertility differentials between the Anglo and the Spanish-surname populations begin in the 15-to-19 age bracket and increase fairly systematically with each age group (Chart 6–10). In the youngest bracket, 997 children were born per 1,000 Mexican-American females as against 706 per 1,000 Anglos. In the 45–49 bracket, the comparable figures are 4,246 as against 2,053. The relatively smaller difference in the lower age group *may* express greater adoption of Anglo norms among young Mexican Americans, but this interpretation is uncertain. Spanish-surname women continue having children at an age when Anglo women generally do not.

As for urban areas, Chart 6–11 shows that, in selected age groups, the fertility rates of Spanish-surname women in the Southwest tend to fall between those of all women in the region and those of all women in urban Mexico. The similarity between the rates for Spanish-name women in the Southwest and the rates for Mexican women becomes greater in the higher age classes. Dissimilarity indexes in all age groups are substantially smaller for Spanish-surname women in the urban Southwest versus women in urban Mexico than they are for Spanish-surname women versus all women in the Southwest.†

One is hard put to find any identifiable United States subpopulation of any numerical consequence in which the Mexican-American record of fertility is matched or even approximated. American Indians show a fertility ratio still higher than that of Mexican Americans,[18] but this is, of course, a very small group in comparison to the Spanish-surname people, and it is predominantly rural. Women of Puerto Rican stock in the continental United States had fertility rates in 1960 substantially below the Mexican-American rates in both urban and rural areas, though above the Anglo rates.[19] Negroes in the Deep South come as close to the Spanish-surname record as any large segment of the population.[20]

DIFFERENCES BETWEEN GENERATIONS

Native and foreign-born Mexican Americans differ sharply in age. The median age of Spanish-surname persons in 1960 progressed from 13.1 years for the natives of natives to 24.1 years for the natives of foreign or mixed parentage to 43.3 years for the

---

*The census data do not permit further refinements in terms of fertility ratios for women of comparable educational and income status.

†For seven age groups, the dissimilarity index for Spanish-surname women versus Mexican women ranges from 4.8 to 22.1, whereas the index for Spanish-surname women versus all women in the Southwest ranges from 7.3 to 32.9.

Chart 6–12.
Median Age of the Spanish-surname Population by Nativity and Parentage, in Urban and Rural Areas of the Southwest, 1960

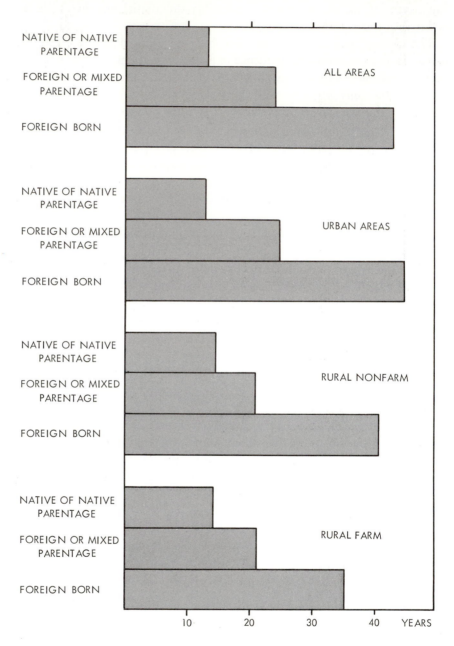

Source: *1950 U.S. Census of Population*, PE no. 3C, table 5; *1960 U.S. Census of Population*, PC(2)–1B, table 2.

136

foreign born (Chart 6–12). These relationships hold broadly in rural as well as urban areas and regardless of sex. Of course, the foreign born include recent adult immigrants—often single adults without children—as well as the surviving immigrants of earlier periods. The natives of foreign parentage are the American-born children of immigrants who have come to this country over a long period of time. The natives of natives have the largest component of children. The age differences correspond to the general experience: the foreign-born population of the United States as a whole is much older than the native born.[21] The sex ratios also differ with nativity status: about 99 males per 100 females among the natives of natives, 103 among the natives of foreign parentage, and nearly 117 among the foreign born.[22] Thus, the excess of males over females is concentrated among the foreign stock.

Table 6–13. Indicators of Family Instability: Spanish-surname Families, by Nativity and Selected Age Groups of Household Heads, Southwest, 1960

NATIVITY AND AGE GROUP	PERCENT OF FAMILIES WITH FEMALE AND "OTHER MALE" HEAD	PERCENT OF WOMEN EVER MARRIED		
		Separated	Divorced	Separated and Divorced
All Ages				
Native of native	14.9	3.5	4.2	7.7
Foreign parentage[a]	13.6	4.1	4.5	8.6
Foreign-born	19.5	3.6	4.2	7.8
20–24				
Native of native	11.0	3.8	3.5	7.3
Foreign parentage[a]	10.6	4.6	3.3	7.9
Foreign-born	17.0	2.9	2.2	5.1
35–44				
Native of native	13.7	3.6	5.0	8.6
Foreign parentage[a]	13.5	4.0	5.1	9.1
Foreign-born	14.3	4.0	5.9	9.9
65 and over				
Native of native	27.9	2.0	2.3	4.3
Foreign parentage[a]	28.4	2.1	3.6	5.7
Foreign-born	29.0	2.6	2.2	4.8

[a] Foreign or mixed parentage.
Source: 1960 U.S. Census of Population, PC(2)–1B, tables 3 and 7.

Unfortunately, nothing can be said about the more subtle question of whether there are discernible differences among first-, second-, and third-generation Mexican Americans with regard to family size or fertility. In all of these cases, the census data are arranged in such form that it is impossible to associate the reported nativity status of children with the reported nativity status of their parents or mothers or of household heads.[23] However, the incidence of family instability in the three generations can be traced by reference to specific age groups, which minimizes the distortions resulting from the great age difference between the nativity classes.*

*However, even the relatively narrow age groups selected for the analysis do not eliminate the influence of age differentials completely. It is possible, for example, that the foreign born among the persons aged 35 to 44 years tend to be older than the native born.

Contrary to what might be expected from the persistence of cultural tradition, *the incidence of other than husband-wife families is highest among the foreign-born Mexican Americans.* As Table 6–13 shows, this is not just a result of their higher average age and the consequent greater probability of wives' remaining widowed, divorced, or deserted. On the other hand, it is difficult to detect any clear association between nativity status and the incidence of separation and divorce.

On the whole, then, the most clear-cut generational differences in the Mexican-American population relate to age and sex, especially to age. These internal differences, as well as the distinctive characteristics of the Spanish-surname group as a whole in comparison with the reference populations, have a bearing on the Mexican Americans' educational and economic status, the subject of the next few chapters.

NOTES TO CHAPTER SIX

1. Because of the great diversity of the nonwhite population in the Southwest and in the individual states composing the region, it would be desirable to present extensive data on the social and economic characteristics of the main subgroups of nonwhites. One could then compare the standing of the Spanish-surname group on a particular characteristic with that of Negroes, Chinese, Japanese, and American Indians separately. The statistics available from the census place severe limitations on such a refinement. The census volumes on social and economic characteristics include few data classified by race within the nonwhite group by state, and these are only for Negroes. In the census report, *Nonwhite Population by Race, 1960 U.S. Census of Population*, PC(2)–1C, the census region is the smallest area for which some characteristics such as those on families are given; the Southwest cuts across two census regions. This report presents state data on general social characteristics by race, but the coverage of races varies from state to state. Statistics by race other than Negro are reported only if the state had 25,000 or more persons of a particular race. Statistics for Negroes are reported only in states where there were 25,000 or more Negroes, and where Negroes represented no more than 75 percent of all nonwhites. Because of these complications, our data for subgroups of nonwhites are fragmentary.

2. For interstate movers, *1960 U.S. Census of Population*, vol. I, parts 4, 6, 7, 33, and 45, table 42; and PC(2)–1B, table 3. Concerning net out-migration, a study using birth, death, and immigration statistics estimates net out-migration of Mexican Americans from Texas in the decade 1950–1960 at 49,000. See Harley L. Browning and S. Dale McLemore, *A Statistical Profile of the Spanish-surname Population of Texas* (Bureau of Business Research, University of Texas, 1964), table 3. While their data do not reveal the destination of the net out-migrants, it is reasonable to assume that a large proportion went to California. In a three-county area of south Texas, where Mexican Americans are a majority of the population, estimated net out-migration to California between 1955 and 1960 was 8,700. Estimate derived from the U.S. Census of Population, PC(2)–2B, *Mobility for States and State Economic Areas* (1963). The counties are Cameron, Hidalgo, and Willacy, which together comprise Texas State Economic Area 15. Gross migration to California is estimated at 10,500, and migration from California to the three-county area at 1,800. The area had a population of 352,000 in 1960, of which 68 percent were Spanish-surname persons. In this case the ethnic composition of the migrants is unknown, but a very high Spanish-surname component can be safely inferred. The evidence for out-migration from the smaller states is wholly inferential. The slow 1950–1960 increase of the Spanish-surname population by

39,000 in Colorado and by little over 20,000 in New Mexico strongly suggests net out-migration.

3. Data from special tabulations of *1960 U.S. Census of Population*, vol. I, parts 4, 6, 7, 33, and 45, table 98, for Spanish-surname persons in the five states. The percentages for Arizona and Colorado were 65 and 72, respectively.

4. The Spanish-surname long-distance internal movers between 1955 and 1960 were 52 percent male. Those moving from abroad were 62 percent male. Long-distance movers are defined by the census as persons 5 years and over who in 1960 lived in a county different from their county of residence in 1955. Source: *1960 U.S. Census of Population*, vol. I, parts 4, 6, 7, 33, and 45, table 100; and PC(2)–1B, table 3.

5. *1960 U.S. Census of Population*, PC(2)–1B, tables 3 and 7.

6. As for the shift away from Texas and Arizona, it is well to remember that by far the largest portion of the Mexican border stretches along these two states. In the earlier periods, they were much more accessible by railroad than was California, both in terms of distance and cost. The route to California was circuitous, and Baja California, the adjoining Mexican area, was so thinly populated that there was no nearby immigration potential of any consequence. Besides, it appears that Texas ranchers used Mexican workers when California's agribusiness could still draw on Chinese, Japanese, and other alien residents. Finally, the data on Mexican stock may overstate the importance of Texas, especially in the earlier periods. San Antonio, Laredo, and El Paso were the most significant ports of entry, and these as well as other Texas cities may have harbored a floating immigrant population residing there for a while but moving on to other states. The same may be true for Arizona, with Nogales, Tuscon, and Phoenix close to the border.

7. See Elizabeth Broadbent, "Mexican Population in the Southwest United States," *Texas Geographic Magazine*, V (Autumn, 1941), pp. 16–24.

8. See Julian Samora and Richard A. Lamanna, *Mexican Americans in a Midwest Metropolis: A Study of East Chicago* (Mexican-American Study Project, Advance Report 8, Graduate School of Business Administration, University of California, Los Angeles, July, 1967), p. 5. Also, Paul S. Taylor, *Mexican Labor in the United States: Chicago and the Calumet Region* (Berkeley, Calif.: University of California Press, 1932), p. 48.

9. California was the only Southwest state in which the rural Spanish-surname population increased between 1950 and 1960. To some extent, the general decline in the rural population is due to the annexation of rural areas by cities. Source for all five states: *1960 U.S. Census of Population*, vol. I, parts 4, 6, 7, 33, and 45; PC(2)–1B, table 1; and *1950 U.S. Census of Population*, PE no. 3C, table 2.

10. The clustering of people in metropolitan areas is in many respects a better indicator of the trend toward cities, because urban places as such range from isolated communities as small as 2,500 population to giants such as Los Angeles. In contrast, the standard metropolitan statistical areas (SMSA's) as defined by the census are counties with large conglomerations of people, often consisting of several cities and towns and having a minimum of 50,000 inhabitants.

11. See *1950 U.S. Census of Population*, vol. II, parts 3, 5, 6, 31, 43, table 2; PE no. 3C, tables 7, 8, and 9; *1960 U.S. Census of Population*, vol. I, part 1, tables S, 42, and 63; parts 4, 6, 7, 33 and 45, tables 13 and 21; PC(2)–1B, table 15; PC(3)–1D, table 1. These data are the sources for Chart 6–3 as well as the figures in the text. Because of varying census definitions in 1950 and 1960 and other statistical complications, the metropolitan area comparisons are estimates derived from the census data.

12. The Guadalajara *municipio*, which is about equivalent to this country's metropolitan area concept, had 740,394 inhabitants in 1960, according to the Mexican Census.

13. See John M. Ellis, "Mortality Differentials for a Spanish-surname Population Group," *The Southwestern Social Science Quarterly*, XL (Mar., 1959), pp. 314–321; and

"Spanish-surname Mortality Differences in San Antonio, Texas," *Journal of Health and Human Behavior*, III (Summer, 1962), pp. 125–127. Also, Browning and McLemore, *op. cit.*, pp. 21–23.

14. The dissimilarity indexes are calculated from the following figures:

Number of Family Members	Percent of All Families		
	U.S. SOUTHWEST		MEXICO
	Anglo	Spanish-surname	
2	35.9	17.9	12.7
3	21.5	17.4	14.0
4	20.6	18.4	14.4
5	12.5	15.5	16.9
6	5.7	11.6	12.3
7 or more	3.8	19.3	29.7

Sources: Southwest: *1960 U.S. Census of Population*, vol. I, parts 4, 6, 7, 33, and 45, table 110; PC(2)–1B, table 5. Mexico: *VIII Censo General de Poblacion, Resumen General*, Cuadro 32.

15. The number of "other relatives" in families cannot be separated from "own children 18 years and over" for the Spanish-surname population. These data are available for the total and nonwhite population. When we estimate the average number of "other relatives and own children 18 years and over" in Spanish-surname families, the results are:

	Average Family Size	Average Number of Other Relatives and Own Children 18 Years and Over	Column (1) Minus (2)
	(1)	(2)	(3)
All families	3.61	.35	3.26
Spanish-surname families	4.72	.62	4.10
Nonwhite families	4.07	.68	3.39

The difference in average family size between all families and Spanish-surname families is 1.11. In turn, the difference between all families and Spanish-surname families in column 2 is .27. Approximately 24 percent of the difference in family size between all families and Spanish-surname families is accounted for by the relatively greater frequency of other relatives and children over 18 in the latter (.27 divided by 1.11). About 76 percent of the difference is associated with the presence of more "own children under 18" in the Spanish-surname group. Derived from *1960 U.S. Census of Population*, vol. I (state volumes), tables 49 and 110; and PC(2)–1B, tables 3 and 5.

16. Comparable census figures for the marital status of males show the percentage of single persons in the Spanish-surname group to be much higher than in the general population. In contrast to females, however, widowers are a little more frequent among Mexican Americans than among Anglos. Mexican-American men are less prone to remarry than either nonwhites or Anglos—the same pattern as that found for women. Of course, the census data on the marital status of Spanish-surname males and females are affected by intermarriage of Mexican Americans with others, which is discussed elsewhere in this volume. Generally, a woman marrying an Anglo loses her statistical Spanish-name identity, while a man taking an Anglo spouse does not.

17. The percentage of families which are not of the common husband-wife type is a useful indicator because by census definition it is directly related to families; but these data fail to show the causes of the uncommon family composition. For example, families may be headed by a woman because the husband has died–an "act of God"– or because he deserted or divorced his wife, an act of man with a definite bearing on family instability. The other indicator, the percentage of married women who are separated or divorced from their husbands, refers to individuals rather than families; a divorcee, for example, may remain un-

married, in which case one can speak of a broken marriage, or she may have five children so that indeed a broken family is involved.

18. The fertility ratio of American Indians in the Southwest in 1960 was 832 as against 709 for Spanish-surname woman, as shown in Table 6–12. From *1960 U.S. Census of Population*, PC(2)–1C, table 51.

19. In 1960, the number of children ever born per 1,000 women born in Puerto Rico or of Puerto Rican parentage was as follows: 1,535 in the 15 to 24 age group, 2,522 in the 25 to 34 age group, and 3,032 in the 35 to 44 age group. Only the figure for the youngest age class even approximates the corresponding number for Spanish-surname women.

20. For example, the number of children ever born per 1,000 ever married Negro women in the age group 35 to 44 years was 4,773 in Mississippi and 4,304 in South Carolina. *1960 U.S. Census of Population*, PC (2)–3A, table 50. Similar high figures are found in other states of the Deep South, such as Alabama and Louisiana.

21. In 1960, the median age of the foreign born in the United States was 57.3 years as against 27.9 years for the native born.

22. *1960 U.S. Census of Population*, PC(2)–1B, table 2.

23. For example, foreign-born household heads are listed with the foreign-born population in households; but foreign-born household heads may have native-born children. These are tabulated under natives of foreign parentage living in households. Similarly, natives of foreign parentage who are heads of households may have children who are native born; these will be tabulated under natives of natives living in households and will inflate the average size of households of natives of native parentage. Computations along these lines produce specious results.

SEVEN

The Education Gap

THIS chapter deals with one of the most widely recognized facts about Mexican Americans: their generally low attainment in formal schooling. Since education has increasingly become the gateway to the more desirable occupations and higher income, the schooling gap is a fundamental cause of the depressed economic condition of the minority.

Mexican Americans concerned with the progress of their group are thoroughly aware of this problem. On initial field tours throughout the Southwest, we often asked which single factor was believed the most important barrier to collective advancement; better education emerged as a standard answer. Many Mexican-American service associations have a long record of educational programs.

The larger society began to show an increasing awareness of the schooling gap in the early 1930s. This concern appeared in teachers' conferences and workshops focusing on the development of special teaching methods and orientation to the general cultural background of the pupils. There were many more such conferences during the period following World War II, as Mexican Americans became more visible in the cities. These efforts, along with preschool programs like Headstart and compensatory and bilingual programs, have continued to proliferate in recent years. A comparison of the discussion topics and recommendations of a conference held immediately after World War II and one held 20 years later, however, reveals little change in content. Though the special programs of the middle and late 1960s have yet to be evaluated, the impact of several decades of educational concern about Mexican-American children on these children's schooling is not clear in light of existing evidence.

It is relatively easy to document the schooling gap; it is far more difficult to explain it. Indeed, it will be shown that any attempt to relate the underattainment of Mexican-American youth to measurable or even clearly identifiable variables inside or outside the school poses perplexing problems, reflecting the state of understanding of the very intricate problems involved.

Table 7–1. Schooling of Spanish-surname Persons Compared with Other Persons, Age 14 and Over, Southwest, 1960 (Males and females combined)

Ethnic Group	Median School Years Completed	PERCENT ATTAINING SCHOOLING LEVEL				
		0–4 Years	5–8 Years	9–11 Years	12 Years	Some College[a]
Anglo	12.0	3.7	22.1	24.3	27.8	22.1
Spanish-surname	8.1	27.6	33.8	20.1	12.8	5.6
Nonwhite	9.7	15.1	29.8	24.7	18.7	11.7
Negro	n.a.	14.1	31.8	26.5	17.4	10.1
Indian	n.a.	32.4	30.9	20.4	11.4	3.9
Japanese	n.a.	4.8	14.9	16.7	39.1	24.5
Chinese	n.a.	23.0	16.9	13.8	19.5	26.7

a Includes complete college education (four years or more) as well as one to three years of college.
Source: 1960 U.S. Census of Population, PC (2)–1B, tables 3 and 7; vol. I, parts 4, 6, 7, 33, and 45, tables 47 and 103. U.S. Census of Population, PC(2)–1C, tables 50, 51, 52, 53. Data for Japanese are unavailable for Arizona and New Mexico. Data for Chinese are unavailable for Colorado and New Mexico.

Even the statistical record is gross. Census data do not take into account differences in the quality of education. They equate six years of schooling in a Texas border town, for example, with six years in Los Angeles. Even in the same city the average quality of education in a highly segregated, poor neighborhood school usually differs sharply from that provided by schools located in areas of higher socioeconomic status. Nevertheless, the record helps to sketch a broad outline of the schooling gap, to indicate the direction of change over time, and to highlight the enormous effort that will be required to narrow that gap.

THE STATISTICAL RECORD

When educational attainment is measured by median years of schooling completed, Mexican Americans in 1960 fell far short of the performance not only of Anglos but also of nonwhites in general (Table 7–1). Only Indians showed still lower attainment. Asians, especially Japanese, were generally better educated than even

Anglos. A higher proportion of Negroes than of Mexican Americans had completed high school or gone on to college. Education is one of the most conspicuous status indicators pointing to a substantially lower position of Mexican Americans in comparison with nonwhites. Taking the Anglo attainment for persons 14 years and older in the Southwest as a norm, the gap was 3.9 school years (or 32 percent) for people of Mexican descent, and 2.3 years (or 19 percent) for nonwhites as a whole.[1] The gap was slightly greater for persons 25 years and over, who had clearly completed their

Table 7–2. Educational Attainment of Spanish-surname Persons Compared with Anglos and Nonwhites, by Age, Southwest, 1960 (Persons with specified attainment as percent of all persons in age group)

Ethnicity and Educational Attainment	Total years 14 and over	AGE GROUPS				
		14–24	25–34	35–44	45–64	65 and over
Anglo						
0–4 years	3.7	1.1	1.2	1.8	4.4	13.0
5–8 years	22.1	18.7	9.6	13.7	29.0	43.7
9–11 years	24.3	39.4	21.2	20.2	21.9	15.6
12 years	27.8	25.6	36.3	36.8	23.8	14.0
Some college[a]	22.1	15.2	31.6	27.5	20.8	13.8
Spanish-surname[b]						
0–4 years	27.6	9.1	21.9	29.0	47.2	66.5
5–8 years	33.8	39.4	31.4	33.4	32.4	23.5
9–11 years	20.1	33.4	20.7	16.5	8.9	3.9
12 years	12.8	14.0	17.6	14.3	7.1	3.8
Some college[a]	5.6	4.2	8.4	6.8	4.3	2.7
Nonwhite						
0–4 years	15.1	4.1	6.5	10.6	25.0	48.6
5–8 years	29.8	24.9	19.9	30.1	41.3	34.6
9–11 years	24.7	39.9	27.0	23.3	15.4	6.9
12 years	18.7	21.0	27.4	22.6	10.5	5.3
Some college[a]	11.7	10.0	19.2	13.4	7.9	4.6

[a] Includes complete college education (four years or more) as well as one to three years of college.
[b] For Spanish-surname persons, the attainment is shown below separately for the 14–19-year and the 20–24-year age groups. No comparable data can be constructed from the census for nonwhites or for Anglos.

Educational Attainment	14–19 years	20–24 years
0–4 years	6.4	13.0
5–8 years	47.5	27.2
9–11 years	38.5	25.6
12 years	6.6	25.2
Some college	1.0	9.0

Source: *1960 U.S. Census of Population*, PC(2)–1B, tables 3 and 7; vol. I, parts 4, 6, 7, 33, and 45, table 103.

schooling. The same generalization holds for people at the extreme ends of educational attainment. Nearly 28 per cent of the Mexican Americans, 15 percent of the nonwhites, and only 4 percent of the Anglos were functional illiterates; that is, they had four years of schooling or less. At the other extreme, only 6 per cent of the Mexican Americans, 12 percent of the nonwhites, but almost 25 percent of the Anglos in the region had had at least some college training by 1960. And even this low rate of college education for Mexican Americans seems to represent something of a breakthrough. According to our interviews throughout the Southwest, the G.I.

[1] Notes for this chapter start on page 171.

Bill of Rights was a major factor in affording Mexican-American veterans an opportunity to go to college in the postwar years.

Sex differences in the over-all educational attainments of both Mexican Americans and Anglos were insignificant in 1960. Anglo men of 14 years and over had completed a median of 11.8 years of school, compared with 12.0 years for Anglo women.

Table 7–3. *School Enrollment of Spanish-surname Persons and all Persons 5 to 21 Years of Age, by Age Groups, Urban and Rural Areas, Southwest, 1960*[a]
(Percent of each age group enrolled)

Type of Area and Age Group	Total	Spanish-surname	Gap
All areas			
5–21	79.0	74.2	4.8
5–6	64.5	55.6	8.9
7–13	97.6	96.0	1.6
14–15	94.3	88.0	6.3
16–17	80.6	66.9	13.7
18–19	41.9	33.2	8.7
20–21	21.2	12.1	9.1
Urban			
5–21	79.9	75.3	2.6
5–6	67.5	58.2	9.3
7–13	97.9	96.4	1.5
14–15	94.8	89.2	5.6
16–17	81.2	68.2	13.0
18–19	43.4	34.0	9.4
20–21	23.3	13.0	10.3
Rural nonfarm			
5–21	74.6	71.1	3.5
5–6	54.2	47.4	6.8
7–13	96.6	94.7	1.9
14–15	92.3	84.9	7.4
16–17	77.1	64.1	13.0
18–19	33.3	30.8	2.5
20–21	12.2	9.6	2.6
Rural farm			
5–21	79.0	67.9	11.1
5–6	44.4	41.3	3.1
7–13	96.8	93.8	3.0
14–15	92.9	82.3	10.6
16–17	82.9	57.9	25.0
18–19	49.3	29.7	19.6
20–21	13.1	7.0	6.1

[a] No separate data for Anglos and nonwhites are available for these age groups in urban and rural areas; hence this table compares Spanish-surname persons with all persons.
Source: *1960 U.S. Census of Population*, vol. I, parts 4, 6, 7, 33, and 45, tables 101, 95; PC(2)–1B, table 4.

Spanish-surname medians were 8.1 years for men and 8.2 for women. Nonwhites showed greater discrepancies: Men in the region had completed a median of 9.3 years, compared with 9.9 for women.[2] These differences were particularly notable among Negroes. A sex disparity also appears between Mexican Americans and Anglos who have gone to college. In 1960 women accounted for 39.1 percent of all Mexican

Chart 7–1.
Percent of Teenagers Enrolled in School: Spanish-surname Persons Compared with Other Population Groups, Southwest, 1960

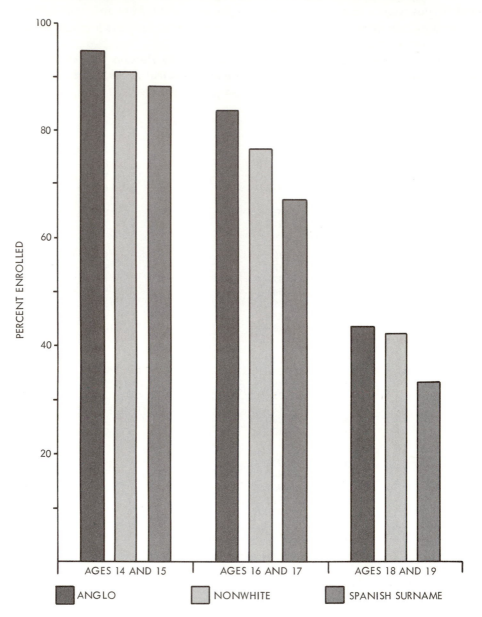

Source: *1960 U.S. Census of Population*, vol. I, parts 4, 6, 7, 33, and 45, tables 44, 94, 101, and PC(2)–1B, table 4.

146

Americans who had attended college (and only 35.4 percent of those who had completed four years or more). By contrast, females accounted for 46 percent of all Southwest college people (and 40 percent of those who had completed four or more years).[3]

The record shows progress when we examine *age differences* in schooling. For all groups, most notably for Mexican Americans and Negroes, people in the oldest age categories are more likely to have poor education. Young people are more likely to have completed high school or to have gone on to college (Table 7–2).[4] Among Anglos, however, adults 25 to 44 years of age show higher educational attainment than younger ones. This relationship is true in each of the five Southwestern states. The gap between Anglos and Mexican Americans is always smaller for persons between 14 and 24 than for persons 25 years and over. The age contrast was particularly great in Texas, where Mexican Americans 14 to 24 years of age had 8.1 years of schooling compared with 4.8 years for those over 25.

These patterns definitely indicate educational progress. Nevertheless, the gaps between Mexican Americans and other population categories in the Southwest remained large in absolute terms. Relative progress does not by any means imply an imminent solution to the Mexican Americans' educational lag. The persistence of this lag is indicated by enrollment figures. Enrollment of Spanish-surname pupils ages 5 and 6 is comparatively low. In other words, schooling typically begins late. The percentage of 7- to 13-year-old Mexican Americans and others enrolled is about the same, but the difference between Mexican-American and total enrollment widens with age from 14 on. At age 20 to 21 only 12.1 percent of the Spanish-surname persons were going to school as against 21.2 percent of all persons in the Southwest (Table 7–3). The pattern is most pronounced in the rural-farm areas, probably reflecting the special problems of the children of migrant farm workers.[5] Enrollment disparities for the strategically important teenage years indicate that dropout problems are most severe in the Mexican-American population (Chart 7–1). The same pattern is repeated in each of the five states.

Educational differences between *Mexican-born and American-born Spanish-surname individuals* are striking. Typically, the foreign-born individual had little more than half the schooling of the second-generation individual (native born of foreign or mixed parentage). But the difference is very slight between the second and the third generations (Table 7–4). Differences by sex are small in all generations. To explore the question whether the observed contrasts between nativity classes are an artifact of age variance, the table shows a special analysis of the young group (14 to 24 years) by nativity. This analysis confirms the general finding, i.e., a sharp difference between native and foreign born, and a minor difference between the second and the third generation.

When we single out high and low achievers (those with high school on the one hand and those with four years or less of schooling on the other), the same generational rank order appears (Table 7–4). With minor exceptions, the greatest divergence is between native and foreign born.

Chart 7–2.
School Enrollment of Spanish-surname Persons 5 to 21 Years of Age, by Nativity, Parentage, and Type of Area, Southwest, 1960
(Percent enrolled)

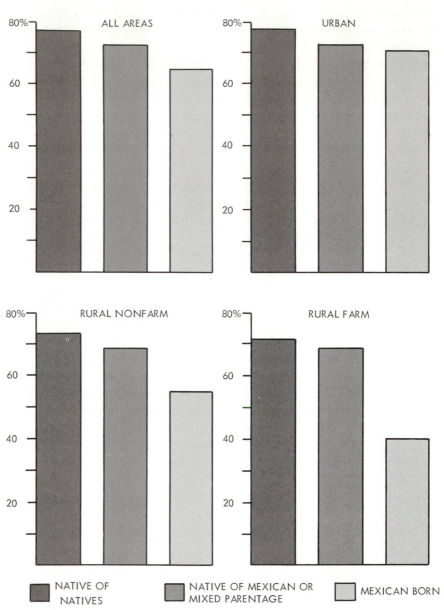

Source: *1960 U.S. Census of Population*, PC(2)–1B, table 4.

School enrollment shows the same general pattern, except that there appears to be greater progress between the second and third generations, as shown in Chart 7–2. This chart also highlights the urban–rural contrasts that appear in all educational statistics. The Mexican born display a drastic decline in enrollment as one proceeds from urban to rural, and especially to rural farm areas. The familiar rank order by generations holds for urban areas, but the range in percent enrolled is small. The range widens in rural nonfarm areas and reaches extremely high proportions in rural farm areas, where just a little over 40 percent of the foreign born were enrolled.[6]

Table 7–4. Educational Attainment of Spanish-surname Persons by Sex, Age, Nativity, and Parentage, Southwest, 1960

Age Group and Nativity	YEARS OF SCHOOL COMPLETED (Percent of all persons in specified age group)					MEDIAN SCHOOL YEARS COMPLETED	
	0–4	5–8	9–11	12	Some College[a]	Male	Female
14 Years and Over							
Native of native parents	18.9	35.3	24.5	14.8	6.5	8.6	8.8
Native of foreign or mixed parents	21.8	34.8	23.1	14.7	5.6	8.6	8.4
Foreign-born	51.7	29.8	8.0	6.4	4.0	4.5	5.0
14–24 Years[b]							
Native of native parents	6.3	40.1	35.6	14.0	4.0	n.a.	n.a.
Native of foreign or mixed parents	6.8	37.9	34.6	16.1	4.5	n.a.	n.a.
Foreign-born	28.6	40.1	18.8	8.1	4.3	n.a.	n.a.
25 Years and Over[c]							
Native of native parents	27.0	32.3	17.3	15.3	8.1	n.a.	n.a.
Native of foreign or mixed parents	28.0	33.3	18.3	14.1	6.0	n.a.	n.a.
Foreign-born	55.7	28.0	6.2	6.0	4.0	n.a.	n.a.

[a] One to three years of college combined with four years or more.
[b] The comparisons for this age group may still be influenced by differences in the age distribution of the various nativity classes. However, the contrast between the native born and the foreign born is so great that more refined data (which are not available) would perhaps reduce the magnitude of the difference but not remove it.
[c] The figures for this larger age group are more heavily influenced by differences in the age distribution of the three nativity classes.
Source: 1960 U.S. Census of Population, PC(2)–1B, tables 3 and 7.

PROGRESS THROUGH TIME AND URBANIZATION

The better educational preparation of younger Mexican Americans evident in the 1960 data conveys a sense of progress. This progress is directly visible when we compare the 1960 and 1950 statistics (Table 7–5). The school years completed by adults increased in all three population groups, but the greatest increase was among Mexican Americans: Their gain was 1.7 years as against 0.8 years for Anglos and 1.2 years for nonwhites. Of course, this gain was achieved from a very low level of attainment in 1950. Nevertheless, the schooling gap was narrowed to a moderate degree.

The relative improvement in the educational standing of Spanish-surname adults in the decade of the 1950s is attributable in part to rapidly increasing urbanization. Educational attainment is generally better in the cities and suburbs than in the country, partly because school facilities and the enforcement of compulsory-education

Table 7–5. Median Years of School Completed by Spanish-surname Persons Age 25 and Over Compared with Other Persons, Five Southwest States, 1950 and 1960

State and Population Group	MEDIAN YEARS COMPLETED		INCREASE 1950–1960	
	1950	1960	Years	Percent
Southwest				
Anglo	11.3	12.1	0.8	7
Spanish-surname	5.4	7.1	1.7	31
Nonwhite	7.8	9.0	1.2	15
Arizona				
Anglo	11.6	12.1	0.5	4
Spanish-surname	6.0	7.0	1.0	16
Nonwhite	5.5	7.0	1.5	27
California				
Anglo	12.0	12.2	0.2	2
Spanish-surname	7.8	8.6	0.8	10
Nonwhite	8.9	10.6	1.7	19
Colorado				
Anglo	11.3	12.2	0.9	8
Spanish-surname	6.5	8.2	1.7	26
Nonwhite	9.8	11.2	1.4	14
New Mexico				
Anglo	11.8	12.2	0.4	3
Spanish-surname	6.1	7.4	1.3	21
Nonwhite	5.8	7.1	1.3	22
Texas				
Anglo	10.3	11.5	1.2	12
Spanish-surname	3.5	4.8	1.3	37
Nonwhite	7.0	8.1	1.1	16

Source: *1960 U.S. Census of Population,* PC(2)–1B, tables 3 and 7; vol. I, parts 4, 6, 7, 33, and 45, tables 47 and 103; *1950 U.S. Census of Population,* PE no. 3C, table 3; vol. II, parts 3, 5, 6, 31, and 43, table 20.

laws are usually superior in the urban and suburban areas. Also, when parents shift from agricultural to urban jobs the impediments to the children's schooling that stem from migrant farm work or seasonal child labor are removed or reduced. As was already shown, the urban-rural contrasts, especially those between the urban and rural-farm areas, were extremely large for Mexican Americans.

Since urbanization has continued during the decade of the 1960s, we may expect the 1970 school attainments to reflect this shift. However, the migration to the cities is just one of many forces bearing on progress. Progress is also visible when the schooling of *urban* Mexican Americans alone is compared for 1950 and 1960. For example, the intercensal increase in median school years completed by urban males 14 to 24 years of age ranges from slightly over half a year in California (where the 1950 figure was somewhat higher than in other states) to a year and a half in Texas.[7] This is true despite the fact that the migrants to cities have come from areas with lower average levels of education. Those who migrated may have had above-average schooling and thereby been more motivated to seek better opportunities in urban environments or to improve their lot by moving from Texas to California.

INTRA-REGIONAL VARIATIONS IN ATTAINMENT

Different states in the Southwest spend vastly different sums on education. This allocation of resources can be an important factor, though it is an oversimplified measure of educational quality. Table 7–6 shows the differences in financial effort and

Table 7–6.   Selected State Statistics on School Input and Output, 1965–66

	Arizona	California	Colorado	New Mexico	Texas
Average daily attendance of children age 5–17	84.7%	93.8%	92.0%	84.6%	83.3%
(Rank among 50 states)	(21)	(5)	(6)	(22)	(24)
Number of children age 5–17 per 100 adults age 21–64	58	49	56	69	56
(Rank among 50 states)	(12)	(43)	(18)	(1)	(18)
Estimated expenditure per average daily attendance	$458	$613	$571	$556	$449
(Rank among 50 states)	(23)	(9)	(22)	(24)	(39)
Public school expenditure as percent of personal income, 1965	5.0%	3.8%	4.6%	5.4%	4.0%
(Rank among 50 states)	(5)	(32)	(10)	(2)	(24)
Pupils per classroom teacher	23.8	26.7	22.3	24.4	24.9
(Rank among 50 states)	(22)	(44)	(12)	(26)	(31)
Estimated average teacher salaries	$7,230	$8,540	$6,625	$6,630	$6,025
(Rank among 50 states)	(15)	(2)	(21)	(20)	(33)
Percent of draftees failing mental tests, 1965	20.5%	15.3%	14.0%	25.4%	23.3%
(Rank among 50 states)	(26)	(25)	(20)	(38)	(35)

Source: *Rankings of the States, 1967*, Research Report 1967–R1, National Education Association, Research Division (Washington, D.C., 1967), p. 12, table 8; p. 21, table 25; p. 25, table 32; p. 26, table 36; p. 32, table 46; p. 54, tables 90 and 92.

related indicators. While no precise judgments can be drawn from such data, certain inferences seem obvious. Among the Southwest states, California spends the most money, pays the highest salaries, has the highest average daily attendance (ADA) percentage, and ranks low in the number of draft rejectees. Texas is at the other extreme, with the poorest ADA, lowest teacher salaries, lowest expenditure per ADA, and next-to-highest percentage failing mental tests for the draft. Although California spends the most money per ADA, it is, however, the lowest of the states in percentage of total personal income used for public education. New Mexico and Arizona, with the largest number of children per adult, seem to be making a strong effort by allocating the highest percentages of total personal income to education.

Except in Colorado, where general educational attainment is high and the gap between minorities and Anglos relatively low, state differences in the schooling attainment of members of the minority groups seem broadly consistent with state differences in the quality of education expressed by their expenditures (Table 7–7). For persons of 25 and over (in other words, persons whose schooling has been largely completed), California shows the smallest schooling gap between Mexican Americans and Anglos (3.6 years) and Texas the largest (6.7 years). In three states—

Table 7–7. Median Years of School Completed by Spanish-surname Persons Compared with Other Persons Age 25 and Over, and Minority/Anglo Schooling Gaps, Five Southwest States, 1960 (Males and females combined)

Ethnic Group	Arizona	California	Colorado	New Mexico	Texas
Anglo	12.1	12.2	12.2	12.2	11.5
Spanish-surname	7.0	8.6	8.2	7.4	4.8
Nonwhite	7.0	10.6	11.2	7.1	8.1
Spanish-surname/Anglo Gap:					
Years	5.1	3.6	4.0	4.8	6.7
Percent[a]	42%	30%	33%	40%	58%
Nonwhite/Anglo Gap:					
Years	5.1	1.6	1.0	5.1	3.4
Percent[a]	42%	13%	8%	42%	30%

[a] Computed as a percent of Anglo median years, i.e., the percentage by which the Spanish-surname or nonwhite number of years falls below the Anglo figure. This calculation is added to provide a common measurement. For example, a difference of three years is equivalent to one-third if the Anglo median is nine years but to 25 percent if the Anglo median is twelve years. Percentages are rounded.
Source: *1960 U.S. Census of Population*, vol. I, parts 4, 6, 7, 33, and 45, tables 47 and 103; PC(2)–1B, tables 3 and 7.

California, Colorado, and Texas—nonwhites as a class had more schooling than Mexican Americans. In New Mexico and Arizona, where the nonwhite category includes a large admixture of American Indians, its schooling record was equal to or lower than that of Mexican Americans. The inclusion of large numbers of highly educated Orientals in California, on the other hand, raised the over-all nonwhite school attainment.

State differences must be interpreted with caution. Because of state-to-state migrations, the statistics on the relative educational attainment of states' inhabitants do not necessarily measure precisely the current attainment levels of groups educated *in* those states: that is, they are not entirely accurate indicators of the relative quality of education in the different states—for instance, California compared with Texas.

Data about the educational level were obtained by the Census Bureau at the 1960 place of residence. If Mexican Americans or, for that matter, others who received their schooling in Texas had moved to California before the census date, the latter state would be credited or debited with schooling that occurred in the former. If those who moved had an above-average education, then all other things being equal California's record would have been raised and that of Texas lowered. This bias will particularly affect the data for the adult population. At the same time, interstate differences with regard to education are so large and consistent that they cannot be explained by state-by-state migrations.

The state-by-state and the urban–rural statistics show greater intra-regional disparities for Mexican Americans (as well as for nonwhites) than for Anglos. The range of disparities is highlighted in the 1960 data for *metropolitan areas* (Table 7–8). Though the state differentials are evident, within-state differences are also notable. For example, Mexican Americans in Fresno, in the heart of California's agricultural Central Valley, had a median attainment of only 6.1 years in 1960. This is below the median attainment of Mexican Americans in many cities of Texas.

Median school attainment for Mexican Americans varied between 10.1 years in Colorado Springs and 3.1 in Lubbock. The range is much smaller for nonwhites, despite the vast differences in the ethnic composition of the nonwhite category from one city to another. And the range is quite narrow for Anglos, with a high of 12.5 in Albuquerque and a low of 10.7 in Fresno and Stockton.

The general lag of Spanish-surname individuals behind nonwhites in average educational attainment is evident in 32 of the 34 areas for which data are available.* Generally, where the educational gap is relatively small for one minority it tends to be small for the other as well. This pattern, which appears in other socioeconomic indicators, suggests the general proposition that the socioeconomic position of all minorities in an area is greatly conditioned by the structure of the dominant society. This proposition will receive support in succeeding analyses. In the present context, we hypothesize that the sharp and usually correlated local variations in the schooling gap for Mexican Americans and for the locally significant nonwhite group reflect the larger social system in each area, of which the school system is an integral part.

Signs of progress for the Spanish-surname population are, again, quite clear from the data for metropolitan areas. The median number of school years completed increased during the 1950s in every one of the areas, even if it was the kind of advance exemplified by Lubbock (from a depressing 1.7 years to the still depressing 3.1 years) or by Stockton and Laredo (where the gains were fractional, from 7.2 to 7.5 years and 5.2 to 5.4 years, respectively). Deficiencies in the 1950 census statistics limit that year's comparison to Spanish-surname persons versus the total population, rather than versus Anglos, and this comparison is influenced by the varying proportions of

---

*In Tucson, the difference between the Spanish-surname and nonwhite minorities is minimal; the proportion of Indians among nonwhites is high, and the proportion of Negroes low. In Beaumont–Port Arthur the difference between the minorities is fairly large: there is a relatively small Spanish-surname population and a large Negro population in this metropolis almost on the border of Louisiana.

Table 7–8. **Median Years of School Completed by Spanish-surname Persons Age 25 and Over Compared with Other Population Groups in 35 Metropolitan Areas, 1950 and 1960**[a]

Standard Metropolitan Statistical Area	1950 Total Pop.	1950 Spanish-surname	1960 Total Pop.	1960 Anglo	1960 Spanish-surname	1960 Non-white	SCHOOLING GAP, 1960, PERCENT[b] Spanish-surname	Non-white
Arizona								
Phoenix	10.6	5.3	11.6	12.1	6.1	8.5	50%	30%
Tucson	11.2	6.5	12.1	12.3	8.0	7.8	35	37
California								
Bakersfield	9.9	6.5	10.8	11.4	7.3	8.5	36	25
Fresno	9.8	5.6	10.4	10.7	6.1	8.8	43	18
Los Angeles–Long Beach	12.0	8.2	12.1	12.3	8.9	11.1	28	10
Sacramento	11.3	7.9	12.2	12.3	9.1	10.9	26	11
San Bernardino–Riverside– Ontario	10.9	6.7	11.8	12.1	8.0	9.8	34	19
San Diego	12.0	8.1	12.1	12.2	8.9	10.7	27	12
San Francisco–Oakland	12.0	8.9	12.1	12.3	9.7	10.2	21	17
San Jose	11.4	8.0	12.2	12.4	8.3	12.0	33	3
Santa Barbara	11.8	7.0	12.2	12.4	8.3	9.9	33	20
Stockton	9.1	7.2	10.0	10.7	7.5	8.2	30	23
Colorado								
Colorado Springs	11.7	8.4	12.3	12.4	10.1	12.1	19	2
Denver	12.0	8.0	12.2	12.3	8.8	11.4	28	7
Pueblo	9.1	6.3	10.2	11.0	8.1	9.2	26	16
New Mexico								
Albuquerque	11.7	7.7	12.2	12.5	8.7	10.9	30	13
Texas								
Abilene	10.1	n.a.	11.7	12.0	4.0	8.8	67	27
Amarillo	11.3	4.7	12.1	12.2	8.1	9.5	34	22
Austin	10.9	3.5	11.7	12.3	4.4	8.6	64	30
Beaumont–Port Arthur	9.7	7.0	10.8	11.7	8.7	7.1	26	40
Brownsville–Harlingen– San Benito	6.3	2.7	7.9	12.3	3.9	9.5	68	23
Corpus Christi	9.4	3.2	10.1	12.2	4.5	8.0	63	34
Dallas	11.0	4.4	11.8	12.1	6.4	8.6	47	29
El Paso	9.2	5.2	11.1	12.4	6.6	11.7	47	6
Fort Worth	10.7	5.4	11.4	11.9	7.7	8.7	35	27
Galveston	9.4	4.9	10.3	11.3	6.9	8.3	39	27
Houston	10.4	5.2	11.4	12.1	6.4	8.8	47	27
Laredo	5.4	5.2	6.7	n.a.	5.4	n.a.	n.a.	n.a.
Lubbock	11.0	1.7	11.6	12.1	3.1	8.3	74	31
Midland	12.1	1.8	12.4	12.6	3.7	8.8	71	30
Odessa	10.4	3.9	11.4	11.8	4.6	8.8	61	25
San Angelo	10.2	2.9	10.7	11.5	4.0	8.0	65	30
San Antonio	9.1	4.5	10.0	12.1	5.7	9.4	53	22
Waco	9.4	2.9	10.3	11.0	5.5	8.2	50	25
Wichita Falls	10.3[c]	4.5[c]	11.4	11.7	6.3	8.7	46	26

[a] No data for the Spanish-surname group are available for 2 of the 37 metropolitan areas in the Southwest; those two areas are omitted.
[b] Computed as in table 7–7.
[c] Numbers for Wichita Falls (Texas) are for Wichita County only, as Spanish-surname data were unavailable for Archer County in 1950.
Source: *1950 U.S. Census of Population*, PE no. 3C, tables 8 and 9; vol. II, parts 3, 5, 6, 31, and 43, table 42; U.S. Bureau of the Census, *County and City Data Book*, 1952, table 2, item 28, and table 3, item 28; *1960 U.S. Census of Population*, PC(2)–1B, table 13; vol. I, parts 4, 6, 7, 33, and 45, tables 73, 77, and 103; Census tracts, PHC (1), various areas, tables P–1, P–4, and P–5.

Mexican Americans and nonwhites included in the total. For this reason, it is inadvisable to trace systematically the 1950–1960 progress in the schooling record of Mexican Americans area by area. Nevertheless, a close look at Table 7–8 discloses that the previous finding of relative, as well as absolute, advance holds for most metropolitan areas as well.[8]

GENERAL SCHOOL PRACTICES

AFFECTING MEXICAN AMERICANS*

In a general way the educational system functions as an agency of socialization and role allocation.[9] The school internalizes in its pupils both commitments to, and capacities for, performance in their adult roles. The effectiveness of the socialization within the school determines the school career of each pupil. In turn, his school career importantly conditions his allocation to major adult roles. How does the Southwest school perform these functions for Mexican-American pupils?

School practices in regard to Mexican Americans in the region are strongly reminiscent of the history of Negro education, but the parallels may easily be exaggerated. *Segregation*, for example, has been an important issue for Mexican Americans as well as Negroes—segregation within schools as well as of schools and of teaching personnel. The long-established practice of segregation, usually justified on pedagogical grounds, was successfully challenged in the courts after World War II. Returning Mexican-American war veterans played a leading part in a series of successful court cases.[10]

California is the only Southwest state that has released data on ethnic concentrations in schools, and since California is socially the most "open" of the five states, conditions elsewhere in the region are in all probability worse. In California, according to a 1966 survey, 57 percent of Spanish-surname children in the eight large districts with enrollment of 50,000 or more attended institutions designated as "minority schools", 28 percent went to "mixed" schools, and only 15 percent went to "majority schools". In a sample of the smaller districts, the figures were 30 percent, 63 percent, and 7 percent respectively, i.e., segregation was less severe in these districts.[11] (Negro segregation was more acute in both types of district, which conforms to the greater residential segregation of this group.) However, the data fail to reveal an important aspect of segregation: The proportion of elementary minority schools is far larger than the proportion of secondary minority schools. This means that the segregation of Spanish-surname children at an early stage of their learning period (the only stage for many of them) is still more severe than the over-all figures

---

*This section is based on Thomas P. Carter, *Mexican Americans in School* (New York: College Entrance Examination Board, in press). Materials from this document have also been used elsewhere in this chapter. Carter's research was sponsored by the Mexican-American Study Project under a grant from the College Entrance Examination Board.

suggest. According to Coleman's recent nationwide study, "a substantial number of Indian-American and Mexican-American first-graders are in schools in which they are the majority group. This is not true of the 12th grade."[12]

The California survey also revealed the extent of segregation in certified teaching personnel. In the eight largest districts, 51 percent of the Spanish-surname teachers were employed in minority schools, 24 percent in mixed schools, and 25 percent in majority schools. For the sample of smaller districts, the corresponding figures were 22 percent, 66 percent, and 12 percent, respectively. The survey also showed a statewide Spanish-surname representation of 2.25 percent for teachers and 1.68 percent for principals, as against 13.69 for Mexican-American pupils enrolled. Approximately 55 percent of the Spanish-surname teachers were in secondary schools, where many of them probably taught only Spanish.[13]

Segregation has continued to the present in the form of certain school practices. Even more than for Negroes, important pedagogical arguments are advanced for the intra-school segregation of Mexican Americans. These arguments include the language handicaps of the Mexican-American child; his more general need to be Americanized before being mixed with Anglos; and his "slowness", which would hold back Anglos. In the past, many educators held that separate schools would help the child overcome his deficiencies of language and culture and protect him from competition with, or discrimination from, Anglo children.[14] Similarly, the assignment of all Spanish-surname children attending mixed schools to "Mexican rooms" was usually justified as necessary for the intensive teaching of English. This type of intra-school segregation seems to be less frequent than in previous years. However, many of the recent compensatory education programs themselves have the unanticipated consequence of isolating the Mexican American. A few schools have set up "opportunity," "second chance," or similarly labeled rooms for their "culturally deprived" children. These often become the modern equivalent of the "Mexican room." The ESL classes, in which English is taught as a second language, are sometimes administered so as to separate the Mexican-American children.[15] Thus modern techniques present something of a dilemma for even the most progressive and well-intentioned educators. If a minority lacks the minimum background to succeed in school, it is good policy to furnish additional training in the English language and other fundamentals. But such additional training may prevent equal-status interaction with Anglos.

Analysis and observation have led to the inescapable conclusion that such separation within the mixed school serves to maintain a caste-like relationship. In one of the few intensive studies of majority–minority relations in a school system, Theodore Parsons reported in 1965 from the small California farming community of "Guadalupe" that

> Ethnically differentiated social patterns and associated stereotypes are learned by village children quite early. After the second grade, Anglo and Mexican-American children increasingly restrict their social choices to members of their own ethnic group. By the time they reach the upper elementary grades, there is virtually complete social separation between the two groups. That the children are aware of Anglo

dominance is reflected in their leadership and prestige choices. Both Anglo and Mexican-American children choose Anglos as sources of prestige and both groups make significant choices of Anglos for positions of leadership.[16]

Teachers responding to questions about the maintenance of separate Anglo and Mexican-American athletic teams often gave replies like " . . . most everything in Guadalupe is set up this way. It just seems like the natural thing to do."[17]

The schools have been in a dilemma with regard to the Mexican Americans' culturally distinctive features. On the one hand, there has been the tendency to remove or suppress certain foreign features, often rather crudely. On the other hand, there has been the tendency to build upon the Mexican culture, often equally crudely. The most obvious form that the former takes is the prohibition of behavioral manifestations of foreignness, including the prohibition of the carrier of the minority culture, the Spanish language.[18] Children's names are changed in teacher-student conversation and sometimes in school records: Jesús, in particular, seems disturbing, and is almost invariably changed to Jesse. Dress codes in high school appear to be more elaborate and more strictly enforced in Mexican high schools than in the same district's mixed or Anglo schools. In some cities these are directed against particular symbols of peer-group identification, which are often defined as alien to school culture and authority. For example, a recent study of a border town in Texas reports a junior high school administrator stating that the Mexican-American children were screened before they were permitted to enroll, and if a boy "wants to stay, he has to get a good haircut, cut off the sideburns." Another concurred: "We try to get the kids' hair cut, get 'em to look like the rest; cut off the *pachuco* style. . . . Down in old Mexico they go around with their shirts unbuttoned all the way down to the navel, and then they tie it around their waist. They think it makes them look sexy. We can't have that here."[19] Secondary schools observed in Texas seemed particularly restrictive with regard to dress and behavior norms. California schools were least so. Nonetheless, in all states the Mexican or mixed schools in lower-class areas appeared less tolerant of unconventional clothing or manners than Anglo institutions in middle-class areas of the same city.

On the other hand, even the most restrictive institutions permit and even encourage some symbols of Mexican culture. Music, art, dances, and festivals in some cases have become significant features of the schools' curricula. Bilingual education, i.e., the teaching of subjects other than the traditional language arts in both Spanish and English, is the most recent large-scale effort to build on elements of the subculture.

Both the dilemmas, of segregation and of culture, are persistent and real. Despite the moderate educational progress evident from the 1960 census materials, few educators interviewed in the Southwest were complacent about their success with Mexican-American pupils. There are far too many visible reminders of the remaining problems, even without pressure from community groups and such ethnic organizations as California's Association of Mexican American Educators. The dropout rates are high, the in-school performance is often frustrating (as we shall detail below for Los Angeles), and Mexican-American children are greatly over-represented in mentally retarded groups. This over-representation is particularly well documented for California public schools in 1966, when 27 percent of the children in special education classes were Mexican American, though they represented only 13 percent of the total student population. Undoubtedly, many factors account for this concentration, but it is interesting to observe that the degree of concentration appears to be related to the proportion of Mexican Americans in the community's population. In the ten counties with the highest proportion of Spanish-surname students, almost twice as many were in special education as their over-all proportion would suggest. In counties with smaller proportions of Mexican Americans, their numbers in special education come closer to their representation in the school population.[20]

There is little systematic information about *educators' general views of Mexican Americans*. And little can be learned from school visits and observations beyond the truism that local teachers tend to represent local views of Mexican Americans, as they do of other features of the local social scene. There is only a sparse literature written for educators and used by the schools as a basis for understanding this group. Schools of Education in the region tend to use general treatises on cultural disadvantage in training future teachers. Few emphasize Mexican Americans.[21] The few recent discussions of Mexican Americans caution the reader that the subculture is changing, but tend to reproduce findings on family structure and general values that are distinctly out of date or of limited relevance beyond restricted geographic areas. One manual, published by a respected educational concern, describes family roles in the most traditional terms.[22] According to another, Mexican-American values are alleged to 1) devalue formal education, especially for women, 2) consider success in terms of non-material rewards, 3) be present-time oriented, 4) be traditionalist, i.e., not desire change, 5) be patient, conformist, and perhaps apathetic, 6) see work as necessary only as a means to satisfy present needs, 7) become imbued with a "mañana" attitude, and 8) be nonscientific.[23]

Such manuals are intended to orient the teacher to culturally different children rather than to provide a guide for curriculum planning. Observation and interviews also suggest that they serve to support and amplify existing conventional diagnoses of the Mexican Americans' educational problems. Generally speaking, teachers interviewed in Southwest schools tend to attribute the problems to the failure of Mexican culture to prepare or motivate the child for school.

To a degree, such a diagnosis may function to exonerate the school for what many teachers and increasingly vocal community associations appear to define as failure. It certainly functions as a rationale for the growing "compensatory education" programs. The availability of greater financial assistance, particularly from Federal sources, and the increasing pressure of outside forces are principally responsible for *recent actions of schools to improve the Mexican Americans' academic standing*. The programs are commonly of two types. One attempts to upgrade poor schools by purchasing new equipment, hiring more and better-trained staff (for example, psychologists), and adding special curricula (vocational or occupational projects). The other, compensatory education, is by far the most common type. These programs attempt to compensate for the child's inadequacies compared to the "standard" middle-class child. The school says, in effect, that "We will prepare you for our school system, we will help you to catch up when you fall behind, we will show you the kinds of lives other kinds of children already know about, and if you get discouraged and drop out, we will try our best to get you back."[24]

Indeed, to the extent that the problem of poor academic achievement lies within the child, compensatory and remedial programs should succeed. Such programs necessitate little institutional modification. In addition, they tend to placate spokesmen for the disadvantaged population, they strengthen the role of school administrators, and they create new functions within the educational establishment. The evidence of the success of such projects is still too incomplete to allow any judgment about how well they are achieving their long-range objectives. Meanwhile, some porgress is being made toward the short-term objectives (for example, reading readiness). Also, there is little doubt that the programs have served to increase teacher enthusiasm and thereby the involvement of their charges.

The prevailing general acceptance in educational circles of the present goals and organization of the school and the prevailing general diagnosis of Mexican Americans' cultural deficiencies as a prime source of their educational problems have apparently prevented radical experimentation with the school itself. Among the few significant exceptions are bilingual schools such as those in Laredo and San Antonio, Texas.[25] Conclusions about the success of these projects must await detailed evaluation. However, school visits indicated that teachers and children were enthusiastic. The participating teachers and principals who were interviewed said that they considered their program as "an answer to a prayer" and that they were confident it would substantially raise the Mexican American's academic performance and his self-esteem as well.

Recently, the ethnic spokesmen's increasing sense of urgency about needed improvements in educational systems has been linked with growing militancy among Mexican-American youth itself. Schools have become the targets of new organizations of Mexican-American college students dedicated to community action. The school year 1968–1969 saw an unprecedented series of school boycotts and sit-ins. Such actions occurred not only in larger cities, such as Los Angeles and Denver, but also in some smaller and highly conservative communities.

This broadening and intensified involvement of Mexican Americans in school policies has alerted school boards and administrators to the need for more speedy action and has already produced some changes in the training of teachers and in school practices. Thus, in the fall of 1969 the Los Angeles Board of Education took the novel step of creating a commission of ethnic leaders to act as an official representative on school problems of Mexican Americans; the commission was an outgrowth of a previous Mexican-American protest organization. The pressures for change are immeasurably greater than only a few years ago, and their effectiveness seems to be increasing.

MEXICAN-AMERICAN YOUTH IN
LOS ANGELES SCHOOLS*

This overview of school practices and dilemmas should be supplemented in the future by a systematic analysis of variations from one part of the Southwest to another. As a beginning, the following section presents a study of Mexican-American and Anglo pupils in Los Angeles. Although the educational resources of Los Angeles give it one of the better school systems of the Southwest, Mexican Americans there follow the Southwest pattern of inordinately high dropout rates and very few individuals in college. One-third of the Mexican Americans enrolled in Los Angeles secondary schools drop out. In some schools only slightly more than half finish.[26]

When we examine in-school performance, we discover the same disparities for the pupils in process as we found for the Mexican Americans and Anglos who had completed their schooling. We discover also that it is extremely difficult to account for the disparities by the usual family and other background correlates of school achievement. Increased research on school practices and procedures is badly needed. Nevertheless, our analysis will provide additional insights by showing how individual school characteristics modify the administratively and culturally determined practices. Although in a large metropolitan system each individual school is constrained toward uniformity by centralized administrative organization, common programs, and comparable financial support and personnel policies, there are counter-influences pressing toward diversity.[27] Pupils are graded and promoted differently in schools serving neighborhoods of different social composition. Schools with higher-status pupils tend to promote on the basis of actual achievement. Schools with lower-status pupils tend to grade and promote on the basis of ascriptive criteria—producing what is sometimes called "social promotion."[28] Lower-status schools, which have more difficulty socializing their students, grant relatively more social promotions, thus moving the cohort (and its problems) on to the next level and clearing the lower levels for new students. A similar contrast in grading and promotion procedures exists between lower and higher grade levels. Emphasis on achievement criteria increases from the elementary grades through the junior and senior high schools.

The combination of "easy" promotion at the lower grade levels and in schools with lower-class pupil populations creates an increasing discrepancy between many students' actual performance and what the school system establishes as performance standards. The maximum discrepancy is reached by the end of the ninth grade. By then most California children have reached the age at which they can legally leave school, and the marginal participants are jettisoned from the system and designated

---

*This section is drawn from C. Wayne Gordon, Audrey J. Schwartz, Robert Wenkert, and David Nasatir, *Educational Achievement and Aspirations of Mexican-American Youth in a Metropolitan Context* (Report No. 36 of the Center for the Study of Evaluation, Graduate School of Education, University of California, Los Angeles, October 1968). This study was supported by the Mexican-American Study Project and by the Center for the Study of Evaluation, and was undertaken in cooperation with the Board of Education of the City of Los Angeles. The condensed version of the study presented here omits many refinements and qualifications in the original work.

by the term "school dropout". They then personally assume the onus of the school's inability to socialize them. A substantial number of marginal achievers do manage to graduate, however, despite inadequate levels of attainment. They become involved with that segment of senior high school social life in which grades are of little importance. Upon graduation, these persons usually go to work; higher education tends to be reserved for those whom the school system has socialized adequately.

The data for this study were provided by 2,979 sixth-, ninth-, and twelfth-grade pupils from the Los Angeles City School District. The basic sampling units were 23 schools stratified on the basis of their ethnic density and the socioeconomic status of the pupils. A detailed discussion of the sample and its construction, and an evaluation of the sample obtained, is provided in Appendix B. Data were collected from cumulative school records (which supplied pupil achievement and selected background data) and pupil questionnaires.

Disparities in Achievement and Aspirations

The recent study by James Coleman and his associates of a national sample of racial and ethnic groups placed Mexican-American pupils fourth among the six groups ranked on a number of achievement tests. Only Puerto Ricans and Negroes scored lower; Anglos, Orientals, and American Indians scored higher. About 85 percent of the Mexican-American pupils in the sample were below the Anglo average. For these pupils, as well as for others from non-English-speaking cultures, the deficit in reading comprehension was greatest through the junior high school. By the ninth grade, the average score of the national Mexican-American sample was three and one-third years behind the average score of the white sample of the Northeastern United States.[29] All minority groups shared a progressive increase in this deficit from grades one through twelve. Mexican-American verbal ability was two years behind Anglo ability at the sixth-grade level. By the twelfth grade the gap had increased to three and one-half years.

On educational and occupational aspirations (which may be important to school achievement), the Coleman study found that relative to other racial and ethnic groups Mexican-American pupils

1. ranked high in their determination to stay in school, be good students, and attend school regularly;
2. planned in fewer numbers to attend college;
3. held equally high occupational aspirations;
4. had a more self-depreciatory self-concept than either Anglos or Negroes;
5. expressed a considerably lower sense of control over the environment than Anglos.[30]

The Coleman report's analysis of factors associated with achievement of Mexican-American pupils concluded that

1. family background is most important for achievement;

2. the association of family background with achievement does not diminish over the years;

3. the influence of school facilities, curriculum, and staff that is independent of family background is small;

4. teachers' characteristics account for most of the differences in school factors that are related to achievement;

5. the social composition of the student body is more highly related to achievement independently of the student's own social background, than is any school factor;

6. attitudes concerning control or responsiveness of the environment are highly related to achievement, but variations in school characteristics have little influence on these attitudes.[31]*

Although our Los Angeles data are not strictly comparable to those of the Coleman study, they cover the same broad topics with reference to Mexican-American and Anglo pupils: achievement differentials, differences in aspirations and values, and the family and school correlates of achievement for each group at the three grade levels.

Mexican-American pupils generally score lower in all four dimensions of achievement analyzed: grades, deportment, achievement test scores standardized against a national norm, and IQ test scores (Appendix C). Particularly notable is the relative score of pupils on the two types of measures standardized against a national norm: the achievement tests and the IQ tests. In both tests, Anglo students score slightly above the national norms and Mexican Americans well below. The discrepancies are greater at the elementary school level in some measures and at the high school level in others.

Similar differences are found in *students' aspirations and expectations* (Appendix C). Contrary to stereotype, the majority of Mexican-American as well as Anglo students aspire to formal education after high school.[32] But the proportion of Anglos with such aspirations is far higher. Among those who aspire to further education, Mexican Americans tend more to aim at trade schools and junior colleges.[33] Anglos tend more toward the four-year colleges. In general, both Mexican-American and Anglo students have lower post-high school educational expectations than aspirations, but, even so, the majority expect to obtain some education after the high school diploma. Again, the proportion of Anglo students who expect more education is almost double the proportion of Mexican-American students with such expectations. The ethnic

---

*The findings of the Coleman report have been questioned on many, principally methodological, grounds. See, for example, Samuel Bowles and Henry M. Levin, "The Determinants of Scholastic Achievement: An Appraisal of Recent Evidence," *The Journal of Human Resources*, Vol. VIII, No. 1, (Winter, 1968), and Professor Coleman's rejoinder in the Spring, 1968 issue of the *Journal*. The questions involve the representativeness of the sample for Coleman's survey in light of total nonresponse by fairly large numbers of schools and of nonresponse (probably not random) on particular questionnaire items. There is reason to believe that this problem is especially acute in the case of Mexican-American pupils covered by the survey. Perhaps more important, the questions involve the validity of indicators used in the survey to measure school resources including teachers' characteristics and the social composition of the student body. The critique by Bowles and Levin concludes that the learning processes by which different influences alter achievement are largely unknown.

differences in expectations are therefore about the same as the differences in aspirations. As with aspirations, the educational expectations of Mexican-American students are considerably higher than one would anticipate on the basis of widely disseminated stereotypes.

The occupational aspirations of all students are also high, with almost nine out of ten students aiming for white-collar rather than blue-collar or manual work. Again, the aim of Anglo students is substantially higher than that of the Mexican-American students. Among those who aspire to white-collar positions, Mexican-American students tend to aim for the lower rungs of the white-collar ladder. Nevertheless, more than half of the Mexican-American teenagers aspire to skilled and professional white-collar positions.

In summary, the school achievements of Mexican-American children tend to be low in absolute terms and relative to those of Anglo children. The aspirations of both ethnic groups are very high. Comparatively, Mexican-American aspirations and expectations are lower than those of Anglos in the same areas.

Significant differences between Mexican-American and Anglo pupils are also apparent at all three grade levels in their responses to questionnaire items pertaining to *attitudes, values and opinions.** Mexican Americans and Anglos are more similar in these regards in the twelfth than in either the sixth or ninth grades. At all three grade levels, however, Mexican Americans are more oriented toward parental control over behavior and toward concern for adult (as opposed to peer) disapproval. Anglos, on the other hand, express more optimism about the future and disapprove more strongly of forceful conflict resolution. At the sixth and ninth grades, the Mexican-American students exhibit a more expressive or positively charged emotional feeling toward school. At the ninth grade, Anglo students show greater faith in human nature.

The differences between Mexican-American pupils of different socioeconomic background are not as great as those between the two ethnic groups. The variation which does exist declines markedly at higher grade levels. In other words, the Mexican-American pupils not only become more similar to Anglos, but become increasingly homogeneous as they progress through school. At the elementary level, the Mexican-American white-collar sample is differentiated from the blue-collar sample by its more instrumental attitude[†] toward the school, by its greater agreement with the formal norms of the school, by its more optimistic orientation toward the future, and by its high faith in human nature. At the junior high level, the two socioeconomic levels are differentiated only by the higher faith in human nature and the more optimistic orientation toward the future of the white collar-pupils. In senior high school there are no significant differences in the values of the two socioeconomic groups within the Mexican-American student population of Los Angeles.

---

*These findings are drawn from Audrey James Schwartz, *Comparative Values and Achievement of Mexican-American and Anglo Pupils* (Report No. 37 of the Center for the Study of Evaluation, Graduate School of Education, University of California, Los Angeles, February 1969).

†The Instrumental Orientation Scale used in the study inquires into the pupil's evaluation of the utility of school-prescribed activity for future benefit. The Expressive Orientation Scale inquires into areas of school activity that yield immediate gratification.

Table 7-9. Explained Variance in Achievement Measures[a] by Pupil and School Characteristics

(Elementary and secondary schools in Los Angeles, 1966)

Pupil and School Characteristics[b]	Elementary				Junior High				Senior High			
	MA		ANGLO		MA		ANGLO		MA		ANGLO	
	I.Q.	Reading Comprehension	I.Q.	Reading Comprehension	I.Q.	Reading Comprehension	I.Q.	Reading Comprehension	I.Q.	Reading Comprehension	I.Q.	Reading Comprehension
Family socioeconomic level	5.26%	.59%	1.48%	0%	.93%	.72%	1.88%	.52%	3.47%	2.80%	7.53%	3.67%
Family educational level	3.00	1.70	9.36	20.50	5.23	6.40	8.94	5.54	6.76	5.24	6.42	10.91
Student attitudes	10.44	12.83	32.13	24.69	3.49	5.75	6.66	9.19	4.86	5.51	4.66	6.45
School social context	0	4.86	0	0	5.16	5.03	0	0	2.52	1.68	.31	0
Teacher attitudes	0	0	0	0	1.07	3.44	1.76	4.36	8.42	6.06	18.98	1.25
Home language	3.69	1.61	1.20	0	3.48	.87	0	0	2.10	1.00	.93	.28
Pupil age and sex	0	0	0	0	.85	0	.62	0	.79	0	.65	.38
Influence of peers	0	0	0	0	0	0	0	0	0	0	.84	0
Total Variance Explained	22.39%	21.59%	44.17%	45.19%	20.21%	22.21%	19.86%	19.61%	28.92%	22.29%	40.32%	22.94%

[a] General abilities as measured by IQ tests, and Reading Comprehension tests.
[b] See Appendix D for components of these variables.
Source: C. Wayne Gordon, Audrey J. Schwartz, Robert Wenkert, and David Nasatir, *Educational Achievement and Aspirations of Mexican-American Youth in a Metropolitan Context* (Report No. 36 of the Center for the Study of Evaluation, Graduate School of Education, University of California, Los Angeles, October 1968), Table 45. All items above zero make a unique contribution to the variance at the .05 level of confidence.

Factors Related to Achievement

Whether or not Mexican-American and Anglo pupils are alike on measures of achievement, aspirations, and other values is one matter. The correlates of actual school and school-related performance is quite a separate matter. To determine whether the same factors explain variation in achievement for the two ethnic groups and the extent to which these factors are similarly ordered, we performed a series of stepwise multiple regressions of the measure of reading comprehension and of IQ scores on variables of pupil and school characteristics.* The analysis examines the relationship of these variables to objective test scores at the elementary, junior, and senior high school levels.

These regressions show that a number of variables are significantly related to reading comprehension and general ability of *both* Mexican-American and Anglo pupils. But a more differentiated result is obtained when the proportions of variation in performance for which each of the variables accounts are combined into *more general factors of pupil and school characteristics.* The proportion of total variation which is explained by these factors differs substantially between the ethnic groups at the same school level and within each ethnic group among the different school levels. A summary of the contribution of the general pupil variables and school variables to performance is shown in Table 7–9. The contribution of the full set of variables included in the regressions is presented in Appendix D.

In summary, the following sources of influence on pupil performance have been observed in the Los Angeles survey:

1. The most consistent and important influence is family educational level as expressed primarily in parental aspirations for pupils' educational attainment. This is apparent for both Mexican-American and Anglo pupils at all three grade levels.

2. Pupil attitudes and values are an important source of influence, again for both ethnic groups at all grade levels. Value orientations supportive of school achievement include *a*) a generalized confidence in mankind, which presumably allows for effective relations in the institutional climate of the school; *b*) personal congruence with the goals toward which the school tasks are directed; *c*) rational rather than emotional orientation toward goal-directed activities—indicated in this study by an instrumental orientation to school and strong disapproval of resolution of conflict by fighting; *d*) an optimistic definition of life in general, which includes the view that goals can be attained through personal effort.[34]

3. School type (a measure of socioeconomic and ethnic composition) substantially affects the performance of Mexican Americans at elementary and junior but not at senior-high level. The performance of Anglo pupils is largely unaffected by school context at any level.

*The IQ tests used were the California Test of Mental Maturity for elementary and junior high school pupils, and the Henmon-Nelson General Aptitude Test for senior high school students. The Reading Comprehension tests used were the California Achievement Test-Reading Comprehension for elementary and junior high school pupils, and the Cooperative English Test-Reading Comprehension for senior high school students.

4. The exclusive use of English as the home language contributes consistently and positively for Mexican-American pupils at all grade levels.

5. Family economic level contributes less to the performance of either ethnic group than does family educational level (whose influence is considerably greater for Anglo than for Mexican-American pupils).

The Influence of the Social Context of the School

We suggested at the outset of this section that the composition of the student body of the individual school (social status and/or ethnicity) affects the educational processes. The regression analysis supports this hypothesis by showing fairly high correlations of school characteristics with achievement—notably for Mexican Americans but not for Anglos.

Table 7–10. Discrepancy Between Expected and Achieved Social Studies Grades, by School Level and Social Context of School, Los Angeles Schools, 1966

Social Studies Grades[a]	SCHOOL SOCIOECONOMIC TYPE			
	Low	Middle	High	Total
Elementary school				
Above expected	50%	33%	25%	34%
Expected	43	57	50	55
Below expected	7	10	25	11
Total number (= 100%)	(101)	(238)	(164)	(503)
Junior high school				
Above expected	64%	55%	40%	53%
Expected	25	33	47	35
Below expected	11	12	13	12
Total number (= 100%)	(374)	(117)	(345)	(836)
Senior high school				
Above expected	30%	25%	24%	27%
Expected	46	47	48	46
Below expected	24	28	28	27
Total number (= 100%)	(349)	(414)	(165)	(928)

[a] Expected social studies grade is based on pupil's performance on the reading comprehension test. Pupils with high scores (7 to 9) are expected to get A's and B's, those with average scores (4 to 6) are expected to get C's, and those with low scores (1 to 3) are expected to get D's and F's.
Source: C. Wayne Gordon et al., *op. cit.,* Table 42.

Even though we did not observe and analyze the pedagogical process itself as it varied by school context, our data suggest how such variation occurs. Specifically, we found in certain schools much less variation between marks given by teachers and scores attained by pupils on standard achievement tests. This discrepancy between the non-local, universalistic measures of mastery provided by achievement tests, on the one hand, and the local evaluations by the teacher, on the other, indicates that different grading standards are applied in schools of different social contexts. The discrepancy is most notable in individual schools having substantial numbers of pupils who do not achieve at national norms; these schools adopt their own criteria of pupil success.

How ascription varies by school type and level is evident from Table 7–10. The table shows for all pupils the discrepancy between the social studies grades expected from the reading comprehension scores and those actually granted. (Social studies grades reflect non-objective criteria to a greater extent than do grades in the more objectively measured mathematics achievement.) At the senior high school level, about half the pupils are graded at the expected level and the remainder equally divided between the above- and below-expected levels. There is little deviation from this pattern by school type. In contrast, more than half of the junior high school pupils attain above-expected grades, and there is greater variation among the three school types. The elementary school distribution is similar to that of the senior high school, where the majority of pupils receive marks in accord with objective measures of ability. However, the middle- and especially the low-status elementary schools grant considerably more grades above the expected level than the higher-status schools.[35]

How grade ascription varies in the different school types becomes even more evident when pupils are grouped by ethnicity and parental occupations (Table 7–11). In senior high school there is a marked decrease in the percentage of Mexican Americans with above-expected grades as the socioeconomic status of the school increases. The percentage of above-expected grades for Anglos, however, does not vary greatly from one school type to another. Since a certain percentage of high school graduates aspire to further education at advanced institutions of national repute, it is to be expected that grades will tend to be granted on the basis of national norms. This is particularly true in the school with pupils of higher socioeconomic status where going to college is a main objective of its student body. In this type of school more Mexican-American pupils receive *below*-expected grades (as predicted by achievement scores) than do Anglos from similar backgrounds. The small number of Mexican-American students in high-status high schools precludes definitive interpretation of this finding. Some pupils may perform poorly in class assignments despite high performance on tests administered outside the classroom.

In contrast, the higher the percentage of Mexican Americans in the school, the lower the proportion of above-expected grades, but more than twice as many of the total junior high pupils as senior high pupils have grades which reflect normative ascription. Grading practices are similar for the two ethnic groups in the lowest-status schools, but in the middle-status schools Mexican-American pupils receive most of the above-expected grades.

Apparently the middle-status school differentiates its student body on the basis of ethnicity. For pupils who are expected to complete high school and perhaps go on to college, it employs a national universalistic criterion to measure achievement; for pupils whose past experience has led to the belief that they will drop from the system, it employs local, particularistic criteria which are functional for these students' emotional well-being and do not rock the educational boat.

The achievement orientation takes over at the high-status schools where all pupils tend to be evaluated by the same yardstick. Forty percent of the pupils get above-expected social studies grades in the high-status junior high schools compared

Table 7-II. Discrepancy between Expected and Achieved Social Studies Grades for Mexican-American and Anglo Pupils, by Parental Occupation and Social Context of School

(Elementary and secondary schools in Los Angeles, 1966)

| Social Studies Grades[a] | Low Socioeconomic Status of Schools | | | | | Middle Socioeconomic Status of Schools | | | | | High Socioeconomic Status of Schools | | | | | Grand Total |
| | MA | | ANGLO | | | MA | | ANGLO | | | MA | | ANGLO | | | |
	BC[b]	WC[c]	BC	WC	Total	BC	WC	BC	WC	Total	BC	WC	BC	WC	Total	
Elementary																
Above expected	48%	59%	—	—	50%	34%	32%	47%	38%	33%	25%	25%	29%	17%	25%	34%
Expected	44	35	—	—	43	56	68	53	50	57	65	50	47	67	50	55
Below expected	8	6	—	—	7	10	—	—	12	10	10	25	24	16	25	11
(Total no. pupils)	(64)	(17)	(0)	(0)	(101)	(86)	(25)	(19)	(8)	(238)	(20)	(4)	(38)	(6)	(164)	(503)
Junior high																
Above expected	65	60	60	60	64	69	71	44	42	55	40	39	44	34	40	53
Expected	24	31	20	20	25	24	29	31	49	33	43	48	46	53	47	35
Below expected	11	9	20	20	11	7	—	25	9	12	17	13	10	13	13	12
(Total no. pupils)	(307)	(57)	(5)	(5)	(374)	(45)	(7)	(32)	(33)	(117)	(89)	(23)	(136)	(97)	(345)	(836)
Senior high																
Above expected	30	28	25	100	30	23	30	24	27	25	15	—	31	24	24	27
Expected	44	54	63	—	46	44	39	51	45	47	31	29	38	57	48	46
Below expected	26	18	12	—	24	33	31	25	28	28	54	71	31	19	28	27
(Total no. pupils)	(271)	(68)	(8)	(2)	(349)	(143)	(23)	(166)	(82)	(414)	(13)	(7)	(52)	(93)	(165)	(928)

[a] Expected social studies grade is based on pupil's performance on the reading comprehension test. Pupils with high scores (7 to 9) are expected to get A's and B's, those with average scores (4 to 6) are expected to get C's, and those with low scores (1 to 3) are expected to get D's and F's.

[b] BC = blue collar.

[c] WC = white collar.

Source: C. Wayne Gordon et al., op. cit, Table 43.

to only 24 percent in the high-status senior high schools. Thus it seems that the junior high school approaches but does not attain as objective a measurement as that attained by the senior high school. At the elementary-school level positive ascription appears for Mexican-American and Anglo pupils equally.

What we have observed is a dual system of evaluation employed by the same school district—first, a local, particularistic system which meets the needs of the individual pupil, the teacher, and the school in dealing with the discrepancy between real and expected learning; and second, a non-local, universalistic system, which meets the needs of the achieving society. Particularistic norms are more frequently employed in the lower-status schools at the junior and the elementary levels, and universalistic norms are common to high socioeconomic schools at all levels.

It seems clear that schools use those grading practices which are felt to be most functional to the projected futures of their pupils. Pupils in schools where most go on to higher education are graded by universalistic achievement measures— measures that are themselves based on assumptions common to similar high-status schools throughout the country. Both the anticipated and the real allocation of individuals by the school is influenced by both the socioeconomic and ethnic qualities of their student populations. Since school social climate is created by the aggregate characteristics of its pupils, schools with student bodies of high ethnic, low socio-economic status utilize particularistic criteria and schools with student bodies of low ethnic, high socioeconomic status utilize universalistic criteria. Schools which have both ethnic groups usually adopt one of these two modes of grading.[36]

When one is aware of this dual evaluation structure, the place of grades in the schools becomes clearer. For those deemed suited for the academic preparation, that is a prerequisite for higher-status positions, a universalistic criterion which can be used for competitive selection and which insures quality control is essential. For those deemed suited for the lower-status positions requiring considerably less academic preparation, grade assignments can be used for attenuating tensions which inevitably arise from achievement pressures. Pupils destined for lower-status futures can be ascribed success without repercussions from the external system. The school can maintain its image of being an effective agency of socialization. The grave dysfunction of particularistic grading is that it obscures the extent of discrepancy between real learning and what is supposed to have been learned. Although ascription of minimal achievement reduces tension between school and community, it is costly to society as well as to many individuals.

SUMMARY

Our analysis of the 1950 and 1960 census data on educational attainment shows Mexican Americans seriously behind Anglos, although there is considerable intra-regional variation in the relative under-attainment of the minority group.

An extraordinary differential existed in 1960 in school years completed, especially for the adult population. The gap was much smaller when the educational attainment of the younger generation or its school enrollment were used as yardsticks. Even by these criteria, however, deficiencies appeared—as evidenced by the relatively late beginning of Mexican Americans' formal education, the widening enrollment differentials as children reached the high school level, and the low percentage of Mexican-American youth who completed high school or college. State and local differences in attainment were far greater for the Spanish-surname group (and nonwhites) than for Anglos.

The gap is attributable in part to intergroup variations in rural–urban background, to immigrant status, and to poverty and other aspects of the home environment. *The extreme disparities in different locales suggests also an hypothesis concerning a strategic determinant in the larger society: the extent to which the local social systems and, through these, the school systems have held the Mexican-American population in a subordinate position.*

But moderate progress was visible in the 1950–1960 comparisons, which showed that the schooling gap relative to Anglos had been narrowed. Progress was also apparent when the educational attainment of the younger generation was contrasted with the schooling of higher age groups. It manifested itself in still another intergenerational advance: from extremely low educational levels of the foreign born to far better performance by the native born, though further improvement between the second and the subsequent generation was evident only in school enrollment. The educational standing of this disadvantaged minority improved, even though slowly, in a period when large-scale Federal aid to education and anti-poverty programs were not yet available. The current programs should serve to accelerate progress. Moreover, as the younger, better-educated Mexican Americans reach parenthood, they will provide a more favorable home environment for the schooling of their own children. Hence one can expect that even modest short-run improvements in educational preparation will have considerable impact in the long run.

Generally speaking, it is the remaining deficiencies rather than the progress that are most evident to educators as well as to Mexican-American spokesmen. In the 1960s increased funds became available for special educational programs for Mexican Americans, but an overview of both past and present school practices reveals serious dilemmas in program planning. Legal though not *de facto* segregation was ended in the 1940s, but intra-school segregation continues. Sometimes it is supported by persuasive pedagogical arguments; perhaps more often it simply reflects ecological and social cleavages in the community. The dilemma lies in ascertaining how much pedagogically justified segregation can be instituted without running the risk of reinforcing status cleavages. Much the same dilemma has been occurring with regard to aspects of Mexican culture, including the Spanish language. Mexican cultural elements were defined by many educators as inhibiting or interfering with school performance. In the past, crude efforts were made to uproot the sources of interference—for example, severe punishment was meted out for speaking Spanish. Today, such practices are less frequent. Instead, programs are being devised to build upon Mexican culture—to make the school experience more congruent with that at home. Both pathways are bordered with problems, and the evidence of the past promises no easy solutions for the future.

A case study of Los Angeles schools indicated the existence of a dual evaluation system that is particularly significant for the school experience of Mexican Americans. Grades higher than warranted by real performance tend to be ascribed especially at younger age levels in the lower-status schools. In coping with undersocialization in this fashion, teachers may mitigate their own problems. But the practice has a costly consequence: There is a drastic accounting at higher grade levels. The pupils with the greatest discrepancy between ascribed grades and actual performance are most likely to drop out.

The study of Mexican-American and Anglo school children in Los Angeles emphasizes both the persistence of problems for Mexican Americans as a category and the difficulties in explaining these problems in a manner satisfactory either to social analysts or to builders of educational programs. The average achievement of Mexican-American students was well below that of Anglos, and though there are a number of factors affecting the achievement of both groups, the ethnic differences in performance are not adequately explained. The findings imply that the highest achievers are those Mexican-American pupils who have been most thoroughly socialized to the dominant American culture both at home and in the school environment. The all-important questions of language introduction and transition, both in family and school experiences, are not adequately answered in this study. It is obvious that language skills will need to be strengthened. More generally our findings confirm the conclusion of other studies that the chances for achievement are greatest when family and school contexts are generally supportive of each other. However, much more research is needed to provide a clearcut direction for those responsible for programs to accelerate the educational progress of this minority.

NOTES TO CHAPTER SEVEN

1. Computed as a percent of Anglo median years, i.e., the percentage by which the Spanish surname of nonwhite number of years falls below the Anglo figure. This calculation was added to provide a common measurement. For example, a difference of 3 years is equivalent to $33\frac{1}{3}$ percent if the Anglo median is 9 years but to 25 percent if the Anglo median is 12 years.

2. *1960 U.S. Census of Population*, PC(2)–1B, tables 3 and 7; vol. I, parts 4, 6, 7, 33, and 45, tables 47 and 103. (A1, tables 3 and 7; A3, tables 47 and 103.)

3. *1960 U.S. Census of Population*, vol. I, parts 4, 6, 7, 33, and 45, table 103.

4. This is the normal relationship between age and number of years of school completed among minorities with substantial proportions of first- and second-generation immigrants compared with a majority with a small proportion of foreign stock. See Conrad and Irene Taeuber, *The Changing Population of the United States* (New York: John Wiley & Sons, Inc., 1958), chapter 10.

5. The educational problems of children of migrant farm workers has given rise to much concern and a number of programs: Entering school late in the term and departing

for a harvest schedule in late May has meant a high dropout rate. The literature on these problems is, however, outside the scope of this study's focus on the urban issues. For recent discussions of the education of migrant children, see Melvin S. Brooks, *The Social Problems of Migrant Farm Laborers: Effect of Migrant Farm Labor on the Education of Children* (Department of Sociology, Southern Illinois University, Carbondale, Ill., Oct., 1960); George H. Haney, *Selected Programs in Migrant Education*, U.S. Office of Education Bulletin no. 35 (1963); and "Educating Migratory Children," *School and Society*, 95 (Dec. 9, 1967), p. 484.

6. The dismal picture in the agricultural regions may in part reflect the inclusion of migrant Mexican workers in the statistics. However, since the enrollment figures are limited to persons between the ages of 5 and 21, the resulting distortion should be of little consequence. More important, the poor record in the farm areas reflects the neglect of schooling among the children of domestic Mexican-American migratory workers, who include a disproportionate number of foreign born. This concentration tends to lower the educational preparation of the entire foreign-born group and, one may add, of the Mexican-American minority as a whole.

7. *1960 U.S. Census of Population*, PC(2)–1B, tables 3 and 7; *1950 U.S. Census of Population*, P-E no. 3C, tables 3 and 6.

8. On the question of the relationship between size of city and educational achievement, the rank correlation of median years of school completed by Spanish-surname persons in 1960 with the total population of each metropolitan area shows a moderate $+0.50$ association. Thus, the case for the size of area being a strategic variable is not a strong one. While the larger places may provide superior schooling opportunities and facilities, many other factors seem to influence the local variations in educational attainment. The case for size of metropolitan area being correlated with schooling record of the Spanish-surname population is stronger in California than in Texas. The rank correlation is $+0.61$ for the metropolitan areas in California but only $+0.45$ in Texas.

9. Talcott Parsons, "The School Class as a Social System: Some of its Functions in American Society," *Harvard Educational Review*, XXIX (Fall, 1959), pp. 297–318. See also Burton C. Clark, "Sociology of Education," in Robert E. L. Faris (ed.), *Handbook of Modern Sociology* (Chicago: Rand McNally & Company, 1964), especially the following statement (p. 739): "Whenever formally differentiated agencies of education [schools] exist, their general social function of training the young for adult roles entails also some part in the assignment of status to individuals and groups. This part grows as education connects more closely to the economy. Education's mediation between the demand and supply of workers entails an expanding mediation in the assignment of social position and status."

10. In 1946, parents, with the support of Mexican-American organizations, initiated legal action against four Southern California elementary school districts. In *Mendez v. Westminster School District et al.*, the plaintiffs claimed that the school districts discriminated illegally against children of Mexican descent by maintaining separate facilities for such children. The plaintiffs contended that such practices violated their constitutionally guaranteed rights to "due process and equal protection of the law." The parents did not employ the "separate but equal" argument: rather, they agreed that the local Mexican schools were as good as, or perhaps superior to, the district's Anglo institutions. (There is much evidence, however, that Mexican schools generally tended to be inferior.) The court ruled in favor of the parents and enjoined the districts from segregating—a decision upheld upon appeal. This case laid the legal groundwork for the subsequent desegregation decisions of the 1950s, which also argued on the First, Fifth, and Fourteenth Amendments to the Constitution. See *Westminster School District of Orange County, et al. v. Mendez et al.*, 161 F. 2d 774 (1947). See too: Henry W. Cooke, "The Segregation of Mexican-American School Children in Southern California," *School and Society* (June, 1948), pp. 417–421, and G. I.

Sanchez, *Concerning Segregation of Spanish-speaking Children in the Public Schools*, *Inter-American Education*, Occasional Papers, no. 9 (Austin, Tex.: University of Texas Press, December, 1951).

The *intent* to segregate was clear in some school districts, where non-Mexican children were transported to their schools by routes which bypassed or even crossed through the zones having schools attended only by Mexican-American children. The *custom* of segregation was clearly revealed in court findings that in some instances, in the place of tests to determine whether a language handicap necessitated provisional segregation, the decision to segregate or not was based mainly on the Latinized or Mexican name of the child.

In 1948 legal redress was sought to end school segregation of Mexican Americans in Texas. In *Delgado v. The Bastrop Independent School District*, a Federal Court ruled that such segregation was illegal. The decision, like that of California, was based on constitutional guarantees. Thus, legally sanctioned segregation was ended.

11. California State Department of Education, *Racial and Ethnic Survey of California's Public Schools, Part One: Distribution of Pupils*, 1967. The method of classifying schools as minority, mixed, or majority schools was as follows:

> A simple integration scale was applied to each of the 2,340 schools in the study groups, comparing each school's percentages of the three largest racial and ethnic groups (Spanish-surname, "other white," and Negro), with the corresponding percentages of the districts in which the school is situated. Allowing a deviation of as many as 15 percentage points above or below the appropriate district percentage, it was possible to classify each school as high concentration, mixed, or low concentration with respect to each of the three racial or ethnic groups. When the basis of comparison was the "other white percentage," the term *majority* school, *mixed* school, or *minority* school could be substituted. (page 25).

12. James S. Coleman et al., *Equality of Educational Opportunity*, U.S. Department of Health, Education, and Welfare (1966), p. 41.

Schools with a high concentration of Mexican-American pupils receive disproportionate numbers of poorly trained teachers. An unpublished study of 1,650 elementary teachers in the Lower Rio Grande Valley of Texas reported that 10 percent had no Bachelor of Arts degree, 13 percent were serving with emergency credentials, and 30 percent had provisional credentials. Only 57 percent were fully credentialed Texas teachers (unpublished survey by A. R. Ramirez of elementary teachers in the Lower Rio Grande Valley, 1966, mimeographed). A Valley superintendent reported that he was forced to employ some teachers with as few as 60 college units of credit. In other areas the situation appears much better. The general shortage of qualified teachers throughout the Southwest thus strongly influences the quality of Mexican-American schooling.

13. *Racial and Ethnic Survey of California's Public Schools. Part Two: Distribution of Employees*. The data refer to certified personnel. In Denver in 1966, only 65 of the 3,687 teachers had a Spanish surname. See Colorado Commission on Spanish-surnamed Citizens, *The Status of Spanish-surnamed Citizens in Colorado* (Greeley, Colo.: Colorado State College, Department of Political Science, 1967). The tendency to assign Mexican-American teachers to minority schools reinforces the isolation of ethnic children. The advocacy of such placement is widespread; the Colorado source recommends:

> Given equal academic or even lower academic qualifications, the Spanish-surnamed teacher applicant deserves special consideration because of two special qualifications he possesses . . . 1) his example or presence in the school can encourage Spanish-surnamed students, and 2) his ability to understand and give special counsel

to many Spanish-surnamed students . . . the second qualification may not always be valid. . . . Mexican-American teachers . . . from upper-middle-class-urban culture may have nothing in common with a poor working class Spanish-surnamed student. (page 62).

In spite of this qualification, such advocacy is usually interpreted to mean the hiring of Mexican-American teachers for Mexican-American children, and administrators tend to act accordingly whenever possible.

14. See Charles Carpenter, "A Study of Segregation Versus Non-segregation of Mexican Children" (unpublished Master's thesis, University of Southern California, 1935); Everett Clinchy, "Equality of Opportunity for Latin Americans in Texas: A Study of the Economic, Social, and Educational Discrimination against Latin Americans in Texas, and of Efforts of the State Government on their Behalf" (unpublished Ph.D. dissertation, Columbia University, 1954); and Paul S. Taylor, *An American-Mexican Frontier* (Chapel Hill, N.C.: The University of North Carolina Press, 1934).

But, as with Negroes, segregation practices in the past had many negative aspects, and they included:

1. The tendency for Mexican schools to have vastly inferior physical facilities, poorly qualified teachers, and larger classes than the Anglo schools.

2. The practice of placing all Spanish-surname children in segregated schools, even though some were fluent in English. The fact that Negro children were sometimes assigned to Mexican schools suggests a racial rather than language basis for segregation.

3. The lack of effort to enforce the often weak attendance laws.

4. The numerous cases of individual children being discouraged from attending school at all, especially in secondary-level institutions.

See Milo Arthur Van Norman Hogan, "A Study of the School Progress of Mexican Children in Imperial County" (unpublished Master's thesis, University of Southern California, 1934); Taylor, *op. cit.*; C. C. Trillingham and Marie M. Hughes, "A Good Neighbor Policy for Los Angeles County," *California Journal of Secondary Education*, XVIII (Oct., 1943), pp. 342–346; Victor B. Lehman, "A Study of the Social Adjustment of the Mexican-Americans in Chino and a Proposed Program of Community Action Under School Leadership" (unpublished Master's thesis, Claremont Graduate School, 1947); "Federal Judge Outlaws Segregation in Public Schools," *Common Ground*, VII (Winter, 1947), pp. 102, 103; V. E. Strickland and G. I. Sanchez, "Spanish Name Spells Discrimination," *Nation's Schools*, XLI (Jan., 1948) pp. 22–24; Carlos I. Calderon, "The Education of Spanish-speaking Children in Edcouch-Elsa, Texas" (unpublished Master's thesis, University of Texas, 1950); Manuel Ceja, "Methods of Orientation of Spanish-speaking Children to an American School" (unpublished Master's thesis, University of Southern California, 1957); and Arthur J. Rubel, *Across the Tracks* (Austin, Tex.: The University of Texas Press, 1966).

15. There is real danger of further unintentional ethnic isolation in actions taken in response to the growing demands that Mexican-American children learn more about their Hispanic cultural heritage and that they be taught non-language subjects in Spanish. On the face of it, the advocates of this procedure present a meritorious argument. See Manuel H. Guerra, "Language Instruction of Inter-group Relations: An Analysis of Language Instruction [Spanish and English] to Spanish-speaking Learners in California Public Schools, in Relation to the Search for Better Inter-group Relations," mimeographed report distributed by the California Department of Education, Sacramento, June, 1967. See also Marcos deLeon, "Wanted: A New Educational Philosophy for the Mexican-American," *California Journal of Secondary Education*, XXXIV (Nov., 1959), pp. 398–402. Congress adopted legislation in 1968 to make Federal funds available for such programs

(90th Congress, first session, H.R. 8000 [Bilingual Educational Opportunity Act] and S. 428.) By August, 1968, no moneys had been appropriated.

However, the implementation of bilingual programs could be used to justify present or future segregation. Many educators would probably reason that if it is best to teach Mexican Americans in Spanish, it is necessary, or most efficient, to place them in separate schools or rooms. Given a choice between continued segregation *with* instruction in Spanish and desegregation *without* it, the latter would seem to be more beneficial to the Mexican-American child and to society.

True bilingual schools, like those presently functioning in Laredo, Texas, where both languages carry the curriculum to Spanish and English speakers in the same classrooms, appear to have an integrative effect. Instead of further separating the children, bilingual institutions of this kind seem to bring the two groups closer together. However, such schools may be possible only under certain conditions, including a fair numerical balance of the student population and positive attitudes of teachers and administrators toward the innovation. For a discussion of these programs, see Charles Stubing (ed.), *Reports: Bilingualism*, Third Annual Conference of the Southwest Council of Foreign Language Teachers (El Paso, Texas, Nov., 1966); *Congressional Record*, vol. 113, Jan. 23, 1967, p. S677, statement of Senator Ralph Yarborough of Texas; and *The Invisible Minority... Pero No Vencibles*, *Report of the NEA-Tuscon Survey on the Teaching of Spanish to the Spanish-speaking*, National Education Association, Department of Rural Education (Washington, D.C., 1966).

16. Theodore W. Parsons, Jr., "Ethnic Cleavage in a California School" (unpublished Ph.D. dissertation, Stanford University, Aug., 1965), pp. 386–387.

17. *Ibid.*, pp. 300, 301. Parsons contends that teachers and administrators "share the general Anglo stereotypes of Mexicans and ... use these as the basis for organizing their perceptions of, and programs for, the Mexican pupils." In his summary he enumerates the following points, among others, that contribute to ethnic differentiation of pupils and stereotyping within the school; 1) the posting of achievement charts—there is a tendency for students to use charts as a basis for judgments about classmates; 2) the sending of Mexican-American pupils who "smell" out of the room; 3) the formal teacher-student relationship between Anglo teacher and Mexican-American student contrasted to the less formal Anglo teacher-student relationship; and 4) the placing of the Mexican-American student in a subordinate position vis-à-vis the Anglo by emphasizing the lack of the former's intelligence —the Mexican American "needs the guidance of Anglos who know better than he does" (pp. 306, 307).

18. The Southwest has a long history of prohibiting Spanish in school. In fact, only presently are state laws that exclude Spanish from utilization as an instructional medium and/or punish its speaking in school being repealed. Educators' arguments for the "no Spanish rule" are well known: 1) English is the national language and must be learned; 2) bilingualism is mentally confusing; 3) the Spanish spoken in the Southwest is a substandard dialect; and 4) teachers do not understand Spanish. Although the validity of the first point cannot be denied, the rejection of Spanish may largely reflect the feeling that the Spanish-speaking child represents a threat to Anglo school authority and control; teachers do not know what Mexican Americans are saying—are they disrespectful or impudent, using foul language, urging their peers to riot and revolt? Speaking Spanish may be seen as a subversive activity, an undeciphered code reflecting hostility and plotting against school authorities.

Although schools are becoming more permissive of Spanish speaking, rigid and strong sanctions are still common, especially in Texas. Many schools no longer prohibit Spanish but rather encourage English. Whether "encouraging" English entails prohibiting Spanish depends on the local situation. The ambiguity of the following instructions in a teachers' manual in a 100-percent Mexican-American junior high school in Texas is obvious:

" . . . encourage the use of English. All teachers are expected to correct students using Spanish on school property." The punishment for speaking Spanish depends on local and school mores. In some schools, up to and including the junior-high grades, students may be spanked; in others they will be merely reprimanded or sent to "Spanish detention." In some Texas schools the persistent speaking of Spanish can and does lead to suspension or expulsion.

19. Rubel, *op. cit.*, p. 11.

20. *Racial and Ethnic Survey of California's Public Schools*, pp. 36–46.

While Mexican Americans are disproportionately represented in classes for the educable mentally retarded, this minority may not be over-represented in the lower ranges of retardation. According to a study of mental retardation in a medium-sized California city,

> There were disproportionately large numbers of persons of Mexican-American and Negro heritage who were labelled as mentally retarded by community agencies. The rates ran almost five times higher for Mexican-Americans and three times higher for Negroes than they did for Anglo-Americans. This was especially true for the public schools, however, it did not hold for persons institutionalized in Department of Mental Hygiene hospitals.
>
> However, when the data were analyzed by I.Q. level, and only those persons with I.Q. scores below 40 were compared, differences between the three groups almost disappeared. Rates for this group of severely and profoundly retarded persons, which consists mainly of individuals who are clearly damaged biologically, were 9.7 per thousand for Anglo-Americans, 16.7 per thousand for Mexican-Americans, and 10.5 per thousand for Negroes. We found exactly the same pattern in our field survey which screened a 10 percent sample of the community population for mental retardation using standardized clinical measures. There were, percentage-wise, no more mental retardates with I.Q.'s under 40 in the Mexican-American and Negro populations than in the Anglo-American populations.
>
> It appears, therefore, that the over-all higher rates among Mexican-Americans and Negroes is accounted for primarily by "undifferentiated" types of mental retardation—the so-called "sub-cultural" varieties which are highly related to cultural difference and economic deprivation. Where there are no organic manifestations, diagnosis rests almost entirely upon performance on psychometric measures normed on the English-speaking Caucasion population, which is primarily middle class. Consequently, persons reared in a different culture and/or from socially and economically deprived circumstances are at a distinct disadvantage.

(Personal communication from Jane R. Mercer of the University of California, Riverside.) The inadequacy of psychometric instruments and techniques, as well as the biases and lack of knowledge of teachers and school psychologists, are likely to account for much of the over-representation. See Uvaldo Hill Palomares and Laverne C. Johnson, "Evaluation of Mexican-American Pupils for EMR Classes," *California Education*, III (Apr., 1966), pp. 27–29. Their small-scale study indicated, among other things, that the psychologist himself, and especially whether he understands Mexican-American subcultures, are important variables in the results of testing.

21. It is a significant part of at least some "progressive" educational ideologies to disregard subcultural differences and emphasize the sameness of all children. See Horacio Ulibarri, "Teacher Awareness of Socio-cultural Differences in Multi-cultural Classrooms" (unpublished Ph.D. dissertation, University of New Mexico, 1959).

22. See Kenneth R. Johnson, *Teaching Culturally Disadvantaged Pupils* (Chicago: Science Research Associates, Inc., Oct. 1, 1966), unit IV, for an example of teacher orientation manuals.

23. See Miles V. Zintz, *Education Across Cultures* (Dubuque, Iowa: William C. Brown Book Co., 1963), especially pp. 200–202.

24. Edmund W. Gordon and Doxey A. Wilkerson, *Compensatory Education for the Disadvantaged* (New York: College Entrance Examination Board, 1966), p. 159.

25. Attempts to effect substantial modifications of the school were undertaken in the past, including efforts to convert existing institutions into community schools by radically modifying the curriculum to eliminate irrelevancy and conflict and by making the school the focal point of community development. The so-called Nambé and Taos projects, both rural experiments in northern New Mexico, are the best known and documented among such projects. See Jesse Taylor Reid, *It Happened in Taos* (Albuquerque, N.M.: The University of New Mexico Press, 1946) and L. S. Tireman and Mary Watson, *La Comunidad: Report of the Nambé Community School, 1937–1942* (Albuquerque, N.M.: The University of New Mexico Press, 1943). We found no such efforts for Mexican Americans being made today. For the Laredo bilingual schools, see sources given in note 15. For San Antonio, cf. Elizabeth H. Ott, "A Study of Levels of Fluency and Proficiency in Oral English of Spanish-speaking School Beginners" (unpublished Ph.D. dissertation, University of Texas, 1967); Robert W. MacMillan, "A Study of the Effect of Socioeconomic Factors on the School Achievement of Spanish-speaking School Beginners" (unpublished Ph.D. dissertation, University of Texas, 1966); Neil A. McDowell, "A Study of the Academic Capabilities and Achievement of Three Ethnic Groups: Anglo, Negro, and Spanish-surname, in San Antonio, Texas" (unpublished Ph.D. dissertation, University of Texas, 1966); and Gloria R. Jameson, "The Development of a Phonemic Analysis for an Oral English Proficiency Test for Spanish-speaking School Beginners" (unpublished Ph.D. dissertation, University of Texas, 1967).

The bilingual school teaches subjects other than the traditional language arts in two languages; that is, such subjects as science, math, and history are taught in Spanish and in English. The teaching of a second language or the use of the children's vernacular as a bridge to facilitate the learning of English may be secondary objectives.

Using models developed earlier by others, Bruce Gaarder differentiates organizationally between "one-way" and "two-way" bilingual schools. The former are institutions where one group of children (Spanish speaking) learns, in two languages, either the national language plus the children's mother tongue or the national language plus a second language. The San Antonio project is such a "one-way" school, with instruction in the mother tongue (Spanish) added. A "two-way" school, exemplified by Laredo, instructs children from two linguistic communities (Spanish and English) in both languages, each learning its own and the other's language. The classes may either be segregated by linguistic group or may be mixed. In the Laredo experiment Mexican-American and Anglo children are mixed in all academic and play activities. A. Bruce Gaarder, "Organization of the Bilingual School," *Journal of Social Issues*, XXIII (Apr., 1967), p. 110.

26. Paul M. Sheldon, "Mexican-Americans in Urban Public Schools: An Exploration of the Drop-out Problem," *California Journal of Educational Research*, XXII (Jan., 1961), pp. 21–26.

27. For a discussion of sources of influence in educational systems which tend to produce uniform standards and those which tend to produce divergence in standards, see Richard P. Boyle, "The Effect of the High School on Students' Aspirations," *American Journal of Sociology*, LXXI (May, 1966), pp. 628–639.

Other studies bearing on the issue include: William H. Sewell and J. Michael Armer, "Neighborhood Context and College Plans," *American Sociological Review*, XXXI (Apr., 1966), pp. 159–168; John A. Michael, "High School Climates and Plans for Entering College," *Public Opinion Quarterly*, XXV (Winter, 1961), pp. 585–594; William H. Sewell and Vimal P. Shah, "Socioeconomic Status, Intelligence, and the Attainment of Higher Education," *Sociology of Education*, XL (Winter, 1967), pp. 1–23; William H. Sewell,

"Community of Residence and College Plans," *American Sociological Review*, LXIX (Feb., 1964), pp. 24–38; Alan B. Wilson, "Residential Segregation of Social Classes and Aspirations of High School Boys," *American Sociological Review*, XXIV (Dec., 1959), pp. 836–845; Coleman *op. cit.*, p. 743.

A lively critical exchange has surrounded those studies. See: Ralph Turner et al., "Communications," *American Sociological Review*, XXXI (Oct., 1966), pp. 698–707; Sewell, "Neighborhood Context and College Plans," *op cit.*, pp. 159–168; Henry M. Levin, "What Difference Do Schools Make?", *Saturday Review*, LI (Jan. 20, 1968), pp. 57–67; and the critique of the Coleman report and the Levin-Coleman exchange in "Letters to the Education Editor," *Saturday Review* (Feb. 17, 1968).

28. Here we will note the dysfunctions of these social promotions. However, observation suggests that failure to promote children, or strict adherence to set grade-level requirements (which seems most frequent in Texas and least frequent in California), produces the problem of "overageness." Children are "kept back" and move through school with their achievement mates rather than with their age mates. "Overageness" is a contributory cause of dropout. Thus, the problem of poor academic achievement is being dealt with differently in each state; however, the problems of the Mexican-American learners are the same in each.

29. Coleman, *op. cit.*, pp. 274–275.

30. *Ibid.*

31. The conclusions presented here are taken verbatim from an analysis of the Coleman report by George W. Mayeske: "Educational Achievement Among Mexican-Americans: A Special Report from the Educational Opportunities Survey," U.S. Office of Education, National Center for Educational Statistics, Technical Note 22 (Jan. 9, 1967). Mayeske's working paper notes that it does not reflect the official policy of the U.S. Office of Education.

32. Similar results to those reported here were obtained by Coleman, *op. cit.*, p. 283, in his national study of American education. He asked a national sample of twelfth-grade students: "How far do you want to go in school?" The following results were obtained for Mexican-American students:

Want to do professional or graduate work	11%
Want to finish college	21
Desire some college training	17
Want to go to a technical school	26
Want to finish high school	19
Do not want to finish high school	5
No response	2

Although these aims are lower than those reported for Anglo students in Coleman's study, they are still very high. In fact, they are somewhat higher than our results (although the questions are worded differently, so the answers are not directly comparable). Also, Coleman's study did not include the Los Angeles school district, which refused access to the U. S. Office of Education, under whose auspices the study was conducted, so our population differs geographically from Coleman's. Despite these differences, the results obtained are remarkably similar.

33. A special note is in order on the Mexican Americans who by 1960 had some college education. True, they were under-represented at this stage of higher learning with regard to the reference populations, but their numbers are not insignificant. Nearly 117,000 Mexican Americans living in the Southwest in 1960 had gone to college. Their number is now undoubtedly much larger. Of the 117,000, however, only 37,128, or 31.7 percent, had four years or more of college. The corresponding percentage for the total Southwest population was 39.9. In other words, relatively fewer members of the Spanish-name group who went to college completed their higher education.

A comment may be added here on the types of institutions of higher learning in the Southwest at which Mexican-American students are concentrated. As in the case of Negroes, these have typically been colleges and universities ranking below top level. Until recently, the students' aspirations tended to reflect these realities of the Mexican Americans' college enrollment pattern. For example, in California 7.4 percent of the junior college students taking regular-credit courses in 1966 had Spanish surnames. See *Racial and Ethnic Survey of California Public Schools*, Part One: Distribution of Pupils. In contrast, Mexican-American students at the University of California represented less than 1.6 percent of all students in the fall of 1968, after a recruitment program was under way for some time. The Berkeley campus had 313 Mexican-American students, and the Los Angeles campus 729 (President's office, University of California; based on the University's ethnic surveys). In New Mexico, too, Mexican Americans are more heavily represented in the smaller, vocationally oriented colleges than at the state university and the land-grant college. See Nancie L. González, *The Spanish Americans of New Mexico: A Distinctive Heritage* (Mexican-American Study Project, Advance Report 9, Graduate School of Business Administration, University of California, Los Angeles, Sept., 1967), pp. 99–101. The same seems to be true for Texas. See the 1958-1959 data presented in Herschel T. Manuel, *Spanish-speaking Children of the Southwest—Their Education and the Public Welfare* (Austin, Texas: University of Texas Press, 1965), p. 61.

34. Other values and attitudes, however, predict success only for Anglos, and still others only for Mexican Americans. For Anglos, success is correlated with high self-esteem (that is, a high evaluation of oneself in general and in relation to others, enjoyment in taking charge of things, independence from or less sensitivity to the opinions of peers, and greater concern for adult than for peer disapproval). For Mexican Americans, it is correlated with independence from family authority, more concern over peer than over adult disapproval, and general autonomy or independence in decision making. It appears, then, that achievement in the context of education requires, at a minimum, the values and attitudes toward school-related activity that were enumerated in the text. For details of the analysis of values, see Schwartz, *op. cit.*

35. The analysis of an experimental program in the teaching of mathematics at the seventh-grade level permits some insight into this process. Many students had already fallen behind in mathematics achievement; they were selected from among the schools represented in the larger study reported in this chapter. The findings show that the teacher may have concentrated less on areas of pupil weakness and more on areas of existing competence. The author suggests that such practices, ensuring some "success," are functional both for frustrated teachers and for under-achieving students. Rod Skager, Los Angeles Model Mathematics Project (Center for the Study of Evaluation, Graduate School of Education, UCLA, 1968, mimeographed report).

36. An exception is the middle-status junior high where Mexican-American pupils are evaluated in the same manner as pupils from the low-status schools, and the Anglos in the same manner as pupils from high-status schools. Another exception is the high-status senior high school where the tendency toward universalistic criteria is reversed for Mexican Americans, who are evaluated more rigidly than any subpopulation in many of the other schools. This final check to the ability of the Mexican Americans to enter the achieving society places an additional obstacle between them and the good life which is more easily available to Anglos with similar academic achievement.

EIGHT

Income Differentials

INCOME differentials express the net result of the many factors causing the material welfare of a minority group to diverge from that of the rest of the population. The differentials reflect intergroup variations in schooling, labor force participation, occupations, and the distribution of workers over low-wage and high-wage industries. They capture the incidence of unemployment or underemployment or even the health, energy, and work discipline of subgroups of the labor force. They show the effects of labor market discrimination that keeps qualified members of a minority out of the more attractive positions, or pays them less than the prevailing wage for the same kind of work, or obstructs their promotion. Hence our economic analysis begins with income.

Intergroup differences in income may also be associated with variations in the sex, age, and locational distribution of subpopulations in the labor force. Women, as a group, usually earn less than men. As a rule, higher earnings come with experience, and experience tends to increase with age. In light of the marked differences in the age composition of Mexican Americans and Anglos, this is a matter of some import.

Wages are lower on farms than in cities. As the analysis proceeds, we shall therefore take sex, age, and locational differences into account.

The next chapters will deal with some of the key factors associated with income differentials, such as the occupational composition of Mexican Americans in the labor force, their relative earnings in comparable jobs, and labor market discrimination.

THE FAMILY-INCOME GAP

Mexican-American families in the Southwest had a median income which was a little less than 65 percent of that of Anglo families but greater than that of nonwhites in 1959, the last year for which census data are available (Table 8–1). Median incomes of all three population groups were higher in the urban areas than in the region as a whole. However, the urban income *differential* between the Spanish-surname group and Anglos was only fractionally smaller than the over-all differential; the same was true for the position of nonwhites relative to Anglos.*

Table 8–1. Median Income of Spanish-surname Families Compared with Other Families, Five Southwest States, 1959

| | | | | Percent of Anglo | |
AREA AND STATE	ANGLO[a]	SPANISH-SURNAME	NONWHITE	SPANISH-SURNAME	NONWHITE
All areas					
Southwest	$6,448	$4,164	$3,644	64.6	56.5
Arizona	6,111	4,182	2,517	68.4	41.2
California	6,990	5,532	4,969	79.1	71.1
Colorado	6,024	4,007	4,504	66.5	74.8
New Mexico	6,287	3,594	2,550	57.2	40.6
Texas	5,635	2,913	2,613	51.7	46.4
Urban areas					
Southwest	6,768	4,465	4,008	65.8	59.2
Arizona	6,278	4,351	3,631	69.3	57.8
California	7,213	5,700	5,061	79.0	70.2
Colorado	6,411	4,443	4,588	69.3	71.6
New Mexico	6,652	4,121	3,696	62.0	55.6
Texas	6,133	3,187	2,913	52.0	47.5

[a] Computed by using $2,000 intervals to match the published figures for Spanish-surname families. The data are not adjusted for intergroup differences in age of family head.
Source: *1960 U.S. Census of Population*, PC(2)–1B, table 5; and vol. I, parts 4, 6, 7, 33, and 45, tables 65 and 139.

The rank order of Anglo, Spanish-surname, and nonwhite family incomes held for four of the five states. Only in Colorado did the nonwhites do better than the Mexican Americans, reflecting the low earnings of the relatively large rural component of Colorado's Spanish-surname population and the predominantly urban orientation of its nonwhite group. The income *gap* between Anglos and Mexican Americans

*In the statistics presented here, income includes not only earnings from work but also returns on property and so-called transfer payments, such as those made under the Federal Old Age and Survivors Insurance program. But earnings from work are by far the most important component of income.

was smallest in California and greatest in Texas. In fact, this gap seems to be inversely related to the general income position of the states. *The greater the over-all state income, the smaller the gap.*[1] The income differentials between nonwhites and Anglos, and between nonwhites and Spanish-surname families, reflect to some extent the diverse composition of the nonwhite group in the several states. The income position of the nonwhite subpopulations will be examined later in an analysis that sharpens the comparisons by holding age, location, and sex constant.

Locational variances in the standing of Mexican Americans, and, for that matter, of nonwhites appear in sharp relief when family incomes in the 16 large metropolitan areas of the Southwest are reviewed. The median income for the Spanish-surname group ranged from $6,308 in the San Francisco Bay area to $3,446, or 55 percent of the former figure, in San Antonio. The median for nonwhites varied between $6,277 in San Jose to $3,039 in Dallas. The range for Anglos was much narrower; the lowest income of $5,829 in San Antonio was 75 percent of the high of $7,758 for San Jose. As one would expect, Mexican-American incomes relative to Anglos also vary widely—from a ratio of almost 84 in San Diego to 59 in San Antonio. Here, as in other measures of socioeconomic standing, minority status means not only a differentiated position generally but one that varies more sharply from one locale to another. Nevertheless, Mexican-American incomes tend to be high in the centers where Anglo incomes are high, and vice versa.[2]

State and local variations in consumer prices may alter some of these differences in money incomes. However, we focus on intergroup differentials in the various states and places, and not on area differentials as such, which apply to all residents. The most pervasive price disparities are probably found between urban and farm areas. For that matter, the earnings reported by persons in the country who receive income in kind, as in crop-sharing, or grow some of their food may be understated. But our analysis addresses itself for the most part to urban places where such distortions are minimal.

Income distributions reveal the difference between majority and minority incomes in more dramatic as well as more instructive fashion than do the medians (Chart 8–1). The distribution curves for all three population groups show the familiar feature of "tails" in the direction of the higher incomes; relatively few families are in the high-income class. However, the distribution for urban Anglos approximates a bell-shaped curve, which means that the bulk of the Anglo population is in the middle-income range. Urban Spanish-surname and nonwhite families show much greater concentration in the low-income brackets. The somewhat better position of Spanish-surname families compared to nonwhites holds throughout the income range. Equally instructive is the contrast in income distributions between urban California and urban Texas (Chart 8–2). The minority families in Texas are far more clustered in the low income brackets than those in California, group for group as well as relative to Anglos.

The concentration of minorities in the low-income class will be examined later. The other side of the coin, or the representation of upper-income families ($10,000

[1] Notes for this chapter start on page 202.

or more) in the three subpopulations, shows similar disparity. *The incidence of such families among Mexican Americans in the Southwest was only about one-third of the Anglo incidence* (Table 8–2). In California, it approached one-half. In Texas, the incidence was about one sixth. In 1960 the Spanish-surname group in the Southwest included 45,799 families with incomes of $10,000 or more. Of these, 32,855, or 72 percent, resided in California. There were fewer well-to-do families among non-whites than among Mexican Americans, except in Colorado.

Chart 8–1.

Urban Income Distribution, Spanish-surname Families Compared with Other Families, Southwest, 1959

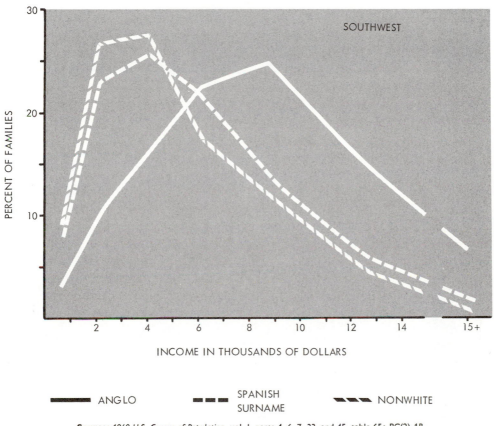

Source: *1960 U.S. Census of Population*, vol. I, parts 4, 6, 7, 33, and 45, table 65; PC(2)–1B, table 5.

For population groups with great divergence in family size, the *income per person in the family* is especially relevant as an indicator of differential restraints on consumption. On this yardstick, the gap between Mexican Americans and Anglos is far greater than the gap in total family income. In the Southwest as a whole, the Spanish-surname group in 1960 had a median income per person in the family *less than half the*

Chart 8–2.
Urban Income Distribution, Spanish-surname Families Compared with Other Families, California and Texas, 1959

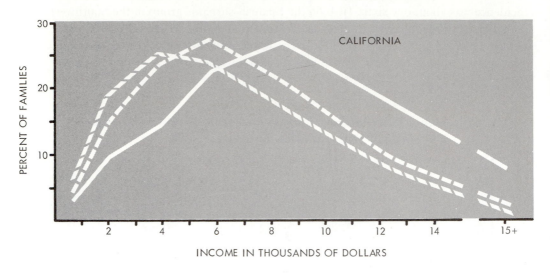

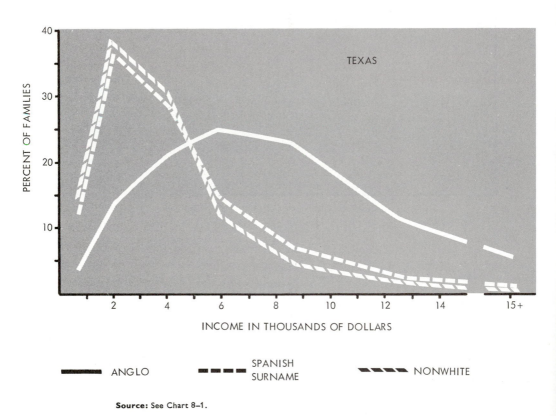

ANGLO ━━━ SPANISH SURNAME ▪▪▪▪ NONWHITE ▰▰▰▰

Source: See Chart 8–1.

184

Anglo figure (Table 8–3). Also, the position of Mexican Americans and nonwhites is reversed on this reckoning. The income per person in the Spanish-surname family is *lower than that of nonwhites*. Only in Arizona and New Mexico are the nonwhites worse off than the Mexican Americans. Nonwhites in these two states include significant numbers of American Indians.

Table 8–2. Urban Spanish-surname Families with Incomes of $10,000 or More Compared with Other Urban Families, 1959 (Percent of all families in each population group)

Area and State	Anglo	Spanish-surname	Nonwhite
Southwest	22.0	7.3	6.3
Arizona	17.6	5.1	4.1
California	25.0	11.3	9.9
Colorado	17.7	5.9	6.7
New Mexico	20.9	5.6	5.0
Texas	17.1	3.0	1.8

Source: *1960 U.S. Census of Population*, PC(2)–1B, table 5; and vol. I, parts 4, 6, 7, 33, and 45, tables 65 and 66.

The effects of family size on per-capita income are not limited to the poor. As shown in Chart 8–3, large differentials in the median size of Spanish-surname and all other families extend over the whole range of incomes. Hence, one would expect

Table 8–3. Median Income per Person in the Family, Spanish-surname Families Compared with Other Families, Five Southwest States, 1959

State and Population Group	Income per Person	Percent of Anglo	State and Population Group	Income per Person	Percent of Anglo
SOUTHWEST			Colorado		
Anglo	$2,047	100.0	Anglo	$1,854	100.0
Spanish-surname	968	47.3	Spanish-surname	915	49.4
Nonwhite	1,044	51.0	Nonwhite	1,317	71.0
Arizona			New Mexico		
Anglo	1,880	100.0	Anglo	1,828	100.0
Spanish-surname	917	48.8	Spanish-surname	882	48.3
Nonwhite	561	29.8	Nonwhite	557	30.5
California			Texas		
Anglo	2,255	100.0	Anglo	1,772	100.0
Spanish-surname	1,380	61.2	Spanish-surname	629	35.5
Nonwhite	1,487	63.7	Nonwhite	755	42.6

Source: *1960 U.S. Census of Population*, vol. I, parts 4, 6, 7, 33, and 45, tables 65 and 110; PC(2)–1B, table 5.

consumption levels of the more well-to-do as well as of the poor Mexican Americans to reflect constraints resulting from the typically large number of persons in the family. The analysis of housing conditions in Chapter 11 will confirm this assumption.

Chart 8–3.
Median Size of Family by Income Class, Spanish-surname Families Compared with All Others, Southwest, 1959

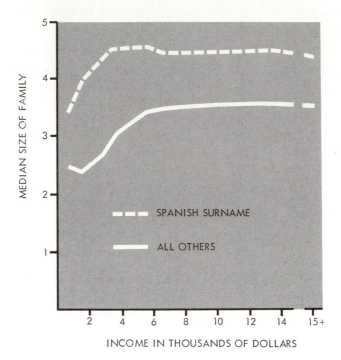

INCOME IN THOUSANDS OF DOLLARS

Source: *1960 U.S. Census of Population,* vol. I, parts 4, 6, 7, 33, and 45, table 141; and special census tabulation of data for Spanish-surname families.

INCOMES OF INDIVIDUALS

The income of individuals in the work force—more precisely, of persons 14 years of age and older who had earnings from any source—reveals most clearly the differential position of Mexican Americans in labor markets. To avoid the distortions that may result from intergroup differences in sex and in urban-rural distributions our analysis will focus on males and, for the most part, on males in urban areas.* Also, the data will be adjusted for age differences between the three populations.

This more refined analysis shows an income gap between Mexican-American and Anglo persons that is even greater than the income gap for families (Table 8–4).

*The pervasive difference between the incomes of men and women appears also in the Spanish-surname group. In 1959, the median for Spanish-surname females in the Southwest was $1,065 as against $2,804 for men (not adjusted for age differences). The comparable figures for the urban Southwest were $1,202 and $3,197, respectively. Our focus on states and urban areas, of course, does not take full account of locational variances. Incomes may vary with the size as well as other characteristics of cities and towns. Nevertheless, the urban–rural dichotomy is meaningful in terms of prevailing occupations and wage levels; besides, it would be too cumbersome to extend the analysis to urban places of varying sizes.

In the Southwest as a whole, Spanish-surname males on the average earned only 57 cents for every dollar earned by their Anglo counterparts, as against 65 cents for families.[3] The relative position of Mexican Americans was somewhat better in urban places. The Spanish-surname income relative to Negroes was about 15 percent higher regardless of whether males in the urban areas or in all areas of the Southwest are included in the comparison.

Table 8–4. Median Income of Spanish-surname Males Compared with Others,[a] Adjusted for Age,[b] Southwest, 1959

Area and State	Anglo	SS[c]	Negro	SS as percent of Anglo	SS as percent of Negro
Southwest					
All areas	$4,815	$2,768	$2,435	57	114
Urban areas	5,134	3,156	2,898	61	109
Urban Areas					
Arizona	4,757	3,236	2,530	68	128
California	5,421	4,275	3,908	79	109
Colorado	4,719	3,240	3,420	69	95
New Mexico	5,276	3,116	2,557	59	122
Texas	4,593	2,297	2,272	50	101

[a] Persons 14 years of age and over with income in 1959.

[b] Age adjustments were computed from index numbers of the following form: $\frac{\Sigma i(X_{is}Y_i)}{\Sigma i(X_{ia}Y_i)}$ where X_{is} refers to the proportion of Spanish-surname males with income in each age class. X_{ia} is the same for Anglos and Y_i is the corresponding median income of all urban males. The index numbers were used to adjust the median incomes of each group. Spanish-surname males with income in 1959 are classified by the census into the following age brackets: 14–19, 20–24, 25–34, 35–44, 45–64, and 65 and over.

[c] SS = Spanish-surname.

Source: *1960 U.S. Census of Population*, PC(2)–1B, tables 6 and 8; vol. I, parts 4, 6, 7, 33, and 45, tables 133 and 134; PC(2)–1C, table 137.

The interstate variations for Mexican Americans, ranging from $4,137 for urban males in California to $2,339 in Texas, are much wider than for Anglos and for Negroes. Spanish-surname urban males earned 76 percent of Anglo incomes in California, and only 51 percent in Texas. Colorado and Arizona came close to the California ratio, and New Mexico, with 62 percent, was in between. Spanish-surname incomes averaged more than Negro incomes in all states except Texas—another indicator of the low status of Mexican Americans in this state.

The income of Mexican Americans does not increase with age as does that of Anglos. Young urban males in the Spanish-name minority come closest to the income "norm," but the income ratio declines steadily with advancing age, at least through the age range of 45–64. Although the data in Chart 8–4 refer only to California they seem to be representative of the Southwest as a whole.[4] Several factors seem to account for this phenomenon. The foreign born, who have typically low incomes, comprise a larger fraction of the older age classes in the Spanish-surname group. Because their main occupations offer more limited job mobility over their working lives, Mexican Americans regardless of nativity do not obtain as sizable increases in earnings as do the members of the majority population. Young Mexican Americans

Chart 8–4.
Median Incomes of Spanish-surname and Nonwhite Males as a Percent of Anglo Males, Urban Areas of California, by Age, 1959

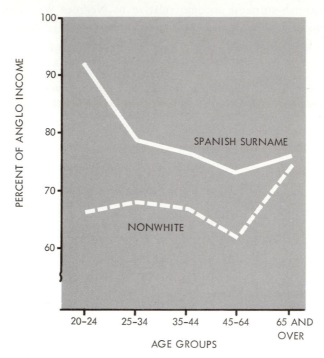

Source: *1960 U.S. Census of Population*, PC(2)–1B, table 8; and vol. I, part 6, table 134.

Table 8–5. Median Income of Spanish-surname Urban Males as a Percent of Selected Nonwhite Groups, 1959

STATE	NEGRO	INDIAN	CHINESE	FILIPINO	JAPANESE
		Not adjusted for age			
Arizona	128	130	84	n.a.	n.a.
California	113	129	109	124	91
Colorado	99	114[a]	n.a.	n.a.	n.a.
New Mexico	123	141	n.a.	n.a.	n.a.
Texas	103	106	70	n.a.	87
		Adjusted for Age[b]			
California	n.a.	122	114	129	94

[a] Based on total rather than urban median income.
[b] See Table 8–4 for method. Age adjustments are presented only for California, which has a sufficiently large number of subgroups of nonwhites to warrant the adjustment procedure. Because of data limitations, the adjustments for age are based on age distributions for males in all areas rather than urban areas alone.
Source: *1960 U.S. Census of Population*, PC(2)–1C, tables 55–59.

are more apt to work full-time; large numbers of young Anglos work only part-time as they continue their education, with the result that the income ratios at age 20 to 24 are unusually favorable for the Spanish-surname group. Also, the decline in the income ratio with higher age corresponds to the greater schooling gap between Mexican Americans and Anglos as age increases.

Lastly, a comparison of Spanish-surname incomes with those of specific groups of nonwhites reveals that Mexican-American urban males in 1959 had median earnings substantially in excess of those of any other minority except for the Japanese in California (Table 8–5). Incomes of urban males among Negroes, Chinese, Filipinos, and especially American Indians were substantially lower.

HAS THERE BEEN PROGRESS?

Mexican Americans have experienced moderate income gains in the decade of the 1950s, gains not only absolute but also relative to the income gains of the majority population.[5] In the Southwest as a whole, the median income of Spanish-surname persons increased by 69 percent as against 57 percent for Anglos. Their advance in the region's urban areas was about the same (Table 8–6). The gains of urban non-whites were substantially smaller than those of Spanish-surname persons. Since Mexican-American incomes increased more than Anglo earnings, *the income gap was somewhat narrowed*.[6]

Although no comparable income data are at hand for previous decades, there is some evidence that the moderate progress between 1949 and 1959 was preceded by advances during the 1940s. As will be shown in the next chapter, the World War II period brought a rather impressive improvement in the occupational position of Mexican Americans, and this change was undoubtedly accompanied by absolute and relative income gains, as was the case for Negroes as well. What seems to emerge, then, is a rise in relative incomes over at least two decades, most likely greater in the 1940s than in the 1950s, when the demand for labor returned to "normalcy" and occupational upgrading was slowing down.

Yet, a sizable income gap remained by 1959 and has unquestionably continued since that time.* Moreover, the income gains of Spanish-surname persons between 1949 and 1959 were unevenly distributed. For urban Mexican Americans, the only substantial gains relative to Anglos occurred in California (where the income gap is also the smallest) and in Colorado. In New Mexico and Texas the median income increased at about the same rate as that of the majority, and in Arizona somewhat less.

---

*According to a special census survey in East Los Angeles, the 1965 median family income in this largely Mexican-American area was about the same as in 1959. However, one can hardly generalize from the record for one large urban neighborhood. The composition of the residents may have changed substantially, especially in light of the evidence of "turnover" in an urban sector that serves as a staging area for immigrants. Nevertheless, the experience in East Los Angeles points to an important phenomenon. While Mexican Americans generally may have become more prosperous, there are large pockets of poverty in cities where the reverse is true. Such a development contributes to the stresses in urban ghettos.

Texas presents a rather distinctive picture. Median incomes of both the Anglo and the Spanish-surname populations are substantially below those of any other Southwest state. Further, the medians rose by only 46 to 48 percent in the 1949–1959 period, as against roughly 57 to 72 percent in the other states. The depressed earnings of both

Table 8–6. Median Income of Spanish-surname Persons
Compared with Others,[a] 1949 and 1959
(Males and females combined)

Area, State, and Population Group	MEDIAN INCOME		PERCENT INCREASE	PERCENT OF ANGLO	
	1949	1959	1949-1959	1949	1959
Southwest					
Anglo	$2,137	$3,351	56.8	—	—
Spanish-surname	1,223	2,065	68.8	57.2	61.6
Nonwhite	1,046	1,777	69.9[b]	48.9	53.0
Urban Southwest					
Anglo	2,279	3,561	56.3	—	—
Spanish-surname	1,385	2,317	67.3	60.8	65.1
Nonwhite	1,268	2,022	59.5	55.6	56.8
Urban					
Arizona					
Anglo	2,051	3,270	59.4	—	—
Spanish-surname	1,406	2,206	56.9	69.6	67.5
Nonwhite	1,162	1,712	47.3	56.7	52.4
California					
Anglo	2,364	3,793	60.4	—	—
Spanish-surname	1,783	3,061	71.7	75.4	80.7
Nonwhite	1,713	2,736	59.7	72.5	72.1
Colorado					
Anglo	1,974	3,154	59.8	—	—
Spanish-surname	1,316	2,176	65.3	66.7	69.0
Nonwhite	1,389	2,296	65.3	70.4	72.8
New Mexico					
Anglo	2,315	3,727	61.0	—	—
Spanish-surname	1,400	2,260	61.4	60.5	60.6
Nonwhite	1,038	1,733	67.0	44.8	46.5
Texas					
Anglo	2,190	3,208	46.5	—	—
Spanish-surname	1,134	1,682	48.3	51.8	52.4
Nonwhite	971	1,349	38.9	44.3	42.1

[a] Persons 14 years and older who received income.
[b] The 1949–1959 increase for nonwhites in the Southwest does not appear to be consistent with the appreciably smaller increase in the urban areas, nor does the excess over the income gain of Anglos seem to be consistent with the fact that only Colorado and New Mexico show such excess. The data are indisputable, and we believe that the results reflect changes in the urban-rural distribution of nonwhites during the 1949–1959 period. The same applies to the Spanish-surname group, except that urban income for this group increased more than that of Anglos in each state except Arizona.
Source: 1950 U.S. Census of Population, PE no. 3C, table 6; 1960 U.S. Census of Population, vol. I, parts 4, 6, 7, 33, and 45, tables 67 and 133; PC(2)–1B, table 6.

Negroes and Mexican Americans in Texas undoubtedly contribute to the state's general low-income standing.

The relative advance of the Spanish-surname population in the Southwest can be in part attributed to the group's migration within the region in response to economic and social opportunities. In 1959, about 49 percent of all Southwest Mexican-American income earners lived in California, compared to only 43 percent in 1949. The increase in the California proportion of *all* Southwest income earners was considerably smaller—from 54 percent in 1949 to 56 percent in 1959.[7] Because California has the highest average income in the region, and Texas the lowest, the shift of the Mexican-American population away from Texas to California would have raised its income relative to the total population regardless of other factors.

Changes in the income position of *Negroes* relative to Mexican Americans also show strong contrasts between California and Texas. After adjustment for differences in age and sex composition of the two groups, the median income of Negroes in California rose from $1,637 in 1949 to $2,656 in 1959, or by 63 percent, compared with an increase from $1,783 to $3,052, or 71 percent, for Mexican Americans. The median income of Negroes in Texas rose from $969 to $1,430, or by 48 percent, compared with an increase from $1,134 to $1,718, or 51 percent, for Mexican Americans.[8] In both states, Spanish-surname incomes advanced more than Negro incomes, but the gain in California was far greater than in Texas.

Progress can be measured also by comparing the incomes of the native-born and the foreign-born at a given moment of time. Improvement in the economic status of ethnic immigrant groups between the first and the second generation is so common that an analyst, on the basis of the 1949 data, referred to Mexican Americans as the one exception to the rule in the United States.[9] If the exception existed in 1949, it did not hold ten years later. As is evident from the cross-sectional comparisons in Table 8–7, the native-born males of foreign parentage in the Southwest earned substantially larger incomes than the foreign-born.* The 1959 difference in median income between the first and the second generation was about $1,000 a year, or 27 percent. But when the native born are further classified by parentage, no continuous progress is discernible. In fact, the natives of native parentage on the average earned a little less than the natives of foreign parentage. (To avoid distortions resulting from the large age differences between the three generational groups, the data refer to urban males 35 to 44 years of age—a group with one of the largest participation rates in the labor force.)

The figures for the five states conform to the overall Southwest pattern, except in Colorado, where all of the three nativity groups show about the same median income.[10] The income benefits from native birth in Texas are also relatively small. This is possibly a reflection of the slow economic growth of south Texas, where Mexican Americans are concentrated, and of labor-market competition from across the border.

In summary, progress is indicated by the moderate increase in relative income between 1949 and 1959 and by the substantial earning differential between the native born and the foreign born in the latter year. Why the natives of native parentage have not advanced in comparison to the second generation remains a matter of

---

*The data for female wage earners in the Spanish-surname group are less indicative partly because income of less than $1,000 is not further classified by amount. Nevertheless, it may be mentioned that the relationships shown for men hold broadly for women as well.

speculation. One might suspect that the absence of such gains could be associated with the large percentage of natives of native parentage in low-income states—Colorado, New Mexico, and Texas. But none of the states, not even California, show improvement beyond the second generation. Consequently, this point does not seem to be of great importance. It seems far more significant that average educational attainment also failed to show any substantial progress beyond the second generation (Chapter 7). Further, discriminatory practices in labor markets may not draw the rather fine distinction between natives of native parentage and those of foreign parentage, but rather may operate against the foreign born in comparison with natives.

Table 8–7. *Median Income of Spanish-surname Urban Males, Age 35–44, and Percent of "High Income" Earners, by Nativity Class, 1959*

Nativity Class	Southwest	Arizona	California
All classes	$4,381	$4,393	$5,252
Foreign born[a]	3,682	3,638	4,315
Natives of foreign or mixed parentage[a]	4,664	4,596	5,543
Natives of native parentage	4,454	4,444	5,524

	Colorado	New Mexico	Texas
All classes	$4,480	$4,360	$3,151
Foreign born[a]	4,549	3,038	2,668
Natives of foreign or mixed parentage[a]	4,563	4,440	3,286
Natives of native parentage	4,452	4,404	3,289

	PERCENT WITH INCOME OF MORE THAN $7,000		
Nativity Class	Southwest	California	Texas
Foreign born[a]	6.1	8.1	2.6
Natives of foreign or mixed parentage[a]	9.6	14.0	3.3
Natives of native parentage	9.7	14.9	5.1

[a] Not available for Mexican-born, but urban males born in Mexico comprise 89 percent of all foreign-born urban males of Spanish surname age 35–44.
Sources: Median-income figures: *1960 U.S. Census of Population,* PC(2)–1B, table 8. Percent with income of more than $7,000: Walter Fogel, *Mexican Americans in Southwest Labor Markets* (Mexican-American Study Project, Advance Report 10, Graduate School of Business Administration, University of California, Los Angeles, October, 1967), Table 35.

In any event, more than three generations seem needed for Mexican Americans to approximate the income status of the general Southwest population. The 1960 median income of natives of natives among Spanish-surname urban males in the 35–44 age bracket was 15 percent less than that of all urban males of like age in California. In Texas the median fell short by 39 percent. The contrast is still greater when "high achievers," defined as urban males of age 35 to 44 who earned more than $7,000 in 1959, are considered. Only 9.7 percent of the Mexican-American natives of native parentage were in this group, as against 37.4 percent of all urban males of comparable age in the Southwest. The fathers of most Mexican Americans in this nativity and age class must have been born in the United States around the turn of the century.

Quite a few of them have been in this country more than three generations. Thus, even 60 years of residency in the United States finds Mexican Americans substantially below the income standing of the general population.

INCOME AND EDUCATION

That there is *generally* a close association between a person's income and his educational preparation has become a universally accepted proposition. As is evident from Table 8–8, the association holds broadly for the Spanish-surname population in the Southwest as well. For example, the level of both schooling and income of Mexican-American males in urban areas is about twice as high as in rural-farm areas. Urban males in the states with the highest and lowest level of educational attainment (California and Texas) also have the highest and lowest incomes. The native-born Spanish-surname people in California show substantially more schooling than the foreign born of comparable age and enjoy substantially higher incomes.

Table 8–8. **Educational Attainment and Income of Spanish-surname Males, Southwest, 1960**

Area, State, and Nativity Class	Median Schooling, Years	Median Income
Southwest[a]		
All areas	8.1	$2,804
Urban	8.4	3,197
Rural nonfarm	6.9	1,871
Rural farm	4.6	1,531
Urban males, by state[a]		
Arizona	8.3	3,269
California	9.2	4,179
Colorado	8.7	3,283
New Mexico	8.8	3,170
Texas	6.7	2,297
Urban males age 35–44 in California		
All nativity classes	9.5	5,252
Native of native parentage	10.8	5,524
Native of foreign or mixed parentage	9.9	5,543
Foreign-born	7.3	4,315

[a] Fourteen years and older.
Source: *1960 U.S. Census of Population*, vol. I, *Detailed Characteristics;* and PC(2)–1B, *Persons of Spanish Surname.* All income data refer to 1959.

But there are exceptions, which means that factors other than schooling influence the levels of income. Urban males of Spanish surname in New Mexico have somewhat lower incomes than those in Arizona and Colorado in spite of slightly better schooling. Although the native born in California show both superior education and earnings in comparison to the foreign born, the relationship between schooling and income becomes equivocal when natives of native parentage and natives of foreign parentage of comparable age are considered. The latter have less education but slightly higher median income than the former.

Table 8–9. Median Incomes of Spanish-surname and Nonwhite Males as a Percent of Anglo Males, Before and After Adjustment for Differences in Schooling, Five Southwest States, 1959[a]

State	SPANISH-SURNAME MALES		NONWHITE MALES	
	Before Adjustment	After Adjustment	Before Adjustment	After Adjustment
Arizona	61	94	41	63
California	73	88	65	72
Colorado	65	78	70	74
New Mexico	55	77	63	56
Texas	47	72	45	56

[a] Age 25 and over, standardized for age. Differences in schooling adjusted in terms of school years completed. The general form of the computation is

$$\frac{\Sigma_i(X_iY_i)}{\Sigma_iX_i}$$

Where X_i = the number of male persons of the ethnic group in the ith school-years-completed class and Y_i = the median income of nonwhite males in the ith-school-years-completed class.

However, the main purpose here is to examine the relationship of income and schooling differences between Mexican Americans and Anglos. This is done in Table 8–9 by a statistical procedure which, in effect, standardizes the educational attainment distributions of Mexican-American and Anglo males of comparable ages. As is evident from the table, much of the income differential between Spanish-surname and Anglo persons is removed when the intergroup differences in schooling are taken into account, but a residual income gap remains in each of the five states. This residual ranges from six percent in Arizona[11] and 12 percent in California to 28 percent in Texas. In other words, income gaps of this magnitude would have existed in 1960 even if Mexican Americans and Anglos had spent the same number of years in school. Differences in the quality of education probably explain part of the remaining income gap between the two populations, as well as the variations of the gap from state to state. But it seems that improved education, though desirable for its own sake, will only go part way in narrowing the income difference.

Chart 8–5 shows income differences between Mexican Americans and Anglos with comparable schooling, for California and Texas. (Because of statistical problems, these data are for urban and rural areas combined and are not adjusted for age differences.) The incomes of Mexican Americans relative to Anglos in each of the two states are quite similar for all levels of schooling. Mexican Americans in California earned nearly four-fifths as much as Anglos with comparable educational preparation; in Texas, they earned only about two-thirds as much. Again, factors other than schooling appear to operate with greater force in Texas than in California. In both cases, however, there is a tendency for income differentials to widen the higher the

Chart 8–5.
A. Median Income of Spanish-surname Males as a Percent of Median Income of Anglos at Different Levels of Schooling, California and Texas, 1959

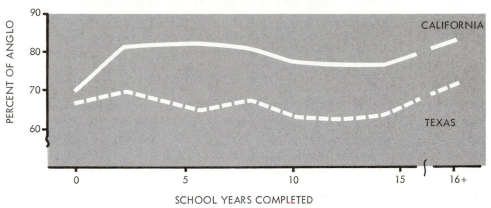

B. Median Income of Spanish-surname Males as a Percent of Median Income of Nonwhites at Different Levels of Schooling, California and Texas, 1959

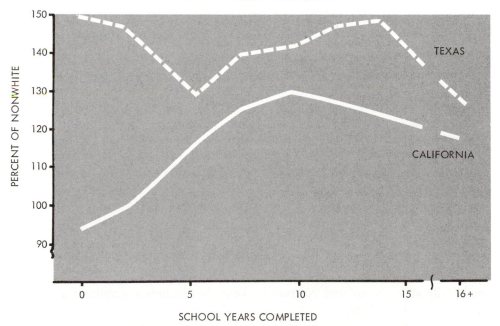

Source: *1960 U.S. Census of Population,* vol. I, part 6, and part 45, table 138. The Spanish-surname data are from a special tabulation of table 138 obtained from the Bureau of the Census. The statistics refer to males with income, age 25 and over, not adjusted for age differences.

educational attainment, except for the groups with the most extensive schooling. For example, Mexican-American males in California who had eight years of schooling earned $1,000, or 19 percent, less than Anglos with equal educational preparation. In Texas, the difference was $1,500, or 33 percent. The median income of Spanish-surname males in California with 12 years of schooling was $1,700, or 24 percent less than that of Anglos of equal educational standing. In Texas, the difference was $2,400, or 38 percent. *That more education fails to improve the income position of Mexican Americans in proportion to that of the majority is a matter of considerable social significance.*

When we compare median incomes of Spanish-surname and nonwhite males with the same amount of schooling, the former show higher incomes at nearly all levels of educational attainment (Chart 8–5). The income differences are substantially greater in Texas than in California. This reflects in part the fact that nonwhites are

Table 8–10. Median Income, School Years Completed, and Income Adjusted for Educational Differences: Selected Ethnic Groups, Five Southwest States, 1959[a] (Males)

	ARIZONA				COLORADO		NEW MEXICO		
	Spanish-surname	Nonwhite	Indian	Negro	Spanish-surname	Nonwhite	Spanish-surname	Nonwhite	Indian
Median Income[b]	$3,132	$2,095	$1,479	$2,612	$3,268	$3,536	$3,061	$2,283	$1,768
Median School Years[c]	6.4	6.7	4.9	8.1	7.9	10.5	7.7	6.9	5.4
Adjusted Median Income[d]	$4,848	$3,223	$2,608	$3,539	$3,881	$3,742	$4,281	$3,485	$2,971

	TEXAS		CALIFORNIA						
	Spanish-surname	Nonwhite	Spanish-surname	Nonwhite	Indian	Negro	Chinese	Filipino	Japanese
Median Income[b]	$2,241	$2,146	$4,238	$3,774	$3,309	$3,716	$4,006	$3,135	$4,703
Median School Years[c]	4.4	7.4	8.2	9.8	9.0	9.3	9.5	9.0	12.3
Adjusted Median Income[d]	$3,416	$2,666	$5,112	$4,170	$3,730	$4,152	$4,516	$3,575	$4,729

[a] "School years completed" refer to 1960.
[b] All median incomes are standardized for the effects of age differences among the populations.
[c] Standardized for age.
[d] Adjusted to Anglo level of educational attainment, with indexes of income computed from the complete schooling distributions in the following form: $\Sigma_i X_i Y_i$ where X_i = the proportion of Spanish-surname (Negro, Chinese, etc.) males aged 14 and over who had completed the ith school year (i = 0 to 16+) and Y_i = the corresponding 1959 median income of nonwhite males (Anglo index = 100).
Source: Walter Fogel, *Mexican Americans in Southwest Labor Markets* (Mexican-American Study Project, Advance Report 10, Graduate School of Business Administration, University of California, Los Angeles, October, 1967), p. 172.

practically synonymous with Negroes in Texas but include a significant admixture of Orientals in California.

Because the nonwhite population in the Southwest states is so heterogeneous, schooling and income are shown for subgroups (Table 8–10). These data are adjusted for the very considerable age differences among the components of the nonwhite population. In general, Mexican-American males have lower educational attainment than Negroes, Chinese, and Japanese. Their income position relative to these ethnic populations, however, is remarkably favorable. Only the Japanese in California and the nonwhites of Colorado score higher earnings, but both also show far superior schooling. Compared to the Spanish-surname males, American Indians have lower incomes and, with the exception of California, inferior educational attainment. Filipinos in California have about the same schooling record but much less income.

When income is adjusted for schooling differentials, in all five states Mexican-American males show larger earnings than any nonwhite group. This is true even in comparison to Japanese in California, who rank high in both education and income. One may infer that Mexican Americans experience less discrimination in labor markets than most nonwhite groups.

THE INCIDENCE OF POVERTY

In spite of some measure of progress, Mexican Americans still bear a highly disproportionate share of the burden of poverty in the Southwest.* When the widely used statistical "poverty line" of a $3,000 family income per year is adopted for 1960, the poverty group in the Spanish-surname population of the Southwest included nearly 243,000 families, or about 35 percent of all families in this national minority (Table 8–11). There were slightly more poor nonwhite families, but the difference is so small and the poverty line so crude as to suggest that the number of poor families in each

Table 8–11. Number and Percent of Poor Families in Various Population Groups in the Southwest, 1960

Population Group	All Families	Poor Families[a]	Percent of Poor in Each Group	Poor in Each Group as Percent Of All Poor
Total	7,356,866	1,451,655	19.7	100.0
White	6,766,367	1,205,729	17.8	83.1
Anglo	6,068,340	962,826	15.9	66.4
Spanish-surname	698,027	242,903	34.8	16.7
Nonwhite	590,299	245,926	41.7	17.0

[a] Families with annual income under $3,000 in 1959.
Source: *1960 U.S. Census of Population*, PC(2)–1B, table 5; vol. I, state volumes, table 65.

of the two minorities is about the same. However, fewer nonwhite families than Spanish-surname families, irrespective of income, resided in the Southwest. Consequently, the incidence of poverty among nonwhites was still greater than among the Mexican Americans. The incidence was much smaller for Anglos. The relative frequency of poverty among Spanish-surname families was well over twice the Anglo rate.[12]

Numerically, however, poor Anglo families far exceeded the poor of both minority groups combined. As the last column of Table 8–11 shows, for every poor

*This section is a condensed version of Frank G. Mittelbach and Grace Marshall's *The Burden of Poverty* (Mexican-American Study Project, Advance Report 5, Graduate School of Business Administration, University of California, Los Angeles, July, 1966).

family in both minorities combined there were almost two Anglo families in the same category. Low income afflicts many Anglos as well as ethnic or racial minorities.

Our data show also the distortion that results from the frequent failure to distinguish between Anglo and Spanish-surname families within the white class. Although the Spanish-surname families represent only 10.3 percent of all white families in the Southwest, irrespective of income, they account for 20.1 percent of the *poor*

Table 8–12. Estimated Number and Percent of Poor Persons in Families, Various Population Groups in the Southwest, 1960[a]

Population Group	All Persons in Families	Poor Persons	Percent of Poor in Each Group	Poor in Each Group as Percent of All Poor
Total	26,524,000	4,731,000	17.8	100.0
Spanish-surname	3,300,000	1,082,000	32.8	22.9
Nonwhite	2,404,000	927,000	38.6	19.6

[a] The estimates in this table and the next understate the dimensions of poverty since they omit persons who are not living in families but rather reside in group quarters and institutions or occupy their own housing units as individuals.
Source: Derived or estimated from *1960 U.S. Census of Population*, vol. I, parts 4, 6, 7, 33, and 45, tables 65, 110, and 141; and PC(2)–1B, tables 3 and 5.

white families. Hence, analyses of poverty in the Southwest that do not separate Spanish-surname persons from Anglos hide the existence of a minority which, on the income criterion used here, is almost as disadvantaged as the nonwhite group.

The problems and consequences of poverty, however, affect individuals just as much as families. Children are a special concern, for poverty tends to be transmitted from one generation to the next. Thus it becomes important to know how many

Table 8–13. Estimated Number and Percent of Poor Children in Families, Various Population Groups in the Southwest, 1960

Population Group	All Children in Families	Poor Children	Percent of Poor in Each Group	Poor in Each Group as Percent of All Poor
Total	10,606,500	1,828,700	17.2	100.0
Spanish-surname	1,620,000	530,000	32.7	29.0
Nonwhite	1,110,220	395,000	35.6	21.6

Source: Derived or estimated from *1960 U.S. Census of Population*, vol. I, parts 4, 6, 7, 33, and 45, tables 94, 96, and 140; and One-In-One Thousand Sample (see Appendix E for description and documentation).

children are included in poor families, as well as the number of individuals regardless of age. The estimates in Tables 8–12 and 8–13 give approximate answers to this question. In 1960, the individuals in poor Spanish-surname families in the Southwest totaled nearly 1,100,000, and those in poor nonwhite families about 927,000. There were 530,000 children below age 18 among the Mexican-American poor and 395,000 among the nonwhite poor. *Thus, about 2 million persons in these minorities, and nearly 1 million children, lived in poverty in the Southwest alone.*

The *incidence* of poverty computed on the basis of persons in families is some-what lower for the Spanish-surname and the nonwhite groups than the incidence computed on the basis of families. On the other hand, the *share* of Spanish-surname and nonwhite persons in the total number of poor individuals is substantially greater than was true for families. These results are related to differences not only in the average family size of the three subpopulations (Chapter 6), but also in the size of poor families. Poor families are typically smaller in all three subpopulations. The poor include an unusually large number of aged couples and broken families. In turn, both minority groups have relatively more such atypical units.[13]

The composition of the poor as a group also changes substantially when indivi-duals and children, rather than families, are considered. Members of the two minori-ties account for nearly 42 percent of poor persons as against 34 percent of poor families. Spanish-surname persons alone represent about 23 percent of total individ-uals as against less than 17 percent of families. Over half the total number of chil-dren in poor families are Spanish-surname or nonwhite.

Not surprisingly, the incidence of poverty among Mexican-American families is inversely related to the general income position of each state. The rank order of the incidence, from low to high, is California, Arizona, Colorado, New Mexico, and Texas (Chart 8-6). And—again not surprisingly—differentials are much greater for the minorities than for Anglos. The proportion of poor families varied between 13 percent in California and 21 percent in Texas for Anglos, between 19 percent and 52 percent for the Spanish-surname group, and between 25 percent and 58 percent for non-whites. The chances of an Anglo family being in the poverty group are about two-thirds greater in Texas than in California; the chances of a Spanish-surname family being in this group are 170 percent greater in Texas than in California. In 1960, nearly 140,000 of the 243,000 poor Spanish-surname families were living in Texas—more than 57 percent of the total. Over 58,000, or 24 percent of the total, resided in California. About 23,000 lived in New Mexico, while Arizona and Colorado had 11,000 each.

The majority of the poor among Mexican Americans were city dwellers. Of the 242,903 Spanish-surname families in the poverty group in the Southwest at the latest census date, 174,651, or 72 percent, were urban, and only 18,034, or a little over 7 percent, lived on farms. The remaining 50,218 were in the twilight zone of rural nonfarm areas which may mean isolated small towns and hamlets or the metro-politan fringe.[14]

Clearly, the poverty of Mexican Americans, as that of most other population groups, has in the main become a city problem. It is much less certain to what extent the differential incidence of poverty is associated with minority status as such. Studies of poverty have shown that minority status is only one of the factors that increase a family's chances of being poor. Characteristics such as age, broken marriage, poor education, and farm employment have the same effect irrespective of ethnicity. The results of a special tabulation of the Spanish-surname poor (Appendix E) can be summed up by saying that family characteristics other than minority status are of considerable importance. The heads of the overwhelming majority of poor Spanish-surname families (over 83 percent) had one or more of six specified characteristics strongly associated with poverty status. In comparison, only 39 percent of the heads of non-poor families showed one or more of these characteristics. The contrast between the poor and non-poor was less noticeable for Spanish-surname individuals not living in families.

Although computations of this kind are imprecise and cannot claim to offer an explanation of poverty, they do emphasize the presence of many factors not directly related to minority status.

Chart 8–6.
Poor Families as a Percent of All Spanish-surname Families in Five Southwest States, 1960

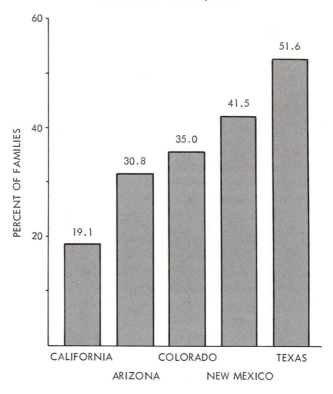

Source: *1960 U.S. Census of Population*, PC(2)–1B, table 5; vol. I (State Volumes), tables 65, 109.

SUMMARY

The income gap between Mexican Americans and Anglos highlights the greatly differentiated economic position of the minority. Depending on the kinds of measurement, the Spanish-surname group is 35 to 50 percent below Anglo income levels in the Southwest. Significantly, the more comparable and refined data for individual incomes show a larger differential than the cruder figures on family incomes. Yet, the standing of Mexican Americans in 1960 reflected moderate progress during the 1950s. Also, the natives did far better than the foreign born.

It appears that, in addition to urbanization, World War II and the GI Bill of Rights have had a major influence on change in the postwar period. In our initial interviews throughout the Southwest, Mexican Americans in the 30- to 50 year age class again and again referred to the new horizons opened up by the war itself and by the postwar educational benefits. War service brought many of the young men from the *barrios* into first contact with large numbers of Anglos of varied origin. Unlike Negroes and Japanese Americans, Mexican Americans were not placed in segregated units. Although discrimination and mistrust or, for that matter, self-segregation were not entirely absent in the armed forces,[15] they were less pervasive or intense than in civilian life. Service abroad exposed Mexican Americans to other peoples and cultures and thus diminished the ethnocentrism related to their previous isolation. Thus, many Mexican-American veterans returned with a new sense of opportunities. The educational benefits of the GI Bill of Rights helped enormously in transforming this awareness of opportunities into reality.

Nevertheless, large income gaps between the Spanish-surname minority and the majority have persisted. According to the detailed analysis for males, income figures adjusted for differences in the amount of schooling still show substantial disparities between Mexican Americans and Anglos. Some though probably not all of these disparities can be explained by variations in the quality of education obtained by the two populations.

In comparison to nonwhites and the various subgroups of nonwhites, the Spanish-surname males have a remarkably favorable earnings position. When income is adjusted for schooling (as well as age) differentials, the Spanish-surname males are ahead of any nonwhite group.

The income of Mexican Americans relative to the majority varies greatly from state to state and among metropolitan areas. The local differences are much larger than those for Anglos. This is true even when the schooling gap is taken into account and the data adjusted so as to control for age, sex, and location (urban). In all of the comparisons, Texas shows the greatest absolute and relative income differences between Mexican Americans and Anglos or the total population. California almost invariably shows the smallest differences.

To some extent, state differentials reflect economic and ecological factors. The Spanish-surname population in Texas is heavily concentrated in the state's low-income Southern region. Job and wage competition from commuters who live across the United States border also seems to affect the large numbers of Mexican Americans living in south Texas more severely than those in any other Southwest area. In Colorado and New Mexico, the Spanish-surname people face the problems of declining regions and declining industries. Jobs in the economic-growth sections of the two states typically require skills which most Mexican Americans have yet to acquire. Continued internal migration to California will help, as it did in the past. Yet, greater gains seem to depend equally if not more on accelerated progress in the present locations of the Mexican-American population.

In the context of the Southwest as a whole, further increases in the relative income of Mexican Americans will require a more rapid shift of people in the labor force from manual to non-manual occupations. Such a shift calls for enormous educational inputs. Only modest gains can be accomplished by moving from unskilled labor jobs into higher-wage manual occupations. The structure of employment is changing in favor of non-manual work. This change limits the opportunities for income gains from upgrading in manual jobs. The implications of these trends for Mexican Americans will become apparent in our analysis of their position in labor markets (Chapter 9).

NOTES TO CHAPTER EIGHT

1. The rank order of the five Southwest states in terms of median family income of their entire populations in 1959 was as follows: 1) California ($6,727), 2) Colorado ($5,780), 3) Arizona ($5,568), 4) New Mexico ($5,371), and 5) Texas ($4,884). The rank order for Spanish-surname family income as a percent of Anglo family income is the same, but the positions of Colorado and Arizona are reversed when the total population is considered and identical for the urban areas of the states. The Colorado-Arizona differences of median income are altogether minor except for nonwhites. For the above figures, see *1960 U.S. Census of Population*, vol. I, part I, table 137.

2. Among the exceptions are Albuquerque and Houston, which rank high in Anglo but quite low in Spanish-surname income, and the San Bernardino and Tucson areas, which rank higher in Spanish-surname than in Anglo income. One of the lowest figures for Mexican Americans is found in Fresno, in wealthy California, where their median family income was barely above San Antonio and a little below El Paso. Source for metropolitan areas: *1960 U.S. Census of Population*, PC(2)–1B, table 14; tract volumes, tables P–1, P–4, P–5; and state volumes, table 140.

3. The greater income gap for individuals than for families is not explained by differences in the number of earners in Mexican-American and Anglo families. The Southwest data for 1960 show that 7.1 percent of the Spanish-surname families had no earner (7.7 percent for Anglos), 49.7 percent had one earner (49.3 percent for Anglos), and 43.2 percent had two earners (43.0 percent for Anglos). Further classifications of the last group are not available for the Spanish-surname population. See *1960 Census of Population*, PC(2)–1B, table 5.

4. In obtaining Anglo figures for Chart 8–4, the Spanish-surname and nonwhite income distributions were substracted from that of all urban males. However, the only nonwhite distribution available was for urban and rural areas combined. Nonwhite medians are also for all areas. In 1960, 89 percent of all California nonwhite males with income lived in urban areas; 8 percent of all urban males with income were nonwhite.

5. The use of benchmark data for single years a decade apart may be open to question for the purpose of measuring income gains during the period. However, general economic conditions in 1949 and 1959 were not substantially different. The former was largely a year of business recession. The latter was a year of business recovery from a preceding recession but still far short of full utilization of resources. Besides, the emphasis is on intergroup

differentials in income changes rather than on absolute levels of change, and the differentials are probably not in any substantial degree affected by the position of the two years in the business cycle.

6. The question arises whether the 1949–1959 comparisons are significantly influenced by changes in the age and sex composition of income earners in the different population groups. (Urban-rural variances have already been eliminated by our focus on urban areas.) To examine this question, the data on median income in 1949 and 1959 were adjusted for differences in age and sex distribution. The combined effects of the adjustments were slight except for some subgroups of the nonwhite population. The two adjustments operate in opposite directions and are thus largely self-cancelling. As for sex, the representation of women in the labor force has increased generally, but the rate of increase has been greater for Spanish-surname females (though their labor force participation remains relatively low in comparison with the rest of the population). Since women generally earn less than men, this factor by itself results in an understatement the of relative income gain of Mexican Americans in our data. The age composition of the Spanish-surname group changed in favor of income-producing ages more than did that of the general population. This factor alone results in an overstatement of the relative income advance of Mexican Americans in the data. See Walter Fogel, *Mexican Americans in Southwest Labor Markets* (Mexican-American Study Project, Advance Report 10, Graduate School of Business Administration, University of California, Los Angeles, Oct., 1967), pp. 52, 53

7. *1960 U.S. Census of Population*, vol. I, parts 4, 6, 7, 33, and 45.

8. Cf. Fogel, *op. cit.*, table 19.

9. Donald J. Bogue, *The Population of the United States* (New York: The Free Press, 1959), p. 372.

10. There were only about 1,300 Mexican-born males in the urban labor force of Colorado in 1960: most urban Mexican Americans in the state are descendants of early settlers who are employed in the mining and metal-fabricating industries. It seems likely that most of the foreign-born persons in Colorado have been able to benefit from the long-standing representation of Mexican Americans in certain industries which have been unionized for some time, for example the steel and hard-rock mine industries. They probably entered the state in response to fairly definite prospects for desirable employment, the information having been communicated to them by relatives or friends already employed in steel production and other manufacturing industries; or else they came with parents who had similar employment opportunities. Thus, small amounts of migration responsive to desirable job opportunities appear to have produced relatively large incomes for foreign-born Mexican Americans in Colorado. In contrast, most of the foreign born in other states had to enter the labor market through low-skilled and low-wage jobs in agriculture or industry.

11. The small residual in Arizona may be explained by the special circumstances there. The educational attainment of Mexican Americans in 1960 was low because of the very low schooling of the many Spanish-surname farm laborers in this state, many of whom had recently migrated from Mexico. Incomes, however, were better than would be expected from the low levels of education; the association between schooling and agricultural earnings appears to be quite weak for Spanish-surname persons. Thus, adjustment for the low education brought a very large increase in Mexican-American relative income. Since 1964, contract labor from Mexico has not been used in Arizona agriculture. Therefore, it is doubtful that the adjustment for education at the present time would "explain" as much of the Mexican-American income position in Arizona as it did in 1960.

12. We refrain from discussing here the conceptual and statistical problems associated with the measurement of poverty. For a summary of them and references to the literature, see Frank G. Mittelbach and Grace Marshall, *The Burden of Poverty* (Mexican-American Study Project, Advance Report 5, Graduate School of Business Administration, University

of California, Los Angeles, July, 1966). As far as measurement is concerned, one of the many difficulties relates to welfare and other "transfer" payments which may raise a family's income above a statistical poverty line of, say, $3,000. But is a family headed by the mother of five children and eligible for aid exceeding $3,000 a year really lifted out of poverty? In the case of minority groups especially, poverty is probably understated for this reason.

13. Since this analysis is based on census data, we must adopt the census definition of a family as two or more persons in the same household who are related to each other by blood, marriage, or adoption. For other definitions and concepts, see Paul C. Glick, *American Families* (New York: John Wiley & Sons, Inc., 1957).

14. The proportion of poor families in urban areas may be overstated in these figures because a uniform poverty line was applied to urban and rural areas. See Mittelbach and Marshall, *op. cit.*, pp. 23–26 and table 7, for a more extensive discussion of urban-rural differences. This source deals also with the problems of applying a uniform poverty line to urban and rural areas.

15. See Raul Morin, *Among the Valiant* (Los Angeles: Borden Publishing Co., 1963).

NINE

Occupations and Jobs

THE present chapter and the next deal with the main labor-market factors that impinge on the income differentials between Mexican Americans and the general population. Here we discuss labor-force participation and unemployment rates, occupations, and changes in the occupational structure of Mexican Americans over time. We examine the characteristics of industries in which Spanish-surname workers are well represented as against those showing under-representation, a subject that lends itself to empirical tests of a number of hypotheses. Finally, we present materials on Mexican Americans in government employment. Job and earnings differentials are analyzed in the next chapter.[1]

LABOR FORCE AND UNEMPLOYMENT

The labor force participation of Mexican Americans is relatively low. In comparison to Anglos the rate is slightly lower for males and much lower for females. This is true both for urban areas alone and for all areas in the Southwest (Table 9–1). On the

[1] Notes for this chapter start on page 227.

basis of age and schooling patterns, one might expect Mexican Americans to show a higher participation rate than Anglos. Why the facts do not bear out the expectations will soon become apparent. Whatever the reasons, the lower participation rate contributes to the lower family incomes of Mexican Americans.

Table 9–1. Labor Force Participation Rates of Spanish-surname Persons Compared with Anglos and Nonwhites, Five Southwest States, 1960[a]

AREA AND STATE	Males			Females		
	ANGLO	SPANISH-SURNAME	NONWHITE	ANGLO	SPANISH-SURNAME	NONWHITE
	Urban and Rural Areas					
Southwest	79.5%	77.5%	74.4%	34.1%	28.8%	42.8%
Arizona	77.4	78.8	59.5	33.1	24.9	27.5
California	79.6	79.9	78.2	35.6	32.2	44.1
Colorado	78.8	70.9	76.4	34.3	25.5	43.1
New Mexico	79.1	69.3	58.4	30.8	23.9	26.6
Texas	79.8	76.9	72.4	31.8	27.0	43.6
	Urban Areas					
Southwest	80.4	78.1	77.6	36.0	30.8	46.4
Arizona	77.5	77.0	71.8	34.6	26.4	40.8
California	80.3	80.0	79.4	36.7	33.3	45.1
Colorado	79.0	71.8	76.0	36.9	28.8	45.4
New Mexico	81.5	74.8	74.7	34.3	28.9	45.3
Texas	81.1	77.0	75.6	34.6	28.9	48.4

[a] Percent of the noninstitutional population 14 years and over in the civilian labor force.
Source: 1960 U.S. Census of Population, vol. I, parts 4, 6, 7, 33, and 45, table 52; PC(2)–1B, table 6.

Relatively few Spanish-surname females are in the labor force in comparison with Anglo and especially with nonwhite women. If low earnings of the family head force women into employment, one would expect the participation rates for both minorities to be relatively high. This difference between nonwhites and Mexican Americans may be attributed to cultural tradition in the latter group: the woman's place is in the home, and the husband's or father's pride would be hurt if a wife or daughter were to hold a job. It is possible also that the large Mexican-American family compels the wife or adult daughter to spend more time caring for small children.

Differences in the economic and social environment seem to have a distinct bearing on labor force participation rates in the several states. California shows about the same rates for Spanish-surname and Anglo males and a small intergroup differential for females. In Colorado and New Mexico, where job opportunities are limited, Mexican-American men and women alike are poorly represented in the labor force. In Arizona, the rates for males are about the same as for Anglos, but the participation of females is exceptionally small. Arizona's industrial structure, at least in 1960, included relatively few light industries suitable for female employment. Mexican Americans in Texas have a comparatively low participation rate regardless of sex. The low rate is probably related to the poor employment prospects of Spanish-surname people in the state's underdeveloped southern region. Competition for jobs by Mexicans crossing the border may also be a factor.

Labor force participation rates are somewhat higher in urban areas for each of the three populations. The contrast between urban and total rates is greatest for non-whites in Arizona and New Mexico, where the group includes substantial numbers of American Indians on rural reservations. The relatively low participation of urban Mexican-American males holds for all age groups (Chart 9–1). Even those in the

Chart 9–1.
Labor Force Participation Rates of Urban Males in the Southwest,
by Age Group, 1960[a]

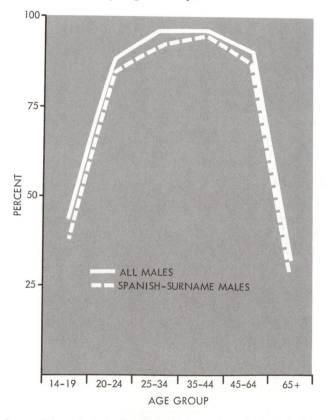

[a] Percent of the noninstitutional population 14 years and older in the civilian labor force.
Source: Walter Fogel, *Mexican-Americans in Southwest Labor Markets* (Mexican-American Study Project, Advance Report 10, Graduate School of Business Administration, University of California, Los Angeles, October, 1967), Table 8.

14–19-year bracket show a lower rate, though they are less likely than others to continue their education and more likely to face the pressures of low family incomes. It seems that young Mexican Americans do not *enter* the labor market in proportion to Anglos of comparable age.

The 1960 *unemployment* rate among urban Mexican–American males in the Southwest, 8.5 percent of the civilian labor force, was nearly twice the Anglo rate (4.5) and just a little lower than the rate for nonwhites (9.1). The condition was worst in Colorado, New Mexico, and Texas, where unemployment among Mexican Americans was about $2\frac{1}{2}$ to 3 times as high as for Anglos.[2] In all probability, the unemployment differentials account at least in part for the relatively low labor force participation of Mexican–American males; job seekers who fail to obtain employment may be so discouraged that they withdraw from the labor force.[3] The differential incidence of unemployment among Mexican Americans extended over the whole range of age groups and was especially great among the young and the aged (Chart 9–2).

Chart 9–2.
Unemployment Rates for Urban Males in the Southwest, by Age Group, 1960[a]

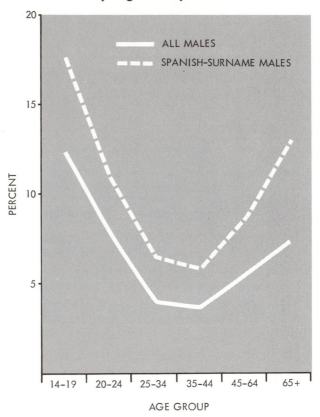

[a] Unemployed persons as a percent of the civilian labor force.
Source: Walter Fogel, *op. cit.*, Table 7.

In addition to higher unemployment, Mexican Americans have experienced a somewhat higher incidence of *underemployment*. For example, only 58 percent of the

Spanish-surname family heads in urban California worked 50 to 52 weeks during 1959, as against 68 percent of all family heads.[4] The contrast would undoubtedly be still greater if the underemployment of Mexican Americans could be compared with Anglos rather than the total population. Above-average underemployment and higher unemployment rates may be associated with job concentration in industries and business firms which do not offer steady work. This matter will be considered shortly. In addition, Mexican Americans may be exposed to layoffs or short hours of work if they have less seniority than other workers or, in the absence of a seniority system, through more haphazard and possibly discriminatory procedures for job termination. In any case, differential underemployment as well as differential unemployment contributes to the income gap.

THE OCCUPATIONAL STRUCTURE

To portray the occupational distribution of various population groups involves a great deal of statistical detail. The shortest census list of occupations shows 12 major categories (including "occupation not reported"). If the differences between males and females, between urban and rural areas, and among the five Southwest states were to be examined for Mexican Americans and the two reference populations, the data would become too voluminous. Consequently, we present merely the Southwest figures for males (Table 9–2) and use "shorthand" expressions, which combine census categories, for the analysis.

Table 9–2. Occupational Distribution of Spanish-surname Males Compared with Other Males, Southwest, 1960[a]

| | URBAN AND RURAL | | | URBAN | | |
Occupational Category	Anglo	Spanish-surname	Nonwhite	Anglo	Spanish-surname	Nonwhite
Professional	13.7%	3.9%	5.5%	15.1%	4.6%	6.1%
Managers and proprietors	13.8	4.3	3.3	14.7	4.9	3.6
Clerical	7.0	4.6	5.3	7.8	5.5	6.1
Sales	8.3	3.4	2.1	9.2	4.1	2.3
Craftsmen	21.0	15.8	10.1	21.5	18.2	10.8
Operatives	15.9	22.9	19.3	15.8	25.4	20.0
Private household	0.1	0.1	0.8	0.1	0.1	0.9
Service, excluding private household	5.0	7.2	16.6	5.4	8.4	18.6
Laborers	4.7	14.4	18.5	4.4	15.8	18.3
Farm laborers	2.1	16.0	6.3	0.6	7.3	2.1
Farm managers	3.9	2.2	3.7	0.7	0.6	1.9
Occupation not reported	4.5	5.1	8.7	4.7	5.1	9.3

[a] Percent of all employed males in each population group.
Source: 1960 U.S. Census of Population, vol. I, parts 4, 6, 7, 33, and 45, table 58; PC(2)–1B, table 6.

One of these expressions is the percentage of persons in white-collar work and the percentage in those manual occupations which require low skill. Another summary expression is a comprehensive index, computed for this study, of occupational position. Each of these methods has its merits and shortcomings, which are explained in Appendix F. Of course, both methods show the occupations in which people are actually engaged, and not necessarily those for which they are potentially qualified. This can make a substantial difference for immigrants and disadvantaged minorities generally.

White-collar and Blue-collar Occupations

In comparison with Anglos, Mexican Americans are grossly under-represented in white-collar occupations; and the extent of under-representation does not vary significantly between urban areas and all areas combined (Table 9–3). Differences between Anglos and Spanish-surname persons are greater for males than for females. This is related to the fact that the white-collar category includes low-paid clerks and sales persons, often females. Within the Southwest, Mexican Americans have the best access to white-collar work in New Mexico, and the worst in Arizona (at least

Table 9–3. Persons in White-collar Occupations[a] as a Percent of All Employed Persons in Each Population Group, Total and Urban, Five Southwest States, 1960

AREA AND STATE	Urban and Rural			Urban		
	ANGLO	SPANISH-SURNAME	NONWHITE	ANGLO	SPANISH-SURNAME	NONWHITE
			Males			
Southwest	42.8	16.3	16.1	46.9	19.0	18.1
Arizona	41.9	11.8	12.0	44.7	15.4	14.5
California	44.1	16.6	22.4	46.3	18.8	23.7
Colorado	41.3	14.3	20.7	47.7	17.5	21.8
New Mexico	43.9	21.2	13.0	50.4	25.8	16.3
Texas	40.9	15.9	9.0	47.8	19.0	10.3
			Females			
Southwest	66.8	36.0	22.0	68.4	37.3	22.8
Arizona	65.3	36.5	20.2	66.4	37.3	18.6
California	66.7	37.8	32.0	67.7	38.4	32.5
Colorado	64.9	30.6	30.6	67.0	31.8	30.2
New Mexico	70.2	42.1	20.7	72.0	43.4	20.1
Texas	67.4	33.4	12.1	70.3	35.5	12.1

[a] Includes the following major occupational categories: professional, managerial, clerical, and sales. Farm managers are excluded, because although it may be considered white-collar, this category comprises an admixture of persons with widely varying degrees of managerial and other functions and of social prestige. The statistical treatment of the category makes little difference in the combined results of this table.
Source: See Table 9–2.

among males). California and Texas show about the same percentage of Spanish-surname men in white-collar occupations, and their representation relative to Anglos is about equally poor. This is one of the few cases where the economic data for the two states do not reveal sharp differences.

Turning to the position of Mexican Americans in comparison to nonwhites, we find that the men in both groups had about the same representation in white-collar occupations in the Southwest as a whole. Mexican-American women, however, had a clear edge over nonwhites. Among the individual states, California and Colorado show far better representation in white-collar jobs among nonwhite than among Spanish-surname males. The reverse was true for New Mexico and Texas.*

In the Southwest as a whole, nearly 61 percent of all employed Mexican-American males in 1960 were in low-skill manual occupations, as against less than 28 percent of Anglos (Table 9–4). The relationship was only slightly better in the urban areas. Here again, the position was somewhat more favorable for Spanish-surname females. And once more, California and Texas show only slight differences in the over-representation of Mexican-American men in low-skill occupations, though somewhat larger variations for females. New Mexico, the "best" state in terms of Spanish-surname persons' access to white-collar work, is also the best by the present criterion. The percentage of Spanish-surname persons in low-skill occupations was lower than in any other state, yet it was about twice that of Anglos.

Table 9–4. Persons of Low-skill Manual Occupations[a] as a Percent of All Employed Persons in Each Population Group, Total and Urban, Five Southwest States, 1960

AREA AND STATE	Urban and Rural			Urban		
	ANGLO	SPANISH-SURNAME	NONWHITE	ANGLO	SPANISH-SURNAME	NONWHITE
			Males			
Southwest	27.8	60.6	61.5	26.3	57.0	60.0
Arizona	28.7	69.8	65.6	26.6	61.8	64.3
California	28.0	59.0	52.4	26.7	56.6	51.4
Colorado	29.1	65.9	55.1	27.5	62.9	55.5
New Mexico	26.8	55.1	58.0	24.4	50.7	54.3
Texas	27.1	61.4	72.2	25.1	57.2	72.0
			Females			
Southwest	26.3	56.0	68.7	25.0	54.7	67.9
Arizona	27.9	56.8	66.6	26.9	55.7	71.2
California	26.5	53.5	57.4	25.6	52.8	57.0
Colorado	28.6	60.1	58.8	27.0	58.4	59.0
New Mexico	24.7	50.7	65.2	23.6	49.7	68.6
Texas	25.4	59.3	80.4	23.0	57.3	80.3

[a] Includes the following major occupational categories: operative; laborer; farm laborer and foreman; and service worker, including private household workers.
Source: See Table 9–2.

Again, the relative position of Mexican-American and nonwhite males was quite similar in the Southwest as a whole. However, nonwhites were less concentrated in low-skill occupations in California and Colorado, and more concentrated in Texas. Relatively more nonwhite than Spanish-surname females were in this occupational grouping throughout the Southwest, except for Colorado.

*Comparisons between nonwhites and Spanish-surname persons must be tentative, because the census data for the former show an unusually large percentage of respondents who failed to report their occupation. The percent of Spanish-surname persons who did not report was also somewhat larger than that of Anglos, but the difference is relatively small. See Table 9–2.

The occupational data presented so far exclude one important category: crafts-men, who are neither white-collar nor low-skill manual workers. *Mexican Americans come close to parity with Anglos in the craft category.* A little over 18 percent of the Spanish-surname males in the urban Southwest were craft workers as compared with 21.5 percent of their Anglo counterparts and only 10.8 percent of the nonwhites (Table 9–2). The nearly equal representation of Mexican Americans in the craft category holds for Texas as well as California. Average earnings in craft occupations are relatively high and labor union organization is relatively well developed. As will be seen in the next chapter, however, this broad occupational class, as well as others, masks important differences in the types of jobs held by Spanish-surname and Anglo workers.

Though the Spanish-surname group has become about as urbanized as the rest of the Southwest population in terms of residence, this is not true for occupation. Even in urban areas a comparatively large proportion of Mexican-American males are employed as farm laborers. In 1960, over 7 per cent were in this type of work as against 0.6 percent for Anglos and 2.1 percent for nonwhites. This disproportionate dependence on agricultural work tends to depress the group's earnings in cities. In many cities of the Southwest, one can observe Mexican-American neighborhoods where "urban" dwellings are no better than rural shacks. These are usually occupied by migrant farm workers who have an urban base and may find only occasional urban employment between agricultural seasons. Phoenix, Bakersfield, and Fresno are examples of larger metropolitan areas which contain such neighborhoods. In 1960, males in farm labor accounted for 45 percent of all employed Mexican-Ameri-can men in Fresno, 44 percent in Phoenix, and 38 percent in Bakersfield. The large proportion of farm workers in urban areas reflects in part the inclusion of *braceros* in the 1960 census data. With the termination of the *bracero* program in 1964, the percentage of agricultural laborers who reside in cities may have declined.

Less than 10 percent of all employed Mexican-American females were in domes-tic service in the urban Southwest as against 33 percent for nonwhites. This type of work has only in recent years become more important for Spanish-surname women, especially young single women. As was already mentioned, cultural factors and the numerous children in Mexican-American families probably have worked against domestic service. So has the language barrier.

Index of Occupational Position

This index provides a single figure for assessing the overall occupational stand-ing of a population group. Technically, the index measures the average value of all occupations held by Mexican Americans and Anglos, the value of each occupation being represented by the average earnings of all workers employed in it. Table 9–5 shows the *ratios* of Spanish-surname occupational indexes to the Anglo indexes.

The indexes and ratios based on "state earnings" are apporpriate for comparing the occupational positions of Mexican–American and Anglo males within each state. In this comparison Mexican Americans have the best relative standing in California and the worst in Texas. The ratio of the Mexican-American to Anglo positions ranges from .84 in California to .77 in Texas.

For purposes of interstate comparisons one must recognize that there are interstate differences in occupational earnings relationships, as well as in occupational distributions of employment. For example, the 1959 median earnings of laborers were

Table 9–5. Occupational Position of Spanish-surname and Anglo Employed Urban Males, Five Southwest States, 1960

Indexes of Occupational Position[a]

| | STATE EARNINGS[b] | | CALIFORNIA EARNINGS[b] | | RATIO OF SPANISH-SURNAME TO ANGLO | |
State	Anglo	Spanish-surname	Anglo	Spanish-surname	State Earnings	California Earnings
Arizona	50.7	40.4	58.6	48.2	.80	.82
California	58.8	49.5	58.8	49.5	.84	.84
Colorado	51.0	42.3	58.9	49.3	.83	.84
New Mexico	52.1	42.7	60.8	52.0	.82	.86
Texas	46.6	36.0	59.3	49.4	.77	.83

[a] The computation form for all indexes computed with state occupational earnings was $\Sigma_i(X_iY_i)/100$ where X_i is the proportion of employed males (either Spanish-surname or Anglo) in the ith occupational category and Y_i is the corresponding 1959 earnings of experienced male workers. This calculation was performed for each state with its own X_i and Y_i. Calculations with the California earnings were identical in form except that the same (California) Y_i was used for all five states.
[b] See text for explanation for the use of two sets of earnings.
Source: Walter Fogel, *op. cit.,* table 14.

35 percent of the median earnings of professional persons in Texas but 52 percent in California. As a consequence, the relative value assigned to laborers, an occupation with an unusually large percentage of Mexican Americans, is smaller in Texas than in California. This difference would cause the relative position of Spanish-surname persons to be lower in Texas even if the proportions of Mexican Americans employed in the laborer and professional groups were the same in each state. To isolate interstate differences resulting solely from variances in occupational distributions, a single set of occupational earnings must be used. California occupational earnings were selected for this purpose.

On this basis, the standing of Mexican Americans relative to Anglos varies little from state to state. The ratio ranges from .86 in New Mexico to .82 in Arizona. It is highest in New Mexico, where the Spanish-surname group has the best representation in white-collar work, and lowest in Arizona, where relatively large numbers of urban Mexican Americans are employed in farm work. And the difference between California and Texas is substantially narrowed. Thus, the relative occupational position of Mexican Americans is better in California than in Texas, but mainly for the reason that in California the earnings in occupations employing many Mexican Americans are higher relative to earnings in occupations where few Mexican Americans are employed. The actual occupational distributions of Spanish-surname persons in comparison to Anglos are essentially the same in both states. It may be added that

213

a corresponding calculation for urban males in the Southwest as a whole resulted in a ratio of .84 for Mexican Americans and .82 for nonwhites, with Anglos standing at 1.00*

On the whole, the occupational experience of Mexican Americans has been far more favorable than their income experience. The difference can be shown by using their relative occupational position to adjust their relative income—in other words, by taking into account the influence of low occupational distribution on income.[5] This rough adjustment removes only about half of the income difference between Mexican Americans and Anglos in Arizona and Colorado, and just one-third in New Mexico and Texas (Table 9–6). The adjustment removes about two-thirds of the difference in California. In other words, their poor occupational position does not fully "explain" the low incomes of Mexican Americans any more than their deficient educational preparation accounted fully for income differentials.

Table 9–6. Income Ratios and Indexes of Occupational Position for Spanish-surname Urban Males, Five Southwest States, 1960

State	Income Ratio[a]	Occupational Position[b]	Adjusted Income Ratio[c]
Arizona	.68	.80	.85
California	.79	.84	.94
Colorado	.69	.83	.83
New Mexico	.59	.82	.72
Texas	.50	.77	.65

[a] From Table 8–4.
[b] Table 9-5, State earnings.
[c] Income ratio divided by occupational position. See note 5 for explanation of the procedure.

Ordinarily one would expect a closer association between the income and the occupational status of a population group. There are two main reasons for the lower association in this case. First, each of the major occupational categories used in the analysis is composed of many different jobs, which vary a great deal in the earnings they provide. As will be shown in the next chapter, Mexican Americans are concentrated in the lower-wage jobs of most of the occupational categories. Second, Mexican Americans tend to earn less than Anglos even when they hold comparable jobs in the same occupational class; Spanish-surname workers are likely to be clustered in industries which provide unsteady employment and in the low-wage firms even in the same industry.

The analysis could be extended to see how the occupational standing of Mexican Americans is related to their schooling. Again, one could standardize the occupational distributions for difference in educational attainment, as was done with respect to income in Chapter 8. However, such an effort would lead us too far afield. It suffices

*These ratios are based on California earnings weights, because earnings for males in the Southwest are not provided by the census.

214

to say here that, in general, schooling explains only part of the inferior occupational position of Mexican Americans, though a larger part than in the case of nonwhites. The unfavorable occupational patterns of both groups result in considerable measure from factors not associated with education.[6]

MEXICAN AMERICANS IN BUSINESS

In the white-collar occupations, Mexican Americans are greatly under-represented among managers and proprietors (or, to use the exact Census term, "managers, officials, and proprietors except farm"). Only 4.9 percent of the Spanish-surname males employed in the urban Southwest were in this category, as against 14.7 percent of Anglos—a ratio of one to three. Yet, economic advancement in business does not depend as clearly on educational achievement as it does in professional work, in which Mexican Americans are equally under-represented (4.6 percent of urban males as against 15.1 percent for Anglos). Historically, entrepreneurship has enabled some of the immigrant groups to make extraordinary progress despite poor schooling. Few of the original founders of some now well-known construction firms or department stores spoke proper or even adequate English. They possessed other abilities that compensated for the lack of formal education.

On field tours for this study we attempted to identify, through our informants, those Mexican Americans in a locality who were "big" businessmen or rich. Relatively few Mexican Americans, given their total numbers, were designated as being in that class—for example, the owner of interests in a television station and other enterprises in Los Angeles, and a family operating a department store in Tucson. Further investigation showed that some of the persons identified ranked in these categories by the standards of the Mexican-American community, but not on general U. S. standards—for example, owners of medium-size tortilla factories or of small real estate brokerage firms. Also, only in recent years were a Mexican-American (though not exclusively ethnic) bank and a savings and loan association established in Los Angeles, with its metropolitan Spanish-surname population of nearly 630,000 (in 1960). To our knowledge, none exist elsewhere. Nor is there a Mexican-American life insurance company, although the Southwest market would seem to provide a sufficient business base. The mutual-benefit type of insurance organization, which has a long history in the Spanish-surname population, is now quite insignificant as a financial institution. In some of the Southwest cities, the credit union has attracted many members of the group. However, the credit unions with large Mexican-American membership usually owe their origin to churches or other external initiators.

Nonwhites in the Southwest show still greater under-representation in business and management occupations than do Mexican Americans (3.6 percent), and this percentage would be even lower for Negroes alone. The Chinese and Japanese have exhibited greater taste or talent for business entrepreneurship and management.

Interestingly, there are quite a few wealthy Mexican Americans among professional persons, such as physicians or attorneys, who have acquired wealth through part-time business and investment activities as well as through their regular occupation. There seem to be more rich men among the professional people than among the businessmen. This situation has its counterpart among Negroes.[7]

One can only speculate about the reasons why so relatively few Mexican Americans have moved into the business occupations. Business itself has changed a great deal since the days when it had offered great opportunities to some immigrant groups. The amount of working capital necessary to start or expand a firm has increased, so that it has become more difficult to enter business with small family savings. Mexican Americans (as well as Negroes) claim that they have had less access to credit (though we have no evidence to that effect). All these factors may combine to prevent businesses originally oriented to an ethnic clientele from breaking out of this limited environment. Further, occupational opportunities in business have tended in the direction of salaried management positions. Formal schooling standards militate against any appreciable number of Mexican Americans obtaining this type of job. In any event, since business is the major vehicle for capital formation, the poor representation of Mexican Americans has meant slow accumulation of wealth that could benefit the group as a whole through internal support of educational, political, and welfare activities.

IMPROVEMENT

IN THE OCCUPATIONAL STRUCTURE

Whether Mexican Americans have improved their occupational standing over time will be examined by reference to urban males in California and Texas, the two states that account for the vast majority of the group's labor force. The data in Table 9–7 reveal slow progress between 1950 and 1960. The percentage of Spanish-surname men in white-collar work increased slightly, the percentage employed in low-skill manual occupations declined, and the all-inclusive occupational indexes show some improvement relative to Anglos. The few available data for nonwhites indicate a slow rate of progress for that group as well.

The 1950–1960 changes, of course, provide only a view of short-term progress. Have there been *long-run* improvements in the relative occupational standing of Mexican Americans? Fortunately, some data are available for answering this question; and they are indeed instructive, for they show how much the advancement of a disadvantaged minority depends on high rates of economic growth. Table 9–8 presents indexes of occupational position for 1930 as well as 1950 and 1960. (Because of limitations of the 1930 data, the indexes for all of the three benchmark years refer to males in urban and rural areas combined, and differ, therefore, from the previous urban indexes for 1950 and 1960.) The data show considerable progress between 1930 and 1950 in California but not in Texas.

In the absence of comparable information for the decade of the thirties alone, one can safely assume little if any occupational upgrading of Spanish-surname workers during the Great Depression. This assumption is supported by research about nonwhites.[8] Thus, what appears as progress between 1930 and 1950 is wholly, or nearly so, a function of the great expansion in employment during the war decade.

Table 9–7. Indicators of Changes in Occupational Structure, Spanish-surname Urban Males Compared with Others, 1950 and 1960

	ANGLO		SPANISH-SURNAME		NONWHITE	
	1950	1960	1950	1960	1950	1960
California						
Percent white collar[a]	n.a.	46.3	16.8	18.8	n.a.	23.7
Percent low skill[a]	n.a.	26.7	64.6	56.6	n.a.	51.4
Occupational index[b]	58.6	58.8	47.7	49.5	45.9	48.2
Ratio of index[c]	—	—	.81	.84	.78	.82
Texas						
Percent white collar[a]	47.4	47.8	17.7	19.0	9.7	10.3
Percent low skill[a]	27.5	25.1	63.3	57.2	80.9	72.0
Occupational index[b]	46.3	46.6	34.2	36.0	28.0	30.6
Ratio of index[c]	—	—	.74	.77	.60	.66

[a] Number of persons in white-collar or low-skill occupations as a percent of all employed persons in each population group.
[b] Index of occupational position computed in the form described in Table 9–5. To obtain the Anglo index for 1950, the occupational distribution of urban nonwhites was estimated from their occupational distribution in urban and rural areas combined.
[c] Spanish-surname or nonwhite to Anglo.
Sources: For percent white collar and low skill in 1960: see tables 9–3 and 9–4. For 1950: *1950 U.S. Census of Population*, vol. II, parts 5 and 43, table 77, and PE no. 3C, table 6. For occupational indexes: Walter Fogel, *op. cit.*, Table 22.

Labor shortages were so great that discrimination in hiring and upgrading was sharply reduced; job qualification standards, especially with regard to formal schooling, were substantially relaxed. This is indeed the recorded experience of Negroes.[9]

The California data in Table 9–8 support these observations. The occupational position of Spanish-surname males improved greatly relative to Anglos between

Table 9–8. Indexes of Occupational Position, Spanish-surname and Anglo Males, California and Texas, 1930, 1950, and 1960[a]

	CALIFORNIA			TEXAS		
Population Group	1930	1950	1960	1930	1950	1960
Spanish-surname (1)	35.8	43.3	46.9	23.8	28.8	33.0
Anglo (2)	53.3	56.6	57.9	34.7	41.5	43.9
Ratio (1)/(2) (3)	.67	.77	.81	.69	.69	.75

[a] Based on gainful workers, age 10 and over for 1930; and on the employed, age 14 and over for 1950 and 1960. Occupational earnings for 1959 in the respective states were used to compute the indexes, as in previous tables.
Source: Walter Fogel, *op. cit.*, table 26.

1930 and 1950, which really means the war years. California, of course, was one of the great centers of war production, and labor market pressures in the state were extremely high.[10] In comparison with the war period, occupational progress of Mexican

Americans from 1950 to 1960 proceeded at a much slower pace. The ratio of the Spanish-surname to the Anglo index of occupational position increased by only 4 percentage points as against 10 in the previous period.

The experience in Texas was quite different. The data show no *relative* improvement for Mexican Americans between 1930 and 1950 in spite of the war years, and moderate improvement in the decade of the 1950s, comparable to that in California. The apparent absence of war effects is not easy to explain. The 1930–1950 figures may mask declines in the relative occupational standing of Mexican Americans during the Depression years and offsetting gains during the 1940s. Also, labor market pressures during World War II were much more moderate in Texas than in California. Increases in employment were smaller, and a large agricultural labor surplus provided a ready increment to the industrial labor supply.[11]

Table 9–9. Occupational Distribution of Spanish-surname Urban Males 35 to 44 Years of Age, by Nativity Class, Southwest, 1960 (Percent of all employed males in each nativity class)

Occupational Category	Foreign-born	Native of Foreign or Mixed Parents	Native of Native Parents
Professional	5.0	5.1	6.5
Managerial	4.5	5.9	7.0
Clerical	3.2	5.6	5.8
Sales	2.8	3.8	3.7
Craft	19.4	24.6	22.3
Operative	24.2	28.3	24.0
Service	7.7	6.5	7.1
Laborer	16.7	14.2	12.2
Farm labor	13.6	3.6	2.5
Farm manager	0.6	0.5	0.4
Not reported	2.3	1.9	8.5
	100.0	100.0	100.0

Source: *1960 U.S. Census of Population*, PC (2)–1B, table 8.

In the 1950s Mexican Americans in Texas did achieve a gain in their comparative occupational position even though employment in the state did not expand as much as in the previous decade. The gain occurred because Mexican Americans moved out of farm jobs as rapidly as the rest of the population. Agricultural employment in Texas continued its decline in this decade (150,000 jobs were eliminated), but now Mexican Americans participated in this decline proportionately. At the same time, Mexican Americans in the nonagricultural sector increased their representation in operative and craft jobs and, to a lesser extent, in white-collar occupations.

As in the case of income, we can also trace progress through intergenerational differences in occupational standing, or a cross-section analysis for 1960 of Spanish-surname persons by nativity. This is done in Table 9–9 for urban males in the Southwest, but with data limited to one age group so as to remove as best we can the possible distortions resulting from age differentials between the three nativity classes.

The native born show an occupational position clearly superior to the foreign born. A larger percentage of the natives were engaged in white-collar work and in craft employment. A considerably smaller percentage held farm-labor jobs, and a moderately smaller proportion were in the laborer category. Here again, the evidence of progression from the natives of foreign parentage to the natives of native parentage is equivocal. Substantial gains are apparent in the professional and managerial categories, but not in craft employment, which is generally a well-paid occupation, nor in the "operative" group. The percentage of natives of native birth in farm and nonfarm labor jobs is somewhat smaller than for the second generation, which is also a sign of progress. The data are difficult to interpret because an unusually large proportion of the natives of native parentage did not report their occupation. But we are inclined to conclude that the occupational data are broadly consistent with the information on income. As indicated in Chapter 8, income failed to show clear evidence of progress between the two native-born groups.

The statistics for California conform to the findings for the Southwest as a whole in every respect. Indeed, they have considerable weight in producing the total Southwest figures. The Texas experience is once again quite different. On the whole, native status in Texas is accompanied by few benefits of occupational upgrading, just as it failed to produce the substantial income gains observed in other states relative to the foreign born.[12]

The occupational standing of persons of Mexican foreign stock in the Southwest was greatly inferior to that of the entire foreign stock in the United States in 1960. The index of occupational position was 33.1 for Mexican-born males as against 48.7 for all foreign-born males, and 42.0 for the native born of Mexican parentage as against 50.1 for all natives of foreign parentage.[13] Moreover, the 1950 census data for the metropolitan areas of Chicago, Los Angeles, and San Francisco show Mexican Americans of foreign stock holding the lowest occupational position of six major nationality groups (no such data exist for 1960).[14] Of course, these are contemporary comparisons for periods when many European immigrants had the education and training to enable them to move rapidly into good jobs. The recent occupational position of the Mexican foreign stock is probably closer to the Europeans' position around the turn of the century.

MEXICAN-AMERICAN EMPLOYMENT

IN VARIOUS INDUSTRIES

One can hypothesize that the representation of Mexican Americans in a given industry would depend on some salient characteristics of that industry. This is a matter of more than theoretical interest. If policies directed at equal employment opportunities are to be more effective, it is of strategic importance to discern the types of industries that are more likely to keep out members of minority groups and to focus remedial efforts on those.

One of the salient characteristics of an industry is the extent and type of *unionization*. Industries where employment hinges on union-administered entry restrictions are especially relevant from this viewpoint. The case *par excellence* is the craft union in the construction industry. It is frequently alleged that craft unions in construction (as well as in other industries) discriminate against members of minority groups by refusing to select them for apprenticeships or failing to admit them to the unions when they possess journeyman skills. That Mexican Americans as well as Negroes have been poorly represented in apprenticeship programs, though they are heavily represented among construction laborers, seems to be borne out by data for California.[15]

The influence of craft unions on the employment representation of Mexican Americans can be discerned by contrasting *construction* with *manufacturing* in California and Texas. Construction craftsmen are extensively organized in craft unions in California and, to a far lesser degree, in Texas. Membership in each union is limited to those skilled in the work traditionally associated with a specific craft. Some craftsmen in manufacturing industries are also members of craft unions, but others belong to industrial unions, which include a variety of workers; and still others, employed mainly in small firms, are not members of any union. Thus, if the charge of discrimination by construction craft unions was true, Mexican Americans would be more poorly represented in this industry than in manufacturing. The comparison of employment representation in Table 9–10 is limited to the same crafts in these two sectors of the economy. Hence the argument that Mexican Americans do not possess the necessary skills is irrelevant.

Table 9–10. Spanish-surname Proportions of Employment in Selected Craft Occupations, California and Texas, 1960
(Percent of all employed males)

Occupation	CALIFORNIA		TEXAS	
	Construction	Manufacturing	Construction	Manufacturing
Carpenters	5.8	8.0	11.3	11.3
Electricians	3.0	5.3	6.6	2.9
Mechanics	5.0	7.5	9.1	6.1
Plumbers	5.5	6.8	11.0	4.3
Sheet-metal workers	8.2	9.9	7.9	7.6
Apprentices	9.3	10.4	12.4	11.0

Source: Walter Fogel, *op. cit.*, Table 53.

Table 9–10 shows the data for six craft jobs in which at least 100 Mexican Americans were employed in both construction and manufacturing in 1960. In California, Mexican-American employment in these jobs was noticeably less frequent in construction than in manufacturing. The reverse was true in Texas. The results for Texas are probably affected by less extensive unionization of the construction industry, so that access of Mexican Americans to jobs cannot be restricted by union practices. These findings give some support to the hypothesis of craft-union discrimination in California, though the evidence is hardly conclusive.

One can establish a number of hypotheses about the influence of *other industry characteristics* on the representation of Mexican-American workers in the labor force of industries. The first hypothesis relates to the size of firms. Employers in small firms may be more willing to hire Mexican Americans because they are able to meet *all* their labor requirements with them. Large firms cannot do so; their Anglo employees may object to work contacts with Mexican Americans. If this reasoning is correct, Mexican Americans will be employed more frequently in industries wherein most firms are small. Second, we may hypothesize that firms enjoying a monopolistic or oligopolistic position find it easier to provide the high wages and fringe benefits that attract a labor supply large enough to enable them to avoid hiring minority workers if they wish to do so, and that firms in the more competitive industries cannot afford this practice. Finally, one can advance a hypothesis related to the previous ones—that Mexican-American employment by industry, as by occupation, is inversely related to levels of earnings. This correlation suggests itself because high wages are associated with large firms and, as was noted, with quasi-monopoly in an industry's product markets.

We can report the results of a statistical investigation of these hypotheses, which is described in detail elsewhere.[16] The analysis was performed for specific occupations in a number of manufacturing industries so that the general level of skill required for employment was held constant. Otherwise, one would merely find that Mexican Americans were most frequently employed in industries where low-skill jobs were relatively numerous, a conclusion already suggested by previous analysis.

As for the size of firm, the evidence confirms the hypothesis that large firms tend to employ a lower proportion of Mexican Americans, especially in such positions as salaried managers, foremen, and engineers. These occupations usually involve the supervision of others. It is a matter of common observation that Anglo tastes are stronger against being *supervised* by minority persons than against working with them as *peers*. In large establishments it is more difficult to limit supervisory relationships to subordinates of the same ethnic group. Besides, management and similar positions in large firms often require a higher level of education.

As for the influence of an industry's competitive structure, Mexican-American workers are more poorly represented in firms that enjoy considerable market power than in businesses that are more competitive. The communications industry, where telephone companies loom large, is a case in point. Even though most firms in the industry are publicly regulated, they hold quasi-monopolistic positions.

But the clearest association is between the relative employment of Mexican Americans and average earnings in an industry. In multivariate analysis with the three variables of firm size, industry competitiveness, and average earnings, the only statistically significant correlations were between earnings and Mexican-American employment in the clerical, craft, foreman, and operative occupations. No significant association was found for laborers. Mexican Americans are probably of such numerical importance in this occupation that even high-wage industries cannot avoid drawing them into employment.

MEXICAN AMERICANS IN GOVERNMENT JOBS

The position of Mexican Americans in public employment warrants special attention—if for no other reason than because the Federal government and most of the state and local governments have at least formally adopted nondiscriminatory policies. These policies have been in effect for some time. To the extent that labor-market discrimination is a barrier to jobs and promotion in the private sector but less prevalent in the public sector, then, members of minority groups should find government employment more attractive. Besides, government is one of the strongest growth industries in this country.

We present, first, 1960 census data on male employees in California, New Mexico, and Texas for all levels of government and, second, more recent information on Mexican Americans in Federal civilian service. The 1960 data may be somewhat obsolete, because government agencies have lowered barriers to the employment of members of minorities since that time. But, as will be seen, the more up-to-date figures on *Federal* jobs confirm the salient findings drawn from the 1960 census data on *all* government jobs.

The 1960 employment representation of Mexican-American males in the public sector shows large variations among the three states included in Table 9–11. Relative to their share in total employment, they are greatly under-represented in California and slightly over-represented in Texas and New Mexico. In the latter state, nearly 30 percent of all government employees are Spanish-surname people. Public employment in all three states has one common characteristic: *The position of Mexican Americans in educational services is generally poorer than in other government work.*

When the various occupations are considered, government employment in California shows substantial under-representation of Mexican-American males in non-manual occupations (as does the private sector) and in manual occupations (the opposite of the private sector). In Texas and New Mexico, the employment share of Spanish-surname males in the public sector exceeds their share in total employment for both manual and non-manual occupations.

Table 9–12 offers further insight into public employment. Among other things, it shows Federal versus state and local government jobs and a comparison of Spanish-surname persons with nonwhites and Negroes. In both California and Texas, the representation of Mexican Americans in Federal administrative jobs is far higher than in state and local governments or in public school systems (which are, of course, under local jurisdiction). In New Mexico, the situation is reversed, although Spanish-surname persons account for 40 percent of the postal service employees in the state.

Here again, the contrast between California and Texas is of special interest. Relative to the employed labor force, Mexican Americans in California are substantially under-represented in all government categories, while Negroes are consistently over-represented, especially in Federal administrative jobs and in the postal service. In Texas, the better over-all position of Mexican Americans in public employment is the result mainly of their large share in Federal administrative jobs. The pattern for

Texas Negroes is more mixed. Relative to the employed labor force, they are over-represented in the postal service and public education but under-represented in Federal and especially state and local administration.

The differences between California and Texas are difficult to explain without further research. The minimum standards of schooling required for most government jobs cannot account for the contrast. As was shown in Chapter 7, the average

Table 9–11. Spanish-surname Males as a Percent of All Male Employees in Government Jobs of Various Types Compared with Their Share in Total Employment, California, Texas, and New Mexico, 1960

OCCUPATIONAL CATEGORY	PUBLIC ADMINISTRATION[a]	PUBLIC EDUCATION	TOTAL PUBLIC	PRIVATE AND PUBLIC
California				
All occupations	5.2	3.7	4.7	8.7
Professional	3.4	2.8	3.0	2.9
Managerial	3.2	1.4	3.1	3.8
Clerical	4.7	4.4	4.6	5.8
Craft	6.9	4.2	6.5	7.0
Craft foremen	7.6	2.3	5.0	6.5
Operative	10.5	6.5	10.1	12.7
Services	4.0	6.2	4.6	8.6
Laborer	11.8	7.9	11.0	26.3
Texas				
All occupations	15.6	7.9	13.4	12.2
Professional	7.0	4.3	5.2	3.9
Managerial	6.5	2.0	6.2	4.9
Clerical	12.4	7.2	12.2	8.9
Craft	26.1	10.5	24.0	10.4
Craft foremen	14.9	1.6	13.3	5.7
Operative	36.5	10.7	34.4	14.9
Services	11.3	19.4	13.6	15.7
Laborer	40.3	24.5	38.5	32.2
New Mexico				
All occupations	31.4	25.9	29.8	24.0
Professional	13.3	19.7	16.8	10.9
Managerial	22.0	4.9[b]	20.8	12.0
Clerical	36.4	20.6[b]	35.8	26.4
Craft	30.3	34.2	30.7	20.0
Craft foremen	30.2	23.1[b]	29.5	14.8
Operative	47.5	23.6[b]	45.2	27.6
Services	44.5	50.6	46.3	42.9
Laborer	62.7	48.3[b]	60.6	50.4

[a] Includes postal service but excludes government educational services.
[b] Based on a small number (less than 100 Mexican Americans).
Source: 1960 U.S. Census of Population, vol. I, parts 6, 33, and 45, table 125, and special census tabulations for Spanish-surname persons.

educational attainment of Mexican Americans is lower in Texas than in California, and the same is true for nonwhites. If the advantage of Negroes over Spanish-surname persons in formal schooling were an important factor, it should have helped Negroes obtain a larger share of government employment in Texas as well as California. Nor can it be said that Mexican Americans are more heavily concentrated in low-wage public jobs in Texas than in California (Table 9–11).

A partial explanation may be the geographic concentration of Mexican Americans in south Texas and of Negroes in other sections of the state.* Thus, the large military installations near San Antonio draw mainly on the Spanish-surname rather than on the Negro minority for jobs. There is no comparable geographic division of the two minorities in California. Also, qualification standards—mainly educational—are possibly higher for state and local government jobs in California than in Texas. As a result, Mexican Americans in California may find it more difficult to obtain such jobs. Finally, the over-representation of Mexican Americans in the public sector in Texas

Table 9–12. Spanish-surname, Nonwhite, and Negro Males in Government Jobs as a Percent of All Male Employees in Such Jobs, by Categories, California, Texas, and New Mexico, 1960

CATEGORY	SPANISH-SURNAME	NONWHITE	NEGRO
	California		
All employment	8.7	7.2	4.5
Public administration	5.2	11.2	8.7
Postal service	4.9	20.6	16.9
Federal public administration	6.2	12.0	9.0
State and local public administration	4.4	6.8	5.2
Public education	3.7	5.4	8.9
	Texas		
All employment	12.2	10.5	10.3
Public administration	6.2	6.2	6.1
Postal service	8.0	12.5	12.4
Federal public administration	23.7	5.7	5.5
State and local public administration	9.9	3.8	3.8
Public education	7.9	12.2	12.0
	New Mexico		
All employment	24.0	4.3	1.3
Public administration	31.5	4.4	.05[a]
Postal service	40.1	1.2	.05[a]
Federal public administration	25.8	5.9	.05[a]
State and local public administration	40.4	2.5	.05[a]
Public education	25.9	2.9	.05[a]

[a] Relatively small numbers.
Source: 1960 U.S. Census of Population, vol. I, parts 6, 33, and 45, tables 129 and 130, with special census tabulations of Spanish-surname data.

may be due to strong discrimination against them in the private sector, which would make government employment relatively more attractive than in California. Indeed, it has been said that Mexican Americans in California are not eager to seek government jobs.[17] If so, this attitude may reflect their expectation of equally good or better prospects in the private sector.

*This geographic division is indeed reflected in the data on public employment in various metropolitan areas of Texas. For example, El Paso and San Antonio show very large shares of Mexican Americans in all government jobs—48 percent and 38 percent, respectively—and relatively insignificant employment of nonwhites. In contrast, Dallas, Houston, and Beaumont–Port Arthur show large shares of nonwhites in all government jobs and relatively insignificant employment of Mexican Americans.

The more recent information on *Federal* employment pertains to both males and females. Mexican Americans in 1966 accounted for one-tenth of all Federal employees in the Southwest. This was in line with their 1960 share in the total labor force (Table 9–13). Negroes also accounted for 10 percent of all Federal employees in the region, but their share in the 1960 labor force was only 7.2 percent. Their representation in Federal government jobs was better than their share in the total labor force.

Table 9–13. Spanish-surname Persons and Negroes Employed by the Federal Government Compared with Their Share in the Total Labor Force, Five Southwest States, 1966

Area and State	SPANISH-SURNAME			NEGRO		
	Number[a]	Percent of Federal Employees[b]	Percent of Labor Force[c]	Number[a]	Percent of Federal Employees[b]	Percent of Labor Force[c]
Southwest	46,414	10.0	9.9	47,292	10.2	7.2
Arizona	1,958	8.9	13.5	637	2.9	3.2
California	11,626	4.7	8.2	32,795	13.3	5.4
Colorado	3,833	9.9	6.7	2,390	6.2	2.2
New Mexico	6,561	26.6	23.7	420	1.7	1.8
Texas	22,436	17.0	11.9	11,050	8.4	12.3

[a] "Identified employees." The numbers fall short of totals to the extent that the ethnic or racial background of a relatively small number of persons could not be identified. For example, 8.2 percent of all Federal employees in the Southwest could not be so identified.
[b] The percent figures in these columns represent Mexican Americans or Negroes as a percent of all Federal employees.
[c] Sum of males in civilian labor force and females in total labor force, from the 1960 census.
Source: *Minority Group Employment in the Federal Government,* U.S. Civil Service Commission, 1967. The Commission's 1968 report for the year 1967 is not used here for comparison because it shifted from a voluntary self-identification technique to visual identification by supervisors. Changes between 1966 and 1967 are therefore difficult to interpret. However, the broad relationships shown in the table hold for 1967 as well.

Among the states, California in 1966 as well as in 1960 showed the greatest under-representation of Mexican Americans in Federal government jobs, and Texas (as well as New Mexico and Colorado) considerable over-representation. Federal agencies in Texas employed about twice as many Mexican Americans as those in California. Federal employment of Negroes in these two states was the reverse of Mexican-American employment. Federal offices and installations in California employed nearly three Negroes for every Mexican American. Those in Texas had about two Mexican Americans on jobs for every Negro. Thus, the more recent data on the Federal sector are broadly consistent with the findings for all levels of government in 1960.

In confirmation of the earlier census data, the Federal jobs of Mexican Americans in the Southwest in 1966 were clustered in blue-collar work. Nearly 54 percent of all jobs held by Mexican Americans were in this class, a little over 29 percent in white-collar employment, 16 percent in the postal field service, and less than 1 percent in the remaining category "all other." Comparable figures for Negroes in the Southwest show a more favorable distribution: only 43 percent in blue-collar work and 28 percent each in white-collar and postal service jobs. In each type of Federal employment, moreover, Mexican Americans were clustered in the low-pay classes. Their representation fades out as pay scales go up (as does that of Negroes).[18]

SUMMARY

In sum, the labor force participation rate of Mexican Americans in the Southwest was somewhat lower than that of the majority population. Their unemployment rate in 1960 was substantially above the Anglo rate though slightly less than for nonwhites. These differentials seem to be continuous, although their magnitude will vary with economic conditions. Together, Mexican Americans and Negroes in the Southwest represent a large portion of the reservoir of labor that can be drawn into jobs in periods of economic expansion and thrown out of work when business contracts. Mexican Americans and Negroes furnish much of the marginal supply of labor.

Marginality in this sense is closely associated with the occupational structure of the Spanish-surname group. The group is greatly over-represented in low-skill manual occupations, particularly in the laborer category, and greatly under-represented in white-collar occupations. The demand for low-skill manual workers is subject to sharp fluctuations.

The occupational distribution of Mexican Americans showed only moderate improvement between 1950 and 1960, but intergenerational progress has been substantial. The occupational structure of the native born is more favorable than that of the foreign born.

In the absence of data, one can only speculate about progress since 1960. In light of the somewhat better schooling record of young Mexican Americans compared to adults, one can assume that those who have entered the labor force since the last census included a larger proportion of persons qualified for better jobs. The fair employment practice committees or agencies may have played a role in diminishing discriminatory procedures in hiring and promotion. Although astonishingly few complaints have been brought to these organizations by Mexican Americans in comparison with Negroes, the mere existence of the agencies and their largely unrecorded, quiet efforts of persuasion may have had some beneficial effect. The same can be said for the enforcement of government rules against discrimination by defense contractors. Nevertheless, whatever improvement has occurred has probably been undramatic.

The legacies of the past cannot be eradicated easily. Their magnitude is illustrated by the large share of Mexican Americans and nonwhites in the total unskilled labor supply of the Southwest. *In 1960, male members of the two minorities together held 57 percent of all farm labor jobs and 43 percent of the nonfarm laborer jobs.* The proportions were even more extreme in Texas—61 percent and 58 percent, respectively. In the not too distant future, Mexican Americans and nonwhites may represent the vast majority of the unskilled labor supply in the Southwest as Anglos continue to move into more desirable occupations.

The demand for unskilled workers relative to the total demand for labor has been declining for some time. Simultaneously, the scramble for jobs of this type has been increasingly concentrated among members of the minorities. The combination of these circumstances presents a major economic dilemma for the Spanish-surname group and for the social stability of the Southwest as well. Americans have thought of their country as one of the few in the world without an identifiable proletariat as a *social class*, that is, a group of people who are and feel permanently relegated to poverty and whose expectations for their children are conditioned by this hopeless outlook. Regardless of the historical validity of this view, the problems posed by a continued existence of an *ethnic* proletariat will be particularly acute in the Southwest with its two disadvantaged minorities.

NOTES TO CHAPTER NINE

1. Chapters 9 and 10 are largely based on Walter Fogel, *Mexican Americans in Southwest Labor Markets* (Mexican-American Study Project, Advance Report 10, Graduate School of Business Administration, University of California, Los Angeles, Oct., 1967).

2. For state data on unemployed persons as a percent of the civilian labor force, see *1960 U.S. Census of Population*, vol. I, parts 4, 6, 7, 33, and 45, table 52; and PC(2)–1B, table 6. Our unemployment data refer only to urban areas. The census figures, the only ones available for intergroup comparison, are for April, 1960. Unemployment rates for a single month may not be representative of unemployment experience over a longer period. This is true especially for labor in rural areas where seasonal variations are pronounced. In addition, the inclusion of *braceros* in census statistics tends to distort the unemployment rates in agriculture. Seasonal influences on farm work even affect the urban unemployment data for Mexican Americans because the percentage of urban residents in this group who work in agriculture is larger than that of the rest of the population. Although the 1960 statistics are out of date, we believe that they reflect continuous structural relationships. The 1950 data show unemployment differentials consistent with those of 1960. Cf. *1950 U.S. Census of Population*, vol. II, parts 5 and 43, table 25; and P-E no. 3C, table 3.

3. Recent research has shown that labor force participation in the United States is inversely related to unemployment rates. See Kenneth Strand and Thomas Dernburg, "Cyclical Variations in Civilian Labor Force Participation," *Review of Economics and Statistics*, XLVI (Nov., 1964), pp. 378–391; and W. G. Bowen and T. A. Finegan, "Labor Force Participation and Unemployment," in A. M. Ross (ed.), *Employment Policy and the Labor Market* (Berkeley, Calif.: University of California Press, 1965), pp. 115–161.

4. *1960 U.S. Census of Population*, vol. I, part 6, table 143, and PC(2)–1B, table 5; also vol. I, Part 6, table 130, and special tabulation of Spanish-surname persons in California, table 130.

5. This adjustment is possible because the indexes of occupational position for each state measure the extent to which the inferior occupational distributions of Mexican Americans cause their earnings to be below those of Anglos. One can approximate an adjustment for the effects of the inferior occupational distributions by dividing the relative income figures by the indexes of occupational position. If, for example, the relative occupational position of Mexican Americans is 80, their average earnings can be adjusted for the effects of their low occupational standing by multiplying average earnings by 1/.80, or 1.25. This procedure provides only a rough adjustment because the occupational indexes are computed with

earnings instead of income valuations, and because the occupational earnings are those for all males instead of Mexican-American males.

6. See Walter Fogel, "The Effects of Low Educational Attainment and Discrimination on the Occupational Status of Minorities," in *The Education and Training of Racial Minorities*, Conference Proceedings of the Center for Studies in Vocational and Technical Education, University of Wisconsin (May 12, 1967).

7. See E. Franklin Frazier, *Black Bourgeoisie* (New York: Collier Books, 1962), especially chap. 11. For a broader discussion of Negroes in business, see Robert H. Kinzer and Edward Sagarin, *The Negro in American Business* (New York: Greenberg: Publishers, Inc., 1950), and Nathan Glazer and Daniel Patrick Moynihan, *Beyond the Melting Pot* (Cambridge, Mass: The M.I.T. Press, 1963).

8. See, for example, Dale Hiestand, *Economic Growth and Employment: Opportunities for Minorities* (New York: Columbia University Press, 1964), chap. 3.

9. *Ibid.*; also, Robert C. Weaver, *Negro Labor* (New York: Harcourt, Brace and Co., 1946), chaps. 7 and 11.

10. During the 1940s, 1.3 million nonagricultural jobs were added in California, and nonagricultural employment increased by nearly 70 percent. Perhaps even more important, almost all the jobs were added in a very short period, between January 1941 and mid-1943. See *Estimated Number of Wage and Salary Workers in Nonagricultural Establishments by Industry, California, January 1939–December 1962*, California Department of Industrial Relations (San Francisco, February, 1963).

11. Total employment in Texas between 1940 and 1950 increased by 30 percent. Nonagricultural employment rose by 57 percent, but this gain was accompanied by a decline of about 200,000 agricultural jobs. Anglos shifted from rural to urban jobs much faster than did Mexican Americans. For more detail, see Fogel, *Mexican Americans in Southwest Labor Markets*, chapter 4, especially p. 72.

12. For state figures for Spanish-surname urban males 35 to 44 years of age, by nativity status, see *1960 U.S. Census of Population*, PC(2)–1B, table 8.

13. Fogel, *Mexican Americans in Southwest Labor Markets*, table 36.

14. *Ibid.*, table 37.

15. For apprenticeship programs, see *Survey of Completed Apprentices*, State of California, Division of Apprenticeship Standards (undated, *ca.* 1962). Mexican-American representation in apprenticeship programs increased in recent years in California. An article by Harry Bernstein in *The Los Angeles Times*, April 29, 1969, quoted the California Director of Industrial Relations as saying that the proportion of Mexican Americans to all active apprentices rose from 8.1 percent in 1967 to 8.8 percent in 1968; the proportion of Negroes rose from 2.5 percent to 3.9 percent. Between 1965 and 1967, however, the proportion of the two minorities had declined.

16. For a more complete statement of the hypotheses and the statistical investigation, see Fogel, *Mexican Americans in Southwest Labor Markets*, pp. 130-136. This source also provides references to the literature.

17. *Proceedings of the Employment Opportunities Education Conference*, Council of Mexican-American Affairs, Los Angeles, Cal. (1962), pp. 25, 26.

18. See *Minority Group Employment in the Federal Government*, U.S. Civil Service Commission (1967).

TEN

Jobs and Earnings

THE unfavorable occupational structure of Mexican Americans, discussed in the preceding chapter, does not fully express their differential position in labor markets. The occupational categories analyzed so far are extremely broad. For example, the professional class ranges from surgeons to medical technicians, the managerial category from the president of a large corporation to the manager of a small restaurant; craftsmen include tool and die makers, whose earnings are relatively high, as well as bakers, whose wages are much lower. The fact is that Mexican Americans tend to hold inferior jobs within almost every major occupational group, and that their earnings are often low relative to those of Anglos in the *same* occupations and jobs. The present chapter will explore in some depth these aspects of the Mexican Americans' standing in labor markets.

229

MEXICAN AMERICANS HOLD THE POORER JOBS

The unfavorable job distributions of Mexican Americans within the major occupational categories are clearly shown in a more detailed classification of occupations from special census tabulations.* Strictly speaking, these are occupational subgroups. For the sake of simplicity we refer to them as "jobs" or "job positions" although these terms often denote an even more specific set of tasks.

Statistical measures of the job positions held by Mexican-American and Anglo males are presented in Table 10–1 for seven major occupational classes for which

Table 10–1. Job Positions within Major Occupations: Indexes for Spanish-surname and Negro Employed Males as Proportions of Anglo Indexes[a], California and Texas, 1960

Occupational Category	SPANISH-SURNAME		NEGRO	
	California	Texas	California	Texas[b]
Professional	.95	.91	.89	.79
Managers and proprietors	.97	.93	.95	.90
Sales	.94	.87	.86	.85
Craft	.98	.91	.95	.88
Operative	.99	.88	.97	.87
Service	.87	.83	.83	.78
Laborer	1.03	.99	1.07	1.06

[a] The computation form for the indexes is the same as described in Table 9–5. State earnings in California and Texas were used for the calculations. The data are not adjusted for differences in age distributions. Such adjustments would be unlikely to change the results significantly. Further, data limitations make it necessary to present indexes for urban and rural males combined. This expedient has probably only minor effects on the job-position indexes included in the table.
[b] Nonwhite population, which is 98 percent Negro, was used in the index computation for Texas.
Source: Walter Fogel, *Mexican Americans in Southwest Labor Markets* (Mexican-American Study Project, Advance Report 10, Graduate School of Business Administration, University of California, Los Angeles, October, 1967), table 46.

sufficient detail was available. In both California and Texas the jobs of Spanish-surname persons are clearly inferior in the white-collar occupations. This reflects the fact, for example, that Mexican Americans in the professional and technical groups are better represented among draftsmen than among architects, among technicians than engineers, among social workers than physicians and lawyers. In the case of managers and proprietors, they are somewhat better represented among self-employed than among salaried persons. Many of the self-employed Mexican Americans are owners of small business firms catering to ethnic communities. Interestingly, the only subgroup of managers whose representation is on a par with Anglos is found in eating and drinking places. People in the Southwest are fond of Mexican food.

The job positions of Mexican Americans in the craft and operative occupations

*For the major occupational categories, see Appendix F, "Note on Occupational Classifications." More detailed census classifications were published for 1960 for the general population, but not for Spanish-surname persons. The latter were obtained for this study through special census tabulations. The tabulations show 150 occupations which in the Census Bureau terminology are intermediate classifications. The 1960 census also provides data for over 400 "detailed" occupational groups. However, this much detail would add little of value to our analysis.

come close to par in California but not in Texas. As for craftsmen, the group is well represented among masons, painters, plasterers, and bakers but not among foremen, electricians, stationary engineers, boilermakers, and tool and die makers. They are greatly under-represented in both California and Texas in such unionized jobs as railroad engineer and fireman and among telephone and telegraph linemen or foremen, despite the fact that the latter jobs are largely free of the influence of union-administered entry restrictions.

In the case of operatives, employment of Mexican Americans is comparatively low in the aircraft, paper, and chemical and petroleum industries, all of which provide well-above-average earnings for this occupational class. It is comparatively high in the furniture, apparel, and textile industries, which pay relatively low wages, and in stone, clay and glass-products manufacture. Relatively large numbers of Mexican Americans are employed as laundry workers, taxi and truck drivers, and packers and wrappers, which are for the most part low-wage jobs.

In service work, the index of job positions for the Spanish-surname group is low in both states—in fact, the lowest among the seven occupational categories. This class includes a great deal of government as well as private employment. On investigation it turns out that the low job positions of Mexican Americans in this class are largely caused by great under-representation in fire and police protection, which pay much better salaries than other service jobs. Their representation in this public sector is better in Texas than in California, possibly because the high proportion of Mexican Americans in some Texas cities results in policies that facilitate their entry into the police and fire departments.

Turning to laborers, we find that the job position of Mexican Americans is nearly on a par with Anglos in Texas and above par in California. The group is well represented in almost all jobs in this low-wage category. Some of the differences in Spanish-surname and Anglo representation probably reflect historical factors. For example, much of the earliest industrial employment of Mexican Americans was on the railroads. In 1960, they still supplied 46 percent of the laborers in this industry in California and 32 percent in Texas.

On the whole, the job position of Spanish-surname males within each major occupation is substantially worse in Texas than in California. The same is true for Negroes. Moreover, Negro job positions are consistently below those of Spanish-surname males in both states, with the one exception of laborers. Negro job positions are especially low in the professional, sales, and service occupations.

HIRING IN THE MANUAL SECTOR

In 1960, Mexican-American males in the urban Southwest held 7 percent of the craft jobs, 13 percent of the operative jobs, and 18 percent of the laborer jobs. The rank order is inverse to earnings in these occupations. Why is it that the lower the pay the greater the Mexican-American representation even in the manual sector? The poor educational attainment of the group provides part of the answer, especially when the quality as well as the years of schooling is considered and the language barrier comes into account. But this explanation is more plausible for non-manual occupations, many of which have very high schooling requirements. In the manual sector, formal education for the most part is not importantly related to job performance because the skills used in manual work are usually not learned in school.[1] The low representation of Mexican Americans in the better-paid manual occupations seems to be associated with the fact that hiring regulations often require job applicants to have more education than the job really calls for. We shall briefly examine job selection procedures to illustrate this point.

The procedure of obtaining a job has been compared to a queuing process where each prospective worker gets in line for the highest paying and otherwise most desirable job that he has a reasonable chance of acquiring.[2] Employers move down the queues, selecting those people who they think will perform best. Workers not chosen for the most desirable jobs must then get in line for the lower-paying and less desirable ones until they are selected for employment. By the nature of this process, employers seeking manual workers for high-wage jobs (and unions controlling entry to such occupations) usually can choose from an ample supply of applicants. The employers' selection problem for high-wage manual jobs thus becomes one of reducing the numbers of applicants to manageable size.[3] In the view of many employers, the most efficient criterion for this purpose has come to be the amount of schooling, frequently a high-school diploma. This is the case not because of a direct *causal* connection between completion of high school and job performance, but rather because employers believe that a high-school diploma increases the probability that an applicant possesses other characteristics related to job performance, such as motivation, perseverance, and stability.

The application of a gross schooling requirement to job queues eliminates a higher proportion of Mexican-American than Anglo applicants and results in a low representation of members of the minority in high-wage manual employment. Consequently, most Mexican Americans must descend the job-wage hierarchy and seek low-wage jobs. Many do not bother to try for those with high earnings because the educational barriers to employment become rather quickly known. In low-wage job queues their schooling compares more favorably with that of Anglos who have been unable to obtain higher-wage positions, and they comprise larger proportions of all applicants. Thus, Mexican-American representation is greater in the low-paying jobs.

Mexican Americans may also be under-represented in high-wage employment because discrimination against hiring them is more acute in these jobs. If employers wish to avoid hiring Mexican Americans or unions wish to exclude them from membership, it is easier to do so in occupations where they are a small fraction of the labor supply. In this respect, the imposition of schooling requirements works hand in

---

[1] Notes for this chapter start on page 246.

glove with a desire to discriminate. Where educational standards are established as employment prerequisites, they eliminate more Mexican Americans than Anglos and thus simplify discrimination.

Using high-school graduation as a prediction of job performance involves the assumption that success in the world of work requires the same personal responses and adaptations as are required for success, or at least perseverance, in the school. It seems that this assumption has never been adequately tested. It is perhaps too much to ask employers to abruptly eliminate schooling requirements in hiring for jobs in which schooling may be of tangential importance. These requirements no doubt eliminate more poor job risks than they let through. In view of the current concern with the disadvantaged status of minorities, however, it would not be unreasonable to ask employers to devote some resources to developing selection procedures that are better predictors of adequate job performance and to apply these to all applicants for work in which schooling requirements are not clearly relevant. Very likely, it would be in the employers' own long-run interest to do so.

We have examined the effects upon Mexican-American employment in 33 craft jobs of differences in schooling actually needed for successful *performance* as distinguished from school requirements for *selection* which have been imposed by employers and unions.[4] Estimates were made of the average school years actually required for successful performance in these 33 jobs. The schooling requisites and the annual job earnings of Anglos were used as independent variables in a linear, least-squares regression analysis to explain the Mexican-American share of employment. Partial correlations of these variables with the Spanish-surname percentage of male employment in California and Texas are given below.

	School requisites	1959 earnings of workers without Spanish surname	
California	−.12	−.47	R^2−.22
Texas	.03	−.63	R^2−.40

Anglo earnings are statistically significant (at the one-percent level) for both states; school requirements are not. The variation in the representation of Mexican Americans in craft jobs is not a function of the schooling necessary to perform these jobs, but it is importantly related to job earnings. Estimates of the schooling necessary for successful performance on operative and laborer jobs could not be obtained. It is unlikely, however, that school requirements have greater influence on Mexican-American employment in these types of jobs than in craft occupations. Simple correlation analysis does show a statistically significant relationship between the proportion of jobs held by Mexican Americans and the job earnings of non-Mexicans for operatives as well as craftsmen (Table 10–2). Thus, the level of earnings is an important factor in determining the Mexican-American share of employment in craft and operative occupations.* Presumably, the earnings variable operates through

*The relationship between employment shares and the level of earnings lends itself to conflicting interpretations. Causality can be considered to be the opposite of the one stated above, i.e., a high Mexican-American share of employment produces low job earnings. For this interpretation, applied to nonwhites, see

the selection process that relegates Mexican Americans more often than Anglos to low-wage jobs in such occupations.

These facts allow an *inference of discrimination*. Mexican-American chances for high-wage manual employment are low because employers give great weight to schooling in the selection of workers for such jobs, even when there is no evidence that the amount of schooling is positively related to performance. This emphasis on formal schooling works against all who are under-educated, but it bears more heavily on minority groups with a disproportionate number of poorly schooled persons—Mexican Americans as well as Negroes.[5]

Table 10–2. *Simple Correlation Coefficients Between Relative Employment of Spanish-surname Males and Annual Earnings of All Other Males in Job Classifications Within Selected Major Occupation Groups, California and Texas, 1960*

	Craftsmen	Operatives	Laborers
California	−.46[a]	−.32[b]	−.27
Texas	−.63[a]	−.60[a]	−.20
Number of Job Classifications	33	42	22

[a] Significant at 1% level.
[b] Significant at 5% level.
Source: Walter Fogel, *op. cit.*, Table 48.

In contrast to the craft and operative groups, employment of Spanish-surname people in laborer jobs does not vary inversely with the earnings that these jobs provide (Table 10–2). It appears that Mexican Americans have equitable access to jobs in this sector. Here, their low educational preparation does not work against them, because schooling requirements are infrequent and would defy common sense. Laborer jobs are at the bottom of the occupational hierarchy, and the supply of high-school graduates for such jobs is not sufficient to permit employers to use the high-school diploma as a screening device. Moreover, employers are less able to discriminate in hiring for laborer jobs because Mexican Americans (and Negroes) constitute large proportions of the unskilled labor supply. The premium wages required to employ only Anglos on such jobs would be excessive, even for employers who would not be otherwise averse to discriminating.

Robert and Patricia Hodge, "Occupational Assimilation as a Competitive Process," *The American Journal of Sociology*, vol. LXXI, no. 3 (November, 1965), pp. 249–264. The analysis of the Hodges implies that white workers in all jobs (within each major occupational category) would have the same earnings (after educational attainment is controlled) if the minority share of employment were the same in all jobs; variation in the minority share of employment causes variation in white earnings. This view of wage determination is not defensible. It seems more realistic to assume, as we do, that minority persons are over-represented on low-wage jobs because the low wages do not attract enough Anglos; and employers, therefore, turn to the minority groups. For further discussion, see Alma F. Taeuber, Karl E. Taeuber, and Glen G. Cain, "Occupational Assimilation and the Competitive Process: A Reanalysis" and the comment by the Hodges in *The American Journal of Sociology*, vol. LXXII, no. 3 (November, 1966), pp. 273–289.

LOW RELATIVE EARNINGS

IN IDENTICAL OCCUPATIONS AND JOBS

Since the Spanish-surname males tend to hold the poorer jobs in nearly all major occupational categories, one would expect them to earn less than Anglos in each occupation. This is indeed the case, as shown by the unadjusted data in Table 10–3. Mexican Americans in California and Texas had lower 1959 earnings than Anglos in all categories except laborers in California. Generally, they obtained the best relative earnings if they were employed as clerks, craftsmen, or operatives, and the poorest if they were managers, sales persons, and farm laborers.

Table 10–3. Occupational Earnings Ratios,
Unadjusted and Adjusted for Differences in Job Positions,
Spanish-surname to Anglo Males,[a] 1959

OCCUPATIONAL CATEGORY	CALIFORNIA	TEXAS	LOS ANGELES–LONG BEACH	SAN ANTONIO
		Unadjusted		
Professional	.84	.60	.82	.72
Managers and proprietors	.80	.59	.75	.58
Clerical	.89	.71	.87	.82
Sales	.83	.53	.85	.49
Craft	.89	.64	.87	.73
Operative	.88	.58	.87	.78
Service except private household	.81	.62	.78	.55
Laborer	1.03	.83	1.15	1.11
Farm Labor	.62	.73	.44	.70
		Adjusted[b]		
Professional	.88	.66	.87	.78
Managers and proprietors	.82	.63	.78	.62
Sales	.88	.61	.90	.56
Craft	.91	.70	.90	.76
Operative	.89	.66	.89	.80
Service	.93	.75	.93	.63
Laborer	1.00	.84	1.07	1.09

[a] Experienced males in the labor force with earnings in 1959. The figures have not been standardized for age; in most cases standardization would have a negligible effect.
[b] Adjusted data obtained from dividing unadjusted ratios by the appropriate figures in Table 10–1. Earnings of persons employed in the clerical and farm occupations could not be adjusted because the job detail available for these categories was not sufficient to justify computation of job positions. In this regard, it should be recognized that the procedure described in the text does not completely adjust Mexican-American occupational earnings for job differences between Mexican Americans and Anglos. To make a full adjustment, one would need employment and earnings data for the hundreds of different work activities that are included within each job classification. Instead, we have used only the "intermediate occupational classification" of the census. Nevertheless, earnings variations within jobs—that is, narrow classifications—logically would seem to be less than the variations existing within broad major occupations. Hence, only a small part of the complete job distribution effect on occupational earnings fails to be reflected in our adjustment procedure. It also seems likely that Mexican Americans are more evenly distributed on work activities within a job classification than on jobs within an occupation.
Source: Walter Fogel, *op. cit.*, Table 54.

After our previous analyses, it is not astonishing to find that relative occupational earnings of Mexican Americans were much lower in Texas than in California. However, the earnings ratios for San Antonio are somewhat larger than for all Texas. The difference suggests that the poor experience in the state as a whole is partly the result of the concentration of this ethnic population in south Texas, where wages are lower than in the rest of the state. But even in San Antonio, the largest metropolitan area in south Texas, earnings ratios of Mexican Americans are lower than in California. In contrast, the California and the Los Angeles ratios are quite similar.

The main part of the analysis relates to the "adjusted" data in Table 10–3. The low relative earnings of Mexican Americans in each major occupation could be solely a function of their over-representation in the poorer jobs, which was already described. It could also be caused by lower earnings in the same or similar jobs. The adjustment makes it possible to separate these factors. The resulting figures indicate how Mexican-American earnings in the respective occupations would compare with Anglos if the proportion of Mexican Americans and Anglos in each job within the occupation were the same.*

Except for laborers, the adjusted earning ratios are larger than the unadjusted ratios. For the most part, however, the differences between the two sets of figures are small. Adjustment of Mexican Americans' relative occupational earnings for the effects of low-job positions reduces the differences in earnings between Anglos and Mexican Americans by rather small amounts. This means that the low earnings of the minority group in most occupations are not so much a result of over-representation on low-wage jobs as of receiving less pay for similar kinds of work. The implications of this conclusion will be discussed shortly.

Managers and sales workers show the poorest (adjusted) earnings of Mexican Americans relative to Anglos. Both occupations require a great deal of verbal communication for purposes of direction or persuasion. This requirement works against those Mexican Americans whose English is inadequate if their clients or subordinates are Anglos. It also works against Mexican Americans if Anglo subordinates resent work contacts with them. Thus, most members of the group are limited to *low-wage* manager and sales positions. One indication of this tendency is the higher incidence of managerial self-employment among Mexican Americans. Half of all Mexican-American managers in both Los Angeles and San Antonio are self-employed, in contrast to one-third of Anglo managers. Self-employed managers earn less than those who work for a salary because so many of the former are dependent upon income from small neighborhood businesses.

The relative earnings of Mexican Americans in the craft group are not significantly higher than those in other occupations. Yet, most craft jobs are extensively organized by unions which attempt to establish a standard wage within metropolitan labor markets or at least a narrow range of rates for all persons employed in each craft

---

*As for the adjustment method, Table 10–1 presents measures of Spanish-surname job positions relative to Anglos within major occupational categories. These measures were derived from indexes (or weighted averages) of job earnings for Mexican Americans and Anglos where the numbers in each group who were employed on each job were used to weight the corresponding annual earnings of all males. Thus, the differences between the Mexican-American index (expressed as a proportion of the Anglo index) and unity provide estimates of the extent to which Mexican Americans have lower earnings in an occupation because of their inability to obtain as much employment in high-wage jobs as do Anglos (job distribution differences). These estimates are used to adjust the ratios shown in the first part of Table 10–3 for the earnings effect of differences in job distributions.

job. Their failure to succeed in this goal is made apparent by the substantial differ‑
ces in earnings of Mexican-American and Anglo craftsmen. If all Mexican-American
craftsmen were employed in unionized establishments they would receive the union
wage, and their earnings would be equal or very close to those of Anglo craftsmen
(unless there were substantial variation in wage rates among unionized establish‑
ments). That this is not the case must be due largely to greater nonunion employ‑
ment among Mexican Americans.

The largest relative earnings are obtained by Mexican Americans in the lowest-
paid occupations—the laborer and service groups. The large relative earnings of
Mexican-American laborers are consistent with the high job position of Mexican
Americans in the laborer group (Table 10–1). If Mexican Americans have access to all
laborer classifications, it is likely that they also have access to high-wage as well as
low-wage employers for these jobs. Spanish-surname persons have comparatively
good access to high-wage employers in service work, except for police and fire
departments.

Generally, then, it appears that within major occupations Mexican Americans
receive lower earnings than Anglos in large part because they work more frequently
for low-wage employers. Nonwhite–Anglo earnings ratios show the same tendency.[6]

HYPOTHESES ABOUT LOW EARNINGS

IN COMPARABLE JOBS

The foregoing discussion suggests a number of hypotheses that may help explain
the low relative job earnings of Mexican Americans. If these hypotheses are valid,
they will enlarge our understanding of the problems to be overcome and the directions
to be taken in surmounting them. Each hypothesis will be examined at least partially
against empirical data in order to see whether the available facts are consistent with
the proposition. For this purpose we use mainly the more detailed job classifications
rather than the major occupations.

1. *Ethnic job dependence is associated with lower relative earnings.* One would
expect the earnings of Mexican Americans relative to Anglos to be lower in job
classifications where Mexican Americans depend upon their own group for em‑
ployment. At first this proposition may seem self-evident, but this is not the case.
Highly competitive labor markets will produce similar earnings for Spanish-surname
persons and Anglos even if most of the former are employed in the Mexican-Ameri‑
can community, as long as their mobility to Anglo firms or to firms with Anglo
customers is not restricted. At the other extreme, in markets where wage controls are
imposed through a union or occupational association, Mexican-American and Anglo
earnings will be similar regardless of the employer's or the clientele's ethnicity. There‑
fore, the proposition should be examined against actual experience. A finding of low
relative earnings in ethnically dependent jobs would imply that there are restrictions

237

on the mobility of Mexican Americans within and between local labor markets because of inferior qualifications, residential segregation, problems of transportation between place of residence and place of employment, or job discrimination.

Some empirical evidence is presented in Table 10–4. Spanish-surname employment in the jobs listed in the table is believed to be heavily dependent upon the Mexican-American community. The hypothesis is confirmed for Texas. In that state, most of the earnings ratios for the ethnically dependent jobs are below the average earnings ratios for all jobs in like occupations. The findings for California are more

Table 10–4. Earnings Ratios for Ethnically Dependent Jobs and Their Major Occupational Categories, Spanish-surname Males to All Other Males,[a] California and Texas, 1959

JOB	JOB EARNINGS RATIO	AVERAGE JOB EARNINGS RATIO FOR MAJOR OCCUPATIONAL CATEGORY[b]
	California	
Clergymen	.74	.93 (professional)
Musicians	.66	.93 ,,
Managers, self-employed		
Construction	.84	.84 (managers)
Manufacturing	.64	.84 ,,
Wholesale trade	.81	.84 ,,
Retail trade	.85	.84 ,,
Insurance agents	.89	.91 (Sales)
Real-estate brokers	.99	.91 ,,
Barbers	.98	.99 (service)
	Texas	
Clergymen	.78	.83 (professional)
Musicians	.38	.83 ,,
Managers, self-employed		
Construction	.58	.65 (managers)
Manufacturing	.65	.65 ,,
Wholesale trade	.47	.65 ,,
Retail trade	.60	.65 ,,
Insurance agents	.72	.70 (sales)
Real-estate brokers	.89	.70 ,,
Barbers	.73	.83 (service)

[a] Based on experienced workers in the labor force.
[b] Unweighted average of job earnings for all jobs in the major occupational category. shown in parenthesis.
Source: Walter Fogel, op. cit., Table 55.

equivocal. This may mean that Mexican Americans employed in these occupations in California are, in fact, not primarily dependent upon their own group for their livelihood, i.e., that their local labor-market mobility in this state is greater than in Texas.

In general, it does appear that Mexican Americans employed in jobs dependent upon their community have lower-than-average earnings ratios. Interestingly, a major exception in both California and Texas is the real-estate broker. The large relative earnings of Mexican-American real-estate agents seem to be associated with their relative scarcity in this field. In both states the proportion of Spanish-surname brokers to all brokers in 1960 was only about one-fourth the proportion of Mexican Americans in the total population. While the record of local real-estate boards in restricting entry of Mexican Americans is mixed, exclusionary practices may in fact have helped to raise the relative earnings of those who are admitted. Another exception is the Mexican-American barber in California, due probably to the minimum prices prescribed by the state licensing agency as well as to mobility of barbers between Anglo and minority establishments.

Support for the "ethnically dependent job" hypothesis comes also from the San Antonio data in Table 10-3. The relative earnings of Mexican Americans in service and sales jobs are lower there than in Texas as a whole. In most other occupational categories, the reverse is true. For managers, the earnings ratios are about the same in the state and the city. In San Antonio, service and sales persons as well as managers are in all likelihood heavily dependent on the Mexican-American community, which in 1960 accounted for 40 percent of the total metropolitan population.

The findings on ethnic job dependence have a larger implication. Some leaders of ethnic or racial minorities advocate a kind of self-sufficient economic system in the hope that it will raise the material welfare of the minority people faster. Ignoring other aspects of the proposition (especially the crucial matter of capital), the evidence on relative earnings, though not entirely clear-cut, serves to question the expectation of greater gains through self-sufficiency.

2. *Wage standardization is associated with high relative earnings.* One would expect the relative earnings of Mexican Americans to be larger than average in job classifications where wage rates are highly standardized.* In these cases, the standard wage rates apply to minority-group workers as to all others, so that Mexican-American earnings would be close to those of Anglos. The jobs listed in Table 10-5 were selected to examine this hypothesis. A high degree of wage standardization is believed to exist in each, either because workers employed in these jobs are extensively unionized or because they work chiefly for large employers.

The California data support the hypothesis. The earnings ratios in most of the jobs listed are larger than those for the major occupations to which the jobs belong. They are also larger than the average earnings ratios in *all* job classifications for which the Census furnishes data. Less support is provided by the Texas data; even so, 10 of 16 job earnings ratios equal or exceed the ratios of the major occupation. Weak unions in Texas may partially account for the low Mexican-American earnings in

---

*Wage standardization—payment of the same wage rate to all persons employed in a job classification—occurs when the labor market for a job includes large institutions which do most of the hiring or strongly influence hiring practices. Trade unions, especially those which consider their appropriate jurisdiction for wage bargaining to include all jobs in a market area rather than just the jobs in a particular bargaining unit, are frequently able to negotiate a wage rate which applies generally to persons working in an occupation. Medium and large-size business firms and government agencies can effect the same result through formal wage administration which provides the same or similar wages to all persons in these organizations who are doing similar work; where a few such organizations employ most members of an occupation, a high degree of market wage uniformity results. Wage standardization will not be as great in job markets where hiring is not concentrated in a few firms and is not strongly influenced by union standardization policies.[7]

some of the craft jobs. Also, Texas is less urbanized and has less large-scale industry than California, so that wage standardization is probably not as prevalent. (It may be noted that intra-state wage differentials do not importantly influence our findings; data for San Antonio, which are not presented here, provide results similar to those for Texas.)

In both states Mexican-American earnings in government jobs—officials and inspectors, mail carriers, firemen and policemen—are comparatively large. This lends

Table 10–5. Earnings Ratios for Standardized Jobs and Their Major Occupational Categories, Spanish-surname Males to All Other Males,[a] California and Texas, 1959

| | CALIFORNIA | | TEXAS | |
Job	Job Earnings Ratio	Job Earnings Ratio in Major Occupational Category[b]	Job Earnings Ratio	Job Earnings Ratio in Major Occupational Category[b]
Engineers, Civil	.97	.93 (professional)	.82	.82
Pharmacists	1.04	,,	.82	,,
Teachers				
Elementary	.97	,,	.78	,,
Secondary	.92	,,	.79	,,
Technicians				
Medical	1.01	,,	.78	,,
Electrical	1.01	,,	.97	,,
Officials and inspectors, state and local gov't.	.88	.84 (manager)	.80	.65
Mail carriers	.96	.90[c] (clerical)	.96	.72[c]
Boilermakers	.94	.92 (craft)	.70	.76
Electricians	.92	,,	.83	,,
Locomotive engineers	.81	,,	—	—
Locomotive firemen	.96	,,	—	—
Plumbers and pipe fitters	.92	,,	.65	.76
Apprentices	1.00	.90 (operative)	.86	.77
Bus drivers	.92	,,	.89	,,
Firemen	.98	.99 (service)	.86	.83
Policemen	.97	,,	.90	,,
Longshoremen	1.00	.97 (laborer)	.74	.89
Earnings Ratios for all jobs (152)[b]	.92		.79	—

[a] Based on experienced workers in the labor force.
[b] Unweighted average of earnings ratios for all jobs in the major occupational category shown in parenthesis.
[c] Ratio for total clerical category; the average ratio for the three job classifications which are available is not meaningful
Source: Walter Fogel, op. cit., Table 56.

significant support for the standardization hypothesis. Wages for comparable work in government service are more uniform than in private industry.

3. *Wage standardization is also associated with low minority-group employment.* There is a corollary to the proposition that Mexican Americans' relative earnings will be large in markets dominated by wage standardization: A high degree of wage standardization will also bring under-representation of Mexican Americans in employment. Standard wages and salaries are almost always accompanied by a set of formal requirements which job applicants must meet to be hired.[8] When earnings are

standardized within a job market, employee qualifications will also be standardized or will at least be adequate to meet educational and other prerequisites for employment. Civil service occupations are outstanding examples of this dual standardization. Civil service employment ensures equal earnings for equal work (holding length of service constant), but to obtain it an applicant must meet a number of formal requirements which pertain to educational attainment, citizenship, and various kinds of knowledge and aptitude. Procedures for private jobs strongly influenced by union practices are different, but the results are often similar.

Table 10–6. Spanish-surname Proportions of Total Male Employment in Jobs with Standardized Wages and Their Major Occupational Categories, Males, California and Texas, 1959

	CALIFORNIA		TEXAS	
Job	Percent of Employment	Percent of Employment in Major Occupation	Percent of Employment	Percent of Employment in Major Occupation
Engineers, civil	2.9	2.9 (professional)	3.7	3.9
Pharmacists	2.5	,,	6.6	,,
Teachers				
Elementary	3.8	,,	9.8	,,
Secondary	3.0	,,	3.3	,,
Technicians				
Medical	4.2	,,	13.8	,,
Electrical	4.0	,,	5.1	,,
Officials and inspectors, state and local gov't.	2.7	3.1 (manager)	5.3	4.7
Mail carriers	4.8	5.8 (clerical)	7.3	9.1
Boilermakers	6.9	7.0 (craft)	4.1	10.6
Electricians	4.4	,,	7.6	,,
Locomotive engineers	1.2	,,	1.9	,,
Locomotive firemen	3.2	,,	1.0	,,
Plumbers and pipe fitters	5.6	,,	10.4	,,
Apprentices	10.3	12.7 (operative)	16.5	15.1
Bus drivers	4.4	,,	10.0	,,
Firemen[a]	4.1	8.7 (service)	9.0	15.9
Policemen[a]	3.4	,,	6.7	,,
Longshoremen	15.7	18.2 (laborer)	9.2	25.6
Spanish-surname percentage of all employment	8.8		12.6	

[a] Qualifications for the fire and police jobs are substantially higher than those for other jobs in the service category; for that reason Mexican-American representation in these two jobs is well below their representation in service employment as a whole. Therefore, Mexican-American representation in total employment is given at the bottom of the table to provide a more meaningful reference, in terms of the hypothesis, for fire and police employment.
Source: Walter Fogel, *op. cit.*, Table 57.

As mentioned in other contexts, the effects of formal requirements for job selection are greater on Mexican Americans than on Anglos. Mexican Americans have less schooling, many have limited command of English, and some are not United States citizens. Their performance on some tests may be adversely affected by the tests' culture orientation, which to a greater or lesser degree is strange to them. Hence, it is hypothesized that Mexican Americans will be under-represented in job markets characterized by wage standardization. This hypothesis is examined in Table 10–6 by reference to the same jobs used previously to test the effects of wage standardization. The table shows comparisons between Mexican-American proportions of employment in jobs and in the major occupational categories which comprise the jobs. In most cases, these comparisons involve similar work activities, so they are not affected by worker qualification differences between the job and its major occupational category.

The table lists 16 jobs for both California and Texas. In only 10 of the 32 possible cases are Mexican Americans better represented in the standardized jobs than in the relevant major occupations. In several of these ten, the qualifications required for the job may be less than the average qualifications required for the major occupation. Only in four jobs is the Spanish-surname proportion of employment larger than their proportion of all employment in California or Texas, even though half the jobs are in the manual sector where the group generally is best represented. Thus, the data lend support to the view that wage standardization has an adverse impact upon the Mexican-American share in employment. *Mexican Americans enjoy the benefits of standardized wages at the price of low employment representation in jobs paying these better wages.*

This finding points up a familiar dilemma. Mexican Americans are most likely to obtain relative equality of earnings in *structured* job markets where wage-rate dispersion is slight. Thus, they have an interest in promoting wage standardization through unionization, government legislation, or industrial concentration. But their chances of employment in structured markets are slim, and, as a result, their rate of improvement in occupational position slows down.[9] As Mexican Americans who have no access to employment in structured markets swell the ranks of job applicants in unstructured markets, unemployment in the latter is increased or wages are depressed.[10]

The assurance of wage equity for those who benefit from wage standardization may be worth the costs imposed on those who do not. However, minority groups bear a disproportionate part of these costs. Hence recent government programs have placed great emphasis on schooling and on job training so that everyone can obtain the formal qualifications necessary for employment in an increasingly structured labor market. At this writing, the question whether such programs will be reasonably effective for disadvantaged minorities, and if so how fast, is yet unsettled.

4. *Earnings ratios vary with the relative supply of Mexican-American labor.* Still another factor bearing on the earnings ratios of Mexican Americans (and other disadvantaged minority groups) could be the relative supply of labor they provide in a job market. Earnings ratios would be high where Mexican Americans represented a large portion of the supply and low where they accounted for a small portion. This hypothesis rests on the premise that it costs employers more money to discriminate against Mexican Americans when they are a large fraction of the labor supply. If employers attempted to avoid hiring Mexican Americans in job markets where minority members are relatively numerous, they would face a greatly reduced supply of

labor from which they must recruit workers. Thus, the wage of Anglo workers would rise sharply. The premium wage necessary to maintain an all-Anglo work force would be greater for most employers than the nonpecuniary costs (psychic or social discomfort) of employing Mexican Americans. Under these conditions, Mexican Americans would be employed by all or most firms in labor markets where they make up a large part of the labor supply, and their earnings would compare favorably with those of Anglos.

In labor markets with few Mexican Americans, most employers could maintain an all-Anglo work force if they chose to do so. In such markets, many employers

Table 10–7. Relative Earnings of Spanish-surname Males and Employment Representation of Spanish-surname and Nonwhite Males, by Occupation, 1960

OCCUPATION	SPANISH-SURNAME RELATIVE EARNINGS[a]	PERCENT OF TOTAL EMPLOYMENT SS[b]	SS AND NW[b]	SPANISH-SURNAME RELATIVE EARNINGS[a]	PERCENT OF TOTAL EMPLOYMENT SS[b]	SS AND NW[b]
	California			Los Angeles		
Professional	.88	2.9	6.9	.87	3.2	7.6
Managerial	.82	3.1	5.8	.78	2.9	5.5
Sales	.88	3.6	6.5	.90	3.4	6.4
Craft	.91	7.0	11.3	.90	7.7	12.0
Operative	.89	12.7	20.7	.89	13.8	23.2
Services	.93	8.7	26.1	.93	8.9	28.2
Laborer	1.00	18.2	34.3	1.07	21.5	39.8
	Texas			San Antonio		
Professional	.66	3.9	7.4	.78	14.6	16.9
Managerial	.63	4.7	6.4	.62	13.9	16.2
Sales	.61	6.7	8.0	.56	20.1	20.7
Craft	.70	10.6	15.2	.76	37.8	41.9
Operative	.66	15.1	27.5	.80	54.0	61.9
Services	.75	15.9	50.0	.63	45.6	69.5
Laborer	.84	25.6	59.0	1.09	70.8	80.3

[a] Spanish-surname to Anglo, adjusted for differences between Spanish-surname and Anglo males in job position within each occupation.
[b] SS = Spanish surname; NW = nonwhite.
Source: Walter Fogel, *op. cit.*, Table 58.

would *not* accept Mexican Americans because they themselves or their Anglo workers or their customers might *not* be averse to discriminating against them. Even if employers were uncertain about the prejudices of their Anglo employees and customers, they would tend to avoid hiring Mexican Americans where their relative supply was small. Few employers in such markets could meet all of their labor requirements with Mexican Americans. Therefore, most would have to pay the prevailing Anglo wage to all workers and would be unable to lower labor costs by hiring Mexican Americans even if other workers and customers turned out to be unprejudiced. (This reasoning assumes that an employer will not establish one wage for Anglos and a lower one for Mexican Americans on the same job.) On the other hand, if Mexican Americans were hired and other workers and customers did turn out to have discriminatory inclinations, the employer would have to pay a premium wage to attract needed Anglo workers (or employ less qualified Anglo workers) and he would also experience the loss of some customers. Hence, in job markets where Mexican Americans compose a small fraction of the labor supply, they would turn to marginal or small employers for jobs. Because such employers offer wages that are unattractive to Anglos, they would hire members of the minority and, as a result, Mexican-American relative earnings would be low.

The available data lend only very limited support to the relative-supply hypothesis. This may be due in part to the difficulty of measuring the supply of Mexican-American labor as a part of total supply.*

A crude examination of the hypothesis is possible by using the Mexican-American proportion of employment in major occupational categories to represent the relative labor supply. Table 10–7 compares these employment proportions with Mexican-American occupational earnings ratios (standardized for job position so that the ratios are largely free of influence from qualification factors). Relative earnings are largest among laborers, where the Mexican-American proportion of employment is also greater than in any other occupation. The next largest relative earnings are in the service group (except in San Antonio). The Spanish-surname fraction of employment in this category is no higher than the Spanish-surname fraction of all employment. However, Mexican-American representation in service employment needs to be viewed together with the very heavy nonwhite representation. When both Mexican Americans and nonwhites are considered, the proportion of minority members among service workers is very substantial, second only to that among laborers. Relative earnings in all other occupations are below those for the service and laborer groups, and Mexican-American employment representation is also lower. In spite of this broad consistency of data with the hypothesis, it is evident that relative earnings for these other occupations do not vary in close conjunction with employment representation. If they did, relative earnings among professionals and craftsmen would be well below those among operatives instead of at approximately the same level.

Thus, it appears that a large proportion of the labor supply provided by Mexican Americans has a salutary effect on their relative earnings only in a very general

---

*Even if one uses the proportion of employment held by Mexican Americans as an imperfect but available surrogate for relative supply, the problem is not solved. The appropriate relative supply to most job classifications is the Mexican-American proportion of employment in the major occupation to which the job belongs, not the proportion of employment in the job classification itself. To illustrate, practically all laborers must be considered as the supply for each job classification in the laborer category, in the sense that almost all laborers are potentially mobile to all laborer jobs because the same skills (or lack of skills) apply to all jobs in the category. Therefore, variation in Mexican-American representation among the jobs in the laborer category must result from influences other than the relative size of the Mexican-American labor supply; the effect of this factor does not vary across the job classification. While skills are less transferable among jobs in the higher-skill occupations, they are sufficiently transferable for arguing that one cannot consider Mexican-American employment in a job classification as the total Mexican-American labor supply for that job.

sense—that is, among major occupational categories, and even there with important exceptions.

This analysis has focused on objectively verifiable factors associated with the low relative earnings of Mexican Americans in comparable occupations and jobs. Of course, job performance may involve factors other than those that are measurable. It is possible, though unlikely, that Mexican Americans as a *group* differ from Anglos on one or more of them, holding socioeconomic factors constant for both populations. In the absence of evidence, it would be exceedingly hazardous to make any sweeping generalizations about differences between Mexican Americans and Anglos in economic productivity.

SUMMARY

Mexican Americans hold inferior jobs in practically all of the major occupations, especially the more desirable ones. In the non-manual occupations, assignment to an inferior job generally results from inability to meet schooling requirements. In the manual occupations, the reason for such assignment is not so obvious. Mexican-American employment in manual jobs is uncorrelated with educational requirements for such employment but is positively correlated with job earnings. Mexican Americans are less likely to hold high-wage craft and operative jobs than Anglos either because fewer of them can meet the employee selection criteria (appropriate or not) which are used for these jobs or because they are the object of direct discrimination. Among industries it was found that Mexican-American employment varied negatively with firm size, degree of product market monopoly, and especially workers' earnings (Chapter 9). Again, it would seem that industry differences in employee-selection criteria are important in bringing about these relationships.

As for earning ratios, job dependency upon the Mexican-American community was an important depressing factor in Texas but less significant in California, where labor market mobility between the Anglo and ethnic sectors seems to be greater. Wage standardization results in more equal pay in similar jobs for Mexican Americans and Anglos. There is the other side of the coin to be noted, however: Relatively few Spanish-surname workers are employed in markets where wages are standardized. The data offered only moderate support for the thesis that the minority's relative earnings would be high in job markets for which Mexican Americans furnish a large percentage of the labor supply, and vice versa. More generally, low job earnings are also associated with the concentration of the Spanish-surname population in low-wage areas, the Lower Rio Grande Valley in Texas being a prime example.

In all probability, the factors considered here do not explain all of the variation in the relative job earnings of Mexican Americans. If data were available for multivariate analysis, one could perhaps more adequately sort out the many influences at work. Even then, however, it would be difficult to account for the elusive and variable taste for discrimination, which operates either in a random fashion on job markets or in systematic ways that are hard to identify. In those occupations and jobs where employers, workers, or consumers have strong tastes for discrimination, Mexican Americans will be under-represented in employment and be able to obtain jobs only in marginal firms and industries, at wages well below Anglo workers. Tastes for discrimination need not be currently pervasive to have an impact on employment and relative wages. It is only necessary that these tastes, past or present, have been projected into hiring practices of employers, admission practices of unions, or shopping habits of consumers.

Apart from tastes for discrimination, however, our analysis indicates that the employee selection system itself tends to depress Mexican-American wages in comparable jobs. The selection process consigns large numbers of Mexican Americans to highly competitive industries, to nonunion employers, and to small firms: Employment in these three types of businesses is characterized by low wage rates and, in many cases, by job insecurity. This allocation results largely from the rejection of Mexican-American job applicants by high-wage employers because the members of the group are unable to meet job-qualification standards. In turn, the standards have been imposed in many cases without reasonable regard for their relevance to performance in manual jobs. Such an allocation system would depress the position of Mexican Americans in the labor markets even if employers did not reject job applicants solely because of their ethnicity.

NOTES TO CHAPTER TEN

1. For a discussion of the acquisition of skills in the building trades, for example, see George Strauss, "Apprenticeship: An Evaluation of the Need," in Arthur Ross (ed.), *Employment Policy and the Labor Market* (Berkeley, Calif.: University of California Press, 1965), pp. 299–332.

2. See report of the National Commission on Technology, Automation and Economic Progress, *Technology and the American Economy* (Washington, D.C.: U.S. Government Printing Office, 1966), p. 23.

3. See Albert Rees, "Information Networks in Labor Markets," *Proceedings, American Economic Review*, LVI (May, 1966), p. 561.

4. Cf. James G. Scoville, "Education and Training Requirements for Occupations," *Review of Economics and Statistics*, XLVIII (Nov., 1966), pp. 387–394. Scoville used the "general educational development" requirements published in *Estimates of Worker Trait Requirements for 4,000 Jobs* (U.S. Department of Labor, 1958), assigned all of the 4,000 job titles to the 221 occupational classifications of the census, and computed the unweighted average of these requirements for each of the 221 classifications. Scoville's work provides a sufficient number of estimates of school requirements to permit an analysis for craft jobs but not for operative and laborer jobs. It is unlikely that school requirements have greater influence on Mexican-American employment in these jobs than in the craft category.

5. We must forego the opportunity to extend the analysis in this chapter to Negroes.

For some relevant comparisons, see Walter Fogel, *Mexican Americans in Southwest Labor Markets* (Mexican-American Study Project, Advance Report 10, Graduate School of Business Administration, University of California, Los Angeles, Oct., 1967), especially chapter 9.

6. *Ibid.*, Appendix A, table 4.

7. On these points see Clark Kerr, "The Balkanization of Labor Markets," in E. Wight Bakke et al., *Labor Mobility and Economic Opportunity* (New York: published jointly by The Technology Press of the Massachusetts Institute of Technology and John Wiley & Sons, Inc., 1954), pp. 97, 98; and same author, "Labor Markets: Their Character and Consequences," *Proceedings, American Economic Review*, XL (May, 1950), p. 283.

8. Kerr, *loc. cit.*

9. This point was already made in 1944 by Gunnar Myrdal in regard to Negroes. See *An American Dilemma* (New York: Harper & Row, Publishers, Inc., 1962; originally published in 1944), pp. 397-401.

10. The findings presented here complement hypotheses about the effects of wage flexibility on unemployment among nonwhites. See the hypotheses as set forth by Harry J. Gilman in his "Economic Discrimination and Unemployment," *American Economic Review*, LV (Dec., 1964), pp. 1077-1096.

ELEVEN

Housing Conditions

INSIGHT into consumption could be as rewarding as the analysis of income. What does the limited spending power of most Mexican Americans mean in terms of nutrition, housing, clothing, children's schooling, medical care, recreation? Do their consumption and saving patterns reflect solely their prevailing low-income status, or do they also show distinctive cultural priorities? Does the charge that "the poor pay more" for equivalent quantities and qualities of goods or services apply to Mexican Americans? Is it true that the ghetto dwellers among them fall victim to door-to-door salesmen of overpriced insurance policies or merchandise and pay inordinately high interest on consumer loans?[1]

No data are available to answer these questions. The U.S. Bureau of Labor Statistics has collected family budget statistics, but the results are usually classified by people's color and therefore reveal nothing about the Mexican-American population.[2] The resources for the present study did not permit any original research of this kind.

[1] Notes for this chapter start on page 267.

Chart 11–1.
Incidence of Overcrowded Housing Units[a],
Southwest Metropolitan Areas, 1960

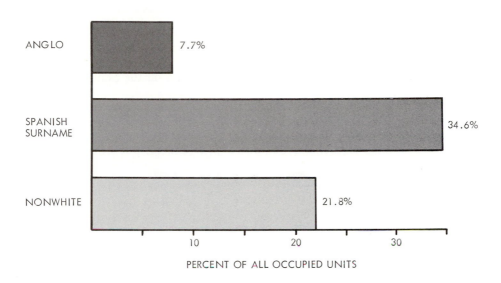

PERCENT OF ALL OCCUPIED UNITS

PERCENT DISTRIBUTION OF ALL
OCCUPIED HOUSING UNITS,
1960

PERCENT DISTRIBUTION OF
OVERCROWDED HOUSING UNITS,
1960

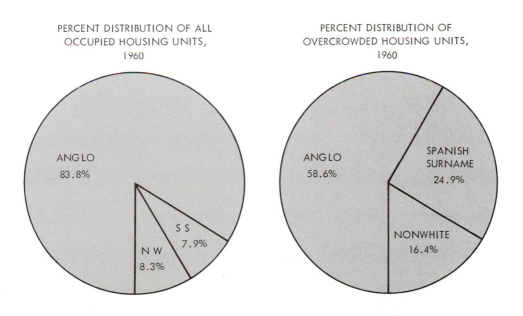

[a] An *overcrowded housing unit* is defined as one which averages more than one person per room.
Source: *1960 U.S. Census of Housing*, HC(1), nos. 4, 6, 7, 33, and 45, tables 15, 37, 38, 40, and 41.

249

However, comparative census data are available on one important aspect of levels of living—housing. These data show unusual deprivation in the Mexican-American population on the yardstick of United States norms. And while the causal nexus between inadequate housing and job performance, physical and mental health, and deviant social behavior is by no means clear (though statistical correlations exist in great abundance), there is a strong presumption that some patterns of poor housing are apt to have an adverse effect on people's opportunities as well as on their immediate well-being.[3]

By way of introduction we note that all of the data on the Southwest and the

Table 11–1. Median Number of Rooms per Housing Unit and Percent of Units with Less Than 5 Rooms, 5 and 6 Rooms, and 7 or More Rooms, Spanish-surname Households Compared with Others, Southwest, 1960[a]

Population Group	Median Number of Rooms	Less than 5 Rooms	5 and 6 Rooms	7 Rooms and over
Total	4.26	44.0%	46.9%	9.1%
Anglo	4.34	41.6	48.6	9.8
Spanish-surname	3.78	55.7	39.1	5.2
Nonwhite	3.73	57.0	36.9	6.1

[a] Metropolitan areas.
Source: *1960 U.S. Census of Housing*, HC(1), nos. 4, 6, 7, 33, and 45, tables 13, 37, 38, 40 and 41.

individual states in this chapter represent summations of census figures for the metropolitan areas of each state. No complete census reports on housing units occupied by Mexican Americans are available on a statewide basis.

THE GREATEST PROBLEM: OVERCROWDING

Mexican Americans are badly overcrowded. When the over-occupancy norm of more than one person per room is adopted,[4] the 1960 rate of overcrowding among the Spanish-surname group was more than four times the Anglo rate (Chart 11–1). In that year an estimated 875,000 Mexican Americans were living in overcrowded dwelling units.[5]

This extraordinary frequency of overcrowding is associated with two factors. One is the large size of Mexican-American families. Even if the dwelling units they occupy were distributed by size (number of rooms) in the same manner as the units occupied by Anglos, the Spanish-surname population would be greatly overcrowded by comparison. Second, Mexican Americans tend to live in smaller housing units (Table 11–1).

Overcrowding among Mexican Americans was also far more frequent than among nonwhites. The higher rate of overcrowding compared to nonwhites was not a function of family income as such. As shown in Chapter 8, the median income of Mexican Americans was somewhat larger than that of nonwhites.

The accompanying chart also indicates the disproportionate burden of over-crowding that falls upon the two minority groups combined. More than 40 percent of all overcrowded housing units were occupied by Spanish-surname and nonwhite households, although the minority households represented only 16.2 percent of all households in the metropolitan areas of the Southwest. One-quarter of the Spanish-surname households were overcrowded, although their over-all share in all metro-politan households was only 7.9 percent.

Interstate variations in the rate of overcrowding in the Spanish-surname group conform closely to the differentials found in our previous analyses. Thus, nearly 47

Table 11–2. Quality Indicators of Housing Occupied by Spanish-surname Households Compared with Other Households, Metropolitan Areas of Five States and Southwest, 1960[a] (Low-quality housing units as a percentage of all housing units occupied by each population group)

State	PERCENT DETERIORATING OR DILAPIDATED			PERCENT WITHOUT EXCLUSIVE BATH OR SHOWER[b]		
	Anglo[c]	Spanish-surname	Nonwhite	Anglo	Spanish-surname	Nonwhite
Southwest	7.5	29.7	27.1	4.4	13.1	12.4
Arizona	6.4	38.3	49.8	3.8	20.1	34.2
California	6.3	21.9	18.9	3.8	5.9	7.4
Colorado	9.2	34.1	29.5	7.8	19.5	12.8
New Mexico	5.0	29.1	27.3	3.7	24.2	23.5
Texas	9.9	41.1	37.6	5.3	24.1	19.2

[a] State figures are calculated for the total of SMSA data available for each state. The data are for 34 of the 37 areas in the Southwest.
[b] Percentage calculated from the figures for "bathtub or shower shared" and "no bathtub or shower" in the 1960 *Housing Census*. Data for bathing facilities are not available for total *occupied* housing units, from which Anglo figures should be calculated. Therefore, the Anglo figures are based on all housing units, which throws all vacant units into the Anglo category. The amount of distortion is probably small.
[c] Anglo figures are calculated by deducting Spanish-surname and nonwhite figures from the total of occupied housing units.
Source: *1960 U.S. Census of Housing*, HC(1), nos. 4, 6, 7, 33, and 45, tables 12, 36, 37, 38, 40 and 41.

percent of the group's metropolitan households in Texas were living in overcrowded housing units. The corresponding figure for California was less than 27 percent. As usual, overcrowding was more prevalent among renters than among home owners.[6]

INCIDENCE OF SUBSTANDARD HOUSING

The physical quality of housing also is inferior to that occupied by Anglos. Since there is no single measure of housing quality, two sets of data are presented in Table 11–2. The results are broadly consistent.* Nearly 30 percent of all

*The census shows a great many characteristics of physical housing quality not included in Table 11–2: sound housing units lacking some or all plumbing facilities; deficient water supply (only cold water inside, water piped outside only, or no piped water); no flush toilets, or flush toilets shared with another household. For four large metropolitan areas (Los Angeles, San Francisco, El Paso, and San Antonio) it is also possible to obtain data on shared access to housing units and shared cooking facilities for units with Spanish-surname heads. There is a high degree of correlation between most of the indicators of low or inadequate quality. Consequently, it would be redundant to show them all.

housing units occupied by Spanish-surname people in the Southwest were dilapidated or deteriorating in 1960, as against 7.5 percent of the units occupied by Anglos. And 13.1 percent of the units with Spanish-surname occupancy were without exclusive baths or showers compared with 4.4 percent of the Anglo units. The incidence of substandard housing was slightly lower for nonwhites than for Mexican Americans. Only in the metropolitan areas of Arizona were nonwhites worse off in this respect.

When the distribution of all the 721,000 dilapidated or deteriorating housing units in metropolitan areas of the Southwest is considered, it becomes apparent how

Table 11–3. Dilapidated Housing Units Occupied by Various Population Groups, Five Southwest States, Urban Areas in 1950 and Metropolitan Areas in 1960

	Urban 1950			Metropolitan 1960[a]		
STATE	ANGLO	SPANISH-SURNAME	NON-WHITE	ANGLO	SPANISH-SURNAME	NON-WHITE
	A. Dilapidated Units as Percent of All Units Occupied by Each Group					
Southwest	3.7	25.5	21.0	1.3	9.0	8.0
Arizona	6.5	29.9	35.2	2.1	14.3	24.6
California	2.7	17.2	11.2	1.1	6.3	4.6
Colorado	3.8	22.7	10.5	1.3	8.1	4.6
New Mexico	5.6	18.2	33.8	1.4	11.0	12.1
Texas	5.8	33.8	28.8	1.9	12.9	12.8
	B. Percent Distribution of All Dilapidated Units Over the Three Groups					
Southwest	48.7	28.0	23.3	44.6	28.8	26.6
Arizona	47.1	37.4	15.5	41.5	30.7	27.8
California	62.4	22.0	15.6	53.6	25.7	20.7
Colorado	72.9	22.1	5.0	65.2	25.6	9.2
New Mexico	42.9	46.7	10.4	27.4	63.5	9.0
Texas	38.4	30.6	31.0	34.7	30.3	35.0

[a] Includes all of the metropolitan areas of the Southwest except Laredo, Tyler, and Texarkana.
Source: *1960 U.S. Census of Housing*, HC(1), nos. 4, 6, 7, 33, and 45, tables 12, 36, 37, 38, 40, and 41. *1950 U.S. Census of Population*, PE no. 3C, table 4; *1950 U.S. Census of Housing*, parts 2, 4, and 6, table 7.

the minority groups are affected. Of these units, 58 percent were occupied by Anglos, and 21 percent each by Spanish-surname and nonwhite households.[7] Thus, *the two minorities had 42 percent of the substandard housing, although they accounted for only 16 percent of the total number of metropolitan households.*

Poor as they were, the housing conditions of Spanish-surname households seem to have improved between 1950 and 1960. The evidence is not as clear-cut as one would wish,[8] but it is convincing. The 1960 incidence of dilapidated housing among *metropolitan* Mexican Americans was far lower than the incidence ten years earlier for *urban* members of the group (Table 11–3). Reflecting the general advance in housing quality, the rate of dilapidation was sharply reduced for Anglos and nonwhites as well. On this yardstick, the housing condition of Spanish-surname households did not improve *relative to Anglos*. In the Southwest as a whole, the rate of dilapidated units occupied by Mexican Americans was about 7 times the Anglo rate in both 1950 and 1960. In Texas, the differential was even greater in 1960 than in 1950. In both census years, dilapidated housing was somewhat more frequent among Mexican Americans in the Southwest than among nonwhites. Only Arizona and New Mexico vary from this pattern, probably reflecting the still poorer housing of urban American Indians.

The absence of relative progress is also reflected in the distribution of all dilapidated housing units over the three population groups. The share of the Spanish-surname households in the Southwest was about the same in 1960 as in 1950, and the share of nonwhites increased.[9]

Absolute but not relative improvement occurred also in density. The incidence of overcrowding was reduced among all three population groups. However, nearly 25 percent of all of the overcrowded housing units in the region's metropolitan areas in 1960 were occupied by Mexican Americans as against 24 percent in urban areas ten years earlier.[10]

THE NEGLECT OF PUBLIC SERVICES

Over and above the quality of the dwelling unit itself, the poor quality or absence of public installations and services is evident in a great many Southwest cities. The transition from Anglo to low-income Mexican-American neighborhoods (and to Negro and other nonwhite areas) is marked by the sudden appearance of dirt roads instead of paved streets. Sewage and garbage collection services become inadequate. Street lighting is poor or nonexistent. Sidewalks are badly maintained. Playgrounds are lacking or inferior, and school buildings tend to be obsolete. The deterioration usually becomes worse as one proceeds from cities to unincorporated areas under county jurisdiction.

In most of the older cities of the East and Middle West, public installations have long become obligations of local governments, which are for the most part met from general revenue. In the Southwest, the special "improvement district" is a frequently used device for relieving local authorities of this responsibility. The burden is shifted directly to the owners and residents of a given area—and this means that the "improvements" are inadequate or are never made in poorer neighborhoods. Even if the residents could afford the special assessments, they often would not know how to establish improvement districts.[11]

The poor quality of public installations and services, as well as the run-down condition of individual buildings, characterizes the Southwest slum even more conspicuously than it does the eastern urban slum. The impact on the observer of the Southwestern variety is usually relieved by low over-all density despite the less visible overcrowding in individual family units, and by more yard space, sun, light and fresh air. But first impressions can deceive. No amount of sunshine and air can offset the human misery inside the shacks. The Mexican-American ghetto south of Buchanan

Street in central Phoenix, comprising about ten square miles close to the railroad tracks, is one of the worst examples of this kind.

Another major influence on the housing condition of Mexican Americans is the vulnerability of their neighborhoods to new freeways, wider highways, and urban renewal. Ethnic communities have been cut to pieces, and large numbers of residents and small businesses unceremoniously displaced. Since slum neighborhoods are the main targets of this process, the poor bear a disproportionate burden of these programs. East Los Angeles is a case in point.

This is a well-known story with regard to Negro ghettos, but Mexican Americans in the Southwest cities are equally affected. Like other ethnic groups, the poorer Mexican-American ghetto residents often have a strong attachment to their familiar neighborhood where they live in close proximity to relatives and friends. Here they rely on an informal labor market for jobs. They use "ethnic" stores as places to gather for talks and diversion as well as to shop. Here, too, more or less organized services have been established to meet their specific needs. No matter how poor the individual housing units may be, the satisfactions derived from familiarity with neighbors, streets, and institutions are so vital that dislocation is a profoundly disturbing experience. Yet, a survey among local renewal officials and others, which was conducted for this study, revealed few instances of organized and effective protest against the destruction of Mexican-American neighborhoods by urban-renewal or other public projects.

Mexican-American (and other minority) informants claim that they receive inadequate compensation for property rights. If the homeowner considers the price offered by the agency exercising the power of eminent domain to be below market value, he can resort to the courts. But this procedure requires outlays for legal and appraisal services, and the outcome is uncertain. Consequently, many Mexican Americans avoid litigation because of the expense as well as because of their apparent reluctance to fight authority. When relocation services are provided they are alleged to be even less effectual for Mexican Americans than for others.[12]

HOME OWNERSHIP

In light of their generally low income, Mexican Americans show a rather high rate of home ownership. Over 53 percent of the Spanish-surname households in Southwest metropolitan areas were home owners in 1960 (upper portion of Chart 11-2). This proportion was lower than the Anglo rate, but so much higher than the nonwhite rate that the differential cannot be explained by the rather small edge of Mexican Americans over nonwhites in income. A more important factor seems to be the larger concentration of nonwhites in the central cities of metropolitan areas. Home ownership in the built-up central cities, where land prices are relatively high and land uses more intensive, is generally less frequent than in the metropolitan fringe areas. Therefore, a population group more clustered in the central cities would be expected

Chart 11–2.
Home Ownership and Owner-occupied Houses Built 1950–1960: Spanish-surname Households Compared with Other Households, Southwest Metropolitan Areas, 1960

OWNER-OCCUPIED UNITS AS A PERCENT OF ALL
HOUSING UNITS OCCUPIED BY EACH POPULATION GROUP

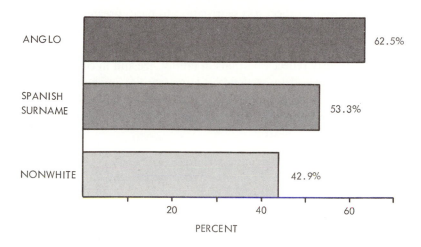

OWNER-OCCUPIED HOUSES BUILT 1950-1960 AS A PERCENT OF ALL
SUCH HOUSES OCCUPIED BY EACH POPULATION GROUP

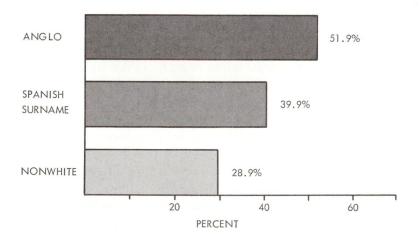

Source: *1960 U.S. Census of Housing*, HC(1), nos. 4, 6, 7, 33, and 45, tables 12, 14, 36, 37, 38, 40, and 41.

to have a lower home-ownership rate. The Mexican-American rate is high relative to nonwhites because a larger proportion of the Spanish-surname population lives on the metropolitan fringe, where home ownership is more common but does not necessarily imply greater economic capacity.

Still another factor associated with the ownership differential between nonwhites and Spanish-surname people may be the degree of residential segregation. As will be seen in Chapter 12, Mexican Americans are generally much less segregated from Anglos than are Negroes. Whatever the complex forces that account for this phenomenon, one would expect less segregation to mean greater freedom of housing choice and easier access to credit for home purchase.

Finally, differential rates of home ownership among groups of about equal standing in income may reflect variations in family size and in consumer preferences. Other things being equal, the prevalence of large families among Mexican Americans would tend to increase their propensity for home ownership. Mexican Americans appear to have a strong desire to own their own homes. Like some earlier European

Table 11–4. **Owner-occupied Housing Units as a Percent of All Units Occupied by Households in Various Population Groups, Southwest, 1950 and 1960 (Urban areas in 1950; metropolitan areas in 1960)**

Population Group	1950, Urban	1960, Metropolitan
Total	54.4	60.9
Anglo	56.3	62.5
Spanish-surname	44.6	53.3
Nonwhite	40.8	42.9

Source: *1960 U.S. Census of Housing,* HC(1), nos. 4, 6, 7, 33, and 45, tables 12, 14, 36, 37, 38, 40, and 41; *1950 U.S. Census of Population,* PE no. 3C, table 4; *1950 U.S. Census of Housing,* vol. I, parts 2, 4, and 6, table 3.

immigrant groups with a large admixture of land-hungry peasants, they tend to yearn for a *casita,* a little house, as they did earlier for a *ranchito,* a small ranch.

In light of these observations, it is interesting to see that the differential in home ownership between Spanish-surname and other households disappears or is even reversed when it is related to income and when the age of the household head is held constant. (Income and age are important determinants of the ownership rate.) Information on this point is limited to two metropolitan areas each in California and Texas. Home ownership among Spanish-name households with male heads 45 to 64 years old is about as frequent in the moderate and upper income brackets as among comparable Anglo households in Los Angeles. In San Francisco, the incidence of home ownership is higher than that of Anglos. In El Paso and San Antonio, Mexican Americans in moderate and higher income groups are more likely to own their homes than the rest of the population of comparable standing (Chart 11–3).

The percentage of home owners among the Mexican-American population increased sharply between 1950 and 1960 (Table 11–4). This increase exceeded the relative rise

Chart 11–3.
Home Ownership of Spanish-surname Households Compared with Others, by Income of Household Head, 1960
(Housing units with male heads age 45–64, owner-occupied as a percent of all occupied units in four metropolitan areas)

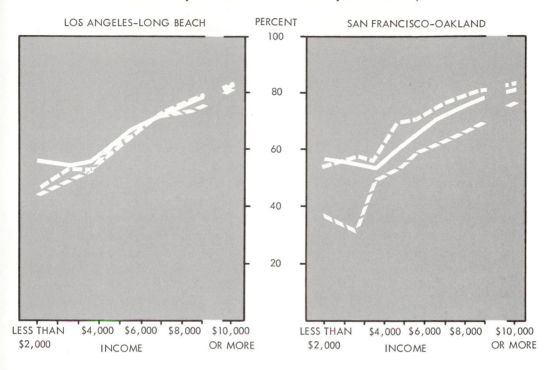

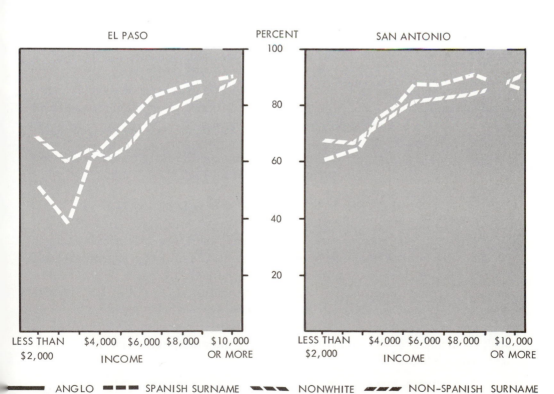

ANGLO   SPANISH SURNAME   NONWHITE   NON-SPANISH SURNAME

Source: *1960 U.S. Census of Housing,* HC(2), parts 60, 104, 156, and 159, tables A–7, A–13, and A–17.

for Anglos despite the fact that the median family income of the Mexican-American group advanced only a little more than that of Anglos (Chapter 8). On the basis of the census data, home ownership of Spanish-surname households in the Southwest rose by 19.5 percent as against 11.0 percent for Anglos and only 5.1 percent for nonwhites. The only flaw in this comparison, as in the earlier analysis of intercensal changes in the physical quality and overcrowding of housing units, is the inconsistency of available data: We are forced to use urban statistics for 1950 and metropolitan statistics for 1960. However, the differences of ownership rates between urban and metropolitan areas are generally small.[13]

It seems that Spanish-surname households find it easier to buy relatively new homes than do nonwhites (see lower panel of Chart 11–2). Most single-family houses constructed during the 1950s were in the suburbs. Consequently, this finding shows something of a trend among Mexican Americans toward suburbia, though not as strong as in the case of Anglos. Again, the ability of Mexican Americans to move to the suburbs seems related to the fact that they experience less severe housing discrimination than do nonwhites.

Altogether, the data suggest that many Mexican Americans have been able to command the credit necessary for the purchase of homes, though we do not know at what cost. Ownership has been also facilitated by the apparently frequent practice of building or acquiring a second house on the same lot: One house is occupied by the owner and the other is rented. This variant of the two-family house so popular in earlier periods in other areas owes its origin to the hope that the income from the rented unit will pay for the owner's unit. The arrangement also has a cultural characteristic: The extra house is often rented to relatives. This practice maintains, in modified form, the traditional pattern of the extended family living in one dwelling unit. Thus, it is an ingenious compromise between the desire for privacy and the need for the security, warmth, and mutual aid provided by the presence of kinfolk. It is interesting to note that a similar arrangement exists among at least one other ethnic group in urban America; many Italian Americans have built or bought small apartment houses and rented the extra units to relatives.

FACTORS BEARING

ON POOR HOUSING CONDITIONS

Some important questions are yet unanswered. Is the generally poor housing of Mexican Americans solely a function of low incomes, or are other factors involved, such as the prevalence of large families and the attendant primary need for other goods or services? Is quality of housing being sacrificed for space? Do Mexican Americans pay more for comparable housing than do others in like income groups? Is their housing worse than that of others in comparable rent classes? The following analysis attempts to deal with these and related questions,[14] although the available information is limited.[15]

Chart 11–4.
Median Value of Owner-occupied Housing Units, by Income, Spanish-surname Households Compared with Others, Four Metropolitan Areas, 1960

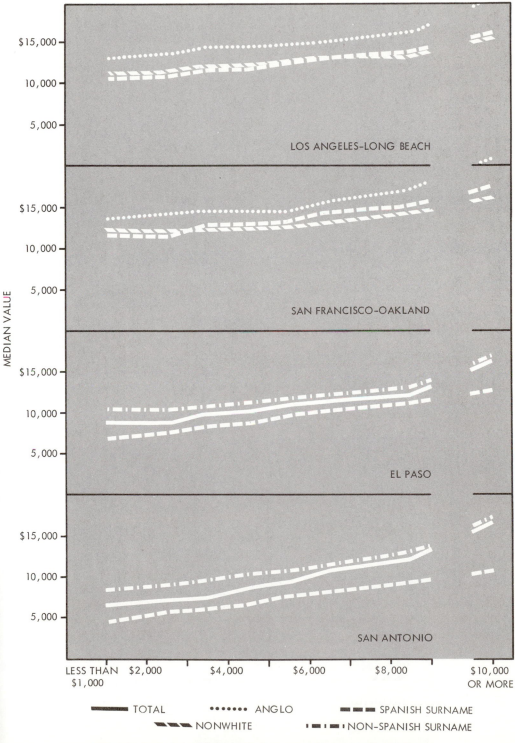

MEDIAN VALUE

LOS ANGELES-LONG BEACH

SAN FRANCISCO-OAKLAND

EL PASO

SAN ANTONIO

$15,000

10,000

5,000

$15,000

10,000

5,000

$15,000

10,000

5,000

$15,000

10,000

5,000

LESS THAN $1,000 $2,000 $4,000 $6,000 $8,000 $10,000 OR MORE

TOTAL   •••••• ANGLO   ■ ■ ■ SPANISH SURNAME
NONWHITE   ∎ ∎ ∎ NON-SPANISH SURNAME

Source: Computed from *1960 U.S. Census of Housing,* HC(2), nos. 60, 104, 156, and 159, tables A–3, A–13 and A–17. Income data pertain to median income of primary families and individuals in 1959.

Chart 11–5.
Median Rent Paid at Different Income Levels, Spanish-surname Households Compared with Others, Four Metropolitan Areas, 1960

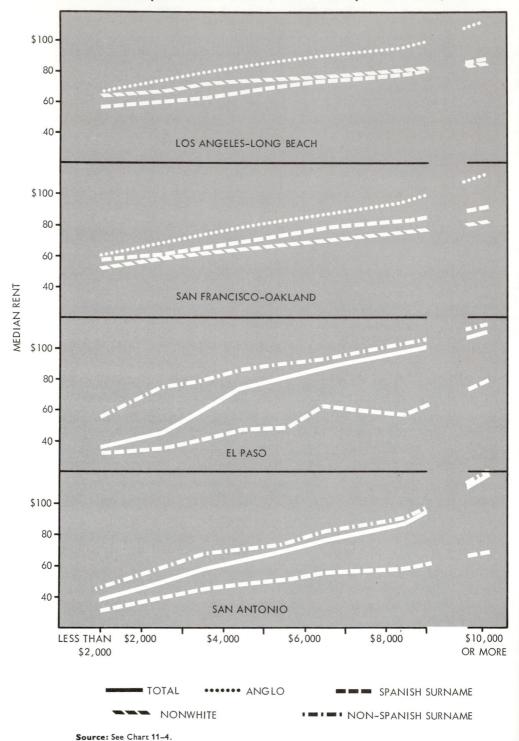

MEDIAN RENT

LOS ANGELES–LONG BEACH

SAN FRANCISCO–OAKLAND

EL PASO

SAN ANTONIO

LESS THAN $2,000 $2,000 $4,000 $6,000 $8,000 $10,000 OR MORE

——— TOTAL   ••••••• ANGLO   ▬▬▬ SPANISH SURNAME

◣◤◢ NONWHITE   ▬▪▬▪▬ NON–SPANISH SURNAME

Source: See Chart 11–4.

House Value or Rent by Income

It is clear from Charts 11–4 and 11–5 that Mexican American home owners and renters pay *less* for housing throughout the range of family incomes. The same is true for nonwhites in the Los Angeles and San Francisco areas, where separate data for this group are available.* As will be seen, the two minority groups in each income bracket occupy units with a larger mixture of inferior quality and less space. *They pay less and get less.*

The relationship between income and housing expenditures for tenants can be examined in terms of the percentage of income spent for rent. Generally, poorer households pay a larger percentage than others. One would expect, therefore, that Mexican Americans spend relatively more for rent than do Anglos. This is not the case when the proportion of Spanish-name households who pay 25 percent or more of their earnings for rent is used as a test (Chart 11–6). In contrast, to judge from the data for the Los Angeles and San Francisco metropolitan areas, the proportion of nonwhites in this category is large in comparison not only with the Spanish-surname group but with the rest of the population. Thus, two generally poor minorities show highly different shares of income devoted to rent. The difference may reflect varying cultural responses to family budget restraints or more limited access of nonwhites, especially Negroes, to housing. Detailed census data show that the intergroup differentials summarized in the chart hold more or less for the entire range of incomes.

Substandard Housing by Income and Rent

The frequency of substandard housing among the Mexican-American population is not solely a function of income. The rate of substandard housing among Spanish-surname households was perceptibly higher than for Anglo or all other households at every level of family income identified by the census (Chart 11–7). The same was true for nonwhites in the two California metropolises for which data were reported. Of course, the more well-to-do among the Mexican Americans, like those among Anglos and nonwhites, occupied better living quarters than the lower-income households. But substantial intergroup differentials persist through the entire range of incomes. The difference is smaller at upper than at lower income levels, but nevertheless it is significant. For example, the chances that a Spanish-surname household in Los Angeles in the $7,000 to $10,000 income class will occupy a substandard housing unit were $4\frac{1}{2}$ times the chances of an Anglo household having the same income. Factors other than income must account at least in part for this discrepancy.

---

*As in all cases where income, age, or rent brackets or median house values are involved, some of the intergroup differences may be explained by uneven distributions within the brackets and be hidden by medians. We have no means of assessing the significance of this potential source of error. However, the findings are so consistent that they would at worst be somewhat modified rather than invalidated by better data. This observation applies to the entire discussion in this section. Further, the only data available for home owners relate income to the value of the housing units they occupy, not to the home ownership expense.

Mexican-American tenants get poorer housing than do others paying comparable rents (Chart 11–8). In each rent class, the percent of substandard units occupied by Spanish-surname households exceeds the percent occupied by Anglos (Los Angeles and San Francisco) or the percent occupied by all other households (El Paso and San Antonio). This situation is more conspicuous in the lower-rent brackets, but a differential persists throughout the range of rents. Even Mexican-American households paying $120 or more per month were more likely to occupy inferior quarters

Chart 11–6.
Tenants Paying 25 Percent or More of Income for Rent:
Spanish-surname Households Compared with Others,
Four Metropolitan Areas, 1960

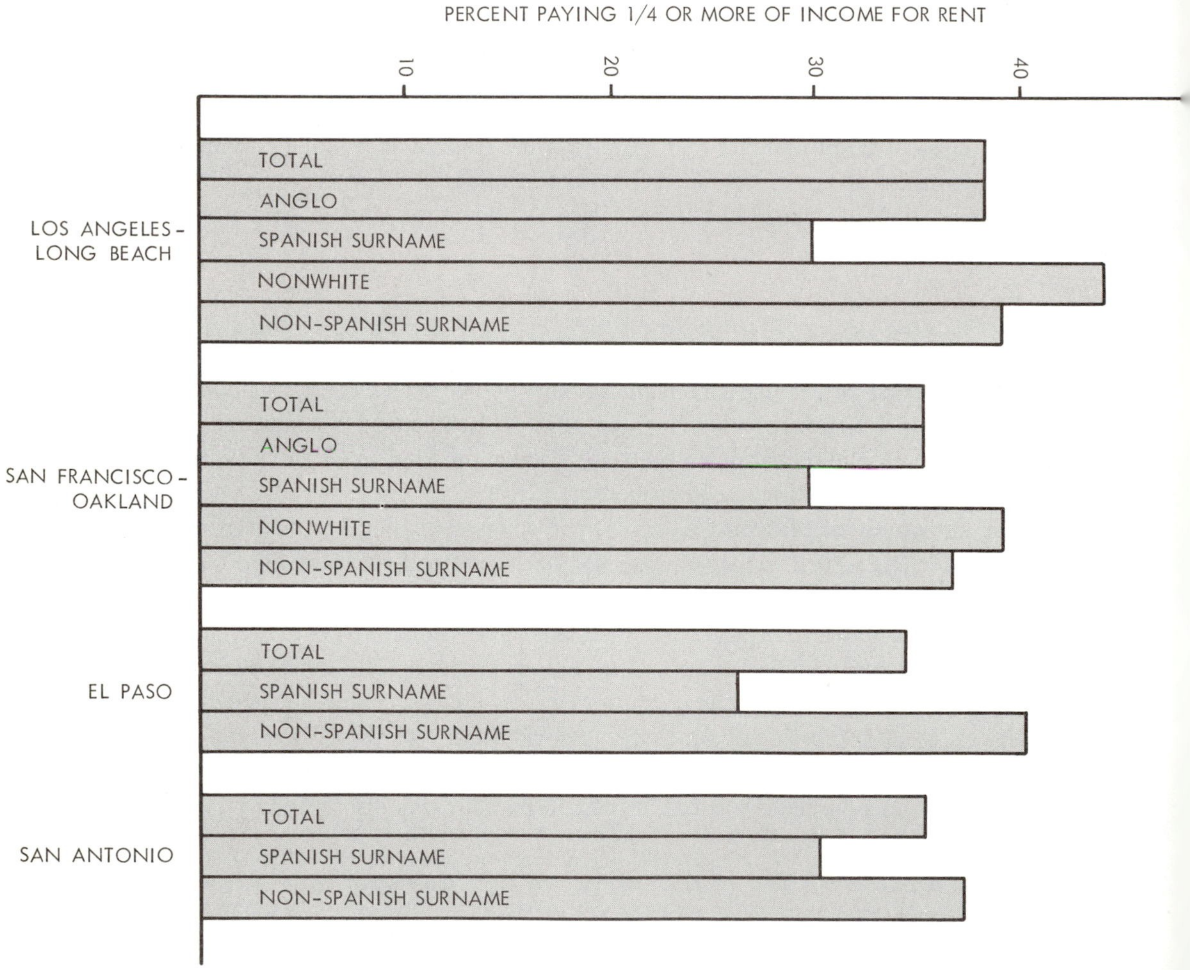

PERCENT PAYING 1/4 OR MORE OF INCOME FOR RENT

	10	20	30	40

LOS ANGELES–LONG BEACH
- TOTAL
- ANGLO
- SPANISH SURNAME
- NONWHITE
- NON-SPANISH SURNAME

SAN FRANCISCO–OAKLAND
- TOTAL
- ANGLO
- SPANISH SURNAME
- NONWHITE
- NON-SPANISH SURNAME

EL PASO
- TOTAL
- SPANISH SURNAME
- NON-SPANISH SURNAME

SAN ANTONIO
- TOTAL
- SPANISH SURNAME
- NON-SPANISH SURNAME

Source: See Chart 11–4.

Chart 11–7.
Dilapidated and Deteriorating Housing Units as a Percent of All Units Occupied by Each Population Group, by Income, Four Metropolitan Areas, 1960

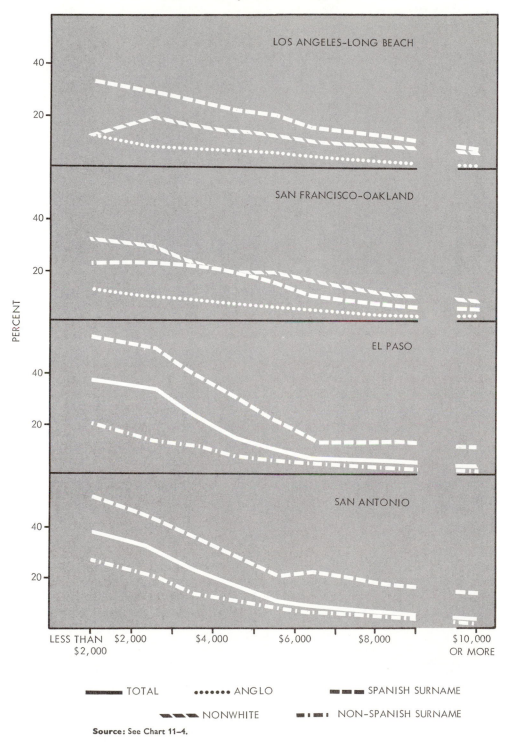

TOTAL　　•••••• ANGLO　　■■■ SPANISH SURNAME

■■■ NONWHITE　　■▪■▪ NON-SPANISH SURNAME

Source: See Chart 11–4.

Chart 11-8.

Dilapidated and Deteriorating Renter-occupied Housing Units as a Percent of All Renter-occupied Units for Each Population Group, by Rent Paid, Four Metropolitan Areas, 1960

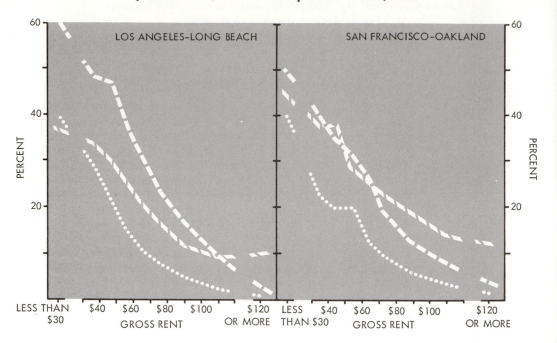

LOS ANGELES–LONG BEACH

SAN FRANCISCO–OAKLAND

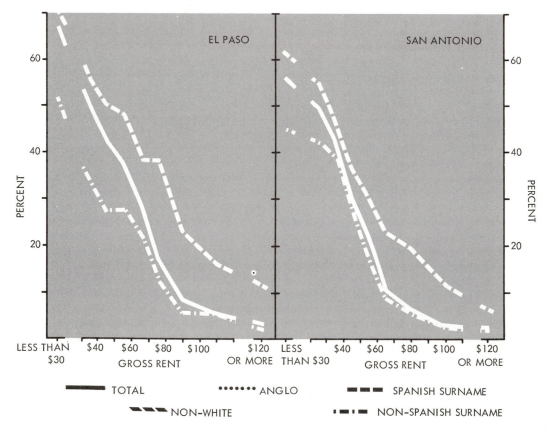

EL PASO

SAN ANTONIO

TOTAL   •••••• ANGLO   ▰▰▰ SPANISH SURNAME

◣◢◣◢ NON-WHITE   ▰▬▰▬ NON-SPANISH SURNAME

a Gross rent is the contract rent plus the average monthly cost of utilities (water, electricity, gas) and fuels, if these items are paid for by the renter.
Source: See Chart 11–4.

than did Anglos (or all others) paying this much. The same tendency prevailed among home owners when houses were grouped by value classes.

Finally, the far greater incidence of overcrowding among Spanish-surname households pervades all income classes (Chart 11–9). Overcrowding generally tends to be greatest in the low-to-moderate income groups, though not in the lowest (which includes large numbers of elderly couples). For Mexican Americans, living in cramped housing is a far more diffused experience. Thus, nearly 27 percent of the Spanish-name households in the $7,000 to $10,000 group in Los Angeles lived in overcrowded quarters as against less than 8 percent of the Anglos and 17 percent of the nonwhites in the same income bracket. In San Francisco, the comparable figures are 15 percent for Spanish-surname households, 6 percent for Anglos, and 18 percent for nonwhites. In El Paso and San Antonio, the Spanish-surname rate of overcrowding in the same income class was four times as high as for the rest of the population.

INFERIOR HOUSING: AN INTERPRETATION

The methods used here impose restraint in interpretation. Our successive two-way classifications of data may fail to disclose fully the multiple determinants of a given condition. Nevertheless, the factors associated with the inferior housing of Mexican Americans as a group may be summarized as follows:

Poverty is clearly one of the strategic determinants, but our analysis serves to place the income variable in better perspective. A significantly higher rate of poor housing quality and overcrowding among Mexican Americans in comparison to the general population extends over the whole range of incomes.[16] In other words, higher earnings do not seem to cure housing or occupancy deficiencies among this minority as effectively as they do for Anglos. We conclude that the budget restraints operating on large numbers of Mexican-American households stem not only from low incomes but from their typically large families. Per-capita income rather than family income sets limits on what households can afford to pay for housing.[17] As shown in Chapter 8, the size of Mexican-American families exceeds by wide margins the size of families in the reference populations throughout the range of incomes recorded in the census.

Income per person in the family also helps explain why the Mexican Americans' housing is in some respects inferior to that of nonwhites. In terms of either median family income or median income of urban males in comparable age groups, Mexican Americans have an edge over nonwhites. In terms of income per person in the family, however, Mexican Americans lag significantly behind nonwhites (Chapter 8). As a consequence, they must make still greater sacrifices of both housing quality and space.

The only statistical evidence bearing on discrimination in the housing market appears in the fact that Spanish-surname households in each rent or house-value class occupy housing with a far greater percentage of substandard units than does the general population. The public record about housing discrimination against Mexican Americans is slim. Field investigations for the U.S. Commission on Civil Rights and

265

Chart 11–9.
Overcrowded Housing by Income, Spanish-surname Households Compared with Other Households, Four Metropolitan Areas, 1960
(Overcrowded units as a percent of all units occupied by each population group)

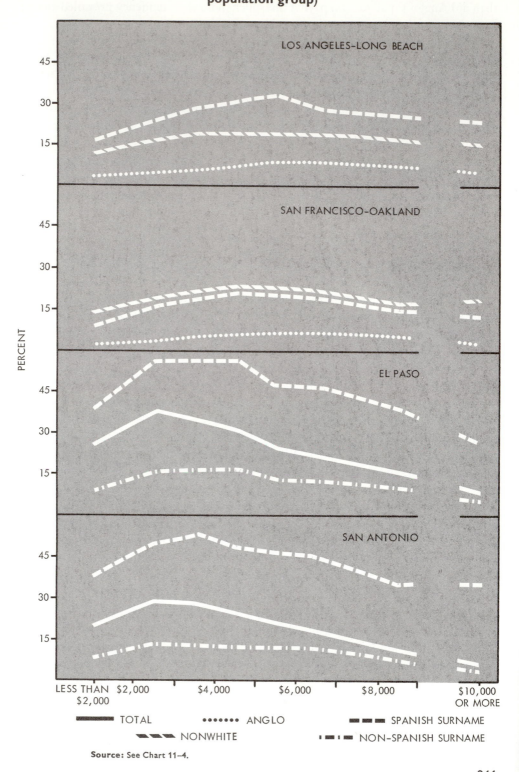

Source: See Chart 11–4.

interviews held for this study indicate, however, that discrimination does exist.[18] But it appears to be less frequent or intense than the discrimination experienced by Negroes. According to an investigator, "one factor playing a generally unspoken but significant role . . . is skin color." Mexican Americans with dark skin are more apt to encounter refusal to sell or to rent than those who are more fair-skinned.[19] As recently as 1955, a real estate board in Los Angeles County expelled members for selling to Mexican Americans.[20] The separation of Mexican-American and Negro minorities from each other is known in public housing,[21] although informants are frequently uncertain whether such segregation is imposed or reflects the preferences of tenants.

NOTES TO CHAPTER ELEVEN

1. See David Caplovitz, *The Poor Pay More* (New York: The Free Press, 1963). In interpreting Caplovitz's and similar findings, one must, of course, bear in mind the high cost of doing business in the urban slums. Among other things, the cost of credit extension to customers whose repayment potential is low, the cost of small-quantity sales in some retail items, and the frequently higher cost of insurance against theft and fire hazards. Competition in many slum areas is reduced by the reluctance of large retail chains to establish branches in these areas. For a small-scale, local study in a low-income Mexican-American area of Los Angeles, see Frederick D. Sturdivant, "Business and the Mexican American Community," *California Management Review*, XI (Spring, 1969).

2. Surveys by the Bureau of Labor Statistics in the 1930s presented separate expenditure data for samples of families designated as "Mexican" in a few selected Southwest cities. These are, of course, too dated to be useful now. See, for example, *Money Disbursements of Wage Earners and Clerical Workers in Five Cities in the Pacific Region, 1934-36*, U.S. Bureau of Labor Statistics Bulletin 639 (1939).

3. See Alvin L. Schorr, *Slums and Social Insecurity*, U.S. Department of Health, Education, and Welfare, Social Security Administration, Division of Research and Statistics, Research Report no. 1 (1963). This author stresses, for example, the adverse consequences of overcrowding (pp. 16–25). Cramped housing quarters make it more difficult to maintain standards of hygiene and health and to prevent the spread of infectious diseases. They can heighten family tension and affect workers' job performance. Lack of privacy makes it harder for children to do their school work. Overcrowding deprives the individual of the sense of privacy that benefits personality development and helps preserve mental health. On the other hand, a longitudinal study matching a group of Negro families who had moved from slums into new housing with a group who had not resulted in more equivocal findings. See Daniel M. Wilner et al., *The Housing Environment and Family Life* (Baltimore: The Johns Hopkins Press, 1962). Both Schorr and Wilner provide substantial references to the literature. See also Leonard J. Duhl (ed.), *The Urban Condition: People and Policy in the Metropolis* (New York: Basic Books, Inc., 1963), part one.

4. As in all cases where certain norms are used, one may debate whether more than one person per room is the correct yardstick for overcrowding. It may be too high when one considers that, say, five persons in a family might live just adequately though not comfortably in a four-room housing unit, depending on the size and layout of rooms and the age of children. A lower standard of overcrowding on which census data are reported is more than 1.5 persons per room. Application of this standard increases the *differential* incidence

of crowding among the three population groups. The Spanish-surname rate for the Southwest is ten times as high as the Anglo rate and remains far greater than the rate for nonwhites. Also, the burden of overcrowding falling upon the minorities is even greater: 60 percent of all overcrowding units for the two combined and 38 percent for the Spanish-surname group alone. The incidence of overcrowded units as such, of course, is reduced for all of the three population groups when the lower standard is applied.

5. Special tabulation of the *1960 U.S. Census of Population*, vol. I, parts 4, 6, 7, 33, and 45, table 110, shows the average family size of Spanish-surname families in the Southwest to be 4.77 persons, and the number of families in overcrowded housing units was 183,374.

6. For metropolitian area data by states, see *1960 U.S. Census of Housing*, HC(2), tables A-3, A-13, and A-17.

7. *1960 U.S. Census of Housing*, HC(1), parts 4, 6, 7, 33, and 45, tables 12, 36, 37, 38, 40, and 41.

8. The most important data problem is the fact that the Bureau of the Census published 1960 figures on dilapidated and overcrowded housing units occupied by Spanish-surname households on a metropolitan-area basis only, while corresponding 1950 figures were given for state totals and for urban areas in each of the five states. Another data problem is posed by the census redefinition of "substandard" housing units. The only consistent census classification of physical condition is "dilapidated," and the comparison is therefore limited to this category. Even so, the change from a two-way classification in 1950 ("dilapidated" versus "not dilapidated") to a three-way classification in 1960 ("sound," "deteriorating," and "dilapidated") may have produced difficulties in comparability. The 1950-1960 comparisons may slightly overstate the decline in the rate of dilapidated units. However, the inaccuracies are probably small. The broad comparability of urban and metropolitan data on dilapidation is indicated by the fact that the rate of dilapidation in 1960 for the United States was 3.24 percent in metropolitan areas and 3.41 percent in urban areas. The rate was almost identical in the two types of areas for housing units occupied by whites. For units occupied by nonwhites the rate was 11.13 percent in metropolitan areas and 12.54 percent in urban areas. See *1960 U.S. Census of Housing*, HC(1), no. 1, tables 9 and 27.

9. The share of all housing units occupied by each of the three population groups in 1950 and 1960 in the Southwest was as follows:

	1950 Urban	1960 Metropolitan
Anglo household head	85.5%	83.8%
Spanish-surname head	7.2	7.9
Nonwhite head	7.3	8.3

The minorities in 1950 occupied 14.5 percent of the housing units but had 51.3 percent of the dilapidated units; in 1960 they occupied 16.2 percent of the units but had over 55 percent of the dilapidated housing. *1960 U.S. Census of Housing*, HC(1), parts 4, 6, 7, 33, and 45, tables 12, 36, 37, 38, 40, and 41. *1950 U.S. Census of Population*, PE no. 3C, table 4; and *1950 U.S. Census of Housing*, parts 2, 4, and 6, table 7.

10. Derived from *1950 U.S. Census of Housing* vol. I, parts 2, 4, and 6, table 11; PE no. 3C, table 4; *1960 U.S. Census of Housing*, HC(1), tables 15, 37, 38, 40, and 41.

11. See findings based on staff investigations of the U.S. Civil Rights Commission, reported by Lawrence B. Glick, "The Right to Equal Opportunity," in Julian Samora (ed.), *La Raza: Forgotten Americans* (Notre Dame, Ind.: University of Notre Dame Press, 1966), pp. 107, 108. Glick's cases include South Tucson, Arizona, a municipality controlled by Mexican Americans.

12. For the urban-renewal survey of the Mexican-American Study Project, see Frank G. Mittelbach and Claudio Arenas, "Mexican Americans in Urban Renewal Areas in the

Southwest," *Journal of Housing*, June 1969. For relocation problems, see also *Relocating the Dispossessed Elderly: A Study of Mexican Americans* (Institute for Environmental Studies, University of Pennsylvania, Feb. 1, 1966). This is a case study of a San Antonio area designated for urban renewal and occupied largely by elderly Mexican Americans. Among other things, the legalistic letters of the local renewal agency that notify the residents of impending relocation are extremely difficult for the addressees to understand, pre-relocation counselling is poor, and the fact that residents can expect aid from the agency is incompletely understood. Moreover, the study found the local welfare agencies to be poorly organized and coordinated for assisting in relocation. The study was made under the general direction of Chester Rapkin.

13. In the United States, the percentage of home ownership in 1960 was 58.3 percent in urban areas and 58.9 percent in metropolitan areas. For whites, it was 60.8 percent in urban areas and 61.7 percent in metropolitan areas. The corresponding figures for nonwhites were 36.2 percent and 35.1 percent, respectively. *1960 U.S. Census of Housing*, HC(1), no. 1, table 9.

14. For similar recent analyses, see Chester Rapkin, "Price Discrimination against Negroes in the Rental Housing Market," in *Essays in Urban Land Economics: In Honor of the Sixty-Fifth Birthday of Leo Grebler* (University of California, Los Angeles, Real Estate Research Program, 1966); Fred E. Case, *Minority Families in the Metropolis*, part 5 of the series called Profile of the Los Angeles Metropolis: Its People and Its Homes (University of California, Los Angeles, Real Estate Research Program, 1966); and Donald L. Foley, Wallace F. Smith, and Catherine Bauer Wurster, "Housing Trends and Related Problems in California," in *Housing in California*, Appendix to the Report of the Governor's Advisory Commission on Housing Problems, April 1963.

15. Most of the relevant census data on Spanish-name households are cross-classified for only four metropolitan areas: Los Angeles–Long Beach, the San Francisco Bay area, San Antonio, and El Paso. These centers, however, accounted for more than half the Spanish-surname population living in Southwest metropolitan areas in 1960. Thus, any general relationships detected in the data are likely to hold for all metropolitan areas combined, though not necessarily for each one. Cross-classifications are available for Spanish-surname, Anglo, and nonwhite households in the Los Angeles and San Francisco metropolitan areas. For El Paso and San Antonio, data can be computed only for all households, Spanish-surname, and all other households. This explains the presentation of materials in this section. The data for El Paso and San Antonio are, of course, influenced by the varying percentage of Spanish-surname households in the total number of households: 37.3 percent in El Paso and 30.1 percent in San Antonio. For an in-depth analysis of intergroup differences in housing conditions related to such variables as age of household head, income, and size of family, three basic methods are available. One is the standardization procedure. Another is multiple regression analysis. Both methods allow statements on the relative importance of a number of independent variables in producing a given outcome—the dependent variable. In the case at hand, the data are insufficient for using either of these procedures. Consequently, the analysis here employs the third method: such cross-classifications as can be computed from the census data. While less rigorous than the other procedures, this method at least permits broad inferences to be made from the evidence.

16. This finding is consistent with Rapkin's nationwide analysis of the Negro rental housing market. See Rapkin, *op. cit*.

17. Our data relate indicators of housing conditions in 1960 to the income in a single year—1959. The concept of "permanent income," as developed by Milton Friedman and applied to housing expenditures by Margaret G. Reid, may conceivably provide an alternative explanation of the quality and quantity of housing occupied by Mexican Americans.

However, data for exploring this possibility are not available. See Milton Friedman, *A Theory of the Consumption Function* (Princeton, N.J.: Princeton University Press, 1957) and Margaret G. Reid, *Housing and Income* (Chicago: The University of Chicago Press, 1962).

18. See Glick, *op. cit.*, pp. 107–110.

19. *Ibid.*

20. Davis McEntire, *Residence and Race* (Berkeley, Calif.: University of California Press, 1960), pp. 241, 242.

21. See statement of Roy B. Yanez, Executive Director, Housing Authority of the City of Phoenix, *Hearings before the United States Commission on Civil Rights*, Phoenix, Ariz., Feb. 3, 1962 (Washington, D.C., 1962), pp. 34–43.

TWELVE

Residential Segregation

THE residential segregation of Mexican Americans in Southwest cities is an important aspect of their housing condition, but it is more than that. The spatial separation of Mexican Americans from Anglos in urban housing is usually correlated with other critical types of separation—in employment, schooling, income, and the affairs of the larger community. Thus, it provides a general indicator of the minority's status in different localities, an indicator of social as well as physical distance from the core group. Social distance is not invariably accompanied by physical distance; in some cities of the South, for instance, Negroes and whites live on the same block, the Negroes living in the poor alley housing once reserved for slaves and the whites occupying the old mansions. But in most American cities, where social distance between subgroups is not so deeply ingrained in all social institutions as in the Old South, residential segregation reflects the realities of social distinctions.

The analysis of residential segregation will once more highlight the enormous local differences in the relative position of the Mexican-American minority. An attempt to specify and quantify the factors associated with varying degrees of segregation in different cities should bring us closer to an understanding of the influence that local milieus have on the condition of the Mexican-American group.

271

In addition, analysis of residential segregation in Southwest cities offers an opportunity to obtain fresh general insights into one of the most pervasive and significant facts of urban life in the United States. For one thing, the region's population includes two large groups generally recognized as disadvantaged minorities: Mexican Americans and Negroes. Hence it is possible to examine how sharply not only one minority but two minorities with different historical relationships to the region are segregated from the dominant population. Second, the unusual ethnic mixture in the Southwest makes it possible to observe still another kind of segregation—that of *minorities from minorities*, or of Mexican Americans from Negroes and from other non-whites (Orientals and Indians). Such comparisons add new dimensions to the usual analysis of residential segregation of a single minority from the dominant population. Finally, since many Mexican Americans are of foreign stock, one can measure the extent of segregation of generations from one another within the same ethnic group.

To date, scholarly work on residential segregation has focused on Negroes versus whites and on ethnic immigrant groups and their children versus natives. As for Negroes, their housing segregation is so pervasive and severe that variations from one city to another are relatively small. Whatever local differences exist are only slightly associated with city size, the proportion of nonwhites in cities, and the region of the country in which the city is located.[1] In contrast, residential segregation of contemporary immigrants and their children is lower and has become much more variable, both across ethnic groups and across communities. Among other things, it is associated with certain characteristics of the foreign-stock population, including in general the degree of their acculturation and in particular their educational attainment and recency of immigrant status.[2] It remains to be seen whether the housing segregation of Mexican Americans conforms to one of these patterns or shows a distinctive pattern of its own.

Apart from the insights into our society that can be obtained from comparative studies of residential segregation, different patterns of distributions of ethnics throughout an urban system have eminently practical implications. They determine the extent of *de facto* school segregation. They influence the potential for ethnic-bloc politics and the chances of minority candidates. They have a bearing on the preservation of ethnic social institutions. In large urban complexes, especially those with poor public transportation facilities (like the Watts area in Los Angeles), ghettoization may place limits on employment opportunities.

HISTORICAL PATTERNS

OF MEXICAN-AMERICAN URBANIZATION

When the image of minority ghettos is evoked, one tends to think of the huge present-day concentrations of Negroes in Northern central-city areas or the earlier clusters of European immigrants in similar—sometimes the same—areas. In these

[1] Notes for this chapter start on page 288.

cases, concentrations of minority-group members have been largely the result of the relatively sudden influx of the group to the city and its settlement in cheap housing, typically located in or near downtown. The facts for Spanish-surname persons do not quite fit this image.[3] The percentage of Mexican Americans living in central cities of the Southwestern metropolitan areas was lower than that of nonwhites (though the percentage of both minorities was higher than of Anglos).[4] More significantly, the proportion of metropolitan Anglos who lived in central cities declined between 1950 and 1960, and the proportion increased for nonwhites—but it remained almost the same for Spanish-surname people. In other words, Mexican Americans generally did not participate in the Anglo exodus to the suburbs, nor did their concentrations in the central cities become more acute.

The differences in central-city concentrations between Mexican Americans and other groups reflect earlier patterns of urban growth. The origins of the Mexican-American *barrios* have been far more varied and complex than those of many other ethnic ghettos. To be sure, the observer sees central-city "downtown" ghettos with large concentrations of Mexican Americans. Their enterprises supply the minority with Mexican food, with movies, with professional services, immigration "experts" and so on. Perhaps the largest of these areas is East Los Angeles which is close to the city center. In 1960, the estimated 135,000 Spanish-surname people in East Los Angeles represented about three-quarters of its total population. In some ways East Los Angeles is like many ethnic sections of Eastern and Midwestern cities. Parts of it were occupied by a succession of different ethnic groups; it has long served as a reception center for Mexican immigrants as well as interstate in-migrants, and it remains a huge pocket of poverty.[5]

However, many areas of Mexican-American concentration have origins quite different from those occupied by nonwhites or other minorities. Quite a few cities in the Southwest were first settled by Mexicans and organized around central *plazas*. With the coming of the railroads and new settlements by Anglos, many of the *plazas*—for example in Albuquerque—were bypassed when transportation terminals, nodes and other central places developed some distance away. With new urban growth concentrating around the nodes and terminals, the *plaza* area remained to form the nucleus of the contemporary Mexican-American "downtown."

Very rapid urbanization of the Southwest absorbed other Mexican-American *barrios* which began as agricultural labor communities. The swift transfer of agricultural land to urban use meant that the resident Mexican-American population moved into the stream of urban activities. The ethnic character of the enclave remained, but the population ceased to be concentrated in agricultural occupations. In Southern California, Pacoima, in the midst of the San Fernando Valley tract developments, is typical of these cases. Pockets in the city of San Diego present the same kind of history. In some places, such as Fresno, agricultural enclaves were established at the fringe of the urbanized parts of metropolitan areas. Many of these still serve as agricultural labor markets. In a few, the population engages partially in urban and partially in agricultural pursuits, holding different jobs in different seasons or working intermittently in both types of occupation. Eventually these communities may also be engulfed.

Still another type of enclave is the former labor camp which brought together a pool of Mexican-American railroad or other gang workers and where a small population remained after the camp had outlived its usefulness. A variant of the worker community is the "company town" established by employers as a permanent community, with family housing, company stores, and other facilities. Such towns were found not only in isolated areas in mining country, but also encapsulated in what are now metropolitan areas.[6]

There are a few cities where Mexican Americans are *not* found in subordinate enclaves but dominate both numerically and socially. This phenomenon is more frequent in small towns, like Rio Grande City and Presidio, Texas, but it characterizes some larger cities as well. Laredo, Texas, is the best illustration. Only in isolated areas—notably Indian reservations—does such a pattern exist for other ethnic groups in mainland United States.

SEGREGATION IN DIFFERENT CITIES

Though the history of Mexican-American urban settlement is not directly apparent in the statistical analysis of this chapter, its distinctive features may well account for some of the regularities discovered.

Table 12–1 shows indexes which measure the degree of residential segregation of various population groups in 35 Southwest cities. In technical terms, these are *indexes of residential dissimilarity*.[7] The index ranges in value from 0 to 100. Crudely, a score of zero means that there is no segregation of a subpopulation from the other, that the members of both populations are randomly distributed throughout the city with respect to each other. A score of 100 means that the two populations are totally segregated, that all of the members of each population are concentrated in separate areas. A detailed discussion of the index and the data sources is presented in Appendix G.

The first three columns of Table 12–1 show segregation indexes for the dominant Anglo population—first, segregation from all others, that is, from both nonwhites and persons of Spanish surname; and then separately from each of the two principal minorities, Mexican-American and Negro. The data indicate that in every city, without exception, Mexican Americans are less segregated from Anglos than are Negroes. In other respects, however, the table highlights sharp differences in extent of segregation of various populations and wide variations from one city to another. For example,

(1) Segregation of the total minority population from Anglos ranges from a low of 39 in Laredo, Texas to a high of 83 in Dallas, Texas.

(2) Segregation of Spanish-surname persons from Anglos ranges from a low of 30 in Sacramento, California to a high of 76 in Odessa, Texas.

Table 12–1. Indexes of Residential Dissimilarity for 35 Southwest Central Cities, 1960

City	Anglo vs. All Others	Spanish-surname vs. Anglo	Negro vs. Anglo	Spanish-surname vs. Negro	Spanish-surname vs. Other Nonwhite[a]	Spanish-surname Foreign-born vs. Native-born
	(1)	(2)	(3)	(4)	(5)	(6)
Arizona						
Phoenix	62.8	57.8	90.0	60.7	40.6	21.6
Tucson	63.9	62.7	84.5	64.1	39.0	18.2
California						
Bakersfield	72.4	53.7	87.7	61.4	49.3	24.6
Fresno	64.4	49.0	92.0	55.2	38.8	19.5
Los Angeles	68.7	57.4	87.6	75.7	50.3	23.8
Oakland	60.0	41.5	72.2	56.4	40.5	21.0
Ontario	52.6	50.6	80.1	32.6	44.3	27.0
Riverside	67.7	64.9	80.8	45.6	48.9	33.8
Sacramento	39.5	30.2	61.9	47.8	38.8	31.4
San Bernardino	70.6	67.9	83.5	35.2	44.6	20.9
San Diego	55.9	43.6	81.1	55.2	34.6	27.5
San Francisco	46.8	38.1	71.5	65.9	60.0	18.8
San Jose	42.5	43.0	64.7	44.4	42.7	17.0
Santa Barbara	48.6	46.5	76.7	37.6	9.8	17.8
Stockton	59.3	52.6	73.0	31.0	39.8	22.0
Colorado						
Colorado Springs	55.4	44.8	74.0	53.8	32.6	50.5
Denver	64.9	60.0	86.8	68.0	39.9	32.9
Pueblo	39.9	40.2	57.0	44.1	44.5	39.4
New Mexico						
Albuquerque	53.0	53.0	81.7	62.4	34.9	26.2
Texas						
Abilene	68.3	57.6	85.1	55.7	64.8	28.1
Austin	62.9	63.3	72.1	66.1	69.9	9.5
Corpus Christi	73.7	72.2	91.3	51.0	46.9	13.2
Dallas	83.2	66.8	90.2	76.1	63.4	23.9
El Paso	52.9	52.9	79.2	59.5	52.8	17.9
Fort Worth	74.8	56.5	85.4	78.1	58.8	29.7
Galveston	58.1	33.3	73.8	52.1	42.3	10.8
Houston	73.2	65.2	81.2	70.9	52.1	14.0
Laredo	39.3	39.4	60.1	43.9	44.7	12.7
Lubbock	74.4	66.0	94.4	89.0	65.8	16.3
Odessa	81.8	75.8	90.5	29.2	68.2	11.8
Port Arthur	81.7	45.9	89.7	76.3	50.3	26.6
San Angelo	67.2	65.7	77.5	75.6	70.6	12.9
San Antonio	63.7	63.6	84.5	77.4	49.9	17.0
Waco	65.7	59.7	74.3	60.6	53.4	20.7
Wichita Falls	76.8	64.8	86.1	47.6	67.8	30.8

[a] Excluding Negroes.
Source: The data in this table and the subsequent tables are calculated from census tract data for the 35 cities.

(3) Segregation of Negroes from Anglos ranges from a low of 57 in Pueblo, Colorado to a high of 94 in Lubbock, Texas.

The lack of uniformity is even more apparent when we examine the segregation of minorities from each other (columns 4 and 5 of the table). This is a very important, though largely neglected issue. In most cities, Mexican Americans are less segregated from "other nonwhites" than they are from Negroes. The table shows that

(4) Segregation of Negroes from Spanish-surname persons ranges from a low of 29 in Odessa, Texas to a high of 89 in Lubbock, Texas.

(5) Segregation of Spanish-surname persons from other nonwhites ranges from a low of 10 in Santa Barbara, California to a high of 71 in San Angelo, Texas.

Of course, the composition of the "other nonwhite" population differs from one area to another: It is predominantly Indian in Arizona and New Mexico, and predominantly Oriental in California cities. Historically, in many parts of the Southwest, it was the "other nonwhites" together with the Mexican Americans who supplied the bulk of cheap labor. In various places, Mexican Americans established not only economic but symbiotic and other special relationships with these "others"—with the Indians, for example, in Tucson and Albuquerque; with the Chinese merchants in Phoenix; and with the Japanese in Los Angeles County.[8] In most places in the region, Negroes are relative latecomers compared with these other minorities.

Finally, the table shows the segregation *within* the Mexican-American minority (the foreign-born from the native-born persons of Spanish surname). It ranges from a low of 9 in Austin, Texas to a high of 50 in Colorado Springs. This type of segregation reflects not only a generational split but intra-minority cultural dissimilarities. The cultural differences are much sharper than the split between generations. We found in further analysis that a *high* order of intra-minority segregation is associated both with a *low* proportion of foreign-born and with a *low* rate of increase in the Spanish-surname population.

Thus, the greatest intra-minority segregation appears in Colorado, and the lowest in the cities of south Texas. Here one must again refer to the different origins of the several segments of the Mexican-American minority. The Spanish-surname population of southern Colorado and northern New Mexico consists predominantly of the descendants of persons who settled in this area before 1848. More recent immigrants from Mexico (such as workers in the beet and melon fields of eastern Colorado) often met hostility from these "Spanish Americans." The greater segregation in Colorado cities probably reflects this cultural rift. On the other hand, the lower indexes in the cities on or near the Mexican border probably reflect the fact that little if any cleavage has developed between first- and second- or third-generation Mexican Americans. Mexican Americans living in border cities seem to visit Mexico on a routine basis, and Mexicans come to the United States side with almost equal casualness. This probably reduces any sense of distance between Americans of Mexican descent and the Mexican-born.

SEGREGATION PATTERNS

A more systematic analysis is presented in Table 12–2, which shows both the average scores for each type of segregation and the standard deviation in the scores.

Negro segregation from Anglos is substantially higher on the average than Mexican-American segregation from Anglos. Also, the variability around the mean of segregation of Negroes from Anglos is smaller than that for Mexican Americans from Anglos. As one would expect in view of these findings, the segregation of the total minority population from Anglos ranks in between the scores for Negroes and for Mexican Americans.

Table 12–2. Indexes of Residential Dissimilarity for 35 Southwest Cities, 1960: Means and Standard Deviations for All Cities

	Mean Dissimilarity	Standard Deviations
Anglo vs. all others	62.5	12.2
Anglo vs. Spanish-surname	54.5	11.4
Anglo vs. Negro	80.1	9.5
Spanish-surname vs. Negro	57.3	15.1
Spanish-surname vs. other nonwhite (excluding Negroes)	48.4	12.9
Spanish-surname foreign-born vs. native-born	22.6	8.7

Further, the table shows a general pattern of inter-minority segregation. The segregation of Mexican Americans from Negroes is greater though more variable than the segregation of Mexican Americans from other nonwhites. Segregation of Mexican Americans from Negroes is also slightly greater on the average than the segregation of Mexican Americans from the dominant population, though far more variable.

Is the segregation of one population systematically related to the segregation of another population in the same city? Yes and no. As Table 12–3 indicates, segregation of Mexican Americans from Anglos is highly correlated with segregation of Negroes from Anglos across the 35 cities. Where one minority is highly segregated the other is also likely to be highly segregated. Neither one, however, is very highly correlated with the inter-minority segregation of Mexican Americans from Negroes. In contrast to what might be observed in a few isolated cases, the extent of a minority's segregation from the dominant group has little to do with the extent of its segregation from another minority. Negroes and Mexican Americans do not necessarily form one big ghetto where either or both are separated from Anglos, nor do they necessarily separate into hostile or competing ghettos where one or both are segregated. Finally, with regard to intra-minority segregation—of foreign-born from native-born persons of Spanish surname—there tends to be an insubstantial but negative correlation with the other forms of residential segregation.

277

We can now proceed to observe how the over-all pattern of minority segregation is distributed from one city to another. Omitting the index for Anglos versus all others, the scores in Table 12–2 show the following general rank order: The highest is for Negroes versus Anglos, the second highest for Mexican Americans versus Negroes, and the lowest for Mexican Americans versus Anglos. According to Table 12–1, this order exists in 26 of the 35 cities. It probably indicates the over-all patterning of social as well as residential distance between the three subpopulations; Anglos and Mexican Americans are generally closer to each other than either group is to Negroes, and Negroes are less distant from Mexican Americans than from Anglos.

Table 12–3. Simple Linear Correlation Matrix Comparing Segregation of Various Subpopulations from One Another, 35 Southwest Cities, 1960 (Items are the same as for numbers in rows)

	1.	2.	3.	4.	5.	6.
1. Anglo vs. All Others	1.00	.83	.76	.38	.53	−.12
2. Negro vs. Anglo		1.00	.67	.38	.24	−.10
3. Spanish-surname vs. Anglo			1.00	.20	.50	−.24
4. Spanish-surname vs. Negro				1.00	.38	−.08
5. Spanish-surname vs. Other Nonwhite (excluding Negroes)					1.00	−.25
6. Native-born vs. Foreign-born Spanish-surname						1.00

However, 9 of the 35 cities show a different ordering of the indexes. In this group, segregation of Negroes from Anglos also scores the highest, but the second highest segregation score is that of Mexican Americans from Anglos, and the lowest is for Mexican Americans versus Negroes. The two minorities—Negroes and Mexican Americans—are both relatively highly segregated from the dominant Anglos, but not from each other.

The differences between the two groups of cities call for further analysis. It seems that the minorities do affect each other's chances for residential (and other) mobility, but more so in the second group of cities than in the first. Can one identify characteristics of the cities that help explain the variations in their pattern of segregation? Though there are too few cities for elaborate analysis, the two groups of cities can be classified into subgroups (Table 12–4). In these subgroups we have tried to take account of the level of segregation in addition to the order of each type of segregation. Thus, if the dissimilarity index for Negroes versus Anglos is above the mean, it is designated "high," or H; if it is below the mean, it is labelled "low," or L. In the HHH group of cities all three major types of segregation scores are above average; in the LLL group all three scores are below average.

This new arrangement of the data shows that, generally, the cities where

Mexican Americans and Negroes are relatively unsegregated from each other are middle-sized or smaller communities. Most of them (six of the nine) fall into one group—HLH—in which segregation of both minorities from Anglos is above average, whereas their segregation from each other is below average. The 26 cities where Mexican Americans are more segregated from Negroes than they are from Anglos present much greater diversity. This group includes not only all of the very large communities but smaller cities as well. Most of the bigger cities are in group HHH, in which all three types of segregation are above average. Nine of the 26 cities

Table 12–4. Classification of Southwest Cities by Level and Order of Segregation, 1960

LEVEL OF SEGREGATION[a]			ORDER OF SEGREGATION	
Negro vs. Anglo	Spanish-surname vs. Negro	Spanish-surname vs. Anglo	Spanish-surname more segregated from Negroes than from Anglos	Spanish-surname more segregated from Anglos than from Negroes
H	H	H	Dallas, Fort Worth, Denver, Houston, Los Angeles, Lubbock, Phoenix, San Antonio, Tucson	None
H	H	L	Albuquerque, Bakersfield, Port Arthur	None
H	L	L	Fresno, San Diego	Ontario
H	L	H	None	Abilene, Corpus Christi, Odessa, Riverside, San Bernardino, Wichita Falls
L	H	L	El Paso, San Francisco	None
L	H	H	Austin, San Angelo, Waco	None
L	L	H	None	None
L	L	L	Colorado Springs, Galveston, Laredo, Oakland, Pueblo, Sacramento, San Jose	Santa Barbara, Stockton

[a] H = above the mean; L = below the mean.

are in this category. However, an almost equally large number (seven) are in group LLL. This order of segregation scores tends to prevail irrespective of the levels of segregation.

Little is known about the general images of these cities held by members of the minority groups.[9] It is clear, however, that certain cities are considered particularly "bad" for Mexican Americans or Negroes, whereas other cities are viewed as relatively "good." There seems to be a general, though not perfect, relationship between the minority image and the pattern of segregation in the city. Our field interviews suggest that many highly segregated cities tend to have a bad reputation among minority-group members for reasons other than residential segregation. Many HLH cities also seem to have a bad reputation. These are the towns where both minorities face more or less the same set of circumstances, and are remote from the dominant Anglos. Several of these communities have a recent history of inter-minority conflict. It may well be that the ecological situation indicated in this pattern represents a distinct factor in generating inter-minority tensions. However, it is for future research to relate our sub-groups of cities more systematically to their reputations among the minorities and to the prevalence or absence of conflict.

CORRELATES OF RESIDENTIAL SEGREGATION

The indexes developed and analyzed so far merely measure the extent of residential segregation. Even when they are arrayed to detect segregation patterns and to establish types of cities grouped by the level and order of segregation of various populations, the indexes do not reveal the causes of diverse degrees of segregation in various cities. Differences in levels of segregation among cities, or in its severity for the two main minority groups examined here, may be determined by a great variety of factors.

Even the casual observer of the urban scene is aware of the complexities involved in determining the causes of residential separation. Yet, one hears in everyday conversation clichés such as these: "People of the same kind like to live together" (voluntary congregation); "people live in separate neighborhoods because they are poor and not because of ethnic or racial segregation" (economic determinism); "ethnic or racial minorities are forced to live in ghettos because of housing discrimination" (involuntary segregation). In each of these statements one, and only one, factor is singled out as *the* explanation of a complicated phenomenon.

Unfortunately, we cannot produce an analysis that will give a clear-cut, neat exposition of cause and effect. Instead, we must be content with sorting out and weighing the factors that seem to be associated with residential segregation of each minority from the dominant group and of each minority from the other. Although these forms of segregation are closely intertwined in specific cities, the analysis can separate them and examine the correlates of each form of segregation as if it were distinct from all others.

Our effort focuses on the three major forms of segregation: of persons of Spanish surname from Anglos, of Negroes from Anglos, and of persons of Spanish surname from Negroes. We begin here with a listing of major factors associated with residential segregation as suggested in the scholarly literature. These factors are cultural, economic, and demographic-ecological.

The relatively conscious *cultural factors* include

a. the acceptability of the subpopulation to the dominant population, or the "taste for discrimination"[10] against a subpopulation; and

b. the cohesiveness of the subpopulation and its desire for assimilation, or the taste for segregation of the subpopulation itself. The literature does not provide much guidance for quantifying the taste for self-segregation, but one would include here such matters as the degree of acculturation of the subpopulation and the extent of traditional values among its members. The "taste for self-segregation" is clearly associated with the "taste for discrimination" though analytically distinct.

The impersonal *economic factors* include

a. the economic position of the subpopulation compared with the dominant population (its relative ability to compete for urban space); and

b. the condition of the housing market (housing supply).

The *demographic and ecological factors* which set limits for the expression of cultural preferences and market operations include

a. the size and density of the population and other physical characteristics of the community which may facilitate segregation; and

b. the size, composition, and growth rates of the minority subpopulations and their concentration in central cities.

THE MAIN FINDINGS ON CORRELATES

In the research process, our first approach to this array of factors or variables was purely exploratory. The purposes, procedures, and results are reported elsewhere,[11] but it should be said here that the exploration yielded a cluster of correlates of residential segregation that clearly warranted further analysis. Such an analysis has several desiderata. First, it should account for each of the types of segregation, that is, isolate those factors that are most highly associated with each form of segregation and that together and individually contribute significantly to an explanation of the variations in segregation of each type. Second, it should indicate why one form of segregation can be more fully explained than another. Third, the analysis should show which of the types of hypothesized factors is most important to each of the three types of segregation. As an example, it could be argued that the most stringent form of segregation is most highly correlated with the relatively conscious cultural factors. It is also possible that it is most closely associated with the more impersonal economic factors. Previous research and theory offer support on either side.

The multiple regression computed for this analysis correlates four independent (or predictor) variables with each type of segregation. These include:

One *cultural* factor: the percentage of minority households with five or more persons, nonwhite or Spanish-surname, as an indicator of traditional familism.*

One *economic* factor: the relative income position of the minority populations. For the equation relating to segregation of the Spanish-surname group from Anglos, we used the ratio of the median income of the total population to Spanish-surname median income. For the equation relating to Negro segregation from Anglos, we applied the ratio of the median income of the total population to nonwhite median

---

*In our exploratory analysis we found this factor to be highly intercorrelated with income and thus far from satisfactory. We made a considerable effort to find new variables which would be less contaminated with economic factors and which would still express the traditional familistic component we were seeking. But such variables, for example differentials in fertility ratios, did not contribute significantly to the correlation coefficients. The contaminated variables did. Therefore, we concluded that household size may reflect an important interaction between traditionalism and the economic status of the minority. When a population is already differentiated in income, large households strengthen the differentiation, and vice versa.

281

income. For the segregation of Spanish-surname persons from Negroes, the equation used nonwhite median income as a percent of Spanish-surname median income. (The substitution of nonwhite for Negro income was dictated by limitations of published census data.)

Two *demographic* factors: 1) size of city—its total population, and 2) ethnic composition of the minority population, expressed as the ratio of Spanish-surname persons to nonwhites, in each city.

The results of the analysis are shown in Table 12–5. The independent variables account most adequately for inter-urban differences in the segregation of Mexican Americans from Anglos, with a coefficient of determination (R^2) of .67. They are moderately successful in regard to the segregation of Negroes from whites (.46). They are least successful in explaining local variations in the segregation of Spanish-surname persons from Negroes, with a coefficient of determination of only .36.

How can the differences in the magnitudes of these coefficients be interpreted? The type of segregation that is most adequately explained, that of Mexican Americans from Anglos, is also the least stringent. The most rigorous level of segregation, that of Negroes from Anglos, is less adequately accounted for in the analysis. This is not unexpected, though it could not have been predicted with confidence. As other sections of this volume indicate, the Mexican-American minority has been experiencing substantial internal changes since World War II. Its residential distribution in a city might therefore be more responsive to situational variables than that of Negroes.

The least adequate explanation is that of the inter-minority segregation of Mexican Americans from Negroes. Our analysis of this form of segregation is novel: Little is known about the separation of minorities from each other. Sociologists have developed descriptive literature on the phenomenon of *succession*, the tendency in Eastern and Midwestern cities for groups to follow one another in the poorer, central-city ghettos.[12] The Lower East Side of Manhattan and the Halstead Street area in Chicago, for example, have seen one wave of immigrants after another living in the same tenements and occupying the same stores—until the current urban renewal. Puerto Ricans settled on the fringe of Negro-occupied Harlem in New York, often succeeding Negroes. Such processes may be quite different in the Southwest. As was mentioned earlier, many cities grew up around originally Mexican nuclei— Anglos succeeding Mexicans at the outset. More recent Mexican-American arrivals to the cities have not always migrated to the central-city ghettos, but have tended to drift to ethnic neighborhoods on the fringes of cities. Negroes, relatively new in the Southwest and attracted by industrial opportunities, have frequently settled in areas quite remote from long-established Mexican-American enclaves.

Finally, a comment is in order on the explanatory power of the independent variables for different kinds of segregation. The *cultural* factor (large households indicating traditional familism) produces significant positive regression coefficients in all equations. This factor is most highly correlated with the segregation of Mexican Americans from Anglos and least correlated with Negro segregation from Anglos.

From the columns showing partial correlations in Table 12–5 it is apparent that, holding other factors constant, familism with its diffuse social and economic attendants is more related to Mexican-American segregation from Anglos and less related to Negro segregation from Anglos than any other factor. To say the same thing in another way: When large proportions of Mexican Americans begin to have small families, they tend to become residentially integrated with Anglos, but this is far less true for Negroes.

The different importance of large families in the segregation of the two minority groups from Anglos probably reflects the greater capacity of Mexican Americans to become assimilated. A decrease in extended-family household arrangements and the beginning of birth-control practices indicates the emergence of a relatively acculturated and more integrable Mexican-American population. This is less clear-cut as an indicator of acculturation among Negroes, who are predominantly non-Catholic. Further, the path from acculturation to integration is undoubtedly far less easy for Negroes than for Mexican Americans.

It is also relevant to note that the size of family is the second most important factor in accounting for inter-minority segregation. This observation suggests that the less the Mexican Americans are acculturated, the more likely they are to share the segregated areas with Negroes.[13] Further, it is the size of the Mexican-American household, not the size of the Negro household, that is correlated with the segregation of Mexican Americans from Negroes.

The *economic* factor (ratio of each minority income to total median income) is very significantly related to the segregation of Negroes from Anglos but only marginally significant for the segregation of Mexican Americans from Anglos. The greater the disparity in income between the minorities and the Anglos, the higher the segregation between them. The income differential is the most important single factor in accounting for the most stringent form of segregation—that of Negroes from Anglos. In the less rigorous segregation of Mexican Americans from Anglos, the economic factor is the least important. The income ratio is not significantly associated with segregation of Negroes from Mexican Americans.

As for the *demographic* factors, the size of the city is significant in all three equations; that is, the larger the city the greater the segregation of all three types. It is the most significant variable "explaining" Mexican-American segregation from Negroes. That the degree of segregation increases with the size of cities seems to contradict common expectations. The impersonality and anonymity of the larger city are assumed to facilitate the social integration of minorities. This may indeed be true for individual members of minority groups, but the larger cities also have many more persons in a minority. Ecological processes can work more freely to sort out various kinds of individuals. The poor can be separated from the less poor. The Mexican-American poor can be separated from the Negro poor. In turn, the segregation of minority individuals into areas with a distinctive social identity (San Francisco's Mission and Los Angeles' Watts) makes the minorities' images even clearer to the dominant group, and it probably facilitates further discrimination against them.

Table 12–5. Coefficients of Determination, Partial Correlations, T-values, Regression Coefficients, and Intercept Values for Variables to Explain Residential Segregation

Independent Variables	Dependent Variables								
	SPANISH-SURNAME VS. ANGLO			SPANISH-SURNAME VS. NEGRO			NEGRO VS. ANGLO		
	Partial Regression coefficient	T-value	Partial correlation	Partial Regression coefficient	T-value	Partial correlation	Partial Regression coefficient	T-value	Partial correlation
Cultural									
Percent SS[a] OHU[b] with 5 persons or more	0.95	3.7c	0.56	0.81	2.6d	0.42	—	—	—
Percent nonwhite OHU with 5 persons or more	—	—	—	—	—	—	0.57	2.0e	0.34
Economic									
Ratio of total median to SS median income	17.61	1.7e	0.29	—	—	—	—	—	—
Percentage of nonwhite to SS median income	—	—	—	−0.30	−1.6	−0.28	—	—	—
Ratio of total median to nonwhite median income	—	—	—	—	—	—	20.03	3.4c	0.53
Demographic									
Total city population	.00001	2.4d	0.40	.00002	3.4c	0.53	.00001	2.1d	0.35
Ratio of SS to nonwhite persons	−0.08	−2.4d	−0.40	−0.07	−1.2	−0.21	−0.09	−2.5d	−0.42
Intercept		−9.2			45.3			32.19	
Multiple R²		.67			.36			.46	

a SS = persons of Spanish surname.
b OHU = occupied housing units.
c Significant at 0.01 level.
d Significant at 0.05 level.
e Significant at 0.10 level.

Such a "snowball effect" in which ecological processes reinforce cultural and psychological processes may generally affect Mexican Americans more than it does Negroes, since Mexican Americans are less rigidly confined to a caste status. The factor is most significant in the case of Mexican-American segregation from Anglos. Negative attitudes of the dominant Anglos may reflect a local association of Mexican Americans with areas of the city known for juvenile delinquency, cheap stores, and generally slummy appearance. Negative attitudes about Negroes, on the other hand, are likely to persist across communities independently of the Negroes' relative socioeconomic status and the particular environment in which the dominant population views the minority. Given the interaction of all these factors in the larger cities, segregation of all groups from each other tends to be high.

The second demographic variable, the composition of the minority, is significant in both equations dealing with the segregation of minorities from the Anglo population. Wherever there are relatively few Mexican Americans in comparison to Negroes, the segregation of either group from Anglos seems to be accentuated. The Mexican Americans may suffer from being classified with the Negro minority in that the greater "taste for discrimination" against Negroes may become diffused to encompass Mexican Americans. Conversely, Negroes may benefit from being associated with Mexican Americans who become defined as "our minority" (as one informant put it) in cities where they predominate; the generally lower taste for discrimination against Mexican Americans may become somewhat diffused to include Negroes. Each minority affects the other's chances for movement in the system.

A NOTE ON DISCRIMINATION

The reader will observe that housing discrimination is not among the factors found to be significant correlates of residential segregation. This omission is not an oversight. Since discrimination is a social reality in housing markets as well as elsewhere, our exploratory efforts attempted to include it in the regression analysis. One of the main problems was to find a *quantifiable* expression for differences in the relative "taste for discrimination" on the part of Anglos against the two minorities, or even an adequate statistical proxy. This problem turned out to be extremely difficult. On the assumption that the percentage of native born among the Spanish-surname population in each city was a measure of the minority's acculturation and that different degrees of acculturation would be associated with variations in the host society's "taste for discrimination," this percentage was tentatively used as an independent variable. However, the variable failed to show any significant relationship to the segregation of Mexican Americans from either Anglos or Negroes. Apart from the difficulty of finding a statistical measure for the "taste for discrimination," very little is known about how a local social climate of prejudice and discrimination operates against one minority, let alone two, and thus generates tensions between the minorities themselves. The largest unexplained variances in our analysis occur for

Spanish-surname versus Negro segregation and Negro versus Anglo segregation, and it is particularly to the former type of separation that variations in the local climate may be most relevant.

The negative outcome does not deny or diminish the importance of discrimination as a factor contributing to residential segregation. It merely illustrates the problem of expressing some facts of life in such form that they lend themselves to quantitative analysis. Yet, at the risk of somewhat incautious interpretation, one can say that the statistical findings do throw light on the relative significance of local variations in the taste for discrimination. To repeat, the regression analysis was able to explain 67 percent of the inter-urban variations in the segregation of Mexican Americans from Anglos. By contrast, the analysis accounted for only 46 percent of the local variations in the segregation of Negroes from whites, leaving over half of the variance unexplained. One cannot tell how much of the unexplained portion represents the elusive factor of discrimination, but the fact that it is far smaller for Mexican-American than for Negro segregation is consistent with general observation of the housing market and with insights from Mexican-American informants. Housing discrimination against the Spanish-surname population is generally portrayed as substantially less severe than that against Negroes. Even though the unexplained portions cannot be taken to measure the inter-city variations in the taste for discrimination, the contrast between the relatively small one for Mexican-American segregation and the relatively large one for Negro segregation may denote varying intensities of discrimination quite adequately.*

SUMMARY

Mexican Americans are differentiated from the larger society in many respects, and the various kinds of differentiation are in all probability highly interrelated. Differentiation in terms of urban residence location reflects not only physical distance from the majority population but this more pervasive social distance as well.

Moreover, segregation patterns in the urban Southwest are of special significance because this region includes two large population groups generally recognized as disadvantaged minorities: Mexican Americans and Negroes. There are also significant numbers of Orientals and Indians in many cities. This constellation makes it possible to examine not only the residential separation of each minority from the members of the dominant society but also the segregation of subordinate groups from each other.

An overview of residential segregation in 35 Southwest cities yields one clear-cut finding. Mexican Americans are without exception substantially less segregated

---

*One hesitates to extend this interpretation to the segregation of Spanish-surname persons from Negroes. For this type of segregation, the multiple regression accounted for only 36 percent of the local variations, leaving 64 percent unexplained. Too little is known about the factors related to inter-minority segregation to consider the large unexplained part as in any way representative of variances in the mutual "taste for discrimination."

from the dominant group than are Negroes, but the level of segregation for both groups has remained high. Focusing only on the two largest minorities, the results show the following general rank order: the most severe segregation exists between Negroes and white Anglos, the next highest degree of segregation is observed between Mexican Americans and Negroes, and the lowest is between Mexican Americans and Anglos. Within the Mexican-American group there is also some segregation between the native born and the foreign born.

However, the degree of segregation varies greatly from city to city as well as between the three population groups in each city. It seems difficult at first to detect any ordering in the indexes of dissimilarity used to measure residential segregation. Cities can, however, be classified by patterns of segregation affecting the minority groups. There are basically two types of patterns. In most cities, segregation of Negroes from Anglos is the highest; segregation of Mexican Americans from Negroes is next; and segregation of Mexican Americans from Anglos is lowest. But in some cities a different pattern emerges in which the order of the last two types of segregation is reversed.

Common observation tells us that residential segregation may be determined by a great variety of factors including but not limited to discrimination in housing markets. The scholarly literature on the subject offers a number of hypotheses on this point; the unusual admixture of minority groups in Southwest cities provides an opportunity to test the general validity of existing explanations and to develop new insights as well.

Some of the factors suggested by previous research have been confirmed as being significantly related to residential segregation. Others have not. Among those which our exploratory work proved to be relatively unimportant as explanatory variables are the absolute income of the minority group, vacancies in the supply of housing, the density of the population, and the concentration of the minority in the central city as contrasted with outlying areas.

We found the following factors important in accounting for segregation:

1. The larger the city, the greater the intensity of segregation in all of its three principal types: Mexican Americans versus Anglos, Negroes versus Anglos, and Mexican Americans versus Negroes.

2. The greater the proportion of large households in the two minorities, the more severe is the residential separation of all three forms. The proportion of large households among minorities, in turn, can be interpreted as an indicator of their acculturation. Here, then, is a significant factor internal to the minority rather than a characteristic of the local milieu.

3. Although residential segregation does not seem to be systematically related to low minority incomes as such, it is associated with income *differentials* between the two minorities and the Anglos. However, the income factor does little if anything to explain the segregation between Mexican Americans and Negroes.

4. The intensity of residential segregation is also a function of the ethnic composition of the total minority population. The separation of either minority from

the dominant group is more pronounced in cities with a large nonwhite population relative to their Mexican-American population, and vice versa. However, these numerical relationships do not seem to influence in any significant measure the segregation of the two minorities from each other.

The strength of the relationships differs from case to case, as it always does in correlation analysis. Some of the factors enumerated above are more clearly associated with the severe forms of residential segregation than others. And there are remaining variances of different magnitudes that are left unexplained by the factors isolated. Several factors which were intuitively believed to be of importance failed to show significant statistical relationships to segregation. Perhaps the most important among these is discrimination of various kinds.

Of course, the conceptual scheme underlying this analysis included what has come to be called the "taste for discrimination." But it turned out to be extremely difficult to find the statistical proxy for discrimination that is necessary for multiple-regression analysis. The statistical measure selected for this purpose failed to show any significant relationships to either inter-city or inter-group segregation. Under these circumstances, one must conclude that the influence of discrimination on differences in the extent of residential segregation is buried in the variances left unexplained by the analysis.

NOTES TO CHAPTER TWELVE

1. See Karl E. Taeuber and Alma F. Taeuber, *Negroes in Cities* (Chicago: Aldine Publishing Company, 1965), and Karl E. Taeuber, "Negro Residential Segregation," *Social Problems*, XII (Summer, 1964), pp. 42–50.

2. See Stanley Lieberson, *Ethnic Patterns in Americans Cities* (New York: The Free Press, 1963).

3. The following section is drawn mainly from Joan W. Moore and Frank G. Mittelbach, with the assistance of Ronald McDaniel, *Residential Segregation in the Urban Southwest* (Mexican-American Study Project, Advance Report 4, Graduate School of Business Administration, University of California, Los Angeles, June, 1966), pp. 10–13.

4. The sequence was 48 percent for Anglos, 60 percent for Mexican Americans, and nearly 75 percent for nonwhites in 1960. From *1960 U.S. Census of Population*, vol. I, parts 4, 6, 7, 33 and 45, tables 13 and 21; PC(2)–1B, table 15; PC(3)–1D, table 1. For the still greater concentration of Negroes in the central cities of metropolitan areas, see Moore and Mittelbach, *op. cit.*, charts A and B.

5. For recent statistical detail on the East Los Angeles area, see "Characteristics of the South and East Los Angeles Areas, November 1965," U.S. Bureau of the Census, Series P–23, no. 18, June 28, 1966.

6. See chapter 16 for details on some of these cases.

7. This index was developed by the Duncans and utilized in Otis Dudley Duncan and Beverly Duncan, "Residential Distribution and Occupational Stratification," *American Journal of Sociology*, LX (Mar., 1955), pp. 493–503. It was also used in the two recent large-scale works on residential segregation cited earlier. See Taeuber and Taeuber, *op. cit.*, and Lieberson, *op. cit.* Irrespective of the merits of alternative measures of segregation (see

Taeuber and Taeuber, *op. cit.*, pp. 195–245), the availability of these two major empirical studies dictated the use of the index of residential dissimilarity in this chapter.

8. See Harry T. Getty, "Interethnic Relationships in the Community of Tucson" (unpublished Ph.D. dissertation, University of Arizona, 1950). Concerning Phoenix, we owe insight into the relationships between Mexican Americans and Chinese to discussion with the late Rose Hum Lee, a Phoenix sociologist of Chinese descent. For Los Angeles we rely on field interviews regarding Mexican-Japanese relationships.

9. For a number of years, the National Urban League has published community surveys which attempt an objective assessment of each city as a place for Negroes to live.

10. See Gary Becker, *The Economics of Discrimination* (Chicago: The University of Chicago Press, 1957), p. 137, for a discussion of this concept.

11. Moore and Mittelbach, *op. cit.*, pp. 25–29 and Appendix C.

12. For a highly analytical treatment of the process of succession, see Otis Dudley Duncan and Beverly Duncan, *The Negro Population of Chicago* (Chicago: The University of Chicago Press, 1957).

13. This finding does not support field observations or comments of informants. However, since it is based on a complete rather than a selective enumeration of the populations involved, it at least strongly suggests that further research on this topic might be useful.

Part four

THE INDIVIDUAL

IN THE SOCIAL SYSTEM

INTRODUCTORY NOTE

The two previous parts have presented the portrait of a population of predominantly low status which is nevertheless beginning to participate in the larger society and to share in the material rewards of participation. It is a population historically isolated in work and residence from the rest of the community, but it is now less segregated. It is a population also isolated by a legacy of overt and more subtle conflict with the dominant system.

The following set of chapters deals with the Mexican-American individual in various contemporary social settings and with his adaptation to urban situations. Most of the materials for the analysis come from interview surveys, conducted in 1965 and 1966 in Los Angeles and San Antonio, of a sample of Mexican-American households. Los Angeles and San Antonio are "capital cities" for this population. Since the experience, behavior, attitudes, and beliefs of the respondents reflect in part the difference in the milieus of the two cities, Chapter 13 presents a brief discussion of Los Angeles and San Antonio as communities for Mexican Americans, as well as basic data on the characteristics of the sample population.

The remaining chapters of Part Four discuss the social class structure; social mobility; the family; social relations with in-group and out-group people; Mexican Americans' perceptions of themselves and others; intermarriage as an index of assimilation; and the tenacity of traditional culture traits, especially those bearing on achievement. In the analysis of many of these subjects, we draw on sociological theory for a conceptual framework and attempt to relate the empirical materials to the theory.

One of our main hypotheses is the existence of a great deal of internal differentiation among the Mexican-American people. To examine the importance and the implications of this differentiation, the interview responses are grouped by social class and, within each social class, by the ethnic composition of the neighborhood in which the interviewees were living. On some salient subjects, we obtain generational differences by comparing the childhood experience of the respondents with their experience as adults and with that of their children. The fact that Los Angeles and San Antonio reflect strong contrasts in the degree of "openness" of the larger society adds still another dimension of differential analysis.

Throughout, social class will emerge as a major differentiating factor. Taking family income as an indicator of social class, we find that the higher-income Mexican Americans show greater acculturation than those of low income, whether the individual's role in the family, the propensity for social relations outside the ethnic community, or the adherence to cultural traditions is involved. Reflecting the more depressed condition of Mexican Americans and the less favorable environment in San Antonio, however, the responses vary a great deal between the two cities. Mexican-American San Antonians are still far more isolated as well as poorer than the Angelenos. In both cities, the ghetto dwellers are less acculturated, partly because they are older, and partly because, as could be expected, they include a large number of people with economic and social problems. On the whole, the relationship between indicators of acculturation and neighborhood ethnicity is more complex than the one existing between indicators of acculturation and social class, partly because the residents of the areas of heavy Mexican-American concentration include higher-income as well as poor people—for reasons discussed in Chapter 14.

The analysis of intermarriages is consistent with the thesis that the Mexican-American population is moving in the direction of integration, at least in the relatively permissive social climate of Los Angeles. In 1963, about one-quarter of all marriages of Spanish-surname persons in the County of Los Angeles involved an individual who married a spouse outside the ethnic group. Although this rate is probably lower in other cities of the Southwest, it can be considered a portent of the future as local systems become more receptive to Mexican Americans and their social status improves.

The analysis of the social-class structure and of social mobility in Los Angeles and San Antonio points up some elements of instability and ambiguity encountered by the Mexican-American achiever. Straddling the ethnic sub-system and the class system of the dominant society, he often finds himself in a status dilemma. Many upwardly mobile persons are still in the process of consolidating their position in the urban structure and feel uncertain about both their accomplishment and their future. In other words, the relatively new middle class exhibits status apprehensions that still reflect the prevailing poverty of their background and memories of discrimination experienced on the way up to the middle class.

THIRTEEN

The Social Worlds
of Mexican Americans

OUR materials on the complex adaptations to city life are based on household sample surveys of Mexican Americans in Los Angeles and San Antonio. These surveys of 1965–1966 are the most comprehensive ever undertaken among this minority group. Los Angeles and San Antonio include about a quarter of all Mexican Americans in the Southwest and 37 percent of those living in metropolitan areas. Nonetheless, even this high numerical representation does not necessarily place the two cities in the full context of social conditions for Mexican Americans. As we shall see, the two cities are very different from each other. Even so, the range of differences between them probably does not represent the total range of living milieus for urban Mexican Americans.

To begin, it is tempting to try to construct some sort of social continuum with these two cities that would range from "folk" to "modern," or from "unacculturated" to "acculturated." If this is done, it must be recognized that Los Angeles and San

Antonio are very diverse within themselves. A more accurate portrait would probably look something like Figure 13–1. Sections of the continuum are broad and tend to overlap. In fact, although the Figure is only the roughest of schematizations, it seems to fit much of the data. Neither the beginning nor the end of this continuum can be clearly marked. Further, there is probably not just one continuum but many. Changes in social environments are so complex and extend into so many dimensions that there is little reason to assume a linear evolution from traditional to modern.

Figure 13–1.

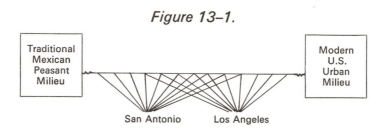

Antonio   Los Angeles

THE LITERATURE OF SOCIAL CONTEXT

This scheme of Fig. 13–1 reflects the controversy between anthropologists and sociologists who have attempted analysis of "folk" and "urban" cultures. The "folk" end of the continuum has always been easy to delineate. According to Redfield, folk systems are small, distinctive, homogeneous, self-sufficient, and slow-changing.[1] But later analysis has shown even this seemingly simple end of the continuum to be less simple.[2] The urban, or modern, end has presented difficulties ever since Wirth's classic statement, complementing Redfield's, of "urbanism as a way of life."[3] One of the current "discoveries" of research in underdeveloped nations is the persistence of folk enclaves or folk relationships in the cities.[4]

These general theoretical problems have exact counterparts in the literature on Mexican Americans. William Madsen's work on a comparatively small, distinctive, and homogeneous community in South Texas presents a clear case of the traditional end of the continuum.[5] It is obvious that this is not entirely a statement of what *exists* in the community he studied, but rather an idealized construct of the essentials of the culture. Thus, Madsen asserts that the "focal values of *la raza*" (such as familism, *machismo*, *envidia*, and similar values) find their "stronghold" in the comparatively isolated lower class. But according to his own analysis this stronghold is embattled and unstable. The middle and even the working classes of the border town of his investigation have already departed from the "pure" Mexican peasant value type. This milieu of the agricultural worker in the lower Rio Grande Valley approximates the traditional end of the continuum, but it is an unstable approximation at best.

[1] Notes for this chapter start on page 312.

The "modern" end of the Mexican-American spectrum is equally equivocal. It has been far less studied than the traditional. Most research on Mexican-American communities and subcommunities has focused on the latter, selecting extremely small towns[6] or the more accessible lower-class areas of large cities.[7] Such procedures are analogous to deriving all knowledge about Negroes from studies in rural Mississippi or in the poorest slums of Harlem, the areas of first settlement for rural in-migrants from the Deep South. Such research obviously introduces a great deal of distortion. To be sure, folk-like or "village" enclaves in large cities indicate some of the alternatives these cities present to Mexican Americans. But the persistence of these ethnic enclaves should not blind the researcher to those individuals who relate more closely to the larger system. In addition, even studies of middle-class urban Mexican Americans tend to place great emphasis on cultural retention and distinctiveness, in part because the researcher has easy access to those who do retain their culture.[8] But the bias makes it difficult to draw an accurate profile of the "modern" Mexican American.

In some respects, the rural-urban continuum presented in Figure 13–1 can be used without pretending theoretical sophistication or operational specificity. That is, if the "modern" end is left undefined and the "traditional" end reconceptualized as "isolation," one gets a closer approximation of an important process involved in social change. As soon as there is the slightest crack in the isolation of a folk society, complex changes take place. In this light, the lower-lower-class Mexican Americans of Hidalgo County described by Madsen and Rubel are very isolated; working-class and middle-class individuals in the same town are less isolated. Similarly, the villages and the urban *barrios* so well portrayed in the literature represent slightly varying degrees of isolation. And the lower-class ghetto areas of San Antonio and Los Angeles are comparatively more isolated than the middle-class neighborhoods in the two cities, whereas the whole milieu of Laredo would be more isolated than that of Los Angeles, despite internal variations. Moreover, the notion of "isolation" is useful in conceptualizing historical as well as contemporary data. In some Midwestern cities, the origins of Mexican-American settlement were conducive to isolation. In Toledo, for example, Mexicans were originally imported as strikebreakers and were hated by Anglo workers.[9]

LOS ANGELES AND SAN ANTONIO AS ECONOMIC MILIEUS

Los Angeles and San Antonio were strikingly different communities for Mexican Americans in the 1960s. The city of Los Angeles was more than five times larger. Mexican Americans were a far less significant proportion of the whole there than in San Antonio; 7 percent of the 1960 Los Angeles central-city population and 9 percent of the SMSA were Spanish-surname, compared with 41 percent of San Antonio.

Even more striking were differences in the material well-being of the Mexican Americans. In 1960 Los Angeles held fifth place among the 35 Southwest cities in median family income for the group ($5,584 for the central cities). San Antonio was twenty-seventh out of 35, with a median family income of $3,474, close to the national poverty level. By the 1960s, Los Angeles had become the major destination for Mexican immigrants and Mexican-American in-migrants from other areas of the Southwest.

The income figures reflect great dissimilarities in the economies of the two cities. Los Angeles had become a national and indeed a cosmopolitan metropolis—the trading, manufacturing, financial, transportation, and recreational center for a vast area, increasingly oriented to international transactions. It was the second largest city in the nation, with the curious combination of urban problems and suburban charms that have made it so fascinating for observers of contemporary American life. San Antonio was a highly specialized metropolis with only slightly over a half million residents, its economy depending in part on a large tourist trade generated by its historic past and in part on its location for a significant amount of regional commerce, but above all on its large military bases.

But only four decades earlier—in 1920, when the first large wave of immigration from Mexico was beginning—there was far less difference between the two cities. Los Angeles was then just on the eve of explosive economic growth. Like San Antonio, it was primarily the regional trading center for a relatively small hinterland.[10] But by 1920 San Antonio was beginning its relative decline. Once the largest and most important city in Texas, it had by that year already lost its leading position. Both cities had comparatively low ratios of manufacturing to trade and professional employment. Both benefited from a considerable volume of tourism. Both cities had an exceptionally vigorous open-shop movement, which meant even weaker labor unions than elsewhere in the nation. In addition, organized labor in California conceived of the Mexicans as a serious threat (Chapter 5).

For Mexicans in both cities in the 1920s this kind of economy meant great insecurity and marginality. In Los Angeles, large numbers of unemployed Mexicans were on public relief.[11] In both cities many were agricultural workers who migrated from an urban base. In Los Angeles they worked primarily as common laborers and domestic servants. Similarly, Mexican Americans in San Antonio during the 1920s suffered from considerable unemployment, a propensity to hold temporary rather than permanent jobs, and heavy concentration in casual agricultural work and other common labor.[12] Not until Los Angeles began to develop an industrial base in the late 1920s did opportunities for Mexicans in the two cities begin to diverge in quality; San Antonio never succeeded in attracting much industry.

During the same years that Los Angeles became a metropolis of national importance, pecan shelling was the most significant industrial development in San Antonio. In most other locations, pecan shelling was mechanized in the late 1920s and early 1930s. In San Antonio, however, the Southern Pecan Company, founded only in 1926 (and thus a latecomer to the industry), began to awaken to the advantages of the cheap Mexican labor supply. In what must be a rare technological reversal in a modern economy, the company rejected the machines and began to shell pecans by hand. This gave it such an edge over its mechanized competitors that by 1935 it dominated the industry. Wages were permitted to decline during the 1930s; the management argued that the workers could eat the pecans.[13] Pecan shelling became the major winter employment of Mexican Americans during the Depression, employing up to 20,000 workers in the peak year of 1934.

On the whole, then, there was comparatively little economic difference for Mexicans between Los Angeles and San Antonio in the 1920s. Equally important, their employment pattern in both places had a heavy admixture of agricultural and other migrant labor and unsteady work in jobs outside agriculture. This tended to isolate Mexican Americans from the rest of the community. As explained in more detail in Chapter 5, it also tended to restrict assimilative opportunities. The large volume of unemployment reinforced isolation. The unremitting hostility of organized labor to Mexicans during the 1920s and early 1930s was another isolating factor common to both cities.[14] In San Antonio, the concentration of Mexicans in the pecan-shelling industry meant continued isolation, since pecans were often shelled at home by the entire family in a revival of cottage industry.

Furthermore, Mexican Americans in both cities were heavily concentrated in service employment. (This is still true in San Antonio.) Commerce and entertainment and recreational services[15] tend to be industries involving direct contact between employee and customer in a relationship of symbolic superiority and subordination. Domestic service, of course, is the prototype of such a relationship. These service jobs may now encompass a fairly wide range of salaries and skills (certainly a greater range than in the 1920s). Nevertheless, they share one feature: Employees must express deference to the customer, who is more often than not an Anglo; and in San Antonio he is often a Texan visiting the Alamo, symbol of Mexico's defeat. Such occupations contrast sharply with those in which the Mexican American is one among many and has no direct contact with customers. On an assembly line, for example, deference is generally expected only in relation to the foreman. Thus the history of the two cities suggests not only isolation but also a distinctive style of interaction between minority and dominant-group members. The occupational milieu of San Antonio is far more likely to perpetuate an etiquette of dominance and subordination than the more industrialized world of present-day Los Angeles.

The populations of the two cities also differ sharply. Los Angeles is far more heterogeneous than San Antonio. Los Angeles had more nonwhites than any other city in the Southwest in both 1950 and 1960; San Antonio had very few. Los Angeles has a large and visible Jewish population, reputedly the second largest in the world; in San Antonio, it is difficult to find a good kosher delicatessen. Los Angeles has the largest Japanese population in the United States; in San Antonio the Japanese are so few as to be invisible. Los Angeles has had many more foreign-born people than San Antonio (Table 13-1). In 1920, when Mexicans were beginning to enter in large numbers, San Antonio had relatively many more American born, and about 58 percent of the total population were native *Texans*. This increased to 65 percent in 1930, contrasted with only 25 percent of the Los Angeles population at both periods who were native Californians.[16] During the last part of the nineteenth century, San Antonio became the major urban destination for Mexicans, just as Los Angeles is now.[17] By 1920, fully 17 percent of San Antonio's population were Mexican-born, compared with only 4 percent of the Los Angeles population. In absolute numbers,

Table 13–1. Total Population and Foreign born as Percent of Total, Cities of Los Angeles and San Antonio, 1930–1960

| | YEAR | | | |
	1930	1940	1950	1960
Los Angeles				
Total population	1,238,048	1,504,277	1,970,358	2,481,456
Foreign born from Mexico as percent of total[a]	4	2	2	2
Non-Mexican foreign born as percent of total	15	12	11	9
San Antonio				
Total population	231,542	253,854	405,442	588,042
Foreign born from Mexico as percent of total[a]	14	9	6	5
Non-Mexican foreign born as percent of total	3	2	2	2

[a] 1930–1950: white persons born in Mexico. 1960: Mexican-born white persons of Spanish surname.
Sources: 1930 and 1940 from *1940 U.S. Census of Population*, vol. 2, part 1 for California and part 6 for Texas, tables B40 and D40; also tables 53 and 64.
1950 U.S. Census of Population, part 5 for California and part 43 for Texas, tables 33. Also PE no. 3A, *Subject report on Nativity and Parentage*, table 13.
1960 U.S. Census of Population, volume 1, part 6 for California and part 45 for Texas, tables 72, also PC(2)–1B, *Persons of Spanish Surname*, table 15.

San Antonio had 28,000 compared with 22,000 for Los Angeles.[18] Since 1920, in San Antonio Mexicans have been the largest foreign population and Mexican Americans the largest minority population, next to which all others are insignificant. San Antonio has almost no distinctive ethnic areas outside of its Mexican "West Side"; there is no Negro Watts, Jewish Fairfax, Little Tokyo, or other ethnic shopping and residential center. In Los Angeles, on the other hand, Mexican Americans have been one among many foreign or minority populations.

COMMON ISOLATION OF MEXICAN AMERICANS UNTIL WORLD WAR II

The composition of its people affects a city's institutions through the values present in its population segments and through the nature of their interaction in various centers of social transaction. Analysis of such effects, of course, involves much speculation. Hard facts are difficult to obtain and it must not be forgotten that both cities exist in a common American frame of reference.

The native-born population of Los Angeles has always been largely Midwestern in origin.[19] Unlike the Texas native who was the typical inhabitant of San Antonio, Americans from the Midwest probably held few strong preconceptions about Mexicans. This might have been some advantage to the Mexicans in Los Angeles. However, according to a recent history of Los Angeles, Midwesterners may have come to Southern California at least in part to escape the urbanization of the developing Midwest, with its implicit threat to traditional values. In particular, they had good reason to fear big-city political machines and worked vigorously to prevent urban political corruption. By 1920, the reformers and progressives had succeeded in undermining any base for organized politics on the lines of Eastern and Midwestern cities.[20] The consequences for politics in the city's minority populations are still being felt.[21]

Apart from effects on the chances of minority politicians for election, the political machines in Eastern cities may have operated diffusely both to move some ethnic groups into jobs and to provide general aid and information. They may have been doing informally very much what some contemporary black movements are demanding that government bureaucracies do formally, that is, giving people jobs not directly contingent on their formal qualifications and cutting through the degrading red tape currently involved in the administration of the welfare state. The machines performed these functions—at least for some groups—as a payoff for political services.

San Antonio had a more traditional political system, but before World War II its politicians did not define Mexicans as an actual or even a potential political clientele. Investigations of the U.S. Public Health Service in 1935, for example, revealed that San Antonio's health services were largely inadequate and were operated entirely as a source of political patronage. Unsanitary living conditions in the Mexican areas were particularly noteworthy, and the city fathers' indifference to them was equally obvious. A 1942 survey of the city's poor, focusing on Mexican Americans, was quashed by the city council.[22] Furthermore, San Antonio displayed its indifference to the welfare of its poverty segment—largely Mexican American— in its relief policies during the Depression. In the late 1930s, for instance,

> San Antonio stood almost alone (among 94 principal United States cities) in refusing relief to its starving residents. . . . Since San Antonio was one of the few cities in the United States that did not dispense general relief, the total per capita relief expenditures from public funds, which included WPA, were also extremely low. In 1937, for example, in only three cities of comparable size were average disbursements lower than San Antonio's $690. . . . With Bexar County avoiding or ignoring its legal responsibility to extend relief to those unable to support themselves, it was left to the state and federal governments and to private charity to prevent the unemployed from starving. The federal government supplied over 98 percent of the funds, first through direct relief, and later through the public works program.[23]

These illustrations are drawn from the Depression years rather than from the

1920s. Nonetheless, they support the point that the politicians of San Antonio could not have been dependent upon or concerned with the Mexican-American segment of the electorate.

In Los Angeles, the combination of political institutions, ecology, and social perceptions meant that the Mexican Americans could long go unnoticed. Because the Anglo population is scattered over a vast area of the county, the Mexican American enclaves could, in effect, vanish from sight. Fogelson dramatically summarizes the situation of minorities in the county: "Unassimilated, unwelcome, and unprotected, these people were so thoroughly isolated that the American majority was able to maintain its untainted vision of an integrated community."[24] Isolation was turned into expulsion for thousands of Mexicans during the next few years as the Los Angeles County Board of Supervisors arranged for their repatriation to Mexico. (For details on the widespread repatriations during the 1930s and their effect on Mexican Americans see Ch. 21.) For those who remained through the Depression years, the onset of World War II brought improving opportunities for urban jobs, greater social interaction in the Armed Forces, and a slow change in their status as outsiders at home. At this point, however, Los Angeles and San Antonio were beginning to diverge more noticeably as milieus for the ethnic population. A large residue of isolation was left in San Antonio. A widening range of choices was provided in Los Angeles. How much the two cities have moved apart in this respect is revealed in the characteristics of our household survey respondents.

DIFFERENCES IN OPPORTUNITY STRUCTURE

Contemporary differences in the opportunity structure of the two cities are evident in the characteristics of the respondents in the Mexican-American households interviewed in 1965–1966.*

The survey distributions of 1965 and 1966 are broadly consistent with the 1960 census data. But it would be fallacious to draw direct comparisons from these and later tables as measurements of structural change over time. Such comparisons are precluded in most cases by sample error and by the differences in definition mentioned in the notes to Table 13–2. Here we focus on a comparison of Mexican Americans in these two cities, rather than on the differences in their relative standing vis-à-vis Anglos or Negroes. In terms of occupations, for example, one can discern significant inter-area variations beneath the surface of the generally low status of the ethnic group (Table 13–2). According to the surveys, San Antonio had a larger proportion of male service workers, unskilled laborers, and clerical and sales personnel. This concentration continues the pattern described for earlier periods. Los

---

*In Los Angeles, the entire county was sampled with 947 respondents. This county includes large sections of Mexican-American concentration outside the city limits. In San Antonio, only the city was sampled, since most Mexican Americans live inside city boundaries; the sample size was 603. See Appendix H for details of sample design and execution. The English version of the questionnaire is reproduced in Appendix I.

Angeles had a larger percentage of males employed as skilled and semiskilled workers (craftsmen, foremen, and operatives) as well as proprietors, managers, and officials.[25]

The differences are even more pronounced in the industry distribution of sample respondents (Table 13–3). The Mexican-American household heads included in the sample survey of Los Angeles were more heavily concentrated in manufacturing and construction. Together these two industries accounted for 54 percent of the employed household heads, as against only 28 percent in San Antonio. In the latter city, on the other hand, trade and nonprofessional service industries (including those connected

Table 13–2. Occupations of Employed Male Heads of Mexican-American Households, Los Angeles and San Antonio Samples, 1965–1966, and Census Figures, 1960

	Los Angeles County	Los Angeles SMSA Census[a]	San Antonio[b]	San Antonio SMSA Census[a]
Professional, technical, and kindred	5%	6%	4%	4%
Proprietors, managers, and officials, including farm	6	4	4	5
Clerical, sales, and kindred	7	9	10	12
Craftsmen, foremen, and kindred	32	19	23	22
Operatives and kindred	28	32	21	24
Service, including private household	9	7	12	10
Laborers	11	17	21	19
Not reported	2	6	5	4
Total number (= 100%)	(665)	(144,422)	(442)	(48,729)

[a] *1960 U.S. Census of Population*, PC(2)–1B, table 12. The census includes all employed males of Spanish surname, whereas the sample includes only household heads. San Antonio's figures are for the standard metropolitan statistical area, whereas the sample survey was limited to the city. However, San Antonio City contains 95 percent of the Spanish-surname families in the metropolitan area (Bexar County). The totals shown for the household surveys of 1965–1966 exclude households with female heads or unemployed male heads.

[b] Weighting procedures were used in the San Antonio sample. This means that total numbers cannot be used as a direct indicator of error. See Appendix H.

with tourism) provided a far greater proportion of total employment than in Los Angeles (25 percent as compared with 18 percent). The same was true for public administration, reflecting the importance for the employment structure of military bases near San Antonio.[26] As was already suggested, these industry distributions make a difference over and above skill levels.

Education also shows strong contrasts between Los Angeles and San Antonio. In 1960, the median schooling of the total population in the latter city was 9.5 years compared with 12.1 years in Los Angeles, and that of the Spanish-surname population was slightly under 6 years as against a little over 8 years. Twenty-nine percent of the male respondents in Los Angeles, compared with 19 percent of their San Antonio counterparts, had completed high school or gone on to college (Table 13–4). A

Table 13–3. Industries in Which Mexican-American Household Heads Worked, Los Angeles and San Antonio Samples, 1965–1966, and Census Figures, 1960

	Los Angeles County	Los Angeles SMSA Census[a]	San Antonio	San Antonio SMSA Census[a]
Agriculture, forestry, mining, fishing	0%	4%	1%	3%
Construction	12	7	8	10
Durable goods manufacture	28	25	11	5
Non-durable goods manufacture	14	16	9	11
Transportation, communication, public utilities	9	6	9	5
Wholesale and retail trade	11	17	11	24
Finance, insurance, real estate	1	3	b	3
Entertainment, recreation, personal, business and repair services	7	9	14	13
Professional and related services	4	5	4	6
Public administration	5	2	16	16
Not reported	9	6	17	4
Total number (= 100%)	(745)	(206,394)	(563)	(67,949)

a *1960 U.S. Census of Population* PC(2)–1B, table 12. See also notes to Table 13–2 of this work.
b 0.5%.

similar contrast is shown for the very poorly educated—those with 4 years or less of schooling. A third of the San Antonio respondents, compared with 17 percent of the Angelenos, had four years of schooling or less—i.e., could be considered functionally illiterate.

Income differences between the two cities are large for the Mexican-American as well as the total population (Table 13–5). According to the household surveys, over 47 percent of the San Antonio Mexican Americans had family incomes of less than $3,000. (Individual incomes were even lower, of course.) At the other end of the

Table 13–4. Education of Male Mexican-American Household Heads, Los Angeles and San Antonio Samples, 1965–1966, and Census Figures, 1960[a]

Years of school completed	Los Angeles County	Los Angeles SMSA Census[b]	San Antonio	San Antonio SMSA Census[b]
No school	4%	7%	10%	17%
1–4 years	13	12	23	25
5–7 years	19	18	21	23
8 years	9	14	9	9
High school, 1–3 years,	26	23	18	11
High school, 4 years,	19	17	14	9
College, 1–3 years	8	6	4	4
College, 4 years or more	2	3	1	2
Total number (= 100%)	(774)	(145,146)	(595)	(50,277)

a Census figures are for males aged 25 and over. The samples are for all male household heads, some of whom are below the age of 25.
b *1960 U.S. Census of Population*, PC(2)–1B, table 10.

income scale, more than 15 percent of the sample families in Los Angeles had incomes of over $10,000, as against less than 3 percent in San Antonio. The sample data conform to the pattern already established in Chapter 6 with regard to the high dependency ratio for the ethnic population. The generally low income of Mexican Americans has to stretch over a larger number of people than the corresponding Anglo income; about a third of the Mexican-American sample families in both cities had more than five members (Chart 13–1). The mean household size for the Mexican-American samples was 4.3 in both Los Angeles and San Antonio, compared with the

Table 13–5. Family Income of Sample Mexican-American Households in 1965–1966 Compared with Family Income of Spanish-surname Families, 1959

	Los Angeles County	Los Angeles SMSA Census[a]	San Antonio	San Antonio SMSA Census[b]
Under $1,000	2%	4%	11%	10%
$1,000–$1,999	5	5	15	15
$2,000–$2,999	7	6	21	18
$3,000–$3,999	9	10	18	17
$4,000–$4,999	11	13	12	14
$5,000–$5,999	13	15	9	11
$6,000–$6,999	14	13	6	5
$7,000–$9,999	24	22	6	7
Over $10,000	15	12	2	3
Total number (= 100%)	(918)	(138,794)	(569)	(50,579)

[a] 1960 U.S. Census of Population, PHC(1), no. 82, table P-5.
[b] 1960 U.S. Census of Population, PHC(1), no. 134, table P-5.

average for the total population of 3.0 in Los Angeles and 3.6 in San Antonio, as reported by the 1960 census.[27]

By one important measure, San Antonio is a far more segregated city. The 1960 census shows only about 10 percent of the Mexican Americans in Los Angeles living in census tracts that were more than three-quarters Mexican, as compared with more than half the Mexican-American San Antonians.[28] This difference in the degree to which Mexican Americans are concentrated in predominantly Mexican areas was important in the analysis of survey data. (Following a terminology elaborated in Chapter 14, we shall hereafter call such areas "Colonies.") We had good reason to expect that at every income level Mexican Americans living in the Colonies would be very different in style of life and outlook from those outside.

The city differences in concentration appear in our statistical definitions of the types of areas. In Los Angeles, our sample households were divided into three equal groups. Replicating the census distributions, one-third of the sample households lived in census tracts with less than 15 percent Mexican Americans. These will be called "Frontier" areas. Another third (Colonies) lived in tracts with more than 43.8 percent Mexican Americans; the remaining third resided in what will be called "Intermediate" areas. In San Antonio, however, the distribution was so skewed by the high proportion living in Colonies that only a two-way classification was possible—the Frontier areas with less than 54 percent Mexican Americans and the Colonies

Chart 13–1.
Number of Persons in Mexican-American Households, Los Angeles and San Antonio Samples, 1965–1966

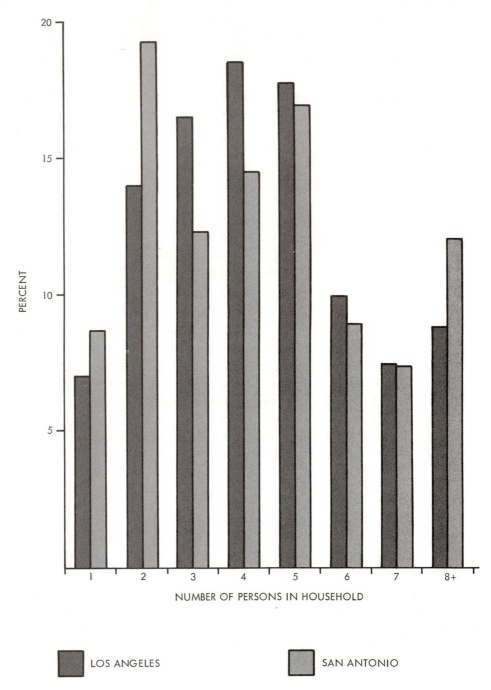

with more than 54 percent. Roughly a third of the sample lived in the Frontiers; two-thirds were in the Colonies. Thus the "Frontier" in San Antonio is roughly equivalent in ethnic composition to the Los Angeles "Frontier" and "Intermediate" categories combined.

Without much exaggeration, one can say that Los Angeles is a place for new-comers; San Antonio is a place of oldtimers. Seventy percent of San Antonio's respondents compared with only 45 percent of the Angelenos had lived in the city at least 20 years. Mobility within the city is also lower in San Antonio (Table 13–6). Greater economic opportunities in Los Angeles probably permit Mexican Americans (as well as others) to change their residence more often.

Table 13–6. Length of Time Survey Respondents Resided in Present Home, by Neighborhood Ethnicity, Los Angeles and San Antonio, 1965–1966

	1 Year	1–5 Years	6–10 Years	11 Years or More	Total Number (= 100%)
Los Angeles[a]					
Frontier	32%	36%	20%	14%	335
Intermediate	27	39	18	16	296
Colony	29	33	20	18	326
San Antonio[a]					
Frontier	15	33	29	23	178
Colony	23	23	16	38	411

[a] In Los Angeles, Frontier = tracts with less than 15.0 percent Spanish-surname individuals; Intermediate = tracts with between 15.0 and 43.8 percent Spanish-surname individuals; and Colony = tracts with more than 43.8 percent Spanish-surname individuals. In San Antonio, Frontier = tracts with less than 54.0 percent Spanish-surname individuals and Colony = tracts with 54.0 percent Spanish-surname individuals.

CITY, *BARRIO*, AND SOCIAL CLASS

Even though there are important objective differences between Los Angeles and San Antonio, it can be argued that these differences are less important for Mexican Americans than some other aspects of the social context. For example, since so many Mexican Americans live in heavily Mexican neighborhoods, is it possible that the quality of life in such *barrios* simply overwhelms the differences in life between the cities?

This question implies something of a distinctive community spirit or community feeling. Mexican neighborhoods are sometimes seen as exceptionally cohesive, as, for example, in San Jose, California:

> They feel most at home within their own neighborhood. . . . In his own barrio more people smile and greet him as he passes, more doors open to him in hospitality, and more people stop him on the streets to ask about his health, his family, his work and his plans for the future. . . . People really care about him.[29]

Another view denies this "folk–culture" conceptualization but also denies the importance of objective differences between cities. It is based on a series of studies of

South Texas towns and emphasizes "contention, invidiousness, and wariness" in relations between neighbors.[30] In other words, the *barrios* are seen as exceptionally *un*cohesive. According to this author, hostile relations with neighbors are interwoven with other cultural features not only of Mexican Americans but of other "atomistically organized" social systems in Latin America and Italy.[31]

Both types of analysis refer to studies of poor *barrios*: Middle-class Mexican Americans are generally recognized as being in a different situation. Our emphasis on objective differences between Los Angeles and San Antonio in this context raises

Table 13–7. Neighboring Behavior, by Income and Neighborhood Ethnicity, Los Angeles and San Antonio Survey Respondents, 1965–1966

	Borrowing Sometimes or Often	Visiting Neighbors Sometimes or Often	Visited by Neighbors Sometimes or Often	Total Number[a] (= 100%)
Los Angeles				
Frontier				
Higher income[b]	21%	49%	59%	182–183
Medium income	11	41	41	76
Low income	11	36	47	78
Intermediate				
Higher income	20	40	50	106
Medium income	17	45	52	98
Low income	20	41	48	75
Colony				
Higher income	19	46	54	78–79
Medium income	14	40	44	124
Low income	16	38	52	122
San Antonio				
Frontier				
Medium income[b]	19	53	56	130–133
Low income	14	27	42	45–47
Colony				
Medium income	18	58	55	188–189
Low income	19	43	40	224–228

[a] There was a slight variation in response rate from question to question: Figures represent the range.
[b] In Los Angeles: higher income = > $6,000; medium income = $3,600–$5,999; low income < $3,600. In San Antonio: medium income = > $2,760; low income < $2,760.

questions of the extent to which milieu characteristics modify the distinctive qualities of life in the *barrios* and also modify social-class distinctions. Our survey questions on neighboring among Mexican Americans suggest some answers.

Mexican Americans fall roughly at the lower end of the range of the 50 to 80 percent of American urban dwellers who engage in borrowing and visiting with neighbors.[32] Somewhat less than half the Angelenos and San Antonians visit or are visited by their neighbors (Table 13–7). These are neither exceptionally friendly nor exceptionally unfriendly neighborhoods, nor is there much difference between Colonies and Frontiers.

Class differences are very noticeable, as they are with other populations.[33] The higher-income respondents in the *barrios* are slightly less pleased with the largely poor neighborhoods (Table 13–8). But in Colonies as well as Frontiers, they have more social relations with their neighbors. The class contrast may stem from such matters as housing differences: The accommodations of the poor probably expose them more acutely to the petty indignities and frictions of a more public life. (When the poor complain about their neighborhood, they tend more than middle-income respondents to emphasize "the people.") They may live in pockets of street rowdiness,

Table 13–8. Positive Perceptions of Neighborhood and Neighbors, by Income and Neighborhood Ethnicity, Los Angeles and San Antonio Survey Respondents, 1965–1966

	Good Influence on Children[a]	Not Many Thefts[b]	Neighbors Would Lend[c]	Total Number[d] (= 100%)
Los Angeles				
Frontier				
Higher income	72%	72%	74%	153–178
Medium income	68	79	59	46–73
Low income	57	71	60	60–77
Intermediate				
Higher income	58	69	64	86–93
Medium income	55	62	65	85–96
Low income	58	62	54	61–75
Colony				
Higher income	37	58	71	65–78
Medium income	55	63	56	101–121
Low income	52	65	43	102–121
San Antonio				
Frontier				
Medium income	85	76	76	97–133
Low income	80	74	72	31–45
Colony				
Medium income	72	58	72	130–186
Low income	68	71	69	160–220

[a] Percent saying neighborhood "very good" influence on children.
[b] Percent saying "not true at all" that there are many thefts in the neighborhood.
[c] Percent saying neighbors would lend them money should the need arise.
[d] There was a variation in response rate from question to question: Figures represent the range.

where repeated incursions of children or unrestrained dogs may in time call forth passionate hatreds, as in the case of many other slum neighborhoods. The frequent appearance of heavy wire chain-link fences—and children and dogs—in Mexican neighborhoods throughout the Southwest would suggest such an interpretation. Chain-link fences are a curious inter-neighbor barrier: They effectively prevent unwanted physical transit, but leave the way open for verbal social exchange. Poverty also precludes some of the normal prescriptions for neighborliness. Summed up for

Americans in general, ideal neighbors are "friendly but not friends," willing to provide emergency aid, mutual assistance, respect for privacy, and "maintenance of collective appearances."[34] Some of these notions are irrelevant to most poverty families.

On the whole, then, Mexican Americans in the two large cities—whether Colony or Frontier—appear to show considerable variation in neighboring with local and personal circumstances, just like other Americans.

Are the *barrios* in San Antonio and Los Angeles more alike than different? Examination of the tables suggest a complicated pattern. With regard to perceptions of the neighborhood (Table 13–8), Colonists of both class levels in San Antonio seem to be more alike than are the middle- and lower-class people *within* the Colonies or Frontiers. But this is not the case in Los Angeles, where class differences are more prominent than neighborhood differences. The latter pattern holds in both cities with regard to actual social relations (Table 13–7).

The contrast between the two cities is notable in another respect. No matter whether we consider differences between Colonists and Frontiersmen or differences between higher- and lower-income respondents, they are greater in Los Angeles than in San Antonio, almost without exception. This observation indicates that the greater opportunity structure of Los Angeles has influenced the behavior patterns of its residents quite perceptibly: There is greater divergence between segments of the Mexican-American population in Los Angeles than in San Antonio.

In summary, analysis of the neighborhood perceptions and relations of San Antonians and Angelenos suggests a considerable modification of the folk-society point of view with regard to Mexican-American *barrios*. Generally, the degree of neighboring does not seem extraordinary by American standards, and residence in the Colonies, especially in Los Angeles, fails to submerge the effect of the increasing social-class differentiation.

Even if Mexican-American culture and a need for belonging were both strong, there would still be every reason to expect differences from one *barrio* to another. All small towns are not the same, nor are all Irish neighborhoods the same. It is naive to assume, without investigation, that all Mexican-American neighborhoods would have the same quality.[35] In many instances, the historical origins are recent enough to leave clear marks on the social structure of the *barrio*. In Los Angeles, for example, some presently Mexican neighborhoods resulted from the invasion of areas occupied by Jews, Russians, Japanese or other existing ethnic colonies. Others resulted from a move into ethnically undifferentiated areas of cheap housing. In the mid–1960s some of these areas, like the major shopping artery of Brooklyn Avenue, still presented a mosaic of merchants and residents of different ethnic backgrounds.

One would expect social relations between Mexican Americans and their neighbors in such areas to be different from those found in neighborhoods which are remnants of former Mexican-American labor camps and in which urbanization followed the initial settlements. Since such areas are fairly common for Mexican Americans and quite unusual for other ethnic groups, some detail may illuminate their special qualities. One such area in Los Angeles County was originally a small walled company town erected by the Simons Brick Company. Workers and their families were recruited by word of mouth from the small town of Penjamo in Guanajuato, Mexico. At the peak in the 1920s, over 1,000 individuals were living in company housing in the enclave outside the town of Montebello. Simons had a company store, its own private police, its "own" church, its "own" school, its own community center, band, and baseball team. Until it burned down in 1952 (it did *not* have its own fire brigade), it was an almost entirely self-sufficient Mexican town, maintained as such by a highly paternalistic management, and a socially isolated enclave, even though Montebello had gradually crept closer, ultimately surrounding it. Years later, the former Simons residents were still distinctive; the young men, for example, were tougher and more "Mexican" in accent and behavior than other Mexican Americans in the adjoining area.[36]

Yet another aspect of this diversity among Mexican-American neighborhoods is illustrated by the medium-sized city of Riverside in California, a citrus center located midway between Los Angeles and Palm Springs. Its Mexican-American population, some 7,000 in 1960, was quite highly segregated from Anglos and predominantly concentrated in the two neighborhoods of Casa Blanca and the Eastside. The two *barrios* were traditionally hostile; fights were common and the atmosphere was tense at a 1965 "intermarriage" of a Casa Blanca boy with an Eastside girl. The areas differed sharply in social structure, both in terms of the long-standing relationships of Mexican-American families with each other and in terms of their relationships with the larger system.

In Casa Blanca an Anglo elementary school principal with decades of service had adopted an extremely paternalistic stance. To some extent he succeeded in becoming the *patrón* of the community, which he managed to isolate from the mainstream of Riverside life. He became the liaison between Casa Blanca and the rest of Riverside. Most Mexican-American business, including most adult business, was reputedly channeled through his office. He adapted the school curriculum to what he perceived to be Mexican culture, spending three months of preparation for a religious Christmas program, establishing a special baseball team, attempting to staff the school with teachers who were his alumni so as to perpetuate the self-sufficiency of this ecological enclave. As in all such cases, including Simons, there were, of course, leakages and dissidents. In particular, children passing on from the Casa Blanca elementary school to the junior high school in a predominantly Anglo district encountered problems. Their dropout rate was exceptionally high.[37]

The Eastside was comparatively more open both ecologically and socially, though it had subareas which were traditionally the "turf" of particular families with special reputations. (One such clan, for example, was distinguished by having a high rate of out-migration impelled mainly by the legal authorities. They were a kind of Mexican Jukes family.) Eastside youngsters had more and friendlier contacts outside the ghetto. Eastside adults were more active politically and helped to elect a Mexican American to the City Council. Eastside adults were less resistant to school desegregation, whereas Casa Blanca parents followed the school and community tradition by firmly resisting elementary-school integration.

Though these illustrations do not cover the range of variation in the origins of neighborhoods, they suggest the significance of local history for the understanding of local social structure and attachments. Some urban districts, like Riverside's Casa Blanca, seem at first glance mysteriously resistant to change and mysteriously retentive of their residents' loyalty. But the mystery tends to evaporate when their recent past is explored, as in the case of Casa Blanca with its rather bizarre ingrown attempts at maintaining cultural dualism. As indicated in earlier chapters, many Southwest cities have recently engulfed such isolated and nearly self-sufficient "folk-like" enclaves. The contemporary residents of the remnant of the Simons brickyard or its counterpart would obviously have a different kind of relationship to their community than the residents of the equally Mexican area a few miles away which resulted from invasion of a formerly Jewish neighborhood.[38] The ethnic composition or the degree of segregation in an area is rarely sufficient to explain its current social structure.

* * *

In sum, the household interview surveys in Los Angeles and San Antonio, which furnish the principal empirical materials for this part of our study, reflect the contemporary position of Mexican Americans in two sharply differing social worlds. It is impossible to tell the place of these two cities in the whole range of urban situations in which the ethnic group finds itself. But it is clear from the recent history of Los Angeles and San Antonio as milieus for the Mexican-American population, and from the educational attainment, the incomes, and especially the occupational distribution of the survey respondents, that social isolation of the minority people is far greater in the Texas metropolis, as is their poverty. This was not always the case. Only a few decades ago the cities offered largely similar opportunity structures to the ethnic group.

A brief discussion of the dichotomy between "folk" and "urban" cultures, which has played a considerable role in social theory and in scholarly literature about Mexican Americans, led us to conclude that these extremes of a wide spectrum are too equivocal to be applied in this study without modification. Instead, a historical analysis of Los Angeles and San Antonio has focused on indicators of social isolation of the ethnic group from the larger communities. The theme of inter-city and intra-city differences in the degree of isolation of the Mexican American will recur in several variations as we proceed to the ethnic individual in his social setting.

NOTES TO CHAPTER THIRTEEN

1. Robert Redfield, *The Little Community* and *Peasant Society and Culture* (Chicago: The University of Chicago Press, 1960), especially chapter 1 of *The Little Community*. Redfield's basic work on the folk society was first published in 1934.
2. See Oscar Lewis, *Life In a Mexican Village: Tepoztlán Restudied* (Urbana, Ill.:

The University of Illinois Press, 1951), for the first extensive criticism of the folk-society concept.

3. Louis Wirth, "Urbanism as a Way of Life," *The American Journal of Sociology*, XLIV (July, 1938), pp. 1–24.

4. For example, cities in Asia are found to retain homogeneous groups with strong group solidarity and personalized, familial, and sacred relationships, to mention just a few. Philip M. Hauser has summarized these and other characteristics of urbanism in less advanced areas in "Observations on the Urban-folk and Urban-rural Dichotomies as Forms of Western Ethnocentrism," in Philip M. Hauser and Leo Schnore (eds.), *The Study of Urbanization* (New York: John Wiley & Sons, Inc., 1965), pp. 503–517.

5. William Madsen, *Mexican-Americans of South Texas* (New York: Holt, Rinehart and Winston, Inc., 1964), p. 31. "Focal values" are described in pp. 17–20.

6. Like "Atrisco," New Mexico, studied by Florence Kluckhohn in "Los Atarqueños: A Study of Patterns and Configurations in a New Mexico Village" (unpublished Ph.D. dissertation, Radcliffe College, Cambridge, Massachusetts, 1941). Her 1951 restudy of the community is reported in Florence R. Kluckhohn and Fred L. Strodbeck, *Variations in Value Orientations* (Evanston, Ill.: Row, Peterson & Company, 1961). Arthur Rubel, in his "Social Life of Urban Mexican Americans" (unpublished Ph.D. dissertation, University of North Carolina, 1963), and *Across the Tracks* (Austin, Tex.: University of Texas Press, 1966) studied a similar community in South Texas–"New Lots," or Weslaco.

7. See Margaret Clark, *Health in the Mexican American Culture* (Berkeley, Calif.: University of California Press, 1959). As for the Midwest, several good unpublished studies exist of Mexican-American communities in Kansas City, Kansas; St. Paul, Minnesota; and Toledo, Ohio: Paul Lin, "Voluntary Kinship and Voluntary Association in a Mexican-American Community" (unpublished Master's thesis, University of Kansas, 1963); Norman Goldner, "The Mexicans in the Northern Urban Area: A Comparison of Two Generations' (unpublished Master's thesis, University of Minnesota, 1959); Barbara J. Macklin, "Structural Stability and Culture Change in a Mexican-American Community" (unpublished Ph.D. dissertation, University of Pennsylvania, 1963). But these are studies of the residual, first-settlement communities, analogous to the Chinatowns or Little Italies of the same cities. Their persistence is interesting, but to generalize from them to all Mexican-American communities is like generalizing from the West-End-Boston Italians studied by Gans to all Italian Americans. See Herbert J. Gans, *The Urban Villagers* (New York: The Free Press, 1962).

8. For example, Sheldon's analysis of middle-class Angelenos is composed of individuals active in Mexican-American associations, who, as will become evident later, are a very unusual group of people. Paul M. Sheldon, "Community Participation and the Emerging Middle Class," in Julian Samora (ed.), *La Raza: Forgotten Americans* (Notre Dame, Ind.: University of Notre Dame Press, 1966), pp. 125–157.

9. Macklin, *op. cit.*

10. Historical material on Los Angeles is derived largely from Robert M. Fogelson, *The Fragmented Metropolis: Los Angeles, 1850-1930* (Cambridge, Mass.: Harvard University Press, 1967), and on San Antonio from Harold Arthur Shapiro, "The Workers of San Antonio, Texas, 1900–1940" (unpublished Ph.D. dissertation, University of Texas, 1952).

11. *Mexicans in California*, Report of Governor C. C. Young's Mexican Fact-Finding Committee (Sacramento, Calif., 1930), pp. 191–194.

12. Shapiro, *op. cit.*, p. 95. Citing a 1927 survey of San Antonio Mexican Americans, Shapiro found that only 30 percent of the American-born and 15 percent of the Mexican-born held permanent jobs. One third of the American-born and half of the Mexican-born performed common labor.

13. *Ibid.*, p. 121. Most of the material in Shapiro on the pecan industry is derived from Selden C. Menefee and O. C. Cassmore, *The Pecan Shellers of San Antonio* (Washington, D.C.: Works Progress Administration, 1940), a careful 1930 survey of the industry, and from contemporary newspaper accounts.

14. For the sake of balance it should be added that Mexicans in both Los Angeles and San Antonio were the major actors in major strikes of the 1930s. See chapter 5.

15. See Otis Dudley Duncan et al., *Metropolis and Region* (Baltimore: published for Resources for the Future by The Johns Hopkins Press, 1961), p. 527, for a description of San Antonio's industrial base.

16. For San Antonio, Shapiro, *op. cit.*, p. 58. For Los Angeles, Fogelson, *op. cit.*, p. 79.

17. San Antonio's foreign immigrants were mainly German rather than Mexican before the turn of the twentieth century, though the Mexican born began to outnumber the German born by 1900. The large influx of Mexicans followed the Mexican Revolution and the American labor shortage of World War I.

18. Shapiro, *op. cit.*, p. 69, derived from U.S. census figures.

19. Fogelson, *op. cit.*, p. 81.

20. *Ibid.*, p. 218. The authority of the local government officials was derived from city-wide rather than ward elections, thus destroying political organization at the neighborhood level. Party strength had been demolished. Politics became a mass affair rather than a personal matter, "placing priority on publicity rather than familiarity and on finances rather than favors."

21. See James Q. Wilson, *Negro Politics* (New York: The Free Press, 1960), for an inter-city analysis of Negro politics, which emphasizes the special features of Los Angeles and its special difficulties for Negro politicians. Of Los Angeles and Negro politics, Wilson says (p. 27):

> Civil service is strong in Los Angeles, and there are few material incentives with which to construct a political organization. There is no citywide organization with a need to attract all segments of the population to support a complete slate of candidates, and hence no group which would have a vested interest in constructing a 'balanced ticket' and distributing 'recognition' to ethnic, religious, and other easily identifiable groups. Politics is largely the province of white, middle-class, Anglo-Saxon Protestants.

The structural factors affected Mexican Americans as well.

22. The questionnaires with information about unsanitary conditions—including inadequate water supply, waste disposal facilities and heating—mysteriously vanished. Shapiro, *op. cit.*, pp. 161–169. A progressive set of building codes was almost totally unenforced, *ibid., p.* 214.

23. *Ibid.*, pp. 241–243. The extent to which San Antonio politicians could ignore the Mexican Americans and their needs is further documented by the city's refusal to pay storage for public surplus food—which was thereupon shipped elsewhere.

24. Fogelson, *op. cit.*, p. 188.

25. A very small proportion of people in either sample were employed as agricultural laborers. This is probably an underestimate of the actual situation in San Antonio, as it is known that approximately 10,000 migrant workers use San Antonio as their home base. The distortion is probably accounted for by two facts. First, interviews were conducted largely in the summer when migrants are in the fields; second, and possibly more important, the migrants are predominantly young (according to one source, largely between the ages of 14 and 20), and are thus not likely to be included in a survey of heads of households. *Economic Base Study of San Antonio and Twenty-seven County Area*, City of San Antonio, City Planning Department (San Antonio, Tex., Apr., 1964), p. 164.

26. San Antonio is the site of four Air Force bases (Brooks, Kelly, Lackland, and Randolph) and of Fort Sam Houston. Kelly is the largest aircraft maintenance and supply depot operated by the United States Air Force. Lackland is the largest USAF training base, the only Air Force basic military training center (annually graduating 100,000 persons), and has the largest USAF hospital. Randolph is also a big installation, the headquarters of the Air Training Command. Two other nearby government facilities are Medina (Atomic Energy Commission) and Leon Springs (Army). In 1960 Kelly alone employed almost 21,000 civilians, making it the largest single employer in the city and accounting for 17 percent of the total employed labor force. Census figures suggest that it accounts for an even larger fraction of Mexican-American workers. Other military installations employed an additional total of 11,000 civilians, *ibid.*, pp. 69 and 74.

27. For San Antonio, *1960 U.S. Census of Population*, PHC(1)-134, p. 13. For Los Angeles, *1960 U.S. Census of Population*, PHC(1)-82, p. 25.

28. See Appendix H in this volume for intervals used in the tenfold classification of census tracts by Spanish-surname density.

29. Clark, *op. cit.*, p. 43. Of the same city, another observer noted the great morale problems that arose when old neighborhoods were shattered by urban renewal (personal communication from Ernesto Galarza).

30. Rubel, *op. cit.*, p. 207.

31. It is Rubel's contention that Mexican Americans are socialized to intense attachment to the nuclear family, the "basic security unit," almost as if familial relationships were the only ones that mattered or would ever matter (*ibid.*, p. 204). He terms this unit an "atomistic social system" and finds counterparts in similar situations in Mexico, Colombia, and southern Italy. His general conclusion is that there is an "association . . . between an atomistically organized social system and the apparent importance of anxiety and disaffection which inhere in extrafamilial relationships" (*ibid.*, p. 237). He cites a negative case, that of the Parisian middle class, whose family is as isolated from others as are the cases he cites, but which is not as semiparanoid as the others.

The traditional belief in witchcraft is related to this perception of neighbors. If witchcraft is conceptualized as a system of projection, whereby socially undesirable impulses are attributed to others, neighbors may be particularly convenient targets.

32. A number of studies are summarized in Theodore Caplow, Sheldon Stryker, and Samuel E. Wallace, *The Urban Ambience* (Totowa, N.J.: The Bedminister Press, 1964), p. 157, including one of Lansing, Michigan; Joel Smith, William H. Form, and Gregory P. Stone, "Local Intimacy in a Middle-sized City," *American Journal of Sociology*, LX (Nov., 1954), pp. 276–284; Morris Axelrod, "Urban Structure and Social Participation," *American Sociological Review*, XXXI (Feb., 1956), pp. 13–18, of Detroit; Wendell Bell and Marion D. Boat, "Urban Neighborhoods and Informal Social Relations," *American Journal of Sociology*, LXII (Jan., 1957), pp. 391–398, of San Francisco; and Scott Greer and Ella Kube, "Urban Worlds" (unpublished manuscript, 1955), of Los Angeles. See summary in Caplow et al., *op. cit.*, pp. 157, 158.

Surprisingly few community studies of Mexican Americans explore how they relate to neighbors. One of the few that venture into the quantitative realm, a study of the Mexican-American *colonia* of Kansas City, reports that "63.3 percent of the 60 respondents do not associate with their neighbors" (Lin, *op. cit.*) Most neighboring is "over the fence" (p. 120), and most Kansas City neighborhoods and indeed most voluntary associations consist of small groups of kin and *compadres*.

33. See Caplow et al., *op. cit.*

34. Ruth Hill Useem, John Useem, and Duane L. Gibson, "The Function of Neighboring for the Middle-class Male," *Human Organization*, XIX (Summer, 1960), pp. 68–76, cited in Caplow et al., *op. cit.*, p. 72.

35. The variations suggested here are reminiscent of an extensive study of half of the *barrios* of San Juan, Puerto Rico. In this study "culture," specifically the family system (the most important variable for Rubel's argument), was held at least roughly constant. Six basic types of neighboring were noted from one *barrio* to another, ranging from a degree of integration called "tribal" to almost complete isolation of families from each other called "anomic." The last type is notably similar to the situation described by Rubel, and character-izes only one of the Puerto Rican *barrios*, the worst and most hopeless slum. The other major slum *barrio* studied showed a pattern of neighboring in inter-related cliques. On the indivi-dual level, greater neighboring was observed among those with favorable housing, income, occupational prestige, and other traits that add up to social and probably personal security. See Caplow *et al.*, *op. cit.*, especially pp. 73–75.

36. Lorenzo Campbell, *Simons: The Brickyard Hacienda: 1910–1952* (unpublished manuscript, 1966).

37. Ernest Robles, "An Analytic Description of Peer-group Pressures on Mobility Oriented Mexican-American Junior High Students" (unpublished Master's thesis, University of Redlands, 1964). The material on the East Side and Casa Blanca is derived from inter-views with Riverside residents and school officials, conducted primarily by Lorenzo Camp-bell, who also contributed to the analysis presented here.

38. Between 1949 and 1958 the Eastside Jewish Community Center in Los Angeles conducted special programs in what had been a Jewish community to provide liaison be-tween incoming Mexicans and outgoing Jews. Once the majority of Jews had left, work at the center was discontinued. This service agency provides an interesting dating for this invasion. Our information was provided by Mark Keats, the former program director of the Eastside Jewish Community Center.

FOURTEEN

Social Class and Social Mobility

OUR analysis of census data has shown an increasing social-class differentiation in such broad statistical measures as education and income. Using the surveys of San Antonio and Los Angeles, we can explore the subject in greater depth.

Earlier studies of the Mexican-American population usually assumed that its lower-status members are confined within their own minority subsystem. Middle-class Mexican Americans, on the other hand, are portrayed in a wider and often conflicting variety of interpretations. Some analysts have concluded that the higher-status Mexican Americans are members of a class within a caste, or the upper level of a stable ethnic subsystem.[1] Another considers them to be the "wave of the future" —a sort of vanguard of an emerging *new* structure which preserves the Mexican identity.[2] Several writers suggest that the process of class mobility dissolves ethnic identity, but they vary in the interpretation of the outcome. In one view, the process

[1] Notes for this chapter start on page 345.

leads to successful acculturation and assimilation.[3] In another, it is held to act in a personally destructive fashion; the middle-class person is seen as deviant. The word *agringado*, referring to acculturation, appears to have a strong pejorative implication. In this latter view, upward mobility entails a painful internalized culture conflict, often manifest in neurotic symptoms.[4]

Such differences in interpretation reflect (among other things) the different milieus in which the research has been done. Over time, the isolation of the Mexican American has declined in most parts of the Southwest. Urban research done in the 1940s mirrors the prejudices of that era that constrained mobile Mexican Americans to remain "Mexican."[5] Acculturation and even assimilation are easier today, and some of the recent urban studies reflect this change.[6] Many mobile Mexican Americans in such cities disappear into the Anglo world, but many *choose* to remain in the group.[7] Some parts of the Southwest, however, still offer limited options to Mexican Americans. Studies of contemporary small-town Texas, with the Texas combination of traditional attitudes and economic inertia, are reminiscent of reports from the 1940s and even the 1930s.[8] For that matter, a study of Mexican-American middle-class life in contemporary *large*-city Texas, such as ours in San Antonio, reveals a continuing high degree of isolation of the minority in the big cities of that state. It is very likely that in such milieus, in which interaction between the Mexican Americans and Anglos is restricted, mobile individuals would experience more severe identity problems and greater marginality with all its symptoms of distress.

This variety of views of what "middle class" means for Mexican Americans echoes themes in studies of other ethnic and racial subgroups in the United States. In general it also reflects the literature on the relationship between ethnicity and social class. For example, the "class within a caste" is found most frequently in Negro communities, especially in the deep South. White and black form almost separate communities, superordinate and subordinate, each with its own class system.

With regard to ethnic groups of European stock, however, the persistence of ethnic systems is itself at issue. According to one theory, the institutionalized class system of the larger society has functioned to dissolve the mobile member's ties to the ethnic group. After more or less difficulty in shifting his identity, the individual winds up as a more or less undifferentiated member of the American middle class. Repeated for enough individuals, this process ultimately works "to destroy the ethnic subsystems and to increase assimilation."[9]

In another theory the incentives of the class system are seen too as a major factor in the acculturation of ethnic minorities, but the ethnic group remains the source of social relationships and identity for the mobile man. Milton Gordon emphasizes the persistence of the ethnic subsystem and the emergence of the "ethclass" system, the "intersection of the ethnic group with the social class."[10] Gordon sees social-class mobility as attainable without separation from the ethclass system, the locus of identity. Marginality bedevils only the ethnic individual who attempts to move into the WASP social-class structure.[11]

Both of these theories appear to overstate their case. The analysis of the assimilationist function of the social-class system was developed at a time when cultural homogeneity was an important American value. It overestimates the extent to which the social-class system subsumes other forms of differentiation, including ethnic differentiation. The pluralistic view of American society, on the other hand, underestimates the continued importance of the superordination of the dominant group. This underestimation is reflected in Gordon's tendency to treat the dominant group—the WASPS—as only one among many ethnic groups.[12] Though this view is attractive in an era when minority groups are struggling for the legitimation of their ethnic status honor, the ideological egalitarianism can blind the analyst to the real subordination of ethnic subgroups, particularly racial, in the United States.[13]

Indeed, it is not necessary to accept either view completely in order to analyze data on Mexican-American stratification. An intermediate position can accept the idea that something like an ethclass system may persist, but that some Mexican Americans, lower-class as well as middle-class, may choose to attempt assimilation into the larger society, and do so with considerable success. A convenient terminology was developed for such a situation by a student of a small colony of Russian Americans. He distinguished between the "Colonists," the conservatives who retained loyalty to the ethnic community, and the "Frontiersmen," who left the ethnic community both spatially and emotionally in the process of occupational mobility. Most of the Colonists were also mobile occupationally, but the Frontiersmen were becoming assimilated while the Colonists maintained more pervasive ethnic attachments.[14] This intermediate formulation emphasizes that the mobile ethnic individual has the option of finding support and identity *either* in the ethnic group or ethclass *or* in the social class or clique outside the ethnic group. The availability of such an option varies from one group to another, and with time and place for any given group. It is greater for the Mexican American now than it was in the past, and greater in large California cities than in small Texas towns.

The social-class system does not completely determine the behavior of mobile individuals. Many members perceive the system primarily in its instrumental aspects, that is, as a narrow reward system, rather than in its broader subcultural and identity-giving aspects. Colonists may view the social-rank structure of the larger society somewhat in the light of a prototype provided in school experiences, that is, as providing relatively specific rewards for performance. The Frontiersman may view the social-class system far more diffusely, as a source not only of specific rewards but also of general self-esteem. For the Colonist, the concept of ethclass may indeed adequately describe his situation. It does not appear to describe the situation of the Frontiersman.

However, the ethnic subsystem is not self-contained.* Potentially, the ethnic individual has a foot in the social-class structure of the dominant society through his

---

*This is true despite the existence of functions in the ethnic community that have no complete counterparts in the society as a whole, e.g., the social worker whose *sole* function is to provide a liaison between Anglo and Mexican-American worlds.

work role. His work role may remind him of the discrepancy between the rewards within the ethnic subsystem and those available in the larger society. A Negro postal clerk may be upper-middle class in his ethnic group but not outside the group. Consequently, the ethclass system at its upper levels is essentially unstable. It is unstable because the middle class includes large numbers of people with constantly renewed status dilemmas. It is also unstable because prestige attaching to high status within the ethnic group is not closely related to status outside the group.[15]

This view of the relationship between social class and ethnicity distinguishes between two aspects of the stratification system—the economic aspect, which provides specific rewards for specific performance, and the identity-giving aspect, which provides more diffuse rewards for performance in a broader spectrum of roles. Here we suggest that social-class subculture (rather than ethnicity) does the most adequate job of providing its members with a focus of positive identity and belonging at its upper level. At lower-class levels, ethnic and religious groups can provide an alternative focus of identity, while the WASP must make his peace with a lower status honor. Our formulation deliberately avoids implying any sort of unequivocal status for the ethnic individual, no matter what his class position. In fact, we suggest that from the Mexican American's point of view the class structure is far more complex, with many more options, than for Anglos. It is more complex than for most other ethnic groups in this society.

ROOTS OF THE CLASS SYSTEM

A good part of the complexity of Mexican-American social-class structure stems from the group's history. The contemporary structure blends features of "typical American" class stratification with residues of class demarcation from Spanish-Mexican times. Before the Americans came, the old Mexican enclaves of the Southwest had developed an elaborate and quite rigid caste system based upon elitism and "purity of blood." This system probably curtailed the mobility chances of latter-day Mexican immigrants to this country. The newcomers to the United States were, in effect, facing two separate class systems—one on the outside and one on the inside. Both made achievement more difficult by making success in part contingent on racial qualities.

The Spanish-Mexican class structure in the Southwest, as in Mexico, was a complicated mixture of colonialism and racism. While Mexico was under Spanish rule—and long after—Spaniards outranked native-born Mexicans of Spanish descent, who in turn outranked *mestizos*, or mixed-bloods, who in turn outranked Indians. Status distinctions were based on "blood,"[16] with Spain allocating "rights and privileges according to 'purity of blood' calculated to 64 to 128 parts."[17] Basic "blood" distinctions were comparatively visible[18] and were further reinforced by originally correlated but increasingly independent distinctions based, for example, on surname and clothing.[19] "Blood" continues to this day to be a status preoccupation in Mexico despite an official ideology emphasizing "Indianism,"[20] and despite the fact that only a small minority of the population is classified as either "pure" Indian or "pure" white.[21]

Social distinctions based on "blood" were increasingly difficult to maintain in Mexico as the population became mixed both genetically and culturally. The sharp distinctions based on wealth and property also slowly changed in response to radical economic and political upheavals. Pre-revolutionary Mexico of 1895 had a tiny elite, a small middle class comprising less than 8 percent of the total population, and an enormous lower class comprising more than 90 percent of the total. Though by 1940 the class structure was beginning to change, the lower classes still accounted for 84 percent of the population. (However, a sizable fraction of these were on their way up. They constituted what could be called, in Warner's terminology, an "upper-lower" class, formerly absent from the structure.) By 1960, it was estimated that the lower classes constituted a still-huge 60 percent of the total, with two-fifths of this 60 percent in the lowest class.[22] One need not accept the precise percentages to consider this portrayal of the class situation as broadly valid.

The first heavy wave of immigration to the United States, in the 1920s, occurred at a time when the class divisions in Mexico were still quite rigid. The cultural heritage transmitted from Mexico with the immigrants included a set of status expectations consonant with a near-feudal and race-conscious system.

The Southwestern version of this Mexican class system is documented in a few places. For example, almost from its start in the early eighteenth century, San Antonio was characterized by a cleavage between the military-missionary settlers and a group of families from the Canary Islands who had been given the title "*hijos dalgo*," formally certifying them as "gentlemen." Though frontier existence did not encourage an aristocratic style of life, the Canary Islanders continued to consider themselves as an elite. The soldiers and farmers in turn resented both the social pretensions of the "*hidalgia*" and their attendant failure to contribute to the survival needs of the colony.[23]

Similar cleavages developed from the outset in other Spanish-Mexican colonies. The variations from place to place depended, among other things, on the stability and density of the settlement, the nature of the agricultural base, the hostility of the Indians, and accessibility to Mexico. In the northern frontier of Texas, for example, grants for cattle ranches were made on the Nueces River. Generally, the grantees were wealthy officials who continued to live as an elite in the comparatively safe river towns while their ranches were run by poorly-paid employees. Because of continual Indian raids, little elaboration of a *ranchero* life was possible in the short Mexican tenure of the area; it was a fortress-like frontier[24] in which the *rancheros* were also military leaders. In California, an even more remote but peaceful frontier, wealth was so concentrated in the missions that it was not until their secularization that a clear class structure developed. The secularization did not really begin before 1831 and was not completed until 1845, just before California's annexation to the United States. The class hierarchy was entirely based on the *ranchos*. There was a tiny elite estimated by one historian to comprise no more than 46 landowners, predominantly *nouveaux riches*, who "ruled California." The laborers were predominantly indigenous Indians. This was a leisured class par excellence, no matter how short its tenure.[25]

The traditional social-class system had its most elaborate Southwestern development in New Mexico, the largest of the northern colonies of Spain and Mexico. Stratification in New Mexico developed from an original three-class system. Spanish aristocrats and officials occupied the top rung, farmers and soldiers the middle, and *mestizos* and Indians the bottom. The upper classes remained largely urban, while village class structure tended to be bifurcated, often with a *patrón* family or two who were somewhat wealthier and tended to dominate decision-making.[26]

THE CLASS STRUCTURE

UNDER ANGLO DOMINATION

Thus Mexican stratification showed great local differences in the early years of the nineteenth century. Although the ideal model of Spanish America—a leisured "Spanish" *hidalgia* and a mass of *mestizo* and Indian laborers—may have existed throughout the northern Mexican colonies, the extent to which this ideal could be realized varied enormously from one area to another. The system was modified with the coming of the Anglos. Almost always, the Spanish-Mexican class structure was headed by a determinedly *white* Spanish group. (San Antonio's Canary Islanders illustrate this point in the early period.) These Spaniards were as hostile to the Indian-Mexican and to the *mestizo* as were the Anglos. The Americans who made initial contact were often traders who sometimes intermarried with the Spanish upper class. In most places, this upper class continued to be accepted in the social life of Anglo Americans even during the periods of greatest discrimination against the lower-class Mexicans. But they were accepted in terms of their perception of themselves, that is, as remnants of a "pure-blood," white aristocracy.

It is far from surprising, therefore, that upwardly mobile Mexican Americans should have called themselves "Spanish" in places where "Mexicans" were considered untouchable.[27] As community studies (even of the recent past) unmistakably indicate, to be Mexican was to be stigmatized. The assumption of "Spanish" identity made it possible to move from a stigmatized caste into a neutral position. This was a status jump that was totally impossible for Negroes (except for those who could pass), or even for most Orientals. Mexican Americans harbor considerable resentment toward those who called themselves Spaniards and thus "denied their heritage." An assumption of Spanish identity meant the usual Latin-American divorcement from the lower classes. And even if he were so inclined, no "Spaniard" could openly take up the cause of the Mexican Americans without jeopardizing his precarious middle-class position. As a result, socially mobile Mexican Americans were lost to potential

322

community leadership as if—let us say—every upwardly mobile Jew would have denied his Jewish identity and become a Christian.

The persistence of a caste-like system in the 1920s, the early years of large-scale Mexican immigration, is detailed in Paul Taylor's study of Corpus Christi, Texas. Corpus Christi had no noticeable "old Spanish" group. Mexicans were "overwhelmingly" laborers in the cotton fields, and definitely lower class. Mexican clerks were hired only to attract the Mexican trade, and the few Mexican-American businessmen almost all served the ethnic population. Mexican Americans went to segregated schools. Restrictive covenant clauses usually confined them to segregated neighborhoods. Discrimination in public accommodations was almost as stringent as it was against Negroes. Mexican Americans were allowed to sit at the drugstore fountain (though not at the tables), while Negroes would not be seated at all. Intermarriage was disparaged and the Anglo member of an intermarrying couple became socially a Mexican. "If a white man marries a Mexican, the Mexicans bring him to their level. People don't associate with him and his children don't mix and usually marry back among the Mexicans. . . . The American from then on is classed as a 'Mexican' by the American community."[28]

Distinctions were made *within* the Mexican caste by both Mexicans and Anglos. Even in the absence of an "old family" upper class in the city, educated "Spaniards" were treated as social equals whereas "Mexicans" were not.[29] The distinction was also related to skin color. One Anglo clerk, for example, refused to serve an apparently "Mexican" man. The man turned out to be the Mexican consul who demanded and received a personal apology. Nativity was also used by some Anglos and most Mexican Americans to place a man, with "Texas-Mexicans" distinguished from the Mexican immigrants. The racial rather than the nativity basis for the cleavage, however, is indicated by the fact that even middle-class, native-born Mexican Americans referred to Anglos as "Americans." Middle-class Mexican Americans were, of course, the most aware of internal distinctions. They often claimed that discrimination was directed *not* against Mexicans per se, but against lower-class appearance and behavior. The denial of categorical discrimination is illustrated by a comment of a Mexican-American middle-class leader of light complexion, who said:

> If you suffer humiliation, don't blame anyone but yourself; you have not been prepared. There is no such thing as race discrimination. . . . Do you expect to be received at the Nueces Hotel in overalls and sombreros? . . . Ninety percent are common laborers, ignorant, and they go to town as they work in the fields.[30]

This attitude was supported by the fact that "Spaniards" *could* live outside of "their own quarter" in Corpus Christi (though not in the smaller towns), and *could* go to the "American" school there (though not in the smaller towns) if they spoke English well and were clean and otherwise "prepared." Upper-status Mexican Americans were *inconsistently* segregated. Thus their exhortations to the lower classes had a basis in fact by the unpredictability with which caste lines were enforced.

The position of Mexican Americans in the local structure differed from place to place even in Texas (even as early as the 1920s). San Antonio, for example, was seen as a relatively open place for the middle classes. There they could gain a modicum of social acceptance that was largely denied in Corpus Christi. The presence of a comparatively large old group of upper-status Mexicans in Laredo (and possibly Brownsville) precluded the establishment of a caste system of the Corpus Christi type. But in most small towns caste lines were very rigid.

San Antonio was studied by Frances Jerome Woods some twenty years after the study of Corpus Christi.[31] The author portrays a situation which was still caste-like in important ways. Particularly noteworthy is the composition of the upper-class group within the Mexican-American community in San Antonio. The most significant elements were old-family members. The descendants of the famous 16 families of Canary Islanders, the would-be *hidalgos* of the eighteenth century, joined with other old families who had lived in the city for several generations or whose ancestors were Spanish land grantees. Another element consisted of upper-status refugees from the Mexican Revolution.[32] This upper class of Mexicans may have been socially acceptable to the Anglos (there were some intermarriages in San Antonio as well as elsewhere), but the extent of real interaction is open to question. There were few social relations between the Mexican upper class and the rest of the Mexicans.

The structure was becoming somewhat less rigid. There are strong indications of ethnic mobility: A *nouveau riche* group was evident, and there was a new upper-middle class of professionals and small businessmen. Both groups had some interaction with Anglos. Nonetheless, the masses (estimated at from 50 to 85 percent of the ethnic population) continued to be seen as largely Indian or *mestizo*, as recent immigrants who were unskilled, uneducated, and spoke a foreign tongue. This lower class was largely isolated from interaction with Anglos. Even more than in Corpus Christi, the lower-class Mexicans in San Antonio were stereotyped as perfectly content with a culture of poverty.[33]

Corpus Christi and San Antonio were both comparatively large cities.[34] If the masses of Mexicans were isolated in such cities, their situation was even more extreme in the labor-camp enclave. Such settlements were often geographically as well as socially isolated. Some were remote even from Anglo settlements. There were few if any middle-class families among the Mexicans to provide role models or liaison with the larger society.

It seems clear that after World War II remnants of caste-like structures in the small cities and towns of the Southwest were being perceptibly modified. Upwardly mobile—or potentially mobile—Mexican Americans are leaving such towns for the cities, rather than remaining to compete for the limited number of middle-class positions within the Mexican community or resigning themselves to caste-like limitations on opportunity. This "leaking caste" situation is an important variant of stratification for Mexican Americans. Though the process does not drastically alter the caste structure (or the relationship between Mexican-American and Anglo subsystems), it does change relationships within the Mexican-American subsystem. Such "leakage" characterizes several small communities studied in the 1950s and

1960s (Del Norte, Colorado; Weslaco, Texas; and Ontario, California) and seems to reflect a process of rapid urbanization.[35]

A third type of class structure appears in large California and certain northern cities. This is a persistent dual system for Mexican Americans and Anglos in which identification with the ethnic community is optional. Such a pattern appears to have become normal in most big cities and some small ones during the recent past. It approximates the historic structure found in eastern cities with large European ethnic groups. Typical of these cases are northern enclaves of Mexican Americans in Kansas City and St. Paul in the late 1950s and early 1960s, and in San Jose and Pomona, California in the 1950s.[36]

Thus, the class situation that has long been the norm for most American ethnic groups of European background has only recently extended to the Mexican Americans. Availability of options characterizes the situation mainly in the larger communities, particularly where Mexican Americans form a comparatively small proportion of the whole population and where their local history does not leave too strong a residue of caste-like structures and attitudes.

THE CLASS SYSTEM TODAY:

SURVEY FINDINGS

With this background, we turn to our survey findings from Los Angeles and San Antonio. We may ask whether the system in these two "capital cities" of the Mexican-American population reveals a movement to voluntarism in ethnic identification (or reference group) on the part of the more mobile ethnics. To use the symbolic labels adopted earlier for people who seek higher status outside or within the ethnic group, what are the status characteristics of "Frontiersmen" and "Colonists" in the two cities? What is the effect of the difference in environment—from relatively open in California to more constricted in Texas? Finding answers to these questions is especially important because the areas of ethnic concentration are so conspicuous that Mexican Americans elsewhere, outside the ethnic enclave, can be easily overlooked. Further, the clamor of the ethnic community is so audible to the scholar that it tends to drown out the softer sound of "leakage" from the ethnic system.

Income

The multiple indicators of social class used in studies of entire communities are inappropriate for the analysis of our survey data from Los Angeles and San Antonio. Instead, *income is here taken as the major indicator of class position*. Not only is income the most general means for the acquisition of most types of status, but the other commonly used indicators (education, occupational level, occupational prestige,

325

neighborhood reputation) are equivocal. Education is an equivocal resource because it is not very closely related to achievement in those few relatively lucrative occupations which cater to the ethnic group. Occupational level or occupational prestige are also equivocal; as was pointed out earlier, occupations of lower general prestige may have high intra-ethnic prestige.* Neighborhood reputation may be a highly equivocal status reward for those who choose to live in a better home "in the old neighborhood" rather than move to an Anglo neighborhood of higher general quality. Thus, of all status indicators available, income appears to be the least biased in terms of the assumptions about the ethnic class system.

In addition to this advantage, income has a positive virtue in the analysis of a predominantly poor population. Comparatively small increments in income make a far greater difference than small increments in education or occupational prestige. For instance, in the lower Rio Grande Valley, and in San Antonio as well, the threat of destitution is so omnipresent that the sharpest status distinctions are said to be made between those with a steady job—or a year-round job—and those limited to a seasonal or otherwise unpredictable source of income.[37] Stratification of the respondent populations into two or three levels of income provides a socially more meaningful distinction than a similar stratification by either educational attainment or occupational prestige score, because both of the latter are so low. It is really only at the highest income level that educational and occupational prestige differences gain any importance.

Some of these points are obvious from the data. Thus, for the Los Angeles respondents there is a correlation of only .57 between earnings of the head of the household and the prestige of his job measured by a standard prestige scale.[38] The correlation between education of the head and family income is even lower (.27), and the correlation between home value and head's income is only .12, reflecting probably the greater importance of multiple incomes as well as other factors. (The correlation with total family income is higher.)

The subsequent analysis considers the residential patterns of respondents in each income class. That is, do they live in a heavily, moderately, or only very lightly "Mexican" area? These are ethnic Colonies, Frontiers, or Intermediate areas, as defined for each city in the previous chapter.

The disparities between San Antonio and Los Angeles were discussed in the previous chapter in terms of differences in segregation. In San Antonio, we could divide the population into only two neighborhood categories, Frontier and Colony. In Los Angeles a greater range permitted us to add a third, intermediate, category. Much the same pattern appeared with regard to income distribution in the two

*Occupations are not only distinguished by the presence of dual prestige systems, casting doubt on the validity of an over-all prestige rating; they are also equivocal for ethnic minorities because most ethnics fall at the bottom of most occupational clusters (see Chapter 9). Thus occupational categories are not even objectively the same in ethnic minorities as in the dominant group. Finally, the relative weight of occupation as against other prestige sources is unknown for most minorities, though several studies of the Negro middle class suggest its lower weight. Thus, status categorization schemes resting on weighting of various status attributes (e.g. Warner's I.S.C. or Hollingshead's multiple factor index) are of questionable validity for an ethnic population.

cities. Dividing the Los Angeles sample into thirds by income of household head, low income is defined as under $3,600, medium as $3,600–$5,999, and higher as $6,000 and over. Even though these incomes are extremely low by American standards for 1965–66, the Los Angeles Mexican-American sample seems prosperous compared with that of San Antonio. Here median income is $2,760, and "low income" is below and "medium income" is above that appalling figure. As with ethnic composition of the neighborhood, only a two-way income division is appropriate in San Antonio.

In both cities, the higher-income people tend to live in the Frontiers and lower-income people in the Colonies, but in both cities there are significant exceptions in each income category (Table 14–1). Thus, although half of the high-income

Table 14–1. Percent of Los Angeles and San Antonio Survey Respondents at Each Income Level Living in Areas of Varying Ethnic Composition, 1965–1966

	LOS ANGELES INCOME			SAN ANOTNIO INCOME	
Neighborhood Ethnicity[a]	Higher > $6,000	Medium $3,600–$5,999	Low < $3,600	Medium > $2,760	Low < $2,760
Frontier	50%	25%	28%	27%	9%
Intermediate	29	33	27	—	—
Colony	21	42	45	73	91
Total (= 100%)	(368)	(298)	(281)	(326b)	(277b)

[a] In Los Angeles, Frontier = tracts with less than 15.0 percent Spanish-surname individuals; Intermediate = tracts with between 15.0 and 43.8 percent Spanish-surname individuals; and Colony = tracts with more than 43.8 percent Spanish-surname individuals. In San Antonio, Frontier = tracts with less than 54.0 percent Spanish-surname individuals, and Colony = tracts with 54.0 percent or more Spanish-surname individuals.
[b] Weighting procedures were used in the San Antonio sample. This means that total numbers cannot be used as a direct indicator of error. See Appendix H.

people in Los Angeles live in predominantly Anglo areas, so do more than a quarter of the low-income people. And although more than two-fifths of the poorest people live in Colonies, so do more than one-fifth of the high-income people. San Antonio shows greater segregation of both poor and middle-income households, although a quarter of the latter live outside the Colonies.

This stratification of respondents by income and neighborhood ethnicity will be utilized not only in this chapter but also in several others. In the present chapter, we use it as a basis for analyzing occupation, sources of income, education, levels of living, personal characteristics, and aspects of social mobility.

Occupation

As expected, people of different income levels show different occupational patterns (Table 14–2). A very small minority of the household heads were white-collar workers. They were clustered in the higher-income categories (of which almost a quarter were white-collar), especially among those living outside the

Colony in predominantly Anglo areas. Most of the higher-income household heads were employed as skilled and semiskilled workers. Even at this income level, more skilled workers were living in the Colony than in the Frontier neighborhoods. Semiskilled and unskilled laborers form the bulk of the medium- and low-income households as well as the majority of households in the predominantly Mexican areas. Generally, there is a slight but persistent tendency at each income level for Colonies to be somewhat more weighted with residents in lower-status occupations.

Table 14-2. Household Head's Occupational Level, Los Angeles and San Antonio Survey Respondents, by Income and Neighborhood Ethnicity, 1965–1966[a]

	White-Collar	Skilled	Semi-skilled	Unskilled	Total Number (= 100%)
Los Angeles					
Higher income[b]					
Frontier	31%	37%	17%	15%	182
Intermediate	19	32	25	24	106
Colony	13	42	27	18	78
Medium income					
Frontier	24	19	35	22	74
Intermediate	13	28	33	26	95
Colony	13	27	38	22	121
Low income					
Frontier	8	17	50	25	24
Intermediate	9	9	29	53	34
Colony	17	17	30	36	46
San Antonio					
Medium income					
Frontier	27	36	16	21	135
Colony	20	24	22	34	189
Low income					
Frontier	6	6	21	67	27
Colony	8	12	18	62	156

[a] Housewives and retired or unemployed heads are omitted from this table.
[b] In Los Angeles: higher income = > $6,000; medium income = $3,600–$5,999; low income < $3,600. In San Antonio: medium income = > $2,760; low income < $2,760.

Each occupation was also assigned a socioeconomic index score reflecting its general prestige in the society as a whole.[39] The occupational prestige of the Mexican-American population is low compared with the nation as a whole. In 1950, for example, the mean prestige score for the male population of the United States was approximately 30 (with a possible range from 0–100), while even 15 years later only 28 percent of the Mexican-American household heads in Los Angeles and only 26 percent in San Antonio had occupations with prestige scores over 30. Thus, despite a general upgrading that probably raised the mean occupational prestige score for the country between 1950 and 1965, Mexican Americans were well below the mean of even the earlier period.

In our samples, within the higher- and medium-income categories the predominantly Mexican Colonies are more filled with low-prestige workers. (The sample has been divided into thirds by prestige score. As with income, the distribution is concentrated at very low levels, and "high" prestige is a rather mixed category.) Mexican Americans living in predominantly Anglo areas include a greater proportion of higher-prestige occupations (Table 14–3). This finding helps to clarify the notion of who are Colonists and who are Frontiersmen. The middle-class Colonists tend to

Table 14–3. Household Head's Job Prestige, Los Angeles and San Antonio Survey Respondents, by Income and Neighborhood Ethnicity, 1965–1966

	PRESTIGE SCORES[a]			Total
	0–9 Low	10–19 Medium	20+ High	Number (= 100%)
Los Angeles				
Higher income				
Frontier	10%	32%	58%	195
Intermediate	13	39	48	106
Colony	19	33	48	79
Medium income				
Frontier	9	47	44	76
Intermediate	15	48	37	98
Colony	22	38	40	124
Low income				
Frontier	70	24	6	79
Intermediate	64	26	10	77
Colony	70	17	13	126
San Antonio				
Medium income				
Frontier	17	16	67	135
Colony	33	21	46	191
Low income				
Frontier	64	28	8	47
Colony	60	20	20	229

[a] Derived from Albert J. Reiss, Jr., *Occupations and Social Status* (New York: The Free Press, 1961), pp. 263–275.

be people who may obtain status rewards from their fellow ethnics on the basis of money (like the skilled workers) while avoiding the possible status deprivation commensurate with their low job prestige in the larger society. For example, a highly-paid truck driver of Mexican descent may be able to get more out of life by staying in a predominantly Mexican area, where both his income and his occupation receive deference because they are above the norm. On the other hand, highly-paid white-collar workers tend to leave the Mexican areas. This may be because both their income and their occupation permit them to be comfortable without the extra prestige support of the ethnic group. As our earlier theoretical analysis suggested, status discrepancies (in this case between income and occupational prestige) can be alleviated by remaining in the ethnically concentrated areas.[40] The plausibility of this interpretation gains in view of the fact that the pattern is most noticeable at higher- and medium-income levels, while at low-income levels very few high-prestige people seem to prefer living in the Colonies. For these people, another kind of income-prestige status discrepancy may be resolved by continued residence in the ghetto.

Table 14–4. *Sources of Family Income: Percent of Los Angeles and San Antonio Survey Households Receiving Income from Selected Sources, by Head's Income and Neighborhood Ethnicity, 1965–1966*

	SOURCE OF INCOME[a]									Total Number of Households
	1	2	3	4	5	6	7	8	9	
Los Angeles										
Higher income										
Frontier	93%	7%	3%	5%	b%	b%	2%	1%	3%	183
Intermediate	99	5	7	6	0	3	1	2	2	106
Colony	97	0	1	6	1	7	1	6	1	79
Medium income										
Frontier	97	4	3	4	1	3	0	0	3	76
Intermediate	98	3	2	3	0	2	0	1	2	98
Colony	95	2	0	4	1	0	1	2	3	124
Low income										
Frontier	60	1	0	1	15	9	0	19	16	79
Intermediate	53	3	1	3	23	4	1	23	14	77
Colony	54	1	0	1	22	7	2	28	18	125
San Antonio										
Medium income										
Frontier	96	7	1	4	0	0	7	1	1	135
Colony	97	4	0	4	1	1	6	1	4	191
Low income										
Frontier	67	0	0	6	8	0	6	37	10	48
Colony	73	2	1	5	9	2	6	27	10	229

[a] Some respondents received income from more than one source. Hence, the percentages in the columns add up to more than 100. Sources of income:
1. Wages and salary.
2. Business.
3. Professional fees.
4. Rents (not lodger).
5. Welfare.
6. Unemployment compensation.
7. Veterans payments.
8. Social Security and other Federal pensions.
9. Other pensions.
[b] 0.5 percent.

Source of Income

At the middle- and higher-income levels Mexican Americans are predominantly wage workers (Table 14–4). Only a small fraction derive their income from business or professional fees. Among the poor, many live on welfare payments or pensions of various kinds, including Social Security and allowances from other Federal programs.

(The proportion deriving income from pensions reflects the greater proportion of the aged among the poor.) The differences between the two cities in the sources of sustenance for the poor are striking. Welfare and unemployment benefits are far more common in Los Angeles than in San Antonio. Because the need in San Antonio is relatively greater than in Los Angeles, the more frequent dependence of Angelenos

Table 14–5. Household Head's Education, Los Angeles and San Antonio Survey Respondents, by Income and Neighborhood Ethnicity, 1965–1966

| | YEARS OF SCHOOL COMPLETED | | | | | Total Number (= 100%) |
	0–4	5–8	9–11	12	12+	
Los Angeles						
Higher income						
Frontier	7%	21%	21%	29%	22%	191
Intermediate	11	23	34	21	11	104
Colony	13	18	37	23	9	78
Medium income						
Frontier	15	32	19	26	8	74
Intermediate	15	32	27	21	5	98
Colony	26	35	26	11	2	121
Low income						
Frontier	18	34	25	13	10	79
Intermediate	56	22	14	5	3	77
Colony	39	29	25	4	3	125
San Antonio						
Medium income						
Frontier	6	22	31	28	14	133
Colony	24	32	21	18	5	185
Low income						
Frontier	46	37	8	7	2	45
Colony	54	33	10	2	1	205

on welfare and unemployment benefits may be due to differences in public policy regarding welfare expenditure or in information accessible to the poor. The greater importance of Social Security and other Federal pension programs in San Antonio possibly reflects Federal employment at military bases like Kelly Field.

Education

Looking only at middle-class Frontiersmen and Colonists, the vast majority of the higher-income families living in the Colonies are headed by persons with less than high school education, while the great majority of higher-income people *with* high school education or more live in more mixed areas (Table 14–5). The relationship between schooling and ghetto concentration is less clear for low-income heads of households. As one would expect, most of the low-income ghetto dwellers show low educational attainment, but this group also includes a fair proportion of people who attended high school.

The analysis of education as well as occupation and prestige of the household head permits further insight into the role of income for Mexican Americans. Those above the poverty line who choose to live in the Colonies tend to be persons whose general status attributes—especially job prestige and education—are relatively low. These are people whose insecurities might be aroused in ethnically mixed areas, with probably better educated neighbors. They might benefit most from the support of their fellow ethnics. Thus income may be best viewed as a catalyst, permitting the expression of underlying sentiments which might influence style of life.

At the higher levels of prestige, there seems to be comparatively little association between occupational standing and education. Some "high-prestige" people in this community have only grade-school education. This phenomenon is possible because ethnic job prestige may not match Anglo standards, because many *comparatively* high-prestige jobs in the ghetto do not require much education, and because of the persistence of ethnic prestige criteria (not measured here) which are unrelated to the amount of schooling.

Personal Characteristics

The age and sex composition of household heads at various income levels sheds light on some of the patterns just described. A high proportion of poverty-level heads are over 50, while the more successful earners tend more to be in the prime of life (Table 14-6). Further, a larger percentage of the poor households are headed by women. In these respects, poor Mexican Americans have much in common with other poverty populations. In Los Angeles, moreover, the proportion of low-income heads of 50 years or older increases with increasing concentration of Mexican Americans, and so does the percentage of female household heads. Here is the familiar pattern of the ethnic ghettos containing a disproportionate number not only of the poor but also of older and broken families.

As one would expect, overt signs of acculturation diminish at the lower economic levels and in the more ghettoized areas. Thus, Spanish fluency is greater and English fluency of respondents is lower in the more predominantly Mexican areas (Chapter 18). And to judge from general impressions of interviewers (for the most part Mexican Americans themselves), the lower the income and the more predominantly Mexican the area of residence the more "Mexican" the respondents appeared to the interviewers (Table 14-7). (Interviewers were asked to rate whether the respondent struck them as very Mexican, moderately, not very, or not Mexican at all.) The relationship of "Mexicanness" to neighborhood ethnicity holds within practically each income category, with the respondents in predominantly Anglo areas consistently appearing less "Mexican" to the interviewer. In part, the large proportion of people who appeared *more* "Mexican" among the low-income respondents in areas of high

Table 14–6. Age and Percent Female of Los Angeles and San Antonio Survey Household Heads, by Income and Neighborhood Ethnicity, 1965–1966

	AGE OF HEAD				Percent Female Heads	Total Number (= 100%)
	Under 30	30–39	40–49	50 and over		
Los Angeles						
Higher income						
Frontier	16%	38%	27%	19%	4%	183
Intermediate	17	38	35	10	1	106
Colony	10	38	41	11	0	79
Medium income						
Frontier	38	29	16	17	16	76
Intermediate	24	37	15	24	11	98
Colony	25	28	25	22	10	124
Low income						
Frontier	18	30	19	33	39	78
Intermediate	17	25	15	43	49	76
Colony	12	21	17	50	49	125
San Antonio						
Medium income						
Frontier	13	39	30	18	5	135
Colony	14	29	26	31	3	191
Low income						
Frontier	9	15	13	63	40	47
Colony	10	16	16	58	37	229

Table 14–7. Interviewers' Ratings of Respondent's "Mexicanness", Los Angeles and San Antonio, by Income and Neighborhood Ethnicity, 1965–1966

	Very Mexican	Moderately Mexican	Not Very and Not at All Mexican	Total Number (= 100%)
Los Angeles				
Higher income				
Frontier	12%	46%	42%	183
Intermediate	22	39	39	102
Colony	28	46	26	79
Medium income				
Frontier	24	49	27	76
Intermediate	36	44	20	96
Colony	37	45	18	123
Low income				
Frontier	31	37	32	78
Intermediate	53	29	18	77
Colony	43	37	20	122
San Antonio				
Medium income				
Frontier	17	58	25	135
Colony	29	50	21	189
Low income				
Frontier	48	37	15	47
Colony	53	39	8	227

ethnic concentration is associated with the greater age of respondents in these areas.

Some of the studies of social class and Mexican Americans emphasize the importance of skin color and "Indianness" of feature. As a result of centuries of genetic mixture the Mexican population shows a great variety of physical attributes. A random selection would include tall, blue-eyed blonds as well as people of clearly Indian and even Negroid type. (Negroes were imported to New Spain and later some American slaves escaped from the South to Mexico. The descendants of these groups tend to be concentrated in coastal areas of the Gulf of Mexico.) Color and its

Table 14–8. Respondent's Skin Coloring, Los Angeles and San Antonio, by Income and Neighborhood Ethnicity, 1965–1966

	Light	Medium	Dark	Total Number (= 100%)
Los Angeles				
Higher income				
Frontier	29%	43%	28%	183
Intermediate	30	44	26	104
Colony	21	46	33	79
Medium income				
Frontier	26	54	20	76
Intermediate	27	40	33	96
Colony	28	40	32	124
Low income				
Frontier	34	38	28	79
Intermediate	34	38	28	77
Colony	25	43	32	124
San Antonio				
Medium income				
Frontier	57	29	14	135
Colony	39	40	21	189
Low income				
Frontier	43	38	19	47
Colony	37	35	28	228

gradations play a role not only in the attitudes of Anglos toward Mexican Americans but within the Mexican-American community itself. There is a rich glossary of terms referring to color, including: *blanco*—white, *guero* and *huero*—blond, *moreno*—brown, *negro*—black, *tisnado*—black, *pecoso*—freckle-face, *prieto*—dark brown, and *trigueño*—light brown. In-group terms for color are complex. The diminutive suffix *-ito*, when added to any of these terms, alters the meaning completely. For example, to identify someone as *prieto* can be simply descriptive, with no value overtones. By identifying the same person as *prietito* a value judgment going beyond identification of color is involved: The diminutive suffix can suggest condescension—a judgment that a person is dark and mentally limited, or it can suggest extreme sympathy and partisanship for the person being identified. In a different vein, the word *prieto*, uttered by itself in a given context and with the proper inflection of the voice, is a clear insult, a call to battle. Other terms like *tisnado*, which also refers to dark skin color, are almost always pejorative. "Hijo de tu tisnada madre" ("You son of a black mother") was a common preface to street combat. Still, by altering context, inflection and/or adding the diminutive suffix, *tisnado* can become quite harmless or very subtly invidious. The complexities of Spanish terms for color are lost in English translation.

The Los Angeles survey found little relationship between color (as rated by the interviewer) and either income or ghettoization (Table 14–8). Most of the respondents had skins of medium or dark color. The minority of light-skinned individuals were not notably concentrated among the higher-income groups, but there was a consistent, though slight tendency for the proportion of dark-skinned individuals to increase in predominantly Mexican areas at all income levels. In San Antonio, the relationship between color and both income and neighborhood ethnicity appeared to be stronger. The respondents with better income included a larger percentage of light-skinned people than those with low income, regardless of whether they lived in areas of small or great Mexican-American concentration. The respondents in the Colonies included fewer light-skinned persons than the Frontier residents, regardless of income. This observation suggests a greater color-caste influence in San Antonio.

The analysis of "Mexicanness" and coloring relies on interviewer judgment and is thus subject to all of the vagaries of this procedure. But it can be broadly accepted as reflecting over-all impressions of predominantly Mexican-American interviewers with college training. The impressions were received in lengthy sessions involving a great deal of interaction.

Neighborhoods and Levels of Living

Reports of the interviewers on how well the respondents lived in material terms generally supported the notion not only of the usual compromise between housing cost and the quality of dwelling and neighborhood but of a "trade-off" of quality for ethnicity. Over-all, the more Mexican the area the lower the quality of the home and neighborhood, holding income constant. For example, traffic nuisances increase with ghettoization almost irrespective of the family's income level in Los Angeles. This is true only of low-income respondents in San Antonio.

The character of predominantly Mexican areas reflects general differences between the two cities. In Los Angeles, the Mexican-American area is mercilessly crosscut by freeways and shows more mixed land use than many other parts of the city. The people in Los Angeles who choose to or can afford to live in the more Anglo areas have a wide range of choice in neighborhood characteristics. In more segregated San Antonio, the heavily Mexican districts include a wide range among themselves. However, in both cities and within each income category, the lower the proportion of Spanish-surname individuals the better the neighborhood reputation. Generally, the Colony tracts are rated comparatively poor by the interviewers, and the higher-income individuals living in these tracts are trading inferior quality features of the ethnic neighborhood for certain advantages provided by its very ethnicity. Some of the occupational and personal characteristics of the relatively high-income people living in the ghettos help explain this choice.

The interviews also suggest an interesting nexus between type of neighborhood, level of income, and journey to work that is different in the two cities. Let us consider a long journey (more than 40 minutes in Los Angeles and 30 in San Antonio) as an indicator of attachment to home and neighborhood. In Los Angeles tolerance for such inconvenience is most likely to be found among two types of respondents: the poor families in the predominantly Mexican areas, and the best-paid families in the predominantly Anglo areas. By contrast, few of the better-paid ghetto household heads and few of the poorest Frontier heads make such a long journey. This is consistent with earlier findings. Poorer Colonists may find the cheaper housing and the diffuse security in the ethnic colony well worth a long trip to a job which probably has little intrinsic reward and little security. Better paid Colonists, who may be financially able to move, probably have an additional reason to remain in the colony if they are closer to work. (Some probably have work that ties them to the ethnic areas.) In San Antonio it is the Colonists at both income levels that travel longer to work than the Frontiersmen. This suggests the generally greater importance of the Colony to the ethnic group. In San Antonio, Frontiersmen at both income levels tend to be very close to work, that is, ten minutes or less.

Direct questions about the neighborhood show that the least satisfied were those who lived in the predominantly Mexican areas of both cities, with little difference in degree of discontent between higher- and lower-income families. The majority of complaints were about the physical environment—dirt, noise, dogs, vermin, freeways, street traffic, ugliness. In San Antonio the physical environment is much worse than in Los Angeles, and it overshadows other sources of irritation. In Los Angeles the poorer respondents in both Frontier and Colony tended to have more complaints about the neighbors themselves, while higher-income respondents were more sensitive to physical environment. What people particularly like is a mirror image of what they dislike. In Los Angeles the physical environment was of most relevance for those who were better off, especially those living in the predominantly Anglo areas, while "people" increased in salience for the poorer respondents.

General status anxiety—keeping up with the Anglo Joneses—as well as more affluence and more attachment to environmental amenities may account for the greater neatness of Mexican houses and yards at all income levels in the predominantly Anglo areas. The indoor furnishings matched the exterior, and were superior and better maintained in predominantly Anglo areas at all income levels. Though these patterns undoubtedly reflect a complicated mixture of economic and attitudinal factors, the fact remains that Mexican Americans in the ethnic Colonies tend to live less well in material terms, irrespective of income level.

Much the same pattern is found for housing features directly concerned with health. Most respondents in both cities had both a bathroom with a flush toilet and hot and cold running water. However, the difference in level of life between the two cities is notable in even these rather crude measures: 10 percent of the San Antonio homes, compared with only 4 percent of the Los Angeles homes, lacked bathroom facilities, and a startling 26 percent of the San Antonio homes, as compared with only 1 percent of the Los Angeles homes, lacked hot running water. Plumbing was slightly more frequent in predominantly Anglo neighborhoods than in predominantly Mexican-American neighborhoods. The vast majority of households in both cities had mechanical refrigeration.

Sharp differences exist between Los Angeles and San Antonio in the ownership of a means of communication with the rest of the community. Almost all Angelenos had a TV set, compared with only 81 percent of the San Antonians. Nearly 80 percent of the Angelenos but only 67 percent of the San Antonians owned cars. (Bus rides in sprawling Los Angeles are longer; a family without a car is seriously isolated.) About three-fourths of the Mexican Americans in Los Angeles were in touch with people outside their homes by household telephone, compared with only 56 percent of the San Antonians. Of course, access to the outside world is a function of income. This is especially true with reference to car ownership; almost half of poverty-level San Antonians, for example, do not own cars. But Frontiersmen at every income level were more likely to possess phones and television sets than were the Colonists.[41]

SOCIAL MOBILITY

Intergenerational Mobility

The occupational level of our respondents' parents was very low. The vast majority in both cities were blue-collar workers, and more than half were unskilled and predominantly agricultural laborers (Table 14–9). Examining the relationships between present income and the skill level of parental occupations yields one interesting finding: Having had a father who was a skilled worker or a white-collar worker seems to have made little difference to the present generation's chances for higher income. Angeleno household heads in higher-income families are almost as likely to have had fathers engaged in unskilled labor as those in low-income families. In San Antonio, however, there is somewhat greater difference in the fathers' occupational background between the poor and the non-poor. But achievement within this generation does not seem to be importantly related to parental achievement in either city.

Present income is somewhat more closely related to parental education than to occupation. One-third of the Angeleno respondents in higher-income families and slightly more of the San Antonians in medium-income families had fathers with more than four years of school. Among the low-income families, only 16 percent in Los Angeles and 24 percent in San Antonio had fathers with more than four years of schooling. Only 6 percent of the Angelenos and 4 percent of the San Antonians had fathers with the equivalent of a high school education; those fathers were not frequent among families with higher incomes. These indicators of parental social-class level are even less associated with the ethnic composition of the respondents' neighborhood.

Another issue related to the family past, however, was less predictable. Pilot interviews with very mobile men had suggested that some kind of "myth of the golden past" (in this case family past) might play a role in social mobility. Such men often reported one of their parents or grandparents as coming from well-to-do

Table 14–9. Occupational Level of Household Heads' Fathers, by Income, Los Angeles and San Antonio Survey Respondents, 1965–1966

| | Head's Income | | |
Father's Occupation	HIGHER	MEDIUM	LOW
		Los Angeles	
Unskilled labor	44%	50%	51%
Semiskilled	18	19	15
Skilled and white-collar	38	31	34
Total number (= 100%)	(192)	(133)	(138)
		San Antonio	
Unskilled labor	—	61%	70%
Semiskilled	—	12	11
Skilled and white-collar	—	27	19
Total number (= 100%)	—	(172)	(159)

families in Mexico, but having lost status through gambling, mésalliance, or other personal problems. (Political problems were seldom mentioned.) Accordingly, one of the items in the questionnaire asked: "Was your father's family in Mexico poor, well-to-do, or what?"

The response patterns show a somewhat stronger association between paternal (and also maternal) reputation and present income than between fathers' occupation and current income. This is also true for neighborhood ethnicity. Within each income level, those who replied "middle class" or "well-to-do" are over-represented in the Frontiers. This is not the case for fathers' occupation and present income.

The data do not allow unequivocal interpretation. One may seriously doubt the objective validity of the responses in view of the data on Mexican stratification presented earlier. There simply were not enough middle-class or well-to-do families to accommodate this many ancestors (almost half of the persons of higher incomes, for example). In one or two instances where the Mexican past is recent and specific, interviewers knowing Mexico City neighborhoods were aware of respondents' upgrading. If this response pattern is largely subjective, it permits at least two interpretations. First, poverty as a virtue (nosotros los pobres) is a Mexican value, and one would expect to find less need to conceal a poor past among people choosing to live in more Mexican areas. This is supported by the survey data. On the other hand, upwardly mobile people in the past have had a strong tendency to claim "Spanish" rather than Mexican ancestry. Though this is not a common pattern in Los Angeles at present, the legitimation of present middle-class status in terms of past middle-class status may represent a residue of this pattern as well as a more general retrospective glow.

Second—and this interpretation goes beyond the symbolic level—if indeed people can recall one member of the family who in the past was something other than the bottom level "peon," it is perfectly possible that association with very lower-class Mexicans in the fields and in the slums was defined as downward mobility. In such circumstances, children might have been discouraged from associating themselves with the values and behavior of those with whom they had to live, but with whom they did not have to identify.[42] This interpretation would also account for the tendency of such individuals to locate in areas outside the Mexican concentrations. However, elaboration of interpretations along such lines would require more extensive life history data than we have available.

Lifetime Mobility

For an overwhelmingly poor and rural population like the Mexicans of only a short time ago, status changes *within* a lower-class level are important. Geographic mobility away from a rural area, away from an area of slow economic growth, away from an area of higher discrimination may have only a small immediate effect on a man's income.* It may result in nothing more than his establishment at the bottom of a metropolitan stratification system. But the difficulty of such establishment should not be underestimated. It is illustrated by one former *bracero* re-interviewed two months after the first interview and three months after his first arrival in Los Angeles. He was on his way to Northern California to work again in the fields. He was aware that agricultural labor "pays little and is much work," but four years of school in Mexico had equipped him for little else in Los Angeles.[43]

Even though geographic mobility is the total extent of their mobility, some respondents feel that the process of uprooting and re-establishment has at least prepared the way for their children to take advantage of the greater opportunities of the metropolis. That they have achieved something of personal significance is shown by contrasting their interviews with those of Los Angeles and San Antonio natives who still occupy low-status jobs. These are people whose parents or grandparents went through the process of uprooting, but who themselves were not able to make further progress. Most were from broken families—some broken in the very process of movement and establishment in the city during the depression years of

---

*The discussion here is based on lengthy interviews held with subsamples of mobile and nonmobile men in the two cities. The analysis was prepared by Lorenzo Campbell, who contributed substantially to this section on social mobility.

the 1930s. Most are painfully conscious of the comparative flatness of their lives in clear contrast with the self-perceptions of those born outside the cities.

There is very little doubt that the current economic status of Angelenos is related to point of origin, especially at the extreme ends. Mexican-born individuals are over-represented in the low-income categories. People born in Los Angeles are over-represented in the higher-income categories (Table 14-10). This is far less true for San Antonio, where those born in the city are not much more likely to live above the poverty level than those born elsewhere in Texas or in Mexico itself. Birth or upbringing in most other areas of the Southwest outside of Los Angeles does not seem to have much relationship to the present income level, except that the Texas-reared are distributed more like the Mexican-bred than are migrants from other areas. (The table shows the much larger hinterland from which Los Angeles draws; in contrast, 99 percent of the San Antonio respondents were either Texans or Mexicans.)

Table 14-10. Birthplace and Present Income of Household Head, Los Angeles and San Antonio Survey Respondents, 1965-1966

		Income	
BIRTHPLACE	HIGHER	MEDIUM	LOW
		Los Angeles	
Mexico	8%	19%	31%
Texas	10	16	14
Arizona, Colorado, New Mexico	25	22	31
California outside Los Angeles	9	9	10
Los Angeles	45	33	20
Elsewhere	3	1	4
Total number (= 100%)	(320)	(233)	(216)
		San Antonio	
Mexico	—	21%	29%
Texas outside San Antonio	—	37	32
San Antonio	—	41	38
Elsewhere	—	1	1
Total number (= 100%)	—	(286)	(277)

The time of life and family context within which moves occur represent additional factors influencing life chances. Among the Mexican-born Angelenos, those who came to the city as children are over-represented in the higher-income group; those who came as adults with dependents are greatly under-represented. Those who came alone as adults are about proportionally represented in all of the three earning brackets (Table 14-11). There is no such pattern in San Antonio, with its far fewer adult immigrants. (Only 37 percent of the Mexican-born San Antonians came as adults, compared with 73 percent of the Mexican-born Angelenos.) The data for Los Angeles give at least a glimpse of the complexities involved in the relationship between time of life and family context at the point of immigration, on the one hand, and economic achievement on the other. Mobility upward from the parental level often entails a sharp break with the family's past: Migrants "leave home" metaphorically as well as literally. Geographic mobility is "a selective mechanism by which the more able are channeled to places where their potential can be realized."[44] Some persons, of course, are upwardly mobile without leaving home physically. In fact, our data suggest that a Los Angeles upbringing encourages upward mobility. Some manage no more than the geographic mobility. For a few, both geographic and occupational mobility are combined. Of course, there are many for whom there has been neither geographic nor occupational mobility from the parental level, and for whom there has been in effect no status change over their lifetime. The survey data on lifetime occupational mobility of the head of the house again reflect the generally low status of the group. Forty percent of all heads in Los Angeles, and more than half in San Antonio started as unskilled laborers, and 15 percent in both cities started as agricultural laborers. Only 14 percent in Los Angeles started work as white-collar workers; a larger percentage in San Antonio claims this beginning occupational status.

Table 14–11. Immigrants from Mexico:
Family Context at Time of Immigration and Current Income,
Los Angeles and San Antonio Survey Respondents, 1965–1966

	Income		
CONTEXT AT TIME OF IMMIGRATION	HIGHER	MEDIUM	LOW
		Los Angeles	
As child with parents	41%	24%	23%
Alone as adult	26	26	21
With spouse or other	33	50	56
Total number (= 100%)	(73)	(109)	(136)
		San Antonio	
As child with parents	—	69%	60%
Alone as adult	—	4	21
With spouse or other	—	27	19
Total number (= 100%)		(46)	(86)

There is only a slight relationship between the present income of a head of household and his (or her) first occupation. White-collar and skilled first jobs are somewhat under-represented in the low-income families and unskilled labor slightly under-represented in higher-income families. Heads who report that their first jobs were white-collar are also more likely (far more likely in San Antonio) to be living in the ethnic frontier areas. There is reason to believe that first jobs are retrospectively upgraded by heads of households in predominantly Anglo areas. Like the possibly glorified family past, this may be a way of claiming acceptance in Anglo and traditional Mexican terms as an atypical Mexican.

341

Because so many of them come from agricultural backgrounds, the Mexican-American poor of Los Angeles include comparatively few household heads with any experience as factory workers. And because of the additional factor of low industrialization, practically none of the San Antonio heads at any income level had worked in a factory. Relatively few respondents among the poor in either city had served in the Armed Forces.

General Problems in the Analysis of Mobility

The data suggest that conventional notions of mobility must be modified in order to understand a population like the Mexican Americans. Many are still in the process of establishing themselves on the bottom rung of the urban stratification system. Agricultural labor is culturally recognized as a means of survival rather than as a desirable occupation. (One respondent, for example, reported a relative as "*desocupado* [unemployed], working in the fields.") Thus, many Mexican Americans themselves see the flight from unskilled agricultural labor as equivalent to a flight from economic and social limbo even though the urban in-migrant may find occupational adjustment to the new milieu difficult.

Even the mobility of some of the higher-income people may be precarious. Thus we find, as have students of other minorities, that highly mobile Mexican Americans frequently do not define themselves as mobile or "successful," as "having made it," or as "middle class." Instead of comparing themselves with their parents and congratulating themselves on how far they have come, they compare themselves with others in the Anglo world and depreciate their accomplishments. Instead of looking ahead to a better future, they often look behind in fear of the abyss from which they have climbed. This tendency is evident at the psychological level,[45] and its strength seems to vary, among other things, among individuals using the Colony and those using the Frontier as their frame of reference. When men in the small subsample of lengthier interviews were asked about their prospects for the next five years, more than a third of those who had been occupationally mobile foresaw no change in the future. Often this prediction was made with considerable apprehension. A dim outlook was much more prevalent among those who had been only geographically mobile or not mobile at all; the latter group showed practically no optimism and great apprehension about the future.

Other observers have noted a similar preoccupation among ethnic people with the maintenance of their status;[46] among the Negro middle class, who face both poverty and increased discrimination if they slide, this preoccupation is so pervasive as to seem almost neurotic.[47] The Los Angeles Mexican Americans have been reared in milieus ranging from permissive to repressive. The greater variability of the Mexican milieu compared with the Negro milieu may mean more variation in the extent of apprehension about status-maintenance in the Mexican-American population. Although better off as a group than Negroes in this respect, Mexican Americans have been generally poorer and exposed to more discrimination than other immigrant groups. Hence they are likely to exhibit more "fear of the abyss" than, say, the Italian Americans. In all probability, the apprehensions associated with a background of poverty (which most Mexicans share) and discrimination (which many Mexicans or their parents share) will become even more variable in the future. For example, the young adult reared in a predominantly Anglo area of Los Angeles by middle-class parents will simply not have had experiences common to most of the present generation of Mexican Americans. Whether this will allay his apprehensive view of the future remains to be seen.

The scarcity of Mexican middle-class role models in previous generations is evident in the lengthier interviews with a subsample of men. One of the questions about the neighborhood where the respondent grew up asked: "Who were the people or families that other people looked up to?" The most frequent response was "no one." (The honorific title "don," for example, was generally used in United States cities only for the aged.) The impact of this situation is underscored by the fact that the occupationally mobile are far more likely to report having been brought up in areas where "the rich" or "the successful" were admired. Whether this is a subjective or objective difference is beside the point. That is, one need not inquire whether the mobile respondents *actually* had rich or successful people around while the non-mobile did not. The point is that the availability of comparatively well-to-do or successful Mexican Americans who *could* serve as role models is far greater now for all Mexican Americans than it was a generation ago when the respondents were growing up. This is true even in the poorer *barrios*: One middle-aged man dramatized the difference between the comparatively affluent poor of today and his own youth by saying "Now you see *bread* lying in the streets. When I was a boy you never saw bread in the streets." Furthermore, the availability of comparatively successful Mexican Americans in the area probably permits more objective evaluation of progress.

In a very literal sense, a population that achieves some collective mobility is anomic or normless. Its norms for self-evaluation are seldom derived from full participation in the general—or any full—social-class system. Rather, these norms come from segmental institutions, such as the schools, or they are conveyed by the mass media (illustrated by the young Mexican who admired "everyone in the United States" before he came). The norms for self-appraisal are as unstable as is the attainment of middle-class status itself. Middle-class position is still precarious and beset with apprehensions over status maintenance and the grim consequences of sliding back. All this may change with a new generation remembering no direct experience of struggle against poverty and discrimination. But only a minority of the Mexican-American youth is being reared in the relative security provided by middle-class parents who live in mixed residential areas. Meanwhile, others who become mobile will in all likelihood go through the same cycle that makes it so hard for the poor and disadvantaged to evaluate their mobility objectively.

343

SUMMARY

The social-class system of the Spanish-Mexican era of what is now the American Southwest was based on sharp distinctions of race and wealth, as was the class system of Mexico itself. Though its small aristocracy maintained high prestige in the American class structure, Mexicans generally tended to be relegated to a caste-like status just a little looser than that of Negroes. These structures have been disintegrating at different rates throughout the Southwest. In some of the larger cities Mexican Americans have almost as much freedom to move their residences as, say, second- and third-generation Italians in Boston. In some—even large—cities restrictions still remain.

These historical residues and milieu differences are reflected in the ways the middle classes are depicted in academic literature. These portrayals, in turn, are reminiscent of variations found in studies of other ethnic groups and the American class system. The controversy about whether social-class differentiation occurs within the ethnic group or dissolves the group can be transcended by acknowledging that both processes may occur simultaneously, depending on the group and the time and the place. Some individuals, the "Frontiersmen," attempt to assimilate into the general system. Others, the "Colonists," attempt to retain ties with the ethnic group. The analysis of survey results in Los Angeles and San Antonio in this and subsequent chapters makes it possible to recognize Mexican-American Frontiersmen and Colonists at various income levels and describe some of their salient characteristics.

Colonists tend at each income level in both cities to have somewhat lower-prestige occupations and educational attainment than Frontiersmen. In personal characteristics, lower-class households (and especially Colonists among them) have a higher proportion of older and of female heads. They were also judged by interviewers to be more "Mexican" in manner in both cities, though the relationship between light skin color and social class was closer in San Antonio than in Los Angeles. The level of living deteriorated as one moved from middle class to lower class and from Frontier to Colony as well. In part this reflects neighborhood characteristics. Colonies, especially in lower-class areas of San Antonio, tended to be rated poor in physical amenities by interviewers and residents alike. Nonetheless, if willingness to endure a long journey to work is an indicator, both middle- and lower-class San Antonio Colonists are attached to their neighborhoods. In Los Angeles it is the Frontiersmen, or at least the middle-class Frontiersmen, who make such a sacrifice of time, apparently for improved neighborhood quality.

The generally lower-class level of the past generation is indicated by parental education and occupation and is also implied by the finding that neither of these factors appears to be importantly related to the level of attainment of the present generation. Being born in the city makes a difference in Los Angeles but not in San Antonio. In Los Angeles the native born attain higher-income levels, and comparatively few of the Mexican-bred reach the middle classes. In San Antonio, those born in the city are not much more likely to live above the poverty level than those born elsewhere in Texas or even in Mexico. The generally lower-class level is also indicated in the work *backgrounds* of the household heads, mostly in unskilled and agricultural labor and only infrequently involving factory experience. Social mobility in such a population is often seen subjectively as precarious, and occupational success as difficult to assess.

NOTES TO CHAPTER FOURTEEN

1. In studying a community in the Lower Rio Grande Valley, Howard G. Raymond uses the term "color caste." "Acculturation and Social Mobility Among Latin Americans in Resaca City" (unpublished Master's thesis, University of Texas, 1952). Similarly, of a California town in Central Valley in the 1940s, Walter R. Goldschmidt comments that "Any social advancement of a Negro or Mexican was within his own group," in *As You Sow* (New York: Harcourt, Brace and Co., 1947), p. 59. San Antonio of the same period is described by Woods as having a "social structure in the Mexican ethnic group" resembling a "pyramid," even though the author discerned a slight tendency for class to become more important than ethnicity. See Frances Jerome Woods, *Mexican Ethnic Leadership in San Antonio, Texas* (Washington, D.C.: The Catholic University of America Press, 1949), pp. 37, 51. A description of the caste situation in McAllen, Texas, in the 1940s concludes that "class lines are much more distinct and sharply drawn within the Mexican group than in the Anglo." See Ozzie Simmons, "Anglo-Americans and Mexican-Americans in South Texas: A Study in Dominant Subordinate Group Relations" (unpublished Ph.D. dissertation, Harvard University, 1952), p. 356.

2. Paul M. Sheldon, "Community Participation and the Emerging Middle Class," in Julian Samora (ed.), *La Raza: Forgotten Americans* (Notre Dame, Ind.: University of Notre Dame Press, 1966). A "kind of stabilized pluralism" was also found to characterize the situation in Tucson durng the post-World War II period. See Harry T. Getty, "Interethnic Relationships in the Community of Tucson" (unpublished Ph.D. dissertation. University of Chicago, 1950).

3. "The measure of Mexican-American mobility is thus an indirect measure of progressive acculturation of the group." Fernando Peñalosa, "Social Mobility in a Mexican-American Community," *Social Forces*, XLIV (June, 1966), pp. 498–505.

4. See, for example, William Madsen, "The Alcoholic Agringado," *American Anthropologist*, LXVI (Apr., 1964), pp. 355–359, for an analysis of the stresses of marginality. The practice of calling middle-class individuals "Spanish" to distinguish them from the "Mexican" lower class also indicates the stresses and marginality produced by mobility.

5. As in Woods, *op. cit.*, for San Antonio, and Ruth Tuck, *Not With the Fist* (New York: Harcourt, Brace and Co., 1956) for San Bernardino, California, both studied during the same period.

6. Peñalosa, *op. cit.*, and "Class Consciousness and Social Mobility in a Mexican-American Community" (unpublished Ph.D. dissertation, University of Southern California, 1963) for a recent study of a city in Los Angeles County.

7. This is true for Sheldon's respondents. See Sheldon, *op. cit.*

8. As in Madsen, *op. cit.*, and Arthur Rubel, *Across the Tracks* (Austin, Tex.: University of Texas Press, 1966).

9. W. Lloyd Warner and Leo Srole, *The Social Systems of American Ethnic Groups*

(New Haven, Conn.: Yale University Press, 1945), p. 283. After analyzing the full range of ethnic and racial groups in the community, the authors conclude that physical and cultural differences between each group and the dominant system combine to affect 1) the group's general position in the over-all class system, i.e., the degree of its subordination; 2) the length of time the group will take to become assimilated; and 3) the strength of its subsystem. (See their chapter 10.)

10. Milton M. Gordon, *Assimilation in American Life* (New York: Oxford University Press, 1964), p. 51. See also Nathan Glazer and Daniel Moynihan, *Beyond the Melting Pot* (Cambridge, Mass.: The M.I.T. Press, 1963).

11. *Ibid.*, pp. 54–59, for a discussion of deviance and marginality. In this respect, the concept of the "ethclass" also provides a competing theory of mobility which differs from that proposed by many writers on stratification in general. Psychologically, the process of mobility has been conceptualized as a process of detachment and reattachment, in which changes in values are accompanied by changes in social relations. See, for example, Peter M. Blau, "Social Mobility and Interpersonal Relations," *American Sociological Review*, XXII (June, 1956), pp. 290–295; W. Lloyd Warner and James C. Abegglen, *Big Business Leaders* (New York: Harper & Brothers, 1955); and Robert K. Merton and Alice K. Rossi, "Contributions to the Theory of Reference Group Behavior," in Robert K. Merton, *Social Theory and Social Structure* (New York: The Free Press, 1957).

12. See, however, E. Digby Baltzell, *The Protestant Establishment* (New York: Random House, 1964), for a more complex view emphasizing the highest status and power groups.

13. The great sociological theorist Max Weber effectively summarized the essential difference between ethnic honor and social-class related honor:

> The sense of ethnic honor is a specific honor of the masses, for it is accessible to anybody who belongs to the subjectively believed community of descent. . . . And behind all ethnic diversities there is somehow naturally the notion of the "chosen people," which is nothing else but a counterpart of status differentiation translated into the plane of horizontal coexistence. The idea of a chosen people derives its popularity from the fact that it can be claimed to an equal degree by any and every member of the mutually despising groups, in contrast to status differentiation which always rests on subordination.

Max Weber, "Ethnic Groups," in Talcott Parsons et al. (eds.), *Theories of Society* (New York: The Free Press, 1961), p. 308. To suggest, as Gordon seems to hope, that the diverse subpopulations of the United States will merge in a new pluralism where "the mutually despising groups" learn mutual respect seems unrealistic.

14. Alex Simirenko, *Pilgrims, Colonists, and Frontiersmen* (New York and London: The Free Press of Glencoe and Collier-MacMillan Limited, 1964).

15. For the deviant adaptations to the discrepancy between in-group and out-group evaluations of performance in the Negro community, see E. Franklin Frazier, *Black Bourgeoisie* (New York: The Free Press, 1957).

16. Hubert Herring, *A History of Latin America* (New York: Alfred A. Knopf, Inc., 1955), cited in Tamotsu Shibutani and Kian M. Kwan, *Ethnic Stratification* (New York: The MacMillan Company, 1965), p. 210.

17. Howard F. Cline, *Mexico: Revolution to Evolution, 1940–1960* (London, New York, and Toronto: Oxford University Press, 1962), p. 88.

18. One ethnologist found a very high correlation between appearance and occupation in Yucatan during the 1920s. See George D. Williams, "Maya-Spanish Crosses in Yucatan," *Papers of the Peabody Museum of American Archaeology and Ethnology*, XIII (1931), cited in Shibutani and Kwan, *op. cit.*, p. 567.

19. Robert Redfield, "Race and Class in Yucatan," *Cooperation in Research* (Washington, D.C.: The Carnegie Institution, 1938), pp. 511–532, cited in *ibid*, p. 75.

20. See, for example, Charles Wagley and Marvin Harris, *Minorities in the New World* (New York: Columbia University Press, 1958), pp. 48–86, and Cline, *op. cit.*, pp. 81–90.

21. *Ibid.*, p. 90.

22. *Ibid.*, p. 124.

23. Woods, *op. cit.*, pp. 11 ff.

24. Paul S. Taylor, *An American-Mexican Frontier* (Chapel Hill, N.C.: The University of North Carolina Press, 1934), pp. 7–13.

25. Material is drawn from Leonard Pitt, *The Decline of the Californios* (Berkeley: University of California Press, 1966). The quotation is from p. 10.

26. Carolyn Zeleny, "Relations Between the Spanish-Americans and the Anglo-Americans in New Mexico: A Study of Conflict and Accommodations in a Dual Ethnic Relationship" (unpublished Ph.D. dissertation, Yale University, 1944).

27. Pitt notes that status loss incurred by the *Californios* when the wave of Mexican and Latin American miners swept California in the late 1840s. All "greasers" were lumped together. Pitt, *op. cit.*, p. 53.

28. Taylor, *op. cit.*, p. 258.

29. *Ibid.*, p. 254.

30. Quoted in *ibid.*, p. 263.

31. Woods, *op. cit.*

32. One source estimates their number as high as 25,000 by 1913. Although many of the refugees returned to Mexico in the 1930s under a general amnesty, their presence for a decade or so reinforced the "Mexicanness" of the elite group, and social relations continued between the repatriates and their San Antonio friends.

33. Woods, *op. cit.*

34. If caste has been the most significant historical form of stratification for Mexican Americans, pluralistic New Mexico in the more recent past was characterized by a fully developed multiple class system, called a "dual hierarchical system" by Zeleny, who studied New Mexico in the 1930s. So isolated were small villages in New Mexico and so ancient are the Spanish-American communities (some dating from the sixteenth century) that a study by Senter in 1946 suggests *three* class systems: "The system of the Anglo populace, the system of the *manitos* Spanish Americans within the state as a whole. . . and that of *manito* villagers. Donovan Senter, "Acculturation among New Mexican Villagers in Comparison to Adjustment Patterns of Other Spanish Speaking Americans," *Rural Sociology*, X (Mar., 1945), pp. 31–47.

35. Julian Samora, "Minority Leadership in a Bi-racial Cultural Community" (unpublished Ph.D. dissertation, Washington University, St. Louis, 1953) for Del Norte; Arthur Rubel, *op. cit.*, for Weslaco; and for Ontario, Ruth Landman, "Some Aspects of the Acculturation of Mexican Immigrants and Their Descendants to American Culture" (unpublished Ph.D. dissertation, Yale University, 1953).

36. For San Jose, Margaret Clark, *Health in the Mexican American Culture* (Berkeley: University of California Press, 1959), p. 43; for St. Paul, Norman Goldner, "The Mexican in the Northern Urban Area: A Comparison of Two Generations" (unpublished Master's thesis, University of Minnesota, 1959); for Kansas, Paul Ming-Chang Lin, "Voluntary Kinship and Voluntary Association in a Mexican-American Community" (unpublished Master's thesis, University of Kansas, 1963); for Pomona, Peñalosa, *op. cit.*, "Class Consciousness and Social Mobility in a Mexican-American Community"; and for San Antonio, Ozzie Simmons, *op. cit.*

37. For Weslaco, see Rubel, *op. cit.*; for San Antonio, personal communication from Buford Farris and Richard Brymer.

38. See Albert J. Reiss, Jr., *Occupations and Social Status* (New York: The Free Press, 1961).

39. *Ibid.*

40. There is a proliferating literature on status discrepancies or inconsistencies of ethnic-group members of different class levels. A primary concern of such studies is how discrepancies between higher status on one dimension—such as income—and lower-status on another dimension—such as occupational prestige—are reconciled for the individual, or alternatively whether unresolved inconsistencies cause discernible stress. See, for example, Gerhard Lenski, *Power and Privilege: A Theory of Social Stratification* (New York: McGraw-Hill, Book Company, 1966). In many of these studies, ethnicity itself is taken as a higher or lower status: Negroes are conceptualized as having lower status, and Negro professionals, for example, are regarded as having status discrepancies between their ethnic and their occupational statuses. The empirical problems in ordering large numbers of ethnic groups into an ethnic-rank system are exemplified in Werner S. Landecker, "Class Crystallization and its Urban Pattern," *Social Research*, XXVII (Autumn, 1960), pp. 308–320.

41. Differences between these figures and comparable data for a rural Texas Mexican-American sample are interesting. Only 34 percent of a rural sample had bathroom facilities, for example, and only 24 percent had hot running water. Fewer had television than either urban sample—only 72 percent—but far more had cars—85 percent—than either urban sample. The data were provided by R. L. Skrabanek, Texas A. & M. University.

42. How a mobile man or woman escapes those bonds of the ethnic group which "keep him back" is a frequent theme in the analysis of ethnic mobility. It is this process, not only of detachment from lower-class childhood associates but from the ethnic group as a whole, that past observers considered part of the mobility process leading to individual assimilation and to the dissolution of the ethnic group. For a description of the ties of the peer group and the strains that such ties impose on the mobile Mexican-American teenager, see Ernest Robles, "An Analytic Description of Peer Group Pressures on Mobility-oriented Mexican American Junior High Students" (unpublished Master's thesis, University of Redlands, 1964).

43. The cultural significance of the move from the farm for Mexicans is indicated in the responses to a Thematic Apperception Test administered to a subsample of men selected from our larger sample. The test card shows a "country scene: in the foreground is a young woman with books in her hand; in the background a man is working in the fields and an older woman is looking on." Henry A. Murray, et al., "Thematic Apperception Test Manual" (Harvard College, Cambridge, Mass., 1943), p. 18. One of the most frequent responses to this card seems to echo the collective and often the individual experience of leaving the rural restrictions. Parenthetically it may be added that the theme of attachment to the soil is extremely rare. Farm work is generally seen either as unrewarding and unremitting toil—as it is here—or as a taken-for-granted feature of the scene, not discussed. For example:

It is a farm scene. The parents are working hard in the field (like we did) so the children can get an education. The daughter will probably be better off if she finished before getting married.

This girl is getting an education while the man is only a common laborer. Woman is expecting a child. Girl has a future, while the older ones can only stay home.

This young girl is wondering how hard it is for her father and mother to work in this field and her mother looks so tired. She looks like she is expecting so she is trying to better herself in life and educating herself to become a person of some profession to help out her parents so she can better themselves and their lives. She believes that their kind of work is not for her future life. She believes that there is a better life ahead than just being a working hand.

This is the sharp difference that there is between the hard life on the field and the intellectual one. This picture represents the new world. The old people have no way out at this point, while the young ones have a chance through school.

This is a man plowing and a young girl holding some books, pregnant woman looks on. But the land is bad; it has too many rocks. The young girl will leave for sure but the couple will stay there. But the land is bad.

44. Peter M. Blau and Otis Dudley Duncan, *The American Occupational Structure* (New York: John Wiley & Sons, Inc., 1967), p. 274. For other studies of Mexican-American migration, see, in particular, Lyle Shannon and Elaine M. Krass, *The Economic Absorption and Cultural Integration of Immigrant Mexican-American and Negro Workers* (Iowa City, Iowa: State University of Iowa, 1964), and several subsequent publications by the same authors. A study of rural migrants to eight Michigan counties is under way at Michigan State University under the direction of Grafton Trout and Harvey Choldin. At the University of Colorado Robert C. Hanson, Ozzie G. Simmons, and William N. McPhee are analyzing the urbanization of rural Spanish-American migrants to Denver. See the following papers by these authors: "Quantitative Analyses of the Urban Experience of Spanish-American Migrants" (Publication 110 of the Institute of Behavioral Science, University of Colorado, Boulder, 1968); and "Time Trend Analyses of the Urban Experience of Spanish-American Migrants" (Publication 112 of the Institute, 1968).

45. William Smelser, the psychologist who analyzed the TAT psychological projective responses from both mobile and non-mobile men, commented on his over-all impression of the entire group: "Themes of survival are much more prevalent than themes of enrichment, *joie de vivre*, expansion, peak, experiences, etc. In a word, security outweighs satisfaction." (Personal communication.)

46. For example, Herbert Gans, *The Urban Villagers* (New York: The Free Press, 1962).

47. See E. Franklin Frazier, *op. cit.*, for one of the most extensive discussions of the stresses of middle-class Negroes.

FIFTEEN

The Family:
Variations in Time and Space

AN understanding of the family is strategic to the understanding of stability and change in any social system. Believed by many to be the most critical socializing agency, the family is, therefore, critical in maintaining a social system by producing and sustaining the kind of individual who is most adapted to it. The special importance of the family structure in a minority population in this regard is underlined by the basic thesis of the Moynihan Report as well as by the controversy that followed its publication.[1] The Report emphasized the relationship between "the traditional Negro matricentric family" and the "unmotivated" male personality in maintaining the *status quo* of large masses of Negroes. Some social scientists question such a simplified causal chain (which has been even further simplified in this condensation).

[1] Notes for this chapter start on page 372.
This chapter draws on an analytic review of the literature prepared by Gerald Rosen.

350

Similar issues are the focus of this chapter about the Mexican-American family. Lower achievement levels of Mexican Americans have often been attributed to some feature of family structure. In the case of Mexican Americans, it is the special male role *within* the family which is supposed to inhibit the achievement of Mexican-American men. The patriarchal ideal and the cultural ideal of masculinity (expressed in *machismo*, which is discussed later in this chapter) are believed to work together to drain energy into expressive rather than instrumental acts.

Furthermore, it is generally believed that Mexican Americans are exceptionally familistic. Familism has been conceived as curtailing mobility by sustaining emotional attachments to people, places and things. It is argued that extreme attachment to the "old homestead," actual or metaphorical, leads the individual to assume burdens that keep him rooted physically and socially. Among Mexican Americans, familism has been adduced as a prime cause not only of low mobility but of resistance to change of all kinds. In the Mexican-American ethos, familism, along with the special male role, is a source of collective pride. Nevertheless, members of the group and others generally believe that familism also deters collective and individual progress, however defined.

This chapter discusses persistence and change in family-life patterns of Mexican Americans in the face of migration, urbanization, and variations in local milieus. The Mexican-American family will be analyzed here in terms of the always useful but ever equivocal continuum from "traditional" to "modern." As with the folk-urban continuum discussed in Chapter 13, neither the beginning nor the ending point of the continuum is clear; nor is the continuum one-dimensional. The "traditional" Mexican family as sketched in much of the literature reflects a mixture of upper-status and lower-status ideals and practices. The mixture was made more complex by the minority's adaptation to varied conditions in the United States and by its comparative isolation. The modern end of the continuum usually becomes "the urban middle-class American family," with all of its own complexities. Whether the urban middle-class Mexican-American family is distinguishable from the urban middle-class Anglo family can be explored with the data available in the Los Angeles and San Antonio surveys. The effects of the greater isolation of Mexican Americans in San Antonio can be assayed at each class level. We can analyze whether the lower-class family in either milieu reflects more traditional relationships and values.

THE IMPORTANCE OF FAMILISM

Along with the special features of the male role, the major theme dominating the classic portrayal of the traditional Mexican family is the deep importance of the family to all its members. The needs of the family collectivity supersede the needs of each individual member.

A number of consequences detrimental to individual achievement may follow. To the extent that the family captures all of the significant social relations of the individual, he becomes *less* capable of absorbing new values and of maintaining relations with new kinds of people. Maintenance of "Mexicanness" of both values and ethnic exclusiveness in social relations is therefore achieved largely through familism. Furthermore, in depictions of families following traditional norms, the kin group is the *only* reliable place of refuge from a hostile world. If this were true, the holding power of the family would be intensified.[2] The benefits of the family's "protection" of its individual members, then, may be gained at the price of lowered individual achievement because of isolation from the larger milieu.

In addition to emotional relationships, kinship ties among Mexican Americans are described as avenues of exchanges of a more instrumental nature, as they are in American society as a whole.[3] Mutual financial assistance, exchange of work and other skills, and advice and support in solving personal problems are ideally available within the extended kin group. Though all of these resources are, normatively, also available within the extended kin network of most Americans, reliance on kin is carried to an extreme in the traditional Mexican-American family system. "A kind of family communism"[4] is expected, and anecdotes are told about promising individuals whose potential mobility was undermined by the financial drain imposed by impecunious relatives. Traditionally, it is felt to be shameful to seek aid outside the family circle. This is true especially when the welfare of aging parents is at stake.[5] Thus, again, familism may be a help to the individual in need, but it may be a serious drain on the mobile or potentially mobile individual.

If these functions of the traditional Mexican-American family were in fact prevalent in the past, they might explain some part of the lower collective achievement of the group. However, the extent to which they exist *today* is unknown. But some indication of their persistence may be found in our data on patterns of household composition and of financial and other dependency. The variations in such patterns by income level also give some indication of how "family communism" is related to achievement or mobility, though only extremely tentative causal imputations can be made from the limited data.

Living Arrangements and Visiting Patterns

Whether members of the extended family—grandparents, sisters, cousins—choose to live with each other is a severe test of familism. Extended-family households were not uncommon in the poor Mexican-American communities of urban areas even in the recent past. But all studies, even of the most traditionalistic individuals, reveal a preference for the separate nuclear family household.[6] However permanent such arrangements may turn out to be, doubling up under the same roof for the Mexican-American family appears to be an *ad hoc* solution to temporary problems rather than a valued goal. A newly married couple might move in with the groom's parents,[7] or a widowed mother or father may move in with a son. And, as in other American households, such *ad hoc* arrangements frequently create tensions.[8]

352

In a modification of the extended-family household, observable in many Mexican-American communities throughout the Southwest, several dwelling units are built on the same lot, housing different families of the same extended kin group.

Today, any but the nuclear household pattern or its broken variant (especially the female-headed household) is rare in either Los Angeles or San Antonio (Table 15–1). Though this finding goes far toward disproving the notion that Mexican Americans are familistic enough to establish joint households in an urban setting, they can still maintain a primary focus on the family, by visiting. In the traditional extended kin group, visiting is especially important for women. For them it is often the major form of recreation, and it tends to be confined to relatives, even to the

Table 15–1. Household Composition of Survey Respondents, Los Angeles and San Antonio, 1965–1966

	Los Angeles	San Antonio[a]
Nuclear family households		
Husband, wife, and children	60%	57%
Husband, wife, no children	10	13
Broken families		
Husband and children	2	3
Wife and children	11	12
Single-person households	7	9
Extended-family households[b]	4[c]	3
All other[d]	6	3
Total number (= 100%)	(947)	(603)

a Weighting procedures were used in the San Antonio sample. This means that total numbers cannot be used as a direct indicator of error. See Appendix H.
b Includes both three-generation households and laterally extended households.
c Two of these households, or 0.2 percent of the total, were joint households with two nuclear families.
d About half of these are single individuals living with a relative. The residual in Los Angeles includes a handful of households with unrelated individuals living with the family, and three households which were extended both vertically and laterally. In both cities, the residual group includes husband-wife families with relatives other than siblings or parents as members of the household.

exclusion of neighbors.[9] Male social relations tend to range more widely and to include non-relatives. While maintaining the kinship system and all of its functions, then, traditional visiting patterns isolate women. Where these patterns survive, they may be important in helping maintain ethnic cohesiveness across potential social distance created by increasing occupational mobility. Any extended kin group is likely to have members scattered over a wide range of jobs and income levels. Thus familism may help prevent a strong social-class cleavage from developing among Mexican Americans. However, several studies have shown that increasing class differentiation within the group does weaken the visiting patterns. And even in homogeneous poor communities, there are generational differences in visiting patterns.[10]

Though our larger interview sample was not questioned about visiting, the smaller subsample was asked where and with whom they spent holidays. In neither San Antonio nor Los Angeles were there consistent patterns. Some families spent the holidays at home, some with extended kin, some with friends, and one cooperated with its kin group to hire a hall for a Christmas party involving some 100 people.

To judge from the limited data on living arrangements and visiting patterns, then, relationships within the extended kinship group among Mexican Americans have declined in importance with increased urbanization, acculturation, and contact with the dominant system. A similar decline has been found in many societies, although cross-cultural research has shown that neither industrialism nor urbanism *depends* on the decline of familism.[11] Thus, the failure of current Mexican-American urban patterns to conform to Mexican tradition is merely noted here without suggesting unequivocal implications.

The Compadrazgo

No discussion of Mexican-American familism would be complete without consideration of the *compadrazgo*. As in all Catholic groups, godparents have a series of implicit and explicit obligations toward their godchildren, but the structural significance of the *compadrazgo* derives more from the relationship established between the child's godparents and his parents (who become *compadres* or *comadres*) than between the godparents (*padrino* and *madrino*) and the child himself. The bond between *compadres* is supposed to be unusually strong; they can make special claims of all kinds on each other. The functional implications of the *compadrazgo* are complex. To follow one implication, its persistence may be taken to mean that Mexican Americans use a kinship prototype for relationships that other Americans differentiate from their kin. Godparents for a newly-born child are chosen (or nominate themselves) from among two kinds of people—those who are already friends and relatives of the parents, or people of higher prestige.[12] *Compadrazgo* between intimates appears to be far more frequent than the upward-directed relationship. Relatives and friends are invited or offer themselves as sponsors of the children, and existing relationships are reinforced.

Several studies have suggested that early in Mexican-American urbanization the *compadrazgo* retarded change by strengthening bonds between kinsmen.[13] However, there is clear evidence that its function has diminished with urbanization. Few cases of godparents actually taking over the care of an orphaned child have been documented in recent years.[14] Among our samples, less than 2 percent of the Los Angeles and 3 percent of the San Antonio respondents had been reared by their godparents. Some research suggests that the mutual obligations of *compadres* are taken far less seriously by younger than by older individuals.[15]

Questions about the *compadrazgo* were asked only of a small subsample of individuals. Relationships with *compadres* were close in some cases but weak in many others, and several respondents had not chosen any godparents for their children. Social mobility did not seem to make much difference in the strength of the bonds. One got the distinct impression that the *compadres* were people with whom the

354

respondents would have had close relationships in any case. Only a handful admitted to having received help from their own godparents; most of them were from Mexico (one explicitly stating, as he told how close he was to his *padrinos*, "Aquí no existe tanto el padrinazgo como en México"—The system of godparents is not as common here as it is in Mexico). In the case of one American-born man, his *padrinos* were his grandparents. Occasionally a respondent would indicate that he felt that his *padrinos* *should have* helped him; one or another complained that they hadn't—"and they were wealthy."

In short, the *compadrazgo*, although undoubtedly still viable, appears to be a minor feature of kinship and community social organization in the major urban centers. It may be changing from an integral feature of the kinship system to an expressive one, beginning to resemble practices found in other Roman Catholic, Greek and Russian Orthodox, and Episcopalian populations in the United States. Its strength among special subgroups of Mexican Americans, such as the politically active, makes the *compadrazgo* interesting. The frequent casual use of the term "*compadre*" among Mexican Americans probably makes the institution more conspicuous than is warranted by its real importance.

Financial Dependency on Kin

If it is the sole resource for financial and other aid (as in the traditional stereotype), the kin group may drain the financial and emotional resources of mobile members. It may also inhibit members from availing themselves of alternative resources in the general society.

As for financial aid, most recent studies show a decline in the sentiment of "family communism" with increasing acculturation and social mobility.[16] The survey data about actual financial exchanges among relatives suggest some interesting amplifications of this statement. Slightly more than half of the Los Angeles respondents admitted having received money from their families—a figure very similar to one found in a general sample of Cleveland.[17] Only about a third of the San Antonio respondents received aid from their families, probably reflecting the city's lower income level, for other data suggest greater traditionalism in San Antonio. On the other hand, about two-thirds of the Los Angeles and about 40 percent of the San Antonio respondents claimed to have *given* financial assistance to their families. The proportion giving increases with the ability to give, that is, with the family's income.

It is difficult to interpret these data as either supporting or refuting the existence of "family communism." Most of those who had either given or received money were involved in more than one such transaction. Families that help one another seem to do so recurrently, as an expected thing, rather than on a one-time emergency basis. Interestingly, though there are no notable age differences in *giving* aid, younger people are far more likely than older ones to admit to having *received* aid. If one accepts these as valid responses (and not as artifacts of some kind of age-related

355

traditionalistic pride in self-sufficiency), they may be explained by the fact that financial aid was simply less available from relatives in the predominantly poverty-stricken past.

Kin as Source of Advice

Another set of responses shows the extent to which the extended kin group competes with other, more general resources in the urban milieu. Respondents were asked where they would go for advice and help on a variety of problems, ranging from "personal" to "bureaucratic" ("advice on where to go in the city government downtown to get something you want"). Less than half of all respondents would turn to kin sources for help in any kind of problem (Table 15-2). Kin sources are more

Table 15-2. Survey Respondents Who Sought Advice or Help From Kin Including Nuclear Family, by Income, Los Angeles and San Antonio, 1965-1966 (Number in parentheses = 100%)

	Personal	Money	Political	City Government[a]
Higher income[b]				
Los Angeles	51%	36%	24%	14%
	(345)	(350)	(280)	(316)
Medium income				
Los Angeles	47	43	32	12
	(289)	(279)	(231)	(239)
San Antonio	45	45	23	10
	(273)	(238)	(203)	(199)
Low income				
Los Angeles	41	44	29	12
	(265)	(252)	(192)	(210)
San Antonio	41	40	19	24
	(232)	(196)	(165)	(156)

[a] "If you needed some advice on where to go in the city government downtown to get something you wanted, who might you go to?"
[b] In Los Angeles: higher income = $\geq$ $6,000; medium income = $3,600-$5,999; low income = < $3,600. In San Antonio: medium income $\geq$ $2,760; low income < $2,760.

popular for personal and financial than for political or bureaucratic problems, and there is little difference between Angelenos and San Antonians at each income level when personal or financial help is involved. In Los Angeles, people's propensity to turn to kin for advice on political and bureaucratic problems varies comparatively little by income. In San Antonio, however, the poor are unexpectedly kin-oriented with regard to maneuvering in city government. Whether people live in predominantly Mexican-American or predominantly Anglo areas makes surprisingly little difference in seeking kinship help for political and bureaucratic assistance, regardless of income level. Women are far more likely than men to turn to kin, most women turning to their husbands.

With regard to financial problems, more than a third of all types of respondents rely on kin. Higher-income people are less likely to do so, however, whether or not they live in a predominantly Mexican colony. (For aid in solving money problems, Colonists are not much different from Frontiersmen at every income level.) Higher-paid people have better credit, and more alternative resources are open to them that permit them to be independent from the kin network. Women are far more likely to turn to family members for financial advice and aid, particularly to their husbands or their children.

On personal problems, family members are particularly frequent sources of advice. However, the survey results show the reverse of what the literature about the

Table 15–3. Percent of Survey Respondents
Turning to Spouse versus Other Kin on Personal Problems,
by Income, Los Angeles and San Antonio, 1965–1966

	Spouse	Other Kin	Non-Kin	Total Number (= 100%)
Higher income				
Los Angeles	27%	24%	49%	345
Medium income				
Los Angeles	23	24	53	289
San Antonio	20	25	56	273
Low income				
Los Angeles	11	30	59	265
San Antonio	7	35	59	232

Mexican family suggests. *High*-income people with problems are more likely to turn to family for advice than *low*-income people. Furthermore, Mexican Americans living in predominantly *Anglo* areas are more likely to turn to kin than those living in the *barrios*. These differences between Frontiersmen and Colonists are found at the middle-class though not the lower-class levels. (Sex differences, interestingly, are inconsequential.) The data might suggest that the psychological salience of the kin group is enhanced as the individual moves up and out, but closer analysis shows that this would be an oversimplification. The more frequent mention of kin as sources of personal advice among higher-income individuals is largely explained by their mention of husband or wife, *not of extended kin*. In fact, higher-income individuals mention extended kin far less frequently (Table 15–3). There are more divorced or single individuals, without a spouse to turn to, in poorer *Colonies*. Nevertheless, there seems little doubt that this is the kind of shift found in studies of upwardly mobile individuals in other groups—that is, away from kinship structures which emphasize one-sex relations in the extended kin group (for example, between mother and daughter, sister and sister) toward emphasis on the husband-wife relationship of the nuclear family.

In general, the data on sources of advice underscore the point that change is not simply distintegration of family bonds. This has been discovered and rediscovered with regard to the American family system as a whole. Mexican Americans share the national experience of complex patterns of change and of shifts in the structure of family relationships. Though most Mexican Americans themselves believe in their extraordinary familism (see Chapter 16 on self-stereotyping), our findings suggest that they may not be reliable informants. They often do not know the larger system, and thus lack comparative context. Their views also often reflect desired states rather than reality in the urban setting.

THE NUCLEAR FAMILY

IN THE PAST GENERATION

The nuclear family—the biological family of husband, wife and children—is the normal household in present-day Los Angeles and San Antonio. All indications are that it has always been the preferred household type among Mexican Americans. We examine first the so-called "family of orientation" of our respondents—the family in which they were brought up. The discussion here reflects the past, and it will show clearly that the past, characterized by poverty in a rural setting, was not devoid of family problems.

Marital Stability

A measure of the strength of the bond between husband, wife, and children is given by the relative proportions of respondents brought up in intact families. Only about two-thirds of our respondents were reared by both parents—slightly more in San Antonio than in Los Angeles. A large proportion of the remainder were brought up by their mothers alone, and the rest predominantly by one or another relative. (The latter group shows a mixed pattern: Grandparents, or the father alone, or a collateral relative on either the mother's or the father's side were almost equally likely to have been responsible for the respondent during his childhood.) A slightly larger percentage of current higher-income respondents than of low-income respondents were brought up in intact families, but the differences are too small for firm interpretation.

The high proportion of individuals not brought up by both parents suggests either an extraordinarily high death rate among men or, what is more likely, a high rate of desertion or divorce in the parental generation. Studies conducted during the 1930s support the latter interpretation; they picture a situation in which desertion was frequent in both rural and urban settings.[18] The Mexican family was not immune to the disorganizing influences of immigration and poverty.

These findings diverge from the widely accepted impression that the Mexican-

American family has been unusually stable.[19] Even those studies which note that divorce is now increasingly common among Mexican Americans contrast the present incidence of divorce with a presumed prior stability,[20] both in the United States among older individuals and in Mexico.[21]

Patriarchy in the Rural Past

The Mexican-American family of the previous generation was primarily geared to rural life. This is evident both from past research and from our analysis based on the subsample of depth interviews in Los Angeles. But neither our analysis nor past research suggest that these families led an idyllic farm life. Many respondents report a substantial amount of instability. Even in cases where the individual was reared by both parents, the father may actually have been absent for long periods of time, either following the crops (which many men did singly, leaving their families at home) or venturing to new locations to prepare the way for the family's arrival later. Nonetheless, the rural past is significant in that some aspects of its family structure and division of roles appear to have persisted even in urban settings.

Large areas of Los Angeles County, for example, had small farms attached to dwelling units as recently as 15 years ago. Mexican-American men brought up in the county frequently recall that they—like their age peers on Mexican or Texan farms—were exempt from household tasks: They cared for the chickens, chopped wood, and did other outside chores. Household tasks were defined as "women's work."[22] Respondents in the subsample who were brought up in such a setting—whether Mexico or Los Angeles—tended to say that their fathers discouraged school in favor of work that yielded immediate benefits to the family. The dubious gains to the individual from finishing high school were far less important than the survival of the family, especially during the Depression, when many of these men were young.

In numerous cases, this kind of family structure adapted itself to the urban setting when the young boy was sent out to work at an early age while the mother and sisters cared for the home. Life histories show many who had part-time jobs, especially in the very poor families or those in which the father had died or deserted. Occasionally, when one parent (especially the mother) had died or left, the boy also helped with household chores, cooking, cleaning, washing dishes. Usually, however, there were enough females around to do the inside chores, and men could grow up firmly convinced of the inherent righteousness of the sexual division of labor. In the intact urban families where there was no need for sons to work, demands were made on them for nothing but trivial errands or help with small household repairs. The sexual division of labor, which is functional in a rural setting, results in a comparatively idle male child and adolescent in a less poverty-stricken urban setting.

The most widely discussed aspect of the sexual division of labor is traditional Mexican patriarchy, in which power and prestige are absolute prerogatives of the male head of the household. When these attributes are delegated, they go through the male line. In the traditional family, the male head makes all important and most unimportant decisions unilaterally, according to the norm.[23] Meanwhile, the submissive wife carries out her husband's decisions unquestioningly or helps to see that they are carried out by the children.[24]

There is considerable evidence that this ideal pattern of decision-making has never been the behavioral norm among Mexican Americans, either in the United States or Mexico, even though it may have been the cultural ideal (at least among men).[25] From the data available on the 27 men in the Los Angeles subsample who were reared in intact families, all but two replied "father" when asked "who ran things" when the respondent was growing up. But this reply was immediately cast in doubt when the same respondents almost universally admitted that their mothers made the day-to-day decisions affecting the children, the running of the household, and so on, and that in most cases decisions about large purchases and similar transactions were made jointly by father and mother.

Further doubt is cast on the image of the patriarch by the fact that only five in the subsample reported that it was the father who normally punished them. In two of these cases the boy worked with the father in the fields, and thus the father had ready access to the miscreant; in certain others, the father was remembered as tyrannical: "My mother practically never spoke; sometimes I wonder how they got married!" In most other cases, either the mother or "whoever was closer" punished the children. Actual power in these families was thus largely situationally determined and was exercised by whoever happened to be around when an action or decision had to be taken. Patriarchal values existed, but the families departed from them as a matter of course.

We might suggest, in fact, that the patriarchal values as well as the belief in the stable family became cultural ideals of the Mexican American at least in part *because* of the weakness of both the family structure and the male role. These values might have represented a yearning for an ideally peaceful state of affairs not readily attainable in the poverty-stricken and unpredictable life of the typical Mexican American of a generation ago.

The family, and particularly the nuclear family of orientation, was certainly the primary reference group of our urban samples. In the responses to questions about "who had more influence" over the respondent when he was 13 or 14 years old, parents overwhelmingly dominate over teachers, age mates, or other relatives. Overt rejection of parental authority was far from normal a generation ago.

But when respondents were asked whether their father or mother had greater influence over them, more than half of the total sample responding (54 percent in Los Angeles and 52 percent in San Antonio) named their mothers. Only 33 percent in Los Angeles and 41 percent in San Antonio named their fathers. Thirteen percent in Los Angeles and eight percent in San Antonio claimed that mother and father had equal influence. Implications of psychological theory to the contrary, the proportion naming father or mother does not vary with present income level in Los Angeles, but higher-income San Antonians are more likely to state that they have been influenced by their mothers. When we look at cross-sex identification, men naming their mothers are more common than women naming their fathers. This indicates the pervasive importance of the mother.

These data, scanty though they are, suggest the overriding significance of situation for family-role patterns and stability. The situations of the past, of course, still exist in pockets throughout the Southwest and in Mexico itself (the sources of in-migrants to the cities). For this reason, the patterns of the future will probably be of the checkerboard kind. It will become increasingly difficult to generalize about "the" Mexican-American family.

THE NUCLEAR FAMILY

OF THE PRESENT GENERATION

The survey data indicate a substantial departure in the contemporary family from the traditional patriarchy. The departure is greatest among the young, the more well-to-do, and those living outside the Mexican colony. There were generally few differences in attitude by sex; men and women tend to be in greater accord than the old and the young.

Patriarchy in the Urban Present

Respondents were asked their opinions on three statements designed to reflect traditional norms. The first related to the wife's role: Did the respondents agree that "the most important thing" that a married woman could do was to have children? The majority in all categories agreed with the statement, but with a notable age differential—71 percent in Los Angeles and 76 percent in San Antonio of those under 30 agreed, whereas 93 percent in Los Angeles and 94 percent in San Antonio of those over 50 years of age agreed. There was also a slightly greater tendency for the respondents living in Colonies, especially low-income persons, to agree.

A second statement expressing a traditional sentiment, "A husband ought to have complete control over the family's income," elicited less agreement. Once again, however, the older respondents were notably more traditional in attitude—59 percent in Los Angeles and 75 percent in San Antonio of those over 50 agreed, compared with only 38 percent in Los Angeles and 53 percent in San Antonio of those under 30. There were substantial, though not systematic, variations among respondents at different income levels in neighborhoods of differing ethnic composition (Table 15–4).

The third question asked whether respondents agreed that a husband should care for the children when the wife wants time for herself. An overwhelming proportion—91 percent—of the respondents agreed that the father should baby-sit. There were only minor variations among people of different ages, income, and so forth in Los Angeles, though age differences were noticeable in San Antonio.

These responses—especially the age-related patterns—suggest a substantial shift in the perception of the norms governing the husband's role, if not the wife's. As mentioned earlier, it is doubtful whether the father's control over family matters, such as the budget, was ever as complete as traditional norms would indicate. The responses indicate that the ideas of younger, better-paid, and less ghetto-bound

Table 15–4. Survey Respondents Agreeing that Husband Ought to Have Complete Control over Family Income, by Income and Neighborhood Ethnicity, Los Angeles and San Antonio, 1965–1966

| | | | TOTAL NUMBER (= 100%) | |
	Los Angeles	San Antonio	Los Angeles	San Antonio
Higher income				
Frontier*a*	24%	—	164	—
Intermediate*a*	51	—	124	—
Colony*a*	43	—	77	—
Medium income				
Frontier	29	44%	93	134
Intermediate	48	—	96	—
Colony	52	67	120	190
Low income				
Frontier	42	72	74	47
Intermediate	64	—	75	—
Colony	64	68	126	227

a In Los Angeles, Frontier = tracts with less than 15.0 percent Spanish-surname individuals; Intermediate = tracts with between 15.0 and 43.8 percent Spanish-surname individuals; and Colony = tracts with more than 43.8 percent Spanish-surname individuals. In San Antonio, Frontier = tracts with less than 54.0 percent Spanish-surname individuals and Colony = tracts with 54.0 percent or more Spanish-surname individuals.

Mexican Americans about the father's role are no longer quite so tenaciously patriarchal as some of the literature suggests. Masculinity is perhaps not quite so associated with dominance as it may have been in the past.

A similar picture emerges in responses to the question as to who performs certain sex-typed household tasks, ranging from painting rooms to washing dishes (Table 15–5). Responses to these questions by Mexican Americans are very similar to those of a 1953 sample of the general population of Detroit, suggesting that in this regard the Mexican Americans are close to "typical Americans."[26]

The Mexican-American responses, especially when compared with the Detroit responses, again suggest that egalitarianism occurs more in the masculine sex-typed tasks than in the feminine, just as there is more loosening in the norms regarding the husband's role than in those regarding the role of the wife. Among Mexican Americans, egalitarianism is generally greater within higher-income families and among those choosing to live outside of predominantly Mexican areas. Such differences are insubstantial, however, and so are differences in responses by age and sex. The most striking finding relates not to internal variations in the departure from traditional sex specialization, but rather to the conspicuous presence of a basically *egalitarian* division of household tasks, with female specialization in a restricted domestic area.

Machismo

In particular, these responses about husband and wife roles in the Mexican-American nuclear family cast doubt on the common notions of *machismo*—at least as expressed within the urban family. The complex of attitudes and identities associated with this ethnic concept of masculinity has been well detailed in the literature. In addition to the dominant theme of sexual virility, *machismo* is also

Table 15–5. Survey Respondents Reporting on Sex Specialization in Family Roles, Los Angeles and San Antonio, 1965–1966

	Who Performs Task							
	HUSBAND (OR HUSBAND MIGHT)		BOTH		WIFE (OR WIFE MIGHT)		TOTAL NUMBER (= 100%)	
	L.A.	S.A.	L.A.	S.A.	L.A.	S.A.	L.A.	S.A.
Painting rooms[a]	41%	37%	52%	57%	7%	7%	919	593
Expensive purchase[b]	22	18	68	74	10	9	910	589
Holiday decision[c]	14	17	80	77	6	5	905	585
Punishing children[d]	12	10	71	76	17	13	892	587
Night care of children[e]	3	4	38	35	59	61	909	587
Washing dishes[f]	6	6	18	11	76	83	900	593

[a] "Painting rooms in the house."
[b] "Picking out more expensive things like furniture or a car."
[c] "Deciding where to go for a holiday or celebration."
[d] "Punishing the children, if necessary."
[e] "Getting up at night to take care of the children if they cry."
[f] "Washing dishes."

intertwined with the traditional patriarchy; masculinity is said to be demonstrated not only by the man's sexuality—particularly extra-marital—and other activities that suggest a phallic preoccupation,[27] but by domination over the affairs of his family and especially over his wife. The female role, which complements this phallic notion of the "strong Mexican husband," is that of the submissive, naive, rather childlike "sainted mother," whose purity is preserved by her husband's refusal to bring the world and its sins into the home. Our data suggest that though the Mexican-American man may still refuse to wash dishes, in the more important aspects of the husband-wife and father-child relationship he is willing to admit that he has ceded control; at the same time he has assumed some of the responsibilities that were traditionally "feminine."

These attitudinal data are, of course, silent on the actual processes of change, which have been touched on in some studies of Mexican-American urban life.[28] The apparently greater persistence of traditionalism with reference to feminine tasks is not surprising; the greater exposure of working men to norms of the larger society may have an indirect influence on their concepts of masculinity. The availability of television at home may reduce the attraction of the corner bar for a tired working man. We also lack data on actual sexual behavior of our male respondents. But *machismo* as traditionally acted out takes at least two to play—the questing man and the alarmed and excited woman. Whatever the similarity in *content* of the extra-marital game in American and in traditional Mexican society, the *rules* of the games are different in the two societies. Acculturation, involving change in self-definition, occurs not only through the inspiration of positive models and interaction conducive to new definitions of appropriate behavior. Such acculturation also occurs in the course of interaction in which expectations are discordant. As isolation declines, the "Mexican" is increasingly in confrontation with the American sex game.

The behavior classified under the label of *machismo* appears to have much in common with lower-class definitions of masculinity, especially youth-culture definitions, across ethnic groups in American society. The complementary *female* roles appear to differ from one subgroup to another. Though the behavior persists and continues to be fun for those participating in it, it is the target of direct attack by the socializing institutions of the American system. (High school dress and conduct regulations throughout the Southwest are specifically directed to curtailing what many administrators designate as "Don Juan" behavior.) It is also the victim of more subtle attacks in the form of the kind of demands placed on the adult man in his work place. Increasingly, also, urban life offers recreational alternatives to the all-male fantasy-creating and occasionally acting-out group of intimates. The continued isolation of the Colony-based Mexican-American nuclear family from families in the dominant system probably permits the preservation of feminine roles and of some intra-family patterns of interaction. These female roles are not too dissimilar from female role expectations in American society at large, and their persistence is undoubtedly reinforced by this fact.

Birth Control

Another issue related to the family's role structure is its size, which involves attitudes toward birth control. Of course, this issue is intimately associated with *machismo* as well as with norms about the role of women. As noted by students of birth control in other lower-class populations,[29] opposition to the use of contraceptives comes frequently from men. Masculine potency and dominance are symbolized by the fact that men can get women pregnant. Though demonstrating one's virility and potency may be especially significant during adolescence, it may continue, by implication, to be meaningful into adulthood and into the familial role. A brief pilot study conducted in a small California community indicates that among traditionalistic lower-class Mexican-American respondents it was more often the husband than the wife who objected to the use of any contraceptive measures, occasionally going to the extreme of taking away or hiding birth-control pills pre-scribed for the wife. And at a more affluent level, one of two pharmacists in this small California town stated in an interview that some Mexican-American women would not permit pill purchases to be put on the family charge account. They insisted on paying cash to conceal the purchase from their husbands despite tax advantages that would accrue from evidence of a legitimate medical expense. The study concluded that when contraception was consistently practiced by Mexican-American families its success depended in large measure on a shift in the husband's

Table 15-6. Attitudes of Survey Respondents Toward Birth Control, by Age, Income, and Neighborhood Ethnicity, Los Angeles and San Antonio, 1965–1966[a]

	PERCENT SAYING ALWAYS RIGHT OR USUALLY RIGHT		TOTAL NUMBER (= 100%)	
	Los Angeles	San Antonio	Los Angeles	San Antonio
Age				
Under 30	73%	64%	217	96
30–39	68	61	290	165
40–49	63	45	213	131
50 and over	50	39	199	207
Income and neighborhood ethnicity				
Colony				
Higher income	69	—	78	—
Medium income	69	53	122	165
Low income	48	45	118	183
Intermediate				
Higher income	71	—	102	—
Medium income	59	—	98	—
Low income	51	—	75	—
Frontier				
Higher income	76	—	175	—
Medium income	62	65	76	109
Low income	56	40	77	135

[a] The item read as follows: "Family planning—or birth control—has been discussed by many people. What is your feeling about a married couple practicing birth control? If you had to decide, which one of these statements best expresses your point of view? It is always right; it is usually right; it is usually wrong; it is always wrong."

perception of his own and his wife's role. The shift may have been motivated in part by the young couple's awareness of the problems experienced by relatives, especially mothers who bore large numbers of children. The manifestations of the change, however, appear to lie in the development of increasing egalitarianism and joint discussion of family problems, including family planning.[30]

Of course, religious scruples as well as husband-wife relationships may set important limits on the use of contraceptives. Lack of knowledge may also be a factor, and prudishness and dignity are threatened in acquiring information about them. Nevertheless, several recent community studies indicate that contraception is far from the unthinkable manipulation implied in some stereotypes of Mexican

Americans.[31] Data from our Los Angeles survey reflect general acceptance of birth control, at least at the level of verbal expression, whereas data from the San Antonio sample show the persistence of a more traditional stance. In Los Angeles, the response of Mexican Americans was, in fact, at least as accepting of birth control as a recent sample of the total United States population asked the same question (See Note *a*, Table 15–6).[32] Sixty-two percent of the total United States sample had no moral compunctions about birth control, compared with 64 percent of the Mexican Americans in Los Angeles and 50 percent of those in San Antonio. As the United States sample included a far larger proportion of Protestants, the response of urban Mexican Americans to the question on birth control is even more striking. (See also discussion in Chapter 19.)

Interestingly, there were no meaningful sex differences in the over-all sample. In both cities, however, there was a pronounced age gradient, with the large majority of respondents under 40—that is, the fertile population—approving birth control (Table 15–6). Acceptance was also strongly related to income and ethnic composition of the neighborhood. Higher-income respondents in both Anglo and Mexican neighborhoods expressed stronger approval than did lower-income persons, and the same was generally true for those living in predominantly Anglo areas, regardless of income. Finally, the Los Angeles respondents remained more accepting of birth control than the San Antonians even when most factors were controlled.[33] (The exception—middle-income respondents in the mixed areas of San Antonio included the very small proportion of high-income respondents who were probably as acculturated as the high-income respondents in Los Angeles.)

The Ideal Child: A Suggestion in the Data

Whether or not children are planned, the literature leaves little doubt that they are welcome in most Mexican-American families. As already noted, the bearing and rearing of children continues to be seen as perhaps the most important function of a woman, symbolizing her maturity.[34]

The actual relationships between parents and children are difficult to describe adequately in any population, as are all important human relationships. It is almost impossible not to exaggerate one or another dimension when the observer must select. The present discussion focuses on the expectations that parents have for children (an aspect relevant to the functioning of the patriarchy).

In the traditional Mexican-American family, particularly in the middle-class, there seems to have been a very distinct ideal of what is appropriate behavior for children. The "well-brought-up" child is a model of respect. He knows his place in the family scheme of things and does not trespass in spheres of life where he has no business. This model extends from family life to other roles. A well-brought-up Mexican-American girl knows enough not to behave like either a boy or a "bad" girl. She does not press for competitive excellence in school. She does not display initiative outside the circumscribed pathways traditionally reserved for girls. If she does, retribution is swift. Traditional Mexican expectations concerning children and, indeed, adults as well are very similar to the traditional expectations of the larger Catholic community. These expectations as regards decorum have extremely constraining effects on children and adults alike. For Mexicans this code of behavior is expressed positively in the term *disciplina*. It is expressed negatively in the term *malcriado*, which is applied to one who is badly brought up.

In view of the non-traditional responses in other spheres, it was rather surprising to find that "*disciplina*" (or its equivalent) was the most frequent response to the question "In your opinion, what are the main things that children need to be taught in the schools today?" (Table 15–7). Further, unlike many other values discussed

Table 15–7. Opinions of Survey Respondents on the Role of the School, by Income, Los Angeles and San Antonio, 1965–1966

| | Income | | | | |
| | HIGHER | MEDIUM | | LOW | |
	Los Angeles	Los Angeles	San Antonio	Los Angeles	San Antonio
Responses emphasizing traditional roles[a]	37%	42%	36%	45%	41%
Responses emphasizing instrumental skills					
Substantive and technical[b]	32	24	38	27	38
Language	3	5	6	5	6
Responses emphasizing social skills[c]	16	16	14	10	9
Diffuse responses[d]	12	13	6	13	6
Total number (= 100%)	(330)	(245)	(287)	(221)	(248)

[a] "Disciplina," obedience, respect, good manners, religious training.
[b] Basic school subject-matter skills and technical skills related to job or occupation.
[c] To get along with others, adapt to society.
[d] E.g. "education"; expression of general satisfaction with the system.

here, this response bore little relationship to the economic or neighborhood status of the parents, or even to their age or sex. The more deprived San Antonians tended at every level to emphasize pragmatic learning more than did Angelenos, but traditional views of child behavior were still held by the plurality.

This response pattern must not be interpreted as indicating no change in the ideals held out for children. It may rather reflect the ways in which parents cope— or fail to cope—with their children's schools. Their response pattern may also reflect their desire to be thought of as law-abiding in the face of being stereotyped as recalcitrant to law and order. Furthermore, higher-income parents in Los Angeles show a somewhat greater tendency than their lower-income counterparts to take an instrumental view of the schools for their children. Respondents in San Antonio, however, regardless of income, were about evenly divided as to whether manners or skills were the most important things taught in school. Finally, there is evidence of a marked departure from traditional norms in responses to the next question in the questionnaire: "Do you feel the same for both boys and girls?" A traditional response would have emphasized a sex difference, but respondents in both cities overwhelmingly rejected sex difference in educational goals (87 percent in Los Angeles and 91 percent in San Antonio). Whatever the education goals of the parents, they were the same for both boys and girls. School enrollment data as given in the U.S. census show little sex disparity.[35]

The traditionalistic response pattern may reflect the persistence of models of behavior for children that are rather inappropriate in a highly competitive urban setting. It suggests processes within many families that discourage behavior deviating from the expected deference. In view of the limitations of survey data on intra-family processes, research on parent-child relations using other methods is badly needed.*

THE FAMILY ROLE IN PERSPECTIVE

This chapter has emphasized those features of the traditional Mexican family life which seem to bear most significantly on the understanding of achievement. In the analysis, we have suggested that the "traditional Mexican family" was in fact far from an integrated whole, and that its fate in the second and third generation involved several kinds of change.

We have suggested that certain aspects of the traditional family might have been the adaptive expedients of a poverty-stricken population with very little access to sources of help in the larger society. These expedients may have acquired a retrospective emotional glow that glorifies the reality. Taking in destitute relatives, and doubling up with other families, for example, were probably felt to be obligations, but the virtual absence of extended-family households in the present, as well as some of the life-history data recorded in our interviews, suggest that the obligations were often felt to be onerous. Poverty emphasizes some kinship obligations, but the general upgrading of material welfare in the population means that the more stressful obligations could be allowed to wither.

We have suggested that in some respects the internal structure of family relationships has been reordered as Mexican Americans have moved more fully into the urban middle-class situation and culture. The family may be no less important now than in the past, but the importance and elaboration of, for example, a woman's relationship to her sister may have declined as the importance of her relationship to her husband became enhanced.

We have suggested the possibility of an actual decline in the importance of some values. These might include the traditional definitions of masculinity as the changing work situation, exposure to new values and models of both masculinity and femininity, and higher levels of living shifted the reward structure. We have suggested that some

---

*For example, data were collected for this study on family sanctioning techniques, but they turned out to be so equivocal that no interpretation was possible.

cultural lags persist—for example, the continuation of the boy's "leisured" household role even after outside chores have vanished in the urban setting. The persistence of traditional values in the face of changing circumstances may also reflect the nostalgia of an uprooted population. It may reflect striving after a dimly remembered upper-class mode of life, as, possibly, in the emphasis on *disciplina* of the young. It may reflect the influence of continued immigration from more archaic rural settings.

In general, we have viewed the family as simultaneously embodying and acting out both a transmitted set of traditional norms and a developing set of adaptive norms.[36] An additional aspect of adaptation to the urban situation is relevant both to the achievement and the roles considered in this chapter. This is the process of mobility away from the lower class. Middle-class role models, mentioned elsewhere in this book, are important in the process. Such role models are, naturally, *outside* the normal lower-class family. But the importance of role models *inside* the lower-class family—and the lessons that may be drawn from the presence of older *non*-achieving household members—may be easily underestimated.*

The possible importance of the class situation for the young person may be illustrated by contrasting the Negro with the Mexican-American family. At least superficially, the similarity between the "product" of each in the behavior of young males is striking. Both fit the stereotype of the "acting-out" man who takes gratification here and now rather than deferring gratification until occupational attainment gives him the income to satisfy his wishes more "rationally." Both Negro and Mexican-American male personalities have been "explained" in terms of ethnic subculture—that is, of a group of particular structures and/or values especially relating to the family and especially concentrated in the ethnic group. Mexican-American families are "too partiarchal, too clannish, with ties that are too strong" for the male role to change or for individual mobility to take place. Negro families are "too matricentric, too disorganized, and too weak" to provide the youth with adequate male role models necessary for achievement. Though this summary vastly simplifies a complex literature, the fact remains that both families are seen as producing basically the same kind of young man—one who drops out of school because he is preoccupied with immediate pleasures—but producing him from radically different structures and values.

This parallel suggests that our analysis of shifts, disintegration, or persistence of traditional Mexican family features would still leave questions about achievement unanswered even if the data were much richer. There may be a process common to lower-class and especially minority lower-class families—whether they are traditionally patriarchal or matriarchal, clannish or disorganized, weak or strong—that presses toward the emergence of a basically similar low-achieving man.

In addition to the familiar discrepancy in total expected lifetime earnings of the well and the poorly educated and of Anglos and minorities, there is a sharp difference in the age-related pattern of earnings, and an equally sharp difference in the age-

*Lorenzo Campbell contributed to this analysis.

369

Chart 15–1.

Age-related Patterns of Earnings and General Social Value, for White Professional College-trained Males Compared with Nonwhite Grade-school Educated Unskilled Laborers

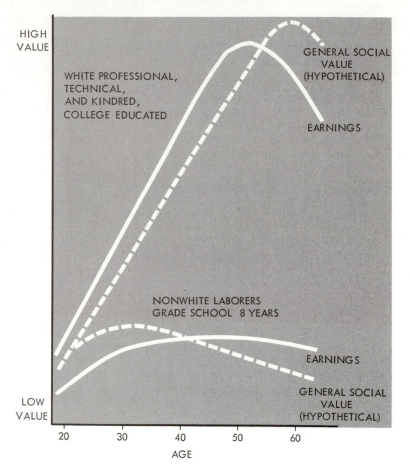

related pattern of access to a general sense of self-esteem based on social evaluations of peers. In Chart 15-1, the age-related earnings pattern of the white college-trained professional is contrasted with that of the nonwhite laborer with an elementary school education.[37] (Comparable data for Spanish-surname males were not available.) Generally the income of the poorly educated laborer does not increase appreciably at higher ages. Graphically, it is closer to a *linear* configuration, indicating lack of variation compared with the clearly parabolic income configuration of the white professionals, who can expect peak earnings in late middle age.

It is, of course, the older men in the family that have experienced either the linear income curve or the parabolic ones. Their experience reflects the opportunity structures of the previous generation without either the economic gains or the civil-rights gains of recent decades. But it is among such older men that today's lower-class young man is reared. The linear income curve may have meant that the family could never "get ahead of itself." The family may be continually vulnerable to unanticipated needs for money because of illness or of unemployment. (Economic disasters are conspicuous in urban minority ghetto life, not only through experiences of relatives and friends, but also in the content of appeals in loan company and insurance company advertisements based on the assumption that economic disaster is just around the corner.) The effect of the contrast between age-and-earnings patterns of the lower and middle classes may be exemplified by the timing of large purchases. For a young laborer of a minority group to make big purchases *before* he acquires the potential burden of a family is "rational," just as it is rational for the young white college man to defer such purchases.

There is also an age-related pattern of more general evaluation. For the middle-class man, the "best years of life" tend to be in middle age. By then he is at the peak of his career and can command maximum general prestige from the community, among other things. On the other hand, for the lower-class man, the "best years of life" tend to be in his youth. At that period, he is just as vigorous and attractive as anyone else—perhaps even more so than the middle-class man of the same age, since he may be more preoccupied with being in good physical condition. General self-esteem is derived more from the world of work for the middle-class man, and more from physical activity for the lower-class man. Although the prestige estimation curve in Chart 15-1 is schematic, both curves do conform to reality. The income curves are based on empirical observations; the "general social value" curves reflect what is known about the timing and the social and psychological meanings of various age statuses to men of different social class levels.[30]

The implication for behavior of the social-evaluation curve may be illustrated, just as the implication of the income curve was illustrated with the timing of large purchases. If a man perceives his greatest chances for access to general prestige to be to those values emphasizing physical attractiveness, then it is rational for him to maximize his attempts to attain these values during youth. On the other hand, if a young man's greatest chances for access to general prestige are those related to occupational success, then he is far more likely to defer immediate gratification during his youth in expectation of future rewards. (The hippie movement—and this may explain the uproar about it—emphasizes norms like those of the lower class: Middle-class hippies act in some ways like lower-class youths.) Neither "decision"— to "act out" or to defer gratification—need denigrate the values inherent in the other. The upper-status individual may envy the lower-class man's *machismo* or its equivalent as much as the latter envies the former's general prestige. In this respect, unlike that concerning income, the poor young man may be the rich young man's equal.

We are suggesting here that lower-class young people, who perceive that their fathers are already old by the time they reach their late fifties, may view things this way. Experiences in the family may suggest the acceleration of life, and the logical conclusion, perhaps never explicit, may be that one should maximize one's enjoyments in youth. The labeling of purchases as "extravagant" or "prudent," the depreciation of "immediate gratification," and the encouragement of "deferred gratification" are parts of a culture which is based on common middle-class experiences with a highly age-patterned income and prestige curve. If lower-class subcultures, irrespective of ethnicity, are based on common experiences with a linear income and prestige curve, they may applaud the decision to spend on comforts earlier in the life cycle. They may also seek more general gratification in the present rather than wait for a probably *less* propitious time. To be sure, in the present social and political climate, lower-class youth following such reasons may be suffering from a cultural lag. Certainly an important factor in the success of policies encouraging ghetto youth is whether such cultural lag exists, and how lower-class and especially minority youth can recognize the new opportunities opening up and respond to them. "To underestimate the extent of these opportunities would mean that some would be lost; to overestimate them would, in the present political climate, be a self-fulfilling prophecy."[39]

This excursus on age expectations is designed to supplement whatever insight into achievement may be gained from the analysis of changes in the Mexican-American family. The attempt to attribute achievement too narrowly to subcultural values and norms—family or other—may run the risk of producing yet another puzzle. On many items, for example, we find Mexican-American respondents to be astonishingly close to "acculturation." But Mexican Americans are not only carriers of an ethnic tradition. Large numbers share the situation of the urban lower-class minority-group members in the United States. The exaggeration of one dimension of their position should not lead to the neglect of the other.

NOTES TO CHAPTER FIFTEEN

1. Lee Rainwater and William Yancey, *The Moynihan Report* (Cambridge: The M.I.T. Press, 1967). This volume includes the text of the Moynihan Report.

2. One of the major theses of a recent study of a border community in Texas, for example, is that the family is the only place of trust and refuge. The family's centrality is one of the Mexican Americans' "core values." See Arthur J. Rubel, "Concepts of Disease in Mexican-American Culture," *American Anthropologist*, LXII (Oct., 1960), p. 812. In this regard, as well as some others, Rubel suggests that Mexican-American rural patterns are strikingly similar to those of other poverty-stricken peasants. See his *Across the Tracks* (Austin, Tex.: University of Texas Press, 1966). The clearest recent portrayal of an urban situation where traditional Mexican familism prevails is of the small Mexican-American community in Toledo, Ohio, whose 600 families are almost competely isolated from the Anglo community. The author comments that this is

> a tradition-directed society where the family still functions much as it has in the past, the ideal patterns of mutual aid and loyalty to family taking precedence over sometimes newly learned values. . . . Any given extended family tends to become enisled within the Toledano community. . . . New cultural items have distinctly limited possibility of being introduced into such discrete groups.

(Barbara June Macklin, "Structural Stability and Culture Change in a Mexican-American Community" (unpublished Ph.D dissertations, University of Pennsylvania, 1963), pp. 151, 267).

3. See Marvin Sussman, "The Isolated Nuclear Family, Fact or Fiction?" *Social Problems*, VI (Spring, 1959), pp. 333–340.

4. Richard Thurston, "Urbanization and Sociocultural Change in a Mexican-American Enclave" (unpublished Ph.D. dissertation, University of California, Los Angeles, 1957), pp. 112–113.

5. See Rubel, *Across the Tracks*, p. 59, and Macklin, *op. cit.*, p. 181, for a traditional view of children's indebtedness. "Parents expect and receive assistance from their grown children," says Simmons of a South Texas community. See Ozzie G. Simmons, "Anglo-Americans and Mexican-Americans in South Texas: A Study in Dominant Subordinate Group Relations" (unpublished Ph.D. dissertation, Harvard University, 1952), p. 73. See also Frances Jerome Woods, *Mexican Ethnic Leadership in San Antonio, Texas* (Washington, D.C.: Catholic University of America Press, 1949), p. 62.

6. In Toledo, Ohio, Macklin found that "although all of the people indicate that they prefer separate households for each biological or nuclear family, in fact, at last a third of the households exhibit some form of extended family. . . . In many cases, extended families occupy residence under the same roof, but with separate facilities," Macklin, *op. cit.*, p. 148. A similar pattern was found by Thurston in Long Beach: "Twenty-eight households, or 29 percent of the total, have additional related persons living with the nuclear family . . . 17 percent are of joint family composition." Thurston, *op. cit.*, p. 66. In rural Texas, Skrabanek found that almost half of the households contained additional members besides parents and children, compared with 37 percent in San Antonio at the same time. Robert Skrabanek, *A Decade of Population Change in Texas* (Lubbock, Tex.: Texas Agricultural Experiment Station, Sept., 1963).

7. Margaret Clark, *Health in the Mexican-American Culture* (Berkeley: University of California Press, 1959), p. 144. See also Mary John Murray, *A Socio-cultural Study of 118 Mexican Families Living in a Low-rent Public Housing Project in San Antonio, Texas* (Washington, D.C.: Catholic University of America Press, 1954), p. 43; Thurston, *op. cit.*, p. 73; and Ozzie G. Simmons, *op. cit.*, pp. 73, 74.

8. William Madsen, *Mexican-Americans of South Texas* (New York: Holt, Rinehart and Winston, Inc., 1964), p. 47; and Rubel, "Concepts of Disease in Mexican-American Culture," p. 810. Even when communities are not quite so poor or traditional, family solidarity is often a significant factor in the choice of a place of residence. In Kansas City, for example, a large proportion of the upwardly mobile were found to leave the *barrio* and the kinsmen there, visiting more or less frequently. But among those Colonists who choose to remain in the *barrio*, related nuclear families tend to live in separate households, very close to each other, sometimes on the same lot or at least within easy visiting distance. Paul Lin, "Voluntary Kinship and Voluntary Association in a Mexican-American Community" (unpublished Master's thesis, University of Kansas, 1963), pp. 78, 86, 120. See also Simmons, *op. cit.*, pp. 73, 74; Frances Jerome Woods, *Cultural Values of American Ethnic Groups* (New York: Harper & Brothers, 1956), p. 329; Thurston, *op. cit.*, pp. 74, 75; and Macklin, *op. cit.*, p. 63.

9. Thurston found that "the most frequent visiting pattern of both generations is a 'family oriented' one, that is, wherein most visits are to relatives" (*op. cit.*, p. 77), and that 60 percent of visiting within this Long Beach *barrio* was with relatives (*ibid.*, p. 75.) In Kansas City, Lin remarks, "Generally speaking, there is little association between un-related individuals even though they are neighbors. . . . Frequency of association between related individuals is high." (Lin, *op. cit.*, p. 121.) In an example of a San Jose couple: "Alicia and Esteban . . . are members of a kinship group of 205 persons living in Santa Clara

County. . . . The couple frequently visits the others at least two or three times a year."
(Clark, *op. cit.*, p. 156). Much the same pattern was found by Simmons in Texas, where
visiting is a major activity on non-working days. (Simmons, *op. cit.*, p. 79.) Rubel, in Texas,
and Landman, in California, found that female visiting was strictly confined to a circle of
female relatives. Rubel, *Across the Tracks*, p. 85; Ruth Landman, "Some Aspects of the
Acculturation of Mexican Immigrants and their Descendants to American Culture" (unpublished Ph.D. dissertation, Yale University, 1953), p. 143.

10. This has been noted for second- and third-generation Mexican Americans in San
Antonio and San Bernardino. See M. Francesca, "Variations of Selected Cultural Patterns
Among Three Generations of Mexicans in San Antonio, Texas," *American Catholic Sociological Review*, XIX (Mar., 1958), p. 30. See also Woods, *Cultural Values of American Ethnic
Groups*, p. 176; and Ruth D. Tuck, *Not With the Fist, Mexican-Americans in a Southwest
City* (New York: Harcourt, Brace and Company, 1956), p. 159. It has been carefully
documented for a poor Mexican-American *barrio* in Long Beach: "A slightly greater
proportion of YG [younger-generation] families as against OG [older-generation] families
. . . visits are primarily to non-relatives." (Thurston, *op. cit.*, p. 77.) Thurston finds that the
visiting of distant relatives is a good way to differentiate between older and younger generation valuation of family ties: "OG families will make visits once or twice a year to relatives
living in towns just across the border in Baja California, and some will make yearly visits to
their 'home' communities in Michoacan," whereas among the younger generation, "Relatives who live outside the visiting range and even many within it are not regularly seen."
(*Ibid.*, pp. 79, 80.)

11. See the analytic summary of such studies in Bert Adams, *Kinship in an Urban
Setting* (Chicago: Markham Publishing Co., 1968).

12. For example, Congressman Roybal of Los Angeles and "Don Miguel" Kleber of
the King Ranch acquired many godchildren. Among political leaders, the *compadrazgo*
becomes an interesting adjunct to the normal play of alliances. *Compadres* may be chosen
and often function to co-opt potentially useful allies or win over potentially harmful competitors or opponents. A *compadre* is more likely to give support or refrain from attack.
For a lower-status person to invite an eminent man to become his child's *padrino* is to express respect and deference toward him, often combined with hope that the great man
might help out. Implicitly, the leader accepts the invitation as a validation and personaliza-
tion of the bond between himself and his follower.

13. Thurston, *op. cit.*, p. 215; Clark, *op. cit.*, p. 160. See also Nancie L. González,
The Spanish Americans of New Mexico: A Distinctive Heritage (Mexican-American Study
Project, Advance Report 9, Graduate School of Business Administration, University of
California, Los Angeles, Sept., 1967), p. 46; and Lin, *op. cit.*, pp. 86 and 89. Macklin, *op cit.*,
pp. 189, 190, discusses the *compadrazgo* by comparison with Mexico. For the Mexican
Americans of South Texas, Rubel believes, the *compadrazgo* functions to ease the conflict
generated by the atomistic social system, which causes one to suspect people outside one's
own family. This conflict is mitigated by a realignment in the relationship, which brings
people who would otherwise be outside the family circle into a social relationship calling for
"respect and deference." Rubel, *Across the Tracks*, p. 81.

14. Thurston, *op. cit.*, p. 86; Macklin, *op. cit.*, pp. 189, 190; Lin, *op. cit.* pp. 85, 86.

15. Thurston, *op. cit.*, p. 87.

16. For the theme of willingness to accept general obligation due parents, which
characterizes the traditional family, see Rubel, *Across the Tracks*, p. 59; Clark, *op. cit.*, p.
144, which cites the pattern whereby a child may move in with parents to aid them financially; and Thurston, *op. cit.*, pp. 119 and 122, which indicates that though no respondents
deny obligation altogether, family exchanges decline among the younger generation, and
there is increasing criticism of the norm of financial obligation to parents.

17. Sussman, *op. cit.*

18. For the rural, see Ruth Alice Allen, *The Labor of Women in the Production of Cotton* (Austin, Tex: University of Texas Press, 1931). For the urban, see Paul S. Taylor, *Mexican Labor in the United States: Chicago and the Calumet Region* (Berkeley, California: University of California Press, 1932). Taylor introduces his volume with a Chicago *corrido*, a ballad in which the singer complains about conditions in America, and particularly of their effect on women:

> Even my old woman has changed on me—
> She wears a bob-tailed dress of silk,
> Goes about painted like a piñata
> And goes at night to the dancing hall.
> . . . .
> I'm going back to Michoacan;
> As a parting memory I leave the old woman
> To see if someone else wants to burden himself.

(p. vii)

19. John Burma, *Spanish-speaking Groups in the United States* (Durham, N.C.: The Duke University Press, 1954), p. 84. See also Madsen, *Mexican-Americans of South Texas*, p. 57.

20. Thurston, *op. cit.*, p. 186; Murray, *op. cit.*, p. 57; Woods, *Cultural Values of American Ethnic Groups*, p. 173; and Lyle Saunders, *Cultural Differences and Medical Care: the Case of the Spanish Speaking People of the Southwest* (New York: Russell Sage Foundation, 1954), p. 94.

21. Thurston, *op. cit.*, p. 184; and Macklin, *op. cit.*, pp. 155, 156. Macklin compares the change in values concerning divorce among residents of Toledo (Ohio), Mexico, and Texas.

22. Thurston, *op. cit.*, p. 161; Murray, *op. cit.*, p. 40. See also Wood, *Cultural Values of American Ethnic Groups*, p. 235; Macklin, *op. cit.*, p. 176; and Tuck, *op. cit.*, p. 115.

23. Beatrice Griffith, *American Me* (Boston: Houghton Mifflin Company, 1948), p. 94; Woods, *Cultural Values of American Ethnic Groups*, p. 233; Clark, *op. cit.*, p. 150; Murray, *op. cit.*, p. 30; Woods, *Mexican-Ethnic Leadership in San Antonio, Texas*, p. 61; Thurston, *op. cit.*, p. 136; Rubel, *Across the Tracks*, p. 63; Macklin, *op. cit.*, p. 157; and Norman S. Goldner, "The Mexican in the Northern Urban Area: A Comparison of Two Generations" (unpublished Master's thesis, University of Minnesota, 1959), p. 81.

24. Griffith, *op. cit.*, p. 95; Woods, *Cultural Values of American Ethnic Groups*, pp. 255, 262; and Thurston, *op. cit.*, p. 136.

25. "The woman who is too submissive, even in Mexico, may be regarded more as a fool than as an ideal." See Woods, *Cultural Values of American Ethnic Groups*, *op. cit.*, pp. 259, 260, for female authority patterns. "My father did the talking . . . but it was my mother who really decided things," one young man is quoted as saying (Tuck, *op. cit.*, pp. 115, 116). See also Griffith, *op. cit.*, p. 94. Macklin (*op. cit.*, p. 158) notes that even in the traditional community the woman "exercies considerable control over the home."

26. Compared with the Detroit sample, Mexican Americans show a somewhat greater tendency for the husband to pick out more expensive items, decide where to go for a family holiday, and punish the children; and a slightly greater tendency for the wife to wash dishes. (Detroit data comparable to the tabulations for San Antonio and Los Angeles were provided through the courtesy of Guy Swanson of the University of Michigan. The questions were drawn from Daniel R. Miller and Guy E. Swanson, *The Changing American Parent* [New York: John Wiley & Sons, Inc., 1958]).

27. See especially Samuel Ramos, *Profile of Man and Culture in Mexico* (Austin, Tex.: University of Texas Press, 1962); also Thurston, *op. cit.*, p. 181; Simmons, *op. cit.*, p. 75; and Madsen, *Mexican-Americans of South Texas*, p. 48.

28. For example, Thurston, *op. cit.*, pp. 216, 217; Goldner, *op. cit.*, p. 95; and Murray, *op. cit.*, p. 112. These touch mainly on intrafamilial interactions; extrafamilial sources of change are largely inferred.

29. See Lee Rainwater and Karol K. Weinstein, *And the Poor Get Children* (Chicago: Quadrangle Books, 1960).

30. Joan Teplow, "Birth Control and the Mexican American in Barstow, California in 1967" (unpublished manuscript).

31. Thurston, *op. cit.*, pp. 61, 62; Landman, *op. cit.*, p. 139; and Clark, *op. cit.*, p. 123.

32. Charles P. Loomis, Zona K. Loomis, and Jeanne E. Gullahorn, *Linkages of Mexico and the United States* (East Lansing, Mich.,: Michigan State University Agricultural Experiment Station, Research Bulletin 14, 1966), p. 68.

33. It is worth noting that most respondents either approved or disapproved; there were few "don't knows" in response to this question. The fact that differences in religious composition compound the difficulty of comparing the Mexican-American and national samples was noted by Lorenzo Campbell, who assisted in the research for this chapter.

34. Simmons, *op. cit.*, p. 65; Macklin, *op. cit.*, pp. 174, 175; Clark, *op. cit.*, p. 119; and Woods, *Cultural Values of American Ethnic Groups*, *op. cit.*, p. 172. In several studies questions have been asked about the number of children desired. Generational differences tend to be notable. Goldner found that second-generation men prefer an average of 5.7 children and third-generation men prefer an average of 4.3. Goldner, *op. cit.*, p. 94; see also Landman, *op. cit.*, p. 140. Thurston found that older-generation women prefer an average of 4 and younger of 3.5. See Thurston, *op. cit.*, p. 56. See also Clark, *op. cit.*, p. 120; and Murray, *op. cit.*, pp. 22, 23. However, generational differences were not apparent in the Los Angeles sample of married respondents answering the question of how many children they planned to have. The modal answer—for all age groups—was between three and four. The average number of the respondents' own children present in the households was 3.4, suggesting less discrepancy between desired and actual family size than has been found previously. Thurston, for example, found a mean household size of 4.4, compared with a preferred size of almost one child fewer. See Thurston, *op. cit.*, p. 55; and Landman, *op. cit.*, p. 140. It should be noted that the total number of children ever born was not ascertained in the Los Angeles sample; the data refer to children living in the household. Furthermore, 52 households, or slightly more than 5 percent of the total, included children who were not born of the existing union.

35. Leo Grebler, *The Schooling Gap: Signs of Progress* (Mexican-American Study Project, Advance Report 7, Graduate School of Business Administration, University of California, Los Angeles, Mar., 1967), p. 43.

36. The frequent pattern of urban settlement of Mexican Americans in laboring areas—sometimes even in company housing—is reminiscent of the so-called urban compounds discussed so frequently in the literature on urbanization in Asia and Africa. Such urban compounds, found particularly among people who are a distinctive minority in a nation, have been described by one authority as "indicative of incipient change, since kin arrangements in the compound tend to differ from those in the home society, while remaining strong.... Normative forms...are replaced in the urban compound by adaptive, or those based on the needs of individuals; that is, traditional forms appear to be changed. ... Such a type is inherently transitional, awaiting the increase of opportunity." Bert N. Adams, "Factors in Modernization and the Adaptations of Kinship Systems" (unpublished paper delivered at the annual meetings of the American Sociological Association, San Francisco, Aug., 1967), pp. 11, 13.

37. For an analysis of age-related patterns of earnings by occupation, education, and color, see Dorothy P. Rice and Barbara S. Cooper, "The Economic Value of Human Life," *Journal of Public Health*, vol. LVII, no. 11 (Nov., 1967), p. 1963.

38. See Bernice L. Neugarten and Joan W. Moore, "The Changing Age-status System," in Bernice L. Neugarten (ed.), *Middle Age and Aging: A Reader in Social Psychology* (Chicago: The University of Chicago Press, 1968).

39. William Petersen, personal communication.

SIXTEEN

Ethnic Perceptions and Relations: Ingroup and Outgroup

A popular belief in the distinctiveness of Mexican Americans has long been widespread in the Southwest. A small-scale survey of Anglos in San Antonio conducted concurrently with this study furnished interesting contemporary illustrations. A young man said, "They have a different way of thought and background: Latins are not so run-run-run," and a young German-born male commented, "Their general outlook on life is different: Mexican Americans are content with less." An elderly woman summed up her views in these words: "Latins are mostly Catholic, very aggressive, emotional, have stronger family ties, are kinder to old people, less progressive." And a retired Air Force officer offered his appraisal by saying, "They think we take advantage of them: We think they're lazy. It's a difference of culture."[1]

As one would expect, such comments verge on or merge into prejudiced stereotypes. It is clear that part of the "folk" explanation for the special status of Mexican

[1] Notes for this chapter start on page 399.

Americans lies in the imputation of a special culture. These contemporary beliefs neither arose nor persist in a social vacuum. They reflect interaction between Anglos and Mexican Americans and are capsule statements of what Anglos have read and been told about the members of the minority group. The ways in which Mexicans and Mexican Americans have been perceived have shifted slightly with the times. Earlier in this century, the supposedly violent nature of the group tended to be somewhat more emphasized during the years of the Mexican Revolution and the border raids by the Villistas.[2] During the debates over the restriction of immigration in the 1920s, racist arguments were vigorously though unsuccessfully invoked to add Mexicans and other Western Hemisphere nationals to the quota system.[3] In later years statements expressing fear of a "mongrel" population tended to recur less frequently, but Mexican cultural characteristics were increasingly seized upon as distinctive—either distinctively bad, because Catholicism and unprogressiveness represented "anti-American values," or distinctively good because, as we shall discuss in Chapter 18, they represented good things lost in materialistic America.

Anglo racism called forth a defensive ethos among Mexican Americans about their "race." Probably the clearest and, at the same time, most extreme argument was forwarded by José Vasconcelos. His concept of *la raza cosmica* was intended to combat "false or erroneous claims of certain racists."[4] Implicit in his work is severe criticism of Anglo-Nordic historians—the products of the "barbarian" society that "conquered" the Mexican people—who induced and validated the social behavior that rejected him and his fellow Mexicans. Vasconcelos contended that scholars kept alive the memory of conquest by force of arms in order to maintain a contemporary relationship in which Mexicans were assumed to be inferior. He wrote:

> Mexicans for the most part considered themselves humiliated and beaten by the defeat suffered at the hands of the North Americans as a result of the Mexican-American war. The yanqui protestantes were feared, hated and envied. In turn, the North Americans thought the Mexican to be inferior and seemed to despise them. There would be no reconciliation of the two cultures, it seemed, as each rejected any gesture offered by the other. One people remained humbled, the other arrogant, but both remained proud.[5]

Vasconcelos found conceptual foundations in the works of such leading exponents of racial doctrines as Montesquieu and Arthur de Gobineau. Their writings satisfied his search for defensive precepts, for the ingredients of an ideology and an indigenous philosophy that would counter the allegations of the hated Nordics. (Ironically, some of the same non-Mexican scholars who were to provide inspiration for Nazi racism furnished intellectual support for Vasconcelos' extreme concept of *la raza cosmica*.) According to Vasconcelos, the *mestizos*, a racially mixed people of the New World with Indian and Mediterranean-European strains, would some day form the "cosmic race," because tropical climates had historically nurtured more of the higher civilizations than did the temperate ones. Ultimately, the *mestizos* of the New World would achieve their rightful place in the universe.[6]

Ethnic political activists have rarely utilized the race concept in Vasconcelos' extreme form.[7] But as recently as the 1930s, the diffuse term *la raza* (whose contemporary implications will be discussed later) still meant racial superiority for some Mexican-American leaders:

> Once you [the Mexican minority] were masters of all you surveyed, and your head of cattle were countless, in south Texas. . . . A Nordic cloud appeared in the north, and slowly but unremorsely, grew into monstrous proportions. You gallantly attempted to stem the tide, but you were swept in the current. . . . Conditions have reached a point where your neighbors say "a white man and a Mexican." Yet, in your veins races the hot blood of adventurous Castilian noblemen, the whitest blood in the world, and the blood of the cultured Aztecs and fierce Apaches, the reddest blood in the world! So why this disrespectful slap in the face? So you can hold your head up with the best, and you should do so in order to keep your ancestors from turning in their graves.[8]

The theme of racial *superiority*, countering Anglo denigration, has tended until recently to diminish in the literature of the ethnic activists. The theme of race *pride*, however, has reappeared with many variations during recent years. Young political activists in particular have taken up an ethnic position resembling Vasconcelos'. Throughout the Southwest, underground newspapers in the late 1960s, for example, stressed *la raza* and *indianismo* in strident tones.

Cultural distinctiveness, and the consequences of centuries of what appears to be defined as "cultural rape," have increasingly been emphasized by Mexican-American spokesmen as the racist themes have declined.[9] According to this view, the years of cohabitation of the two cultures have not resulted in happily integrated offspring, but rather in recurrent violation of the subordinate group, especially in the schools, which have produced generation after generation of self-denigrating and confused Mexican Americans. Action programs have been offered and funded to advance cultural pluralism, particularly bilingualism, at least in part on the conviction that such programs would preclude yet another generation of "cultural rape."[10]

La raza is a term frequently taken by Anglos to refer to race solidarity. However, its meaning for Mexican Americans is far more vague, appealing to the sense of "peoplehood" that comes from the group's common past. At its broadest, *la raza* refers to all Latin Americans, the people who experienced the Spanish conquest. In the American Southwest, however, it is used to refer specifically to the Mexicans and is reminiscent of terms like "volk" and "soul brothers." The term began to appear prominently in the literature of Mexican-American organizations in the late 1940s. It became particularly significant in the 1950s and 1960s, as Mexican Americans began to strive for political unity across the Southwest. *La raza* has remained a deeply evocative term—stronger than "Mexican American," appealing simultaneously to a sense of solidarity with the most vulnerable of the group—the exploited and unacculturated—and with the most successful members of the group, all of whom reflect glory on *la raza*. Its vagueness is particularly functional as a term of solidarity with a group whose cultural and genetic diversity in Mexico and historical and inter-regional diversity in the United States make more specific symbols of cohesiveness difficult. For example, the Mexican national holidays which celebrate Mexico's liberation from Spain and France are not understood or observed by the Spanish Americans of New Mexico and Southern Colorado, whose ancestors lived in what is now the United States long before Mexico's struggle for independence from either France or Spain. Nonetheless, both old-family Spanish Americans and the Mexican-born share a broad heritage in the Spanish conquest and in the experience in the United States that can potentially transcend such specifics.

MEXICO AND THE "MEXICAN WAY OF LIFE"

Attitudes toward Mexico are difficult to describe. Obviously, immigrants have left for *some* reason; if they had unequivocally favorable attitudes toward all aspects of their home country they would presumably still be there. (Logically, this holds true for political refugees as well as for opportunity seekers.) In the case of Mexicans, however, there are many indications of an extraordinary attachment to the motherland. The extremely low rate of naturalization has been interpreted at least in part as an effect of attachment, sentimental and/or pragmatic, to the homeland (Chapter 23). The colors of the Mexican flag and the Aztec eagle appear frequently in store displays in Mexican-American areas. The Mexican national holidays—May 5 and September 16—are widely celebrated in Texas, Arizona and California. There are parades, fiestas, queen contests in Mexican-American associations, and the entire community—Mexican *and* Anglo—may be temporarily saturated with a strong Mexican flavor. Following the practice in Mexico itself, both holidays celebrate rebellions remote in time—one against France and the other the liberation from Spain. These symbolic celebrations of the solidarity of *la raza* avoid potential cleavages arising from the more recent upheavals in twentieth-century Mexico. The celebrations also permit local officials and sympathetic Anglos to demonstrate their respect for the Mexican tradition, and middle-class leaders in the Mexican-American community to receive a dual legitimation of their status. The visible symbols of loyalty to Mexico, therefore, must be interpreted with reference to their functioning for Mexican Americans in *this* country, as well as their functioning for Mexicans vis-à-vis their motherland. The same holds for the low rate of naturalization.

The actual nature and extent of devotion to Mexico have barely been touched on in this research. There remain many significant questions in the unusual situation that exists for this minority in the Southwest. We do not know, for example, whether the focus of sentiment is on Mexico itself or to one's home state in Mexico. Los Angeles formerly had soccer and other clubs organized on a Mexican-state basis. We have strong indications that much migration occurred in clusters from the same town or province. But we have no systematic data on the persistence of what among Italian Americans might be called the "*paisano* pattern." Another facet of which there are curious hints in many interviews is the symbolic significance of particular Indian

381

strains. Being part Tarahumara is very different in meaning from being part Tarras-can, just as Hopi is from Sioux. These differences in meaning would be more strongly felt in Indian-conscious Mexico, of course, than in the United States. But it is also a matter of special interest in the United States among a population whose legal "whiteness" is symbolically important.

Another question on which we have little data is Mexican Americans' perceptions of the revolutions in twentieth-century Mexico. Accounts of the time suggest that Mexican politics was very much a topic of concern among even the very poor and illiterate immigrants of the revolutionary era. Indeed the dramatic presence of conflict along the border in Douglas and Nogales, Arizona, Columbus, New Mexico, and El Paso, Texas, would have generated interest in most contemporaries. Much of the concern probably had to be covert among immigrants to a country at war with Mexico, but its presence is unquestionable. Its extent and quality and its persistence into the second and third generation is a subject for future research. The rediscovery of a revolutionary history among present-day young militants is another matter of interest.

The suppression of nationalism early in the immigrant generation is not common in the experience of immigrants to this country. (The cases of German Americans in World War I and of Japanese Americans in World War II are quite special.) With Mexicans, this suppression may have had important consequences for their later political participation. Nationalism was probably useful in the creation of solidary political blocs among various foreign-born groups, but such nationalism did not become overt among Mexican Americans. We have some evidence that Mexican refugees with leadership qualities were too involved with events in Mexico itself to provide leadership for the Mexican Americans. The potential leadership among the lower-class Mexican Americans may have been stifled by a general feeling that it was dangerous in the borderland United States to evoke Mexican solidarity for American goals. The events meant an underground tradition of Mexican nationalism that was expressed in *corridos* (topical ballads) and local myths. The underground tradition, also anti-*gringo*, could not serve as a bridge to collective movement in American politics and society at large.

Such issues are only peripherally touched upon in our questionnaire data. There are only two questions even remotely relating to perceptions of Mexico. The first elicited the overwhelming consensus that "In old Mexico it was more difficult to get ahead than here in the United States," with 88 percent of the Angelenos and 90 percent of the San Antonians agreeing. There is little tendency to romanticize *that* part of "old Mexico."

However, 55 percent of the Angelenos and 44 percent of the San Antonians denied that "In Mexico, it is harder for a man to get along if he is an Indian." This low rate of denial suggests romanticization. Ideologically, to be sure, Mexico is committed to a policy of glorification of the Indian heritage. Despite this ideology, however, "to be an Indian in Mexico . . . is still to be a member of the most depressed segment of Mexican society. . . . Like other minority groups, they are subject to

382

prejudices."[11] In both Los Angeles and San Antonio, it is the better off and those living in more Anglo areas that tend most to defend Mexico against charges of discriminating against Indians. One might surmise that the poor who live in the ethnic colonies have a more realistic view of Mexico and its discrimination. The more well-to-do, even if they are dark-skinned, are shielded from experiences with discrimination in contemporary visits to Mexico and are less likely to be in touch with recent lower-class immigrants from Mexico.

This odd relationship between romanticism and achievement does *not* extend to feelings about actual immigration from Mexico. When asked about the statement "The U.S. should allow Mexicans from Mexico to come to this country to work as freely as possible," only 57 percent of the higher-income Angelenos agreed. Eighty-seven percent of the medium- and low-income respondents agreed. In San Antonio, where there are many fewer recent immigrants, there was generally less support for immigration. Only 43 percent of the medium-income and 57 percent of the low-income respondents approved of unrestricted immigration. Although this is predominantly an income-related response, there is also a tendency for Frontiersmen in both cities to respond negatively.

The data are too meager to make firm interpretations, but the incongruities between responses on the two items suggest that a Mexican American of higher status may romanticize the racial policy of a remote country. But then, possibly, when he is faced with opening the gates of immigration to people who might threaten the collective status of the group in the United States, the romanticism disappears. That lower-income Mexicans are willing to receive potential competitors is also noteworthy. Many of these, of course, are themselves Mexican-born.

The border is only a few hours' drive from either Los Angeles or San Antonio, and more than three-quarters of the respondents had visited Mexico at least once. More than half had visited within the preceding five years. The significance of such visits appears to differ slightly for residents of the two cities: The part of Mexico south of Los Angeles is largely a tourist service area and immigrant waiting station, populated only near the border itself and along the coasts, with roads that degenerate into barely navigable sand trails in the inland areas. Many Angelenos have visited only this part of Mexico, which in addition to the attraction of the specialized border cities, like Tijuana, has offered a cheap, accessible and uncrowded vacation, utilized by Anglos as well as Mexicans from southern California. San Antonio, on the other hand, has access to the only part of borderland Mexico which is relatively densely settled, as well as far easier access to the heartland of Mexico. Middle-class Mexican Americans retain memberships in country clubs "on the Mexican side," visit night clubs in Monterrey, and generally seem to be more integrated with the life "south of the border" than their Angeleno counterparts. The difference in relationship is illustrated by the mournful comment of one Angeleno who regularly visits the beaches of Baja California that he "had never been to Mexico."

Perhaps an even more useful indication of the attachment Mexican Americans feel toward Mexico and its culture is their response to the question: "Is there anything about the Mexican way of life that you would particularly like to see your children follow?" By this measure, slightly over 15 percent in Los Angeles but 28 percent in San Antonio could be called assimilationist, denying that they wanted to preserve anything (Table 16-1). "When in Rome, . . ." one respondent put it; another said, "I owe no other country allegiance"; and still another, "We're American, not Mexican." Some were less rejecting: "I've been brought up American, I wouldn't know." The higher proportion of assimilationists in the overtly more "Mexican" San Antonio strongly indicates that when Mexicanism is a liability it will be rejected more frequently.

Table 16-1. **What Children Should Keep of the Mexican Way of Life[a]:** **Los Angeles and San Antonio Survey Respondents, 1965-1966**

	Los Angeles	San Antonio[b]
Spanish language	51%	32%
Manners and customs	33	38
Religion	12	10
Food, music, art	10	6
Identity as Mexican	5	3
Patriotism, Mexican nationalism	2	1
Nothing	15	28
Total number	(759)	(543)

[a] Both first and second mentions were combined in this table. Therefore, percentages add up to more than 100%, since some respondents mentioned more than one item.
[b] Weighting procedures were used in the San Antonio sample. This means that total numbers cannot be used as a direct indicator of error. See Appendix H.

Among those who want their children to retain something of Mexican culture, by far the most desirable feature was the Spanish language. (Not surprisingly, this was especially common among the respondents who chose to conduct their interviews in Spanish.) Counting first and second mentions, a plurality of respondents of all types (San Antonio or Los Angeles, poor or better off, living in Mexican or Anglo neighborhoods) wanted their children to speak Spanish. However, language was *less* often mentioned among the poor than among the better off. The diffuse categories "manners and customs" (including respect for one's parents, dating patterns, and so on) and religion were the second and third most popular. "Patriotism," or Mexican nationalism, was one of the least frequently mentioned traits.

The lack of variation in themes by socioeconomic status of the respondents suggests a certain stereotype in the ways in which Mexican Americans think of the culture of Mexico. Perhaps it may be due to a suppression of parts of the actual heritage, as suggested earlier. Perhaps respondents have difficulty in conceptualizing for themselves what it is that they are attached to, apart from the obvious, like language. Analysis of the kinds of people that are attached to different aspects of Mexican culture, however, is precluded by the very diffuse and generalized quality of the attachment. In this respect our data suggest that the Mexican American, while far from rejecting the "Mexican" aspect of himself, is also far from clear as to what he wants to retain. This is not surprising in a population of this kind. "Mexican culture" has become a rallying cry for generations of politicians. Its ambiguity is indicated not only by these responses but by the near-distress of young Mexican Americans whose first prolonged exposure to the "old country" leaves them with the shock of discovery of their own Americaness, and their lack of Mexicaness, even when they believed that they had retained "their culture."

SELF-PERCEPTIONS OF MEXICAN AMERICANS

The Battle of the Name

Mexican Americans are not the first group of immigrants to the United States to be sensitive about being "hyphenated Americans,"[12] but they fight the battle of the name with special passion. It was impossible for the Mexican-American Political Association to merge with the Political Association of Spanish-Speaking Organizations largely because of the ideological commitment of each regionally based group to its own name. Californians stood firm for use of the word "Mexican-American." The Texans were resolutely in favor of "Spanish-speaking" as a pragmatic gesture to include name-sensitive Texans. Even more sensitive is the reaction of the descendants of colonial New Mexicans, who often reject the term "Mexican" altogether, insisting on some version of "Spanish." This might be "Spanish American," "Hispano" or "Spanish-surname," as the population is known in parts of Colorado. A request to adopt the equivocal term "Spanish-surnamed Americans" in Washington officialese[13] in 1967 reflects these sensitivities.

The question of names has been especially important to many of the more mobile individuals. As discussed earlier, Mexican Americans originally were something of a caste within a caste, with a so-called "Spanish" upper class which was by and large acceptable to the Anglos. Perhaps because of this historical background, becoming "Spanish" was for a time almost the equivalent of Negro "passing." Interestingly, it could be accomplished without actual name changing. Much of the "battle of the name" also has racial implications. The battle *against* the designation "Mexican"—particularly in official statistics—was often explicitly a battle against the implied exclusion of Mexican Americans from the "white race" with all its rights and privileges. Mexican Americans were legally white. Thus, it was a Mexican American who in 1948 challenged successfully the California law against miscegenation; the plaintiff, who married a Negro, claimed that the statute illegally denied the couple the sacrament of marriage. Likewise, exclusion of Mexican Americans from public facilities deprived them of their rights as whites. But the struggle against this kind of exclusion has been carried on generally with far less direct conflict than in the case of the Negro, perhaps because light-skinned Mexican Americans could "pass" into theaters and restaurants labeled "no Mexicans or dogs."

Thus at least three names out of the many alternatives have had distinct status implications. "Spanish" implied upper-class pretensions. "Mexican" implied suppressed color-caste. "Spanish American" has referred traditionally to the status-sensitive residents of New Mexico and has been used to distinguish these colonial descendants from the more recent—and lower status—Mexican immigrants.[14]

Other names have arisen in other circumstances. The term "Latin American," in widespread use in Texas as a "nice" word for Mexicans, has been in existence at least since the 1920s, when the League of Latin-American Citizens was formed. But in a book written in the 1920s, replete with quotations from Anglos and Mexican

Table 16–2. Self-designation in Spanish and English, by Income,[a] Los Angeles and San Antonio Survey Respondents, 1965–1966

	LOS ANGELES			SAN ANTONIO	
	Higher Income	Medium Income	Low Income	Medium Income	Low Income
English name preference					
Mexican	40%	51%	58%	21%	32%
Mexican American	34	25	18	7	9
American	15	7	7	7	3
Latin American	4	7	5	61	50
Spanish-speaking	5	6	6	4	5
Spanish American	1	2	4	0	0
Other	1	2	2	0	1
Total number (= 100%)	(343)	(286)	(262)	(316)	(259)
Spanish name preference					
Mexicano	54	61	56	30	49
Mexico-Americano	24	24	19	14	15
Americano	11	5	11	3	0
Latino	6	5	6	46	28
Hispano	2	2	5	2	2
Other	4	3	3	5	6
Total number (= 100%)	(274)	(176)	(123)	(227)	(151)

[a] In Los Angeles: Higher income = > $6,000; Medium income = $3,600–$5,999; Low income = < $3,600. In San Antonio: Medium income = > $2,760; Low income < $2,760.

Americans alike, there is no reference to "Latin Americans" outside of the name of this and its successor organization, the League of United Latin-American Citizens.[15] Sometime between the late 1920s and the early 1940s, the term "Latin American" became a genteel Texas designation for Mexican American, neatly enshrined in official statistics and widely used by Mexican Americans and Anglos alike.

These three names—"Mexican," "Spanish American," and "Latin American"— are the three designations about which there has been the greatest status battle. "Mexican American" (with or without hyphen) is increasingly used at least in California and Arizona as acceptable and honorable. An increasing number of bold American-born individuals risk the negative implications of calling themselves "Mexicans." In recent years, *chicano* (diminutive of *mexicano*) has come into increasing use as a self-referent, notably among the young and especially among the militant. Several genteelisms, e.g. "Spanish-speaking" or "Spanish descent," persist but have never gained conventional acceptance. Some Mexican Americans altogether reject the "Mexican" designation, refusing to be known other than as "Americans."

Collective self-designation—the battle of the name—is carried on in the political and official arena. But individual self-designation reflects the wide variety of considerations that plague the definition of ethnic identity. They range from definitions of the self available in ethnic ideology (or political associations) to definitions of the self that become available in the course of routine interaction with others—what Cooley has called "the looking-glass self." The sensitivity of self-designation to socioeconomic status factors is shown by the comparatively close relationship between self-designation (Mexican, Mexican American, Latin American) and income level (Table 16-2). The much lower sensitivity of *intra-ethnic* self-definition in Los Angeles is evident in the greater consensus on self-designation in Spanish as compared with English. Though not all Mexican Americans call themselves *mexicano* in Spanish, as has been sometimes claimed, there *is* less variability in Spanish self-designation in Los Angeles. However, in San Antonio the Spanish genteelism *latino* has come into wide use, with the plurality of respondents above the poverty level preferring it. (Interestingly, it is also preferred by women respondents.) Self-referents, sensitive as they are to rapidly shifting ethnic ideology, change rapidly. Within five years, a totally different configuration might appear. Yet it, too, would reflect social class, age, and locational variations.

Self-stereotyping

Mexican Americans' vision of themselves is often tinged with a wry, self-depreciatory humor reminiscent of Jewish anti-Semitic jokes and Catholic anti-Catholic jokes. The "typical Jew" as seen by the upper-status Jew, the "typical Negro" as stereotyped by some Negro college students have counterparts in the "typical Mexican" as seen by Mexican Americans. The "typical Mexican" (or "T.M." as he is known by at least one subcommunity) has many traits that are not perceived by Anglos, and include many non-lower-class mannerisms, and many that are rather endearing or at least neutral as well as some that are irritating or deprecated as boorish. ("*Chicano*-style" or "*a lo chicano*" also connotes similar style.)

Collective self-perception of both the corrosively self-critical and more tolerant varieties obviously comes about in the course of interaction with other kinds of people as well as interaction within the ethnic group. Ethnocentric exaggeration of positive traits also results largely from contact. It may be either defensive or—like that of the Chinese and ancient Greeks—a real assumption of an innate superiority. In the case of the Mexicans, positive ethnocentrism appears to be a mixture of the two, in which the superior qualities of parts of Hispanic culture are touted both defensively and with conviction. At least one author persuasively argues that both varieties of collective self-conceptualization tend to occur in the process of status change. He concludes that negative self-perceptions would occur most often among those in the process of assimilation and positive self-perceptions most often among those advocating plural-ism.[16]

Our respondents were presented with a set of statements about Mexican Americans (Table 16–3). Five of these statements were derived from a study in which Los Angeles Mexican Americans were asked about traits that characterized their own group and traits which characterized Anglos.[17] Two were taken from a study in which they were used as indicators of Negro self-hatred.[18] Both studies concluded generally that rejection of the ingroup is associated with rejection of the outgroup, i.e., that anti-Anglo Mexican Americans also tended to project negative views of Mexican Americans and that anti-Negro Negroes also tended to be anti-white.

Among survey respondents with positive attitudes toward Mexican Americans, there is very little variation by age or sex in the degree of favor. (Table 16–3 is

Table 16–3. Favorable Self-stereotypy by Mexican Americans, by Income, Los Angeles and San Antonio Survey Respondents, 1965–1966

| | INCOME | | | | |
| Question[a] and Response | Los Angeles | | | San Antonio | |
	Higher	Medium	Low	Medium	Low
1. Emotional—agree	81%	80%	80%	86%	86%
2. Stronger family ties—agree	73	67	57	75	72
3. Anglos materialistic—agree	60	58	57	65	63
4. Shout for rights—disagree and don't know	56	54	51	43	42
5. Work hard—agree	44	50	55	68	90
6. Anglos progressive— disagree and don't know	34	31	33	39	31
7. Blame others—disagree and don't know	31	33	29	38	34
Total Number (= 100%)[b]	(360–368)	(293–298)	(274–280)	(321–325)	(271–275)

[a] Statements 1–3, 5, and 6 are derived from Anthony Dworkin, "Stereotypes and Self-Images Held by Native-Born and Foreign-born Mexican-Americans," *Sociology and Social Research*, XLIX (January, 1965), pp. 214–224. Statements 4 and 7 are replications of items used in Robin Williams et al., *Strangers Next Door* (Englewood Cliffs, N.J.: Prentice-Hall, Inc., 1964), p. 284. The full statements are:
1. "Generally speaking, people of Mexican background are very emotional."
2. "Mexican Americans tend to have stronger family ties than most other Americans."
3. "Generally, other Americans are more materialistic than Mexican Americans are."
4. "Mexican Americans often shout about their rights but don't have anything to offer."
5. "Other Americans don't work as hard as Mexican Americans."
6. "Other Americans tend to be more progressive than Mexican Americans."
7. "Mexican Americans often blame other Americans for their position, but it's really their own fault."
[b] Response rates varied slightly from question to question. Numbers represent the range.

arranged so that all responses are positive.) The greatest consensus is on personal qualities. In some statements where responses vary with income of household head, there may well be a real difference in the phenomena perceived. Thus, low-income people *are* likely to work harder. If a Mexican American observes his friends working like *camellos* (or camels, which is a distinct virtue), he may well interpret it ethnocentrically as applying to all Mexican Americans.

The notably greater degree of positive sentiments expressed in San Antonio calls for comment. Only on one item ("Mexican Americans often shout about their rights but don't have anything to offer") are San Antonio Mexican Americans less favorable toward their own group than Los Angeles respondents. It would be convenient to be able to interpret these city differences as we have interpreted inter-class differences. In some instances (such as hard work) there may indeed be a real difference between the two cities, considering the occupational distributions of San Antonio and Los Angeles. But other factors must also be adduced. Mexican Americans in San Antonio are far more traditional on many indicators, and traditional values (e.g. of family solidarity) may be expressed in these self-concepts. Furthermore, Mexican Americans in this city are far more isolated than Angelenos, and these responses undoubtedly reflect a considerably greater quantity of ethnocentrism.

The data suggest that self-stereotypes may be more pervasive when they refer to personal qualities than to social behavior. They also seem in a complicated way to reflect the combination of opportunity structure, traditionalism, and isolation which increase differentiation between ethnic group and out-group. The least consensual and least favorable self-perceptions seem to occur when some implications of discrimination appear in the statements. Most respondents in both cities and at all income levels, for example, feel that Mexican Americans project the cause of their own failures onto the shoulders of Anglos. Presumably it follows that the Anglos are more successful because they are more "progressive," a sentiment which the majority of respondents also thought was true.

PERCEPTIONS OF DISCRIMINATION

A set of questions probed directly the perceptions of discrimination or the "problems" Mexican Americans face in competition. More than half of the respondents in Los Angeles and an overwhelming majority in San Antonio felt that Mexican Americans have to work harder, especially in politics. This is particularly believed by the poorer respondents in the predominantly Mexican areas, although the relationship of this definition of the situation to income disappears for respondents living in predominantly Anglo neighborhoods. (Interestingly, language ability in English is related to perception of discrimination in business though not in politics.)

Prejudice has been a loaded topic of conversation in any Mexican-American community. Indeed, merely calling Mexican Americans "a minority," and implying that the population is the victim of prejudice and discrimination, has caused irritation among many who prefer to believe themselves indistinguishable white Americans. As mentioned earlier, there are light-skinned Mexican Americans who have never experienced the faintest discrimination in public facilities, and many with ambiguous surnames have also escaped the experiences of the more conspicuous members of the group. A curious phenomenon noticed early in the research probably reflects the great milieu variations: Quite a few respondents who *have* experienced discrimination fail to generalize their resentment about it, but continue to particularize incidents and places and times. Finally, there is the inescapable fact that, as stated

389

in Chapter 14, even comparatively dark-skinned Mexicans—such as some consular officials or tourists—and also the United States-born middle-class "Spanish" could get service even in the most discriminatory parts of Texas a generation or two ago. All of these equivocations, inconsistencies and changes in the actual position of Mexican Americans have meant a long and bitter controversy among middle-class Mexican Americans about defining the ethnic group as disadvantaged by any other criterion than individual failures. The recurring evidence that well-groomed and well-spoken Mexican Americans can receive normal treatment has continuously undermined either group or individual definition of the situation as one entailing discrimination.

Thus the data presented here are in some respects important testimony to the present collective definition of the Mexican Americans as a minority. The positive outlook of the population is evident in the fact that more than three-quarters of the respondents felt that discrimination had lessened within the preceding five years. Political awareness and participation, and interaction with others in the society, are increasing. Collective self-definitions are changing. Mexican Americans will probably increasingly come to view themselves as a minority with rectifiable grievances. However, they are not yet ready to merge with the other large minorities in political coalition (Chapter 23).

GENERAL FEELINGS
ABOUT ANGLOS AND NEGROES

There are many opinions but few data about the extent of anti-Anglo and anti-Negro prejudices among Mexican Americans. We do have clear evidence that they live in Anglo and in Negro neighborhoods (Chapter 12). We know they have married Anglos but not Negroes (Chapter 17). Such behavioral data are much more relevant to the lives of people than any possible study of attitudes.[19]

From the Anglo side, long-range data are available on Anglo perceptions of Mexicans and Mexican Americans. In 1926, 1946, 1956 and 1966 Emory Bogardus administered approximately the same instrument to measure "social distance" felt by college students. The groups ranged from "English" to Negroes and Turks; on all four occasions, the respondents (presumably mostly Anglo) were asked about Mexicans. On the last three administrations they were asked also about Mexican Americans. Though the samples were limited and the instrument unsubtle, it is rather surprising that there has been little change over time in the relative accepta-bility of Mexicans and their descendants. In 1926, Mexicans were ranked 21st out of 30 ("English" ranked first). In 1946 Mexicans were ranked 24th out of 30 groups and Mexican Americans ranked 22nd. In 1956 and 1966 Mexicans ranked 28th out of 30, while Mexican Americans ranked 22nd in 1956 and 23rd in 1966. The absolute social-distance scores for all groups "improved" over the 40-year period; all groups were more acceptable in 1966 than they had been in 1926.[20]

390

There are very few studies of the feelings about social distance and nearness felt by members of minority groups toward the dominant group and between one minority group and another. This is clearly an issue of a different sort from that of social distance felt by Anglos toward ethnic minorities. A handful of studies of Negroes has emphasized psychological dynamics and so-called identity problems in prejudice, although the relationship between a racial identity problem and a Negro's feelings about whites, foreigners, or Jews, for example, is far from simple.[21]

An extensive study of inter-ethnic relations (by Robin Williams and associates) included data on mutual perceptions of Mexican Americans, Anglos, and Negroes. In Table 16–4 data from their Bakersfield, California sample are compared with

Table 16–4. Social Distance:
Los Angeles and San Antonio Mexican American Respondents, 1965–1966, and Bakersfield Mexican Americans, Negroes, and Anglos[a]

A. Percent Finding It Distasteful "to Eat at the Same Table with:"

	ANGLOS		NEGROES		MEXICANS	
	Percent	Total Number (= 100%)	Percent	Total Number (= 100%)	Percent	Total Number (= 100%)
Los Angeles Mexican Americans	9	929	18	878	—	—
San Antonio Mexican Americans	9	589	34	581	—	—
Bakersfield Mexican Americans	4	130	11	128	—	—
Bakersfield Negroes	10	227	—	—	7	227
Bakersfield Anglos	—	—	51	315	23	313

B. Percent Finding It Distasteful "to Go to a Party and Find that Most People Are:"

	ANGLOS		NEGROES		MEXICANS	
	Percent	Total Number (= 100%)	Percent	Total Number (= 100%)	Percent	Total Number (= 100%)
Los Angeles Mexican Americans	12	912	53	901	—	—
San Antonio Mexican Americans	18	583	54	570	—	—
Bakersfield Mexican Americans	9	130	43	127	—	—
Bakersfield Negroes	23	226	—	—	20	226
Bakersfield Anglos	—	—	80	316	57	317

[a] Source for Bakersfield, Calif. data: Robin Williams et al., *Strangers Next Door* (Englewood Cliffs, N.J.: Prentice-Hall, Inc. 1964), p. 52.

data from our Los Angeles and San Antonio Mexican-American samples. There is comparatively little distaste expressed by any Mexican-American sample about eating with Anglos or going to an Anglo party. Mexican Americans are distinctly less uncomfortable at the prospect of going to an Anglo party than Bakersfield's Negroes, though most people in all minority samples were willing to socialize with the white Anglos.

Social-distance attitudes toward Anglos among our Los Angeles and San Antonio respondents are presented in greater detail in Table 16–5. One cannot easily interpret these data as indicating strong "anti-gringo" sentiment. Most respondents find it no more distasteful to marry an Anglo than to go to an Anglo party. (Twelve percent of the Angelenos would find such a party distasteful and 13 percent would find marriage distasteful. Both figures were 18 percent in San Antonio.) "Anti-Anglo" feeling expressed in the responses to these questions may represent a large component of discomfort as well as, or instead of, distaste. Women are no more reluctant than men to marry Anglos, and the old not much more so than the young. However, older people are more reluctant to go to Anglo parties, possibly reflecting greater anxiety. This is also true for women as compared to men. In any event, there is only minimal dis-

Table 16–5. Social Distance from Anglos, by Income and Neighborhood Ethnicity, Los Angeles and San Antonio Survey Respondents, 1965–1966

	PERCENT FINDING IT DISTASTEFUL TO:				Total Number (= 100%)[a]
	Eat with	Dance with	Party with	Marry	
Los Angeles					
Frontier[b]					
Higher income	2	6	17	13	83–86
Medium income	5	5	21	11	111–115
Low income	6	8	10	14	96–102
Intermediate[b]					
Higher income	2	2	10	13	107–109
Medium income	4	6	15	16	127–131
Low income	4	1	11	13	82–85
Colony[b]					
Higher income	1	1	3	11	96–98
Medium income	3	4	10	9	67–70
Low income	2	4	11	14	132–136
San Antonio					
Frontier[b]					
Medium income	4	10	11	21	131–134
Low income	9	21	30	18	45–46
Colony[b]					
Medium income	6	13	11	15	183–188
Low income	14	20	23	22	218–221

[a] Response rates varied from question to question. Numbers represent the range.
[b] In Los Angeles, Frontier = tracts with less than 15.0 percent Spanish-surname individuals; Intermediate = tracts with between 15.0 and 43.8 percent Spanish-surname individuals; and Colony = tracts with more than 43.8 percent Spanish-surname individuals. In San Antonio, Frontier = tracts with less than 54.0 percent Spanish-surname individuals and Colony = tracts with 54.0 or more percent Spanish-surname individuals.

comfort and/or distaste with regard to Anglos. The responses show no strong or consistent pattern by income or neighborhood ethnicity in Los Angeles, but negative feelings increase notably among the poor in San Antonio in both ethnic Colony and Frontier. The relevance of these feelings to actual patterns of interaction with Anglos will be discussed shortly.

The picture of general tolerance changes sharply when we turn to Mexican-American attitudes toward Negroes. True, Mexican Americans in the three cities of Bakersfield, San Antonio, and Los Angeles are less prejudiced than Bakersfield

Anglos (Table 16–4). Bakersfield Mexican Americans show the least prejudice and San Antonians the greatest. But Mexican Americans in all three cities accept Negroes less than Bakersfield Negroes do Mexican Americans in all social contexts. And, notably, most Mexican Americans in all three cities were opposed to party sociability. The San Antonio and Los Angeles respondents were overwhelmingly opposed to intermarriage with Negroes.

Table 16–6. Social Distance from Negroes, by Income and Neighborhood Ethnicity, Los Angeles and San Antonio Survey Respondents, 1965–1966

	PERCENT FINDING IT DISTASTEFUL TO:				Total Number (= 100%)[a]
	Eat with	Dance with	Party with	Marry	
Los Angeles					
Frontier					
Higher income	22	47	52	72	83–87
Medium income	19	49	52	82	109–113
Low income	22	50	49	80	96–101
Intermediate					
Higher income	14	49	58	87	103–105
Medium income	21	47	56	79	128–130
Low income	16	42	51	84	81–83
Colony					
Higher income	13	48	52	88	92–97
Medium income	10	33	49	88	65–70
Low income	15	50	55	82	124–138
San Antonio					
Frontier					
Medium income	23	69	61	92	119–129
Low income	29	76	66	90	44–45
Colony					
Medium income	30	65	59	88	184–188
Low Income	41	66	61	90	214–220

[a] Response rates varied from question to question. Numbers represent the range.

Table 16–6 amplifies these data by income and neighborhood ethnicity. The greater expression of prejudice in San Antonio, where there are comparatively fewer Negroes and very few opportunities for interaction with them, is understandable if we view these San Antonians as acculturated to the Southern ethos. (There is additional evidence to support such an interpretation. In a study of social-distance attitudes of poverty-level Mexican Americans in Los Angeles, the Texas-born were more prejudiced than those born elsewhere.[22]) The racial basis of these prejudices in San Antonio is indicated by the fact that there were more respondents who were reluctant to dance with Negroes than to go to a party with them, though this was not the case in Los Angeles. Body contact is involved in dancing, but not necessarily in parties where only sociability and hostility need to be managed. Sex differences in responses to the item on dancing are greater than in responses to the item on marriage. In San Antonio, 72 percent of the women compared with 58 percent of the men would find it distasteful to dance with a Negro. But there is a spread of only 4 percentage points between men and women in response to the marriage question. In Los Angeles, the same sex discrepancy is evident, though at a lower level of prejudice, with 53 percent of the women and 38 percent of the men finding it distasteful to dance with a Negro. (It may also be, of course, that the style of dancing in Los Angeles is more "modern," which meant in 1965 and 1966 that it involved less body contact and more remote gesturing and arm-waving.) Angelenos show no sex difference in response to the intermarriage question.

Mexican-American attitudes toward Negroes vary with income and neighborhood, though the variations are small. Holding neighborhood ethnicity constant, the poor are in some responses more xenophobic than those better off, especially in San Antonio, but the pattern is mixed. There is little relationship with neighborhood ethnicity; the people in the Colonies and the Frontier do not show consistent differences in the degree of prejudice.

There is really no substantial reason, apart from claims of some spokesmen, to expect Mexican Americans to be particularly tolerant toward Negroes. The Mexican tradition is not one of tolerance: A recent study of a rural sample in Mexico shows feelings of great social distance not only toward Negroes, but also toward Protestants, Jews, and Indians.[23] The Texas and for that matter the California tradition probably does little to ameliorate racism. The inter-city differences in attitudes toward Negroes also underline the fact that Mexican Americans learn much from the other Americans around them.

SOCIAL RELATIONS
WITH INGROUP AND OUTGROUP

In addition to data on attitudes, the survey results reveal patterns of social relations in a broad range of contexts. The larger society has long believed that Mexican Americans form a very cohesive population and do so by their own choice. In this view, they are most comfortable "with their own kind."

Our analysis of the social-class structure (Chapter 14) has already indicated that such a pattern of social relations would be far more likely for the Colonists than for the Frontiersmen. We would also expect ethnic exclusiveness to be more characteristic of the past than of the present. And, generally, we would expect relations in intimate contexts to be more closely confined to fellow Mexican Americans than relations in more formal contexts.

The data do show such patterns.* In the temporal dimension, the majority of

---

*The sampling procedure, which called for both spouses to be Mexican American, systematically biased the respondent population against those with the greatest amount of intimate social relationships with Anglos—the intermarried. This procedure was adopted before we discovered the comparatively high frequency of intermarriage in Los Angeles (Chapter 17). Since they exclude the most assimilated segment of the Mexican-American population, the survey responses reported here tend to understate the extent of inter-ethnic interaction.

respondents report that their friends during childhood were all or mostly Mexican American (Chart 16–1). This was less true for schoolmates. In addition, the difference between Los Angeles and San Antonio respondents was notable even in the past, particularly in the primary-group context of friendship.

The generational shift can be traced from the respondents' childhood through their present associates to their children's associates. A definite assimilative trend is evident. Taking the primary-group dimension of friendship, in each successive generation there is less ethnic exclusiveness and, generally, an increasing proportion with predominantly Anglo friends. Differences between the cities remain throughout the generational span. Comparatively few people in Los Angeles are confined to their own ethnic group for friends. In San Antonio, 55 percent of the respondents reported having an entirely Mexican-American friendship circle. The same generational shift, even stronger, is shown with regard to associates in more formal settings such as school and work. The inter-city differences pertain to secondary-group as well as primary-group associates.

Apart from shifts and variations in the extent of ethnic exclusiveness or integration, the level of ethnic exclusiveness might be considered high by comparison with some sort of idealized norm of American assimilation, especially in San Antonio. A third of the children of our San Antonio respondents were exclusively confined to fellow Mexican Americans. But the level appears low—especially in Los Angeles—compared with expectations derived from the literature. Less than 10 percent of the children were confined to other Mexican-American schoolmates. (This conforms with findings from an ethnic survey of Los Angeles schools; there are few all-Mexican or nearly all-Mexican schools and there are very few schools in the county without some Mexican-American pupils.) Children's friends reflect their schools' ethnic composition. At work, only a small minority of the respondents in Los Angeles, though nearly a third in San Antonio, were in an all-Mexican environment. At the other extreme, more than half of the Angelenos worked with a predominantly Anglo group, though only a minority had predominantly Anglo friends. However, a sizable proportion of their children were in school with and formed friendships with a predominantly Anglo circle.

Even more dramatic differences appear when the respondents are divided by income and by the ethnicity of neighborhood (Table 16–7). Anglos are the vast majority of fellow workers and of children's schoolmates and friends for the Angelenos who live in predominantly Anglo areas. San Antonio again reveals greater ethnic exclusiveness, but there are still notable variations by type of neighborhood. Persons who live in Frontier areas are more heavily involved with Anglos not simply in the neighborhood but also in other aspects of their lives. Respondents living in Colonies, on the other hand, report much less association with non-ethnics; Anglo representation among the friends and schoolmates of their children is not much greater than that of the respondents themselves a generation ago.

The relationship between respondents' present economic status and Anglo associates is also strong except among the Colonists. The higher-income people

Chart 16–1.
Ethnicity of Associates, Los Angeles and San Antonio Survey Respondents, 1965–1966

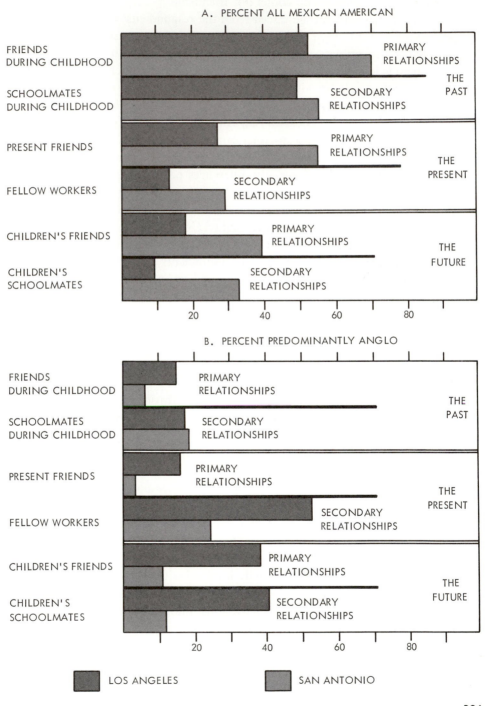

A. PERCENT ALL MEXICAN AMERICAN

B. PERCENT PREDOMINANTLY ANGLO

LOS ANGELES   SAN ANTONIO

almost invariably show a larger percentage reporting predominantly Anglo associates. The proportions again are greater in Los Angeles than in San Antonio, but the class differentiation is obvious in both cities. For Colonists, however, the neighborhood influence seems to swamp the influence of income. There is a strong relationship between income and neighborhood characteristics, on the one hand, and the Anglo associations of the respondents' children, on the other. Some of the intergenerational differences in this respect are extraordinary. In Los Angeles, for example, 70 percent of the respondents living in predominantly Anglo neighborhoods (compared with

Table 16–7. Associates of Survey Respondents and Their Children, by Income and Neighborhood Ethnicity, Los Angeles and San Antonio, 1965–1966

PERCENT HAVING PREDOMINANTLY ANGLO ASSOCIATES

	Respondents' Childhood Friends	Respondents' Childhood Schoolmates	Respondents' Friends	Parish Members	Fellow Workers	Children's Friends	Children's Schoolmates	Priest (non-Mexican-American)	Supervisor (non-Mexican-American)
Los Angeles									
Higher income									
Frontier	26%	34%	31%	57%	68%	69%	75%	87%	83%
Intermediate	12	17	13	21	52	38	47	79	78
Colony	13	18	9	4	50	12	19	57	83
Medium income									
Frontier	21	30	18	45	74	50	68	71	89
Intermediate	10	10	11	17	39	36	28	74	86
Colony	6	6	7	6	36	11	11	41	68
Low income									
Frontier	13	17	35	53	89	63	61	89	78
Intermediate	8	6	9	12	52	26	26	52	75
Colony	11	13	7	5	25	13	18	57	71
Total number (= 100%)	918	891	915	908	421	723	636	702	400
San Antonio									
Medium income									
Frontier	12	17	13	38	45	40	38	92	75
Colony	6	10	2	4	19	10	9	71	83
Low income									
Frontier	11	17	8	31	23	18	22	88	61
Colony	4	11	0	1	25	4	6	57	74
Total number (= 100%)	603	536	597	544	270	568	552	454	240

only 12 to 16 percent of those in Mexican neighborhoods) say that their children's friends and schoolmates are (or were) predominantly Anglo. But only about a quarter of the respondents themselves grew up with predominantly Anglo friends and schoolmates (compared with about 10 percent of those living in predominantly Mexican neighborhoods). Both figures, especially the contemporary, are lower in San Antonio.

Nevertheless, in both cities, the generational disparity in ethnic composition of the associates is far greater in the predominantly Anglo areas than in the Colonies. For Frontiersmen, the social world is becoming increasingly Anglo. For Colonists, it has remained predominantly Mexican. There is one exception, however. Even respondents living in predominantly Mexican areas report their supervisors to be mostly non-Mexican, though there is less chance that fellow workers will be Anglo.

In short, these data show unequivocally that the degree of reported social interaction with members of the larger society or of confinement to the ethnic group is closely related to present living arrangements. In fact, the ethnic composition of associates may be more strongly related to the ethnic makeup of the neighborhood than to income. This could be anticipated because the ethnicity of the neighborhood both reflects preferences and itself has an influence on the ethnic makeup of, for example, the schoolmates of a man's children. In general, neighborhood ethnicity is extremely significant, particularly for children's associates, when income is held constant. Though income differences exist within Colonies as well as within Frontiers, they are generally smaller than those between Colonists and Frontiersmen. Interestingly, there are few significant sex differences. Women tend to be somewhat more confined in social interaction to other Mexicans than men, but sex variances even in friendship are not substantial. Differences between respondents of different age are also not substantial, except in two instances. One is their children's associates, presumably reflecting change over time. The other pertains to workmates: The older the worker, the more likely his present workmates are to be predominantly Mexican. Undoubtedly, this reflects the greater occupational diffusion of the younger persons.

These relationships reflect preferences as well as given factors in the social world of the respondent. The data illuminate not only the kinds of people who inhabit the ethnic Frontiers and Colonies, but also the processes that maintain the Colonies once they are established. Indeed, Colonists turn to fellow Mexican Americans for most of their social relations, almost irrespective of income. They occupy positions in an "ethclass" system, in which their work relations may be with Anglos (though even that is dubious) but in which their leisure relations are with fellow Mexican Americans. Their choice in this regard in turn evidently affects the social relationships of their children. The persistence of the Colony over time thus partly reflects a choice on the part of its inhabitants. But its dependence upon external circumstances as well is illustrated by the contrast between San Antonio and Los Angeles. San Antonio is a more "Mexican" milieu for higher- as well as lower-income levels, and for Frontier and Colony alike.

SUMMARY

This chapter deals both directly and indirectly with critical issues surrounding the integration of Mexican Americans into American social life. This group has generally been perceived by others in the society as distinctive racially and culturally, though the racist perception has been waning and the cultural perception increasing. In response, Mexican-American spokesmen have advanced arguments defending and even extolling *la raza* and things Mexican on both genetic and cultural grounds.

Evidence about the Mexican-American attitude toward Mexico is scanty. Most respondents in both cities had visited the country at least once, and more than half had done so recently. Whether "visiting Mexico" entails a renewal of Mexican culture for the visitor is another question, however. Some data suggest that this is more true for San Antonians than for Angelenos, whose experiences tend to resemble those of the typical American tourist. Though somewhat vague about "Mexican culture" apart from language, most respondents hoped to see something Mexican persist in American life.

The designation "Mexican" when applied to members of the ethnic group has held pejorative overtones for many members. What Mexican Americans call themselves or want to be called in English and in Spanish is a matter of considerable sensitivity. The data suggest that self-designation reflects the environment: The euphemistic terms, such as "Latin American" and "*latino*," are preferred in San Antonio, while "Mexican" is accepted by a large proportion even of middle-class Angelenos.

There is considerable agreement among Mexican Americans that their people are more emotional and less materialistic, work harder, and have stronger family ties than Anglos. These are the major positive stereotypes, to which many Anglos also subscribe. However, many Mexican Americans agree with hostile stereotypes as well; they think that Mexican Americans are less progressive and more prone to blame others for their problems. Nonetheless, a plurality in both cities, and a vast majority in San Antonio, believed that Mexican Americans suffered from discrimination.

Mexican Americans are generally far more prejudiced against Negroes than against Anglos. Respondents in San Antonio express more prejudice against both.

One of the most significant findings relates to the respondents' reports of the ethnicity of their associates—in their childhood and at present—and of their children's associates. There has been a striking generational shift, compounded by social-class differences, away from exclusively Mexican associates. San Antonians remain far more confined to members of their own group, and Angelenos have far more social relations with Anglos. The importance of these findings for the future generation, represented here in their parents' reports, depends, of course, on many unpredictable changes in American society. But the data point unequivocally in the direction of integration.

NOTES TO CHAPTER SIXTEEN

1. Quotations are from interviews in a study conducted by Richard Brymer and Buford Farris under a grant from the Hogg Foundation. We are grateful for their willingness to make these materials available to us.

2. In 1912, a sociology student at the University of Southern California conducted a

study of Mexicans in Los Angeles that was published in a Methodist mission magazine which reflected the general view of Mexicans. His writings appeared at a time when border raids by Pancho Villa were common topics of conversation. A few excerpts illustrate aspects of the majority group's perception of the Mexican people, many of which recur through the years.

> It is generally estimated that there are from 20,000 to 40,000 Mexicans within the city boundaries. . . . Economic reasons are of the greatest influence in causing them to come to the United States. . . . Very few of the Mexicans are naturalized, due in the main to their ignorance of the possibility and somewhat to their prejudice against Americans and American customs. . . . The Mexican laborer is generally regarded as *less efficient* than other labor. . . . The chief fault found with the Mexican laborer is his *irregularity and uncertainty*. Much of this is caused by drunkenness . . .
>
> The Mexican *plane of living is probably the lowest* of any race in the City. . . . There is general antipathy for the Mexicans, and they are looked down upon by all races. The Mexicans meet this attitude with one of haughty indifference. . . .The social life of the Mexicans is meager in the extreme. Occasionally, dances are held. . . . The next social institution of importance . . . is the *Plaza*. Here the men congregate in large number and loaf, when unemployed. . . . A more or less heated argument is always in progress among them, the usual subject being *the Revolution in Mexico*. Supporters of all factions are to be found among them, and frequently, *I.W.W. adherents* may be heard in the general discussion. . . .
>
> The Mexicans furnish more than their proportion of *criminals*. . . . These people are non-moral rather than immoral, but their conditions are immoral from the viewpoint of Christian civilization and are a perpetual challenge to us to improve them. . . . The small children attend the public school . . . but as soon as it is possible for them to do so, *they quit school and go to work*. The small children are very bright, quick, attentive and responsive, but, after reaching the fifth grade, they become slow and dull. A general cause of this mental condition is more or less irregular attendance, due to home conditions. When in school their memory is remarkable, and they are generally well liked by their teachers. . . . The problems presented by this *race of ignorant, illiterate and non-moral people, complicated by their low plane of living, their tendency to crime, and their bad housing conditions*, are serious in the extreme and urgently demand the attention of all Christian reformers and social workers. . . . [Emphasis added]

El Mexicano, I (November-December, 1913); II, (January, 1914, and April, 1914). See also Cecil Robinson, *With the Ears of Strangers* (Tucson, Ariz.: University of Arizona Press, 1965), for a comprehensive view of how Mexicans were defined in earlier periods.

3. Congressman John Box of Texas, who sponsored a bill in 1926 to include the Western Hemisphere countries under the quota law, stated that Mexican immigrants stemmed from "a mixture of Mediterranean-blooded Spanish peasants with low grade Indians who did not fight to extinction but submitted and multiplied as serfs." For details and documentation see Ronald Wyse. "The Position of Mexicans in the Immigration and Nationality Laws," in Leo Grebler, *Mexican Immigration to the United States: The Record and Its Implications* (Mexican-American Study Project, Advance Report 2, Graduate School of Business Administration, University of California, Los Angeles, Jan., 1966), pp. D-9 to D-11. Likewise, Senator John B. Kendrick observed "that of all the alien races they [the Mexicans] amalgamate the least with the white man; they live entirely in a separate way," but he added that they are really an orderly people in our country. See U.S. Senate Hearings, *Restriction of Western Hemisphere Immigration*, p. 71

Apprehension that the American stock would be diluted by Mexicans was expressed by Robert F. Foerster, a Princeton professor of economics, in these words: "It is a deplorable fact that numerous, intelligent and enterprising one hundred percent Americans, to say nothing of other brands, are busy in helping along this insidious elimination of their own breed in favor of the progeny of Mexican peons who will continue to afflict us with an embarrassing race problem." See Robert F. Foerster, *The Racial Problems Involved in Immigration from Latin America and the West Indies to the United States* (U.S. Department of Labor, 1925), pp. 330, 331.

Not all views articulated during the 1920s were so negative. For example, one writer stressed that Mexicans could become good citizens if they were treated well.

> Let it be said that there is no doubt as to the ultimate ability of the Mexican to become a good citizen. Pay him a living and stable wage which will enable him to raise his family to the American standard, and put him in an American community which opens its schools and other friendly agencies to him, and he soon surprises and silences his detractors.

Charles A. Thomson, "What of the Bracero?" *Survey*, LIV (June 1, 1925), p. 292. Another believed that the Mexican peon was not such a bad fellow even though he was "hopelessly more alien to the United States than any European." Richard Lee Strout, "A Fence for the Rio Grande," *Independent*, CXX (June 2, 1928), p. 520. Still another observer concluded that Mexicans were confused in their own minds as to whether they were or were not Americans. Helen W. Walker, "Mexican Immigrants and American Citizenship," *Sociology and Social Research*, XIII (May-June, 1929), p. 470.

4. For a thorough discussion of the philosophy and works of Jose Vasconcelos see Nicandro Juarez, "José Vasconcelos' Theory of the Cosmic Race" (unpublished Master's thesis, University of California, Los Angeles, 1965).

5. Quoted in *ibid.*, pp. 9 and 12.

6. Juarez suggests that Vasconcelos was influenced by the *indianismo* that prevailed in Mexico during the 1920s, much of which is reflected in the writings of Manuel Gamio. In fact, Manuel Gamio joined Vasconcelos in the writing of *Aspects of Mexican Civilization* (Chicago: The University of Chicago Press, 1926), which attempts to refute the notion of Mexican racial inferiority. Vasconcelos' effort to elevate the *mestizaje* of the New World was in the same tradition that prompted Lázaro Cárdenas in the mid-1930s to emphasize the honor of being *indio mexicano*. Race was invoked to invalidate the notion of Anglo-Nordic superiority. Vasconcelos' thought is perhaps the clearest case of the use of a Mexican-American ideology as a defense mechanism.

7. Exhortations to feel pride in the race, numerous through the 1930s, were invariably stressed in a mimeographed magazine called the *Mexican Voice*, which appeared in the Los Angeles area prior to World War II. In an early issue, the *Voice* carried accounts of young Mexican Americans who had achieved success in various fields. Most of the reported achievers were high-school athletes. The few others were identified with success in the Anglo business world. All stories were presented with forceful appeals to racial pride. For example, "just realize—a Mexican did all this, a Mexican like you and me, a Mexican with the same kind of blood as you and I." Manuel de la Raza, "Nosotros," *Mexican Voice*, July, 1938, p. 2.

The Vasconcelos argument for the superiority of the Mexican race mixture is reflected in the following exhortation expressed in the 1930s:

> Why are we so afraid to tell people that we are Mexican? Are we ashamed of the color of our skin, the shape and build of our bodies, or the background from which we have descended?

...A Mexican must be a Mexican. His heritage of rich Aztec and Spanish blood has provided him with characteristics born of a high cultural civilization. When this rich background has been tempered with the fires of the Anglo-Saxon understanding and enlightenment, you will have something which will be the envy of all.

Manuel Ceja, "Are We Proud of Being Mexicans?" *Mexican Voice*, Aug., 1938, p. 9.

8. Rodolfo A. de la Garza, "Who Are You?" *LULAC News*, II (Sept., 1932). Quoted by Frances Jerome Woods in *Mexican Ethnic Leadership in San Antonio, Texas* (Washington, D.C.: The Catholic University of America Press, 1949), p. 30.

9. The term "cultural rape" accurately reflects statements made in speeches delivered in the late 1960s. Earlier literature emphasizing the distinctiveness of Hispanic culture was not quite so extreme in tone. Arturo Campa, for example, emphasized that the differences between the Anglo and the Spanish language and culture were important enough to influence the school performance of Mexican Americans. The distinct nature of each culture makes the emergence of a blended culture difficult, he argues ("Cultural Variations in the Cultures of the Southwest," a paper delivered at the Migrant Bilingual Education Workshop, 1963). This kind of writing, emphasizing the problems experienced in the region, along with the black culture movement, undoubtedly prepared the way intellectually for the more aggressive contemporary stance. Mexican-American militants, far more than American Negroes, can point to "their own culture."

10. Perhaps the most dramatic step in this direction was the approval by Congress in 1967 of Federal assistance for bilingual school instruction in other than language courses. Interestingly, the bills were sponsored by both Mexican-American and Anglo legislators. To judge from the Congressional hearings, Mexican Americans and Anglos alike can agree on the merits of bilingual education: the concreteness of the programs derived from the theme of cultural distinctiveness can give both dominant and subordinate systems a sense of real progress and accomplishment. In addition, cultural pluralism has the advantage of appealing to both liberal and conservative; the proposed legislation was supported by conservative members of the Congressional committees (such as Senator George Murphy of California), as well as liberals (such as Senator Ralph Yarborough of Texas). See *Bilingual Education*, Hearings on S. 428 before the Special Subcommittee on Bilingual Education of the Committee on Labor and Public Welfare, United States Senate, 90th Congress, first session, June 24 and July 21, 1967. The constellation also applies to the House hearings on the accompanying H.R. 8000.

11. Charles Wagley and Marvin Harris, *Minorities in the New World* (New York: Columbia University Press, 1958), p. 84.

12. See John Higham, *Strangers in the Land* (New York: Atheneum Publishers, 1966), especially chapter 8. In the case of Mexican Americans, the removal of the hyphen, suggested in a Washington conference early in 1967 and followed in this manuscript, appears magically to have removed the stigma of social "hyphenation," though that stigma is certainly perceived differently by today's Mexican-American spokesmen than it was by, say, their German-American counterparts in 1914. This is an interesting illustration of the reification and subsequent shift in meaning of a relatively minor symbol.

13. The history of the U.S. census designation is detailed in Appendix A. The 1967 designation was requested by Vicente Ximenes, Chairman of the Inter-Agency Committee on Mexican American Affairs, to obtain data on all Hispanic Americans, including Puerto Ricans.

14. Age of lineage in New Mexico is almost as significant a status differentiator as prestige of lineage, within certain broad limits. One of the most widely consulted status guides in the state, for example, is Fray Angélico Chavez, *Origins of New Mexico Families* (Santa Fe, N. Mex.: The Historical Society of New Mexico, 1954), which lists the "original

settlers" along with brief biographies of the family founders. These include, as would be expected, a fair number of horse thieves and murderers as well as solid settlers. But the arrangement and the use of "the book" make it clear that it is *when* the family founder came—i.e., in the original Oñate (1598–1693) or subsequent (1693–1821) waves—rather than *who* he was that is the prestige point. In the case of "Spanish Americans" not only the categorical name, but also individual lineage names, e.g. Chavez, Baca, Roybal, are significant status indicators.

15. Paul Taylor, *An American-Mexican Frontier* (Chapel Hill, N.C.: The University of North Carolina Press, 1934).

16. Tamotsu Shibutani and Kian M. Kwan, *Ethnic Stratification* (New York: The Macmillan Company, 1965), especially chap. 18.

17. Anthony Gary Dworkin, "Stereotypes and Self-images Held by Native-born and Foreign-born Mexican-Americans," *Sociology and Social Research*, XLIX (Jan., 1965), pp. 214–224. See also Ozzie G. Simmons, "The Mutual Images and Expectations of Anglo-Americans and Mexican-Americans," *Daedalus*, XC (Spring, 1961), pp. 286–299.

18. Robin Williams et al., *Strangers Next Door* (Englewood Cliffs, N.J.: Prentice-Hall, Inc., 1964), p. 284.

19. Attitudinal and behavioral discrimination are not necessarily related, either in individuals or communities. For example, one study of regional differences in prejudice and discrimination finds that the whites in a Western city are less prejudiced toward Negroes—but notably more discriminatory—than whites in a city in the state of New York. *Ibid., p.* 50.

20. Emory S. Bogardus, *A Forty Year Racial Distance Study* (Los Angeles, California: University of Southern California), p. 28. In an earlier version of his study, Bogardus commented on these findings as follows:

> The Mexicans fell in rank order and received an increased distance score in 1946. By 1956 they slipped down again in rank order, but were given a decreased distance score, which may mean that other racial groups received an even greater decrease in distance. The publicity given in the press in the western part of the United States to the large number of Mexicans who have allowed themselves in recent years to be enticed to come across the Border illegally to work on farms chiefly, and who had been labeled "wetbacks," aroused adverse reactions. Some respondents think of Mexicans as "wetbacks," "peons," and "unclean laborers."
>
> The second-generation Mexican, that is, Americans of Mexican parentage, received a higher rank order and a better nearness score in 1956 than they did ten years earlier. Many respondents distinguished between Mexicans and the second generation of Mexican-Americans, in favor of the latter.

Emory S. Bogardus, *Social Distance* (Yellow Springs, Ohio: The Antioch Press, 1959), p. 36.

21. One source summarizes its findings:

> Uncertainty about their personal identities, in relation to their perceptions of themselves as members of an oppressed, prestigeless, historically inferior group, is important for *most* of these students regardless of their classification by the Bogardus test. They seem, however, to deal with this uncertainty in different ways. Thus the more hostile and prejudiced students . . . avoided contact with people, especially strange ones, tended to be preoccupied with the inferior status of Negroes and were not significantly involved in the Negroes' group movement toward political and social parity with whites. In general, they seemed to maintain their group identity on the basis of shared negative characteristics. . . . Those with the least marked anti-foreign and anti-Semitic prejudice . . . appear to have dealt with their underlying

conflicts . . . by espousing pro-Negro and prohumanistic causes. These individuals seem to have achieved a group identification on the basis of shared positive sociopolitical aspirations, rather than shared negative, unwished for characteristics.

Eugene B. Brody and Robert L. Derbyshire, "Prejudice in American Negro College Students: Mental Status, Antisemitism and Antiforeign Prejudice," *Archives of General Psychiatry*. IX (Dec., 1963), pp. 619–628. Similar conclusions were drawn from a less intensive analysis of prejudiced minority-group students in which the author distinguished between "ethnocentric" prejudice, which is based on intensive loyalty to one's own group, and "out-group prejudice," which is based on hatred for one's own group because of its low status: Such hatred is displaced to out-groups, the author argues. Gerhard W. Ditz, "Outgroup and Ingroup Prejudice among Members of Minority Groups," *Alpha Kappa Deltan*, XXIX (Spring, 1959), pp. 26–31. See also Kenneth Clark, "Racial Prejudice Among American Minorities," *UNESCO Social Science Bulletin*, II (Winter, 1950), pp. 506–513; Nathan Glazer, "Negroes and Jews: the New Challenge to Pluralism," *Commentary*, XXXVIII (Dec., 1964), p. 29; and Richard L. Simpson, "Negro-Jewish Prejudice: Authoritarianism and Some Social Variables as Correlatives," *Social Problems*, VII (Fall, 1959), pp. 138-146.

22. Joan W. Moore, "Mutual Perceptions of Mexican Americans and Negroes" (unpublished manuscript, Mexican-American Study Project, based on 272 interviews with unemployed or recently unemployed Mexican Americans).

23. Jeanne E. Gullahorn and Charles P. Loomis, "A Comparison of Social Distance Attitudes in the United States and Mexico," *Studies in Comparative International Development*, vol. II, no. 6, original series 020, Washington University, Social Science Institute, St. Louis, Mo., 1966.

SEVENTEEN

Intermarriage as an
Index of Assimilation

THE preceding chapters indicate that the options of Mexican Americans for social interaction and personal association with the outgroup have been enlarging over time. Progressive urbanization and movement into middle-class status and out of the *barrios* to less segregated neighborhoods have been important factors in this process. Also, the younger people seem to have more opportunity for developing relations with the dominant group than the older generation, or they have been more willing to seize the opportunity, or both.

These findings are amplified by a study of intermarriage among Mexican Americans in Los Angeles County for the year 1963.[1] The pattern of ingroup and outgroup marriages is perhaps the most crucial indicator of the degree of social distance between an ethnic minority and the majority population. Exogamy creates *new* primary-group relationships at the same time that it upsets or disrupts existing ones that have cemented the cohesiveness of the ethnic population. For these reasons, the analysis of intermarriage adds an important dimension to our earlier discussion of social interaction and personal association.

For most ethnic groups in the United States and elsewhere, the incidence of exogamous marriages has been a reliable guide to the extent and speed of assimilation —their blending with the larger society. Conversely, endogamy can be viewed as a reflection of the rigidity of boundaries around the subpopulation, regardless of whether the boundaries are drawn by majority prejudice against the ethnics or by the social and cultural cohesion of the subgroup itself. Empirical studies of intermarriage *between* subpopulations in this country—for example, analyses of Negro endogamy —have in some cases emphasized the significance of external barriers imposed by prejudice. In research on upper-class endogamy and that of American ethnic populations of European stock, much of the literature assumes ingroup solidarity to be the important factor.

Table 17-1. Percent Exogamous Marriages of Mexican Americans, Various Places and Times

| | LOS ANGELES | | ALBUQUERQUE | | | SAN ANTONIO |
	1924–1933 (Panunzio)[a]	1963 (MASP)[b]	1924–1940 (Zeleny)[c]	1953 (González)[d]	1964	1940–1955 (Bradshaw)[e]
For individuals	9	25	8	13	19	10
For marriages	17	40	15	23	33	17

[a] Derived from Constantine Panunzio, "Intermarriage in Los Angeles, 1924–1933," *American Journal of Sociology*, XLVII (1942), 690–701.
[b] Mexican American Study Project, UCLA, based on original records of marriage licenses in Los Angeles County.
[c] Derived from Carolyn Zeleny, "Relations between the Spanish-Americans and the Anglo-Americans in New Mexico" (unpublished Ph.D. dissertation, Yale University, 1944).
[d] Derived from Nancie L. González, *The Spanish American of New Mexico: A Distinctive Heritage* (Mexican-American Study Project, Advance Report 9, Graduate School of Business Administration, University of California, Los Angeles, September 1967).
[e] Derived from Benjamin Spencer Bradshaw, "Some Demographic Aspects of Marriage: A Comparative Study of Three Ethnic Groups" (unpublished Master's thesis, University of Texas, 1960).

The Mexican-American minority has often been portrayed as unassimilated and characterized by a strong tendency to maintain its cultural distinctiveness. The unusual strength of ingroup cohesiveness, combined with a long history of conflict with and prejudice and discrimination by Anglos, should manifest itself in a low rate of intermarriage. The few previous studies of Mexican-American exogamy (summarized in Table 17-1) support this notion. For instance, Panunzio's research on individuals who were born in Mexico and were married in Los Angeles between 1924 and 1933 showed exogamy for only 9 percent of the individuals (and 17 percent of the marriages).[2] An analysis of Spanish-surname persons in Albuquerque, from 1924 to 1940, indicated that only 8 percent of the individuals (and 15 percent of the marriages) involved exogamous choices; however, outgroup marriages were more prevalent after 1930 than before.[3] Finally, a more recent study of Spanish-surname persons who were married in San Antonio between 1940 and 1955 showed exogamy rates of no more than 10 percent for individuals (and 17 percent for marriages) in any of the years sampled.[4]

That the passage of time is an important variable is also shown by later figures for Albuquerque. According to González, exogamy rates for native-born Spanish-surname persons in that city were approximately 13 percent in 1953 and 19 percent in 1964 for individuals (and 23 percent and 33 percent, respectively, for marriages).[5] Considering that many of the spouses in Albuquerque, and probably in San Antonio, were native born of native parents, the impression of a low propensity for intermarriage among Mexican Americans seems to be validated. Moreover, in view of the fact that the studies were conducted in different places and at different times, the notion that the low rate of exogamy is due to unusual strength of ingroup bonds seems to be confirmed.

Our findings in previous chapters on the emerging class structure of the Mexican-American population, the relationships between this minority and the larger society, and the minority's perceptions of the majority have cast doubt on the great strength of boundary-maintaining tendencies usually attributed to the group, as well as on the tenacity of its resistance to assimilation. Among other things, we stressed the growing differentiation *within* the Mexican-American population and the great diversity of its standing in various local milieus. The study of intermarriages in Los Angeles County serves to support a view of this minority that is at variance with past conceptions and compatible with our over-all conclusions with regard to the emerging status of the group. The rate of exogamy in 1963 was substantially higher than the rates found in former studies. In addition, our analysis—by age, sex, occupation, and generation—affords insights into some of the characteristics of those members of the ethnic group who do or do not intermarry.

THE LOCALE AND THE DATA

Because our findings are confined to Los Angeles County, one must bear in mind the social environment of this metropolitan area as well as the characteristics of the local Mexican-American population. As shown in Chapter 13, contemporary Los Angeles is far less hostile to Mexican Americans and offers much greater economic opportunity than do most of the other large Southwest metropolitan communities. These features of the external system are apt to affect the boundary maintenance of the ethnic group and facilitate its interaction with the larger community.

The data which form the basis for the analysis consist of 7,492 marriage licenses issued in Los Angeles County during 1963, from a total of over 47,000 licenses. The 7,492 licenses include all marriages in which one or both spouses carried a Spanish surname.[6] By the name definition adopted, a total of 9,368 Mexican-American individuals were identified. Of these 2,246, or 24 percent, were first-generation or were born in Mexico; 3,537, or nearly 38 percent, were second-generation natives, with one or both parents born in Mexico; and 3,585, or a little over 38 percent, were third-generation, defined as Spanish-surname individuals whose parents were born in one of the five Southwest states.[7]

As shown in Table 17–2, two-fifths of the 1963 *marriages* involving Mexican Americans were exogamous, and 25 percent of Mexican-American *individuals* married outside their ethnic group. These rates are strikingly higher than those reported in the earlier studies both for Los Angeles and for other cities.[8] Although various demographic factors influence the extent of exogamy, it is most unlikely that they account for any appreciable portion of the marked difference.[9] Interestingly, the recent Mexican-American exogamy rate in Los Angeles County was about the same as that of the Italian and Polish ethnic populations in Buffalo, New York a whole generation ago.[10]

Table 17–2. Endogamous and Exogamous Marriages of Mexican Americans, Los Angeles County, 1963

	Total	Endogamous	Exogamous	Exogamous as Percent of Total
Number of marriages involving Mexican Americans	5,869	3,499	2,370	40.4
Number of individuals	9,368	6,998	2,370	25.3
Number of grooms	4,579	3,499	1,080	23.6
Number of brides	4,789	3,499	1,290	26.9

SEX AND GENERATIONAL DIFFERENCES

The exogamy rates for Mexican-American men and women are also shown in Table 17–2. Women are more exogamous than men, with rates of 27 percent and 24 percent, respectively. This kind of differential is duplicated among other low-status populations.[11]

Intermarriage rates for men and women *by generation* are presented in Table 17–3. The generational gradient suggests that exogamy will probably increase in the future as relatively more Mexican Americans move out of immigrant status. The most exogamous are third-generation women (32 percent) and the least exogamous are first-generation men (13 percent). The generational gradient is steady (row 4). Sex differences are maintained within each generation, with women continuing to be more exogamous than men. Similar findings were discovered in a recent two-generational analysis of Puerto Rican exogamy, which interpreted the results within a social class context,[12] as will be done here.

Significantly, there is a pattern of endogamy *within* each generation. Individuals of each generational status tend to marry those with the same generational background. In Table 17–3 the generationally endogamous cells are shown in italic.

It is also noteworthy that marriages of second- and third-generation Mexican Americans are *assimilationist*. Both men and women are more likely to marry Anglos than immigrants from Mexico. And among third-generation men and women, the chances are actually higher that they will marry Anglos than either first- or second-generation Mexican Americans. Further evidence related to this finding is presented in Table 17-4, where persons with foreign or mixed parentage are sorted out into those with both parents born in Mexico and those with only one parent born there. Clearly, Mexican-American men and women with two Mexican-born parents are

Table 17-3. Percent of Endogamous and Exogamous Marriages of Mexican Americans, by Sex and Nativity, Los Angeles County, 1963

	MEXICAN-AMERICAN GROOMS			MEXICAN-AMERICAN BRIDES		
Spouse	Mexican-born (1)	Natives of Mexican or Mixed Parentage (2)	Natives of Native Parentage (3)	Mexican-born (4)	Natives of Mexican or Mixed Parentage (5)	Natives of Native Parentage (6)
(1) Mexican born	51.9	13.8	6.8	48.5	14.5	6.9
(2) Mexican or mixed parentage	22.8	34.5	23.8	21.8	36.7	27.0
(3) Natives of native parentage	12.2	28.4	38.9	9.7	23.2	33.8
(4) Total endogamous	86.9	76.7	69.5	80.0	74.4	67.7
(5) Hispanic foreign or mixed parentage[a]	2.9	1.5	0.8	4.0	1.6	1.3
(6) Other exogamous[b]	10.2	21.9	29.8	15.9	24.0	31.1
(7) Total exogamous	13.1	23.3	30.5	20.0	25.6	32.3
Total number (= 100%)	(1,086)	(1,826)	(1,667)	(1,160)	(1,711)	(1,918)

[a] Excludes foreign stock from Mexico; includes foreign stock from Central and South America, the Philippines, and Spain.
[b] Includes natives of native parentage with Spanish surnames whose parents were born outside the five Southwestern states; natives of native parentage without Spanish surnames throughout the United States; and people of foreign stock from outside Mexico or other Hispanic countries.

Table 17-4. Percent of Endogamous and Exogamous Marriages of Second-generation Mexican Americans, by Nativity, Los Angeles County, 1963

	NATIVE GROOMS OF MEXICAN OR MIXED PARENTAGE[a]			NATIVE BRIDES OF MEXICAN OR MIXED PARENTAGE[a]		
Spouse	Mexican Parents	Mexican Father	Mexican Mother	Mexican Parents	Mexican Father	Mexican Mother
Mexican born	17.9	10.7	9.1	18.1	11.9	9.8
Mexican or mixed parentage	36.5	31.5	34.0	38.6	34.2	36.6
Natives of native parentage	24.1	33.8	30.0	17.8	28.8	26.8
Total endogamous	78.5	76.0	73.1	74.5	74.9	73.2
Hispanic Foreign or Mixed Parentage	1.2	1.2	2.5	2.1	1.5	0.7
Other	20.3	22.8	24.4	23.4	23.6	26.1
Total exogamous	21.5	24.0	26.9	25.5	25.1	26.8
Total number (= 100%)	(885)	(588)	(353)	(811)	(605)	(295)

[a] χ^2 significant past .001 for grooms and brides.

more likely than those with mixed parentage to marry first-generation or second-generation spouses, and less likely to choose third-generation partners. By this indicator, the social distance between different generations of Mexicans is greater than the social distance between some categories of Mexican Americans and Anglos.

The apparently low degree of solidarity within the ethnic group is not only contrary to widespread popular opinion but also to sociological assumptions about the group.

This three-generational gradient and the intra-Mexican–American type of variations may well exist in other ethnic groups, but to our knowledge it has not been previously demonstrated. The findings on intermarriage offer a clue to the processes that take place as the assimilation of a subordinate population progresses. The data suggest, for example, that foreign-born members of an ethnic group become less attractive to the native born to the extent that they appear to be more "ethnic." On the other hand, as differentiations between members of the minority and the majority diminish, exogamy is increased.

THE INFLUENCE OF OCCUPATIONAL STATUS

Some of the factors aiding this tendency toward assimilation are suggested by the occupational gradient in Mexican-American marriages. The only indicator of general social-class standing available on Los Angeles applications for marriage licenses is the indicated occupation of the bride and the groom; the occupations of their parents is not reported. Because women's occupations are notoriously poor indicators of their social-class position, we examine here only the groom's occupation; that is, both brides and grooms are grouped according to the occupational status of the groom. Obviously, this grouping has different implications for the analysis of the status of brides and of grooms. For the former, it expresses the new family's class standing; for the latter, it shows the class standing of both the individual (the groom) and the new family. The emphasis on the new family's status in both cases conforms to the fact that in our society it is the husband's occupational status that generally determines the social-class standing of the family. This grouping yields data consistent with data from earlier studies and, in addition, allows comparison with findings for other subpopulations (for example, Fitzpatrick's analysis of Puerto Rican marriage patterns).

The analysis reaffirms the social-class context of exogamy (Table 17–5). Generally, the higher the socioeconomic status of the groom (or the new family) the greater the rate of exogamy. As for Mexican-American brides, slightly more than half of those who married high-status grooms were exogamous. Here, too, as with generation, the gradient is remarkably steady. The most exogamous are women marrying high-status men; this observation conforms to Fitzpatrick's findings for Puerto Ricans, and his interpretation that "It is likely that . . . women are marrying up as they marry out"[13] applies in all probability to Mexican-American women as well. The least exogamous were the women who married low-status men.

Within each occupation group, exogamy increases as the spouse is further removed from immigrant status; this is true for both brides and grooms. Further, within each generational group exogamy tends to increase with the socioeconomic status of the husband. This holds for each generation of brides. It also holds for first- and second-generation grooms, but not for the third generation. Although the lowest rate of ingroup marriage for men appears among the third-generation of high status, the percentage of endogamy in the middle-status group far exceeds the ingroup marriage of the lower-status individuals.

In most cases, Mexican-American women show a higher rate of exogamy than do the men. This is so even when both generation and occupational level of the new family is held constant. The only exceptions appear among second- and third-generation individuals in families of low status, where Mexican-American men

Table 17–5. Ingroup Marriages Among Mexican Americans, by Occupational Status of Groom, Los Angeles County, 1963 (Number of cases in parentheses)

Occupational status of Groom	Generation	GROOMS: Percent ingroup	BRIDES: Percent ingroup
High[a]			
Mexican born		66.2	57.6
Native of Mexican or mixed parentage		63.1	49.3
Native of native parentage		51.4	44.6
Total, 3 generations		59.6	49.3
		(399)	(483)
Middle[b]			
Mexican born		87.5	75.3
Native of Mexican or mixed parentage		76.0	74.1
Native of native parentage		75.6	69.0
Total, 3 generations		77.9	71.9
		(1,989)	(2,155)
Low[c]			
Mexican born		88.7	87.3
Native of Mexican or mixed parentage		80.4	82.1
Native of native parentage		65.6	71.3
Total, 3 generations		78.6	80.3
		(2,029)	(1,986)
All[d]			
Mexican born		86.9	80.0
Native of Mexican or mixed parentage		76.7	74.4
Native of native parentage		69.5	67.7
Total, 3 generations		76.4	73.1
		(4,579)	(4,789)

[a] High: Includes professional, technical and kindred workers, managers, officials, and proprietors (except farm).
[b] Middle: Includes clerical, sales and kindred workers, craftsmen, foremen and kindred workers, and farm owners and managers.
[c] Low: Includes operatives and kindred workers, non-household service workers, private household workers, laborers, and farm workers.
[d] All marriages include also those where occupation was not reported, unemployed persons, students, and others with no occupation.

marry out of their ethnic group more than do women. This is not particularly surprising, because, among other reasons, lower-class women are most restricted in their chances to form social relationships outside the narrow limits of kinship or of friendships usually formed in the ethnic community.

The results tabulated in Table 17–5 show on the whole that both generation and occupation are relevant in Mexican-American exogamy, just as they were in the Puerto Rican study.[14] To gain some insight into the relative importance of occupation or generation in influencing the intermarriage rate, the percentages in Table 17–5 are ranked by these two variables, and the actual rankings are compared with hypothetical ones (Table 17–6). If occupation is more important than generation in exogamy, the rank order will emphasize occupation (with the generation ordered within each occupation, as in column 4); if generation is more relevant, it will emphasize generation (with the occupation ordered within each generation, as in column 5). The results show that actual rankings conform much more closely to the hypothetical rank order emphasizing occupation.[15]

Table 17–6. Rank Order of Exogamous Marriage Rates, by Sex, Occupation, and Generation, Los Angeles County, 1963

(1)	(2)		(3)		(4)		(5)	
	ACTUAL		ACTUAL		HYPOTHETICAL		HYPOTHETICAL	
					Rank if Occupation More Important than Generation		Rank if Generation More Important than Occupation	
Rank from Most to Least Exogamous	Rank, Males		Rank, Females					
	Occ'n	Gen.	Occ'n.	Gen.	Occ'n.	Gen.	Occ'n.	Gen.
1st	High	3rd	High	3rd	High	3rd	High	3rd
2nd	High	2nd	High	2nd	High	2nd	Middle	3rd
3rd	Low	3rd	High	1st	High	1st	Low	3rd
4th	High	1st	Middle	3rd	Middle	3rd	High	2nd
5th	Middle	3rd	Low	3rd	Middle	2nd	Middle	2nd
6th	Middle	2nd	Middle	2nd	Middle	1st	Low	2nd
7th	Low	2nd	Middle	1st	Low	3rd	High	1st
8th	Middle	1st	Low	2nd	Low	2nd	Middle	1st
9th	Low	1st	Low	1st	Low	1st	Low	1st

Table 17–6 shows two departures from the hypothetical ranking among the men and one among the women. Interestingly, both Mexican-American men and women in the third-generation group of low status have a greater propensity for marrying out than is hypothesized from the influence of social class (or occupational status) alone. Possibly members of this group are more acculturated, and therefore feel more comfortable with Anglos than their occupation alone might suggest. Perhaps for the man the effect of being native born of native-born parents counteracts the cultural isolation of a low status blue-collar job. The exception may also be associated with age. Third-generation persons of low status may marry earlier than middle- and higher-status persons in the same generation. (No firm conclusions could be reached on this point because cross tabulations by generation, occupation, and age unavoidably reduced sample sizes in the cells to small and often insignificant numbers.)

Despite the few departures from the hypothesized rank orders, the data warrant the general conclusion that occupation is more significant than generation in explaining exogamy for both men and women of Mexican descent. The findings also support the proposition that women who married exogamously probably associated with upwardly mobile people.

According to Fitzpatrick, the pattern is somewhat different for Puerto Rican men, whose outgroup marriages apparently show generational rather than occupational primacy. This contrast seems to reflect important differences in the position of the Mexican Americans of Los Angeles and the Puerto Ricans of New York. Mexican Americans are a long-established minority in Los Angeles, whereas Puerto Ricans are relative newcomers to New York. It is quite possible, therefore, that Mexican Americans have made more substantial gains in social and occupational status than Puerto Ricans.[16] Consequently, occupational status may be more important in the case of Mexican-American men, as is suggested by the wide variations in accordance with occupation as shown in Table 17–5.

It is also possible that the so-called "Anglos" whom Puerto Ricans marry include many Negroes. The closeness of Puerto Rican and Negro areas of settlement in New York would support this interpretation.[17] Thus, some out-marriages of New York's Puerto Ricans may occur within a basic ghetto context in which linguistic facility is important but acceptability by the dominant white system unnecessary. By contrast, the incidence of marriage with Negroes is insignificant among Mexican Americans.[18] In any case, the higher population density in New York may allow much greater intermingling of English-speaking Puerto Ricans with members of other ethnic groups and tend to reduce social distance.

Another important difference bearing on the comparison of Mexican Americans and Puerto Ricans in the matter of intermarriage is the fact that our data include three generations of Mexican Americans, and those for Puerto Ricans only two. When the third generation of Mexican Americans is omitted and the comparison limited to two generations in each ethnic group, one finds *generational primacy* to be as important to Mexican Americans in their marriage patterns as it is to Puerto Ricans. This modification suggests that, in addition to the real differences in the social position of Mexican Americans and Puerto Ricans, the results of intermarriage studies will vary depending on whether minorities are viewed in terms of two-generational or three-generational populations. Relations between first- and second-generation ethnics are distinctive for most American subgroups.[19] In time, as a third generation begins to be important in the Puerto Rican population, the social-class influence on exogamy may assert itself more markedly.

It is plain that within an ethnic population consisting largely of immigrants and their children, the culture and the kinship relations are closely interwoven, and this is true whether or not a third generation is present (as it is in the case of Mexican Americans) or absent (as in the Puerto Rican study). With the addition of a third generation, other kinds of social relationships and distinctions undoubtedly become more important. Consequently, it is not surprising that occupational status is so significant in the relatively open social system of Los Angeles.

AGE AT MARRIAGE

Research has shown that the age of a man or woman at marriage is definitely patterned by ethnic and social-class subcultures. It is reasonable, then, to expect that Mexican Americans in Los Angeles would show such patterns. The aggregate data for all cases where neither party had been previously married indicate that the median age is 22.0 for Mexican-American grooms and 20.3 for brides (Table 17–7). These figures are slightly below the figures for the nation as a whole.[20]

Table 17–7. Median Ages of Grooms and Brides, by Nativity, Los Angeles County, 1963
(Neither party previously married)

Bride	GROOM'S MEDIAN AGE AND GENERATION			
	Mexican Born	Native of Mexican or Mixed Parentage	Native of Native Parentage	Not Mexican American[a]
Mexican born	25.9	26.1	22.0	23.3
Native of Mexican or mixed parentage	24.0	23.2	21.3	23.1
Native of native parentage	21.8	21.2	20.8	21.8
Subtotal:				
Mexican American	24.9	22.3	21.1	n.a.
Not Mexican American	22.4	22.0	21.0	n.a.
Over-all	24.7	22.2	21.1	n.a.
(All Mexican-American grooms—22.0)				

Groom	BRIDE'S MEDIAN AGE AND GENERATION			
	Mexican Born	Native of Mexican or Mixed Parentage	Native of Native Parentage	Not Mexican American[a]
Mexican born	23.7	22.1	19.4	19.8
Native of Mexican or mixed parentage	22.6	21.0	19.3	19.5
Native of native parentage	20.7	19.8	19.1	19.0
Subtotal:				
Mexican American	22.4	20.6	19.2	n.a.
Not Mexican American	21.7	21.5	19.9	n.a.
Over-all	22.3	20.8	19.4	n.a.
(All Mexican-American brides—20.3)				

[a] Persons of non-Mexican Hispanic stock omitted.

However, the aggregate data conceal important generational differences. First- and second-generation Mexican Americans tend to be notably older and third-generation spouses notably younger than the average American at time of marriage. This gradient is not entirely unexpected in light of the variations in age composition of the first, second, and third generations. For example, in the Los Angeles metropolitan area in 1960, only 13 percent of the Spanish-surname population born in Mexico and over 15 years old were in the age group of 15 to 24. In contrast, individuals with native or Mexican-born parents accounted for 36 and 26 percent of this age group, respectively.[21]

Given the generational differences in age composition, one finds that, among persons of every generation, the lower the generation of the bride or groom, the older the spouse. One might conclude that persons who choose marriage partners close to immigrant status are marrying into an older population and are themselves likely to be older than those who marry native-born Mexican Americans. But further examination reveals that this is not a sufficient explanation.

Table 17–8 holds both age and generation constant for Mexican-American grooms and examines the distribution of marriages by ethnicity and generation of brides. The data suggest that in any particular generation of grooms, *age* has a stronger influence on differential mate selection by Mexican-American men within the ethnic community than on the over-all endogamy rate. In every one of the three generations, older Mexican-American men tend to marry women close to immigrant status.

Table 17–8. Percent of Endogamous and Exogamous Marriages of Mexican Americans, by Age of Groom, Los Angeles County, 1963

Brides	GROOMS, MEXICAN BORN, BY AGE GROUP			GROOMS, NATIVE OF MEXICAN OR MIXED PARENTAGE, BY AGE GROUP			GROOMS, NATIVE OF NATIVE PARENTAGE, BY AGE GROUP		
	Under 25	25–34	Over 34	Under 25	25–34	Over 34	Under 25	25–34	Over 34
Mexican born	42.1	56.4	61.6	8.0	18.1	24.8	5.8	8.9	14.1
	(49.7)	(63.1)	(71.0)	(10.3)	(24.3)	(32.4)	(8.2)	(12.9)	(26.7)
Natives of Mexican or mixed parentage	23.0	24.8	19.8	30.5	37.7	40.7	23.6	25.8	20.0
	(27.2)	(27.7)	(22.8)	(39.2)	(50.6)	(53.1)	(33.4)	(37.4)	(37.8)
Natives of native parentage	19.6	8.2	5.3	39.3	18.7	11.1	41.2	34.2	18.8
	(23.0)	(9.2)	(6.1)	(50.5)	(25.1)	(14.5)	(58.4)	(49.6)	(35.5)
Subtotal— endogamous	84.7	89.4	86.7	77.8	74.5	76.6	70.6	68.9	52.9
	(100.0)	(100.0)	(100.0)	(100.0)	(100.0)	(100.0)	(100.0)	(100.0)	(100.0)
Foreign or mixed stock, Hispanic	2.0	3.7	3.4	0.5	2.6	2.6	0.8	0.7	1.2
Other exogamous	13.3	6.9	9.9	21.7	22.9	20.8	28.6	30.4	45.9
Total number (= 100%)	(444)	(379)	(263)	(973)	(546)	(307)	(1,280)	(302)	(85)

Note: Percentages in parentheses are based on endogamous marriages only.

The Mexican-American men in our sample who married Anglo women tended to be somewhat younger than the men who married first- or second-generation brides, and older than those who took third-generation brides, although the differences were minor. Among the brides who married Anglo men the pattern was more mixed, although neither for brides nor grooms are there strong reasons to believe that the exogamous spouses were necessarily older (Table 17–7). The explanation for these patterns might be cultural or demographic. Regrettably, data for clarifying this matter are not available.

Our findings are somewhat contrary to those of other studies, which concluded that men who marry outside their ethnic group tend to be older.[22] This conclusion is usually taken as a reflection of some fairly complicated changes in the life of the out-marrying individuals who have not followed what is assumed to be the path of least resistance; rather, it is suggested, they go to considerable trouble to upset a normal pattern of close relationships inside their group and to establish new relationships with the larger community. Such an atypical preference may be interpreted as alienation or perhaps maturation, but in either case the process presumably takes so much time that the individual does not marry until he is older than his fellows. We cannot accept this idea as a complete explanation of our own findings, because the degree of "foreignness" of the spouse seems to weigh heavily in marriage selection.

Why, then, are younger Mexican Americans as likely to marry exogamously as are older persons? It is possible that the younger people are more antitraditionalist in their orientation than the older. This hypothesis is supported by the results of our field surveys, which show the prescriptive marriage age of Mexican-American men to be rather high, and it would argue that the *young* are departing from the age norms of the ethnic community. It is possible also that other studies, which found the rate of exogamy to rise with age, dealt with groups in which the prescriptive age for marriage is low—where those who defer marriage until they are economically and socially established are breaking with their group's traditions. Moreover, the opportunities for wide contacts and social mobility appear to be much greater among the young. Our cross-sectional study of intermarriages captures persons in different age brackets. Thus, the 21-year-old Mexican American marrying an Anglo in 1963 may have had social experiences quite different from those of the 31-year-old marrying a Mexican-born bride in the same year. In other words, relationships of the minority with the larger society had changed considerably in the relevant ten-year period.

SUMMARY AND IMPLICATIONS

The marriages involving Mexican Americans in Los Angeles County in 1963 showed a much greater rate of exogamy than was expected from earlier studies. Outgroup marriages were more frequent for women than for men and increased with removal from immigrant status. Those who married within the ethnic group tended to select spouses of the same generation. Exogamy was more prevalent among higher-status individuals; with a few exceptions, the groom's occupation was a better predictor of outgroup marriage than generation. The data suggest, in fact, that social distance between the various generations of Mexican Americans may be as important in marriage as is the social distance between Mexican Americans and Anglos. Generally, the older the groom the more "Mexican" is the spouse, but the pattern is not the same for brides.

These findings suggest an assimilative potential of the Mexican-American population greater than has been commonly assumed, provided that external barriers are comparatively low. Of course, a three-generational cross-section analysis does not take the place of a longitudinal study; the internal differences in exogamy rates imply that the assimilative potential is related to nativity and rate of economic advancement in the group, and both of these may shift.

Further, the analysis strongly supports the responsiveness of Mexican Americans, along with other ethnic groups, to the external milieu—that is, to variations in both prejudice and opportunities, which themselves are interrelated. The importance of the milieu emerges from the comparison of Los Angeles intermarriage rates with those found in previous studies.

More generally, the data can be interpreted as indicating underlying processes that occur in the breakdown of ethnic solidarity in an increasingly open system. Mexican Americans have long maintained unusually strong ethnic boundaries in part because their initial contact with Anglos tended to isolate and antagonize the group. The many isolating experiences have been historically accompanied by a considerable if not exclusive reliance on kin as a source of emotional and other support and also by considerable homogeneity in outlook and style of life. However, the extent of isolation is generally declining—only slightly in some parts of the Southwest, more substantially in others. Los Angeles, of course, is an example of the latter trend.

As isolation diminishes and as both social and geographic mobility becomes more common, the minority exhibits greater diversity in style of life. Most importantly, primary-group relations decline in functional importance, and they even cease to be maintained mechanically, that is, by style of life. Thus, the socializing and identity-maintaining structures of the ethnic group, and particularly the family, are structurally weakened.

This interpretation seems applicable particularly to the *third generation* among the large Mexican-American community of Los Angeles County, a metropolitan area with a relatively open opportunity structure. The strong propensity toward mixed marriage among members of this generation is related to their increased contact with the larger system, and to especially rewarding experiences that have decreased the role of the ethnic group as the prime source of identity. The movement outward and away from the primary group in turn has weakened its control on the social relations of this generation of Mexican Americans.

NOTES TO CHAPTER SEVENTEEN

1. This chapter is based on a paper by Frank G. Mittelbach and Joan W. Moore, "Ethnic Endogamy—The Case of Mexican Americans," in *The American Journal of Sociology*, LXXIV, (July, 1968), pp. 50–62. For an earlier and more extended version, see *Intermarriage of Mexican-Americans* (Mexican-American Study Project, Advance Report 6, Graduate School of Business Administration, University of California, Los Angeles, Nov. 1966), by the same authors. The literature of intermarriage is extensive. For this theoretical discussion we have drawn on many sources, prominently on the classic analyses by Kingsley

Davis, "Intermarriage in Caste Societies," *American Anthropologist*, XLIII (1941), pp. 376–395, and Robert K. Merton, "Intermarriage and Social Structure: Fact and Theory," *Psychiatry*, IV (1941), pp. 361–374, as well as on the recent extensive discussion by John Finley Scott, "Endogamy in Industrial Societies" (unpublished manuscript, University of California, Sociology Department, Davis).

2. Constantine Penunzio, "Intermarriage in Los Angeles, 1924–1933," *American Journal of Sociology*, XLVII (1942), pp. 690–701. Calculations based on the number of marriages and on the number of persons involved in marriages can vary considerably. Studies reporting one without the other add greatly to the confusion in the understanding of intermarriage. The formula for calculating the ingroup marriage for persons is $2E/E+N$, where E is the number of ingroup marriages and N is the total number of marriages involving the subpopulation in question. We are indebted to Richard Griego for calling our attention to this relationship. See also Hyman Rodman, "Technical Note on Two Rates of Mixed Marriages," *American Sociological Review*, XXX (1965), pp. 776–778.

3. Derived from Carolyn Zeleny, "Relations between the Spanish-Americans and the Anglo-Americans in New Mexico" (unpublished Ph.D. dissertation, Yale University, 1944), p. 334.

4. Benjamin Spencer Bradshaw, "Some Demographic Aspects of Marriage: A Comparative Study of Three Ethnic Groups" (unpublished master's thesis, University of Texas, 1960). John Burma, in "Interethnic Marriage in Los Angeles, 1948–1959," *Social Forces*, LXII (1963), pp. 156–165, also reports on the ethnicity of the partners of exogamous Mexican Americans.

5. Nancie L. González, *The Spanish American of New Mexico: A Distinctive Heritage* (Mexican-American Study Project, Advance Report 9, Graduate School of Business Administration, University of California, Los Angeles, Sept., 1967), pp. 110–116.

6. To identify "Spanish surname," the U.S. Census Bureau's "long" list, which includes more than 7,000 names, was used. However, for classifying persons as first- or second-generation, nativity as recorded on the marriage license was given priority. For details, see Mittelbach and Moore, Advance Report 6, Appendix A.

7. The third-generation Spanish-surname persons with parents born outside the Southwest were defined as "non-Mexican Americans." This definition seemed appropriate in light of the relatively high probability that such persons might be of other than Mexican descent. However, analysis of the data using such a reclassification did not importantly affect the rate of endogamy. Exploratory research suggests that name changing is not frequent among Mexican Americans. Also, it can be noted that among the foreign-stock Mexican Americans in our sample population only 5.8 percent did not have a Spanish surname. This low percentage could be the result of intermarriage on the part of one of the parents, name changing, or incompleteness of the census list of Spanish surnames. The relative role of these factors is indeterminate, but it seems to be insignificant for the period of our study.

8. The Los Angeles rate of intermarriage does not appear to be much higher than the exogamy rate of 19 percent found by González for 1964 in Albuquerque. However, González included only native-born Spanish-surname persons in her analysis. Native-born Mexican Americans in Los Angeles showed a rate for individuals of 31 percent. Thus, our conclusion stands unchallenged by existing data. The only qualification is that the share of Mexican Americans in the Albuquerque population is much greater than in Los Angeles, though the absolute numbers of marriageable Mexican Americans available in Los Angeles are enough to maintain complete endogamy.

9. For a detailed analysis of the demographic factors that bear on the rate of intermarriage, see Mittelbach and Moore, Advance Report 6, Appendix B. The number and proportion of the ethnic group, as well as the sex ratios, may influence the extent of exogamy. These factors may be neutral, or they may reinforce or cancel each other. For a

recent discussion on some of the issues involved, see Paul H. Besanceney, "On Reporting Rates of Intermarriage," *American Journal of Sociology*, LXX (1965), pp. 717–721.

10. B. R. Bugelski, "Assimilation through Intermarriage," *Social Forces*, XL (1961), pp. 148–153. The 1930 rates of endogamy were 71 percent for Italians and 70 percent for Poles, but the 1960 rates were 27 percent for Italians and 33 percent for Poles. If one estimates the mid-1890s as the high point of Polish and Italian immigration and the 1920s as the crest of Mexican immigration, the 60–70 percent endogamy rates occurred for both populations approximately 40 years after their highest immigration rate.

11. See Scott, *op. cit.*

12. Joseph P. Fitzpatrick, "Intermarriage of Puerto Ricans in New York City," *American Journal of Sociology*, LXXI (1966), pp. 395–406.

13. *Ibid.*, p. 400.

14. *Ibid.* Data on occupation were calculated so as to be comparable with Fitzpatrick's.

15. An analysis of variance of the data in Table 17–5 shows the following results.

Source of Variation	Sum of Squares	D.F.	Mean Square
Generation	0.041	2	0.0205
Occupation	0.070	2	0.0350
Interaction	0.040	4	0.0100

These data provide further support for the hypothesis that occupation contributes more to the variation in rates of intermarriage than does either generation or the interaction between these variables. (On the assumption that the results represent a sample from a larger universe, we calculated F-ratios. These suggested that all the mean squares were significant at the .01 level.)

16. Given the many difficulties of comparing two ethnic groups in different environments, no firm conclusion can be reached on relative social status and economic achievement. Census data for 1960 on occupation and income indicate that in Los Angeles 19 percent of the Mexican Americans held white-collar occupations as compared with 17 percent of the Puerto Ricans in New York. Also, 19 percent of the Mexican Americans were skilled workers as compared to 10 percent of the Puerto Ricans. The income of Mexican Americans in Los Angeles was considerably above that of the Puerto Ricans in New York.

17. This interpretation is supported by other reports on Puerto Ricans. For a summary of this material, see Nathan Glazer and Daniel Patrick Moynihan, *Beyond the Melting Pot* (Cambridge, Mass.: The M.I.T. Press, 1963), pp. 129–142.

18. See Burma, *op. cit.*

19. The Japanese appear to be something of an exception. See Harry Kitano, *The Japanese-American* (Englewood Cliffs, N.J.: Prentice-Hall, Inc., 1969).

20. U.S. Bureau of the Census, *Statistical Abstract of the United States* (1964), p. 65. Nationally, the median age at first marriage, in 1963, was 20.4 for women and 22.8 for men.

21. *1960 U.S. Census of Population*, PC(2)–1B, table 9.

22. See, for example, John Burma, "Research Note on the Measurement of Interracial Marriage," *American Journal of Sociology*, LVII (1951), pp. 249–255. Burma's findings generally agree with ours on exogamous Mexican-American men.

EIGHTEEN

The Tenacity of Ethnic Culture

THE theme of cultural distinctiveness appears in many variations in the social science literature about Mexican Americans. Some writers transmute their culture into a fancied high Hispanic culture and contrast it with perceived cultural deficiencies in the United States:

> Some positive values are in the process of being lost, and . . . life may become less satisfying as a result. Some of these values may be precisely those which are best preserved in Hispanic culture; values associated with the poetization of life, with the personalization of human relationships, with the full perception of the present, with the completeness and adequacy of the individual, with unquantifiable human experience, with a greater range of inner freedoms, and with a serenity which accepts what is, to make the most of it rather than restlessly and continuously searching for something different. If these values are worth preserving, we can *best preserve them in those persons for whom they are native*, persons from a background which for centuries has been a matrix for those values.[1] [Emphasis supplied].

[1] Notes for this chapter start on page 439.

Others view the distinctive culture primarily as an impediment to the group's material progress:

> Social scientists in describing and analyzing Spanish-American life have demonstrated a high level of agreement. . . . By reasons of their history and the opportunity structure of their present environment Spanish-Americans in the Southwest are a poor, proud, stable and cohesive group, with a value orientation strongly emphasizing interpersonal relations rather than ideas, abstractions or material possessions. . . . Despite prolonged contact with Anglo norms, Spanish-American values have been influenced only to a slight degree by the Anglo social environment. . . . Very few Spanish-Americans adopt the Anglo's competitive, materialistic orientation that could be of assistance to them in rising above their present underprivileged position. . . .
>
> Furthermore, Spanish-Americans in business or the professions also tend to be automatically suspect in the eyes of their compatriots because they do not perform "honest labor" which, according to Spanish-Americans, is work commonly requiring physical strength, tenacity, and dexterity. A traditional example of this is agricultural labor.[2]

Such generalizations are based on a large research literature and accurately represent its content. However, several *caveats* are in order about this literature. Most of the best known and widely read research monographs are based on studies in rural areas, especially among the Spanish Americans of New Mexican villages; or they are old and therefore relate to Mexican Americans of a generation or more ago; or they are confined to the poorest *barrios* in urban areas, the repositories of the largest number of unacculturated ethnics. Although the research findings may be entirely valid in each of these contexts, they are often used indiscriminately for generalizations on contemporary Mexican Americans in an urban environment. Cultural distinctiveness is a question for investigation, not for unwitting projection.

One of the methodologically most elaborate studies, for example, was undertaken in 1951 by Florence Kluckhohn and her associates in a small village in northern New Mexico, comparing the value patterns of the Spanish Americans with those of neighboring Texan, Mormon, Zuni, and Navaho settlements. The authors develop a set of "universal problems of evaluation." These problems call forth alternative cultural responses, all of which are present in all cultures, but only one dominates:

1. innate human nature may be evaluated as good, neutral or evil;

2. man's relation to nature may entail seeing man as subjugated to, master over, or in harmony with nature;

3. the proper temporal focus of human life may emphasize past, present or future;

4. the best modality of human activity may value being, doing, or being-in-doing; and finally

5. the most desirable relationship of men to each other may be individualistic, collateral, or lineal.

Applying this framework in the analysis of the five culture patterns, Kluckhohn's major findings include:

(1) the highly distinctive position of the Spanish-American group as a culture which stands apart from all of the others; (2) the great . . . similarity of the two English-speaking communities which as a unity stand at the opposite pole from the Spanish-Americans. . . . The strength of the preference of the Spanish-American for the Present *time* orientation, the Being alternative of the *activity* orientation, and the Subjugated-to-Nature position on the *man-nature* orientation made it possible to separate the group off and call it the most unique of the five cultures.[3]

This strong statement of cultural distinctiveness (in which Spanish Americans are seen as more different from Anglos than are either Zuni or Navaho Indians) appears much modified in Kluckhohn's work in the same book on *changes* in the Spanish-American culture, based on a comparison of her experiences in 1939 and 1951. Compared with the earlier period in which she did not rely on a standardized instrument, she felt that a major shift had occurred in the values around problem (5) above—that of the proper relationship of men to each other. She found a shift from hierarchical "lineality" to greater individualism, as well as some other minor shifts in values. She suggests that further changes will follow:

At the present time the changes to be noted are . . . the superficial ones made necessary by the demands of adaptation, and they have as yet scarcely touched the deeper convictions of the people. But however superficial these changes may now appear to be relative to Spanish-American *dominant* value orientations, they nonetheless indicate that basic changes in the total value system are to be expected. There can be no turning back by these people, given the fact that they are firmly held within the borders of the United States and are increasingly subjected to dominant Anglo American culture as one by one the small villages like Atrisco decay and the inhabitants of them move off to urban centers. A majority of the people we tested in 1951 were still firm in their value choices of the Subjugated-to-Nature, the Present and the Being orientation in matters having to do with recreation and religion, but year by year the patterns which support these values wither away.

Two alternative end results appear possible. One is that of a greater acculturation of a majority of the group. . . . The other prospect is a fairly thoroughgoing disorganization. . . . At the moment the first of the two prospects seems the more likely.[4]

A very important point to be derived from this significant study, therefore, is that as long ago as 1951 the author predicted "basic changes" in the distinctive features of Spanish-American culture—even in this remote village. However, the general literature dealing with Mexican Americans tends to seize upon her findings about the "uniqueness" of the New Mexican Spanish-American culture and to extend them to Mexican Americans generally, without paying much attention to Kluckhohn's incisive qualifications.

Other research monographs, like that by Margaret Clark, pertain to the least acculturated lower-class segments of urban areas and add a special warning against generalizing the findings.[5] Still others, like Rubel's, concern small towns along the Mexican border.[6] A third group of studies, like Tuck's,[7] though performed in a large city, portray conditions of the generation of the 1940s. None of these contexts allows universal conclusions. Although many basic findings of the studies are in considerable accord, they tend to reflect the less acculturated milieus in time or place or both.

Enough has been said in the preceding chapters to indicate that despite common structures and values, urban Mexican Americans display a wide range of variation in behavior, attitudes, and beliefs. The range of responses of Los Angeles and San Antonio respondents was shown to be generally *within* the range of American cultural values in such critical arenas of life as family, neighboring, and social class. Some aspects of traditional Mexican culture were placed in the perspective of contemporary urban life. Thus, we discussed *machismo* in the context of the family, and attachment to *la raza* in the context of ethnic perceptions. To sum up this material crudely, we found quite a few Mexican Americans to be "typical Americans" in all but a few areas of special knowledge or opinion, and not very many who could be said to have a truly distinctive culture. Of course, the people included in our household surveys were living in two of the largest cities of the Southwest—cities with highly complex economic, social, and political institutions. The stereotyped Mexican peasant with all his distinctive culture traits could not survive in such an environment without change. Indeed, in 1951, the Spanish-American villager was already modifying *his* peasant culture. Further, few of our respondents are Mexican peasants, but are rather the children, grandchildren, and great-grandchildren of Mexicans.

There has been a tendency to overgeneralize from special times and places to the whole range of milieus. There is also a tendency to overgeneralize the culture itself. Certainly, Mexican-American culture is not now an integrated whole. Eroded, altered, and shifted by its exposure to the American experience, it has been transformed into an amalgam. This point has been made repeatedly in previous chapters with regard to major values and structures of relationships.

This chapter employs survey data from Los Angeles and San Antonio in an attempt to put into perspective two aspects of the culture that are particularly relevant to an understanding of *achievement*. We are concerned first with language and second with those values which are related to performance in work—often considered the most important characteristic separating the Mexican-American from the Anglo-American culture. Both sets of values have been grossly romanticized. Both sets of values have been seen as major handicaps to full participation in American society. At the same time, both sets of values are viewed by some as so worthy that they should be preserved by the larger society.

THE PERSISTENCE OF SPANISH

An extensive study of "language loyalty" among ethnic groups in the United States shows conclusively that Spanish is the most persistent of all foreign languages, and the one with the greatest prospects of survival.[8] It is the Mexican Americans who are the main contributors to this tendency; they appear to have diverged substantially from the usual pattern of dissolution of old-country language use over succeeding generations in the United States.

As we expected, many people in both the Los Angeles and San Antonio samples were bilingual. Fluency in conversation with fully bilingual interviewers was judged to be an adequate and appropriate indicator. No formal tests of fluency in English and Spanish were administered. Though it probably does not measure capacity to converse at higher levels of abstraction or with upper-status vocabulary or pronunciation, conversational fluency is enough to rate language competence for normal social functioning. By this measure 56 percent of the Los Angeles sample and 55 percent of the San Antonio sample were bilingual—that is, they could get along comfortably in either language. A very small fraction, less than 1 percent in Los Angeles and 4 percent in San Antonio, were unable to converse comfortably in either language. They had heavy accents and small vocabularies in both languages. The small numbers so rated by the interviewers contradict the frequent assertion that *many* Mexican Americans are unable to speak either language.

More respondents were comfortable in Spanish than in English; 84 percent of the Los Angeles sample and 91 percent of the San Antonio sample could get along comfortably in Spanish, but only 71 percent of the Los Angeles sample and a low 57 percent of the San Antonio sample could get along comfortably in English. Of the subsample of those comfortable in English, 79 percent in Los Angeles and 95 percent in San Antonio could also speak Spanish without notable handicap. Thus, the chances were greater in San Antonio than in Los Angeles that a Mexican American comfortable in English could also get along in Spanish. Of the subsample of respondents comfortable in Spanish, however, only 66 percent in Los Angeles and 59 percent in San Antonio could also converse in English.

At least some fluency in Spanish characterizes most of the respondents at all income levels. By contrast, almost half of the low-income Angelenos and even more in San Antonio have trouble with English. Linguistic competence—especially in English—varies by income within neighborhoods of similar ethnic composition (Table 18–1). Even in the predominantly Mexican-American areas, upper-income people have far less trouble with English than lower-income respondents. Despite the persistence of these social class differences in language ability, there is evidence that justifies treating the predominantly Mexican, heavily lower-class Colonies as special language milieus for Mexican Americans. Spanish is spoken more frequently in the Colonies, as the higher proportions of individuals handicapped in English attest. Even the linguistic environment within the family is not independent of that of the neighborhood. In Los Angeles slightly more than half and in San Antonio an even higher proportion of the poorer Colonists report that they prefer using Spanish with their children. The proportion of the more well-to-do Frontiersmen using all or mostly Spanish declines to about 10 percent in Los Angeles and only slightly more in San Antonio (Table 18–2). In Los Angeles, we find a high negative correlation between the proportion in the neighborhood speaking Spanish with their children and the proportion speaking English (rank order correlation of $-.81$).

There is an almost equally high negative correlation between the proportion speaking Spanish and the proportion speaking a mixture of languages ($R = -.67$), but a small positive correlation between the proportion speaking English and the proportion speaking a mixture ($R = .23$).

There is good reason to believe that neighborhood and social class factors as well as the individual's fluency in either language would have an independent effect on language use at home.* Mexican-American children in predominantly Anglo

Table 18-1. *Survey Respondents Conversationally Handicapped in Spanish and English, by Income[a] and Neighborhood Ethnicity, Los Angeles and San Antonio, 1965-1966*

| | BROKEN OR NO ENGLISH | | BROKEN OR NO SPANISH | |
	Percent	Total Number[b] (= 100%)	Percent	Total Number[b] (= 100%)
Los Angeles				
Frontier[c]				
Higher income	9	181	23	178
Medium income	25	75	24	74
Low income	30	77	15	78
Intermediate[c]				
Higher income	12	105	17	102
Medium income	29	96	12	93
Low income	58	72	7	73
Colony[c]				
Higher income	18	79	14	77
Medium income	40	119	9	122
Low income	51	120	10	124
San Antonio				
Frontier[c]				
Medium income	9	129	6	135
Low income	51	41	0	47
Colony[c]				
Medium income	28	180	0	188
Low income	62	202	12	221

[a] In Los Angeles: higher income = > $6,000; medium income = $3,600–$5,999; low = < $3,600. In San Antonio: medium income = > $2,760; low income < $2,760.
[b] Weighting procedures were used in the San Antonio sample. This means that total numbers cannot be used as a direct indicator of error. See Appendix H.
[c] In Los Angeles, Frontier = tracts with less than 15.0 percent Spanish-surname individuals; Intermediate = tracts with between 15.0 and 43.8 percent Spanish-surname individuals; and Colony = tracts with more than 43.8 percent Spanish-surname individuals. In San Antonio, Frontier = tracts with less than 54.0 percent Spanish-surname individuals and Colony = tracts with 54.0 percent or more Spanish-surname individuals.

areas (who, it will be recalled, tend more to have Anglo associates) come home speaking English. Even poor or otherwise isolated parents in such areas are forced into the use of English in the home. This "use of English" may be only the pattern familiar in many other immigrant groups, where parents retain the foreign tongue

*The following section draws on material prepared by Lorenzo Campbell.

and children respond in English or else a "gemixste pickles" blend of both languages is spoken by both parents and children.[9]

Fishman has suggested that the typical immigrant to a new country systematically shifts in language use as he gradually penetrates into increasing numbers of spheres (or domains) where the new language is desirable or necessary. In the first stage of acculturation in the United States, English is used only in a few spheres, such as work, where the mother tongue cannot be used; in the second stage, immigrants

Table 18–2. Survey Respondents Using Spanish or English with Their Children, by Income and Neighborhood Ethnicity, Los Angeles and San Antonio, 1965–1966

| | LANGUAGE USED WITH CHILDREN | | | |
	Spanish— All or Most	English— All or Most	Both	Total Number (= 100%)
Los Angeles				
Frontier				
Higher income	10%	50%	40%	166
Medium income	27	30	43	63
Low income	33	38	29	73
Intermediate				
Higher income	14	39	47	99
Medium income	29	32	39	83
Low income	58	18	24	66
Colony				
Higher income	22	36	42	73
Medium income	40	17	43	108
Low income	51	25	24	106
San Antonio				
Frontier				
Medium income	13	23	64	125
Low income	46	9	45	42
Colony				
Medium income	38	9	53	180
Low income	73	4	23	200

not only use English in an increasing number of spheres, but it begins to creep into their casual conversation; in the third stage there is maximum overlap between languages and spheres of life; and in the final stage, English has almost entirely displaced the mother tongue.

Applied to Mexicans, the initial stage also characterizes the newcomer to an urban area who needs to use English only in "official" situations, such as contacts with government or employer. However, if the supervisor or government official is bilingual, as Anglos often are, it is unnecessary for an immigrant to learn much English even in "official" situations, especially if he lives in a Colony area.

In many "language islands,"[10] such as the villages of northern New Mexico, this first stage has persisted over many generations. The Spanish-speaking population is relatively isolated, and the agents of the dominant language are not actively attempting to discourage the use of Spanish. Though Spanish Americans of the area frequently charge that their privileges as a "charter member" minority (Chapter 3) are not recognized in practice, the use of Spanish is legitimated by the New Mexico state constitution. A clause guarantees that "the right of any citizen of the state to vote, hold office, or sit upon juries, shall never be restricted, abridged, or impaired on account of religion, race, language or color, or inability to speak, read, or write in English or Spanish languages."[11] Even in the absence of such guarantees elsewhere in the Southwest, the history of the region has produced many Spanish-speaking islands in the rural areas and even in some larger cities. Supervisory positions in such areas are commonly reserved for the bilingual, and their availability may serve as an incentive for a few to learn English. But the masses of Mexican Americans in such areas, which usually have restricted mobility opportunities, experience little pressure to learn English, especially if the *patrón* is a Mexican American or bilingual Anglo. In such situations, the school is often perceived as a foreign element, and its use of the "foreign tongue" of English is little reinforced outside the classroom.

This suggests that for Mexican Americans the shift from Spanish to English is most fruitfully considered not only in terms of generational and chronological changes in language usage of the individual, but also in terms of a community milieu which may inhibit or enhance the possibilities of retaining Spanish or adding English.[12]

In the second stage discussed by Fishman, "more immigrants know more English and therefore can speak to each other in mother tongue or in English (still mediated by mother tongue) in several domains of behavior."[13] This is a transitional stage in which the immigrant's contacts with the dominant group increase. The domains are still separate, that is, the native language is still used in the more *gemeinschaft* surroundings of home, church, friendship, etc., and English in *gesellschaft* situations such as dealing with government and employment bureaucracies and schools. As with the first stage, this is also a relatively enduring condition for many Mexican-American communities. In some locales, jobs demanding English proficiency are scarce, but Mexican Americans need some English for everyday use. Mass media and schools are primarily English. The "second stage" may long persist in such areas, which include the *barrios* of San Antonio or El Paso where Mexican Americans must rub shoulders with the English-speaking community in a *gesellschaft* context. Such milieus are less totally isolated than those represented by the first stage, but lack of job opportunities in general makes it possible for many Mexican Americans to avoid contact with employers who demand fluent English. It is also in milieus such as this that the interference of the two languages results in the use of *pochismos*—the jargon referred to earlier.

In the third stage outlined by Fishman, "the languages function independently of each other," but "both domains overlap and the number of bilingual individuals is at its maximum." This stage is exemplified by low-income Mexican Americans living in predominantly ethnic areas in cities such as Los Angeles, which provide relatively ample opportunities for job mobility. In such settings, English is an important economic resource. Its importance is underscored by the fact that few employers, except in special occupations, feel the need of a bilingual foreman to interpret instructions. The use of English penetrates into domains which were formerly exclusively Spanish, as Mexican Americans also have more contact with Anglos in other spheres. The language at home and with friends may be either English or Spanish, or both, as friends and relatives begin to vary in ethnicity. The "stabilized interference" noted by Fishman as characteristic of the third stage is represented by the more or less standard Southwest vocabulary of *pochismos*. The generational shift is notable in such areas in cases where domestic life is still primarily a domain of Spanish for adults, but has become a domain of English for children. It is also seen in the symbolic use of Spanish among otherwise English-speaking friends or associates and the increasing ideological significance of language use.

The fourth stage for the individual would be represented by the non-Spanish-speaking *agringado*, the Mexican American who has reached the point where he is in contact only or primarily with English speakers. Such a person would also live in a predominantly Anglo neighborhood. The logical extension of the Mexican American who knows so little Spanish that it has been necessary for him to learn it in public school through the mediation of English is the Mexican American who is mono-lingual in English—the urban Mexican American whose parents already spoke primarily English. This is the ethnic living and working so predominantly with Anglos that he needs only English to compete and survive. Spanish has become as foreign to him as English is to the isolated pocket of Mexican Americans in the first stage.

REASONS FOR THE PERSISTENCE OF SPANISH

Mexican Americans depart from the typical immigrant pattern of succession through these stages in one or two generations for a variety of reasons, and these reasons are rooted in their special qualities as a minority in our society. Unlike European immigrants to the Northern cities, Mexican Americans started out as a "charter-member" minority whose only or dominant language was Spanish. Even the immigrant fresh from Mexico entering Los Angeles is affected by this past; he is under less compulsion to learn English than was the counterpart greenhorn from Europe who entered New York City two generations ago.[14]

As the isolation of the Mexican Americans began to crack, the use of English became more frequent but never quite conformed to Fishman's sequence. The Anglo owner of the King Ranch in Texas, for example, still speaks Spanish with "his *Kineños*," but the Los Angeles aerospace supervisor probably does not. With the decline in isolation there has been a decline in the institutionalized go-between functions and their agents (the *patrones*, the labor agents, and other bilinguals who arranged life for the Mexicans), and the pressure to speak English has increased. But, as indicated by the King Ranch illustration, these conditions are not by any means universal for Mexican Americans. The symbolic meanings of language use vary widely. Thus, a young Mexican-American Vista volunteer from Los Angeles County who was assigned to the *barrios* of San Antonio was mercilessly ridiculed for his clumsy Spanish. On the other hand, the new "TJs" (immigrants from Tijuana) are equally ridiculed by young Los Angeles Mexican Americans for their ineptness in English. In Tucson in the 1940s "pupils seem to have an almost irresistible impulse to revert to the informal Southern Arizona dialect at play,"[15] while in Los Angeles in the 1960s grandparents complain of their grandchildren's inability to carry on a conversation in Spanish. Another interesting case of the symbolic importance of language (as well as its utility) is that of the Mexican-American achiever who wants to act as a spokesman for his ethnic group and makes a laborious effort to improve his Spanish in order to be able to appeal to his constituency.

The individual's social environment may be further permeated by ethnicity when he uses Spanish rather than English mass media for information and entertainment. Associated with the persistent use of Spanish is an impressive array of Spanish media, especially radio broadcasting. According to an authoritative source, Spanish accounted for 66 percent of the total foreign language broadcasting in the United States in 1960 and 86 percent of the total in the West.[16] Its strength "could not have been predicted on the basis of either the number of Spanish mother tongue claimants in the American population or the circulation of the Spanish press."[17] In 1960, Spanish was the only foreign language in which some radio stations broadcast *all* their programs, as well as the only one used in all-day broadcasting. And it was the only one strong in relatively small cities. Advertising revenues are substantial, with Mexican specialties put out by major American companies (like Masa Harina, distributed by Quaker Oats) and producers of standard products like Pepsi-Cola making special efforts to capture the large Mexican-American market. Spanish-language television is also growing in the major cities, with a network hooked in with a Mexican network and running two American stations in 1967 (Los Angeles and San Antonio) and five border stations. Many of these stations are VHF, and so many viewers must purchase converters to receive their broadcasts. Despite the inconvenience and expense, however, these stations' appeal is notable; programming is predominantly imported from Mexico and includes tapes of sports events in Mexico—not only bullfighting[18] (which also attracts Anglo viewers) but also high-quality boxing and soccer—and dramatic serials and musical variety shows as well.

Data on media preferences in the home supplement the previous discussion of language environment in home and neighborhood (Table 18–3). In the predominantly Mexican neighborhoods of Los Angeles, for example, more people prefer the Spanish-language radio stations (there are two major stations) than the English-language stations, and this preference also holds for poorer respondents in intermediate neighborhoods. The story is somewhat different for television: The Spanish channel is usually the favorite only among poorer families in predominantly Mexican areas. This is a particularly interesting commentary on the marginal utility of language; these viewers are the poorest, but they are the most willing to spend money

**Table 18–3. Preferences of Survey Respondents for Spanish-language Media,
by Income and Ethnicity of Neighborhood,
Los Angeles and San Antonio, 1965–1966**

A. FAVORITE RADIO STATION

	Spanish Language	English Language	No Preference	No Radio	Total Number (= 100%)
Los Angeles					
Frontier					
Higher income	18%	56%	24%	2%	175
Medium income	25	58	16	1	73
Low income	25	30	26	19	77
Intermediate					
Higher income	22	54	22	2	100
Medium income	35	34	25	6	97
Low income	56	16	22	6	73
Colony					
Higher income	47	39	11	3	78
Medium income	57	28	14	11	124
Low income	52	27	13	8	119
San Antonio					
Frontier					
Medium income	23	52	25	0	134
Low income	52	12	28	8	46
Colony					
Medium income	44	32	20	4	187
Low income	58	19	14	9	222

B. FAVORITE TELEVISION STATION

	Spanish Language	English Language	No Preference	No Television	Total Number (= 100%)
Los Angeles					
Frontier					
Higher income	14%	54%	31%	1%	179
Medium income	16	59	22	3	74
Low income	21	43	33	3	79
Intermediate					
Higher income	10	76	14	0	97
Medium income	23	50	24	3	97
Low income	37	32	23	8	74
Colony					
Higher income	30	47	23	0	78
Medium income	34	42	23	1	124
Low income	40	36	18	6	123
San Antonio					
Frontier					
Medium income	5	63	32	0	130
Low income	26	36	24	14	46
Colony					
Medium income	18	59	19	4	198
Low income	27	35	19	19	221

Table 18–3 (cont.)

C. FAVORITE NEWSPAPER

	Spanish Language	English Language	No Newspaper	Total Number (= 100%)
Los Angeles				
Frontier				
Higher income	4%	82%	14%	180
Medium income	13	72	15	75
Low income	15	63	22	78
Intermediate				
Higher income	2	93	5	101
Medium income	19	65	16	98
Low income	31	33	36	72
Colony				
Higher income	14	80	6	79
Medium income	30	56	14	122
Low income	25	51	24	122
San Antonio				
Frontier				
Medium income	1	96	3	179
Low income	1	82	17	47
Colony				
Medium income	4	65	31	190
Low income	4	58	38	222

on a VHF television converter. In San Antonio, the preference for Spanish radio stations is strong among people in the Colony regardless of income and also among the poor living in predominantly Anglo areas. But this is not true for television. Generally, preference for Spanish media is positively related to "Mexicanness" of neighborhood, irrespective of income, and to low income irrespective of neighborhood ethnicity.

The point has been made for other ethnic groups that "Many natural supports for language use are cut off in America. . . . Even before school, television is in the home, and with it, the language of television."[19] The language heard over the airwaves at home or in the car is at least as likely to be Spanish as English in the predominantly Mexican areas of Los Angeles and San Antonio, and in this regard the younger generation of Mexican Americans (like the Puerto Ricans in New York) are less exposed to English in the home or other settings in which the personal use of the medium may be emphasized. To be sure, individual factors other than the neighborhood language milieu are related to media preferences. Women and the aging, for example, are far more likely to listen to Spanish-language radio and watch Spanish-language television, regardless of neighborhood milieu. But the major point is that the small world of the neighborhood is highly consistent in maintaining ethnic relations and ethnic exclusiveness.

A sidelight is that almost all announcers on Spanish-language stations—radio and television—are imported from Mexico or other Latin-American countries. The complaint is that the American version of Spanish is either too *pocho* (i.e., too inter-mixed with English words or constructions) or too "peasanty" (i.e., agricultural terms are used in discussing non-agricultural subjects). Local Mexican Americans are usually utilized only in "personality" spots.

Spanish-language newspapers are not as significant as the spoken or visual media. A comparatively high proportion of respondents, especially the poorer ones, have no newspaper preferences or take no newspaper. Preferences for the Spanish-language paper—*La Opinión* in Los Angeles—are smaller than those for either Spanish radio or television. Once again, Spanish is the only foreign language in which there are daily Southwest papers entirely in the language, but failures are common and circulation is unimpressive. As was true for many earlier immigrants to this country, the Mexicans were isolated from the literate tradition in Spanish, whether of Spain or Latin America.[20] In Mexico, literacy drives were instituted *after* the invention and wide use of radio, and radio communication in that country—and in this country for the Mexican immigrant—has burgeoned probably at the expense of newspaper reading. In any event, our data show that the Spanish-language press is not a serious competitor for the English-language press in these two cities.

A final manifestation of the pervasiveness of the Spanish language in mainly Mexican neighborhoods is the existence of a substantial market for Mexican films, with some dozen theaters exhibiting in Los Angeles, for example. Mexican cowboy musicals and Mexican comedies, especially those starring Cantinflas, draw large audiences. Downtown theaters also show first-run Hollywood films with Spanish captions dubbed in for first-generation audiences, which include increasing numbers of immigrants to Los Angeles from other Latin-American countries as well as from Mexico. Though Mexican movies are probably not a dominant feature of the leisure life of the Mexican Angeleno, their availability adds further strength to the Spanish-language milieu of the *barrio*.

VALUES RELATED TO PERFORMANCE

There is extensive research and theoretical literature dealing with the cultural and personal correlates of achievement. The most widely known is the seminal work of Max Weber, *The Protestant Ethic and the Spirit of Capitalism*, in which the Western cultural emphasis on achievement is traced to a psychological dynamic stemming from religious sources. Some of Weber's intellectual heirs have pursued this theme by studying the subconscious "need" for achievement as a personality characteristic. The personality correlates of low or high attainment, however, are as likely to be consequences of the status as causes of it, and for this as well as other reasons, many scholars interested in the psychocultural correlates of achievement have shifted attention to children and adolescents. Some, for example, have studied subgroup differences in child-rearing practices on the assumption that they affect personality and thus influence subgroup differences in achievement. Others have explored differences in values and attitudes of adolescents of different class levels and ethnic groups.[21]

In this study, our purposes are more specific; we are seeking to answer questions relating to the distinctiveness of Mexican-American culture rather than questions about the psychological correlates of achievement in general.

Values Related to Work

In a major study by Lenski of Catholics, Protestants, and Jews that stems directly from Weber's *Protestant Ethic*, systematic differences were found between these subgroups when they were asked about what factors were important in a man's job. Significantly, the study revealed that internalized gratification from work (the factor most closely related to Weber's *Protestant Ethic*) was most frequently found to be important to occupationally mobile individuals. Extrinsic values—including income or chances for advancement—were far less significant.[22]

Table 18–4. Survey Respondents Saying Specified Job Feature Is "Very Important," by Income, Los Angeles and San Antonio, 1965–1966

	Job Feature[a]							
	STATEMENTS CONGRUENT WITH PROTESTANT ETHIC[b]			STATEMENTS CONTRADICTING PROTESTANT ETHIC[c]		PRESUMED MEXICAN VALUES[d]		Total Number[e] (= 100% in each cell)
	1	2	3	4	5	6	7	
Los Angeles								
Higher income	56%	43%	64%	57%	13%	36%	46%	362–366
Medium income	52	56	60	56	11	35	47	291–297
Low income	53	51	58	52	13	28	47	267–276
San Antonio								
Medium income	60	62	69	61	15	45	48	320–324
Low income	47	57	67	64	20	40	47	264–268

[a] Questions 1–5 are adapted from Gerhard Lenski, *The Religious Factor* (Garden City, N.Y.: Doubleday and Co., Inc., 1963). See text discussion.
[b] Statements congruent with Protestant Ethic:
    1. The work is important and gives a feeling of accomplishment.
    2. High income.
    3. Chances for advancement.
[c] Statements contradicting Protestant Ethic:
    4. No danger of being fired.
    5. Working hours are short, lots of free time.
[d] Presumed Mexican values:
    6. You get a feeling of belonging.
    7. People take you as you are.
[e] Figures represent the range of responses given by each subcategory to each of the 7 items.

The questions used by Lenski have been modified for our survey. For each of seven work rewards, each respondent was asked whether he felt the reward to be very important, important, or not important. The percent finding each job feature to be "very important" is presented in Table 18–4.

Each of the rewards can be conceptualized in relation to the ostensibly achievement-producing Protestant Ethic. According to Lenski, the first statement, that "the work is important and gives a feeling of accomplishment", "best expresses the classic Weberian understanding of the term," i.e., of "Protestant Ethic". The second statement—"high income"—expresses the "current popular understanding of the term," while the third—"chances for advancement"—"occupies a middle ground between the other two. A concern with chances for advancement is consistent with both classical and current usages." With regard to the fifth statement, "working hours are short, lots of free time," Lenski comments that "it was designed to express a view completely in opposition to any conception of the Protestant Ethic," as was the fourth—"no danger of being fired"—though the latter's relation to the Protestant Ethic is more ambiguous.[23] The fifth alternative—"working hours are short . . ."—will be familiar to those acquainted with the stereotypes of Mexican Americans; it is also recognizable as a value prized by the so-called "target worker" who quits his job when he has made enough to satisfy some particular need. The sixth and seventh values were added in the Mexican-American surveys because they reflect other, significant, though perhaps friendlier stereotypes of Mexican Americans: "You get a feeling of belonging" and "people take you as you are."

Although our questions were not identical with Lenski's, it seems that the Mexican-American responses are well within the "normal" American range of value patterns as represented by his Detroit sample. The first three values relating to the Protestant Ethic are generally affirmed by the respondents, as they are by Lenski's random sample of Detroit, and the fifth, representing the opposite of the Protestant Ethic, is rated very low, as is also the case among the Detroiters. Security (statement 4) ranks relatively high among our respondents—a not unexpected finding for this group. The sixth statement reflects the "value orientation strongly emphasizing interpersonal relations."[24] It receives moderate support from our respondents. The final statement, "people take you as you are" is given a rather high rating, though it may have been interpreted as much as a plea for an end to prejudice as it is a "typically Mexican" value.

Generally, the differences between San Antonio and Los Angeles responses tend to reinforce our earlier analysis of Mexican Americans in these two cities, especially among the low-income respondents. In addition to valuing more highly the "Mexican" feeling of belonging, San Antonians, living as they do in a milieu which is not only more "Mexican" but offers more reason to worry about job security, value job security more than do Angelenos. In one respect, the San Antonio data present a surprising finding. Chances for advancement are generally *less* valued among Angelenos and most valued among the San Antonians—higher as well as lower income. This anomaly is not easily explainable, but it may reflect a much lower beginning point in San Antonio, with a consequent greater need to "advance." For example, advancement in San Antonio may mean a change from a part-time to a full-time job, rather than mobility up the status ladder as it is usually conceived.

Income differences are not noteworthy in most responses (nor are other differences, e.g. age or ghettoization of residence). In other words, the work-related values are fairly pervasive at all class levels in each of the two cities. This somewhat unexpected finding makes the similarity with Lenski's observations for Detroit even more significant.

Some of the perceptions of the job world by Mexican Americans seem to differ from those of other Americans. To probe into this aspect of cultural values, we asked a question that had been used with a nationwide sample in 1946, namely, "What occupation would you advise a promising young man to enter?"[25] Admittedly, the comparative data represent the United States of a generation ago, but even so, differences between Mexican Americans and the national sample appear to be far greater than the time gap alone might produce (Table 18–5). Mexican Americans were more professionally oriented and much less attracted to the entrepreneurial occupations—the last especially in the case of San Antonio. This may indeed reflect something of the time difference between the two surveys, since professional occupations have come into greater prominence in recent years. But it also reflects the low participation of Mexican Americans and other minorities in any but small and mainly "ethnic" businesses (Chapter 9). If indeed Mexican-American cultural preferences currently militate against business in favor of professional work, the importance of education is heavily underscored.

Table 18–5. Occupation Toward Which a Promising Young Man Should Aim, National Sample of 1946 and Los Angeles and San Antonio Mexican-American Samples of 1965–1966, by Income Level

	Professional	Managerial and Proprietorial	Craftsmen and Foremen	Clerical and Sales	Other	Depends on Person, Don't Know	Total Number (= 100%)
National Sample, 1946[a]							
Prosperous	58%	12%	5%	7%	10%	8%	514
Middle-class	54	10	12	8	9	7	1531
Poor	38	11	19	7	17	8	856
Los Angeles Mexican Americans							
Higher income	65	4	4	6	5	16	339
Medium income	51	6	9	7	7	20	250
Low income	46	3	6	6	4	35	218
San Antonio Mexican Americans							
Medium income	63	7	1	4	7	18	272
Low income	45	11	2	14	11	17	196

a Figures are derived from Albert J. Reiss, Jr., *Occupations and Social Status* (New York: The Free Press, 1961), p. 27.

Obviously, the responses to a single question can do little more than raise issues, but these differences appear to call for further exploration. The Mexican-American response pattern also shows extraordinary particularism. Far more than any other subgroup in the national sample, Mexican Americans responded to the occupational preference question with some statement implying that job choice depends on the person and is an individual matter. The particularistic response was given by almost half the Mexican-American women and 18 percent of the men as compared with only 7 percent of the national 1946 sample. It was quite a common response among low-income Mexican Americans as well, and among both the oldest and youngest respondents. These responses may reflect the time gap and some general social trend toward more particularism in advising the young toward the future. Again, the differences are of such magnitude that they bear further investigation.

Table 18–6. Responses to "Activism" and "Integration With Relatives" Scale Items: Four Samples
(Percent disagreeing with statement)

	Item Number[a]							Total Number[b] (= 100% in each cell)
	ACTIVISM				INTEGRATION WITH RELATIVES			
	1	2	3	4	5	6	7	
Los Angeles Mexican Americans (household heads and spouses)								
Higher income	65	75	74	4	93	80	79	344–359
Medium income	51	64	76	28	85	66	64	282–292
Low income	37	59	65	20	74	52	59	233–277
San Antonio Mexican Americans (household heads and spouses)								
Medium income	54	71	83	41	85	76	71	283–317
Low income	43	52	62	31	65	51	43	228–248
Los Angeles poverty-area sample (household heads)[c]								
Mexican American	57	n.a.	71	n.a.	74	n.a.	n.a.	165–218
Negro	59	n.a.	66	n.a.	89	n.a.	n.a.	332–352
Other	58	n.a.	75	n.a.	91	n.a.	n.a.	40–62
Mexico City sample (males)[d]	54	55	64	34	75	73	40	737–740

[a] Items:
Activism-mastery
1. Making plans only brings unhappiness because the plans are hard to fulfill.
2. It doesn't make much difference if the people elect one or another candidate, for nothing will change.
3. With things as they are today, an intelligent person ought to think only about the present, without worrying about what is going to happen tomorrow.
4. The secret of happiness is not expecting too much out of life and being content with what comes your way.

Integration with relatives
5. When looking for a job, a person ought to find a position in a place located near his parents, even if that means losing a good opportunity elsewhere.
6. When you are in trouble, only a relative can be depended upon to help you out.
7. If you have the chance to hire an assistant in your work, it is always better to hire a relative than a stranger.

[b] Figures represent the range of responses to the seven items.
[c] See note 26 for source. Items were worded somewhat differently.
[d] Data provided courtesy of Joseph A. Kahl, Washington University.
Source for items: Joseph A. Kahl, "Some Measures of Achievement Orientation," *American Journal of Sociology*, LXX May, 1965), pp. 680–681.

General Value Patterns Related to Achievement

There are several approaches to the study of the values underlying an achievement orientation or, as some scholars perceive it, of the "components" of achievement orientation. This analysis focuses on two value clusters which have been found to be significantly related to achievement in other populations. One concerns attitudes toward "mastery" or "activism," that is, taking active control over the environment by planning. The other value cluster concerns attitudes toward independence from relatives or feelings about whether or not people should cling to their kin. The two value clusters are formulated in seven statements which are reproduced at the bottom of Table 18–6.

Since the same seven questions were used in a study conducted in Mexico City,[26] international comparison is possible on this issue of "acculturation" to American achievement values. In the Mexico City study, the two value scales—with additional items—produced correlation coefficients with socioeconomic status of .49 and —.46, respectively. These were the two highest correlation coefficients obtained of four scales tested. Inferences from the comparison must be limited, however. Among other things, only males were included in the Mexico City sample. Similar short questions were asked in an early survey by the Mexican-American Study Project of people of several ethnic groups living in Los Angeles poverty areas.[27] Hence, we can also extend the comparison to the heads of poor Negro, Mexican-American and Anglo households for an inter-ethnic analysis of "acculturation."

In almost all items, most respondents of whatever ethnicity, city, or country *disagreed* with both the passive stance of the statements in the Activism scale and with the affiliative stance of the Integration-with-Relatives scale (Table 18–6). The only exception was their response to the statement "The secret of happiness is not expecting too much out of life, and being content with what comes your way."

This finding is at wide variance with the notion that Mexican Americans are extraordinarily passive and attached to relatives to the detriment of achievement. The responses are especially noteworthy when it is recalled that the Los Angeles and San Antonio Mexican-American samples are half female, and that women tend to be more traditionalistic in such response patterns than men. Furthermore, the results cast serious doubt on the notion of *Mexican* culture as being distinctive; men in Mexico City sound at least as "acculturated" as most Mexican-American respondents on all but two of the seven items. One (number 7) refers to nepotism, which is more readily accepted in Mexico City than by people of Mexican descent in either Los Angeles or San Antonio, and the other (number 2) refers to the efficacy of the electoral process, about which men in the Mexican capital appear to be more pessimistic. Of course, the findings in Mexico City may not hold for the entire country any more than those for Angelenos and San Antonians hold for rural Texas or New Mexico. The tenacity of cultural values in Mexico seems to vary greatly between cities and rural areas and among cities of different size and economic growth, and there are indications that rural Mexican-American values may be still more retentive of traditional elements than even their Mexican counterparts. Be this as it may, the comparison of Mexico City with Los Angeles and San Antonio is a comparison of large cities and therefore quite revealing.

The essential similarity in the central tendencies of these responses reaffirms many findings on the basic cultural similarity of industrialized nations, whether European or non-European in tradition. As one writer comments: "Men's environment, as expressed in the institutional patterns they adopt or have introduced to them, shapes their experience, and through this their perceptions, attitudes and values, in standardized ways which are manifest from country to country, despite the counter-vailing randomizing influence of traditional culture patterns."[28] If *international* studies of values show such similarity, it seems logical to expect that inter-ethnic studies would do likewise. Granted, there are marked differences between individuals of various social-class levels and between groups who live in various general social settings. In fact, degree of ghettoization as well as income seems to affect the response patterns as it does language behavior. But the data show no support whatsoever for the notion that Mexican Americans are culturally unique with regard to two value clusters significant to achievement: their belief in potential mastery of their environment (activism) and their attitudes toward independence of or integration with relatives.

SUMMARY

Cultural and especially language distinctiveness have often been seized upon by Mexican-American spokesmen to support their claims to special attention for their people. Many ideologues have emphasized "cultural maintenance." Their arguments find echoes in the literature of the social sciences. They are found both in research reports and in more general statements, including those in which an attempt is made to offer a cultural explanation for the low collective attainments of the Mexican Americans. Most of the research documents, however, provide findings too limited for generalizations. Many of the more general statements suffer from the deficiencies of the basic research data.

In large part because of the loyalty of Mexican Americans to their mother tongue, Spanish is indeed the language with the greatest prospects for survival among all of the languages represented in the United States. Its persistence among Mexican Americans reflects the unusual and long-lasting degree of isolation of large segments of the group from interaction with the larger society, as well as the relative recency of mass migrations and the continuous arrival of newcomers. Our surveys showed more Mexican Americans speaking inadequate English than speaking inadequate Spanish, especially among the poor in predominantly Mexican areas and particularly in San Antonio. There was far less of a language handicap in English among those living in mixed neighborhoods. Language use at home is also related to neighborhood ethnicity and social class. Spanish-language radio is more popular than Spanish-language television, and Spanish-language newspapers reach comparatively few respondents. The Spanish-language media are most popular among the poor, those living in ethnic Colonies, women, and older people.

Mexican Americans do not appear to possess distinctively traditional values of the kind frequently attributed to them. Much like other Americans, and probably much like other urbanites in industrial countries, most want to get ahead in their work; they want work that gives them intrinsic satisfactions; many hope for job security and higher income. Consonant with the actual composition of the Mexican-American upper income group (Chapter 9), they would tend—somewhat more than most other Americans—to aim their young people toward professional jobs, though many would hesitate to guide the occupational choice of the young. On the whole, Mexican Americans are not notably more passive, nor do they value integration with relatives more than most other populations on which data were available. However, passivity and desire for integration with relatives increases among the poor and is generally somewhat greater in San Antonio than in Los Angeles.

On the two critical points of language use and cultural values related to achievement, the data analyzed here, as elsewhere in this volume, provide the beginnings of a reassessment of the Mexican American in the contemporary world. A large body of literature has stressed the cultural distinctiveness of the ethnic group, but most of it concerns studies which were made in such isolated places or are so dated that their findings are almost irrelevant to an understanding of the present-day person of Mexican descent in an urban milieu. As usual, the popularizers of the research literature, including many Mexican-American spokesmen, have drawn generalizations from work related to a particular place and time, and have sometimes ignored cautions advanced by the scholars themselves. Unfortunately, there is a danger that policy at the national and local levels may be formulated from the simplistic popular versions instead of from the more complex originals.

The ostensibly distinctive cultural traits of Mexican Americans vary within the urban milieus, with social class and neighborhood factors playing a very significant role. Generally, however, the ethnic values bearing on achievement seem to be far less tenacious and far less pervasive than the main literature and its principal users suggest. At the same time, Mexican Americans have remained highly distinctive in their loyalty to their mother tongue. Our analysis makes it clear that ethnic culture perhaps more than any other area warrants continuing intensive research directed toward the urban native-born Mexican American, now the major element among all Mexican Americans.

NOTES TO CHAPTER EIGHTEEN

1. Jane McNab Christian and Chester C. Christian, Jr., "Spanish Language and Culture in the Southwest," in Joshua A. Fishman, et al., *Language Loyalty in the United States* (The Hague, London, and Paris: Mouton & Co., 1966), p. 315.

2. Robert G. Hayden, "Spanish-Americans of the Southwest," *Welfare in Review*, IV (Apr., 1966), pp. 14, 15. Secondary analyses of the distinctive Mexican-American culture, often quite detailed, are found in Ruth Landes, *Latin Americans of the Southwest* (New York: McGraw-Hill Book Company, 1965) and Celia S. Heller, *Mexican-American Youth* (New York: Random House, Inc., 1966), among others.

3. Florence Rockwood Kluckhohn and Fred L. Strodtbeck, *Variations in Value Orientations* (Evanston, Ill.: Row, Peterson & Company, 1961), p. 353.

4. *Ibid.*, p. 257. It might be noted that Kluckhohn's intent in this monograph was *not* to understand Mexican Americans but rather to understand cultural variation. Taking findings about a particular culture out of the comparative context, therefore, can lead to confusion: The Spanish Americans were "the most unique" in comparative context, but examined separately they showed an increasing tendency toward similarity with the dominant culture.

5. Margaret Clark, *Health in the Mexican-American Culture* (Berkeley: University of California Press, 1959). Clark describes the neighborhood which is the site of her study as follows (p. 43):

> *San Jose Sal si Puedes* differs from representative neighborhoods of the Mexican-American colony in three important ways: First, it is populated almost entirely by Spanish-speaking people; thus its residents are more isolated from Anglo customs and beliefs than most Mexican-American neighborhoods in San Jose. Second, partly as a result of social insulation, more Mexican patterns of life are retained in *Sal si Puedes* than in other *barrios*. Third, it is one of the poorer neighborhoods within the colony.

6. Arthur J. Rubel, *Across the Tracks: Mexican-Americans in a Texas City* (Austin, Tex.: University of Texas Press, 1966).

7. Ruth D. Tuck, *Not With the Fist: Mexican-Americans in a Southwest City* (New York: Harcourt, Brace and Company, Inc., 1956).

8. Joshua A. Fishman and John E. Hofman, "Mother Tongue and Nativity in the American Population," in Joshua Fishman et al., *op. cit.*, p. 37. Using survey data from several cities, including San Antonio, Robert Hayden makes much the same point with regard to Mexicans' use of Spanish in "Some Community Dynamics of Language Maintenance," in the same volume.

9. Joshua A. Fishman et al., "Language Maintenance and Language Shift as a Field of Inquiry," in *ibid.*, appendix B.

10. See Heinz Kloss, "German American Language Maintenance Efforts," in *ibid*.

11. State Constitution of New Mexico, Article VIII, Section 3 (New Mexico Bluebook: 1921, p. 21). Of contemporary New Mexico, Nancie González remarks that "The Spanish language . . . is still the primary symbol of the cultural dichotomy between Anglos and those of Spanish and/or Mexican heritage." Nancie L. González, *The Spanish Americans of New Mexico: A Distinctive Heritage* (Mexican-American Study Project, Advance Report 9, Graduate School of Business Administration, University of California, Los Angeles, Sept., 1967), p. 17.

12. The distinction between individual and community analysis of bilingualism is made in Joshua A. Fishman, "Bilingualism With and Without Diglossia; Diglossia With and Without Bilingualism," *Journal of Social Issues*, XXIII (Apr., 1967) pp. 29–38. "Bilingualism" here refers to the individual level of analysis and "diglossia" to the communal language use.

13. Fishman, *op. cit.* p. 434.

14. The importance of the general shift in language use over time, however, is indicated by the fate of the "Spanish mother tongue" criterion of classifying respondents as Mexican American in the U.S. census. A number of serious questions were raised about the validity of this technique after it was used in the 1940 census. By 1950, enough objections had been voiced to cause the shift to identification by Spanish surname.

15. George C. Barker, "Social Functions of Language in a Mexican-American Community," *Acta Americana*, V (July-Sept., 1947), p. 199.

16. Mary Ellen Warshauer, "Foreign Language Broadcasting," in Fishman et al., *op. cit.*, p. 80.

17. *Ibid.*, p. 86.

18. According to the executive vice president of Los Angeles' KMEX, some 3,800 protest letters were received when the FCC threatened to suppress broadcasts of bullfights.

19. Nathan Glazer, "Process and Problems of Language-Maintenance," in Fishman et al., *op. cit.*, p. 367.

20. See Robert E. Park, *The Immigrant Press and Its Control* (New York: Harper &

Brothers, 1922) for an analysis of this type of situation and its consequences in Europe for the linkage between nationality consciousness and use of the vernacular.

21. The literature in this field is voluminous and controversial, and it is outside the scope of this study to add to the theoretical issues. Only a few of the more significant works will be mentioned here. A general work focused on the personality need for achievement gave rise to a large literature on the so-called "n-ach." See David C. McClelland, *The Achieving Society* (Princeton, N.J.: D. Van Nostrand Company, Inc., 1961). Bert Kaplan (ed.), *Studying Personality Cross-culturally* (Evanston, Ill., Row, Peterson & Company, 1961), presents several discussions relevant to this topic, most notably one comparing Russian and American personality data. On the generally greater impulsivity, etc., of lower-status individuals, Oscar Lewis, *The Children of Sanchez* (New York: Vintage Books, Inc., 1961) is probably the most influential general work, though his focus is on the "*culture of poverty*" rather than on its psychological correlates. See Ralph Turner, *The Social Context of Ambition* (San Francisco: Chandler Publishing Co., 1964) for an analytic review of the literature on social class and adolescence. Concerning literature relating to social class and Negro-white child-rearing differences, one of the earliest and most influential studies is Allison W. Davis and Robert J. Havighurst, "Social Class and Color Differences in Child-rearing," *American Sociological Review*, XI (Dec., 1946), pp. 698–710. Urie Bronfenbrenner has synthesized much of the controversial research literature on social-class differences in child rearing in "Socialization and Social Class Through Time and Space," in E. E. Maccoby, T. M. Newcomb, and E. L. Hartley (eds.), *Readings in Social Psychology* (New York: Henry Holt & Co., 1958).

22. Gerhard Lenski, *The Religious Factor* (Garden City, N.Y.: Doubleday & Company, Inc., 1963), pp. 89–92.

23. Quotations in this paragraph are from *ibid.*, p. 89.

24. Christian and Christian, *op. cit.*

25. This is the "North-Hatt" study fully analyzed in Albert J. Reiss, Jr., *Occupations and Social Status* (New York: The Free Press, 1961).

26. Discussed in Joseph A. Kahl, "Some Measures of Achievement Orientation," *American Journal of Sociology*, LXX (May, 1965), pp. 669–681.

27. The scales employed by Kahl in his Mexico City study were derived from a "V-scale," or value scale, which was developed for a study of relative achievement of Italian and Jewish teenagers. See Fred L. Strodtbeck, "Family Interaction, Values and Achievement," in David C. McClelland et al., *Talent and Society* (Princeton, N.J.: D. Van Nostrand Company, Inc., 1958). Before Kahl's modification of this scale was published in May, 1965, the Mexican-American Study Project had added two short sets of questions to an already funded study of extreme-poverty tracts in heavily Negro and Mexican-American areas. Three of the items used in this poverty area sample were employed (with modifications in wording) by Kahl in his Latin American research. The original wording of the items used in the Los Angeles poverty area study was as follows:

1. Planning only makes a person unhappy since your plans hardly ever work out anyway.

2. Nowadays, with world conditions the way they are, the wise person lives for today and lets tomorrow take care of itself.

3. When the time comes for a boy to take a job he should stay near his parents, even if it means giving up a good job opportunity.

None of the items is precisely comparable with Kahl's, but the correspondence seems great enough to warrant inclusion of the responses in our discussion.

28. Alex Inkeles, "Industrial Man," *American Journal of Sociology*, LXVI (July, 1960), p. 2, cited in Kahl, *op. cit.*, p. 677.

Part five

THE ROLE OF CHURCHES

INTRODUCTORY NOTE

The next two chapters analyze how the Roman Catholic Church and the Protestant denominations in the Southwest have been functioning for the Mexican-American population. Churches are viewed here as organizations that can act as agencies of socialization of values in childhood and of social control over values and conduct throughout the individual's life span. Churches are, of course, also institutions of the larger society, that is, they are agents of inter-ethnic as well as intra-ethnic contact. How they operate within a distinctive minority reflects the societal milieu as well as religious or ethical norms. Thus, the impact of the churches on a culturally different and socially subordinate population such as the Mexican Americans can be highly significant to that population's adaptation to American society. Because most people in this group consider themselves Catholic, the impact of the Roman Catholic Church is especially relevant.

This kind of institutional analysis is rare either in the standard literature on religion or, for that matter, in the writings about Mexican Americans. There are a great many cultural descriptions of Mexican-American religious customs, practices, and attitudes. One reads of the cleavage between the Mexican American and the Anglo American due to religious differences, with indications that Roman Catholic parishes have reflected ethnic cleavage in their congregations. Immigration to the United States is said to result in conversions to "normal, non-fanatic Catholicism" or to Protestantism, or in indifference or unbelief. Recent writers have explored the function of religious conversion in upward-mobility striving, or the organization, ceremonies, and religious practices in a *barrio* parish. Because churches have been rarely analyzed as social organizations, our approach involved the development of a considerable amount of original research materials.

The religious institutions of the Southwest, Protestant and Catholic, began to be concerned with the Mexicans very early—at a time when schools, government agencies, and political institutions were ignoring them or, at best, tolerating their presence. For decades before the schools or government agencies thought of Mexican Americans as a "problem," Protestants and Catholics alike were organizing missions and haranguing each other about the best way to "reach" these people. In the long view, their struggles seem prototypical of later work by Anglo institutions.

First, both the Catholic Church and the Protestant denominations felt a special religious imperative to reach out to the Mexican Americans. Religious care was the first and primary mandate of the institutions. This was especially significant for the Roman Catholic Church, of which most Mexicans were members (even though their membership, because of pagan remnants and later because of the anti-church orientation of the Mexican Revolution, was in "jeopardy"). The much fainter religious obligation of the Protestants to the pagan—Mexican or other non-Christian— was reflected in their much weaker attempts to reach these people. Later, nonreligious institutions similarly developed their own special obligations toward the ethnic group.

Second, as institutions of the larger society both Catholic

and Protestant churches had the secular mission to Americanize the Mexicans. For the Catholic hierarchy in the United States, Americanization was an important strategy for institutional survival during much of the time considered here. For the Protestants, until very recently, the task of Americanizing foreigners was an explicit part of the overall home mission ideology. The Americanization theme is also common among non-religious institutions in their later contacts with Mexicans.

Both Catholic and Protestant churches in the Southwest have operated under conditions of organizational weakness and lack of funds. For both, the areas of the Southwest were in a sense "frontiers." We have suggested earlier that this weakness and poverty characterized many Southwest institutions.

Both Catholic and Protestant churches have operated also under over-all conditions of change in Christianity, and particularly in American Christianity, that have been near-revolutionary. Beginning at the turn of the century, value shifts have pushed both Catholics and Protestants in the direction of increasing social emphasis combined with a more differentiated pastoral emphasis. Both churches have become increasingly flexible in their structure. For the Protestants, ecumenism seriously challenges denominational boundaries; for the Catholics, internal structures throughout the Church are undergoing radical upheavals.

Under these broadly similar general and local conditions, then, it is not surprising that both Catholics and Protestants evolved many parallel organizational roles and units as well as similar values supporting their dealings with Mexicans. Furthermore, since the religious institutions of the Southwest shared many features with other institutions, some of these values and organizational elements are paralleled in other reaching-out efforts. (Of course, the parallels should not obscure the separate institutional constraints any more than parallels between Catholics and Protestants should obscure the very real differences.)

Organizationally, both the Catholic and Protestant churches have had "Mexican mission specialists"—religious orders such as the Claretians and Oblates among the Catholics, and special mission bodies among most of the Protestant denominations. These were groups organized within the larger church bodies. Of course, a large proportion of the Catholic effort was conducted under the regular hierarchy, and only some of the Protestant effort was conducted under regular congregational aegis. Most of the members of these mission groups were probably "Mexicanists," that is, Mexican Americans or others who had a special interest in or aptitude for "reaching" Mexicans, and who became interpreters of these people to their institution as a whole. Thus, there was specialization on both the organizational and the individual role levels in efforts to turn Mexicans into practicing members of these American institutions. And as a notable institutional strategy, both Catholics and Protestants have utilized segregated bodies—more often on a *de facto* basis among Catholics, as in all-Mexican parishes, and more often on a conscious *de jure* basis among Protestants. In all probability, such segregated bodies served as intermediate structures for individual Mexican Americans who were becoming acculturated to the institution.

Perhaps the most useful perspective from which to view the parallels between Catholic and Protestant activities among the Mexican Americans, then, is one which considers the churches as institutions of American society. In this perspective, the structures evolved over time and the rationales supporting these structures bear striking similarities to non-religious institutions. For example, the schools, like the churches, have developed "Mexicanists" who specialize in working with Mexican-American children, interpreting them to Anglos and preparing them to enter the larger system; the schools, like the churches, have utilized the device of segregation to cope with the Mexicans; the schools, like the churches, present a shift of values from emphasis on Mexican-American conformity to existing institutional norms, to emphasis on institutional adaptation to the local social structure of the Mexican-American group. The churches, however, were among the first social institutions to develop these patterns of relationship with the Mexicans.

In the value sphere, the continuum from a conservative tradition to a liberal position will be noted in the analysis of both Catholic and Protestant. If one abstracts from the purely religious content of this continuum (that is, from pastoral-social action for Catholics or from evangelical-social gospel for Protestants), it can be generalized to the analysis of other institutions. The conservative tradition requires that the "client" should become totally immersed in the values of the institution; the liberal position maintains that the institution is there to serve the "client." Of course, neither position is mutually exclusive, and the difference between the conservative and the liberal is a matter of emphasis. Thus, the religious liberals argue that the social gospel is an enlarged concept of evangelism. Adherence to values at either end of the continuum will be shown to imply special stances toward Mexican Americans—from paternalism through self-determination, from priority on conformity to the institution's norms of conduct through priority on the institution's assistance to the client in his non-institutional roles. The value continuum suggests a fundamental difference: the institution as an end versus the institution as a means.

In light of this conceptualization of the conservative-liberal value continuum, it is not surprising to see that the individuals and groups within both Protestantism and Catholicism who have been most prone to the liberal position are those who are *structurally* liberated from the institution. The liberals among both Catholics and Protestants, for example, have worked in cooperation with non-religious agencies such as labor unions, the Office of Economic Opportunity, and other groups that are explicitly or implicitly designed to change the general status quo within which the religious institutions function. It appears a plausible hypothesis that in non-religious institutions as well it will be the individuals and groups on the institutional *margin* rather than those at the *core* who will be able to undertake more flexible programs for members of ethnic groups.

447

NINETEEN

Dynamics of the Catholic Church: From Pastoral to Social Concern

THE role of the Catholic Church in the lives of Mexican Americans has been importantly conditioned by two factors. One is the clergy's prevailing view of these people as uninstructed in the faith and deficient in their adherence to the general norms of Church practice. The other is the inadequacy of resources available to the Church in the Southwest. Mexican immigration placed the resources, scarce to begin with, under special strain, for the clergy was faced with immigrants from a country that had gone through a protracted struggle between church and state.

The historic conflict between the Church and government in Mexico had grave consequences for the Southwest Church. It resulted in a chronic shortage of priests in

Thanks are due to the officials of the California Province of the Society of Jesus, who made it possible for Patrick H. McNamara to engage in the study incorporated in this chapter; to Edmundo Cardenas for valuable assistance in the historical research; to Joan Foley and Carmen Carillo, who coded diocesan newspaper accounts used in the content analysis; and to the Rev. Francis J. Weber, archivist of the Archdiocese of Los Angeles.

Mexico that became even more acute after the Revolution.[1] Consequently, many of the nominally Catholic immigrants were ignorant about their religion, with only tenuous loyalties to the institutional Church and formal Catholicism. There had never been many parochial schools in Mexico and they were finally outlawed by the Constitution of 1912.[2] The textbooks and teaching programs in public education had an anti-religious flavor.[3] Hence, some immigrants brought to their new environment an anticlerical upbringing.

Further, most of the immigrants came from the lower classes and the agricultural areas in which the influence of the Church in Mexico had been weakest. The religiosity of the Mexican lower classes was different from the ecclesiastically accepted and sanctioned Catholicism expressed in regular Mass attendance, frequent reception of the sacraments, and some articulate knowledge of basic doctrine.[4] Their "folk Catholicism" combined some aspects of normal Catholic practice with pagan (Indian) rites. Thus, the typical Mexican immigrant was not a strongly practicing "Mass-and-Sacraments Catholic."

All of this meant that the clergy in the Southwest had to spend an extraordinary amount of effort to fulfill its prescribed role of ministering to the needs of a rapidly increasing flock. Contrary to the notion that the immigrant would seek the Church for support and comfort during the trying interval of adjusting to a new country, a notion valid for most Catholic immigrants to the East, in the Southwest the Church had to reach out for the newcomer if it was to perform its function. This would have been difficult under the best of circumstances; the poor resources at the command of the Southwest Church made it an overwhelming task.

THE LEGACY OF POOR RESOURCES

When the present Southwest was annexed to the United States in the mid-nineteenth century, the Roman Catholic Church there lay in a state of near collapse. The decay was partially attributable to the Spanish and Mexican "decrees of secularization" of the mission churches, the backbone of the Catholic presence in the Southwest. The liberal governments of Spain, and later of Mexico, were hard pressed financially to continue their support of the missionary enterprise under provisions of the *patronato real* (royal patronage).[5] Attempting to disengage the traditional alliance of church and state, the governments issued decrees providing that the wealth accumulated during the ten years prior to their issuance be distributed equitably among the neophyte Indians of the missions. All other property, including church buildings and priests' quarters, was turned over to the bishop, who, in turn, was to appoint parish priests. Thus, the mission disappeared and gave way to a regular parochial church.[6]

However, no diocesan priests were available to take over the churches. For many years, the mission churches in Texas were practically abandoned.[7] New Mexico

[1] Notes for this chapter start on page 478.

450

and Arizona were not much better off.[8] In California, Bishop Garciadiego graphically portrayed the moribund state of the Church in 1846:

> San Solano, San Rafael, San Francisco, San Antonio, San Juan Capistrano, etc., are without . . . funds, without tithes, without priests, and without the hope that any may want to come, since they are aware how those fare who are here, without schools, and without the means to establish them. In short, without anything upon which to base hope, it is impossible to advance, and so the diocese is on its way to destruction.[9]

The personal inadequacies of some of the priests emphasized the shortage of competent clergy. Historians, biographers, and diarists all comment on the "scandalous conduct" of certain clergymen.[10] Bishop Lamy of Santa Fe had to excommunicate five native priests shortly after his installation.[11] In addition, he had to cope with conflicts between the native Spanish priests and the French clergy whom he had brought to New Mexico.[12]

Historically, religious-order priests were usually the first to enter "unevangelized" territory. The Oblate Fathers of Mary Immaculate came from France to South Texas in 1847, and for several decades they constituted the majority of priests in this vast area. Spanish Franciscans founded and staffed the California missions. Even after the formal establishment of the dioceses in the Southwest, bishops plagued by a shortage of diocesan priests invited religious-order priests to staff parishes and schools. Spanish Claretian Fathers came to both San Antonio and Los Angeles in the early 1900s. Orders arriving subsequently to work with Mexican-American Catholics included Immaculate Heart Mission Fathers, Vincentian Fathers, and Piarist Fathers, to name but a few. In 1966, 18 of 26 pastors of Mexican-American parishes in San Antonio were members of religious orders. Los Angeles, on the other hand, had only six religious order pastors among 26.

Until recent years, when American-born priests began to fill the ranks of religious orders, priests born in Spain were a majority of the religious-order priests assigned to work with Mexican Americans. A fairly widespread impression depicts Spanish priests as relatively authoritarian in such pastoral concerns as sexual morality, financial contributions, and attendance at parochial schools, and somewhat wary of Americanization programs which, they felt, jeopardized the "faith" of the Mexican American. Additional research is necessary on this topic.

The Roman Catholic Church of the Southwest contrasted sharply with the well-established, even flourishing (though at times persecuted) Church whose parishes stretched from Boston to St. Louis.[13] Over this wide expanse, the Church grappled quite successfully from 1840 to 1900 with Catholic immigrants coming from over twenty different countries. It developed an urban organization equipped with church buildings, schools, and agencies of general charity. Irish Catholics were the earliest to arrive in large numbers—over a million and a half by 1870.[14] Priests came with them, and the Irish have supplied the majority of members of the American hierarchy ever since. The importance of their leadership lies in their efforts to establish the Catholic Church in the Midwest and East as "genuinely American" and to defend it against the attacks of the Know-Nothings, the American Protective Association and, later in this century, the Ku Klux Klan. The Americanization crusade was the chosen instrument of this defensive and self-legitimating strategy.

Catholics who spoke no English developed their own national parishes, which became "a powerful factor in conserving group solidarity within the ethnic tradition."[15] However, the Irish bishops made sure that these parishes were not perpetuated indefinitely, but rather encouraged American citizenship and the learning and use of English. The Church had not only to survive, as the hierarchy saw it; it had to grow as an institution fully accepted on and adapted to the American scene. The Irish clergy "were men qualified by their aptitude for politics and their knowledge of English, and by the dominant position they occupied in the Church, for just this work."[16]

As the immigrants made economic progress, the Church in the East and Midwest became financially more secure than it had ever been in Europe. The conditions under which the Church functioned in the Southwest were quite different. In contrast to the Catholics in the Northeast and Midwest, those of Mexican background formed a subordinate population quickly dominated by largely Protestant Yankees who settled in the area during the latter part of the nineteenth century. Their Catholicism was just another cultural characteristic setting them apart from and, in many instances, sharply against the Anglo Americans. In turn, Anglos aggravated antagonisms by bringing with them a crusading Protestant zeal for converting the "poor ignorant Mexicans."[17] As early as 1850, Bishop Odin of Texas expressed concern about the activities of the Bible Society of New York, with "the fatal poison of their contagious doctrines."[18] As will be seen in the next chapter, such fears were quite exaggerated in light of the actual weakness of Protestant proselytism.

Institutionally, too, the Southwest Church differed significantly from the established Catholicism of the East. No firmly structured Church existed to mediate the encounter of the Mexican and Anglo cultures. No equivalent of an Irish hierarchy was present to see to it that churches and schools were provided and foreign-language priests appointed. The new American bishops were not ruling over large, relatively compact and populous urban centers. They were literally *padres* on horseback,[19] responsible for isolated settlements of rural Spanish-speaking Catholics. They received practically no financial support. Unlike their counterparts in Chicago, Philadelphia, and New York, they were plagued with a severe shortage of clergy that lasted well into the twentieth century.[20] Furthermore, the new bishops were not Americans, nor was English their native tongue, and they could scarcely perform the "bridging role" of an Archbishop Ireland of St. Paul or a Cardinal Gibbons of Baltimore. The vast majority of bishops in Texas and New Mexico, until very recent times, were French, and they recruited priests from their native land.[21]

Priests of other nationalities arrived eventually, particularly in Texas, but they settled among the Bohemian, Polish, and German communities formed by immigrants in the latter part of the nineteenth century. In any event, their ethnic composition was such that Catholicism in Texas "suffered under the label of being a foreign Church"[22]—the very designation the Irish hierarchy in the East and Midwest had feared and could combat more effectively.

Roman Catholicism among immigrants in the Midwest and East was generally strong enough to resist Protestant proselytizing efforts.[23] But the shortage of priests and the lack of funds for parochial schools left Spanish-speaking Catholics in the Southwest open to secularizing and also to Protestant influence. Warner and Srole point out that the parochial schools in Yankee City functioned "to orient the child to the American social system," as well as to transmit cultural elements of the ethnic group.[24] The scarcity of parochial schools in the earlier decades of this century seriously inhibited this function in the Southwest.[25]

The major structural liability of the Southwest Church, the relative shortage of priests, is summarized in Appendix J.

PASTORAL CARE VERSUS SOCIAL ACTION

The Church we have seen so far is best described as a missionary institution whose most appropriate symbol is the *padre* on horseback. His saddlebags laden with Mass kit, holy oils, and catechism, a rosary dangling from his belt or cincture, the *padre* rides on an emergency mission, saying Mass in a rural chapel, baptizing and confirming, validating civil marriages with the Church's blessing, instructing, bringing sacramental comfort to the sick and dying. He represents an institution serving a "clientele" perceived as floundering in an emergency situation; Mexican immigrants are woefully uninstructed and non-practicing by standards of the missionary *padres*. They must be provided with the religious essentials. But what are the essentials? This question introduces the crucial problem of the goals and goal priorities of the Church.

The Church is a normative organization. It strives for the intense commitment of its members to the means necessary to achieve its basic objective—their eternal salvation and indeed that of all human beings. These means are well summarized by Joseph Fichter:[26]

> Certain truths must be believed by all members of the Church. These constitute the Christian creed. There are also certain patterns of conduct, called "the Christian code of behavior," as outlined basically in the Ten Commandments, the counsels of Christ, and the precepts of the Church. Third, the Christian cult, or form of worship, comprises the sacramental, liturgical, and devotional system of the Church. Finally, the Christian communion of all members with one another idealizes the essential social nature of the Church.

When these necessary means are conceptualized as goals in their own right, they constitute "pastoral goals" or "pastoral orientation," the first type of goal considered here. In saying Mass, preaching, administering the sacraments, in assisting "those in his parish who are ill, especially those who are near death,"[27] the priest is carrying out his fundamental pastoral mandate, set down in Canon Law and sanctioned by Church tradition.

The mandate is fundamental in the sense that priests and bishops accept these functions as their primary duty. They are so trained from their earliest years in the seminary. Pastoral goals are institutionalized as first-rank functions. They take precedence over other possible activities in which Church representatives may engage, and this precedence is embedded in their consciences and in responsibilities before superiors.

An important consequence of this primacy is that other goals can receive little, if any, attention as long as pastoral needs are urgent. The Church defined the Mexican Americans of the Southwest as a religiously deprived "target population." The large numbers of immigrants coming into a region already understaffed served only to perpetuate the primacy of the pastoral response—"as long as the emergency lasts," and it has lasted, with intra-regional variations, to the present day. As Warner and Srole imply in their analysis of the Church in a different environment,[28] other goals became important only after the emergency pastoral needs were met.

It is not enough, then, to say that the Church is a multi-purpose organization. The more significant point is to determine the conditions which permit a variety of functions to be performed. Parochial schools and the Americanization crusade were already mentioned as characterizing the East-Midwest axis of the American Catholic Church. As will be seen, the Southwest Church, too, has its history of functioning beyond the pastoral goals. It has at times provided extensive welfare services for the Mexican-American community, has sponsored citizenship classes and youth organizations, has engaged in anticommunism campaigns, and has recently seen some of its clerical representatives demonstrate in picket lines on behalf of striking Mexican-American farm workers, directing antipoverty programs, and testifying on minimum-wage legislation before Congressional committees.

However, such activities in behalf of a deprived minority have varied a great deal in time and location. Much of our discussion will be devoted to these variations. It will also indicate *how* the goals of the Church came to be more differentiated and will lay the basis for defining the relationship between pastoral and non-pastoral goals.

Maintaining the focus of other parts of this volume, we deal principally with the Roman Catholic Church in the archdioceses of Los Angeles and San Antonio. Not only is the Spanish-surname population highly concentrated in these two areas, but the other dioceses of the Southwest, with the exception of Santa Fe and Tucson, were originally sections of these two major archdioceses. Their present archbishops have played an important role in the selection of bishops within their respective jurisdictions. Thus, the traditions and policies of these two major archdioceses exert considerable influence on their surrounding dioceses.

PASTORAL GOALS: SOUTH TEXAS, 1920–1940

Despite the scarcity of resources available to the Church, some members of the Catholic hierarchy in Texas succeeded in going beyond strictly pastoral care. Thus, between 1914 and 1941 Bishop Anthony J. Schuler of El Paso established hospitals, clinics, orphanages, and day nurseries, largely with help received from the Catholic Extension Society.[29] However, these efforts were not intended to effect far-reaching changes in the levels of living of the Mexican-American population. The climate of public opinion in the region was not conducive to social reform, and a Church just beginning to grow and sponsor allied institutions for the benefit of the community was not likely to challenge the status quo.

It made no difference in ecclesiastical policy, then, that the papal social encyclical *Rerum Novarum*, promulgated by Leo XIII in 1891, urged an equitable wage level and defended the right of workingmen to form organizations to improve their bargaining power.[30] What mattered was the Church's teaching as stressed at that time in Texas. For example, in 1921 an editorial in the *Southern Messenger*, a Catholic newspaper serving all the dioceses of Texas, reminded "the would-be economist" who searched for "a panacea for the social and economic ills of society" that "the main business of the Church on this earth is concerned with the individual soul." At the same time, it asserted that the Catholic Church "stands firm behind all true labor unionism." Catholic writers "never hesitate, in season and out of season, to urge its importance and necessity."[31] Yet, in a region where immigrant Mexican laborers worked under desperate conditions, no hint was given that the Church's social teaching might apply to them directly.

But the conditions of Mexican Americans did not go unnoticed by the priest-missionaries struggling with their pastoral labors. In the pages of *Mary Immaculate*, a small monthly published by the Oblate Fathers of Mary Immaculate (who, until recently, provided the majority of priests in the Corpus Christi diocese), detailed diary-like accounts were published in almost every issue. Six articles appearing between 1928 and 1934 indicated a remarkable awareness of the Mexican Americans' problems.

One missionary commented on the changes brought about by irrigation. Where only Mexican settlers existed before, now a "prosperous American community, largely Protestant . . . devote their energies and their money to the development of the country." The Mexicans are laborers "who carry out the industrial part of the work." The result is that "we have, in fact, two absolutely distinct people, two classes of society as widely apart as the castes of India."[32] Another priest wrote of "the sordid huts, set back in intricate obscure lanes." Mexicans "work for a pittance," suffer and endure "their sufferings as only Mexicans can, with barely enough to eke out a miserable existence."[33] A third, writing of Crystal City, Texas, noted that the winter harvests there brought in, annually, "thousands of Mexicans from elsewhere, to divide or take away entirely, at lower prices, the work from the home population.

Occupation and a fair wage for 8,000 people hardly means more than tortillas and coffee for 16,000."[34]

A later writer told his readers that Mexican immigrants are "often subject to very unfair discrimination and contempt." Because they know no English and belong "to the very humble class of the cheapest day laborers, they are regarded with scorn." The "middle-class Mexicans," especially, "deeply resent the fact that they are treated as an inferior race." They suffer "bitterly as a result of social and racial prejudices of which they are the victims."[35]

Despite the awareness of social injustices, however, there were no indications in the Catholic press that it might be incumbent upon Catholics, laity and clergy, to work toward a change in these conditions. They were viewed as evil, but accepted as part of a given framework within which one's pastoral duties were performed.

The conditions that militated against the Church's orientation toward social-action goals were a stress on pastoral functions within the operative teaching of the Church at this time in Texas; a continuing shortage of priests and financial weakness; a climate of laissez-faire in the larger society, reflected in emphasis on the individual in local interpretations of Catholic social teaching; and a population of Mexican immigrants and previous settlers considered woefully in need of the pastoral essentials. Given these conditions, it was highly unlikely that priests would assume the role of social reformers. To play such a role would have seemed at best futile and at worst directly subversive of pastoral efforts.

A social-action orientation, however, may arise in service of pastoral goals themselves. Such an orientation would legitimize and secure the pastoral goals in the face of attacks from hostile forces, e.g., Protestant missionaries. A strategy particularly favored by Church authorities has been participation in various Americanization programs of governmental or other agencies, or the adoption of Church programs for the same purpose. Yet, this strategy carries within it the seeds of conflict. The attempt to "make Americans" out of the foreign born may be interpreted as a threat to the religious welfare of the group, exposing it to American "materialism" and, worst of all, Protestantism. The following sections illustrate 1) social action adopted as a defensive strategy and 2) the resulting intra-Church conflict.

SOCIAL ACTION
IN SERVICE OF PASTORAL GOALS:
LOS ANGELES, 1920–1949

In the present Archdiocese of Los Angeles, comprising Los Angeles, Orange, Santa Barbara, and Ventura Counties, Mexican Americans represent a large part of the Roman Catholic population. Despite the importance of this group to the Church (and vice versa), no literature exists on the role of the Church among the Mexican-American population. However, the weekly diocesan newspaper is an important source of information and insight. *The Tidings*, the official organ of the Archdiocese, has reflected in its news articles and editorials the shifts in official concern with this minority. To mine this primary source of data systematically, a content analysis procedure was applied (Appendix J). Generally, though, articles on the Mexican Americans are quite rare. This population was obviously not a central concern to the archdiocese.

The earliest noteworthy themes in *The Tidings* in the first quarter of the century were the fear of Protestant proselytism and the need to Americanize the Mexicans. In contrast to the clergy's efforts in Texas, where the Church was still struggling to bring the Mass and sacraments to a scattered rural population, Los Angeles Catholic social workers and benefactors had established two settlement houses as early as 1905. As an article in 1910 clearly indicates, these activities were prompted not only by pastoral concern but also by the fear of Protestant proselytism.[36] In November 1918, $50,000 was allotted by the National Catholic War Council to Bishop Cantwell of Los Angeles for "Americanization work." In recruiting teachers for the program, a *Tidings* article stressed that Americanization (focused primarily on Mexicans) was pre-eminently a Catholic responsibility.[37]

Between 1920 and 1929, only 17 *Tidings* articles dealt with Mexican immigrants and the Church. Americanization as such was deemed important in only 4 of the 56 themes in these articles. But half of the themes dealt with activities, such as youth work and vocational and citizenship programs, that indirectly demonstrated the Church's interest in helping the Mexican immigrant adapt to American patterns.

These major themes of *The Tidings* also appeared in the annual reports of the Bureau of Catholic Charities, which was organized in 1919. The Bureau's work was handicapped by financial struggles until 1924, when it became a charter member of the new Community Chest of Los Angeles. This affiliation indicated increasing integration of the Church with the larger society, and it had a striking concomitant. As soon as the Community Chest began contributing to the Bureau, references to combatting Protestant proselytism ceased. Americanization themes continued, however. The 1926 Report spoke of the failure of efforts to have Mexican aliens take out citizenship papers—"only 3 percent of the Mexican people become citizens"—and it recommended that English and civics be studied "so that in time the settlement members as a whole might have a wholesome influence on the governmental practices of the community."[38]

Church officials recognized the larger problems that lay at the root of the continuing poverty of the Mexican immigrant population. Bishop John J. Cantwell, quoting papal teachings, preached a "living wage" for the Mexican laborers and advocated organization of "artisans and laborers . . . to tell . . . their problems and troubles."[39] However, the bishop avoided mention of *union* organization specifically. This was a time when labor unions were in disfavor in Los Angeles. A Church still

457

viewed with concern and suspicion by many in the dominant society was unlikely to incur the risk of advocating institutionalized conflict.

Significantly, the 1930–1932 issues of *The Tidings* contained only one short article on the repatriation of tens of thousands of Mexicans from Los Angeles, which took place during this period.[40] Content analysis of ten articles appearing between 1933 and 1941 shows continuing emphasis on pastoral care. Six of 11 themes classified as "major" dealt with strictly religious activities—four with special religious instruction classes for adult Mexicans, reflecting the problem of religious socialization whose origin we have seen in Mexican history. The pastoral emphasis is underscored strongly in a 1937 editorial, which points out that too many Catholics were asking the Church to be concerned with "merely human and worldly objects" and continues:

> The business of the church is divine. To seek the things of the next world, not of this. . . . Christ did not found the Church to be a mere humanitarian institution. The Church is a teacher. She works to bring God's grace to the souls of men. . . . She has, in fact, plenty to do to attend to her own business.[41]

In the late 1940s, youth problems became increasingly serious in East Los Angeles. The content analysis of 17 *Tidings* articles between 1942 and 1948 shows that 6 out of 15 major themes dealt with juvenile problems. The Catholic Youth Organization attempted to work inside the Mexican gangs, recruiting leaders to become "youth directors." The public presentation of these efforts by *The Tidings* was cast so as to rehabilitate the image of the Mexican-American teenager. An article in 1943 pointed out that "in a district which was once condemned by the public press as a hotbed of juvenile delinquents," the local parish had developed "normal" youth activities. The writer comments, "Public condemnation fell upon all of the Mexican youths, and not just the few who were at fault."[42]

In the immediate postwar years, the communist threat became an important theme. Reprinting an article by Louis Budenz, *The Tidings* attempted to alert its readers to the danger of communist exploitation of Mexican-American grievances. Budenz expressed alarm that "the Reds were able to attract almost 10,000 Mexican Americans to hear Henry Wallace speak in Spanish at Los Angeles during the 1948 election campaign."[43] The Communist movement was seen as a threat to Catholic allegiances and loyalties. The *barrio* dwellers were pictured as happy families, needing not social reformers but ministers of the gospel.[44]

Nevertheless, there was some recognition of other ways of "saving people for the Church." A *Tidings* article in 1948 reports the founding of the Catholic Labor School in East Los Angeles, with evening classes in industrial ethics, parliamentary procedure, and public speaking. It seems that this effort was prompted in part by concern over reported communist infiltration of the movie industry. The Mexican-American men who began to attend the school lost interest in most of the classes except those for citizenship, which were encouraged by Mexican-American political figures who envisioned increased voting strength in the community.[45]

AMERICANIZATION: LOS ANGELES, 1949–1967

In the postwar era, the Church's concern shifted increasingly away from purely pastoral care to other subjects, notably to efforts at Americanization and to a massive program of parochial school building. The stress on Americanization may have been related to the return of Mexican-American GIs who were pressing for full acceptance in Anglo society. This postwar concern for helping integrate the Mexican American into the larger society and protecting him from subversive forces appears in the content analysis of 25 *Tidings* articles between 1949 and 1967. Only 6 of 25 major themes dealt with strictly religious topics. Youth work was the subject of eight articles; others focused on citizenship classes, anticommunism and, in the last few years, on antipoverty programs.

The building of parochial schools in the Mexican-American community has been an outstanding feature of the Los Angeles Archdiocese during the past two decades. The general policy of the Catholic Church in the United States has been to place responsibility for parochial schools with each parish. This policy necessarily leaves poorer parishes at a disadvantage. It is not surprising, then, that only 30 percent of the Los Angeles parishes in heavily Mexican-American areas had parochial schools in 1948 as against 58 percent of all other parishes (according to data in the *Catholic Directory*).

The prime motivation for building additional schools in Mexican-American parishes seemed to be a strong suspicion of public education. Monsignor Thomas J. O'Dwyer, a prominent spokesman on social issues for the Archdiocese, expressed this concern:

> Many who attend public schools have tended to regard themselves as superior to their Mexican-born parents . . . and to repudiate all that they stood for, beginning with the Catholic Faith. . . . There has been a tendency to identify freedom as freedom from the so-called shackles of Catholic dogma and doctrine, and progress towards a wholly secularist outlook and the concept that religion is purely a private matter and scarcely a primary matter at any rate.[46]

Building Catholic schools was the obvious answer. Shortly after his installation, Archbishop J. Francis McIntyre proposed that several million dollars earmarked by his predecessor for construction of a new cathedral be used for parochial schools. In 1948, he referred to "the large numbers" of the "future citizens of this fair city" who will come "from the children of this eastern area of the city today." Parochial schools, he hoped, would provide a "safeguard in their traditions" and preserve them "from an American brand of liberalism."[47] By 1960, practically every parish in East Los Angeles had a parochial school.

The familiar Americanization theme was another motive in the archbishop's promotion of parochial schools for Mexican Americans. In a 1949 address to a largely Mexican-American audience, he said: "We look to the Mexican people to take leadership in American ideals, to take their places in the government." The Church, he assured them, would do all it could "to further their opportunity."[48] In a dedication ceremony for a parochial school in a Mexican area, the Spanish-born pastor in 1953 echoed the archbishop in proclaiming the patriotic value of the parochial school. "Apart from being a true protection against juvenile delinquency," he said, the school "has opened . . . the doors to genuine American life with its integral sense of the human person as a child of God, Christian and democratic."[49]

The school building program, then, was an important manifestation of a twofold strategy adopted by the Los Angeles Church leadership and to some extent by other Church officials in the Southwest: 1) to preserve and defend the Catholic faith of the Mexican American and his offspring against Protestant influence and, later, against communism, moral "liberalism" and "secularism"; 2) to exhibit the Church to the larger society as an institution instilling American ideals into its laity of Mexican background, i.e., only under Catholic auspices and supervision could Mexicans be made into good, loyal Americans.

This strategy was seriously challenged in 1947 even before the school building program got underway. A notable illustration of goal conflict within the Catholic Church, the challenge was contained in a memorandum "Religious Assistance to the Mexicans in the United States." The letter was addressed not to a local superior, but directly to Pope Pius XII. In an unusual departure from normal procedure, the Apostolic Delegate in Washington forwarded the document to each of the Southwest bishops, with a request for comment.[50]

Though unsigned in the version transmitted to each bishop, the memorandum leaves the impression of being written by a priest of Mexican background. In describing the "problems of religious assistance to the Mexicans residing in the United States," the writer adduces four "fundamental reasons underlying the problem:" 1) the "psychological race differences" between Anglo-Saxon and Mexican people; 2) the differences between and consequent difficulties of the Spanish and English languages; 3) the strong attachment of the Mexicans to their national traditions; 4) the almost unanimous determination of the "North Americans" to Americanize the various groups of immigrant residents in the United States.

Space does not permit detailed analysis of this document, but its message is clear. A vast majority of the Southwest's Spanish-speaking people "today live for the most part far from the practice of their religion." The susceptibility of Mexicans to Protestant proselytizers (with Methodists and Pentecostals especially mentioned) is blamed on the American Catholic hierarchy. The solution attempted by the hierarchy, continued the document's author, has been Americanization, but this "is usually equivalent to loss of the Catholic Faith."

The writer proposed that "priests and religious of the Spanish tongue" should be "put in charge of these churches," since "experience teaches that American priests find it most difficult to learn Spanish well enough to speak in public." Besides, "the Mexican does not go willingly to churches frequented by Americans" but prefers instead to "assist at the functions celebrated according to the customs of his country with much song and long discourses."

Three bishops voiced strong objections to the document. Archbishop Lucey of San Antonio was less defensive and admitted that "educational and social care . . . does not suffice in the case of the Mexicans." All of the responses minimized or failed to answer directly the charge that Americanization contributed to conversions to Protestantism.[51]

SOCIAL ACTION AS A COORDINATE GOAL

The preceding sections discussed two types of Church goals: strictly pastoral, and social involvement in service of pastoral concerns. Yet another type of goal calls for social action in its own right. Three developments illustrate this orientation: the Bishops' Committee for the Spanish-Speaking, the San Francisco Spanish Mission Band of 1949–1962, and the more recent activities of priests in California and Texas in helping Mexican-American farm workers to organize.

It is always difficult to date goal reorientation of a large organization precisely. Nevertheless, one does not go far wrong in designating World War II as the period in which social action for its own sake began to be adopted in the Southwest Church, at least by parts of its administrative hierarchy. The Nazi ideology had brought racial questions to the forefront internationally. On the domestic scene, riots in Detroit and elsewhere involving in-migrant Negro and white war workers pointed up our own racial problems. The zoot-suit riots in Los Angeles were even closer to home. The Office of War Information issued brochures on ethnic groups in the United States to minimize social friction among people moving from place to place for military service or industrial war work. One of these brochures, authored by George I. Sanchez, dealt with the "Spanish-American people."[52] At the same time, the conditions of the migratory workers who came from Mexico to help harvest America's war crops caused problems of direct concern to the Church.

The Bishops' Committee for the Spanish-Speaking

In 1943, the Social Action Department of the National Catholic Welfare Conference called a meeting of 70 Church and civil leaders from areas with large Mexican-American populations. This meeting, in San Antonio, was "the first general conference ever held by Catholic leaders at work among the Spanish-speaking people of the Southwest."[53] In his keynote address, Archbishop Lucey referred to the Federal and state governments as allies:

> We no longer stand alone. The administration in Washington, through the Office of the Coordinator of Inter-American Affairs, is showing an intelligent and helpful interest in these problems. State officials and citizens generally are aroused over the lethargy and mistakes of the past.

461

Archbishop Lucey emphasized social reform. Poverty and discrimination "have robbed many [Mexican Americans] of educational opportunities. . . . In normal times they are given the worst jobs with the lowest pay." Conditions in Texas were singled out in these words:

> A very general lack of labor organizations, the absence of good legislation and the greed of powerful employers have combined to create in Texas dreadful and widespread misery. The evil men who are driving tens of thousands of our people into a slow starvation will be held to strict accountability by the God of eternal justice.

The archbishop recommended an organization on the state or interstate level to "analyze and attack our problems of industry, agriculture, relief, housing, race discrimination" and the development of leaders "among the Spanish Americans themselves."[54]

Action was taken in January 1945. The American Board of Catholic Missions, based in Chicago, agreed to underwrite a "Bishops' Committee for the Spanish-Speaking."

The Committee's work over the years is indeed indicative of a change in orientation from strictly pastoral to social action.[55] For example, the Committee supported the termination of the *bracero* program. On other matters, it was more cautious. Thus, union organization was first recommended in terms of the *right* to organize; only in the early 1960s, when public opinion seemed to swing in favor of farm workers' unions, did the Committee call for actual organizing efforts. One of the less tangible results of the Bishops' Committee was increased interaction of Catholic laity and clergy interested in the Spanish-speaking people both pastorally and socially. This interaction occurred at a time when a number of the dioceses had enough priests to release some of them for full-time work among this population, again illustrating the dependence of social action on resources. Nevertheless, it is questionable whether the Bishops' Committee has improved the lot of the Spanish-speaking significantly. Pastors asked about this subject expressed divided views about the Committee's influence.[56]

The Spanish Mission Band, 1949–1962

Stimulated by their attendance at a Regional Conference of the Bishops' Committee in 1948, two priests of the Archdiocese of San Francisco persuaded the hierarchy to release four clergymen from territorially based parishes. These men were to work exclusively with Mexican farm laborers in some of the counties of central and northern California. Traveling from settlement to settlement, the priests used portable altars to say evening Mass, trained catechists to instruct adults and children, recited the Rosary with families, and heard confessions "under the open sky, in the station wagon, or in a car." In other words, their work began with strictly pastoral functions.

Soon, however, the priests began to expand beyond these functions. In April 1954, one of them asked permission "to explain the teachings of the Church on labor-management cooperation." The letter in which he made this request was carefully guarded, and so was the response which granted the request.[57] No reference was made to advocacy of union organization. In California's social milieu of 1954, the time was not ripe for such a direct approach. But this correspondence and the subsequent events demonstrated growing awareness by the Mission Band priests of the conditions which kept so many Mexican families at a poverty level and which they came to define as injustice.

In 1959, however, Father McDonnell, the priest who had initiated the new type of work, spoke of the clergy's efforts to encourage "both producers and workers to organize into associations and unions. . . . Legislators have been called upon to include all workers, especially those employed in agriculture, under the jurisdiction of the National Labor Relations Act" and extend to them other legal protection (including the termination of the *bracero* program). Finally, "we have urged Catholic laymen to undertake with courage at this crucial time the immense work of organizing the desperately needed farm unions."[58]

The priests now were not simply preaching social justice, but were taking action to advance it. Though they had begun their Spanish-speaking apostolate with pastoral perspectives, social-action goals had emerged.[59] Such an involvement was apt to lead to complications. As the priests attended union meetings to explain the social teachings of the Church concerning the right to organize, opposition developed among the growers and ranch owners. The local parish clergy received letters from growers challenging the priests' authority to speak as representatives of the Catholic Church. Pressures reached a climax in 1958 and 1959, when large numbers of growers in the Stockton area sent the Bishop a signed statement saying that unless he halted "this thing and pulled his priests out of it. . . . The Church should be registered as a lobbyist and . . . denied tax-free status."

Eventually the Mission Band priests were assigned to various parishes with Spanish-speaking Catholics. By the time the Archdiocese of San Francisco was divided into three separate dioceses (1962) the work of the Mission Band as such had ceased.

Evidence on the role of pressure from growers in the dissolution of the Mission Band is difficult to obtain. The priests interviewed for this study seemed vague on the matter. The division of the archdiocese meant, of course, that the priests would be located in different jurisdictions, each of which might evolve its own policy with regard to work among the Spanish-speaking. When the *bracero* program came to an end in 1964, the number of Mexican migrants diminished, and the respective bishops apparently felt that existing parishes could serve the predominantly resident Mexican-American population without the help of "specialists."

Despite its short history, however, the Mission Band illuminated a general evolution. Until the early 1950s, the pastoral needs of the Mexican agricultural laborers in the San Francisco archdiocese were not adequately met through the common parish structure. The creation of priest specialists was the answer. But in the process of focusing almost exclusively on Mexican Catholics, these priests became aware of a range of problems beyond the strictly pastoral. By identifying themselves with the plight of the migrants, they assumed responsibilities beyond those perceived by the average parish-based pastor. This development became a common pattern; one of the necessary conditions for moving from pastoral concern to social action among Mexican Americans was the release of priests from a territorially based parish. The consequent day-to-day involvement with Mexican farm laborers created a heightened sensitivity to the larger socioeconomic issues which were seen to under-lie their religious condition. The involvement, in turn, brought intense opposition in the larger society that created serious difficulties for the Church.

THE PRIESTS' ROLE IN STRIKES

Shortly after the Spanish Mission Band was dissolved, the direct involvement of priests in social action took a new and more dramatic form, first in the Delano grape strike and later in attempts to organize farm labor in south Texas. These struggles, beginning in September 1965, have received more nationwide attention than almost any other news concerning Mexican Americans. Scarcely an article or news account on the subject fails to mention the role of the churches, Protestant and Catholic.

Again, "outside priests" were the first to support the Delano strike. The meeting of the committee which unexpectedly voted to strike was held in the local Catholic parish hall. The pastor, a Spaniard by birth, had consented to the use of the hall for a union meeting, but in Cesar Chavez' words, "he told me later that a day before the meeting, he began to get calls every 15 minutes from the growers for hours and hours, just one after the other. . . . You know, a planned harassment against him."[60]

Shortly after the meeting, the pastor went to Spain, but when he returned the pressure was resumed. At this point, two priests from a northern California diocese joined the picket lines: the pastor and the assistant of a Mexican parish who were also prominent priest-directors in their diocese's Cursillo Movement. Despite Chavez' friendly warning to the two clergymen that the local Roman Catholic bishop wanted no priests on the picket line, the two continued to demonstrate. One result was a letter of the local bishop to the bishops in California asking that no clergy from other dioceses come into the Delano area. Another consequence was opposition by em-ployers. Growers wrote and telephoned chancery offices, labeling the priests as "outside agitators." When they returned to their diocese, the two priests were taken to task, and under pain of suspension from priestly duties they were enjoined to refrain from association with all persons connected with the strike and from all statements regarding the issues, including the fact that they had been disciplined. They were not to leave the diocese.

Though the two priests were silenced, action continued at higher levels. A "Committee of Religious Concern" composed of eleven nationally prominent church representatives, Protestant, Catholic, and Jewish, visited Delano in December 1965. In a statement made at the conclusion of their visit, they deplored the failure of local growers, clergy, and community leaders to appear at a scheduled meeting. They called upon the strikers to continue their walkout until "their just demands were recognized," asked Governor Brown and the State Legislature to pass legislation ensuring the right of collective bargaining, and urged President Johnson and Congress "to enact Federal legislation extending the provisions of the National Labor Relations Act so that it includes agricultural workers."[61]

In a personal statement one of the committee members, the Reverend James L. Vizzard, S.J., Executive Secretary of the National Catholic Rural Life Conference, insisted that the strikers had a right to expect moral support from the Catholic Church. However,

> Church authorities often are frozen with fear that if they take a stand with the workers the growers will punish them in the pocketbook. . . . Church institutions do not exist for their own sake. Nor does the Church itself exist solely for the comfortable, affluent, and powerful who support those institutions. Christ had a word to say about the shepherd who, out of fear and because the sheep weren't his, abandoned the sheep when they were under attack.[62]

Though Father Vizzard's statement brought a strong rebuttal from the Bishop of Monterey-Fresno, nothing was done officially to censure the priest-executive. His national post insulated him—a protection that has been important in more than one instance. Nor did the interfaith statement elicit any replies from the Catholic leadership of the area. The local bishop almost two months later set forth his own, more cautious views. The Church, he said, "has attempted to create an atmosphere of Christian justice and charity in which to search out an equitable solution. But she has not taken sides. The Church supports the theories and concepts of social justice which groups may set forth. She does not, however, endorse or align Herself with a particular union, owner organization, or other secular enterprise."[63]

The Mexican-American field worker, however, did not view the Church's position in the same light. Chavez said in an interview that his biggest worry during the first six months of the strike was to keep his men from picketing the bishop or the local church, or picketing during Mass. "I just put my leadership on the line and said it's not going to be done and I'm not even going to explain why, but there are certain things where someone has to have respect." Chavez added, however, that the strikers stopped attending Church.

Shortly thereafter, clergy intervened on behalf of Mexican Americans in the Rio Grande Valley area of Texas. Archbishop Lucey of San Antonio, who had always supported labor organization and minimum-wage legislation, had long fostered a climate legitimating social action on behalf of Mexican Americans. In the spring of 1966, when a movement paralleling the Delano strike began in the lower Rio Grande Valley, two priests of the Archdiocese of San Antonio, the Reverend William Killian, executive editor of the archdiocesan weekly, and the Reverend Sherill Smith, the social-action director of the archdiocese, went south to Brownsville, the scene of a developing labor conflict. The priests joined the field workers in picketing, attended several rallies, and marched in an eight-mile "pilgrimage." Father Killian addressed the strikers on the steps of the Rio Grande City Courthouse: "The priests are here from San Antonio to show the power structure that these people are not apart. They must receive dignity and respect. . . . The people will march and march until they have their rights."[64]

The subsequent pilgrimage march featured the American flag, the flag of the National Farm Workers Association, and banners of Our Lady of Guadalupe. According to a newspaper report, "the religious atmosphere was inescapable. Three Catholic priests marching with the people signified the Church's presence."[65]

The situation was complicated by an interim regime in the Diocese of Brownsville due to the bishop's death. During the interregnum, local pastors expressed opposition to the activities of the visiting priests. The San Antonio priests were "intruders who did not speak for the Church." The strikers did not need a union "but if they ever do, and if they go about it properly, they will receive all the support they need." When asked whether he thought that Catholic social principles were involved in the dispute, a local monsignor replied, "I am not able to say. I was ordained to offer Mass and bring the Sacraments to the people."[66]

When the new prelate, Bishop Humberto Medeiros, took over, he assumed a "balancing role." In an address to both field workers and growers he stated that "a minimum wage necessary for a citizen to live like a human being is $1.25 per hour." He defended the right of union organization, yet also that of "any other group of men who need to unite in order to protect and defend their right against the unjust demands of either management or labor." The role of priests, he continued, was "to preach the justice and charity of the Gospel and urge both sides to listen to the voice of reason and faith and adjust their differences in a friendly way for the good of all."[67] The bishop gave $1,500 to a local pastor for "needy families in the area."

As in Delano, the local clergy refrained from committing themselves or were somewhat hostile to the strike. With both field workers and growers constituting their congregations, the local priests felt caught in the middle.[68]

At the hierarchial level, Bishop Medeiros reportedly made it clear to Archbishop Lucey that he wanted no more "outside priests" coming into his diocese. The diocese could "handle its own problems." However, the Archbishop continued to support the workers' demands.[69] Meanwhile, opposition from growers was mounting. For example, to Ray Rochester, the general manager of the La Casita farms, the largest of those being struck, "those two priests (Fathers Smith and Killian) were acting as labor organizers, actively organizing and using their position of the priesthood."[70] When three priests (Father Killian and Father Smith among them) visited the strike area again in January 1967 against orders to the contrary, they were arrested by Rio Grande City authorities for trespassing on private property, released on their own cognizance, and sent back to San Antonio. The Archbishop ordered Fathers Killian and Smith to New Mexico for a mandatory retreat. When his action was publicly protested by four other priests in the city's leading daily, the four were suspended from their priestly duties.

Unlike their fellow-priests of the Archdiocese of San Francisco ten years earlier, then, the social-action clergy of the mid-1960s was operating in a climate of social protest related to far-reaching changes in the external world affecting the Church. The civil-rights movement sensitized them to conditions affecting minority groups and influenced their attitude toward ecclesiastical authority. But the more decisive social-action orientation was also determined by internal changes in the Roman Catholic Church. One of these was the rapid development of the Cursillo Movement.

THE INFLUENCE OF THE CURSILLO MOVEMENT

The Cursillo Movement, initiated in Spain in 1947 and brought to the United States ten years later, has provided definite impetus to social involvement. It has already had an impact on the Mexican-American community of the Southwest. Cesar Chavez and other prominent Mexican Americans are *cursillistas.*

Cursillistas meet for three-day periods of intense religious renewal and dedication. The movement brings together lay persons and priests in an atmosphere remote from daily concerns and from the parish-oriented contacts between the clergy and the laity. Perhaps more important to our subject, Mexican-American and Anglo Catholics meet in an environment dissociated from social conflict and emphasizing common membership in "the People of God." The three days of the Cursillo are packed with techniques of both group dynamics and the old-fashioned frontier revival. Lay persons usually give fifteen of the major talks, the priest-director only five. "Christ's message" of dynamic self-reform and responsibility for others is woven into presentations of traditional doctrinal themes. The intended result is a lifetime commitment to active Christianity within the Roman Catholic Church. One of the special facets of the movement is its attempt to recruit men first. Only after a group of men has made the Cursillo are their wives invited. This approach counteracts the "Latin" bias against male religious commitment and participation.[71]

Most Cursillo directors, priests and laymen, do not conceive the movement as directly oriented to social action. *Cursillistas* are urged to join existing parish and diocesan organizations and explicitly warned against forming their own ingroup. But it is hardly an accident that all of the social-action priests named in the previous section and many Mexican-American laymen prominent in the farm-worker struggle and other reform movements are *cursillistas.* It seems, then, that the Cursillo attracts action-oriented Catholics and that it may motivate its members toward social involvement.

Accompanying the action dynamic, however, is insistence on obedience to legitimate Church authorities, from pastor to bishop. Thus, the degree of social involvement often depends on the orientation of a particular Cursillo priest-director. Nevertheless, it appears that the movement has been a significant intra-institutional change within the Church. It has made active participation in Church life respectable for Mexican-American men and laid the basis for a social apostolate contrasting with the individualistic piety in much of Latin religious worship.

These changes in the direction of greater involvement in problems of the world, together with the protest climate created by the civil rights movement, have meant that social-action priests could count on new sources of support and sympathy within as well as outside the Church. The public press and the liberal sector of the larger society, always suspicious of the Roman Catholic Church as a reactionary social institution, responded favorably to the non-traditional roles assumed by the priests. Such support, in turn, has generated fresh expectations for the involved clergy, now anxious to demonstrate that the Church is indeed on the side of social progress, particularly in its work for a minority group predominantly poor and Roman Catholic.

THE CHANGING STANCE
OF MEMBERS OF THE HIERARCHY

Another significant change within the Church is the support for social action at the higher levels of the hierarchy, which are protected by their organizational position and insulated from the pressures of the larger society. As was shown earlier, the striking Mexican-American field workers obtained the support of the Church at the national level (the Committee of Religious Concern). The same was true at the state level. The bishops of California[72] and Texas, acting as representatives of the Church throughout their respective states, endorsed the right of farm workers to organize unions, and, in Texas, advocated statewide minimum-wage legislation. But, with the exception of San Antonio, the Church did not take sides on the diocesan level.

Priests and laymen speaking and acting on behalf of the Church on "higher levels" protected by organizational structures can continue to act on behalf of Mexican-American farm workers. Thus, the Reverend John McCarthy, field representative of the Bishops' Committee for the Spanish-Speaking, said at an official conference in 1967:

> The role of the Church in this area is to be a prophet, to scream loud and clear where there are injustices. The Church should be a free agent and not involved in the vested interests of the socioeconomic structure. But it is a point of fact that the Church has been indifferent and pretty much a part of the over-all scenery in South Texas.[73]

Supporting Father McCarthy was a report of the Social Action Committee of the Texas Catholic Conference (composed of all the bishops of Texas), whose members had toured the strike area in the spring of 1967. The Social Action Committee recommended "that the Catholic Church in Texas establish and maintain wherever needed a special ministry to the '*campesino*,' and that this program be worked in conjunction with the local ordinary and the state office of the Bishops' Committee for the Spanish-Speaking."[74]

Such recommendations were not the anguished protests of individual priests acting on their own and contravening established procedure. Father McCarthy spoke as the incumbent in a recognized, episcopally supported post. The Social Action Department was authorized by the bishops of Texas collectively. Its members had been invited to the Brownsville area as representatives of the bishops' Texas Catholic Conference. Although there could have been protests against such intervention, those responsible for it were not vulnerable to being labelled "intruders" or to the sanctions levelled against individual priest-protestors.

Yet, the social-action priests have been catalysts. Following their initiative and spurred by the attention they focused on a problem, the Church on higher levels supported action involving, in recent years, collaboration with Protestant and other non-Catholic groups. The insulation provided by organizational structures has enabled spokesmen of the Church to persist in their greater involvement in social reform. Individual bishops, on the other hand, have been prone to stress balance, harmony, and the right of both sides. This emphasis has reflected both papal teaching and awareness of the local power milieu; a bishop, like a parish-based pastor, has Catholics of all socioeconomic classes in his territorial flock. His pastoral training teaches him to be concerned with all and to antagonize none; his financial responsibilities tell him that his cherished pastoral projects depend on support from the more affluent. The less financially secure the diocese or parish, the greater will be the impact of these pressures.

One recent and potentially significant form of social action has been the participation of the Southwest Church in the War on Poverty programs. Some bishops and priests were quick to see possibilities of Catholic involvement in these activities. In the Southwest, the Mexican American would obviously be among the chief beneficiaries.

Though episcopal initiative in submitting proposals for anti-poverty programs has varied greatly, our inquiries indicate that practically all of the Southwest dioceses had one or more programs directed by a priest. In the smaller towns, the priest was the natural spokesman for a community overwhelmingly Catholic by religious affiliation and overwhelmingly poor. His status as a priest facilitated local support and reduced the amount of opposition. In the larger cities, such as San Antonio, the priest-director was usually allied with other community groups and agencies.

THE URBAN MEXICAN-AMERICAN PARISH

The trends described in the preceding sections do not mean that the Southwest Church is undergoing a sweeping social-action orientation toward the Mexican-American population. The individual territorial parish remains the Church's basic unit of contact with the people. The vast majority of Mexican Americans know the Church through their local parish. Even if many do not attend Sunday Mass regularly, baptisms, marriages, and funerals bring a majority to the Church at one time or another. The chances are that they will meet not the social-action *padre*, much less the bishop, but a traditional parish priest.

Because the parish priest is so important, interviews were held with pastors of Mexican-American parishes in Los Angeles and San Antonio. The main purpose was to test the hypothesis that pastors in Mexican-American parishes, as a group, exhibit status-quo preferences and emphasize strictly pastoral concerns. Fifty-two pastors, 26 in each city, were interviewed between September 1966 and April 1967.

In detail, the interview questionnaire was designed to test the five propositions stated below together with a summary of the responses of those interviewed.[75]

1. *Pastors tend to depreciate suggestions of prejudice and discrimination against Mexican Americans in the larger society*. This proposition was not borne out. A majority of pastors in both cities acknowledged the existence of prejudice and discrimination in the local system, and the majority was greater in San Antonio than in Los Angeles. Instances of past discrimination within the Church were acknowledged by both sets of pastors. "Mexicans were told by 'Anglo' pastors to go to their own church." A few cited instances of a "Mexican church" constructed close to a larger church "so the Mexicans would have some place to go—obviously they weren't wanted in the big church." But denial of present-day discrimination within the Church was practically unanimous.

2. *Pastors are hostile to Protestant churches and view them as the chief enemy in the definition of their jobs*. No pastor interviewed seemed to take Protestant proselytizing seriously. "Not important" and "negligible impact" were opinions commonly expressed. Only 14 pastors in both cities admitted that Protestant efforts attracted "some converts," but very few—and only because of material benefits offered (several spoke of "rice Christians").

3. *Pastors have had little exposure to the social teachings of the Church and preach on this topic infrequently if at all*. In Los Angeles, 73 percent of the pastors said they had had no exposure to social teachings of the Church in the seminary. In contrast, only 8 percent of the San Antonio pastors reported no such exposure. Thus, the responses confirm this part of the hypothesis for one locale but not the other. The large discrepancy may be explained partly by the age differentials between the two groups of priests. The Los Angeles pastors were older and may therefore not have been exposed to changed seminary curricula, which include courses in the social encyclicals of recent popes. Also, the majority of San Antonio's clergy consisted of religious-order priests. Religious-order candidates for the priesthood have longer seminary training than diocesan seminarians and are therefore more likely to have had specific courses in social justice.

Acquaintance with this teaching is no guarantee that the priest will preach it. In fact, the majority in both cities did not preach on topics of social justice, confirming the second part of the proposition. When questioned about the reasons, Los

Angeles pastors claimed mainly lack of suitable occasions, or that other topics were more important. San Antonio pastors felt that the people were "not ready" to understand the teaching. This inter-city difference may reflect the lower level of Mexican-American educational attainment in San Antonio. Most of the relatively few priests in both cities who stated that they preached "quite often" on the social teachings of the Church did so because it was "prescribed by the Archdiocese."

These findings support the proposition that parish-based priests on the whole do not invest social questions with the urgency felt by their social-action counterparts. In the case of the Mexican American, particularly, they preferred to emphasize "doctrinal and moral" sermons as best meeting the needs of a population poorly instructed in religion.

4. *Pastors take little part in state, civic, or neighborhood organizations and activities.* Generally, this hypothesis is borne out by the responses in Los Angeles but not those in San Antonio. The San Antonio Neighborhood Youth Organization (SANYO), the major war-on-poverty agency in this city, accounts largely for the fact that practically all of the pastors interviewed there mentioned some socioeconomic welfare programs or activities sponsored by the parish. Only 35 percent of Los Angeles pastors mentioned parallel programs. One Los Angeles parish had a war-on-poverty program initiated by the pastor. Credit unions were mentioned with some frequency, although several pastors in San Antonio reported the failure some years before of a parish credit union.

The pastors in San Antonio showed more participation in state, civic, and neighborhood organizations than those in Los Angeles—54 percent and 19 percent, respectively, reporting "some participation." An important factor here may be that more civic leadership is expected of the pastors in San Antonio because there are relatively few qualified lay participants from the Mexican-American community. The wider leadership base of more highly educated Mexican-American laymen in Los Angeles probably diminishes the expectation of clerical representation there. Almost half the nonparticipants in both cities gave no reason for their inactivity; about a third alleged "no time due to pastoral duties;" and the remainder listed "no interest."

No dramatic social protest involving Mexican Americans occurred in Los Angeles to match the "March on Austin" of striking Mexican-American farm workers from the Rio Grande Valley in the late summer of 1966. The marchers came through San Antonio on their way to Austin. They were greeted by Archbishop Lucey and a group of social-action priests. We used this event to probe the San Antonio pastors' attitudes toward a controversial social protest involving Mexican Americans. Only 10 of the 26 San Antonio pastors mentioned the march from the pulpit (all favorably). Four of the sixteen who did not professed to be "confused" about the issues or to lack adequate understanding. Six others expressed disapproval of "the method—not the cause." Some were so annoyed by the social-action priests' participation that this factor qualified their approval of the march.

5. *Pastors show preference for traditional parish societies as contrasted with social-action organizations.* This hypothesis was confirmed by the responses in both cities. Organizations ranked first in importance by the pastors stress traditional parish societies, with some emphasis on the Confraternity of Christian Doctrine which in each diocese is responsible for religious instruction programs for Catholic students in public schools. Doctrinal instruction was given high priority because of the large numbers of Mexican-American elementary and high school students attending public schools.

Generally, then, the interview results confirm the over-all assumption that parish-based priests tend to have a narrower view of their functions and to be wary of new and possibly disruptive activities. At the same time, the responses highlight once more the inter-area variations which have been stressed in many other contexts throughout this volume. The general findings may in part reflect the demands on the

Table 19–1. Frequency of Sunday Mass Attendance, Mexican-American and National Sample Surveys

	Percent Attending Once a Week or More	Percent Attending Less than Once a Week	Percent Never Attending	Total Number (= 100%)
Los Angeles Mexican-American survey respondents, 1965–1966	47	47	6	852
San Antonio Mexican-American survey respondents, 1965–1966	58	41	1	569[a]
U.S. Catholics, 1966[b]	67	20	13	n.a.
U.S. Catholics, 1957[c]	72	24	4	1,270

[a] Weighting procedures were used in the San Antonio sample. This means that total numbers cannot be used as a direct indicator of error. See Appendix H.
[b] Gallup Survey, reported in the *Catholic Digest*, July, 1966, p. 27.
[c] Survey Research Center at the University of Michigan, reported by Bernard Lazerwitz, "Religion and Social Structure in the United States," in Louis Schneider (ed.), *Religion, Culture and Society* (New York: John Wiley & Sons, Inc., 1964), p. 430.

time of priests staffing the low-income parishes in Mexican-American areas. In addition to the strictly religious functions, acute financial problems require close attention to management, particularly in San Antonio where the Archdiocese has not been in a position to subsidize low-income parishes.

The parish priest's round of here-and-now activities tends to absorb his time and constrict his perspective, leaving little room for expanding his vision to larger problems in the community. Also, preoccupation with parochial duties means limited contacts with organizations and activities outside the parish. He may be impatient, too, with the protracted discussions of neighborhood and community meetings, for he is used to making decisions on his own and making them rapidly.

RELIGIOUS PRACTICE AND ATTITUDES

OF MEXICAN AMERICANS

Finally, pastors' concern with strictly religious functions is understandable in light of the religious practice and attitudes of Mexican Americans. What was said previously about the clergy's historical perception of the Mexican immigrant applies to contemporary Mexican Americans as well. Large numbers of Catholics in this population do not conform to the norms of the Church. This is evident from our survey data on Mexican-American religious practice and attitudes in Los Angeles and San Antonio.

Table 19-2. Frequency of Mass Attendance, by Sex,
Mexican-American Survey, National Survey, and Schuyler Study

	PERCENT ATTENDING ONCE A WEEK OR MORE		PERCENT ATTENDING LESS THAN ONCE A WEEK		TOTAL NUMBER (= 100%)	
	Men	Women	Men	Women	Men	Women
Los Angeles Mexican-American survey respondents, 1965–1966	39	52	61	48	365	488
San Antonio Mexican-American survey respondents, 1965–1966	56	60	44	40	230[a]	339[a]
Schuyler study,[b] 1960	73	82	27	18	7,354	
U.S. Catholics, 1957[c]	67	75	33	25	1,270	

[a] See note [a] in preceding table.
[b] Joseph B. Schuyler, S.J., *Northern Parish: A Sociological and Pastoral Study* (Chicago, 1960), p. 2020.
[c] See note[c] to preceding table.

Mexican Americans in the two cities fall substantially below the national average in weekly Mass attendance (Table 19-1). According to a recent national survey, even respondents with no Catholic schooling attend Mass more regularly than Mexican Americans (for whom Catholic schooling is not reported). Mexican-American women attend Mass more frequently than do men, but both range well below Catholics in other surveys (Table 19-2). Similar differences appear when age is controlled, with Mexican-American attendance in Los Angeles markedly low in the 20–29 year age group (Table 19-3). San Antonio Mexican Americans score consistently higher on Mass attendance by age and sex groupings than do Los Angeles Mexican Americans.

National surveys reveal a positive correlation between Mass attendance and education, with a sharp increase for those who have completed high school. San Antonio Mexican Americans generally follow this pattern, while a more complicated pattern holds for Mexican Americans in Los Angeles (Table 19–4). Los Angeles Mexican Americans living in more segregated neighborhoods appear to practice somewhat more regularly than those in mixed areas, though San Antonio reveals the opposite. Poorer people among Los Angeles Mexican Americans practice more regularly, but income makes little difference in the case of San Antonio Mexican Americans (Table 19–5). Though no exactly comparable national survey data are available, Lazerwitz' sample cited in the tables indicates an opposite pattern: Roman Catholic professionals and other white-collar persons show 81–83 percent regular Sunday Mass attendance; the attendance of unskilled workers drops, but

Table 19–3. *Percent Attending Mass Weekly or More Often, by Age and Sex, Mexican-American Survey and Schuyler Study (Sample size in parentheses)*

| | Mexican Americans, 1965–1966 | | | | | | | | SCHUYLER STUDY[a] |
| | LOS ANGELES | | | | SAN ANTONIO | | | | |
Age Group	Men		Women		Men		Women		Men and Women
20–29	28%	(76)	41%	(129)	42%	(38)	57%	(51)	76%
30–39	39	(113)	51	(152)	42	(62)	61	(81)	69
40–49	44	(97)	51	(98)	69	(49)	69	(71)	76
50 years and older	42	(74)	69	(95)	65	(77)	67	(96)	80
Total		(360)		(474)		(226)		(299)	(7,354)

[a] See note [b] in Table 19–2.

only to a level of 62 percent, or more than 10 percentage points above low-income Mexican Americans in Los Angeles.

Further, a study of marriages in Los Angeles County in 1963 revealed a low percentage of Mexican-American marriages originally performed before a Catholic priest (Table 19–6). This may not be surprising in the case of the foreign born. Mexican law recognizes only a civil marriage, which customarily precedes Church marriage in Mexico. Hence, the foreign born may be ignorant of American practice. However, any impact of American Catholic socialization should appear in an increased percentage of original Church marriages among the native born. This is true for the second generation, but initial Church marriages drop again among natives of native parentage. (Of course, these data do not indicate the proportion of civil marriages later validated within the church.)

Agreement with the teachings of the Church on birth control was far less widespread among the sample of Mexican Americans interviewed in Los Angeles and San Antonio than among a national sample. About 33 percent of the Mexican Americans expressed agreement as against 68 percent of the national survey respondents who had complete Catholic schooling, 52 percent who had some Catholic schooling, and 44 percent without any Catholic schooling.[76] Moreover, even those Mexican

Americans who attend Mass each Sunday or more often were divided in their opinion on birth control; in Los Angeles only 49 percent expressed conformity to the position of the Church. Disagreement in both cities was particularly striking among those under 30 (65 percent) and those who had attended college (67 percent).

The relatively low levels of religious practice and of adherence to some of the fundamental teachings of the Church are at least partially related to the Mexican Americans' low degree of Catholic socialization. This is most evident in their attendance of parochial schools and their participation in religious instruction at public schools. According to estimates for 1966–1967, only 15 percent of the Spanish-surname school population in grades 1 to 6 were enrolled in the parochial schools of high-density Mexican-American areas of Los Angeles; and only 57 percent received either parochial schooling or so-called CCD instruction (named after the Con-

**Table 19–4. Percent Attending Mass Weekly or More Often,
by Sex and Educational Attainment,
Mexican-American Survey Compared with National Survey
(Sample size in parentheses)**

	Mexican Americans, 1965–1966							
	LOS ANGELES				SAN ANTONIO			NATIONAL SURVEY[a]
School Years Completed	Men		Women		Men		Women	Men and Women
0–8 years	49%	(164)	57%	(232)	58%	(139)	60% (191)	63% (436)
Some high school	25	(81)	42	(144)	38	(39)	64 (60)	67 (256)
Four years of high school	30	(67)	48	(77)	62	(34)	72 (28)	80 (397)
One or more years of college	38	(45)	38	(45)	73	(11)	100 (7)	83 (181)
No response		(3)		(5)		(5)	(22)	
Total		(360)		(503)		(228)	(308)	(1,270)

[a] Bernard Lazerwitz, "Religion and Social Structure in the United States," in Louis Schneider (ed.), *Religion, Culture and Society* (New York: John Wiley & Sons, Inc., 1964), table 6, p. 431.

fraternity of Christian Doctrine). For grades 7 to 12, the corresponding figures were 23 percent and 32 percent. At the junior high and high school level, the Mexican-American participation in CCD classes alone was far below the level for all Catholic students in the same grades. In the city of San Antonio, the Mexican-American enrollment in Catholic schools was only 21 percent in grades 1 to 8 as against 30 percent for all Catholic students in these grades, and 14 percent in grades 9 to 12 as against 23 percent for all Catholic students. However, their participation in CCD classes matched the general level more closely.[77]

Thus, the parish priest can indeed point to an enormous need for pastoral concern with his Mexican-American flock and rationalize his preoccupation with this

Table 19-5. Frequency of Mass Attendance in Los Angeles and San Antonio, by Residential Density and Income, Mexican-American Survey, 1965–1966 (Sample size in parentheses)

Frequency of Mass Attendance	Residential Density[a]					Income of Head of Household[b]				
	COLONY		INTERMEDIATE	FRONTIER		HIGH	MEDIUM		LOW	
	L.A.	S.A.	(L.A. only)	L.A.	S.A.	L.A.	L.A.	S.A.	L.A.	S.A.
Once a week or more	52% (159)	57% (220)	46% (116)	40% (120)	69% (111)	35% (70)	48% (81)	59% (92)	51% (234)	61% (225)
One to three times a month	25 (77)	30 (113)	22 (56)	30 (89)	24 (40)	30 (60)	28 (47)	28 (44)	23 (108)	28 (104)
Few times a year or less	18 (54)	10 (39)	24 (62)	21 (63)	6 (9)	25 (51)	21 (36)	11 (18)	19 (88)	8 (30)
Never	5 (16)	2 (7)	6 (15)	8 (25)	1 (1)	9 (19)	2 (4)	1 (2)	7 (32)	1 (5)
Total number (= 100%)	(306)	(379)	(249)	(297)	(161)	(200)	(168)	(156)	(462)	(364)

[a] In Los Angeles, Frontier = tracts with less than 15.0 percent Spanish-surname individuals; Intermediate = tracts with between 15.0 and 43.8 percent Spanish-surname individuals; and Colony = tracts with more than 43.8 percent Spanish-surname individuals. In San Antonio, Frontier = tracts with less than 54.0 percent Spanish-surname individuals, and Colony = tracts with 54.0 percent or more Spanish-surname individuals.

[b] In Los Angeles, high income = > $6,000; medium income = $3,600–$5,999; low income = > $3,600. In San Antonio, medium income = > $2,760; low income = < $2,760.

task. As was true in earlier periods, the Church cannot assume that the Mexican American will turn to her for comfort and support. Rather, the Church must reach out for him if it is to perform its spiritual role.

Table 19–6. Percent of Marriages Involving Mexican Americans with Catholic Ceremony, Los Angeles County, 1963 (Neither party previously married)

BRIDES	GROOMS		
	Foreign Born, Mexico	Mexican or Mixed Parentage	Natives of Native Parentage
Foreign born, Mexico	46.7	47.1	43.6
Mexican or mixed parentage	38.6	55.2	52.4
Natives of native parentage	33.3	48.7	45.8

Source: Frank G. Mittelbach, Joan W. Moore, and Ronald McDaniel, *Intermarriage of Mexican-Americans* (Mexican-American Study Project, Advance Report 6, Graduate School of Business Administration, University of California, Los Angeles, November, 1966), Table V–4, p. 43.

SUMMARY

The role of the Roman Catholic Church among the Mexican-American people of the Southwest shows a gradual and uneven trend toward a more involved Church trying to improve their social condition as well as their Church loyalty and their adherence to the norms of religious practice. At the beginning, the legacy of extremely poor resources and the demands made on the Church by the waves of Mexican immigrants necessitated an emphasis on pastoral care. It took considerable time before the Church could turn to social concern.

The study of the dynamics of Church activities suggests that social-action goals may have one of two possible relationships to pastoral goals:

1. Social-action goals may be adopted to further pastoral goals, defending them, legitimating them, making the position of the institutional Church (and therefore its right to exercise its primary religious mission) more acceptable in the larger society. The Archdiocese of Los Angeles, with its relatively early programs to further the Americanization and education of Mexican Americans, is a good illustration of this relationship.

2. Social-action goals may also be adopted as ends in themselves. In this view they are direct concerns of the Church. The betterment of working conditions, housing, health, education, and so forth is not simply a means to achieve pastoral goals, or a bait to attract new members and re-enlist those who have fallen away. The social-action priests invest their activities with a significance paralleling that of the pastoral concerns. For such priests, encouraging labor-union organization may be no less important than saying Mass.

The most effective and continuous goal reorientation, however, has occurred at the upper levels of the Church hierarchy–statewide bishops' committees and national agencies–as well as in ecumenical groups. For the Church on the parish level is interdependent with the local power centers and subject to immediate constraints, and so is the diocese—it takes a bishop of unusual courage and conviction to resist the strong pressures which can be brought to bear upon him. In contrast, administrative officials operate behind the bulwarks of their multi-faceted institutions.

Most of the parish priests have remained preoccupied with purely pastoral concerns. This explains why writers concentrating on typical parish activities have conveyed the impression of little change in the role performed by the Church. Conversely, an analysis of policies at the upper levels of the hierarchy suggests a cautious revision of the notion that the Church, being basically a conservative force, has retarded the assimilation of Mexican Americans.[78]

NOTES TO CHAPTER NINETEEN

1. "Furthermore, the Mexican Constitution of 1917 forbade the training of native priests in seminaries, which were expropriated and closed. Finally, the legislatures fixed the maximum number of priests, and these had to be licensed." Joseph H. L. Schlarman, *Mexico, A Land of Volcanoes* (Milwaukee: The Bruce Publishing Company, 1950), p. 504. Cuevas underlines the unbalanced distribution of priests at the turn of the nineteenth century—a relatively heavy concentration in the central plateau (e.g., Mexico City and Puebla) and progressively fewer as one moved northward. The distribution was "disproportionate even when population differences are considered." There is no evidence that this imbalance was repaired during succeeding decades up to and including the Revolution era (1910–1930); see Mariano Cuevas, S.J., *Historia de la Iglesia en Mexico*, 5 vols. (El Paso, Tex.: Editorial "Revista Catolica," 1928), vol. V, p. 35. Hayner contrasts the 8,500 priests for a total population of 4,400,000 in 1767 with 3,863 for an estimated population of 22,000,000 in 1946. Norman S. Hayner, *New Patterns in Old Mexico: A Study of Town and Metropolis* (New Haven, Conn.: College and University Press, 1966), p. 153.

2. Karl M. Schmitt, "Catholic Adjustment to the Secular State: The Case of Mexico, 1867–1911," *Catholic Historical Review*, XLVIII (1962–1963), p. 194. The Catholic schools which did operate had their problems:

> Hopes and aspirations always far surpassed achievements. Nowhere, not even in Mexico City or Guadalajara, was there general satisfaction among Catholics with the quality and extent of their school system. In the poorer dioceses the obstacles were insuperable . . . in Chiapas . . . the bishop was still trying, not so much to establish a primary school system, but simply to erect adequate religious training centers.

> . . . .

> Also, . . . between November 11, 1931 and April 28, 1936, four hundred and eighty Catholic churches, schools, orphanages, and hospitals were closed by the government or converted to other uses, and . . . the National Preparatory School was formerly a Jesuit college, built in the eighteenth century.

Joseph H. L. Schlarman, *op. cit.*, pp. 193, 194, 415.

3. Charles S. MacFarland, *Chaos in Mexico* (New York and London: Harper and Bros., 1935), p. 71. MacFarland, sent to Mexico by the American Presbyterian Church to observe the persecution of the Catholic Church in the late 1920s, remarks (p. 102) of the textbooks used in the schools:

> There are two distinct elements in most of them: a tendency to set class against class . . . and anti-Church or anti-religious slants, or both. . . . Occasional motion pictures are widely advertised as bearing upon the past history of the Church. One depicting the atrocities of the Inquisition would have the effect on the child of horror for the Church and for the priesthood.

4. "Among the lower social and economic classes, Mass and the regular receiving of the Holy Eucharist are replaced by other religious customs. These may or may not be pleasing to God, but it is certain that they have little to do with the priests, and that they lie outside the regular functions of the Church." Robert E. Quirk, "Religion and the Mexican Social Revolution," in W. V. D'Antonio and F. B. Pike (eds.), *Religion, Revolution, and Reform: New Forces for Change in Latin America* (New York: Frederick A. Praeger, Publishers, 1964), p. 62.

5. Under terms of the *patronato*, the Spanish government erected and endowed churches, supported missionary priests, and provided army protection for the missions. In return, the Spanish monarchs could regulate "the procedure of the ecclesiastical courts, the manner and the time of worship, and rules for lay and clerical behavior, even to cause of excommunication and lifting of same. They were masters of all local patronage and of the presentation of every incumbent, as they also guided his choice of policies and his local movements from that time onward." W. Eugene Shiels, S. J., *King and Church: The Rise and Fall of the Patronato Real* (Chicago: Loyola University Press, 1961), p. 7.

6. Carlos M. Castaneda, *Our Catholic Heritage in Texas*, 7 vols., vol. V: *The Mission Era: The End of the Spanish Regime, 1780–1810* (Austin, Tex.: Von Boeckman-Jones, 1936–1958), p. 35.

7. Carlos M. Castaneda, "Pioneers of the Church in Texas," *Archdiocese of San Antonio, 1874–1949* (San Antonio: The Alamo Messenger Press, 1949), p. 14.

8. The second Bishop of Santa Fe, writing in the late 1890s, reported that Bishop Lamy found only nine priests residing in the Territory of New Mexico when he arrived in 1850, and that they "were altogether unable to meet the spiritual wants of all the population, scattered over the Territory." Most Rev. J. B. Salpointe, *Soldiers of the Cross: Notes on the Ecclesiastical History of New Mexico, Arizona, and Colorado* (Banning, Calif.: St. Boniface's Industrial School, 1898), p. 206.

Arizona, too, had suffered. The Jesuits had been expelled by the Spanish government in 1767, and the Franciscans met a similar fate at the hands of the Mexican government in 1828. In 1858 and 1859, Bishop Lamy sent Father Macheboeuf on a tour of this territory. The Friars and Jesuits had done their work well, for he "found the inhabitants almost all Catholics" who desired to "receive the Sacraments of the Church, a benefit they had been deprived of a long time" (*ibid.*, p. 226).

9. Rev. Gerald J. Geary, *The Secularization of the California Missions* (Washington, D.C.: Catholic University of America, 1934), p. 187.

10. Hubert Howe Bancroft, *History of Arizona and New Mexico* (San Francisco: The History Company, 1889), p. 777.

11. Warren A. Beck, *New Mexico: A History of Four Centuries* (Norman, Okla.: University of Oklahoma Press, 1962), p. 215.

12. *Ibid.* According to Beck, the French clergy "had little respect for the native priests. The latter, in turn, looked upon Lamy as a foreign usurper who was out to destroy their position."

13. Even in the early nineteenth century, the Roman Catholic Church was surprisingly well organized on the frontier. In 1820 Bardstown, Kentucky, had 25 priests and 35 churches to serve 40,000 Catholics. Raphael N. Hamilton, "The Significance of the Frontier to the Historian of the Catholic Church in the United States," *Catholic Historical Review*, XXV (1939–40), pp. 160–178.

14. Colman J. Barry, O.S.B., *The Catholic Church and German Americans* (Milwaukee: The Bruce Publishing Company, 1953), p. 6. See also Oscar Handlin, *The Uprooted* (New York: Grosset & Dunlop, Inc., 1951), especially chapter 10, "The Shock of Alienation"; and Marcus Lee Hansen, *The Immigrant in American History* (Cambridge, Mass.: Harvard University Press, 1948), especially chapter 6, "Immigration and American Culture." For views of these and other historians, see the bibliographical essay by Vincent P. De Santis, "The American Historian Looks at the Catholic Immigrant," in Thomas T. McAvoy, C.S.C. (ed.), *Roman Catholicism and the American Way of Life* (Notre Dame, Ind.: Notre Dame University Press, 1960), pp. 225–234.

15. Thomas J. Harte, "Racial and National Parishes in the United States," in C. J. Nuesse and Thomas J. Harte (eds.), *The Sociology of the Parish* (Milwaukee: The Bruce Publishing Company, 1951), p. 155.

16. Theodore Maynard, *The Story of American Catholicism* (New York: The Macmillan Company, 1941), p. 504.

17. See, for example, the lively account of Melinda Rankin, *Twenty Years Among the Mexicans: A Narrative of Missionary Labor* (Cincinnati: Chase and Hall, 1875).

18. Carlos M. Castaneda, *Our Catholic Heritage in Texas*, vol. VII, *The Church in Texas Since Independence: 1836–1950*, p. 117.

19. Rev. P. F. Parisot, O.M.I., *The Reminiscences of a Texas Missionary* (San Antonio, Tex.: Press of Johnson Bros. Printing Co., 1899).

20. "When Timon (John Timon, C.M., first Apostolic Visitor to Texas) and Odin (John M. Odin, first Bishop of Texas) parted . . . both . . . agreed that the greatest obstacle to the spread of the Faith in Texas was the need of financial aid and personnel. In the spring of 1841 there were only six priests, counting Odin, to care for the 10,000 scattered Catholics throughout Texas." Castaneda, vol. VII, *op. cit.*, p. 66.

21. With reference to Texas, Archbishop Lucey states that "In the majority of these places it was a Frenchman who was the pioneer missionary and builder." In 1874, of the 63 secular priests, 42 were from France. During the nineteenth century, at least 75 secular priests in Texas were from France. Archbishop Robert E. Lucey, "The Catholic Church in Texas," in Louis J. Putz, C.S.C. (ed.), *The Catholic Church, U.S.A.* (Chicago: Fides Publishers Association, 1956), pp. 228, 229.

22. *Ibid.*, p. 230.

23. For example, although accurate figures are difficult to obtain, one estimate places the number of Italian Protestants, in 1916, at only 53,073—out of a total of over two million Italian immigrants then in the United States. Rev. Gerald Shaughnessy, S.M., *Has the Immigrant Kept the Faith?: A Study of Immigration and Catholic Growth in the United States, 1790–1920* (New York: The Macmillan Company, 1925), p. 262.

24. W. Lloyd Warner and Leo Srole, *The Social Systems of American Ethnic Groups* (New Haven, Conn.: Yale University Press, 1945), p. 236. The performance of this "bridging function" was positively related to the length of time the ethnic group had been in the city. Schools of the French-Canadians, one of the more recently arrived groups, maintained a curriculum including French-Canadian elements, whereas "The Irish parochial school, like the Irish church, can no longer be said to be Irish in its content." (p. 241).

25. In 1930, Baltimore and St. Louis could boast 179 and 212 parochial schools for Catholic populations of 305,490 and 440,000, respectively. Los Angeles and San Diego had 79 schools for 301,775 Catholics; El Paso, 12 schools for 119,623; Corpus Christi, 27

schools for 247,760. *The Catholic Directory* (New York: P. J. Kenedy & Sons, 1930).

26. Joseph H. Fichter, S.J., *Dynamics of a City Church* (Chicago: The University of Chicago Press, 1951), p. 5.

27. Lincoln T. Bouscaren, S.J., and Adam C. Ellis, S.J. (eds.), *Canon Law: Text and Commentary* (Milwaukee: The Bruce Publishing Company, 1946), Canon 468, paragraph 1, p. 216.

28. Warner and Srole, *op. cit.*

29. Castaneda, vol. VII, *op. cit.*, pp. 153, 154.

30. "On the Rights and Duties of Capital and Labor," encyclical letter of Pope Leo XIII, in Etienne Gilson (ed.), *The Church Speaks to the Modern World: The Social Teachings of Leo XIII* (Garden City, N.Y.: Image Books, 1954), pp. 200–244.

31. "The Church and Society," *The Southern Messenger*, Jan. 20, 1921, p. 4.

32. Fourth Report of the Oblate Fathers, "Mary Immaculate," San Antonio, Oct., 1929, p. 284.

33. "The Condition of the Mexicans in 1911," *ibid.*, Jan., 1929, p. 13.

34. "An Appeal," *Ibid.*, Aug.–Sept., 1931, p. 241.

35. "Mexicans Migrate North of the Rio Grande," *ibid.*, Dec., 1933, p. 327.

36. "Deeply impressed with the knowledge that a larger number of the poor Mexican children of Los Angeles were being proselytized and weaned away from the faith of their fathers, on May 5, 1897, a number of Catholic women banded themselves together, under the patronage of the late Most Rev. George Montgomery, for the purpose of devising ways and means of saving these little wanderers from the fate that threatened them." "El Hogar Feliz—The Happy Home," in *The Tidings*, 7th Annual Edition (1910), p. 80.

37. "Americanization Work in Los Angeles," *The Tidings*, Nov. 21, 1919, p. 10.

38. Bureau of Catholic Charities of the Diocese of Los Angeles, *Annual Report*, 1926, p. 20 (from the Archives of the Archdiocese of Los Angeles, hereafter abbreviated as AALA).

39. "Sermons and Addresses of The Most Reverand John J. Cantwell," unpublished manuscript, AALA.

40. Catholic Welfare Bureau representatives attending a meeting of the Social Workers' Club of San Diego, "a non-sectarian organization," were told by a speaker that "great care should be taken that justice may be served and technicalities eliminated in decisions of officials handling deportation cases." *The Tidings*, Dec. 5, 1930, p. 12.

41. "The Business of the Church," *The Tidings*, Oct. 22, 1937, p. 8.

42. *The Tidings*, Apr. 2, 1943, p. 5.

43. "How Reds Lure L.A. Workers," *The Tidings*, Aug. 4, 1950, p. 1.

44. An article in *The Tidings* of Sept. 12, 1947 about the low-income Mexican parish of Dolores Mission, just east of Los Angeles' downtown area, declared (p. 3):

> They're working people, and as any second-string Communist will tell you, they're plenty busy with the problem of making a living. But don't misunderstand, they're not malcontents.... The Flats may not look much like a movie set from "Fiesta," but on a warm summer evening when folks are on their front porches you'll often hear a guitar ... singing coming from genuine people, happy by nature.

"There are meddlers in the Flats," the article continued,"—certain types of welfare 'experts' who attempt to solve all problems from wages to housing with the stereotype suggestion: birth control." By contrast, the article praises the catechistic and family visiting practices of the Sisters. They inquire "about baptism of children, the status of marriages, and the general condition of the people." "No one," the writer concludes, "will ever write anything as ridiculous as 'Miracle of the Flats' because, you see, a miracle isn't needed down in the Flats. Just ordinary hard work and understanding are necessary to save the people of the Flats for the Church."

45. Interview with Msgr. Thaddeus Shubsda, 1967. By 1965, the Catholic-sponsored citizenship schools in East Los Angeles had graduated approximately 2,700 Mexican-born men and women in programs begun in 1953.

46. Rt. Rev. Msgr. Thomas J. O'Dwyer, "Catholic Charities and Mexican Welfare," a partial collection of speeches given by Rt. Rev. Thomas J. O'Dwyer, from the AALA. (It has not been possible to ascribe an exact date to this speech, which was given sometime in the 1950s.)

47. Files of the sermons and addresses of James Francis Cardinal McIntyre, AALA. The Cardinal's continuing misgivings about public education appeared in a memorandum sent to Bishop Manning in September, 1957. Referring to a conversation in New York with the Apostolic Delegate "regarding the Mexican situation here," the Cardinal notes that "he was quite interested in the summary and suggested I write him a memorandum of our experience for his records." Bishop Manning is requested to submit his own memorandum on this topic. The Cardinal states, among other points, "I emphasize ... the influence ... of Catholic education upon them as compared to the influence of public education and Communistic forces." By 1957, 22 parochial schools had been constructed, at a cost of over $4,700,000, in predominantly Mexican-American areas. (Files of the Most Reverend Timothy Manning, Auxiliary Bishop of Los Angeles, AALA).

48. *The Tidings*, Nov. 4, 1949, p. 4.

49. *The Tidings*, May 22, 1953, p. 11.

50. The Memorandum was discovered in the Archives of the Archdiocese of Los Angeles by Patrick H. McNamara when he conducted the research for this chapter. Professor McNamara asked the Southwest diocesan chanceries for copies of the bishops' comments on the Memorandum. Copies were furnished by the following dioceses: Fresno, Los Angeles, San Antonio, and San Diego.

51. Thus, the San Diego reply reflects that "there are also defections from the faith among the Mexican people, but not any more so than are found in the average American parish." The Monterey-Fresno report assures the Delegate that "the Protestants are no real threat to the faith among Mexicans in this diocese. They have struggling churches in Bakersfield, Fresno, Hanford, and Visalia, the very places where our concentration on Mexican work has been greatest." McGucken of Los Angeles is less reassuring:

> The clergy are inclined to underestimate the success of the Protestant proselytizing agencies. Yet, the results of the Protestant efforts are not commensurate with the vast sums of money expended or the large number of workers in this field. Too, many of the Mexicans, even the Ministers who have graduated from their seminaries, give up Protestantism and become indifferent to the practice of any religion.

52. U.S. Office of War Information, *Building America*, vol. VIII, no. 5 (Feb., 1945).

53. *The Spanish-speaking of the Southwest and West* (Washington, D.C.: National Catholic Welfare Conference, 1943), pp. 3, 4.

54. *Ibid.*, pp. 15–18.

55. See Brother Albeus Walsh, C.S.C., "The Work of the Catholic Bishops' Committee for the Spanish-speaking in the United States" (unpublished Master's thesis, University of Texas, 1952), p. 25. See also Rosemary E. Smith, "The Work of the Bishops' Committee for the Spanish-speaking on Behalf of the Migrant Worker" (unpublished Master's thesis, The Catholic University of America, 1958).

56. When interviewed on this subject, two highly placed church officials in Los Angeles remarked that the archdiocese "has always taken care of its own problems" with regard to the Mexican-American population, and never needed the services of the Bishops' Committee. Only eight of twenty-six San Antonio pastors affirmed that the Committee's

programs affected the parish, and two of the eight respondents in this category expressed negative criticism of the committee ("A lot of reports and resolutions mailed to you, but they didn't do anything here in the parish").

57. The letter asking Auxiliary Bishop Hugh A. Donahue of San Francisco for permission to go beyond pastoral care is of sufficient interest to be quoted:

Your Excellency, April 4, 1954

A group of Mexican-American field workers from the East San Jose community around the Our Lady of Guadalupe Center have invited me to give them an explanation of the teachings of the Church on management-labor cooperation as a background for the solution of their economic problems. In forming their association to accept the responsibility for educating and representing their vocational group, they wish the guidance of religious teaching.

A check on the background of the spokesman, Mr. Ernesto Galarza . . . reveals that he is a well-known figure in this field and that he has no connection with any communistic or subversive group.

In the hope that such guidance may be useful and opportune for the promotion of Christian Social Teaching on the duties of Mutual Cooperation, I submit this request to you for consideration.

Accordingly, I ask permission to be a consultant when requested at their meetings.

Yours in Christ,
Fr. Donald McDonnell

In his reply, Bishop Donahue allowed Father McDonnell to be a "consultant" and "to explain the teachings of the Church on management-labor cooperation." From the Archives of the Archdiocese of San Francisco, "Spanish-speaking Apostolate."

58. Quotations are from a radio speech.

59. An interview in 1967 with one of the priests involved, Father Thomas McCullough, indicated this development graphically:

During the first few years, our main concern was that they were being lost to the Church; our concern with poverty was . . . that through poverty they were becoming morally disorganized . . . hurting themselves and losing the Faith.

Q. What caused the shift in your perception to the larger structural problems?

A. The historical event was the organization of the strike by Ernesto Galarza of the tomato workers of the Tracy area. And we were just in the process of going in to arrange for a Mass the next day, when there was this disturbance. People were running around . . . hollering "Huelga." . . . We were very interested; we recalled some of Father Munier's teachings and some of the things we had read about the early strikes, and so we began following this thing . . . and going to the union meetings and listening to them.

This was all done with ecclesiastical approval. Father McDonnell wrote . . . to the Bishop to ask if we could attend the meetings of the union workers and if we could say anything. The reply . . . was yes. We shouldn't take sides, but we certainly could read the social encyclicals and present their teachings; that was the thing to do.

60. Interview, 1967.

61. Quoted in Jerome B. Ernst, "Worthy of His Hire," *Extension Magazine*, June, 1966, p. 12.

62. News release, National Catholic Rural Life Conference, Washington, D.C. office, Dec. 10, 1965.

63. "The Delano Strike: The Democratic Solution," *Central California Register*, June 23, 1966, p. 1.

64. *Brownsville Herald*, June 17, 1966, p. 1.

65. *Alamo Messenger*, June 24, 1966, p. 10.

66. *Ibid.*

67. *Brownsville Herald*, Feb. 5, 1967, pp. 1 and 12-A.

68. In an interview, a local priest remarked: "I never mentioned the strike or the problem we were having in relation to the field worker and the farmer. I was afraid to mention it from the pulpit because I knew that whatever I would say would be misinterpreted because of the thinking of the people either on the farmer's side or the field worker's side."

69. The *Alamo Messenger* of Sept. 2, 1966 reported (p. 11):

> He [Archbishop Lucey] bluntly told the marching Mexican-American field workers when they reached San Antonio: "It is with a large measure of reluctance and regret that we endorse and approve your demand for an hourly wage of $1.25. No sane man would consider that a fair wage in these days when the high cost of living requires a much better return for your labor . . . a wage of $1.25 is ghastly recompense for exhausting labor under the burning sun of Texas. This explanation and this apology to the nation are necessary because I have approved this brutal wage scale."

70. *San Antonio Express News*, Feb. 4, 1967, p. 12-A.

71. Figures on the number of *cursillistas* are difficult to obtain. See Rev. Anthony Soto, O.F.M., "Cursillo Movement in the West," and Rev. Victor Goertz, "Brief History of the Cursillo Movement," *Proceedings of the Eleventh Conference of the National Catholic Council for the Spanish-speaking* (Milwaukee: National Catholic Council for the Spanish speaking, 1962), pp. 81–94. The Archdiocese of Los Angeles, in the words of one prominent churchman interviewed, has "just tolerated" the movement, for reasons not made altogether clear. Information given by the Cursillo director in Los Angeles revealed that nearly 1,200 persons, 600 with Spanish surnames, had made the Cursillo by October 1967. Of the Spanish-surname persons, half were men.

72. In March of 1966, Bishop Hugh A. Donohue of Stockton appeared before the U.S. Senate Subcommittee on Migratory Labor, meeting in Delano. His statement, approved by all the bishops of California, reaffirmed the right of farm laborers "not to be looked down upon as outside agitators." Their organizations "must be protected by law." It would be "unjust for . . . grower organizations to strive to prevent by reprisal the legitimate efforts of farm laborers to form worker associations or unions." *Central California Register*, Mar. 17, 1966, p. 1.

73. *Alamo Messenger*, June 22, 1967, p. 3. The statement was made at a conference sponsored by the Texas Advisory Committee of the U.S. Civil Rights Commission.

74. *Ibid.*, p. 1.

75. A more detailed analysis is presented in Patrick H. McNamara, "Bishops, Priests, and Prophecy: A Study in the Sociology of Religious Protest" (unpublished Ph.D. dissertation, University of California, Los Angeles, 1968).

76. For the national survey, see Andrew M. Greeley and Peter H. Rossi, *The Education of Catholic Americans* (Chicago: Aldine Publishing Co., 1966). The questions about birth control in the Los Angeles–San Antonio surveys and in the national sample survey differed in language, but their general thrust was similar enough to justify broad comparison. The question asked of respondents in Los Angeles and San Antonio was "Family planning—or

birth control—has been discussed by many people. What is your feeling about a married couple practicing birth control? If you had to decide, which one of these above statements best expresses your point of view?" The 33 percent given in the text combines "It is always wrong" and "It is usually wrong" responses. The item in Greeley-Rossi read as follows: "A married couple who feel they have as many children as they want are really not doing anything wrong when they use artificial means to prevent conception." The percentages in the text represent combined "Disagree somewhat" and "Strongly disagree" responses.

77. The data are from Patrick H. McNamara, *op. cit.*

78. Cf. Leonard Broom and Eshref Shevky, "Mexicans in the United States: A Problem in Social Differentiation," *Sociology and Social Research*, XXXVI (Jan., 1952), p. 157. See also Ruth Tuck, *Not With the Fist: Mexicans in a Southwest City* (New York: Harcourt, Brace and Company, Inc., 1956), pp. 155–163 and 203; Ruth Landes, *Latin-Americans of the Southwest* (New York: McGraw-Hill Book Company, 1965), p. 84; Griffith, *American Me* (Boston: Houghton Mifflin Company, 1948), p. 186.

TWENTY

Protestants and Mexicans

Iꜰ it is true that contact with the religious values of a dominant society helps a minority acculturate and achieve, then in the United States Mexican conversions to Protestantism may be exceedingly important. As commonly advanced, such an argument involves at least two assumptions. It assumes that the "Protestant ethic" and its achievement-oriented values are far more conducive to success in American society than the Mexican-Catholic ethos. It assumes also that the values of the "Protestant ethic" are more closely held by Protestants than by members of other religions.

Evidence on the Protestant contribution to acculturation of ethnic groups in the United States is rather equivocal, to say the least. Protestant immigrants (as shown in the *Handbook of Denominations*[1]) try very hard to retain *national* forms of Protestantism; the Lutherans are a case in point. Protestantism does not seem to have contributed much to Negro "acculturation," although the importance of the Negro church as a "race institution" is unquestioned. Nevertheless, Protestantism is still seen by scholars and the community as a possible acculturation agent.[2] This

[1] Notes for this chapter start on page 507.

is also a rationale for Protestant activists. And apart from the question of value acculturation, the network of Protestant churches has been perhaps the single most important voluntary association of white America. Its ideology emphasizes the participation of all men. The nature, conditions, and success of Mexican-American participation are therefore intrinsically interesting. The conditions of their participation in Protestant churches may also cast some light on problems of participation in other American institutions.

DENOMINATIONAL STATISTICS

Statistically, Protestantism is not important in the Mexican-American population. Our Los Angeles and San Antonio survey data show that only 5 percent of those professing a religion are Protestant. According to a 1960 survey for the United States, slightly over 113,000 "Spanish" persons, or less than 3 percent of the Mexican-American population, were members of Protestant denominations (Table 20–1). Mexican-American Protestants are quantitatively as insignificant in Protestantism as Protestantism is generally insignificant to the Mexican Americans. With nearly 10 million Protestants in the five Southwest states (in 1960),[3] a scant 100,000 or so Mexican-American Protestants are not worth much special attention. Most Mexican-American activists in Protestant denominations know this.

It is extremely difficult to obtain reliable data on the distribution of Mexican Americans among the various Protestant denominations. Beyond the usual severe difficulties with religious statistics in the United States (for example, the lack of data on discrepancies between members *claimed* by denominations and those actually participating as members), there are other troubles. In the most general estimate available from the survey conducted by the National Council of Churches, Mexican Americans are not distinguished from all "Spanish Americans." A rough estimate of Mexican-American churches is available from data covering those states in which Mexican Americans are concentrated, but such an estimate is doubtless far from accurate. Second, these and other statistics from the churches refer only to the segregated Mexican-American congregations and their members. Mexican Americans attending *integrated* churches are not enumerated. A third problem is the incomplete enumeration of denominations. The abovementioned survey by the National Council of Churches, which is summarized in Table 20–1, includes only 13 denominations, as compared with the 100-odd listed in the *Handbook of Denominations*. Only one of the Pentecostal bodies—the Assemblies of God—is represented. Jehovah's Witnesses, also active among Mexican Americans, are omitted from this survey. Surveys of Mexican-American congregations conducted in three cities under the auspices of the Texas Council of Churches show variable ratios of such sectarian groups to major denominational congregations.[4]

Fourth, membership alone does not determine the denomination's interest in or work with Mexican Americans. In some instances, social work among the poor has largely replaced the attempt to convert more members for the denomination. This fact is reflected in the discrepancy between the rank order of membership (column 1 in Table 20–1) and total annual budget (column 4). Thus the United Presbyterian Church ranks second in amount of money spent but only fifth in membership. The 30 United Presbyterian institutions include 21 community centers and one hospital serving primarily the "Spanish." These expensive activities hardly reflect the size of church membership.[5]

Table 20–1. Distribution of Protestant Religious Efforts Among the "Spanish," by Denomination, 1960[a]

	(1)	(2)	(3)	(4)	(5)
	Total Number of Members[b]	Total Number of "Spanish" Churches in the U.S.	Percent of "Spanish" Churches that are in the West and Southwest[c]	National Annual Budget, 1960	Denominational Institutions[d] Serving the "Spanish"
Assemblies of God	29,054	392	77.0	$ [e]	3
Methodist Church	28,000[f]	221	81.7	781,575	18
Southern Baptist Convention	28,000[f]	559	95.3	601,561	3
American Baptist Church	7,950[f]	106	54.7	46,000	6
United Presbyterian, U.S.A.	6,604	94	74.5	690,796	30
Seventh Day Adventists	5,000	68	64.7	n.a.	8
Presbyterian Church in the U.S.	2,842	38	100.0	64,891	1
Disciples of Christ	1,851	18	50.0	53,174	2
Lutheran Church—Missouri Synod	1,245	7	100.0	60,476	3
Evangelical United Brethren	972	14	78.6	237,332	10
United Lutheran Church	604	4	0.0	15,000	n.a.
Congregational—Christian Churches	543[f]	7	71.4	9,349	n.a.
Church of God (Anderson, Indiana)	465	7	100.0	16,000	n.a.
Total	113,130	1,535	81.4%	$2,576,154	84

[a] Derived from Glen W. Trimble, "Responses to the Brief Survey of Church Related Spanish American Work in The Continental United States," National Council of Churches, unpublished manuscript.
[b] Includes only those in "Spanish-American" congregations.
[c] Includes 1,225 churches in the five states with sizable Mexican-American populations, and 24 churches in the other Western and Southwestern states, where "Spanish" most probably means Mexican American, i.e., Washington, Oregon, Idaho, Montana, Oklahoma, Utah, and Wyoming.
[d] E.g., Hospitals, schools, community centers.
[e] "Entirely indigenous."
[f] Estimated by denominational official.

It is evident from the statistics that denominations differ markedly in their concern with Mexican Americans.[6] Nor does the denomination's numerical strength in American society reflect accurately its importance among Mexican Americans, except in the cases of Methodists and Southern Baptists.[7]

In this chapter we trace the larger Protestant denominations—Methodist, Presbyterian, and Baptist—as they have passed through three stages in their activities with Mexican Americans.* The first was the missionary phase. This stage was

*Obviously there are differences in attractiveness to Mexican Americans of the various denominations, depending on the social and cultural distance between the denomination and the local Mexican-American system. But for purposes of this discussion we shall treat this fact as given, and discuss denominational initiative only.

The materials presented in this chapter are drawn from published and unpublished data (often kindly provided by denominational sources) and from interviews.

usually led by Anglo missionaries and totally separated from the denomination's other activities. Working conceptions of "Mexicans" and of an appropriate involvement depended largely on the times and on the relationship of the missionary to the dominant cultural goals of his denomination. The segregated phase came second. Here Mexican Americans had come to constitute a large enough group within the denomination to form a separate conference, presbytery, or convention. These were not only separate congregations, but separate administrative bodies within the church structures. Last came the integrated phase. "Mexican" Protestant churches were abolished and no formal distinctions were made between Mexican-American members and/or any other members of the church.

We shall compare Texas with California. To follow this comparison it is essential to remember that different branches of each of the denominations are under consideration. Methodists split into a Northern and a Southern branch in 1844 and reunited in 1939. Presbyterians split in similar fashion in 1861 and still remain separate in the mid-1960s. The Baptists split in 1845 and also remain separate in the mid-1960s. Although the issue of slavery precipitated all three splits, there were usually major theological and organizational disagreements as well. In general, the Southern branch of each denomination tended to be the more conservative.[8] In the case of major denominations, these distinctions were of real significance with regard to their activities among Mexican Americans. One can follow the interplay of competing values and the influence of different denominational organizational structures on these activities. We shall also touch upon the work done under the auspices of the National Council of Churches, which serves as an interdenominational rallying point for many Protestant liberals; the role among Mexican Americans of Pentecostal sects, which are significant numerically but pose more difficult research problems than a study of this scope can resolve; and the work of the Mormon Church. The Mormon Church is of particular interest not only because of the special position of Mexicans in Mormon theology and history but also because of the manner in which Mormons cope with the economic and social problems of their converts.

MISSIONARY BEGINNINGS
IN THE MAJOR DENOMINATIONS

The Presbyterians

In Texas, missionary work among the Mexicans by the three major denominations started well before the Civil War. Presbyterians were active in Texas as early as 1838 and in the lower Rio Grande Valley by 1850.[9] Melinda Rankin, the principal Presbyterian missionary, reported meeting her Methodist counterpart in the 1850s—just after the war with Mexico. Almost all missionaries from the three denominations held beliefs and conducted activities that would now be considered theologically conservative. Sin and salvation were seen as matters touching the individual soul alone, for man is seen as born full of sin. This is not a "humanistic" or "social" view of man or of God's kingdom. The sacred and the secular are perceived as realms apart, and the only strategy appropriate for the attainment of salvation (or for spreading the blessings of salvation) is to instill religious sentiments in individual believers. Faith is the important central concept—a direct responsibility of man to God. This is a *Bible* faith, and those not in a "Bible religion" are felt not to be Christian. Indeed, Roman Catholicism is defined by such conservatives as a major perverter of Bible faith and therefore actually as "non-Christian."

Miss Rankin's interest in the Mexicans was typical of the missionary's preoccupation with his special potential flock. She was clearly aware of her deviation from the general Anglo attitude: "I did not feel, as many others have expressed, that the sight of a Mexican was enough to disgust one of the whole nation."[10] Characteristically, her principal approach was evangelism—the conversion of individuals to the personal knowledge and use of the Bible as self-evident truth. The Mexicans were defined as pagans, and she justified her mission to other Protestants, and especially to her Eastern sponsors, as that of combating Catholicism. She emphasized the presence of newly-arrived French priests. Yet she faced strong prejudices in her efforts to rally financial and moral support among Anglo Protestants:

> The idea of establishing a Protestant institution upon that papal frontier was regarded as chimerical and absurd in the extreme. . . . Even ministers of the gospel said to me, "We had better send bullets and gunpowder to Mexico than Bibles." . . . My zeal and efforts were regarded as a sort of insanity, and I more dreaded meeting a Protestant Christian in my round of Bible distribution than I did a Romish priest. . . . Some went so far as to say, "The Mexicans have a religion good enough for them, and we had better let them alone."[11]

Presbyterian missionary work was not solidly established in Texas until well after the Civil War. By then the anti-Mexican hostility engendered by the Mexican wars had diminished somewhat. In the 1880s, the Reverend Walter Scott, a Mexican-reared son of Scottish refugees from the Civil War, was ordained "evangelist to the Mexicans." He remained the principal activist among the Mexicans until the mission phase of Southern Presbyterian work ended in 1908 with the founding of the Texas-Mexican Presbytery.[12] As with the work started in the last quarter of the century in California by the Northern Presbyterians, camp meetings and revivals were held in addition to door-to-door evangelism. A handful of Spanish-language churches ministered almost exclusively to new immigrants, using predominantly Mexican-born and Mexican-trained ministers under the direction of Anglo evangelists. Like most missions, the Mexican Presbyterian mission practiced segregation from the outset—at first because of Anglo hostility to Mexicans, and later because it was considered the easiest way of accomplishing the mission.

A final point, generally true of the missionary phase, is also illustrated by the Presbyterians. Although the rationale for mission work is a Christian imperative to evangelize pagans, support from the larger church body is often urged because of *social* benefits to be obtained from the conversion of Mexicans. The missionaries suggest that conversion makes worthy American citizens out of "typical" Mexicans.[13]

The Methodists

Methodist activity among the Mexicans began in Texas in 1834. By 1859 an Anglo missionary—Miss Rankin's acquaintance—was given the title "Missionary to the Mexicans of the Rio Grande Valley."[14] In sharp contrast to other denominations, Methodists at first evangelized from within existing Anglo congregations, though the practice was neither common nor long-lasting. By 1874 a regular mission district was established by the Southern Methodists. Special materials were prepared in Spanish; Mexican ministers were hired, and an all-Mexican congregation was established in San Antonio.

"Sporadic and lethargic" activity[15] was carried on by the Methodists in Southern California beginning in 1879. An effort was made to bring Mexicans into the Los Angeles Anglo congregations, which were just getting established.[16] In 1911 a new superintendent of the Spanish and Portuguese Mission District, the Reverend Vernon McCombs, was appointed. His training and outlook reflected new currents in Protestant ideology.

A form of theological liberalism known as the "social gospel" had appeared. It was particularly strong in the Methodist church. This view saw sin as institutionally transmitted and not always a failing of the individual. Social institutions rather than individuals became the target of efforts at salvation.[17] The social gospel was a response to the visible cleavages evident in the industrializing cities of America. Social reform was a manifest goal. Individual conversions became relatively meaningless. Tactically, the social gospelists did not evangelize, but engaged in activities ranging from "institutional" (or multifunction) churches to the founding of settlement houses. Theologically, the liberal thought of human nature as fundamentally good or at least not inevitably sinful. He felt a strong sense of responsibility to men. His most important symbolic concept is "harmony" rather than "faith." Social-gospel ideologies attempted to combine secular and religious concerns: The sacred and the profane were not seen as antithetical, as they were in conservative ideologies.

McCombs was a son of missionaries and had attended seminary during the period when the social gospel movement was the major religious trend of the time. He represented an interesting transitional blend of missionary evangelism and social-gospel ideology. In defining the objects of his attention, he was the traditional missionary, with what might be called a vocation for one particular people—the Mexicans. He saw them as "noble, as history shows, but . . . many of them are sinful, anarchistic, and dangerous, if the truth be told."[18] "Anarchy" and "danger" referred not only to the Mexican Revolution, then passing through its most violent epoch just across the border, but also to the visible and audible presence of the "Wobblies" (International Workers of the World) among Mexicans.[19] As did other Protestant missionaries, McCombs tended to define Roman Catholicism as the source of many of the problems of Mexicans in the United States and of Mexico itself. And in common with other Protestant missionaries who had preceded him, he employed Mexican and Mexican-American evangelists.[20]

The McCombs method was that of the social gospel. His ideal was the so-called "institutional" church, that is, the extension of the church into welfare, recreational, and educational activities.[21] As part of this ideal, he raised money to construct the Plaza Community Center in what was then the heart of Los Angeles' Mexican area. Thus, McCombs used an expanded concept of the mission provided by social gospel to minister to "his" people, the Mexicans.

The Baptists

Although the Northern Baptists were active in South Texas among Mexicans as early as the 1840s, their work, like that of the Methodists, had virtually disappeared by the end of the Civil War.[22] Baptist work in Texas did not revive until the 1880s. It came then under the aegis of the Southern Baptists, who were using Anglo missionaries with experience in Mexico.[23] Thus, the beginnings of Baptist activities date from approximately the same time as those of the other two major denominations and were conducted under similar circumstances. By 1890, the work had been declared a mission, and this phase lasted for twenty years—until 1910.

In Southern California, Baptist missionary efforts did not start until the twentieth century, and in 1910—a year before the appointment of the Methodist Vernon McCombs—the Home Mission Society of the American (i.e., Northern) Baptist Church appointed a former overseas missionary couple as superintendents of Mexican Baptist missions in the Southwest.[24] This couple functioned much as did the McCombses. They recruited other missionaries, both Mexican and Anglos, like the man nicknamed, significantly, "Mexican" Brown. The first recorded hiring of a Mexican evangelist, however, did not occur until 1925, two years after the establishment of the segregated Baptist convention for Mexican Americans in Southern California. Like the Methodists of a previous era, the early Baptist missionaries debated appropriate missionary techniques. Their emphasis was entirely evangelistic, and their concern was with the "quality" of conversions. Some wanted to avoid the "half-baked material" produced by revivals, which they felt would particularly attract the "naturally emotional" Mexicans.[25] The Baptists (much more conservative than either Presbyterians or Methodists) never felt the impact of the social gospel during this missionary phase, although the extreme poverty of the Mexican Americans sometimes impelled them to social welfare activities.

Adaptations in Missionary Work

Thus in all three denominations discussed, theological ideas were extremely important, even during the early mission stage. Work in the early nineteenth century seems to reflect the predominant evangelistic emphasis of most denominations. But by the twentieth century, denominational differences were beginning to make themselves felt even in this mission outpost field. The Methodists altered both philosophy and strategy, whereas the Baptists retained essentially the same philosophic and organizational approach that the Presbyterians and Methodists had used at the border nearly a hundred years earlier. (In the "purely" evangelistic approach, particular techniques—door-to-door Bible distribution, camp meetings, revivals—depend both on the degree to which the missionary believes in the omnipotence of the Bible [an index of his conservatism] and on his conception of his potential flock.)

Regardless of the particular theological stance of the missionary, the missionary movement—especially the domestic mission—has generally been radical in terms of the major denominations. First, as Miss Rankin illustrates, missionary activity may become an expensive extension of the institution to a pariah group. In this respect, the missionary always acts as a *social* liberal regardless of theology. Second, the missionary's work generally seems to involve taking the acceptability of the Word (the omnipotent Bible) to a wide public. He preaches not to the convinced, but to those outside the flock. He must learn and adapt to the ways of the "outside" world. In the past, for a young man in seminary training in one of the major Protestant denominations, it meant rejecting the normality of the well-educated minister ready for service in the church and also acquiring a considerable degree of secular (non-scriptural) learning. It denies the denomination's unique claim to universal wisdom and substitutes for it a compromised version in which, though the denomination has supreme wisdom, the outside world has useful knowledge. (The contemporary missionary getting an advanced degree in anthropology is an example.) Such a revision is a compromise, an adaptation, that is liberal in effect, particularly in theologically conservative denominations. (The missionary operations of the Jesuits offer an interesting parallel in the Roman Catholic Church.) Thus, the missionary is impelled to innovate in order to deal with people outside the "normal" denominational frame of reference. These innovations may appear perilously close to secularism and even heresy to the conservative church member. With special reference to Protestant missions to Mexicans, cultural innovations combined with attention to *local* outcasts (rather than remote overseas missions) probably were particularly distasteful to Southwest congregations.

Finally, all Protestant domestic missions generally stated their dedication to "Americanization through evangelization."[26] The small numbers involved in the mission to the Mexicans, though alarming to Catholic observers, meant a minimal impact. The cultural and social isolation of Mexican-American Protestants within the denominations continued throughout the next phase of segregated organizational activities as well, further reducing their impact.

SEGREGATED ORGANIZATIONS

AND THE PROBLEM OF INTEGRATION

After the mission phase, the three major denominations passed through an organizational stage in which activities among the Mexican Americans were more or less run by Mexican Americans themselves. In almost all denominations, the segregated presbytery, conference, or convention survived somewhere in the Southwest until very recently. Although the segregated "Texas-Mexican Presbytery" of the Southern Presbyterians (founded in 1908) was dissolved, and though the Methodists' separate Southern California Conference was merged with the larger body (in 1956), Texas Methodists retained through the late 1960s their segregated Rio Grande Conference and the American Baptists their segregated Southern California Baptist Convention (Spanish-speaking).*

All of these segregated bodies are conservative theologically and socially, irrespective of denominational affiliation. Mexican Americans who are members of churches in these segregated bodies are so much alike that differences between the denominations are obscured. The segregated bodies are poor and congregationally oriented. They have had a largely ill-educated ministry. They retain the missionary philosophy characteristic of their origin—anti-Catholicism, asceticism, and fundamentalism with strict separation of the sacred and the secular.

Among both Northern and Southern branches of the Mexican-American Baptists, anti-Catholicism is maintained with a fervor that has largely disappeared in official statements and among denominational officials elsewhere. As one Mexican-American Baptist minister stated in an interview:

> The Catholic Church, of course, is—conservatively speaking—not Christian. There are people within the Catholic Church that I have known who *are* actually following Christ and not the priests. But amongst our Spanish-speaking people most of the Catholic practice is idolatrous, and it's not truly a Christian practice, so anyone in that position would be a prospect for us.†

The Baptists are more explicit than other denominations, but interview sources report similar contemporary refusals of segregated Methodists and Presbyterians to recognize Catholics as "Christians."

With regard to asceticism, a segregated Texas Presbyterian source commented in 1951:

> One minister expressed the fear that if his elders should attend [the Anglo] Presbytery and see other elders smoking, he would return to his church with the feeling

---

*This body was established in 1923, despite the fact that it was not until the 1930s that a few Mexican churches began to establish financial independence.

†In addition to the conception of Mexican Catholicism as semi-pagan, reflected in this contemporary statement, Baptist literature is replete with references to Mexican Americans as largely "unchurched," or "nominal," Catholics. These two themes were common in early missionary statements as a justification for their work.

that all moral restraint was now removed—Christians and non-believers were now the same—and the inevitable consequences would be drinking, dancing, and finally prostitution and adultery. There is no question that these churches stand squarely in the tradition of puritanism within our church.[27]

Generally, these congregations, along with other theological conservatives, whether Catholic or Protestant, rigidly separate sacred from secular matters. This orientation is accompanied by strong emphasis on the individual congregation, as illustrated for Baptists in the following statement from an interview:

> The Spanish people are trained to serve *their church*, not the Kingdom of God. We find faithful people who come to church three days a week. They serve the church; they come and clean it; they bring flowers to the church; they cook for the church; they do everything for the church—the local congregation. But they never serve in the community.

As T. Scott Miyakawa remarks, there are many similarities between these congregations and frontier Anglo-Protestant congregations of the mid-nineteenth century. The major—and important—difference is the latter's encouragement of communal participation of its members.[28] This kind of congregation has a familistic quality which was even more apparent in the earlier mission phase. "At one time most of the Spanish-speaking [Baptist] churches were formed by large family units; one church in California had only seven families represented in its congregation of ninety-two members."[29]

These themes of anti-Catholicism, asceticism, separation of the sacred and the secular, and congregationalism characterize conservative Protestantism everywhere. Their contemporary persistence simply underlines the fact that the separate presbyteries, conventions and conferences in the major denominations insulated their Mexican-American members from liberal trends of thought in the main body of each denomination.

Typically, churches in the segregated bodies are small, first-generation, and very poor. A 1947 report of the annual budgets (including pastoral salary and mission quota) of the twelve self-supporting Mexican-American churches in three Baptist conventions showed only one with an annual budget of over $4,250.[30] A more recent survey in Southern California (in 1965) showed a mean pastoral salary of $4,755—probably the highest for Mexican-Baptist churches in the Southwest.[31]

The problem of a badly-educated ministry is also well illustrated by the Baptists. A survey of 300 ministerial delegates attending three Mexican Baptist conventions in the late 1940s showed only 25 percent who had received high school, college, or seminary training. Among the 300 delegates 30 percent had received no education at all.[32] "Jack-leg preachers" who worked part or full time in secular occupations were common in nominally "self-supporting" congregations.[33] By the 1960s pastors of churches receiving mission support from the Baptists' Southern California Commission on Spanish Work were "expected to give undivided time to their pastoral duties and not engage in secular employment, except by special arrangement

495

with the Commission."[34] But it is likely that this rule was occasionally violated by the impoverished clergy.

In 1921, the American Baptists opened a Spanish-American seminary, the only such institution ever provided by any major denomination.[35] It offered only an undergraduate program, however, and thus was the only unaccredited seminary in the denomination. It was closed in 1960. In 1964, special lower requirements for Mexican ministers were finally abandoned by the Baptists.

Until recently, training requirements also were lower among the Methodists for Mexican-American (and Indian) ministers. Ministers were badly needed and Mexican-American congregations could rarely afford to pay a minister enough to attract a college graduate. In recent years, there has been more pressure to normalize educational standards for Mexican-American clergy. Second-generation Protestants are more likely to refuse to attend second-rate churches and are thus lost to both Spanish and Anglo branches.[36] Finally, a vicious circle is established by poor education. As one informant commented:

> There have been double standards in the preparation of [Presbyterian] ministers. . . . Most Mexican and other Spanish-speaking members are lower class, and the denominations tended to feel that "anybody" could minister to them. This is one of the reasons for the poor job being done with them—poor ministers. . . . Then for a poor man the prestige of being "Reverend" in his community keeps him from wanting more education.

Theological conservatism and the rather low educational standards of the majority of Mexican-American ministers have resulted in an exceptional willingness to cross denominational boundaries. Many cities have had associations of Protestant ministers of all denominations trading pulpits with each other and with Pentecostal ministers with an *élan* unthinkable to most "proper" Presbyterian, Methodist, and Baptist clergy.

All of these structural and philosophical characteristics add up to the fact that the Mexican-American membership in these segregated bodies has been largely remote from the currents of change in American Protestantism. It has also been socially remote from Anglo-American Protestants. Obviously, this latter distance would occur in some denominations and in some locales without formal segregation. For example, according to a recent survey,[37] there are comparatively few Mexican Americans in Texas Anglo congregations. By contrast, in California, a Baptist source reports comparatively high social integration: "We have sixteen Spanish-American Baptist churches, yet the English-speaking Baptist churches have more members of Mexican background than these sixteen put together."

These trends make the segregated body increasingly a problem within the denomination. Segregation survives largely in order to provide for churches serving the unacculturated, non-English-speaking members. In the past, the segregated conference represented a career line for the comparatively uneducated ethnic minister. It also provided a special *power* for the minority within the denomination, very easily lost with integration. Thus, there is often substantial opposition to the dissolution of segregated bodies by the minority members themselves, as in the case of the Texas-Mexican Presbytery. Sometimes it is long before the mergers significantly affect social integration of Mexican Americans. After a dozen years of integrated operations in Texas at least two Mexican-American ministers were appointed to Anglo Presbyterian churches, and sentiment for integration seemed to be generally favorable. But after almost a decade of combined work the California Methodist merger was viewed less favorably: "Some of the Spanish-speaking pastors feel the conference was merged too quickly. Others feel the process of merger was not fully accomplished. The congregations and the ministers have somehow not been drawn completely into the total work of the conference."[38]

The Baptists in Southern California illustrate the dilemmas in either maintaining or terminating segregated bodies. The small ethnic church is a problem to the denomination. Its shabbiness and naiveté alienate the increasingly sophisticated native-born member. Further, clergy who can meet denominational requirements cannot be expected to minister contentedly to such congregations. They thus remain increasingly outside the denominational mainstream. In California, such congregations are still seen as mission outposts for recently immigrated Mexicans. Native-born members are seen as possible members of Anglo congregations. But this policy runs the risk of reducing even further the potential ministry, as a Baptist official suggested:

> Transfer from a Spanish-speaking congregation to an English-speaking congregation means they are lost in a sense to our Spanish ministry and church. And these are the people we need because they are the leadership material. . . . One of our main problems is the recruitment and training of able personnel for our pastorate. . . . Most of them are born in Mexico or another country in Latin America. Very few native-born Americans have become ministers in our Spanish-speaking churches.

Explicitly disavowing their exclusively Mexican orientation, the segregated Baptist convention changed its name in 1964 from "*La Convención Bautista Mexicana*" to "*La Convención Bautista*." Churches are encouraged to remove the "Mexican" identification from their names. These steps are meant to retain those second- and third-generation Mexican Americans who prefer not to be identified as "Mexican" and also to attract immigrants from other Latin American countries. Similar attempts are made to manipulate the Spanish-language services. Some congregations alternate Spanish and English sermons. Others provide a pastor adroit enough to deliver a bilingual sermon that communicates to both language groups without excessive redundancy. It is interesting to note that the generational issue here is the familiar one of education and acculturation of the young contrasting painfully with the traditionalism and "foreignness" of the old.

The theological conservatism of the segregated bodies means a retreat from concern with the worldly fate of the poorer Mexican Americans. This phenomenon takes on a new aspect when members of a segregated congregation achieve a degree of upward social mobility. One Texas Presbyterian minister reported his frustration at the constricted view of his church's mission held by the elders in a predominantly middle-class congregation located in a poverty area. He commented angrily, "I am the servant of the Lord in this neighborhood and that means more than being the pastor of this particular church." Theological conservatism appeared to combine with an identification of Protestantism with middle-class respectability. Resistance to church extension into the surrounding poverty pocket seemed to be caused as much by status anxiety as by religious ideology.

COMMUNITY ACTIVITIES
OF THE MAJOR DENOMINATIONS

These conservative, narrowly religious themes by no means exhaust Protestant activities among the Mexican Americans in the mid-1960s. It is outside the (continuing) missionary work and segregated bodies that denominational differences in theology and organization are most important. This unstructured field also provides scope for individual initiative and is frequently the scene of the most rapid innovation. United (Northern) *Presbyterians* began to shift from an evangelistic emphasis in their work among Mexican Americans shortly after World War I. Until that time, the population was defined exclusively in religious terms. It was felt that until Mexicans became Presbyterians they were outside serious concern. By the mid-1960s, community centers represented a major activity among the Presbyterians.[39] They increasingly fell under the jurisdiction of departments involved with inner-city work and became subject to a liberal influence. Many community centers continued to function traditionalistically as referral agencies (or with one or two part-time social workers attempting the heroic task of coping with the problems of thousands of individuals), but the thrust was toward the communal, toward the creation of power blocs among the dispossessed. Urban Mexican Americans were thus becoming the objects of basically change-oriented, though very small-scale, movements. Increasingly, urban Mexican Americans came to be treated not just as a particular people but as victims of society's collective failure. They had come to be one of many social problems in the purview of the "prophets" in the denomination. This was in contrast to an earlier period when interest in them was a special concern of "Mexican specialists," both Mexican-American and Anglo.

Methodist non-evangelistic activity during the same period was even more bound to the traditional settlement-house approach. In the past as well as the present, the degree of this approach depended greatly on the local situation and individual initiative. The social gospel is carried on in Los Angeles in three agencies (all founded in the mission decade 1910–1920). In 1965 and 1966 these agencies had a combined operating budget of slightly less than half a million dollars. The largest settlement house conducted community-organization projects and provided group and individual services and referrals. The second largest provided similar social and community work on a smaller scale and operated a clinic. The third was a residence for Latin-American boys. "Methodist out-reach in social service to the disadvantaged" has grown notably in other areas. The Wesley Community Center in San Antonio illustrates this growth potential: One of twelve community centers in Texas in 1952, by 1966 it had three branches, had extended its scope to include basic research (under foundation grants), had undertaken action work with violent gangs, had established liaison with VISTA volunteers (Volunteers In Service to America), and had become involved with local OEO programs and planning groups. Heavily committed to a wide variety of social activities, its evangelistic work was now virtually non-existent. The small chapel in the newest building was used almost exclusively by visiting Anglo-Methodist laymen who provided a major source of funds. The center grew entirely as social agency; its religious affiliations were almost invisible. The same was true for Methodist centers in Los Angeles. (A Catholic employee of one of the Los Angeles centers was warned by his priest to avoid the center—a surprise to the man, who had thought the center was totally without religious ties.) In San Antonio, the agency played an increasing role partly because of the comparative vacuum in social, recreational, and research services and facilities, and partly because of the initiative taken by its director, a Methodist home-missionary reared and trained in the social gospel.

The non-evangelistic Methodist work among the Mexican Americans illustrates the importance of both ideology and individual initiative. Individual initiative in this work has meant success in mobilizing contemporary local resources (in and out of Methodism) to serve the Mexican-American population. In the early years of the century, this appeared to mean primarily intra-denominational efforts. More recently, it seems to mean successful maneuvering in the increasingly complex world of social welfare, including politics. Methodist work in Texas may be somewhat slowed down by the predominant social conservatism in the area: Methodism is one of the churches of the establishment in Texas. Its lay leaders may not be able to tolerate much more than a moderately traditional settlement approach to Mexicans.

Baptist work, on the other hand, continues to reflect conservative Baptist theology and organization. Social concerns are avoided; an effort is made to remain evangelistic and congregational. But there is some indication that even these conservative evangelists were in the past impelled to "relief work" despite their inclinations.[40] One California Baptist minister recalled: "During the Depression what you would mostly see in a Mexican community would be dire need of a material nature. . . . Now you go to a Mexican community and this need is not so apparent. So the churches have sort of pulled out of this type of approach."

Relief work was regarded as necessary before evangelism, but as intrinsically undesirable. It is still seen as intruding and occasionally substituting an instrumental for a spiritual motivation for membership. One source recounts a Depression-period anecdote about a Los Angeles mother who complained to a missionary that the priest wanted ten dollars to bury her child. When the missionary offered to bury the child without payment, the mother indignantly refused a "pagan" ceremony; she just wanted the Protestant to give her the ten dollars to pay the priest. This source estimated that at that time "between 10 and 15 percent of those who have joined the church through relief work must be discounted as belonging to the category of people who come for what they can get."[41] The assumption behind this comment is made explicit in a mission source: "Our fathers emphasized the hope of a reward for the faithful in the by and by; the present generation desire to cash in their expectations in the here and now."[42] It accounts for the pattern of responses in the mid–1940s by Mexican-Baptist ministers to the statement: "The social gospel is for the welfare agencies and has no part in the program of the church". Among three hundred delegates to the segregated conventions (American Baptist), half of those responding concurred.[43]

The Mexican-Baptist churches withdraw from relief work not only because they "can afford" to do so in locations of relative affluence, but because it is repugnant to them. It not only brings in the "wrong kind of people" (that is, the instrumentally oriented) but may also corrupt the "truly religious."[44] One pastor recalled his church's withdrawal from community work: "Our church had started a community center, but it had become so community minded. They danced and did a lot of things we didn't approve of, so we didn't work with them. We let them be a social agency, and we did our work from house to house."

Notably, most work among the Mexican Americans conducted by the Baptists appears, as in the case just quoted, to be carried on by the local congregations rather than by a central coordinating department. Among the American Baptists, inner-city work has been relatively weak and has had even less strength in the Southwest than elsewhere in the country.* Initiative is taken, therefore, by the locals. Usually these are conservative Mexican-American ministers and congregations that may be even more traditionalistic than their denomination. And the work has tended to be confined to "house-to-house" evangelism, often in "competition" with the Pentecostalists.

INTERDENOMINATIONAL WORK

Migrant Ministry

The most liberal of the contemporary Protestant ideologies is represented by the community-organization movement which departs from the physical shell of the institutional church into free-swinging work among the poor. It is most clearly

*The Baptists represent a curious anomaly. They have an increasingly liberal intellectual wing within the denomination which may or may not occupy positions of power within the church organization. However, its influence is limited because of the historic congregationalist ideology. There is little indication that the Baptists have any less resources in their central apparatus than other large denominations. But Baptists have been much less willing to exercise authority—even informally—over their congregations. Decisions taken in convention appear, much more than with other nominally congregationalist denominations, to reflect grass-roots sentiment. The American Baptists' lack of participation in the Protestant ecumenical movement of the mid-1960s is a good illustration of this trend.

present in the *Migrant Ministry*, whose clergy are supported by the interdenominational National Council of Churches of Christ in the U.S.A. Its state branches attract the most liberal ministers. The Migrant Ministry is dedicated to a view of humanity that emphasizes the "wholeness of the community."[45] Many NCC officials are ministers who have struggled personally with more restricted views of Christian fellowship in their denominations and, more poignantly, in their own congregations—tasting "the emptiness of an insulated congregation."[46] Many NCC ministers appear to follow a career line defined as deviant by their more conservative peers. These ministers eschew mobility within the denomination for interdenominational efforts. At best these efforts are only lightly supported, and at worst they get only token financial support.

The Migrant Ministry was founded in 1920, after a survey revealed "very acute problems of housing, sanitation, and morals" among farm workers.[47] It is a comparatively large effort (with a 1966 budget of slightly over a million dollars) and is an extremely ambitious attempt to deal with the social problems (including health, education, and recreation) of a neglected segment of the population.*

Not all of the Migrant Ministry's attention is directed to Mexican-American migrant workers, but its most controversial and symbolically significant work in the mid–1960s was helping the labor organizations in the vineyards of Delano, California and the melon fields of South Texas. This ministry exemplifies the view that the Christian community must extend beyond the confines of the local congregation. Their communitarianism is paramount; Mexican Americans have been the means for expressing it.[48] Reactions of local churchmen to the Migrant Ministry in California and Texas alike tended to be quite hostile.[49] The work of the Migrant Ministry takes on special meaning in the light of the profound and very visible Roman Catholic attributes of most of the strikers and of the labor movement led by Cesar Chavez. Commenting on the Protestant ministers, Chevez told an interviewer:

> The Protestant Church has some of the same pressures, yet they have been with us every day we have been on strike and they have been identifying with us and not asking us for anything in return. They are not saying, "Look, become a Protestant," and not proselytizing because that is one of the rules that we set, and we didn't have to set it but just so that the score would be clear. And so the [Catholic] Church really has a lot of catching up to do.

The Migrant Ministry's involvement in union activities began in the early 1960s, reflecting a desire to extend its work to more critical areas of the migrants' life. This strong version of the community action movement has flourished within an interdenominational structure which permits ministers to operate outside the constraints of their particular denomination. Thus the migrant ministers are structurally free in two respects: from denomination, and from the localism of a

*Many of their service programs have been taken over by state or Federal agencies. In 1966, 38 state committees were coordinated and guided by the national office of the Migrant Ministry. This made it, at that time, the most extensive interdenominational field program in Protestantism, according to their publications.

particular congregation. No minister within a denominational structure is quite so free to experiment with ideas or with action. As suggested earlier, within the denominations these tend to be men outside the congregational career line and oriented toward experiment. They appear on the staffs of presbyteries and in the social work centers rather than in pastoral roles.

Council on Spanish-American Work (COSAW)

Though the Migrant Ministry reflects the National Council of Churches' concern with social justice, this interdenominational body has also been involved in evangelistic endeavor. Its Council on Spanish-American Work (COSAW) was established in 1912, not long after the founding of the National Council of Churches itself. Set up for the purposes of "cooperative mission planning and action,"[50] COSAW's activities have been extremely restricted.

In the early 1960s, COSAW sponsored a review of Spanish-language missionary literature put out since 1900 by six major denominations. This review served the purpose of appraising and reorienting the missionary effort of these denominations. It found that most literature was directed to existing members, and practically none to the upper-status "sophisticated frontier."

Perhaps COSAW's most important function has been in providing "the only interdenominational experience some of its members have known. It is an ecumenical witness in spirit and purpose in an area where the true meaning of ecumenicity is not known."[51]

A recent review by COSAW of its own work shows an awareness of the liaison functions performed by Mexican-American clergy vis-à-vis the regular denominational officials. It urges the development of "grass roots ecumenism" as part of the churches' broader (nonreligious) role in adjusting Spanish Americans to United States society. It urges that the acculturative and integrative functions of the mission church be "strengthened," leaving it up to the separate denominations to implement these and other recommendations. This review also clearly reflects the difficulty of a bureaucratic approach to evangelism.

THE MAJOR DENOMINATIONS: AN ASSESSMENT

Contemporary work among the Mexican Americans by the three major denominations—both separately and jointly through the National Council of Churches—thus appears to cover the full range of ideologies in Protestantism. At the conservative end, the Baptists do no more "social work" than they consider absolutely necessary for their primary task of evangelism. This body is not only the most theologically conservative of the groups considered here, but also the most congregationally oriented. At the other extreme is the organizational work done by the Migrant Ministry among the grape and melon workers. Here the rationale is not the needs of organized religion but of social justice. The group attracts the theologically liberal and is removed from the constraints of congregationalism and of denominationalism.

The work done among Presbyterians and Methodists lies between these extremes. Though evangelism continues in both denominations, it is accompanied by activities that are not overtly religious, with the degree of social gospel or evangelistic flavor dependent on individual initiative. The settlement house activities of the Methodists show considerable complexity and seem to bear out one authority's contention that "This denomination sees service and witness as paralleling ministries. . . . Service must sometimes precede witness. . . . Service and witness are Siamese twins."[52] The ideological linkage between evangelism and the social work of the Methodist settlements is apparent in notes prepared by the director of a settlement house that totally avoids overt evangelism:

> In the Wesleyan tradition, salvation or the relationship of man to God has been defined as a developmental process. John Wesley talked of this using the analogy of the porch, door and the house. In this sense the community center is or at least is a part of the buildings of the porch. . . . We work largely with the "implicit" . . . church. The members who join the community center are in a sense joining the Methodist Church.[53]

This quotation makes explicit one of the major dilemmas of Protestant denominations in dealing with the Mexican Americans. Until recent ecumenicism, the work of the denominations has been focused on caring for their own members—those already "in the house." However, the Christian ideology carries a mandate for the continued expansion—and ultimately the universality—of membership. Most Protestants have never taken this mandate seriously, but they must recognize its legitimacy for those few (that is, the missionaries) who do.

Protestant denominations are simultaneously institutions of the dominant society and also religious bodies. The Mexican is a nonmember, but he must be seen as a potential member. However, access to membership for the Mexican American is made difficult because he is not simply a *non*believer, but has an *erroneous* (that is, Roman Catholic) attachment. To destroy this attachment, the evangelist must also struggle with the "potential Christian's" special Mexican characteristics. The Mexican people have been to a degree pariahs. In order to cope with them or overcome the distaste caused by "Mexicaness," the evangelist must either be Mexican himself or have a special liking for or "vocation" for these people (which is often defined as rather peculiar). This extension of the church to the "pagan Mexican" is thus *not* an extension of the church as an institution, but only of those within it who (rather absurdly, perhaps, to the mundane Southwestern Protestant) are committed to its religious mandate to extend membership. Simple conversion does not succeed in making Mexican Americans into Anglo Protestants—it just makes them "Christian" rather than pagan.

This tendency on the part of the dominant group to separate the converts is matched by a parallel tendency on the part of the Mexican-American congregations and segregated bodies. Mexican Americans join as converts; their commitment is not to the total Protestant American institutional church with its Swiss, Scottish, English or colonial traditions. Their commitment is to Bible Christianity. The mission process does not incorporate them into the diffuse culture of the denomination, but only into the culture surrounding its stated ideology. And the mandate to include the pariah in Christian communion is handled in such a way and by such people that the fellowship rarely entails a serious social confrontation for the ordinary Protestant parishioner who is insulated both from the somewhat deviant mission movement and from the slum-based settlement houses. One Presbyterian source makes this explicit:

> In the past, Christian mission attempted to meet the needs of the Spanish Americans largely through social service. . . . The main reason for this approach is that these people were looked down upon as the object of mission. Hence, charity was paramount and social service the main concern.[54]

This statement means something more than the anti-welfare Baptists meant, that is, that social welfare is irrelevant to the religious. What it implies is that the welfare activities act as a conscience palliative to the Anglo Presbyterians. By donating money to such endeavors they formally fulfill the Christian mandate to extend fellowship to a people who were pariahs to Miss Rankin's fellow Presbyterians in the mid-nineteenth century and who remain pariahs today.

It seems highly likely that the "Americanizing" goals of the early missionaries would have required a major effort on the part of the denominations to include the Mexican Americans. Neither the original religious goal of extending Christianity to the "unchurched" nor the secondary social goal of acculturating the foreigners has been or can be substantially accomplished by activities that are peripheral to the goals of the organizations as these activities must necessarily be. Denominational goals are being subsumed to ecumenical goals, which will surely weaken the organizational structure of Christianity for some years to come. This "new hope" of religious liberals therefore appears to offer limited possibilities to pariah peoples for their inclusion into the important social institution of the dominant society that Protestantism once was.

OUTSIDE THE MAINSTREAM: AUTONOMY AND INTEGRATION

Pentecostals: Church Autonomy

Pentecostal sects are found quite generally in Mexican-American and other disadvantaged areas, both in cities and small towns. These sects are named after the experience of the Apostles—who were given the "gift of tongues" on Whitsunday, or

Pentecost. In general, the sects try to recapture this experience of the descent of the Holy Spirit, which is considered the most significant single event in primitive Christianity.

Not all Pentecostal sects share congregationalist doctrines, but the general trend among Pentecostal groups has been a rapid splintering of church bodies. For Mexican Americans this has meant concentration into their own church groups. The splintering is not a result of church policy. There is every indication that the congregations within these sects tend toward homogeneity, largely because the Pentecostalists have a distinctive familistic quality. The atmosphere is one of total acceptance: Personal and family troubles are made public for congregational help through prayer; embraces between pew neighbors at the close of a service enhance the sense of a warm and all-encompassing community. Pentecostal groups tend far more than the classic denominations to reach the hard-to-reach in a meaningful fashion.

Materials about the Pentecostal groups were especially difficult to obtain, but it seems generally true that social-gospel activities, especially of an economic nature, have been rare. This is probably due to a lack of ready funds for such work as well as the lack of ideological support.

The Apostolic Assembly is the predominant Mexican-American Pentecostal sect. Others, such as the Assemblies of God and the Church of the Nazarene, have also been active among Mexican Americans, but none appears to be as large although comparative statistics are unavailable. The Apostolic Assembly is highly distinctive because it is quite self-contained and is operated by Mexican Americans. The ministers are certified by a Mexican who lives in Texas. Anglos are urged to join the sister United Pentecostal Church. Negroes are urged to join the Pentecostal Assemblies of the World, also a sister church. The dominant ideology among these churches maintains that each church is responsible for its own welfare and success, that each should care for its own members, and that each should operate within ethnic boundaries. The three churches are bound by a common theology.

We have suggested in our general discussion of major Protestant denominations that the more paternalistic, such as the Presbyterians, have implicitly tended to exclude Mexican Americans from equal-status participation in the church. In denominations like the Baptists, on the other hand, in which denominational practice vacillates between paternalism and self-determination, the equality of Mexican-American members is a serious and difficult issue within the denomination. The ethnic exclusiveness and sectarian autonomy of the Apostolic Assembly mean, at the least, that there is no problem about equality of status in this group.

Mormons: A Policy of Integration

The Church of Jesus Christ of Latter-Day Saints (the Mormons) is especially significant among Protestant efforts, although it does not officially classify itself as a Protestant Church. Uniquely identified with the history of the Americas, the

Mormons have both a special place in their ideology for Mexicans and also a long historical relationship with Mexicans.

Ideologically Mexicans are defined by the Mormons as predominantly of American-Indian stock. Mexicans are bluntly classified as among the descendants of the Lamanites. These are described in the Book of Mormon as a people of Hebraic origin who were marked with "dark" skins as "a curse upon them because of their transgression and their rebellion against their brethren."[55] The Mormons had a special obligation to reconvert the Indians to the true faith, so that "their scales of darkness shall begin to fall from their eyes. . . . They shall be a white and delightsome people."[56]

The Mormons have been part of Western history since the war between the United States and Mexico. (It was on July 24, 1847, that Brigham Young decided to settle in the Great Salt Lake Valley.) Though their settlements have only peripherally overlapped traditional Mexican areas, in the last quarter of the nineteenth century a number of Mormons who wanted to continue polygamy fled to the Mexican border states of Chihuahua and Sonora, where they established about eight colonies.[57] In most of the rural areas in the United States in which Mexican Americans and Mormons have met, there appear to be the same kinds of problems as those between Mormons and Indians. Despite the special place in Mormon theology for Mexicans, the Mormons developed what one author has called a "pioneer attitude,"[58] in which the "subordinate peoples" continue to occupy a subordinate position.

Mormon missionary activity among Mexican Americans has been continuous since the 1870s. As with some other Protestant denominations, the first work was performed under the aegis of the Mexico City mission rather than the United States mission. But at the present time there are two branches of the "Spanish American Mission"—one in San Antonio and one in East Los Angeles. A few of the missionaries are Mexican Americans (the number varies, year to year). More are Anglos (often descendants of the Mexican colonists) who have a special knowledge of Mexicans. If they cannot support themselves, they are assisted by their local stakes. To fill missionary vocations, young men are apparently sent with equal ease to canvass fields in Mexico or the United States. Within the United States they have been sent freely to both urban and rural areas. They are frequent visitors to migrant camps, for example. In recent years, however, work has concentrated on the urban mission. In any case, most of the work has been conducted among the poorer Mexican Americans. Some 15,000 members are claimed, which would make the Mormons one of the largest denominations among Mexican Americans.

Mormon missionary activities are purely evangelistic, and the aim is converting non-members to the one church. Individual missionaries are often concerned about the physical well-being of their flock, but material assistance is not systematically extended to non-members. Part of the rationale for not offering welfare activities lies in their typically evangelistic belief that conversion involves a turning about, a reorientation of the convert's life that will lead to a better, healthier, more moral, and probably more prosperous existence. The church "discourages the taking of unearned benefits from public or other sources."[59] Its own welfare plan is available only to members, and indeed only to members considered worthy. Missionaries seeking converts are taught never to mention it, and several steps are necessary before even a long-standing member receives substantial material assistance. The purpose of the assistance is to restore the value of work in the eyes of the destitute members. Elaborate precautions are taken by means of the Mormon rules to avoid instrumental pseudo-conversions. An elaborate structure of controls keeps the member's behavior from deviating too far from the desired norm. Each member is encouraged to better himself. As in all strongly sectarian groups, the support of individuals by the group is dependent on their strong commitment to the group's values.

Though their theological justification for attention to Mexican Americans is entirely idiosyncratic, the Mormons are more consistent than the major denominations in their demands that, once converted, the Mexican Mormon conform to the diffuse culture of the denomination. This is indeed the diffuse, achievement-oriented culture of the Protestant ethic.

Further, the Mormon pattern of coping with other cultural dissimilarities of the Mexican-American converts departs radically from the ambivalence displayed by many Protestant denominations, or the ethnic autonomy of the Pentecostal sects. It is distinctive enough to warrant the following statement by an official of the church:

> Initially in each area a separate church is established [for the Mexican Americans], for the principal reason of teaching these people in their own tongue. Within the same area, English speaking churches are established and these people are free to go to whichever they choose, and then ultimately there is a consolidation and in these churches English is the language which is spoken. . . . The policy of the Church over the years, throughout its history, has been that English is the language of this country and that as fast as people can learn the language there need not be any separation between them and other members of the Church.[60]

Thus the Mormon Church body is theologically conservative, with a special niche for the Mexican Americans that seems to exaggerate the patronizing tendencies implicit in other evangelizing Protestant sects and denominations. But its rigorous adherence to certain norms of procedure seems more effective in attaining the objective to "Americanize through evangelization" than the policies of denominations which in the past made this an explicit goal.

NOTES TO CHAPTER TWENTY

1. Frank S. Mead, *Handbook of Denominations in the United States* (New York and Nashville: Abingdon Press, 1965).

2. See, for example, Delbert Lee Gibson, "Protestantism in Latin American Acculturation" (unpublished Ph.D. dissertation, University of Texas, 1959) for the argument that Protestantism attracts people well on their way to acculturation and accelerates the

process. See also Fernando Peñalosa, "Class Consciousness and Social Mobility in a Mexican-American Community" (unpublished Ph.D. dissertation, University of Southern California, 1963) for a test of the hypothesis.

3. *Churches and Church Membership in the United States: An Enumeration and Analysis by Counties, States and Regions*, National Council of Churches in the U.S.A., Bureau of Research and Survey, Series A-E (New York: National Council of Churches, 1956–1958).

4. In Corpus Christi, there were 19 congregations of the "classic" denominations, with 14 sectarian groups. In Lubbock the pattern is reversed, with only 6 denominational and 17 sectarian congregations. In Midland, there were three of each type. Although the sectarian congregations tend to be smaller than the denominational, this is not invariably true: Several of the sectarian groups in Lubbock had 200 members—comparatively large memberships. (Data were provided through the courtesy of Leo D. Nieto, Texas Council of Churches.) Estimates from Mormon sources claim some 15,000 members. (Mormons do not consider themselves a Protestant denomination, and do not belong to the National Council of Churches.)

5. For a further discussion of these methodological problems, see also Kyle Haselden, *Death of a Myth* (New York: Friendship Press, Inc., 1964). The "myth" which the author hopes will die is that Mexican and other Spanish Americans are devout Catholics.

6. Most Protestants are accustomed to ignoring not only Catholics but also Protestants in other denominations. T. Scott Miyakawa points out that this indifference is a heritage of the sectarian origin of most American Protestant denominations; even the denominations with establishmentarian origins, such as the Episcopalians and some branches of the Lutheran Church, have "become sectarianized in this country" (personal communication). This characteristic of American Protestantism qualifies its conceptualization as an institution of the dominant society, and, as George Cole commented in a personal communication, such a conceptualization must be further qualified in the Southwest by the comparative weakness of mainline denominations. In this latter respect, Southwest Protestantism is similar to Southwest Catholicism.

7. The rank-order correlation between denominational prominence among Mexican Americans and the United States population for 13 denominations is only .34. The more sectarian groups (such as Assemblies of God and Seventh-Day Adventists) are greatly over-represented among Mexican Americans compared with the total populations. Lutherans are under-represented.

8. The Methodist split has been described as an exception to this norm. As one source puts it: "It was a split that concerned neither doctrine nor policy: it was purely political and social," Mead, *op. cit.*, p. 149. Northern and Southern Presbyterians and Baptists differ because of: "1) differences in the concept of the mission of the church which involve participation or nonparticipation in civic, social, economic, and political questions and controversies; 2) differences in theological (conservative vs. liberal) opinion; and 3) ... the racial question," *ibid.*, p. 180. In addition, Baptists were split on the issue of denominational organization, with the Southern group favoring more centralized coordination of missionary and publication efforts, *ibid.*, p. 37.

9. *Flying Chips: Latin-American Presbyterianism in Texas* (published for the Synod of the Texas Presbyterian Church, U.S., Executive Committee of Home Missions, by the Wallace Engraving Company, no date).

10. Melinda Rankin, *Twenty Years Among the Mexicans: A Narrative of Missionary Labor* (Cincinnati: Chase and Hall, 1875), p. 36.

11. *Ibid.*, pp. 46, 51, 58, 59.

12. *Flying Chips: Latin-American Presbyterianism in Texas*, pp. 2–12.

13. The following quotation from a Texas evangelistic source suggests this theme:

These Mexican Presbyterian Christians are making records for themselves. The storekeepers have to "carry" many families through the crop-making period. From different localities merchants have volunteered testimony as follows: "We have never lost a dollar by carrying one of your Presbyterian Mexican families; we have had one or two who were slow, but they *always pay up*." A rancher tells of a Mexican riding back five miles after dark to "make it right." After reaching his camp, and much painful "figuring," he discovered he had been overpaid "six bits," and could not sleep until it was "fixed." (*ibid.*, p. 40).

14. Our historical material on Texas Methodism is derived primarily from David C. Harrison, "A Survey of the Administrative and Educational Policies of the Baptist, Methodist, and Presbyterian Churches Among Mexican-American People in Texas" (unpublished Master's thesis, University of Texas, 1952); on Southern California Methodism, the material is largely derived from the collection of Mrs. Vernon McCombs and from interviews with others concerned.

15. As described by a later missionary in an interview, 1966.

16. In Los Angeles, "the Catholic church remained the only organized religious body until 1854, when a Yankee preacher launched the first Protestant congregation in a converted saloon." Leonard Pitts, *The Californios* (Berkeley: University of California Press, 1966), p. 126.

17. See Charles Howard Hopkins, *The Rise of the Social Gospel in American Protestantism: 1865–1915* (New Haven: Yale University Press, 1940), and Richard M. Cameron, *Methodism and Society in Historical Perspective* (Nashville, Tenn.: Abingdon Press, 1961).

18. *El Mexicano*, I (1913), p. 6. This was a Methodist periodical.

19. The "Wobblies," whose influence among the Mexicans was documented in *El Mexicano*, were feared as a serious threat.

20. Increasingly, these men were his own converts. One important minister was Ambrosio Gonzales, the grandson of a man who was both "the first Protestant Mexican in New Mexico and the first Mexican preacher in the United States" (*El Mexicano*, II [1914], p. 4), and brought from Albuquerque in 1912. Methodist work in New Mexico was begun in 1850 by E. G. Nicholson (who was remembered by Rev. Gonzales' grandfather). The purpose of the work, according to a 1952 release by El Buen Samaritano Methodist Church of Albuquerque, was "to establish a new mission for American traders and soldiers and for the newly-acquired populations of Mexicans and Indians." In 1871, Rev. Thomas Harwood came to New Mexico to organize and develop Methodist churches and schools, working with both Spanish-speaking and Anglo Methodists. Ultimately, the two phases of Methodist work were separated, and the Texas-based Rio Grande Conference became responsible for Spanish-language work in New Mexico.

McCombs also recruited several men in Mexico. One of them came to work with him in a less orthodox way, as recalled by Mrs. McCombs in an interview:

> Let me tell you about Mr. Quintinilla. He had just come up from Mexico, having been in the battle under Villa. He came to Pasadena with a bottle and a knife in his pockets, and our Mexican minister there, Rev. A. C. Gonzales, saw him and invited him to come to church. The boy—18 years old—laughed and said, "Church! What do I want church for?" But he did go, and he heard a message there about forgiveness and salvation and the Bible. He went out a changed man. . . . He was ordained.

A total of nine Mexican ministers worked with McCombs between 1912 and 1920. Their circuits were large: One, for example, was responsible for Pasadena, San Francisco, and Sacramento. It should be noted that, in many respects, these Mexican ministers appear to have been far more traditional in their view of their mission than was McCombs. For example, one of the most notable, Rev. Olazabel, later became a Pentecostal evangelist.

21. See James Hastings Nichols, *History of Christianity, 1650–1950* (New York: The Ronald Press Company, 1956), pp. 278 ff. for a discussion of the institutional church and the related notion of the church-run settlement house.

22. Samuel M. Ortegon, "Religious Thought and Practice among Mexican Baptists in the United States: 1900–1947" (unpublished Ph.D. dissertation, University of Southern California, 1950), pp. 70–73.

23. *Ibid.*, pp. 70–73, and also Harrison, *op. cit.*, note 16.

24. Jackie Hinson, "A History of American Baptist Spanish-speaking Work in Southern California" (unpublished manuscript, 1964), and Adam Morales, *American Baptists with a Spanish Accent* (Valley Forge, Chicago, and Los Angeles: The Judson Press, 1964), are the principal sources for this historical material on the American Baptists.

25. Quoted in Hinson, *op. cit.*, p. 12.

26. Theodore Abel, *Protestant Home Missions to Catholic Immigrants* (New York: Institute of Social and Religious Research, 1933), p. 3. Mexicans were one of the five Catholic nationality groups on whom the Protestant home mission focused (p. x).

27. Quoted in Harrison, *op. cit.*, p. 29.

28. Personal communication. See also his *Protestants and Pioneers* (Chicago: The University of Chicago Press, 1965) for an analysis of Protestant congregations in the early nineteenth century.

29. Morales, *op. cit.*, p. 105, note 25.

30. Ortegon, *op. cit.*, p. 127. The poorest church in San Antonio had a budget of $1,150. Per capita contributions, 1945–47, amounted to $13.84.

31. Jackie Hinson, "The Economic and Political Organization of Spanish-speaking Work" (unpublished manuscript, 1964), p. 11.

32. Ortegon, *op. cit.*, p. 212.

33. Morales, *op. cit.*, pp. 60 and 65, note 25.

34. Hinson, *op. cit.*, p. 16.

35. Morales, *op. cit.*, p. 73, note 25.

36. Harrison, *op. cit.*, pp. 67, 68; also several interviews.

37. "There does not appear to be any sizable number of Mexican-Americans in the Anglo churches. . . . There are one or two, perhaps more families." Leo Nieto, "Spanish Speaking Texans" (unpublished manuscript, Texas Council of Churches, 1964), pp. 14, 15.

38. Allen B. Rice, "A Peaceful Invasion," *Adult Student*, XXIV (May, 1965), p. 28. But another source pointed out the increase in income and improvement in the quality of leadership resulting from the merger.

39. This appears to have been true for all areas except Texas. In Texas, the United Presbyterians are a minority, and seem to adjust their strategy to the stronger Southern Presbyterians—or perhaps just the Southern ethos. As a result, their work in Texas tends to be heavily evangelistic. Southwest mission programs are summarized for 1966 in the periodical *Up To Date*, X, 1966, The United Presbyterian Church in the U.S., Board of National Missions, New York. The programs show a social-gospel emphasis in Mexican-American programs in every state except Texas, though the United Presbyterians began in 1967 to contribute to the labor-organizing efforts of the Valley Ministry in South Texas.

40. Abel., *op. cit.*, pp. 27 ff.

41. *Ibid.*, p. 32.

42. Quoted in *ibid*.

43. Ortegon, *op. cit.*, p. 228.

44. A 1933 source, Abel, *op. cit.*, pp. 63, 64, reiterates this theme, which is found throughout evangelistic Protestantism:

The Italian minister of an institutional church declared: "The churches are stooping down to do social work during the week, but their real work is done on Sunday. . . . "I think," exclaimed a Mexican missionary, "that our church with its few members has done a hundred times more for the Kingdom of God among Mexicans than our Christian center with its thousands of participants." Some state that they are opposed to a social program because it "destroys the wholesomeness of the church atmosphere."

45. "Christian Concern and Responsibility for Economic Life in a Rapidly Changing Technological Society," statement adopted by the General Board of the National Council of the Churches of Christ in the U.S.A., Feb. 24, 1966 (New York: National Council of the Churches of Christ in the U.S.A., Department of Publication Services, 1966).

46. Gibson Winter, *The Suburban Captivity of the Churches* (Garden City, N.Y.: Doubleday & Company, Inc., 1961), p. 170.

47. Louisa R. Shotwell, *The Harvesters: The Story of the Migrant People* (Garden City, N.Y.: Doubleday & Company, Inc., 1961), p. 176.

48. As the writings of one of them show, migrant ministers are interested in mending social cleavages.

Most of our churches are separated from the realities of the farm workers' world. . . . The farm workers are separated from the established institutions, including the churches. . . . The Migrant Ministry's efforts in Delano must be seen in the context of the Church's historic failure to serve low income people and in the context of deep cleavages in the life of the community. Being with farm workers would not be controversial if there was not a festering wound in the life of the community that results in suspicion and hostility on the part of the farm workers and guilt and fear on the part of established citizens. . . . The Church must be willing to risk its life to live out the urgent message we proclaim.

Our corporate sin against farm workers is so great that the only word that can now be heard is the incarnate word—the word proclaimed by deeds of justice and mercy. In doing of those deeds, Christians may discover those forms of corporate life that can include men on both sides of the track.

Rev. Wayne C. Hartmire, Jr., "The Church and the Delano Grape Strike—A Partial Report" (unpublished, California Migrant Ministry, 1966), pp. 5, 7, and 10; and by the same author, "The Plight of Seasonal Farm Workers," *Christianity and Crisis*, XXV (Oct. 4, 1965), 207.

49. The *Los Angeles Times* of Feb. 12, 1967, reported, for example:

Dr. Reed, pastor of the First Baptist Church and a spokesman for the Delano Ministerial Assn., said last year that 'no moral issue is involved' and that the migrant ministers of the Southern California Council seemed to suddenly know more about the situation than local ministers who had been around for years.

Some angry words were tossed back and forth between Dr. Reed and Rev. Wayne Hartmire, the Migrant Ministry director.

With regard to the strike and march of the melon workers of Starr County, Texas, the October, 1966 issue of the *Texas Presbyterian* commented:

Some clergymen in Rio Grande City and the immediate area, recognizing that they could not take a public stand and expect to remain in their pulpits, welcomed outside assistance from the Texas Council of Churches' Migrant Ministry. Others viewed those who came as "intruders," "imposters," "outsiders who have no business here." One pastor is quoted as saying "In my parish we have no social problems."

Though it received less nationwide attention than the Delano strike, the march from Rio Grande City to Austin, occurring in a far more conservative milieu, caused even greater conflict for the Texas Protestant churches than did similar activities for the churches in California. The clash was highlighted by the 1967 suit filed by the Texas Council of Churches asking for "an injunction to prevent the Texas rangers and law enforcement officers of Starr County from interfering" with the work of their clergy in the strike area. *New York Times*, July 5, 1967.

50. Conrad Hoyer, "Christian Mission Among Spanish Americans," address given at Silver Bay, New York, 1964.

51. Byron L. Spice, "The Present and Future of the Council on Spanish American Work" (unpublished manuscript, Jan. 23, 1966).

52. Haselden, *op. cit.*, pp. 1–7. The author reports 31 settlements and 14 clinics among the Methodists.

53. Buford Farris, "Implications of Church Relations" (unpublished manuscript, Wesley Community Centers, San Antonio, Texas, 1966).

54. Alfonso Rodriguez, "Program," in *Guidelines for a Program Concerning Our Mission among the Spanish Americans in the U.S.A.* (New York: Board of National Missions, United Presbyterian Church in the United States, General Department of Mission Strategy and Evangelism, 1965), p. 1.

55. *The Book of Mormon* (Salt Lake City, Utah: The Church of Jesus Christ of Latter-Day Saints, 1964), p. 201.

56. *Ibid.*, p. 102.

57. Thomas F. O'Dea, *The Mormons*, (Chicago: The University of Chicago Press, 1957), p. 87.

58. *Ibid.*, p. 256.

59. Richard L. Evans, "These Are the Mormons," *Deseret News Press*, no date, p. 12.

60. Donald E. Matthews, Mission president, San Antonio, 1967, personal communication.

Part six

POLITICAL INTERACTION

INTRODUCTORY NOTE

Sooner or later each of the large ethnic or racial minorities has sought to influence its environment through the political process; the Mexican Americans have only recently begun this effort. There were several reasons for the late start. First, a rapid growth of population (including a population shift toward California) has only recently given them potential strength outside New Mexico and south Texas. There is now a broader electoral base, with more native-born citizens. This means more potential voters. Second, their rapid urbanization since World War II and the growth of a middle class improved the chances for political socialization. Third, Mexican-American veterans of World War II and the Korean War provided new leadership and were instrumental in forming new, action-oriented ethnic organizations.

Political interaction between this minority and the larger system is just beginning. Much of the analysis in Part Six deals with past and current impediments to interaction in this sphere of life. Some are imposed by the larger society and some are rooted in the minority. The history of conflict between Mexicans and Anglos in the Southwest has not favored political cooperation. No other ethnic group has labored under a similar handicap of hostility, mistrust, and suspicion as the result of an historical struggle with the dominant society.

The very real dimensions of this handicap become clear when one examines the contact of Mexican Americans with governmental agencies in the United States (Chapter 21). The relationship between the minority group and government has been strained. Mexican Americans have tended to fear public agencies. Even the agencies designed to serve the individual and help redress inequality have represented to him the coercive power of the state.

Government agencies that had an especially negative impact on Mexican Americans include the Border Patrol and the celebrated Texas Rangers. United States citizens as well as aliens were caught up in massive repatriations during the Great Depression. The roundup of "illegals" in Operation Wetback, in the 1950s, often was accompanied by humiliating tests of the citizenship of people who were required to prove that they were not deportable. Such harassment occurs more or less continuously as the Border Patrol attempts to meet its responsibility for detecting illegal entrants.

Friction between police and Mexican Americans has been frequent and often intense. There is evidence through recent times that big-city as well as small-town policemen make universalized racist assumptions about members of the group. For a long time the narcotics problem in the Southwest was defined as a Mexican problem. On the whole, then, Mexican Americans have perceived and indeed experienced government in such a way that they have not felt encouraged to seek political participation.

Internal forces in the Mexican-American population also have retarded the political socialization of this minority group. Its mixture of voluntary ethnic associations, beginning with the mutual-aid and purely social type and later branching out to foster education and citizenship, has only recently been augmented by organizations with a more definite political orientation (Chapter 22). With few exceptions, they have not obtained, and have even shunned, outside help with money and organizational expertise. They have rarely adopted the strategy of political coalition with other groups that is fairly common among ethnic minorities in the East.

Political interaction with the majority is handicapped by a highly complex pattern of leadership, parochialism, and a high degree of individualism. It is handicapped also by the familiar problem of dual validation of leaders by the ethnic clientele and the dominant system. Most of these issues are not unique to the group, but they are especially acute. Furthermore, most organizations have not yet made themselves widely known among the Mexican-American population.

The final chapter in this part attempts to measure political effectiveness. Mexican-American political influence has been restricted by gerrymandered election districts and other external restraints and by the extremely low rate of naturalization of the foreign born. Yet, the data reveal once more the minority's assimilative potential in a relatively open system. Our survey respondents in Los Angeles show a substantially higher rate of voting participation (in the general elections of 1964) than those in San Antonio. The difference reflects the greater isolation and poverty of Mexican Americans in San Antonio as well as the more restrictive voting laws and practices prevailing in Texas.

Although Texas ranks lower than California on almost every measure of the socioeconomic position of Mexican Americans, it ranks higher in terms of their political representation in the state legislature and in the United States Congress. This contrast reflects the large proportion of Mexican Americans in south Texas—a proportion that has no counterpart in California. Low voting participation in the Rio Grande Valley can still result in considerable voting strength. In local government, however, this minority is still greatly under-represented both in California and in Texas (with a few exceptions). The recent episode of Crystal City, Texas, in which Mexican Americans with outside support took over the city government but were unable to maintain control illustrated once more the group's difficulty in activating and sustaining its political potential.

TWENTY-ONE

Contact with
Governmental Agencies

Fᴏʀ many new immigrants from Mexico the only contact with the Anglo world beyond the employer has been with a government agency. Historically, this contact has nearly always been strained. Whatever the present degree of tension— and it varies from place to place and agency to agency—an understanding of the distinctive quality of these contacts is important for an understanding of the total experience of Mexican Americans.

Since the inception of the modern nation-state, the functions of Western governments have increasingly expanded in a direction that counters the inequalities of social class and race. Basic civil rights were acknowledged early. Political rights were enlarged as suffrage was extended legally in the nineteenth and twentieth centuries, as T. H. Marshall has pointed out.[1] Social rights were expanded as publicly supported education, health, and welfare functions were adopted. Civil, political, and social

---

[1] Notes for this chapter start on page 537.

rights attaching to every citizen, without regard for the advantages of birth, remain an important element in the egalitarian ideology of American society. In theory, such rights open the opportunity for citizens born to lower-status parents to overcome the handicaps and reduced life chances of their birth.

The important question for Mexican Americans is how civil, political and social rights have functioned or not functioned in an egalitarian fashion. For this reason, we have been much concerned with two major institutions which, in theory, counteract inequalities in the distribution of power and privilege. These are the educational institutions (Chapter 7) and the political institutions (Chapter 23). Our analysis underscores the persistent gulf between the egalitarian stance of our society and its practices.

But some of the most critical encounters of Mexican Americans with government have been outside the political arena or the public schools. Despite the unevenness of the available data, the importance of the topic as it emerged in field interviews and observations demands attention. This is clearly an area in urgent need of research, particularly since it is an area in which American society can act quickly to ameliorate at least some of the problems of Mexican Americans.

Generally, Mexican Americans have made very few attempts to modify the government agencies' operation. There have been school desegregation cases, and, as we shall discuss below, some suits against law enforcement agencies. But this slender record of challenge to authority does not mean that the Mexican Americans have defined the administration of government programs as just. In part, the quietude has stemmed from a widespread and diffuse fear of authority. Challenging even a "helping" agency such as the school may bring—and has brought—criminal indictments. Also, in the past the Mexican government has concerned itself with certain violations of civil or social rights of Mexican Americans, and this interest by a foreign government created an ambiguous atmosphere.

This chapter suggests that lower-status Mexican Americans developed a generalized subcultural "coping pattern" in their contact with official agencies. It is a pattern that emphasized withdrawal. The few cases that came to *be* cases (in the sense that a dialogue was established with the agency) were in fact deviant cases, illuminating the larger "coping pattern" by their exceptional quality.

These observations may apply to any subordinate group. Hence, our discussion draws on the general literature on the relationship between low-status people and government agencies or bureaucracies. Government agencies, of course, *are* bureaucracies, and it has been cogently argued that the rationality, impersonality and specificity of *all* bureaucracies in dealing with lower-class individuals in some ways exacerbate the problems they are designed to cure.[2] Problems of communicating the agency's desiderata—always present with lower-class clientele—are aggravated when the bureaucrat speaks no Spanish and the client no English. These persistent problems have been aired in the past literature. Government agencies, in addition, have the implicit coercive power of the society behind them. This also probably affects all subordinate groups. However, the Mexican-American experience shows some special qualities stemming both from the high visibility of many of the poor and from the fact that poor Mexican Americans are often defined by Anglos—notably government officials—as "probably foreign." In fact, the propensity of government officials to question their legal status—and their special relations with a Federal agency devoted to testing citizenship—form an important part of this Mexican-American experience.

THE BORDER PATROL

From the earliest part of the twentieth century Mexican immigrants were viewed as only temporary visitors to American society. They were seen as people who could benefit the Southwest by providing labor and who in return would ask nothing more than a small paycheck as they went contentedly home to Mexico. (Whether or not they perceived of Mexico as "home" was rarely questioned.) The growers during the 1920s firmly believed that Mexicans returned home after their stint in the fields.[3] Those who did not go back to Mexico or who wanted to be in the United States at an inconvenient time or place were handled by a variety of local and Federal agencies. Of these the U.S. Border Patrol was the most important.

The first Federal efforts to patrol the Mexican border began in 1904 to combat the illegal entry not of Mexicans but mainly of Chinese, who were then excluded from coming to the United States. With increasing restrictions on immigration the original token force of the Border Patrol, not more than 75 mounted men, was expanded by legislation coincident with the national quotas act of 1924. The Patrol's authority to apprehend illegal immigrants was clarified by Federal statute in 1925 and expanded somewhat by subsequent legislation as recent as the Immigration and Nationality Act of 1952. The agency is empowered to interrogate aliens suspected of being illegally in the country, to search boats, trains, cars, trucks, or planes, to enter and search private lands within 25 miles of the border, and to arrest so-called "illegals" and also those committing felonies under immigration laws.[4]

Border Patrol operations have become not only technically but also socially more sophisticated. Basically, however, they are of three kinds. First is the watch over the border itself, which now involves complex methods of tracking, with air and ground observation of sand traps and drag trails (smoothed-out surfaces in strategic areas to show footprints), traffic checks, transportation-terminal checks, and so on. All of these techniques are designed to apprehend aliens at entry. The second operation is an elaborate set of apprehension activities after entry. Finally, of course, there is the deportation of illegal entrants.

The illegal migrant Mexican attempts to maximize his chances of entry—with the help of relatives or friends in the United States or of professional smugglers; alone or in groups; sometimes with documents forged in locations as far south as Guadalajara; with the help of whatever information or rumor he can garner from whatever sources are available to him; or with whatever ingenuity he can devise in the mode of transportation. Despite the issuance of a visa to a prospective immigrant by the United States Consul in his homeland, the Immigration and Naturalization

Service re-examines his admissibility when he presents himself at the border. The possession of a visa is not sufficient to ensure an alien's admission. Nor is the possession of either a United States birth certificate photostat or a "green card" sufficient proof of the legality of the claimant's status in the United States. (A "green card" is the common name given to an alien registration card, permitting permanent residence in the United States.)

If the border inspector has any doubts as to the admissibility of a would-be immigrant, he denies access, and the individual is then held for a hearing before a Special Inquiry Officer. If the decision is still against the applicant, he may file an administrative appeal.

In contrast to most legal procedures in the United States, the burden of proof is on the individual claiming admission to the United States. The harshness of this procedure stems from a very real dilemma. Persons born in the United States are of course to be admitted, but documentary proof of birth is often extremely difficult to obtain. A man may have been told that he was born in the United States while his parents worked in the fields, for example. To deny access to such a person without a hearing would certainly be a deprivation of due process, because the Fourteenth Amendment grants citizenship to all persons born in the United States. But to require the government to disprove his claim would virtually throw open the border to any person who claimed citizenship. The hearing and appeal procedure with the initial burden of proof on the individual has demonstrably denied legitimate claims, and there is evidence that it has intimidated others from attempting entry. Interestingly, there is no such appeal procedure from Consular decisions, which is inconsistent with the administrative review allowed of decisions by immigration officials.[5]

Mexican Americans appear to feel no special hostility to the Border Patrol in its role as guardian at the border. Would-be illegal entrants know the risks and take their chances. However, the circumstances of operations at the border mean that United States citizens of Mexican descent are subject to harassment. Indignant stories about this harassment are extremely common, particularly among middle-class Mexican Americans who try to come back to the United States from a trip across the border to Mexico. The term "harassment" is not used loosely; hours of delay and embarrassing and degrading questions may be entailed. Resentment and resistance are taken as suspicious conduct. (There is always, particularly at the border, the problem of contraband and suspicion of contraband, especially narcotics, to complicate the problem of legality of entry.) This experience can be particularly upsetting when it occurs to a third-generation Mexican American. To the Border Patrol official such procedures, and the search of ranch and farm lands near the border, appear fully justified. To the law-abiding Mexican American they often do not.

It is their apprehension of illegal entrants that has made the Border Patrol synonymous with obtrusive Anglo authority for many Mexican Americans, primarily because it involves raids and interrogations in areas of heavy Mexican-American concentration which also normally harbor large numbers of illegal aliens. At present these checks occur mainly in two kinds of areas—those with many work opportunities, such as agricultural centers, and those which are transportation nexuses. Riverside, California, for example, for years represented an outer limit to which a "blue-card" holder could extend his visit to the United States. It also represented a point at which such a holder could board a labor-contractor's bus and thus, by entering a forbidden area, become an illegal alien. It was therefore a center of Border Patrol activities. (The blue card entitles a border crosser to stay in the United States for a limited period and within a restricted area.)

Raids and interrogations are also conducted in settled urban communities, with many Mexican Americans stopped and queried closely about their nativity status. Informers are used to locate "illegals"—hardly a practice that makes for intra-ethnic solidarity. The close queries have a reason; in addition to document forgeries, there are many sales to illegal aliens of legitimate U.S. documents.[6] One Patrol official recalls a case in central California in which an officer seemed to feel that a birth certificate presented by a Mexican American was familiar. When he checked at the state capital, he found that in the recent past a total of 23 copies of the birth certificate had been requested by the original owner, who had been busy making a profit on their sale. "Green cards" can be reissued to the owner at a replacement cost of $5—and then can be tampered with for any illegal alien who is willing to pay a price.

The most extensive effort to apprehend illegal entrants was known as Operation Wetback.[7] By the early 1950s it had become evident that large numbers of Mexicans were continuing to cross the border illegally, despite the existence of the *bracero* program. Growers strenuously resisted proposals to make it a crime to employ "illegals," and normal control measures did not seem to work. Widespread alarm about the "wetback invasion" led to official recommendations to Congress that the United States Army be called upon to "stem the tide."[8] In fact, Operation Wetback was conducted by a retired general, and was organized with military precision by an expanded and better-equipped Border Patrol. The roundup effort—raids and interrogations—got under way in June 1954. A special mobile force concentrated first on California and then on Texas, and extended to points as far from the border as Spokane, Chicago, Kansas City, and St. Louis.

Expulsions under this program reached vast proportions. The number of apprehensions rose from 875,000 in the fiscal year 1953 to 1,035,282 the next year. As Operation Wetback was phased out, it fell to 256,290 in 1955 and 90,122 in 1956.[9] In mid-1955, the Immigration and Naturalization Service reported that "for the first time in more than ten years, illegal crossing over the Mexican border was brought under control."[10] In the first half of the 1950s as many as 3.8 million expulsions of Mexican aliens were recorded. (These include multiple counts of men who had entered and been expelled more than once.)

The sweep included persons of long residence in this country as well as those of only a few weeks' tenure. United States-born children were known to have been expelled with their parents. Many American-born adults were stopped and asked for proof of citizenship in cities far removed from the border—and some, reacting with anger as well as amazed incredulity, came into conflict with the officers. Because of its large scale and allegations of rough treatment, Operation Wetback became one of the most traumatic recent experiences of the Mexican Americans in their contacts with government authority. No Mexican-American community in the Southwest remained untouched.

But it should be noted that growers and other employers resented the stepped-up activities of the Border Patrol almost as much as the Mexican Americans. In a heavily satirical article, Bill Helmer, a native of one of the Texas border cities, comments on the "passing of the Valley's happy wetbacks" and shows the importance of the wetbacks in the economy—and ideology—of the lower Rio Grande Valley.

> Before the big Border Patrol crackdown in the early 1950's wetbacks were as contraband and commonplace as liquor in Mississippi. They picked the cotton and citrus, harvested the vegetable crops, dug the irrigation ditches, cut the weeds, cleaned up the messes, trimmed the palms, and kept the Valley's lawns pretty. They didn't cost much, either. A dollar or two a day kept them in beans and tortillas; if you paid them more than that they would just go out and spend it foolishly. Anyhow, it was more than they could make in Mexico, God knows, and they were happy.[11]

Wetbacks were often found and deported, but the "deportation" was usually just a drop across the Rio Grande, and

> the Valley people thought it quite amusing the way a wetback could get back "home" so quickly after being deported. Some could make it back the same day they were taken across. This pleased anyone who employed wetbacks; it meant the system was working smoothly and dependably, and that his wetbacks liked him, which was important to the community conscience. It justified the breaking of the law and the paying of low wages. It was also a good joke on the unpopular Border Patrol.[12]

The journalist's report of the Anglo's view of the Border Patrol illustrates the complexity of the "contact" between Mexican and Border Patrol. It underscores the point that the Anglo employer—usually an exploiter of wetback labor—was also deeply involved. It further emphasizes the important point that the Border Patrol *was not subject to local controls*:

> Nobody liked the Border Patrol, and the Border Patrol didn't like nobody either. . . . I remember they were a surly bunch who always kept to themselves, wouldn't tell tales, and wouldn't wave back at kids on bicycles the way other cops would. . . . The Patrol was frequently accused of mistreating wetbacks and of using Gestapo tactics, but the accusations didn't even have lurid stories to go with them, and I suspect they were largely false. In some ways, the Patrol even helped wetbacks. One day, to everyone's surprise, they instituted a policy of making employers pay off arrested wetbacks . . . before deporting them. This was intended to discourage unscrupulous employers from hiring a flock of wetbacks and then instigating a deportation raid to avoid paying them, which was said to happen from time to time.
> . . . The tougher the Border Patrol got, the more people liked wetbacks. . . . Immigration officials, conceding it was pointless to deport wetbacks across the river if they would only swim right back again, hit upon an idea that outraged the entire Valley. . . . Wetbacks would be . . . transported by planes to the interior of Mexico

so they counld't get back so easily. Such a scheme not only jeopardized the Valley's economy and (therefore) the nation's welfare, but was *inhumane*. . . . The newspapers and the public closed ranks in righteous opposition to the green-clad devils who were sweeping down on the helpless wetbacks.[13]

Although the transportation of Mexicans deep into Mexico was not new in the 1950s, it was not until September 1956 that Mexicans were airlifted to points from which the Mexican Government could return them to their home towns. By the end of 1956, 81,078 persons had been airlifted to Guanajuato, and 107,939 moved by train to Chihuahua.[14] This procedure greatly reduced the number of repeaters.

Helmer's ironic report on the wetbacks concludes with these words on the aftermath:

> By the time I left the Valley in 1954 . . . the wetback was nearing extinction. A few survived on isolated farms and ranches as permanent help, but the migratory wetbacks, depended on to pick the seasonal crops, were too conspicuous to escape the Patrol's suddenly efficient efforts. The new Bracero program kept Valley crops from "rotting in the fields," but Braceros weren't as loyal and trustworthy and hardworking as the good old wetbacks, and also they cost more. They kept the cotton farmers in business just long enough to equip themselves with cotton-picking machines.[15]

Despite the increasing mechanization of Southwestern agriculture, the economic significance of the wetback is indicated in Helmer's conclusion that the 1966 melon strike in the Rio Grande Valley would have been inconceivable during the era of wetback labor. Organizers in that strike actually welcomed Border Patrolmen searching for wetbacks (who were working as strikebreakers). The union itself launched a boat to patrol the Rio Grande for wetbacks, just as in an earlier agricultural strike unions had mounted their own guards to close the California border. Organized or organizing labor has generally been in alliance with the Border Patrol, whereas growers' associations are reported to have lobbied in Washington to keep the agency's budget as small as possible.[16] That organizing labor is often Mexican American means that their feelings about the Border Patrol's activities are deeply ambivalent: On the one hand, wetbacks jeopardize union efforts, but on the other hand many have wetback relatives and friends. The same deep and probably unresolvable ambivalence is evident in many Mexican Americans' discussions of restricting even legal immigration from Mexico.

THE WELFARE REPATRIATIONS

OF THE DEPRESSION

Operation Wetback may have been even more traumatic because it echoed a similar experience of some twenty years earlier. The equivocal citizenship status of Mexican Americans and the consequences for their relations with governmental authority are nowhere more evident than in the actions of welfare agencies during the Great Depression of the 1930s. During those years of sharply curtailed immigration, many individuals returned to Mexico. Some went entirely by their own volition, and many were deported as Federal authorities responded to unemployment by increasing the raids and other enforcement activities of the Border Patrol. But there was another kind of return movement, organized by local authorities in conjunction with private welfare agencies and assisted by the Republic of Mexico itself. During this period, many American cities were perilously close to bankruptcy. It became evident that money could be saved in relief expenditures by removing Mexicans from the welfare rolls. Massive efforts were undertaken to send Mexican welfare recipients back to Mexico. This strategy was congruent with the general American view of the time that Mexicans were really better off "home," irrespective of the wishes or legal standing of the individuals involved. In many cases these individuals were actually United States citizens—a possibility that was apparently never conceived of at the time.

In Los Angeles, unemployed Mexicans had been a burden on the local relief budgets as early as the late 1920s.[17] Many more applied after 1929. The city's economic rationale for "repatriating the Mexicans" is vividly described by Carey McWilliams, who observed the process at close range:

> It was discovered that, in wholesale lots, the Mexicans could be shipped to Mexico City for $14.70 per capita. The sum represented less than the cost of a week's board and lodging. And so, about February 1931, the first train-load was dispatched, and shipments at the rate of about one a month have continued ever since. A shipment, consisting of three special trains, left Los Angeles on December 8. The loading commenced at about six o'clock in the morning and continued for hours. More than twenty-five such special trains had left the South Pacific Station before last April.
>
> The repatriation programme is regarded locally as a piece of consummate states-craft. The average per family cost of executing it is $71.14, including food and transportation. It cost Los Angeles County $77,249.29 to repatriate one shipment of 6,024. It would have cost $424,933.70 to provide this number with such charitable assistance as they would have been entitled to had they remained—a saving of $347,468.41.[18]

Between 1931 and 1934 the Los Angeles Department of Charities launched 15 special trainloads averaging 1,000 Mexicans each.[19] The records of the Los Angeles County Board of Supervisors—their negotiations with Mexican railroads, their careful accounting—cover many pages. There is practically no mention in these pages of the reaction of Mexicans involved—nor of their friends and relatives, who witnessed the "repatriations." Some of our field interviews with Mexican Americans, however, have suggested the depth of the shock, and perhaps even more important, of the sense of impotence and helplessness among those affected.

We have a record of the procedures involved in only one case, the city of Detroit. There the Department of Public Welfare established a Mexican Bureau in 1932. All Mexicans applying for aid were referred to the Bureau. The policy was instigated at the suggestion of and enthusiastically supported by the Mexican Consul and Diego Rivera, who was in Detroit at the time. The Mexican Bureau chartered trains to carry Mexicans to the border at $15 a person including food. The movement was far from benevolent. On the basis of case records, Humphrey comments:

> At the "Mexican Bureau" discussion occurred which was designed to evince a forthright declaration of the intentions of the Mexican family head regarding his return to Mexico. When knowledge of the actual functions of this agency became widespread in the colony, resistance appeared even to the point of refusals to go to the agency. . . . Referral was made to the Mexican Bureau, despite frequent protestations by families that repatriation was not desired. . . . Persons who were naturalized citizens, and children who were born citizens, were subjected to scrutinizing inquiry for purposes of "repatriation." In one case the worker strongly insisted that the possibility of continued dependence was grounds for repatriation, despite the fact that the head of the family had been naturalized. . . . Children might oppose this move for the same reason. . . . The rights of American-born children to citizenship in their native land were explicitly denied or not taken into account.[20]

Pressures exerted by the Detroit case workers included "threats of deportation, stoppage of relief (wholly or in part, as, for example, in the matter of rent), or trampling on customary procedures. Thus, placing a family on the 'cafeteria list' meant that it would not receive 'out-door relief' in its home, but would have to troop to a commissary for meals."[21]

Such detail is not available for other cities, but many of the same general processes (implicit and explicit threat by welfare officials, rumor in the *colonia*, and cooperation of Mexican officials) appear to have taken place elsewhere. In St. Paul, Minnesota, for example, Goldner suggests that because relief authorities had deported 328 Mexicans in 1934 many Mexicans stopped applying for relief.[22] In 1934 Bogardus wrote that "it takes only an insinuation from an official in the United States to create widespread fear among the Mexican immigrants of deportation if they apply for relief."[23]

To the present-day observer, the procedure of those days, with all of its bureaucratic overlay, is painfully reminiscent of the later removal of the Japanese from the West Coast during World War II. There was no institution aiding those who wanted to stay in the United States. Almost no voice of contemporary dissent by Anglos was heard. The ethnic community seems to have been so intimidated that there is no record of organized protest. Only the informal record—for example, of *corridos* (epic ballads)—suggests the depth of the distress.[24]

It is impossible even to arrive at an estimate of the numbers of individuals involved, or even of all of the cities that instituted the procedure. The unusual situation led the Commissioner General of Immigration to comment in 1931:

> An unrecorded but impressive number of Mexicans have returned home in the past year, with the help of the Mexican Government itself or through the efforts and aid of cities, towns, and charitable organizations. . . . The Immigration Service had not the facilities to keep count of this hegira, but with the purpose of laying the

groundwork for future readmission without expense or trouble, many of the aliens sought to impress upon our officers that they were leaving the country but temporarily. It is certain that nearly all will seek to return when employment and business conditions improve.[25]

The scale of the exodus is indicated by a decline in the Mexico-born United States population from 639,000 persons in 1930 to little over 377,000 in 1940.

In fact, many individuals did try to return to the United States. Among those "repatriated" were United States citizens, and if they had had the resources or the information, they could have challenged their removal on constitutional grounds. Later such cases led to an important reinterpretation of United States nationality laws.[26]

Mexican Americans born in the United States of Mexican parents are particularly susceptible to vagaries of the nationality statutes. They are likely to be "dual" nationals—United States citizens by virtue of birth in this country, but nationals of Mexico by virtue of their parents' citizenship. The United States has traditionally taken the position that American citizenship should be withdrawn if a dual national exercises his other nationality. Children deported with their parents, who did not know that they had a claim to United States citizenship or that their birthright could be threatened by acts consummated in Mexico, would serve in the Mexican Army or vote in a local election. Either act was then sufficient to deprive them of United States citizenship. When they later attempted to return to this country, some would find their claim to United States citizenship challenged. Eventually, after many administrative and lower-court decisions, a few persistent individuals were able to argue their cases before the United States Supreme Court in a series of actions beginning in 1955. As a result of these cases (almost all of which involved United States-born Mexicans "repatriated" in the 1930s), the special handicaps of dual nationals have been largely removed. United States citizenship cannot be "lost" inadvertently; it must be relinquished.

The welfare repatriations of the 1930s differ legally and economically from Operation Wetback in the 1950s. During the Depression the focus was on the indigent Mexican; in the 1950s it was on the "illegal" Mexican. But both deportation programs shared important functional characteristics. Both emphasized the foreignness of the Mexican Americans. This was particularly evident during the Depression, when it was an operating assumption of the welfare agencies that the people they deported were aliens. It was further evident in their alacrity to reject Mexican Americans as part of the normal American community welfare obligation. (Of course, this did not apply in the case of the charter-member "Spanish Americans" in Colorado and New Mexico, where "the majority . . . became directly dependent upon the Federal government" during the Depression.[27]) Both programs were massive in their impact, removing not isolated individuals but large groups. Both involved Mexican as well as United States authorities. Both were grim reminders that for low-status members of the group a claim to the rights of citizenship is always subject to question.

WELFARE, HEALTH, AND CONSERVATION

Little information is available on how the equivocal status of their citizenship affects Mexican-American willingness to use the social agencies of local and state governments. That Mexican Americans now turn to welfare agencies for money is evidenced in the surveys of Los Angeles and San Antonio: Approximately six percent of the Los Angeles respondents and five percent of the San Antonio respondents received welfare payments from local sources (exclusive of unemployment and Federal Social Security benefits). But the evidence on more general attitudes is scanty except for a notable concern with what social workers and ethnic spokesmen define as "failures to reach" the Mexican-American clientele. Most frequently, such shortcomings of welfare, health, and other social agencies are interpreted as failures of cultural communication. It is seen as the clash of the rational culture of the bureaucrat and the personalism of the Mexican. Few bureaucrats or researchers realize that these agencies exercise coercive as well as "helping" power. Among those few are the authors of a small-scale study of Anglo-Latin problems perceived by Texas public service personnel. In addition to many attributions of cultural difference, the study mentions that "several workers reported . . . a 'fear of authority,' which . . . created, seemingly, a barrier of suspicion and distrust toward all outsiders."[28] Suspicion and distrust may also be based on demonstrated abuses by the agency of its functions. In recent years, for example, state employment service branches dealing with agricultural labor have offered jobs at below-minimum wages. Rumors about such corruptibility of government-agency officials in the service of growers and at the expense of Mexicans play an important role in the reluctance to utilize agency services.[29]

Another illustration may be drawn from the public health agencies. The problems of these agencies with Mexican-American clientele are severe enough to have generated a number of research studies. By and large the studies focus on the "chasm" in cultural understanding between the folk-like poor Mexican American and the Anglo health practitioner. However, amongst the description of cultural conflict about the causes and treatment of disease appears a usually underplayed but recurrent theme—the sense of distrust of Anglo authority and fear of Anglo power represented by the health worker. Though there are many hints in the literature and in our own field interviews that the problems of cultural conflict are being ameliorated, partly through the recommendations of studies such as Saunders', Hanson's, and others,[30] some of the sources of distrust are evident. For example, tuberculosis cases can be hospitalized, that is, removed from the home and taken to a remote place despite family feelings. Immunization programs (which the Mexican-American poor resist far less than the Negro poor in Los Angeles[31]) cause pain and show no apparent benefit. The past "failures" of the public health agencies, interpreted generally in terms of violation of cultural beliefs, can also be interpreted as violation of norms regarding social relations. Mexican Americans often lack conviction about the helping power of such programs, and in the absence of such conviction the latent coercive power of the agency becomes more salient. Implicitly recognized in many studies, this point is made explicit by Margaret Clark:

> Several factors of the public health worker's status maintain social distance between him and the people with whom he deals: First, he is a government worker and as such is related to other government workers—law enforcement officers, tax assessors, immigration authorities, truant officers, building inspectors, FBI agents, and public prosecutors—all of whom are viewed as potential threats to the security of barrio people.
>
> . . . The second factor which maintains the gulf between medical workers and Spanish-speaking clients is that most public health people are Anglos. Aside from the communication barriers that result from this difference, there are also conflicts resulting from historical group tensions between Anglos and Mexican Americans in California and parts of the Southwest.
>
> . . . Those who are not actually hostile may at least feel uncomfortable with English-speaking persons, fear discriminatory treatment, and remain acutely sensitive to Anglo criticism.[32]

Among the many service agencies coming in contact with Mexican Americans, the U.S. Forest Service would hardly appear to be a source of friction. Yet, the discrepancy between the minority view and the general view of the agency is enormous. To the middle-class Anglo, the Forest Ranger in his flat hat immediately calls up images of Smoky the Bear, surrounded by redwoods, birds, and lovable small animals. To the New Mexican villager, however, according to one among many responsible observers, "it is not uncommon for the native population to see the forest ranger in his olive drab uniform as an American occupational trooper guarding the spoils of the Mexican-American War. The injustices of the past are manifested in the attitudes of the northern New Mexican commoner. There is an enemy in those hills. It is that forest ranger."[33] A service agency to most Anglos, the Forest Service is a coercive agency to the Spanish Americans.

As discussed extensively by Nancie González,[34] the charter-member Spanish-American minority of northern New Mexico came into conflict with conservationists early in the history of their contact with the American society. The villagers were not attuned to conservationist arguments and saw not the overgrazing of their ancestral lands (the Anglos' point) but the erosion of their livelihood as grazing permits in national forest areas were reduced or as the grazing season was shortened. Their almost total dependency on the forest lands for subsistence led to desperate measures, as in the attempt to burn and regain parts of the Carson National Forest in 1967. Resentment against the Forest Service and its personnel reached a peak when it was "learned that forest personnel were used to guide police and National Guard patrols searching for Spanish Americans involved" in the short-lived "Tijerina Rebellion" in Tierra Amarilla, New Mexico.[35]

Though this illustration may seem bizarre to middle-class Anglos accustomed to the recreational use of national forest lands, it is precisely the recreational use that adds insult to the injury perceived by Spanish-American people. Throughout the

528

Southwest, the Forest Service's expenditures for recreation surpass by a wide margin its expenditures for range and revegetation purposes, and the implication is clear to the Spanish-American villager that the rich men play while he starves.[36] The villager is dispossessed, he feels, not for the cause of conservation but for the pleasure of the Anglo. The rifle fire and arson encountered by the Forest Rangers in the forests of New Mexico and Colorado is a consequence of this perception; accurate evaluation of their weak bargaining position makes some ethnic leaders feel that violence is their only means of reaching beyond the government agency to the wider audience of American public opinion. Tijerina's actions and many similar though less broadly organized protests are the desperate expedients of angry rural people who see a "helping" agency as an intransigent opponent of what they define as their collective welfare.

In brief, if service agencies worked ideally they would perform functions that would help counteract the inegalitarian forces in society. The heritage of suspicion attaching to *all* government services, however, probably inhibits their effectiveness. Such agencies not only provide services but they possess and exercise coercive power. For a population whose right to live in this society has been continually under question, the heritage of suspicion of government agencies is justified in those agencies' current operations. Even if their programs were designed for a minimum of *cultural* friction, their effectiveness in "reaching" Mexican Americans would depend on their effectiveness in changing their operations so as to reduce the actual exercise of coercive power.

LOCAL POLICE AGENCIES

If the coercive power of the state is implicit or latent in the operations of service bureaucracies, it is explicit in the case of local police agencies. In general, law enforcement units operate in a spirit of rather diffuse morality. This is perhaps more true in the Southwest with its recent vigilante tradition than elsewhere. Enforcing the law, of course, means protecting or avenging the law-abiding. Very early in the history of most law-enforcement agencies came the discovery that the probability of locating a law-breaker is maximized if attention is focused on the poorer areas of the towns.[37] Thus, suspicion is attached to those who are or look poor. In the case of the visible minorities, such as Negroes and Mexican Americans, the suspicion is easily extended to all members of the group. There has long been a widespread conviction that Mexican Americans are not only poor, but also inherently prone to violence and thus particularly dangerous.

This conviction appears in its pseudoscientific form in the so-called Ayres Report prepared for the Los Angeles County Grand Jury in 1942 after the zoot-suit riots which gave rise to exceptional tension between the police and the Mexican-American population. It said that ". . . his (the Mexican's) desire is to kill, or at least let blood. . . . This inborn characteristic . . . has come down through the ages."[38]

This racist report was endorsed by the chief of the Los Angeles Police Department in a letter to the foreman of the Grand Jury: "Lieutenant Ayres of the Sheriff's Department, gave an intelligent statement of the psychology of the Mexican people, particularly, the youths. He stated many of the contributing factors that caused the gang activities."[39]

The persistence of a racist perception of Mexican Americans among police is indicated by the testimony of the chief of the Los Angeles Police Department as recently as 1960:

> The Latin population that came in here in great strength were here before us, and presented a great problem because I worked over on the East Side when men had to work in pairs—but that has evolved into assimilation—and it's because of some of these people being not too far removed from the wild tribes of the district of the inner mountains of Mexico. I don't think you can throw the genes out of the question when you discuss behavior patterns of people.[40]

In addition to the fact that Mexicans thus obviously qualify as members of the "poor and dangerous" classes, police have had two special reasons for close scrutiny of Mexican Americans. For one thing, the suspects may be "illegal." Second, until very recently the traffic in narcotics was defined in many areas of the Southwest almost entirely as a Mexican problem. Thus, Mexican-American lower-class communities have been liable to generalized suspicion on three grounds, and by three law enforcement agencies concerned respectively with general crime, narcotics, and illegal aliens. The latter two frequently conduct raids and use informers. All three agencies often work together.

The effects of such vulnerability on the relations of Mexican Americans with law enforcement agencies must be seen in historical context.* The longest contact has been with the Texas Rangers, a group of law enforcement officers organized in 1835 to protect the frontier and reduced to a token force of 40 men exactly 100 years later. Despite its present-day numerical insignificance, the Texas Rangers ("*los Rinches*") remain a symbol of Anglo control, perceived by the Texas Mexican Americans as "a force which was *designed* to curb and crush any sign of progress or independent action" by Mexican Americans.[41] Its reputation was earned not only during the frontier conflicts of the nineteenth century, but by incidents in the twentieth century as well. The border region of Texas was in constant turmoil in the years 1912–1920, during the Mexican Revolution. German propaganda efforts in Mexico during World War I raised the old questions of Mexican-Americans' loyalty to the United States. As Webb comments in his definitive history of the Rangers: "After the troubles developed the Americans instituted a reign of terror against the Mexicans. . . . In the orgy of bloodshed that followed, the Texas Rangers played a prominent part. . . . The reader would not be interested in a list of a hundred or more clashes, raids, murders, and fights that occurred between 1915 and 1920."

*The historical portions of this section were developed from materials prepared by Paul Fisher and John V. Kelly.

But he goes on to supply the context: "In passing judgment one must not forget the psychology of fear and racial antagonism that made the Rio Grande a battle-line and the border a battle field. On one side of the river the slogan was 'Kill the Gringos,' on the other it was 'Kill the Greasers.' "[42] The atrocities committed by the Rangers against Mexican Americans finally came under fire from a Mexican-American state legislator, J. T. Canales—one of the rare instances in which this population has met excesses with something other than withdrawal. Among the effects of the Canales investigation was the decision to reduce the size of the Rangers.[43]

In the second and third decades of this century Mexican Americans were also having problems in Colorado and Arizona. Professional law enforcement agencies capable of handling labor disputes in remote mining areas were conspicuously absent from the state and local government apparatus. County sheriffs were the chief law enforcement officials in rural areas, but few had enough trained, full-time deputies to cope with emergencies.

Thus, in potentially explosive situations demanding the attention of a large police force, officials relied upon the assistance of hastily recruited amateurs—in short, vigilante groups. Most importantly, there were no restrictions on who could organize a vigilante committee, and employers who did not control the sheriff or the governor frequently created and paid armed civilian forces to work for them in labor disputes. Civil rights were grossly violated.[44]

In the 1920s an investigation revealed that basic legal rights were often denied to Mexican Americans arrested in communities of the Southwest. Informants in the Rio Grande Valley reported to Paul S. Taylor that police practiced a double standard of law enforcement, protecting the rights of arrested Anglos while treating their Mexican counterparts with violence.[45] In complete subversion of Texas law, Dallas police frequently made arrests without cause, denied prisoners legal counsel and maintained a cell in which prisoners were indefinitely held incommunicado. Denver police adopted similar procedures, and Los Angeles police were accused of employing various third-degree tactics ranging from beatings to marathon interrogation sessions.[46]

In the 1930s the vigilante tradition came to life again in the troubled agricultural areas, most notably in California. The San Joaquin Valley cotton strike of 1932 is representative of these encounters between growers and striking workers, and most particularly of the role of the police as a force intervening in a partisan manner. In this strike Mexicans accounted for approximately three-quarters of the work force. As the strike gained enough support to disrupt the harvest, growers began arming themselves. With deputies at their sides, they evicted strikers from farm labor camps. Local police assured the growers of their right to protect their property and undertook a program to keep the peace by strictly enforcing anti-picketing ordinances and arresting strike agitators. Strikers were unarmed; the growers were never disarmed, and local sheriffs deputized additional local officers. Of these new deputies an analyst comments: "The special deputies which numbered more than a hundred in the three counties were even more inexperienced in handling strikes than the sheriffs and their judgment was continually in danger of being warped by their prejudices. Many of the deputies were ranchers, ranch managers, and gin employees."[47]

In the violence which shortly broke out, several strikers were killed. To prevent further bloodshed the Governor of California ordered a large contingent of the State Highway Patrol into the area. The subsequent investigations concluded that "without question, civil rights of strikers have been violated."[48] A local under-sheriff revealed the basic assumptions of the law-enforcement forces about local social structure and about their own role: "We protect our farmers here in Kern County. They are our best people. They are always with us. They keep the county going. They put us here and they can put us out again so we serve them. But the Mexicans are trash. They have no standard of living. We herd them like pigs."[49]

The tradition of law enforcement by "emergency forces" of untrained and partisan men recurs in the history of Mexican-American labor disputes in isolated mining communities during the early years of the twentieth century, and in the fields beginning with the 1928 strike of the *Confederación de Uniones Obreras*, and subsequent strikes in 1934, 1936, and 1941.[50]

Conflict between police and workers has been endemic in the most recent and well-publicized of the agricultural strikes. In the 1966–1967 melon strike in Rio Grande City, Texas, the ubiquitous Rangers appeared to "protect the harvest." Their indulgence in violence led to considerable public protest. In California, the Delano police chief went so far as to change the color of his officers' uniforms so that grape strikers could distinguish between the "friendly" local men and the "less considerate" officers from other forces.[51] Early in 1968, resentment among the grape strikers against law enforcement officers hovered increasingly close to violence. Cesar Chavez, in a remarkable effort to reaffirm the nonviolent nature of the movement, went on a prolonged fast, with serious after-effects on his health. It is probably due largely to his personal influence that this most long-drawn-out, most widely known of the agricultural organizing efforts has been so notably free of violence between police and strikers.

These cases reflect the situation in small communities. Strikes represent a very real threat to the established social system; they vehemently call into question the rationales and the mutual myths by which local ethnic stratification is maintained. Whether or not civilians are deputized in such strikes, the local law-enforcement agencies know, in the words of the earlier-mentioned Kern County under-sheriff, "who put them there," and they know who are the "best" people and who are "trash."

Large city police operate under different circumstances. Far more bureaucratized, they may share the racist assumptions of the small-town policemen, as the earlier quotations indicate, but their operating procedures differ. Mexican Americans did not begin to flock to the cities in large numbers until comparatively recently, and it is difficult to put their experiences there in meaningful perspective. The sense of outrage, the continual references to police brutality, the anecdotes, the picketing, the many harrowing incidents which never become formal cases and thus never permit any chance of redress—all of these give an overwhelming impression of the problems in police relations with Mexican Americans in one city after another. But the police system in cities is far more complex, and its relation to the larger system is far more difficult to disentangle than it is in the smaller towns.

Police tactics in Los Angeles, documented in connection with Mexican-American youth activities in the late 1930s and early 1940s, definitely appear to have departed from tactics used in dealing with other populations. According to one study, "prejudicial treatment" and arrest procedures which employed "indiscriminate, wholesale . . . 'dragnet' methods" were widely used. These procedures, in turn, helped account for a higher arrest-conviction ratio among minorities. Thus, in 1938 the Los Angeles Superior Court records showed a ratio of 5.3 arrests to each felony conviction for Mexican Americans, compared with only 2.7 for Anglos. Furthermore, the same study showed that Anglos, if convicted, had almost three times as good a chance for probation as Mexican-American offenders.[52] Mass arrests continued to be a major police tactic in Los Angeles during the increasingly serious race tensions of the 1940s. It was a major means of control used to suppress what police in 1942 defined as an "imminent" crime wave by youth gangs, which in 1943 "broke out" in the "zoot-suit riots." (Both situations were clearly entangled with racial issues. The zoot-suit riots, in particular, were definitely Anglo-initiated race riots, though the media at the time did not define them as such.[53]) The tactic of mass arrests, which was widely publicized, was felt by a relatively detached observer to "almost inevitably intensify the already serious bitterness between the Mexican colony and the remainder of the community."[54] In Los Angeles, intensive police control procedures were used against a population of which a large proportion was comparatively new on the urban scene and which had neither self-help institutions nor influence on the political process. A number of interviews have suggested that the zoot-suit riots, with the accompanying sensationalized news, left a deep residue of shame and anger among Mexican Americans. Their importance clearly transcended Los Angeles.

It is perhaps significant that in the late 1940s and early 1950s Mexican-American war veterans, age peers of those who had been arrested in the early 1940s, were prominent among those who formed the Los Angeles Community Service Organization (CSO), one of the earliest political associations in the area. And it is also significant that one of the CSO's principal activities was to marshal complaints of police malpractice: It conducted 35 formal investigations between 1947 and 1956.[55] During the same period, another major Mexican-American organization, the Alianza Hispano Americana, developed a program to initiate court action in civil rights violations throughout the Southwest. In the 1960s, the Los Angeles-based Council on Mexican-American Affairs took up the cause. Numerous *ad hoc* groups were formed—and are still formed—in communities when particularly outrageous events occurred. Thus, in 1966, one such group, the Citizens' Committee for Justice, attained unusual success, and the local gun law was changed after a Riverside policeman had killed a fleeing youth. In late September 1966 the American Civil Liberties Union opened a "police malpractice complaint center" in the Mexican-American area of East Los Angeles. The ACLU accepted about ten cases a month in their first two years of operation.[56] However, tangible outcome in the way of change in police practice, including the recruitment and training of officers and the disciplining of offending officers, has been inconsequential. These non-judicial channels have been so unsatisfying that in late 1968 the ACLU joined with the University of Southern California's Western Center for Law and Poverty in a suit directed against the Los Angeles Police Department for harassment of minority citizens—an indication of the complexities and of the difficulties in instituting reform. Efforts to achieve more responsible law enforcement thus have moved from "normal" channels to political organization to judicial relief—all without much effect. The condition in the Los Angeles area is duplicated in many places throughout the Southwest.

The problem is compounded by the unwillingness of Mexican Americans to file complaints. As a document issued by the Council on Mexican-American Affairs concludes, Mexican-American "complainants were very reluctant to take their grievances to law enforcement."[57] This is substantiated by the fact that of 1,328 complaints alleging police brutality presented to the U.S. Department of Justice between January, 1958 and June, 1960, only ten were from persons known to be of Mexican descent.[58]

Information on day-to-day details of police practice in areas of heavy Mexican concentration is very poor. A study in the mid-1960s showed Mexican Americans in San Diego to believe that

> In San Diego police "exist for the protection of the . . . Anglo community," and they have only "restraining and punitive" functions [in the minority areas]. . . . Several police practices were singled out for unfavorable comment. It was felt that police are discriminatory, condescending, and paternalistic. This is evidenced by indiscriminate stopping and frisking of both minority adults and juveniles; the use of degrading terms, such as "pancho," "muchacho," and "amigo"; and excessive patrolling within the Mexican-American community.[59]

These complaints, according to our interviews, barely scratch the surface of discontent with the police: Condescension may be irritating, but brutality terrifies and enrages.

Post-arrest judicial processes, in turn, are almost totally unanalyzed.[60] At this writing, a motion challenging the constitutionality of indictments returned by the Los Angeles County Grand Jury was being heard; it attacked the jury as grossly under-representing the Mexican-American population. The many complexities of court procedure and of lawyer-client interaction, so critical to the outcome of a case, have barely been studied. These processes, interestingly, have *not* been a significant source of protest by Mexican-American groups. Thus, the operations of the courts, one of the most sensitive government functions, must be left unexplored, though it may be one of the potentially explosive points of contact between Mexican Americans and the government.

534

IMPLICATIONS OF GOVERNMENT CONTACT

The data available on Mexican-American contact with government agencies are least deficient for those agencies which are directly concerned with law enforcement. Accordingly, we have concentrated on these agencies. It may be objected that data on police practices do not give information about Mexican relationships with "helping" agencies. But the coercive power explicit in the law-enforcement agencies, such as the police and the Border Patrol, has always intruded into the so-called "helping" agencies. This intrusion was most dramatic during the Depression, when many of the city welfare agencies became functionally indistinguishable from law-enforcement agencies directly involved in deportation. The intrusion is continuously latent in all government agencies. Frequently it is manifest. We suggested at the outset of this chapter that many immigrants from Mexico have had contact with American society only through their employers and through government agencies. (Government agencies have, of course, proliferated during the twentieth century and are far more significant in the experience of the present-day newcomer to the United States than they were to the nineteenth-century immigrants coming from Europe.) If our analysis in this chapter is borne out by further research, the confusion of welfare and police functions in the operation of government agencies might be a very significant element in the historical reluctance of Mexican Americans to become attached to this society. Further, it may help explain the alienation and "hard-to-reach" orientation of many Mexican Americans in the present. Thus the Border Patrol and its actions cannot be dismissed as merely of historical interest. Its past activities have, indeed, left a residue of hatred that influenced all subsequent relationships of Mexican Americans to other agencies. This residue continues to affect the Border Patrol because the Patrol still has much to do with the lives of individuals and the conditions of life in Mexican-American communities. On the other hand, the welfare "repatriations" of the 1930s are of more historical than contemporary relevance. But their rationale and their procedures have a contemporary echo, and they remind us that though the administration of social-welfare funds in the present is not so blatantly coercive as in the past, it nonetheless carries a coercive and degrading quality.

Until World War II government agencies easily could, and did, define Mexican Americans as "probably foreign." Along with most citizens of the Southwest, they added to this legal definition the notion that Mexican Americans were permanently "alien" in behavior. It was this combined definition that permitted the welfare repatriations of the 1930s as a similar definition of another ethnic group, the Japanese Americans, "legitimated" even more extreme government action in California a decade later. It is this legal and social definition that continues to permit the Border Patrol to examine Mexican Americans to see if indeed they *are* foreign and deportable. The "probably foreign" definition of Mexican Americans thus has exposed them to harassment of a very special nature. It has also exposed them to unusual administrative arbitrariness. Under the immigration rules, the burden of proof of citizenship is on the individual rather than on the government. As court cases involving the nationality laws attest, the amount of administrative discretion in this crucial matter is extraordinary. More than most law-enforcement agencies, the Border Patrol initiates action; it does not merely react to citizen complaints.[61] Administrative arbitrariness also characterizes much contact with police and other law-enforcement agencies and has frequently resulted in special discrimination against Mexican Americans.

This chapter has been concerned primarily with government bureaucratic functions and with some of the special relations of Mexicans to these bureaucracies. In recent years the meaning of government to minorities has been changed by the proliferation of a variety of *ad hoc* agencies, particularly those funded by the Office of Economic Opportunity (OEO). They have appeared in local neighborhoods as special-function agencies for minorities, and they have appeared at the state-wide and regional level with similar special mandates to serve hitherto neglected citizens. As such they have provided in some instances a real impetus for local change; in other instances their impact at the local level has been insignificant. But in many places and situations they have provided a specific focus for minority discontent with government agencies in general. Thus, the beginning of an upsurge of militancy among Mexican-American associations coincided with a mass walkout of Mexican-American representatives to a 1966 meeting called by the Equal Employment Opportunities Commission. The meeting, paradoxically, was called by the Commission in response to previous complaints that there had not been enough attention to Mexican-American needs in administration of antidiscriminatory regulations. The Cabinet-level meetings held on Mexican-American problems in 1967 met essentially the same reception from a wide variety of Mexican-American leaders. Failure to meet minority needs is especially irritating in an agency whose sole job it is to meet those needs. However, such special-function agencies do permit the legitimation of protest by minority members. The protest can then spill over to other agencies of government.

An analysis of the role of such agencies in focusing the more diffuse anxiety and resentment of Mexican Americans vis-à-vis government agencies in general would be very useful. In rare instances, such as that of the California Rural Legal Assistance offices, OEO programs have even provided the means for modifying the operations of "normal" local government agencies.[62] Because the roles of government at all levels are changing so rapidly, our discussion here can provide no more than a prolegomenon to research in this highly significant area as well as to policy intervention in the status of minorities.

Inquiries into such ostensibly egalitarian institutions as the schools and the welfare agencies generally show persisting structural relations that maintain social inequalities as well as those that work toward their eradication. This is particularly true when these inequalities are related to social visibility, as with poor Mexican Americans. Recently the politicization of contacts between client and agency has shown how clearly the client sees the agency as a combination of welfare and coercion.

This politicization has appeared nationally with the welfare rights organizations. It can be viewed as the client counterpart of the agency's combination of welfare and coercion. It has not yet advanced very far among Mexican Americans. In time this politicization, combined with direct political action, may begin to find the solutions to minority problems that men such as T. H. Marshall felt were to come from American society at large as natural extensions of the citizenship role.

NOTES TO CHAPTER TWENTY-ONE

1. T. H. Marshall, "Citizenship and Social Class," in his *Class, Citizenship and Social Development* (Garden City, N.Y.: Doubleday & Company, Inc., 1964). See also H. L. Wilensky and C. N. LeBeaux, *Industrial Society and Social Welfare* (New York: Russell Sage Foundation, 1958) for the notion of social welfare as having a "residual" function operating when normal social structures fail, and an "institutional" function.

2. Sjoberg, Brymer, and Farris discuss these problems in an analytic review of the literature which includes illustrations from a long-range study of Mexican Americans in San Antonio. Gideon Sjoberg, Richard A. Brymer, and Buford Farris, "Bureaucracy and the Lower Class," *Sociology and Social Research*, L (Apr., 1966), pp. 325–337.

3. See Carey McWilliams, *Factories in the Field* (Boston: Little, Brown and Company, 1939).

4. *The Border Patrol: Its Origin and Its Work*, U.S. Department of Justice, Immigration and Naturalization Service (1965).

5. See Ronald Wyse, "The Position of Mexicans in the Immigration and Naturalization Laws," in Leo Grebler et al., *Mexican Immigration to the United States: The Record and Its Implications* (Mexican-American Study Project, Advance Report 2, Graduate School of Business Administration, University of California, Los Angeles, Jan., 1966), Appendix D.

6. As an illustration, in the month of November, 1967, there were in the Southwest region 41 such "green-card misuses," 43 nonresident "blue-card" misuses, 65 individuals presenting invalid documents to claim United States citizenship, 65 individuals presenting unsupported oral claims to United States citizenship, and 298 aliens apprehended who had been smuggled in by 58 smugglers. Information provided by Richard Wischkaemper of the Border Patrol Regional Commissioner's office, San Pedro, California, who kindly supplied much other information on Patrol operations.

7. This discussion was developed from Leo Grebler et al., *op cit.*, pp. 33–35.

8. *Reorganization of the Immigration and Naturalization Service*, Hearings before the Subcommittee on Legal and Monetary Affairs of the Committee on Government Operations, House, 84th Congress, first session, March 9 and 17, 1955, p. 3.

9. *Annual Report of the Immigration and Naturalization Service*, 1956, p. 8.

10. *Annual Report of the Immigration and Naturalization Service*, 1955, p. 10.

11. Bill Helmer, "The Valley's Happy Wetbacks," *The Texas Observer*, LVIII (Dec. 9, 1966), pp. 6–8. See also Lyle Saunders and Olen E. Leonard, "The Wetback in the Lower Rio Grande Valley of Texas," Inter–American Education Occasional Paper no. 7 (Austin, Tex.: University of Texas Press, 1951).

12. Helmer, *op. cit.*, p. 6.

13. *Ibid.*, p. 7.

14. *Annual Report of the Immigration and Naturalization Service*, 1956.

15. Helmer, *op. cit.*, p. 8.

16. Ernesto Galarza, *Merchants of Labor: The Mexican Bracero Story* (San Jose, Calif.: The Rosicrucian Press, Ltd., 1965), p. 61.

17. *Mexicans in California: Report of Governor C. C. Young's Mexican Fact-finding Committee* (Sacramento: 1930), pp. 191–194.

18. Carey McWilliams, "Getting Rid of the Mexicans," *American Mercury*, XXVIII (Mar., 1933), pp. 322–324.

19. We are indebted to Ronald Lopez for calling our attention to the records of the Los Angeles County Board of Supervisors, from which these figures are drawn. Interestingly, simultaneous efforts were made to get Mexicans on the city's relief rolls into agricultural labor. In 1933, the *Los Angeles Citizen* (an AFL official publication) noted that 4,000 Mexican families on welfare had been shipped to the valleys to harvest the cotton crop, which growers contended was in danger of loss from the winter rains (issue of Nov. 10, 1933).

20. Norman D. Humphrey, "Mexican Repatriation from Michigan—Public Assistance in Historical Perspective," *Social Service Review*, XV (Sept., 1941), pp. 505, 507, 509.

21. *Ibid.*, p. 505.

22. Norman S. Goldner, "The Mexican in the Northern Urban Area: A Comparison of Two Generations" (unpublished Master's thesis, University of Minnesota, 1959), p. 36.

23. Emory L. Bogardus, *The Mexican in the United States* (Los Angeles: University of Southern California Press, 1934), p. 95, cited in Ronald Lopez, "Los Repatriados" (unpublished manuscript), p. 11. We are indebted to Ronald Lopez for calling attention to a number of details of Mexican repatriation from cities throughout the nation.

24. See the *corrido* "El Deportado," reproduced in Nellie Foster, "The Corrido: A Mexican Culture Trait Persisting in Southern California" (unpublished Master's thesis, University of Southern California, 1939), p. 182, cited in Armando Morales, *Historical and Attitudinal Factors Related to Current Mexican American Law Enforcement Concerns in Los Angeles* (mimeographed manuscript, Council of Mexican American Affairs, 1967), p. 9. The welfare repatriations were connected in the Mexican-American definition of the situation with the stepping up of raids by immigration authorities, according to Foster (p. 8).

25. *Annual Report of the Commissioner-General of Immigration* for the fiscal year 1931, p. 9.

26. The material here is developed from Wyse, *op. cit.*

27. Nancie L. González, *The Spanish Americans of New Mexico: A Distinctive Heritage* (Mexican-American Study Project, Advance Report 9, Graduate School of Business Administration, University of California, Los Angeles, Sept., 1967), p. 88.

28. Glenn V. Ramsey and Beulah Hodge, "Anglo Latin Problems as Perceived by Public Service Personnel," *Social Forces*, XXXVII (May, 1959), p. 346.

29. Ismael Dieppa, lecture at the University of California, Riverside, 1969, referring to such abuses in Santa Cruz County, California.

30. Lyle Saunders, *Cultural Difference and Medical Care* (New York: Russell Sage Foundation, 1954); Robert C. Hanson and Lyle Saunders, with the collaboration of Marion Hotopp, *Nurse-Patient Communication—A Manual for Public Health Nurses in Northern New Mexico* (Boulder, Colo. and Santa Fe, N. Mex.: Bureau of Sociological Research, Institute of Behavioral Science, University of Colorado and New Mexico State Department of Public Health, 1964). See also A. Taher Moustafa and Gertrud Weiss, *Health Status and Practices of Mexican Americans* (Mexican-American Study Project, Advance Report 11, Graduate School of Business Administration, University of California, Los Angeles, Feb., 1968).

31. Glenn D. Mellinger, Dean I. Manheimer, and Marianne T. Kleman, "Deterrents to Adequate Immunization of Preschool Children" (Los Angeles County Health Department, 1967), p. 26.

32. Margaret Clark, *Health in the Mexican American Culture* (Berkeley, Calif.: University of California Press, 1959), pp. 232, 233.

33. Tomas C. Atencio, "The Forest Service and the Spanish Surname American," presented at Cabinet Committee Hearings on Mexican American Affairs, El Paso, Tex., 1967.

34. González, *op. cit.*

35. Clark S. Knowlton, "Recommendations for the Solution of Land Tenure Problems Among the Spanish American," presented at Cabinet Committee Hearings on Mexican American Affairs, El Paso, Tex., 1967.

36. Atencio, *op. cit.*

37. See Allan Silver, "The Demand for Order in Civil Society: A Review of Some Themes in the History of Urban Crime, Police and Riot," in David J. Bordua (ed.), *The Police: Six Sociological Essays* (New York: John Wiley & Sons, Inc., 1967). Silver discusses the development of techniques—urban and rural—for dealing with the "dangerous classes" of nineteenth-century England. He comments that the "vigilantism" of rural England at the time exacerbated the latent class conflict, and that the urban pressure for the bureaucratization of police functions operated to insert a "third force," the force of the state, into the situation of developing class cleavage.

38. Cited in Carey McWilliams, *North from Mexico* (New York: J. B. Lippincott Company, 1949), p. 234.

39. C. B. Horrall, letter to Foreman Oliver.

40. *Hearings before the United States Commission on Civil Rights*, San Francisco, Jan. 27, 1960 (Washington, D.C., 1960).

41. Arthur J. Rubel, *Across the Tracks* (Austin, Tex.: University of Texas Press, 1966), p. 47; emphasis added.

42. Walter Prescott Webb, *The Texas Rangers: A Century of Frontier Defense* (Boston: Houghton Mifflin Company, 1935), pp. 479 and 486.

43. *Ibid.*, pp. 513–515.

44. Some of the more dramatic cases of law "enforcement" by vigilantes occurred in the mining country of Arizona. One was a strike by Mexican-American workers at Ray in 1915. Almost immediately after the walkout began, carloads of armed men left Phoenix for the camp "to restore order," even though the local sheriff had not requested aid because the strikers were generally peaceful in making their demands. Violence was averted when the mine manager agreed to a wage increase. Another, even more dramatic case was the Bisbee deportation in 1917. The IWW Bisbee Miners Union called a walkout, ostensibly over wages and hours. The sheriff of Cochise County, believing that the strike was intended to embarrass the United States war effort, conspired with a company vigilance committee to deport all workers suspected of Wobbly affiliation. A "posse" of civilians marched them into the ball park. Telephone and telegraph offices were guarded by the sheriff, and company officials censored all Associated Press dispatches. Those corralled in the park, some 1,200 persons, were then loaded into boxcars and shipped to Columbas, New Mexico, 114 miles from Bisbee. Normal government operations in the area collapsed. Armed men guarded entrances to the district, keeping out "undesirables." The company created a court staffed with their own men who went about passing upon the "fitness" of workers who were allowed to remain in the district, resulting in further deportations. These paragovernmental institutions lasted for four months. Vernon H. Jensen, *Heritage of Conflict: Labor Relations in the Nonferrous Metals Industry Up to 1930* (Ithaca, N.Y.: Cornell University Press, 1950), pp. 364, 365 (for Ray), pp. 401–406 (for Bisbee).

45. Paul S. Taylor, "Crime and the Foreign Born: The Problem of the Mexican," in National Commission on Law Observance and Enforcement, *Report on Crime and the Foreign Born* (Washington, D.C., 1931), VI, p. 219.

46. National Commission on Law Observance and Enforcement, *Lawlessness in Law Enforcement* (Washington, D.C., 1931), XI, p. 138 (Dallas), p. 141 (Denver), and pp. 143, 144 (Los Angeles).

47. Paul S. Taylor and Clark Kerr, "Documentary History of the Strike of the Cotton Pickers in California—1933," in U.S. Congress, Senate, *Education and Labor Committee Hearings: Violation of Free Speech and Rights of Labor; Part 54, Agricultural Labor in California*, 1940, p. 19947.

48. *Ibid.*, p. 20005.

49. *Ibid.*, p. 19992. Also quoted in McWilliams, *op. cit.*, p. 191, whose treatment of labor troubles reflects the progressive biases of his era.

50. Galarza, *op. cit.*, p. 39.

51. John Gregory Dunne, *Delano* (New York: Farrar, Straus & Giroux, 1967), p. 114.

52. Edwin M. Lemert and Judy Rosberg, "The Administration of Justice to Minority Groups in Los Angeles County," in R. L. Beals, Leonard Bloom, and Franklin Fearing (eds.), *University of California Publications in Culture and Society*, vol. II (Berkeley, Calif.: University of California Press, 1948), pp. 3, 12.

53. See McWilliams, *op. cit.*, for an analysis of both the Sleepy Lagoon arrests and the later zoot-suit riots.

54. Paper by Guy T. Nunn, field representative of the Minority Groups Service of the War Manpower Commission (read in a meeting of the Special Mexican Relations Committee of the Los Angeles County Grand Jury, Oct. 8, 1942), p. 17. This was two months following the arrest of more than 600 Mexican youths following the Sleepy Lagoon incident. Nunn also reported the hysterical Anglo reaction to the exaggerated news reports:

> Shortly after the mass arrests of several weeks ago complaints began to reach my agency from communities over a hundred miles away, alleging a sudden increase in discrimination against Spanish-speaking people; many times in localities relatively free of it in the past, as a direct out-growth of events in Los Angeles and of the sensational publicity accorded them. Mexicans were denied access to movies, public parks, and recreational facilities, restaurants. At the same time there was a sharp increase in employment discrimination (*ibid.*).

55. Morales, *op. cit.*, p. 12.

56. Major causes of complaint involve the failure of officers to show warrants before searching private homes and cars, the failure of officers to identify themselves, and the use of ethnic slurs by officers (*ibid.*, pp. 17–19). Morales notes that several of the officers against whom complaints were lodged were themselves Mexican Americans. He goes on to comment that the "common request on the part of some Mexican Americans . . . that officers learn to speak Spanish and that they hire more Mexican American officers . . . does not necessarily insure a good 'product' " (p. 20). Morales also cites several instances in which epileptic and other convulsive seizures suffered by Mexican Americans were interpreted by police officers as evidence of the use of narcotics, and strongly suggests that the Mexican Americans are victims of the long-standing belief that, as one law enforcement officer put it in an interview, "narcotics problems are Mexican problems." The Police Commission, charged with the responsibility of investigating malpractice charges, is itself a source of complaint in Los Angeles because of the long period of time usually elapsing between the submission of a complaint and its processing, the poor feedback of the outcome of the complaint to the complainants, and the light punishments felt to be imposed on officers found guilty of abuses.

57. Morales, *op. cit.*, p. 15.

58. *1961 Report of the U.S. Commission on Civil Rights*, U.S. Department of Justice.

540

59. Joseph D. Lohman et al., *The Police and The Community*, U.S. President's Commission on Law Enforcement and Administration of Justice, Field Survey no. 4 (Berkeley, Calif.: 1966), p. 55.

60. A study of court personnel and procedures and an analysis of arrest, arraignment, and bail records has been under way at the University of Southern California. The study, conducted by the Western Center on Law and Poverty, was sponsored by the United States Civil Rights Commission, and included six places—East Los Angeles, San Bernardino, San Diego, Fresno, San Jose, and Monterey County.

61. See Albert J. Reiss, Jr. and David J. Bordua, "Environment and Organization: A Perspective on the Police," in Bordua, *op. cit.*, for an analysis of the consequences of the predominantly reactive strategy of most police work. Proactive strategy is made difficult in most police work since it usually entails access to private places. Reiss and Bordua argue that the reactive nature of police work means that the social system of the complainer dominates their work. The difference between normal police work and Border Patrol work, where there is usually no complainant, is evident. The consequence has generally been to expand the license of the Border Patrol as its mandate is enlarged to that of enforcing a national ideal.

62. For an account of the operations of the California Rural Legal Assistance in central California—largely on behalf of Mexican Americans—see Calvin Trillin, "U.S. Letter: McFarland," *New Yorker*, XLIII (Nov. 4, 1967), pp. 173–181.

TWENTY-TWO

Ethnic Organizations and Leadership

THE voluntary associations of Mexican Americans owe their origin to a large variety of circumstances, and they have highly diverse goals. In some instances, organizations formed in response to a galvanizing event and then expanded their activity. For example, the American G.I. Forum was established when a funeral home in Texas refused to bury the body of a Mexican-American soldier, a World War II casualty. When the organization's protest led to the soldier's burial in Arlington Cemetery, it continued with a varied program of social action. However, most associations that were formed in reaction to a specific grievance vanished once the abrasiveness of the offense was removed or forgotten.

The first voluntary associations were of the mutual-benefit type so common among immigrant groups: *La Alianza Hispano Americana* (1894); *La Camara de Comercio Mexicana ; La Sociedad Progresista Mexicana y Recreativa*, and *La Sociedad Mutualista Mexicana*, all organized about 1918; and *La Sociedad Union Cultural*

Mexicana (1924). These associations performed a limited welfare role. They were in part also substitutes for Anglo organizations which Mexican individuals could not easily join. Large numbers of Mexican-American clubs and similar associations performed purely social functions, and they still do. In addition, hundreds of Catholic organizations were established in the early part of this century to serve Mexican-American communities.

Organizational activity increased greatly during the 1920s, the period of the first mass immigration. Some of the associations formed at that time reflected the presence of urban Mexican-American achievers. The organizations met their members' status needs and made an effort to validate the group before the larger society. The most notable, lasting association of this period is the League of United Latin American Citizens (LULAC), which developed a number of educational programs. The 1920s witnessed also the establishment of more militant organizations, such as the Mexican-American Liberation Front. These were active mainly in agricultural areas and mining towns, but they were quickly repressed by employers.

A new era of general organizational activity began in the period after World War II. The war years had brought Mexican Americans into closer contact with American society, particularly in the cities. Increased urbanization produced some material benefits but little other change. Discrimination continued, housing conditions were poor, and access to places of public accommodation remained restricted. The tension of this period reached a climax in the Los Angeles *pachuco* riots of 1943. Old-line associations, such as the *Alianza Hispano Americana* and the *Spanish-American Recreational Committee*, proved incapable of providing social defense. Hence, new organizations were established to meet new needs. In this process, Mexican-American war veterans, bringing back new perceptions of opportunities and of discrimination in civilian life, played an important part.

The new groups formed since the end of World War II include the Community Service Organization (CSO), the American G.I. Forum, the Mexican American Political Association (MAPA), and the Political Association of Spanish-Speaking Organizations (PASSO). In contrast to the earlier associations of urban achievers, these organizations are not limited to the middle class, nor do they exclude the foreign born or require English as the official language.

INCREASING POLITICAL ORIENTATION

Despite the difficulty of classifying voluntary ethnic organizations, it can be said that the goals of Mexican-American associations have unquestionably changed in the direction of social action and political intent. The Community Service Organization, for example, undertook in the 1950s the first massive voter-registration drive among the Mexican Americans in Los Angeles. The American G.I. Forum has shifted from a nonpartisan civic-action program to an increasingly political position. It launched intensive get-out-the-vote drives and "Pay Your Poll Tax" campaigns and continued voter registration efforts after the repeal of the poll tax. Forum members were encouraged to run for political office; many did and won.

Upon its formation in 1958, the Mexican American Political Association declared as its overriding concern 1) "the election and appointment to public office of Mexican Americans and other persons sympathetic to our aims" and 2) the need "to take stands on political issues and to present and endorse candidates for public office." In a statewide drive in 1962, the organization reminded the Mexican-American electorate that it did not yet have its "proper share of elected or appointed government officials." This under-representation has been a continuing theme in the group's activities. The Political Association of Spanish-Speaking Organizations, a Texas group formed in 1960, is comparable to California's MAPA, and its goals are quite similar. PASSO members attempt to place Mexican Americans in public office by participating directly in Federal, state, and local elections. They stress voter registration and get-out-the-vote drives.

But there are at least two notable differences between MAPA and PASSO. One is regional setting: PASSO adopted a euphemistic name, whereas MAPA chose the more explicit Mexican-American designation. Another difference is the degree of ethnocentrism. MAPA is an intensely "Mexican" organization; only in 1967 did it reach out for non-Mexican allies by inviting a national coalition of Mexican Americans and Puerto Ricans. PASSO, on the other hand, has adopted the Eastern practice of ethnic political associations seeking alliances with other groups. For example, in 1962 the organization joined with the Teamster's Union and Anglo liberals in an attempt to capture political control of Crystal City, Texas. In San Antonio and Houston, PASSO members allied themselves with Negro organizations in political campaigns to elect "one of our own."[1]

It is an interesting commentary on the regional diversity of Mexican Americans that MAPA, in the comparatively open social environment of California, is at once more clearly Mexican and less disposed to seek allies outside the Mexican-American community. PASSO, on the other hand, operating in the more restrictive milieu of Texas, pragmatically adopted a euphemism for a label and proceeded to form political coalitions. It is another interesting commentary that actual political representation of Mexican Americans is far greater in Texas than in California, as will be seen in the next chapter. Of course, the different stance of the two organizations may be only a minor factor contributing to this result.

Under the influence of new leaders and the competitive pressures of new organizations, some of the older associations also have changed their objectives. For example, the League of United Latin American Citizens in the 1960s joined other groups in court suits challenging discrimination in jury selection, fought school segregation, and helped to defeat the poll tax. However, LULAC's efforts to increase civic participation of Mexican Americans stops short of political partisanship. The organization does not support individual political candidates. Although many of its

[1] Notes for this chapter start on page 555.

members participated in the Viva Kennedy movement for the election of John F. Kennedy, LULAC avoided direct involvement.

In recent years, antipoverty and related programs have prompted ethnic associations to become more clearly oriented to social action. By sponsoring proposals to Federal agencies, they have been instrumental in securing funds for activities geared directly to large segments of the Mexican-American population. Notable among these efforts is SER (service, education, redevelopment), a regionwide agency sponsored jointly by LULAC and the American G.I. Forum in cooperation with other organizations. The agency has obtained substantial funds from the Office of Economic Opportunity and the U.S. Department of Labor. It parallels a program aimed at Negroes that is sponsored by the Urban League.

No matter how diverse their goals may be, most Mexican-American organizations share a common political rhetoric. An important part of the rhetoric is their emphasis on loyalty to the United States. This has been a stance common to many immigrant groups in the United States before they became fully accepted by the larger society. In the case of Mexican Americans, the need for such a defensive ethos has been especially acute because of the widespread rejection of the group as a "foreign" element. The two-way migrations of Mexicans across the border reinforced the doubts of the larger community about "where these people belong." For a long time, the need of Mexican Americans to demonstrate their patriotism was accentuated by the loyalty pull exerted from Mexico and by the influence of Mexican consulates in the Southwest on some segments of the population. Mexican Americans often turned to the consuls for redress of grievances when they could not obtain help from United States agencies. The consuls were not always judicious in their perception of their role, especially in the aftermath of the Mexican Revolution.[2] However, there has never been an irredentist movement of any consequence among Americans of Mexican descent—not even during the episode of the "Zimmerman Telegram" in World War I.[3]

Another common theme in the organizations' political rhetoric is that of "historical primacy." This theme has been articulated most forcefully by George I. Sanchez:

> [People of Spanish-Mexican descent] began coming here from Spain and New Spain as long ago as the sixteenth century, and have continued to come from Mexico. Unlike such groups as the Italians, the Irish, the Poles, the Spanish Mexicans of the Southwest are not truly an immigrant group, for they are in their traditional home. . . . It should be unnecessary to have to underscore the perfectly elementary concept that we Americans of Mexican descent have the rights of Americans and that, if historical precedence is to be the criteria, our rights and needs have priority over those of other nationality groups.[4]

The argument that "we were here first" is prominent in numerous pamphlets and speeches by organizational spokesmen.

COMMON PROBLEMS OF ORGANIZATIONS

One of the perpetual problems of Mexican-American organizations has been the inadequacy of resources, both money and staff. Fund raising is not a well-developed art among the voluntary associations of this minority. There are relatively few wealthy Mexican Americans. In the past, many of the upwardly mobile individuals left the community spiritually as well as geographically. The main support has come from the developing middle class of professional people and small businessmen who have limited financial resources and are often still anxious about the permanence of their new status. Until recently, no single Mexican-American association could afford full-time staff for any length of time. Organizational expertise was poorly developed. Practically all work was performed by a handful of dedicated persons in their spare time.

Rarely have voluntary associations obtained funds and expertise through outside assistance. Until 1968, there was no equivalent of the NAACP or the Urban League, which are joint efforts of the minority and the majority. One of the few cases of help coming from outsiders was the Community Service Organization, which in the 1950s obtained financial and personnel support from the Chicago-based Industrial Areas Foundation. This support made it possible to organize the voter registration drive in Los Angeles that was already mentioned. When the Industrial Areas Foundation withdrew its assistance in favor of a rural program, the CSO was unable to sustain its efforts and remained moribund for several years.

In 1968, the Ford Foundation helped to establish a separate agency that could perform more effectively some of the functions previously assumed by ethnic associations in a haphazard and discontinuous fashion. The foundation provided an initial grant of $2.2 million for a Legal Defense and Educational Fund for the Mexican Americans of the Southwest, "modeled generally after the NAACP Legal Defense and Education Fund." Simultaneously, additional money was allocated for support of the legal education of students from minorities—Mexican Americans as well as Negroes and Indians. Finally, the Foundation announced its support of a "Southwest Council of La Raza."[5]

A problem common to the politically orientated Mexican-American organizations is the overwhelming commitment of this population to the Democratic party. This is a hotly debated issue among Mexican-American leaders. According to one argument, the Democratic party is so sure of the group's support that its office holders need not go out of their way to accede to ethnic demands. The Republicans, on the other hand, are conscious of the futility of appeals to the Mexican-American electorate and therefore make only halfhearted gestures in promising programs on their behalf. Some of the leaders feel that this problem must be overcome by playing the political game with both parties more astutely. Others are convinced that Mexican Americans have no choice and must work within the Democratic party to attain their objectives. In the Southwest context of politics, the commitment of the electorate to one party has probably weakened the group's interest in political activity and its influence on public affairs. Since voting is unlikely to change matters, this dilemma has reinforced the belief of many Mexican Americans that politics had best be left alone.

These frustrations are similar to those faced generally by dissidents in one-party states, as in Texas. In order to effectuate social change, political bargaining must take place within the structure of a single party.

Perhaps the greatest problem of most ethnic organizations is their relative obscurity among the people they intend to serve. The household surveys conducted

Table 22–1. Awareness of Major Ethnic and Other Organizations, Mexican-American Survey Respondents, Los Angeles and San Antonio, 1965–1966

| | LOS ANGELES | | | |
	Very Familiar or Belongs	Heard of It	Never Heard of It	Total Number (= 100%)
Alianza Hispano Americana	10%	32%	58%	940
American G.I. Forum	4	20	76	943
Community Service Organization	2	13	85	935
Democratic Clubs	10	42	48	939
League of United Latin American Citizens	4	10	86	939
Mexican American Political Association	5	23	72	940
Political Association of Spanish Speaking Organizations	1	5	94	938
Republican Clubs	8	33	59	938
Viva Johnson Clubs	4	19	77	935
	SAN ANTONIO[a]			
	Very Familiar or Belongs	Heard of It	Never Heard of It	Total Number (= 100%)
Alianza Hispano Americana	1%	14%	85%	592
American G.I. Forum	8	43	49	596
Community Service Organization	1	7	92	589
Democratic Clubs	5	36	59	596
League of United Latin American Citizens	15	59	26	598
Mexican American Political Association	1	5	94	584
Political Association of Spanish Speaking Organizations	6	42	52	593
Republican Clubs	3	29	68	591
Viva Johnson Clubs	4	33	63	594

[a] Weighting procedures were used in the San Antonio sample. This means that total numbers cannot be used as a direct indicator of error. See Appendix H.

in 1965 and 1966 in Los Angeles and San Antonio provide some indication of the standing of major ethnic associations among the rank and file of Mexican Americans (Table 22–1). Interestingly, Democratic and Republican clubs seemed to be about as well known as most of the ethnic associations. Among the latter, the G.I. Forum, PASSO, and LULAC stand out in San Antonio; MAPA and the Alianza Hispano

Americana are rather more familiar organizations in Los Angeles. In neither city, however, have the associations been able to penetrate the Mexican-American population in great depth. Much of the membership is duplicative, that is, those interested in ethnic organizations are likely to belong to more than one. Thus, a relatively small group of the same people can be seen at conventions and other gatherings of most associations. Studies of the general population show that membership in voluntary associations increases with economic status.[6] Since most Mexican Americans are poor, this factor alone may help explain their low participation in ethnic organizations.

LEADERSHIP PATTERNS

The complexity of leadership patterns in the Mexican-American population is illustrated in the accompanying typology. Any such attempt to compress and simplify observations made in the rough and tumble of community life must be tentative. Yet, the typology highlights some useful distinctions.

One function common to most leaders is the strategically important intermediation between the minority and the dominant system. Even when internal leaders are confined to activity within the *barrio* they usually perform some intermediary function. What Gunnar Myrdal has said of Negroes and whites[7] tends to apply here as well: The minority and majority live like two foreign nations dealing with each other through the medium of plenipotentiaries (though not of equal power). The external leaders—either Anglos who come from outside or Mexican Americans who return to the *barrio* to help the minority—may also function as intermediaries, but usually in connection with particular programs.

As intermediaries, the economic achievers and social leaders face several problems. They are usually the first to be tapped by Anglos who seek indigenous leaders. Yet, they are rarely in close touch with the community that they ostensibly interpret for people who represent Anglo power. Because of a generational or class cleavage, or both, their perception of the *barrio's* reality is usually clouded. Few of them are completely comfortable when the Anglos turn to them for advice. Nevertheless, some of these leaders have made important contributions to the group by launching and supporting political candidates, movements, and organizations.

Intermediaries who are associated with the labor movement are in almost all instances validated by Anglos who control workers' organizations. The labor intermediary owes his existence to the fact that the Anglo labor hierarchy also seeks faithful interpreters and reliable advisers about the Mexican-American people. Some labor intermediaries perform this function in the shops, where they may hold a union position, such as that of steward. Others serve as intermediaries between unions and the Mexican-American people in general. In addition to their union work, they are active in civic organizations and are officers of ethnic associations. Their credentials enable them to move into sectors outside the Mexican-American

548

community as well as outside the labor movement. Though not elected by the community, they often become ethnic spokesmen.

TYPOLOGY OF MEXICAN-AMERICAN LEADERSHIP

I. Internal Leaders

(a) *Social*

1. Heads of ethnic clubs and societies
2. The economically secure

(b) *Economic*

1. Merchants whose economic base rests in the *barrio*
2. Professionals (lawyers, doctors, etc.) who depend upon the *barrio* for income
3. Labor

(c) *Religious*

1. Priests or ministers
2. Laymen

(d) *Political*

1. Party committeemen
2. Professional politicians
3. Field representatives of professional politicians

(e) *Professional*

1. Teachers
2. Social workers
3. Police officers
4. Other civil servants

(f) *Informal social workers*

A man or woman who has a reputation for solving social problems

II. External Leaders

(a) *Anglos*

1. Social organizers from labor, community, and church groups
2. Experts from government, universities, and political groups

(b) *Mexican Americans*

1. "Subsidized leaders" employed by local state, or Federal agencies
2. Independent individuals

The few Mexican-American labor intermediaries who operate at the national level have played important roles in recent years. They have made the labor movement aware of the Mexican Americans' problems and have aligned the economic aspirations of the group with those of other American workers. In the Delano grape strike, for example, a Mexican-American labor intermediary was instrumental in obtaining support of the AFL-CIO for Cesar Chavez' National Farm Workers Association— the kind of support that had not been forthcoming in earlier efforts to organize farm labor.

Many of the professional persons who act or could act as intermediaries are in a dilemma. Teachers, social workers, and policemen may win approval of their intermediary role in the Mexican-American community, but at the risk of losing their standing with Anglo colleagues. Conversely, they may gain status with the Anglos in their profession at the risk of losing their following among the Mexican-American group. The problems of validation within the *barrio* and outside seem to be most severe for ethnic social workers and policemen. Both function in areas of social deviance from the norm. This circumstance alone tends to limit their ability to view the realities of their group in broad perspective. More important, the work of both involves sanctions, that is, the power to withhold aid and services in the case of the social worker and to suspend the liberty of an individual in the case of law-enforcement officers. Because of this power, social workers and policemen are forever on trial before their community, their peers, and even themselves.

The "informal social workers" listed in the typology warrant special comment. These are individuals who have the respect and trust of people on the neighborhood level.[8] They are the persons to whom local residents turn for guidance when they want community projects, or when they need translations from English and from the special language of bureaucracy. They are in many ways the most "natural" of all the ethnic intermediaries. They live among the people and yet hold no formal positions. They are not appointed or elected. They draw no salaries and they are not even called leaders.

Many such informal social workers are women. In a small study of an East Los Angeles community, when people were asked how things could be improved in their communities, women figured prominently in the responses.[9] These women were rarely members of formal organizations. Their important role may be partly explained by the fact that women stay at home and are therefore more intensively involved in the daily life of the neighborhood. Also, the urban setting is more likely to subject the man to social stress that undermines his self-confidence and his traditional position as arbiter. Women are less exposed to these ego-debilitating forces.

The group of informal social workers includes also small businessmen, some priests, and the notary public. The latter's position in the community stems partly from the fact that the *notario* in Mexico is a full-fledged attorney. Hence, many immigrants believe that the title has the same meaning in the United States. The notary public often assists people with immigration and other legal problems and may refer his clients to the proper governmental agency. High fees and chicanery are not uncommon.

Among external leaders, Anglos may operate overtly or by indirection. As overt leaders they take charge of campaigns, programs, and other activities without reservation or equivocation—almost as if they were Mexican Americans. Overt leaders often put in focus and clarify issues that affect Mexican Americans. Thus, a Mexican-American community may be enlightened that the loss of a nearby public park means neglect of the needs of the poor by the establishment. In contrast, the behind-the-scenes Anglo leaders qualify their role in the community as "friends of the Mexican people." They emphasize the need for indigenous spokesmen and recruit and train ethnic leaders.

External leaders of Mexican descent are often economic achievers. They return to the *barrios* to provide services as government employees or to seek ethnic validation. Government employees constitute important cadres of such external leadership. The community calls them, tongue-in-cheek, "subsidized" because many are former internal leaders who now perform similar functions on public salaries. The typology lists also the independent individual who is neither a government official nor wealthy —for example, young Mexican-American college professors or school teachers. They are less encumbered than is the older generation of activists by memories of past hurts in contacts with the larger society. Often they bring a fresh viewpoint to community action and organizational programs.

Some of the Mexican Americans who rejoin the community turn to it for personal prestige. They may seek status appointments in government in a fashion consonant with the practices of their Anglo peers, and may bring themselves to public attention by furnishing the mass media with statements about the problems of their ethnic group and suggest solutions. Others make it their business to be seen and heard in order to impress Mexican Americans and Anglos at a variety of public functions. Although some of these individuals may return to the community only to touch base with the *barrio* en route to greater glory, others are motivated by genuine concern.

PROBLEMS OF LEADERSHIP

The foregoing discussion has already touched on some issues in the development and maintenance of leadership. One is the problem of validation: the built-in conflict between acceptance in the dominant society and approval by the Mexican-American community. Another issue is the high degree of fragmentation and parochialism that results from the many varieties of organizations and leaders. In addition, Mexican-American leadership is not exempt from the familiar generational conflict.

The fragmentation of leadership is often singled out as the most crucial difficulty. However, the existence of multiple bases of leadership as such is not the foremost problem, nor is it unique to Mexican Americans. Members of the dominant society who often insist on a "united front" within a minority as a precondition for fruitful dialogue or action seem to forget that pluralistic organization and leadership is basic to their own way of doing things.

Validation of Leadership

Although most types of leaders face the problem of dual validation, the political leader is in the most serious dilemma both before and after he attains his position. He must have the approval of those who receive him in the larger society. He may be validated by the ethnic community itself as he emerges in one of the categories of internal leadership, but when he appears before those who control society he must be acceptable in order to be an effective intermediary.

More often than not the political leader is recruited by Anglos. This process of selection is likely to create initial problems of validation: The ethnic emissary may be fully approved by the Anglo establishment but rejected by Mexican Americans. Further problems arise as the political leader begins to officiate. Acquiring the viewpoint (and the workload) of a Federal or state legislator, for example, he may fail to live up to the community's expectation that he will make *its* welfare his main or exclusive concern. Or he may maintain good credentials with his Mexican-American clientele but act in such manner that he incurs the displeasure of the Anglo establishment.

The problem of the leader's validation in the Mexican-American community is often complicated by mistrust. The masses feel that spokesmen do not necessarily represent the people's interests. Past experience lends some credence to this view. Further, it is said that Mexican Americans begrudge success to their leaders. An ingroup anecdote on this point among political activists is attributed to a Mexican-American lawyer from San Antonio: "If a Mexican and an Anglo were both trying to climb greased poles with prizes at the top, the Anglos would clap when the Anglo reached the top, but when the Mexican got near the prize the Mexicans would pull the fellow down by his breeches."[10]

Generally, it is much harder for the ethnic minority than for the Anglo establishment to withdraw its support from political intermediaries. When such intermediaries fall into disrepute among Mexican Americans, they retain many of the trappings and even the rewards of leadership long after the community has rejected them. "We have very few people who can talk to the Anglos," a Mexican American observed. Therefore, "we cannot afford to punish them too severely."

Fragmentation and Parochialism

Mexican-American leaders are highly individualistic and competitive or often even hostile to one another. These characteristics add to political disunity. Some of the ethnic organizations represent the special view of only a few individuals or their urge for recognition. When these persons are dislodged from an association, they often go on to establish another. Many persons who belong to the elite seem to be unwilling to recognize the leadership of other members of the elite and share it. So common is this trait that the authors, at the beginning of their study, were warned by insiders to use the term "key people" rather than "leaders" in exploring questions of leadership. It would seem that it is easier to share the reputation of being a "key person" than a "leader."

Among the reasons for this fragmentation is the highly differentiated composition of the Mexican-American group, which has been stressed throughout this volume. Also, the condition of deprivation keeps the poor wary and suspicious of all who offer to help them—including their own kind. Always in search of the "ultimate" leader, the large masses of Mexican Americans seem to be quickly dissatisfied with existing leadership.[11] Equally if not more salient is the prevailing parochialism of Mexican-American leaders.

Most of the leaders are men and women whose experience has been almost exclusively limited to one part of the Southwest. Their parochial commitments involve narrow views about the identity of the group and about its social problems. Parochialism inhibits the discovery of ethnic commonalities and agreement on national issues. It manifests itself, among other things, in dissension among the leaders about such basic issues as what to call the ethnic group, what are the main social problems that face the group, and what strategies should be pursued to resolve the few questions upon which the leaders do agree. Disagreement over the name of an organization reflects the more pervasive "battle of the name" that plays such a large role in the self-perceptions of Mexican Americans (Chapter 16).

National or regional meetings where Mexican-American leaders attempt to present a united front before Anglo society or build internal group unity are often threatening to some of the leaders. The exposure of issues is felt to reflect upon their efficacy or their knowledge of conditions in their communities. The difficulty is compounded by conflicting pluralistic or assimilationist stances taken by spokesmen.

Parochialism and poor communication among leaders across the Southwest reinforce one another. There is no national or regional medium of communication. The ethnic press is largely localized and has a low circulation. The journals published by some of the Mexican-American associations serve more or less as organizational house-organs.

The Generational Split

The classic conflict between the young and the old has become more acute in the Mexican-American elite, as elsewhere. The established leaders have been generally slow in recruiting young people for leadership roles. On the other hand, young Mexican Americans, like other youth, consider themselves to be more in tune with present reality than are their elders, and so they impatiently clamor for change. Age, long a basis for authority among the Mexican-American people, is now often the target of youthful contempt. In this sense, the young in this group are like other Americans—products of the forces that disturb our whole society. But their search for roles in political or social action is often complicated by their simultaneous search for personal identity, or the meaning of being a real Mexican inside the American system.

The Black Power movement has served to widen the generational gap by providing models of militant action for young Mexican Americans who aspire to leadership. The past few years have witnessed the formation of a number of militant youth organizations, largely among Mexican-American students. One such group calls itself the Brown Berets. Mexican-American students at colleges and even high schools have staged walk-outs, sit-ins, and boycotts, and they have occasionally used violent techniques of protest. Demands for Mexican-American study programs and for greater recognition in history books of Hispano-Mexican cultural contributions to the Southwest have been proliferating. This ferment among young Mexican Americans cuts across social class and regional lines, uniting high-school dropouts, college students, and ex-convicts in a loosely articulated network of action groups. This has become a true social movement, known among its members as the *chicano* movement.

SUMMARY

Many minorities in the United States have been able to improve their position by organizing themselves for community and political action and thus exerting some influence on their social environment. Although voluntary associations among Mexican Americans have a long history, it was only after World War II that organizations oriented to this type of action were formed. Since the war, too, some of the older organizations have changed their goals in favor of greater social or political involvement. Until recently, most of these efforts were handicapped by scanty financial resources, a lack of staff and organizational expertise, and only sporadic help coming (often because it was not encouraged to come) from outside the community. The household surveys in Los Angeles and San Antonio revealed a low level of awareness of most ethnic organizations among the respondents.

A typology of Mexican-American leaders shows a very complex pattern, though perhaps not any more complex than that of other minority groups. Leadership may be associated with economic accomplishment, Anglo acceptance, command of the English language, election to public office (often by both Anglo and Mexican voters), or professional work (as in the case of teachers, social workers and police officers). In most cases, leadership involves formal roles, but there are also the informal leaders at the neighborhood level, often women, who owe their influence to their reputation for "getting things done."

Among the main problems of Mexican-American leadership is the need for dual validation by the ethnic clientele and the dominant system. Without this dual validation, leadership roles can rarely be attained or preserved. Yet, approval by one source of power often entails rejection or mistrust by the other. (Again, this problem may not be any greater for Mexican Americans than for other kinds of ethnic leaders.) The generational conflict, too, is pervasive, but it may be felt more deeply among adult Mexican Americans because their tradition invests age with authority and respect.

The most serious problem of Mexican-American leadership is its fragmentation and parochialism. After decades of organizational activity, regional unity is still a distant goal. Although some of the ethnic associations have penetrated beyond their original base, usually Texas or California, each still has its main strength in the state in which it was formed. Whether attempts to establish a Southwest super-organization will succeed is uncertain at this writing. The difficulties posed by multiple bases of leadership have diminished the political effectiveness of many other minorities, but they appear to be especially acute among Mexican Americans.

NOTES TO CHAPTER TWENTY-TWO

1. Interview with Al Pena, Commissioner of Bexar County, Texas.

2. As late as in 1938, the Mexican Consul of Los Angeles told a group of young Mexican Americans that "A Mexican will always be a Mexican. . . . Those who desire to become American citizens should drain their blood, dye their hair blond and change the color of their eyes . . . " Consul Trujillo, quoted by Manuel de la Raza in the *Mexican Voice*, Los Angeles, Calif., November, 1938, p. 16.

3. To prevent the United States from entering the war, Alfred Zimmerman, the German Foreign Minister, offered the Republic of Mexico an alliance with Germany (and Japan) that would enable Mexico to recover large parts of the American Southwest. See Barbara W. Tuchman, *The Zimmerman Telegram* (London: Constable and Company Ltd, 1959). When Zimmerman's offer became known in the United States, questions arose about the loyalty of the Mexican-American population; and the position of the minority was threatened as was that of the Japanese Americans during World War II. There is no evidence of any subversive activity by Mexican-Americans in connection with the abortive German proposal. However, a Mexican-American writer reported many years later that Mexicans in World War I were considered security risks because of fears that the United States might be attacked from the South. See Raul Morin, *Among the Valiant: Mexican-Americans in World War II and Korea* (Los Angeles: Borden Publishing Company, 1963), p. 15.

4. George I. Sanchez, *Chicago Jewish Forum*, vol. 20 (1961-1962), p. 3.

5. Ford Foundation, news release of May 1, 1968. The Legal Defense and Educational Fund is described in the release as designed "to attack problems of discrimination and segregation through legal channels." The grant in support of the legal education of students from minority groups was made to the Fund for Public Education of the American Bar Association. Information regarding a "Southwest Council of La Raza" was received in a letter (June 3, 1968) from an official of The Ford Foundation addressed to Leo Grebler.

6. See Charles R. Wright and Herbert H. Hyman, "Voluntary Association Memberships of American Adults: Evidence from National Sample Surveys," *American Sociological Review*, XXIII (1958), pp. 284-294.

7. Gunnar Myrdal, *An American Dilemma: The Negro Problem and Modern Democracy* (New York: Harper & Row, Publishers, Inc., 1962), p. 724.

8. The notion of a reputational leader comes from Floyd Hunter's *Community Power Structure* (Chapel Hill, N.C.: The University of North Carolina Press, 1953).

9. Ralph C. Guzman, Beaman Patterson, and Dewey Park, "Comparative Access to Government: Three Minority Groups in Los Angeles County" (seminar paper, University of California, Los Angeles, Department of Political Science, Spring, 1962).

10. Quoted by Frances Jerome Woods in *Mexican Ethnic Leadership in San Antonio, Texas* (Washington, D.C.: The Catholic University of America Press, 1949), p. 52.

11. The idea that minority groups search for a messiah to lead them out of their social problems is developed by James Q. Wilson in *Negro Politics: The Search for Leadership* (Chicago: The University of Chicago Press, 1960).

TWENTY-THREE

Political Effectiveness

DISUNITY of the leadership—the concluding theme of the previous chapter—is only one of several debilities that have diminished the collective influence of Mexican Americans in politics. Other conditions, varying in time and space, have had similar effects. People of low educational and economic attainment tend to be less active politically regardless of ethnicity.[1] Also, many Mexican Americans who moved from rural areas to the cities in the past generation have probably maintained a rural outlook on their role in political life. This outlook is usually very limited and apprehensive.

In no sphere was the isolation of this minority group from the dominant society as great as in the political system of the small towns and rural areas of the Southwest. At best Mexican Americans could attempt to penetrate the tightly organized local governments by indirection, through Anglos who expected to be rewarded for such service. As a consequence of such dependency on Anglo go-betweens, the political sociaizaltion of the group was greatly retarded. Another pattern of dependency evolved from the *patrón*, or boss, system within Mexican-American communities.

[1] Notes for this chapter start on page 570.

The *patrón* usually owed his economic status to the local Anglo powers, and one of his functions was to enlist the Mexican-American voters on the right side. This kind of rural *patronismo* has carried over into urban centers, especially in cities like Fresno, San Jose and Riverside where Mexican-American agricultural workers depend upon ethnic bosses for work and favorable treatment by growers.

The political participation of Mexican Americans has been limited by election laws and rules that tend to affect most severely the poor and the uneducated. The poll-tax imposed by Texas was only declared unconstitutional in 1966. English literacy tests are bound to exclude more Mexican Americans than others. Only in New Mexico does the state constitution guarantee that the right to vote cannot be denied because of illiteracy (in either English or Spanish).

How voter registration is organized can also make a difference. In Texas, for example, voters were usually required to register with the county tax assessors who were in charge of collecting the poll-tax. Often, this meant a visit to the county courthouse, difficult to arrange for poor people without automobiles and threatening because the building was associated with the feared governmental authority. Also, voters in Texas must re-register each year during limited periods. In California, registration is open year round, and almost any registered voter can become a deputy registrar. Deputy registrars station themselves in many convenient places to provide service to all who qualify. Once a person registers in California he remains eligible to vote unless he fails to exercise the franchise in a general election, or moves, or changes his political affiliation. Other Southwest states are less rigid than Texas but more strict than California.

Gerrymandering has been a pervasive technique for preventing the designation of election districts in which racial or ethnic minority groups would predominate in the electorate.

THE LOW RATE OF NATURALIZATION

In addition to these limitations, which are more or less common to disadvantaged groups, the political potential of Mexican Americans has been reduced by the low naturalization rate of the foreign born. Although the foreign born make up a relatively small portion of the Mexican-American population, in 1960 there were 576,000 Mexican-born persons living in the United States, 502,000 in the Southwest alone. Perhaps not all of them were legal residents, nor were all legal residents of voting age. Nevertheless, the numbers are large enough to suggest that the low propensity of Mexican aliens for naturalization has contributed to political ineffectiveness. Conversely, their apparent indifference to formal citizenship may indicate indifference to full participation in American society.

Table 23–1 shows the naturalization rate of Mexican immigrants in comparison with all other immigrants who came at the same time and had the same length of residency in this country. *Between 1959 and 1966, only from 2.4 to 5.0 percent of the*

Mexican immigrants who became eligible each year obtained citizenship papers, as against about 26 to 35 percent of all other immigrants. These data may exaggerate the difference between the newcomers from Mexico and from other countries,[2] but even a generous allowance for statistical understatement of the Mexican naturalization rate would still leave a sizable gap. A low propensity for naturalization is also indicated by the long period of residency in the United States preceding the acquisition of citizenship by Mexican aliens.[3]

Table 23–1. Naturalization Rates of Mexican Immigrants and of All Other Immigrants, 1959–1966[a]

NUMBER OF IMMIGRANTS ADMITTED			NUMBER OF PERSONS NATURALIZED BY JUNE 30			PERCENT NATURALIZED	
Period	Mexico	All Other	Year	Mexico	All Other	Mexico	All Other
1950–1953	41,267	849,591	1959	2,051	288,350	5.0	33.9
1951–1954	71,882	777,966	1960	2,837	276,004	3.9	35.5
1952–1955	116,282	765,639	1961	3,896	257,532	3.4	33.6
1953–1956	171,729	766,297	1962	4,956	262,054	2.9	34.2
1954–1957	202,429	892,030	1963	5,211	293,202	2.6	32.8
1955–1958	191,685	947,862	1964	4,608	304,916	2.4	32.2
1956–1959	163,974	998,469	1965	3,938	295,682	2.4	29.9
1957–1960	131,611	974,605	1966	3,248	253,354	2.5	26.0

[a] The method used in this table treats the immigrants of, say, the calendar years 1956–1959 as a cohort group and shows how many of them had become naturalized by June 30, 1965, a maximum of nine and a half years later. The method is adapted from Gertrude D. Krichevsky, "Naturalization Rates of Immigrants," *Immigration and Naturalization Reporter* (U.S. Immigration and Naturalization Service), April, 1963. However, the article is limited to one year and uses calendar-year figures on immigration not available elsewhere. In contrast, the above table shows fiscal-year data on immigration, and the number of naturalized persons is derived from published figures showing naturalizations by *calendar year* of the immigrants' entry. This is a minor blemish which should not affect the results in any significant manner. For example, the Krichevsky article arrives at a naturalization rate for Mexican immigrants of 2.5 percent in 1962, as against 2.9 percent in the above table. The number of persons naturalized by the dates shown is a cumulative figure. For example, the figure of 4,608 Mexican immigrants who had become naturalized by June 30, 1964 is composed of those reported naturalized during the fiscal year 1964 after having entered in the calendar years 1955–1958; those reported naturalized during the fiscal year 1963, after having entered in the calendar years 1955–1958; and so forth. Although immigrants are generally required to be in continuous residence for at least five years before petitioning for naturalization, this is not necessary for certain excepted classes. Consequently, the cumulation of the number of naturalized persons by year of entry was carried back to the year of admission—e.g., to 1955 in the case of the cohort group of 1955–1958 immigrants who had become naturalized by June 30, 1964.

Source: Annual Reports of the Immigration and Naturalization Service.

Naturalization rates declined in the 1960s for all aliens, including Mexicans. This is probably associated with two provisions of the Immigration and Nationality Act of 1952. The Act gave legal residents of foreign birth who were 50 years of age or over the privilege of qualifying for naturalization in their native language. It permitted aliens, under certain conditions, to legalize their status if there was doubt about the legality of their entry. Large numbers of immigrants, and especially Mexican immigrants, took advantage of these provisions. Among other things, naturalization enabled them to qualify for Old Age Assistance if they met other eligibility requirements. Consequently, the naturalization rate reached exceptionally high levels *before* the period covered in Table 23–1.

The Mexicans' indifference to citizenship was debated as early as the 1920s, when the Congress considered changes in immigration laws. As mentioned in Chapter 19, the subject received attention in connection with the efforts of the

Roman Catholic Church to Americanize the Mexican immigrant. Thus, the low naturalization rate is a problem of long standing.

At first, this seems to be a case of interacting forces in the minority and the larger society producing a vicious circle. Mexican aliens have been indifferent to citizenship because of their social isolation and because they failed to see the usefulness of such formal allegiance to the United States, which meant formal severance from Mexico: "Why should I become an American citizen? Anglos will still treat me as a Mexican." In turn, the failure of so many Mexican aliens to seek naturalization reinforced the negative views of Mexicans held in the larger society: "They do not even want to be citizens." What is notable here is the absence of change, which means that "vicious circle" describes the situation more adequately than does Myrdal's "principle of cumulation."[4]

However, the vicious-circle argument is somewhat shaken when we compare experiences in Texas and California. In the 1961–1966 period Texas accounted for a far larger share of all naturalizations of Mexican aliens than one would anticipate from its share of Mexican-born persons (Table 23–2); the opposite was true for California. This is an unexpected finding. As previous chapters have shown, Mexicans

Table 23–2. Percentage Distribution of Mexican Immigrants Naturalized Compared with Percentage Distribution of Mexican-born Persons, by States

State or Area	1961	1962	1963	1964	1965	1966	Percent Born in Mexico in 1960[a]
Southwest	87.6	89.1	86.9	85.6	84.6	87.5	87.4
Arizona	5.1	3.0	3.9	4.2	5.6	4.1	6.2
California	36.8	31.5	31.3	30.9	30.6	29.9	43.2
Colorado	2.3	1.3	1.6	1.4	1.5	1.1	0.8
New Mexico	3.1	1.4	1.2	1.5	0.6	1.4	1.9
Texas	40.3	51.9	48.9	47.6	46.3	51.0	35.3
Other	12.4	10.9	13.1	14.4	15.4	12.5	12.6
Total	100.0	100.0	100.0	100.0	100.0	100.0	100.0

[a] From the 1960 U.S. Census of Population.
Source: Annual Reports of the Immigration and Naturalization Service.

in Texas encountered a host society less favorable to their full acceptance than did Mexicans in California. Hence one would anticipate that the Texan Mexicans considered naturalization even more futile and were therefore less eager to take out citizenship papers. Also, the educational and economic standing of foreign-born Mexican Americans is generally a great deal lower in Texas than in California. The language barrier to successful performance of the literacy test for naturalization is certainly not any less formidable in Texas. Since the propensity for citizenship seems to be associated with the alien's socioeconomic position, one would expect California to be in the lead.

It is possible that the inferior position of Mexicans in Texas has stimulated rather than retarded naturalization. In a hostile environment, citizenship status may help to open doors that are closed to aliens. Consequently, immigrants may be more eager to become naturalized in a milieu where the advantages of citizenship are more clearly evident. In the more open social system of California, the acquisition of a "defense document" may not seem to be equally urgent. Also, Mexican-American organizations in Texas have made a more continuous effort in preparing immigrants for citizenship. This has been a traditional goal of the League of United Latin American Citizens (LULAC), one of the oldest organizations with particular strength in Texas.[5]

In earlier years, indifference to naturalization seems to have been reinforced by efforts of Mexican consuls to maintain the immigrants' identification with the homeland.[6] To the consuls, United States citizenship meant that Mexicans would lose the limited protection provided by their offices. When naturalized Mexicans could not obtain the full protection of United States institutions, redress through the consuls would be impossible. These practical considerations, together with patriotic and cultural ideologies, served to orient consular activities toward sustaining the bonds between Mexican residents in the United States and their homeland. But this situation seems to have changed a great deal.

If the theory of the vicious circle offers a somewhat dubious explanation of the low naturalization rate, the educational and economic status of Mexican aliens provides a far less equivocal interpretation. The rate of naturalization has been found to be associated generally with schooling and occupation.[7] For this reason alone, one would expect the naturalization rate of Mexican aliens to be lower than that of other contemporary immigrants. Our data compare Mexican immigrants with others in recent years, when illiteracy was virtually nonexistent in most European nations and Canada. In contrast, illiteracy is still widespread in Mexico. Most of the European immigrants are on a higher socioeconomic level than the Mexicans.

The need for historical perspective on this point is suggested by the public debate of several decades ago about the apparent difficulty of assimilating the New Immigrants to the United States (such as Italians, Poles, and Russians) as compared to the Old Immigrants (who were mainly from England, Ireland, Germany, and the Scandinavian countries). One piece of evidence used to "prove" the slow assimilation of the New Immigrants was their low rate of naturalization. However, studies that investigated naturalization among both New and Old Immigrants demonstrated that length of residence, educational attainment, occupation, and income—rather than country of origin—were the main determinants of differences in their rate of naturalization.[8]

MEXICAN-AMERICAN LEGISLATORS

One measure of political effectiveness is Mexican-American representation in the legislature at various government levels. In 1968, the United States Senate had one Mexican-American member: Joseph M. Montoya of New Mexico, which has a long tradition of active political participation by the indigenous population. (Dennis Chavez served as United States Senator from New Mexico in the 1930s and 1940s.) The United States House of Representatives had three Mexican Americans: Edward R. Roybal of California and Henry B. Gonzales and Eligio de la Garza, both from Texas.

Mexican-American representation in the legislatures of the five Southwest states was highly uneven (Table 23–3). As in the case of naturalization, California and Texas show a contrast that is at variance with practically all other indicators of the relative position of this minority in the two states. California in 1967 had no single state legislator of Mexican-American ancestry. Before the Republican landslide of 1966 in California, there was just one Mexican-American Assemblyman. In the general election of that year, 14 ethnic candidates divided the votes by running against each other in districts with a heavy concentration of Mexican-American people, thus ensuring their defeat in the primaries or in the final election. Despite the relative openness of the dominant society in this state, Mexican Americans have failed to muster enough strength and unity for sustained representation in the legislature.

Table 23–3. State Legislators of Mexican-American Ancestry,[a] Five Southwest States, 1967

	LEGISLATURE		MEXICAN-AMERICAN DEMOCRATS		MEXICAN-AMERICAN REPUBLICANS		
	Total House Members	Total Senate Members	House	Senate	House	Senate	Total Mexican Americans in Both Houses
Arizona	60	30	3	1	—	—	4
California[b]	80	40	—	—	—	—	—
Colorado	65	35	—	1	—	—	1
New Mexico	70	42	18	11	1	3	33
Texas	150	31	9	1	—	—	10
Total	425	178	30	14	1	3	48

[a] Legislators who identify themselves as Mexican American (or Spanish American in the case of New Mexico) or who are so identified by others. A number of these elected officials do not have Spanish surnames.
[b] A Mexican American was elected in 1968 to the California State Assembly.

Texas, with a Spanish-surname population about as large as California's, shows a far more favorable picture—despite the fact that Texas ranks far lower than California on almost any yardstick of socioeconomic position for this group, despite the fact that its social system generally is more hostile to Mexican Americans, and despite voting procedures that militate against its minority populations. In 1967, ten members of the Texas legislature were Mexican Americans, and one of them was a senator. Both Arizona and Colorado had some ethnic representation in their legislatures. New Mexico is the only state with proportional representation; Mexican-American members of the state Senate and House accounted for almost 30 percent of all legislators.

The commitment of Mexican Americans to the Democratic party that was discussed in the previous chapter as a leadership problem appears clearly in the affiliation of state legislators. The only exception is New Mexico, where 4 of 33 ethnic legislators were Republicans. Historically, the Spanish Americans in this state have been more divided in their party preference than their counterparts in other Southwest states. According to a widespread story, New Mexico families used to split their affiliation to be assured of some patronage regardless of which party was in power.

The gerrymandering of election districts has had a special impact on the minority's political representation at the local level. For example, district lines in East Los Angeles are so drawn that the possibilities of bloc voting are minimized. No Mexican American has ever been on the Board of Supervisors of the County of Los Angeles. The election of Edward R. Roybal to the Los Angeles City Council in 1949 broke a long record of Anglo exclusiveness. And since 1962, when Roybal became a United States Congressman, the large Mexican-American population of Los Angeles has again been without representation in the city council. The increasing residential dispersion of Mexican Americans may also weaken the potentials of ethnic bloc voting, although this is not entirely clear.[9] Finally, infighting among their candidates for local office, usually exacerbated by the larger number of competing office seekers, results in low representation for Mexican Americans. Infighting as well as gerrymandering accounted for the community's failure in Los Angeles to elect a Mexican-American councilman to succeed Edward Roybal.

In many of the smaller cities and rural areas of Texas, Arizona, and California, Mexican Americans are such a large proportion of the total population that they could wield considerable political influence. But this potential is rarely activated. Pauline Kibbe's observations in Texas more than twenty years ago are still valid: With rare exceptions, Mexican Americans are without due representation on school boards, city councils, or other governmental or quasigovernmental units.[10] And her analysis of the reasons for this state of affairs is also sound today:

> Anglo politicians in most cities having a sizable Latin American population appear to have promulgated an effective, but unwritten, law which, while consenting to the appointment or election of Latin Americans to minor political posts, forbids and prevents their securing a top-ranking post. Thus, when an ambitious and capable Latin American announces for office in opposition to an Anglo incumbent or candidate (who is in all probability the candidate of the local machine), Anglo politicians follow the tried-and-true formula of "divide and conquer." They immediately sponsor the candidacy of another Latin American, preferably a personal enemy of the man who has previously announced, and thereby split the Latin American vote and assure the election of the Anglo candidate.[11]

Kibbe adds that this practice could not prevail were it not for the "exaggerated individualism" of Mexican Americans and their lack of intra-ethnic cooperation.[12]

One of the recent exceptions to the rule of exclusion from local government occurred in Crystal City, Texas, a tiny agricultural center said to be the "spinach capital of the world." Mexican Americans account for the vast majority of the total population (9,101 in 1960), as is true in many places in south Texas, but the small

Anglo group had always wielded exclusive political power. Mexican Americans, for the most part migrant agricultural workers or employees of the dominant vegetable cannery, were too intimidated by economic pressure to dare seek a voice in local government. However, in the early 1960s the Teamsters Union and the Political Association of Spanish Speaking Organizations joined forces to organize labor in the processing plant. In conjunction with this effort, the Mexican Americans, supported by the Teamsters' Union, gained all five seats on the city council in 1963 and virtually took over the local government. Although this upset occurred through the regular political process, it was dubbed a "rebellion." So unusual was this event in an obscure small Texas community that it received nationwide publicity as a possible harbinger of things to come—an "example of the power of the ballot box for politically underprivileged groups."[13]

But the "rebellion" was short-lived. Once in power, the group was unable to maintain political unity and discipline, and the opposition used the internal dissension to its advantage. In rapid succession three of the five Mexican-American councilmen were removed from their office for nonpayment of taxes and utility bills. The mayor and other officials were subjected to threats and harassment by Texas Rangers. The Teamsters lost interest. The Anglos who had previously been in the saddle without making much of an effort organized themselves for political action, and they managed to obtain the cooperation of some of the more affluent Mexican Americans, who were promptly labeled Uncle Toms in their own community. In 1965, a new slate of Anglos and Mexican Americans was elected, and the Mexican-American city manager resigned.

On balance, a coalition government may well be a net gain for the ethnic group in Crystal City. Anglos can no longer be certain of their political dominance. However, the Crystal City case highlighted the fact that an urban style of politics in an essentially rural setting with a feudalistic tradition is unlikely to bring durable success. The attainment of governmental control without other ingredients of power is not enough.[14] Also, this episode demonstrated once more the dependence of effective political action by the minority on outside forces. When the Teamsters Union withdrew its support, the Mexican-American electorate's chances of sustaining its control of Crystal City were greatly reduced.

VOTING BEHAVIOR
IN LOS ANGELES AND SAN ANTONIO

To obtain further insight into the political participation of Mexican Americans, our questionnaire for the household surveys in Los Angeles and San Antonio included a number of items on voting and political attitudes.

Solely on the basis of the persistent greater isolation of Mexican Americans and their more limited opportunities in San Antonio (Chapter 13), one would expect a lower level of political participation than in Los Angeles. On the other hand, Mexican Americans in San Antonio are more heavily concentrated in one area, the Westside, and such clustering is often believed to be conducive to organization and the acquisition of political power. The population in Los Angeles is more scattered, although there are large concentrations in areas such as Boyle Heights, Lincoln Heights, Belvedere, and East Los Angeles. The index of residential segregation from Anglos in 1960 was 57.4 for the central cities of the Los Angeles metropolis as against 63.6 for the central city of San Antonio (Chapter 12). These figures understate the differ-

Chart 23–1.

Percent of Mexican-American Survey Respondents Reporting Voter Registration and Voting in the 1964 General Elections, Los Angeles and San Antonio

(Percent of respondents eligible to vote)

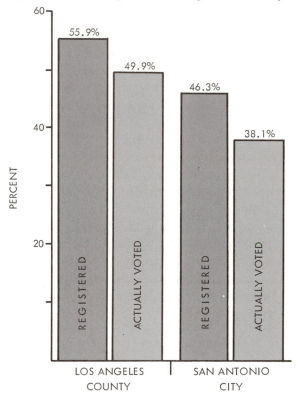

ence. Fairly large numbers of Mexican Americans live in Los Angeles County areas outside the central cities, whereas relatively few live in fringe areas outside the city of San Antonio. Our interview data relate to the county in the case of Los Angeles and the city in the case of San Antonio. The interview questions pertained to the general elections of 1964.

The responses show voter registration and actual voting at a substantially higher level in Los Angeles than in San Antonio (Chart 23–1). The better socioeconomic position of Mexican Americans and the greater "openness" of the system in Los Angeles are indeed associated with a higher rate of political participation. The larger geographic concentration of Mexican Americans in San Antonio may offer political advantages, but this factor seems to be swamped by their social isolation and lower economic level. However, when the 1964 registration rates of our respondents are compared with the general rates reported for the two cities in 1960, one notes an interesting contrast of a different kind. The 56 percent rate of our Los Angeles respondents is far below the 77 percent reported for the general population of this city. The 46 percent rate of the San Antonio respondents is a little higher than the 43 percent reported for the total population.[15] The discrepancy may reflect the acceleration of political activity of Mexican Americans in San Antonio in the first half of the 1960s.

As shown in Table 23-4, voter registration among the respondents increased with age and dropped off beyond the 50-and-over age group, a pattern not unlike the general pattern in the United States.[16] And voter registration is positively related to income, as it is in the general population (Table 23-5).

Table 23-4. Voter Registration, by Age Group, Survey Respondents in Los Angeles and San Antonio, 1965-1966

Age Group	LOS ANGELES (COUNTY) Number of Respondents in Age Group	Percent Registered	SAN ANTONIO (CITY)[a] Number of Respondents in Age Group	Percent Registered
Under 29	225	40	94	38
30–39	298	60	164	47
40–49	218	68	134	64
50 and over	204	55	210	39
Total	945	56	602	46

[a] Weighting procedures were used in the San Antonio sample. This means that total numbers cannot be used as a direct indicator of error. See Appendix H.

Where people register to vote tells much about the access of citizens to the franchise. This is especially relevant in light of the difference between Texas and California in providing registration facilities. When asked where they were registered to vote, 54 percent of the San Antonio respondents named a local government building, most likely the courthouse, or a bank. Los Angeles registrants, on the other hand, reported numerous locations among which homes and supermarkets were equally prominent.

In terms of voting itself, Mexican-American participation was below the national norm in Los Angeles and even still lower in San Antonio. Nationally, actual voters have typically accounted for more than 60 percent of those eligible to vote.[17] For our survey respondents, the corresponding figures were 50 percent in Los Angeles and 38 percent in San Antonio. More men than women went to the polls, as is true for the general population.[18] However, the sex difference in voter participation was far greater in San Antonio than in Los Angeles. In San Antonio, only 27 percent of the eligible female respondents voted as against 55 percent of the male respondents. In Los Angeles, 45 percent of the women and 57 percent of the men voted in the general election of 1964. Altogether, these data confirm the notion of a low rate of political participation more definitely than did the registration figures. They point up again

Table 23–5. Voter Registration, by Income Category[a],
Survey Respondents in Los Angeles and San Antonio, 1965–1966

	Percent Registered	Total Number (= 100%)
Los Angeles (County)		
Higher	73	367
Medium	49	298
Low	40	280
San Antonio (City)		
Medium	55	326
Low	32	276

[a] In Los Angeles: high income = > $6,000; medium income = $3,600–$5,999; low income = < $3,600. In San Antonio: medium income = > $2,760; low income = < $2,760.

the greater isolation of Mexican Americans in San Antonio. The persistance of traditionalism in the latter city is revealed in an extremely low voting rate for women.

The low rate of Mexican-American voting in San Antonio compared with Los Angeles *seems* to suggest something of a paradox. Assuming that these urban complexes are reasonably good proxies for urban Texas and urban California, how is it possible for Mexican Americans to achieve substantial representation in the state legislature of Texas as against none in California, and to send two Congressmen to Washington as against one from California? The ecology of the Mexican-American population of Texas provides a sufficient though perhaps not the entire explanation. As was mentioned in other contexts throughout this book, the population is heavily concentrated in south Texas. Its numerical strength in this region enables the group to elect Mexican-American officials despite its lower rate of voting participation. In 1960, the 257,000 Spanish-surname people in Bexar County (in which San Antonio is located) accounted for more than 37 percent of the total population. In Los Angeles County, the 577,000 persons of Spanish surname were only a little over 9 percent of the total. A 40 percent voter-participation rate in Bexar County would give the Mexican Americans far greater political muscle than would a 60 percent rate in Los Angeles County. The concentration of minority groups in city ghettos has often been cited as a condition favorable to bloc voting. In the case of Texas, we find a similar condition for a larger region within the state. The advantage of concentration has been great enough to overcome the adversity of the social milieu and of the more stringent election rules in Texas.[19]

The preference of our survey respondents for the Presidential candidate in the

1964 general elections confirmed the overwhelming commitment of Mexican-American voters to the Democratic party. About 95 percent voted for Lyndon B. Johnson in both Los Angeles and San Antonio.

ATTITUDES TOWARD POLITICS

Responses to attitudinal questions revealed a great deal of ambivalence about politics among Mexican Americans. On the one hand, 80 to 81 percent of the survey respondents in both Los Angeles and San Antonio agreed that "voting decides what happens." On the other hand, an about equally large majority said that politics was "too complicated" and presumably to be avoided (79 percent in San Antonio and 75 percent in Los Angeles). The level of confidence in the political process is quite low. In Los Angeles, 55 percent of the respondents felt that people like themselves have a great deal to say about government, and 35 percent expressed a negative view. In San Antonio, only 44 percent gave a positive answer, and 40 percent were negative. (The remainder did not answer this question or said "don't know"). That the Mexican Americans' confidence in their ability to influence political affairs is so much lower in San Antonio reflects, in all probability, their greater social isolation as well as the procedural obstacles to political participation that were mentioned earlier in this chapter.

Table 23–6. Support of and Opposition to Ethnic Unity by Survey Respondents, Los Angeles and San Antonio, 1965–1966

Reason for Support	Los Angeles (County)	San Antonio (City)
(1) Attain political influence	25%	35%
(2) Achieve social influence	34	24
(3) Create cultural unity	17	11
(4) Establish Mexican-American dominance	6	12
(5) "It's a good idea"	11	11
(6) Other[a]	7	7
Subtotal: In favor of unity (= 100%)	757	482
Opposed to unity	178	52
Total	935	534

[a] Includes "to provide educational opportunity" (which evoked a surprisingly small response), "we must unite," and other miscellaneous reasons.

Confidence in public officials is low. When they were asked whether officials care about their constituents, only 44 percent of the Los Angeles respondents gave a positive answer, and an equal proportion held the opposite view. In San Antonio, only 36 percent believed that officials "cared," 47 percent expressed a negative opinion, and relatively more interviewees than in Los Angeles failed to answer or said "don't know." Again, the inter-city differences are consistent with the greater degree of isolation of Mexican Americans in San Antonio and the consequent alienation.

The sample survey included a number of questions designed to explore the acceptance of the notion of ethnic unity. As shown in Table 23–6, the vast majority of the respondents in both cities supported the notion. This was true despite the low level of awareness of Mexican-American organizations. The support was somewhat greater in San Antonio (90 percent) than in Los Angeles (81 percent). The residential concentration of Mexican Americans in San Antonio and their depressed status are

Table 23–7. Percent of Survey Respondents Favoring Political Unity of Mexican Americans and Political Alignment with Negroes,[a] by Income and Neighborhood Ethnicity, Los Angeles and San Antonio, 1965–1966

	UNITY OF MEXICAN AMERICANS		UNITY WITH NEGROES	
	Percent	Total Number (=100%)	Percent	Total Number (=100%)
Los Angeles				
Frontier[b]				
Higher income	50	173	17	175
Medium income	60	171	18	72
Low income	61	67	21	74
Intermediate[b]				
Higher income	58	102	16	102
Medium income	61	92	21	95
Low income	76	67	28	68
Colony[b]				
Higher income	60	73	20	76
Medium income	68	120	27	115
Low income	71	108	24	109
San Antonio				
Frontier[b]				
Medium income	59	123	21	121
Low income	63	41	32	40
Colony[b]				
Medium income	66	181	27	163
Low income	81	196	12	187

[a] The question asked if the respondent agreed or disagreed with the statements "Mexican Americans should get together politically" and "...should get together with Negroes politically."

[b] In Los Angeles, Frontier = tracts with less than 15.0 percent Spanish-surname individuals; Intermediate = tracts with between 15.0 and 43.8 percent Spanish-surname individuals; and Colony = tracts with more than 43.8 percent Spanish-surname individuals. In San Antonio, Frontier = tracts with less than 54.0 percent Spanish-surname individuals, and Colony = tracts with 54.0 percent or more Spanish-surname individuals. For income: In Los Angeles, High income = > $6,000; Medium income = $3,600–$5,999; Low income = < $3,600. In San Antonio: Medium income = > $2,760; Low income = < $2,760.

probably more conducive to ethnic awareness and may make appeals to unity more effective. The lower the income of the respondent and the more Mexican his neighborhood—in other words, the more disadvantaged and Mexican his way of life—the more he approved ethnic political solidarity (Table 23–7).

Only 25 percent of the respondents who supported ethnic unity in Los Angeles, and 35 percent of those in San Antonio, named the attainment of political influence as a reason. About the same percentages of the respondents named the achievement of social influence as the reason for favoring ethnic unity, though the order of the two cities in this response is reversed. Cultural unity did not seem to loom large in the minds of the respondents. In both cities, this reason was named by fewer respondents than either political or social influence. Interestingly, though, the idea of cultural unity had greater appeal to the Angelenos than the generally poorer San Antonians. Relatively few Mexican Americans subscribed to the notion of unity in order to establish Mexican dominance, and this notion met greater approval in San Antonio than in Los Angeles. Among the reasons most frequently given for opposing the notion of ethnic unity was "pride in the United States" and "the idea is without value"—the latter perhaps expressing strong individualism.

Political alignment with *Negroes* was rejected by about three-quarters of the respondents in both cities (Table 23–7). Interestingly, the poorer respondents in mixed neighborhoods were more likely to favor an interminority coalition. This was not true in the city areas with large concentrations of Mexican-American people, suggesting that the ethnic identity of these people is stronger than any feeling of class solidarity with Negroes. A variety of reasons were offered by those who rejected a coalition of minorities. Most of the negative responses were based on the distinctiveness of Mexican Americans and/or prejudice against Negroes; others stressed the difference in the problems faced by the two groups. A fairly high proportion in Los Angeles (but not San Antonio) rejected Negro militant strategy as distasteful to the Mexican-American tradition of "quiet fighting." The degree of Negro militancy in the two cities differed sharply at the time of the surveys. Attitudes towards minority coalitions, however, can change with circumstances and leadership, just as Mexican Americans can change their definition of themselves as a minority.

SUMMARY

The political effectiveness of the Mexican-American minority in the Southwest has been handicapped by internal disunity, by external restraints imposed through voting laws and procedures, and by the gerrymandering of election districts. In addition, many urban Mexican Americans are relatively recent migrants from rural areas and have probably maintained the limited view of their potential role in political life that was derived from their experience in small towns and in the countryside. The low naturalization rate of Mexican aliens has been an important factor in keeping the political effectiveness of the whole group below its potential.

When political effectiveness is measured by Mexican-American representation in the national and state legislatures, the most startling result is the strong contrast between California and Texas. This contrast is the opposite of practically all other indicators of the relative position of Mexican Americans in the two states. The Texans have far better representation than the Californians, despite their approximately equal numerical strength, despite the less open social system, despite more stringent election laws and rules, and despite their substantially lower rate of voter participation revealed by the household surveys in San Antonio and Los Angeles. The great concentration of the Mexican-American population in the Rio Grande Valley explains much if not all of this difference between Texas and California.

That Mexican Americans are indifferent to exercising their right to vote is one of the most widely accepted clichés among Anglos and one of the most common self-stereotypes among ethnic spokesmen. Our survey results provide perspective on the truth of this allegation. In Los Angeles County, the rate of voter registration among our respondents was within the range of United States norms, and the actual voting rate was not much below par. Here, as in other parts of our study, the assimilative potentials in a relatively open milieu are clearly evident. Lower participation rates in San Antonio are consistent with the greater isolation of Mexican Americans and their depressed economic status in this city.[20]

The ideas of ethnic unity generally and political solidarity especially met with overwhelming approval of the respondents. Political coalition with Negroes was overwhelmingly rejected.

At the same time, respondents in both Los Angeles and San Antonio expressed divided opinions about the political process and about their ability to change their social environment through participation in the process. Possibly the experience of Mexican Americans in their contacts with governmental authority (Chapter 21) causes many members of the group to feel ambivalent if not apprehensive about politics. Nevertheless, the political socialization of the Mexican-American population no longer appears to be as dubious or difficult as it did a generation ago. In the wake of recent decisions of the United States Supreme Court, the larger society is removing some of the external restraints on more effective political participation by this as well as other minority groups. As shown in the previous chapter, Mexican-American organizations have been adopting a clearer political orientation geared to the variety of political action found in the United States. If they were to step up their efforts to prepare Mexican aliens for citizenship, they would strengthen the political potential of the group and at the same time remove one of the lingering causes of the dominant society's apprehensions about Mexican Americans.

NOTES TO CHAPTER TWENTY-THREE

1. Angus Campbell, Phillip E. Converse, Warren E. Miller, and Donald E. Stokes, *The American Voter* (New York: John Wiley & Sons, Inc., 1960), chap. 17.

2. The data relate the number of naturalized persons in a given year to the number of legal immigrants in a previous period sufficiently distant to make them eligible for citizenship. This cohort method, the only one available for measuring the rate of naturalization, assumes that the immigrants remained in this country and then, normally after five years of residence, could have applied for citizenship papers. As pointed out in chapter 4, this assumption is more dubious for Mexicans than for others. To the extent that Mexicans had a greater than average tendency to return to their homeland, immigrants who were "statis-

tically" eligible for citizenship had no real claim because they had left the United States before they could file their papers. Consequently, the statistical base on which the naturalization rate is computed is in all probability overstated, and the rate itself is understated. Another possible error in the comparison of naturalization rates for immigrants from different countries can arise from varying age distributions within immigrant groups. Obviously, older immigrants may die before they are eligible for citizenship, and the incidence of such cases may differ for people from various countries of origin. Further, an applicant for naturalization must generally be at least eighteen years old. Younger children derive citizenship from the naturalization of their parents. If Mexican immigrants have had an unusually large number of foreign-born children who by the time of their parents' naturalization were less than eighteen years old, the naturalization rate for the group would have appeared to be relatively low. The children had been counted in immigration statistics but were not included in the figures on naturalization.

3. For example, 79 percent of the Mexican aliens who were naturalized in 1966 had resided in this country ten years or more, as against 34 percent among all aliens acquiring citizenship in that year; and nearly one third had entered this country before 1940 as against only 6 percent of all persons naturalized. The figures for earlier years indicate equally long periods of residency for Mexican aliens before they obtained citizenship, except that the percentage of those who had entered before 1940 has declined, as one would expect. Several studies have used the speed of naturalization as an index of acculturation of immigrants from different countries or of different socioeconomic positions. For example, see Witold Krassowski, "Naturalization and Assimilation-proneness of California Immigrant Populations" (unpublished Ph.D. dissertation, University of California, Los Angeles, 1963).

4. Gunnar Myrdal, *An American Dilemma* (New York, Evanston, and London: Harper & Row, Publishers, Inc., 1962), pp. 75–78. In his analysis of the Negro problem, Myrdal prefers the "principle of cumulation" to the theory of the "vicious circle" because interaction between the minority and the majority can work in an "upward" desirable direction as well as in a "downward" undesirable direction.

5. Area variations in the rate of naturalization may also be associated with differences in the age distribution of Mexican aliens and in the length of their residence in the United States. It is very unlikely that these factors would explain the large difference between Texas and California. For the age and sex distribution of Mexican and all aliens who were naturalized in recent years, see Leo Grebler, "The Naturalization of Mexican Immigrants in the United States," *The International Migration Review*, I (Fall, 1966), pp. 17–32.

6. This point is made in the sparse earlier writings on the naturalization of Mexican immigrants. See Norman D. Humphrey, "The Detroit Mexican Immigrant and Naturalization," *Social Forces*, XXII (Dec., 1943), pp. 332–335, and the still earlier sources cited there. The meager literature is based on more or less casual observations.

7. For a recent study confirming this observation, see Gertrude D. Krichevsky, "Naturalization Rates of Immigrants," *Immigration and Naturalization Reporter* (U.S. Immigration and Naturalization Service), Apr., 1963; also, William S. Bernard, "Cultural Determinants of Naturalization," *American Sociological Review*, I (Dec., 1936), pp. 943–953.

8. See William S. Bernard, *op. cit.* For length of residence see also Stanley Lieberson, "The Old-New Distinction and Immigrants in Australia," *American Sociological Review*, XXVIII (Aug., 1963), pp. 550–565, and literature cited there.

9. See Michael Parenti, "Ethnic Politics and the Persistence of Ethnic Identification," *The American Political Science Review*, LXI (Sept., 1967), pp. 717–726.

10. Pauline R. Kibbe, *Latin Americans in Texas* (Albuquerque, N.M.: The University of New Mexico Press, 1946), p. 227.

11. *Ibid.*, p. 228.

12. *Ibid.*, p. 228.

13. " 'Latinos' Govern Tense Community," *New York Times*, Sept. 19, 1963.

14. This story of Crystal City is based on a field tour, on news reports in *The Texas Observer*, published in Austin, and on an unpublished study by Professor Sugiyama Iutaka of the University of Rio de Janeiro while he was temporarily attached to the Institute of Latin American Studies at the University of Texas. The Crystal City case was not entirely unique. In 1965, an "action party" made up of a large part of the Mexican-American population and a small group of Anglos won the city elections in Mathis, a town of 6,000 people 35 miles northwest of Corpus Christi. *Texas Observer*, Sept. 17, 1965.

15. General rates of voter registration in 1960 are analyzed for 104 cities by Stanley Kelley, Jr., Richard E. Ayres, and William G. Bowen, "Registration and Voting: Putting First Things First," *American Political Science Review*, LXI (June, 1967), pp. 359–379. Our comparison of the general registration rates for 1960 in this source with the 1964 rates reported by our respondents ignores, of course, differences in voter registration between these two dates. Our 1964 data may be influenced by sampling variance.

16. Campbell et al., *op. cit.*, p. 494.

17. See *Politics in America, 1945–1966* (Washington, D.C.: Congressional Quarterly Service, 1967), p. 84. See also Angus Campbell et al., *op. cit.*, p. 89.

18. Campbell et al., *op. cit.*, pp. 483–489. The authors found that the voter participation rate among women in their sample was consistently 10 percent below that of men when their figures were adjusted for the numerical relationship between men and women in the adult population.

19. This is true also for some localities in Texas, such as Laredo, where Mexican Americans have always been a numerical and social majority. Cf. Kibbe, *op. cit.*, p. 227.

20. Voting registration and participation of Mexican Americans in California may be raised by a decision of the State Supreme Court of March 24, 1970. The court held that literate Spanish-speaking citizens may vote in state elections even though they cannot read English, provided they can demonstrate access to political information in their own language. *Los Angeles Times*, March 25, 1970, Part I, p. 3.

Part seven

SUMMARY AND

CONCLUSIONS

TWENTY-FOUR

Past Trends and
Future Outlook

THIS book has been an inquiry into social change. That to study the life of Mexican Americans means to study social change is indeed one of the main findings suggested by our research. Such emphasis on the dynamics of this minority's condition departs from convention. Neither scholars nor policy makers, nor the general public, nor even Mexican-American leaders themselves have seen Mexican people in the United States as being importantly involved in change.

Only a generation ago the most crucial hypothesis about Mexican Americans postulated that they would never assimilate. Scholarly studies tended to support this notion by focusing on people living in urban ghettos or remote rural areas. Yet, we have observed throughout this volume that Mexican Americans are showing a growing potential for participation in the larger society. The minority's relation to the larger system has been profoundly altered by the greater internal diversity of the subpopulation and by its rapid urbanization. Also, the social environments of Mexican Americans in the Southwest have become more highly differentiated. As Mexicans moved into the cities and to California, they encountered a far greater variety of local social systems than they had known in the rural areas. Today, their milieus range from relatively accepting to traditionally rejecting.

Accordingly, this concluding chapter is couched in terms of social change. It will summarize the directions of change in both the minority population and the larger society, stress the unevenness of change in different spheres of life and different locales, and attempt to identify the forces involved in the process of change. Finally, the chapter will probe the critical question of whether the trends observed in the past can be projected into the future.

THE ETHNIC COLLECTIVITY

Following tradition, some parts of this book compared Mexican Americans with other population groups. This is a useful heuristic device and conforms to long-established sociological practice. Studies of the assimilation of ethnic groups have been conducted for decades, and they have generated a number of important theories about the process of assimilation. Thus, several sociologists have hypothesized a "race-relations cycle" from the initial contact between two peoples to their final amalgamation.[1] The cycle as originally formulated assumed internal homogeneity of the confronting groups. In the mid-1940s Warner and Srole suggested a timetable for the assimilation of American ethnic groups, the length of time depending on racial and cultural similarities to the basic WASP stock.[2] Their detailed analysis of the processes of assimilation would be distorted by a simple summary. But they seemed to assume at the time that all American groups would *eventually* be assimilated; one important part of the process was the dissolution of ethnic solidarity as members became absorbed into the larger system. Recently, some sociologists have attempted to reconceptualize the American system in light of theories of pluralistic societies. Thus, Milton Gordon challenges the assumption of the eventual assimilation of all groups and suggests that assimilation may stop before it becomes complete.[3] Cultural or value assimilation may occur without full amalgamation.

It must be recognized, however, that the term "pluralism" has many meanings. It can be interpreted in almost as many ways as there are national varieties of relationships between cultural groups. Research in Canada as well as in the United States has suggested that the national ideal or myth justifying a particular form of pluralism may not at all conform to reality. The "mosaic" of Canadian ethnic sub-populations was recently shown to be a "vertical mosaic," with sharp differences in power and privilege between the groups.[4]

These and other difficulties in conceptualizing the processes of coexistence of distinctive cultural or racial groups are illustrated by Shibutani and Kwan's massive

[1] Notes for this chapter start on page 596.

attempt to analyze pluralism (which they label "ethnic stratification") in a variety of countries. Shibutani and Kwan repeatedly acknowledge the significance of intra-ethnic diversity and the processes creating such differentiation.[5] Our findings for Mexican Americans in the United States support this emphasis.

To fit Mexican Americans into a scheme that assumes ultimate full assimilation is no more profitable than to force them into a pattern that assumes no assimilation whatever. The classification of an ethnic group as a collective entity serves the limited purpose of enabling one to see the group's problems in the perspective of the problems of other groups; such an approach is especially useful in the case of a little-known minority. Thus, we have shown that Mexican Americans share with Negroes the disadvantages of poverty, economic insecurity, and discrimination. Problems of acculturation, especially the difficulty of acquiring an adequate command of English, were experienced by many other immigrant groups. Like all those who are poor and uneducated, Mexican Americans have the frustrations of coping with bureaucracy even of the benevolent kind, especially in the modern world of imper-sonal government forms, documents, and computers. Their ethnic-minority status has been compounded by religious-minority status, as was that of Catholic immigrants from Italy and Ireland. Like other subordinated groups, past and present, they have experienced obstacles to attaining political influence at all levels of government.

In many cases, our analysis could *measure* the severity of problems of Mexican Americans in comparison with other identifiable subpopulations. For example, throughout the major Southwest cities Mexican housing segregation from Anglos is significantly less extreme than the segregation of Negroes from whites. Since residential location is a fairly reliable indicator of general social segregation, this find-ing assumes added importance in defining the place of Mexican Americans in our society. On the other hand, Mexicans fall well below other minorities on measures of acculturation. They include a high proportion of first- and second-generation persons, and the naturalization rate among the foreign born is low. Except for the Puerto Ricans, Mexican Americans retain their native language more persistently than any other major ethnic population on the United States mainland. Their average school attainment is substantially poorer than that of Negroes and notably below that of Asians.

Mexican-American family and individual incomes tend to be higher than non-white or Negro incomes. Their occupational structure is also less depressed than that of Negroes. But Mexicans are plagued by all of the problems of a population with a large proportion of low-skilled workers: a high rate of unemployment and under-employment, and declining or flat income with advancing age. Their *per capita* income is far lower than that of nonwhites or Negroes—a consequence of one of the most distinctive characteristics of this population: exceedingly high fertility (and, by implication, a high birth rate) and the prevalence of unusually large families. Low income per person in the family, in turn, accounts for an extremely high incidence of poor, overcrowded housing and probably a great many other serious consumption deficiencies (which we were unable to identify and measure).

In comparison with other immigrants, even the Southern and Eastern European immigrants of the late nineteenth and early twentieth centuries, Mexican Americans have had little time for acculturation. Moreover, their initial concentration in rural areas and agricultural work contrasts sharply with the earlier immigrants' direct movement to the cities and urban employment. Rural concentration limited their opportunities to become acculturated. Rural settlement retarded the education of their children, made it far more difficult for them to consolidate their position through labor organization, restricted their job mobility, and kept them from attaining political influence.

THE DIVERSITY
OF THE MEXICAN-AMERICAN PEOPLE

Nearly every one of the similarities between Mexican Americans and other minorities is modified by distinctive features of the subpopulation, or of its experience in the United States, or of local social settings. These distinctive features have important consequences. They determine in large measure the choices available to Mexican-American individuals seeking their place in society. For example, social and economic discrimination against members of the group is significantly influenced by the great variations in their physiognomy and skin color. Discrimination is not as categorical as in the case of Negroes.

Public policy can be seriously misguided if it overlooks the fact that a category consists of subcategories and individuals with varying motivations and aspirations. Mexican Americans, like any other category of people defined as "disadvantaged," are indeed objects of social action, but they are at the same time *subjects* in the social process.[6] Their behavior as subjects, as actors, in this process is far more complex and ambiguous than any collective classification might suggest. In their personal choices in such strategic matters as the selection of a career or a spouse, individual values and preferences are beginning to dissolve the categorical boundaries imposed by the larger system or marked off by ethnic spokesmen. Ethnic identity is becoming more differentiated, though it may never disappear altogether.

Because of these complexities, our analysis has emphasized differentiation *within* the Mexican-American collectivity. A systematic though brief review will show the numerous manifestations of internal diversity and relate them to past and current social change.

Generational Differentiation

Mexican Americans are both the oldest and the newest minority in the United States. Except for the Indians, colonial settlers coming from Mexico were the earliest inhabitants of what is now the United States. Yet in the historical perspective of immigration to this country, Mexicans also represent the most recent wave of new-comers. This dual position has had important implications.

When mass immigration began after the Mexican Revolution and World War I, the Mexicans in this country were a small, old-stock population facing a rapidly growing new immigrant population. In contrast to this early bimodal distribution, the Mexican-American people now show far greater generational differentiation. In addition to the old stock, they include a large component of native-born children and grandchildren of immigrants. Although immigration from Mexico still continues at a substantial rate, the foreign-born component is declining. The proportion of native born was already 85 percent in 1960 and has certainly increased since the last census date. Identifiable descendants of the colonial settlers still form a very small group; the Spanish-surname populations of New Mexico and Colorado in 1960 accounted for less than one-eighth of the total Mexican-American population in the Southwest.[7] But this small group now confronts large numbers of second- and third-generation people as well as "greenhorns" fresh from Mexico.

The old settlers, the "charter-member" segment, have shown astonishingly little collective assimilation in more than four generations of life in the United States. And this fact permeates much thinking about Mexican Americans and their difficulties in acculturation. Beliefs about the "inassimilability" of Mexicans have always reflected, directly or by implication, the continuing attachment of the people of New Mexico to their linguistic and cultural tradition.

Further, the split between the old stock and the immigrants and their children has been an important social distinction within the Mexican-American population. This great gap is largely unrecognized by Anglos both inside and outside the South-west. The "Spanish Americans" have exhibited a persistent (though perhaps now diminishing) desire to dissociate themselves from those who came across the border in recent decades. "Mexicans" were held to be inferior, and their presence was considered a status threat. On the other hand, the preoccupation of the traditional New Mexican with proper family lineage and his somewhat archaic customs and Spanish idioms represent quaint curiosities to most Mexican Americans and their children. Few Mexican Americans outside of New Mexico and Colorado seem to know much about this variant of their culture which (like the Elizabethan songs in Appalachia) was preserved by centuries of rural isolation.

Locational Differentiation

That this minority, once predominantly rural, has become predominantly urban is probably the most significant change in the Mexican-American population. Furthermore, the move to the cities has often been a move to California. Both shifts increased the range of opportunities and have begun to alter the style of life. Not only have new immigrants been moving to the cities without interim sojourns in rural areas, but those Mexicans with a longer experience in the United States have increasingly joined the movement to urban and, indeed, large metropolitan places. Thus, the urban populations of Mexican-American origin now consist of large numbers of people *born* in cities, as well as United States-born migrants and newcomers from Mexico.

Although the movement to the city continues, for most Mexican Americans urban life today is no longer a new experience. This means that the problems of Mexican Americans have become more nearly identical with the problems of American urban society. Yet, most Anglos continue to define the difficulties of this minority as failures of rural, unacculturated people new on the complex urban scene. And Mexican Americans themselves continue to respond to definitions of their situation that also fail to reflect contemporary metropolitan life. One of the first elements to appear in Mexican-American ideology was the concept of the "conquered people." The ideological impact of this notion has traveled far beyond New Mexico and the New Mexican villagers who still live with the effects of the conquest by the United States. Even the children and grandchildren of Mexican immigrants can identify with such a claim on American society. It is on this basis, for example, that some spokesmen have been demanding a reallocation of lands in the Southwest. Apart from specifics, the ancient outrages have great ideological appeal. The notion of "conquered people" seems to give Mexican Americans in the cities an important moral wedge by which they can drive home demands for the redress of grievances. Such demands are analogous to the Negroes' moral demands based on their history of slavery.

The continuing appeal of a rural ideology is easily understandable. The rural battles in New Mexico, in the vineyards of California, and in South Texas are close to people urbanized so recently. Furthermore, the rural-based struggles are dramatic and present clearly delineated issues involving clearly definable oppressors. They also offer the Mexican American a semblance of "pure" ethnic values and virtues, and charismatic leaders who have no peers on the urban scene.

Thus, the shift from rural to urban areas, and especially to cities in California, has brought the Mexican-American people some socioeconomic improvements but not, so far, an ideology adapted to their urban condition. For the minority group, this cultural lag means that much of their ideology is divorced from reality. The majority group, in turn, suffers from its own cultural lag by assuming that the problems of Mexican-American newcomers to cities will disappear in time, as did those of earlier migrants from rural to urban areas.

Increasing Social-class Differentiation

The social-class structure of Mexico and of the early Mexican settlers in the United States was based on rigid distinctions of race and wealth. Thus, Mexican immigrants entered a dual class system, one within and the other outside the ethnic community. The two systems used sometimes congruent and sometimes conflicting criteria for the allocation of prestige. Of course, the vast mass of Mexicans were at the bottom of both systems; the present-day urban, middle-income Mexican American most likely has come from a lower-class family. The contemporary class structure of Mexican Americans is still characterized by status discrepancies. Some of these are resolved by reference-group commitments to the larger society and others by commitments to the Mexican-American subsystem. Either choice tends to entail different scales of prestige and accompanying styles of life as well as considerable ambiguity.

Over time, increasing numbers of Mexican Americans have been able to break out of the bottom range of the social stratification system. Yet, the minority's over-all occupational profile still indicates penetration primarily at working- and lower-middle-class levels. Past improvements in educational attainment have been too slow to permit the massive change from manual to non-manual occupations that is required for more substantial gains in income and social status. College recruitment programs that are currently reaching out to Mexican Americans in some parts of the Southwest offer limited promise of accelerating the move to greater representation at middle-class levels.

Increasing differentiation in the social-class subsystem has had different consequences for Mexican Americans in different parts of the region. Even middle-class Mexican Americans still find themselves in a caste-like position in parts of Texas; in these areas, an increase in the number of middle-class individuals has meant little for collective integration. In other areas and especially in the large cities, social status and economic position have become more congruent.

Increasing Differentiation in Social Relations

Mexican Americans were long confined to largely ethnic neighborhoods. More recently urbanization and occupational upgrading have brought increasing interaction with Anglos. This is evident among our survey respondents, who report many more contacts with Anglos now than in their childhood. Their children have even more contacts with Anglos as schoolmates and friends. As one would expect, relations with Anglos are more frequent among middle-class than among lower-class individuals and among those living in mixed neighborhoods than among ghetto residents. Also, Mexican Americans in Los Angeles show a greater degree of social integration than do their counterparts in the less open system of San Antonio.

That the options of Mexican Americans for social interaction with the outgroup have been enlarged over time is highlighted by our data on intermarriages in Los Angeles County. In the relatively permissive climate of Los Angeles, outgroup marriages were much more frequent than would be expected on the basis of earlier studies: About 25 percent of the Spanish-surname persons who married in 1963 selected Anglos as mates. Here, too, social class was an important determinant. Higher-status individuals were most likely to marry outside the ethnic collectivity. Also, outgroup marriages increased with removal from immigrant status. Again, the extent of ethnic exclusiveness seems to diminish in a milieu that permits social interaction. With more interaction, the roles of the ethnic group and especially the family as prime sources of identity may be weakened.

Increasing Differentiation in Family Types

Our study shows the Mexican-American family to be quite different from the traditional patterns suggested in the literature. The extended family household is extremely rare. The role of the *compadrazgo* has diminished. A high incidence of broken families indicates that the Mexican-American family possesses no extra-ordinary capacity to resist the strains of poverty and of rapid social change. The data do not permit us to judge whether there has been drastic change over time, or whether earlier writings, by emphasizing norms rather than reality, may have ideal-ized the existing situation.

Specifically, the roles of husband and wife in today's nuclear, urban family differ greatly from the cliché of the dominant man and the submissive woman. Decisions on spending and the division of household tasks are comparatively egalitar-ian, as in Anglo families of similar social-class level, although the female retains some specialized functions in a restricted domestic area. This departure from alleged ethnic norms is found most frequently among higher-income families.

Birth control meets with far greater approval, at least in interview responses, than would be expected from a Catholic population. In Los Angeles, the rate of acceptance by Mexican Americans was as high as in a recent nationwide sample, but San Antonio showed a lower rate. Birth-control practice may be so recent that its results can only be seen in the future.

Increasing Differentiation in Cultural Maintenance

The pervasive cultural distinctiveness of Mexican Americans is a favorite theme of earlier studies. It is also strongly emphasized by some ethnic spokesmen, perhaps largely as a defense against ideas of a superior Anglo-Saxon culture in the larger society. The facts are far more complex.

Values related to work and individual achievement and the parents' aspirations for their children do not differ sharply from those held in the dominant society. Much like other people, most Mexican Americans want satisfying work, wish to get ahead in their jobs, and hope for security and steady income. They want their children to take up careers in the professions, though quite a few are reluctant to guide the occupational choice of the young. Our surveys do not support the notion that Mexican Americans generally are extraordinarily passive and that they are attached to relatives to the detriment of personal achievement. Values related to work and achievement vary with income, as they do in the general population, and with neighborhood ethnicity.

Cultural distinctiveness appears more strongly in the Mexican emphasis on *disciplina* as an important part of school teaching for their children. This emphasis cuts across the age of parents and their economic or neighborhood status, and holds about equally for boys and girls. Cultural maintenance appears most strongly in the Mexican Americans' loyalty to their mother tongue. The persistent use of Spanish reflects in part the historical isolation of large segments of this population, but it is probably reinforced by the recency of mass immigration and by the continuous arrival of newcomers from Mexico. Higher-income people and those living in mixed neighborhoods are more likely to speak English. Hence, this manifestation of cultural maintenance may change if Mexican Americans extend and consolidate their economic progress and as new immigrants account for a diminishing proportion of the group.

On the whole, then, cultural tenacity is neither as strong nor as uniform as is often suggested in the literature or by ethnic spokesmen.

Increasing Differentiation in Ingroup and Outgroup Perceptions

Mexican Americans see themselves and others in an increasingly complex fashion. Many subscribe to both positive and negative stereotypes. They tend to believe that Mexican Americans are more emotional, less materialistic, work harder, and have stronger family ties than Anglos. They also believe that Mexicans are less progressive and more inclined to blame their problems on others. A majority see the outside world as discriminatory but believe that discrimination has lessened. There seems to be little feeling against social interaction with Anglos. Social interaction with Negroes is rejected more strongly and uniformly.

What Mexican Americans call themselves or want to be called is a matter of considerable sensitivity. Here the notions of the minority itself interact strongly with those held in the dominant society. Conforming to a pattern of prejudice in the larger American system as well as to the heritage of racism in Mexico itself, socially mobile individuals have tended to avoid identification as "Mexican" by adopting "Spanish" ancestry. American racism is clearly reflected in the first attempt by the Census Bureau to classify people of Mexican ancestry; and continuing negative attitudes are evidenced by the measure of social distance consistently applied by Emory Bogardus over 40 years, in which Anglos continued to rank Mexicans near the bottom of ethnic groups. Interestingly, as more Mexican Americans move into the middle class, the traditional genteel denial of Indian heritage is being replaced by attempts to explore the meaning of Indianness and its relationship to ethnic identity. But it is still true that self-designation largely reflects the local environment. Euphemistic terms such as "Latin American" or "latino" prevail in Texas, and the term "Spanish American" is a must in New Mexico; but "Mexican American" has come to be increasingly accepted in California and, more recently, *chicano* has emerged as a term of self-reference among the young activists in all states.

The "battle of the name" has contributed to the Mexican Americans' difficulty in achieving political solidarity in the Southwest. Yet recent years have witnessed a remarkable shift in self-concept from an ethnic-cultural group seen in local contexts to a national minority group. Increasingly, Mexican Americans are defining their problems as malfunctions of society rather than as consequences of cultural distinctiveness. This trend is still impeded by traditional parochialism, and it may yet be deflected by the new resurgence of ethnic consciousness.

Increasing Political Differentiation

Finally, during the past few years Mexican-American political tactics have become more diverse. Except in New Mexico, this minority until recently had developed little political "muscle," considering their potential strength in many Southwest areas. Characteristically, Mexican activists (and some Anglo liberals) referred to Mexican Americans as the "sleeping giant," with the implied warning to the larger system to beware of the minority's political awakening. But a low voting rate, a great deal of intra-ethnic disunity, and the commitment of Mexican Americans to the Democratic Party made the warning an empty gesture. Anglo politicians—especially on the local level—could continue to rely on private negotiation as the preferred tactic of middle-class spokesmen. Anglos could also continue to validate "manageable" ethnic leaders.

All this is changing. Today, Mexican Americans exhibit a far greater variety of political techniques that range from the tradition of "quiet fighting" to outright militancy. They are increasingly learning the politics of soical protest and adopting the standard tactics of strikers and of the Negro civil-rights movement: picketing, walkouts, sit-ins, street demonstrations, school strikes, and the rest. Militancy is most notable among young people, but it has an echo in the political stance of established leaders.

The new militancy is not just a simple imitation of Negro protest; it can be seen also as a resurgence of the historic conflict between Mexican Americans and Anglos in the Southwest. Tijerina's rebellion in New Mexico represents a modern counterpart of earlier guerrilla warfare and border clashes. The fact that Cesar Chavez undertook a lengthy fast to keep the strikers in the Delano vineyards from violence indicates the amount of barely suppressed rage of some Mexican Americans at the bottom of the socioeconomic ladder. Although the militancy of Tijerina and Chavez differs a great deal, these two men, along with Mexico's revolutionary leaders, have become symbols of social protest for many Mexican Americans throughout the Southwest.

Paralleling the new black consciousness, Mexican-American youth, especially college and high-school students, are involved in a renewed search for ethnic identity. Whether this movement will counteract the previous trend toward a weakening of ethnic cohesiveness is uncertain. Together with the increasing range of political tactics, the reawakening of "brown" awareness does mean that the conduct of this minority in the arena of political and social action has become less predictable. The "giant" may indeed be stirring. The outcome will be deeply affected by the capacity of the larger system to respond to the Mexican Americans' definitions of their problems and to solve the economic and social issues that underlie the unrest.

584

THE LARGER SOCIETY:

TRANSFORMATION AND INERTNESS

Some of the forces in the larger system of the Southwest that have facilitated social change among Mexican Americans are easily identified. Without question, the region's progressive industrialization and its rapid rate of urbanization were of strategic importance in opening up new job opportunities. The impact of this change on isolation, political socialization, education, and the beginning social mobility of Mexican Americans has already been summarized.

The urbanization of Mexican Americans, nearly equal to that of the general Southwest population in 1960, has continued, and it will probably increase in the future. The mechanization of agriculture (perhaps accelerated by recent successes in unionizing farm labor) will displace substantial numbers of rural people, whose foothold in the urban labor market will be even more precarious than for the earlier arrivals. The problem of changing labor force requirements, already a serious handicap for much of the present minority population in the cities, will become even more acute for the new migrants from rural areas. Shifts in labor demand will place a premium on effective programs for manpower training and retraining and require far greater efforts in English-language education for adults. The children of recent and future migrants as well as of the urban poor will need much better schooling to prepare them for desirable or even for readily available jobs. Thus, Mexican Americans in the Southwest will probably be increasingly involved in what has come to be labeled "the urban crisis."

The Checkered Pattern of Social Change

It is harder to assess developments in the larger society that bear more generally on the Mexican-American position. Civil-rights legislation, statutes to assure minorities of equal access to housing and employment opportunities, court decisions dealing with the gerrymandering of election districts and other obstacles to fair political representation of minority groups, the ban on *de jure* school segregation, and antipoverty programs are clearly visible parts of the record. The record of actual practice is far more obscure, the evidence of change mixed. And practice rather than precept confronts the individual member of a minority and determines his view of the larger system.

The history of conflict between the Mexicans and the majority in the Southwest has extended to the present day. A special Southwestern brand of Anglo racism permeates much of this history. The zoot-suit riots in Los Angeles and the subsequent hostile interpretation of "racial" features of the Mexican-American population, only a generation old, are echoed in statements of the 1960s and in similar assumptions deeply embedded in the institutions of the Southwest. We have not tested directly the extent of changes in hostility or feelings of racial superiority on the part of Anglos. But certain indirect indicators point to some decrease. Thus, Mexican Americans now have better access to public accommodations in most areas of the Southwest. The sign "No Mexicans or dogs allowed" can rarely if ever be seen even in Texas. The fact that fairly large numbers of Mexican Americans are living in mixed or even predominantly Anglo neighborhoods and that social contacts with Anglos have increased over time suggests that categorical rejection by the majority is diminishing. The militancy of some of the young is based more on the persistence of overwhelming problems of poverty and continuing repression of the collectivity with which they identify than on grievances derived from personal experience.

The contacts of Mexican Americans with governmental authority have remained precarious to this day. The early categorical definition by government agencies of this group as "probably alien" by legal status and "innately alien" in behavior is not yet extinct. Some of the activities of the Border Patrol, especially "Operation Wetback" in the mid-fifties, as well as actions of the Texas Rangers, have continued a tradition of repression. The minority group's relation to government, particularly to agencies with a large degree of administrative discretion, is still characterized by a great deal of mutual suspicion. And this suspicion extends to the agencies offering social services and thus reduces their effectiveness for Mexican Americans. New public organizations, notably those administering antipoverty programs and especially designed to meet minority needs, may alter this condition by drawing larger numbers of Mexican Americans into policy decisions and administrative tasks, but it is too early to assess their influence. The persistent difficulty in establishing a trusting relationship to government is apparent at the level of the elite as well as at the grass roots.

The larger system has not been completely unresponsive. The termination of the *bracero* program in 1964 was a signal victory of Mexican-American organizations which had joined with labor unions and civic groups to argue for this action. When Congress in 1967 adopted the Bilingual Education Act providing funds for teaching non-language skills in a foreign tongue and when state laws prohibiting such instruction were modified at about the same time, another significant step was taken to adapt the system to the needs of this minority. (Only a few years earlier, even in some California communities, Mexican-American schoolchildren were forbidden to speak Spanish during recess periods.) Appointments of Mexican Americans to responsible Federal posts are beginning to answer one of the most persistent demands of minority spokesmen. Colleges and universities throughout the Southwest are actively recruiting and supporting promising Mexican-American as well as Negro students.

Yet, even when the larger society has responded, its actions have often been of the "too little" variety as well as late. For example, the modest authorization of $30 million for the Bilingual Education Act was whittled down to a meager appropriation of $7.5 million. At the local level, it was only in 1969 that the Board of Education of Los Angeles, a relatively sophisticated institution functioning in a relatively open social climate, recognized the culture bias of IQ tests and abolished such tests in the first two grades. Representations by a Mexican-American community organization played a considerable role in this action.[8] Institutions of higher learning have been much slower in relaxing their admission standards for minority students than for athletes. When the *bracero* program was terminated, the beneficial effects on Mexican Americans were partially offset by allowing increasing numbers of Mexican nationals to cross the border as commuters or illegal migrants. Effective control of border movements is still blocked by inadequate budgets for the immigration authorities or lack of will, or both. Appointments of Mexican Americans to important Federal positions were made only in response to extraordinary political pressures. Thus, inertness as well as transformation has continued to characterize the larger society.

Our evidence of social change is weakest for specific social institutions. The public school is one of the most important agencies of socialization and role allocation. Accordingly, we undertook two school studies. One dealt with school practices affecting Mexican Americans in the Southwest; the other analyzed the performance and aspirations of Mexican-American youth in Los Angeles schools compared to other pupils and in the context of neighborhood ethnicity and parental socioeconomic status.

The survey of Southwest schools revealed many communities where traditional practices of intra-school as well as inter-school segregation and of rejection of the Mexican-American child continued unchanged. In other places the schools had instituted superficial and rather ritualistic modifications. In some cities minority protest was bringing a somewhat bewildered search for the "answers," often verbalized rather than transformed into action. In yet other areas the school systems were undertaking minor structural changes. Major innovations were under way in only a few communities. It is increasingly apparent that the educational institution is poorly understood and that its interaction with Mexican-American pupils and parents will continue to be problematic. What seems to be needed is a major experimental effort extending throughout the entire system from teacher training to administration.

Our society is unquestionably able to finance such an effort. However, given the fiscal constraints of local and state governments and the unwillingness of taxpayers to appropriate more money for school systems from traditional revenue sources, experimentation combined with research requires substantial Federal funding. Even then, the chances are that localism of the centralized or the decentralized variety (in large urban systems) would prevail in the future. Whatever the general merits of localism in the administration of schools, this would mean adaptations continuously restrained by local social structures and the professional rationalizations of teachers and school administrators that reflect these structures. There is little reason to believe that Mexican Americans would gain much in the process, the least in those places where change is most needed.

Our Los Angeles study of Anglo and Mexican-American youngsters, like the almost concurrent national study conducted by James Coleman, highlighted the complexity and difficulty of explaining the problems of minority children. It also illuminated the present gap between the concepts and tools of the social scientist and the program needs of educators. The study confirmed the conclusion that

Mexican-American children—like others—have the best chance for achievement when family and school contexts are generally supportive of each other. But this is not much help in building programs. Assuming that the question is not to locate "blame" for problems but to understand the educational process in order to improve it, we are woefully short of the knowledge necessary for changing the schools.

The churches have also acted as acculturative agencies for Mexican Americans. They were concerned with this group before some of the other institutions of society, including the schools, began to be involved. Americanization has played an important role in the activities and goals of both the Catholic Church and various Protestant denominations. Shifts from segregation to integration and from paternalism to greater self-determination, the development of institutional structures and church specialists for coping with the group's needs, the growing emphasis on social action— all of these trends mirror significant changes in the larger society. In fact, one can read the history of the churches' role among the Mexican-American people as an illustration of social change in this country. It spotlights the slowness and difficulty of institutional adaptation. Change in basic institutional *assumptions* (for example, questioning of established values, addition of new values) has been under way for close to three generations, with only recent signs of change in institutional *functioning*. This conclusion is the main contribution of the two chapters devoted to the churches.

No area needs more research and thought than the relationship between Mexican Americans and social institutions. Among the institutions that require thorough analysis are the law enforcement agencies, public health services, the Social Security Administration, the organizations dealing with employment and labor standards, the trade unions, the immigration authorities (including the Border Patrol), and the schools and colleges. Our work in this area has only scratched the surface. Further research will not only tell us more about Mexican Americans but provide insight into the actual functioning of American institutions as distinguished from their avowed objectives. It will help find operational solutions to the persistent problem of alienation of parts of the Mexican-American population. It will also contribute to the improvement of vital social services.

As an example, it seems that many Mexican Americans do not claim the social security benefits and welfare support to which they are entitled. Among the reasons given for their not doing so are ignorance, fear of government, and uncertainty over their legal status. But such suppositions have never been tested on any meaningful scale, and the remedies are therefore quite unclear. Research could form the basis for efforts to bring social security and welfare services closer to the intended level. Or, to identify a problem affecting practically all major institutions, imaginative innovation is needed to reconcile the application of modern technology (exemplified by automation and the "systems" approach to institutional operations) with the maintenance of a satisfactory personal relationship between the individual and the organization. The increasing impersonality in dealings between the individual and institutions is particularly offensive to many Mexican Americans.

The Diversity of Local Conditions

The checkered pattern of social change in the larger system is most clearly visible in the local milieus affecting the life of Mexican Americans. The diversity of local milieus seems to have increased rather than diminished over time. This is true even for the two large cities, Los Angeles and San Antonio, which were the objects of special study. As recently as the 1920s the two cities were not too different as social environments for the minority. Today, they show startling and pervasive contrasts in level of poverty, social isolation, and attachment to ethnic traditions. Yet neither of these cities can be said to represent an extreme in the range of social environments. Moreover, when smaller towns and rural areas are considered as well as big cities, even the present-day status of Mexican Americans varies between semi-caste and comparatively integrated, with a great deal of internal differentiation in the larger communities especially. The migration of Mexican Americans to California has unquestionably helped to improve their collective position and that of many individuals who moved. However, the effects of this migration on the Mexican Americans left behind in New Mexico, Arizona, and the poorer sections of Texas are difficult to assess.

Of course, such diversity of local conditions affects not only Mexican Americans. Negroes in Mississippi are worse off relative to whites than those in Chicago, both economically and socially. But the absence of an overview for Mexican Americans has too often led to generalizations based on local studies. Hence, we have stressed that minority status means not only pervasive differentiation from the majority but enormous area-to-area variations in the condition of Mexican Americans relative to Anglo Americans.

It would be unrealistic to expect these variations to change greatly in the foreseeable future. The local diversities are rooted partly in the economic structure of regions, and an economic base can rarely be altered swiftly. They reflect deep-seated differences in attitudes of the general population and in local power constellations. These, too, change at a slow pace. Cases of rural political challenges, illustrated in Chapter 23 by the story of Crystal City, Texas, serve to highlight the difficulty of social change in areas of traditional Anglo domination even when the minority has vast numerical superiority and manages to obtain formal access to government. Hence, it is not enough to say that the larger society, perceived as an aggregate, must accelerate the rate of change in order to remove its barriers to fuller participation by Mexican Americans. Remedial action must take into account not only the differences in the functioning of various social institutions but also the need for highly differentiated approaches in various locales.

General policies and programs coming from Washington or even from state capitals will remain ineffective in many areas unless they are accompanied by a concerted effort to transform them into action at the local level. Most of the crucial encounters of the Mexican American with the larger society occur in a local context: in the reception rooms of government and private agencies or in schoolrooms, or with individual members of the Border Patrol, clerks in employment offices or health centers, social workers, police officers on the beat, and so forth. These contacts, rather than the abstract principles embodied in the mission of social institutions or in well-intentioned programs, condition the individual's relation to the social system.

AN INSIDE VIEW OF NEEDED ACTION

That inertness of the social system accounts for most grievances of the Mexican-American people is apparent from a recent comprehensive record: the Cabinet Committee Hearings on Mexican American Affairs in 1967. The hearings gave ethnic spokesmen a rare opportunity to articulate public policies needed to improve the condition of this minority, and they provided the Federal government and society at large with a highly instructive view of "what Mexican Americans want." Most of the testimony was quite specific, and represented a nuts-and-bolts approach. As such, it was useful because, as was already emphasized, it is the nuts and bolts of the social institutions that confront the individual who must deal with them. Testimony at the hearings was presented by 51 persons, all but two or three of whom were Mexican Americans, and ranged over such critical issues as education, jobs, housing, antipoverty programs, economic and social development, welfare and health, and the group's special problems in rural areas.[9]

True, some Mexican-American leaders chose to boycott the hearings because they felt that only "safe" spokesmen were invited to testify. The record of the hearings may indeed represent the demands of the Mexican-American "establishment" laid before the larger "establishment." Quite a few witnesses were members of governmental commissions or boards or in charge of publicly financed programs and were therefore members of the system that was being criticized. However, their roles within the system enabled them to better understand its weaknesses and malfunctions. (Incidentally, that the Mexican-American community could marshal so much knowledgeable talent for the hearings testifies to its emerging strength; such a performance would have been impossible a generation ago.) The spokesmen's prevailing style was one of persuasion and polite pleading. At the same time, the content does not at all suggest that the presentations to the Federal officials were diluted. Even though the more militant or radical voices may have been muted, the hearings still provided remarkable insights into the Mexican Americans' point of view.

Several themes are common to the testimony. One is that most social institutions and governmental programs do not operate in accordance with their mission. A vast gap between intent and practice raises doubts about the policy makers' sincerity: "Those trapped in the cycle of poverty no longer trust the establishment." "We . . . are profoundly skeptical." "We are very disappointed with the performance of all levels of government." "In many cases, major industry's participation in jobs for the poor has resulted in little more than 'window dressing'. . . ."[10] What is at stake, then, is the inertness of social institutions or the inefficacy of action programs and the consequent loss of confidence in their functioning for the Mexican-American population. Even the dramatic proposal for a "Marshall Plan for Mexican Americans" in the Southwest would merely call for a new scale of educational, economic, and technological aid. And another unorthodox idea—that the Federal government should act as an employer of last resort—is held not only by representatives of the poor.[11]

The Cabinet Committee Hearings provide ample testimony on the gap between promise and fulfillment in governmental operations. We do have a Federal program of food distribution for the poor, including free school lunches for children. But the good intent is negated by the nonparticipation of many local governments in counties with large Mexican-American populations,[12] a charge duplicated by the shocking discoveries of a Congressional committee investigating the program at about the same time. We do have an agricultural extension service that is the envy of the world, but the requirement that local governments must share the cost leaves the poorer counties underserved—and the rural Mexican Americans are concentrated in those counties.[13] We do have laws against housing discrimination generally and especially against discrimination by builders who use Federally insured or guaranteed loans, but the regulations are seldom enforced.[14] We do have a Federal program for the support of compensatory education, but the appropriated funds are so meager that only half the eligible children are getting "a little bit of not enough."[15] One could extend the list indefinitely.

Another, related theme is the failure of social institutions and government programs to "reach the Mexican American." This failure is portrayed partly as a function of insufficient funding or gross neglect. Public health (including mental health) is a case in point. We lack data to assess the health needs of this minority; we lack even rudimentary vital statistics. Further, unless programming and funding are coordinated at the Federal level, "programs will not be implemented effectively on the state and local level"[16]—an observation applying to unemployment insurance and welfare programs as well. Health services available to Mexican Americans are highly inadequate, especially in rural areas and for migrant workers and their families. But failure to reach this group is attributed mostly to the Anglos' inability to "understand" Mexican Americans and their culture, and specifically to the scarcity of Spanish-speaking personnel. The communication barrier, cultural as well as merely linguistic, appears as a common thread in the testimony,[17] and so does the prescription: the employment of more Mexican Americans in agencies dealing with jobs, welfare, health, housing, and similar services. To overcome the paucity of human resources, the witnesses recommend recruitment programs, stipends and scholarships for training, and greater resort to subprofessional personnel.

A third theme is discrimination. "Many companies maintain an employment policy requiring a high school education for employment. Many of the jobs to be filled require no such level of education."[18] Even people applying for the recently developed on-the-job training programs find it difficult to overcome the hurdle of tests unrelated to job qualifications.[19] Apprenticeship training controlled by labor unions and employers still bars minorities in favor of "friends and relatives only."[20]

In contacts with government agencies having a large degree of administrative discretion, Mexican Americans share with other poverty groups a special type of discrimination: the extraordinary difficulty of seeking redress through the courts. Chapter and verse on this point are cited with regard to the Social Security Administration and the Texas Department of Public Welfare.[21]

Most of the basic policies needed to meet the problems of Mexican Americans, as seen in the Cabinet Committee Hearings, are already at hand or under consideration. And most of the demands by ethnic spokesmen concern widely recognized defects of our social system. This is true even for what may appear to be self-seeking demands, such as the call for more Mexican-American personnel in institutions and agencies dealing with the minority people, coupled with some relaxation of employment standards. Social critics have become increasingly concerned over excessive reliance on educational standards: "We have become a credential society, where one's educational level is more important than what he can do."[22]

As for schooling, the Mexican-American experts at the Cabinet Committee Hearings offer a variety of familiar solutions: more Federal money allocated more flexibly; the retraining of school administrators and teachers in community relations and Hispano-Mexican culture; Federal support for meeting the high cost of school desegregation through busing children and constructing new schools; funds for bringing more teachers and parents together in a learning situation and greater efforts to involve Mexican-American parents generally; bilingual and bicultural projects, with special emphasis on the early teaching of English as a second language.[23] One spokesman would want to see the Federal authority (or power of the purse) invoked more forcefully so as to compel changes at the local level.[24] Suggested policies for higher education include several steps already initiated in recent years, such as seeking out potential college students in high school, modifying admission standards, providing tutorial assistance and special counseling, revising curricula to give proper attention to Hispano-Mexican cultural contributions, and offering more financial support. They include also the unorthodox proposal to "reflect ethnic composition of the community in student college population as a basic principle of college life."[25] Only one spokesman, concerned with manpower training rather than education, hints at the complexities of the schooling problem by quoting Robert Hutchins: "The decisive factors in education appear to be beyond the control of the schools. They are such matters as poverty, discrimination, family background—the circumstances of daily life."[26]

Special policy issues affecting Mexican Americans appear in the Cabinet Committee Hearings mostly in the context of rural life: extension of the Fair Labor Standards and National Labor Relations laws to farm workers; cooperative labor pools instead of the governmental farm-placement services which are said to be employer-oriented; housing for migrant labor; more attention to the needs of small farmers in agricultural research and extension services; and the failings of the Forest Service (which were discussed in Chapter 21).[27] Some spokesmen advocate more extensive government-assisted rural development programs to stem the tide of migration to the cities.[28] This approach, whatever its merits, conforms to a growing general sentiment that it may be more productive to spend money on making rural areas more attractive to potential out-migrants than to spend it on the costly and difficult problem of providing for new migrants to the cities.

Another issue of special importance to Mexican Americans is the commuter system that allows people who live in Mexico to cross the border for more or less regular work. The testimony is unanimous in calling for a halt to this arrangement.[29] Our discussion of benefits and costs in Chapter 4 did indeed find the commuter system to be highly inequitable to domestic workers, most of whom are of Mexican descent.

PROJECTING TRENDS

On the whole, then, the "inside" view shows pressing claims for a place in American society and great frustration at the slow pace at which the larger system is making room. The charges levelled against the system are broadly consistent with our own analysis of lags in institutional adaptation. The charges are also largely consistent with our analysis of the meaning of "social disadvantage" in Chapter 2. Despite the institutional lags and the very real obstacles, however, Mexican Americans have demonstrated considerable capacity to enter the larger society. Are we justified in projecting this trend into the future?

Projecting the dynamics of the past is always hazardous. This is especially true when unstable relationships and emergent rather than long-standing social structures are involved. The task is further complicated by the present condition of American society. Even long-standing social structures are confronted with unprecedented challenges to basic values and norms. Minorities—black, Mexican American, Puerto Rican, American Indian—are importantly involved in these challenges. Under such circumstances, projection becomes extraordinarily risky.

The scholar may overreact to evidence of structural change and overlook certain basic continuities. A generation ago, when Gunnar Myrdal was speculating on the future position of Negroes, he could expound strong confidence in the capacity of our system to solve social problems through practical formulas. Such a pattern conformed to the American pragmatic approach to problems. Myrdal could point to the society's demonstrated openness to criticism as one source of his optimism about its future ability to cope with social strain. He could try to "discern the gamut of possibilities for the future" from knowledge of past trends.[30] He could express trust that the findings of social science would be taken as guides to social betterment. Yet most of Myrdal's expressions of hope for the future turned out to be wrong. They were wrong in part because he assumed that certain American values were more than values—that they were (or would soon become) operative norms. He erred in emphasizing the *potential* for integrative change that was inherent in American values and in scanting the basic continuities in the operating norms of discrimination. His error is evidenced by the stubborn resistance in the South to school desegregation and to making constitutional rights operative for all citizens, and by worsening race relations in Northern and Western cities with rapidly growing Negro populations.

No student of American minorities today can be as optimistic as Myrdal was in 1944. One cannot ignore the continuity of conflict which caused the Commission on Civil Disorders in 1968 to speak of a growing division of American society into "two societies, one black and one white, increasingly separate and scarcely less unequal"—a finding reiterated in a 1969 follow-up report.[31] If such a trend were to continue, it would produce a society radically different from any in our past. At the extreme, the trend might include the possibility of a black revolution.[32] Mexican Americans could hardly remain untouched by such developments.

On the other hand, the scholar may overreact to the present turmoil and underestimate the capacity of the American system to accelerate social change. Continuity in the basic egalitarian value system of society is manifest despite glaring failures in converting it into operative norms. The increasing recognition of structural problems beneath the surface of general prosperity has called forth fresh ideas for social change, as well as programs to combat poverty and urban decay and more stringent laws to remove inequality in civil rights, employment opportunities, and housing. Proposals such as national standards for welfare benefits, considered quite unorthodox only a few years ago, are now endorsed by a Republican Administration. The growing support of the once-heretical notion of "minimum income maintenance," in the form of a negative income tax, or a guaranteed annual income, or family or children's allowances, shows a change of values embedded in one of the fundamental structures of society—its social-class system. That such an idea meets with approval by traditionalists as well as reformers signifies a remarkable shift in a society whose core value only forty years ago was "nobody owes you a living." The resistances to change are formidable, and they are reinforced by manifestations of unrest which threaten to divert public attention from the underlying maladies to the symptoms of conflict. But the moral and political forces that propel the American system toward change are also strong.

Whether one leans toward an optimistic projection of the historic resilience of American society or toward a pessimistic projection of the more recent condition of unresolved conflict, it is clear that our institutions will need to change far more rapidly than in the past to cope with the new social forces among which Mexican Americans are destined to play an increasing role. American pluralism can assume true validity as a national ideal only if our major institutions can transform themselves speedily and ensure the participation of minority members in the process. Only then can the term "minority" shift in meaning from the present almost inevitable connotation of "disadvantaged group."

As for cultural identity, the larger system can broaden the range of options for the Mexican-American individual by fully recognizing the value of Hispano-

Mexican culture. History can be rewritten to place the contributions of this culture to the Southwest in a truer perspective. School texts and courses can be revised. At institutions of higher learning, research centers and institutes for the study of Mexican Americans can fill gaps in our knowledge of this population and provide emotional support for Mexican-American students who seek ethnic identity. However, such study centers must be developed at a pace consistent with the present scarcity of human resources available for scholarly work.

But the main task is the removal of obstacles which the larger system has placed in the path of socioeconomic improvement for the Mexican-American people. Five years ago, when we began our research, our most significant discovery seemed to be the evidence of social change in a subpopulation widely held to be immune to change. As we proceeded, the enormous local differences in the social milieus in which the minority encountered American society emerged as a strategic variable. But this finding could be transformed into an important thesis for social action: If the more open local systems provide an environment conducive to the minority's progressive integration, a change from relatively closed to relatively open local systems will do much to solve the problems of Mexican Americans. As our research moved on to an exploration of just how the institutions of the larger society function for the minority, we found so much institutional resistance to change that this inertness came to affect our conclusions in significant measure. Only utopias claim no discrepancy between promise and fulfillment. In comparison with the realities in other countries, American society may still represent a relatively open system. It has been notably successful in absorbing European immigrants. It has been far less successful in absorbing Mexican Americans, who are now the second largest minority.

One basic assumption of American ideology has been that social mobility is potentially available to all members of society. On this assumption, no sizable and readily identifiable groups of people were to be permanently subordinated. Such a social system would be without a permanent proletariat. The ideology has always ignored the condition of most Negroes and American Indians and, as this volume has demonstrated, the condition of most Mexican Americans as well. All three groups were long considered beyond the pale. But the ideology conformed to the experiences of enough other people to be perceived as broadly valid.

Today, however, the dominant society has become painfully conscious of the large number of people who live under the dual handicap of ethnic or racial minority status and poverty. These people themselves have become far more aware of their disadvantage, their social aspirations have been immeasurably heightened, and they insist on more rapid and more effective remedial action. Hence, the past in this case is not a prologue to the future in any deterministic or probabilistic sense. Rather, the challenge is to impart a new thrust to the future—to create the conditions in which the Mexican-American people can become ever more active participants in our society, can develop their individual abilities without hindrance, and are free to make personal choices with regard to their cultural identity.

NOTES TO CHAPTER TWENTY-FOUR

1. Robert E. Park proposed a universal cycle of "contact, competition, accommodation and eventual assimilation" in *Race and Culture* (New York: The Free Press, 1949), p. 150. Parks' theory of the race relations cycle, originally proposed in the early part of the century is the best known; there are several others—all falling equally short of empirical validation.

2. W. Lloyd Warner and Leo Srole, *The Social Systems of American Ethnic Groups* (New Haven, Conn.: Yale University Press, 1945).

3. Milton M. Gordon, *Assimilation in American Life* (London: Oxford University Press, 1964).

4. John Porter, *The Vertical Mosaic: An Analysis of Social Class and Power in Canada* (Toronto: University of Toronto Press, 1964).

5. Tamotsu Shibutani and Kian M. Kwan, *Ethnic Stratification* (New York: The McMillan Company, 1965).

6. See Everett C. Hughes, "A Note on Georg Simmel," *Social Problems*, vol. XIII (Fall, 1965), pp. 117, 118, and Georg Simmel, "The Poor," in the same issue, pp. 118–140.

7. This count is diluted by immigrants and their children. On the other hand, it excludes the descendents of original settlers living in other Southwest states in 1960.

8. "Testing of IQs in L.A. Primary Grades Banned," *Los Angeles Times*, Jan. 1, 1969. According to the *Los Angeles Times*, pressure for the action came from the Educational Issues Coordinating Committee formed in East Los Angeles.

9. Inter-Agency Committee on Mexican American Affairs, *The Mexican American: A New Focus on Opportunity*, Testimony Presented at the Cabinet Committee Hearings on Mexican American Affairs, El Paso, Texas, Oct. 26–28, 1967 (Washington, D.C.). Subsequently referred to as Hearings.

10. Hearings, pp. 3, 41, 51, 192.

11. For the "Marshall Plan," *ibid.*, p. 212. For the Federal government as employer of last resort, p. 58. We are not concerned here with an appraisal of the merits of any particular policy recommendation, or with the validity of complaints presented at the Hearings.

12. *Ibid.*, pp. 9–15. The testimony refers to Texas.

13. *Ibid.*, p. 5.

14. *Ibid.*, p. 219.

15. *Ibid.*, p. 108. The statement refers to California.

16. *Ibid.*, p. 123.

17. *Ibid.*, pp. 20, 42, 43, 53, 135, 136.

18. *Ibid.*, pp. 45, 58.

19. *Ibid.*, p. 50.

20. *Ibid.*, p. 58.

21. *Ibid.*, pp. 127–136. Among other things, attorneys' lack of interest in such small claims, the paucity of legal aid programs (in Texas), and the lack of Spanish-speaking agency personnel mean that poorly qualified middlemen and interpreters can abuse the poor by charging high fees (p. 136).

22. S. M. Miller, "Credentialism and the Education System" (paper delivered at the meeting of the American Orthopsychiatric Association, Washington, D.C., Mar. 23, 1967). Miller refers to (among other things) a study by Ivar Berg, which "discovered that at every occupational level the high-educated have a poorer record than the low-educated: more absenteeism, turnover, dissatisfaction, and probably lower productivity." For another aspect of the credential society, the tendency of professional associations to control entry requirements, see Richard N. Farmer and Harold H. Kassarjian, "The Right to Compete," *California Management Review* (published by the University of California Press for the Graduate Schools of Business Administration at Berkeley and Los Angeles), VI, 1, (Fall,

1963), pp. 61–68. The authors present a formidable list of licensing requirements in California that controls the entry of individuals into occupations and the entry of firms into business.

23. Hearings, pp. 97–118.

24. *Ibid.*, p. 241.

25. *Ibid.*, p. 99.

26. *Ibid.*, pp. 56, 57.

27. *Ibid.*, pp. 17, 18, 21, 27, 35.

28. *Ibid.*, pp. 3, 31.

29. *Ibid.*, pp. 2, 63, 64, 69–77, 91, 92.

30. Gunnar Myrdal, *An American Dilemma* (New York: Harper & Row, Publishers, Inc., 1962), p. 998. Our statements are based on chapter 45.

31. Urban America, Inc., and The Urban Coalition, *One Year Later—An Assessment of the Nation's Response to the Crisis Described by the National Advisory Commission on Civil Disorders* (1969).

32. Lewis M. Killian, *The Impossible Revolution? Black Power and the American Dream* (New York: Random House, Inc., 1968).

Appendixes

DERIVATION OF DATA
ON MEXICAN AMERICANS
FROM THE U.S. CENSUS

CHANGES IN CENSUS IDENTIFICATIONS

Before 1930, the census data on persons of Mexican descent were limited to counts of those born in Mexico and those of Mexican or mixed parentage. This classification was consistent with the traditional attention in U.S. census statistics to the foreign stock in the white population, and it has been maintained to the present time.

The first effort to identify Mexican Americans more broadly to include the native born of native parentage as well as the foreign stock was made in 1930. The classification selected by the Census Bureau was "Mexican," and it was placed in the larger rubric "other races" which also included Indians, Negroes, and Orientals. This definition made clear that Mexicans were not considered whites. Census enumerators were instructed to classify as Mexicans all persons of Mexican origin, whether of old colonial stock or immigrants and their children, who were not definitely white, Negro, Indian, or Oriental.

Records in the United States Archives reveal that the 1930 census definition of Mexicans evoked "unfavorable reactions" from the Mexican government and the U.S. Department of State. Besides, the classification proved to be highly inadequate. Among other things, it resulted in a gross undercount of native persons of Mexican descent, especially in New Mexico. There is reason to believe that enumerators failed to include Mexican Americans of lighter complexion, especially when they had middle-class or upper-class status.

In 1940 the Bureau of the Census turned to mother tongue as a means of identification —the language other than English spoken in earliest childhood. This was part of a general attempt to obtain information on the spoken mother tongue from a sample of the entire population. However, the results turned out to be of dubious value for statistical identification of national minorities. For example, about seven percent of the native population of Mexican parentage in the United States reported English as their mother tongue in 1940, and this percentage was probably much higher for natives of native parentage.

When the 1950 census was prepared, the Bureau of the Census decided to use the "Spanish-surname" identification, and the same method was applied in 1960 with very minor modifications. Significantly, Spanish-surname persons were now classified in principle as whites; they were called "white persons of Spanish surname." Thus, the statistical identification had run full circle from a subcategory of "other races" to a subgroup of the white population. How the Spanish-surname definition came to be developed is not entirely clear. But the record indicates that social scientists in the Southwest pressed for more adequate data on Mexican Americans and that Census Bureau statisticians had already used a surname technique informally for other purposes.[1] In any event, the changing classifications confine systematic comparisons of census data to the years 1950 and 1960.

THE SPANISH-SURNAME DEFINITION

The Spanish-surname definition is probably as good as any that can be devised for broad statistical purposes. The Bureau of the Census uses surnames based on a list of about 7,000 originally prepared by the U.S. Immigration and Naturalization Service in 1936. The census coders are instructed to classify a name as Spanish only if it appears in the list. Other names of apparent Spanish origin are referred to specialists trained to distinguish Spanish surnames from surnames in other Romance languages.[2]

There may be questions about the completeness and accuracy of any such list of surnames. On the other hand, this method has the considerable advantage that it can be applied to any non-census set of records which list surnames. For example, it was the basis for the compilation of statistics on intermarriages which are reported in this volume. The technique was also used as a screening device for the selection of Mexican-American households in our Los Angeles and San Antonio sample surveys. Its application is facilitated by the fact that the Bureau of the Census has prepared an abbreviated list of about 700 Spanish surnames that appear with greatest frequency—a source sufficient for statistical approximations.

The Spanish-surname method is certainly superior to most of the identification procedures employed by state and local government agencies for record-keeping purposes. Altogether too often receptionists or other clerks have been given the responsibility of defining a person as Mexican, and they do so on the basis of superficial impressions which, in turn, may reflect their own prejudices or the visitor's class status. The Spanish-surname technique, if properly applied, lends itself to far more accurate local investigations in such fields as health, welfare, education, and law enforcement. If these potentials are to be utilized, more methodological work is needed to identify Spanish surnames and their frequency in different areas and localities, and computer programs to extract Spanish surnames must be further developed.[3]

The Spanish-surname definition does not identify Mexican Americans directly. The

---

[1] The surname technique had been helpful in distinguishing between French Canadians and other Canadians in the United States and in allocating persons in the United States to the several countries formed after the breakup of the Austrian empire in the aftermath of World War I. This account of changing census classification is based on the "Definitions and Explanations" provided in the 1950 and 1960 Census volumes on persons of Spanish Surname, on discussion with Census Bureau staff members, and on a review of minutes (in the United States Archives) of the meetings of the Census Bureau's Technical Advisory Committees. For a local survey designed to test the differences in results obtained from applying the Spanish-surname technique, the mother-tongue criterion, and the test of Spanish ancestry of household heads, see William W. Winnie, Jr., "The Spanish Surname Criterion for Identifying Hispanos in the Southwestern United States," *Social Forces*, XXXVIII (May, 1960), pp. 363–366.

[2] See the "Definitions and Explanations" in the census volumes referred to in note 1.

[3] See, for example, Robert W. Buechley, "A Reproducible Method of Counting Persons of Spanish Surname," *Journal of the American Statistical Association*. LVI (March, 1961), pp. 88–97. This article includes some suggestive ideas for using a highly abbreviated list of Spanish surnames. See also the same author's "Characteristic Name Sets of Spanish Populations," *Names*, XV (March, 1967), pp. 53–69.

following minimum adjustments are required for transforming the number of Spanish-surname people to the number of Mexican Americans: (1) Deduct persons of Spanish surname who are not of Mexican origin; (2) Add persons who are of Mexican origin but have surnames other than Spanish.

As for the first group, for example, persons of Spanish surname include immigrants from Spain and their descendants as well as individuals of Latin American stock other than Mexican, such as Cubans, Puerto Ricans, and people from Central or South America.

The second group is mainly composed of (a) persons who simply changed their name, say from Moreno to Brown or from Rey to King (which involves a relatively simple procedure in this country), and (b) Mexican-American females who married Anglos and the progeny of such unions. It seems that legal name changes have been relatively infrequent among Mexican Americans, but no substantial data are available on this point. However, the statistical disappearance of Mexican-American females from the Spanish-surname group through intermarriage has been quite significant, and it may become increasingly significant in the future. On the other hand, intermarriages of Spanish-surname males with Anglo females produce statistical increments to the Spanish-surname group. Census counts based on the surname identification of the household head include the wife and children.

As ethnic identification reaches back in time, one enters the never-never land of highly mixed origins which characterize so large a segment of our total population. The intermarriage in 1925 of a Spanish-surname male and an Anglo female may have produced a son who married an Anglo girl of Italian stock, a daughter who married a Mexican American, another daughter who entered matrimony with a Jew, and so forth.

Some analysts have concluded that the census statistics understate the number of Spanish-surname persons in the Southwest, and they have more or less arbitrarily added 10 percent.[4] The assumption of an undercount is reinforced by the fact that the census has failed to enumerate Negroes as completely as whites. It is possible that some of the difficulties that account for this failure apply to Spanish-name persons as well. Besides, fear of governmental authority or dubious legality of residence status among Mexican Americans may have resulted in a disproportionate amount of statistical "slippage." Nevertheless, we abstain from making corrections for which there is no sufficient factual basis.[5] As was already indicated, any adjustment of the census data to allow for persons of non-Spanish surname must also exclude Spanish-surname people who are not of Mexican origin—if the objective is to arrive at an estimate of Mexican Americans. Moreover, the analysis here

---

[4] See, for example, Herschel T. Manuel, *Spanish-Speaking Children of the Southwest* (Austin, Tex.: University of Texas Press, 1965), pp. 21 and 22. One of the reasons given for the "correction" is the fact that Mexican Americans may not have Spanish surnames although they identify themselves historically and culturally with the Mexican-American population. This argument, however, ignores the Spanish-surname persons who are not of Mexican origin and do not identify themselves with Mexican Americans.

[5] Post-enumeration studies by the U.S. Bureau of the Census after the 1950 and 1960 censuses have revealed substantial underenumeration of the total population. Depending on the methods used, the estimates of "missed" persons range up to 4.7 percent of the total population in 1960. Of particular interest here is a greater-than-average underenumeration of people in slum areas and of nonwhites. By inference, one would expect underenumeration to be greater than average for Spanish-surname persons as well. However, the post-enumeration studies were not specifically addressed to this segment of the population. Since the census data in this volume are mainly used for comparing the socioeconomic characteristics of the Spanish-surname population with Anglos and nonwhites in the Southwest, the post-enumeration studies provide no sufficient basis for statistical corrections. For a technical discussion of census underenumeration, see the following papers delivered at the annual meeting of the American Statistical Association in 1966 (American Statistical Association, *Proceedings of the Social Statistics Section*): Eli S. Marks and Joseph Waksberg, "Evaluation of Coverage in the 1960 Census of Population through Case-by-Case Checking," and Jacob S. Siegel and Melvin Zelnik, "An Evaluation of the Coverage in the 1960 Census of Population by Techniques of Demographic Analysis and by Composite Methods."

focuses on socioeconomic characteristics of this segment of our population in comparison to other population groups; and it would be impossible to assign any additional or reduced numbers to subgroups of Mexican Americans differentiated by age, sex, educational attainment, occupation, income, urban or rural residence, and so forth. For these purposes, one has no choice but to use the census data on Spanish-surname persons as they come.

However, the numerical differences between Spanish-surname people and Mexican Americans do complicate the analysis of socioeconomic characteristics. For example, if the Spanish-surname females who married Anglos and were therefore lost in the census count were typically more educated than other Spanish-surname females, had a higher labor-force participation rate, and were engaged in more skilled occupations, the socioeconomic position of Mexican-American females as shown in census data would be lower than otherwise. Or, if the socioeconomic status of Spanish-surname persons of other than Mexican origin was typically better than that of Mexican Americans, the census figures would paint a brighter picture than was warranted for Mexican Americans alone.

Another complicating factor is the inclusion of farm workers from Mexico in the census figures on Spanish-surname persons, despite the fact that they are not permanent residents. This procedure, rarely recognized in the literature, affects not only the numbers and the age and sex distributions but should tend to lower the socioeconomic status of the group as a whole.[6] It produces no serious distortions when large aggregates of people are involved, but it can create more substantial defects in data for certain age or sex groups or for small areas where temporary agricultural workers may represent a significant portion of the Spanish-surname population.[7]

It is generally recognized that the accuracy of census data can be affected by response errors. Whether response error is more frequent for Spanish-surname persons than for others is a moot question, but people with an insufficient command of English and a low level of schooling may misunderstand census questions.

Finally, the 1960 census data on Spanish-surname persons are based on a 25 percent sample, whereas the general population count was designed to be complete. Most of the socioeconomic characteristics of both the general and the Spanish-name population are derived from a 25 percent sample. Although a sample of this size is adequate for most purposes, the errors resulting from sampling variability are greater the smaller the number of persons in a particular group or area. Altogether, the limitations of census data and procedures suggest caution in the interpretation of the results.

[6] According to the *Enumerators' Reference Manual* of the Bureau of the Census, the enumerators are instructed to include, among others, citizens of foreign countries living in the enumeration district who are employed in the United States even if they do not expect to remain here, as well as members of their families living with them in this country. Instructions pertaining to "persons with no usual residence" specify that persons in camps for migratory agricultural workers are to be enumerated. Our interpretation of these instructions was verified by the U.S. Bureau of the Census as follows: "You are correct in your assumption that *braceros* living in the United States when the 1960 Census was taken were to be enumerated and were counted as Spanish-surname persons when their surname so indicated. They were also included in the twenty-five percent sample." (From a letter to Leo Grebler, Director of the Mexican-American Study Project, dated June 22, 1966, by Howard G. Brunsman, U.S. Bureau of the Census.) The 25 percent sample covers most of the socioeconomic characteristics of the population.

[7] In April 1960, when the census was taken, nearly 70,000 Mexican contract workers were employed on farms, according to figures supplied by the U.S. Department of Labor (House Committee on the Judiciary, *Study of Population and Immigration Problems*, Special Series No. 11, 1963, table 7, p. 45). Of the 70,000 a little over 33,000 were in California, nearly 24,000 were in Texas, 10,000 were in Arizona, and 3,100 were in New Mexico. These numbers are quite low relative to the total Mexican-American population in the Southwest or the various states. However, when smaller statistical aggregates are involved, such as males in certain age groups or occupations, or when limited areas such as rural segments in Arizona and New Mexico are analyzed, the inclusion of migratory farm workers may affect the figures more significantly.

AN ESTIMATE OF THE NUMBER
OF MEXICAN AMERICANS IN 1960 *

Although the adjustments of Spanish-surname counts for an estimate of the Mexican-American population are fairly clear conceptually, as shown in the preceding section, they are difficult to perform in practice.

Two sets of 1960 census data can be used for estimating the Mexican-American population in the United States. One of these pertains to "white persons of Spanish surname" who were enumerated in the five states designated here as the Southwest: Arizona, California, Colorado, New Mexico, and Texas. In addition to totals for this group, the census reports details from which may be derived the number of persons comprising the *foreign stock* of Spanish surname, i.e., persons born abroad or of foreign or mixed parentage, by country of origin, and, separately, the number of persons of *Mexican* stock in this group. Further, the census data make it possible to derive the number of persons who are of Mexican stock but have no Spanish surname or are classified as other than white. These elements have been used for estimating the number of Mexican Americans in the Southwest.

The other set of census data pertains to persons of Mexican stock in the balance of the United States. These data will be used for estimating the number of Mexican Americans outside the Southwest, including natives of native parentage as well as persons of foreign stock.

The census reports that there were 3,464,999 white persons of Spanish surname (WPSS) in the Southwest in 1960. This figure excludes Mexican Americans with non-Spanish surnames and/or classified as nonwhite, and it includes Puerto Ricans, Cubans, and other Spanish-surname people who are not of Mexican descent. The estimation task for the Southwest is to include the former and exclude the latter. In addition, the ratio of foreign-stock population to natives of natives in the Southwest can be applied to an estimate of Mexican Americans in the balance of the United States.

The estimating procedure for the *Southwest* is as follows:

A	Mexican stock without regard to surname or color (census)	1,511,058
B	Mexican stock, WPSS (census)	1,386,298
C	Mexican stock other than WPSS (A−B)	124,760
D	Foreign stock, WPSS (census)	1,565,597
E	Percent of WPSS foreign stock that came from Mexico (B/D)	88.548%
F	Natives of natives, WPSS (census)	1,899,402
G	WPSS natives of natives from Mexico (ratio E applied to F)	1,681,882
H	Percent of Mexican stock that are WPSS (B as percent of A)	91.744%
I	Mexican natives of natives without Spanish surname or nonwhite (G/H−G)	151,352
J	Estimated number of Mexican Americans (B+C+G+I)	3,344,292

The resulting number is only 120,707 less than the 3,464,999 white persons of Spanish surname reported by the census. The difference of less than 3.5 percent from the census figure is the result of largely offsetting items. We have added persons of Mexican descent but without Spanish surname (C and I), and deducted from the WPSS those who are not of Mexican descent (F−G for natives of natives, and D−B for foreign stock).

*This section and the concluding section were prepared by Frank G. Mittelbach and Grace Marshall.

The resulting estimate is useful for a variety of purposes. First, if the underlying assumption is reasonable, the result indicates that the number of WPSS can be used in further census analysis as a proxy for Mexican Americans in the Southwest and its major subdivisions without significant distortion. Second, the ratios shown by the census for the population of foreign stock are of considerable substantive interest. Only a little over 11 percent of the persons of foreign stock among the WPSS group were of non-Mexican descent, and only 8.26 percent of the persons of Mexican stock did not have a Spanish surname (or were nonwhite). These percentages indicate general margins of error involved in using any original sets of data classified by Spanish and other surnames. Finally, the results show details on the composition of the Mexican-American population.

To estimate the number of Mexican Americans *outside the Southwest*, we assume that the relationship between the number of natives of natives and the number of persons of Mexican stock, which is reported by the census for the Southwest, holds for the United States. This is a necessary but probably more questionable assumption than any of those made for the Southwest estimate. Nothing is known about the differential characteristics of Mexican Americans who have migrated to areas outside the Southwest (except for foreign stock), and differential birthrates alone could produce substantial variation in the numerical relationship between foreign stock and natives of natives. However, this is the only relationship available for the purpose. The estimating procedure is as follows:

A Mexican stock in Southwest, without regard to surname or color
(census) · 1,511,058

B Estimated number of Mexican Americans in the Southwest (J in
estimate for Southwest) · 3,344,292

C A as a percent of B · 45.183%

D Mexican stock in the balance of the United States, without regard
to surname or color (census) · · · · · · · · · · · · · · · · · · · 224,934

E Estimated natives of natives in the balance of the United States
(D/C−D) · 272,895

F Estimated number of Mexican Americans in the balance of the
United States (D+E) · 497,829

The results for the *United States* may be summarized as follows, in round numbers:

	Natives of Natives	Mexican stock	Total Mexican Americans
Southwest	1,833,200[a]	1,511,100[b]	3,344,300
Balance of U.S.	272,900[c]	224,900[d]	497,800
Total	2,106,100	1,736,000	3,842,100

[a] G+I in estimate for the Southwest.
[b] A in estimate for the Southwest.
[c] E in estimate for the balance of the United States.
[d] D in estimate for the balance of the United States.

When the procedures used in the estimate for the Southwest are applied to each individual state, it turns out that the estimated difference between Spanish-surname persons and Mexican Americans in 1960 was very unevenly distributed. In California and Colorado, Spanish-name persons were in substantial excess over Mexican Americans, that is, there was a relatively large population in the WPSS group that was not of Mexican descent. Most of this population was concentrated in California. In the remaining three states, the estimated number of Mexican Americans exceeded the Spanish-surname persons, reflecting the fact that people of Mexican stock do not necessarily have a Spanish surname. Although the data in the following table are only as good as the estimating procedures, they are offered as material for further research.

**Table A–1.   Estimates of White Persons of Spanish Surname
and of Mexican Americans, Five Southwest States, 1960**

State and Region	White Persons of Spanish Surname	Mexican Americans	Excess of WPSS over MAs	Excess of MAs over WPSS
Arizona	194,356	207,791	—	13,435
California	1,426,538	1,289,008	137,530	—
Colorado	157,173	144,218	12,955	—
New Mexico	269,122	274,531	—	5,409
Texas	1,417,810	1,448,744	—	30,934
Southwest	3,464,999	3,364,292[a]	150,485	49,778

[a] The small discrepancy between this figure and the figure of 3,344,292 shown in the earlier estimate for the Southwest is the result of estimating procedures.

AN ESTIMATE OF THE NUMBER
OF MEXICAN AMERICANS IN 1970

Data available for Mexican Americans permit only the crudest sort of projections. Nothing is known of their age-specific birth or death rates. No numbers are compiled on their interstate migrations. Neither the Federal government nor the various state governments prepare estimates of their number or projections of their future numbers.

The Southwest

One of the two methods used in this estimate for 1970 is a straight-line projection. It assumes that the rate of increase of Spanish-surname persons in the Southwest between 1950 and 1960 continued in the decade of the 1960s. The increase from 2,289,550 in 1950 to 3,465,000 in 1960 was 51.34 percent. Applied to the 1960–1970 period, this rate produces an increment of about 1,779,000 persons and a total Spanish-surname population of 5,244,000 in the Southwest in 1970.

The other method takes account of the fact that the 1950–1960 rate of increase of the United States population as a whole fell sharply in the 1960–68 period. The decline occurred in both the white and nonwhite segments of the population. The estimates and projections of the U.S. Bureau of the Census in its *Current Population Series, Population Estimates*, P–25 have been revised downward from its previous expectations several times during the 1960s. The revisions were due to the drastic decline in the birth rate. Immigration and death rates have remained almost unchanged. For interstate migration, the movement is still predominantly westward, but at reduced rates. Decreases occurred in the rate of migration to Arizona and California as well as to other states in the West.

None of these observations applies specifically to persons of Spanish surname. Intercensal data for this group are not available. However, to take account of the generally declining rate of increase of the population, the second method of estimation is based upon the proportion of persons of Spanish surname in the total population of the Southwest. It starts with the revised census projections of the total resident population. The arithmetic average of the four census series for 1970 (as given in Series P–25, No. 388) is 37,216,500 persons in the Southwest, as follows:

Arizona	1,811,500
California	20,830,000
Colorado	2,110,000
New Mexico	1,085,000
Texas	11,380,000
Southwest	37,216,500

607

To estimate the percentage of Spanish-surname persons in the total population in 1970, we use a projection of the 1950 and 1960 relationships:

Spanish surname, 1950	10.87%
Spanish surname, 1960	11.82
Spanish surname, 1970 (est.)	12.69

On this basis, the Spanish-surname population in the Southwest would be 4,722,800 in 1970—a figure substantially below the estimate derived from straight-line projection. The lower figure assumes that the Spanish-surname population also is growing at a declining rate.

The two methods of projection, then, give a range of 4,723,000 to 5,244,000 Mexican Americans in the Southwest in 1970.

The United States

The starting point for the following projection is the number of Mexican Americans in the United States in 1960, as presented previously. When the 3,842,000 Mexican Americans estimated for 1960 are multiplied by the rate of increase for Spanish-surname persons in the Southwest between 1950 and 1960, 51.34 percent, the resulting increment is 1,972,483, or a total in 1970 of about 5,814,500. This method merely projects ten years into the future the trend defined by the growth of the Spanish-surname population from 1950 to 1960. The procedure assumes that the rate of increase of the Mexican-American population outside the Southwest was the same as in the Southwest. It is subject to the same reservation that applied to the straight-line estimate for the Southwest. As we noted earlier, the United States population growth rate has generally been slowing down; hence one would expect any straight-line projection to err on the high side.

A second method of projection is somewhat similar to the second estimating method applied to the Southwest, but it necessitates even more assumptions. Foreign-stock Mexican Americans declined from 51.2 percent of all Mexican Americans in 1950 to 45.2 percent in 1960. We estimate that this proportion will be about 40 percent in 1970. By using the census projections of the total United States population for 1970, this method reflects the decline in the rate of growth of the general population. The computation is as follows:

	White Stock from Mexico	White Population of United States	Stock from Mexico as a Percent of Total White Population
1950	1,342,542	135,149,629	.9934
1960	1,724,838	158,831,732	1.0860
1970	2,134,757 (est.)	181,030,432 (est.)	1.1792 (est.)

Applying the projected 40.0 percent ratio of Mexican stock to the total Mexican-American population, the method yields a projected Mexican-American population in the United States of 5,336,900 (dividing 2,134,757 by .400) by 1970.

The two methods of projection, then, produce a range of 5,340,000 to 5,800,000 Mexican Americans in the United States in 1970. This range is broadly consistent with a census sample survey of November 1969. The census estimate, based on respondents' self-indentification, arrived at 5,073,000 people of Mexican descent. Another 1,582,000 indentified themselves as "other Spanish Americans" (not of Mexican, Puerto Rican, Cuban, or Central and South American descent). Some of these persons were unquestionably Mexican Americans by our definition. See U.S. Bureau of the Census, *Current Population Reports*, Series P–20, No. 195, Feb. 20, 1970.

SAMPLE DESIGN FOR

THE LOS ANGELES SCHOOL STUDY*

The study was conducted in 1966. The sample included equal proportions of Mexican-American and Anglo pupils enrolled in the schools of the Los Angeles City School District. The selection of schools took into account the socioeconomic status and the ethnic composition of their student populations as well as their geographic location. Much of this information was supplied by materials based on the 1960 census, which show the ethnic density and the socioeconomic status of the census tracts serviced by each of the District's 560 school units.[1] District personnel supplied additional information about recent changes in the composition of the student body.

Twenty-three schools were chosen as sampling units. Non-probability selection techniques were preferred over random techniques for several important reasons:

1. Random sampling throughout the District would have included schools in which few Mexican-American pupils were enrolled, thereby loading the sample with a disproportionate number of Anglo pupils.

2. The District requested that as few school units as possible be sampled and that the total number of pupils surveyed be restricted to 4,500. To gain access to pupils in schools with the desired socioeconomic status and ethnic densities, school units had to be selected with care.

3. Analytic advantages can be derived from choosing elementary, junior, and senior high schools from the same geographic areas of the District.

The social rank and the ethnic density of the schools selected are presented in Tables B–1 and B–2.

The method of selecting pupils from the sixth, ninth, and twelfth grade classes within the school units was strongly influenced by District policy. The following conditions were stipulated: (a) questionnaires are to be administered to entire classrooms of pupils rather

---

*This appendix and the tables presented in Appendixes C and D are derived from C. Wayne Gordon, Audrey J. Schwartz, Robert Wenkert and David Nasatir, *Educational Achievement and Aspirations of Mexican-American Youth in a Metropolitan Context*, Occasional Report No. 36 (Center for the Study of Evaluation, Graduate School of Education, University of California, Los Angeles), October, 1968.

[1] See Eshref Shevky and Wendell Bell, *Social Area Analysis* (Stanford, California: Stanford University Press, 1955), for the social rank index employed as a measure of school socioeconomic status; see Vincent I. Correll, Jr., "Effect of School District Size Upon Public Interest in Schools," unpublished Ed. D. Dissertation, University of California, Los Angeles, 1963, for the social rank index of each census tract.

than to randomly selected individuals, (b) data collection in any one school is to be completed in a single day, and no provisions are to be made for a later survey of pupils who were absent on that day, and (c) signed parental consent forms are to be received from pupils prior to the administration of questionnaires and the collection of data from cumulative record files.

The classes in which questionnaires were administered had been randomly selected from mandatory State or District courses. This gave each pupil at the desired grade level an equal chance to be represented in the sample. In anticipation of sample loss through pupil absence or lack of parental consent, additional classes were added to the sample. Data collection was most successful in the sixth grade, where the return rate was 82 percent. The rates were 71 percent at the ninth grade level and 59 percent at the twelfth grade level. There was also considerable variation in the rates of different schools, especially among the high schools.

Table B–I. Los Angeles School Study Sample, by Grade Level, Ethnicity, and Socioeconomic Status[a] (Elementary schools and junior and senior high schools)

	ELEMENTARY (10 SCHOOLS)		JUNIOR (8 SCHOOLS)		SENIOR (5 SCHOOLS)	
	Mexican-American	Anglo	Mexican-American	Anglo	Mexican-American	Anglo
Upper white collar	0.3%	8.3%	2.3%	14.4%	2.1%	16.8%
Intermediate white collar	2.1	10.4	3.6	13.0	4.1	13.6
Lower white collar	8.0	18.7	7.7	14.0	10.1	9.6
Upper blue collar	19.9	27.1	21.7	31.4	23.4	34.3
Lower blue collar	62.2	31.2	50.3	23.9	50.1	21.8
Unknown	7.3	4.2	14.6	3.6	10.4	4.3
Total number (= 100%)	(286)	(96)	(899)	(558)	(667)	(473)

[a] The occupational classifications are composed of the following:
Upper White Collar—professional and managerial occupations, owners of large businesses
Intermediate White Collar—skilled non-manual occupations, owners of small or medium-sized businesses
Lower White Collar—semiskilled non-manual occupations
Upper Blue Collar—skilled manual occupations, foremen, self-employed craftsmen
Lower Blue Collar—unskilled and semiskilled manual occupations

From field observations it seems clear that differences in return rates stem primarily from differences in the amount of effort expended by principals and teachers in asking pupils to have their parents sign the consent forms. Among the high schools and, to a lesser extent, among the elementary schools, there is a relation between the size of the school and the return rates—the bigger the school, the lower the rate. Also, individual teachers differed in the extent to which they stressed the return of parental consent forms.

Inasmuch as the schools studied were not selected by random or probability techniques, as was also true of some aspects of the pupil selection process, the results of this inquiry cannot be extended to the entire Mexican-American and Anglo pupil populations of the Los Angeles Metropolitan School District. On the other hand, the Mexican-American and Anglo samples appear to be similarly affected by any biases which the pupil selection process might have engendered. The data can be used without reservation for comparing the different subpopulations of pupils, and this is the main purpose of the analysis.

Two sets of indices were developed to classify the schools. One, the socioeconomic measure, was created from the Shevky-Bell Social Rank Index and from the mean socioeconomic level of the sample obtained from each school. Pupil socioeconomic level was

610

Table B–2. Characteristics of Los Angeles School Study Sample

School Type and School	Shevky-Bell School Social Rank	Mean SES Level of School Sample	Socioeconomic Rank Order of Sample	Percent Anglo School Census	Percent Anglo Rank Order of Sample	Percent Spanish Surname Rank Order of Sample
ELEMENTARY SCHOOLS						
Low Ethnic, High SES						
A	19.7	2.07	1	60	1	8.5
B	14.1	2.17	2	27	3	8.5
C	17.0	2.04	4	12[a]	8	7
D	18.5	1.86	3	46	2	10
Medium Ethnic, Medium SES						
E	5.8	1.58	5	25	6	5
F	9.0	1.65	6	4	7	3
G	8.3	1.52	7	13	5	4
H	4.9	1.59	8	13	4	6
High Ethnic, Low SES						
I	1.0	1.24	9	1	9.5	1.5
J	1.0	1.24	10	1	9.5	1.5
JUNIOR HIGH SCHOOLS						
Low Ethnic, High SES						
A	18.1	2.47	2	63	1	7.5
B	10.4	2.48	1	56	2	6
C	10.4	2.27	3	53	3	5
Medium Ethnic, Medium SES						
D	8.9	2.23	4	35	5	7.5
E	8.4	2.15	5	32	4	4
High Ethnic, Low SES						
F	5.5	1.84	6	4	6	3
G	5.0	1.66	8	4	7	2
H	2.8	1.73	7	1	8	1
SENIOR HIGH SCHOOLS						
Low Ethnic, High SES						
A	13.5	3.23	1	65	1	5
Medium Ethnic, Medium SES						
B	11.4	2.05	3	47	2	4
C	11.3	2.03	4	34	3	3
High Ethnic, Low SES						
D	8.7	2.06	2	3	4	2
E	5.4	1.67	5	5	5	1

[a] The official school census reports 51 percent Oriental pupils for this school

611

derived from the occupational prestige rank of the main support of the family. These ranks range from lower blue collar to upper white collar (Table B–1).

The other index, the ethnic density measure, was computed from official school data pertaining to the ethnic composition of each school and the ethnic distribution of the sample obtained from each school. Schools with 50 percent or more Anglo pupils were coded "low ethnic," those with 30 to 49 percent Anglos "medium ethnic," and those with less than 30 percent Anglos "high ethnic" (Table B–2).

The relationship between the school socioeconomic status measures and the ethnic density measures should be noted. For most schools there is a perfect inverse relationship between the two so that the low ethnic density schools are also schools of high socioeconomic status, the medium ethnic density schools have medium socioeconomic status, and the high ethnic density schools have low socioeconomic status.

It also should be noted that schools classified as high socioeconomic status are high only in comparison with other schools in the sample. For example, the school with the highest status has a mean SES score of 3.23, which indicates that the parents of its student body tend toward lower white collar occupations. Had this school been compared with schools typically attended by children from professional and upper white collar homes, it would have been classified differently. The school SES type, then, describes its position only among the schools sampled, and not its position in a larger universe of schools.

SUPPLEMENTAL TABLES
ON THE LOS ANGELES
SCHOOL STUDY

*Table C–I.   Recorded Marks in History (Elementary School)
and Social Studies (Secondary School),
by Grade Level and Ethnicity, Los Angeles School Study*

	Mexican-American	Anglo
Elementary school		
Percent A and B	21.3%	44.4%
Percent C	62.1	39.7
Percent D and F	16.6	15.8
Total number (= 100%)	(272)	(83)
Junior and senior high school combined[a]		
Percent A and B	28%	48%
Percent C	40	32
Percent D and F	32	20
Total number (= 100%)	(1,154)	(738)

[a] These data are based on slightly less than three-quarters of the total sample. For the remainder, parental permission allowing access to cumulative records was not granted.

*Table C–2.   Recorded Marks in Arithmetic (Elementary School)
and Mathematics (Secondary School),
by Grade Level and Ethnicity, Los Angeles School Study*

	Mexican-American	Anglo
Elementary school[a]		
Percent A and B	27.4%	36.4%
Percent C	45.3	37.4
Percent D and F	27.3	26.2
Total number (= 100%)	(274)	(88)
Junior high school[a]		
Percent A and B	21%	34%
Percent C	48	37
Percent D and F	31	28
Total number (= 100%)	(595)	(340)
Senior high school[a]		
Percent A and B	26%	44%
Percent C	33	32
Percent D and F	41	24
Total number (= 100%)	(383)	(163)

[a] See Note [a], Table C–1.

Table C–3. Recorded Deportment Marks by Grade Level and Ethnicity, Los Angeles School Study

| | FOR WORK HABITS | | FOR CITIZENSHIP | |
	Mexican-American	Anglo	Mexican-American	Anglo
Elementary school				
Percent A and B	36.8%	50.6%	49.6%	57.4%
Percent C	43.5	32.2	38.2	29.9
Percent D and F	19.7	17.2	12.2	12.7
Total number (= 100%)	(280)	(87)	(280)	(87)
Junior and senior high schools combined[a]				
Percent Excellent	35%	42%	49%	61%
Percent Satisfactory	46	42	43	33
Percent Unsatisfactory	19	16	8	6
Total number (= 100%)	(1,161)	(752)	(1,161)	(751)

[a] See Note [a], Table C–1.

Table C–4. English and Mathematics Achievement Test Results, by Grade Level and Ethnicity, Los Angeles School Study (In stanines[a])

| | MEXICAN-AMERICAN | | ANGLO | |
	English	Math	English	Math
Elementary school				
Markedly above and above average	7%	15%	23%	34%
Average	41	49	52	51
Below and markedly below average	53	36	25	15
Total number (= 100%)	(261)	(261)	(82)	(82)
Junior high school				
Markedly above and above average	8%	7%	25%	24%
Average	39	36	52	53
Below and markedly below average	53	57	23	23
Total number (= 100%)	(571)	(571)	(323)	(323)
Senior high school				
Markedly above and above average[b]	10%	8%	39%	38%
Average[c]	54	55	50	49
Below and markedly below average[d]	36	37	11	13
Total number (= 100%)	(534)	(534)	(392)	(392)

[a] These categories are constructed on the basis of the normal curve, and are usually referred to as "stanines." An "average" performance (stanines 4, 5, and 6) should account for 54 percent of a normal population; "above average" and "below average" performances (stanines 7 and 8, and 2 and 3) should account for 38 percent of a normal population; and "markedly above average" and "markedly below average" performances (stanines 9 and 1) should account for the remaining 8 percent of a normal population. Tests are constructed on the basis of national samples. The distribution is based on the standard deviations of the normal curve. For secondary schools, see Note [a], Table C–1.
[b] Expected national norm: 23 percent.
[c] Expected national norm: 54 percent.
[d] Expected national norm: 23 percent.

Table C–5. Intelligence Test Results, by Grade Level and Ethnicity, Los Angeles School Study (In stanines[a])

	Mexican-American	Anglo
Elementary school[b]		
Markedly above and above average	8.4%	33.0%
Average	50.6	47.5
Below and markedly below average	41.0	19.5
Total number (= 100%)	(261)	(82)
Junior high school[b]		
Markedly above and above average	3%	22%
Average	50	64
Below and markedly below average	47	14
Total number (= 100%)	(571)[c]	(323)[c]
Senior high school[b]		
Markedly above and above average	2%	25%
Average	58	65
Below and markedly below average	40	10
Total number (= 100%)	(536)[c]	(392)[c]

[a] See Note [a], Table C–4.
[b] Among senior high school students, the Henmon-Nelson Test was used; among junior high and elementary school students, the California Test of Mental Maturity was used.
[c] See Note [a], Table C–1.

Table C–6. Educational Aspirations, by Grade Level and Ethnicity, Los Angeles School Study

	Mexican-American	Anglo
Elementary school students		
Quit school	2.5%	5.3%
Finish high school	33.2	22.9
Go to school after high school	56.5	69.7
Don't know	7.8	2.1
Total number (= 100%)	(283)	(96)
Junior and senior high school students combined		
Go to graduate school after college	4%	12%
Go to a four-year college	27	38
Go to a junior college	20	18
Go to a trade school	12	8
Graduate from high school	31	18
Quit school as soon as possible	1	1
Don't know	5	5
Total number (= 100%)	(1,551)	(1,027)

Table C–7. Educational Expectations by Ethnicity, Los Angles School Study
(Junior high and senior high students combined)

	Mexican-American	Anglo
Go to a graduate school after college	2%	7%
Go to a four-year college	17	31
Go to a junior college	28	32
Go to a trade school	13	7
Graduate from high school	35	20
Quit school as soon as possible	1	0
Don't know	4	3
Total number (= 100%)	(1,550)	(1,025)

Table C–8. Occupational Aspirations by Ethnicity, Los Angeles School Study
(Junior high and senior high students combined)

	Mexican-American	Anglo
Upper white collar	28%	44%
Intermediate white collar	33	34
Lower white collar	18	9
Upper blue collar	10	8
Lower blue collar	4	1
Don't know	7	4
Total number (= 100%)	(1,363)	(977)

MULTIPLE REGRESSION ANALYSIS OF FACTORS RELATED TO ACHIEVEMENT (LOS ANGELES SCHOOL STUDY)

Table D–I. *Unique Contribution of Pupil and School Characteristics to the Variance in Pupils' Reading Comprehension, Secondary Schools, Los Angeles School Study*

Pupil and School Characteristics	JUNIOR		SENIOR	
	Mexican-American	Anglo	Mexican-American	Anglo
A. Family Socioeconomic Level				
Mother Lives in Home	—	—	.0022	—
Father Lives in Home	—	—	.0080	—
Length of Family Residency in Los Angeles	.0050	—	.0050	—
Number of Siblings	.0022	—	.0061	.0053
Number of Different Schools Attended	—	—	.0067	—
Family SES Index	—	.0052	—	.0314
Total	.0072	.0052	.0280	.0367
B. Family Educational Level				
Parents' Grade Expectations of Pupil	.0020	—	—	.0787
Parents' Educational Aspirations for Pupil	.0565	.0159	.0247	.0087
Amount of Adult Homework Help	.0055	.0190	.0072	.0047
Dictionary in the Home	—	—	—	.0029
Amount of Education of Mother	—	.0205	.0077	.0041
Proportion of Relatives/Parents, Friends Gone to College	—	—	—	.0068
English Newspaper in the Home	—	—	—	.0032
Encyclopedia in the Home	—	—	.0128	—
Total	.0640	.0554	.0524	.1091

Table D-1 Continued

Pupil and School Characteristics	JUNIOR		SENIOR	
	Mexican-American	Anglo	Mexican-American	Anglo
C. Affectivity Orientations				
Faith in Human Nature Scale	.0304	.0058	.0098	—
Occupational Values—Social	.0115	—	.0021	.0029
Occupational Values—Reward	—	.0098	—	—
Independence from Peers	—	—	.0015	—
Index of Self-Esteem	.0032	—	—	.0044
Idealized School Goals	.0053	—	.0027	.0035
Futuristic Orientation	.0071	.0763	.0210	.0430
Expressive Orientation	—	—	.0033	—
Orientation to Family Authority	—	—	.0147	.0107
Total	.0575	.0919	.0551	.0645
D. School Social Context				
School Ethnic Composition	—	—	.0168	—
School Socioeconomic Composition	.0503	—	—	—
Total	.0503	0	.0168	0
E. Teacher Attitudes				
Teachers' Grade Expectations of Pupil	.0344	.0436	.0606	.0125
Total	.0344	.0436	.0606	.0125
F. Language Usage				
Language Most Spoken in Home	.0034	—	—	.0028
Proportion of Friends Who Speak Spanish	.0053	—	.0100	—
Total	.0087	0	.0100	.0028
G. Pupil Characteristics				
Sex	—	—	—	.0038
Total	0	0	0	.0038
H. Influence of Peers	0	0	0	0
(r^2) Total Proportion of Variance Explained	.2221	.1961	.2229	.2294
Sample Size	(889)	(558)	(667)	(473)
Multiple Correlation Coefficient	0.4713	0.4428	0.4721	0.4790
Standard Error of Estimate	1.3028	1.2919	1.4587	1.4449

618

Table D–2. *Unique Contribution of Pupil and School Characteristics to the Variance in Pupils' I.Q., Secondary Schools, Los Angeles School Study*

Pupil and School Characteristics	JUNIOR		SENIOR	
	Mexican-American	Anglo	Mexican-American	Anglo
A. Family Economic Level				
Mother Lives at Home	.0058	.0118	.0027	.0061
Father Lives at Home	—	—	.0053	.0021
Length of Family Residency in Los Angeles	.0020	.0033	—	.0062
Number of Siblings	.0015	—	.0169	—
Number of Different Schools Attended	—	.0037	.0066	—
Longest Pupil Residency (Rural-Urban)	—	—	.0032	.0019
Family Socioeconomic Status	—	—	—	.0590
Total	.0093	.0188	.0347	.0753
B. Family Educational Level				
Parents' Grade Expectations of Pupil	—	—	.0037	.0137
Parents' Educational Aspirations for Pupil	.0380	.0517	.0418	.0341
Amount of Adult Homework Help	.0111	.0223	.0100	.0073
Dictionary in the Home	.0032	.0069	—	—
Amount of Education of Mother	—	.0085	.0121	—
Relatives and Parents' Friends with College Education	—	—	—	.0091
Total	.0523	.0894	.0676	.0642
C. Affectivity Orientations				
Faith in Human Nature Scale	.0156	.0187	.0092	—
Occupational Values—Social	.0045	—	—	—
Occupational Values—Reward	.0020	.0059	—	.0064
Independence from Peers Scale	.0020	.0041	—	—
Index of Self-Esteem	.0070	—	—	.0055
Index of Idealized School Goals	.0015	—	—	—
Instrumental Orientation	.0023	—	.0043	—
Futuristic Orientation	—	.0346	.0175	.0149
Expressive Orientation	—	.0033	.0019	—
Orientation to Family Authority	—	—	.0157	.0198
Total	.0349	.0666	.0486	.0466
D. School Social Context				
School Ethnic Composition	—	—	.0252	.0031
School Socioeconomic Composition	.0516	—	—	—
Total	.0516	0	.0252	.0031
E. Teacher Attitudes				
Teachers' Grade Expectations of Pupil	.0107	.0176	.0842	.1898
Total	.0107	.0176	.0842	.1898

Table D-2 Continued

Pupil and School Characteristics	JUNIOR Mexican American	Anglo	SENIOR Mexican-American	Anglo
F. **Language Usage**				
Language Most Spoken at Home	.0093	—	.0210	.0054
Proportion of Friends who Speak Spanish	.0255	—	—	.0039
Total	.0348	0	.0210	.0093
G. **Pupil Characteristics**				
Age	.0056	.0062	.0079	.0040
Sex	.0029	—	—	.0025
Total	.0085	.0062	.0079	.0065
H. **Influence of Peers**				
Proportion of Friends with High Educational Aspirations	—	—	—	.0084
	0	0	0	.0084
(r^2) Total Proportion of Variance Explained	.2021	.1986	.2892	.4032
Sample Size	(899)	(558)	(667)	(473)
Multiple Correlation Coefficient	0.4496	0.4457	0.5378	0.6350
Standard Error of Estimate	1.1468	1.1062	1.0315	1.2169

Table D–3. Unique Contribution of Pupil and School Characteristics to the Variance in Pupil Achievement Measures—I.Q. and Reading Comprehension, Elementary Schools, Los Angeles School Study

Pupil and School Characteristics	I.Q. Mexican-American	Anglo	READING COMPREHENSION Mexican-American	Anglo
A. **Family Socioeconomic Level**				
Mother Lives at Home	.0432	—	—	—
Number of Different Schools Attended	.0094	—	—	—
Length of Family Residency in L.A.	—	.0148	.0059	—
Total	.0526	.0148	.0059	0
B. **Family Educational Level**				
Amount of Education of Father	.0116	—	.0170	.0405
Amount of Education of Mother	.0079	—	—	—
Dictionary in the Home	.0105	—	—	.0125
Parents' Grade Expectations of Pupil	—	.0804	—	.0518
Encyclopedia in the Home	—	.0132	—	.0520
Parents Educational Aspirations for Pupil	—	—	—	.0482
Total	.0300	.0936	.0170	.2050

Table D-3 Continued

Pupil and School Characteristics	I.Q. Mexican-American	Anglo	READING COMPREHENSION Mexican-American	Anglo
C. Affectivity Orientations				
Good Fight Best Way to Settle Arguments	.0343	—	.0124	—
Usually Enjoy Classes at School	.0084	.0279	—	—
Pupil's Educational Aspirations	.0086	.0274	.0204	.0752
Main Enjoyment of School Is Friends	.0141	.0500	.0097	.0299
Parents Should Not Disallow Seeing Friends, Even If They Disapprove	.0097	—	—	—
Doing Schoolwork Makes Future Easier	.0177	—	.0570	—
School Will Not Help Future	.0062	.0154	—	—
Generally Like School	.0054	—	.0057	.0224
Would Not Mind Being Thought "Oddball"	—	.0171	—	—
School Will Not Help Get Better Job	—	.0993	—	.0486
Rather Be Someone Different Than Self	—	.0376	—	—
Times When I Think I'm No Good at All	—	.0113	—	.0128
How Important to Get Good Grades	—	.0192	—	.0135
People Should Not Expect Too Much of Life So They Will Not Be Disappointed	—	.0161	—	.0312
Most People Help Others Before Selves	—	—	.0092	—
Never Act Only for Esteem from Others	—	—	.0074	—
Teacher Usually Right, Even When Punishing Entire Class	—	—	.0065	—
Children Should Obey All Parents' Rules	—	—	—	.0133
Total	.1044	.3213	.1283	.2469
D. School Social Context				
School Socioeconomic Composition	—	—	.0486	—
Total	0	0	.0486	0
E. Teacher Attitudes				
Total	0	0	0	0
F. Language Usage				
Proportion of Friends Who Speak Spanish	.0369	—	—	—
You Speak Spanish	—	.0120	—	—
Language Most Spoken in Home	—	—	.0161	—
Total	.0369	.0120	.0161	0

Table D-3 Continued

Pupil and School Characteristics	I.Q.		READING COMPREHENSION	
	Mexican-American	Anglo	Mexican-American	Anglo
G. Pupil Characteristics				
Total	0	0	0	0
H. Influence of Peers				
Total	0	0	0	0
(r²) Total Proportion of Variance Explained	.2239	.4417	.2159	.4519
Sample Size	(286)	(96)	(286)	(96)
Multiple Correlation Coefficient	0.4732	0.6646	0.4647	0.6722
Standard Error of Estimate	1.6311	1.5666	1.4786	1.4598

ESTIMATES OF THE CHARACTERISTICS

OF POOR AND OF NON-POOR

SPANISH-SURNAME FAMILIES

AND INDIVIDUALS IN THE

SOUTHWEST, 1960

Table E–1 provides estimates derived from special census tabulations and from a step-by-step procedure that allows the multiple characteristics of families or individuals to be ordered in a systematic fashion. The six characteristics are: employment of the family head in farm work, aged family head (65 years and over), broken family (indicated by female being the family head), underemployment (including unemployed), family headed by person under 25 years, and functional illiteracy of family head.

When the individual characteristics are considered, farm employment greatly increased a Mexican-American family's chance of being poor. After eliminating this factor, old age further raised the risk of being poor. When these two characteristics are accounted for, poverty was next most likely to occur among broken families. But there is little difference between the poor and non-poor among Mexican Americans when the step-by-step analysis proceeds to underemployment, youth of the family head, and highly deficient education. Separately, these characteristics do not account for substantially more poor than non-poor families. After eliminating families with heads who were farmers, senior citizens, or females, 25 percent of the poor and 24 percent of the non-poor families had the remaining three characteristics. But underemployment and functional illiteracy are probably highly correlated with farm residence and age and are therefore already accounted for in these categories.

For families, the six specified characteristics together account for 83 percent of the poor but only 39 percent of the non-poor. For persons *not* in families, the six specified characteristics together account for 93 percent of the poor and 71 percent of the non-poor individuals. Thus, the methodology adopted here is more efficient in distinguishing the characteristics of poor families from those of other families than it is in respect to individuals not in families.

This Appendix was prepared by Frank G. Mittelbach and Grace Marshall.

Table E-1. Estimates of Characteristics of Poor and Non-poor Spanish-surname Families and Individuals,[a] 1960 (Families and individuals counted only once)

	Families[b]	Members of families	Head's Children under 18	Persons not in families[c]
The poor				
Head farmer or farm laborer	23.2%	28.7%	29.6%	31.4%
Head 65 years and over	14.1	9.1	2.3	16.2
Female family head	20.3	17.8	18.6	22.9
Head employed less than 13 weeks[d]	4.6	5.1	6.5	3.8
Head under 25 years	6.6	4.8	3.6	15.2
Head 0–4 years education	13.7	15.0	17.3	3.8
Other	17.4	19.6	22.2	6.7
Total Number	241,000	1,092,000	527,000	105,000
Total percent	100.0	100.0	100.0	100.0
The non-poor				
Head farmer or farm laborer	5.4%	6.6%	6.9%	12.0%
Head 65 years and over	5.2	4.1	0.6	9.3
Female family head	4.6	4.1	3.7	18.7
Head employed less than 13 weeks[d]	4.3	4.9	5.4	8.0
Head under 25 years	6.9	5.2	4.8	10.7
Head 0–4 years education	12.6	14.7	14.9	12.0
Other	61.0	60.4	63.9	29.3
Total number	461,000	2,233,000	1,007,000	75,000
Total percent	100.0	100.0	100.0	100.0

[a] Individuals not living in families.
[b] Poor families are defined as having income of less than $3,000 in 1959. Number of families equals number of family heads.
[c] Individuals are classified as poor if their income in 1959 was under $1,500. Inmates of institutions are excluded.
[d] Includes unemployed.
Source: See Tables 8–11, 8–12, and 8–13.

The estimates are derived from information contained in the One-in-One Thousand Sample drawn from the 1960 censuses of population and housing.[1] The users of these data are obliged to include the following notation: "Certain data used in this publication were derived by the authors from a computer tape file furnished under a joint project sponsored by the U.S. Bureau of the Census and the Population Council and containing selected 1960 Census information for a 0.1 percent sample of the population of the United States. Neither the Census Bureau nor the Population Council assumes any responsibility for the validity of any of the figures or interpretations of the figures published herein based on this material."[2]

The procedure for preparing the estimates was as follows: First, the record was searched to determine if the head of the family had the occupation of farmer or farm worker. If so, the family was recorded in this group and other characteristics were disregarded. If not a farmer or farm worker, the records were searched further to establish if the head was 65 years old or over. Again, if the answer was positive the family was classified under "head 65 years and over" and other characteristics were disregarded. The search continued in this manner until all families had been classified under one of the six specified categories in the order indicated in Table E-1. If they did not fit any of these classifications the families were placed in the "other" group. This procedure was applied to both poor

[1] For a detailed discussion, see Bureau of the Census, *U.S. Censuses of Population and Housing*, "1/1,000, 1/10,000, Two National Samples of the Population of the United States, Description and Technical Documentation," and supplements thereto.

[2] *Ibid.*, Supplement 1, p. 10.

and non-poor families as well as persons not in families. While the ordering is subjective, it is not without rationale.[3]

The file of the One-in-One Thousand Sample includes information on Spanish-surname persons in the five Southwest states. In all, 3,498 white persons of Spanish surname entered the sample, and one can compare this to estimates based upon the 25 percent sample of 3,464,999 such persons in the five Southwest states. In other words, the sample approximates .001 of the control total.

We should note that not all persons in families whose heads have a Spanish surname will necessarily have a Spanish surname. Conversely, white persons of Spanish surname may be present in families without a Spanish-surname head. The One-in-One Thousand Sample includes non-Spanish-surname persons in families with a Spanish-surname head but excludes Spanish-surname persons in families without a Spanish-surname head.[4]

The estimates are based on a small sample and are therefore subject to some random error. Chi-square tests were prepared to determine if the families with heads having the indicated characteristics represent a significantly higher percentage among the poor than among all families. Similarly, these tests were applied to establish whether or not a significantly higher percentage of the families with the respective characteristics are poor compared to the proportion of poor families generally in the total sample of families with a Spanish-surname head.

In all but two cases, the poor with the specified characteristics varied significantly at the 0.05 level from the group with which they were compared. The poor families with a head less than 25 years of age did not vary significantly from the control groups. In other words, the percentage of poor families with heads under 25 was not significantly higher than the percentage of poor Spanish-surname families at large. Similarly, families with heads under 25 did not represent a significantly higher percentage of all the poor than their proportion in the population at large.

---

[3] See Herman P. Miller, *Rich Man, Poor Man* (New York: Thomas Y. Crowell Company, 1964), pp. 64–70.

[4] For details on this matter, see Frank G. Mittelbach and Grace Marshall, *The Burden of Poverty* (Mexican-American Study Project, Advance Report 5, Graduate School of Business Administration, University of California, Los Angeles, July 1966).

A NOTE ON

OCCUPATIONAL CLASSIFICATIONS

The U.S. Bureau of the Census shows the following major occupational categories:

1. Professional, technical, and kindred workers
2. Managers, officials, and proprietors, except farm
3. Clerical and kindred workers
4. Sales workers
5. Craftsmen, foremen, and kindred workers
6. Operatives and kindred workers
7. Private household workers
8. Service workers, except private household
9. Laborers, except farm and mine[1]
10. Farm laborers and farm foremen
11. Farmers and farm managers
12. Occupation not reported

The census shows also much greater detail under each of these headings, and our analysis in Chapter 10 uses some of this detail.

As for groupings of the above occupations, our *white-collar* classification includes the first four—professional, managers and proprietors, clerical and sales. It omits farm managers, who often perform a large variety of functions ranging from complex farm management to chores more akin to those of foremen or blue-collar farm workers. In any case, their omission does not affect our results in any substantial degree.

The proportion of white-collar workers is a useful indicator of occupational standing, especially in terms of social prestige. Also, the white-collar–blue-collar distinction comes so close to manual versus non-manual occupations that we can use these designations interchangeably. While average earnings are higher in white-collar than in blue-collar work, this is not true for all major occupational groups. Clerical and sales persons, for example, generally have lower incomes than craft workers, who are classified as blue collar. Nor does the traditional division between white collar and blue collar necessarily reflect differing skill levels, as is again exemplified by the contrast between craft and clerical workers. Moreover, if 20 percent of a population group are employed in white-collar work, this does not necessarily mean that exactly 80 percent hold blue-collar jobs. The main reason is the ambiguous occupational category "service exclusive of private household." This class is not included in the white-collar group. Yet, it comprises, for example, firemen

---

[1] All mine workers are included in some occupational category other than laborer.

and policemen as well as janitors, elevator operators, and waiters. Consequently, it does not fit easily into the division by the "color of the collar" or the manual versus non-manual classification.

The proportion of persons in those manual occupations which require low skill comes closer to a classification by skill level. This group includes the census categories 6 through 10 in the above list: operatives, service workers in private households and other service workers, laborers, and farm laborers. The degrees of skill, of course, vary among these categories. Generally, however, the categories denote unskilled or semi-skilled work. Again, the dichotomy is not complete. Many sales and clerical persons are also characterized by low skill in terms of the time and effort that it takes to train them. But these white-collar persons usually must possess a level of literacy in oral and written communication that is not required in the low-skill manual occupations. The dichotomy is also blurred by the inclusion in the low-skill manual occupations of such "service" workers as firemen and policemen, as well as janitors and cleaning personnel for office.

The *index of occupational position* avoids the degree of arbitrariness involved in the two preceding classifications. It therefore provides a more complete measure of the standing of various population groups. The advantage of the index lies in its simplicity—it furnishes a single number—and in the fact that it is based on the entire distribution of the major occupational categories of the census. Its shortcomings are those of all index numbers. The computation of the index is explained in the text and the note for Table 9–5.

THE INDEX OF RESIDENTIAL

DISSIMILARITY AND PROBLEMS

OF ITS USE IN THIS STUDY

The formula used for calculating the index of dissimilarity is as follows:

$$D_{jk} = \tfrac{1}{2} \sum_{i=1}^{n} \left| \left(\frac{N_{ij}}{T_j} - \frac{N_{ik}}{T_k} \right) \right|$$

where $D_{jk} =$ The index of dissimilarity between ethnic groups j and k in a city
$n =$ the total number of areas in a city
$i =$ the particular subareas of a city, which for purposes of this study are census tracts
$N_{ij} =$ number of people in area i of ethnic group j
$N_{ik} =$ number of people in area of ethnic group k
$T_j =$ total population in a city of ethnic group j
$T_k =$ total population in a city of ethnic group k

The indexes were computed on the basis of census-tract data for the 35 cities. Unfortunately, no data on areas smaller than tracts were available for the Spanish-surname population, which for our purposes was here defined as the universe of Mexican Americans. As a consequence, the data have several weaknesses, which are identified below and whose importance we have made some attempt to evaluate.

The first and most important weakness is the possibility that census-tract boundaries have been aligned so as to separate ethnic and/or racial groups. We found a rank-order correlation coefficient of .56 between D's for Negro versus "other" computed on a block[1] and on a tract basis for 15 of our 35 cities. This suggests that analysis of segregation by tracts may be confounded by administrative decisions the consequences of which cannot be assessed.

A second issue is that the typical size of census tracts varies between cities. As has been shown empirically,[2] the smaller the area units the higher the indexes of segregation are likely to be. Therefore, two cities would probably show differences in residential segre-

[1] As presented in Karl E. Taeuber and Alma F. Taeuber, *Negroes in Cities* (Chicago: Aldine Publishing Company, 1965), pp. 39–41. Fifteen of the cities analyzed by the Taeubers using block data are in the Southwest.

[2] *Ibid.*, p. 230.

Table G-I. Coefficients of Determination, Partial Correlations, T-values, Regression Coefficients, and Intercept Values for Variables to Explain Residential Segregation

Independent Variables	SPANISH-SURNAME vs. ANGLO			SPANISH-SURNAME vs. NEGRO			NEGRO vs. ANGLO		
	b	T-value	Partial Correlation	b	T-value	Partial Correlation	b	T-value	Partial Correlation
Cultural									
Percent SS[a] OHU[b] with 5 persons or more	0.95	3.7[c]	0.56	0.81	2.6[d]	0.42	—	—	—
Percent nonwhite OHU with 5 persons or more	—	—	—	—	—	—	0.57	2.0[e]	0.34
Economic									
Ratio of total median to Spanish-surname median income	17.61	1.7[e]	0.29	—	—	—	—	—	—
Percentage of nonwhite to Spanish-surname median income	—	—	—	−0.30	−1.6	−0.28	—	—	—
Ratio of total median to non-white median income	—	—	—	—	—	—	20.03	3.4[c]	0.53
Demographic									
Total city population	.00001	2.4[d]	0.40	.00002	3.4[c]	0.53	.00001	2.1[d]	0.35
Ratio of Spanish-surname to nonwhite persons	−0.08	−2.4[d]	−0.40	−0.07	−1.2	−0.21	−0.09	−2.5[d]	−0.42
Intercept	−9.2			45.3			32.19		
Multiple R²	.67			.36			.46		

a SS: Persons of Spanish surname
b OHU: Occupied housing units
c Significant at 0.01 level
d Significant at 0.03 level
e Significant at 0.10 level
Source: 1960 census tract data for 35 Southwest cities.

gation even if they were similar in every other respect, provided that they were divided into different numbers of census tracts. To determine the extent to which our indexes were influenced by this element, the average population size of census tracts in our 35 cities was correlated with the *D*'s. The correlations were insignificant, and this element also proved insignificant in later step-wise regression analysis.

A third problem arising from the use of tract data stems from the fact that many of the cities in the Southwest have a relatively small number of tracts. There existed the possibility of confounding the *D* by the number of tracts. This problem can be illuminated with a hypothetical illustration. Assume that all tracts in all cities have exactly 5,000 persons. A city of 5,000 persons would thus have only one tract; one with 10,000 would have two tracts, and so on. The indexes of segregation are likely to increase with city size up to a certain point, beyond which the addition of another area unit will have little or no impact on the final result. Our finding that greater segregation is associated with larger population size may be slightly influenced by this element as well as by real differences.

The analysis of 35 tracted cities is cross-sectional and limited to 1960. The sharp changes in many city and tract boundaries between 1950 and 1960 preclude the preparation of indexes that could be compared for both benchmark years—a procedure feasible only where block data are available. (Analysis prior to 1950 is even less feasible due to changing census definitions of Mexican Americans.) Further, a large number of these cities were not tracted until 1960.

There is another technical matter with respect to the preparation of the indexes of segregation: Indexes were calculated for both central cities and for Standard Metropolitan Statistical Areas. In some cases the differences between the two indexes were substantial. However, the SMSA indexes were not always higher, as one might expect if the minority population were uniformly concentrated in older central sections of the urban areas.[3] The reason is that in certain SMSA's of the Southwest (as, for example, in San Bernardino), the central cities are surrounded by extensive rural territory, where large numbers of Mexican Americans (and smaller numbers of Negroes) are concentrated in small enclaves and shacktowns close to agricultural employment opportunities. In other cases, such as Los Angeles, the SMSA reflects the limits of urbanized areas more accurately than the central city. Lacking strong indications to the contrary in our data, we confined our analysis to the central cities, thus avoiding the introduction of agricultural elements. The correlations between the metropolitan and city indexes were high enough to consider them as substitutes for one another.

The cities included in the study are all central cities in SMSA's in 1960. However, a number of central cities in the five Southwestern states were excluded for several reasons. No census tract data were available for a few areas and relevant indexes of dissimilarity could not be calculated. Also, central cities with less than 2,000 Spanish-surname persons or with less than 2.5 per cent of the population having Spanish-surname persons were not included. As a result, the central cities of Long Beach (California) and Amarillo, Beaumont, Texas City, Midland, Texarkana, and Tyler (all in Texas) did not enter into the analysis.

[3] The correlation coefficients between city and SMSA indexes were as follows: White Persons of Spanish Surname vs. Anglo = .92; WPSS vs. Negro = .85; Negro vs. Anglo = .78.

SAMPLE DESIGN AND SELECTION

PROCEDURES FOR

MEXICAN-AMERICAN HOUSEHOLD

INTERVIEW SURVEYS IN

LOS ANGELES AND SAN ANTONIO*

The purpose of the surveys was to reach the full range of Mexican Americans living in Los Angeles and San Antonio, the two cities which accounted for about one quarter of the total Mexican-American population in 1960. As usual, resources for the study were limited, and a sampling plan had to be devised that would enable the survey to fulfill its analytic function—comprehensive coverage of Mexican-American life—and that would take account of the vast disparities in living standards between the two cities. The sampling design maintained the characteristics of a probability sample, in that every Mexican-American household had an equal chance of selection. It added the analytic desiderata, in that it ensured the inclusion of Mexican-American households of middle- as well as lower-class status and of households in predominantly Anglo as well as predominantly Mexican-American areas of the city.

The surveys were undertaken in 1965 and 1966. The target was to obtain 1,000 interviews in Los Angeles and 625 in San Antonio, with interviewees stratified in both places by (1) location in terms of "density" of the Spanish-surname population, i.e., percent of total population, and (2) socioeconomic status.

*The Mexican-American Study Project is greatly indebted to Professor Raymond J. Jessen of the Graduate School of Business Administration at the University of California, Los Angeles, for his generous assistance in developing the sample design and selection procedures and his continuous interest in the execution of procedures in the field. See R. J. Jessen, "Some Methods of Probability Non-Replacement Sampling," *The Journal of the American Statistical Association*, LXIV, No. 325, March 1969; and the same author's "Probability Sampling with Marginal Constraints," to be published in a subsequent issue of the same journal. Frank G. Mittelbach, in consultation with Ralph C. Guzman, worked out the details and checked the performance of interviewers against instructions. This Appendix was prepared by Mr. Mittelbach and Ronald McDaniel.

LOS ANGELES COUNTY

No estimate of the number of Mexican Americans living in Los Angeles at the time of the survey was available. The closest surrogate was the 1960 number of white persons of Spanish surname (SS). In the Southwest, this statistic can be accepted as including most Mexican Americans. To eliminate non-Mexican Americans in the Spanish-surname population, field personnel were instructed to ascertain whether households coming into the sample were Mexican American before interviews were taken.

The 1960 census enumerated 576,716 SS persons in the 1,297 census tracts of Los Angeles County. The first step in the sampling procedure was to classify all 1,297 tracts into a 10 × 10 matrix whose dimensions were density of the SS population and imputed home value. (Table H–1). The intervals on the axes were chosen to keep all marginal totals as closely equal as possible, given the fact that census tracts are relatively large discrete units.

Table H–1. Number of White Persons of Spanish Surname and Number of Tracts by Cell, Los Angeles County, 1960[a]

SPANISH-SURNAME PERSONS AS PERCENT OF TOTAL POPULATION

Imputed Home Value ($)	0– 3.6	3.7– 6.2	6.3– 9.9	10.0– 15.1	15.2– 21.9	22.0– 32.3	32.4– 43.8	43.9– 64.1	64.2– 74.4	74.5– 94.0	Totals
6,625 or less	695 16	1,189 7	1,551 5	3,960 12	3,645 7	9,199 12	6,031 6	7,691 6	6,903 3	16,823 5	57,687 79
6,626– 7,239	616 10	1,481 6	1,064 4	3,703 9	5,332 6	4,731 4	4,831 3	19,708 8	6,017 2	7,703 2	55,186 54
7,240– 7,750	740 11	379 2	3,690 11	3,293 6	3,067 5	3,554 3	9,567 6	7,583 3	17,534 4	7,622 2	57,029 53
7,751– 8,287	1,129 11	1,768 10	1,736 5	6,059 13	7,986 8	3,424 4	2,468 2	7,540 5	9,493 2	16,612 4	58,215 64
8,288– 9,197	1,896 21	3,993 16	8,294 23	10,526 18	2,647 4	2,878 3	6,890 5		13,801 4	7,764 2	58,689 96
9,198– 10,129	2,695 32	5,937 27	8,630 20	4,583 8	12,145 12	5,618 4	11,992 7	3,622 2	2,908 1		58,130 113
10,130– 11,270	5,816 45	7,009 26	9,490 24	9,237 19	3,332 4	8,413 6	4,303 2	10,769 4			58,369 130
11,271– 12,565	6,694 53	9,001 35	10,406 26	7,342 11	10,068 10	3,123 3	10,095 4	1,107 1			57,836 143
12,566– 14,504	11,113 89	11,412 43	6,734 17	4,118 9	8,522 10	14,526 9	1,265 1				57,690 178
14,505– 35,673	27,015 269	16,659 82	6,929 21	5,560 12	833 2	889 1					57,885 387
Totals	58,409 557	58,828 254	58,524 156	58,381 117	57,577 68	56,355 49	57,442 36	58,020 29	56,656 16	56,524 15	576,716 1297

[a] All tables pertaining to the Los Angeles sample are derived from *1960 US Censuses of Population and Housing*, Final Report PHC(1)–82, Census Tracts Los Angeles–Long Beach, Calif.

Substantive as well as technical reasons led to the adoption of density and imputed home value as major strata in the sample design. On the technical side, it was recognized that selection procedures in areas of low SS density would have to be different from those followed in areas of high density. Substantively, it seemed reasonable to hypothesize that density would be a significant aspect of the milieu in which the subject population lived. Imputed home value, the other dimension, was chosen as a proxy for socioeconomic status. The objective was to sample across as broad a group as possible, while maintaining equal probability of selection for each Spanish-surname housing unit. A further consideration was the effect of a stratified design in reducing sampling variances for strata exhibiting relative internal homogeneity.

Imputed home value (V_j) was computed according to the following formula:

$$V_j = \frac{H_j^o V_j + H_j^r \, 100 \, R_j}{H_j^t}$$

where H_j = number of occupied housing units in the jth census tract. Superscripts o, r, and t designate owner, renter, and total number of occupied housing units with R_j = median contract rent in renter-occupied units for the jth tract.

Selection of Primary Sampling Units (Census Tracts)

From the total of 1,297 census tracts in Los Angeles County, 50 were selected as primary sampling units (PSU's). These tracts were chosen with probabilities proportional to size, with the measure of size being the number of Spanish-surname persons living within the tract in 1960. A more desirable measure of size would have been the number of Spanish-surname households within the PSU's. However, this statistic was not available for all tracts.

Table H–2 shows the probabilities of selection for each cell of the 10 × 10 matrix. The primary sampling units (PSU's) were selected so that five tracts would enter the sample from each row and column of the matrix. To maintain this balance, some tracts were drawn with certainty. Table H–3 shows the particular tracts that were chosen according to this scheme.

The PSU's were divided into four categories depending on WPSS density: (1) "High" density—43.9 percent or more; (2) "Medium" density—15.2 percent through 43.8 percent; (3) "High-low" density—6.3 percent through 15.1 percent, and (4) "Low-low" density —less than 6.3 percent.[1]

Selection of Secondary Sampling Units

In tracts for which data were available, census or street blocks, or street segments constituted secondary sampling units, or SSU's (Table H–3). In high- and medium-density tracts for which no census data on blocks were published, field personnel cruised the area, identified the blocks, and made visual estimates of the number of occupied housing units in each designated block. The blocks were then chosen to enter the sample as SSU's with

[1] In our discussion of Los Angeles in Chapter 13, we combine categories (3) and (4) into one and use three categories: High-density tracts with more than 43.8 percent Spanish-surname individuals, designated Colony; medium-density tracts with 15.0 to 43.8 percent Spanish-surname individuals, designated Intermediate; and low-density tracts with less than 15.0 percent Spanish-surname individuals, designated Frontier. In San Antonio, Colony = tracts with 54.0 percent or more Spanish-surname individuals, and Frontier = tracts with less than 54.0 percent Spanish-surname individuals.

Table H–2. Quotas and Sample Numbers of Tracts by Cell, Los Angeles County

SPANISH-SURNAME PERSONS AS PERCENT OF TOTAL POPULATION

Imputed Home Value ($)	0–3.6	3.7–6.2	6.3–9.9	10.0–15.1	15.2–21.9	22.0–32.2	32.4–43.8	43.9–64.1	64.2–74.4	74.5–94.0	Totals
6,625 or less	.06*	.10	.13	.34	.32	.80*	.52	.67*	.60*	1.46[a]*	5.00 / 5
6,626–7,239	.05	.13	.09	.32*	.46	.41	.42*	1.71[a]**	.52	.67*	4.78 / 5
7,240–7,750	.06	.03	.32	.29	.27*	.31	.83*	.66	1.52[a]**	.66*	4.95 / 5
7,751–8,287	.10	.15	.15*	.52	.69	.30*	.21	.65*	.82*	1.44[a]*	5.03 / 5
8,288–9,197	.16	.35*	.72	.91*	.23	.25	.60*		1.20[a]*	.67*	5.09 / 5
9,198–10,129	.23	.51	.75*	.40*	1.05[a]*	.49*	1.04[a]*	.31	.25		5.03 / 5
10,130–11,270	.50*	.61*	.82	.80*	.29*	.73	.37	.93*			5.05 / 5
11,271–12,565	.58	.78*	.90*	.64	.87*	.27*	.88*	.10			5.02 / 5
12,566–14,504	.96*	.99*	.58*	.36	.74*	1.26[a]*	.11				5.00 / 5
14,505–35,673	2.34[a]**	1.44[a]*	.60*	.48*	.07	.08					5.01 / 5
Totals	5.04 / 5	5.09 / 5	5.06 / 5	5.06 / 5	4.99 / 5	4.90 / 5	4.98 / 5	5.03 / 5	4.91 / 5	4.90 / 5	49.96 / 50

* Cells from which one tract was chosen
** Cells from which two tracts were chosen
[a] Certainty cell (10 in all)

probabilities proportional to size, where the measure of size was the number of occupied housing units, derived either from census data or from the visual estimates.

In high-low areas, the SSU's were street segments. Again, the tracts were cruised to determine the names of the streets within the boundaries of the tracts and their exact limits in terms of house numbers. Reverse telephone directories were then used to list all Spanish-surname households (with telephones) in the PSU. Thus, street segments were chosen as SSU's with probabilities proportional to the number of Spanish-surname households.

In the low-low areas, there were no SSU's. Sampling proceeded directly from the PSU to the occupied housing unit as outlined under "Selection of Tertiary Sampling Units," to be discussed shortly.

An implicit assumption in the high- and medium-density areas was proportionality of Spanish-surname persons in each block to total housing units in the block. Obviously, this would not hold invariantly from one block to another, but the limited resources of the study precluded refinements. In the high-low areas, as just outlined, selection of the SSU's

Table H–3. Census Tracts Used as Primary Sampling Units, Los Angeles County (1960)

HIGH DENSITY

Tract Number	Number of WPSS[a]	Percent WPSS[a]	Imputed Home Value	Location	Blocked (B) or Unblocked (U)
2032	2,917	77.2	$8,297	LA City	B
2038	2,744	76.1	7,243	LA City	B
2043	3,004	64.1	6,983	LA City	B
2049	2,507	76.2	7,836	LA City	B
2071	1,991	50.4	5,682	LA City	B
2081	1,866	67.4	4,447	LA City	B
4043	3,018	48.7	8,117	LA County (uninc.)	U
5027	4,362	54.9	10,667	LA County (uninc.)	U
5305	5,511	88.4	6,516	East LA (uninc.)	U
5308	6,020	74.3	8,297	East LA (uninc.)	U
5311	6,222	89.3	7,177	East LA (uninc.)	U
5313	5,608	72.0	7,240	[b]	U
5315	5,593	72.2	7,594	East LA (uninc.)	U
5316	4,906	64.7	8,098	East LA (uninc.)	U
5415	2,528	55.2	7,090	LA County (uninc.)	U

MEDIUM DENSITY

Tract Number	Number of WPSS[a]	Percent WPSS[a]	Imputed Home Value	Location	Blocked (B) or Unblocked (U)
1046	1,700	38.7	$10,073	LA City	B
1047	1,900	39.9	7,178	LA City	B
2011	1,295	31.2	9,509	LA City	B
2051	1,910	35.8	7,278	LA City	B
2242	809	29.8	5,658	LA City	B
2311	421	18.7	7,267	LA City	B
2676	406	15.8	13,701	LA City	B
4006	809	21.3	10,492	LA County (uninc.)	U
4015	1,382	42.2	8,351	LA County (uninc.)	U
4077	1,329	25.7	12,099	LA County (uninc.)	U
4323	720	18.0	11,918	LA County (uninc.)	U
4811	2,939	38.7	11,297	LA County (uninc.)	U
5023	1,866	27.6	12,787	LA County (uninc.)	U
5432	987	15.5	9,712	[c]	B
5426	1,756	31.5	7,758	Compton	B

LOW DENSITY[d]

Tract Number	Number of WPSS[a]	Percent WPSS[a]	Imputed Home Value	Location	
High-low					
1215	288	9.8	$14,571	LA City	
1832	486	7.9	9,328	LA City	
2133	742	15.0	7,207	LA City	
2932	684	11.2	10,138	LA City	
2969	492	9.2	7,922	LA City	
4051	566	10.5	9,591	Baldwin Park	
4085	504	8.6	11,564	LA County (uninc.)	
4823	1,078	13.2	8,959	South San Gabriel	
4828	586	14.2	15,541	Monterey Park	
5436	678	8.7	13,010	Carson (uninc.)	
Low-low					
1284	96	2.3	15,466	LA City	
1812	109	4.1	14,924	LA City	
2699	272	3.9	10,437	LA City	
3107	335	4.7	8,781	Burbank	
4058	362	6.2	12,833	LA County (uninc.)	
4816	440	4.6	12,014	Alhambra	
5704	73	0.9	10,910	[e]	
5716	99	3.5	4,813	LA County (uninc.)	
5774	41	1.1	13,236	Long Beach	
6005	149	2.5	17,480	Inglewood	

[a] WPSS = white persons of Spanish surname.
[b] Tract split between East Los Angeles (uninc.) and Los Angeles County (uninc.).
[c] Tract split between Compton and Los Angeles County (uninc.). Partially blocked.
[d] Blocked or unblocked is not relevant in the case of low density.
[e] Tract split between Los Angeles County (uninc.) and Long Beach.

was directly related to Spanish-surname population in each street segment, derived from the reverse telephone directory. All the inherent defects of using a telephone directory as a frame were present, but a procedure, which will be outlined shortly, was adopted to select phoneless households at the tertiary level.

From each tract five SSU's—i.e., five census or street blocks or five street segments—were selected. However, if the "expected" number of Spanish-surname households (that is, the number obtained by extrapolating 1960 census data to the time of the survey) fell below 5.2 in any SSU, one or more blocks were added.

Selection of Tertiary Sampling Units

The goal of the survey was 1,000 interviews from Mexican-American households (an average of four interviews per SSU, or twenty per tract). To allow for various losses due to non-response, non-Mexican households, etc., the sampling rate was set to obtain 4.8 Spanish-surname households per SSU. However, after interviewing began in the summer of 1965 it became apparent that this figure was too low. Accordingly, the rate was raised to 5.2.

The basic sampling scheme for the tertiary units, or occupied housing units, was systematic, with a random start. The sampling interval was calculated according to the following formula:

$$SI = \frac{H_i \times S_j^c / H_j^c \times K_j}{5.2}$$

where H_i = number of occupied housing units in ith SSU, 1960 census
S_j^c = number of housing units occupied by WPSS (white persons of Spanish surname) in jth PSU, 1960 census
H_j^c = number of occupied housing units in the jth PSU, 1960 census
K_j = WPSS/population, jth PSU, 1960 census

When no census data by blocks was available, H_i was calculated as follows:

$$H_i = H_j^c / H_j^f \times H_i^f$$

where H_j^c = total number of occupied housing units in the jth PSU from the 1960 census (c)
H_j^f = the number of occupied housing units in the jth PSU as determined by field cruises (f) in June, 1965
H_i^f = the number of occupied housing units in the ith secondary sampling unit as determined from field surveys in June, 1965

Selection of Sample Points in High-density Tracts. The general procedure in high density areas was to list and interview simultaneously. The interviewer was given a map of the SSU (block) and a form on which lines had been drawn according to a random start–systematic sampling scheme. Commencing at the northwest corner, he proceeded to list all occupied housing units in the block or street segment. He then attempted to obtain interviews at the points indicated by the lines on the listing sheet after identifying the household as Mexican American.

Selection of Sample Points in Medium-density Tracts. In the medium-density tracts, a listing was made of Spanish-surname households in the SSU's (blocks) prior to selection of sample points. The sources for this listing were reverse telephone directories and field surveys. The plan was to have field personnel visit the SSU's and list the Spanish-surname households not in the reverse telephone directories, but this procedure failed to produce a complete inventory of the housing units. Furthermore, SSU's with less than 4.8 expected Spanish-surname households entered into the sample without supplementation. As in the high-density tracts, the sample in a number of SSU's was too small.

A systematic scheme was used to select the sample points, as in high density tracts, but the basis for calculating sample intervals was shifted to Spanish-surname households obtained through the listing process.

Selection of Sample Points in High-low–Density Tracts. As in medium-density tracts, listings of Spanish-surname households were made in the high-low areas using the reverse telephone directory. The target was four interviews per SSU. Additionally, field personnel were asked to list and interview at addresses not in the directory to help correct for the bias implicit in using a telephone directory as a frame. In practice, the techniques in the field tended to degenerate into quota sampling of households on the reverse telephone directory lists. Non-directory addresses were interviewed only if the quota could not be met from the list. Lack of resources precluded a complete re-sample, so some compromises were made, but these did not conflict substantially with the goal of equiprobability of selection.

Selection of Sample Points in Low-low–Density Tracts. As noted before, there were no SSU's in the low-low tracts. The sampling intervals were calculated by dividing total imputed Spanish-surname households per tract by 26 (5×5.2). The total Spanish-surname households were obtained from the reverse telephone directories.

Evaluation of Results

Interviewing began in the early summer of 1965. Toward the end of the summer, when 757 of the intended 1,000 interviews had been administered, the field work was suspended because it appeared that field personnel had deviated from the prescribed sampling rules in a number of instances, resulting in too few or too many sample points from the standpoint of maintaining equiprobability. A careful check revealed that errors arose from arbitrary changes of the sample rate. A few interviews were removed, and the sample ratio was increased from 4.8 to 5.2.

The interviews necessary to meet the target and to substitute for discarded interviews were administered in the early summer of 1966. The delay was caused by our need to review the 1965 field work and by the desirability of employing the trained field staff, consisting mostly of students. Advisable as it was, however, the delay may have influenced the results of the survey. For example, the Watts riots in Los Angeles occurred in August 1965, shortly before the interviewing was suspended. Some of the responses in the 1966 group of interviews may have been colored by this event.

Altogether, the procedure laid out for the sample turned up a total of 1,116 "eligible" Mexican-American households, from whom 949 usable interviews were obtained. This outcome is within the range of reasonable expectations. These results are shown in Table H–4, together with other "coverage data" (that is, data indicating the adequacy with which the sampling procedure designated the number of housing units, Spanish surnames, etc., as compared with some established benchmarks found in the 1960 Census of Housing).

According to the survey, total households (any surname) increased by an estimated 13.7 percent (± 4.1)[1] since 1960, which can be compared with an 18.1 percent increase in

---

[1] The figure in parentheses is the estimated standard error. There is a 0.67 probability that the value which would have been obtained by 100 percent coverage is within plus or minus 1 standard error of the estimate.

total housing units (occupied and unoccupied) given by the Los Angeles Regional Planning Commission for the period April, 1960 to October, 1965. The same organization estimates a population increase of 14.5 percent for the same period.

It may also be noted in Table H–4 that we estimate from the survey that households with Spanish surname increased about 20.4 percent (± 6.7). This seems to be a reasonable estimate. The fraction of Spanish-surname households meeting our criteria for "Mexican American" is estimated from the survey as 71.8 per cent (± 1.6) and is also within a reasonable range.

Table H–4. Summary of Coverage Data, Los Angeles[a]

Density Decile	OHU Expected 1960	OHU's Observed 1965	1965 as Percent of 1960	OHU Expected 1960	SSOHU's Observed 1965	1965 as Percent of 1960	MA-SS's Observed 1965	1965 MA/SS, Percent
1	7,034	7,294	103.7	121	149	123.1	72	48
2	2,804	3,175	113.2	130	147	113.0	80	54
3	1,266	2,114	170.0	130	193	148.4	128	66
4	1,048	1,319	125.9	130	199	153.0	144	72
5	705	757	107.4	130	81	62.3	69	85
6	445	557	125.2	130	173	133.0	155	90
7	330	361	109.4	130	99	76.1	86	87
8	236	225	95.3	130	195	150.0	109	56
9	183	188	102.7	130	174	133.8	147	84
10	155	167	107.7	130	144	110.7	126	88
Totals	14,206	16,157	113.7	1,291	1,554	120.4	1,116	71.8%
Standard errors		± 4.1			± 6.7		± 105.2	± 1.6

[a] OHU's = occupied housing units; SS = Spanish surname; MA = Mexican American.

When one examines some of the above characteristics by density class, several anomalies are apparent. These include declines in Spanish-surname household units (SSHU's) in two deciles (5 and 7) and the unexpectedly low fraction of Mexican Americans in another decile (8). The explanations for these anomalies might include actual changes in population and its composition, poor search procedure in the survey, sampling errors, errors in the 1960 Census of Housing, or some combination of these. Interestingly, the proportion of Mexican Americans in Spanish-surname households increases almost invariably with density.

SAN ANTONIO

In 1960, the San Antonio SMSA (Bexar County) included 247,090 white persons of Spanish surname, or 37.4 percent of the total population of 687,151. The overwhelming majority is located within the city limits of San Antonio. The population outside the city is largely rural or concentrated on military bases. Since the study was primarily concerned with Mexican Americans in an urban environment, and no data were available for census blocks outside the city, it was decided to confine sampling to San Antonio City.

The bases for sampling, therefore, were the 244,430 white persons of Spanish surname located in the 92 tracts of San Antonio in 1960 plus four tracts in the enclaves of Alamo Heights, Terrell Hills, Olmos Park, and Castle Hills.

Selection of Primary Sampling Units (Census Tracts)

The procedures for selecting tracts in San Antonio were identical to those used in Los Angeles. The tracts were organized in a 10×10 matrix, with density of Spanish-surname population in tracts on the horizontal axis and imputed home value on the vertical. The objective again was to obtain a distribution in which the Spanish-surname persons in each summed row and column would be approximately the same (Table H–5). From the 96 tracts in the cells, 25 were selected as presented in Table H–6. Sample cells are shown with an asterisk. The methods of selecting sample cells were the same as in the case of Los Angeles.

In addition to the 25 original PSU's from which the basic sample was drawn, an additional eight tracts were selected from strata with imputed home values of more than $6,000. This group of tracts was designated the "over-sample" and was drawn for the following reasons:

Table H–5. Number of White Persons of Spanish Surname and Number of Tracts by Cell, San Antonio, 1960[a]

SPANISH-SURNAME PERSONS AS A PERCENT OF TOTAL POPULATION

Imputed Home Value ($)	0–22.5	22.6–38.1	38.2–54.0	54.1–65.0	65.1–78.9	79.0–85.0	85.1–89.0	89.1–93.5	93.6–95.0	95.1–100.0	Totals
4,300 or less								8,738 1	6,956 1	11,803 1	27,497 3
4,301–4,399					4,500 1			19,855 2			24,355 3
4,400–4,650			1,529 1						13,743 2	8,455 1	23,727 4
4,651–4,900					4,948 1	2,010 2	17,656 2				24,614 5
4,901–5,300		2,113 2	9,083 3	1,227 1	4,183 1	9,716 1					26,322 8
5,301–6,000	979 1			8,909 1	2,016 1	7,636 1			6,122 1		25,663 5
6,001–6,400	215 1	5,582 3	4,224 1		4,453 1	3,136 1	8,729 1				26,339 8
6,401–7,300	2,583 4	8,402 6		12,183 3							23,168 13
7,301–8,600	6,322 8	7,193 4	11,042 4	2,784 1							27,341 17
8,601 and over	13,517 29	1,887 1									15,404 30
Totals	23,616 43	25,177 16	25,878 9	25,103 6	20,100 5	22,499 5	26,385 3	28,593 3	26,821 4	20,258 2	244,430 96

[a] All tables pertaining to the San Antonio sample are derived from *1960 US Censuses of Population and Housing*, Final Report PHC(1)–134 Census Tracts San Antonio, Texas.

639

Table H–6. Quotas and Sample Numbers of Tracts by Cell, San Antonio, 1960

Imputed Home Value ($)	0–22.5	22.6–38.1	38.2–54.0	54.1–65.0	65.1–78.9	79.0–85.0	85.1–89.0	89.1–93.5	93.6–95.0	95.1–100.0	Totals
4,300 or less								.89*	.71*	1.21*	2.81 3
4,301–4,399					.46		2.03**				2.49 2
4,400–4,650			.16					1.41**	.87*		2.44 3
4,651–4,900					.51	.21	1.81**				2.53 2
4,901–5,300		.22	.93*	.13	.43*	.99*					2.70 3
5,301–6,000	.10			.91*	.21	.78*			.63		2.63 2
6,001–6,400	.02	.57	.43*a		.46*	.32*	.89a				2.69 3/2
6,401–7,300	.27	.86*a		1.25*a							2.38 2/2
7,301–8,600	.65*a	.74*a	1.13*	.29a							2.81 3/3
8,601 and over	1.38*a	.19*									1.57 2/1
Totals	2.42 2	2.58 3	2.65 3	2.58 2	2.07 2	2.30 3	2.70 2	2.92 3	2.75 3	2.08 2	25.05 25
	2	2	1	2		1					8

* Cells from which one tract in the basic sample was drawn.
** Cells from which two tracts in the basic sample were drawn.
a Cells from which over-sample was drawn.
Italic numbers denote the number of tracts in the over-sample in row or column.

1. the probability of including Mexican Americans of high and middle socioeconomic status in the sample was expected to be much lower in San Antonio than in Los Angeles;

2. given this fact, there might not be enough interviews from the higher strata to allow comparisons with lower strata;

3. hence, it was expected that the over-sample (with proper weighting, as described below) would solve this problem of inference. Tracts in the basic sample and over-sample are shown in Tables H–7 and H–8. Contrary to the situation in Los Angeles, no low density tracts entered the basic sample.

Selection of Secondary Sampling Units

The selection of secondary sampling units in San Antonio was simplified by the availability of census data for all blocks. Consequently, there was no need to identify street segments or blocks by means of field cruises or the reverse telephone directory.

Table H–7. Census Tracts in San Antonio Included in Basic Sample

	HIGH DENSITY				MEDIUM DENSITY		
Tract Number	Number of WPSS[a] (1960)	Percent WPSS[a] (1960)	Imputed Home Value (1960)	Tract Number	Number of WPSS[a] (1960)	Percent WPSS[a] (1960)	Imputed Home Value (1960)
33	8,738	89.7	$4,263	16	2,182	21.3	$8,524
34	9,716	79.0	4,973	21	3,302	54.0	8,419
37	2,360	93.7	4,614	23	998	19.7	8,908
39	3,136	82.4	6,027	35	8,909	62.8	5,556
40	8,455	96.4	4,400	48	2,067	33.7	6,454
41	8,038	88.8	4,870	54	5,146	53.9	5,014
42	11,383	94.5	4,445	62	2,056	38.1	7,628
43	12,845	93.2	4,380	80	4,224	48.3	6,277
44	6,956	93.9	2,802	81	3,688	55.3	6,934
56	7,637	81.6	5,430	85	1,887	23.7	8,623
58	11,803	95.4	4,167				
60	7,010	92.9	4,382				
64	4,453	76.9	6,086				
65	4,183	71.9	5,282				
79	9,618	88.6	4,733				

[a] WPSS = white persons of Spanish surname.

Six census blocks were selected in each of the 25 tracts of the basic sample, while five blocks per tract were chosen in the over-sample (Tables H–9 and H–10). The procedures for selecting SSU's were exactly the same as in the case of Los Angeles.

Selection of Tertiary Sampling Units

The sample rate in SSU's for the basic sample was 3.6; for the over-sample it was 4.8. The expected rate of interviews was three and four respectively for the basic and over-sample after allowing for non-response.

A comprehensive updated city directory was available for listing Spanish-surname households in the census blocks. Hence, the inherent biases of using a reverse telephone directory as a frame were not a problem. Since there were no SSU's which could be classified as "low" density, the calculation of sampling intervals was exactly as specified previously for high- and medium-density areas in Los Angeles.

Table H–8. Census Tracts in San Antonio Included in Over-sample

Tract Number	Number of WPSS[a] (1960)	Percent WPSS[a] (1960)	Imputed Home Value (1960)
9	1,105	10.4	$8,355
26	2,126	30.9	8,381
57	2,784	61.6	7,374
59	8,729	85.4	6,116
77	1,984	32.0	6,638
80[b]	4,224	48.3	6,277
81[b]	3,688	55.3	6,934
88	589	6.6	9,685

[a] WPSS = white persons of Spanish surname
[b] Included in both basic and over-sample

Table H–9. Census Blocks in San Antonio Included in Basic Sample

HIGH DENSITY

Tract Number	Block Number	OHU's[a] 1960	Tract Number	Block Number	OHU's[a] 1960
33	8	13	40	3	17
	24	37		18	27
	43 (44)	53 (0)		35	21
	65	62		51	18
	84	21		69	20
	114	67		84	16
34	8	40	41	2	18
	34	47		15	23
	52	20		30	135
	75	48		37	374[b]
	97	29		37	374[b]
	131	22		51	24
37	3	8	42	20	14
	13 (14)	3 (0)		49	24
	18 (19)	42 (0)		63	14
	22	28		84	17
	25	25		107	135
	28	22		125	32
39	11	51	43	20	23
	14	31		51	16
	21	29		78	60
	26	21		99	58
	31	21		118	27
	35	31		132	19
44	7	42	60	4	38
	18	34		5 (6)	264 (0)
	31	44		21	16
	40	64		36	27
	50	61		52	30
	68	57		62	27
56	9	41	64	11	114
	22	58		21	22
	31	97		36	15
	42	11		51	23
	63	24		67	11
	83	17		77	19
58	11 (12)	23 (0)	65	3	45
	42	61		12	14
	68	18		33	44
	89	35		43	38
	96	200		53	37
	107	28		61	43
	—	—	79	14	15
	—	—		38	19
	—	—		55	21
	—	—		74	16
	—	—		59	26
	—	—		114 (115)	21 (0)

Table H–9   Continued

LOW DENSITY

Tract Number	Block Number	OHU's[a] 1960	Tract Number	Block Number	OHU's[a] 1960
16	27	27	54	7	39
	65	17		31	16
	104	20		65	18
	135	30		70	20
	174	36		86 (87)	394 (0)
	203	25		103	28
21	2	26	62	2	32
	11	41		13	18
	25	37		23	22
	33	14		34	43
	54	24		48	17
	70	11		61	18
23	7	36	80	30	15
	25	25		53	26
	37	20		73	8
	49	23		101	34
	57	22		122	36
	70	22		135	31
35	22	17	81	29	9
	51	10		65	16
	79	54		106	48
	111	15		113[c]	27
	152	13		124	7
	190	15		142	37
48	15	14	85	3	32
	39	23		8	59
	65	27		14	29
	81	29		20	35
	107	10		24	27
	126	19		31	22

[a] OHU = occupied household units.
[b] This block enters twice into the sample.
[c] This block is also included in the over-sample.

Numbers in parentheses show blocks adjacent to those sampled. The adjacent blocks had no housing units in 1960. They were included to give housing units which might have been built in such blocks between 1960 and 1965 a chance to be selected.

Merging the Basic Sample with the Over-sample

As was mentioned previously, there was no low-density area in the San Antonio sample as there was in Los Angeles. Yet, previous experience had indicated that Spanish-surname density would be inversely correlated with the general socioeconomic level of an area, which meant that Mexican Americans of higher income levels might not enter the basic sample in sufficient numbers to allow valid inferences. Consequently, an over-sample was taken. The boundary between "high" and "low" socioeconomic status was set at an imputed home value of $6,000. The over-sample was drawn entirely from census tracts whose home values were imputed at $6,000 or more. The tracts falling into this category are shown in Table H–10.

However mandatory the substantive reasons for resorting to the over-sample, this procedure raised the problem of weighting, since the over-sample caused sampling fractions to be different in the two imputed home-value strata. In effect, a Mexican American in

Table H–10. Census Blocks in San Antonio Included in Over-sample

Tract Number	Block Number	OHU's[a] 1960	Tract Number	Block Number	OHU's[a] 1960
9	37	17	77	2	49
	92	14		15	19
	140 (141)	27 (0)		29	17
	188	19		47	22
	236	19		59	71
26	14	21	80	18 (19)	8 (0)
	30	28		45	18
	50	32		70	12
	69	20		102	13
	96 (97)	32 (0)		126	19
57	4	33	81	5 (6)	11 (0)
	18 (19, 20)	38 (0)		49	10
	35	15		103 (104)	29 (0)
	61 (62)	20 (0)		113[b]	27
	73	25		127	32
59	5	165	88	4	44
	19	50		18 (19)	22 (0)
	39	44		35	31
	50	51		65	24
	69 (70)	10 (0)		86	30

[a] OHU's = occupied household units.
[b] This block is also included in basic sample.
For explanation of numbers in parentheses, see note to Table H–9.

the higher stratum had a higher probability of being interviewed than one in the lower. To correct for this bias, a formula was devised for merging the two sub-samples. The formula for estimating any mean attribute for the target population (sampled tracts) was as follows:

$$\hat{\bar{Y}} = \bar{y}_w = \frac{\hat{Y}}{M} = \frac{\hat{Y}_1 + \hat{Y}_2}{M_1 + M_2}$$

$$= \frac{M_1}{M}\bar{y}_1 + \frac{M_2}{M}\bar{y}_2 = \frac{\sum_{i=1}^{m_1} y_{1i}}{m_1} + \frac{\sum_{i=1}^{m_2} y_{2i}}{m_2}$$

$$= \frac{1}{M}\left[\frac{\sum_{i=1}^{m_1} y_{1i}}{f_1} + \frac{\sum_{i=1}^{m_2} y_{2i}}{f_2}\right]$$

where M = total Mexican-American population in the survey census tracts

M_1 = total Mexican-American population in the survey stratum of less than $6,000 imputed home value

M_2 = total Mexican-American population in the survey stratum of $6,000 or more imported home value

m_1 = number of interviews in the stratum below $6,000

m_2 = number of interviews in the stratum of $6,000 or more

f_1 = sampling fraction in the stratum below $6,000

f_2 = sampling fraction in the stratum $6,000 or more

$\bar{y}_w$ = weighted sample mean, two strata combined

$\bar{y}_1, \bar{y}_2$ = sample mean in strata 1 and 2, respectively

$\hat{Y}_1, \hat{Y}_2$ = population aggregate for some attribute (e.g., a binomial count) in strata 1 and 2, respectively

y_{1i}, y_{2i} = observation of the ith interview within the indicated stratum.

Estimates of parameters in the formula were derived as shown below:

$\hat{M}_i$ = number of Spanish-surname persons in survey census tracts (stratum i) as shown in 1960 Census of Population

$\hat{M} = \hat{M}_1 + \hat{M}_2$

Table H–11 lists all the census tracts in the San Antonio sample, identifies them as to stratum (U = upper, L = lower), and indicates the number of interviews along with the total number of Spanish-surname persons in each tract (1960 census). From this tabulation we aggregated the numbers of interviews and Spanish-surname persons *within each stratum*. Note that all parameters were based on the target population alone, i.e., the tracts that entered the sample as PSU's. The actual figures follow:

$m_1 = 300$
$m_2 = 303$
$M_1 = 122{,}797$
$M_2 = 45{,}310$
$f_1 = m_1/M_1 = 0.002443 \qquad 1/f_1 = 409.333$
$f_2 = m_2/M_2 = 0.006687 \qquad 1/f_2 = 149.544$

Table H–11. Census Tracts in San Antonio with Interview and Related Data

Census Tract	Number of Interviews	Socioeconomic Stratum[a]	Number of Spanish-surname Persons
9	15	U	1,105
16	13	U	2,182
21	16	U	3,302
23	14	U	998
26	16	U	2,126
33	17	L	8,738
34	13	L	9,716
35	17	L	8,909
37	23	L	2,360
39	28	U	3,136
40	20	L	8,455
41	17	L	8,038
42	22	L	11,383
43	20	L	12,845
44	23	L	6,956
48	13	U	2,067
54	5	L	5,146
56	24	L	7,637
57	16	U	2,784
58	20	L	11,803
59	25	U	8,729
60	22	L	7,010
62	16	U	2,056
64	21	U	4,453
65	35	L	4,183
77	16	U	1,984
79	22	L	9,618
80	28	U	4,224
81	36	U	3,688
85	15	U	1,887
88	15	U	589

[a] U = upper; L = lower.

Table H–12 shows how the formula was used to obtain aggregate (adjusted) numbers of persons falling into various income categories from raw sample data. There was no final division in this case by M, since only aggregates were desired.

Results Obtained

With 625 interviews targeted in San Antonio, 603 usable interviews were obtained. These interviews were administered in the period June 1965 to October 1966. The total was distributed over the various density classes as shown in Table H–13.

*　　*　　*

Finally, it was important in both San Antonio and Los Angeles to obtain interviews distributed between male and female respondents. Consequently, field personnel were instructed to interview heads of households and spouses alternately, from one sample point to the next. In each SSU, a random selection was made of the first person to be interviewed. Exceptions were made in households not consisting of husband and wife. In such cases, the household head was interviewed regardless of sex.

Table H–12. Estimated Numbers of Spanish-surname Persons in Various Income Categories for the Sampled Population in San Antonio

STRATUM I (IMPUTED HOME VALUE BELOW $6,000)[a]

Income Category (Monthly)	(2) Number of Respondents	(3) (2) Times $1/f_1$
No reported income	94	38,477
$100–199	51	20,875
$200–299	82	33,565
$300–399	40	16,373
$400–499	14	5,730
$500–599	14	5,730
$600–699	3	1,227
$700–799	1	409
$800–899	1	409
	300	122,795

STRATUM II (IMPUTED HOME VALUE ABOVE $6,000)[b]

Income Category (Monthly)	(2) Number of Respondents	(3) (2) Times $1/f_2$
No reported income	51	7,626
$100–199	25	3,738
$200–299	69	10,318
$300–399	57	8,524
$400–499	37	5,533
$500–599	40	5,981
$600–699	15	2,243
$700–799	6	897
$800–899	2	299
$900+	1	149
	303	45,308

646

Table H-12   Continued

FINAL ESTIMATES – SUM OF COLUMN (3), EACH INCOME CATEGORY[c]

Income Category	Y	Percent
No reported income	46,103	27.4
$100–199	24,613	14.6
$200–299	43,883	26.1
$300–399	24,897	14.8
$400–499	11,263	6.7
$500–599	11,711	7.0
$600–699	3,470	2.1
$700–799	1,306	.8
$800–899	708	.4
$900+	149	.1
	168,103	100.0

[a] Weight = 409.333 = $1/f_1$
[b] Weight = 149.544 = $1/f_2$
[c] Discrepancy with sum of 1960 census figures due to rounding error.

Table H–13.   Distribution of Households Interviewed in San Antonio, by Density Classes

Density Decile	Number of Interviews
1	53
2	76
3	52
4	66
5	54
6	84
7	63
8	63
9	51
10	41
Total	603

Appendix I
Chapter 13

QUESTIONNAIRE FOR HOUSEHOLD SURVEYS IN LOS ANGELES AND SAN ANTONIO

UNIVERSITY OF CALIFORNIA

LOS ANGELES, CALIFORNIA 90024

1965

Job Number _ _ _ _

Case Number _ _ _ _

(OFFICE USE ONLY)

City ☐ 1 LA ☐ 2 SA ☐ 3 Alb

Interviewer

Tract Number _ _

Block Number _ _

WPSS Density   1 2 3 4 5 6 7 8 9 0

Imp. Home Value 1 2 3 4 5 6 7 8 9 0 _

Time Start _ _ _ _   Time Finish _ _ _ _   Time Elapsed _____ (18)

Respondent's Name _____ Sex _____ ☐ 1 Sp
First (19)   Last (20)   (21)   ☐ 2 Non-Sp

Address _____ Position in Household (22) ☐ 1 Head   ☐ 1 Sp
(Number)   (Street)   ☐ 2 Spouse   ☐ 2 Non-Sp

Phone Number _ _ _ - _ _ _ _   ☐ 1 M
☐ 2 F

Hello, my name is _____ and **I**'m with the University of California, Mexican-American Study Project. We're doing a study in which we're talking to Americans of Mexican descent to find out how they feel about important things like schools, jobs, and housing. The only way conditions can be improved is to actually talk to the people and find out how they feel about things. You have been selected in a scientific manner to represent thousands of people like yourself who do many of the same things you do and feel as you do about important matters. Your answers will be strictly confidential and no one will see them except the scientific workers who count up the different answers.

Now as I have explained, this is a study of people of Mexican descent. Is this a Mexican or Spanish-American household?
If YES: Proceed with interview

☐ 0 No
☐ 1 Yes

If NO: Of what descent are most of the members of this household? _____

IF DEFINITELY NON-MEXICAN, COMPLETE A NON-INTERVIEW FORM

Now I would like to ask you about the people who live here in this household in order to determine who to interview. You see, in different households we talk to different people. In this way we talk with some men, some women, some younger people and some older people. I would like to ask who the head of this household is.

INTERVIEWER: FILL OUT CHART BELOW ASKING FOR EACH PERSON:
(1) Name, (2) Relationship to head (specify if adopted children), (3) Age, (4) Sex, (5) Marital Status: M-Maried; Sin-Single; Sep-Separated; W-Widow; D-Divorced.

Relationship to HEAD	Sex M F	Age	Marital Status NM M Sp W D NR	Present Occupation	Prestige	Education	Permanent? P T NA DK	Earnings
Head								

Have we missed anyone who usually stays here but is away temporarily?

If YES: (List above). How about children or babies, have we missed any?

Our questions cover several different kinds of things. Some of them give us background facts about the community. On others, we just want to know how you feel about different things. It is not a test, and there are no right or wrong answers. Please feel free to stop and ask me questions at any time.

As we go around talking with people in this community, we find that some people prefer to call themselves:

Spanish-speaking ☐

Latin-Americans ☐

Mexicans ☐

Mexican-Americans, and ☐

By other terms _____ ☐
(specify)

How do you prefer to be identified?

IF IDENTITY GIVEN IN ENGLISH, ASK IN SPANISH:
¿Como prefiere Usted ser identificado en Español?

Mexicano ☐

Mexico-Americano ☐

Latino ☐

Hispano ☐

Other _____ ☐
(specify)

INTERVIEWER CHECK

Understood Spanish ☐

Did not understand Spanish ☐

I have questionnaires in both Spanish and English. Would you prefer that we talk in

Spanish, or in ☐

English ☐

IF SPANISH, SWITCH TO SPANISH QUESTIONNAIRE.

How long altogether have you been living in the Los Angeles (San Antonio) area?

Less than 6 months ☐

6 months to one year ☐

1 - 5 years ☐

5 - 10 years ☐

11 - 20 years ☐

More than 20 years ☐

NA or NR ☐

DK ☐

Born here ☐

Since pre-16 years ☐

Moved as adult ☐

NA or NR ☐

DK ☐

IF NOT IN LOS ANGELES (SAN ANTONIO) ALL HIS LIFE:

Where did you live just before you moved to Los Angeles (San Antonio)?

_____ _____
(State)   (Country)

Why did you decide to move here?

Economic or occupational reasons ☐

Family reasons ☐

Community reasons ☐

Other (RECORD BELOW) ☐
☐
_____ ☐
_____ ☐
_____
_____
_____

NA ☐

DK ☐

And how long have you been living here in this house (apartment)?

Less than 6 months ☐

6 months to 1 year ☐

1 to 5 years ☐

5 to 10 years ☐

11 to 20 years ☐

More than 20 years ☐

NA or NR ☐

DK ☐

IF LESS THAN THREE YEARS (CIRCLE)
In all, how many times have you moved (changed addresses) in the last three years?

1   2   3   4   5   6   7   8   9+
0 = NR or DK

About how long does it take you (primary earner) to get to work from here?

Minutes _____

☐ 00 NA

-2-

	Yes	DK	No	NR
Now I would like to ask you some questions about the kinds of people that live around here.				
In case of sudden need, do you think your neighbors would help you?				
Do your neighbors quarrel with you?				
Do you think your neighbors would lend you money should the need arise?				

	Often	Some-times	Rarely/Never	NR
How often do you borrow anything, such as food, household goods, or clothing from your neighbors?				
How often do you visit with your neighbors?				
How often do the neighbors visit you?				

Now I would like to read some statements to you. For each statement, please tell me if it is very true, somewhat true, or not true at all for your neighborhood.

	Very True	Some-what True	Not True	NR
There are many thefts in this neighborhood.				
You can get along best in this neighborhood by being friendly and nice.				
This neighborhood is a good influence on children.				

Now we are going to talk to you a little bit about your relatives. IF HEAD IS MARRIED, WIDOWED OR DIVORCED: Do you have any children who have left home?

☐ No

☐ Yes

IF YES, Where do they live now?

What kind of work do they do?

(INT: ENTER ON CHART BELOW)

(IF R'S PARENTS ARE NOT MEMBERS OF HOUSEHOLD)

Where are your parents living now?

(INT: ENTER ON CHART BELOW)

Where are your brothers and sisters living?
What kind of work do they do?
(INT: ENTER ON CHART BELOW)

Relationship			Sex		Location	Occupation
Child	Parent	Sibling	Male	Female		

Job Number _ _ _ _
Case Number _ _ _ _

People have different ideas about how family members should act toward each other. Will you please tell me whether you agree or disagree with the following statements?
(CHECK ONLY ONE RESPONSE FOR EACH STATEMENT)

	Agree	DK	Dis-agree	NR
Having children is the most important thing that can be done by a married woman.				
A husband ought to have complete control over the family's income.				
A mother leaves her young children two afternoons a week while she goes shopping and visiting.				
A father should take care of the children when the mother wants some time to herself.				

Here are some things that might be done by a husband or wife. As I read each of these to you I would like you to tell me if, in your home, it is usually done by you, by your husband (wife) or by both of you.
IF NEITHER: If it were done by one of you, which would it be?

	Husband	Wife	Both	Neither H Might	Neither W Might	DK
Painting rooms in the house						
Getting up at night to take care of the children if they cry						
Deciding where to go for a holiday or celebration						
Punishing the children, if necessary						
Picking out more expensive things like furniture or a car						
Washing dishes						

IF R HAS ANY CHILDREN:
Now please think about a time when one of your children was (will be) 10 years old. He has just done something which you feel is very good, or he has been particularly good. What would you do at these times? (CHECK ONE)

Psychic reward ☐
Verbal praise ☐
Special privileges ☐
Material reward ☐
Demonstrations of love ☐
Other (specify) _____ ☐
_____
_____
_____

Now, please think about that same time when one of your children was (will be) 10 years old. He has just done something you feel is very wrong, something that you have warned him against ever doing. What you do at such times? (CHECK ONE)

Psychic punishment ☐
Verbal scolding ☐
Withdrawal of privileges ☐
Material deprivation ☐
Demonstrations of withdrawal of love ☐
Other (specify) _____ ☐
_____
_____
_____

Now we would like to talk about schooling and education.

First, could you tell me how much schooling you have had--what was the last grade in school that you completed? How about __(rest of family in turn)__ ?
(COLLECT FOR ALL MEMBERS OF HOUSEHOLD AND ENTER IN HOUSEHOLD CHART, ON COVER SHEET. FOR ANY MEMBERS STILL IN SCHOOL, RECORD GRADE)

Now we'd like to ask some questions about your family when you were growing up. Were you raised by your parents or by somebody else? (IF SOMEBODY ELSE: WHO WAS THAT?)

Both parents ☐
Mother only ☐
Father only ☐
Grandparents ☐
Collateral--father's side ☐
Collateral--mother's side ☐
Godparent ☐
Non-relative ☐
Institution ☐
Other and NA ☐

IF FATHER IS NOT A MEMBER OF THE HOUSEHOLD:
Is your father still living? What was your father's education? (How many years of school completed) _____
FOR ALL: And where was that? _____

IF MOTHER NOT A MEMBER OF THE HOUSEHOLD:
Is your mother still living? What was your mother's education? _____
FOR ALL: And where was that? _____

When you were a child, around 13 or 14 years old, who had more influence on you:

Your parents (or whoever raised R) or ☐

Your teachers? How about: ☐

Your parents (or whoever raised R) or ☐

Friends your own age? ☐

Your parents (or whoever raised R) or ☐

Some other relative? ☐

(IF "Other relative"): Which one?

_____

Your father, or ☐

Your mother? ☐

When you were that same age, 13 or 14 years old, how many of your schoolmates at that time were of Mexican background?

All of them ☐

Most of them ☐

A few of them ☐

None of them ☐

And how many of your friends at that time were of Mexican background?

All of them ☐

Most of them ☐

A few of them ☐

None of them ☐

(IF R HAS ANY CHILDREN WHO ATTEND OR HAVE ATTENDED SCHOOL):
Now, how about your children? (Do)(Did) they go to:

Public, ☐

Catholic, or ☐

Other private elementary school? ☐

(IF ANY OF THESE CHILDREN HAVE ANY HIGH SCHOOL):
And (do) (did) they go to:

Public ☐

Catholic, or ☐

Other private high school? ☐

(IF R HAS ANY CHILDREN):
How many of your children's friends are (or when they were young were) of Mexican background?

All of them ☐

Most of them ☐

A few of them ☐

None of them ☐

And how many of their schoolmates are (or when they were young were) of Mexican background?

All of them ☐

Most of them ☐

A few of them ☐

None of them ☐

You can't always tell about how things will work out, but if you had your wish, about how much schooling would you (have) like(d) your child(ren) to have (had)?

_____

Now I would like to get your opinion concerning the schools for children. In your opinion what are the main things that children need to be taught in the schools today?

_____
_____
_____
_____

Do you feel the same for both boys and girls?

No ☐

Yes ☐

ASK OF PARENTS WITH CHILDREN IN SCHOOL:
Have you gone to the school within the past year?

No ☐

IF YES, Who did you talk with?

Principal ☐

Teacher ☐

Counsellor ☐

Other ☐

What about?

_____
_____
_____
_____

Now, I would like to ask you some questions about your housing here.

(IF R LIVES IN ANYTHING OTHER THAN A SINGLE-FAMILY HOUSE):

How many apartments are there in this building?

1 - 2 ☐

3 - 4 ☐

5 - 9 ☐

10 - 20 ☐

21 or more ☐

Do you own this home, or pay rent, or what?

Owns ☐

Rents ☐

Other (Specify)_____ ☐

IF "OWNS": Are you buying on a sales contract, buying on a mortgage (trust deed), or is your house fully paid-up?

Contract ☐

Mortgage ☐

Paid-up ☐

IF "MORTGAGE": How much do you still owe on your mortgage(s) (liens)?

First Mortgage $_____

Second Mortgage $_____

Third Mortgage $_____

IF "CONTRACT": How much do you pay on that?

$_____ per month

Could you tell me what the present value of this house is--I mean about what would it bring if you sold it today? $_____

IF "RENTS": How much rent do you pay a month?

$_____

How many rooms are there in this (House) (Apartment), including the kitchen, but not counting bathroom or hall? _____

(IF ONE ROOM IS DIVIDED INTO TWO FUNCTIONAL AREAS BY SCREEN, RECORD AS ONE ROOM.)

Now I would like to find out about things you have like a TV, a refrigerator, and so on. Would you tell me which of the following things you have that are in working order?

	No	Yes--How many?		
Do you have a television set?	0	1	2	3
A refrigerator?	0	1	2	3
IF NO--An icebox?	0	1	2	3
An automobile?	0	1	2	3
A telephone?	0	1	2	3
A sewing machine?	0	1	2	3

Do you have a bathroom with a flush toilet?

IF YES, How many do you have?

IF ONE, Do you share that with any other families?

No	☐
One--Private	☐
1-1/2--private	☐
1-3/4--private	☐
2 or more	☐
One--Shared	☐

Do you have running water here?

IF YES, Is that both hot and cold?

No	☐
Yes, both	☐
Yes, cold only	☐

What kind of heat do you have here?

None	☐
Gas furnace	☐
Gas space heater	☐
Electric space heater	☐
Wood stove	☐
Kerosene or oil	☐
Other--explain _____	☐

Job Number _ _ _ _

Case Number _ _ _ _

We have been talking about your family, your neighborhood, and your home. Now we'd like to talk a little bit about family situations. For example, some people feel that a person should be able to call on his family for anything, while other people think this is a bad idea.

Have you ever helped out any member of your family financially?

No	☐
Yes	☐

IF YES, Who? _____

Has any member of your family ever helped you out financially?

No	☐
Yes	☐

IF YES, Who? _____

Sometimes people need money and they can't get it from family or from friends. Apart from a mortgage or insurance, do you now owe any money to anyone, such as a bank, finance company, stores, credit union, and so on?

No ☐
Yes ☐

IF YES, Altogether, how much do you owe?

$_____

What is your total monthly payment every month on these debts?

$_____

Does your family now have five hundred dollars or more in savings?

No ☐
Yes ☐

IF NO--Does your family now have one hundred dollars or more in savings?

No ☐
Yes ☐

IF NO--Does your family have any savings at all?

No ☐
Yes ☐

Now I would like to talk with you about some of the things you would like to have for the future. For example,

Some people feel that 50 years from now Mexican-Americans will be exactly the same as everybody else in the United States. Do you

Agree ☐
Disagree ☐

Do you feel such a thing would be

Good ☐
Not so good ☐

Why do you say that? _____
_____
_____
_____

What about your own children? Is there anything about the Mexican way of life that you would particularly like to see them follow? _____
_____
_____
_____
_____

What language do you use when you talk with your children?

Spanish only ☐
Mostly Spanish ☐
English only ☐
Both languages ☐

Here are some statements that people have different opinions about. Please tell me, for each statement, whether you (1) agree, or (2) disagree.
(INT: CIRCLE ONE)

	A	DK	D
Mexican-Americans tend to have stronger family ties than most other Americans			
Other Americans don't work as hard as Mexican-Americans			
Generally, other Americans are more materialistic than Mexican-Americans are			
Generally speaking, people of Mexican background are very emotional			
Other Americans tend to be more progressive than Mexican-Americans			
Mexican-Americans often blame other Americans for their position, but it's really their own fault			
Mexican-Americans often shout about their rights but don't have anything to offer			

It has frequently been said that people of Spanish-speaking background in the Southwest have to work a lot harder to get ahead than Anglo-Americans.

	Very true	Somewhat true	DK	Not very true	Not true at all	NR
How true is that in this community?						
How about in business?						
How about in politics or government?						

Do you feel that this situation has become better, worse or what, in the past five years?

Better ☐
About the Same ☐
Worse ☐

Now I'd like to talk to you about some of the experiences you and your family have had at work and in trying to get work.

Are you (head) working now?

No ☐
Yes ☐

What kind of work do you (head) do? (Specific as possible)

Job_____
_____
_____

Do you (head) have any additional jobs at this time?	
No	☐ 0
Yes	☐ 1

IF YES: What is that?

_____

_____

Is that:	
Full	☐
Part time	☐

Is it:	
Seasonal	☐
Full Year	☐

How much do you (head) earn on your job (jobs)?

First Job: _____ hour

_____ week, or

_____ month

Second Job: _____ hour

_____ week, or

_____ month

What kind of business is that?

First Job: _____
(firm name or type of business)

Second Job: _____
(firm name or type of business)

Job Number ‗ ‗ ‗ ‗

Case Number ‗ ‗ ‗ ‗

How long have you (head) had this job? (First Job)

Less than 6 months	☐
6 months to one year	☐
1 - 2 years	☐
3 - 4 years	☐
5 - 6 years	☐
7 - 8 years	☐
9 - 10 years	☐
11 - 19 years	☐
20 years or more	☐
NA, NR, DK	☐

How long have you (head) had this job? (Second job)

Less than 6 months	☐
6 months to one year	☐
1 - 2 years	☐
3 - 4 years	☐
5 - 6 years	☐
7 - 8 years	☐
9 - 10 years	☐
11 - 19 years	☐
20 years or more	☐
NA, NR, DK	☐

Have you (head) had any different jobs with this company since you (he) started working for it? IF YES: Get as precise job progression as possible from beginning with firm to present for each job.

First Job: _____

Second Job: _____

Third Job: _____

Fourth Job: _____

Fifth Job: _____

How or from whom did you (head) first happen to hear about this job?

_____

INT: QUESTIONS IN COLUMN CODES 28 THROUGH 67 ARE ASKED OF HEAD ONLY

About how many of the people with whom you work closely on the job are of Mexican background?

All	☐
Most	☐
Few	☐
None	☐

(IF R IS NOT SELF-EMPLOYED) And how about your supervisor or boss--what is his language or racial background?

Mexican	☐
Anglo	☐
Negro	☐
Other	☐

Now I would like to ask you (head) about some jobs you have held in the past. What was your first full-time job?

Occupation _____

Industry _____

Location _____

Metropolitan	☐
Non-Metropolitan	☐

How old were you then? _____

What were some of the reasons you went to work at that time? _____

_____

_____

Have you (head) received any special job training other than learning on the job?

No	☐
Yes	☐

IF YES, For what kind of work? From Whom? How long ago was that?

(INT: ENTER RESPONSES IN TABLE BELOW)

Kind of Work	Source (Apprentice, trade school, etc.)	Dates

IF ARMED FORCES NOT MENTIONED:
Was any of your training in the Armed Forces?

No ☐

Yes (Kind of work) _____

How long ago? _____

Have you (head) ever worked as an agricultural laborer?

No ☐

Yes ☐

IF YES, When was that? _____

Have you (head) ever served in the armed forces?

No ☐

Yes ☐

IF YES, When was that? _____

Have you (head) ever worked in a factory?

No ☐

Yes ☐

IF YES, When was that? _____

ASK OF HEAD ONLY:
Do you now belong to a Union?

No

Yes

Job Number _ _ _ _

Case Number _ _ _ _

Were you (head) out of work at all during the past 12 months?

No ☐

Yes ☐

IF YES, Please tell me for each time you (head) were not working, (1) why you were not, and (2) for how many weeks were you without work?

Period	Why?	Number of Weeks
1st		
2nd		
3rd		
4th		

How did your family support itself during the times you (head) were out of work?

_____

_____

Who else in the household earns any money now?

_____

_____

_____

FOR EACH: How much does he earn?

(INT: ENTER IN TABLE ON COVER)

ASK OF HEAD: Generally speaking, how satisified are you with your present job?

Very ☐

Pretty much ☐

Not Very ☐

Not at all ☐

How would you rate your chances of promotion on your present job?

Very good ☐

Good ☐

Not very good ☐

Poor ☐

Suppose you knew a really outstanding young man here in the neighborhood--what one occupation do you think you would advise him to aim toward?

_____

What would you say is the most important single thing for a young man to consider when he is choosing his life's work?

_____

Now I am going to read to you some statements about the things some people like on jobs. Tell me, for each one, whether you think it is (1) Very Important, (2) Important, (3) Don't Care.

	Very Imp	Imp	Don't Care
High Income			
No danger of being fired			
Chances for advancement			
The work is important and gives a feeling of accomplishment			
Working hours are short, lots of free time			
You can really have a feeling of belonging to an organization			
People take you as you are			

We've been talking about your experiences and your family's experiences at work, and about what you think of work in general. We have found that people with different incomes feel differently about such things, so, in order to better classify your answers, we'd like to have some idea of your income. As you know, this is completely confidential.

Does your family income right now come from wages, welfare, social security, or what?
(INT: CHECK AS MANY AS APPLY)

	No	Yes
Wages or salary		
Professional fees		
Vet's payments		
Unemployment benefit		
Welfare		
Social Security		
Other pensions		
Rent or Board from someone living here		
Other Rents (What?)_____		
Income from business		
Income from farm		
Interest, dividents		

I would like you to listen as I read this list. Counting rents, interests, wages, salary, and things like that, in which one of these categories did your family's total income fall last year before taxes?

Under $1,000 a year or under $20 a week	☐
$1000 to $1499 a year or $20 to $28.50 a week	☐
$1500 to $1999 a year or $29 to $37.50 a week	☐
$2000 to $2499 a year or $38 to $47.50 a week	☐
$2500 to $2999 a year or $48 to 57.50 a week	☐
$3000 to $3999 a year or $58 to $76.50 a week	☐
$4000 to $4999 a year or $77 to $95.50 a week	☐
$5000 to $5999 a year or $96 to $115.50 a week	☐
$6000 to $6999 a year or $116 to $134.50 a week	☐
$7000 to $999 a year or $135 to $192.50 a week	☐
$10,000 to $14,999 a year or $193 to $288.50 a week	☐
$15,000 and over a year or $289 and more a week	☐

How many people are supported by this income?

_____

Part of our understanding of how people live is understanding their problems of health and sickness. We're interested in all kinds of illness, whether serious or not. As in all of this interview, your answers here are strictly confidential.

About how long has it been since you have seen or talked to a doctor?

Under 6 months	☐
6 - 11 months	☐
1 - 2 years	☐
3 + years	☐
Never	☐
Unknown	☐

Job Number _ _ _ _
Case Number _ _ _ _

When did you have your last chest X-ray?

Within past year   ☐

More than 1 year ago   ☐

Never   ☐

DK   ☐

Now we would like to switch the subject and talk about the groups you belong to:

Do you have a religious preference? That is, are you

Catholic	☐
Protestant, or	☐
Something else? (specify)_____	☐
No preference	☐

IF PROTESTANT, What denomination is that?

_____

IF ANY PREFERENCE, Have you always been a

_____
(NAME DENOMINATION)?

No	☐
Yes	☐

IF NO, What was your religious preference previously? _____

When did you make the change?

_____

IF MARRIED, How old were you when you got married?

_____

IF MARRIED, And how many children do you plan to have altogether? _____

Family planning--or birth control--has been discussed by many people. What is your feeling about a married couple practicing birth control? If you had to decide, which one of these statements best expresses your point of view? (INT: READ ALL STATEMENTS EXCEPT "DON'T KNOW." IF R WILL NOT CHOOSE, CODE IN "DON'T KNOW" CATEGORY).

It is always right	☐	1
It is usually right	☐	2
Don't Know	☐	3
It is usually wrong	☐	4
It is always wrong	☐	5

How important is religion to you, would you say it is:

Very important	☐
Somewhat important	☐
Not very important	☐
Not at all important	☐
DK	☐

About how often, if ever, have you attended religious services in the last year? (CARD) I will read from my list; please follow me on the list I give you and tell me which one applies.

Once a week or more	☐
Two or three times a month	☐
Once a month	☐
A few times a year or less	☐
A special day only, e.g., Easter	☐
Never	☐

What nationality background is your priest (or minister)? Do you know?

Mexican	☐
Spanish	☐
Irish	☐
Other foreign	☐
Native	☐
DK	☐

About how many of the members of your parish are of Mexican background?

All	☐
Most	☐
Few	☐
None	☐
DK	☐

We are interested in some particular health problems. Would you tell me if you agree with the following statements or not? (CIRCLE ONE):

	True	DK	Not True
I am nervous often			
I am nervous sometimes			
I feel that I am the "worrying type"			
Sometimes I feel weak all over			
I often feel such restlessness that I can't sit long in a chair			
I am bothered by a sour stomach several times a week			
I often feel that nothing turns out right for me			
Personal worries often get me down physically			

Most of the time I am in:

High spirits	☐
Low Spirits	☐
Very low spirits	☐

What is the name of that parish? _____

None	☐
Mexican Pastor	☐
Spanish	☐
Irish	☐
Other foreign	☐
Native	☐
DK	☐

INTERVIEWER:	Yes	No	DK
IS A SHRINE VISIBLE?			
VIRGIN OF GUADELOUPE?			
OTHER RELIGIOUS ART?			
PERSONAL RELIGIOUS JEWELRY?			

Are you a member of any organizations that meet more or less regularly, such as societies, fraternal organizations, educational groups, or recreational organizations, or unions?

No	☐
Yes	☐
DK	☐

IF YES, ASK FOLLOWING QUESTIONS AND ENTER ON CHART BELOW:

What are their names?

What kind of group is that? (IF NOT CLEAR FROM NAME)

FOR EACH: About how many of the members are of Mexican background?

Name	Kind of Group		All	Most	Few	None
		(63)				
		(67)				
		(71)				
		(75)				

Job Number ____
Case Number ____

Here is a list of organizations which people tell us are around here. I will read them from my list. Please follow me on the list I gave you. Tell me if (1) you never heard of the organization; (2) if you heard of the organization somewhere; or (3) if you are very familiar with the organization. (OMIT ANY GROUP MENTIONED BY R AS HIS MEMBERSHIP GROUP IN QUESTION, 63-75, but CHECK COLUMN 4)

	Never	Heard	Familiar	Belongs
G. I. Forum				
P.T.A.				
Alianza Hispano-Americana				
Republican Clubs				
Democratic Clubs				
Viva Johnson Clubs				
MAPA				
PASO				
LULAC				
CSO				
LAPA				

This list of Mexican-American organizations is incomplete. Many organizations are not listed here. Would you care to name a few more?

_____

_____

Out of all these organizations, which one do you think is the best?

_____

Why? _____

_____

In talking to people about voting we find that a lot of people were not able to vote because they were not registered or they were sick or they just did not have time. How about you? Are you registered to vote?

No	☐
Yes	☐

IF YES, WHERE did you get registered to vote?

_____

IF NO, Why was that? _____

_____

IF YES, Did you vote in the last Presidential election?

No	☐
Yes	☐

IF NO, Why was that? _____

_____

IF YES, "DID VOTE, " Who did you vote for for President?

Johnson ☐

Goldwater ☐

Somebody else ☐

If somebody else, Who? _____

How many people living in this household are citizens of the United States?

_____

How many people living in this household are registered to vote?

_____

Some people say that all people of Mexican background should get together politically, and other people disagree. Which would you say?

Agree ☐

Disagree ☐

Other _____ ☐

Why do you say that? _____

_____

_____

Some people say that all people of Mexican background should get together with Negroes politically, but others don't agree. Which would you say?

Agree ☐

Disagree ☐

Other _____ ☐

Why do you say that? _____

_____

_____

The following statements are simply to ask you about your outlook on life in general. As far as we are concerned, there are no right or wrong answers to these questions. We are merely interested in what you think. Would you agree or disagree with the following statements?

	A	DK	D
I don't think public officials care much what people like me think.			
The way people vote is the main thing that decides how things are run in this country.			
Voting is the only way that people like me can have any say about how the government runs things.			
People like me don't have any say about what the government does.			
Sometimes politics and government seem so complicated that a person like me can't really understand what's going on.			

Now can we go back to some things about your family and when you were growing up?

Where were you born? _____

                       (city)   (state)

United States ☐

Mexico ☐

IF NOT BORN IN LOS ANGELES (SAN ANTONIO), Where did you spend most of your childhood?

_____

(city)   (State)   (Country)

Was that:

In a big city ☐

A small town ☐

A village, or ☐

On a farm? ☐

IF BORN IN MEXICO: When did you come to the United States?

_____

Who did you come with?

Alone ☐

Child with parents ☐

Other (specify) _____ ☐

Why did you happen to come? _____

_____

_____

Are you now a citizen of the United States?

No ☐

Yes ☐

IF NO: Under what provision are you here?

IF NOT BORN IN MEXICO: When did the first member of your family come to the United States from Mexico?

_____

What was your father's regular occupation when you were growing up?

_____

IF DK FATHER'S OCCUPATION: What was your mother's regular occupation when you were growing up?

_____

Was your father's family in (New) Mexico:

Poor ☐

Well-to-do ☐

Other (specify) _____ ☐

DK ☐

Was your mother's family in (New) Mexico:

Poor ☐

Well-to-do ☐

Other (specify) _____ ☐

DK ☐

When was the last time you were in Mexico for a visit?

Date: _____

We are interested in your views about Mexico. What about this statement--would you agree or disagree?

	A	DK	D
The United States should allow Mexicans from Mexico to come to this country to work as freely as possible			
In old Mexico it was more difficult to get ahead than here in the United States.			
In Mexico it is harder for a man to get along if he looks Indian.			
In the United States it is harder for a Mexican-American with dark skin to get along than one of light skin.			

Job Number _ _ _ _
Case Number _ _ _ _

Now I'd like you to think about another important thing. Some people like to be with people from different backgrounds, and some people don't like it at all.

Do you think you would ever find it a little **distasteful**:

	Distasteful	Not Distasteful	Other
To eat at the same table with an Anglo?			
To dance with an Anglo?			
To go to a party and find that most of people were Anglo?			
To have an Anglo person marry someone in your family?			
To eat at the same table with a Negro?			
To dance with a Negro?			
To go to a party and find that most of people were Negro?			
To have a Negro person marry someone in your family?			

How many of your friends are of Mexican background?

All ☐
Most ☐
Few ☐
None ☐

At some time or other, almost everybody feels the need for somebody to talk things over with. If you needed help or advice about money matters, who might you go to? (IF NAME NOT GIVEN, ASK: Is he of Mexican descent?

Mexican-American ☐
Non-Mexican-American ☐

Why would you go there? What is there about that person (or place) that would make you feel you would get good advice?

If a person, does he (she) live around here?

Local ☐
Non-local ☐

How about for advice or information about politics? Who might you go to?

Is he of Mexican descent, or ☐
Non-Mexican descent ☐

Why would you go to him? (there)

If a person, does he (she) live around here?

Local ☐
Non-local ☐

How about for advice on personal problems? Who might you go to?

_____

Is he (she) of Mexican descent, or ☐

Non-Mexican descent ☐

_____

Why would you go (to him) there?

_____

If a person, does he (she) live around here?

Local ☐

Non-local ☐

How about if you needed some advice on where to go in the city government downtown to get something you wanted, who might you go to?

_____

Is he (she) of Mexican descent, or ☐

Non-Mexican descent ☐

_____

Why would you go (to him) there?

_____

If a person, does he (she) live around here?

Local ☐

Non-local ☐

Now, there are a few more things I would just like your opinion about. Once again, there are no right answers and no wrong answers; we would just like to get your opinion. For each of the following statements, would you tell me whether you (1) Agree, or (2) Disagree.

	A	DK	D
Making plans only brings unhappiness because the plans are hard to fulfill.			
It doesn't make much difference if the people elect one or another candidate for nothing will change.			
With things as they are today, an intelligent person ought to think only about the present without worrying about what is going to happen tomorrow.			
The secret of happiness is not expecting too much out of life and being content with what comes your way.			
When looking for a job, a person ought to find a position in a place located near his parents, even if that means losing a good opportunity elsewhere.			
When you are in trouble, only a relative can be depended upon to help you out.			
If you have the change to hire an assistant in your work, it is always better to hire a relative than a stranger.			

Finally, to wind up, could you tell me about what you read and see on television?

What is your favorite television station?--the one you watch most often? _____

Mexican ☐

Mexican-US origin ☐

Network ☐

Other ☐

No favorite ☐

No TV ☐

NR ☐

What is your favorite radio station   -the one you listen to most often? _____

Mexican ☐

Mexican-US origin ☐

Network ☐

Local or other ☐

No favorite ☐

No Radio ☐

NR ☐

And what newspaper do you read most often?

_____

Mexican ☐

Mexican-US Origin ☐

Major Daily Newspaper ☐
(in S. A.--Light)

(in S. A.) Express-News ☐

Neighborhood ☐

No newspaper ☐

NR ☐

And what magazines do you read or subscribe to?

_____

_____

_____

_____

Thank you very much. Your opinions have been very valuable to us. Should it be necessary, may we come back and talk to you again at some future time?

No ☐

Yes ☐

Job Number _ _ _ _
Case Number _ _ _ _

INTERVIEWER: FILL OUT IMMEDIATELY AFTER LEAVING

HOUSING ASSESSMENT

Condition of yard

Landscaped, professional or nearly professional ☐

Neat, attractive ☐

Neglected ☐

Cluttered, filled with miscellany ☐

No yard (include corral) ☐

Type of structure in which respondent lives

Trailer ☐

Detached single family home ☐

Not detached single family home ☐

Apartment in a partly commercial structure ☐

Apartment house (5 or more units, not public housing) ☐

Apartment house (5 or more units, public housing ☐

Detached 2 - 4 family house ☐

Corral ☐

Other (specify) _____ ☐

Condition of house exterior

Above average ☐

Sound, average, in good shape (paint, porch, screens) ☐

Deteriorating (needs paint or repair) ☐

Dilapidated (disrepair, falling apart) ☐

Condition of house interior

Expensive furniture and decor ☐

Medium-priced but clean well-kept furniture like new ☐

Orderly but furniture shows wear from usage by working people and children ☐

Disorder, furniture adequate and in general repair ☐

Disorder, furniture scanty and in general disrepair ☐

Type of art work

	No	Yes
Mexican		
American		
Religious		
None		
Other (describe)		

_____

DWELLING AREA

Does the stree on which respondent lives have

Heavy through traffic, including commercial vehicles ☐

Light through traffic, mainly private cars going to and from houses ☐

Mainly local residential traffic ☐

Other (describe) _____ ☐

_____

Is the street on which the respondent lives

Mainly residential ☐

Mainly residential and commercial ☐

Mixed residential and industrial ☐

Mixed commercial and industrial ☐

Is the neighborhood reputation

Very high (home of the "400" etc.) ☐

High--better suburbs and apartment house areas, houses with spacious yards, etc. ☐

Above average, larger than average space around houses, areas all residential, apartment areas in good condition, etc. ☐

Average, residential, no deterioration in area ☐

Below average, area not quite holding its own, beginning to deteriorate, business entering, etc. ☐

Low, considerably deteriorated, run down and semi-slum ☐

Very low, slum ☐

PERSONAL CHARACTERISTICS OF R

Skin and hair color

Light skin and hair ☐

Light, black hair ☐

Medium skin and black hair ☐

Dark skin and black hair ☐

Very dark skin and black hair ☐

How did the respondent strike you

Very Mexican ☐

Moderately Mexican ☐

Not very Mexican ☐

Not at all Mexican ☐

Fluency in language (vocabulary, etc.)

Spanish

Very fluent ☐

Normally fluent ☐

Broken Spanish ☐

English

Very fluent ☐

Normally fluent ☐

Broken English ☐

BASIC SAMPLE _____ ☐

OVERSAMPLE _____ ☐

ACTUAL PERCENTAGE WPSS _____

Did you have difficulty convincing R that he (she) should be interviewed?

No ☐

Yes ☐

IF YES, What kind of difficulty did you have?

_____

How did you overcome the difficulty? What did you say?

_____

Was R eager, not too eager or very cautious about answers?

Eager ☐

Not too eager ☐

Very cautious ☐

Why do you think R acted that way?

_____

Would you say that this was a poor interview, a fair interview, or an excellent interview?

Poor interview ☐

Fair interview ☐

Excellent interview ☐

Why do you say that?

_____

What other comments do you have that might help other interviewers?

_____

SUPPLEMENTAL MATERIALS

ON THE ROMAN CATHOLIC CHURCH

This appendix explains the content-analysis procedure that was used for articles in diocesan newspapers about Mexican Americans and presents data on the meager resources of the Roman Catholic Church in the Southwest.

CONTENT ANALYSIS

Using the procedure employed in Sanford Dornbusch and Louis Schneider, *Popular Religion* (Chicago: The University of Chicago Press, 1958), the categories in the present analysis were established after a careful reading of the newspaper articles. (The author's own knowledge of the subject matter was helpful also.) Each individual article was treated as a unit; each was rated on every one of the categories in terms of the following evaluative scheme: 0 = missing or insignificant; 1 = some attention given to this theme; 2 = considerable attention given to this theme; 3 = major theme of the article.

Two coders, working independently, evaluated each article. A total of 73 disagreements occurred out of a possible 2,724 evaluations. The author took the responsibility of making the final evaluation in such cases after considering both coders' evaluations and the content of the articles in question.

A. Religious Status, Practices, Programs of or for Mexican Americans:
    A1. Mexican Americans are practicing their religion satisfactorily
    A2. Mexican Americans face dangers/obstacles to practice of religion from
        A2.1 Protestant proselytism
        A2.2 Ignorance of their religion
        A2.3 Lack of priests/sisters
        A2.4 Unfavorable, threatening social/cultural environment
    A3. Mexican-American children receive catechistic instruction
    A4. Mexican-American adults receive religious instruction
    A5. Mexican Americans have Mass made available to them
    A6. Mexican Americans have mission/retreat planned or conducted for them
    A7. Mexican Americans attend special religious celebrations (processions/fiestas, etc.) arranged by/for them
    A8. Strictly religious organizations: for "Catholic action," to promote piety, for the study of Catholicism, to promote devotions, etc.
    A9. Charitable visiting of sick, families in their homes; bringing people to Church, etc.

This Appendix was prepared by Patrick H. McNamara.

B. Social Welfare Programs or Activities for Mexican Americans
   B1. Adult vocational, job-placement programs, home-making classes, etc.
   B2. Labor school classes
   B3. Citizenship classes
   B4. Programs designed for youth when delinquency NOT mentioned; social clubs, services provided, special classes (music, athletics, etc.)
   B5. Delinquency prevention specifically mentioned as objective of organization or group
   B6. Civic welfare organizations: community councils, veterans
   B7. Mutual-benefit societies (insurance, burial, etc.)
   B8. Family counselling programs, services
   B9. Classes in English for children
   B10. Classes in English for adults
   B11. Medical care/clothing given, distributed
   B12. Parochial schools for Mexican Americans

C. The Mexican as Foreigner, Immigrant
   C1. Efforts to Americanize the Mexican immigrant
   C2. Surveys conducted on numbers of Mexican immigrants
   C3. Voter registration
   C4. Anticommunist organization or movement

D. Social Justice
   D1. Social reform advocated: working conditions, community organization, etc.
   D2. Social reform regarded as secondary to piety, religious practice, etc.

E. War on Poverty
   E1. War on Poverty programs carried on under diocesan or parish auspices

RESOURCES OF THE SOUTHWEST CHURCH

The shortage of personnel in the Southwest Church is illustrated in Table J–1. Dioceses closest to the Mexican border have experienced the most pronounced shortage of priests (in terms of the number of Catholic persons per priest). Los Angeles and San Antonio have fared better, particularly the former. But all the Southwest dioceses taken together contrast strongly with those in the East and Midwest, represented in the table by the dioceses of Baltimore and St. Louis. Even when Southwest dioceses were divided—as was Santa Fe between 1940 and 1950, or Corpus Christi in 1965—there was little relief. The Brownsville diocese, carved out of Corpus Christi, exhibited in 1967 the highest ratio—3,012 persons to one priest—of any of the dioceses in question, a ratio nearly six times that of the dioceses of Baltimore in the same year. The data on "square miles per priest" tell practically the same story, although they must be viewed in light of the relatively low population density of most Southwest areas. Again excepting Los Angeles and San Antonio, the Southwest dioceses, even in 1967, did not come close to matching the square-miles-per priest figures for Baltimore in 1880 and St. Louis in 1903.

The ratio of Spanish-surname priests to all priests has always been lower than the ratio of Spanish-surname people to the total Catholic population. Taking the few instances in which Catholics of Mexican background were enumerated separately in the *Catholic Directory*, we find that in 1921 94 percent of the Catholics in the Corpus Christi diocese were listed as "Mexican"; Spanish-surname priests constituted 17 percent of all priests. The archdiocese of San Antonio in 1930 classified 68 percent of its Catholic population as "Mexican"; Spanish-surname priests made up only 14 percent of all priests. San Diego in 1940 included 60 percent "Mexican" Catholics; Spanish-surname priests totalled a mere 4 percent of all priests in the diocese. Even today, the Spanish-surname population of the Southwest supplies comparatively few priests. The majority are missionaries from Mexico and Spain. New Mexico is an exception, suggesting that a less mobile population with deeper historical roots may provide more fertile soil for vocations to the priesthood (Table J–2).

Table J–1. Total Catholic Population and Number of Priests in Selected Roman Catholic Dioceses, 1880–1967

SAN ANTONIO[a]

Year	Catholic Population[b]	Square Miles	No. of Priests	No. of SS[c] Priests	Persons to one Priest	Square Miles per Priest
1880	47,000	116,000	45	0	1,044	2,577
1890	50,000	116,000	45	0	1,111	2,577
1903	78,000	116,000	74	3	1,054	1,567
1910	85,000	116,000	89	12	955	1,303
1921	146,596	60,810	165	16	888	368
1930	181,776	39,272	207	28	878	189
1940	195,326	39,272	255	26	765	154
1950	259,908	39,272	302	29	860	109
1960	380,230	33,025	382	23	995	86
1967	506,084	33,025	427	42	1,185	77

CORPUS CHRISTI (BROWNSVILLE)[d]

Year	Catholic Population[b]	Square Miles	No. of Priests	No. of SS[c] Priests	Persons to one Priest	Square Miles per Priest
1880	40,000	17,720[c]	22	0	1,818	805
1890	44,550	17,720	19	0	2,342	932
1903	68,000	17,720	25	4	2,720	708
1910	82,000	17,720	30	3	2,733	590
1921	146,596	22,391	44	8	2,068	508
1930	247,760	22,391	85	27	2,914	263
1940	160,973	22,391	115	24	1,399	194
1950	454,000	22,391	144	17	3,109	155
1960	524,500	22,391	213	24	2,462	105
1967	196,058	18,165	159	35	810	75

EL PASO[e]

Year	Catholic Population[b]	Square Miles	No. of Priests	No. of SS[c] Priests	Persons to one Priest	Square Miles per Priest
1921	112,504	68,395	64	25	1,757	1,068
1930	119,623	62,395	89	49	1,344	701
1940	120,161	62,910	112	42	1,072	561
1950	144,591	64,434	115	27	1,257	560
1960	200,000	64,434	159	36	1,257	405
1967	170,470	64,434	137	47	1,244	470

SANTA FE[f]

Year	Catholic Population[b]	Square Miles	No. of Priests	No. of SS[c] Priests	Persons to one Priest	Square Miles per Priest
1880	110,000	104,168	52	5	2,134	2,003
1890	100,000	104,168	48	3	2,083	2,170
1903	133,000	104,168	59	3	2,254	1,765
1910	127,000	104,168	66	1	1,925	1,578
1921	141,573	104,168	96	7	1,474	1,085
1930	142,934	104,168	104	12	1,374	1,001
1940	165,454	104,168	158	14	1,047	659
1950	205,000	74,860	188	19	1,090	398
1960	275,000	74,860	245	24	1,122	305
1967	255,463	74,860	442	41	577	169

Table J–I Continued

ARIZONA—TUCSON[g]

Year	Catholic Population[b]	Square Miles	No. of Priests	No. of SS[c] Priests	Persons to one Priest	Square Miles per Priest
1880	60,000	131,212	13	0	4,615	10,093
1890	20,000	131,212	19	2	1,052	6,905
1903	40,000	131,212	27	1	1,481	4,859
1910	48,500	131,212	36	0	1,347	3,644
1921	51,000	133,058	62	0	822	2,146
1930	95,472	133,058	80	27	1,193	1,663
1940	100,000	52,369	78	17	1,282	671
1950	115,000	52,369	121	16	950	432
1960	276,000	52,369	159	21	1,735	329
1967	412,000	52,369	319	23	1,291	164

LOS ANGELES[h] (MONTEREY AND SAN DIEGO)

Year	Catholic Population	Square Miles	No. of Priests	No. of SS Priests	Persons to one Priest	Square Miles per Priest
1880	21,000	80,000	39	12	538	2,051
1890	40,000	80,000	62	9	645	1,290
1903	58,000	80,000	101	8	574	792
1910	95,000	80,000	188	15	505	425
1921	190,000	80,000	248	21	766	322
1930	301,775	44,350	490	59	615	90
1940	317,549	9,508	601	40	528	15
1950	832,375	9,508	770	54	1,081	12
1960	1,297,584	9,508	1,135	75	1,143	8
1967	1,640,167	9,508	1,496	108	1,096	6

SAN DIEGO

Year	Catholic Population	Square Miles	No. of Priests	No. of SS Priests	Persons to one Priest	Square Miles per Priest
1940	120,161	35,879	136	6	898	263
1950	160,000	35,879	257	11	622	139
1960	376,716	35,879	391	21	963	91
1967	330,999	35,879	451	28	733	79

BALTIMORE					ST. LOUIS				
Year	Total Catholic Population	Persons to 1 Priest	Square Miles	Square Miles per Priest	Year	Total Catholic Population	Persons to 1 Priest	Square Miles	Square Miles per Priest
1880	200,000	766	12,862	49	1880	145,872	561	32,348	124
1890	220,000	709	12,862	41	1890	280,000	989	32,348	114
1903	250,000	631	12,862	32	1903	220,000	503	32,348	74
1910	260,000	485	12,862	24	1910	375,000	728	32,348	62
1921	276,000	453	12,862	21	1921	425,692	700	27,092	45
1930	305,490	379	12,862	15	1930	440,000	630	27,092	38
1940	384,710	296	12,862	9	1940	440,000	614	27,092	37
1950	397,546	470	44,801	7	1950	433,442	442	27,092	27
1960	410,714	590	44,801	6	1960	451,958	477	5,968	6
1967	478,370	660	44,801	6	1967	518,142	492	5,968	5

[a] The total district of San Antonio was successively reduced by the creation of the following dioceses from the original district: Corpus Christi in 1912; El Paso in 1914; San Angelo in 1950.

[b] Catholic population data for the years 1880 through 1910 are of dubious accuracy. Later figures are based on more accurate censuses, but the reliability of the data cannot be determined.

[c] SS = Spanish-surname.

[d] The original Vicariate-Apostolic of Brownsville became the Diocese of Corpus Christi in 1912. In 1965, the Brownsville Diocese was created from the four southernmost counties of Corpus Christi.

[e] The Diocese of El Paso was created in 1914.

[f] The Archdiocese of Santa Fe lost parts of its district to the new Diocese of Gallup in 1940.

[g] The original Vicariate-Apostolic of Arizona became the Diocese of Tucson in 1897. The district of the diocese was reduced in 1940 by the creation of the Diocese of Gallup.

[h] The total district of Monterey–Los Angeles was successively reduced by the creation of the following dioceses from the original district: Monterey–Fresno in 1922; San Diego in 1936.

Source: The Catholic Directory for 1880, 1890, and 1903, published by D. & J. Sadlier & Company, New York. The Directory for 1910 was published by M. H. Wiltzius Company, New York. Succeeding issues of the Directory have been published by P. J. Kenedy and Sons, New York. The Directory for the years 1900, 1901, 1902, and 1920 were unavailable at the Los Angeles Archdiocesan Archives, making it impossible to present data for precise ten-year intervals.

Table J–2. Number of Spanish-surname Priests, by Area of Birth, Selected Dioceses of the Southwest, 1967

| Diocese | AREA OF BIRTH | | Totals |
	United States	Mexico or Spain	
San Antonio	8	21	29
El Paso	12	35	47
Santa Fe	37	4	41
Brownsville	7	15	22
	—	—	—
Totals	64	75	139

Sources: The chancery offices of the several dioceses.

PERSONS INTERVIEWED INFORMALLY
ON FIELD TOURS
AND IN LOS ANGELES

Throughout this study, and especially in its formative stages, the authors and contributors benefited greatly from interviews and discussions with a great many persons, most of them Mexican Americans. We acknowledge gratefully their valuable assistance in the following list, which, unfortunately, is compiled from incomplete records. Besides those omitted through inadvertency, it omits the interviewees in our structured household surveys in Los Angeles and San Antonio, certain persons interviewed by our collaborators, and members of our advisory committees (the latter are listed in the Preface). Of course, the persons listed are in no way responsible for our findings and interpretations.

ARIZONA

Charles Bartlett
Tony Carillo
Robert B. Choate, Jr.
Jose Del Castillo
Grace Gil-Olivarez
Lester Goldberg
Alex Gonzalez
William O. Johnson
Rose Hum Lee
Gene Marin

Lou Martinez
Mrs. Jerry Massiem
Gilberto Mantañez
Harriett Rainwater
The Reverend M. Salinas
Currin Shields
R. J. Small
Grace Urquidas
Jesse Ybarra

CALIFORNIA

Fermin Alvarez
Ben Amador
Manuel Aragon
Roberto Aragon
Burt S. Avedon
Nick Avila

Helen Bailey
Thomas Blaisdell
William Blea
Carlos F. Borja, Jr.
JoAnn Braighwaite
John Buggs

CALIFORNIA—*continued*

Paul Bullock
Lorenzo Campbell
Manuel Carlos
R. J. Carreon
Arthur Carstens
Felix Castro
Salvador Castro
Ruth Chance
César Chavez
The Reverend George Cole
Joseph L. Connaughton
Bert N. Corona
Eugene Cota-Robles
James Cruz
Alfredo Cuellar
Marcos de Leon
Edward Elliott
Hector Enriques
Fred Felix
Trinidad Flores
Helen Foley
John Anson Ford
George Foster
The Reverend John Gabrielson
Ernesto Galarza
Herman Gallegos
Lynn Gardner
Maurice I. Gershenson
Nathan Glazer
Cesar Gonzaléz, S.J.
Jesse Gonzaléz
Manuel Guerra
William Gutierrez
George P. Hammond
Aileen Hernandez
Max Hernandez
The Reverend William Hervey
Kendall Jenkins
Nicandro Juaréz
Leonard Kerner
Charles Kolisher
Carl Lara
Yolanda Araiza Leaf
Richard Leiva
Dwight Lindholm
The Reverend César Lizarraga
Harvey Locke
A. P. Lopez
Leo Lopez

Lino Lopez
Ron Lopez
Hazel Love
Josie Lozano
Daniel Luevano
The Reverend Vahac Mardirosian
Ben Martinez
The Reverend César Mascareñas
Mrs. Vernon M. McCombs
Ronald McDaniels
David McEntire
Augustin Medina
Nicolee Miller
Gonzalo Molina
George J. Monica
Max Mont
Rachel Montenegro
Sal Montenegro
The Reverend Adam Morales
Armando Morales
J. Hector Moreno
Julian Nava
The Reverend Mardoqueo L. Olivas
Hilario Pena
Hugh Pingree
Albert Pinon
Ralph Poblano
Eduardo Quevedo
Arthur Rendon
Anthony P. Rios
Ernest Robles
Armando Rodriguez
J. J. Rodriguez
Raymond Rodriguez
Octavio Romano
Keith Romney
Fred Ross
Lillian Roybal Rose
Manuel Ruiz
Max Ruiz
George Russell
The Reverend Ruben Saenz
Ruben Salazar
Phil Sanchez
Harvey Schechter
Hope Mendoza Schechter
Fred Schmidt
Maria Talavera Schutz
Antonio Serafin

672

CALIFORNIA—*continued*

Father Shubste
Frank M. Sifuentes
The Reverend David Stirdivant
Abe Tankenson
Paul S. Taylor
John Ulene

Richard Vasquez
Rafael Vega
Robert Villalobos
Willard W. Williams
Malcom Wise
Alex Zambrano

COLORADO

Ted Baros
George Bateman
C. Allen Blomquist
Ed Byles
Arthur Campa
James R. Carrizan
Mr. and Mrs. Roy Davidson
Manuel Diaz
Leonard Flores
Tim Flores
Rudolph Gonzalez
Gary Larsen
Steve Maldonado
Mary Martinez

David Mejia
Edward Miller
The Reverend Charles J. Murray
Rachel B. Noel
Roberto Ornelas
Helen L. Peterson
George Roybal
Manuel Salinas
Ozzie Simmons
J. H. Stenmark
John B. Tiger
Bernard Valdez
Walter R. Valdez
Ben Velasquez

NEW MEXICO

Tomás C. Atencio
Fred F. Baca
Helen Blumenschein
Stanley J. Brasher
José A. Chacon
A. B. Chavez
Fabian Chavez
Dorothy Cline
James Cooper
E. C. de Baca
Concha Ortiz y Pino de Kleven
Edward Devereux
Larry P. Frank
Richard Griego
Charles R. Griffith
G. C. Hafbauer
David Hamilton
Alvin Hardie
Marion Hotopp, M.D.
Frederick Irion
Myra Ellen Jenkins
Spud Johnson
State Senator Anthony Lucero
Eddy Martinez

Palemon Martinez
J. B. McCoy
Stephen Mitchell
Robert Mondragon
Joseph M. Montoya
Theodore Montoya
Leo T. Murphy
Lynne T. Murphy
John F. Otero
Miguel Pijoan, M.D.
Richard J. Pino
Antonio Rey
Alfonso Rodriguez
Tom Sasaki
Nan Smith
Billie Sponseller
P. T. Therkildsen
Reies Tijerina
D. W. Varley
Leandro Vigil
T. P. Wolf
C. E. Woodhouse
Bert Zippel

TEXAS

Richard Adams
John Alaniz
Paul Andow
Hector Azios
Ivan Belknap
Tony Bonilla
Willy Bonilla
Stephen Bosio
Harold Braun
Father Briganti
Leonard Broom
Harvey Brown
Miguel Bustamente
Carlos Calderon
Cleofas Calleros
W. M. Calnan
The Reverend Henry Casso
Ramiro Casso, M.D.
Mr. and Mrs. Chester Christian
Nada Collins
Governor John Connally
Juan Cornejo
Fred Crawford
Alfred Cuellar, Sr.
Erasmo Endrade
Buford Farris
Clea Garcia, M.D.
Gerardo García
Hector Garcia, M.D.
J. A. Garcia
Glen Garrett
Manuel Garza
Noe Garza
Reynaldo Garza
Jack Gibbs
Cruz Gonzales
Henry B. Gonzales
Joaquin D. Gonzales, M.D.
Valdemar Gonzales
Hector Gonzalez
Alfred J. Hernandez
Gilbert Herrera

Wayne Holtzman
Lamar B. Jones
The Reverend James Killian
Clark S. Knowlton
Oscar Laurel
Bert Lavine, M.D.
Mary LeBlanc
Sheridan Lewis
Honoré Ligarde
Manuel Lopez
Joe Mares
Ray Marshall
Arnulfo Martinez
W. L. Maxwell
Dale McLemore
Wayne Metzgar, M.D.
M. T. Miles
Joe B. Montez
Henry Muñoz
Eastin Nelson
Gilberto Nuirello
David Olson
Robert Peck
Albert Peña
Ignacio Perez
The Reverend Eduardo Quevedo, Jr.
Edna Reyes
Israel R. Reyes
Oscar Reyna
John Richards
George I. Sanchez
Robert Sanchez
Mr. and Mrs. Gideon Sjoberg
The Reverend Sherrill Smith
Victor Sumner
Felix Tijerina
Carlos Truan
Frank Valdez
The Reverend John Wagner
John Widenthal
Samuel D. Young, Jr.

PERSONS OUTSIDE THE SOUTHWEST

Julia Cellini
Jesse Escalante
Joshua A. Fishman

Eli Ginzburg
Douglas Glick
The Reverend Donald Headley

PERSONS OUTSIDE THE SOUTHWEST
—*continued*

John Hobgood
Elaine Kup
Carmen Mendoza
David North
The Reverend Robert Reicher
Armando Rodriguez

Joel Rogge
Joan W. Roxborough
Clarence Senior
Edward Torres
Victor Wright
Vicente Ximenes

Bibliography

I. BOOKS, PAMPHLETS, AND GOVERNMENT PUBLICATIONS

Abel, Theodore. *Protestant Home Missions to Catholic Immigrants.* New York: Institute of Social and Religious Science, 1933.

Adler, Herman, Frances Cahn, and Stuart Johannes. *The Incidence of Delinquency in Berkeley, 1928–1932.* Berkeley, Calif., University of California Press, 1934.

Allen, Ruth Alice. *The Labor of Women in the Production of Cotton.* Texas University. Bureau of Research in the Social Sciences Study no. 3. Austin, Tex.: University of Texas Press, 1931.

Allport, Gorden W. *The Nature of Prejudice.* Cambridge, Massachusetts: Addison-Wesley, 1954.

American Council on Race Relations. *Intergroup Relations in San Diego: Some Aspects of Community Life in San Diego Which Particularly Affect Minority Groups, with Recommendations for a Program of Community Action.* Prepared by Lawrence I. Hewes and William Y. Bell. San Francisco, 1946.

American Friends Service Committee. *Farm Workers and the Law: A Report on* the Illegal Treatment of Farm Workers in California. Farmworkers Opportunity Project, n.p., 1967.

American GI Forum of Texas and Texas State Federation of Labor (AFL). *What Price Wetbacks?* Austin, Tex., 1953.

American Public Welfare Association. *Public Welfare Survey of San Antonio, Texas, a Study of a Local Community.* Chicago, 1940.

Anderson, Henry Paul. *The Bracero Program in California, with Particular Reference to Health Status, Attitudes and Practices.* Berkeley, Calif.: University of California, School of Public Health, 1961.

Andrews, Wade H., and Saad Z. Nagi. *Migrant Agricultural Labor in Ohio.* Research Bulletin 780. Wooster, Ohio: Ohio Agricultural Experiment Station, Sept. 1956.

Apodaca, Anacleto. "Corn and Custom: The Introduction of Hybrid Corn to Spanish-American Farmers in New Mexico," in Edward H. Spicer, ed., *Human Problems in Technological Change*, pp. 35–39. New York: Russell Sage Foundation, 1952.

Arnold, Elliot. *The Time of the Gringo.* New York: Alfred A. Knopf, 1954.

Ashworth, Mae Hurley, ed. *Who? Spanish-speaking Americans in the U.S.A.* New York: Friendship Press, 1953.

Atkins, James A. "A Cultural Minority Improves Itself," in *Human Relations in Colorado*, pp. 91–105. Denver, Colo.: Colorado State Department of Education, 1961.

Atwater, Ernesta E. *A Tabulation of Facts on Conditions Existent in Hick's Mexican Camp.* El Monte, Calif.: Published by the author, 1942.

Banfield, Edward C. *Big City Politics.* New York: Random House, 1965.

Barker, George C. *Pachuco: An American-Spanish Argot and Its Social Functions in Tucson, Arizona.* Tucson, Ariz.: University of Arizona Press, 1958.

Barron, Milton L., *American Minorities.* New York: Alfred A. Knopf, 1957.

Beals, Ralph, and Norman Humphrey.

No Frontier to Learning. Minneapolis, Minn.: University of Minnesota Press, 1957.

Beck, Warren. *New Mexico: A History of Four Centuries.* Norman, Okla.: University of Oklahoma Press, 1962.

Becker, William L. *Report to Governor Edmund G. Brown: Second Ethnic Survey of Employment and Promotion in State Government.* Sacramento: State of California Governor's Office, 1965.

Bexar County Tuberculosis Association. *Like a Sore Thumb.* San Antonio, Tex.: 1945.

Bishops' Committee for the Spanish-speaking. *Pilot Project—Merrill Trust Fund.* San Antonio, Tex.: Jan. 1962.

Blair, Bertha, Anne O. Lively, and Glen W. Trimble. *Spanish-speaking Americans: Mexicans and Puerto Ricans in the United States.* New York: Home Mission Research Unit, Bureau of Research and Survey, Home Missions Division, National Council of Churches of Christ in the United States of America, 1959.

Bogardus, Emory S. "Attitudes and the Mexican Immigrant," in Kimball Young, ed., *Social Attitudes*, pp. 291–327. New York: Henry Holt, 1931.

———. "The Mexican Immigrant," in Emory S. Bogardus, ed., *Essentials of Americanization*, pp. 264–271. Los Angeles: J. R. Miller, 1920.

———. *A Forty Year Racial Distance Study.* Los Angeles, Cal.: University of Southern California, 1967.

———. *Immigration and Race Attitudes.* New York: D. C. Heath and Co., 1928.

———. *The Mexican Immigrant.* Los Angeles: Council on International Relations, 1929.

———. *The Mexican in the United States.* Los Angeles: University of California Press, 1934.

———. *The Survey of Race Relations on the Pacific Coast.* Los Angeles: Council on International Relations, Information Service, May, 1926.

Bolton, Herbert E. *The Spanish Borderlands.* New Haven, Conn.: Yale University Press, 1921.

———. *Spanish Exploration in the Southwest, 1542–1706.* New York: A. S. Barnes and Noble, 1959.

Bresette, Linna E. *Mexicans in the United States.* Washington: National Catholic Welfare Conference, 1930.

Broom, Leonard. *Sociology. Second Edition*, pp. 461 and 470. Evanston, Ill.: Row, Peterson and Co., 1958.

Browder, Walter G. *The Pattern of Internal Mobility in Texas: A Subregional Study.* Austin, Tex.: University of Texas Press, 1944.

Brown, Francis J., and Joseph S. Roucek. *One America: The History and Contributions and Present Problems of Our Racial and National Minorities.* New York: Prentice-Hall, 1946.

Browning, Harley L., and S. Dale McLemore. *A Statistical Profile of the Spanish-surname Population of Texas.* Austin, Tex.: Population Research Center, University of Texas, June 9, 1964.

Buechel, F. A., and E. R. Dedeke. *"Family Expenditures in Twenty-one Texas Communities,"* Texas University, Bureau of Business Research. Progress Report No. 2. Austin, Tex.: University of Texas, 1942.

———, and ———· *"Family Expenditure and Per Capita Consumption in Nine Texas Communities,"* Texas University, Bureau of Business Research. Progress Report No. 1. Austin, Tex.: University of Texas, 1942.

Bunker, Robert, and John Adair. *The First Look at Strangers.* New Brunswick, N.J.: Rutgers University Press, 1959.

Bureau of Business and Social Research, University of Denver. *Housing Trends in Denver, 1939–1949.* University of Denver Reports, vol. 25 (Nov., 1949).

Burma, John. "The Civil Rights Situation of Mexican-Americans and Spanish-Americans," in Jitsuichi Masuoka and Preston Valien, eds., *Race Relations: Problems and Theory.* Chapel Hill, N.C.: University of North Carolina Press, 1961.

———. "Spanish-speaking Children," in Eli Ginzberg, ed., *The Nation's Children*, pp. 78–102. New York: Columbia University Press, 1960.

———. *Spanish-speaking Groups in the United States.* Durham, N.C.: Duke University Press, 1954.

Burris, Quincy G. "Latin-Americans," in Francis J. Brown and Joseph Slabey Roucek, eds., *One America.* New York: Prentice-Hall, 1945.

California Committee for the Study of Transient Youth. *Transient Youth in California: A National, State and Rural Problem: Report and Recommendations.* Los Angeles, 1948.

California Department of Employment. *Mexican Nationals in California Agriculture, 1942–1959.* Sacramento, Calif., 1959.

California Department of the Youth Authority, Division of Research. *Characteristics of California Youth Authority Wards.* Sacramento, Calif., June 30, 1963.

———. *Employment Trends among California Youth Authority Wards on Parole, 1948–1962*, Research Report no. 34. Sacramento, Calif., Jan. 16, 1963.

———. *Characteristics of the California Youth Authority Parole Caseload.* Sacramento, Calif., 1963.

California Department of the Youth Authority, Youth and Adult Corrections Agency. *Annual Statistical Report, 1961.* Sacramento, Calif., 1962.

California, Division of Criminal Law and Enforcement. *Guide to Community Relations for Peace Officers.* Sacramento, Calif., March 31, 1958.

California, Governor's Committee to Survey the Agricultural Labor Resources of the San Joaquin Valley. *Agricultural Labor in the San Joaquin Valley: Final Report and Recommendations.* Sacramento, Calif., 1951.

California Governor's Office, Selected California Newspaper Publishers, and the State Personnel Board. *Negroes and Mexican-Americans in the California State Government*, a cooperative project conducted by the Office of Governor Edmund Brown, selected California newspaper publishers, and the State Personnel Board, 1965.

California State Committee for the Study of Transient Youth. *Transient Youth in California: Police-Minority Relations*, n.p., Aug., 1963.

California State Department of Corrections, Research Division, Administrative Statistics Section, *California Prisoners, 1960*. Sacramento, Calif., 1961.

California State Department of Education. *Teachers' Guide to the Education of Spanish-speaking Children*, Sacramento, Calif., Bulletin 21, no. 14, Oct., 1952.

———, Biennial Report, 1930–1932, Sacramento, Calif.

California State Department of Industrial Relations. *Mexicans in California*, Sacramento, Calif., 1930.

California State Department of Public Health, Bureau of Child Hygiene. *Report of the Mexican Demonstration, July 1, 1936–June 30, 1938: Maternal and Child Health Among the Mexican Groups in San Bernardino and Imperial Counties*, n.d.

———. *Report of Migratory Demonstration, July 1936–June 1937: A Study of the Health of 1,000 Children of Migratory Agricultural Workers in California*. Sacramento, Calif., n.d.

California State Fair Employment Practice Commission. *Annual Reports*, 1961–1968. Sacramento, Calif., 1961–1968.

———. *Californians of Spanish Surname*. Sacramento, Calif., May, 1964.

———. *Negroes and Mexican-Americans in South and East Los Angeles: Changes between 1960–1965 in Population, Employment, Income and Family Status*. An Analysis of a U.S. Census Survey of November, 1965. San Francisco, Calif., 1966.

California State Relief Administration. *Migratory Labor in California*. San Francisco, 1936.

Campa, Arthur L. "Spanish, Mexican, Native: The Problem of Nomenclature," in his *Spanish Folk-poetry in New Mexico*, pp. 12–16. Albuquerque, N. Mex.: University of New Mexico Press, 1946.

Case, Fred E., and James H. Kirk. *The Housing Status of Minority Families: Los Angeles, 1956*. Los Angeles, University of California, Real Estate Research Program and the Los Angeles Urban League, 1958.

Castaneda, Carlos E. *Our Catholic Heritage in Texas, 1519–1936*. Austin, Tex.: Von Boeckmann-Jones Co., 1936.

Cerwin, Herbert. *These Are the Mexicans*. New York: Reynal & Hitchcock, 1947.

Chapman, Charles E. *The History of California: The Spanish Period*. New York: The Macmillan Co., 1921.

Chavez, Fray Angelico. *Origins of New Mexico Families*. Santa Fe Historical Society of New Mexico, 1954.

Chramosta, Sharon. *Directory of Community Services in the Southwest Area of San Antonio, Texas*. San Antonio: Bishop's Committee for the Spanish-speaking, 1961.

Christian, Jane, and Chester Christian, Jr. "Spanish Language and Culture in the Southwest," in Joshua A. Fishman, ed., *Language Loyalty in the United States: The Maintenance and Perpetuation of Non-English Mother Tongues by American Ethnic and Religious Groups*, pp. 280–317. The Hague: Mouton and Co., 1966.

Citizens' Committee for the Defense of Mexican-American Youth. *The Sleepy Lagoon Case*. Los Angeles, 1942.

Clark, Elmer Talmage. *The Latin Immigrant in the South*. Nashville, Tenn.: Cokesbury Press, 1924.

Clark, Elmer Talmage, and Harvey C. Spencer. *Latin-America, U.S.A.* New York: Joint Division of Education and Cultivation, Board of Missions and Church Extension, the Methodist Church, 1942.

Clark, Margaret. *Health in the Mexican-American Culture. A Community Study*. Berkeley, Calif.: University of California Press, 1959.

Cleland, Robert Glass. "Aliens and Nomads," in his *California in Our Time*, pp. 242–264. New York: Alfred A. Knopf, 1947.

Clifford, Roy A. *The Rio Grande Flood: A Comparative Study of Border Communities in Disaster*, Disaster Study no. 7. Washington, D.C.: Committee on Disaster Studies, National Academy of Science and National Research Council, 1956.

Clinton, Ione L. *Children in Migratory Agricultural Families.* Washington, D.C.: Federal Security Agency, 1946.

Cole, Stewart G., and Mildred Wiese Cole. *Minorities and the American Promise: The Conflict of Principle and Practice.* New York: Harper & Brothers, 1954.

Coleman, Algernon. *English Teaching in the Southwest: Organization and Materials for Instructing Spanish-speaking Children.* Washington, D.C.: American Council on Education, 1940.

Collins, Henry Hill. *America's Own Refugees: Our 4,000,000 Homeless Migrants.* Princeton, N.J.: Princeton University Press, 1941.

Colorado Commission on Spanish Surnamed Citizens. *The Status of Spanish Surnamed Citizens in Colorado: Report to the Colorado General Assembly*, Jan., 1967. Greeley, Colo., 1967.

Colorado Legislative Council. *Migratory Labor in Colorado.* Report to the Colorado General Assembly, Research Publication no. 72, Dec., 1962.

Colorado State Anti-Discrimination Commission. *Seventh Annual Report: 1960–1961.* Denver, Colo., 1961.

Colorado State Department of Employment. *The Cultural Background of Spanish-speaking People*, n.p., Mar. 10, 1958.

Colorado State Department of Institutions. *A Report of Spanish-Americans in Correctional Institutions and on Parole*, n.p., 1943.

Commission on Race and Housing. *Where Shall We Live? Report of the Commission on Race and Housing.* Los Angeles and Berkeley: University of California Press, 1958.

Commission on Social and Economic Factors, Home Missions Council. *A Study of Social and Economic Factors Relating to Spanish-speaking People in the United States*, n.p., 1928.

Committee on Mexican Labor in California. *The Governor Young Report.* Sacramento, Calif., 1930.

Cooke, W. Henry. *Peoples of the Southwest.* Anti-Defamation League of B'Nai B'rith Freedom Pamphlets. New York, 1951.

Coordinator of Inter-American Affairs. *Spanish-speaking Americans in the War: The Southwest.* Washington, D.C.: Coordinator of Inter-American Affairs and Office of War Information, 1943.

Costilla County, Colorado. *Overall Economic Development Plan*, n.p., 1962.

Council of Mexican-American Affairs. Proceedings of Employment Opportunities Education Conference, sponsored by the Council of Mexican-American Affairs, n.p., Mar. 31, 1962.

Cramp, Kathryn, Louis F. Shields, and Charles A. Thomson. *Study of the Mexican Population in Imperial Valley.* New York: Council of Women for Home Missions, 1926.

Crawford, Fred R. *The Forgotten Egg: A Study of the Mental Health Problems of Mexican-American Residents in the Neighborhood of the Good Samaritan Center, San Antonio, Texas.* San Antonio, Tex.: Good Samaritan Center, 1961.

Crofoot, W. G., ed. *Flying Chips: Latin-American Presbyterianism in Texas.* Austin, Tex.: The Executive Committee of Home Missions of the Synod of Texas of the Presbyterian Church in the United States, 1949.

Curl, E. F. *Southwest Texas Methodism.* San Antonio, Tex.: Inter-Board Council of the Southwest Conference of the Methodist Church, 1951.

D'Antonio, William V., and William H. Form. *Influentials in Two Border Cities: A Study in Community Decision-making.* Notre Dame, Ind.: University of Notre Dame Press, 1965.

Davila, Jose M. *The Mexican Migration Problem.* Los Angeles: Pan Pacific Progress, 1929.

Davis, E. E. *A Report on Illiteracy in*

Texas. Bulletin no. 2328. Austin, Tex.: University of Texas, July 22, 1923.

——. *A Study of Rural Schools in Travis County, Texas.* Bulletin no. 67. Austin, Tex.: University of Texas, Dec. 1, 1916.

—— and C. T. Gray. *A Study of Rural Schools in Karnes County.* Bulletin no. 2246. Austin, Tex.: University of Texas, Dec. 8, 1922.

Davis, W. W. H. *El Gringo, or New Mexico and Her People.* Chicago: Rio Grande Press, 1962.

Dawber, Mark A. "The Mexican Immigrant," in *Our Shifting Population,* chapter 11. New York: Home Missions Council, 1941.

Delaney, Eleanor C. and George I. Sanchez, *Spanish Gold.* Macmillan Inter-American Series. New York: The Macmillan Co., 1946.

Dobie, J. Frank. *A Vaquero of the Brush Country.* Dallas: Southwest Press, 1929.

Dodson, Jack E. "Minority Group Housing in Two Texas Cities," in Nathan Glazer and Davis McEntire, eds., *Studies in Housing and Minority Groups: Special Research Report to the Commission on Race and Housing.* Los Angeles: University of California Press, 1960.

Donnelley, Thomas C. "New Mexico: An Area of Conflicting Cultures," in Thomas C. Donnelley and Arthur N. Holcombe, eds., *Rocky Mountain Politics.* Albuquerque, N. Mex.: University of New Mexico Press, 1940.

Dunne, John G. *Delano: The Story of the California Grape Strike.* New York: Farrar, Straus and Giroux, 1967.

Du Prey, Virginia H. *A Technique of a Minority Bi-lingual Group.* New York: The Macmillan Co., 1955.

Eaton, Joseph, and Kenneth Polk. *Measuring Delinquency: A Study of Probation Department Referrals.* Pittsburgh, Pa.: University of Pittsburgh Press, 1961.

Edmundson, Munro. *Los Manitos.* New Orleans: Middle American Research Institute, Tulane University, 1957.

Edwards, Alba M. *A Social-Economic Grouping of Gainful Workers of the*

United States. Washington, D.C.: U.S. Bureau of the Census, 1938.

El Paso Public Schools. *Workshop for Developing Teaching Aids for Non-English-speaking Children.* El Paso, Tex., Sept. 1945.

Federal Inter-Agency Committee. *Migrant Labor: a Human Problem.* Washington, D.C.: U.S. Department of Labor, 1947.

Federal Works Agency, Works Progress Administration, Division of Research. *Migratory Cotton Pickers in Arizona,* Washington, D.C., 1939.

Feery, Allison B. *A Planned Community for Migratory Farm Workers.* Bishops' Committee for the Spanish-speaking, San Antonio, Tex., Jan., 1962.

Feldman, Herman. "Mexicans and Indians," in his *Racial Factors in American Industry,* pp. 104–118. New York: Harper & Brothers, 1931.

Fergusson, Erna. *New Mexico: A Pageant of Three Peoples.* New York: Alfred A. Knopf, 1955.

——. *Our Southwest.* New York: Alfred A. Knopf, 1940.

Fergusson, Jarvey. *Rio Grande.* New York: William Morrow and Co., 1955.

Fisher, Lloyd H. *The Problem of Violence: Observations on Race Conflict in Los Angeles.* Chicago: American Council on Race Relations, 1946.

Fogel, Walter. *Education and Income of Mexican-Americans in the Southwest.* Advance Report 1, Mexican-American Study Project. Los Angeles: University of California, 1965.

——. *Mexican Americans in Southwest Labor Markets.* Advance Report 10, Mexican-American Study Project. Los Angeles: University of California, 1967.

Forbes, Jack. *Apache, Navaho and Spaniard.* Norman, Okla.: University of Oklahoma Press, 1960.

Frost, Joe L., and Glen R. Hawkes, eds. *The Disadvantaged Child: Issues and Innovations.* Boston: Houghton Mifflin Co., 1966.

Fuller, Elizabeth. *Mexican Housing Problems in Los Angeles.* Sociological Monograph no. 17, Los Angeles: University of Southern California, Southern California Sociological Society, 1920.

Galarza, Ernesto. *Merchants of Labor : The Mexican Bracero Story*. San Jose, Calif.: Rosicrucian Press, 1965.

———. *Strangers in Our Fields*. Washington, D.C.: Joint U.S.—Mexico Trade Union Committee, U.S. Section, 1956.

Gallardo, Lloyd. *Mexican Green Carders : Preliminary Report*. Washington, D.C.: U.S. Department of Labor, Bureau of Employment Security, July 10, 1962.

Gamio, Manuel. *The Mexican Immigrant : His Life Story*. Chicago: University of Chicago Press, 1931.

———. *Mexican Immigration to the United States*. Chicago: University of Chicago Press, 1930.

———. *Preliminary Survey of the Antecedents and Conditions of the Mexican Immigrant Population in the United States and the Formation of a Program for a Definite and Scientific Study of the Problems*. New York: Social Science Research Council, 1928.

———. *Quantitative Estimate of Sources and Distribution of Mexican Immigration into the United States*. Mexico City: Talleres Graficos, 1930.

Garber, Paul N. *The Gadsden Treaty*. Philadelphia: Philadelphia Press of the University of Pennsylvania, 1924.

Garner, Claud. *The Wetback*. New York: Coward-McCann, 1947.

Getty, Harry T. "Ethnic History of Tucson, Arizona," in Erik K. Reed and Dale S. King, eds., *For the Dean*. Santa Fe, N. Mex.: Hokoham Museum Association and Southwestern Monuments Association, 1950.

———. *Mexican Society in the Community of Tucson, Arizona*. Tucson: Arizona State Museum Library, University of Arizona, 1949.

Goldschmidt, Walter. *As You Sow*. New York: Harcourt, Brace and Co., 1947.

Goldstein, Marcus. *Demographic and Bodily Changes in Descendants of Mexican Immigrants : With Comparable Data on Parents and Children in Mexico*. Austin, Tex.: Institute of Latin-American Studies, University of Texas, 1943.

Gonzales, Isabel. *Step Children of a Nation*. New York: American Committee for Protection of the Foreign Born, 1947.

Gonzales, Jovita. "Latin-Americans," in Frances J. Brown, and Joseph Roucek, eds., *Our Racial and National Minorities : Their History, Contributions and Present Problems*, pp. 497–509. New York: Prentice-Hall, 1937.

———. *League of United Latin-American Citizens : Regulations and By-laws*. Brownsville, Tex.: Recio Brothers, 1933.

González, Nancie L. *The Spanish Americans of New Mexico : A Distinctive Heritage*. Advance Report 9, Mexican-American Study Project. Los Angeles: University of California, 1967.

Governor's Committee on Migrant Labor. *Report on Domestic Migratory Labor in Ohio*. Columbus, Ohio: Heer Printing Co., 1958.

Gray, Edward D. McQueen. "Spanish Language in New Mexico: A National Resource." *University of New Mexico Bulletin*, Sociological Series, vol. 1, no. 2, 1912.

Grebler, Leo. *Mexican Immigration to the United States : The Record and Its Implications*. Advance Report 2, Mexican-American Study Project. Los Angeles: University of California, 1966.

———. *The Schooling Gap : Signs of Progress*. Advance Report 7, Mexican-American Study Project. Los Angeles: University of California, 1967.

Greene, Shirley E. *The Education of Migrant Children : A Study of the Educational Opportunities and Experiences of Agricultural Migrants*. Washington, D.C.: Department of Rural Education, 1964.

Greer, Scott. *Last Man In*. Glencoe, Ill.: The Free Press, National Council on Agricultural Life and Labor, 1959.

Gregg, Robert. *Influence of Border Disorders on Relations Between the United States and Mexico, 1871–1910*. Baltimore: Johns Hopkins Press, 1937.

Griffith, Beatrice. *American Me*. Boston: Houghton Mifflin Co., 1948.

Group for the Advancement of Psychiatry, Committee on the Family. *Integration and Conflict in Family Behavior*. Topeka, Kans., 1964.

Guzman, Ralph. "Politics and Policies of the Mexican-American Community," in Eugene Dvorin and Arthur Misner, eds., *California Politics and Policies*, pp. 350–381. Los Angeles: Addison-Wesley, 1966.

———. *Rights Without Roots: A Study of the Loss of Citizenship by Native-born Americans of Mexican Ancestry*. Los Angeles: Fund for the Republic, Inc. and Southern California Chapter, American Civil Liberties Union, 1955 (mimeographed).

———. *The Socio-Economic Position of the Mexican-American Migrant Farm Worker*. Washington, D.C.: National Advisory Commission on Rural Poverty, 1967.

Hacker, D. B., and others. *A Study of Food Habits in New Mexico, 1949–1952*. Bulletin 384, State College, New Mexico, New Mexico A&M Agricultural Experiment Station, 1954.

Hafen, Lewis. *Colorado and Its People*. New York: Historical Publishing Co., 1948.

Haines, Helen. *History of New Mexico from the Spanish Conquest to the Present Time, 1530–1890*. New York: New Mexico Historical Publishing Co., 1891.

Handlin, Oscar. *Race and Nationality in American Life*. Boston: Little, Brown and Co., 1957.

———. *The American People in The Twentieth Century*. Cambridge University Press, 1954.

Handman, Max S. "Preliminary Report on Nationality and Delinquency: The Mexican in Texas," in *Report on Crime and the Foreign Born*, pp. 245–264. Washington, D.C.: National Commission on Law Observance and Enforcement, 1931.

Hanson, Earl. *Los Angeles County Population and Housing Data: Statistical Data from 1940 Census*. Los Angeles: Haynes Foundation, 1944.

Hanson, Robert C., and Lyle Saunders. *Nurse-Patient Communication: A Manual for Public Health Nurses in Northern New Mexico*. Santa Fe, N. Mex.: New Mexico State Department of Public Health, 1964.

Harper, Allan G., Andrew Cordova, and Kalervo Oberg. *Man and Resources in the Middle Rio Grande Valley*. Albuquerque, N. Mex.: University of New Mexico Press, 1943.

Heller, Celia Stopnicka. *Mexican-American Youth: Forgotten Youth at the Crossroads*. New York: Random House, 1966.

Henderson, Alice Corbin. *Brothers of Light: The Penitentes of the Southwest*. New York: Harcourt, Brace and Co., 1937.

Henry, Robert S. *Story of the Mexican War*. Indianapolis, Ind.: Bobbs-Merrill, 1950.

Hidalgo, Earnesto. *La Proteccion de Mexicanos en los Estados Unidos*. Mexico City: Secretaria de Relaciones Exteriores, 1940.

Hiestand, Dale L. *Economic Growth and Employment Opportunities for Minorities*. New York: Columbia Univ. Press, 1964.

Hill, George W. *Texas-Mexican Migratory Agricultural Workers in Wisconsin*. Madison, Wis.: Agricultural Experiment Station, University of Wisconsin, May, 1948.

Hill, Gladwin. "The Political Role of Mexican-Americans," in Arnold M. Rose and Caroline B. Rose, eds., *Minority Problems*. New York: Harper & Row, 1965.

Hill, Merton Earle. *The Development of an Americanization Program*. Ontario, Calif., Board of Trustees of Chaffey Junior College, 1928.

Hinman, George W. *Report of Commission on International and Interracial Factors in the Problem of Mexicans in the United States*. Philadelphia: Home Missions Council, 1927.

Hollum, William E. *The Southwest: Old and New*. New York: Alfred A. Knopf, 1961.

Holmes, Jack Ellsworth. *Party, Legislature*

and Governor in the Politics of New Mexico. Albuquerque, N. Mex.: University of New Mexico, 1967.

Horn, Calvin. New Mexico's Troubled Years: The Story of the Early Territorial Governors. Albuquerque, N. Mex.: Horn and Wallace, 1963.

Hudson, Wilson M. The Healer of Los Olmos. Dallas, Tex.: Texas Folklore Society, 1951.

Hughes, Elizabeth Ann. Living Conditions for Small-wage Earners in Chicago. Chicago: City of Chicago, Department of Public Welfare, 1925.

Hughes, Marie, and George Sanchez. Learning a New Language. Association for Childhood Education International, Bulletin 101. Washington, D.C., 1948.

Hutchinson, E. P. Immigrants and Their Children: 1850-1950. New York: John Wiley & Sons, 1956.

Inter-Agency Committee on Mexican-American Affairs. The Mexican American: A New Focus on Opportunity. Testimony Presented at the Cabinet Committee Hearings on Mexican American Affairs, El Paso, Texas, Oct. 26-28, 1967. Washington, D.C., n.d.

Jaco, E. Gartley. "Mental Health of the Spanish-American in Texas," in Marvin K. Opler, ed., Culture and Mental Health, pp. 467-488. New York: The Macmillan Co., 1959.

Johnson, Elizabeth S. Welfare of Families of Sugar Beet Laborers. Washington, D.C.: U.S. Department of Labor, Children's Bureau, 1939.

Johnston, Edgar G. The Education of Children of Spanish-speaking Migrants in Michigan. Paper of the Michigan Academy of Science, Arts and Letters, vol. 32, 1946.

Jones, Robert C. Mexican War Workers in the United States: The Mexico-United States Manpower Recruiting Program, 1942-1944. Washington, D.C.: Pan American Union, 1945.

Jones, Robert, and Louis R. Wilson. The Mexican in Chicago. Chicago: Comity Commission of the Chicago Church Federation, 1931.

Karpas, Melvin R. Mexican-American and Cultural Deprivation. Chicago: Chicago Teachers College, Juvenile Delinquency Research Projects, 1963-1964.

Karracker, Cyrus H. Agricultural Seasonal Laborers of Colorado and California. Pennsylvania Citizens Committee on Migrant Labor, n.p., n.d.

Kelley, Arthur Randolph. Physical Anthropology of a Mexican Population in Texas: A Study in Race Mixture. New Orleans: Middle American Research Institute, Tulane University, 1947.

Key, V. O. Southern Politics, pp. 271-274, 614-615. New York: Random House, 1949.

Kibbe, Pauline R. "The Economic Plight of Mexicans," in E. C. McDonough and E. S. Richards, eds., Ethnic Relations in the United States, pp. 189-200. New York: Appleton-Century-Crofts, 1953.

———. Latin-Americans in Texas. Albuquerque, N. Mex.: University of New Mexico Press, 1946.

Kingrea, Nellie W. History of the First Ten Years of the Texas Good Neighbor Commission. Fort Worth, Tex.: Texas Christian University Press, 1954.

Kluckhohn, Florence, and Fred Strodtback. Variation in Value Orientation. Evanston, Ill.: Row, Peterson & Co., 1961.

Koch, Helen L., and Rietta Simmons. A Comparative Study of the Performance of White, Mexican and Negro School Children in Certain Standard Intelligence Tests, vol. 4, part 2, pp. 193-233. Austin, Tex.: Texas Educational Survey Commission, 1925.

——— and ———. "A Study of the Test Performance of American, Mexican, and Negro Children," Psychological Monographs, vol. 35, no. 5, 1926.

Larson, Olaf L. Beet Workers on Relief in Weld County, Colorado. Fort Collins, Colo.: Works Progress Administration, Division of Social Research, Rural Section, Colorado State Experimental Station, 1937.

League of United Latin-American Citizens. *Lulac in Action: A Report on the "Little School of the 400."* n.p., 1960.

Lemert, Edwin M., and Judy Rosberg. *The Administration of Justice to Minority Groups in Los Angeles County.* University of California Publications in Culture and Society, vol. 2, no. 1. Berkeley, Calif.: University of California Press, 1948.

Leonard, Olen, and Charles P. Loomis. *Culture of a Contemporary Rural Community: El Cerrito, New Mexico.* Washington, D.C.: U.S. Department of Agriculture, 1938.

——— and———. *Standards of Living in an Indian-Mexican Village on a Reclamation Project.* Washington, D.C.: U.S. Department of Agriculture, 1938.

Little, Wilson. *Spanish-speaking Children in Texas.* Austin, Tex.: University of Texas Press, 1944.

Lobart, Edward. *The Career of Dennis Chavez as a Member of Congress, 1930–1934.* Albuquerque, N. Mex.: University of New Mexico Press, 1958.

Lockwood, George. *Supplement to Manual of Immigration: Spanish Personal Names.* New York: U.S. Immigration and Naturalization Service, 1936.

Loomis, Charles. *Social Relationships and Institutions in Seven New Rural Communities.* Social Research Report XVIII. Washington, D.C.: U.S. Department of Agriculture, Farm Security Administration and Bureau of Agricultural Economics, 1940.

Lopez, Lino M., ed. *Colorado Latin-American Personalities.* Denver: A. M. Printing Co., 1959.

Los Angeles County, Commission on Human Relations. *The Urban Reality: A Comparative Study of the Socioeconomic Situation of Mexican-Americans, Negroes, and Anglo-Caucasians in Los Angeles County.* Los Angeles, 1965.

Los Angeles County Committee on Human Relations. *Survey of Medical Care Facilities for Minority Groups.* Prepared by Dale Gardner. Los Angeles, Dec., 1946.

Los Angeles County Probation Office

Summary of Recommendations and Progress to Date of the Special Committee on Older Youth Gang Activity in Los Angeles and Vicinity: Statistical Report of Juvenile Delinquency Among Children of Latin-American Ancestry. Prepared by Robert Scott. Los Angeles, Dec. 28, 1942.

Los Angeles County Tuberculosis and Health Association, Social Studies Division. *Tuberculosis High Incidence Area: Focus at Central Los Angeles.* Los Angeles, June, 1947.

Lummis, Charles Fletcher. *Spanish Songs of Old California.* Los Angeles: C. F. Lummis, 1923.

McClatchy, V. S. *Increase in Mexican Population.* Bulletin no. 316. San Francisco: California Joint Immigration Committee, 1933.

McCleneghan, Thomas J., and Charles R. Gildersleeve. *Land Use Contrasts in a Border Economy.* Special Study no. 23, Bureau of Business and Public Research, Tucson, Ariz.: University of Arizona, June, 1964.

McCombs, V. M. *From Over the Border.* New York: Council of Women for Home Missions, 1925.

McConnell, Weston Joseph. *Social Cleavages in Texas: A Study of the Proposed Division of the State.* New York: Columbia University, 1925.

MacCurdy, Raymond R. *A History and Bibliography of Spanish-language Newspapers and Magazines in Louisiana, 1808–1949.* Albuquerque, N. Mex.: University of New Mexico Press, 1951.

McDonagh, Edward C., and Eugene S. Richards. "Mexicans," in their *Ethnic Relations in the United States,* pp. 174–189. New York: Appleton-Century-Crofts, 1953.

McDowell, John. *A Study of Social and Economic Factors Relating to Spanish-speaking People in the United States.* Philadelphia: Home Missions Council, 1927.

McEntire, Davis. *Leisure Activities of Youth in Berkeley, California.* Berkeley, Calif.: Council of Social Welfare and University of California, 1952.

————. *The Population of California : A Report of a Research Study Made by Authorization of the Board of Governors of the Commonwealth Club of California.* San Francisco: The Commonwealth Club, 1946.

————. *The Problem of Segregation.* San Francisco: American Council on Race Relations, 1946.

————. *Residence and Race: Final and Comprehensive Report to the Commission on Race and Housing.* Berkeley, Calif.: University of California Press, 1960.

McLean, Robert M. *The Northern Mexican.* New York: Home Missions Council, 1930.

————. *That Mexican.* New York, Fleming H. Revell Co., 1928.

McLean, Robert N., and Charles A. Thomson. *Spanish and Mexican in Colorado: A Survey of the Spanish Americans and Mexicans in the State of Colorado.* New York: Board of National Missions of the Presbyterian Church in the U.S.A., Department of City Immigration and Industrial Works, 1924.

————. and Grace Williams. *Old Spain in New America.* Issued by the Council of Women for Home Missions. New York: Associated Press, 1916.

McWilliams, Carey. *Factories in the Field.* Boston: Little, Brown and Co., 1934.

————. "The Forgotten Mexican," in his *Brothers Under the Skin.* Boston: Little, Brown and Co., 1944.

————. *Ill Fares the Land: Migrants and Migratory Labor in the United States.* Boston: Little, Brown and Co., 1942.

————. *North from Mexico: the Spanish-speaking People of the United States.* New York: J. B. Lippincott Co., 1949.

Madsen, William. *The Mexican-Americans of South Texas.* San Francisco: Holt, Rinehart and Winston, 1964.

————. *Society and Health in the Lower Rio Grande Valley.* Austin, Tex.: Hogg Foundation for Mental Health, 1961.

Manuel, Herschel T., *The Education of Mexican and Spanish-speaking Children in Texas.* Austin, Tex.: University of Texas, 1930.

————. *The Preparation and Evaluation of Inter-language Testing Materials.* Cooperative Research Project no. 681. Austin, Tex.: University of Texas, 1963.

————. *Spanish and English Editions of Stanford-Binet in Relation to the Abilities of Mexican Children.* Austin, Tex.: University of Texas, 1935.

————. *Spanish-speaking Children of the Southwest: Their Education and the Public Welfare.* Austin, Tex.: University of Texas Press, 1965.

Marcus, Lloyd. *The Treatment of Minorities in Secondary School Textbooks.* New York: Anti-Defamation League, 1961.

Marden, Charles F. *Minorities in American Society.* New York: American Book Co., 1952.

Marden, Charles F., and Gladys Meyer. *Minorities in American Society.* Second ed. New York: American Book Co., 1962.

Martin, Roscoe C. *The Defendant and Criminal Justice.* Study no. 9. Austin: Bureau of Research in the Social Sciences, University of Texas, 1934.

Martinez, Rafael V. *My House is Your House.* New York: Friendship Press, Jan., 1964.

Martyn, Kenneth A. *Increasing Opportunities for Disadvantaged Students: A Report Prepared for the Coordinating Council on Higher Education.* Sacramento, Calif., 1967.

————. *Report on Education to the Governor's Commission on the Los Angeles Riots.* Los Angeles, 1965.

Mead, Margaret, ed. *Cultural Patterns and Technical Change.* Paris: United Nations Educational, Scientific, and Cultural Organization, 1953.

Menefee, Seldon C. *Mexican Migratory Workers of South Texas.* Washington, D.C.: U.S. Works Progress Administration, 1941.

———— and Orin C. Cassmore. *The Pecan Shellers of San Antonio,* Washington, D.C.: Works Progress Administration, Division of Research, 1940.

Merrill, John Calhoun. *Gringo: The*

American as Seen by Mexican Journalists. Gainesville, Fla.: University of Florida Press, 1963.

Metzler, William H., and Frederic Sargent. *Incomes of Migratory Agricultural Workers.* Bulletin 950. College Station, Tex.: Texas Agricultural Station, Mar., 1960.

Mexico, Departmento de Informacion para el Extranjero. *Advice to the Mexican Laborers Who Go to the United States.* Contracted by the War Food Administration. Mexico, 1944.

Mexico, Department of State For Foreign Affairs, Bureau of International News Service, by C. R. Stevenson and Ezequiel Padilla. *The Good Neighbor Policy and Mexicans in Texas.* Mexico, D.F., National and International Problems Series, no. 17, 1943.

Meyers, Frederic. *Spanish-name Persons in the Labor Force in Manufacturing Industry in Texas.* Inter-American Education Occasional Papers, VIII. Austin, Tex.: University of Texas, 1951.

Minnesota, Governor's Interracial Commission. "The Mexican in Minnesota," in *Race Relations in Minnesota,* Reports of the Commission. St. Paul, Minn., 1948 and 1953.

Mittelbach, Frank G. and Grace Marshall. *The Burden of Poverty.* Advance Report 5, Mexican-American Study Project. Los Angeles: University of California, 1966.

————, Joan W. Moore, and Ronald McDaniel. *Inter-marriage of Mexican-Americans.* Advance Report 6, Mexican-American Study Project. Los Angeles: University of California at Los Angeles, 1966.

Montiel, Olvera J., Ed. *Year Book of the Latin-American Population of Texas.* Mexico City: Published by the author, 1939.

Moore, Joan W., and Frank G. Mittelbach. *Residential Segregation in the Urban Southwest.* Advance Report 4, Mexican-American Study Project. Los Angeles: University of California, 1966.

Morgan, Patricia. *Shame of a Nation: A Documented Story of Police-state Terror Against Mexican-Americans in the U.S.A.* Los Angeles: Los Angeles Committee for the Protection of Foreign Born, 1954.

Morin, Raul. *Among the Valiant.* Alhambra, Calif.: Borden Publishing Co., 1963.

Morton, John A. *The Mexican-American in School and Society.* Los Angeles: Los Angeles State College, Institute for American Studies, n.d.

Moustafa, Taher A., and Gertrud Weiss. *Health Status and Practices of Mexican Americans.* Advance Report 11, Mexican-American Study Project, Los Angeles: University of California at Los Angeles, 1968.

Murray, Sister M. J. *A Socio-cultural Study of 118 Mexican Families Living in a Low Rent Housing Project in San Antonio, Texas.* Washington, D.C.: Catholic University of America Press, 1954.

National Catholic Welfare Council, Department of Social Action. *The Spanish-speaking of the Southwest and West.* Washington, D.C., 1944.

National Commission on Law Observance and Enforcement, U.S. Report on Crime and the Foreign Born, Publication no. 10, Washington, D.C., 1931. *Part III, Mexican Immigrant, Section II, The Mexican in Texas.*

National Conference on Educational Opportunities for Mexican Americans. *Proceedings, April 25–26, 1968.* Austin, Tex.: Southwest Educational Development Laboratory, n.d.

National Council for the Spanish-speaking. *1964 National Council for the Spanish-speaking: Its Needs . . . Its Goals . . . Its Program.* n.p., 1964.

————. *Résumé of the Villa Coronado Study,* n.p., 1964.

National Opinion Research Center. *The Spanish-speaking Population of Denver: Housing, Employment, Health, Recreation, Education.* Denver, Colo.: Denver Unity Council, 1946.

O'Brien, Robert. *Survey on Mexicans and*

Crime in Southern California, 1926–1927. Claremont, Calif.: Lawson Roberts Publishing Co., 1928.

Ortega, Joaquin. *The Compulsory Teaching of Spanish in the Grade Schools of New Mexico: An Expression of Opinion.* Albuquerque, N. Mex.: University of New Mexico Press, 1941.

Ortiz, Martin. *The Mexican-American in the Los Angeles Community.* Community Intelligence Bulletin no. 3. Los Angeles: Community Relations Educational Foundation, Nov., 1963.

Otero, Miguel Antonio. *My Nine Years as Governor of the Territory of New Mexico, 1897–1906.* Albuquerque, N. Mex.: University of New Mexico Press, 1940.

Otero, Nina. *Old Spain in Our Southwest.* New York: Harcourt, Brace and Co., 1936.

Oxnam, G. Bromley. *The Mexican in Los Angeles: Los Angeles City Survey.* Interchurch World Movement of North America, n.p., 1920.

Padfield, Harland, and William E. Martin. *Farmers, Workers and Machines: Technological and Social Change in Farm Industries of Arizona.* Tucson, Ariz.: University of Arizona Press, 1965.

Palomares, U. H., and Emery J. Cummins. *Assessments of Rural Mexican-American Pupils: Preschool and Grades One Through Six: San Ysidro, California.* Sacramento, Calif.: California State Department of Education, Mexican American Research Project, 1968.

Panunzio, Constantine. *How Mexicans Earn and Live.* A Study of the Incomes and Expenditures of One Hundred Mexican Families in San Diego, California, by the Heller Committee for Research in Social Economics. Berkeley, Calif.: University of California Publications in Economics, vol. 13, no. 1, 1933.

Paredes, Americo. *With His Pistol in His Hand.* Austin, Tex.: University of Texas Press, 1958.

Parker, Carleton. *The Casual Laborer and Other Essays.* New York: Harcourt, Brace and Howe, 1920.

Paschall, F. C., and Louis R. Sullivan. "Racial Differences in the Mental and Physical Development of Mexican Children." *Comparative Psychological Monograph no. 3,* 1926.

——— and———. *Racial Influences in the Mental and Physical Development of Mexican Children.* Baltimore: Williams and Wilkins, 1925.

Patric, Gladys Emelia. *A Study of Housing and Social Conditions in the Ann Street District of Los Angeles, California.* Los Angeles Society for the Study and Prevention of Tuberculosis, 1917.

Peak, Horace. "Search for Identity by a Young Mexican-American," in his *Clinical Studies in Culture Conflict.* New York: Ronald Press Co., 1958.

Peixotto, Ernest Clifford. *Our Hispanic Southwest.* New York: Charles Scribner's Sons, 1916.

Perales, Alonso S., Comp. *Are We Good Neighbors?* San Antonio, Tex.: Artes Graficas, 1948.

———. *El Mexico Americano y Politica del Sur de Texas.* San Antonio, Tex.: n.p., 1931.

Perrigo, Lynn I. *Our Spanish Southwest.* Dallas: Banks Upshaw and Co., 1960.

Perry, Everett L. *Presbyterian U.S.A. Educational Work in New Mexico.* New York: Board of National Missions of the Presbyterian Church in the U.S.A., Field Office Survey, Nov., 1957.

Perry, Louis B., and Richard S. Perry. *A History of the Los Angeles Labor Movement, 1911–1941.* Los Angeles: University of California Press, 1963.

Pesotta, Rose. *Bread Upon the Waters.* New York: Mead and Co., 1944.

Peyton, Green. *San Antonio: City in the Sun.* New York: McGraw-Hill, 1946.

Pijoan, Michel. *Certain Factors Involved in the Struggle Against Malnutrition and Disease.* Albuquerque, N. Mex.: University of New Mexico Press, 1943.

———, and R. W. Roskelley. *Nutrition and Certain Related Factors of Spanish-Americans in Northern Colorado.* Denver, Colo.: Rocky Mountain Council on Inter-American Affairs, 1943.

Pitt, Leonard. *The Decline of the Californios: A Social History of the Spanish-speaking Californians, 1846–1890.* Los Angeles: University of California Press, 1966.

Potter, Marguerite. *Grass Roots Diplomat.* Leo Potisham Foundation, Texas Christian University, n. p., 1961.

Presbyterian Church in the United States, Synod of Texas, and Interim Committee on Latin-American Work. *Latin-American–Presbyterian Churches in Texas.* Austin, Tex., 1952.

President's Commission on Migratory Labor. *Migratory Labor in American Agriculture.* Washington, D.C., 1951.

Pueblo Regional Planning Commission. *The Socio-economic and Physical Characteristics of the Various Neighborhoods in Pueblo.* Pueblo, Colo., Mar., 1965.

Pulse, Inc. *A Pulse Report: The Spanish Market.* Survey conducted for the National Spanish Language Network, n.p., June, 1962.

Rademaker, John A. *These Are Americans.* Palo Alto, Calif.: Pacific Books, 1951.

Rahm, Harold J., and J. Robert Weber. *Office in the Alley: Report on a Project with Gang Youngsters.* Austin, Tex.: Hogg Foundation for Mental Health, University of Texas Printing Division, 1958.

Rak, Mary Kidder. *Border Patrol.* Boston: Houghton Mifflin Co., 1938.

Record, Wilson. *Minority Groups and Intergroup Relations in the San Francisco Bay Area.* Berkeley: University of California at Berkeley, Institute of Governmental Studies, 1963.

Reid, J. T. *It Happened in Taos.* Albuquerque, N. Mex.: University of New Mexico Press, 1946.

Reynolds, Annie. *The Education of Spanish-speaking Children in Five Southwestern States.* Bulletin no. 11. Washington, D.C.: Office of Education, U.S. Department of the Interior, 1933.

Riggings, Rachel T. *Educational Background of Spanish-American Students in Tucson Public Schools.* Tucson, Ariz.: University of Arizona, 1947.

Robertson, Jack. *A Study of the Youth Needs and Services in Dallas, Texas.* Washington, D.C.: American Youth Commission, 1938.

Robinson, Cecil. *With the Ears of Strangers: The Mexican in American Literature.* Tucson, Ariz.: University of Arizona Press, 1963.

Rose, Arnold M., ed., *Race Prejudice and Discrimination: Readings in Intergroup Relations in the United States.* New York: Alfred A. Knopf, 1951.

——, and Caroline Rose. "Mexicans and Other Latins," in their *America Divided*, pp. 50–53. New York: Alfred A. Knopf, 1953.

Rosenquist, Carl M., and Walter G. Browder. *Family Mobility in Dallas, Texas, 1923–1938.* Austin, Tex.: University of Texas, 1942.

—— and——. *Family Mobility in Houston, Texas, 1922–1938.* Austin, Tex.: University of Texas, 1942.

Roskelley, R. W. *Beet Labor in Colorado.* Fort Collins, Colo.: Colorado State Agricultural College, 1940.

Rubel, Arthur J. *Across the Tracks: Mexican-Americans in a Texas City.* Austin, Tex.: University of Texas Press, 1966.

Rusinar, Irving. *A Camera Report on El Cerrito, A Typical Spanish-American Community in New Mexico*, Misc. Publication no. 479. Washington, D.C.: U.S. Dept. of Agriculture, Bureau of Agricultural Economics, 1942.

Salinas, José Lazaro. *La Emigracion de Braceros.* Mexico City: "Cauh Temoc," 1955.

Samora, Julian, ed. *La Raza: Forgotten Americans.* Notre Dame, Ind.: University of Notre Dame Press, 1966.

——. "The General Status of the Spanish-speaking People in the Southwest", in *Summary of Proceedings of the Southwest Conference on "Social and Educational Problems of Rural and Urban Mexican-American Youth,"* sponsored by the Rosenberg Foundation at Occidental College, Apr. 6, 1963.

—— and Richard A. Lamanna. *Mexi-*

can-Americans in a Midwest Metropolis: A Study of East Chicago. Advance Report 8, Mexican-American Study Project. Los Angeles: University of California, at Los Angeles, 1967.

San Antonio City Planning Department. Economic Base Study of San Antonio and Twenty-seven County Areas. San Antonio, Tex., Apr., 1964.

San Antonio Housing Authority. San Antonio Housing Survey. San Antonio, Tex., 1939.

San Antonio Social Welfare Association, Educational Committee on Relief Needs. 8,000 Families Go Hungry Today in San Antonio. San Antonio, Tex., n.d.

Sanchez, George I. Concerning Segregation of Spanish-speaking Children in the Public Schools. Inter-American Education Occasional Papers, IX. Austin, Tex.: University of Texas, Dec., 1951.

———. The Equalization of Educational Opportunity—Some Issues and Problems. New Mexico University Bulletin, Educational Series, vol. 10, no. 1. Albuquerque, New Mexico, 1939.

———. Forgotten People: A Study of New Mexicans. Albuquerque, N. Mex.: University of New Mexico Press, 1940.

———. "Spanish in the Southwest," in Summary of the Proceedings of the Southwest Conference on Social and Educational Problems of Rural and Urban Mexican-American Youth, sponsored by the Rosenberg Foundation at Occidental College, Apr. 6, 1963.

Santibanez, Enrique. Ensayo Acerca de la Inmigracion Mexicana en los Estados Unidos. San Antonio, Tex.: The Clegg Co., 1930.

Saunders, Lyle. Anglos and Spanish-speaking: Contrasts and Similarities. Denver, Colo.: University of Colorado School of Medicine, 1959.

———. Cultural Differences and Medical Care: The Case of the Spanish-speaking People of the Southwest. New York: Russell Sage Foundation, 1954.

———. "Healing Ways in the Spanish Southwest," in E. Gartley Jaco, ed., Patients, Physicians and Illness, pp.

189–206. Glencoe, Ill.: The Free Press, 1958.

———. The Spanish-speaking Population of Texas. Austin, Tex.: University of Texas Press, 1949.

——— and Julian Samora. "A Medical Care Program for Colorado County," in Benjamin D. Paul, ed., Health, Culture and Community: Case Studies of Public Reactions to Health Programs. New York: Russell Sage Foundation, 1956.

——— and Olin E. Leonard. The Wetback in the Lower Rio Grande Valley of Texas. Inter-American Education Occasional Papers (III). Austin, Tex.: University of Texas Press, 1951.

Schermerhorn, R. A. "Mexicans and Spanish-speaking Americans: A Mixed Culture," in his These Our People: Minorities in American Culture, chap. 9, pp. 175–198. Boston: D. C. Heath and Co., 1949.

Schrieke, B. Alien Americans. New York: The Viking Press, 1936.

Scotford, John R. Within these Borders: Spanish-speaking Peoples in the U.S.A. New York: Friendship Press, 1953.

Seckel, Joachim P. Employment and Employability Among California Youth Authority Wards: A Survey. Research Report no. 30. Department of the Youth Authority, Division of Research, Sacramento, Calif., Aug. 21, 1962.

Shannon, Lyle W. The Assimilation and Acculturation of Migrants to Urban Areas. n.p., University of Wisconsin Urban Program, 1963.

Shevky, Eshref, and Marilyn Williams. Social Areas of Los Angeles. Berkeley, Calif.: University of California Press, 1949.

Sickels, Alice L., and Henry L. Sickels. The Mexican Nationality Community in St. Paul in February, 1935. St. Paul, Minn.: International Institute, 1935.

Simpson, George E., and J. Milton Yinger. "Mexican-American Children in the Public Schools," in their Racial and Cultural Minorities, pp. 565–573. New York, Harper & Brothers, 1953.

Simpson, L. S., *Many Mexicos*. Berkeley, Calif.: University of California Press, 1967.

Skrabanek, R. L. *A Decade of Population Change in Texas*. College Station, Tex.: Texas Agricultural Experiment Station, Sept., 1963.

Smith, Howard E. Proceedings of the U.S.–Mexico Border Health Conference, Ciudad Juarez, Chihuahua, Mexico, and El Paso, Texas, May 30–June 1, 1944.

Smith, Justin. *The Annexation of Texas*. New York: Barnes & Noble, 1941.

Social Welfare and Fact-Finding Committee. *Starvation in San Antonio*. San Antonio, Tex., 1940.

Sorenson, Roy. *Recreation for Everybody: A Community Plan for Recreation and Youth Service for Los Angeles*. Report of a survey conducted by the community surveys associated under the auspices of Community Chests and Councils, Inc., for the Welfare Council of Metropolitan Los Angeles, June 1, 1946.

Soukup, James R., Clifton McClesky, and Harry Holloway. *Party and Factional Division in Texas*. Austin, Tex.: University of Texas Press, 1964.

Southwest Texas State Teachers College. *Art Activities for Latin-American Children in Elementary Grades*. San Marcos, Tex., 1944.

———. *Building Better School-Community Relations in Latin-American Communities*. San Marcos, Tex., 1944.

Spicer, Edward. *Pasqua: A Yaqui Village in Arizona*. Chicago: University of Chicago Press, 1940.

Stambaugh, J. Lee, and Lillian J. *The Lower Rio Grande Valley of Texas*. San Antonio, Tex.: The Naylor Co., 1954.

Stegner, Wallace. *One Nation*. Boston: Houghton Mifflin Co., Riverside Press, 1945.

Steiner, Edward Alfred. *On the Trail of the Immigrant*. New York: F. H. Revell, 1906.

Steiner, Paul E. *Cancer, Race and Geography: Etiological, Environmental, Ethnological, Epidemiological and Statistical Aspects*. Baltimore: Williams and Wilkins Co., 1954.

Stephenson, Nathaniel W. *Texas and the Mexican War*. New Haven, Conn.: Yale University Press, 1921.

Stilwell, Hart. *Border City*. London: Hurst & Blackett, 1945.

Stowell, J. S. *The Near-side of the Mexican Question*. New York: Home Missions Council, 1921.

———. *A Study of Mexicans and Spanish-Americans in the United States*. New York Home Missions Council, 1920.

Sullivan, Mary, and Bertha Blair. *Women in Texas Industries*. Women's Bureau Bulletin no. 126. Washington, D.C.: U.S. Department of Labor, 1936.

Talbert, Robert H. *Spanish-name People in the Southwest and West*. Fort Worth, Tex.: Potishman Foundation, Texas Christian University, 1955.

Tanner, Myrtle L. *Handbook: Good Neighbor Commission of Texas*. Austin, Tex.: Good Neighbor Comm., 1954.

Taylor Paul S. *An American-Mexican Frontier*. Chapel Hill, N.C.: University of North Carolina Press, 1934.

———. "Crime and the Foreign-born: The Problem of the Mexican," in *Report on Crime and the Foreign-born*, pp. 199–244. Washington, D.C.: National Commission on Law Observance and Enforcement, 1931.

———. *Mexican Labor in the United States: Bethlehem, Pennsylvania*. Berkeley, Cal.: University of California Publications in Economics, vol. 7, no. 1, 1930.

———. *Mexican Labor in the United States: Chicago and the Calumet Region*. Berkeley, Cal.: University of California Publications in Economics, vol. 7, no. 2, 1932.

———. *Mexican Labor in the United States: Dimit County, Winter Garden District, South Texas*. Berkeley, Cal.: University of California Publications in Economics, vol. 6, no. 5, 1930.

———. *Mexican Labor in the United States: Imperial Valley*. Berkeley, Cal.: University of California Publications in Economics, vol. 6, no. 1, 1928.

———. *Mexican Labor in the United States: Migration Statistics, part 1.* Berkeley, Cal.: University of California Publications in Economics, vol. 6, no. 3, 1929.

———. *Ibid.*, part 2, vol. 12, no. 1, 1933.

———. *Ibid.*, part 3, vol. 12, no. 2, 1933.

———. *Ibid.*, part 4, vol. 12, no. 3, 1934.

———. *Mexican Labor in the United States: Racial School Statistics.* Vol. 6, no. 4. Berkeley and Los Angeles: University of California Publications in Economics, University of California Press, 1929.

———. *Mexican Labor in the United States: Valley of the South Platte-Colorado.* Berkeley, Calif.: University of California Publications in Economics, vol. 6, no. 2, 1929.

———. "Songs of the Mexican Migration," in Frank J. Dobie, ed., *Puro Mexicano*, pp. 221–245. Austin, Tex.: Texas Folk-Lore Society, 1935.

Texas State Department of Education. *State-wide Survey of Enumeration, Enrollment, Attendance and Progress of Latin-American Children in Texas Public Schools.* Austin, Tex., 1943–1944.

Texas State Department of Health, Division of Maternal and Child Health. *The Latin-American Health Problem in Texas.* Austin, Tex., Aug., 1940.

Texas State Department of Health, Division of Mental Health. *A Study of the Mental Health Problems of Mexican-American Residents.* Austin, Tex., 1961.

Texas Education Agency, Division of Research. *Report of Pupils in Texas Public Schools Having Spanish Surnames, 1955–1956.* Austin, Tex., 1957.

Texas Good Neighbor Commission, Austin. *Texas: Friend and Neighbor.* Austin, Tex.: Von Boeckmann-Jones, 1961.

Texas State Department of Health. *Latin-American Health Problems in Texas.* Austin, Tex., 1940.

Thadden, J. F. *Migratory Beet Workers in Michigan.* Agricultural Experiment Station Special Bulletin no. 319, Michigan State College, 1942.

Thomas, E. L. *Latin-American Markets for Soaps and Soap Ingredients.* Trade Promotion Series no. 121. Washington, D.C.: U.S. Department of Commerce, 1961.

Thomas, Howard E., and Florence Taylor. *Migrant Farm Labor in Colorado: A Study of Migratory Families.* New York: National Child Labor Committee, 1951.

Tireman, Lloyd Spencer. *Spanish Vocabulary of Four Spanish-speaking Pre-first-grade Children.* Albuquerque, N. Mex.: University of New Mexico Press, 1948.

———. *Teaching Spanish-speaking Children.* Albuquerque, N. Mex.: University of New Mexico Press, 1948.

——— and Mary Watson. *Report of Nambe Community School.* Albuquerque, N. Mex.: University of New Mexico Press, 1943.

Topete, Jesus. *Aventuras de un Bracero.* Mexico City: Editora Grafia Moderna, S.A., 1961.

Towe, Emily. *Methodism and Latin-Americans in the United States.* New York: Board of Missions and Church Extension of the Methodist Church, 1949.

El Tratado de Guadalupe Hidalgo 1848—Treaty of Guadalupe Hidalgo: A Facsimile Reproduction of the Mexican Instrument of Ratification and Related Documents. Telefact Foundation in cooperation with the California State Department of Education, 1968.

Tuck, Ruth D. *Not with the Fist: Mexican-Americans in a Southwest City.* New York: Harcourt, Brace and Co., 1956.

Ulibarri, Horacio. *The Effect of Cultural Differences in the Education of Spanish-Americans.* Albuquerque, N. Mex.: University of New Mexico, 1958.

U.S. Bureau of the Census. "Characteristics of the South and East Los Angeles Areas: November, 1965." *Current Population Reports*, Series P–23, no. 18, Washington, D.C., 1966.

———. "Mother Tongue of the Foreign-Born White Population," in *Fifteenth Census of the United States: 1930*, vol. 2, chap. 7. Washington, D.C.: United

States Government Printing Office, 1932.

———. *Nativity and Parentage of the White Population: Mother Tongue by Nativity, Parentage, Country of Origin, and Age for States and Large Cities, Part of Sixteenth Census of the United States.* Washington, United States Government Printing Office, 1943.

———. *Population of Spanish Mother Tongue. Part of Sixteenth Census of the United States: 1940 Population.* Washington, Government Printing Office, 1942.

———. *Special Report on Foreign-Born White Families by Country of Birth of Head with an Appendix Giving Statistics for Mexican, etc., Families. Part of Fifteenth Census of the United States: 1930 Population,* Washington, Government Printing Office, 1933.

U.S. Bureau of Employment Security, Farm Placement Service. *Information Concerning Entry of Mexican Agricultural Workers into the United States.* Washington, D.C., 1952.

United States Civil Service Commission. "Mexican-American and Total Employment in Selected States and Standard Metropolitan Statistical Areas," Part of *Study of Minority Group Employment in the Federal Government.* Prepared for the President's Committee on Equal Employment Opportunity, June, 1963.

———. "Spanish-speaking and Total Employment in Selected Agencies," in *Study of Minority Group Employment in the Federal Government.* Prepared for the President's Committee on Equal Employment Opportunity, June, 1963.

U.S. Commission on Civil Rights. *The Concentration of Spanish Surname Persons in the Five Southwestern States.* Washington, D.C., 1962.

———. *The 50 State Report Submitted to the Commission on Civil Rights by the State Advisory Committees, 1961.* Washington, D.C., 1961.

———. *Hearings before the U.S. Commission on Civil Rights, Feb. 3, 1962, held in Phoenix, Arizona.* Washington, D.C., 1962.

———. *Hearings in Los Angeles and San Francisco Before the U.S. Commission on Civil Rights (Jan., 1960).* Washington, D.C., 1960.

U.S. Commission on Civil Rights, California Advisory Committee. *Police Minority Group Relations in Los Angeles and the San Francisco Bay Area.* Washington, D.C., 1963.

U.S. Congress, House. Immigration and Naturalization Committee. *Seasonal Agricultural Laborers from Mexico, Hearing,* 69th Congress, 1st Session, Jan. 28–Feb. 23, 1926, on H.R. 6741, H.R. 7559, H.R. 9036, 1926. Hearing No. 691.

———. *Immigration from Latin America, The West Indies, and Canada: Hearings before Subcommittee on Immigration and Naturalization,* 83rd Congress, 2nd session on S.3660 and S.3661, July 12–14, 1954.

U.S. Congress, House. Committee on Education and Labor, *Report on the Farm Labor Transportation Accident at Chailar, California, on September 17, 1963.* 88th Congress, second session, Washington, D.C., 1964.

U.S. Congress, Senate. Committee on the Judiciary. *To Control Illegal Migration. Hearings Before the Subcommittee on Immigration and Naturalization of the Committee on the Judiciary.* Senate Documents 3660 and 3661, 83rd Congress, second session, July 12–14, 1954.

U.S. Department of Agriculture. *Preliminary Report on Concho.* Regional Bulletin no. 29, Conservation Economics Series no. 2. Albuquerque, N. Mex., 1935.

———. *Village Dependence on Migratory Labor in the Upper Rio Grande Area.* Regional Bulletin no. 47, Conservation Economics Series no. 20, n.p. 1937.

———. Economic Surveys Division, vol. II. *The Spanish-American Villages.* Tewa Basin Study, Albuquerque, N. Mex., 1939.

U.S. Department of Agriculture, Soil Conservation Service. *Destruction of Villages at San Marcial.* Regional

Bulletin no. 38, Conservation Economics Series no. 11, Albuquerque, N. Mex., 1937.

U.S. Department of Labor, Bureau of Labor Statistics. "Mexican Families in Los Angeles," in *Money Disbursements of Wage Earners and Clerical Workers in Five Cities in the Pacific Coast Region, 1934–1936*, pp. 85–109. Washington, D.C., 1939.

U.S. Immigration Commission. *Immigrants in Industries* (in 25 parts), part 25, vol. 3. Washington, D.C., 1911.

U.S. Inter-Agency Committee on Mexican American Affairs. *The Mexican American: A New Focus on Opportunity*. El Paso, Tex., Oct. 26–28, 1967. Washington, D.C., 1968.

U.S. Office of Education. *Learning English Incidently: A Study of Bi-lingual Children*. Bulletin 1937, no. 15. Washington, D.C., 1938.

———. *Young Spanish-speaking Children in our Schools*. Elementary Education Series no. 30. Washington, D.C., 1951.

U.S. Treasury Department. *Immigration into the United States from 1820 to 1930*. Washington, D.C., 1930.

University of New Mexico. *Barelos Community Center Social Training Program*. Albuquerque, N. Mex., 1942.

University of Texas, Bureau of Business Research. *Comparison of Family Income and Expenditures for Five Principal Budget Items in Twenty Texas Cities*. Austin, Tex., Apr., 1943.

University of Texas, Bureau of Research in the Social Sciences. *Population Mobility in Austin, Texas, 1929–1931*. Austin, Tex.: University of Texas Press, 1941.

———. *Texas' Children: The Report of the Texas Child Welfare Survey*. Austin, Tex., 1938.

University of Texas, Department of Government, Election Research Project Committees. *Texas Votes: Selected General and Special Election Statistics, 1944–1963*. Austin, Tex., 1964.

Valdes, Daniel T. *The Spanish-speaking People of the Southwest*. Bulletin WE-4.

Denver, Colo.: Works Progress Administration Program of Education and Recreation of the Colorado State Department of Education, 1938.

Van der Erden, Sister Lucia M. *Maternity Care in a Spanish-American Community of New Mexico*. Anthropological Series 13. Washington, D.C.: Catholic University of America Press, 1948.

Vander Zanden, James Wilfred. *American Minority Relations: The Sociology of Race and Ethnic Groups*. New York: Ronald Press Co., 1963.

Vickery, William E., and Stewart G. Cole. *Intercultural Education in American Schools*. New York: Harper & Brothers, 1943.

Walter, Paul, Jr. *Population Trends in New Mexico*. Albuquerque, N. Mex.: University of New Mexico, Department of Government, Division of Research, Publication no. 10, 1947.

Walter, Paul A. G., Jr. *Race and Cultural Relations*, pp. 325–341. New York: McGraw-Hill Book Co., 1952.

———. and Ross Calvin. *The Population of New Mexico*. Albuquerque, N. Mex.: University of New Mexico Press, 1947.

Warnships, Paul L. "Crime and Criminal Justice Among the Mexicans of Illinois," in *Report on Crime and the Foreign-Born*, pp. 265–329. Washington, D.C.: National Commission on Law Observance and Enforcement, 1931.

Watson, Walter T. "Mexicans in Dallas," in S. D. Meyers, Jr., ed., *Mexico and the United States*, pp. 231–250. Dallas: Institute of Public Affairs, Southern Methodist University, 1938.

Webb, Walter Prescott. *The Texas Rangers: A Century of Frontier Defense*. Austin, Tex.: University of Texas Press, 1965.

Weeks, O. Douglas. *Texas Presidential Politics in 1952*. Austin, Tex.: Institute of Public Affairs, University of Texas, 1953.

Weschler, Louis F., and John F. Gallagher. "Viva Kennedy," in Rocco J. Tressolini and Richard T. Frost, eds., *Cases in American National Government and*

Politics, pp. 51–61. Englewood Cliffs, N.J.: Prentice-Hall, 1966.

Wharburton, Amber A., Helen Wood, and Marian Crane. *The Work and Welfare of Children of Agricultural Laborers in Hidalgo County, Texas*. Publication 298. Washington, D.C.: U.S. Department of Labor, Children's Bureau, 1943.

White House Conference. "The Mexican In California," *White House Conference on Child Health and Protection of Dependent and Neglected Children*, Section 4. New York: D. Appleton-Century Co., 1933.

Wiley, Tom. *Public School Education In New Mexico*. Albuquerque, N. Mex.: University of New Mexico, Division of Government Research, 1965.

Winters, Jet C. *A Report on the Health and Nutrition of Mexicans Living in Texas*. Study no. 2. Austin, Tex.: University of Texas, Bureau of Research in the Social Sciences, 1931.

Witacre, Jessie. *The Diet of Texas School Children*. Bulletin 489. College Station, Tex.: Texas A&M Agricultural Experiment Station, 1934.

———. *Some Body Measurements of Texas School Children*. Bulletin 567, College Station, Tex.: Texas A & M Agricultural Experiment Station, 1939.

Wood, L. D. *Manual for Summer Workers*. San Antonio, Tex.: Convencion Boutista Mexicana de Texas, 1952.

Woods, Sister Frances J. *Cultural Values of American Ethnic Groups*. New York: Harper & Brothers, 1956.

———. *Mexican Ethnic Leadership in San Antonio, Texas*. Washington, D.C.: Catholic University of America Press, 1949.

Works, G. A. "The Non-English Speaking Children and the Public School," in *Texas Educational Survey Report*, vol. 8, pp. 207–226. Austin, Tex.: Texas Education Survey Commission, 1925.

Young, Donald. *Research Memorandum on Minority Peoples in the Depression*. Bulletin No. 31. New York: Social Science Research Council, 1937.

Young, Kimball. *Mental Differences in Certain Immigrant Groups*. Eugene, Ore.: University of Oregon Publications, vol 1, no. 11, 1922.

II. JOURNAL ARTICLES

"Across the Tracks." *Time*, 42:25 (Sept. 6, 1943).

Albig, William. "Opinions Concerning Unskilled Mexican Immigrants." *Sociology and Social Research*, 15:62–72 (Sept., 1930).

Alexander, L. "Texas Helps Her Little Latins." *Saturday Evening Post*, 243:30–31 (Aug. 5, 1961).

Alisky, Marvin. "The Mexican-Americans Make Themselves Heard." *Reporter*, 36:45–48 (Feb. 9, 1967).

Allen, Gary. "The Grapes: Communist Wrath in Delano." *American Opinion*, 9:1–14 (June, 1966).

Allen, Ruth A. "Mexican Peon Women in Texas." *Sociology and Social Research*, 16:131–142 (Nov., 1931).

Almazan, Marco A. "The Mexicans Keep 'em Rolling." *Inter-American*, 4:20+ (Oct, 1945).

Altus, William D. "The American Mexican: The Survival of a Culture." *Journal of Social Psychology*, 29:211–220 (May, 1949).

Alvarado, E. M. "Mexican Immigration to the United States." *Proceedings of National Conference of Social Work*, 1930:479–480.

Alvarez, Jose Hernandez. "A Demographic Profile of the Mexican Immigration to the United States, 1910–1950." *Journal of Inter-American Studies*, 8:471–496 (July, 1966).

Americana Corporation. "Our Minority Groups: 2. Spanish-speaking People."

Building America, vol. 8, no. 5 (1943).

Andrus, Ethel Percy. "Workshop Studies —Education of Mexican-Americans," *California Journal of Secondary Education*, 18:328–330 (Oct. 1943).

"Another Civil-rights Headache: Plight of Mexican-Americans, Los Angeles." *U.S. News and World Report*, 60:46–48 (June 6, 1966).

Applegate, Betty. "Los Hermanos Penitentes." *Southwest Review*, 17:100–107 (1931).

Aragon, Manuel. "Their Heritage—Poverty." *Agenda*, 2:9–13 (July, 1966).

Arias, Ronald. "The Barrio." *Agenda*, 2:15–20 (July, 1966).

Armour, D. T. "Problems in the Education of the Mexican Child." *Texas Outlook*, 16:29–31 (Dec., 1932).

Arnold, R. D. "English as a Second Language." *Reading Teacher*, 21:634–639 (Apr., 1968).

Austin, Mary Hunter. "Mexicans and New Mexico." *Survey Graphic*, 66:141–144, 187–190 (May, 1931).

"Authentic Pachuco." *Time*, 44:72 (July 10, 1944).

Bailey, Wilfred C. "Problems in Relocating the People of Zapata, Texas." *Texas Journal of Science*, 7:20–37 (Mar., 1955).

Bamford, Edwin F. "Industrialization and the Mexican Casual." *Proceedings of Southwestern Political and Social Science Association*, Austin, Tex., Mar., 1924.

———. "Mexican Casual Labor Problem in the Southwest." *Journal of Applied Sociology*, 8:363–371 (July, 1924).

Banay, Ralph S. "A Psychiatrist Looks at the Zoot Suit." *Probation*, 22:81–85 (Feb., 1944).

Barker, George C. "Growing up in a Bilingual Community." *Kiva*, vol. 17, nos. 1–2 (Nov.–Dec., 1951).

———. "Social Functions of Language in a Mexican-American Community." *Acta Americana*, 5:185–202 (July–Sept., 1947).

Batten, James H. "The Mexican Immigration Problem." *Pan Pacific Progress*, 8:39+ (1928).

———. "Mexico's Program: An Opportunity." *World Tomorrow*, 12:36–39 (Jan., 1929).

———. "New Features of Mexican Immigration: The Case Against Further Restrictive Legislation." *Pacific Affairs*, 3:956–966 (Oct., 1930).

Beals, Ralph. "Culture Patterns of Mexican-American Life." *Proceedings of the Fifth Annual Conference on Education of Spanish-speaking Peoples*, George Pepperdine College, Los Angeles, Calif., 1951.

Beegle, J. Allan, Harold F. Goldsmith, and Charles Y. Loomis. "Demographic Characteristics of the United States–Mexican Border." *Rural Sociology*, 25:106–162 (Mar., 1960).

Beshoar, Barron B. "Report from the Mountain States." *Common Ground*, 4:22–30 (spring, 1944).

Biddick, Mildred L., and Esther A. Harrison, "Helping Spanish-American Children Achieve Status." *Intercultural Education News*, 8:1 + (winter, 1947).

Blair, William C. "Spanish-speaking Minorities in a Utah Mining Town." *Journal of Social Issues*, 8, no. 1:4–9 (1952).

Blatt, G. T. "The Mexican-American in Children's Literature." *Elementary English*, 45:446–451 (Apr., 1968).

Bloch, Louis. "Facts About Mexican Immigration Before and Since the Quota Restriction Laws." *Journal of the American Statistical Association*, 24:50–60 (Mar., 1929).

Blumenfeld, A. A. "Effects of New Mexico's Social and Economic Structure upon Governmental Expenditures." *New Mexico Business*, 14:3–10 (Aug., 1961).

———. "Trends in Personal Income in New Mexico and the United States." *New Mexico Business*, vol. 14:3–12 (Oct., 1961).

Bogardus, E. S. "Changes in Racial Distances." *International Journal of Opinion and Attitude Research*, 1:58 (Dec., 1947).

———. "Current Problems of Mexican Immigrants." *Sociology and Social Research*, 25:166–174 (Nov., 1940).

———. "Gangs of Mexican-American Youth." *Sociology and Social Research*, 28:55–66 (Sept., 1943).

———. "The Mexican Immigrant." *Journal of Applied Sociology*, 11:470–488 (May, 1927).

———. "The Mexican Immigrant and the Quota." *Sociology and Social Research*, 12:371–378 (Mar., 1928).

———. "The Mexican Immigrant and Segregation." *American Journal of Sociology*, 13:74–80 (July, 1930).

———. "Mexican Repatriates." *Sociology and Social Research*, 18:169–176 (Nov., 1933).

———. "Race Reactions by Sexes." *Sociology and Social Research*, 43:439–443 (July, 1959).

———. "Racial Distance Changes in the United States During the Past Thirty Years." *Sociology and Social Research*, 43:127–137 (Nov., 1958).

———. "Racial Reactions by Regions." *Sociology and Social Research*, 43:286–290 (Mar., 1959).

———. "Resident Immigrant Problem." *Proceedings of the Institute of International Relations, Fifth Session*, Los Angeles, 1930, pp. 196–197.

———. "Second Generation Mexicans." *Sociology and Social Research*, 13:276–283 (Jan., 1929).

Bogen, David. "Concerning Zoot Suit Gangs." *Community Coordination*, 11:1–3 (Jan.–Feb., 1943).

Borah, Woodrow, and Sherburne F. Cook. "Marriage and Legitimacy in Mexican Culture: Mexico and California." *California Law Review*, 54:946–1008 (May, 1966).

Bostwick, Prudence. "They Speak the Same Language." *Progressive Education*, 19:26–28 (Jan., 1942).

Boyd, D. L. "Bilingualism as an Educational Objective." *Educational Forum*, 32:309–313 (Mar., 1968).

Braddy, H. "Pachucos and Their Argot." *Southern Folk-lore Quarterly*, 24:255–271 (Dec., 1960).

Bradford, H. F. "The Mexican Child ... In Our American Schools." *Arizona Teacher-Parent*, 27:198–199 (Mar., 1939).

Branigan, J. "Education of Over-age Mexican Children." *Sierra Educational News*, 29:25–29 (Dec., 1929).

Bratt, Charles. "Profiles: Los Angeles," in "Race Relations on the Pacific Coast." *Journal of Educational Sociology*, 19:179–186 (Nov., 1945).

Bratten, James H. "The Mexican Immigration Problem." *Pan Pacific Progress*, 8:39–52 (1928).

Britton, Gertrude Howe, and Kate Constable. "Analysis of Mexican Patients at Chicago Dispensary." *Nation's Health*, July, 1925, p. 453.

Broadbent, Elizabeth. "Mexican Population in Southwestern United States." *Texas Geographic Magazine*, vol. 5, no. 2 (1941).

Brookshire, Marjorie S. "Some Notes on the Integration of Mexican-Americans Since 1929, Nueces County, Texas." *Industrial Relations Research Association Annual Proceedings*, 1955, pp. 356–361.

Broom, Leonard, and E. Shevky. "Mexicans in the United States." *Sociology and Social Research*, 36:150–158 (Jan., 1952).

Broom, M. E. "Sex and Race Differences Discovered by Certain Mental Tests." *El Paso School Standard*, 16:29–32 (Nov., 1938).

Brown, Edwin R. "The Challenge of Mexican Immigration." *Missionary Review of the World*, 49:192–196 (Mar., 1926).

Browning, Harley L., and S. Dale McLemore. "The Spanish Surname Population of Texas." *Public Affairs Comment*, Institute of Public Affairs, University of Texas, vol. 10, no. 1 (Jan., 1964).

Bryan, Samuel. "Mexican Immigrants in the United States." *Survey*, 28:726–730 (Sept., 1912).

Buechley, Robert W. "A Reproducible Method of Counting Persons of Spanish Surname," *Journal of the American Statistical Association*, 56:88–97 (Mar., 1961).

———, John E. Dunn, George Linden,

and Lester Breslow. "Excess Lung-Cancer-Mortality Rates Among Mexican Women in California." *Cancer*, 10:63–66 (Feb., 1957).

Bullock, Paul. "Combating Discrimination in Employment." *California Management Review*, 3:18–32 (summer, 1961).

———. "Employment Problems of the Mexican-American." *Industrial Relations*, 3:37–50 (May, 1964).

——— and Robert Singleton. "The Minority Child and the Schools." *Progressive*, 26:33–36 (Nov., 1962).

——— and ———. "What To Do with the Drop-out?" *New Republic*, 147:17–18 (Oct. 20, 1962).

Burbeck, Edith. "Problems Presented to Teachers of Bi-lingual Pupils." *California Journal of Elementary Education*, 8:49–54 (Aug., 1939).

Burgess, Rev. Thomas. "On the American Side of the Rio Grande." *Missionary Review of the World*, 50:689–692 (Sept., 1927).

Burma, John H. "Interethnic Marriage in Los Angeles, 1948–1959." *Social Forces*, 42:156–165 (Dec., 1963).

———. "The Present Status of the Spanish-Americans in New Mexico." *Social Forces*, 28:133–138 (Dec., 1949).

———. "Research Note on the Measurement of Interracial Marriage." *American Journal of Sociology*, 57:587–589 (May, 1952).

——— and Janet Jorgenson. "The Push of an Elbow; Civil Rights and Our Spanish-speaking Minority." *Frontier*, 11:10–12 (July, 1960).

Burnhill, James. "The Mexican People in the Southwest." *Political Affairs*, 32:43–52 (Sept., 1953).

———. "The Mexican-American Question." *Political Affairs*, 32:50–63 (Dec., 1953).

Burris, Quincy Guy. "Institute of the Air." *New Mexico School Review*, Sept., 1943, pp. 4, 5.

———. "Juan, a Rural Portrait." *Survey Graphic*, 33:499–503 (Dec., 1944).

Busey, J. L. "The Political Geography of Mexican Migration." *Colorado*

Quarterly, 2:181–190 (autumn, 1953).

Cabrera, Y. A. "Schizophrenia in the Southwest, Mexican Americans in Anglo-land." *Claremont Reading Conference Yearbook*. 31:101–106 (1967).

Caldwell, Floyd F., and M. D. Mowry. "Sex Difference in School Achievement Among Spanish-American and Anglo-American Children." *Journal of Educational Sociology*, 8:168–173 (Nov., 1934).

——— and ———. "Teacher Grades as Criteria of Achievement of Bilingual Children." *Journal of Applied Psychology*, 18:288–292 (Apr., 1934).

California Department of Public Health. "Health of Mexicans in California." *Weekly Bulletin*, 17:105–106 (July, 1938).

Callcott, Frank. "The Mexican Peon in Texas." *Survey*, 44:437–438 (June 26, 1920),

Camblon, Ruth. "Mexicans in Chicago." *Family*, 7:207–211 (Nov., 1926).

Campa, Arthur L. "Mañana is Today." *New Mexico Quarterly Review*, 9:3–11 (Feb., 1939).

Carl, May. "Our Anti-social Mexican Class." *Los Angeles County Employee*, 2:12+ (1929).

Carlson, Helding S., and Norman Henderson. "Intelligence of American Children of Mexican Parentage." *Journal of Abnormal and Social Psychology*, 45:544–551 (Apr., 1952).

Carlson, Olen E. "Community Organization Turns a Corner." *Sociology and Social Research*, 32:782–786 (Mar., 1948).

Carpenter, W. "Ferment in the Lettuce Fields in Imperial Valley." *Nation*, vol. 180, Apr. 9, 1955, inside cover.

Carter, Hugh, and Bernice Doster. "Residence and Occupation of Naturalized Americans from Mexico." *U.S. Immigration and Naturalization Service Monthly Review*, 8:47–53 (Oct., 1950).

——— and ———. "Social Characteristics of Aliens from the Southwest Registered for Selective Service During World War II." *U.S. Immigration and*

Naturalization Service Monthly Review, 8:88–94 (Jan., 1951).

———— and ————. "Social Characteristics of Naturalized Americans from Mexico: Age and Marital Status." *U.S. Immigration and Naturalization Service Monthly Review*, 8:35–39 (Sept., 1950).

Carter, T. P. "Negative Self Concepts of Mexican American Students." *School and Society*, 96:217–219 (Mar. 30, 1968).

Chambers, R. L. "The New Mexico Pattern." *Common Ground*, 9:20–27 (summer, 1949).

"Child Labor and the Work of Mothers in the Beet-Sugar Industry." *School and Society*, 17:554–556 (May 19, 1923).

Clark, Margaret. "Social Functions of Mexican-American Medical Beliefs." *California's Health*, 16:153–155 (May, 1959).

Clark, Victor. "Mexican Labor in the U.S." *Labor Bulletin no. 78*, U.S. Dept. of Commerce, 17:466–522 (1908).

Coalson, George O. "Mexican Contract Labor in American Agriculture." *Southwestern Social Science Quarterly*, 33:228–238 (Dec., 1952).

Coers, W. C. "Comparative Achievement of White and Mexican High School Pupils." *Peabody Journal of Education*, 12:157–162 (Jan., 1934).

Cohn, J. "Integration of Spanish-speaking Newcomers in a Fringe Area School." *National Elementary Principal*, 39:29–33 (May, 1960).

Coindreau, Josephine. "Teaching English to Spanish-speaking Children." *National Elementary Principal*, 25:40–44 (June, 1946).

"Concentrations of Foreign Stock in the United States." *Congressional Quarterly*, 14:49–55 (Sept. 28, 1956).

Conway, T. F. "The Bi-lingual Problem in the Schools of New Mexico." *Alianza*, 36:13+ (Feb., 1942).

Cook, J. M., and Grace Arthur. "Intelligence Rating of 97 Mexican Children in St. Paul." *Journal of Exceptional Children*, 18:14–15 (Oct., 1951).

Cooke, W. Henry. "The Segregation of Mexican-American School Children in Southern California." *School and Society*, 67:417–421 (June 5, 1948).

Cordasco, F. M. "Challenge of the Non-English-speaking Child in American Schools." *School and Society*, 96:198–201 (Mar. 30, 1968).

Cox, I. J. "The Early Settlers of San Fernando." *Texas State Historical Association Quarterly*, 5:142–160 (Oct., 1901).

Crawford, W. Rex. "The Latin-American in Wartime United States." *Annals of the American Academy of Political and Social Science*, 223:123–131 (Sept., 1942).

Culbert, James I. "Distribution of Spanish-American Population in New Mexico." *Economic Geography*, 19:171–176 (Apr., 1943).

D'Antonio, William V., and Eugene C. Erickson. "The Reputational Technique as a Measure of Community Power: An Evaluation Based on Comparative and Longitudinal Studies." *American Sociological Review*, 27:362–375 (June, 1962).

———— and Julian Samora. "Occupational Stratification in Four Southwestern Communities: A Study of Ethnic Differential Employment in Hospitals." *Social Forces*, 41:17–25 (Oct., 1962).

————, William H. Form, Charles Loomis, and Eugene C. Erickson. "Institutional and Occupational Representations in Eleven Community Influence Systems." *American Sociological Review*, 26:440–446 (June, 1961).

Darcy, Natalie T. "A Review of the Literature on the Effects of Bi-lingualism upon the Measurement of Intelligence." *Journal of Genetic Psychology*, 82:21–57 (1953).

Daustin, Helen. "Bettering Inter-American Relations in One Small Elementary School." *California Journal of Elementary Education*, 12:107–111 (Nov., 1943)

Davenport, E. L. "The Intelligence Quotients of Mexican and non-Mexican Siblings." *School and Society*, 36:304–306 (Sept. 3, 1932).

Davidson, Cecelia Ragovsky. "Mexican Laborers Imported into the United

States." *Interpreter Releases*, 20:298–300 (Oct. 18, 1943).

Davis, Harold E. "Education Program for Spanish-speaking Americans." *World Affairs*, 8:43–48 (Mar., 1945).

Davis, Kingsley, and Clarence Senior. "Immigration from the Western Hemisphere." *Annals of the American Academy of Political and Social Science*, 262: 70–81 (Mar., 1949).

Davis, Thomas M. "Assessments During the Mexican War: An Exercise in Futility." *New Mexico Historical Review*, 41:197–216 (1966).

Dawson, Joseph Martin. "Among the Mexicans in Texas." *Missionary Review of the World*, 50:757–758 (Oct., 1927).

De Huff, Elizabeth Willis. "People of the Soil." *New Mexico Magazine*, 18:26+ (June, 1940).

de La Rose, L. "Ministry of Public Health and Welfare of Mexico on Sanitary Problems of Mexicans Living in the United States." *Boletin de la Oficina Sanitaria Panamericana*, Washington, D.C., 27:752–755 (Aug., 1948).

De Leon, Marcos. "Wanted: A New Educational Philosophy for the Mexican-American." *California Journal of Secondary Education*, vol. 34:398–402 (Nov., 1959).

Delmet, D. T. "Study of the Mental and Scholastic Abilities of Mexican Children in the Elementary School." *Journal of Juvenile Research*, 14:267–279 (Oct., 1930).

Demos, George D. "Attitudes of Mexican-Americans and Anglo Groups Toward Education." *Journal of Social Psychology*, 57:249–256 (Aug., 1962).

De Vargas, D. "Teaching Mexicans an English Vocabulary." *Elementary English Review*, 14:31 (Jan., 1937).

Dickerson, R. E. "Some Suggestive Problems in the Americanization of Mexicans." *Pedagogical Seminary*, 26: 288–297 (Sept., 1919).

Dobie, J. Frank. "The Mexican Vaquero of the Texas Border," *Southwestern Political and Social Science Quarterly*, 8: 15–26 (June, 1927).

———. "Ranch Mexicans." *Survey Graphic*, 66:167–170 (May, 1931).

Donnelley, Thomas C. "Educational Progress in New Mexico and Some Present Problems." *New Mexico Quarterly Review*, 16: 305–317 (autumn, 1946).

Dotson, Floyd. "Decrease of the Mexican Population in the U.S. According to the 1950 Census." *Mexican Sociological Review*, vol. 17, 1955.

Drolet, Godias J. "Discussion of Paper Presented by Benjamin Goldberg, M.D., on 'Tuberculosis in Racial Types with Special Reference to Mexicans.'" *American Journal of Public Health*, 19:285–286 (Mar., 1929).

Dublin, Louis I. "The Mortality from Tuberculosis Among the Racial Stocks in the Southwest." *American Review of Tuberculosis*, 45:61–74 (Jan., 1942).

Dworkin, Anthony Gary. "Stereotypes and Self-images Held by Native-born and Foreign-born Mexican-Americans." *Sociology and Social Research*, 49:214–224 (Jan., 1965).

Dymek, D. T. "Spanish Students." *Sierra Educational News*, 34:20 (Nov., 1938).

"Education for Spanish-American Children in San Antonio, Texas." *School and Society*, 50:824 (Dec. 23, 1939).

Ellis, John M. "Mortality Differentials for a Spanish-surname Population Group." *Southwestern Social Science Quarterly*, 39: 314–321 (Mar., 1959).

———. "Spanish Surname Mortality Differences in San Antonio, Texas." *Journal of Health and Human Behavior*, vol. 3, no. 2 (summer, 1962).

Emch, Tom. "The Two 'Ls'—Latins, Labor and Two Young Men from McAllen," in *The Valley Story*. Special issue of the *Houston Chronicle*, Dec. 1, 1963, pp. 12–14.

———. "There's a Restlessness Along the River, A Stirring of New Life," in *ibid*.

Encisco, F. B. "Rights and Duties of a Mexican Child." *Progressive Education*, 13:123 (Feb., 1936).

Erickson, E. H. "Concept of Identity in Race Relations: Notes and Queries."

Daedalus, 95:145–171 (winter, 1966).

Eulau, Heinz F. "Sinarquismo in the U.S.A." *Mexican Life*, 20:17+ (May 1, 1944).

Faltis, J. "Understanding Our Student of Mexican Extraction." *California Teachers Association Journal*, 47:11 (Feb., 1951).

"Farm Workers Map Fight." *American Federationist*, 58:5, (Dec., 1951).

Fergusson, Erna. "New Mexico's Mexicans." *Century* 116:437–444 (Aug., 1928).

———. "The New New Mexico." *New Mexico Quarterly Review*, 19:417–426 (winter, 1949).

"Few Spanish-speaking Children in High School in Southwest." *School and Society*, 94:376+ (Nov. 12, 1966).

Fisher, Reginald. "Hispanic People of the Rio Grande: A Statement of a Program of Research Being Planned in the Conservation of Human Resources." *El Palacio*, 49:157–162 (1942).

Forbes, Jack D. "Race and Color in Mexican-American Problems." *Journal of Human Relations*, 16:55–68 (first quarter, 1968).

Form, William, and William D'Antonio. "Integration and Cleavage Among Community Influentials in Two Border Cities." *American Sociological Review*, 24:804-814 (Dec., 1959).

Foster, George M. "Relationships Between Spanish and Spanish-American Folk Medicine." *Journal of American Folklore*, 66:201–217 (July, 1953).

———. "Relationships Between Theoretical and Applied Anthropology: A Public Health Program Analysis." *Human Organization*, 11, no. 3: 5–16 (1952).

———. "Working with People of Different Cultural Backgrounds." *California's Health*, 13: 107–110 (Jan., 1956).

Francesca, Sister M. "Variations of Selected Cultural Patterns Among Three Generations of Mexicans in San Antonio, Texas." *American Catholic Sociological Review*, 19:24–34 (Mar., 1958).

Francis, E. K. "Multiple Intergroup Relations in the Upper Rio Grande Region." *American Sociological Review*, 21:84–87 (Feb., 1956).

Frank, Eva A. "The Mexicans Simply Won't Work." *Nation*, 125:155–157 (Aug. 17, 1927).

Frazier, E. Franklin. "Ethnic and Minority Groups in Wartime, with Special Reference to the Negro." *American Journal of Sociology*, 48: 369–377 (Nov., 1942).

Fuller, Roden. "Occupations of the Mexican-born Population of Texas, New Mexico, and Arizona, 1900–1920." *Journal of the American Statistical Association*, 23:64–74 (Mar., 1928).

Galarza, Ernesto. "Big Farm Strike at the Di Giorgio's," *Commonweal*, 48:178–182 (June 4, 1948).

———. "Life in the United States for Mexican People: Out of the Experience of a Mexican." *National Conference of Social Work Proceedings of 1929*, 1929: 399–404.

———. "Mexican Ethnic Group." *California Elementary School Principals' Association, 17th Yearbook*, 1945, pp. 34–35.

———. "Program for Action." *Common Ground*, 9, no. 4:27–38 (summer, 1949).

———. "They Work for Pennies." *American Federationist*, 59:10–13 (Apr., 1952).

———. "Without Benefit of Lobby," *Survey*, 66:181 (May 1, 1931).

Gamble, Leo M. "The Mexican: An Educational Asset or an Educational Liability." *Educational Research Bulletin*, Dec., 1925, pp. 9–12.

Gamblon, Ruth S. "Mexicans in Chicago," *Family*, 7:207–211 (Nov., 1926).

Gamio, Manuel. "Migration and Planning." *Survey Graphic*, 66:174–175 (May 1, 1931).

Garnett, William E. "Immediate and Pressing Race Problems of Texas." *Proceedings of the Southwestern Political and Social Science Association*, Austin, Tex., 1925, pp. 31–48.

Garretson, O. K. "A Study of Causes of Retardation among Mexican Children in a Small Public School System in

Arizona." *Journal of Educational Psychology*, 19:31–40 (Jan., 1928).

Garth, Thomas R. "A Comparison of the Intelligence of Mexican and Mixed and Full Blood Indian Children." *Psychological Review*, 30: 388–401(1923).

———. "The Industrial Psychology of the Immigrant Mexican." *Industrial Psychology*, 1:183–187 (1926).

———. "The Intelligence of Mexican School Children." *School and Society*, 27:791–794 (June 30, 1928).

——— and E. Candor. "Musical Talent of Mexicans." *American Journal of Psychology*, 49:298–301 (Apr., 1937).

——— and Harper D. Johnson. "The Intelligence and Achievement of Mexican Children in the United States." *Journal of Abnormal and Social Psychology*, 29:222–229 (July, 1934).

———, T. H. Elson, and M. N. Morton. "The Administration of Non-language Intelligence Tests to Mexicans." *Journal of Abnormal and Social Psychology*, 31: 53–58 (Apr. 1936).

———, W. M. Holcomb, and I. Gosche, "Mental Fatigue of Mexican School Children." *Journal of Applied Psychology*, 15: 675–680 (Dec., 1932).

Gilbert, F. de B. "New Mexican Diets." *Journal of Home Economics*, 34:668–669 (Nov., 1942).

Gill, L. J. and B. Spilka. "Some Non-intellectual Correlates of Academic Achievement Among Mexican-American Secondary School Students." *Journal of Educational Psychology*, 53:144–149 (June, 1962).

Gillin, John. "Magical Fright." *Psychiatry*, 11: 387–400 (1948).

Gilmore, N. R. and G. W. Gilmore. "Bracero in California." *Pacific Historical Review*, 32:265–282 (Aug., 1963).

Ginsburg, Ruth. "A New Program in Spanish for Los Angeles." *California Journal of Secondary Education*, 18: 347–348 (Oct. 1943).

Goldberg, Benjamin. "Tuberculosis in Racial Types with Special Reference to Mexicans." *American Journal of Public Health*, 19:274–286 (Mar., 1929).

Goldschmidt, Walter R. "Class Denominationalism in Rural California Churches." *American Journal of Sociology*, 49:348–355 (Jan., 1944).

Gonzales, Eugene. "Mexican-American in California." *California Education*, 3:19–22 (Nov., 1965).

———. "Mexican-American Parents Respond to Bilingual Questionnaires." *California Education*, 3:10+ (Sept., 1965).

Gonzales, M. C. "Our Spanish-speaking Parent-Teacher Groups and Their Problems." *Texas Outlook*, 27:23–24 (June, 1943).

Gonzalez, Jovita. "The Americans Invade the Border Towns." *Southwest Review*, 15:469–477 (summer, 1930).

Gould, David M. "Mass X-ray in San Antonio." *Public Health Reports*, 60: 117–126 (Feb. 2, 1945).

Granneberg, A., "Maury Maverick's San Antonio." *Survey Graphic*, 28:420–426 (July, 1939).

Grebler, Leo. "The Naturalization of Mexican Immigrants in the United States." *International Migration Review*, 1:17–32 (fall, 1966).

Green, William. "Our Own Forgotten People." *American Federationist*, 57: 20–22 (Dec., 1950).

Greer, Scott. "Situational Pressures and Functional Role of the Ethnic Labor Leader." *Social Forces*, 32:41–45 (Oct., 1953).

Gregg, R. "Medical Examination and Vaccination of Farm Laborers Recruited from Mexico." *Public Health Reports*, 65: 807–809 (June 23, 1950).

Griffiths, Beatrice W. "The Pachuco Patois." *Common Ground*, 7 no. 4:77–84 (summer, 1947).

———. "Viva Roybal—Viva America." *Common Ground*, 10 no. 1:61–70 (autumn, 1949).

Guerra, M. H. "Why Juanito Doesn't Read." *California Teachers Association Journal*, 61:17–19 (Oct., 1965).

Guzman, Ralph. "The Hand of Esau: Words Change, Practices Remain in Racial Covenants." *Frontier*, 7:7+ (June, 1956).

———. "How El Centro Ended Segregation." *Frontier*, 7:13+ (Feb., 1956).

———. "Mexican-Americans on the Move." *Agenda*, 2:2–8 (July, 1966).

——— and Joan Moore. "The Mexican-Americans: New Wind from the Southwest." *Nation*, 202: 645–648 (May 30, 1966).

Gwin, J. B. "Immigration Along our Southwest Border." *Annals of the American Academy of Political and Social Science*, 93:126–130 (Jan., 1921).

———. "Social Problems of Our Mexican Population." *Proceedings of the National Conference of Social Work*, 1926:327–332.

Hadley, Eleanor M. "A Critical Analysis of the Wetback Problem." *Law and Contemporary Problems*, 21:334–357 (spring, 1956).

Hall, Martin. "400,000 Mexican-American Voters." *Chicago Jewish Forum*, 14:19–25 (fall, 1955).

———. "Roybal's Candidacy and What It Means." *Frontier*, 5:5–7 (June, 1954).

Handman, Max S. "Economic Reasons for the Coming of the Mexican Immigrant." *American Journal of Sociology*, 35:601–611 (Jan., 1930).

———. "The Mexican Immigrant in Texas." *Southwestern Political and Social Science Quarterly*, 7:33–40 (June, 1926).

———. "Nationality and Delinquency: The Mexicans in Texas." *Proceedings of the National Conference of Social Work*, 1930:133–145.

———. "San Antonio: The Old Capital City of Mexican Life and Influence." *Survey*, 6: 163–166 (May 1, 1931).

Hanna, Agnes K. "Social Services on the Mexican Border." *Proceedings of the National Conference of Social Work*, 1935: 692–702.

Hanson, Robert C. "The Systematic Linkage Hypothesis and Role Consensus Patterns in Hospital-Community Relations." *American Sociological Review*, 27:304–313 (June, 1962).

——— and Mary J. Beech. "Communicating Health Arguments Across Cultures." *Nursing Research*, 12 (fall, 1963).

Harby, L. C. "Texan Types and Contrasts." *Harpers*, 81:229–246 (July, 1890).

Harvey, Louise F. "Delinquent Mexican Boy." *Journal of Educational Research*, 42:573–585 (Apr., 1948).

Haught, B. F. "The Language Difficulty of Spanish-American Children." *Journal of Applied Psychology*, 15: 92–95 (Feb., 1931).

Hawley, Florence, and Donovan Senter. "Group Designed Behavior Patterns in Two Acculturating Groups." *Southwest Journal of Anthropology*, 2: 133–151 (1949).

Hayes, Edward F. "Operation Wetback: Impact on the Border States." *Employment Security Review*, 22:16–21 (Mar., 1955).

Hayne, Coe. "Studying Mexican Relations at El Paso." *Missionary Review*, 50: 110–112 (Feb., 1927).

Heald, J. H. "Mexicans in the Southwest." *Missionary Review*, 42:860–65 (Nov., 1919).

Heer, David M. "The Marital Status of Second Generation Americans." *American Sociological Review*, 26:233–241 (Apr., 1961).

Heffernan, Helen. "Some Solutions to the Problems of Students of Mexican Descent." *National Association of Secondary School Principals*, 39:43–53 (Mar., 1955).

Heffernan, Helen, ed. *Teacher Guide to the Education of Spanish-speaking Children*. Bulletin of the California State Department of Education, vol. 21, no. 14, Sacramento, Calif., 1952.

Heller, C. A. "Regional Patterns of Dietary Deficiency: Spanish-Americans of New Mexico and Arizona." *Annals of the American Academy of Political and Social Science*, 225:49–51 (Jan., 1943).

Hernandez, Juan. "Cactus Whips and Wooden Crosses." *Journal of American Folklore*, 76:216–224 (July, 1963).

Hernandez, Luis F., "The Culturally Disadvantaged Mexican-American Student." *Journal of Secondary Education*, 42: 59–65 (Feb., 1967).

Herr, S. E. "Effect of Pre-first Grade Training upon Reading Readiness and Reading Achievement Among Spanish-American Children." *Journal of Educ. Psychology*, 37:87–102 (Feb., 1946).

Herriott, M. E. "Administrative Responsibility for Minorities." *California Journal of Secondary Education*, 18:362–364 (Oct., 1943).

Hewes, Gordon, "Mexicans in Search of the 'Mexican'". *American Journal of Economics and Sociology*, 13:209–223 (Jan., 1954).

Hilding, C. B., and N. Henderson. "The Intelligence of American Children of Mexican Parentage." *Journal of Abnormal and Social Psychology*, 45:544–551 (July, 1950).

Hill, G. "Two Every Minute Across the Border." *New York Times Magazine*, Jan. 31, 1954, p. 13.

Hill, J. E. "El Chamizal." *Geographical Review*, 55:510–522 (Oct., 1965).

Hobart, Charles W. "Underachievement Among Minority Group Students: An Analysis and a Proposal." *Phylon*, 24, no. 3, 184–196 (summer, 1963).

Hoben, N., and J. T. Hood. "Help the Language Handicapped." *Texas Outlook*, 50:28+ (Mar., 1966).

Hollister, Arthur C., Jr., and Others. "Influence of Water Availability on Shigella Prevalance in Children of Farm Labor Families." *American Journal of Public Health*. 45:354–362 (Mar., 1955).

Holmes, Samuel J. "Perils of Mexican Invasion." *North American Review*, 227:615–623 (May, 1929).

Hoover, G. E. "Our Mexican Immigrants." *Foreign Affairs*, 8:99–107 (Oct., 1929).

Houghton, John. "Always a Brave River." *Southwest Review*, 50:345–354 (1965).

Huddleston, Ruth B. "New Mexico—la Tierra de Mañana." *Public Health Nursing*, 29:421–424 (July, 1937).

"Huelga! Tales of the Delano Revolution." *Ramparts*, 5:37–50 (July, 1966).

Hull, Harry E. "Protective Immigration." *American Labor Legislation Review*, 20:97–98 (Mar., 1930).

Humphrey, N. D. "El Campesino Mexicano en Detroit." *Review of Mexican Sociology*, 7:403–416 (1945).

———. "The Changing Structure of the Detroit Mexican Family." *American Sociological Review*, 9:622–625 (Dec., 1944).

———. "The Concept of Culture in Social Case Work." *Sociology and Social Research*, 26:53–59 (Sept., 1941).

———. "The Detroit Mexican Immigrant and Naturalization." *Social Forces*, 22:332–335 (Mar., 1944)

———. "Education and Language of Detroit Mexicans." *Journal of Educational Sociology*, 17:534–542 (May, 1944).

———. "Employment Patterns of Mexicans in Detroit." *Monthly Labor Review*, 61:913–923 (Nov., 1945).

———. "The Housing and Household Practices of Detroit Mexicans." *Social Forces*, 24:433–437 (May, 1946).

———. "The Integration of the Detroit Mexican Colony." *American Journal of Economics and Sociology*, 3: 155–166 (Jan., 1944).

———. "Mexican Repatriation from Michigan: Public Assistance in Historical Perspective." *Social Service Review*, 15:497–513 (Sept., 1941).

———. "Migration and Settlement of Detroit Mexicans." *Economic Geography*, 19: 358–361 (Oct., 1943).

———. "On Assimilation and Acculturation." *Psychiatry*, 6:343–345 (Nov., 1943).

———. "Some Dietary and Health Practices of Detroit Mexicans." *Journal of American Folklore*, 58: 255–258 (July, 1945).

———. "Some Marriage Problems of Detroit Mexicans." *Applied Anthropology*, 3:13–15 (Dec., 1943).

———. "The Stereotype and the Social Types of Mexican-American Youths." *Journal of Social Psychology*, 22:69–78 (Aug., 1945).

Huser, C. W. "San Antonio Educates Little Mexico." *Adult Education Bulletin*, 3:13–16 (Apr., 1939).

"Integration and Mal-integration in Spanish-American Family Patterns." Group for the Advancement of Psychiatry, *GAP Reports*, no. 27, Aug., 1954, pp. 12–15.

"Invisible Minority: Attitude of Schools Toward Spanish-speaking Pupils." *Newsweek*, 68:46 (Aug., 29, 1966).

Jaco, E. Gartley. "Social Factors in Mental Disorders in Texas." *Social Problems*, 4:322–328 (1957).

———. "The Social Isolation Hypothesis and Schizophrenia." *American Sociological Review*, 19:567–577 (Oct., 1954).

Jacobs, Paul. "The Forgotten People." *Reporter*, 20:13–20 (Jan. 22, 1959).

Jamieson, Stuart. "Labor Unionism in American Agriculture." *U.S. Bureau of Labor Statistics Bulletin* no. 836, 1945.

Janow, Seymour J., and Davis McEntire. "Migration to California." *Land Policy Review*, 3:24–36 (July–Aug., 1940).

Jeidy, Pauline. "First Grade Mexican-American Children in Ventura County." *California Journal of Elementary Education*, 15:200–208 (Feb. and May, 1947).

Jensen, Arthur R. "Learning Abilities in Mexican-American and Anglo-American Children." *California Journal of Educational Research*, 12:147–159 (Sept., 1961).

Johansen, Sigurd. "Family Organization in a Spanish-American Culture Area." *Sociology and Social Research*, 28:123–31 (1943).

———. "The Social Organization of Spanish-American Villages." *Southwestern Social Science Quarterly*, 23:151–159 (Sept., 1942).

Johnson, Edgar G. "Michigan's Stepchildren." *University of Michigan School of Education Bulletin*, 15:1–6 (Oct., 1943).

Johnson, J. B. "The Allelujahs: A Religious Cult in Northern New Mexico." *Southwest Review*, 22: 131–139 (Jan., 1937).

Johnson, L. W. "A Comparison of the Vocabularies of Anglo-American and Spanish-American High School Pupils." *Journal of Educational Psychology*, 29:135–144 (Feb., 1938).

Jones, Anita Edgar. "Mexican Colonies in Chicago." *Social Service Review*, 2:579–597 (Dec., 1928).

Jones, H. J. "An All Mexican School." *Sierra Educational News*, 36:17 (Nov., 1940).

Jones, O. L. Jr., "The Conquest of California." *Journal of the West*, 5: 187–202 (1966).

Jones, Robert C. "Ethnic Family Patterns: The Mexican Family in the United States." *American Journal of Sociology*, 53:450–453 (May, 1948).

———. "Integration of the Mexican Minority in the United States into American Democracy." *Events and Trends in Race Relations*, 4:175–177 (Jan., 1947).

———. "The Latin-American Problem." *School and Society*, 58:441–443 (Dec., 4, 1943).

———. "Mexican-American Youth." *Sociology and Social Research*, 32:793–797 (Mar., 1948).

———. "Mexican Youth in the United States." *American Teacher*, 28:11–15 (Mar., 1944).

Karcik, W. "Wetback Story." *Commonweal*, 54:327–329 (June 13, 1951).

Kelley, E., and others. "Segregation of Mexican-American School Children in Southern California." *American Journal of Public Health*, 38:30–35 (Jan., 1948).

Kelley, J. B. "The Deportation of Mexican Aliens and Its Impact on Family Life." *Catholic Charities Review*, 37:169–171 (Oct., 1954).

Kelley, V. H. "The Reading Abilities of Spanish and English-speaking Public School Pupils." *Journal of Educational Research*, 29:209–211 (Nov., 1935).

Keston, M. J., and C. A. Jiminez. "A Study of the Performance on English and Spanish Edition of the Stanford-Binet Intelligence Test by Spanish-American Children." *Journal of Genetic Psychology*, vol. 85:263–269 (1954).

Kibbe, Pauline R. "The American Standard—For All Americans." *Common Ground*, 10 no. 1:19–28 (autumn, 1949).

Kirk, William. "Cultural Conflict in Mexican Life." *Sociology and Social Research*, 15:352–364 (June, 1931).

Kiser, Clyde V. "Cultural Pluralism." *Annals of the American Academy of Political and Social Science*, 262:117–130 (Mar., 1949).

Kluckhohn, Florence R. "Cultural Factors in Social Work Practice and Education." *Social Service Review*, 25:40–45 (Mar., 1951).

Knowlton, Clark. "Changes in the Structure and Roles of Spanish-American Families of Northern New Mexico." *Proceedings of the Southwestern Social Science Association*, vol. 15 (Apr., 15–17, 1965).

———. "The New Mexican Land War." *Nation*, 206:792–796 (June 17, 1968).

———. "Patron-Peon Pattern Among the Spanish-Americans of New Mexico." *Social Forces*, 40:12–17 (Oct., 1962).

———. "The Spanish-Americans in New Mexico." *Sociology and Social Research*, 45:448–454 (July, 1961).

Kress, Dorothy M. "The Spanish-speaking School Child in Texas." *Texas Outlook*, 18:24 (Dec., 1934).

Krueger, A. O. "Economics of Discrimination." *Journal of Politics and Economics*, 71:481–486 (Oct., 1963).

Lamb, E. "Racial Differences in Bimanual Dexterity of Latin and American Children." *Child Development*, 1:204–231 (1930).

Landazuri, Elena. "Why We are Different." *Survey*, 52:159–160 (May 1, 1924).

Lasker, Gabriel W. "The Question of Physical Selection of Mexican Migrants to the U.S.A." *Human Biology*, 26:52–58 (Feb., 1954).

——— and F. G. Evans. "Age, Environment, and Migration: Further Anthropomorphic Findings on Migrant and Non-migrant Mexicans." *American Journal of Physical Anthropology*, 19:203–211 (1961).

"The League's Investigations and Arizona's Demands Concerning Mexican Immigration." *Municipal League of Los Angeles Bulletin*, 5:1–3 (Apr., 1928).

Leary, Mary E. "As the Braceros Leave." *Reporter*, 32:43–45 (Jan., 28, 1965).

Lee, John D. "Diary of the Mormon Battalion Mission." *New Mexico Historical Review*, 42:165–209 (1967).

Leibson, Art. "The Wetback Invasion." *Common Ground*, 10 no. 1:11–19 (autumn, 1949).

Leifeste, Sam. "Skill in Public Relations and a Command of Spanish Help in Selling to Texas' 1,000,000 Latin-Americans." *Texas Business Review*, Dec., 1955, pp. 15–17.

Leland, R. G. "Medical Care for Migratory Workers." *Journal of the American Medical Assoc.*, 114:45–55 (Jan. 6, 1940).

Leonard, William E. "Where Both Bullets and Ballots are Dangerous." *Survey*, 37:86–87 (Oct. 28, 1916).

Leroy, Georges P. "Contribution to the Study of the 'Wetback' Problem: Illegal Mexican Immigration to the United States." *Revue Trimestrielle, Population*, 7:334–337 (Apr.–June, 1952).

Lescohier, Don D. "The Vital Problem in Mexican Immigration." *Proceedings of the National Conference of Social Work*, 1927:547–554.

Levenstein, H. A. "AFL and Mexican Immigration in the 1920's: An Experiment in Labor Diplomacy." *Hispanic American Historical Review*, 48:206–219 (May, 1968).

Lewis, H. P., and E. R. Lewis. "Written Language Performance of Sixth-grade Children of Low-Socio-economic Status from Bilingual and from Monolingual Backgrounds." *Journal of Experimental Education*, 33:237–242 (spring, 1965).

Locke, Harvey J., Georges Sabah, and Mary Thomas. "Interfaith Marriages." *Social Problems*, 4:329–333 (Apr., 1957).

Loeffler, H. W. "San Antonio's Mexican Child." *Texas Outlook*, 29:28 (Mar., 1945).

Lofstedt, Christine. "The Mexican Population of Pasadena, California." *Journal of Applied Sociology*, 7:260–268 (May, 1923).

Longmore, T. W. and Homer L. Hitt. "A Demographic Analysis of First and

Second Generation Mexican Population of the United States." *Southwestern Social Science Quarterly*, 24:138–149 (Sept., 1943).

Loomis, Charles P. "El Cerrito, New Mexico: A Changing Village." *New Mexico Historical Review*, 33:53–75 (Jan., 1958).

———. "A Cooperative Health Association in Spanish-speaking Villages." *American Sociological Review*, 10:149–157 (Apr., 1945).

———. "The Development of Planned Rural Communities." *Rural Sociology*, 3:385–409 (Dec., 1938).

———. "Ethnic Cleavages in the Southwest as Reflected in Two High Schools," *Sociometry*, 6:7–26 (Feb., 1943).

———. "Informal Groupings in a Spanish-American Village." *Sociometry*, 4:36–51 (Feb., 1941).

———. "Systematic Linkage of El Cerrito." *Rural Sociology*, 24:54–57 (Mar., 1959).

———. "Wartime Migration from the Rural Spanish-speaking Villages of New Mexico." *Rural Sociology*, 7:384–395 (Dec., 1942).

——— and Nellie H. Loomis. "Skilled Spanish-American War-industry Worker from New Mexico." *Applied Anthropology*, 2:33–36 (Oct.–Nov.–Dec., 1942).

Lopez, Henry. "Here They Come Again." *Frontier*, 6:13–14 (May, 1955).

Lopez, Lino M. "Spanish-Americans in Colorado." *America*, 91:585–587 (Sept., 18, 1954).

Lopez, Malo Ernesto. "The Emigration of Mexican Laborers." *Ciencias Sociales*, 5:220–227 (Oct., 1954).

Lucey, Robert E. " 'Christianizing' Mexican Catholics." *America*, 77:541–542 (Aug. 16, 1947).

———. "Justice for the Mexicans." *Commonweal*, 49:117 (Nov. 12, 1948).

———. "Migratory Workers." *Commonweal*, 59:370–373 (Jan. 15, 1954).

Lugo, A. "So You Are Teaching Spanish-American Children." *Arizona Teacher-Parent*, 29:9 (Mar., 1941).

McAnulty, Ellen Alice. "Achievement and Intelligence Test Results for Mexican Children Attending Los Angeles City Schools." *Los Angeles Research Bulletin* (Mar., 1932).

Macaulay, R. K. "Vocabulary Problems for Spanish Learners." *English Language Teachers*, 201:131–136 (Jan., 1966).

McCammon, Eleanore L. "Study of Children's Attitudes Toward Mexicans." *California Journal of Elementary Education*, 5:119–128 (Nov., 1936).

McCully, John. "The Spanish-speaking: North from Mexico." *Reporter*, 3:25–28 Dec. 26, 1950).

McDonagh, Edward C. "Attitudes Towards Ethnic Farm Workers in Coachella Valley." *Sociology and Social Research*, 40:10–18 (Sept., 1955).

———. "Status Levels of Mexicans." *Sociology and Social Research*, 33:449–459 (July, 1949).

McEntire, Davis, and N. L. Whetten. "Recent Migration to the Pacific Coast." *Land Policy Review*, 2:7–17 (Sept.–Oct., 1939).

McGinnis, John H. "Cities and Towns of the Southwest: III." *Southwest Review*, 13:36–47 (Oct., 1927).

McGonay, William E. "The Needs of a Mexican Community." *California Journal of Secondary Education*, 18:349–350 (1943).

McGovney, D. O. "Race Discrimination in Naturalization." *Iowa Law Bulletin*, 8:129–211 (1923).

McKenney, J. Wilson. "The Dilemma of the Spanish Surname People of California." *California Teachers Association Journal*, 61:17+ (Mar., 1965).

McKinnon, William, and Richard Centers. "Authoritarianism and Urban Stratification." *American Journal of Sociology*, 61:610–620 (May, 1956).

McLean, Robert N. "Goodbye, Vicente!" *Survey*, 66:182+ (May 1, 1931).

———. "The Mexican Return." *Nation*, 135:165–166 (Aug., 1932).

———. "Mexican Workers in the United States." *Proceedings of the National Conference of Social Work*, 531–538 (1929).

———. "Rubbing Shoulders on the Border." *Survey*, 52:184–185 (May, 1924).

———. "Tightening the Mexican Border." *Survey*, 64:28+ (Apr., 1930).

McLemore, S. D. "Ethnic Attitudes Toward Hospitalization: An Illustrative Comparison of Anglos and Mexican-Americans." *Southwestern Social Science Quarterly*, 43:341–346 (Mar., 1963).

McNamara, Patrick H. "Mexican-Americans in the Southwest: Mexican-American Study Project." *America*, 114:352–354 (Mar. 12, 1966).

McWilliams, Carey. "America's Disadvantaged Minorities: Mexican-Americans." *Journal of Negro Education*, 20:301–309 (summer, 1951).

———. "California and the Wetback." *Common Ground*, 9 no. 4:15–20 (summer, 1949).

———. "The Forgotten Mexican." *Common Ground*, 3 no. 3:65–78 (spring, 1943).

———. "The Los Angeles Archipelago." *Science and Society*, 10:41–53 (1946).

———. "Los Angeles 'Pachuco' Gangs." *New Republic*, 108:76–77 (Jan. 18, 1943).

———. " 'The Mexican Problem,' " *Common Ground*, 8 no. 3:3–17 (spring, 1948).

———. "Mexicans to Michigan." *Common Ground*, 2 no. 1:5–17 (autumn, 1941).

———. "They Saved The Crops." *Inter-American*, 2:10–14 (Aug., 1943).

———. "Zoot-suit Riots." *New Republic*, 108:818–820 (June 21, 1943).

Madsen, William. "The Alcoholic Agringado." *American Anthropologist*, 66:355–361 (Apr., 1964).

Mahikian, Charles. "Measuring the Intelligence and Reading Capacity of Spanish-speaking Children." *Elementary School Journal*, 39:760–768 (June, 1939).

Maisel, Albert Q. "The Mexicans Among Us." *Readers Digest*, 68:177–178 (Mar., 1956).

Manning, J. C. "Linguistic Approach to the Teaching of English as a Foreign Language." *Instructor*, 75:81 (Mar., 1966).

Manuel, H. T. "Comparison of Spanish-speaking and English-speaking Children in Reading and Arithmetic." *Journal of Applied Psychology*, 19:189–202 (Apr., 1935).

———. "The Mexican Population of Texas." *Southwestern Social Science Quarterly*, 15:29–51 (June, 1934).

———. "Physical Measurements of Mexican Children in American Schools." *Child Development*, 5:237–252 (Sept., 1934).

———. "Recruiting and Training Teachers for Spanish Speaking Children." *School and Society*, 96:211–214 (Mar., 30, 1968).

———. "Spanish-speaking Child." *Texas Outlook*, 14:21 (Jan., 1930).

——— and Lois Hughes. "The Intelligence and Drawing Ability of Young Mexican Children." *Journal of Applied Psychology*, vol. 16, no. 5 (Aug., 1932).

Marie, Sister Jean. "Summer School for Pre-first Grade for Mexican-American Children." *Catholic School Journal*, 65:34–35 (June, 1965).

Martindale, G. "Teaching English to Mexican Boys." *Elementary English Review*, 6:276–278 (Dec., 1929).

Martinez, Paul G. "Teaching English to Spanish-speaking Americans in New Mexico." *New Mexico School Review*, 13:22–23 (Sept., 1933).

Meany, George. "Peonage in California." *American Federationist*, 48:3+ (May, 1941).

Meriam, Junius L. "An Activity Curriculum in a School of Mexican Children." *Journal of Experimental Education*, 1:304–308 (June, 1933).

———. "Learning English Incidentally: A Study of Bi-lingual Children." *United States Office of Education Bulletin*, 1937, no. 15:1–105.

"The Mexican-American." *Economist*, 156:1139–1140 (June 18, 1949).

"The Mexican-Americans: Their Plight and Struggles; Resolution on [Communist] Party Work Among the Mexican-American People." *Political Affairs*,

28:71–80 (May, 1949); 28:75–84 (July, 1949).

"Mexican-Immigrants in El Paso." *Interpreter Release Clip Sheet*, Foreign Language Information Service, 7:44–46 (July 18, 1930).

"Mexican Immigration." *Transactions of the Commonwealth Club of California*, 21:1–34 (Mar., 1926).

"Mexicans in Los Angeles." *Survey*, 44:715–716 (Sept. 15, 1920).

"The Mexicans of Imperial Valley." *Interpreter Release*, Foreign Language Information Service, 6:85–91 (May 15, 1929).

Mexican Voice. A magazine published by Mexican-American college and high school students from 1938 to 1944(?) in Los Angeles.

"Mexico-United States Farm Labor Agreement." *Bulletin of the Pan American Union*, 82:411–412 (July, 1948).

Meyers, Frederic. "Employment and Relative Earnings of Spanish-name Persons in Texas Industries." *Southern Economic Journal*, 19: 494–507 (Apr., 1953).

Miller, R. R. "The Mexican Dependency Problem." *Municipal League of Los Angeles Bulletin*, Mar. 6, 1929.

Miller, William. "Developing Status for Members of a Minority Group." *National Association of Secondary School Principals. Bulletin*, 39:58–62 (Mar., 1955).

Milor, J. H. "Problems of a Junior High for Mexicans." *California Journal of Secondary Education*, 16:482–484 (Dec., 1941).

Mintz, Sidney, and Eric R. Wolf. "An Analysis of Ritual Co-Parenthood (Compadrazgo)." *Southwestern Journal of Anthropology*, 6:341–368 (winter, 195 ̄).

Mitchell, A. J. "The Effect of Bi-lingualism on the Measurement of Intelligence." *Elementary School Journal*, 28: 29–37 (1937).

Mitchell, H. L. "Unions of Two Countries Act on Wetback Influx." *American Federationist*, 61:28–29 (Jan., 1954).

Montoya, A. "Removing the Language Difficulty." *American Childhood*, 17: 12–15 (Mar., 1932).

Moore, Joan, and Ralph Guzman. "The Mexican-Americans: New Wind from the Southwest." *Nation*, 202:645–648 (May 30, 1966).

Morgan, Thomas B. "The Texas Giant Awakens." *Look*, 27:71–75 (Oct. 8, 1963).

Morrill, D. B. "The Spanish Language Problem." *New Mexico Journal of Education*, 14:6–7 (May, 1918).

———. "Teaching the Spanish-American Child." *New Mexico Journal of Education*, 13:8+ (Apr., 1917).

Mott, Frederick D. "Health Services for Migrant Farm Families." *American Journal of Public Health*, 35:308–314 (Apr., 1945).

Mulky, Carl. "Program for Tuberculosis Control Among Spanish-speaking People." *New Mexico Health Officer*, 11: 13–16 (Sept., 1943).

———. "Tuberculosis in the Spanish Population of New Mexico." *Southwestern Medicine*, 25: 165–166 (1941).

Muls, Ernest E. "The Labor Movement in New Mexico." *New Mexico Business Review*, 4:137–140 (1935).

Muny, Charles Curtis. "Awakening in the Coral." *New Masses*, 31:10–12 (Apr. 18, 1939).

Murphy, L. F. "Experiment in Americanization." *Texas Outlook*, 23:23–24 (Nov., 1939).

Murray, Katherine Mary. "Mexican Community Service." *Sociology and Social Research*, 17:545–550 (July, 1933).

Nall, Frank. "Role Expectations: A Cross Cultural Study." *Rural Sociology*, 27:28–41 (Mar., 1962).

Nelson, Lowry. "Speaking of Tongues." *American Journal of Sociology*, 54:202–210 (Nov., 1948).

Netzer, H. E. "Teaching Mexican Children in the First Grade." *Modern Language Journal*, 25:322–325 (Jan., 1941).

Neumeyer, M. H. "Joint Meeting of the Pacific Sociological Society, Southern Division, and Alpha Kappa Delta on Race Relations, 1944, University of Southern California." *Sociology and*

Social Research, 29: 58–62 (Sept., 1944).

"New Census Returns and Education of Our Spanish-speaking Population." *Education for Victory*, 1:7–8 (July 15, 1942).

Newcomb, W. Fred. "Caring for Children of Seasonal Workers in Ventura County Schools." *California Journal of Elementary Education*, 6: 54–59 (Aug., 1937).

New Mexico Writers' Project, Works Progress Administration. "Spanish-American Baptismal Customs." *El Palacio*, 49:59–61, 1942).

———. "Spanish-American Wedding Customs." *El Palacio*, 49:1–6 (1942).

Norman, Arthur. "Migration to Southwest Texas: Peoples and Words." *Southwestern Social Science Quarterly*, 37:149–158 (Sept. 1, 1956).

Northrup, H. R. "In the Unions: Racial Politics." *Survey Graphic*, 36:54–56 (Jan., 1947).

———. "Race Discrimination in Trade Unions: The Record and Outlook." *Commentary*, 2: 124–131 (Aug., 1946).

O'Brien, Robert W. "That Northern Mexican." *Pomona College Magazine*, Oct., 1931, pp. 29–33.

Officer, James E. "Barrier to Mexican Integration in Tucson." *Kiva*, 17:7–16 (Nov.–Dec., 1951).

———. "Historical Factors in Interethnic Relations in the Community of Tucson." *Arizoniana*, 1:12–16 (fall, 1960).

Otero, Adelina. "My People." *Survey Graphic*, 66:149–151 (May 1, 1931).

Oxnam, G. Bromley. "Mexicans in Los Angeles from the Standpoint of the Religious Forces of the City." *Annals American Academy of Political and Social Science*, 93:130–133, (Jan., 1921).

Panunzio, Constantine. "Intermarriage in Los Angeles, 1924–1933." *American Journal of Sociology*, 47:690–701 (Mar., 1942).

Paredes, A. "Estados Unidos, Mexico y el Machismo." *Journal of Inter-American Studies*, 9:65–84 (Jan., 1967).

Paredes, Americo. "Texas' Third Man: The Texas-Mexican." *Race*, 3–4:49–58 (May, 1963).

Pasamanick, Benjamin. "The Intelligence of American Children of Mexican Parentage: A Discussion of Uncontrolled Variables." *Journal of Abnormal and Social Psychology*, 46:598–602 (Oct., 1951).

Peck, Robert F. "Intelligence, Ethnicity and Social Roles in Adolescent Society." *Sociometry*, 25: 64–72 (Mar., 1962).

Peñalosa, Fernando. "The Changing Mexican-American in Southern California." *Sociology and Social Research*, 51:405–417 (July, 1967).

——— and Edward C. McDonagh. "Social Mobility in a Mexican-American Community." *Social Forces*, 44: 498–505 (June, 1966).

Perry, George S. "The Gonzalezes of San Antonio." *Saturday Evening Post*, 221: 24+ (Oct. 2, 1948).

Peters, L. S. "New Mexico Medicine." *New Mexico Quarterly Review*, 11:322–329 (Aug., 1941).

Petterson, I., and H. M. Johnson. "Methods for Mexicans: Informal Method vs. Textbook Method for Mexican Children." *Sierra Educational News.* 33:12 (Sept., 1937).

Phillips, Herbert. "The School Follows the Child." *Survey*, 66:493–495 (Sept., 1931).

Phillips, L. H. "Segregation in Education: A California Case Study." *Phylon*, 10 no. 4:407–413 (winter, 1949).

Pierson, G. K. "Analysis of Population Changes in New Mexico Counties." *New Mexico Business*, 14:2–8 (Nov., 1961).

Pijoan, Michael. "Food Availability and Social Function." *New Mexico Quarterly Review*, 12: 419–423 (Nov., 1942).

Pinkney, A. "Prejudice Toward Mexican and Negro Americans: A Comparison." *Phylon*, 24, no. 4:353–359 (winter, 1963).

Pintner, R. R., and S. Arsenia. "The Relation of Bilingualism to Verbal Intelligence and School Adjustment."

Journal of Educational Research, 31: 255–263 (1937).

Polifroni, M. "Including Our Spanish Speaking Neighbors." *Young Children*, 20:351–356 (summer, 1965).

Prado, E. L. "Sinarquism in the United States." *New Republic*, 109:97–102 (July 26, 1943).

Rael, Juan B. "The New Mexican Alabado." *Stanford University Publications University Series Language and Literature*, vol. 9, no. 3. Stanford, Calif.: Stanford University Press, 1951.

———. "New Mexican Spanish Feasts," *California Folklore Quarterly*, 1:83–90 (Jan., 1942).

Raisner, A. "New Horizons for the Student of Spanish Speaking Background: Science Spanish Research Experiment." *High Points*, 48: 19–23 (fall, 1966).

Ramsey, Glenn U., and Beulah Hodge. "Anglo-Latin Problems as Perceived by Public Service Personnel." *Social Forces*, 37:339–348 (May, 1959).

"Reaching Mexicans in the United States." *Missionary Review*, 50:50–51 (Jan., 1927).

Rebolledo, Antonio. "Shall Language Groups Be Segregated for Teaching Spanish?" *New Mexico School Review*, 22:1+ (Dec., 1942).

———. "Teaching of Spanish in Elementary Grades." *New Mexico School Review*, 19:2–3 (Mar., 1940).

Redfield, Robert. "Antecedents of Mexican Immigration to the United States." *American Journal of Sociology*, 35:433–438 (Nov., 1929).

Reynolds, Quentin. "Girls at Camp: Spanish-American Girls are Taught a New Way of Life in Camp Capitan, Lincoln County, New Mexico." *Colliers*, 103:16 (Mar., 4, 1937).

Rice, Roy C. "Intergroup Relations in Arizona." *Journal of Educational Sociology*, 21:243–249 (Dec., 1947).

Richards, Eugene S. "Attitudes of White College Students in the Southwest Toward Ethnic Groups in the United States." *Sociology and Social Research*, 35:22–30 (Sept., 1950).

Risdon, R. "Study of Interracial Marriages Based on Data for Los Angeles County." *Sociology and Social Research*, 39:92–95 (Nov., 1954).

Robinson, Cecil. "Spring Water with a Taste of the Land; The Mexican Presence in the American Southwest." *American West*, 3:6–15 (summer, 1966).

Robinson, Norma J. "The Public Health Program for Mexican Migrant Workers." *Public Health Reports*, 73: 851–860 (Sept., 1958).

Rodriguez, A. M. "Speak up Chicanos: Fight for Educational Equality." *American Education*, 4:25–27 (May, 1968).

Rodriguez, N. E., and J. Y. Boyle. "Opportunity Classes Help Spanish-speaking Pupils." *Chicago School Journal*, 43:228–231 (Feb., 1962).

Rogde, M. "Learning to Speak English in the First Grade." *Texas Outlook*, 22: 40–41 (Sept., 1938).

Rogers, John. "Poverty Behind the Cactus Curtain." *Progressive*, 30:23–25 (Mar., 1966).

Romano, O. I. "Charismatic Medicine, Folk Healing and Folk-Sainthood." *American Anthropologist*, 67:1151–1173 (Oct., 1965).

Romano, V., and I. Octavio. "Donship in a Mexican-American Community in Texas." *American Anthropologist*, 62: 966–976 (Dec., 1960).

Rooney, James F. "The Effects of Imported Mexican Farm Labor in a California County." *American Journal of Economics and Sociology*, 20:513–521 (Oct., 1961).

Rosaldo, R. "De Mayoria a Minoria." *Hispania*, 51:18–28 (Mar., 1968).

Rosenfeld, Albert. "Modern Medicine Where 'The Clock Walks.'" *Colliers*, 137:24–29 (Feb. 3, 1956).

Rosenquist, Carl M. "Differential Responses of Texas Convicts." *American Journal of Sociology*, 38:10–21 (July, 1932).

Rosing, B. "Where Overcrowding and the Open Prairie Rub Elbows." *Survey*, 23: 362–364 (Dec. 11, 1909).

Ross, J. C. "Industrial Education for the

Spanish-speaking People." *New Mexico Journal of Education*, 7:19–21 (Feb., 1911).

Ross, Malcolm. "Those Gringos." *Common Ground*, 8 no. 2:3–13 (winter, 1948).

Rubel, Arthur J. "Concepts of Disease in Mexican-American Culture." *American Anthropologist*, 62:795–814 (Oct., 1960).

——. "The Mexican-American Palomilla." *Anthropological Linguistics*, 7: 92–97 (Apr., 1965).

Ruiz, Manuel. "Latin-American Juvenile Delinquency in Los Angeles, Bomb or Bubble!" *Crime Prevention Digest*, vol. 1, no. 13 (Dec., 1942).

Russel, Daniel. "Problems of Mexican Children in the Southwest." *Journal of Educational Sociology*, 17:216–222 (Dec., 1943).

Russell, John C. "Racial Groups in the New Mexico Legislature." *Annals of the American Academy of Political and Social Science*, 195:62–71 (Jan., 1938).

——. "State Regionalism in New Mexico." *Social Forces*, 16:268–272 (Dec., 1937).

Samora, Julian. "Conceptions of Health and Disease Among Spanish-Americans." *American Catholic Sociological Review*, 22:314–323 (winter, 1961).

——. "Educational Status of a Minority." *Theory and Practice*, 2:144–150 (June, 1963).

——, and Richard F. Larson. "Rural Families in an Urban Setting: A Study in Persistence and Change." *Journal of Human Relations*, 9:494–503 (1961).

——, Lyle Saunders, and Richard F. Larsen. "Knowledge About Specific Diseases in Four Selected Samples." *Journal of Health and Human Behavior*, 3:176–184 (fall, 1962).

——, ——, and ——. "Medical Vocabulary Knowledge Among Hospital Patients." *Journal of Health and Human Behavior*, 2:83–92 (summer 1961).

Sanchez, A. M. "The Spanish-speaking Child and the English Language." *New Mexico Educational Association Journal and Proceedings*, 22nd Annual Meeting, 1947.

Sanchez, George I. "The Age-grade Status of the Rural Child in New Mexico, 1931–1932." *Educational Research Bulletin*, New Mexico State Department of Education, vol. 1, no. 1 (Nov., 1932).

——. "The American of Mexican Descent." *Chicago Jewish Forum*, 20:120–124 (winter, 1961–1962).

——. "Bi-lingualism and Mental Measurement." *Journal of Applied Psychology*, 18:765–772 (Dec., 1934).

——. "The Default of Leadership." *Summarized Proceedings IV, Southwest Council on the Education of the Spanish-speaking People*, Fourth Regional Conference, Albuquerque, N. Mex., Jan. 23–25, 1950.

——. "Group Differences and Spanish-speaking Children: A Critical Review." *Journal of Applied Psychology*, 16:549–558 (Oct., 1932).

——. "The Implications of a Basal Vocabulary to the Measurement of the Abilities of Bi-lingual Children." *Journal of Social Psychology*, 5:395+ (1934).

——. "New Mexicans and Acculturation." *New Mexico Quarterly Review*, 11:61–68 (Feb., 1941).

——. "North of the Border." *Texas Academy of Science Transactions*, Houston, Tex., 25:77–85 (1941).

——. "Pachucos in the Making." *Common Ground*, 4 no. 1:13–20 (autumn, 1943).

——. "Spanish-speaking People in the Southwest—A Brief Historical Review." *California Journal of Elementary Education*, 22:106–111 (Nov., 1953).

Sandoval, A. D. "New Mexico County Industrial Composition and Levels of Living." *New Mexico Business*, 16:3–10 (May, 1963).

Santiago, Hasel D. "Mexican Influence in Southern California." *Sociology and Social Research*, 16:68–74 (Sept., 1931).

Saunders, Lyle. "The Education of Spanish-Americans." *Colorado School Journal*, 60:12–15 (Jan., 1945).

——. "The Social History of Spanish-speaking People in Southwestern United

States Since 1846." *Proceedings of the First Congress of Historians from Mexico and the United States*, 1950, pp. 152–165.

———. "*Sociological Study of the Wetbacks in the Lower Rio Grande Valley.* Proceedings of the Fifth Annual Conference on the Education of Spanish-speaking People, George Pepperdine College, Los Angeles, Calif., 1951.

——— and G. Hewes. "Folk Medicine and Medical Practice." *Journal of Medical Education*, 28: 43–46 (Sept., 1953).

Schaupp, Karl L. "Medical Care of Migratory Agricultural Workers." *California and Western Medicine*, 60:1–12 (May, 1944).

"School Bias Toward Mexican-Americans." *School and Society*, 94:378+ (Nov. 12, 1966).

Schulman, Sam. "Rural Health Ways in New Mexico," in Vera Rubin, ed., *Culture, Society and Health*, Annals of the New York Academy of Sciences, 84:950–959 (Dec., 1960).

Scott, Florence Johnson. "Customs and Superstitions Among Texas Mexicans." *Publications of the Texas Folk-Lore Society*, 2:75–85 (1923).

Scruggs, O. M. "Texas and the Bracero Program." *Pacific Historical Review*, 32:251–264 (Aug., 1963).

———. "Texas, Good Neighbor?" *Southwestern Social Science Quarterly*, 43:118–125 (Sept., 1962).

Senter, Donovan. "Acculturation Among New Mexican Villagers in Comparison to Adjustment Patterns of Other Spanish-speaking Americans," *Rural Sociology*, 10: 31–47 (Mar., 1945).

——— and Florence Hawley. "The Grammar School as the Basic Acculturating Influence for Native New Mexicans." *Social Forces*, 24:398–409 (May, 1946).

Servin, Manuel P. "The Pre–World War II Mexican American: An Interpretation." *California Historical Society Quarterly*, 45: 325–338 (1966).

Shaftel, G. A. "The Needs and Anxieties of Spanish-speaking Students." *California Journal of Secondary Education*, 28:160–170 (Mar., 1953).

Shannon, Lyle W., and Elaine M. Krass. "The Economic Absorption of Immigrant Laborers in a Northern Industrial Community." *American Journal of Econ. and Sociology*, 23:65–84 (Jan., 1964).

——— and ———. "The Urban Adjustment of Immigrants: The Relationship of Education to Occupation and Total Family Income." *Pacific Sociological Review*, 4:37–42 (spring, 1963).

——— and Kathryn Lettau. "Measuring the Adjustment of Inmigrant Laborers." *Southwestern Social Science Quarterly*, 44:139–148 (Sept., 1963).

——— and Patricia Morgan. "The Prediction of Economic Absorption and Cultural Integration Among Mexican-Americans, Negroes, and Anglos in a Northern Industrial Community." *Human Organization*, 25:154–162 (summer 1966).

Shapiro, Harold A. "The Pecan Shellers of San Antonio, Texas." *Southwestern Social Science Quarterly*, 32:229–243 (Mar., 1952).

Sheldon, W. H. "The Intelligence of Mexican Children." *School and Society*, 19:139–142 (Feb., 1924).

Sherif, Carolyn W. "Self Radius and Goals of Youth in Different Urban Areas." *Southwestern Social Science Quarterly*, 42:259–267 (Dec., 1961).

Shontz, Orfa. "The Land of Poco Tiempo: A Study of Mexican Family Relationships in a Changing Environment." *Family*, 8: 74–79 (May, 1927).

Shotwell, Anna M. "Arthur Performance Ratings of Mexican and American High-grade Mental Defectives." *American Journal of Mental Deficiency*, 49:445–449 (Apr., 1945).

Silva, Luciano V. "Characteristics of Mexican Immigration." *12th Annual Conference Journal*, Los Angeles Committee for the Protection of the Foreign Born, 1962, pp. 14–16.

———. "Recent Developments in Mexican Immigration." *13th Annual Conference Journal*, Los Angeles Committee for the

Protection of the Foreign Born, 1963, pp. 17–20.

Simmons, Ozzie G. "The Mutual Images and Expectations of Anglo-Americans and Mexican-Americans." *Daedalus*, 90:286–299 (spring, 1961).

Simpson, R. E. "Migrant Children— Fresno County Conducts a Significant Project." *California Teacher's Association Journal*, 50:19+ (Jan., 1954).

Singleton, Robert, and Paul Bullock. "Some Problems in Minority-group Education in the Los Angeles Public Schools." *Journal of Negro Education*, 32:137–145 (spring, 1963).

Sisk, William O. "The Mexican in Texas Schools." *Texas Outlook*, 14:10+ (Dec., 1930).

Slayden, J. L. "Some Observations on Mexican Immigration." *Annals of the American Academy of Political and Social Science*, 93:121–126 (Jan., 1921).

Smith, R. M. "The Problem of Tuberculosis Among Mexicans in the U.S." *Transactions of the National Tuberculosis Association*, 34:247–253 (1938).

Solien De Gonzalez, Nancie L. "Family Organization in Five Types of Migratory Wage Labor." *American Anthropologist*, 63: 1264–1280 (Dec., 1961).

Sommers, Vita S. "The Impact of Dual Cultural Membership on Identity." *Psychiatry*, 27:332–344 (Nov., 1964).

"Spanish-Americans in Politics." *Congressional Quarterly Weekly Report*, June 23, 1961, pp. 1042–1043.

Spaulding, Charles B. "The Mexican Strike at El Monte, California." *Sociology and Social Research*, 18:571–580 (July, 1934).

Spicer, Edward. "Indiginism in the United States, 1870–1960." *America Indigena*, 24:349–363 (Oct., 1964).

Spiess, Jan. "Feudalism and Senator Cutting." *American Mercury*, 33:371–374 (Nov., 1934).

Spilka, Bernard, and Lois Gill. "Some Non-intellectual Correlates of Academic Achievement Among Spanish-American Students." *School Counselor*, 12:218–221 (May, 1965).

Stanley, Grace C. "Special Schools for Mexicans." *Survey*, 44: 714–715 (Sept. 15, 1920).

Stemmler, A. O. "Experimental Approach to the Training of Oral Language and Reading." *Harvard Education Review*, 36:42–58 (winter, 1966).

Stevenson, Emma Reh. "The Emigrant Comes Home." *Survey*, 66:175–177 (May 1, 1931).

Stevenson, Philip. "Deporting Jesus." *Nation*, 143: 67–69 (July 18, 1936).

Stilwell, Hart. "The Wetback Tide," *Common Ground*, 9 no. 4:3–15 (summer, 1949).

Stone, Robert C., and others. "Ambos-Nogales: Bi-cultural Urbanism in a Developing Region." *Arizona Review of Business and Public Administration*, 12: 1–29 (Jan., 1963).

Storm, O. P. "Teaching Spanish-American Children How to Speak, Read and Write English." *New Mexico School Review*, 17:26–27 (May, 1938).

Stowell, J. S. "The Danger of Unrestricted Mexican Immigration." *Current History*, 28:763–768 (Aug., 1928).

Strout, Richard Lee. "A Fence for the Rio Grande." *Independent*, 120:518–520 (June 2, 1928).

"Study of Socio-cultural Factors that Inhibit or Encourage Delinquency Among Mexican-Americans." *It's News*, Welfare Planning Council, Los Angeles Region, 10:9 (Feb., 1958).

Sturges, Vera L. "Mexican Immigrants." *Survey*, 46:470–471 (July 2, 1921).

———. "The Progress of Adjustment in Mexican and United States Life." *Proceedings of the National Conference of Social Work*, 1920:481–486.

Sullenberger, T. Earl. "The Mexican Population of Omaha." *Journal of Applied Sociology*, 8:289–293 (Mar.–Apr., 1924).

Sumner, Margaret. "Mexican-American Minority Churches U.S.A." *Practical Anthropology*, 10:115–121 (May–June, 1963).

Swickard, D. L., and B. Spilka. "Hostility Expression in Spanish-American and

Non-Spanish White Delinquents." *Journal of Consulting Psychology*, 25:216–220 (1961).

Taylor, Mrs. J. T. "The Americanization of Harlingen's Mexican School Population." *Texas Outlook*, 18:37–38 (Sept., 1934).

Taylor, Paul S. "Contemporary Background of California Farm Labor." *Rural Sociology*, 1: 401–419 (1936).

———. "Employment of Mexicans in Chicago and the Calumet Region." *Journal of the American Statistical Association*, 25:206–207 (June, 1930).

———. "Mexicans North of the Rio Grande." *Survey Graphic*, 66:135–140 (May 1, 1931).

———. "Migratory Agricultural Workers on the Pacific Coast." *American Sociological Review*, 3:225–232 (Apr., 1938).

———. "More Bars Against Mexicans." *Survey Graphic*, 64:26–27 (Apr. 1, 1930).

———. "Note on Streams of Mexican Migration." *American Journal of Sociology*, 36:287–288 (Sept., 1930).

———. "Some Aspects of Mexican Immigration." *Journal of Political Economy*, 38:609–615 (Oct., 1930).

——— and Clark Kerr. "Uprisings on the Farms." *Survey Graphic*, 24:19–22 (Jan., 1935).

——— and Edward Rowell. "Patterns of Agricultural and Labor Migration Within California." *Monthly Labor Review*, 47:980–990 (Nov., 1938).

——— and Tom Vasey. "Drought Refugee and Labor Migration to California, June–Dec., 1935." *Monthly Labor Review*, 42:312–318 (Feb., 1936).

Teel, Dwight. "Preventing Prejudice Against Spanish-speaking Children." *Educational Leadership*, 12:94–98 (Nov., 1954).

Tercero, D. M. "Workers from Mexico." *Bulletin of the Pan American Union*, 78: 500–506 (Sept., 1944).

Tetreau, E. D. "Arizona Farm Laborers." *Agricultural Experiment Station Bulletin*, Tuscon, Arizona, 163:293–336 (1934).

———. "The Impact of War on Some Communities in the Southwest." *American Sociological Review*, 8:249–255 (June, 1943).

———. "Social Aspects of Arizona's Farm Labor Problems." *Sociology and Social Research*, 24:550–557 (July, 1940).

Thomas, John L. "The Factor of Religion in the Selection of Marriage Mates." *American Sociological Review*, 16:487–491 (Aug., 1951).

Thompson, A. N. "Mexican Immigrant Worker in Southwestern Agriculture." *American Journal of Economics*, 16:73–81 (Oct., 1956).

Thompson, Merrell E., and Claude D. Dove. "A Comparison of Physical Achievement of Anglo and Spanish-American Boys in Junior High School." *Research Quarterly*, Oct., 1942.

Thomson, Charles A. "Cooperative Broadcasting to the Mexicans in the United States." *Missionary Review of the World*, 48:937–943 (Dec., 1925).

———. "The Man from Next Door." *Century*, 111:275–282 (Jan., 1926).

———. "Mexicans—An Interpretation." *Proceedings of the National Conference of Social Work*, 1928, pp. 499–503.

———. "Restriction of Mexican Immigration." *Journal of Applied Sociology*, 11:574–578 (July, 1927).

———. "What of the Bracero?" *Survey*, 54:291–292 (June 1, 1925).

Thunder, J. A. "Feature X: System of Mexican Contract Laborers." *America*, 89:599–600 (Sept. 19, 1953).

Tipton, Elis M. "The San Dimas Intercultural Program." *California Elementary School Principals' Association Yearbook*, 17:93–99 (1945).

———. "What We Want is Action: Relations of Americans and Mexicans in San Dimas, California." *Common Ground*, no. 1:74–81 (1946).

Tireman, L. S. "Discovery and Use of Community Resources in the Education of Spanish-speaking Pupils." *National Education Association Dept. of Rural Education Yearbook*, 1939, pp. 72–85.

———. "The Education of Minority

Groups, Bi-lingual Children." *Review of Educational Research*, 11:340–352 (1941).

——. "New Mexico Tackles the Problem of the Spanish-speaking Child." *Journal of Education*, 114:300–301 (Nov., 1931).

——. "School Problems Created by the Foreign-speaking Child." *Texas Outlook*, Nov., 1942, pp. 19–20.

—— and Marie Hughes. "Reading Program for Spanish-speaking Pupils." *Elementary English Review*, 14:138–140 (Apr., 1937).

—— and V. E. Woods. "Aural and Visual Comprehension of English by Spanish-speaking Children." *Elementary School Journal*, 40:204–211 (Nov., 1939).

Trillingham, C. C., and Marie M. Hughes. "A Good-neighbour Policy for Los Angeles County." *California Journal of Secondary Education*, 18:342–346 (Oct., 1943).

Tuck, Ruth D. "Behind the Zoot-Suit Riots." *Survey Graphic*, 32:313+ (Aug., 1943).

——. "Mexican-Americans: A Contributory Culture." *California Elementary School Principals' Association Yearbook*, 17:106–109 (1945).

——. "Sprinkling the Grass Roots." *Common Ground*, 17 no. 3:80–83 (spring, 1947).

Turner, Ralph H., and Samuel J. Surace. "Zoot-suiters and Mexicans: Symbols in Crowd Behavior." *American Journal of Sociology*, 62:14–20 (July, 1956).

"Twenty-eight Important Mexicans." *Commonweal*, 47:436–457 (Feb. 13, 1948).

U.S. Department of Labor, Bureau of Labor Statistics. "Increase of Mexican Labor in Certain Industries in the United States." *Monthly Labor Review*, 32:81–83 (Jan., 1931).

——. "Increase of Mexican Population in the United States, 1920–1930." *Monthly Labor Review*, 37:46–48 (July, 1933).

——. "Labor and Agricultural Migra-
tion to California, 1935–1940." *Monthly Labor Review*, 53:18 (July, 1941).

——. "Labor and Social Conditions of Mexicans in California." *Monthly Labor Review*, 32:83–89 (Jan., 1931).

——. "Mexican Labor Colony at Bethlehem, Pennsylvania." *Monthly Labor Review*, 33:74–78 (Oct., 1931).

——. "Mexican Labor in the Imperial Valley, California." *Monthly Labor Review*, 28:59–65 (Mar., 1929).

——. "Minority Groups in California." *Monthly Labor Review*, 89:978–983 (Sept., 1966).

——. "Results of Admission of Mexican Laborers Under Departmental Order for Employment in Agricultural Pursuits." *Monthly Labor Review*, 11:1095–1097 (Nov., 1920).

——. "Wages, Employment Conditions and Welfare of the Sugar-beet Laborers." *Monthly Labor Review*, 46:322–333 (Feb., 1938).

"United States and Mexico Reach Agreement on Agricultural Workers." *United States Department of State Bulletin*, 24:300, (Feb. 19, 1951).

Urquidez, Marie. "Spanish for the Spanish Speaking—Implications for Teachers in the Spanish Southwest." *Arizona Teacher*, 55:6–9 (Sept., 1966).

"U.S. Latins on the March." *Newsweek*, 67:32–36 (May 23, 1966).

Villareal, Jose Antonio. "Mexican-Americans in Upheaval." *West*, Sept. 18, 1966, pp. 21–30.

Vivas, Gustavo E. "Our Spanish-speaking U.S. Catholics." *America*, 91:187–188 (May 15, 1954).

Walker, Helen W. "Mexican Immigrants and American Citizenship." *Sociology and Social Research*, 13:465–471 (May, 1929).

——. "Mexican Immigrants as Laborers." *Sociology and Social Research*, 13:55–62 (Sept., 1928).

Wallis, Wilson D. "The Mexican Immigrant of California." *Pacific Review*, 2:444–454 (Dec., 1921).

Walter, Paul. "Octaviano Ambroisio Larrazolo." *New Mexico Historical Review*, 7:97–104 (Apr., 1932).

————. "The Spanish-speaking Community in New Mexico." *Sociology and Social Research*, 24: 150–157 (Nov., 1939).

Ward, Stuart R. "The Mexican in California." *Transactions of the Commonwealth Club of California*, 21: 4–10 (Mar., 1926).

Waters, Lawrence Leslie. "Transient Mexican Agricultural Labor." *Southwestern Social Science Quarterly*, 22: 49–66 (June, 1941).

Watson, James B., and Julian Samora. "Subordinate Leadership in a Bicultural Community: An Analysis." *American Sociological Review*, 19:413–421 (Aug., 1954).

Watson, Kendrick W. "Zoot Suit, Mexican Style." *Intercollegian*, 61:7+ (Sept., 1943).

Weeks, O. Douglas. "The League of United Latin-American Citizens: A Texas-Mexican Civic Organization." *Southwestern Political and Social Science Quarterly*, 10:257–258 (Dec., 1928).

————. "The Texas-Mexican and the Politics of South Texas." *American Political Science Review*, 24:606–627 (Aug., 1930).

Weir, E. P. "The Mexican Child." *Texas Outlook*, 20:23 (June, 1936).

West, Guy A. "Race Attitudes Among Teachers in the Southwest." *Journal of Abnormal and Social Psychology*, 31: 331–337 (Oct.–Dec., 1936).

Wharburton, Amber. "Children in the Fields." *Survey*, 80:13–15 (Jan., 1944).

Wilder, Mrs. L. A. "Problems in the Teaching of Mexican Children." *Texas Outlook*, 20:9–10 (Aug., 1936).

Wilder, M. A. "Santos: Religious Folk Art of New Mexico." *American West*, 2:37–46 (fall, 1965).

Williams, Faith M., and Alice C. Hanson. "Mexican Families in Los Angeles", in *Money Disbursements Of Wage Earners and Clerical Workers in Five Cities in the Pacific Region*, 1934–1936. U.S. Bureau of Labor Statistics Bulletin 639:85–109 (1939).

Winne, William W. "The Spanish Surname Criterion for Identifying Hispanos in the Southwestern United States: A Preliminary Evaluation." *Social Forces*, 38:363–366 (May, 1960).

Winters, Allen. "Peonage in the Southwest." *Fourth International*, 14:43–49, (Mar., 1953); 14:74–78 (May, 1953).

Witherspoon, Paul. "A Comparison of the Problems of Certain Anglo and Latin-American Junior High School Students." *Journal of Educational Research*. 53:295–299 (1960).

Wolman, Marianne. "Cultural Factors and Creativity." *Journal of Secondary Education*, 37:454–460 (Dec., 1962).

Wonder, J. P. "The Bilingual Mexican-American as a Potential Teacher of Spanish." *Hispania*, 48:97–99 (Mar., 1965).

Wood, Samuel E. "California Migrants." *Sociology and Social Research*, 24: 248–261 (Jan., 1940).

Woods, Sister Frances Jerome. "Cultural Conditioning and Mental Health." *Social Casework*, 39:327–333 (June, 1958).

Woolsey, A. W. "What are We Doing for the Spanish-speaking Student?" *Hispania*, 44:119–123 (Mar., 1961).

Wright, Carrie E., and H. T. Manuel. "The Language Difficulty of Mexican Children." *Journal of Genetic Psychology*, 36:458–468 (1929).

Yarbrough, C. L. "Age-grade Status of Texas Children of Latin American Descent." *Journal of Educational Research*, 40:14–27 (Sept., 1946).

Yinger, J. M., and G. E. Simpson. "Integration of Americans of Mexican, Puerto Rican, and Oriental Descent." *Annals of the American Academy of Political and Social Sciences*, 304: 124–127 (Mar., 1956).

Zurcher, L. A., and others. "Value Orientation, Role Conflict, and Alienation from Work: A Cross-cultural Study." *American Sociological Review*, 30:539–548 (Aug., 1965).

III. UNPUBLISHED DISSERTATIONS

Ackerman, R. E. "Trends in Illiteracy in New Mexico." Master's, University of New Mexico, 1933.

Ajubita, Maria Juisa. "Language in Social Relations with Special Reference to the Mexican-American Problem." Master's, Tulane University, 1943.

Allstrom, Erik W. "A Program of Social Education for a Mexican Community in the U.S." Master's, University of Arizona, 1929.

Allwell, Patrick J. "Mexican Immigration into the United States." Master's, University of Missouri, 1928.

Anderson, Mary. "A Comparative Study of the English-speaking and Spanish-speaking Beginners in the Public Schools." Master's, University of Texas, 1951.

Armstrong, John M., Jr. "A Mexican Community: A Study of the Cultural Determinants of Migration." Ph.D., Yale University, 1949.

Arnold, Charles A. "The Folklore, Manners, and Customs of the Mexicans in San Antonio, Texas." Master's, University of Texas, 1928.

Ashton, Richard Price. "The Fourteenth Amendment and the Education of Latin-American Children in Texas." Master's, University of Texas, 1949.

Atkinson, Rosa M. "The Educational Retardation of the Spanish-speaking Child and Recommendations for Remediation." Master's, University of Texas, 1953.

Baca, Fidel Garcia. "Bi-lingual Education in Certain Southwest School Districts." Ph.D., University of Utah, 1956.

Baker, Margaret T. "An Analysis of Significant Factors Related to Incapacity of Parents in Families Receiving Aid to Dependent Children in Texas on the Basis of Deprivation of Parental Support Through Physical or Mental Incapacity." Master's, University of Texas, 1954.

Barfell, Lawrence Otto. "A Study of the Health Program Among Mexican Children with Special Reference to the Prevalence of Tuberculosis and Its Causes." Master's, University of Southern California, 1937.

Barker, George C. "Social Functions of Language in a Mexican-American Community." Ph.D., University of Chicago, 1947.

Batista y Calderon, Judith. "A Study of Counter-prejudice in a Mexican-Spanish Community in the Surroundings of Des Moines, Iowa." Master's, Drake University, 1948.

Baugh, Lila. "A Study of Pre-school Vocabulary of Spanish-speaking Children." Master's, University of Texas, 1933.

Baur, Edward Jackson. "Delinquency Among Mexican Boys in South Chicago." Master's, University of Chicago, 1938.

Beard, E. Alice. "A Study of the Mexican Pupils in Fremont Junior High School." Master's, Claremont College, 1941.

Beebe, A. A. "An Analysis of Racial Reactions of a Select Group of Mexican Children." Master's, University of Southern California, 1941.

Bishop, Hazel Peck Campbell. "A Case Study of the Improvements of Mexican Homes Through Instruction in Homemaking." Master's, University of Southern California, 1937.

Blackman, Robert D. "The Language Handicap of Spanish-American Children." Master's, University of Arizona, 1940.

Blayeck, Leda F. "Food Habits and Living Conditions of Mexican Families on Farm Income Levels in the Upper Rio Grande Valley." Master's, University of Texas, 1938.

Blum, Owen W. "Some Aspects of the Latin-American Market of Austin, Texas with Emphasis on the Radio as a Means of Reaching This Market." Master's, University of Texas, 1952.

Booker, Margaret. "A Study of the Dietary Habits of Mexican Families in Tucson, Arizona." Master's, University of Arizona, 1937.

Booth, Leroy, L. J. "A Normative Comparison of the Responses of Latin-American and Anglo-American Children to the Children's Apperception Test." Ph.D., Texas Technological College, 1953.

Bowen, Jean Donald. "The Spanish of San Antonio, New Mexico." Ph.D., University of New Mexico, 1952.

Bradshaw, Benjamin S. "Some Demographic Aspects of Marriage: A Comparative Study of Three Ethnic Groups." Master's, University of Texas, 1960.

Brewer, Sam A., Jr. "Latin-America in Texas High Schools." Master's, University of Texas, 1952.

Broadbest, Elizabeth. "The Distribution of Mexican Populations in the United States." Master's, University of Chicago, 1944.

Brookshire, Marjorie. "The Industrial Pattern of Mexican-American Employment in Nueces County, Texas." Ph.D., University of Texas, 1954.

Broom, Perry M. "An Interpretative Analysis of the Economic and Educational Status of Latin-Americans in Texas, with Emphasis on the Basic Factors Underlying an Approach to an Improved Program of Occupational Guidance, Training and Adjustment for Secondary Schools." Ph.D., University of Texas, 1942.

Brown, Willie L. "Knowledge of Social Standards Among Mexican and Non-Mexican Children." Master's, University of Texas, 1934.

Browning, Horace N. "A Comparison of the Spanish-speaking Children in Nine Schools over a Four-year Period." Master's, University of Texas, 1944.

Buckner, H. A. "A Study of Pupil Elimination and Failure Among Mexicans." Master's, University of Southern California, 1935.

Bustrillos, M. R. "Decision Making Styles of Selected Mexican Homemakers." Ph.D., Michigan State University, 1963.

Bynum, H. E. "Inequality of Educational Opportunity in New Mexico." Master's, University of Southern California, 1936.

Cabaza, Berta. "The Spanish Language in Texas: Cameron and Willacy Counties, District 10A." Master's, University of Texas, 1950.

Cabrera, Y. Arturo. "A Study of American and Mexican-American Culture Values and Their Significance in Education." Ed.D., University of Colorado, 1963.

Calderon, Carlos I. "The Education of Spanish-speaking Children in Edcouch-Elsa, Texas." Master's, University of Texas, 1950.

Campbell, Donald T. "The Generality of an Attitude." Ph.D., University of California, Berkeley, 1947.

Cantwell, George C. "Differential Prediction of College Grades for Spanish-American and Anglo-American Students." Master's, University of New Mexico, 1946.

Caraway, Corine D. "A Study of the Attitudes of Latin-American Mothers Toward Juvenile Probation Officers." Master's, University of Texas, 1961.

Carney, John P. "Leading Factors in the Recent Reversal of U.S. Policy Regarding Alien Contract Labor Agreements." Master's, University of Southern California, 1954.

————. "Postwar Mexican Migration: 1945–1955, with Particular Reference to the Policies and Practices of the United States Concerning its Control." Ph.D., University of Southern California, 1957.

Carpenter, C. C. "Mexicans in California: A Case Study of Segregation Versus Non-segregation of Mexican Children." Master's, University of Southern California, 1934.

Carrillo, Stella Leal. "Importancia Economica y Social de la Polbacion Mexicana en Estados Unidos de Norteamerica." Master's, Mexico City: Universidad Nacional Autonoma de Mexico, Escuela Nacional de Economica, 1963.

Carter, Carrol J. "History of Sacred Heart Parish." Master's, Adams State College, 1961.

Chang, D. K. "A Guide for the Understanding and Teaching of Mexican-American Adolescents." Master's, University of Southern California, 1957.

Chappelle, A. M. "Local Welfare Work of Religious Organizations in San Antonio, Texas." Master's, University of Texas, 1939.

Chavez, David Julian. "Civic Education of the Spanish-American." Master's, New Mexico Institute of Mining and Technology, 1923.

Clark, David Hendricks. "A Comparison of the Factors Related to Success in Problem Solving in Mathematics for Latin-American and Anglo-American Students in a Junior High School." Master's, University of Texas, 1938.

Clark, Madeline. "A Preliminary Survey of Employment Possibilities of the Spanish-American Girls Receiving Commercial Training in the San Antonio Secondary Schools." Master's, University of Texas, 1936.

Clark, Margaret. "Sickness and Health in Sal si Puedes: Mexican-Americans in a California Community." Ph.D., University of California, Berkeley, 1957.

Clements, Harold M. "An Analysis of Levels of Living of Spanish-American Rural and Urban Families in Two South Texas Counties." Master's, Agricultural and Mechanical College of Texas, 1963.

Clinchy, Everett Ross. "Equality of Opportunity for Latin-Americans in Texas: A Study of the Economic, Social and Educational Discrimination Against Latin-Americans in Texas, and of the Efforts of the State Government on Their Behalf." Ph.D., Columbia University, 1954.

Coan, Bartlett E. "A Comparative Study of the American and Mexican Children in the 'Big Bend' Area for 1935–36." Master's, University of Texas, 1936.

Cobb, Wilbur K. "Retardation in Elementary Schools of Children of Migratory Laborers in Ventura County, California." Master's, University of Southern California, 1932.

Condit, Eleanor Daly. "An Appraisal of Certain Methods of Treating Bi-lingualism in the Claremont Elementary School." Master's, University of Southern California, 1946.

Connell, Earl Monroe. "The Mexican Population of Austin." Master's, University of Texas, 1925.

Coole, Mrs. Ruth. "A Comparison of Anglo-American and Latin-American Girls in Grades V-XI with Reference to Their Vocational, Academic and Recreational Preferences and Aversions . . . " Master's, University of Texas, 1938.

Coon, Mary W. "The Language Difficulty in Measuring the Intelligence of Spanish-American Students." Master's, University of New Mexico, 1927.

Cooper, Elizabeth K. "Attitude of Children and Teachers Toward Mexican, Negro and Jewish Minorities." Master's, University of California, Los Angeles, 1955.

Cornelius, John Scott. "The Effects of Certain Changes of Curriculum and Methods on the School Achievement of Mexican Children in a Segregated School." Master's, University of Southern California, 1941.

Corona, Bert Charles. "Study of Adjustment and Interpersonal Relations of Adolescents of Mexican Descent." Ph.D., University of California, Berkeley, 1955.

Cox, L. M. "Analysis of the Intelligence of Sub-normal Negro, Mexican and White Children." Master's, University of Southern California, 1938.

Crain, Forest Burr. "The Occupational Distribution of Spanish-name People in Austin, Texas." Master's, University of Texas, 1948.

Crasilneck, Harold Bernard. "A Study of One Hundred Latin-American Juvenile Delinquents in San Antonio, Texas." Master's, University of Texas, 1948.

Cromack, Isabel Work. "Latin-Americans: A Minority Group in the Austin Public

Schools." Master's, University of Texas, 1949.

Cromer, Sturgeon. "Transciency and Its Effect upon the Progress of Pupils . . ." Master's, University of Arizona, 1941.

Cruz, Maria Angelita. "Spanish-speaking Children's Expressed Attitudes Toward Money Values." Master's, University of Texas, 1942.

Culp, Alice Bessie. "A Case Study of the Living Conditions of Thirty-five Mexican Families of Los Angeles with Special Reference to Mexican Children." Master's, University of Southern California, 1921.

Cunningham, Sister Mary, R.S.M. "A Descriptive Study of 100 Families Registered at Madonna Neighborhood Centers, March 1962—March 1963." Master's, University of Texas, 1963.

Curran, Harriett Edgar. "New Approach to Health and Physical Education Instruction for Mexican Children." Master's, Southern Methodist University, 1940.

Daniels, Herbert Scott. "Cultural Aspects in the Behavior of the Mexican Schizophrenic Patient." Master's, University of Southern California, 1949.

D'Antonio, William. "National Images of Business and Political Elite in Two-border Cities." Ph.D., Michigan State University, 1958.

Davenport, Everard L. "A Comparative Study of Mexican and Non-Mexican Siblings." Master's, University of Texas, 1931.

Davis, Ethelyn Clara. "Little Mexico: A Study of Horizontal and Vertical Mobility." Master's, Southern Methodist University, 1936.

Davis, Howard Wingfield. "An Analysis of Current Patterns in Human Resource Development in San Antonio, Texas." Ph.D., University of Texas, 1966.

Deal, Gerald V. "A Study of the Vocational Opportunities in Pomona Valley for Mexican-Americans: A Study in Counseling." Master's, Claremont Graduate School, 1951.

Dearman, Cecil J. "A Socio-economic Study of Latin-American Farm Migrants in Texas." Master's, Texas A & M College, 1947.

De Hoyos, Arturo. "Occupational and Educational Levels of Aspiration of Mexican-American Youth." Ph.D., Michigan State University, 1961.

De La Vega, Marguerite. "Some Factors Affecting Leadership of Mexican-Americans in a High School." Master's, University of Southern California, 1951.

Delmet, Don T. "A Study of the Mental and Scholastic Abilities of Mexican Children in the Elementary Schools." Master's, University of Southern California, 1928.

Des Marais, Alice. "Environmental and Cultural Factors Associated with Infant Diarrhea in San Antonio, Texas." Master's, George Warren Brown School of Social Work, Washington University, 1949.

Dodd, Elmer Cecil. "A Comparison of Spanish-speaking and English Children in Brownsville, Texas." Master's, University of Texas, 1930.

Dodson, Jack Elwood. "Differential Fertility in Houston, Texas, 1940–1950: A Study of Recent Trends." Ph.D., University of Texas, 1955.

Doerr, Marvin F. "Problems of the Elimination of Mexican Pupils from School." Master's, University of Texas, 1938.

Douglas, Helen Walker. "The Conflict of Cultures in First Generation Mexicans in Santa Ana, California." Master's, University of Southern California, 1928.

Drake, Rollen H. "A Comparative Study of the Mentality and Achievement of Mexican and White Children." Master's, University of Southern California, 1927.

Drennan, Davy D. "The Progress in Reading of Fourth Grade Spanish-speaking and English-speaking Pupils." Master's, University of Texas, 1937.

East, Mary Elizabeth. "A Comparison of the Reading Achievement of Mexican and American Children on the Gates Silent Reading Tests." Master's, University of Southern California, 1942.

722

Edmonson, Munro S. "Los Manitos: Patterns of Humor in Relation to Cultural Values." Ph.D., Harvard University, 1952.

Elliot, Robert S. "The Health and Relief Problems of a Group of Non-family Mexican Men in Imperial County, California." Master's, University of Southern California, 1939.

Ellis, Christine E. "The Relation of Socio-economic Status to the Intelligence and School Success of Mexican Children." Master's, University of Texas, 1932.

Ellis, Ivan. "Origin and Development of Baptist Churches and Institutions in Southern California." Master's, University of Southern California, 1938.

Ellis, John M. "Mortality in Houston, Texas, 1949–1951: A Study of Socio-economic Differentials." Ph.D., University of Texas, 1956.

Ellis, Phyllis. "A Comparative Study of Two Methods of Teaching Retarded First Grade Mexican Children to Read." Master's, Southern Methodist University, 1938.

Elms, James Edwin. "Attendance of Mexican and Anglo Students in Two Austin, Texas Schools." Master's, University of Texas, 1950.

Emerson, Ralph Waddell. "Education for the Mexican in Texas." Master's, Southern Methodist University, 1929.

Ethell, Ora Gjerde. "A Study of Fifty Spanish-speaking and Mexican Families in Denver County Granted Aid to Dependent Children from April to October, 1936 and Receiving Grants Continuously to June, 1942." Master's, University of Denver, 1943.

Farmer, William Andrew. "The Influence of Segregation of Mexican and American Children upon the Development of Social Attitudes." Master's, University of Southern California, 1937.

Faunce, Leo Warrington. "An Analysis of Vocational and Avocational Pursuits of Mexican Men . . . " Master's, University of Arizona, 1940.

Fellows, Lloyd Walder. "Economic Aspects of the Mexican Rural Population in California with Special Emphasis on the Need for Mexican Labor in Agriculture." Master's, University of Southern California, 1929.

Felter, Eunice Beall. "The Social Adaptations of the Mexican Churches in the Chicago Area." Master's, University of Chicago, 1941.

Fickinger, Paul L. "A Study of Certain Phases of the Language Problem of Spanish-American Children." Master's, University of New Mexico, 1930.

Finney, Floy C. "Juvenile Delinquency in San Antonio, Texas." Master's, University of Texas, 1932.

Flores, Zella K. Jordan. "The Relation of Language Difficulty to Intelligence and School Retardation in a Group of Spanish-speaking Children." Master's, University of Chicago, 1926.

Fogartie, Ruth Ann Douglas. "Spanish-name People in Texas with Special Emphasis on Those Who Are Students in Texas Colleges and Universities." Master's, University of Texas, 1954.

Fraga, Felix, and John J. Kennedy. "A Study of the Recreational Needs of the Senior Latin-American in San Antonio, Texas." Master's, Our Lady of the Lake College, 1954.

Fussell, William Durwood. "Comparable Norms for Anglo and Latin-American Pupils on a Scholastic Aptitude Test." Master's, University of Texas, 1940.

Gadd, Milan W. "Significant Problems of Spanish-speaking Persons and a Study of Their Registrations in the Denver Office of the Colorado State Employment Service." Master's, University of Denver, 1941.

Garza, Edward D. "LULAC: League of United Latin-American Citizens." Master's, Southwest Texas State Teachers College, 1951.

Getty, Harry T. "Interethnic Relationships in the Community of Tucson." Ph.D., University of Chicago, 1950.

Gibson, Delbert L. "Protestantism in Latin-American Acculturation." Ph.D., University of Texas, 1959.

Gibson, Mary Ellen. "Some Important

Problems in Teaching Spanish Culture Children." Master's, Texas College of Arts and Industry, 1940.

Gilbert, Ennis H. "Some Legal Aspects of the Education of Spanish-speaking Children in Texas." Master's, University of Texas, 1947.

Gillette, George Curtiss. "A Diagnostic Study of the Factors Affecting the Low Scores of Spanish-speaking Children on Standardized Tests." Master's, University of Southern California, 1941.

Ginn, A. "Mexicans in Belvedere, California: The Social Implications." Master's, University of Southern California, 1947.

Goldkind, Victor. "A Comparison of Folk Health Beliefs and Practices Between Ladino Women of Denver, Colorado and Saginaw, Michigan." Master's, Michigan State University, 1959.

——. "Factors in the Differential Acculturation of Mexicans in a Michigan City." Ph.D., Michigan State University, 1963.

Goldman, Mary. "A Study of the Adequacy and Economy of Some Mexican Dietaries." Master's, University of Texas, 1929.

Goldner, Norman. "The Mexican in the Northern Urban Area: A Comparison of Two Generations." Master's, University of Minnesota, 1959.

Gonzales, Aurora M. "A Study of the Intelligence of Mexican Children in Relation to Their Socio-economic Status." Master's, University of Texas, 1932.

Gonzales, Jovita. "Social Life in Cameron, Starr and Zapata Counties." Master's, University of Texas, 1932.

Gonzales, Kathleen. "The Mexican Family in San Antonio, Texas." Master's, University of Texas, 1928.

Goodman, John K. "Race and Race Mixture as the Basis of Social Status in Tuscon, Arizona." B.A., Yale University, 1942.

Goree, Audrey C. "The Distribution of Food Money by Two Thousand Texas Families." Master's, University of Texas, 1935.

Goribund, Antonio. "Food Patterns and Nutrition in Two Spanish-American Communities." Master's, University of Chicago, 1943.

Goulard, Lowell Jack. "A Study of the Intelligence of Eleven and Twelve Year Old Mexicans by Means of the Leiter International Performance Scale." Master's, University of Southern California, 1949.

Gould, Betty. "Methods of Teaching Mexicans." Master's, University of Southern California, 1932.

Graeber, Lillian Kernaghan. "A Study of Attendance at Thomas Jefferson High School, Los Angeles, California." Master's, University of Southern California, 1938.

Graham, Leon R. "A Comparison of the English-speaking and Latin-American Students in the Mercedes, Texas Schools." Master's, Southern Methodist University, 1938.

Graves, Theodore. "Time Perspective and the Deferred Gratification Pattern in a Tri-ethnic Community." Ph.D., University of Pennsylvania, 1961.

Greer, Scott. "The Participation of Ethnic Minorities in the Labor Unions of Los Angeles County." Ph.D., University of California, Los Angeles, 1952.

Guerra, Irene. "The Social Aspirations of a Selected Group of Spanish-name People in Laredo, Texas." Master's, University of Texas, 1959.

Guertin, Carol. "Perceived Life-chances in the Opportunity Structure: A Study of a Tri-ethnic High School." Master's, University of Colorado, 1962.

Gutierrez, Emeterio, Jr. "A Study of School Attendance of Migrant Students in Grulla, Texas." Master's, University of Texas, 1952.

Hall, Faye Benson. "A Study of the Educational Progress of Graduates of Chaffey Union High School." Master's, University of Southern California, 1931.

Hall, Gilbert Ennis. "Some Legal Aspects of the Education of Spanish-speaking Children in Texas." Master's, University of Texas, 1947.

Hall, William C. "A Study of 281 Farm Labor Families of South Texas." Master's, Texas College of Arts and Industries, 1942.

Hanson, Edith Josephine. "A Study of Intelligence Test Results for Mexican Children Based on English and Mexican Test Forms." Master's, University of Southern California, 1931.

Hanson, Stella E. "Mexican Laborers in the Southwest." Master's, Pomona College, 1926.

Harris, James K. "A Sociological Study of a Mexican School in San Antonio, Texas." Master's, University of Texas, 1927.

Harrison, David C. "A Survey of the Administrative and Educational Policies of the Baptist, Methodist, and Presbyterian Churches among Mexican-American People of Texas." Master's, University of Texas, 1952.

Harrison, I. A. "Health Needs and Interests of Spanish-speaking Children of Intermediate Grades." Master's, University of California, Los Angeles, 1957.

Harvey, Louise Fawcett. "The Delinquent Mexican Boy in an Urban Area, 1945." Master's, University of California, Los Angeles, 1947.

Hayden, Jessie. "The La Habra Experiment in Mexican Social Education." Master's, Claremont College, 1934.

Hayes, James U. "An Analysis of Latin-American Partial Attendance and Dropouts in the Elementary Schools of Eagle Pass, Texas, in Recent Years." Master's, University of Texas, 1952.

Heller, Celia Stopnicka. "Ambitions of Mexican-American Youth: Goals and Means of Mobility of High School Seniors." Ph.D., Columbia University, 1964.

Henderson, Norman B. "A Study of Intelligence of Children of Mexican and Non-Mexican Parentage." Master's, Occidental College, 1948.

Hernandez, Arcadia. "A Study of Retarded Spanish-speaking Children in the Second Grade . . . " Master's, University of Texas, 1938.

Hernandez, Elias Vega. "Reading Retardation of Children in Zavala School, Austin, Texas." Master's, University of Texas, 1954.

Herr, Selma E. "The Effects of Pre-first-grade Training upon Reading Readiness and Reading Achievement Among Spanish-American Children in the First Grade." Ph.D., University of Texas 1944.

Herriman, G. W. "An Investigation Concerning the Effect of Language Handicap on Mental Development and Educational Progress." Master's, University of Southern California, 1932.

Hill, Marguerite W. "A Proposed Guidance Program for Mexican Youth in the Junior High School." Master's, Claremont College, 1945.

Hill, Merton E. "The Development of an Americanization Program." Ph.D., University of California at Berkeley, 1928.

Hoffman, Howardine G. "Bi-lingualism and Oral and Written Expression of Fifth Grade Children." Master's, University of Southern California, 1938.

Hogan, Milo Arthur Van Norman. "A Study of the School Progress of Mexican Children in Imperial County." Master's, University of Southern California, 1934.

Holliday, Jay Newton. "A Study of Non-attendance in Miquel Hidalgo School of Brawley, California." Master's, University of Southern California, 1935.

Horner, Edward. "A Recreation Director in a Mexican-American Community." Master's, University of California, Los Angeles, 1945.

Horton, Frances. "Food Habits and Living Conditions of Mexicans Dwelling in the Rio Grande Valley Between Roma and Mercedes." Master's, University of Texas, 1936.

Houle, Bettie E. "Some Significant Characteristics Associated with Popularity in American and Mexican Elementary School Children." Ph.D., University of Chicago, 1954.

Howard, Donald Stephenson. "A Study of the Mexican, Mexican-American and

Spanish-American Population in Pueblo, Colorado, 1929–1930." Master's, University of Denver, 1932.

Howard, Raymond G. "Acculturation and Social Mobility Among Latin-Americans in Rasaca City." Master's, University of Texas, 1952.

Howe, Anna L. "Proposals for the Organization and Administration of a Program of Special Education to Improve the English Speech of Certain Spanish-speaking Pupils." Master's, University of Texas, 1952.

Hufford, Charles Henry. "The Social and Economic Effects of the Mexican Migration into Texas." Master's, University of Colorado, 1929.

Hughes, L. S. "A Comparative Study of the Intelligence of Mexican Children." Master's, University of Texas, 1928.

Hughes, Marie Morrison. "The English Language Facility of Mexican-American Children Living and Attending School in a Segregated Community." Ph.D., Stanford University, 1952.

Hunt, William Andrew, Jr. "Migration and Population Changes and Their Educational Implications." Master's, University of Texas, 1941.

Hurt, Wesley. "Manzano: A Study of Community Disorganization." Master's, University of New Mexico, 1941.

Hurta, J. Conrad. "Educational Trends and Utilization of Education by Spanish-American Children in the Scottsbluff Public School System." Master's, Nebraska State Teachers College, 1959.

Hymer, Elizabeth. "A Study of the Social Attitudes of Adult Mexican Immigrants in Los Angeles and Vicinity." Master's, University of Southern California, 1924.

Irion, Clyde. "A Study of Neighboring in Dallas." Master's, Southern Methodist University, 1940.

Irish, Dorothy C. "An Experiment to Determine the Value of Use of the Mother-Tongue in Teaching a Beginning Class of Spanish-speaking Children." Master's, University of New Mexico, 1945.

Jackson, Dorris G. "Educational Status of Mexican Children in a Texas Elementary School." Master's, University of Texas, 1952.

Jackson, Lucile Prim. "An Analysis of the Language Difficulties of the Spanish-speaking Children of the Bowie High School, El Paso, Texas." Master's, University of Texas, 1938.

Jarvis, Gertrude O. "A Study of the Relation of Achievement in Spanish to Achievement in English." Master's, University of Texas, 1953.

Jerden, Cecil M. "A Study in Racial Differences in the El Paso Public Schools." Master's, Southern Methodist University, 1939.

Johansen, Sigurd. "Rural Social Organization in a Spanish-American Culture Area." Ph.D., University of Wisconsin, 1941.

Johns, Bryan Theodore. "Field Workers in California Cotton." Master's, University of California, Berkeley, 1948.

Johnson, B. E. "Ability, Achievement, and Bi-lingualism: A Comparative Study Involving Spanish-speaking and English-speaking Children at the 6th Grade Level." Ph.D., University of Maryland, 1962.

Johnson, C. G. "The Effectiveness of Light Singing Instruction for Mexican and Negro Children." Master's, University of Southern California, 1938.

Johnson, Henry Sioux. "Ethnic Group Differences in Certain Personal, Intellectual, Achievement and Motivational Characteristics." Ph.D., University of Southern California, 1964.

Johnson, Roberta M. "History of the Education of Spanish-speaking Children in Texas." Master's, University of Texas, 1932.

Jones, Anita Edgar. "Conditions Surrounding Mexicans in Chicago." Master's, University of Chicago, 1928.

Jones, Hubert Ledyard. "A Comparison of Physical Skill and Intelligence of Negro and Spanish-American Boys of Junior High School Age." Master's, University of Denver, 1940.

Jonson, Carl R. "A Study of the Spanish-

American Normal School at El Rito." Master's, University of New Mexico, 1939.

Juarez, Nicandro. "José Vasconcelos' Theory of the Cosmic Race." Master's, University of California, Los Angeles, 1965.

Kadechi, James U. "A Study of Mexican Education in Altascosa County with Special Reference to the Pleasantown Elementary School." Master's, University of Texas, 1938.

Kaderli, Albert T. "The Educational Problem in the Americanization of Spanish-speaking Pupils of Sugarland, Texas." Master's, University of Texas, 1940.

Kelsey, Ruth M. "The Comparison of Scholastic Standing Among Children of Native Born Parents with Children of Foreign Parents." Master's, University of Denver, 1932.

Kienle, John Emmanuel. "Housing Conditions Among the Mexican Population of Los Angeles." Master's, University of Southern California, 1912.

King, Genevieve. "The Psychology of a Mexican Community in San Antonio, Texas." Master's, University of Texas, 1938.

King, John Randle. "An Inquiry into the Status of Mexican Segregation in Metropolitan Bakersfield." Master's, Claremont Graduate School, 1946.

Kingrea, Nellie Ward. "History of the Good Neighbor Commission in Texas." Master's, Texas Christian University, n.d.

Kluckhohn, Florence. "Los Atarquenos: A Study of Patterns and Configurations in a New Mexico Village." Ph.D., Radcliffe College, 1941.

Knopf, Arthur Carlyle. "Some Mexican Characteristics and Their Educational Significance." Master's, University of Southern California, 1943.

Knox, William J. "The Economic Status of the Mexican Immigrant in San Antonio, Texas." Master's, University of Texas, 1927.

Krassowski, Witold. "Naturalization and Assimilation Proneness of California Immigrant Populations." Ph.D., University of California, Los Angeles, 1963.

Kresselman, Harold B. "A Study of 100 Male Latin-American Juvenile Delinquents in San Antonio." Master's, University of Texas, 1948.

Kurth, Myrtle. "A Study of Four Racial Groups in a Pasadena Junior High School." Master's, University of Southern California, 1941.

Landman, Ruth. "Some Aspects of the Acculturation of Mexican Immigrants and Their Descendants to American Culture." Ph.D., Yale University, 1953.

Lanigan, Mary C. "Second Generation Mexicans in Belvedere." Master's, University of Southern California, 1932.

Lasswell, Thomas E. "A Study of Status Stratification in Los Angeles." Ph.D., University of Southern California, 1952.

Lehman, Victor Boyd. "A Study of the Social Adjustment of the Mexican-Americans in Chino and a Proposed Plan of Community Action Under School Leadership." Master's, Claremont Graduate School, 1947.

Leifeste, Sam A. D. "Characteristics of the Texas Latin-American Market." Ph.D., University of Texas, 1954.

Leis, Ward William. "The Status of Education for Mexican Children in Four Border States." Master's, University of Southern California, 1932.

Leonard, Olen E. "The Role of the Land Grant in the Social Organization and Social Processes of a Spanish-American Village in New Mexico." Ph.D., Louisiana State University, 1943.

Lin, Paul Ming-Chang. "Voluntary Kinship and Voluntary Association in a Mexican-American Community." Master's, University of Kansas, 1963.

Linthicum, John Buren. "The Classification of Spanish-American Beginners in an Albuquerque Public School." Master's, University of Southern California, 1929.

Lipshultz, Robert J. "American Attitudes Toward Mexican Immigration, 1924–

1952." Ph.D., University of Chicago, 1962.

Lofstedt, Anna C. "A Study of the Mexican Population in Pasadena, California." Master's, University of Southern California, 1922.

Loftin, J. O. "Mexican Secondary Education as Developed in the Sidney Lanier Junior High School of San Antonio, Texas." Master's, Texas State Teachers College, 1927.

Loomis, Nellie Holmes. "Spanish-Anglo Ethnic Cleavage in a New Mexican High School." Ph.D., Michigan State University, 1955.

Lyon, L. L. "Investigation of the Program for the Adjustment of Mexican Girls to the High Schools of San Fernando Valley." Master's, University of Southern California, 1933.

Lyon, Richard Martin. "The Legal Status of American and Mexican Migratory Farm Labor: An Analysis of U.S. Farm Labor Legislation, Policy and Administration." Ph.D., Cornell University, 1954.

MacCarthy, Carrie Bell Hooper. "A Survey of the Mexican Hardship Cases Active in the Los Angeles County Department of Charities, Los Angeles, California." Master's, University of Southern California, 1939.

McCary, Mallie Muncy. "These Minorities in our Midst: With Emphasis on Latin-Americans in Texas." Master's, University of Texas, 1953.

McClendon, Juliette Jane Canfield. "Spanish-speaking Children of Big Spring—An Educational Challenge." Ph.D., University of Texas, 1964.

McEuen, William. "A Survey of the Mexican in Los Angeles." Master's, University of Southern California, 1914.

McGarry, Sister Francesca. "A Study of Cultural Patterns Among Three Generations of Mexicans in San Antonio, Texas." Master's, University of Texas, 1957.

McGregor, Mrs. R. P. "The Elimination of Eighth Grade Graduates Among the Mexicans from the High Schools of a Certain Small City in California." Master's, University of Southern California, 1940.

McLean, Robert J. "A Comparative Study of Anglo-American and Spanish-name Children in the Austin Public Schools over a Seven Year Period." Master's, University of Texas, 1950.

McLennan, LeRoy. "A Comparison of the Spanish-speaking and English-speaking Children in Nine Schools over a Five-year Period." Master's, University of Texas, 1936.

McNamara, Patrick H., S. J. "Mexican-American Families in Los Angeles County." Master's, Saint Louis University, 1957.

McNaughton, Donald Alexander. "A Social Study of Mexican and Spanish-American Wage-earners in Delta, Colorado." Master's, University of Colorado, 1942.

McNiel, Guy Brett. "A Pre-first-grade Oral-English Program as Related to the Scholastic Achievement of Spanish-speaking Children." Ph.D., University of Colorado, 1958.

Macklin, Barbara J. "Structural Stability and Culture Change in a Mexican-American Community." Ph.D., University of Pennsylvania, 1963.

Madril, Ernest. "Social Participation in Relation to the Acculturation of the Spanish-speaking People of Del Norte, Colorado." Master's, Washington University, 1952.

Manzo, Ricardo. "Difficulties of Spanish-speaking Children in the Fundamental Number Combinations." Master's, University of Arizona, 1939.

Marcoux, Fred Wesley. "Handicaps of Bi-lingual Mexican Children." Master's, University of Southern California, 1961.

Marsh, Elizabeth F. "Dietary Studies of Families on Relief." Master's, University of Texas, 1935.

Martinez, Arnulfo S. "A Study of the Scholastic Census of the Spanish-speaking Children of Texas." Master's, University of Texas, 1944.

Martinez, Ruth Lucretia. "The Unusual

Mexican: A Study in Acculturation." Master's, Claremont Graduate School, 1942.

Mason, Florence Gordon. "A Case Study of Thirty Adolescent Mexican Girls and Their Social Conflicts and Adjustment Within the School." Master's, University of Southern California, 1928.

Massey, Ellis Leonard. "Migration of the Spanish-speaking People of Hidalgo County." Master's, University of Texas, 1953.

Matzigkeit, Wesley Winifred. "The Influence of Six Mexican Cultural Factors on Group Behavior." Master's, University of Southern California, 1947.

Meador, Bruce Staffel. "Minority Groups and Their Education in Hay County, Texas. Ph.D., University of Texas, 1959.

——. "Wetback Labor in the Lower Rio Grande Valley," Master's, University of Texas, 1951.

Meguire, K. H. "Educating the Mexican Child in the Elementary School." Master's, University of Southern California, 1938.

Meier, Harold C. "The Oral Communication of Health-disease Beliefs in a Serial Reproduction Experiment." Ph.D., University of Colorado, 1963.

——. "Three Ethnic Groups in a Southwestern Community." Master's, University of Colorado, 1955.

Mendenhall, W. C. "A Comparative Study of Achievement and Ability of the Children in Two Segregated Mexican Schools." Master's, University of Southern California, 1937.

Merryweather, Rose. "A Study of the Comparative Ability of the Mexican and American Children in the Upper Elementary Grades." Master's, University of Southern California, 1937.

Michea, Claude Angus. "The Intelligence of Nine and Ten Year Old Mexican Children as Measured by the Leiter International Performance Scale." Master's, University of Southern California, 1941.

Miller, Bonnie Belle. "Meeting the Needs of the Spanish-speaking Migrant in the Coahoma Elementary School, Howard County, Texas, 1950–1953." Master's, University of Texas, 1954.

Miller, Curtis R. "A Typology of Spanish Surname Census Tracts in Los Angeles County." Master's, University of Southern California, 1960.

Mitchell, Nan J. "An Evaluation of Provisions for the Education of the Spanish-speaking Children in San Marcos, Texas." Master's, University of Texas, 1946.

Mitchell, Q. B. "Comparative Achievements of White, Mexican, and Colored Children in Elementary Public Schools." Master's, University of Kansas, 1926.

Montez, Philip. "Some Differences in Factors Related to Educational Achievement of Two Mexican-American Groups." Master's, University of Southern California, 1960.

Moore, Luella. "The Administration of the Social Welfare Program in Several Typical Foreign Schools in Los Angeles City." Master's, University of Southern California, 1935.

Morales, Armando. "A Study of Recidivism of Mexican-American Junior Forestry Camp Graduates." Master's, University of Southern California, 1963.

Moran, Mattie Belle. "A Study of the Oral and Reading Vocabularies of Beginning Spanish-speaking Children." Master's, University of Texas, 1940.

Morrison, Charlotte Amos. "A Comparison of the Achievement of Mexican Pupils in Learning English in a Segregated School and in a Non-segregated School, 1952." Master's, University of Oregon, 1952.

Morrison, Ethel M. "A History of Recent Legislative Proposals Concerning Mexican Immigration." Master's, University of Southern California, 1929.

Moya, Benjamin S. "Superstitions and Beliefs Among the Spanish-speaking People of New Mexico." Master's, University of New Mexico, 1940.

Mullins, Martha Mersman. "The Personality Differences Between Unilingual and Bi-lingual Ninth Grade Students in Depressed Areas." Master's, University of New Mexico, 1961.

Munoz, Rosalio Florian. "Differences in Drop-out and Other School Behavior Between Two Groups of Tenth Grade Boys in an Urban High School." Ph.D., University of Southern California, 1957.

Munson, John. "Intelligence Ratings for Ninety-seven Mexican Children in St. Paul, Minnesota." Ph.D., University of Minnesota, 1950.

Nall, Frank. "Levels of Aspiration of Mexican-Americans in El Paso Schools. Ph.D., Michigan State University, 1959.

Nami, Julia. "A Study of the Family Life, in Its Relation to Education, of Pupils in the Second Grade of the Anthony Margil School, San Antonio, Texas." Master's, University of Texas, 1940.

Nathan, Jerome M. "The Relationship of English Language Deficiency to Intelligence Test Scores of Mentally Retarded Mexican-American Children." Master's, University of California, Los Angeles, 1955.

Neal, Joe W. "The Policy of the United States Toward Immigration from Mexico." Master's, University of Texas, 1941.

Newell, Elizabeth Virginia. "The Social Significance of Padua Hills as a Cultural and Educational Center." Master's, University of Southern California, 1938.

Nicoll, James Stewart. "A Comparison of the Physical Development, Motor Capacity and Strength of Anglo-American and Spanish-American Boys." Master's, University of Southern California, 1943.

O'Brien, Mary Ross. "A Comparison of the Reading Ability of Spanish-speaking with Non-spanish-Speaking Pupils in Grade 6A of the Denver Public Schools." Master's, University of Denver, 1937.

Officer, James E. "Sodalities and Systemic Linkage: The Joining Habits of Urban Mexican-Americans." Ph.D., University of Arizona, 1964.

Ortegon, Samuel Maldonado. "The Religious Status of the Mexican Population of Los Angeles." Master's, University of Southern California, 1932.

———. "Religious Thought and Practice among Mexican Baptists of the U.S., 1900–1947." Ph.D., University of Southern California, 1950.

Osborne, Marie A. S. "The Educational Status of Intra-state Migrants in Texas, 1935–40." Master's, University of Texas, 1954.

Page, Mrs. Dorothy. "Performance of Spanish-American Children on Verbal and Non-verbal Intelligence Tests." Master's, University of New Mexico, 1931.

Painter, Norman Wellington. "The Assimilation of Latin-Americans in New Orleans, Louisiana." Master's, Tulane University, 1949.

Palace, Arthur Lawrence. "A Comparative Description of Anglo-white and Mexican–white Boys Committed to Pacific Colony." Master's, University of Southern California, 1950.

Parsley, Rosa Frances. "A Study of the Expenditure for Food of Some Urban Latin-American Families on Work Relief in Austin, Texas." Master's, University of Texas, 1935.

Parr, Eunice P. "A Comparative Study of Mexican and American Children in the Schools of San Antonio, Texas." Master's, University of Chicago, 1926.

Parsons, Theodore William. "Ethnic Cleavage in a California School." Ph.D., Stanford University, 1965.

Peek, R. B. "The Religious and Social Attitudes of the Mexican Girls of the Constituency of the All Nations Foundation in Los Angeles." Master's, University of Southern California, 1929."

Peñalosa, Fernando. "Class Consciousness and Social Mobility in a Mexican-American Community." Ph.D., University of Southern California, 1963.

Perez, Soledad. "Mexican Folklore in Austin." Master's, University of Texas, 1949.

Perry, Josef Henry. "Economic Characteristics of Texas Intrastate Migrants." Master's, University of Texas, 1961.

Peters, Mary M. "The Segregation of Mexican-American Children in the Elementary Schools of California: Its Legal and Administrative Aspects." Master's, University of California, Los Angeles, 1948.

Pipes, Karl M. "A Study of the Failures and Drop-outs in the San Benito High School." Master's, University of Texas, 1950.

Pitt, Leonard Marvin. "The Foreign Miners' Tax of 1850: A Study of Nativism and Antinativism in Gold Rush California." Master's, University of California, Los Angeles, 1955.

———. "Submergence of the Mexican in California, 1846–1890: A History of Culture Conflict and Acculturation." Ph.D., University of California, Los Angeles, 1958.

Porter, Charles Jesse. "Recreational Interests and Activities of High School Boys of the Lower Rio Grande Valley of Texas." Master's, University of Texas, 1940.

Pratt, P. S. "A Comparison of the Social Achievement and Socio-economic Background of Mexican and White Children in a Delta, Colorado Elementary School." Master's, University of Southern California, 1938.

Press, Ernest. "The Mexican Population in Laramie." Master's, University of Wyoming, 1946.

Putman, Howard L. "The Relation of College Programs of Community Services to the Needs of the Spanish-speaking People." Ph.D., University of Texas, 1956.

Randals, Edwyna Henrietta. "A Comparison of the Intelligence Test Results of Mexican and Negro Children in Two Elementary Schools." Master's, University of Southern California, 1929.

Ranker, Jesse E. Jr., "A Study of Juvenile Gangs in the Hollenbeck Area of East Los Angeles." Master's, University of Southern California, 1958.

Ramirez, Emilia S. "Wetback Children in South Texas." Master's, University of Texas, 1951.

Ream, Glen O. "A Study of Spanish-speaking Pupils in Albuquerque High School." Master's, Yale University, 1930.

Reeves, Grace Elizabeth. "Adult Mexican Education in the United States." Master's, Claremont College, 1929.

Rendon, Gabino. "Voting Behavior in a Tri-ethnic Community." Master's, University of Colorado, 1962.

Renner, Richard Roy. "Some Characteristics of Spanish-name Texans and Foreign Latin-Americans in Texas Higher Education." Ph.D., University of Texas, 1957.

Reyes, Ignacio. "A Survey of the Problems Involved in the Americanization of the Mexican-American." Master's, University of Southern California, 1957.

Reynolds, Evelyn Dolores. "A Study of Migratory Factors Affecting Education in North Kern County." Master's, University of Southern California, 1932.

Rice, Theodore D. "Some Contributing Factors in Determining the Social Adjustments of the Spanish-speaking People of Denver and Vicinity." Master's, University of Denver, 1932.

Riggins, Rachael T. "Factors in Social Background Which Influence the Mexican Child." Master's, University of Arizona, 1946.

Robertson, Clyde R. "A Comparative Study of the Progress of American and Mexican Pupils in Certain Elementary Schools in Texas." Master's, University of Texas, 1935.

Robles, Ernest A. "An Analytic Description of Peer Group Pressures on Mobility-oriented Mexican-American Junior High Students." Master's, University of Redlands, 1964.

Rogers, Robert B. "Perception of the Power Structure by Social Class in a California Community." Ph.D., University of Southern California, 1962.

Rogers, Thomas Guy. "The Housing Situation of the Mexicans in San Antonio, Texas." Master's, University of Texas, 1927.

Roots, Floy. "Methods and Materials for Teaching Spanish to Spanish-speaking Students in Texas High Schools." Master's, University of Texas, 1937.

Ross, William T. "Social Function of the Mexican-American Godparent System in Tucson." Master's, University of Arizona, 1953.

Rubel, Arthur Joseph. "Social Life of Urban Mexican-Americans." Ph.D., University of North Carolina, 1963.

Ruby, Carrie L. "Attitudes Toward Latin-Americans as Revealed in Southwestern Literature." Master's, University of Texas, 1953.

Russell, John C. "State Regionalism in New Mexico." Master's, Stanford University, 1938.

Saenz, Alfredo N. "A Field Study of Two Programs Designed for Preparing the Resident, Non-English-speaking Child of Spanish Culture to Meet First-grade Requirements in One Year." Ph.D., University of Houston, 1957.

Saint John, Berea Edith. "Spanish-speaking Delinquents of the Denver Juvenile Court." Master's, University of Denver, 1939.

Salcedo, Consuelo. "Mexican-American Socio-cultural Patterns: Implications for Social Casework." Master's, University of Southern California, 1955.

Samora, Julian. "The Acculturation of the Spanish-speaking People of Fort Collins, Colorado, in Selected Culture Areas." Master's, Colorado A&M College, 1947.

———. "Minority Leadership in a Biracial Cultural Community." Ph.D., Washington University, 1953.

Sanchez, George I. "A Study of the Scores of Spanish-speaking Children on Repeated Tests." Master's, University of Texas, 1931.

———. "The Education of Bi-linguals in a State School System." Ph.D., University of California, Berkeley, 1934.

Sanchez, Luisa Guerrero G. "The 'Latin-American' of the Southwest: Backgrounds and Curricular Implications." Ph.D., University of Texas, 1954.

Sandoval, T. Joe. "A Study of Some Aspects of the Spanish-speaking Population in Selected Communities in Wyoming." Master's, University of Wyoming, 1946.

Sargis, Albert L. "Networks of Discord: A Study of the Communications System Between Spanish-speaking Organizations and Their Community." Master's, San Francisco State College, 1966.

Sauter, Mary C. "Arbol Verde: Cultural Conflict and Accommodation in a California Mexican Community." Master's, Claremont College, 1933.

Schneider, Virginia. "Abilities of Mexican and White." Master's, University of Southern California, 1931.

Schroff, Ruth. "A Study of Social Distance Between Mexican Parents and American Teachers in San Bernardino, California." Master's, University of Southern California, 1936.

Shannon, Fain Gillock. "A Comparative Study of Desirable Teacher Traits as Listed by Anglo-American and Latin-American Pupils." Master's, University of Texas, 1939.

Shelton, Edgar Greer. "Political Conditions Among Texas Mexicans Along the Rio Grande." Master's, University of Texas, 1946.

Shybut, John. "Delayed Gratification: A Study of Its Measurement and Its Relationship to Certain Behavioral, Psychological and Demographic Variables." Master's, University of Colorado, 1963.

Simmons, Ozzie G. "Anglo-Americans and Mexican-Americans in South Texas: A Study in Dominant-Subordinate Group Relations." Ph.D., Harvard University, 1952.

Sininger, H. "New Mexico Reading Survey." Master's, University of New Mexico, 1930.

Sion, Alvin P. "Mentally Deficient Mexican-American Delinquent Boys Who Made Good After Institutional Care: An Analysis of Six Cases." Master's, University of Southern California, 1951.

Sjoberg, Gideon. "Culture Change as Revealed by a Study of Relief Clients of a Suburban New Mexico Community." Master's, University of New Mexico, 1947.

Skendzel, Eduardo Adam. "La Colonia Mexicana en Detroit." Master's, Saltillo Coahuila, Mexico, 1961.

Smith, Alva Louis. "A Comparative Study of Facts and Factors Affecting and Effecting the Retardation of Bi-lingual Children." Master's, University of Texas, 1952.

Smith, Avis Dowis. "A Comparative Study of Some Attitudes and Interest of Latin-American and Anglo-American Boys." Master's, University of Texas, 1940.

Smith, Clara Gertrude. "The Development of the Mexican People in the Community of Watts, California." Master's, University of Southern California, 1936.

Smith, Helen P. "Health and Nutrition of Mexican Infants and Pre-school Children." Master's, Univ. of Texas, 1930.

Smith, J. B. Jr. "A Survey of Pupil Failure in the La Feria School with Suggested Remedial Measures." Master's, University of Texas, 1939.

Soffer, Virginia M. "Socio-cultural Changes in the Lives of Five Mexican-American College Graduates." Master's, University of Southern California, 1958.

Sowell, Emmie I. "A Study of Boys' Clubs in Texas, with Special Reference to San Antonio." Master's, University of Texas, 1940.

Spielberg, Joseph. "Social and Cultural Configurations and Medical Care: A Study of Mexican-Americans' Responses to Proposed Hospitalization for the Treatment of Tuberculosis." Master's, University of Texas, 1959.

Sprinkle, Eunice Caroline. "A Comparative Study of the Reading Interests of Mexican and White Children." Master's, University of Southern California, 1941.

Starkey, R. J. "A Synthesis and Interpretation of Research Findings Which Pertained to Teaching Spanish-speaking Children." Ph.D., Texas Technological College, 1961.

Steinike, David G. "Population Characteristics of Dallas by Census Tracts." Master's, Southern Methodist University, 1938.

Summers, Helen. "An Evaluation of Certain Procedures in the Teaching of Non-English-speaking Mexican Children." Master's, University of California, Los Angeles, 1939.

Swalestuen, E. D. "A Comparative Study of the Mexican and White Child in Ninth Grade Algebra." Master's, University of Southern California, 1933.

Taylor, Harry Franklin. "The Musical Abilities of Spanish-American Children." Master's, Denver University, 1934.

Taylor, Juanita Faye. "A Comparison of First and Second Generation Mexican Parents." Master's, University of Southern California, 1943.

Taylor, M. C. "Retardation of Mexican Children in the Albuquerque Schools." Master's, Stanford University, 1927.

Thurston, Richard G. "Urbanization and Socio-cultural Change in a Mexican-American Enclave." Ph.D., University of California, Los Angeles, 1962.

Tinsley, Willa Vaughn. "Building Better School Community Relations in Latin-American Communities." Master's, Southwest Texas State Teachers College, 1949.

Treff, S. L. "The Education of Mexican Children in Orange County." Master's, University of Southern California, 1934.

Trujillo, Luis M. "Diccionario del Espanol del Valle de San Luis de Colorado y del Norte de Nuevo Mexico." Master's, Adams State College, 1961.

Tubbs, Lowell L. "A Survey of the Problems of Migratory Mexicans." Master's, University of Texas, 1952.

Ulibarri, Horacia. "Teacher Awareness of Socio-cultural Differences in Multicultural Classrooms." Ph.D., University of New Mexico, 1959.

Ullman, Paul S. "An Ecological Analysis of Social Variables of Mexican-Americans in Los Angeles County." Master's,

University of Southern California, 1953.

Valdes, Daniel T. "A Sociological Analysis and Description of the Political Role, Status and Voting Behavior of Americans with Spanish Names." Ph.D., University of Colorado, 1964.

Valerius, John B. "The Spanish-speaking Population of Texas 1954–1955: Estimates and a Study of Estimation Methods." Master's, University of Texas, 1956.

Van der Erden, Sister Lucia. "Maternal Care in a Spanish-American Community in New Mexico." Ph.D., Catholic University of America, 1947.

Van Velzer, Francis. "Race Relation Problems of 50 Normal Adolescent Mexican-American Boys in Los Angeles." Master's, University of Southern California, 1936.

Villarreal, Eduardo. "A Study of Group Processes in Two Small Natural Groups of Latin-American Adolescents." Master's, University of Texas, 1962.

Vincent, Henrietta H. "A Study of Performance of Spanish-speaking Pupils on Spanish Tests." Master's, New Mexico State Teachers College, 1933.

Von Elm, Sister Theodore Mary. "An Appraisal of Participation in the Group Work Services Offered at Guadalupe Community Center." Master's, University of Texas, 1963.

Waddell, Jack. "Value Orientations of Young Mexican-American Males as Reflected in Their Work Patterns and Employment Preferences." Master's, University of Texas, 1962.

Wagoner, Delmer William. "Recent Migration of Young Males into Houston, Texas." Master's, University of Texas, 1957.

Walker, Helen W. "The Conflict of Cultures in First Generation Mexicans in Santa Ana, California." Master's, University of Southern California, 1928.

Wallis, Marie Pope. "A Study of Dependency in One Hundred Cases Taken from Files of Bureau of County Welfare. Catholic Welfare Bureau, Los Angeles County Relief Administration." Master's, University of Southern California, 1935.

Walsh, Brother Albeus. "The Work of the Catholic Bishops' Committee for the Spanish-speaking People in the United States." Master's, University of Texas, 1952.

Walter, Paul A. "A Study of Isolation and Social Change in Three Spanish-speaking Villages of New Mexico." Ph.D., Stanford University, 1938.

Walton, Roger M. Vernon. "A Study of Migratory Mexican Pea-pickers in Imperial Valley, August, 1940." Master's, University of Southern California, 1941.

Wells, Gladys. "Factors Influencing the Assimilation of the Mexican in Texas." Master's, Southern Methodist University, 1941.

White, Jean Dempewolf. "Time Orientation as a Factor in the Acculturation of Southwestern Spanish-speaking Groups." Master's, University of Texas, 1955.

Whitten, Chester Irwin. "An Experimental Study of the Comparison of 'Formal' and 'Progressive' Methods of Teaching Mexican Children." Master's, University of Southern California, 1939.

Whitwell, Inez Margaret. "A Homemaking Course for Mexican Girls Who Will Be Unable to Attend High School." Master's, University of Southern California, 1937.

Whitworth, Wallace. "School Drop-outs: A Comparison of Interest in School with Peer and Authority Relationship." Master's, Worden School of Social Service, Our Lady of the Lake College, 1964.

Williams, Coleen. "Cultural Differences and Medical Care of 10 Mexican Migrant Families in San Antonio, Texas." Master's, University of Texas, 1959.

Williams, Dean L. "Some Political and Economic Aspects of Mexican Immigration into the United States since 1941, with Particular Reference to This Immigration into the State of California." Master's, University of California, Los Angeles, 1950.

Wilson, Frank E. "El Cerrito: A Changing

Culture." Master's, New Mexico Highlands University, 1949.

Wilson, Joe H. "Secondary School Dropouts with Special Reference to Spanish-speaking Youths in Texas." Ph.D., University of Texas, 1953.

Wilson, William Nathan. "Analysis of the Academic and Home Problems of the Pupils in a Mexican Junior High School." Master's, University of Southern California, 1938.

Winchester, Gertrude K. "Achievements, Social Concepts and Attitudes of Three Racial Groups." Master's, Whittier College, 1944.

Withers, Charles Dinnijes. "Problems of Mexican Boys." Master's, University of Southern California, 1942.

Wolf, N. "Standardization of a Spanish Translation of the Davis-Eells Games (Elementary A) on Mexican-American Children in the Elementary Schools in Los Angeles County." Master's, University of California, Los Angeles, 1955.

Wood, Herbert Sidney. "A Pupil Survey of James A. Garfield High School, Los Angeles." Master's, University of Southern California, 1937.

Woodward, Dorothy. "The Penitentes of New Mexico." Ph.D., Yale University, 1935.

Wright, Frank M. "Survey of the El Monte School District." Master's, University of Southern California, 1930.

Ybarra, Jesse R. "A Study to Determine Why Spanish-speaking Children Drop out of School in Junior and Senior School in a Particular Community in San Antonio, Texas." Master's, Trinity University, 1955.

Ynigo, Alexander. "Mexican-American Children in an Integrated Elementary School: An Investigation of Their Academic Performance and Social Adjustment." Master's, University of Southern California, 1957.

Zeleny, Carolyn. "Relations Between the Spanish-Americans and the Anglo-Americans in New Mexico: A Study of Conflict and Accommodation in a Dual Ethnic Relationship." Ph.D., Yale University, 1944.

IV. OTHER UNPUBLISHED MATERIALS

Adams State College, Center for Cultural Studies. "Readings for Understanding Southwestern Culture." Alamosa, Colo., Center for Cultural Studies, 1963.

Almanza, Arturo S. "Mexican-Americans and Civil Rights." Los Angeles County Commission on Human Relations, 1964.

Alvarado, Luis. "Employment Opportunities Questionnaire Summary." Report distributed by the Catholic Bishop's Committee for the Spanish-speaking, San Antonio, Tex., March 14, 1961.

Barraza, Robert B. "Helping Mexican-American Children Become More Socially Productive Citizens." Project report, University of Southern California, May, 1955.

Battey, Viola. "The Mexican Situation in St. Paul." From the files of the International Institute, St. Paul, Minn.' 1925.

Belden, Joe. "Market Characteristics of San Antonio Latin-Americans." Dallas, Tex., Joe Belden and Associates, 1952.

———. "The Latin-American Population in Texas: Estimates by Counties." Dallas, Tex., Joe Belden and Associates, 1951.

———. "Radio Listening, Buying Power, Brand Preferences of the Latin-American Market in the Lower Rio Grande Valley of Texas." Dallas, Tex., Joe Belden and Associates, 1952.

———. "The Latin-American Audience and Market of Austin, Texas." Dallas, Tex., Joe Belden and Associates, 1951.

Bellesteros, L., V. Lopez, and A. P. Herman. "Study of an Eleven Year Old

Mexican-American Boy." California State Department of Education, n.d.

Bexar County Tuberculosis Association. "Annual Report for 1939." San Antonio, Tex., 1940.

――――. "Tuberculosis and Its Control—Facts and Figures in San Antonio and Bexar County." Bexar County Tuberculosis Association in Cooperation with the Alamo Tuberculosis Control Council and the Junior Chamber of Commerce, San Antonio, Tex., 1939.

Bullock, Paul. "Occupational Distribution by Major Ethnic Groups and by Labor Market Areas, Selected Government Contractors, Los Angeles Metropolitan Area." Institute of Industrial Relations, University of California, Los Angeles, 1963.

Calexico Unified School District, Calexico, Calif. "Teaching English as a Second Language to Pupils of Foreign Born, Mexican Heritage." Imperial County Education Center, 1963–65.

California Citizens' Committee on Civil Disturbances in Los Angeles. "Report and Recommendations." San Francisco, Bay Area Council Against Discrimination, 1943 (mimeographed).

California Commission of Immigration and Housing. "A Community Survey Made in Los Angeles City." San Francisco, 1919[?].

California Department of Industrial Relations, Division of Apprenticeship Standards. "Preliminary Report on Survey of Active Apprentices." Apr., 25, 1962.

California Fair Employment Practice Commission. "Los Angeles City Schools," Preliminary Report. October, 1964.

California Federation for Civic Unity. "Get Out If You Can: The Saga of Sal si Puedes." An account by Fred W. Ross of an American Friends Service Committee project among Mexican-Americans in a Northern California community. San Francisco, 1953.

"Careers for Youth." Report of the Mexican-American Education Conference. Phoenix, Arizona, Jan., 1963.

Carmelia F., and F. W. Kratz. "Tuberculosis Control in Los Angeles City." Los Angeles Department of Health, 1940.

Chamber of Commerce of the United States, Immigration Committee. "Mexican Immigration." Washington, D.C., 1930.

"Committee Reports of the Conference on Educational Problems in the Southwest with Special Reference to the Educational Problems in Spanish-speaking Communities." Conference held at Santa Fe, New Mexico, Aug. 19–24, 1943 under the auspices of the University of New Mexico, New Mexico Highlands University, and the Coordinator of Inter-American Affairs.

Community Service Organization, Educational Committee. "Report of the Advisory Committee on Human Relations to the Board of Education." 1951.

Community Service Organization, Education Standing Committee. "Guidelines for Use by Chapter Education Committees," Mar. 23, 1957.

Coordinator of Inter-American Affairs. "Committee Reports of the Conference on Educational Problems in the Southwest with Special Reference to the Educational Problems in Spanish-speaking Communities." Washington, D.C., Coordinator of Inter-American Affairs, 1943.

Council of Mexican-American Affairs. "Report on Housing Discrimination." Los Angeles, Mar. 14, 1956.

Dal Pozzo, Dorris. "A Consideration of Carpinteria's Provision for the Education of Its Minority Group." Research paper in Education, Claremont Graduate School, May, 1945.

Denver Area Welfare Council. "The Spanish-speaking Population of Denver," 1950.

Denver University National Opinion Research Center. "The Spanish-speaking Population of Denver." Denver, Colo., Denver Unity Council, 1946.

Donahue, Mary P. "A Suggested Plan for Improving the Academic Achievement of Mexican-American Students in a Specific High School." University of Southern California, School of Education, 1965.

Dworkin, Anthony Gary. "Popular Stereotypes and Self-images of the Anglo-American and Mexican-American." Honors thesis in Sociology, Occidental College, 1964.

Ewing, T. W. "A Report on Minorities in Denver: The Spanish-speaking People in Denver." Denver, Colo., Mayor's Interim Survey Committee on Human Relations, 1947.

Facci, Joseph A. "Rehabilitation for Mexican Farm Laborers." Manuscript in Haines Hall Library, University of California, Los Angeles, Nov. 18, 1939.

Farris, Buford, and William M. Hale. "A Method and Approach to Working with the 'Mexican-American' Boy and His 'Gang.'" Wesley Community Centers, San Antonio, Tex., n.d.

Farris, Buford. "Mexican-American Conflict Gangs—Observations and Theoretical Implications." Research and Educational Report no. 1, San Antonio, Tex., Wesley Community Center, n.d.

Far West Surveys. "A Report of the Latin-American Population Living in Los Angeles, California." Prepared for Radio Station KALI, Los Angeles, 1962.

Foster, George M. "Problems in Intercultural Health Programs." Memorandum to the Committee on Preventive Medicine and Social Science Research, Social Science Research Council, New York, 1958.

Friend, Reed E., and Samuel Baum. "Economic, Social and Demographic Characteristics of Spanish-American Wage Workers on U.S. Farms." U.S. Department of Agriculture, Economic Research Service, Economic and Statistical Analysis Division.

Fuller, Varden, John W. Mainer, and George L. Viles. "Domestic and Imported Workers in the Harvest Labor Market, Santa Clara County, California, 1954." Report no. 184, Giannini Foundation of Agricultural Economics, University of California, Berkeley, 1951.

Gamio, Manuel. "Number, Origin, and Geographic Distribution of the Mexican Immigrants in the United States." Institute of Pacific Relations, 1929.

Garcia, Mrs. M. "Report on Relocation Progress, August 1961—May 1964." Study made by the case work director of the San Antonio Urban Renewal Agency, May 13, 1964.

Greer, Scott, and Henry Baggish. "Chavez Ravine: Urbanization and Occupational Mobility in a Mexican-American Enclave." Research report, Department of Anthropology, University of California, Los Angeles, 1949.

Grisham, Glen. "Basic Needs of Spanish-American Farm Families in New Mexico." U.S. Department of Agriculture, Farm Security Administration, Albuquerque, N. Mex. On file at Farm Security Administration Office, n.d.

Grossman, Mitchell. "Multi-factional Politics in San Antonio and Bexar County, Texas." University of Texas, 1959.

Guzman, Ralph. "The Mexican-American Population: An Introspective View." Palm Springs, Calif., Western Governmental Research Association, Aug., 1966.

Hanson, Robert C. "The Structure and Content of Health Belief Systems." New Mexico Rural Health Survey Files, University of Colorado, 1961.

Heffernan, H. "The Implications of the White House Conference for the Education of Spanish-speaking Children." Southwest Council on the Education of Spanish-speaking People, Los Angeles, Pepperdine College, 1951.

Hill, George W. "Texas-Mexican Migratory Agricultural Workers in Wisconsin." Bulletin no. 6. Madison, Wisconsin Agricultural Experiment Station, 1948 (mimeographed).

Hoehler, Fred K., and others. "Public Welfare Survey of San Antonio, Texas." Chicago, American Public Welfare Association, 1940.

Home Missions Council. "Notes for

Report of Commission on International and Interracial Factors in the Problem of Mexicans in the United States." New York, 1926.

Hughes, Marie M., and Reuben R. Palm. "Los Angeles County Schools Workshop in Education of Mexican and Spanish-speaking Pupils." Los Angeles, Office of the County Superintendent of Schools, Nov., 1942.

Jorgenson, Janet M., David E. Williams, and John H. Burma. "Migratory Agricultural Workers in the United States." Grinnell College, 1960.

Keating, Stephen J. "Vocational Opportunities for Mexican and Negro Youth in the Clanton Street Area, June 20, 1941." Manuscript in the Anthropology-Sociology Departmental File, University of California, Los Angeles, 1941 [?].

Kerrick, Jean S. "Preliminary Report—Attitudes of Migrant Farm Population in Santa Barbara County." Research report on attitudes toward health, School of Public Health, University of California, Los Angeles, Sept. 8, 1964.

Kritzer, Edith. "St. Paul Report on Mexican Study." From the files of the International Institute, St. Paul, Minn., 1929.

Landes, Ruth. "Counselling the Mexican-Americans." Claremont Graduate School, 1960.

———. "Integration of Minorities." Claremont Graduate School, 1960.

Loomis, Charles P. "Relations of Anglo-Latino Groups with Hospitals and Communities." Report prepared under the auspices of the U.S. Department of Health, Education and Welfare, Michigan State University, n.d.

Los Angeles Chamber of Commerce, Research Department. "General Data Regarding Mexican Population of Los Angeles City, 1933, 1934, 1936." In Los Angeles Chamber of Commerce Library, n.d.

———. "Mexican Repatriation from California During 1931, 1932 and 1933." Statistical report in the Los Angeles Public Library.

Los Angeles City Health Department. "Data on Mexicans Compiled from Records of the Los Angeles City Health Department." 1929.

Los Angeles City Planning Commission. "Chavez Ravine, Community Redevelopment." 1948.

Los Angeles Committee on Scholarships. "The Need for a Scholarship Fund for Students of Mexican Ancestry." Report on a questionnaire answered by fifty students of Mexican Ancestry at East Los Angeles Junior College, 1954.

Los Angeles County Bureau of Inspections, Division of Housing and Sanitation. "Housing and Sanitation Survey of Active Tuberculosis Cases in Belvedere Health District." By Charles G. Kalhert, Los Angeles, Aug. 31, 1937.

Los Angeles County Commission on Human Relations. "A Comparative Statistical Analysis of Minority Group Population for Los Angeles County from April, 1950 to July 1, 1959." 1959.

———. "Minority Groups in Los Angeles County." 1959.

——— "Population and Housing in Los Angeles County: A Study in the Growth of Residential Segregation." 1963.

Los Angeles County Committee for Interracial Progress. "Racial Breakdown of the County and City Housing Authority Development, March–April, 1946." 1946.

Los Angeles County Coordinating Councils, Information Division. "Some Notes on the Mexican Population in Los Angeles County." In Citizens Committee for the Defense of Mexican-American Youth, Archive (107/6), University of California, Los Angeles, n.d.

Los Angeles County Department of Charities, Office of the Superintendent. "Analysis of Mexican Repatriation Trains, 1934." In Los Angeles County Public Library, n.d.

Los Angeles County Grand Jury. "Final Report of the Los Angeles County Grand Jury, 1943."

———, Special Mexican Committee. "Papers Read in Meeting Held October

8, 1942, Called by Special Mexican Relations Committee of the Los Angeles County Grand Jury."

Los Angeles County Youth Committee. "The Echo Park Study: A Social Analysis of an Urban Area, with a Description of the Study Method." Los Angeles, 1950 [?].

Los Angeles Region Welfare Planning Council, Research Department. "Report on the Survey of Unsponsored Youth Groups in the East Central Areas." Jan. 24, 1958.

Lukens, Eleanor. "Factors Affecting Utilization of Mental Health Services by Mexican-Americans." Working paper no. 47, Research Department, Welfare Planning Council, Los Angeles Region, June, 1963.

McMillan, Oliver. "Housing Deficiencies of Agricultural Workers and Other Low Income Groups." Report to the Division of Housing for the Governor's Advisory Commission on Housing Problems, San Francisco, Nov. 27, 1962.

McWilliams, Carey. Carey McWilliams Collection no. 2. Government and Public Affairs Reading Room, Haines Collection, University of California, Los Angeles.

———. "Memorandum on Housing Conditions among Migratory Workers in California." Prepared for California Department of Industrial Relations, Division of Immigration and Housing. Los Angeles, Mar. 30, 1939.

———. "Report Covering the Activities of the Division of Immigration and Housing, 1939–1942." In the Los Angeles Public Library.

———. "Testimony Before L.A. County Grand Jury, October 8, 1942." Re: Mexican Zoot-suiters. Research resources storage file, the Urban League, Los Angeles.

Marquez, Mary N., and Consuelo Pacheco. "Parteras in Northern New Mexico: A Descriptive Review of Selected Practice in Midwifery." U.S. Public Health Research Project, grant no. GM 05615, n.d.

Mercer, Jane. "A Social and Economic Study of Ethnic Groups in Riverside." Research Department, Pacific State Hospital, 1963 [?].

Moore, Joan W. "Mexican-Americans, Problems and Prospects." Washington, D.C., Office of Economic Opportunity, 1966.

National Catholic Welfare Conference, Administrative Board. "Comprehensive Report of the Office of the Bishop's Committee for Migrant Workers." Washington, D.C., n.d.

Nelson, Robert. "The Churches in Ignacio." Tri-ethnic Research Project, Institute of Behavioral Science, University of Colorado, Jan., 1963.

Ortiz, Martin. "Mexican-Americans in the Los Angeles Region." East Central Area Welfare Planning Council, 3232 Estrada Street, Los Angeles 23, Calif., Aug., 1962.

Rendon, Gabino. "Objective Access in the Opportunity Structure: The Assessment of Three Ethnic Groups with Respect to Quantified Social Structural Variables." Report no. 20, Tri-ethnic Research Project, Institute of Behavioral Science, University of Colorado, June, 1963.

"Report on the Survey of Unsponsored Youth Groups in the East Central Areas." Edited by Research Department of the Welfare Planning Council, Los Angeles Region, Jan. 24, 1958.

Roybal, Edward. "Papers, 1953–1962." In Special Collection Library, University of California, Los Angeles. Includes correspondence, notes, manuscripts, photographs, and related printed material concerning Roybal's activities as a Los Angeles city councilman.

Samora, Julian. "The Spanish-speaking People in the United States." U.S. Commission on Civil Rights, staff paper, Washington, D.C., 1962.

San Antonio Public Health Department. "Vital Statistics in San Antonio, 1960–1964." San Antonio, Tex., 1964 [?].

San Antonio Urban Renewal Agency. "A Relocation Housing Market Study of the

San Antonio Standard Metropolitan Statistical Area." Bexar County, Tex., Oct., 1963.

Sanchez, George. "The American of Mexican Descent." State of Colorado Anti-discrimination Commission, Denver, n.d.

—— and Lyle Saunders. "Wetback: A Preliminary Report." University of Texas, 1949.

Saposs, David J. "Report on Rapid Survey of Resident Latin-American Problems and Recommended Program." Washington, D.C., Office of the Coordinator of Inter-American Affairs, Apr. 3, 1942.

Saunders, Lyle. "Cultural Factors Affecting Public Health Programs in a Border Agricultural Area." Prepared for the fourteenth annual meeting of the U.S.-Mexico Border Public Health Association, Calexico-Mexicali, Apr. 13–16, 1956.

Shannon, Lyle, and Elaine M. Drass. "The Economic Absorption and Cultural Integration of Immigrant Mexican-Americans and Negro Workers." Progress report on grouped-value assimilation among immigrant workers, National Institutes of Health project, Department of Sociology and Anthropology, State University of Iowa, 1964.

Sheldon, Paul M. "Mexican-Americans in Urban Public High Schools: An Exploration of the Drop-out Problem." Rosenberg Foundation of San Francisco and Laboratory of Urban Culture, Occidental College, 1959.

Simmons, Ozzie G., Robert C. Hanson, and Jules J. Wanderer. "Urbanization of the Migrant: Processes and Outcomes: A Research Proposal." Boulder, Colo., Institute of Behavioral Science, Bureau of Sociological Research, Jan. 14, 1964.

Sleepy Lagoon Defense Committee, Los Angeles. 1942–1945. Records of committee materials, correspondence, office memo file, petitions, materials on the Mexican minority, information about defendants, clippings, case records. In Special Collections library, University of California, Los Angeles.

Smith, Clara Gertrude. "The Effect of the Culture of the United States upon Some of the Mexican Immigrants in the Watts District." Research report, Jan., 1931.

Sommer, Charles G. "A Study of the Increase in Mexican Immigration to the U.S." Mexico City, U.S. Embassy Report, 1956.

Southwest Texas State Teachers College. "Final Report. Program in the Southwest: School and Community Cooperation. Special School-community Project in Inter-American Affairs." San Marcos, Tex., July, 1944 (mimeographed).

Texas Committee on Migrant Farm Workers and the Good Neighbor Commission of Texas. "Proceedings of the Conference on Education for Adult Migrant Workers." Austin, 57th Texas Legislature, 1962.

Texas Council on Migrant Labor. "Mechanization and the Texas Migrant." Feb., 1963.

——. "Texas Migrant Labor During 1962: Overall Summary." Mar., 1963.

Texas Education Agency. "Estimated Number of Potential School Dropouts for Children and Average Daily Attendance in Public Schools in 1960 and of Current Dropouts as of 1960 for School Age Children with Percent of Population Who Are Latin-American and Non-white Population." Austin, Tex., 1961.

——. "Handbook for the Instructional Program for Pre-school Age Non-English Speaking Children." Austin, Tex., 1960.

——. "Report on the Educational Needs of Migrant Workers." Study prepared for the House Interim Committee on Migrant Labor, 57th Texas Legislature, 1962.

——. "The Texas Project for Migrant Children: An Evaluation of First Year Operation of a Pilot Project in Five School Districts." Austin, Tex., 1964.

Texas Employment Service, Farm Placement Service Division. "Origins and Problems of Texas Migratory Farm Labor." Austin, Tex., 1940.

Texas State Board of Education. "Statement of Policy Pertaining to Segregation of Latin-American Children." Austin, May 8, 1950.

Thompson, Edyth T. "Public Health Among the Mexicans." Pomona College, Claremont, California, 1928.

———. "A Statistical Study of Sickness among Mexicans in the Los Angeles Hospital." California State Board of Health, 1925.

———. "Survey of Mexican Cases Where Tuberculosis is a Problem." California State Board of Health, 1926.

Trimble, Glen W., Director, Home Missions Research Bureau of Research and Survey, National Council of Churches. "Responses to the Brief Survey of Church Related Spanish-American Work in the Continental United States." Jan. 10, 1960.

Underhill, Bertha. "A Study of 132 Families in California Cotton Camps with Reference to Availability of Medical Care." California State Department of Social Welfare (Manuscript in Haines Library, University of California, Los Angeles), 1941 [?].

United States Commission on Civil Rights. "Spanish-speaking Peoples." Staff paper, Feb. 5, 1964.

U.S. Farm Security Administration. "A Study of 6,655 Migrant Households Receiving Emergency Grants." Farm Security Administration, Washington, D.C., 1938.

U.S. Federal Writers' Project, Works Progress Administration. "Organization Efforts of Mexican Agricultural Workers," Oakland, Calif. [?], 1938 [?].

U.S. Public Health Service. "Public Health Survey of San Antonio, Texas, with Particular Regard to Tuberculosis and Venereal Disease Control." U.S. Public Health Service, n.d.

University of California, Los Angeles, Department of Education. "Summary of Proceedings of Conference on Educational Problems of Students of Mexican Descent." Los Angeles, Mar. 26, 1955.

University of New Mexico, School of Inter-American Affairs. "Recent Educational and Community Experiments and Projects in New Mexico Affecting the Spanish-speaking Population." Report prepared in connection with the Conference on Problems of Education Among Spanish-speaking Populations of Our Southwest, Santa Fe, N. Mex., Aug. 19–24, 1943.

Valdez, Bernard. "Contrasts Between Spanish Folk and Anglo Urban Cultural Values." California, Department of Institutions, Department of Social Welfare, n.d.

———. "Implications of Spanish-American Culture on Family Life." California, Department of Institutions, Department of Social Welfare, n.d.

Whitaker, Neely, and Carl J. Burk. "Summary Report of the Study of Dropouts in the Three Senior High Schools, Compton Union High School District." Los Angeles, Office of the Los Angeles County Superintendent of Schools, 1960.

Woods, Marion J. "Employment Problems of the Mexican-American." Presentation by Marion J. Woods, State Supervisor of the Minority Employment Program, before the Assembly Subcommittee on Special Employment Problems, East Los Angeles College Auditorium, Jan. 10, 1964.

Zamora, Ted. "Survey of Mexican Families and Individuals Served by the Neighborhood House." St. Paul, Minn., Apr. 1941.

V. BIBLIOGRAPHIES

American Council on Race Relations. *Mexican-Americans: A Selected Bibliography.* Bibliography Series no. 7. Chicago, 1949.

Bogardus, Emory S. *The Mexican Immigrant: An Annotated Bibliography.* Los Angeles: Council on International Relations, 1929.

Cook, Katherine M., and Florence E. Reynolds. *The Education of Native and Minority Groups: A Bibliography, 1923–32.* Bulletin 12. Washington, D.C.: U.S. Department of the Interior, Office of Education, 1933.

Cumberland, Charles C. "The United States–Mexican Border: A Selective Guide to the Literature of the Region." Supplement to *Rural Sociology*, vol. 25, no. 2 (June, 1960).

Dobie, J. Frank. *Guide to Life and Literature of the Southwest.* Austin, Tex.: University of Texas Press, 1943.

Guzman, Ralph, and staff. *Revised Bibliography.* Advance Report 3, Mexican-American Study Project. University of California, Los Angeles, 1967.

Jones, Robert C. *Mexicans in the United States—A Bibliography.* Washington, D.C.: Pan American Union, 1942.

——. *Selected References on Labor Importation Program Between Mexico and the United States.* Washington, D.C.: Pan American Union, 1948.

Lavell, C. B., and others. "Annotated Bibliography on the Demographic, Economic and Sociological Aspects of Immigration," in *Report on World Population Migration as Related to the United States of America: An Exploratory Study of Past Studies and Researches on World Population Migration,* pp. 269–275, 353–359. Washington, D.C.: George Washington University, 1956.

Pan American Council. *Suggested References on the Mexican Immigrants in the United States.* Chicago, 1942.

Potts, Alfred M. *Knowing and Educating the Disadvantaged: An Annotated Bibliography.* Alamosa, Colo.: Center for Cultural Studies, Adams State College, 1965.

Riemer, Ruth. *An Annotated Bibliography of Material on Ethnic Problems in Southern California.* Los Angeles: The Haynes Foundation and Department of Anthropology-Sociology, University of California, 1947.

Sanchez, George I. and Howard Putnam. *Materials Relating to the Education of Spanish-speaking People in the United States: An Annotated Bibliography.* Austin, Tex.: Institute of Latin-American Studies, University of Texas, 1959.

Saunders, Lyle. "A Guide to the Literature of the Southwest." A regular bibliographic feature in the *New Mexico Quarterly Review,* 1942–1955.

——. *A Guide to Materials Bearing on Cultural Relations in New Mexico.* Albuquerque, N. Mex.: University of New Mexico Press, 1944.

——. *Spanish-speaking Americans and Mexican-Americans in the United States.* New York: Bureau for Intercultural Education, Jan., 1944.

Sonnichsen, C. L. *The Southwest: The Record in Books.* El Paso, Tex.: Texas Western College, 1961.

U.S. Department of Labor. *Selected Reference on Domestic Migratory Agricultural Workers, Their Families, Problems and Programs, 1955–1960.* Bulletin no. 225, Washington, D.C., 1961.

Lists of Tables, Charts, Maps, and Figures

I. LIST OF TEXT TABLES

748

II. LIST OF APPENDIX TABLES

III. LIST OF CHARTS, MAPS, AND FIGURES

Index

Index

A

social mobility under domination of, 322-325
  in Southwest (1910-1960), 46-48
    19th-century, 43-44
  unemployment rate of (1960), 20
Anti-Catholicism of Baptists, 494-495
Anticommunism of Catholic Church, 454, 458
Antipoverty programs:
  church participation in, 454, 468
  effects of immigration on, 75
Arizona:
  educational attainment in, 152, 154
  family income in, 185
  housing conditions in, 251-252
  income differentials in, 189, 193-194, 196, 199
  individual income in, 187
  labor force participation in, 206
  occupational structure in, 214
  population in: growth of, 108-109
    by population groups, 106-107
  residential segregation in, 274-276
Asceticism, Protestant, 494-495
Aspirations, disparities in, 161-164
Assimilation:
  geographic mobility and, 83-84
  intermarriage and, 293, 405-418
    age factor and, 414-416
    disparaged, 323
    generational differences in, 408-410
    occupations and, 410-413
    percentage of, 406
    social distance and, 392, 394, 405
  occupational structure and, 86
  in pluralistic societies, 576-577
  potential for, 9-12, 575
  through social relations, 396
    (*See also* Social relations)
  steps toward, 84
  work and settlement patterns and, 89-95
    (*See also* Acculturation;
      Americanization through churches)
Associations (*see* Ethnic organizations)
Attainment (*see* Education; Schooling;
  Schools)
Attendance (*see* Mass attendance;
  Schools)
Austin, Stephens, 40

Authority (*see* Patriarchy)
Automation, skilled labor and, 71
Automobiles, ownership of, 337
Average daily attendance (ADA), 151-152
Ayres Report (1942), 529

B

Baptists:
  missionary work of, 492-493
  segregation and, 494-496
Baptists' Southern California Commission
  on Spanish Work, 495-496
Barrios:
  class differences in, 309
  history of, 273
  of Los Angeles and San Antonio,
    compared, 310-312
  uncohesiveness of, 307-308
  (*See also* Ghettos; Housing conditions;
    Residential segregation)
Behavior, neighboring, 308-309
Beveridge, Albert, 45
Bilingual Education Act (1967), 586
Birth certificates, sale of, 521
Birth control:
  attitudes toward, 9, 135, 364-366, 582
  machismo and, 364
  position of Church on, 474-475
Birth rates, comparative (1960), 135
Bishop's Committee for the
  Spanish-speaking, 461-462, 468
Black Power movement, 553
"Blood," status distinctions based on,
  320-321
Blue-collar occupations, 210-211, 225
Bogardus, Emory L., 390, 525, 583
Boilermakers, Machinists and Railway
  Carmen Union, 91
Border:
  control of, 66
    (*See also* Border Patrol; Texas
      Rangers)
  evolution of Southwestern, 40-42
Border Patrol, 519-523
  disliked, 522-523, 586
  effects of, 535-536
  functions of, 519-520
  Operation Wetback and, 521-522

O

U

V

W